Praise for *101 Middle Eastern Tales and Their Impact on Western Oral Tradition*

"From *Belling the Cat* to *A Pound of Flesh,* an absolute master of comparative folklore identifies the Middle Eastern narratives that have entered the Western oral tradition in the past millennium. Ulrich Marzolph's mastery of classical Persian, Arabic, and Ottoman Turkish sources shines through this volume and will engage the expert and entertain the lay reader."

—MAHMOUD OMIDSALAR, consulting editor in folklore for the Encyclopaedia Iranica and resident scholar at Dr. Samuel M. Jordan Center for Persian Studies at the University of California, Irvine

"A bold contribution founded on intimate knowledge of European and Middle Eastern folk narrative scholarship."

—HASAN EL-SHAMY, professor emeritus in the Departments of Folklore and Ethnomusicology and Near Eastern Languages and Cultures, Indiana University, Bloomington

"This book is an endlessly fascinating 'story of our stories,' tracing the resonant linkage between individual tales preserved in Middle Eastern literary traditions and their later lives, as they were transmitted to the West and then circulated orally across Europe and beyond. Marzolph's erudition and appetite for literary treasure hunts are unsurpassed."

—MARGARET MILLS, author of *Rhetorics and Politics in Afghan Traditional Storytelling*

101 MIDDLE EASTERN TALES

101 Middle Eastern Tales and Their Impact on Western Oral Tradition

Ulrich Marzolph

WAYNE STATE UNIVERSITY PRESS
DETROIT

ISBN 978-0-8143-4773-7 (paperback);
ISBN 978-0-8143-4774-4 (case);
ISBN 978-0-8143-4775-1 (ebook)

Library of Congress Cataloging Number: 2019948753

Published with the assistance of a fund established
by Thelma Gray James of Wayne State University for
the publication of folklore and English studies.

Wayne State University Press
Leonard N. Simons Building
4809 Woodward Avenue
Detroit, Michigan 48201–1309

Visit us online at wsupress.wayne.edu

On cover: Two illustrations from the thirteenth-century
copy of the *Maqāmāt* by al-Ḥarīrī (d. 1122) preserved in the
Bibliothèque Nationale de France, Arabe 5847

Cover design by Lindsey Cleworth

CONTENTS

Introduction 1

1. The Fox Rids Itself of Fleas (ATU 63) 29

2. Belling the Cat (ATU 110) 34

3. The Bird Promises to Give Its Captor Three Pieces of Advice (ATU 150) 38

4. The Faithful Animal Rashly Killed (ATU 178A) 45

5. The Cat and the Candle (ATU 217) 49

6. The Princess and Her Secret Affair (ATU 306) 52

7. The Unfaithful Wife Transforms Her Husband into a Dog (ATU 449) 59

8. The Two Hunchbacks (ATU 503) 68

9. The Unpromising Rascal Makes His Fortune with the Help of a Magic Object (ATU 561) 74

10. The Mechanical Flying Gadget (ATU 575) 86

11. The Husband Buried Alive Together with His Deceased Wife (ATU 612) 95

12. The Contending Lovers Are Challenged to Acquire the Rarest Thing in the World (ATU 653A) 105

13. The Sensitive Brothers and Their Clever Deductions (ATU 655) 111

14. Years of Experience in a Moment: The Man is Transformed into a Woman (and Back Again) (ATU 681) 125

15. The Chaste Woman Coveted by Her Brother-in-Law (ATU 712) 132

16. The Three Old Men (ATU 726) 140

17. The Foolish Couple Waste the Three Wishes They Have Been Granted (ATU 750A) 147

18. The Subaltern Does Not Want to Sell the House to the Ruler (ATU 759E) 154

19. The Treasure Finders Murder One Another (ATU 763) 161

20. Greed Makes the Cheater Admit His Misdemeanor (ATU 785) 170

21. God Willing! (ATU 830C) 178

22. The Greedy Man Is Blinded and Falls into Misery (ATU 836F*) 181

23. Drinking Leads to Committing Serious Crimes (ATU 839) 186

24. The Princess Whose Suitors Will Be Executed if They Fail to Solve Her Riddles (AT 851A) 192

25. The Entrapped Would-Be Seducers Have to Work to Earn Their Food (ATU 882A*) 203

26. The Prince Learns a Profession (ATU 888A*) 213

27. A Pound of Flesh as Security for a Loan (ATU 890) 221

28. The Lowly Man Shrewdly Responds to the King's Unanswerable Questions (ATU 922) 225

29. The Treacherous Treasure Hunter (ATU 936*) 231

30. The Robbers Hiding Their Treasures in a Magic Cavern (ATU 954) 237

31. Whose Was the Noblest Action? (ATU 976) 243

32. The Villager in the Town of Rogues (ATU 978) 252

33. The Dishes of the Same Flavor (ATU 983) 255

34. The Fool Guards the Door by Taking It Along (ATU 1009) 261

35. The Fools Try to Keep the Bird from Escaping (ATU 1213) 266

36. Trying to Please Everyone (ATU 1215) 271

37. The Fool Doubles the Load by Counterbalancing the Wheat with Stones (AT 1242B) 275

38. Making a Hole in the Ground to Deposit the Soil from the Previous Digging (ATU 1255) 279

39. Warming Oneself on a Distant Fire (ATU 1262) 282

40. The Fool Forgets to Count the Donkey He Is Sitting on (ATU 1288A) 287

41. The Scholar and the Ferryman (El-Shamy 1293C*) 292

42. Freeing the Part of the Body Stuck in the Jar by Cutting It Off (ATU 1294) 295

43. The Fox Fears It Might Be Taken for a Camel (El-Shamy 1319N*) 298

44. Accidental Cannibalism (ATU 1339G) 302

45. The Thieves Find Nothing to Steal in the Poor Man's House (ATU 1341C) 305

46. The House without Food or Drink (ATU 1346) 309

47. The Liar Sows Discord between a Married Couple (ATU 1353) 314

48. The Frightened Person Withdraws the Vow to Die Instead of a Close Relative (ATU 1354) 320

49. The Weighed Cat (ATU 1373) 325

50. Test of Self-Composure: Small Animal Escapes When Lid of Vessel Is Lifted (ATU 1416) 329

51. The Tricky Lover Regains the Gift He Gave for Intercourse (ATU 1420G) 337

52. The Enchanted Tree (ATU 1423) 343

53. The Men Realize That They Will Never Manage to Control Women's Sexuality (ATU 1426) 349

54. Ignorance Concerning the Use of Flour (ATU 1446) 356

55. The Burglar's Lame Excuse: The Sound Will Be Heard Tomorrow Morning (Jason 1525*T) 359

56. The Swindler Leaves an Uninformed Person as Security for His Purchase (ATU 1526) 363

57. The Thief Claims to Have Been Transformed into a Donkey (ATU 1529) 367

58. The Subaltern Is Made Lord for a Day (ATU 1531) 375

59. The Clever Man Privileges Himself When Carving the Roast Chicken (ATU 1533) 385

60. Quoting the Scripture to Gain an Advantage at the Meal (ATU 1533A) 392

61. Hanging by Proxy (ATU 1534A*) 396

62. The Accused Wins the Lawsuit by Feigning to Be Dumb (ATU 1534D*) 400

63. The Exigent Dreamer (ATU 1543A) 403

64. Promising to Sell the Large Farm Animal for a Trifle Amount (ATU 1553) 409

65. The Rogue Trades Water for Wine (ATU 1555B) 414

66. Welcome to the Clothes (ATU 1558) 418

67. "Think Thrice before You Speak!" (ATU 1562) 422

68. The Sham Threat (ATU 1563*) 426

69. The Trickster Relieves His Itching with a Trick (ATU 1565) 430

70. The Prankster's Ambiguous Dream (ATU 1572M*) 433

71. The Thievish Tailor's Terrifying Dream of the Patchwork Banner (ATU 1574) 436

72. The Drink Served in the Pisspot (ATU 1578A*) 441

73. The Adviser Is Duped with His Own Advice (ATU 1585) 444

74. The Inanimate Object Allegedly Gives Birth and Dies (ATU 1592B) 450

75. The Courtiers Force the Bearer of a Present to Share His Anticipated Award (ATU 1610) 455

76. The Greedy Banker Is Deceived into Delivering the Disputed Deposit (ATU 1617) 463

77. The Pauper Regains His Buried Money (ATU 1617*) 468

78. The Imaginary Tissue (ATU 1620) 474

79. The Lowly Man Posing as Soothsayer (ATU 1641) 482

80. The Miracle Cure (ATU 1641B) 491

81. Who Stole?—The Thieves! (ATU 1641B*) 497

82. The Dream of Finding One's Fortune Somewhere Else (ATU 1645) 500

83. The Dreamer Marks the Treasure with His Excrements (ATU 1645B) 507

84. The Clever Man Privileges Himself When Distributing Food Items among Several Persons (ATU 1663) 513

85. Anticipatory Beating (ATU 1674*) 518

86. The Animal Will Not Know How to Make Proper Use of the Meat (ATU 1689B) 521

87. The Clever Woman Has the Entrapped Would-Be Lovers Publicly Humiliated (ATU 1730) 525

88. The Clever Culprit Pretends That His Sword Has Been Transformed to Wood (ATU 1736A) 534

89. The Preacher Cleverly Avoids Delivering a Sermon (ATU 1826) 541

90. The Numskull Thinks That a Name Ages (ATU 1832N*) 546

91. How the Preacher's Sermon Makes a Member of His Parish Cry (ATU 1834) 550

92. The Simpleton Is Not Able to Perform a Seemingly Easy Mental Task (ATU 1835D*) 554

93. The Illiterate Fool's Reckoning of Time Is Ruined (ATU 1848A) 558

94. The Rider Goes Where His Bolting Mount Takes Him (ATU 1849*) 562

95. The Greater Bribe Wins (ATU 1861A) 566

96. Diagnosis by Observation (ATU 1862C) 570

97. The Liar Reduces the Size of His Lie (ATU 1920D) 574

98. The Trickster Forces His Challenger to Admit That He Is Telling a Lie (ATU 1920F) 577

99. A Nonsense Introduction to the Fairy-Tale World (ATU 1965) 582

100. Mouse-Maid Marries Mouse (ATU 2031C) 585

101. The Climax of Horrors (ATU 2040) 589

Works Cited 597

Index of Narrators and Collectors 671

Index of Names and Motifs in the Tales 676

General Index 689

101 MIDDLE EASTERN TALES

INTRODUCTION

Since antiquity, the "Orient" constitutes the quintessential Other vis-à-vis the European cultures. While delineation against this Other served to define and reassure the Self, the "Orient" also constituted a constant source of fascination, attraction, and inspiration.[1] Probably the most instructive historical example for this ambiguous attitude toward the "Orient" is the narrative appropriation of "Oriental" realms in the *Romance of Alexander.*[2] Particularly since the advent of Islam in the seventh century CE and ensuing cultural contacts between the Muslim world and Christian Europe, tales were a vital part of the intellectual goods that traveled East to West.

Several collections of tales transmitted a considerable number of "Oriental" tales to the West, initially in Latin as the medieval lingua franca of learning, and increasingly since the early modern period in the European vernacular languages. The most prominent of these collections are

- the Arabic *Kalīla wa-Dimna* (Kalīla and Dimna), an adaptation of the Sanskrit *Panchatantra* (Five [Books of] Wisdom), whose Hebrew version was translated to Latin in John of Capua's twelfth-century *Directorium vitae humanae* (A Guide for Human Life);[3]
- the originally Persian *Sendbād-nāme* (Book of Sendbād [the Sage]), variously adapted in the West, most prominently as *Historia septem sapientum* (Story of the Seven Sages);[4]
- Petrus Alfonsus's early twelfth-century *Disciplina clericalis* (The Scholar's Guide), conceived in the multicultural and multireligious atmosphere of medieval Spain;[5]
- the Arabic *Alf layla wa-layla* (The Thousand and One Nights) in Antoine Galland's adapted and enlarged French translation *Les Mille et une nuit* (1704–17) that unwittingly and contrary to the author's well-meaning intentions contributed to the rise of Orientalism, the sweepingly uncritical and exploitative perception of the "Orient";[6] and
- the Ottoman Turkish *Ferec baʿd eş-şidde* (Relief after Hardship), a selective adaptation of which Galland's colleague and competitor François Pétis de la Croix published as *Les Mille et un jours* (The Thousand and One Days; 1710–12).[7]

In addition, numerous single tales or small clusters of tales originating from or adapted by Muslim tradition found their way into Western tradition through a variety of less prominent written or literary instances in the West, such as learned treatises, the sermons of medieval preachers, late medieval *fabliaux*, the works of Italian Renaissance writers or Spanish authors of the *Siglo de oro*, early modern chapbooks, or modern calendar literature, newspapers, and magazines. At all times, and particularly in areas and periods of intense cultural contacts between the Muslim world and the West, such as the Crusades,[8] medieval Spain, or trade with the Levantine countries, oral tradition likely served as a powerful medium of transmission, especially of short and often jocular tales that were comparatively easy to remember and retell. Although both East and West regarded themselves as relatively closed homogenous entities, numerous cultural contacts and occasions for narrative transfer existed. Initially, these contacts predominantly occurred in the Iberian Peninsula, Sicily, Palestine and the Levant, and Byzantium[9] and, later, in the Ottoman Empire in North Africa and the Balkans. Particularly from the Enlightenment period onward, the enthusiastic reception of "Oriental" literatures in such genres as the "Oriental Miscellany" added yet another powerful opportunity of mediating tales to the West.[10] Whether the tales were originally part of learned, instructive, or entertaining discourses in literature or whether they originated from popular contexts in oral performance, through oral retellings numerous "Oriental" tales eventually became an integral part of European oral tradition, from which folklorists would eventually record the tales in the nineteenth and twentieth centuries. Already in the late Middle Ages and early modernity, in the European context tales of "Oriental" origin would travel as far as Scotland[11] or Iceland.[12] Whereas, temporally, the Western reception of "Oriental" tales thus covers more or less the second millennium CE, geographically it spans the whole of Western tradition in Europe and the Americas.

This book focuses on the originally "Oriental" tales that became part and parcel of modern Western oral tradition. Against the methodological backdrop of the academic discipline of historical and comparative folk narrative research, it surveys in detail the history, dissemination, and characteristics of 101 narratives transmitted to Western tradition from or by the Middle Eastern Muslim literatures, that is, authored written works in Arabic, Persian, and Ottoman Turkish. In order to be considered, a given tale would fulfill two criteria. First and foremost, the tale would originate from or at least be transmitted by a Middle Eastern source. This criterion is generally considered as given if a tale's Middle Eastern version predates the same tale's earliest attested version in a Western language. As a rule, such a Western version would postdate the year 1000, that is, belong to the high or late Middle Ages. Tales the Middle Eastern Muslim literatures share with Greek or Roman antiquity, including a fair variety of fables and short jocular tales, are excluded by definition, as it is more likely that the medieval and early modern European versions of those tales were mediated through the reception of the ancient classics since the Renaissance period rather than by way of the respective tales' corresponding texts in the Middle Eastern Muslim literatures. And second, in order to be considered, a tale would be documented from recent oral tradition in the West, that is, it would, as a rule, be recorded from a Western narrator's oral performance in the course of the nineteenth or twentieth centuries.

The rationale behind these restrictive definitions is predicated on my main intention. Rather than providing a comprehensive history surveying the general impact of "Oriental" narrative culture in the West or surveying tales Middle Eastern tradition shares with Greek or Latin antiquity, I am concerned with the long-lasting effect some of the "Oriental" narratives exercised in Western popular tradition. Numerous "Oriental" tales that were transmitted to and adapted in the Western medieval and early modern literatures never transcended the learned or pedagogical contexts in which they initially appeared. Today, many of those tales are more or less forgotten or are at least relegated to a body of historical literature that is primarily the domain of specialists. In other words, those tales never became pervasively popular in the sense of being listened to and being told or retold by "the people," that is, "ordinary" folks without a formal education who often could not read nor write. The practical argument for deciding whether or not a given tale became popular is whether or not it was recorded from Western oral tradition, regardless of the recording's time or place. Although this argument involves a number of pitfalls, it is hoped that the data investigated are comprehensive enough to ascertain that no substantial occurrence of a given tale in oral tradition has been overlooked. It is particularly instructive to study the adaptation and appropriation of originally "Oriental" tales in Western oral tradition, as these tales reveal a dimension of the Western narrative heritage that is not consciously perceived as such. Modern Western narrators were often not aware of the "alien" origins of the tales they told, since over time the tales in addition to being accessible in terms of language had been closely assimilated to their own local, regional, or national contexts without any obvious indications of their originally being imported. In other words, those tales were often not only adapted but also literally adopted into Western tradition. In present times, when national narcissisms often acquire the status of strongholds delineating the Us against the Other, it is imperative to distinguish, document, visualize, and discuss the extent to which the West is not only indebted to the Muslim world, but rather shares common features with Muslim narrative tradition. The present study is a modest contribution to this debate.

The Study of "Oriental" Tales

The interdisciplinary academic discipline of historical and comparative folk narrative research relies on a history of about two centuries. The following short survey of the state of the art focuses on questions relevant for my approach, that is, the awareness of the "Oriental" component of tales prevalent in Western oral tradition.[13] As used here, the term "Orient" implies the geographical region extending from North Africa and the Iberian Peninsula, formerly for several centuries under Muslim dominion, via the Balkans to the Levantine countries and the Middle East. In contemporary research, this region is at times abbreviated as MENA (= Middle East and North Africa), and will here be referred to in short as the Middle East. The narrative traditions of Muslim regions in South and Southeast Asia are largely irrelevant, as I am mainly concerned with Muslim narrative tradition in its historical dimension and only inasmuch as it had an impact on Western narratives. Although it might be unnecessary to say so, it should be mentioned that my work by no means attempts a general assessment of any of the narrative traditions concerned, as the 101 narratives surveyed represent just a minute fraction of narratives available or current in either Middle Eastern or Western tradition. My main concern is the historical dimension of Arabic, Persian, and Ottoman Turkish tales of the Muslim period. Indian narrative tradition is relevant insofar as it sometimes documents early versions of narratives whose Muslim adaptations were mediated to the West, particularly of complex narratives of a fairy-tale character.

Throughout, the terms "Orient" and "Oriental" are placed in quotation marks. Although some of the large international learned societies devoting their efforts to the study of the "Orient" still prefer to keep the term or similar terms in their name, such as the American Oriental Society or the German Deutsche Morgenländische Gesellschaft, the impact of Edward Said's book *Orientalism* (1978) made the general public understand that the "Orient" is not a homogenous unit but rather a conglomerate of highly divergent cultures, each of which deserves to be identified and studied in its own right. Meanwhile, neither Said nor his many critics[14] ever studied vernacular and/or popular culture, and so my study adds a (folk) narrative dimension to achieve a more nuanced perception of "Oriental" cultures. Today, the denomination "Orient" at best serves as a post-colonial umbrella term for the Asian and African Other. Even so, the term is equally common in both scholarship and public discourse. Although the term "Muslim World" used here is, in some ways, equally generalizing, as it suggests a non-existent cultural homogeneity in a region governed by a common majority religion, it is part of the conventionally employed terminology and is here exclusively applied to denominate the regional narrative traditions as specified above.

The founders of the discipline of historical and comparative folk narrative research, the German brothers Jacob and Wilhelm Grimm, published the first edition of their *Kinder- und Hausmärchen* (Children's and Household Tales) in two volumes in 1812 and 1815. Already at the beginning of the nineteenth century, when comparative studies of literature were in their infancy, the Grimms had a certain awareness of the fact that the tales they took to be German often relate to the narrative traditions of other regions or cultures. A section of their general commentary to the collection is even devoted to discussing *The Thousand and One Nights* that the Grimms had read in Jean Jacques Antoine Caussin de Perceval's enlarged French edition (1806). Although today their discussion is unsatisfactory due to the limited amount of critical information available to the Grimms in their day,[15] it deserves to take pride of place as a first in comparative folk narrative studies. A fair amount of ensuing nineteenth century research was devoted to studying the dissemination and presumed origin of tales from the East. Influential in this respect was German scholar of Indic studies Theodor Benfey (1809–1881)[16] with his two-volume edition and commentary of the Sanskrit *Panchatantra* (1859).[17] Benfey advocated the so-called Indian theory, that is, the hypothesis that the ultimate origin of the majority of European folktales was to be sought in Indian tradition.[18] Although the exclusivity of Benfey's theoretical approach to the dissemination of folktales is no longer tenable, works of Indian Sanskrit literature, and particularly the *Panchatantra* (Five [Books of] Wisdom), the *Śukasaptati* (Seventy [Tales of a] Parrot), and the *Kathāsaritsāgara* (The Ocean of Streams of Stories), hold an important historical position in documenting early instances of narratives that later traveled to other regions and cultures. In the United Kingdom, widely read scholars such as William Alexander Clouston (1843–1896)[19] contributed to creating an awareness for the relevance of "Oriental" narratives in their relation to Western narrative tradition.[20]

A milestone in amassing data assessing the role of Arabic tradition in transmitting tales to Western tradition is the work of Belgian Orientalist scholar Victor Chauvin (1844–1913).[21] In his multivolume "Bibliography of Arabic Works or Works Pertaining to the Arabs" (1892–1922),[22] he devoted particular attention to the monumental collections "Kalîlah" (*Kalīla and Dimna* and fable literature; vol. 2), "Les Mille et une nuits" (*The Thousand and One Nights* and related collections; vols. 4–7), and "Syntipas" (The *Sendbād-nāme/Story of the Seven Sages* complex; vol. 8). Even though modestly titled a bibliography, Chauvin's work is much more, since for all of the above-mentioned collections he supplies detailed summaries of the tales they include as well as a tremendous wealth of references pertaining to similar tales or elements of tales in other sources. Still today, Chauvin's *Bibliographie* remains unrivaled as the indispensable starting point for any serious in-depth study of the impact of "Oriental" narratives in the West. In 1918, German Orientalist scholar Mark Lidzbarski (1868–1928) called attention to the "Desideratum" that "the numerous smaller novellas, narratives and anecdotes contained in Arabic literature of an entertaining character . . . should be made available to comparative studies of literature."[23] As a timely, though most probably indirect response to this call for attention, French Arabist and folklorist René Basset (1855–1924)[24] published three volumes of "A Thousand and One Arabic Tales, Stories, and Legends" (1924–26).[25] Equally important as Chauvin's *Bibliographie*, though largely disregarded in nonfolklorist research as a mere anthology of texts, Basset's work contains extensive comparative annotation on both the Middle Eastern and the European dimensions of the cited tales. By the beginning of the twentieth century, Orientalist scholars had thus made a considerable amount of data available that would potentially contribute to creating a detailed awareness of the narratives Middle Eastern tradition shares with European tradition. Folk narrative scholarship would also profit from this.

When Finnish folklorist Antti Aarne (1867–1925)[26] first published his numerical system for the classification of internationally attested tale types, the *Verzeichnis der Märchentypen* (Index of Fairy-Tale Types; 1910),[27] he did so not only to propose an internationally applicable system of cataloguing and retrieving widely known tales in the large archival collections of narratives recorded from oral tradition that had been amassed all over Europe. Aarne also intended to supply a systematic handbook useful for the approach of the then prominent historic-geographic method whose goal was to trace the dissemination of folktales in the Indo-European tradition with the ultimate goal of identifying the tales' "Urform."[28] In their endeavor to identify or reconstruct a given tale's ultimately "original" form, the researchers of the Finnish school at the end of the nineteenth and the beginning of the twentieth century, above all Walter Anderson (1885–1962),[29] tended to regard Middle Eastern narrative traditions essentially as an intermediary between the Indian and the Western traditions of secondary or even negligible relevance. Lacking the linguistic competence and, consequently, the ability to access the relevant sources in their original languages prevented most folklorists from exploring this question in due detail. At the beginning of the twentieth century, Orientalist scholars largely shared this prevailing attitude. Although they possessed the linguistic competence to arrive at a more nuanced evaluation, Orientalist scholars largely denied Arabic (and, by extension, Muslim) narrative tradition its creative potential. An inglorious case in point is the statement by which Danish scholar Johannes Oestrup introduced his entry on *The Thousand and One Nights* in the first edition of the *Encyclopaedia of Islam* (1913): "Like all Orientals the Arabs from the earliest times enjoyed imaginative stories. But the intellectual horizon of the true Arabs being rather narrow, the material for these entertainments was mainly borrowed from elsewhere, from Persia and India."[30] The deplorable longevity of this denigrating and unjustified assessment is evidenced by its almost verbatim repetition in German scholar Enno Littmann's corresponding entry in the second edition of the *Encyclopaedia of Islam* (1960).[31] The only attenuating detail Littmann adduces is his specification of the "true Arabs" as being those "in ancient times before the rise of islam."

It was Austrian journalist Albert Wesselski (1871–1939),[32] a self-taught folklorist, who prominently drew the attention of international folk narrative scholars to the crucial role of Arabic and Persian tradition, both as intermediaries and producers of tales that eventually migrated to Western tradition. Wesselski published a number of extensively annotated translations of early modern Italian and German compilations of jocular tales and two anthologies of tales excerpted from medieval works in Latin. A publication deserving particular mention is his extensively annotated edition of 555 jocular tales that are attributed or related in one way or another to the Turkish trickster Nasreddin Hodja and his several alter egos in the Mediterranean world.[33] Moreover, drawing on his admirably wide reading, Wesselski published a considerable number of exemplary case studies exploring the historical developments of specific narratives.[34] Altogether, Wesselski's unequivocal advocacy for the pivotal, although not necessarily exclusive, role of written sources for a given tale's permanence in tradition had a strong impact on subsequent research that still today awaits its due recognition.[35] Another important contribution to be mentioned is Hungarian scholar Bernhard Heller's (1871–1943)[36] comprehensive survey of "Arab fairy tales" in the fourth volume of the "Annotations to the Grimm Brothers' Children's and Household Tales," compiled and edited by German scholar Johannes Bolte and his Czech colleague Georg (Jiří) Polívka,[37] later supplemented by the same scholar's survey of "Arabic motifs in German fairy tales and fairy-tale compilations."[38] Today, the general awareness of folklorist scholars about the "Oriental" components of European narrative tradition is prominently attested by the fact that American folklorist Stith Thompson (1885–1976)[39] included references to both Chauvin and Basset in his *Motif-Index of Folk-Literature* (1955–58)[40] and his revised edition of the English translation of Antti Aarne's *The Types of the Folktale* (1961),[41] two of the major reference works of comparative folk narrative research. Some thirty years ago, Lidzbarski's "Desideratum" inspired my two-volume study *Arabia ridens* (1992), a comprehensive comparative discussion of short jocular prose tales attested in classical Arabic literature before the sack of Baghdad by the Mongol conquerors and the extinction of the Abbasid caliphate (1258).[42] Introduced by an assessment of the relevant Arabic source material and its study, the first volume of *Arabia ridens* surveys the impact jocular tales attested in classical Arabic literature had on the Arabic, Persian, Asian, and European literatures. The study concludes with a chapter discussing theoretical aspects of tradition, in particular the substantiated assumption that traveling tales need to adapt to the changing cultural contexts in which they are performed in order to be appreciated by the respective audiences and thus stay alive in tradition. The work's second volume presents summaries of altogether 1,247 short jocular narratives together with their documentation in several thousand single versions. It is a matter of course that my present work is heavily indebted to the data I formerly assembled for *Arabia ridens*.

Orientalist expertise was a major cornerstone of the Göttingen-based *Enzyklopädie des Märchens*, a handbook of historical and comparative folk narrative research, published in 15 volumes under the auspices of the Göttingen Academy of Humanities and Sciences from 1975 to 2015. Originally, this expertise was supplied by the prominent scholar of Islamic studies Otto Spies (1901–81).[43] From the very beginning of this major encyclopedic enterprise, Spies suggested entries for the list of the encyclopedia's subject headings. Later he contributed a number of important surveys such as sections of the entry on Egyptian narrative tradition,[44] the comprehensive entry on narrative themes, motifs, and tales in Arabic-Islamic tradition,[45] and the entry on tales in Arabic zoographer al-Damīrī's fifteenth-century encyclopedia *Ḥayāt al-ḥayawān* (The Life of Animals).[46] After Spies's demise in 1981, I joined the editorial team of the encyclopedia in 1986, from then on both editing and contributing myself a considerable number of entries relating to or dealing with the narrative culture of the Muslim world. Since 1995, Egyptian American folklorist Hasan El-Shamy published several catalogues assessing folktales from Arabic tradition according to the international systems of both motif and tale-type classification,[47] thus supplying additional data for studying the relations between "Oriental" and Western traditions. El-Shamy's work complements the assessment of tale types and motifs in Middle Eastern Muslim traditions as presented for modern Turkish[48] and Persian[49] folklore that is soon to be rounded off by a tale-type index for Kurdish narrative tradition.[50] Several tale-type and motif indexes assess Jewish-Oriental narrative lore that, although specific in its kind, is also relevant for a comprehensive study of the region's Muslim narrative heritage.[51] Of particular relevance for the current research project are also the contributions by scholars of Spanish narrative literature such as Fernando de la Granja,[52] Maxime Chevalier,[53] or María Jesús Lacarra Ducay,[54] most of which have rarely been taken into account in international comparative folklorist research.

Methodology of the Present Study

The 101 tales discussed here correspond to international tale types, and the arrangement of the relevant essays follows the numerical arrangement of ATU (Aarne, Thompson, and Uther), the third and most recent revision of the international tale-type index.[55] Without entering into the methodological debates about the system's usefulness or its shortcomings, the tale-type system is here applied for purely pragmatic reasons. Each tale type is more or less unambiguously identified by a number essentially ranging between 1 and 2400. Tale types 1–299 denote animal tales, 300–749 tales of magic, 750–849 religious tales, 850–999 realistic tales, 1000–1199 tales of the stupid ogre, 1200–1999 anecdotes and jokes, and 2000–2399 formula tales. By referring to a given tale's number in the international tale-type catalogue or, for that matter, any regional catalogue applying the same system, interested readers gain access to a wealth of comparative references that, once identified and verified, further flesh out a tale's role in historical and modern tradition. In the present work, the distribution of tale types and genres results from the assessment of the available data and not from ideological or methodological preference. About two thirds of the "Oriental" tales that exercised a noticeable impact on Western narrative tradition pertain to the genre of jocular prose. Rather than simply constituting "laughing matter," many, if not most, of these tales imply a "serious" message of an instructive or edifying intent, although the message might be as simple and straightforward as warning the audience against a character's overt gullibility or silliness. Even so, the genre's overwhelming dominance demonstrates that short jocular prose narratives constituted a favorite genre of traditional Arabic, and by extension, Muslim narrative culture.[56] Like anecdotes and jokes, the short genre of animal tales or fables was also widely appreciated in the traditional Muslim literatures. But as most "Oriental" narratives of this genre either originate from Greek or Indo-Persian antiquity[57] or were simply never recorded from Western oral performance, they are not considered here in detail. Internationally documented narratives pertaining to the categories of "tales of magic" or "realistic tales," on the other hand, constitute a comparatively rare phenomenon in classical Arabic literature, and most of the instances discussed here were transmitted to the West at a relatively late date, either by way of the late fourteenth- or fifteenth-century Ottoman Turkish collection of Persian origin, *Ferec ba'd eş-şidde* (Relief after Hardship), or through their inclusion in the final volumes of Antoine Galland's *Mille et une nuit*, being adapted from the early eighteenth-century performance of the talented Syrian Christian narrator Ḥannā Diyāb. Jocular tales of "Oriental," and most often of Arabic origin, on the other hand, were often transmitted to Western tradition in the Middle Ages or early modernity, and the originally Latin texts were later adapted to chapbooks in the European vernaculars from whence they potentially passed on to oral tradition.

As mentioned above, the historical discussion of a given tale's tradition focuses on the tale's appearance in reliably documented written sources. This is, however, never meant to exclude the possibility of the tale's transmission by way of oral tradition, as many authors might not have adapted their tales directly from a written source available to them but might rather have written down a text they heard orally. In the medieval Muslim cultures, tales were often told in learned gatherings, and the content of previously published books was, as a rule, learned by heart before the original author would grant his permission to pass the book's content on. When medieval European authors such as Jacques de Vitry claim to have heard a given tale, their statement might mirror actual circumstances, as this particular author resided in the Eastern Mediterranean for many years and likely came into contact with local tradition bearers. At the same time, and particularly during the Romantic period, a European author's claims of relying on an oral performance often served to authenticate a given tale as originating from a supposedly unspoiled and pure "folk" tradition. Even in written tradition, a given tale is rarely cited in exactly the same wording, and it is virtually impossible to decide whether an author changed the wording himself or whether he relied on a single oral intermediary or a chain of oral intermediaries. As the historical transmission of a given tale by oral tradition can neither be verified nor excluded for sure, a tale's occurrence in written sources constitutes the historically only verifiable instance. Although I have explicitly endeavored to take this feature into account in some of the essays, its lacking mention in other essays is thus not meant to indicate a bias against a given tale's potentially existing transmission by oral tradition.

The 101 essays essentially follow a common structure that varies only occasionally. An essay usually begins with the discussion of a tale's occurrence in Western oral tradition, mentioning the tale-type number and title and assessing in detail a representative selection of the recorded versions from a variety of regions. For reasons of space, the discussion is never intended to be as exhaustive as focused studies such as the relevant entries in the *Enzyklopädie des Märchens*, cited in the notes, would aim to be. The tale's introduction is followed by a condensed summary of its historical dimension, at the very least mentioning the tale's earliest appearance in Western written tradition, but often also listing its most important verifiable potential instances of transmission to oral tradition. Having concluded a tale's discussion in Western sources, the essay would turn to "Oriental" tradition, most often initially referring to the tale's oldest documented occurrence in the Arabic, Persian, or Ottoman Turkish traditions. Since a tale's oldest occurrence is not necessarily the one that was transmitted to the West, the ensuing discussion details the tale's citations in subsequent sources, if any, again in Arabic, Persian, and Ottoman Turkish. If tales are known to exist in ancient Indian or Greek sources, the relevant versions are at least mentioned and, sometimes, discussed in detail. Although the interface between "Oriental" and Western tradition can at times be pinned down with relative certainty, particularly in the case of narratives appearing in early Andalusian tradition, I usually prefer to refrain from hypothesizing about direct adaptations, mainly for two reasons. First, it is futile to speculate from which "Oriental" work a given European author adapted a specific narrative, as not a single author would mention his sources. And second, any additional source identified in the future might add to the present findings, detailed as they are, by suggesting other and more specific instances of transmission. As the "Oriental" literatures in question have not been explored to a satisfactory extent, new findings are bound to change and detail the picture at any time. What should become clear when reading through the essays, is the fact that the Middle Ages and early modernity were periods of intensive cultural exchange during which Western authors time and again had recourse to "Oriental" narratives that they adapted to the specific requirements of their own cultural context. As the implications of the tales' history and dissemination are often the same, I equally refrained from adding repetitive statements, at times rather preferring to discuss some of the tale's striking features.

As practical advice, the present book is not necessarily meant to be read from cover to cover in one go. Readers might prefer to browse through the essays by title or topic, or else directly look up the information they need by way of the indexes. Since each of the essays constitutes an independent unit, the notes to every essay contain full bibliographical information, to spare readers the effort of having to flip back and forth between the text and the cumulative bibliography at the end of the book.

Sources of the Present Study

The main body of Middle Eastern sources assessed here consists of works in Arabic, Persian, and Ottoman Turkish. First and foremost, the data pertain to classical and postclassical or premodern Arabic literature. For a nonspecialist Western audience, it might be useful to note that the specification of periods commonly identified for the literatures of the Muslim world does not correspond to the one they might be used to from historical studies of the Western cultures. The history of Arabic literature is conventionally divided into three periods. It starts with a classical period from the early days of written literature after the advent of Islam at the beginning of the seventh century CE to the downfall of the Abbasid caliphate in the middle of the thirteenth century. This is followed by an intermediary period often labeled as postclassical or premodern and mainly comprising the literatures of the Mamluk and Ottoman periods, that is, the periods from the middle of the thirteenth to the beginning of the sixteenth and roughly from the fourteenth to the end of the eighteenth centuries.[58] In older scholarship, this intermediary period is at times equated with the Middle Ages. But while the European Middle Ages are usually seen as a period of stagnation and decline that was only resolved with Renaissance and Enlightenment, the intermediary period of Arabic literature is characterized by a vibrant production.[59] Although many of the works written during the intermediary period might justly be critiqued for citing, compiling, and rearranging material from the classical period, many of them are quite original. Moreover, many works hold a special value for preserving material from the classical period that is otherwise lost. The third and modern period of Arabic literature, largely irrelevant for the present topic, conventionally begins at the end of the eighteenth century when Napoleon's Egyptian expedition ushered in a new period of cultural exchange with Western concepts and ideas.

From the beginning of Arabic literature, narratives played a crucial role in a genre that is conventionally termed *adab* literature, a term that translates best as "belles-lettres."[60] Originally, the term *adab* means "proper behavior," and thus *adab* literature implies a literature whose knowledge is desirable, useful, and necessary to participate in a learned discussion in an educated manner while displaying a supreme command of all kinds of subjects, including suitable narratives to illustrate one's point. As Robert Irwin recently put it, *adab* literature "provided the sort of information that could inform a civilized conversation over dinner."[61] For the present purpose, *adab* literature constitutes a literary genre that aims to both instruct and entertain, at all times employing narratives to substantiate its arguments while at the same time consciously avoiding a focus on narratives as an end in itself. To a certain extent, the genre is ruled by the

Arabic equivalent of the Horacian device *prodesse et delectare* that essentially calls for a suitable mixture of instruction and entertainment. Rendered in Arabic as *al-jidd wa-'l-hazl* (earnestness and jocularity),[62] the principle is succinctly expressed by twelfth-century author Ibn al-Jawzī (d. 1201) who justified his compilations of anecdotes and jokes by arguing, "The mind (*nafs*) tends to get annoyed when staying earnest for too long, and it delights in admissible pastime (*al-mubāḥ min al-lahw*)."[63] As the general audience will not necessarily be acquainted with the Arabic, Persian, and Ottoman Turkish works quoted in the essays, the following passages outline the phenomenon, highlighting some of the authors and works that are most relevant for the present considerations. In the age of the Internet, interested readers will easily manage to find general information about all of the quoted authors, and standard reference works such as the *Encyclopedia of Arabic Literature* offer quick and reliable information.[64]

The most important early representative of *adab* literature is polymath ʿAmr ibn Baḥr al-Jāḥiẓ (d. 868), one of the highly versatile authors of classical Arabic literature. His magnum opus, the *Kitāb al-Ḥayawān* (Book of Animals), not only "assembles all sorts of curious, instructive and entertaining information about the animal kingdom" but also serves "the fundamental aim of demonstrating the uniqueness of man as a moral being endowed with free will."[65] Al-Jāḥiẓ's book on misers and mendicants, *al-Bukhalā'*, belongs to a popular subgenre of *adab* literature whose representatives deal with stereotypical characters or professions. Also pertaining to the early stages of *adab* literature are Abū Muḥammad ʿAbdallāh ibn Muslim Ibn Qutayba al-Dīnawarī's (d. 889) *ʿUyūn al-akhbār* (Quintessential Reports) and Andalusian author Abū ʿUmar Aḥmad ibn Muḥammad Ibn ʿAbd Rabbih's (d. 940) *al-ʿIqd al-farīd* (The Unique Necklace). The latter author is particularly relevant as a potential intermediary to later Western tradition, as some of his narratives were later adapted in the work of Andalusian author Abū Bakr ibn ʿĀṣim al-Gharnāṭī ("from Granada;" d. 1426), *Ḥadā'iq al-azāhir* (Flower Gardens).[66]

About a third of the jocular tales presently surveyed find an early attestation in Abū Saʿd Manṣūr ibn al-Ḥusayn al-Ābī's (d. 1030) *Nathr al-durr*. Whereas the word *durr* means "pearls," the term *nathr* can be translated either as a "scattering" or as denoting the genre of prose (as opposed to *naẓm* or poetry). The title can thus be translated both as "The Scattering of Pearls," (implying the presentation of a generous selection of exquisite narratives) or "The Prose of Pearls," (implying a selection of prose narratives, in contrast to verse narratives). With a certain poetic license, I render the title as "Pearls of Prose." Al-Ābī's compilation is a most unusual work of classical Arabic literature as it is a veritable encyclopedia of anecdotes and jokes comprising thousands of items in its seven volumes.[67] The narratives are presented without any comment or interpretation. The book's chapters vaguely follow a chronological arrangement, ranging from the basic principles of Muslim religion and the early days of Islam via the Omayyad (661–744) and Abbasid (since 750) dynasties to general topics, such as women (vol. 4), extraordinary characters of Muslim history (vol. 5), and Bedouins (vol. 6). Whereas the author usually starts by discussing "serious" topics, toward the end of each volume and even more so in the later volumes of his compilation, he takes pleasure in jocular tales and does not shy away from embracing even disputed or morally objectionable topics, as in the chapters on extramarital sexual activities (bk. 4, ch. 10), male prostitutes, transvestites, and homosexuals (bk. 5, ch. 14–16), or loud and silent farters (bk. 6, ch. 16). Altogether, al-Ābī's encyclopedia is an often highly amusing anecdotal cultural history of early Muslim society, and his exhaustive access to traditional narratives is matched by an equally fascinating tolerance for the many facets of human life. In addition to documenting thousands of anecdotes from Arabic tradition, al-Ābī's encyclopedic compilation also constitutes a potential intermediary to Christian "Oriental" tradition, as a selection of its tales was adapted to Syriac Christian literature in the *Laughable Stories* compiled by Grīgōr Abū 'l-Faraj Bar ʿEḇrāya (d. 1286), better known as Bar Hebraeus or in Latin Abulpharagius, the *maphrian* or deputy of the Jacobite church's patriarch.[68] The degree to which Bar Hebraeus's adaptation of al-Ābī's compilation impacted subsequent Christian tradition in general appears to be, however, limited.

Similarly wide reaching, and to some extent overlapping with al-Ābī's work are Abū Ḥayyān al-Tawḥīdī's (d. 1023), *al-Baṣāʾir wa-'l-dhakhāʾir* (Deep Insights and Treasures), al-Ḥusayn ibn Muḥammad al-Rāghib al-Iṣfahānī's (d. 1108) *Muḥāḍarāt al-udabāʾ* (Conversations of the Educated), Maḥmūd ibn ʿUmar al-Zamakhsharī's (d. 1144) *Rabīʿ al-abrār* (Spring of the Pious), and Muḥammad ibn al-Ḥasan Ibn Ḥamdūn's (d. 1167) *al-Tadhkira al-ḥamdūniyya* (The Aide-Mémoire [by Ibn Ḥamdūn]). Toward the end of the twelfth century, the principle of *al-jidd wa-'l-hazl* increasingly degenerated into a lip service, as the historian and preacher Abū 'l-Faraj ʿAbd al-Raḥmān ibn ʿAlī Ibn al-Jawzī (d. 1201) compiled his three relatively short books of anecdotes and jokes, *Akhbār al-Adhkiyāʾ* (Tales of Clever People), *Akhbār al-Ḥamqā wa-'l-mughaffalīn* (Tales of Stupid and Silly People), and *Akhbār al-Ẓirāf wa-'l-mutamājinīn* (Tales of Subtle People and Jesters).[69] Although justifying his anecdotal approach by detailed introductions in which he would, for instance, theorize about the creator's wisdom in distributing mental capacities in dramatically differing ways, Ibn al-Jawzī's compilations are the earliest examples of outright jestbooks in Arabic, equaling in scope and hilarity both the ancient Greek *Philogelos* and the early modern European jestbooks. In the postclassical period, Shihāb al-Dīn Aḥmad ibn ʿAbd al-Wahhāb al-Nuwayrī's (d. 1332) comprehensive *Nihāyat al-arab fī funūn al-adab* (The Ultimate Ambition in the Arts of Erudition)[70] contains a considerable number of jocular narratives, as does Shihāb al-Dīn Muḥammad ibn Aḥmad al-Ibshīhī's fifteenth-century encyclopedia of all kinds of knowledge an educated person should command, *al-Mustaṭraf fī kull fann mustaẓraf* (The Exquisite Elements from Every Art Considered Elegant).[71] The position of al-Ibshīhī's work for mediating data from classical literature to subsequent tradition is particularly prominent, as it served as a kind of "Hausbuch" until quite recently, at times constituting a household's only available book besides the Koran. In the seventeenth century, Muḥammad ibn Aḥmad ibn (al-)Ilyās al-Ḥanafī's *Nuzhat al-udabā'* (Entertainment of the Educated) is another veritable jokebook whose sometimes fairly coarse contents require a conscious effort to appreciate them against the backdrop of the book's contemporary cultural context, that of the Ottoman period.[72]

Although *adab* literature supplied the bulk of the material studied here, numerous works of other genres of Arabic literature were considered whenever pertinent to the historical discussion. These include, to mention but a few, collections of proverbs and related tales such as those by al-Mufaḍḍal ibn Salama (d. after 903) and al-Maydānī (d. 1124); historical works such as al-Ṭabarī's (d. 923) *Tārīkh al-rusul wa-'l-mulūk* (History of the Prophets and Kings), al-Mas'ūdī's (d. 956) *Murūj al-dhahab wa-ma'ādin al-jawhar* (The Meadows of Gold and Mines of Gems), or Ibn 'Asakir's (d. 1176) *Tārīkh madīnat Dimashq* (History of the City of Damascus); al-Tha'labī's (d. 1038) and al-Kisā'ī's (12th c.) collections of *Qiṣaṣ al-anbiyā'* (Tales of the Prophets); theologian, philosopher, and mystic al-Ghazzālī's (d. 1111) magnum opus *Iḥyā' 'ulūm al-dīn* (The Revival of the Religious Sciences); al-Qazwīnī's (d. 1286) cosmography *'Ajā'ib al-makhlūqāt* (The Wonders of Creation) and other works of a geographical nature; the biographical dictionaries compiled by Ibn Khallikān (d. 1282), Ibn Shākir al-Kutubī (d. 1361), or al-Ṣafadī (d. 1363); and al-Damīrī's (d. 1405) zoographical encyclopedia *Ḥayāt al-ḥayawān* (The Life of Animals), the latter work constituting an influential composition until the modern period. In short, wherever relevant narratives were to be found, I aim to mention and document them in translations from the original language.

As might be imagined, a substantial quantity of narratives in Western tradition were mediated by or are, at least, also attested in that famous Arabic collection of tales, *Alf layla wa-layla* (The Thousand and One Nights), that was introduced to Western and world literature by way of its adapted French translation prepared by Antoine Galland at the beginning of the eighteenth century. In terms of global impact second only to the Bible, *The Thousand and One Nights* barely needs an introduction here, as the work's history and content can easily be accessed in a number of comprehensive reference works.[73] As a monumental compendium of all kinds of tales, the Arabic *Nights* draw on the repertoire of older narrative traditions, including those of Greece, India, and Persia as well as Jewish lore. In several cases, the impact of the *Nights* on Western tradition predates Galland, but it was Galland's adapted and enlarged translation of the *Nights'* oldest surviving manuscript, dating from the fifteenth century, that inspired Western and international tradition, both written and oral, beyond comparison. In addition to some of the tales in the work's Arabic manuscript tradition, tales from the *Nights* that strongly impacted Western tradition are mainly those Galland introduced as adapted from the oral storytelling of young Syrian Christian Ḥannā Diyāb. It is this talented storyteller to whom Galland owed the collection's world-famous tales of Aladdin and Ali Baba, both of which in popular perception came to be regarded as the acme of "Oriental" storytelling. Galland never acknowledged Ḥannā Diyāb's contribution to his success in public, and the true dimensions of the narrator's role and qualification as the most influential early modern storyteller and as an artist in his own right are only recently being explored in detail.[74]

Second in importance is Persian literature for which Jan Rypka's *History of Iranian Literature* offers comprehensive surveys.[75] Although the Persian cradle of *The Thousand and One Nights* dating from before the ninth century, the *Hezār afsān* (A Thousand Tales of Magic), is irretrievably lost, the recently (re-)discovered *Munes-nāme* (The Book as an Intimate Friend), compiled by a certain Abu Bakr ibn Khosrow al-Ostād around the year 1200[76] offers an equally influential compilation of fantastic tales, even though their impact on Western tradition relates to the work's late fourteenth- or fifteenth-century Ottoman Turkish adaptation *Ferec ba'd eş-şidde* (Relief after Hardship).[77] In its regional context, the *Munes-nāme* resulted in numerous anonymous adaptations in Persian commonly known under the generic label *Jāme' al-ḥekāyāt* (Collection of Stories) that served to disseminate its stories in Iran as well as Middle and South Asia. Persian literature is also the cradle of the *Sendbād-nāme* (Book of Sendbād) whose European adaptations feature as the tradition of *The Seven Sages*.[78] Fictional tales of the marvelous and the strange are also contained in the early Persian adaptations of the Indian Sanskrit *Śukasaptati* (Seventy [Tales of a] Parrot), the *Javāher al-asmār* (Jewels of Evening Tales), written in 1314 by a certain 'Emād ibn Moḥammad, and Żiyā' al-Din Nakhshabi's (d. 1350) *Ṭuṭi-nāme* (Book of the Parrot). In addition to tales of Persian or Indian origin, Persian literature also excels in the creative adaptation of anecdotes and jokes from Arabic literature, as evidenced particularly in the works of the Persian mystical poets, Farid al-Din 'Aṭṭār (d. 1221)[79] and Jalāl al-Din Rumi (d. 1273). Compilations of anecdotes and jokes similar to those encountered in Arabic literature, and comprising a considerable amount of originally Arabic material, include Sadid al-Din Moḥammad 'Awfi's (d. ca. 1232) *Javāme' al-ḥekāyāt* (Collections of Stories), a compilation that comprises more than 2,100 single items,[80] and Fakhr al-Din 'Ali Ṣafi's (d. 1532) *Laṭā'ef al-ṭavā'ef* (Jocular Tales from the Various Strata of Society).

The Ottoman and modern Turkish literatures are mainly relevant here as mediating narratives from Persian and Arabic literature that, resulting from many centuries of Ottoman dominion, exercised a particular impact on Balkan tradition. On a wider international scale, several tales from the *Ferec ba'd eş-şidde*, largely adapted from the Persian *Munes-nāme*, were introduced to European tradition by way of François Pétis de la Croix's *Les Mille et un jours* (The Thousand and One Days; 1710–12).[81] The attribution of numerous anecdotes and jokes to the main protagonist of Turkish jocular prose, Nasreddin Hodja, supplied a powerful instance for mediating these items to Balkan and international tradition as they were adapted, translated, and published frequently in a fair variety of languages.[82] Documented since the sixteenth century, already the early Ottoman Turkish manuscript tradition of Nasreddin's jests integrates tales from Arabic tradition. In the compilations published in the nineteenth century, the repertoire of Nasreddin's stories was not only consciously merged with that of the Arabic jester Juḥā but also expanded by integrating tales from a variety of sources so that the originally quite limited repertoire of several dozen tales has since then been blown up to more than 1,600 jests attributed to Nasreddin,[83] documenting the character's function as a focusee of jocular prose[84] in the Turkish world and beyond.

Indian Sanskrit literature, although not of prime relevance here, is at times referred to as supplying the oldest documented occurrences of tales that were adapted to Persian literature, and sometimes to Arabic. Compilations mentioned several times include the Indian *Panchatantra* (Five [Books of] Wisdom), a mirror for princes whose lost Pahlavi (Middle Persian) translation served as the basis for Ibn al-Muqaffaʿ's early eighth-century Arabic *Kalīla wa-Dimna*, named after the two jackals that play a prominent role in the collection's frame tale. Mediated to the West by various influential adaptations in Hebrew and Latin, the fables and wisdom tales contained in that collection exercised a considerable impact on medieval and early modern European written tradition, although their lasting influence in Western oral tradition is limited. The tales of the equally anonymous *Śukasaptati* (Seventy [Tales of a] Parrot) mainly treat the wiles of women, as a lonely woman looks for ways to visit her lover but is warned by the parrot to consider the potential consequences of her action. The collection experienced two adaptations in fourteenth-century Persian literature, mentioned above. Eventually, tales from the collection were potentially mediated to the European literatures by way of the seventeenth-century Ottoman Turkish adaptation prepared by Sari ʿAbdallāh Efendi.[85] Second in influence only to the *Panchatantra* is Somadeva's eleventh-century *Kathāsaritsāgara* (The Ocean of Streams of Stories),[86] an extensive compilation of tales that to some extent derive from the ancient *Bṛhatkathā* (The Great Narrative). In addition to several jocular tales, the *Kathāsaritsāgara* is also relevant for some of the complex tales of wonder and magic.

"Oriental" Tales in Western Tradition

The reception of "Oriental" tales in Western tradition largely begins during the crusades, that is, in the twelfth and thirteenth centuries.[87] Early instances of reception are documented for the Latin works of clerics such as Jacques de Vitry (1160/70–1239/40),[88] Odo of Cheriton (ca. 1185–ca. 1246),[89] Stephen of Bourbon (1190/95–1261),[90] John Gobi (d. ca. 1350),[91] John Bromyard (14th c.),[92] or San Vicente Ferrer (1350–1419).[93] The *Disciplina clericalis* by Petrus Alfonsus (d. after 1121), an Andalusian author converted from Judaism to Christianity, is a major Latin instance credited with transmitting "Oriental" tales to the West,[94] here in the multicultural context during the *reconquista*, the Christian reconquest of Andalusia from the Arab and Berber Muslim conquerors that culminated with the vanquishing of the kingdom of Granada in 1492. Early compilations in the European vernacular languages drawing to a certain extent on "Oriental" tradition include the French genre of *lai*, such as those compiled by twelfth-century French author Marie de France,[95] and Chaucer's fourteenth-century *Canterbury Tales*.[96] In the late Middle Ages, some of the relevant tales are first encountered in the works of a number of Spanish and Italian authors, such as Don Juan Manuel's *El conde Lucanor* (1330–1335),[97] the anonymous *Cento novelle antiche*, compiled at the end of the thirteenth century,[98] or the works of Italian novelists Giovanni Boccaccio (1313–1375),[99] Franco Sacchetti (d. 1400),[100] or Giovanni Sercambi (1348–1424).[101] Numerous European authors of subsequent centuries, including Geoffrey Chaucer (d. 1400), William Shakespeare (1564–1616) and many other well-known authors, treat tales originating from "Oriental" tradition at times. Beginning with the sixteenth century, chapbooks in the European languages played a major role in mediating tales from written to oral tradition as they were distributed in previously unprecedented print-runs, reprints, and various editions. In English, a late popular representative of this genre is the chapbook *Joe Miller's Jests*, first published in 1739. From the eighteenth century onward, *The Thousand and One Nights* and the subsequent genre of "Oriental Miscellanies" opened a new window for the reception of "Oriental" narratives. In the nineteenth- and twentieth centuries newspapers, journals, calendars, and magazines functioned similarly to early modern chapbooks in disseminating popular narratives both on a national scale and internationally.

A detailed survey of the various sources and instances that contributed to the transmission of tales from "Oriental" tradition would be nothing short of a history of the European literatures, and the rough sketch given above barely indicates a few of the major or most popular instances. Exhaustive references for the transmission of specific tales are given in the relevant surveys, as each and every case has something special to offer, whether in terms of a tale's earliest attestations, regional or national reception, intensity of documentation, or media of transmission.

A necessary caveat in relation to the present study's comprehensiveness concerns the state of the art, that is, the scholarly exploration of European works of literary and written tradition with respect to the popular narratives they contain and potentially mediated to oral tradition. To name but a few prominent examples, German scholar Johannes Bolte (1858–1937) compiled a number of invaluable editions of early modern German chapbooks, usually including extensive comparative annotation;[102] Hungarian scholar Lajos György (1890–1950) authored a comprehensive study on the history and universal connections of jocular tales from Hungarian written tradition;[103] Romanian scholar Sabina Cornelia Stroescu (1912–1989) compiled an exhaustive catalogue of jocular tales in Romanian journals and magazines;[104] German-American scholar of German and Medieval literature, Frederic (Fritz) Christian Tubach (b. 1930) published an extensive survey of narratives in medieval Latin exempla literature;[105] for German tradition, Elfriede Moser-Rath (1926–1993), a long-term collaborator first of Kurt Ranke, and then of the *Enzyklopädie des Märchens*, compiled two admirably detailed studies, the first one concerning popular narratives in German compilations of sermons, and the second on chapbooks of the baroque period.[106] To the same extent as some areas of European popular narratives are thus historically well explored, numerous other areas have not been studied in detail or have, at best, been surveyed selectively, including chapbook literature in English, French, and many other European languages, and, on an almost international scale, newspapers and magazines. As the heyday of comparative folk narrative studies with its groundbreaking surveys appears to be over, much of the comparative work to be done for a truly comprehensive assessment of a given narrative's tradition relies on a scholar's scrutiny and sleuthing of individual sources, as the relatively easy access to comparative annotation in published surveys often only allows a glimpse at the top of the iceberg of tradition.

A Note on Oral Tradition

Since my study is exclusively concerned with tales from "Oriental" sources documented from Western oral tradition during the nineteenth and twentieth centuries, a short word on the underlying perception of oral tradition is in order. Oral tradition initially gained scholarly attention during the period of romanticism, that is, toward the end of the eighteenth and during the first half of the nineteenth century. Authors and scholars of the period were fascinated with oral tradition as they regarded it as the unspoiled and pure expression of "the folk" that had been preserved from times of old and that itself would preserve "original" and "authentic" cultural concepts.[107] In modern usage, the term "romantic" has gained the meaning of "characterized by, or suggestive of an idealized view of reality."[108] In the romantic period, this idealized view comprised the notion of the folk as a homogenous entity, a notion that relieved scholars studying and publishing tales collected from the oral performance of folk narrators from specifying their sources, as a tale would ideally be part of anonymous folk tradition and thus presumably be more or less the same regardless of which individual of the anonymous folk performed it. Narrators were regarded as simply being spokespersons of the folk, those who expressed folk tradition without having an agenda of their own. Twentieth-century scholarship, to the contrary, demonstrates beyond reasonable doubt that popular storytellers are artists in their own right, thus betraying the cultural arrogance of romantic scholars toward the creativity of the subaltern. Even so, and until today, popular audiences are quite satisfied enjoying the folktales of a specific region or country without being informed about the tales' performers. And still today, folk narrative scholars would often voice judgmental statements qualifying folktales as pure or "contaminated,"[109] as either originating from old and genuine oral traditions or otherwise constituting mere retellings from authored literature. With the exception of studies devoted to specific narrators,[110] folktales are rarely appreciated as the pieces of verbal art each and every performance constitutes, as each performance arises from the effort of the storyteller to the best of her or his capacities. Therefore, I explicitly mention the names and personal details of the individuals from whom the cited folktales were recorded, whenever this information has been published. Although folktales are commonly considered as originating from or residing in popular tradition and lacking identifiable authors, each folktale and each of its performances have a specific author, that is, the tale's performer. Folktales only originate from anonymous tradition insofar as researchers consciously make them anonymous by denying their authors the right to be identified as what they are—the individual creators or performers of traditional tales in their own right. By excluding the narrators' names, one denies them not only individuality and an agenda of their own, but even their sheer existence. Rather than merely being a matter of style whether we allow folktales to be quoted and published anonymously, it is a matter of respect to give due credit to the tales' original performers, at least as much as the available data permit.

Acknowledgments

This book draws on the author's forty years of occupation with the Muslim world's narrative culture, both in its regional context and its impact on European and world tradition. More than my own humble efforts, it is indebted to those *qui ante nos in mundo fuere*. Above all, it rests on the shoulders of the numerous scholars of folk narrative research and comparative literature who devoted their time to exploring specific compilations, narratives, or narrative traditions. This book would not have been possible without my three decades of editorial work at the Göttingen *Enzyklopädie des Märchens* that strengthened my expertise for comparative folk narrative studies. The assessment of the tales' European dimension owes much to the institution's specialized library and its archives that contain hundreds of thousands of easily retrievable photocopied texts arranged according to the international tale-type system. Moreover, the short surveys of a given tale's history in my work are often much indebted to the studies of specific tales and narrative traditions published in the encyclopedia's entries. In addition to the comprehensive holdings of the Göttingen libraries and the generous services of the German interlibrary loan system, the tremendous wealth of scanned texts available on the Internet enabled me to assess and verify a great number of references with comparatively manageable effort.

In terms of collaboration with other colleagues in the field, I am particularly grateful to the two international colleagues who accompanied the present project from its beginning, Aboubakr Chraïbi and María Jesús Lacarra Ducay, both of whom contributed valuable advice. Special thanks are due to Margaret Mills, who read, edited, and critiqued all of the book's text with untiring efforts, occasionally adding encouraging remarks and always reminding me not to fall into the trap of forgetting to acknowledge the potential role of oral tradition. During our regular cordial meetings, Joachim Strube's patient endurance of my infatuation reassured me that my work might also be useful for a non-specialist audience. Various other colleagues assisted with advice or critique over time, including Helga Anetshofer-Karateke, Nasrin Askari, Cristina Bacchilega, Dan Ben-Amos, Regina Bendix, Lina Būgienė, Mustafa Duman, Valdimar Hafstein, Don Haase, Bill Hansen, Lauri Harvilahti, Galit Hasan-Rokem, Barbara Hillers, Aurélie Houdebert, Robert Irwin, Moḥammad Jaʿfari Qanavāti, Heda Jason, Rella Kushelevsky, Kai Lämmerhirt, Amir Lerner, Desirée López Bernal, Patricia Lysaght, Wolfgang Mieder, Shahnaz Nadjmabadi, Sadhana Naithani, Dorothy Noyes, Mahmoud Omidsalar, Marilena Papachristophorou, José Manuel Pedrosa, Ravshan Rahmoni, Joseph Sadan, Gregor Schoeler, John Shaw, Rósa Þorsteinsdóttir, Roberto Tottoli, David Wacks, Romina Werth, and Annette Zgoll. It should not be left unmentioned that my work owes some of its inspiration to William F. Hansen's now classical *Ariadne's Thread: A Guide to International Tales Found in Classical Literature* (2002). For three years, the Deutsche Forschungsgemeinschaft funded my position in the framework of my research project "The Orient Within: Narratives from the Muslim World in Western Oral Tradition," enabling me to research and write in relaxed economic conditions. The Academy of Sciences and Humanities at Göttingen, under whose auspices I had been working for the *Enzyklopädie des Märchens* for almost three decades, took care of the project's administrative dimension. Graduate research assistant Barbara Danti worked with the project for some time, enabling me to focus on the actual research questions. My gratitude also extends to the staff of Wayne State University Press and its collaborators for their efforts in publishing the present book. Donald Haase kindly agreed to include my work in his "Series in Fairy-Tales Studies," while acquisitions editor Marie Sweetman and editorial, design, and production manager Kristin Harpster saw the book through the production process. I would also like to acknowledge my appreciation to the three anonymous readers whose supportive comments and suggestions helped to make the book better. While I sincerely appreciate the share these individuals and institutions have in the project's successful completion, all remaining mistakes and shortcomings are my own.

My wife, Michaela Fenske, herself an established scholar of European Ethnology, served as my audience and critic at all times. It is to her that I affectionately dedicate the results of my occupation with the Western world's Middle Eastern narrative heritage.

Notes

1. References in the following are often to the entries in the German language *Enzyklopädie des Märchens.* Although the entries in the encyclopedia's first volumes are somewhat dated, all of them focus on the narrative aspects of the authors or works concerned that are most relevant for the present context. Whenever necessary, more recent studies are listed.

2. Köhler, Ines, and Rudolf Schenda, "Alexander der Große," in *Enzyklopädie des Märchens,* vol. 1 (1977), cols. 272–291.

3. Grotzfeld, Heinz and Sophia, and Ulrich Marzolph, "Kalila und Dimna," ibid., vol. 7 (1993), cols. 888–895; Falk, Harry, "Pañcatantra(m)," ibid., vol. 10 (2002), cols. 497–505; Kühne, Udo, "Johannes von Capua," ibid., vol. 7 (1993), cols. 580–583.

4. Lundt, Bea, "Sieben weise Meister," ibid., vol. 12 (2008), cols. 654–660.

5. Lacarra Ducay, María Jesús, "Petrus Alfonsus," ibid., vol. 10 (2002), cols. 797–802.

6. Irwin, Robert, *The Arabian Nights: A Companion,* London: Allen Lane, 1994; Marzolph, Ulrich, and Richard van Leeuwen, *The Arabian Nights Encyclopedia,* 2 vols., Santa Barbara: ABC-Clio, 2004.

7. Marzolph, Ulrich, *Relief after Hardship: The Ottoman Turkish Model for* The Thousand and One Days, Detroit: Wayne State University Press, 2017.

8. Tenberg, Reinhard, "Kreuzzüge," in *Enzyklopädie des Märchens,* vol. 8 (1996), cols. 413–419.

9. Ranelagh, Elaine L., *The Past We Share: The Near Eastern Ancestry of Western Folk Literature,* London: Quartet, 1979; Stohlmann, Jürgen, "Orient-Motive in der lateinischen Exempla-Literatur des 12. und 13. Jahrhunderts," in Zimmermann, Alfred, and Ingrid Craemer-Ruegenberg, eds., *Orientalische Kultur und lateinisches Mittelalter,* Berlin: De Gruyter, 1985, pp. 123–150.

10. Duggan, Anne E., "Oriental Tales," in Duggan and Donald Haase, eds., *Folktales and Fairy Tales: Traditions and Texts from around the World,* vol. 2, Santa Barbara: Greenwood, 2016, pp. 747–751; Marzolph, Ulrich, "The Literary Genre of 'Oriental Miscellany'," in Bauden, Frédéric, Aboubakr Chraïbi, and Antonella Ghersetti, eds., *Le Répertoire narratif arabe médiéval: transmission et ouverture,* Geneva: Droz, 2008, pp. 309–319.

11. Hillers, Barbara, "The Abbot of Druimenaig: Genderbending in Gaelic Tradition," *Proceedings of the Harvard Celtic Colloquium* 15 (1995), pp. 175–197; Ó Síocháin, Tadhg, *The Case of The Abbot of Drimnagh: A Medieval Irish Story of Sex-Change,* Cork: University College Cork, 2017.

12. Strömbäck, Dag, "En orientalisk saga i fornnordisk dräkt," in *Donum Grapeanum: festskrift tillägnad överbibliotekarien Anders Grape,* Uppsala: Almqvist & Wiksell, 1945, pp. 408–444; Strömbäck, "Uppsala, Iceland, and the Orient," in Brown, Arthur, and Peter Foote, eds., *Early English and Norse Studies Presented to Hugh Smith in Honour of His 60th Birthday,* London: Methuen, 1963, pp. 178–190; Mundt, Marina, *Zur Adaptation nordischer Bilder in den Fornaldarsögur Norðrlanda: Materialien zu einer neuen Dimension altnordischer Belletristik,* Frankfurt: Lang, 1993.

13. For comprehensive approaches to the lineages of narrative research history and attendant paradigms, see, e.g., Holbek, Bengt, *Interpretation of Fairy-Tales: Danish Folklore in a European Perspective,* Helsinki: Suomalainen Tiedeakatemia, 1987; Dégh, Linda, *Folktales and Society: Story-telling in a Hungarian Peasant Community,* Bloomington: Indiana

University Press, 1989; Niles, John D., *Homo narrans: The Poetics and Anthropology of Oral Literature*, Philadelphia: University of Pennsylvania Press, 1999; Merkel, Johannes, *Hören, Sehen, Staunen: Kulturgeschichte des mündlichen Erzählens*, Hildesheim: Olms, 2015.

14. From the vast body of literature on Said and Orientalism, I just refer to two of my favorites, Polaschegg, Andrea, *Der andere Orientalismus: Regeln deutsch-morgenländischer Imagination im 19. Jahrhundert*, Berlin: De Gruyter, 2005; Irwin, Robert, *For Lust of Knowing: The Orientalists and Their Enemies*, London: Allen Lane, 2006.

15. Marzolph, Ulrich, "Grimm Nights: Reflections on the Connections between the Grimms' 'Household Tales' and 'The Thousand and One Nights'," *Marvels & Tales* 28.1 (2014), pp. 75–87, 161–166.

16. Simson, Georg von, "Benfey, Theodor," in *Enzyklopädie des Märchens*, vol. 2 (1979), cols. 102–109; Belcher, Stephen, "Benfey, Theodor," in Duggan and Haase, eds., *Folktales and Fairy Tales*, vol. 1, p. 118.

17. Benfey, Theodor, *Pantschatantra: Fünf Bücher indischer Fabeln, Märchen und Erzählungen*, 2 vols., Leipzig 1859 (reprint Hildesheim: Olms, 1966).

18. Mehner, Maximilian, *Märchenhaftes Indien: Theodor Benfey, die indische Theorie und ihre Rezeption in der Märchenforschung*, Munich: Kirchheim, 2012.

19. Dorson, Richard M., *The British Folklorists: A History*, London 1968, pp. 257–265; Newall, Venetia, "Clouston, William Alexander," in *Enzyklopädie des Märchens*, vol. 3 (1981), cols. 79–80; Whittaker, Gareth, "William Alexander Clouston (1843–96), Folklorist: Introduction and Bibliography," *Folklore* 115.3 (204), pp. 348–362.

20. Clouston, William Alexander, *A Group of Eastern Romances and Stories from the Persian, Tamil, and Urdu*, Glasgow: privately printed, 1889; Clouston, *Flowers from a Persian Garden and Other Papers*, London: David Nutt, 1890; Clouston, *The Book of Noodles: Stories of Simpletons; or, Fools and Their Follies*, London: Elliot Stock, 1903; Clouston, *The Book of Sindibād; or The Story of the King, His Son, His Damsel, and the Seven Vazīrs: From the Persian and Arabic*, Glasgow: privately printed, 1884; Clouston, *Popular Tales and Fictions: Their Migrations and Transformations*, ed. Christine Goldberg, Santa Barbara: ABC-Clio, 2002.

21. Wehr, Hans, "Chauvin, Victor," in *Enzyklopädie des Märchens*, vol. 2 (1979), cols. 1268–1271.

22. Chauvin, Victor, *Bibliographie des ouvrages arabes ou relatifs aux arabes [...]*, 12 vols., Liège: H. Vaillant-Carmanne, and Leipzig: O. Harrassowitz, 1892–1922.

23. Lidzbarski, Mark, "Ein Desideratum," *Der Islam* 8 (1918), pp. 300–301.

24. Lacoste-Dujardin, Camille, "Basset, René," in *Enzyklopädie des Märchens*, vol. 1 (1977), cols. 1319–1322.

25. Basset, René, *Mille et un contes, récits et légendes arabes*, Paris: Maisonneuve, 1924; ibid., ed. Aboubakr Chraïbi, 2 vols., Paris: Corti, 2005 (previously published in 3 vols., Paris: Maisonneuve, 1924–26).

26. Rausmaa, Pirkko-Liisa, "Aarne, Antti Amatus," in *Enzyklopädie des Märchens*, vol. 1 (1977), cols. 1–4; Apu, Sato, "Aarne, Antti," in Duggan and Haase, eds., *Folktales and Fairy Tales*, vol. 1, pp. 1–2.

27. Aarne, Antti Amatus, *Verzeichnis der Märchentypen, mit Hülfe von Fachgenossen ausgearbeitet*, Helsinki: Suomalainen Tiedeakatemia, 1910.

28. Röhrich, Lutz, "Geographisch-historische Methode," in *Enzyklopädie des Märchens*, vol. 5 (1987), cols. 1012–1030; Apu, Sato, "Historic-Geographic Method," in Duggan

and Haase, eds., *Folktales and Fairy Tales*, vol. 2, pp. 453–455; Boden, Doris, "Urform," in *Enzyklopädie des Märchens*, vol. 13 (2011), cols. 1259–1262.

29. Ranke, Kurt, "Anderson, Walter," in *Enzyklopädie des Märchens*, vol. 1 (1977), cols. 493–494.

30. Oestrup, Johannes, "Alf laila wa-laila," in *Encyclopaedia of Islam*, vol. 1, Leiden: Brill, 1913, pp. 252–256, at p. 252.

31. Littmann, Enno, "Alf laila wa-laila," in *Encyclopaedia of Islam*, 2nd ed., vol. 1, Leiden: Brill, 1960, pp. 358–364, at p. 358.

32. Marzolph, Ulrich, "Wesselski, Albert," in *Enzyklopädie des Märchens*, vol. 14 (2014), cols. 652–656; Marzolph, "Wesselski, Albert," in Duggan and Haase, eds., *Folktales and Fairy Tales*, vol. 3, pp. 1100–1101.

33. Wesselski, Albert, *Der Hodscha Nasreddin*, 2 vols., Weimar: Duncker, 1911.

34. Wesselski, Albert, *Erlesenes*, Prague: Gesellschaft Deutscher Bücherfreunde in Böhmen, 1928.

35. Kiefer, Emma Emily, *Albert Wesselski and Recent Folktale Theories*, Bloomington: Indiana University Press, 1947.

36. Fröhlich, Ida, "Heller, Bernhard," in *Enzyklopädie des Märchens*, vol. 6 (1990), cols. 799–802.

37. Heller, Bernhard, "Das hebräische und arabische Märchen," in *Anmerkungen zu den Kinder- und Hausmärchen der Brüder Grimm*. ed. Johannes Bolte and Georg Polívka, 2nd ed., vol. 4, Leipzig: Dietrich, 1929 (reprint Hildesheim: Olms, 1963), pp. 315–418.

38. Heller, Bernhard, "Arabische Motive in deutschen Märchen und Märchendichtungen," in *Handwörterbuch des deutschen Märchens*, ed. Lutz Mackensen, vol. 1. Berlin: De Gruyter, 1930, pp. 93–108.

39. Goldberg, Christine, "Thompson, Stith," in *Enzyklopädie des Märchens*, vol. 13 (2010), cols. 515–519.

40. Thompson, Stith, *Motif-Index of Folk-Literature: A Classification of Narrative Elements in Folktales, Ballads, Myths, Fables, Mediaeval Romances, Exempla, Fabliaux, Jest-Books and Local Legends*, 6 vols. (Helsinki, 1932–1936), rev. and enl. ed. Copenhagen: Rosenkilde and Bagger, 1955–1958 (reprint Bloomington: Indiana University Press, 1965).

41. Aarne, Antti, *The Types of the Folktale: A Classification and Bibliography. Antti Aarne's Verzeichnis der Märchentypen (FF Communications No. 3) Translated and Enlarged*, ed. Stith Thompson, Helsinki: Suomalainen Tiedeakatemia, 1928; Aarne, *The Types of the Folktale: A Classification and Bibliography. Antti Aarne's Verzeichnis der Märchentypen (FF Communications No. 3) Translated and Enlarged*, ed. Stith Thompson, 2nd Revision, Helsinki: Suomalainen Tiedeakatemia, 1961.

42. Marzolph, Ulrich, *Arabia ridens: Die humoristische Kurzprosa der adab-Literatur im internationalen Traditionsgeflecht*, 2 vols., Frankfurt: Klostermann, 1992.

43. Marzolph, Ulrich, "Spies, Otto," in *Enzyklopädie des Märchens*, vol. 12 (2008), cols. 1048–1051.

44. Spies, Otto, and Nabila Salem, "Ägypten," ibid., vol. 1 (1977), cols. 175–227.

45. Spies, Otto, "Arabisch-islamische Erzählstoffe," ibid., vol. 1 (1977), cols. 685–718.

46. Spies, Otto, "Damīrī," ibid., vol. 3 (1981), cols. 219–223.

47. El-Shamy, Hasan, *Folk Traditions of the Arab World: A Guide to Motif Classification*, 2 vols. Bloomington: Indiana University Press, 1995; El-Shamy, *Types of the Folktales in*

the Arab World: A Demographically Oriented Tale-Type Index, Bloomington; Indiana University Press, 2004; El-Shamy, *A Motif-Index of "The Thousand and One Nights*," Bloomington: Indiana University Press, 2006; El-Shamy, *Motific Constituents of Arabic-Islamic Folk Tradition: A Cognitive Systemic Approach*, 2 vols., IUScholarWorks; https://scholarworks.iu.edu/dspace/handle/2022/20938; (accessed July 23, 2018).

48. Eberhard, Wolfram, and Pertev Naili Boratav, *Typen türkischer Volksmärchen*, Wiesbaden: Steiner, 1953.

49. Marzolph, Ulrich, *Typologie des persischen Volksmärchens*, Beirut: Deutsche Morgenländische Gesellschaft, 1984.

50. Amani, Mohammad Sina, *Typologie des kurdischen Volksmärchens*, PhD dissertation University of Göttingen (forthcoming).

51. Jason, Heda, "Types of Jewish-Oriental Tales," *Fabula* 1 (1964/1965), pp. 115–224; Jason, *Types of Oral Tales in Israel*, Jerusalem: Israel Ethnographic Society, 1975; Jason, *Folk Tales of the Jews of Iraq: Tale-Types and Genres*, Or-Yehuda: Babylonian Jewish Heritage Center, 1988; Haboucha, Reginetta, *Types and Motifs of the Judeo-Spanish Folktales*, New York: Garland, 1992; Soroudi, Sarah Sorour, *The Folktale of Jews from Iran, Central Asia and Afghanistan: Tale-Types and Genres*, Dortmund: Verlag für Orientkunde, 2008.

52. Granja, Fernando de la, *Precedentes y reminiscencias de la literatura y el folklore árabes en nuestro Siglo de Oro*, Madrid: Real Academia de la Historia, 1996.

53. Chevalier, Maxime, *Cuentos folklóricos en la España del Siglo de Oro*, Barcelona: Crítica, 1983; Chevalier, *Cuentecillos tradicionales en la España del Siglo de Oro*, Madrid: Gredos, 1975.

54. Lacarra Ducay, María Jesús, *Cuentos de la edad media*, Madrid: Castalia, 1986; Lacarra Ducay, *Cuento y novela corta en España*, Barcelona: Crítica, 1999; Lacarra Ducay, *Cuentos medievales: de Oriente a Occidente*, Madrid: Fundación José Antonio de Castro, 2016.

55. Uther, Hans-Jörg, *The Types of International Folktales: A Classification and Bibliography, Based on the System of Antti Aarne and Stith Thompson*, 3 vols., Helsinki: Suomalainen Tiedeakatemia, 2004.

56. Marzolph, Ulrich, "The Muslim Sense of Humor," in *Humour and Religion: Challenges and Ambiguities*, ed. H. Geybels and W. Van Herck, London: continuum, 2011, pp. 169–187.

57. Brockelmann, Carl, "Fabel und Tiermärchen in der älteren arabischen Literatur," *Islamica* 2 (1926), pp. 96–128; Rosenthal, Franz, "A Small Collection of Aesopic Fables in Arabic Translation," in Macuch, Maria, Christa Müller-Kessler, and Bert Fragner, eds., *Studia semitica necnon Iranica: Rudolpho Macuch septuagenario ab amicis et discipulis dedicata*, Wiesbaden: Harrassowitz, 1989, pp. 233–256; Marzolph, Ulrich, "Fable," in *Encyclopaedia of Islam*, 3rd ed., Leiden: Brill, 2016, fasc. 1, pp. 100–106.

58. Allen, Roger, and D.S. Richards, eds., *Arabic Literature in the Post-Classical Period* (*The Cambridge History of Arabic Literature*), Cambridge: Cambridge University Press, 2006.

59. See, e.g., Lowry, Joseph E., and Devin J. Stewart, eds., *Essays in Arabic Literary Biography, 1350–1850*, Wiesbaden: Harrassowitz, 2009.

60. Ashtiany, Julia, T.M. Johnstone, J.D. Latham, R.B. Serjeant, and G. Rex Smith, eds., *'Abbasid Belles-Lettres (The Cambridge History of Arabic Literature)*, Cambridge: Cambridge University Press, 1990.

61. Irwin, Robert, *Ibn Khaldun: An Intellectual Biography*, Princeton: Princeton University Press, 2018, p. 10.

62. Pellat, Charles, "Seriousness and Humour in Early Islam," *Islamic Studies* 3

(1963), pp. 353–362; Marzolph, Ulrich, "Prodesse et delectare," in *Enzyklopädie des Märchens*, vol. 14 (2014), cols. 1800–1803.

63. Ibn al-Jawzī, Abū 'l-Faraj ʿAbd al-Raḥmān ibn ʿAlī, *Akhbār al-Ḥamqā wa-'l-mughaffalīn*, ed. Kāẓim al-Muẓaffar, al-Najaf: al-Maktaba al-ḥaydariyya, 1386/1966, p. 2; see Marzolph, Ulrich, "'Erlaubter Zeitvertreib': Die Anekdotensammlungen des Ibn al-Ǧauzī," *Fabula* 32 (1991), pp. 165–180, at p. 171.

64. Meisami, Julie Scott, and Paul Starkey, eds., *Encyclopedia of Arabic Literature*, 2 vols., London: Routledge, 1998.

65. Sergeant, D.S., "al-Jāḥiẓ," in Meisami and Starkey, *Encyclopedia*, vol. 1, pp. 408–409, at p. 409.

66. López Bernal, Desirée, *Los Ḥadāʾiq al-azāhir de Abū Bakr ibn ʿĀṣim al-Garnāṭī: Traducción y estudio de una obra de adab de la Granada nazarí*, 2 vols., Ph.D. thesis University of Granada, 2016.

67. Marzolph, *Arabia ridens*, vol. 1, pp. 38–43; Marzolph, "Ābī, Abū Saʿd Manṣūr ibn al-Ḥusain al-," in *Enzyklopädie des Märchens*, vol. 14 (2014), cols. 1477–1481.

68. Marzolph, Ulrich, "Die Quelle der Ergötzlichen Erzählungen des Bar Hebräus," *Oriens Christianus* 69 (1985), pp. 81–125.

69. Marzolph, "'Erlaubter Zeitvertreib';" Marzolph, "Ibn al-Ǧauzī," in *Enzyklopädie des Märchens*, vol. 7 (1993), cols. 1–7.

70. Muhanna, Elias, *The World in a Book: Al-Nuwayri and the Islamic Encyclopedic Traditon*, Princeton: Princeton University Press, 2018; Nuwayri, Shihab al-Din al-, *The Ultimate Ambition in the Arts of Erudition: A Compendium of Knowledge from the Classical Islamic World*, transl. and ed. Elias Muhanna, New York: Penguin, 2016.

71. Marzolph, Ulrich, "Ibšīhī," in *Enzyklopädie des Märchens*, vol. 7 (1993), cols. 6–10; Marzolph, "Medieval Knowledge in Modern Reading: A 15th Century Arabic Encyclopedia of *omni re scibili*," in *Pre-modern Encylopaedic Texts: Proceedings of the Second COMERS Congress, Groningen, 1–4 July 1996*, ed. Peter Binkley, Leiden: Brill, 1997, pp. 407–419; Marzolph, *Arabia ridens*, vol. 1, pp. 60–66; Tuttle, Kelly, "al-Ibshīhī," in Lowry and Stewart, eds., *Essays*, pp. 236–242.

72. Flügel, Gustav, "Einige bisher wenig oder gar nicht bekannte arabische und türkische Handschriften," *Zeitschrift der Deutschen Morgenländischen Gesellschaft* 14 (1869), pp. 527–546, at pp. 534–538; Marzolph, *Arabia ridens*, vol. 1, pp. 67–71; Marzolph, "Nuzhat al-udabāʾ," in *Enzyklopädie des Märchens*, vol. 10 (2002), cols. 166–169.

73. Irwin, *The Arabian Nights*; Marzolph and Van Leeuwen, *The Arabian Nights Encyclopedia*; Chraïbi, Aboubakr, *Les Mille et une nuits: Histoire du texte et Classification des contes*, Paris: L'Harmattan, 2008; Grotzfeld, Heinz und Sophia, *Die Erzählungen aus* Tausendundeiner Nacht, 2nd rev. ed., Dortmund: Verlag für Orientkunde, 2012.

74. Bottigheimer, Ruth B., "East Meets West: Ḥannā Diyāb and The Thousand and One Nights," *Marvels & Tales* 28.2 (2014), pp. 302–324; Bottigheimer, and Claudia Ott, "The Case of the Ebony Horse, part 1," *Gramarye* 5 (2014), pp. 8–20; Bottigheimer, "The Case of the Ebony Horse, part 2: Hannā Diyāb's Creation of a Third Tradition," *Gramarye* 6 (2014), pp. 7–16; Bottigheimer, "Flying Carpets in the Arabian Nights: Disney, Dyab … and d'Aulnoy?" *Gramarye* 13 (2018), pp. 19–34; Horta, Paulo Lemos, *Marvellous Thieves: Secret Authors of The Arabian Nights*, Cambridge: Harvard University Press, 2017, pp. 17–54; Marzolph, Ulrich, "The Man Who Made the *Nights* Immortal: The Tales of the Syrian Maronite Storyteller Ḥannā Diyāb," *Marvels & Tales* 32.1 (2018), pp. 114–129; Bottigheimer, Ruth B., "Ḥannā Diyāb's Tales in Antoine Galland's Mille et

une nuit(s): I. New Perspectives on Their Recording; II. New Conclusions about Western Sources within Nights Texts," in Bauden, Frédéric, and Richard Waller, eds., *Antoine Galland (1646–1715) et son Journal: Actes du colloque international organisé à l'Université de Liège (16–18 janvier 2015) à l'occasion du tricentenaire de sa mort*, Louvain: Peeters, 2019, pp. 53–74; Marzolph, Ulrich, "Ḥannā Diyāb's Unpublished Tales: The Storyteller as an Artist in His Own Right," ibid., pp. 75–92.

75. Rypka, Jan, "History of Persian Literature Up to the Beginning of the 20th Century," in Rypka, ed., *History of Iranian Literature*, ed. Karl Jahn, Dordrecht: D. Reidel, 1968, pp. 69–351; Cejpek, Jiří, "Iranian Folk-Literature," ibid., pp. 607–709.

76. Meredith-Owens, G.M., "An Early Persian Miscellany," In *Iran and Islam: In Memory of the Late Vladimir Minorsky*, ed. C.E. Bosworth, Edinburgh: University Press, 1971, pp. 435–441; Askari, Nasrin, "A Mirror for Princesses: *Mūnis-nāma*, A Twelfth-Century Collection of Persian Tales Corresponding to the Ottoman Turkish Tales of the *Faraj ba'd al-shidda*," *Narrative Culture* 5.1 (2018), pp. 121–140.

77. Marzolph, *Relief after Hardship*.

78. Perry, Ben Edwin, "The Origin of the Book of Sindbad," *Fabula* 3 (1960), pp. 1–94; Belcher, Stephen, "The Diffusion of the Book of Sindbad," *Fabula* 28 (1987), pp. 34–58.

79. Ritter, Hellmut, *The Ocean of the Soul: Man, the World and God in the Stories of Farīd al-Dīn 'Aṭṭār*, transl. John O'Kane, Leiden: Brill, 2003.

80. Niẓámu'd-dín, Muḥammad, *Introduction to the Jawámi'u'l-ḥikáyát wa lawámi'u'r-riwáyát of Sadídu-dín Muḥammad al-'Awfí*, London: Luzac & Co., 1929.

81. Tietze, Andreas, "Das türkische Ferec ba'd eş-şidde als Medium der Wanderung orientalischer Stoffe ins Abendland", in *Proceedings of the Twenty-Second Congress of Orientalists Held in Istanbul, September 15th to 22nd, 1951*, ed. Zeki Velidi Togan, vol. 2, Leiden: E.J. Brill, 1957, pp. 412–420; Baldauf, Ingeborg, "Freude nach Bedrängnis? Literarische Geschichten zwischen Osmanisch, Persisch und Tatarisch", in *Armağan: Festschrift für Andreas Tietze*, ed. Ingeborg Baldauf, Suraiya Faroghi, and Rudolf Veselý, Prague: enigma, 1994, p. 29–46; Hazai, György, and Andreas Tietze, eds., *Ferec ba'd eş-şidde: "Freud nach Leid " (ein frühosmanisches Geschichtenbuch)*, 2 vols., Berlin: Klaus Schwarz, 2006; Hazai, György, and Heidi Stein, transl., "Proben aus dem *Ferec ba'd eş-şidde* in der deutschen Übersetzung von Andreas Tietze," *Archivum Ottomanicum* 30 (2013), pp. 49–104; Marzolph, *Relief after Hardship*.

82. Wesselski, *Der Hodscha Nasreddin*; Marzolph, Ulrich, and Ingeborg Baldauf, "Hodscha Nasreddin," in *Enzyklopädie des Märchens*, vol. 6 (1990), cols. 1127–1151; Marzolph, Ulrich, "Zur Überlieferung der Nasreddin Hoca-Schwänke außerhalb des türkischen Sprachraumes," in *Türkische Sprachen und Kulturen: Materialien der 1. Deutschen Turkologen-Konferenz*, ed. Ingeborg Baldauf, Klaus Kreiser, and Semih Tezcan, Wiesbaden: Harrassowitz, 1991, pp. 275–285; Marzolph, *Nasreddin Hodscha: 666 wahre Geschichten*, Munich: C.H. Beck, 1996; Başgöz, İlhan, and Pertev Boratav, *I, Hoca Nasreddin, Never Shall I Die: A Thematic Analysis of Hoca Stories*, Bloomington: Indiana University Press, 1998.

83. Duman, Mustafa, *Nasreddin Hoca ve 1555 fıkrası*, Istanbul: heyamola, 2008 (2nd, enl. ed. titled *Nasreddin Hoca ve 1616 fıkrası*, Istanbul: Everest, 2018).

84. Marzolph, Ulrich, "'Focusees' of Jocular Fiction in Classical Arabic Literature," in *Story-telling in the Framework of Non-fictional Arabic Literature*, ed. Stefan Leder, Wiesbaden: Harrassowitz, 1998, pp. 118–129.

85. Marzolph, Ulrich, "Papageienbuch," in *Enzyklopädie des Märchens*, vol. 10 (2002), cols. 526–531.

86. Somadeva, *The Ocean of Story: Being C.H. Tawney's Translation of Somadeva's Kathā Sarit Sāgara (or Ocean of Streams of Stories)*, ed. N.M. Penzer, 10 vols. (2nd ed. London: privately printed, 1923–1928), reprint Delhi: Motilal Banarsidass, 1968.

87. Marzolph, Ulrich, "Orientalisches Erzählgut in Europa," in *Enzyklopädie des Märchens*, vol.10 (2002), cols. 362–373.

88. Bremond, Claude, "Jacques de Vitry," ibid., vol. 7 (1993), cols. 387–394.

89. Berlioz, Jacques, "Odo of Cheriton," ibid., vol. 10 (2002), cols. 219–225.

90. Schenda, Rudolf, "Etienne de Bourbon," ibid., vol. 4 (1984), cols. 511–519.

91. Polo de Beaulieu, Marie Anne, "Johannes Gobi Junior," ibid., vol. 7 (1993), cols. 596–601; Gobi, Jean, *La Scala coeli*, ed. Marie-Anne Polo de Beaulieu, Paris: Centre National de la Recherche Scientifique, 1991.

92. Rehermann, Ernst Heinrich, and Fritz Wagner, "Bromyard, John," in *Enzyklopädie des Märchens*, vol. 2 (1979), cols. 797–802.

93. See, e.g., Pedrosa, José Manuel, "Más reescrituras del cuento de El tesoro fatal (AT 763): del Orto do esposo, Vicente Ferrer y Hans Sachs a eça de Queiroz, William Faulkner y Max Aub," *Revista de poética medieval* 5 (2000), pp. 27–43.

94. Spies, Otto, "Arabische Stoffe in der Disciplina Clericalis," *Rheinisches Jahrbuch für Volkskunde* 21 (1973), pp. 170–199; Schwarzbaum, Haim, "International Folklore Motifs in Petrus Alphonsi's 'Disciplina clericalis'," in Schwarzbaum, *Jewish Folklore between East and West: Collected Papers*, ed. Eli Yassif, Beer-Sheva: Ben-Gurion University of the Negev Press, 1989, pp. 239–358; Lacarra Ducay, "Petrus Alfonsus."

95. Gier, Albert, "Marie des France," in *Enzyklopädie des Märchens*, vol. 9 (1999), cols. 332–336.

96. Mehl, Dieter, "Chaucer, Geoffrey," ibid., vol. 2 (1979), cols. 1255–1268.

97. Briesemeister, Dietrich, "Juan Manuel, Infante Don," ibid., vol. 7 (1993), cols. 668–671.

98. Rossi, Luciano, "Novellino," ibid., vol. 10 (2002), cols. 129–134.

99. Spinette, Alberte, "Boccaccio, Giovanni," ibid., vol. 2 (1979), cols. 549–561.

100. Mordeglia, Caterina, "Sacchetti, Franco," ibid., vol. 11 (2005), cols. 967–971.

101. Rossi, Luciano, "Sercambi, Giovanni," ibid., vol. 12 (2008), cols. 594–598.

102. Lixfeld, Hannjost, "Bolte, Johannes," ibid., vol. 2 (1979), cols. 603–605.

103. Sándor, István, "György, Lajos," ibid., vol. 6 (1990), cols. 334–336; György, Lajos, *A magyar anekdota története és egyetemes kapcsolatai*, Budapest: Studium, 1934.

104. Datcu, Iordan, ed., *Sabina Cornelia Stroescu*, Bucarest: Grai şi suflet, 2011; Stroescu, Sabina Cornelia, *La typologie bibliographique des facéties roumaines*, 2 vols., Bucharest: Académie de la République Socialiste de Roumanie, 1969.

105. Goldberg, Christine, "Tubach, Frederic (Fritz) Christian," in *Enzyklopädie des Märchens*, vol. 13 (2011), cols. 996–998; Tubach, Frederic C., *Index exemplorum: A Handbook of Medieval Religious Tales*, Helsinki: Suomalainen tiedeakatemia, 1969.

106. Tomkowiak, Ingrid, "Moser-Rath, Elfriede," in *Enzyklopädie des Märchens*, vol. 9 (1999), cols. 939–943; Moser-Rath, Elfriede, *Predigtmärlein der Barockzeit: Exempel, Sage, Schwank und Fabel in geistlichen Quellen des oberdeutschen Raumes*, Berlin: De Gruyter, 1964; Moser-Rath, *"Lustige Gesellschaft:" Schwank und Witz des 17. und 18. Jahrhunderts in kultur- und sozialgeschichtlichem Kontext*, Stuttgart: J.B. Metzler, 1984.

107. On the notion of authenticity in folkloristics, see Bendix, Regina, *In Search of Authenticity: The Formation of Folklore Studies*, Madison: University of Wisconsin Press, 1997.

108. https://en.oxforddictionaries.com/definition/romantic (accessed August 6, 2018).

109. Shojaei Kawan, Christine, "Kontamination," in *Enzyklopädie des Märchens*, vol. 8 (1996), cols. 210–217.

110. Dégh, Linda, "Erzählen, Erzähler," ibid., vol. 4 (1984), cols. 315–342.

CHAPTER 1

The Fox Rids Itself of Fleas (ATU 63)

Tales that enjoy such great popularity as to be known as "folktales" are not necessarily long and complex narratives. In particular, some of the tales catalogued as animal tales, that is, tale types ATU 1–299, are short and ostensibly realistic observations about the life of animals. These tales contrast with structured fictitious narratives such as fables, in which animals speak and act as metaphorical representatives of human characters, often stereotypical ones. Referring to the need for a clear distinction between the two types of animal tales, identified by Carl Wilhelm von Sydow,[1] the compilers of the catalogue of French folktales discussed the short tale classified as tale type ATU 63: *The Fox Rids Himself of Fleas.*[2] According to the tale, the fox would take a small object such as a piece of moss into its mouth and then slowly immerse its body into the water, tail first. To avoid being drowned, the fleas would gradually mount the fox's body up to its head. Finally, when the fox would submerge its head in the water, they would save themselves by jumping onto the piece of moss. The fox would then abandon the floating object and be rid of the fleas.

Some of the tale's versions documented from European oral tradition in the twentieth century are extemely short, such as the one in German dialect recorded by J. Schwebe from the oral performance of Christoph Lemke (b. 1866), a former farmer in Lüchow, Lower Saxony, in 1958.[3] Although this version does not even mention an object on which the fleas rescue themselves, the action is virtually the same as summarized above.

> The fox is full of fleas. It goes backward into the water with its tail first until the fleas jump off his nose. Thus it gets rid of the fleas.

Other versions, such as an Estonian text, authenticate the alleged observation by embellishing it into a lengthy narrative in which a man collecting wood at the shore of a river on a hot summer day observes the fox perform the said action.[4] The Estonian text ends by mentioning that the narrator did not understand what the fox had actually done until he picked up the bundle of hay the fox had held in its mouth. It was so full of fleas that the narrator could not get rid of them himself. John Campbell's version from the Scottish Highlands presents the observation as fact, claiming that the fox "was seen in the sea near the Caithness hills."[5] Similarly, the Irish narrator Mac Thuathaláin, aged 60, claimed his version to be a factual report, saying that Máirtín Ó Loideáin saw a fox "draw a mouthful of wool from a sheep, go into the river and swim to the foot of a waterfall and back" three times.[6]

In the nineteenth and twentieth centuries, the tale was repeatedly published as a factual report in newspapers. In a short notice in the May 4, 1911, issue of *Nature*, Bohuslav Brauner from Prague recounted the tale as told by his father almost fifty years earlier.[7] Instead of wool or hay, the fox here sacrifices a tuft of his own fur to collect the fleas. The narrator further emphasized the fox's ingenuity by stating "the effect was superior, for the fleas could creep into the hair without noticing any change of medium during the water trick." In the United States, the December 22, 1900, issue of the *Pacific Rural Times* quoted the tale from the *Baltimore Sun*, referring to "an old hunter and naturalist of local repute" who told the tale, confirming it "as absolutely true and trustworthy."[8] Asserting that he never heard or read of the tale, the hunter related the events as "observed in the waters of the Patapsco River." In this version, when the fox hurried away, the "object left floated near to the observer, and he hauled it ashore with a stick. Fleas literally swarmed through the object, which was found to be a bit of raw rabbit fur."

Historically, the tale was popularized for many centuries by its mention in a fair variety of European works of a scientific, educative, and sometimes entertaining, nature.[9] These include, to list but a few, Scots-Irish novelist William Hamilton Maxwell's 1833 book on sports and pastimes of the United Kingdom;[10] eighteenth-century German encyclopedian Johann Heinrich Zedler's influential comprehensive dictionary "of all sciences and arts;"[11] German author Hilarius Salustius' chapbook *Melancholini wohl-aufgeraumter Weeg-Gefärth* (The Melancholic's Well-tempered Companion; 1717);[12] Sir Kenelm Digby's *Two Treatises: Of Bodies and of Man's Soul*, the "first comprehensive philosophical work in the English language,"[13] initially published in 1644;[14] Swedish historian and naturalist Olaus Magnus's *Historia de gentibus septentrionalibus* (A History of the Northern People; 1555);[15] Swiss physician and naturalist Conrad Gesner's *Historia animalium* (History of Animals; 1551);[16] and a number of sixteenth-century Spanish works.[17] The ultimate source of these authors likely was Albertus Magnus's (d. 1280) *De animalibus* (On Animals) who quoted the tale from the obscure medieval author known as Jorach or Jorath ("Iorach dicit . . . ").[18] The earliest-known mention of the fox's clever trick in the European literatures is attested in the Latin *Otia imperialia* (Recreation for an Emperor), compiled by Gervase of Tilbury at the beginning of the thirteenth century.[19]

More than three centuries prior to Gervase of Tilbury, the narrative is recounted from "popular tradition" (*ḥadīth al-ʿāmma*) in the *Kitāb al-Ḥayawān* (Book of Animals) written by the Arab polymath al-Jāḥiẓ (d. 868).[20] Here, the action is presented more or less as a scientific observation with the fox taking a tuft of wool into its mouth and slowly submerging its body into the water until the fleas gather on the wool, at which point the fox suddenly abandons the wool and leaves. Being a critical observer, al-Jāḥiẓ added a commentary saying, "If this was true, then there would be nothing more amazing. And if it was not true (*bāṭil*), then the people would have attributed it to the fox only because of the animal's demonstrated excellence in cunning and cleverness (*al-khubth wa-'l-kays*)."

Repeatedly mentioned in Arab learned and entertaining literature of the following centuries,[21] albeit with a shorter and slightly different wording, the narrative is cited in such influential compilations as al-Damīrī's (d. 1405) zoographical encyclopedia *Ḥayāt al-ḥayawān* (The Life of Animals)[22] or al-Ibshīhī's popular fifteenth-century encyclopedia *al-Mustaṭraf fī kulli fann mustaẓraf* (The Exquisite Elements from Every Art Considered Elegant).[23] Still in the seventeenth century, Muḥammad ibn Aḥmad ibn (al-)Ilyās al-Ḥanafī included the tale in his compilation of amusing tales, *Nuzhat al-udabā'* (Entertainment of the Educated).[24] Although in particular al-Ibshīhī's work was widely read until the twentieth century,[25] the tale has apparently not been recorded from contemporary Arab oral tradition.[26]

At the beginning of the twenty-first century, the tale is presented in Western children's books[27] and various Internet websites.[28] As the first European author citing the tale did not bother to mention his (most likely Arabic) source, and as the tale fits neatly into the well-known corpus of Aesopic fables, Western tradition readily adopted it into its own historical tradition. Although the tale's veracity was discussed ever since its first appearance, even many centuries of critical distance do not prevent contemporary narrators from claiming to actually have witnessed the event.

Notes

1. Von Sydow, Carl Wilhelm, *Selected Papers on Folklore*, ed. Laurits Bødker, Copenhagen: Rosenkilde & Bagger, 1948, p. 138.

2. Delarue, Paul, and Marie-Louise Tenèze, *Le conte populaire français*, vol. 3, Paris: Maisonneuve et Larose, 1976, pp. 30–32; see Uther, Hans-Jörg, "Fuchs und Flöhe," in *Enzyklopädie des Märchens*, vol. 5 (1987), cols. 484–486.

3. Zentralarchiv der deutschen Volkserzählung, Marburg, no. 41299.

4. Loorits, Oskar, *Estnische Volkserzählungen*, Berlin: De Gruyter, 1959, p. 26, no. 17.

5. Campbell, John Francis, *Popular Tales of the West Highlands*, new ed., vol. 1, Edinburgh and London: Edmonston & Douglas, 1890, p. 276, no. 2.

6. Mac Giollarnáth, Seán, "Trí sgéal ar an sionnach," *Béaloideas* 2.1 (1929), pp. 90–94, at pp. 93–94, no. III.

7. *Nature* 86.312 (May 4, 1911); available at https://www.nature.com/articles/086312b0 (accessed June 1, 2018).

8. *Pacific Rural Times*, December 22, 1900, p. 399; available at https://cdnc.ucr.edu/cgi-bin/cdnc?a=d&d=PRP19001222.2.27 (accessed June 1, 2018).

9. For a detailed survey of the tale's historical sources see Marzolph, Ulrich, "'Ceci n'est point une fable:' Tale Type ATU 63, *The Fox Rids Himself of Fleas*, from Popular

Tradition to Natural History (and Back Again)," in *Contexts of Folklore: Festschrift for Dan Ben-Amos*, ed. Simon Bronner and Wolfgang Mieder, Frankfurt: Lang, 2019, pp. 193–204.

10. Maxwell, William Hamilton, *The Field Book: Or, Sports and Pastimes of the United Kingdom*, London: Effingham Wilson, 1833, p. 205.

11. Zedler, Johann Heinrich, *Grosses vollständiges Universal-Lexicon Aller Wissenschaften und Künste*, vol. 51, Halle: Zedler, 1747, col. 1278.

12. Salustius, Hilarius, *Melancholini wohl-aufgeraumter Weeg-Gefärth*, s.l., 1717, p. 289.

13. Digby, Kenelm, *Two Treatises: Of Bodies and of Man's Soul*, ed. Paul S. MacDonald, s.l.: The Gresham Press, 2013, p. 5.

14. Digby, Kenelm, *Two Treatises: In the One of Which The Nature of Bodies; In the Other, the Nature of Man's Soule, Is Looked Into: In Way of Discovery of the Immortality of Reasonable Soules*, London: Iohn Williams, 1645, p. 377 (ch. 36); Digby, *Two Treatises: Of Bodies and of Man's Soul*, pp. 388–389.

15. Magnus, Olaus, *Historia de gentibus septentrionalibus*, ed. Peter Foote, vol. 3, London: Hakluyt Society, 1998, p. 922 (bk. 18, ch. 39); quoted from Bentham, Jeremy, *The Book of Fallacies*, ed. Philip Schofield, Oxford: Clarendon Press, 2015, p. 68, note 2.

16. Gesner, Conrad, *Historia animalium*, vol. 1, Zurich: Froschover, 1551 (reprint ed. Olaf Breidbach, Hildesheim: Olms-Weidmann, 2012), pp. 957–958.

17. Fradejas Lebrero, José, "Apostillas al catálogo tipológico del cuento folklórico español," *Estudos de literatura oral* 11–12 (2005–2006), pp. 113–128, at pp. 113–119.

18. Albertus Magnus, *Thierbuch*, transl. Walther Hermann Ryff, Frankfurt: Jacob, 1545, s.p., s.v. Vulpes; Albertus Magnus, *Beati Alberti Magni, Ratisbonensis Episcopi, Ordinis Prædicatorum, Opera*, vol. 6: *De Animalibus lib. XXVI*, ed. Pierre Jammy, Lugduni: Claude Prost, 1651, p. 609; Albertus Magnus, *On Animals: A Medieval Summa Zoologica*, transl. and ed. Kenneth F. Kitchell Jr. and Irven M. Resnick, Baltimore: Johns Hopkins University Press, 1999, vol. 2, p. 1541; quoted from Bentham, *The Book of Fallacies*, p. 68, note 2.

19. Gervase of Tilbury, "Gervasii Tilberensis Otia Imperialia [. . .]." in *Scriptores rerum Brunsvicensium*, ed. Gottfried Wilhelm Leibniz, Hannover: Förster, 1707, p. 983 (bk. 3, ch. 68); Gervase of Tilbury, *Otia imperialia: Recreation for an Emperor*, ed. and transl. S.E. Banks and J.W. Binns, Oxford: Clarendon Press, 2002, p. 690 (Latin), 691 (English).

20. Jāḥiẓ, ʿAmr ibn Baḥr al-, *Kitāb al-Ḥayawān*, ed. ʿAbd al-Salām Muḥammad Hārūn, 3rd ed., Beirut: al-Majmaʿ al-ʿilmī al-ʿarabī al-islāmī, 1388/1969, vol. 6, p. 306.

21. Marzolph, *Arabia ridens*, vol. 2, p. 30, no. 110. See also Waṭwāṭ, Muḥammad ibn Ibrāhīm al-, *Mabāhij al-fikar wa-manāhij al-ʿibar*, ed. ʿAbd al-Razzāq Aḥmad al-Ḥarbī, Beirut: al-Dār al-ʿarabiyya lil-mawsūʿāt, 1420/2000, p. 229.

22. Damīrī, Kamāl al-Dīn al-, *Ḥayāt al-ḥayawān al-kubrā*, s.l.: al-Maktaba al-islāmiyya, s.a., vol. 1, p. 175.

23. Ibshīhī, Shihāb al-Dīn Muḥammad ibn Aḥmad Abū 'l-Fatḥ al-, *al-Mustaṭraf fī kull fann mustaẓraf*, ed. Mufīd Qumayḥa, Beirut: Dār al-Kutub al-ʿilmiyya, 1403/1983, vol. 2, p. 229.

24. Ḥanafī, Muḥammad ibn Aḥmad ibn (al-)Ilyās al-, *Nuzhat al-udabāʾ*, Gotha, Ms. Orient A 2706, fol. 113b–114a.

25. Marzolph, Ulrich, "Medieval Knowledge in Modern Reading: A Fifteenth-Century Arabic Encyclopedia of *omni re scibili*," in *Pre-modern Encyclopaedic Texts*, ed. Peter Binkley, Leiden: Brill, 1997, pp. 407–419.

26. El-Shamy, *Types*, p. 28, no. 0063.

27. Fox, Baedron, *The Fox and the Fleas*, 2018; available at https://www.storyjumper.com/book/index/29378656/The-Fox-and-the-Fleas# (accessed June 4, 2018).

28. https://1517ad.wordpress.com/2009/10/18/do-you-know-how-a-fox-gets-rid-of-its-fleas/ (accessed June 4, 2018).

CHAPTER 2

Belling the Cat (ATU 110)

In English, and in corresponding versions in other European languages, the (currently not very common) proverbial expression "Belling the Cat" is used to denote the performance of a risky, dangerous, or simply impossible task.[1] In other words, something that is easier said than done. A representative modern way to use the proverb in context is, for instance, "Who's going to bell the cat and tell mom we wrecked the car?"[2] The fable that gave rise to the proverb features a council of mice who decide that in order to protect themselves from the cat, they ought to hang a bell around the cat's neck. Although all of the mice agree that this is a great idea, none of them is willing to actually perform the task. Classified as tale type ATU 110: *Belling the Cat*, the fable relies on a documented history spanning about a millenium and a half, originating in the context of Middle Eastern adaptations of the ancient Indian mirror for princes, the *Panchatantra* (Five [Books of] Wisdom).[3]

The fable is attested with little variation in numerous short versions recorded from Western oral tradition, including texts in German,[4] Lithuanian,[5] Bulgarian,[6] Greek,[7] Italian,[8] Spanish,[9] and several other languages.[10] The fable's history in the European literatures is as rich as its frequency in oral tradition, comprising dozens of texts in influential collections of *exempla* and fables since the late Middle Ages.[11] Similar to tale type ATU 63: *The Fox Rids Himself of Fleas* (see essay **1, *The Fox Rids Itself of Fleas***), in contemporary popular perception, the tale is usually presented as belonging to the ancient European corpus of Aesopic fables.[12] As a matter of fact, however, the fable is at best in the Aesopic style, since its first occurrence in a European source dates to early in the thirteenth century when Odo of Cheriton (d. ca. 1246) included it in his *Liber parabolorum* (Book of Parables).[13] Odo, who was educated and worked as a cleric, appended an interpretation to the fable, comparing the debate of the mice to one of clerics and monks wanting to depose a bishop, prior, or abbot. As none of them is actually willing to stand up in open opposition to their superior, the situation remains at it is. With a touch of resignation, Odo concludes, "And it is thus that men of lower station allow those higher up to live on and prevail over them."[14]

Prior to its European versions, the fable's oldest attestation appears not in the Sanskrit *Panchatantra* itself, but in the sixth-century Syriac translation of the *Panchatantra*'s lost Middle Persian adaptation, albeit in the particular form included in the story of "The King of the Mice and His Ministers."[15] The tale is not a regular constituent of the manuscripts of *Kalīla wa-Dimna*, the Indian collection's influential Arabic translation prepared by ʿAbdallāh Ibn al-Muqaffaʿ in the first half of the eighth century.[16] Of the collection's medieval European translations, it features only in the Greek version.[17] Considering this fact, the story of "The King of the Mice and His Ministers" was probably added by Burzōe, the collection's translator from Sanskrit to Middle Persian. In the story of "The King of the Mice and His Ministers," the fable of "Belling the Cat" is just one of the solutions proposed to protect the mice from the cat. As soon as the king's first counselor presents his suggestion, however, the second counselor rejects it as he doubts they will find anybody to perform the task.[18] Although the story of "The King of the Mice and His Ministers" likely played a role in transmitting the fable of "Belling the Cat," the tale's specific appearance in that context suggests a different historical precursor for Odo of Cheriton's succinct version in which the council of mice comes to the conclusion that said is easier than done.

A likely candidate for this precursor whose wording is much closer to that given by Odo of Cheriton is the tale's version in the collection of proverbs and their tales compiled by the Arabic author al-Mufaḍḍal ibn Salama (d. after 903).[19] Referring to times of old, the Arabic text introduces the rodents holding council discussing how to protect themselves effectively from the cat. Although they all agree that fastening a bell (*juljul*) on the cat's neck is a great idea, there is no solution to the question of who is going to perform that act. Finally, one of the mice comes up with the phrase that became a proverb in Arabic, saying "*baqiya shadduhu*." As the Arabic term *shadd* can denote both, the act of fastening (*shadda*) and something difficult (*shadīd*), the phrase could mean "The act of fastening remains" as well as "The most difficult part remains." The tale's ending in al-Maydānī's (d. 1124) collection of proverbs opts for the latter reading, as the phrase *baqiya ashaddu* ("The most difficult part remains," for which the author gives *baqiya shadduhu* as an alternative) is explained as relating to a task whose most difficult (*aṣʿab*) or most detested (*ahwan*) aspect remains to be completed.[20] Al-Maydānī also presents another similar tale interpreting a verse alluding to the fable that is attributed to the Arab poet Abū 'l-Najm (d. after 724), "Except for a man who attaches the bell's band."[21] In the corresponding tale, a numskull advises the members of his Bedouin tribe, the Banū ʿIjl, to protect their animals from a ferocious lion by attaching a bell to the lion's neck. Moreover, classical Arabic literature knows yet another fable with a similar moral that is attested in several compilations dating to the eleventh century.[22] In that tale, the fox refuses to deliver a letter to the dog, arguing, "The reward is abundant, but the task is too dangerous."

Originating from Middle Eastern tradition, the history of the fable of "Belling the Cat" demonstrates convincingly first, how a succinct tale is boiled down to a meaningful proverb, and second, how this proverb acquires a long life in international tradition, all the while transporting the tale as its backdrop. Moreover, the tale's historical dissemination serves as a strong argument for its adaptability to universal contexts in which mice and cats are as ubiquitous as the tale's moral is appealing. In addition to these general considerations, the tale is a telling example for the appropriation of an originally "alien" narrative and its integration into Western tradition to such an extent that its origin from Middle Eastern tradition is completely obscured.

Notes

1. Wander, Karl Friedrich Wilhelm, *Deutsches Sprichwörter-Lexikon: Ein Hausschatz für das deutsche Volk* (1867), Augsburg: Weltbild, 1987, vol. 2, cols. 1185–1186, no. 402.

2. https://idioms.thefreedictionary.com/bell+the+cat (accessed May 4, 2018).

3. Baum, Paul Franklin, "The Fable of Belling the Cat," *Modern Language Notes* 34 (1919), pp. 462–470 (also in Carnes, Pack, ed., *Proverbia in Fabula*, Bern: Lang, 1988, pp. 37–46); Marzolph, Ulrich, "Katze mit der Schelle," in *Enzyklopädie des Märchens*, vol. 7 (1993), cols. 1117–1121.

4. Kooi, Jurjen van der, and Theo Schuster, *Märchen und Schwänke aus Ostfriesland*, Leer: Schuster, 1993, pp. 270–271, 358, no. 209.

5. Range, Jochen D., *Litauische Volksmärchen*, Munich: Diederichs, 1981, pp. 21–22, 269, no. 7.

6. Ognjanowa, Elena, *Märchen aus Bulgarien*, Wiesbaden: Drei Lilien, 1987, pp. 192, 491, no. 59.

7. Loukatos, Demetrios, *Neoellēnika laographika keimena*, Athens: Zakharopulos, 1957, pp. 25–26, no. 4.

8. Pitrè, Giuseppe, *Fiabe, novelle e racconti popolari siciliani*, Palermo: Lauriel, 1875, vol. 1, p. 391, no. 118.

9. Rael, Juan B., *Cuentos españoles de Colorado y Nuevo Méjico: Spanish Originals with English Summaries*, Stanford: Stanford University Press, 1940, vol. 2, pp. 586–587, 811, no. 497 (87).

10. Dähnhardt, Oskar, *Natursagen: Eine Sammlung naturdeutender Sagen, Märchen, Fabeln und Legenden*, vol. 2, Leipzig: Teubner, 1907 (reprint Hildesheim: Georg Olms, 1983), pp. 145–147.

11. Pauli, Johannes, *Schimpf und Ernst*, ed. Johannes Bolte, Berlin: Herbert Stubenrauch, 1924, vol. 1, p. 351; vol. 2, pp. 393–394, no. 634; Tubach, *Index exemplorum*, p. 48, no. 566; Dicke, Gerd, and Klaus Grubmüller, *Die Fabeln des Mittelalters und der frühen Neuzeit: Ein Katalog der deutschen Versionen und ihrer lateinischen Entsprechungen*, Munich: Fink, 1987, pp. 567–569, no. 483.

12. See, e.g., Paxton, Tom, and Robert Rayevsky, *Belling the Cat and Other Aesop's Fables*, New York: Morrow Junior Books, 1990.

13. Perry, Ben Edwin, *Babrius and Phaedrus: Newly Edited and Translated into English, Together with an Historical Introduction and a Comprehensive Survey of Greek and Latin Fables in the Aesopic Tradition*, Cambridge: Harvard University Press, 1965, p. 545, no. 613; Odo of Cheriton, *The Fables*, transl. John C. Jacobs, Syracuse, NY: Syracuse University Press, 1985, pp. 129–130, no. 80; Adrados, Francisco Rodríguez, *History of the Graeco-Latin*

Fable, vol. 3, *Inventory and Documentation of the Graeco-Latin Fable*, Leiden: Brill, 2003, pp. 722–723, no. M308.

14. Odo of Cheriton, *The Fables*, p. 130.

15. Chauvin, *Bibliographie*, vol. 2 (1897), pp. 109–110, no. 74.

16. De Blois, François, *Burzōy's Voyage to Indian and the Origin of the Book of Kalīlah wa Dimna*, London: Royal Asiatic Society, 1990, pp. 13–14.

17. Krönung, Bettina, "The Wisdom of the Beasts: The Arabic *Book of Kalīla and Dimna* and the Byzantine *Book of Stephanites and Ichnelates*," in Cupane, Carolina, and Bettina Krönung, eds., *Fictional Storytelling in the Medieval Eastern Mediterranean World and beyond*, Berlin: De Gruyter, 2016, pp. 427–461, at p. 431.

18. Nöldeke, Theodor, "Die Erzählung vom Mäusekönig und seinen Ministern: Ein Abschnitt der Pehlewî-Bearbeitung des altindischen Fürstenspiegels," *Abhandlungen der Königlichen Gesellschaft der Wissenschaften zu Göttingen* 25.3 (1879), pp. 1–68, at pp. 44 (Syriac), 45 (Arabic).

19. Mufaḍḍal ibn Salama, *al-Fākhir*, ed. Charles A. Storey, Leiden: Brill, 1915, pp. 147, no. 292; ed. ʿAbd al-ʿAlīm al-Ṭaḥāwī and Muḥammad ʿAlī al-Najjār, Cairo: ʿĪsā al-Bābī al-Ḥalabī, 1380/1960, pp. 179, no. 292; see Brockelmann, Carl, "Fabel und Tiermärchen in der älteren arabischen Literatur," *Islamica* 2 (1926), pp. 96–128, at p. 110.

20. Maydānī, Abū 'l-Faḍl Aḥmad ibn Muḥammad ibn Aḥmad ibn Ibrāhīm, *Majmaʿ al-amthāl*, ed. Muḥammad Abū 'l-Faḍl Ibrāhīm, Cairo: ʿĪsā al-Bābī al-Ḥalabī, 1398/1978, vol. 1, p. 147, no. 490.

21. Maydānī, *Majmaʿ al-amthāl*, vol. 3, pp. 209–210, no. 3694; Brockelmann, "Fabel und Tiermärchen," pp. 110–111.

22. Marzolph, *Arabia ridens*, vol. 2, pp. 147–148, no. 599.

CHAPTER 3

The Bird Promises to Give Its Captor Three Pieces of Advice (ATU 150)

Tale type ATU 150: *The Three Teachings of the Bird* is a straightforward warning about the devastating effects of greed.[1] The tale introduces a small singing bird, often a nightingale or lark, that has been caught by a man, who is sometimes specified as a gardener or hunter. Since the bird refuses to sing in captivity and since it is too small to satisfy the captor's hunger, the bird suggests that it will give its captor three pieces of advice in return for being released. The advice the bird gives is of a commonplace nature, such as "Never grieve for anything that you cannot change any more," "Never believe things that are impossible," or "Never try to attain the impossible." Set free, the bird mocks the man for his stupidity, as it claims to have precious stones in its belly. The man believes the bird's claim and regrets not having killed it while it was in his possession. Again the bird mocks the man, this time for his greed that makes him lose his common sense. After all, the bird is so small that its body could not possibly hold the alleged jewels.

Widely spread in literature, the tale has rarely been recorded from European oral tradition, and even the few texts presented as folktales often lack an unambiguous identification of origin from oral performance. In a Ukrainian version, the man catches a nightingale.[2] The bird gives three pieces of advice in return for the promise of being set free. The pieces of advice are "Never eat anything that is not good for you," "Never grieve for anything you cannot change," and "Do not believe in things impossible." Set free, the bird wants to test whether the man heeds its advice and tells him that it holds a huge pearl inside its body. When the man hears this, he regrets having set the bird free and tries to convince it to come back. But the bird mocks the man for his stupidity, as its tiny body could never hold the alleged large pearl.

In a Flemish text, the bird claims to have a precious stone larger than an ostrich egg in its body.[3] In an early twentieth-century German version from Lissa, today Leszno in Poland, the bird mentions a diamond as large as a hen's egg.[4] The latter tale details the man's argument to entice the bird to come back to him. The man alludes to the dire winter conditions the bird will have to suffer through, in contrast to which it would have an easy life being well fed in captivity. But first the bird mocks its captor because of his alleged stupidity for setting it free, and then it laughs about the man's incapacity to heed the given advice. The Albanian tale told to Martin Camaj by Halit Shala in February 1974 has the hunter set the bird free before it gives its advice.[5] The bird then first mentions three jewels in its crop before warning the man not to believe in what the world says. The bird's final advice is to never let go anything you hold in your hand. An early twentieth-century French version, collected by Georges Thibault, introduces the tale with the lengthy description of a poor farmer's toils.[6] A warbler wants to console him with its melodies, but—as "a hungry belly does not have ears"[7]—the farmer prefers to catch the bird in a trap. The bird promises to give the farmer three pieces of advice if set free immediately. The first and only advice it gives is "It is foolish to let go whatever you have in your hands, because one thing you have is better than two you may or may not have in the future." When the farmer is deeply grieved at having set the bird free, the bird mocks him by claiming to have a large jewel inside its head worth two hundred écus. And when the farmer curses his own stupidity, the bird goes into a lengthy exhortation. At the end, the bird adds the satirical advice that the stupid farmer should from now on eat thistles, as stupid donkeys do, and flies away.

The tale's numerous versions in the European literatures were frequently discussed in twentieth-century research, particularly in relation to influential texts such as those included in the legend of *Barlaam and Josaphat*, an early medieval adaptation of the legends of the Buddha,[8] in Petrus Alfonsus' (d. after 1121) *Disciplina clericalis* (The Scholar's Guide),[9] and in the medieval French *lai L'Oiselet* (The Little Bird).[10]

One of the tale's oldest preserved versions is given in the legend of *Barlaam and Josaphat* contained in an Arabic manuscript that presumably dates from the ninth century. Here, the owner of a garden sees a sparrow (Arabic *ʿuṣfūr*) eat the fruit of the trees and catches it. The bird's three pieces of advice (*kalimāt*) are "Do not regret what you have lost," "Do not long to attain the impossible," and "Do not believe the impossible." Set free, the bird tells the man about a pearl in its body as big as a goose egg.[11] In the version of the *Disciplina clericalis*, the second text that was influential for subsequent European tradition, a man catches a bird in his garden. The bird does not want to sing, nor does it want to be eaten. Instead, it promises three pieces of advice and is set free. The pieces of advice are "Do not believe in everything people say," "What you possess will be yours," and "Do not grieve over anything you have lost." The jewel the bird then claims to have inside its body is said to weigh a pound. The two versions influential in European tradition and their derivatives were classified according to a model that identifies their most obvious difference in the fact whether the bird is set free after (as in *Barlaam and Josaphat*) or before (as in *Disciplina clericalis*) giving its advice.[12] Surveys of the tale's historical versions include the reference to the *Laughable Stories* compiled by thirteenth-century Syriac Christian author

Bar Hebraeus (d. 1286).[13] As Bar Hebraeus's compilation largely constitutes an ingenious adaptation of material from Arabic Muslim author al-Ābī's (d. 1030) encyclopedia of jokes and anecdotes, *Nathr al-durr* (Pearls of Prose),[14] the reference opens up a window to the tale's specific and richly documented tradition in the Middle Eastern Muslim literatures.[15]

In the tenth century, the version from *Barlaam and Josaphat* is still cited in Ibn Bābawayh (Bābōyah) al-Ṣaddūq's (d. 991) *Kamāl al-dīn wa-tamām al-niʿma* (The Perfection of Religion and the Completeness of Grace).[16] It finds a distant reflection in the ornate prose text in Barkhordār ibn Maḥmud Farāhi's late sixteenth- or early seventeenth-century Persian work *Maḥbub al-qolub* (The Hearts' Beloved).[17] Meanwhile, at least as of the first half of the tenth century, Arabic and, subsequently, Persian tradition knows a specific version that is usually attributed to the famous Arab traditionist al-Shaʿbī (d. ca. 728). The earliest-known mention of this version, in Andalusian author Ibn ʿAbd Rabbih's (d. 940) *al-ʿIqd al-farīd* (The Unique Necklace),[18] moreover presents the events as occurring to an Israelite man,[19] thus probably indicating the origin of this version from Jewish tradition.[20] The tale's "Muslim" version has a specific variation that adds additional attraction to the plot. The bird is a lark (Arabic *qubbara* or *qunbura*) that promises three pieces of advice (*khiṣāl, kalimāt*, or *fawāʾid*). The bird says that it will give the first advice while still held in its captor's hand; the second one after being released and sitting in a tree; and the third one from a hilltop (*jabal*). The first advice is usually "Do not mourn for anything you have irretrievably lost," and the second one "Do not believe in anything impossible." Then, from a safe distance on the hilltop, the bird mentions a large pearl or two pearls in its body. And finally, when the man grieves about not having kept and slaughtered the bird so as to procure the precious pearls, the bird chides him and refuses to give the third piece of advice, as he obviously did not heed the two previous ones.

This version is cited in a fair number of works from the pre- and post-Mongol periods, including al-Ābī's (d. 1030) *Nathr al-durr* (Pearls of Prose),[21] from which Bar Hebraeus (d. 1286) adapted it in his Christian Syriac compilation;[22] Abū Nuʿaym al-Iṣfahānī's (d. 1038) *Ḥilyat al-awliyāʾ* (The Decoration of the Saints);[23] al-Ghazzālī's (d. 1111) *Iḥyāʾ ʿulūm al-dīn* (The Revival of the Religious Sciences);[24] Ibn Ḥamdūn's (d. 1167) *al-Tadhkira* (The Aide-Mémoire);[25] Ibn al-Jawzī's (d. 1201) *Akhbār al-Adhkiyāʾ* (Tales of Clever People);[26] al-Sharīshī's (d. 1222) *Sharḥ Maqāmāt al-Ḥarīrī* (Commentary on the *Maqāmāt* of al-Ḥarīrī);[27] Yāqūt al-Ḥamawī's (d. 1229) *Muʿjam al-udabāʾ* (Dictionary of Learned People);[28] Ibn Abī 'l-Ḥadīd's (d. 1258) *Sharḥ Nahj al-balāgha* (Commentary on *Nahj al-balāgha*, a collection of traditions attributed to ʿAlī ibn Abī Ṭālib);[29] al-Damīrī's (d. 1405) zoographical encyclopedia *Ḥayāt al-ḥayawān* (The Lives of Animals);[30] Andalusian author Ibn ʿĀṣim's (d. 1426) *Ḥadāʾiq al-azāhir* (Flower Gardens);[31] and one of polymath al-Suyūṭī's (d. 1505) historical works.[32] The only notable variation occurs in al-Suyūṭī's text where the sequence of locations is inverted (hill is second, and tree is third), and where the third advice "Do not rejoice because of things that have not yet happened" is added. This version also adds an explicit short moral pointing out that this is what happens to excessively greedy people. Versions of the tale are also included in recent Arabic compilations of tales and manuscripts of *The Thousand and One Nights*.[33]

Probably al-Ghazzālī's (d. 1111) Persian work *Kimiyā-ye sa'ādat* (The Elixir of Happiness) achieved the tale's transmission to the Persian context.[34] The little bird who gives the pieces of advice (Persian *sokhan*) here is a sparrow (*gonjeshk*), and the author adds the short moral that the greedy believe everything. Versified versions of the tale were offered by two famous Persian mystics, in Farid al-Din 'Aṭṭār's (d. 1221) *Elāhi-nāme* (Book of God)[35] and Jalāl al-Din Rumi's (d. 1273) mystical *summa*, the *Masnavi-ye ma'navi*.[36] Whereas 'Aṭṭār's rendering was read as a tale of blind greed, exemplifying the "consequences of lacking a sense of contentment with little, of not being satisfied with what one has,"[37] Rumi expounds the uselessness of trying to educate stupid people with the phrase "to give counsel to a sleepy ignoramus is to scatter seed in nitrous soil,"[38] that reminds one of the biblical expression "to cast pearls before swine" (Matthew 7:6). The prose version in Sadid al-Din Moḥammad 'Awfi's (d. ca. 1232) *Javāme' al-ḥekāyāt* (Collections of Stories) introduces a market scene in which the man who caught the sparrow sells it to another man.[39] The three places from which the bird gives its advice are from within the cage, on its owner's hand, and from a tree. After the final admonition, the bird has pity on its former owner. As a token of gratitude for releasing it from captivity, the bird tells the man to dig up a jar full of gold from under the tree on which it is sitting. A similar ending is also given in an undated (and presumably fairly recent) Arabic manuscript version.[40] The tale's version in the first Persian adaptation of the Sanskrit *Śukasaptati* (Seventy [Tales of a] Parrot), the *Javāher al-asmār* (Jewels of Evening Tales), compiled in 1314 by a certain 'Emād ibn Moḥammad, supplies additional everyday flavor to the introductory scene by specifying that the bird's new owner attaches a cord to its foot so as to give it to the children, presumably to play with.[41] The tale is not contained in the *Śukasaptati*'s second Persian adaptation, Żiyā' al-Din Nakhshabi's (d. 1350) *Ṭuṭi-nāme* (Book of the Parrot).[42]

Textual evidence demonstrates that the tale's two versions that were most influential for medieval and modern European tradition are related to each other. In other words, the version of the *Disciplina clericalis* with its introductory scene of a garden appears to be modeled on the version of the legend of *Barlaam and Josaphat*. The tale's Arabic and Persian versions, on the other hand, most prominently through the lack of the bird's third advice, betray a distinct adaptation that developed independently. In this respect, although the Arabic versions of *Barlaam and Josaphat* played a role in transmitting the tale East to West, the distinct "Muslim" version constitutes a distant relative to its European relations.[43]

Notes

1. Marzolph, Ulrich, "Lehren: Die drei L. des Vogels," in *Enzyklopädie des Märchens*, vol. 8 (1996), cols. 883–889; see also Lerner, Amir, "Two Amalgamated Ancient Bird Fables in Classical Arabic Literature and Their Shape in Later Popular Prose Tradition: A Comparative Study and Critical Edition," *Al-Qantara* 39.2 (2018), pp. 321–351.

2. Popov, Pavel Nikolayevich, *Ukraïns'ki narodni kazky, legendy, anekdoty*, Kyïv: Vid. Khudozhno i literaturi, 1957, p. 404.

3. Joos, Amaat, *Vertelsels van het Vlaamsche volk*, vol. 1, Brugge: Standaard, 1889, pp. 142–144, no. 82.

4. Knoop, Otto, *Ostmärkische Sagen, Märchen und Erzählungen*, Lissa i. P.: Eulitz, 1909, pp. 147–149, no. 72.

5. Camaj, Martin, and Uta Schier-Oberdorffer, *Albanische Märchen*, Düsseldorf: Diederichs, 1974, pp. 192–193 no. 57.

6. Thibault, Charles, *Contes de Champagne*, Paris: Quatre jeudis, 1960, pp. 117–120.

7. Ibid., p. 118.

8. Chauvin, *Bibliographie*, vol. 3 (1898), pp. 103–104, no. 14; Tyroller, Franz, *Die Fabel von dem Mann und dem Vogel in ihrer Verbreitung in der Weltliteratur*, Berlin: Felber, 1912, pp. 74–113; Lackner, Irmgard, "Barlaam and Josaphat," in *Enzyklopädie des Märchens*, vol. 1 (1977), cols. 1243–1252; see also Dicke, Gerd, and Klaus Grubmüller, *Die Fabeln des Mittelalters und der frühen Neuzeit: Ein Katalog der deutschen Versionen und ihrer lateinischen Entsprechungen*, Munich: Fink, 1987, pp. 652–657, no. 570.

9. Chauvin, *Bibliographie*, vol. 9 (1905), p. 30, no. 20; Tyroller, *Die Fabel*, pp. 23–73; Schwarzbaum, Haim, "International Folklore Motifs in Petrus Alphonsi's 'Disciplina clericalis'," in Schwarzbaum, *Jewish Folklore between East and West: Collected Papers*, ed. Eli Yassif, Beer-Sheva: Ben-Gurion University of the Negev Press, 1989, pp. 239–358, at pp. 305–307, no. 22; Spies, Otto, "Arabische Stoffe in der Disciplina Clericalis," *Rheinisches Jahrbuch für Volkskunde* 21 (1973), pp. 170–199, at p. 191–192, no. 22.

10. Paris, Gaston, *Légendes du moyen âge*, Paris: Hachette, 1903, pp. 225–291; Cock, Alfons de, "De vogelaar en de nachtigaal," [1904], in *Studien en essays over oude volksvertelsels*, Antwerp: De Sickel, 1919, pp. 51–75; Campbell, Marie, "The Three Teachings of the Bird," in *Studies in Biblical and Jewish Folklore*, ed. Raphael Patai, Francis Lee Utley, and Dov Noy, Bloomington: Indiana University Press, 1960, pp. 95–107; Wolfgang, Lenora D., *Le Lai de l'oiselet: An Old French Poem of the Thirteenth Century*, Philadelphia: American Philosophical Society, 1990; Galmés de Fuentes, Álvaro, "Un cuento árabe y el *Lai* francés del *Oiselet*," in *Homenaje al profesor Jacinto Bosch Vilá*, vol. 2, Granada: Universidad de Granada, 1991, pp. 729–737; also in *Romania arabica: Estudios de literatura comparada árabe y romance*, vol. 2, Madrid: Real Academia de la Historia, 2000, pp. 57–69.

11. Hommel, Fritz, *Die älteste arabische Barlaam-Version*, Vienna: Alfred Hölder, 1887, p. 46.

12. Wolfgang, *Le Lai de l'oiselet*, pp. 34–37.

13. Tyoller, *Die Fabel*, pp. 158–159; Wolfgang, *Le Lai de l'oiselet*, p. 35, no. C6; Bar Hebraeus, Mâr Gregory John, *The Laughable Stories*, transl. E.A. Wallis Budge, London: Luzac and Co, 1897, p. 93, no. 382.

14. Marzolph, Ulrich, "Die Quelle der Ergötzlichen Erzählungen des Bar Hebräus," *Oriens Christianus* 69 (1985), pp. 81–125.

15. Brockelmann, Carl, "Fabel und Tiermärchen in der älteren arabischen Literatur,"

Islamica 2 (1926), pp. 96–128, at p. 108; Tyroller, *Die Fabel*, pass.; Marzolph, *Arabia ridens*, vol. 2, p. 92–93, no. 369; Marzolph, "Lehren."

16. The text I have consulted is available at http://books.rafed.net/view.php ?type=c_fbook&b_id=262, pp. 609–610 (accessed March 1, 2017).

17. Clouston, William Alexander, *A Group of Eastern Romances and Stories from the Persian, Tamil, and Urdu*, Glasgow: privately printed, 1889, 448–452; Tyroller, *Die Fabel*, pp. 131–134, 302–305.

18. Ibn ʿAbd Rabbih, Abū ʿUmar Aḥmad ibn Muḥammad, *Kitāb al-ʿIqd al-farīd*, ed. Aḥmad Amīn, Aḥmad al-Zayn, Ibrāhīm al-Abyārī, 3rd ed., Cairo: Lajnat al-taʾlīf wa-ʾl-tarjama wa-ʾl-nashr, 1372/1952, vol. 3, p. 68.

19. The Arab polymath al-Suyūṭī (d. 1505) in his *Badāʾiʿ al-zuhūr fī waqāʾiʿ al-duhūr* (Wondrous Flowers, about the Events of Past Eras) later elaborates this by specifying an Israelite man in the times of the Prophet Solomon; see Ibn Iyās al-Ḥanafī, Muḥammad ibn Aḥmad [recte Suyūṭī, Jalāl al-Dīn ʿAbd al-Raḥmān], *Badāʾiʿ al-zuhūr fī waqāʾiʿ al-duhūr*, Cairo: ʿIsā al-Bābī al-Ḥalabī, s.a., pp. 167–168.

20. For the tale's Jewish dimension, see Bin Gorion, Micha Joseph, *Mimekor Israel: Classical Jewish Folktales, Abridged and Annotated*, ed. Emanuel Bin Gorion, prepared by Dan Ben-Amos, Bloomington: Indiana University Press, 1990, pp. 455–456, no. 245.

21. Ābī, Abū Saʿd Manṣūr ibn al-Ḥusayn al-, *Nathr al-durr*, ed. Muḥammad ʿAlī Qarna et al., vol. 7, Cairo: al-Hayʾa al-miṣriyya al-ʿāmma lil-kitāb, 1991, p. 277–278.

22. Bar Hebraeus, *The Laughable Stories*.

23. The consulted edition Beirut: Dār al-kitāb al-ʿarabī, 1405, is available in both pdf and doc format at shamela.ws, part 5 (accessed March 1, 2017).

24. Ghazzālī, Abū Ḥāmid Muḥammad al-, *Iḥyāʾ ʿulūm al-dīn*, Cairo: Dār al-Kutub al-ʿarabiyya al-kubrā, s.a., vol. 3, pp. 207–208.

25. Ibn Ḥamdūn, Muḥammad ibn al-Ḥasan ibn Muḥammad ibn ʿAlī, *al-Tadhkira al-ḥamdūniyya*, ed. Iḥsān ʿAbbās and Bakr ʿAbbās, Beirut: Dār Ṣādir, 1996, vol. 8, pp. 239–240, no. 715.

26. Ibn al-Jawzī, Abū ʾl-Faraj, *Akhbār al-Adhkiyāʾ*, ed. Muḥammad Mursī al-Khūlī, s.l. 1970, p. 253–254; see Tyroller, *Die Fabel*, pp. 157–158, 322–323.

27. Galmés de Fuentes, "Un cuento árabe," pp. 57–58; see Lūwīs Shaykhū, *Majānī al-adab fī ḥadāʾiq al-ʿarab*, p. 126 (ch. 5), available at alwaraq.net (accessed March 1, 2017).

28. The consulted text is available at shamela.ws/browse.php/book-9788/page _1477 (accessed March 1, 2017).

29. The consulted text is available at alwaraq.net [page 2017] (accessed March 1, 2017).

30. Damīrī, Kamāl al-Dīn al-, *Ḥayāt al-ḥayawān al-kubrā*, s.l.: al-Maktaba al-islāmiyya, s.a., vol. 2, p. 241; see Tyroller, *Die Fabel*, pp. 324–325.

31. Ibn ʿĀṣim al-Andalusī, Abū Bakr ibn Muḥammad, *Ḥadāʾiq al-azāhir*, ed. ʿAfīf ʿAbd al-Raḥmān, Beirut: al-Masīra, 1401/1981, p. 295; López Bernal, Desirée, "Los cuentos de Ibn ʿĀṣim (m. 1426): precedentes peninsulares de relatos españoles y del folklore universal en el s. XV," *Boletín de literatura oral* 9 (2019), pp. 35–52, at p. 40, no. 32.

32. Ibn Iyās al-Ḥanafī [recte Suyūṭī], *Badāʾiʿ al-zuhūr*, pp. 167–168.

33. Chauvin, *Bibliographie*, vol. 6 (1902), pp. 110–111, no. 275; Basset, *Mille et un contes*, vol. 2, pp. 65–72, no. 39.

34. Ghazzālī, al-, *Kīmiyā-ye saʿādat*, ed. Aḥmad Ārām, Tehran: Ketābkhāne va chāpkhāne-ye markazi, 1319/1940, pp. 541–542

35. Ritter, Hellmut, *The Ocean of the Soul: Man, the World and God in the Stories of Farīd al-Dīn ʿAṭṭār*, transl. John O'Kane, Leiden: Brill, 2003, p. 97 (ch. 13, no. 13); see Ṣanʿatiniyā, Fāṭeme, *Maʾākhez̲-e qeṣaṣ va tams̱ilāt-e mas̱navihā-ye ʿAṭṭār-e Neishāburi*, Tehran: Zavvār, 1369/1990, pp. 66–68.

36. Rumi, Jalāl al-Din, *The Mathnawí of Jalálu'ddín Rúmí*, transl. Reynold A. Nicholson, London: Luzac & Co., 1934, vol. 2, pp. 396–397 (bk. 4, verses 2245–2265); Foruzānfar, Badīʿ al-Zamān, *Maʾākhez̲-e qeṣaṣ va tams̱ilāt-e Mas̱navi*, 3rd printing, Tehran: Amir Kabir, 1362/1983. pp. 144–145, no. 163. A modern prose rendering of Rumi's verse is given by Arberry, Arthur John, *More Tales from the Masnavi*, London: Allen & Unwin, 1963, p. 56, no. 119. Tyroller, *Die Fabel*, pp. 130–131, 300–302, discusses and quotes a fourteenth-century versification by a certain Jalāl al-Din Jaʿfar ibn Farkhāni (*apud* Hammer-Purgstall, Joseph von, *Geschichte der schönen Redekünste Persiens*, Vienna, 1818, p. 222).

37. Ritter, *The Ocean of the Soul*, p. 97.

38. Rumi, *The Mathnawí*, vol. 2, p. 397, verse 2264.

39. ʿAwfi, Sadid al-Din Moḥammad, *Gozide-ye Javāmeʿ al-hekāyāt*, ed. Jaʿfar Sheʿār, Tehran: Sāzmān-e entesharāt va āmuzesh-e enqelāb-e eslāmi, 1363/1984, p. 363–364; see also Niẓāmuʾd-dín, *Introduction*, p. 243, no. 1923 (bk. 4, ch. 13).

40. Tyroller, *Die Fabel*, pp. 150–151.

41. ʿEmād ibn Moḥammad [al-S̱aghari], *Ṭuṭi-nāme: Javāher al-asmār*, ed. Shams al-Din Āl-e Aḥmad, Tehran: Bonyād-e farhang-e Irān, 1352/1973, pp. 93–94, no. 10.

42. Hatami, Mahroo, *Untersuchungen zum persischen Papageienbuch des Naḫšabī*, Freiburg: Klaus Schwarz, 1977, p. 19.

43. In addition to several texts not discussed in the present context, Tyroller, *Die Fabel*, following p. 328, presents a family tree of the tale's versions known at the beginning of the twentieth century.

CHAPTER 4

The Faithful Animal Rashly Killed (ATU 178A)

A modern legend popular in Western European tradition in the 1990s tells of a man who takes his little son and dog along in the car when doing the shopping one Saturday morning.[1] As he puts the goods in the car, the man notices that he has forgotten to dispose of the empty bottles. Leaving his son and the dog in the car, he goes to take care of the bottles. When the man returns, his son has blood all over his face and cries frantically. As the dog's snout is soiled with blood, the man thinks that the dog attacked the child. In a fit of rage, he pulls the dog out of the car and throws it to the ground so violently that it dies instantly. Only then does the man notice what actually happened. A rat hidden in the sack of potatoes he had bought had attacked the child, and the dog had defended the child, killing the rat. Contributed to the collector, presumably in written form, by secretary Angelika Kühn, aged 38, from Peine in the German federal state of North Rhine-Westphalia, the legend is a typical "foaf-tale." Allegedly retelling a true event, foaf-tales are a genre of contemporary legends about events that rarely happened to the actual teller. Instead, these tales relating allegedly true events rely on the narration of a "friend of a friend," an informant whose existence is only vaguely vouchsafed and whose reliability cannot be verified. In the present case, the legend was told to the contributor by a neighbor whose friend claimed to have witnessed the event in person. The tale's nature as a legend is substantiated by the fact that it was published in a Belgian newspaper a few years earlier.[2] Further, a very similar tale was told in the Southern United States.[3] That tale features a hunter and trapper whose wife had died, leaving him alone with his little son. The attacking animal here is a wolf that the hunter's faithful part-wolf sled dog had killed. Misunderstanding the situation when returning home late one afternoon, the hunter splits the dog's head with his axe. Although the narrator claimed, "they's things that to us are unbelievable now that are actually real and did happen back then," this version likely derives from the publication by popular author Rex Beach in the July 1942 issue of *Reader's Digest*.[4] In an attempt to supply additional credibility to the depicted events, the characters in Beach's version are identified as young trapper Peter Dobley and his dog Prince.

In fact, however, the tale is "one of the world's most travelled tales."[5] Classified as tale type ATU 178A: *The Innocent Dog*, the tale's internationally documented history spans more than two millennia.[6] Mainly published in literary works of an educative nature, the tale was rarely recorded from contemporary oral tradition, and the few available oral versions display a considerable variation. A Spanish folktale narrated by farmer Antonio Pernía, aged 58, from Olvera in the Andalusian province of Cádiz introduces a couple out in the fields harvesting olives.[7] In the afternoon, the couple's five-year old son lets their dog loose and follows it. Attacked by wolves at dusk, the dog defends the little son. When both finally return home, the father at first wants to punish the dog. But when the mother indicates that the dog would never go astray all by itself, the parents find out what actually happened. A German version of the tale was recorded in August 1962 from the oral dialect narration of Irma Gerstenberger originating from Beresina in the Eastern European region of Bessarabia, today part of Ukraine and Moldavia.[8] In this version, the father is out in the fields and the mother leaves the infant child alone for a while as she goes to weed the potato field. When a snake is about to attack the baby in the cradle, the cat attacks and kills it, being bitten and killed itself by the snake. When the mother returns home, she finds the dead animals and realizes that the cat saved her child. A nineteenth-century Welsh tale current in Anglesea (Anglesey) relates the story to Gelert, Prince Llewellyn of Carnavonshire's faithful dog.[9] Out hunting one day, Llewellyn happens to miss the dog that would usually answer the call of his horn. Returning home, the prince finds Gelert lying by the overturned cradle and there is blood all over the room. Presuming that the dog killed his child, the prince runs his sword through the dog, only to find out soon after that the child is safe as the faithful dog slew the wolf that had attacked it. Gelert dies licking his grieving master's hand and is buried in a regular grave. From then on, the place is known as Beth-Gelert, Gelert's Grave.

In European tradition, full-fledged versions of the tale are rendered in a large variety of medieval and early modern collections.[10] Already in the Middle Ages, the tale was attributed to a named individual dog. A particularly fascinating version was told by the thirteenth-century Dominican preacher and inquisitor Stephen of Bourbon (Étienne de Bourbon) who criticized the contemporary popular pilgrimage to the grave of Saint Guinefort, presumably the greyhound killed by his master due to a misinterpretation of the situation.[11] Warning against the consequences of rash action, early sixteenth-century German author Johannes Pauli advised his readers to first count the 24 letters of the alphabet before proceeding to act.[12]

The tale was mediated to European tradition by Latin translations of two of the most influential Middle Eastern collections of tales, the Arabic *Kalīla wa-Dimna* and the Persian *Sendbād-nāme* (The Book of Sendbād [the Sage]).[13] In

ʿAbdallāh Ibn al-Muqaffaʿ's eighth-century *Kalīla wa-Dimna*, the faithful animal is a weasel.[14] In Moḥammad ibn ʿAli Ẓahiri Samarqandi's *Sendbād-nāme*, compiled around the middle of the twelfth-century, it is a cat.[15] The complicated filiation of the medieval European translations was discussed in considerable detail by Jean-Claude Schmitt.[16] Rabbi Joël's mid-thirteenth-century Hebrew translation of the Arabic *Kalīla wa-Dimna* was in turn translated to Latin in John of Capua's *Directorium vitae humanae* (A Guide for Human Life) between 1263 and 1278. The latter later formed the basis for various translations into the European vernacular languages such as Anton von Pforr's German *Buch der Beispiele der alten Weisen* (Book of the Examples of the Old Sages), prepared around 1470. A second strand of tradition derives from the *Sendbād-nāme*, commonly known in European research as the book of *The Seven Sages*. In addition to the book's ancient Syriac, Greek, Hebrew, and Persian versions, the tale has recently also been identified in the book's Arabic version contained in the *Mi'at layla wa-layla* (The Hundred and One Nights), the North African sibling collection of *The Thousand and One Nights* whose oldest preserved manuscript may or may not have been written in the thirteenth century.[17] From the French translations of *The Seven Sages* prepared in the twelfth and thirteenth centuries onward, the present tale, in international research labeled *canis* (The Dog), is included in the collection's numerous European versions. Except for changing the brave animal to a dog, the tale's European versions show little variation.

The texts contained in both Middle Eastern collections ultimately derive from the Sanskrit mirror for princes, the *Panchatantra* (Five [Books of] Wisdom) whose roots go back to the third century BCE.[18] In the *Panchatantra*, the faithful animal is a pet mongoose. Versions of the tale are also given in a variety of other ancient Indian compilations,[19] including a selection of *Panchatantra* tales contained in Somadeva's eleventh-century *Kathāsaritsāgara* (The Ocean of Streams of Stories).[20]

Similar to tale type ATU 1339G: *The Relative in the Urn* (see essay **44, *Accidental Cannibalism***), the present tale's historical analysis traces the updating of a traditional tale in the genre of contemporary legend. This updating often includes the mention of individualized characters and specified informants, although the latter remain fairly vague. Both features aim to supply credibility to the tale at least to the degree that the narrated events could possibly have occurred. At the same time, the tale's adaptation to the context of modern societies obscures the tale's origin in the medieval and ancient literatures while still serving as an instructive warning against hasty action whose timelessness is documented by the tale's remarkable history.

Notes

1. Brednich, Rolf Wilhelm, *Die Ratte am Strohhalm: Allerneueste sagenhafte Geschichten von heute*, Munich: C.H. Beck, 1996, pp. 134–135, no. 100.
2. Portnoy, Ethel, *Broodje aap met*, Amsterdam: de Harmonie, 1992, p. 53.

3. Burrison, John A., *Storytellers: Folktales and Legends from the South*, Athens: University of Georgia Press, 1989, pp. 62–63, 236.

4. Brunvand, Jan Harold, *The Choking Doberman and Other "New" Urban Legends*, New York: W.W. Norton & Company, 1984, pp. 33–34.

5. Blackburn, Stuart, "The Brahmin and the Mongoose: The Narrative Context of a Well-Travelled Tale," *Bulletin of the School of Oriental and African Studies* 57 (1996), pp. 494–507, at p. 494.

6. Schmitt, Jean-Claude, "Hundes Unschuld," in *Enzyklopädie des Märchens*, vol. 6 (1990), cols. 1362–1368.

7. Río Cabrera, Juan Antonio del, and Melchor Pérez Bautista, *Cuentos populares de animales de la Sierra de Cádiz*, Cádiz: Universidad de Cádiz, 1998, pp. 144–145, no. 48.

8. Cammann, Alfred, *Deutsche Volksmärchen aus Russland und Rumänien: Bessarabien, Dobrudscha, Siebenbürgen, Ukraine, Krim, Mittelasien*, Göttingen: Schwartz, 1967, pp. 364, 443, no. 129.

9. Emerson, Peter Henry, *Welsh Fairy-Tales and Other Stories*, London: D. Nutt, 1894, pp. 19–21.

10. Tubach, *Index exemplorum*, p. 139, no. 1695; Schmitt, Jean-Claude, *Der heilige Windhund*, Stuttgart: Klett-Cotta, 1982, pp. 61–70.

11. Étienne de Bourbon, *Anecdotes historiques, légendes et apologues tirés du recueil inédit d'Étienne de Bourbon*, ed. A. Lecoy de la Marche, Paris: Renouard, 1877, pp. 325–328, no. 370; Schmitt, *Der heilige Windhund.*

12. Pauli, Johannes, *Schimpf und Ernst*, ed. Johannes Bolte, Berlin: Herbert Stubenrauch, 1924 (reprint Hildesheim: Olms, 1972), vol. 1, pp. 163–164; vol. 2, p. 321, no. 257.

13. Chauvin, *Bibliographie*, vol. 2 (1879), pp. 100, no. 59; vol. 8 (1904), pp. 66–67, no. 31.

14. Cheikho, Louis, *La version arabe de Kalîlah et Dimnah ou Les fables de Bipai*, (Beirut 1905) reprint Amsterdam: Philo Press, 1981, pp. 176–177.

15. Samarqandi, Moḥammad ʿAli Ẓahiri, *Sendbād-nāme*, ed. Moḥammad Bāqer Kamāl al-Dini, Tehran: Mirāṯ-e maktub, 1381/2002, pp. 109–112.

16. For detailed references to the European works, see Schmitt, *Der heilige Windhund*, pp. 61–70; Schmitt, "Hundes Unschuld."

17. Marzolph, Ulrich, "The *Hundred and One Nights*: A Recently Acquired Old Manuscript," in *Treasures of the Aga Khan Museum: Arts of the Book & Calligraphy* (Exhibition Catalogue), ed. Margaret S. Graves and Benoît Junod, Istanbul: Aga Khan Trust for Culture and Sakip Sabancı University and Museum, 2010, pp. 206–215, at p. 214, no. 13.14; Fudge, Bruce, ed. and transl., *A Hundred and One Nights*, New York: New York University Press, 2016, pp. 254–257.

18. Clouston, William Alexander, *Popular Tales and Fictions: Their Migrations and Transformations*, ed. Christine Goldberg, Santa Barbara, CA: ABC-Clio, 2002, pp. 363–374; Blackburn, "The Brahmin."

19. Blackburn, "The Brahmin;" Hertel, Johannes, *Indische Märchen*, Düsseldorf: Diederichs, 1953, p. 278, no. 58.

20. Somadeva, *The Ocean of Story: Being C.H. Tawney's Translation of Somadeva's Kathā Sarit Sāgara (or Ocean of Streams of Stories)*, ed. N.M. Penzer, (2nd ed. London: privately printed, 1923–1928) reprint Delhi: Motilal Banarsidass, 1968, vol. 5, pp. 138–139, no. 140.

CHAPTER 5

The Cat and the Candle (ATU 217)

In his assessment of Occitan narrative tradition in Southern France, Daniel Fabre published a short tale recorded from the oral performance of a certain Mélanie, aged 66, who was born in the region and still lived there at the time of recording. The tale is about the owner of a certain hotel who trained a cat to sit still and hold a candle. Although the text does not mention this explicitly, the candle is assumed to be lit. The cat's owner makes a lot of money by people betting, without success, that they could make the cat drop the candle. One day, however, a young man is advised by his father to take along a rat. When the young man lets the rat run loose, the cat immediately drops the candle and chases the rat. That way the young man wins the bet.[1]

The tale corresponds to tale type ATU 217: *The Cat with the Candle*. It is rather short and clearly structured, and so there is little variation in versions recorded from oral tradition in Europe or elsewhere. At times, the situation is introduced by the cat's owner expressing his conviction that education trumps natural inclination, as in texts from Denmark[2] or Ireland.[3] The Irish tale elaborates on the situation to some extent by challenging the cat with a total of three mice one after the other. While the cat does not quiver on seeing the first and second mouse, it finally throws away the candle and hunts the third one. Most, if not all, of the tale's European texts likely derive from the tale's first attestation in the late twelfth-century Latin tale of *Solomon and Marcolf* and its vernacular versions published in several European languages. Although many of the texts collected from modern oral tradition attribute the events to the famous ancient ruler and his court fool,[4] the action was often adapted to other characters who enjoyed a similar prominence in their regional, ethnical, or linguistic contexts. These characters include, for instance, the twelfth-century Jewish philosopher Maimonides and a Christian ruler, the fifteenth-century Italian jester Arlotto Mainardi, and an unnamed philosopher, or the Prussian ruler Frederick II (r. 1740–1786) and his court fool Kion.[5]

Although French folklorist Emmanuel Cosquin adduced vague parallels in arguing for the tale's origin from ancient Indian literature,[6] the earliest-known Indian version is given in Hēmavijaya's *Kathāratnākara* (The Sea of Tales), completed in 1600.[7] Johannes Hertel opined that the tale might have passed into Muslim literature from Jain narrative literature in North-Western India,[8] but other than frequently documented versions in modern Indian tradition there is no evidence to support his claim. Similarly, folklorist Haim Schwarzbaum mentioned the narrative motif of "absurd attempts to change animal nature" (Mot. J1908) from the context of Aesopic literature that may or may not have a genetic connection to the tale under consideration.[9]

The tale's oldest-known version is attested in the book *al-ʿIqd al-farīd* (The Unique Necklace) compiled by the Andalusian Arab author Ibn ʿAbd Rabbih (d. 940).[10] Ibn ʿAbd Rabbih's text is framed by the tale of an unspecified Persian king who used to follow the advice of his wise vizier. When the king dies and his son takes over, the latter does not ask the advice of his father's vizier any more, instead claiming that he himself would prove the vizier to be wrong. The young ruler challenges the vizier, asking him whether he deems education (*adab*) or natural inclination (*ṭabīʿa*) to be stronger. As the vizier argues that natural inclination will always trump education, the ruler invites him to a meal where light is supplied by a number of cats holding candles in their paws. Proudly referring to the cats' extraordinary training, the ruler asks the vizier to admit his defeat. The vizier, however, prefers to remain silent for the time being. Instead, he asks a servant to catch some mice and brings them along the next night. As soon as the cats have taken their position, the vizier releases the mice, and the cats chase them, abandoning the candles and in the resulting mess almost setting the room on fire. Witnessing the situation, the ruler admits that he himself was wrong and reinstalls the vizier in his previous position. The book's author closes his argument by referring to a Koranic passage (38:86) implying that any constraint to abandon one's natural inclinations is blameworthy as nature is bound to gain the upper hand, just as heated water will get cold again, and just as the bitter fruits of a tree will remain bitter, even though one might apply honey to its trunk.

In Arabic, the tale is later cited in al-Sharīshī's (d. 1222) commentary to al-Ḥarīrī's (d. 1122) *Maqāmāt*[11] and, almost verbatim, albeit in a somewhat shorter form and without the author's concluding observations, in the book *Ḥadāʾiq al-azāhir* (Flower Gardens), compiled by Ibn ʿĀṣim (d. 1426), an author who likewise lived in Muslim Spain.[12] In the nineteenth century, a much-condensed version of the tale is contained in al-Shirwānī's (d. 1840) anthology *Nafḥat al-Yaman* (A Breeze from Yemen).[13]

The tale's reference to a Persian ruler and the scene's setting in a palace (*bayt*) with a lavishly laid dinner suggest a cultivated setting in a sedentary culture. The message conveyed by the tale's simple, yet striking demonstration finds a close equivalent in an ancient Arabic tale whose context refers to Arab Bedouin tradition.[14] Here, a man raised a wolf cub on sheep's milk. Even so, the grown-up wolf attacks and kills the sheep. First attested in the ninth century, this tale remained popular with a variety of Arabic authors up to the nineteenth century.[15]

Notes

1. Fabre, Daniel, and Jacques Lacroix, *La tradition orale du conte occitan*, vol. 2: *Les Pyrénées Audoises*, Paris: Presses Universitaires de France, 1973, p. 363, no. 64.

2. Kristensen, Evald Tang, *Molbo- og aggerbohistorier samt andre dermed beslægtede fortællinger*, vol. 2, Århus: Forfatterens Forlag, 1903, p. 140, no. 518.

3. Ó Duilearga, Séamus, *Seán Ó Conaill's Book: Stories and Traditions from Iveragh*, Baile Átha Cliath: Comhairle Bhéaloideas Éireann, 1981, pp. 5–6, no. 10.

4. See, e.g., Allardt, Anders, and Selim Perklén, *Nyländska folksagor och -sägner*, Helsingfors: Nyländska afdelningen, 1896, p. 231, no. 184; Kristensen, *Molbo- og aggerbohistorier*, pp. 140–142, no. 519; Jegerlehner, Johannes, *Sagen und Märchen aus dem Oberwallis*, Basel: Helbig & Lichtenhahn, 1913, pp. 127–129, no. 146; Liungman, Waldemar, *Sveriges samtliga folksagor i ord och bild*, vol. 2, Stockholm: Lindfors, 1950, pp. 47–48; Schier, Kurt, *Schwedische Volksmärchen*, 2nd ed., Düsseldorf and Cologne: Diederichs, 1971, pp. 244–245, no. 81; Van der Kooi, Jurjen, and Theo Schuster, *Der Großherzog und die Marktfrau: Märchen und Schwänke aus dem Oldenburger Land*, Leer: Schuster, 1994, p. 367, no. 255.

5. For references to these and other characters see Marzolph, Ulrich, "Katze mit der Kerze," in *Enzyklopädie des Märchens*, vol. 7 (1993), cols. 1113–1117, at col. 1115.

6. Cosquin, Emmanuel, "Le conte du chat et de la chandelle," in Cosquin, *Études folkloriques*, Paris: Édouard Champion, 1922, pp. 403–495.

7. Hēmavijaya, *Kathāratnākara: Das Märchenmeer. Eine Sammlung indischer Erzählungen*, transl. Johannes Hertel, vol. 2, Munich: Georg Müller, 1920, pp. 292–295, no. 223.

8. Hertel, Johannes, "Altindische Parallelen zu Babrius 23," *Zeitschrift für Volkskunde* 22 (1912), pp. 244–252, at p. 252.

9. Schwarzbaum, Haim, *The Mishle Shu'alim (Fox Fables) of Rabbi Berechiah ha-Nakdan*, Kiron: Institute for Jewish and Arab Folklore Research, 1979, pp. 169–170.

10. Ibn ʿAbd Rabbih, Abū ʿUmar Aḥmad ibn Muḥammad, *Kitāb al-ʿIqd al-farīd*, 3rd ed., ed. Aḥmad Amīn, Aḥmad al-Zayn, Ibrāhīm al-Abyārī, Cairo: Lajnat al-ta'līf wa-'l-tarjama wa-'l-nashr, 1372/1952, vol. 3, pp. 4–5; see Marzolph, *Arabia ridens*, vol. 2, p. 91, no. 365.

11. See Basset, *Mille et un contes*, vol. 2, p. 171, no. 157.

12. Ibn ʿĀṣim al-Andalusī, Abū Bakr ibn Muḥammad, *Ḥadā'iq al-azāhir*, ed. ʿAfīf ʿAbd al-Raḥmān, Beirut: Dār al-Masīra, 1401/1981, p. 373; see López Bernal, Desirée, "Los cuentos de Ibn 'Asim (m. 1426): precedentes en la península ibérica de relatos españoles y del folklore universal en el siglo XV," *Hispanic Review* 85.4 (2017), pp. 419–440, at pp. 428–429.

13. Rescher, Oskar, *Die Geschichten und Anekdoten aus Qaljûbî's Nawâdir und Schirwânî's Nafhat el-Jemen*, Stuttgart: W. Heppeler, 1920, p. 267, no. 111.

14. Nöldeke, Theodor, "Das Gleichnis vom Aufziehen eines jungen Raubtiers," in ʿAǧab nāma: *A Volume of Oriental Studies Presented to Edward G. Browne*, ed. Thomas W. Arnold and Reynold A. Nicholson, Cambridge: University Press, 1922, pp. 371–382.

15. Marzolph, *Arabia ridens*, vol. 2, p. 26, no. 96.

CHAPTER 6

The Princess and Her Secret Affair (ATU 306)

Tale number 133 in the Grimm brothers' *Kinder- und Hausmärchen* (Children's and Household Tales) is titled "Die zertanzten Schuhe" (The Shoes That Were Danced to Pieces).[1] Essentially, the tale is about an upper-class girl's illicit and clandestine nocturnal amusement the nature of which a clever man finds out, hereby earning the reward promised by the girl's father. Contributed by Jenny von Droste-Hülshoff, the sister of German poet Annette von Droste-Hülshoff (1797–1848),[2] the Grimms' tale is a version of the international tale type ATU 306: *The Danced-Out Shoes.*

> Every night, the king guards his twelve beautiful daughters in a locked room, only to find their shoes danced to pieces in the morning. The king has a herald announce that whoever finds the solution to the enigmatic events will be allowed to take one of the princesses as his wife. Should he fail, however, his life is forfeited. Many princes try their luck, but all of them fall asleep at night and lose their lives.
>
> Aided by an old woman, a poor soldier finally tries his luck. The woman advises him not to drink the wine he is offered at night and also gives him a coat that would make him invisible. At night, the soldier feigns drinking the wine and then pretends to fall fast asleep. As soon as the princesses feel safe, they leave the room through an underground corridor the entrance to which is hidden under one of the beds, and the soldier follows them invisibly. Although he steps on the coat of the youngest princess and makes noise breaking twigs from the silver, golden, and diamond trees they pass on the way, the magic coat prevents the soldier from being discovered. In the end, the twelve princesses meet twelve princes who take them in their boats to a castle on an island where they dance until early the next morning. All the while, the soldier watches them. Finally, the princesses return to their own castle. As the soldier hurries home before them, the princesses find him snoring loudly. Having been granted another two days respite, the soldier witnesses the same events during the following nights. In order to prove his allegations later, he takes along a cup from the island castle.

> On the fourth day, the soldier discloses his discovery to the king and shows him the twigs and the cup as proof. The princesses have to admit their misdemeanor, and the soldier is married to the eldest princess.

With considerable variations in details, although not in structure, the tale is documented in a fair number of texts from nineteenth- and early twentieth-century oral tradition in Europe and the Americas.[3] Almost 30 versions are attested from Greece alone.[4] The version performed by Maria Ostwald, aged 17, from the German community in the Hungarian village of Hajos, reads like a close retelling of the Grimm text, albeit with a different ending.[5] As in the Grimm tale, in Ostwald's version the princes are enchanted, and their meeting with the princesses serves gradually to disenchant them. When in Ostwald's version the king allows the old man who solved the princesses' secret to marry one of them, the old man choses the eldest daughter, as in the Grimm version. Here, however, the princess refuses to marry a beggar, as she claims that the princes with whom they spent the night will be disenchanted in just another three days. Accordingly, all of the princesses leave through the trapdoor, and however much the king searches for them, they never come back. François Gagnepain, honorary vice director of the Natural History Museum in Paris, knew the French version he narrated in 1950 from his mother, an illiterate peasant woman.[6] Even so, his tale is again very similar to the Grimm version. The fact that the old soldier La Ramée receives advice and the gift of a coat from a fairy that makes him invisible is motivated by the alms he gave her previously as the fairy appeared to him in the guise of an old beggar. At night, the king's only daughter is joined by another eleven princesses who appear through a trapdoor. When the soldier discloses the events to the king the next day, the princess rejoices, as he has broken the spell that would have kept her forever in the company of the other dancing princesses. Anna Charlotte Nilsson, born 1843, whose Swedish version her daughter Emelie Jonson recorded in 1925, knew the tale from her parent's house.[7] Here, a princess has to dance with a troll every night until she has danced seven pairs of shoes to pieces. A young man determined to disenchant the princess tricks three giants out of their magic objects, a pair of magic boots, a cloak that makes its bearer invisible, and a lantern that would show its owner where the troll is. With the help of the lantern, the young man is able to follow the troll and the princess at night. The boots enable him to cross over to the island where the troll and the princess are merrymaking, and with the help of the cloak he partakes in their meal without being seen. The next day, the young man proves his allegations about where the princess has been by showing the king a number of objects he collected. As the princess is now disenchanted, she is married to the young man. The late nineteenth-century Romanian version collected by Georgi Ruseski from his mother in Stara Zagora introduces a dragon who is in love with the tsar's daughter and who collects her every night to play with her for some time.[8] A clever man stands up to the challenge to find out what happens after many others failed. The morning after witnessing the events, he tells the king "how the dragon took the princess to his premises, where they talked and frolicked." As he shows a number of objects collected from the otherworld as proof, the princess confesses that all of the clever man's allegations are true. With little variation, the tale was also recorded from various other European countries. Versions from the Americas include those narrated by Adela Aguilar Sánchez from Chaquiago Alto, Andalgalá, in Argentina;[9] by an unnamed travel guide from Ubá, Minas Gerais, in Chile;[10] by Francisco Coronado from Ignao, Valdivia, in Chile;[11] and by Celia Álvarez from Mezcala in Mexico.[12]

The present tale is one of the rare items for which no versions predating the period of intensive recording activities in nineteenth-century Europe are known. Consequently, discussions of the tale's historical development are equally rare, although a (somewhat vague) "Oriental" origin was suggested.[13] In Western tradition, the Grimm version appears to have been influential, although by no means exclusively so. The following discussion of the tale's "Oriental" versions is built on an assumption. This assumption implies that the excessive dancing in the course of which the shoes are danced to pieces as mentioned in most of the tale's Western versions in connection with the princess' illicit and clandestine nocturnal amusement is a euphemism for sex, since fancy shoes and dancing in folktales often serve as a metaphor for sexual activities.[14] Assuming that the tale's Western versions are domesticated to make suitable entertainment for a juvenile audience, a tale performed by the Syrian narrator Ḥannā Diyāb for Antoine Galland, the French scholar who introduced *The Thousand and One Nights* to world literature, presents an interesting precursor.[15] Ḥannā Diyāb told his tale to Galland on May 15, 1709, presumably in French, and the latter took it down in shorthand in his diary.[16] Although Galland later included elaborations of most of the Syrian narrator's tales in his *Mille et une nuit*, the present tale was never published, probably due to its explicit content of illicit sexual practices that risked shocking Galland's contemporary audience.

A king has his three sons brought up and educated in a secluded atmosphere. When the princes finally become aware of the world, one after the other gains their father's permission to travel. At first, the eldest son reaches a palace whose princess offers herself in marriage if her suitor can present a satisfactory solution to her question. If not, he will be beheaded. When the prince agrees to the condition, she asks him where the City of Gold is located. As he does not know the answer, they cut off his head. Through a token of life, his father learns about his son's death. The same happens to the second son. As the king is reluctant to let his youngest son set out, the prince leaves secretly. Meeting the princess, he pretends to know where the City of Gold is located and is granted forty days respite to prove his assertion.

Not exactly knowing where to go, the prince rests at the foot of a mountain. He saves the chicks of the giant bird Roc from a serpent's attack, and

> upon their return the grateful birds take him to the City of Gold. From his hiding place in the palace, he sees a flock of birds transform themselves into human beings, the princess and an old female magician in their midst. The company enjoys dinner and dancing, and then a black man and the princess retreat to sleep together. The prince kills the sleeping black man and puts his head in a bag, together with the princess's jewelry. Burning a feather the Rocs had given him, he then summons the helpful birds who take him back to the princess's palace.
>
> The following day, the princess has also returned. The prince shows proof of his knowledge about the events to the king who puts the princess's fate in the young man's hands. The prince obliges the princess to resuscitate his brothers, and all of them leave for home. On the way, the prince puts the mischievous princess to death.

Although Ḥannā Diyāb's tale reads like a distant relative of the tale's Western versions, it displays essentially the same content and structure. Specific points corresponding in both forms of the tale are the challenge to solve an enigma on pain of death, the sexually inflected adventure of the princess in an otherworldly context, the prince solving the enigma with the help of supernatural creatures, and his bringing back tangible objects as proof of his experience. At the same time, the two forms differ decisively in terms of implicit moral. Most Western versions take the princesses' conduct at face value, at best implicitly commenting on their unacceptable conduct by preventing them from continuing their habit. Some versions explicitly excuse their violation of moral decency and their transgressive clandestine amusement by saying that the princesses were under a spell and thus were not responsible for their action. In terms of moral judgment, this feature even serves to justify their cruelly indifferent stance toward the many men who are killed on their behalf and whose involvement they sometimes comment upon with emotionally detached sarcasm. In Ḥannā Diyāb's version, the princess herself is a magician, and it is probably not so much her consciously enacted sexual transgression for which she is punished in the end but the fact that she practices sorcery. Essentially, both a potential continuation of the princesses' dancing habits and the magician's sorcery pose a permanent danger to male supremacy.

Ḥannā Diyāb's tale, in its turn, is closely related to an ancient Indian tale contained in Somadeva's eleventh-century *Kathāsaritsāgara* (The Ocean of Streams of Stories). This is the "Story of the Golden City," narrated by the supernatural being Śaktivega, the former Brāhman Śaktideva, as his own series of adventures.[17] In relation to the Indian tale, Ḥannā Diyāb's version was heavily critiqued for being "badly motivated," for constituting a "clumsy contamination" including various unrelated elements and, in general, for being "a badly founded reinterpretation of the elements supplied by the Indian tale."[18] Justified as this judgment may or may not be from the vantage point of a modern Western literary critic, it disregards the storyteller's creativity as well as the fact that he did not intend to "retell" the Indian tale but rather presented his own specific interpretation after a period of several hundred years of, probably oral, transmission.

> Śaktivega's "Story of the Golden City" introduces the extraordinarily clever and knowledgeable princess Kanakarekhā who will only agree to marry "whatever Brāhman or Kshatriya has succeeded in seeing the city called the Golden City." At first, the good-for-nothing spendthrift Śaktideva simply pretends to have seen the Golden City, but his fraud is easily discovered. Following this experience, Śaktideva is determined to actually find the Golden City. He goes through a series of adventures involving repeated shipwreck, being swallowed by a huge fish, overhearing a bird conversation, and being saved from a tree at the side of a maelstrom by clinging to a giant bird before reaching his destination. From his host, the beautiful female supernatural being Chandraprabhā, he learns that her three sisters are under a spell to live as humans for annoying a hermit. When his host is away, Śaktideva transgresses Chandraprabhā's order not to ascend the palace's middle terrace and happens to find the lifeless bodies of three maidens, princess Kanakarekhā being one of them. When he attempts to mount a horse standing on the bank of a beautiful lake, the horse flings him into the lake, and as he emerges, he finds himself in the middle of a garden lake in his own city. Presenting himself to the princess, Śaktideva furnishes a token to prove his speaking the truth when he asks her to explain why he saw her lying dead on a sofa in the Golden City and yet sees her here alive. Although princess Kanakarekhā acknowledges that he solved the enigma, he has now broken her spell, and she leaves her human body.
>
> In the further series of events, which are of no relevance for the present discussion, Śaktideva again travels to the Golden City, eventually marries all of the four supernatural sisters (and a couple of other women) and is himself transformed into the supernatural being Śaktivega.

Numerous other Arabic tales build on the enigma of a woman's illicit nocturnal sexual activity, demonstrating the motif's tremendous creative power. One of the better-known stories is the "Tale of the Ensorcelled Prince" that is contained in the core corpus of *The Thousand and One Nights* as documented in the oldest preserved manuscript dating to the fifteenth century.[19] Here, the woman herself is a sorcerer who drugs her husband unconscious at night so as to be able to visit her lover. When the husband one night does not drink the soporific she serves him and stays awake, he surprises his wife with her lover. After he has seriously wounded the lover in an attempt to kill him, the woman turns her husband's lower half into stone (thus abolishing his sexual authority), turns his kingdom into a lake, and puts a spell on its inhabitants who are transformed into fishes of different colors (hereby vitiating his political power). As part of the *Nights'* core corpus, the tale reflects the motif of adultery and revenge in the collection's frame tale.[20]

Although the "Oriental" tales discussed above have never been discussed in relation to the Western tales of the shoes that were danced to pieces, particularly Ḥannā Diyāb's tale suggests that the latter constitute domesticated versions of the former. As additional historical evidence for the tale's stages of transmission in literary sources is lacking, oral tradition with its tremendously creative impetus supplies the strongest argument for the tale's numerous variations and adaptations. This evaluation applies to both the differences between the "Oriental" and Western strands of tradition and the multiple variations encountered in the tale's Western versions whose exact filiation still needs to be unraveled.

Notes

1. Bolte and Polívka, *Anmerkungen*, vol. 3, pp. 78–84, no. 133.

2. Grimm, Jacob and Wilhelm, *Kinder- und Hausmärchen: Ausgabe letzter Hand mit den Originalanmerkungen der Brüder Grimm*, ed. Heinz Rölleke, Stuttgart: Philipp Reclam Jun., 1980, vol. 3, p. 495, no. 133.

3. Köhler-Zülch, Ines, "Schuhe: Die zertanzten S.," in *Enzyklopädie des Märchens*, vol. 12 (2008), cols. 221–227.

4. Papachristophorou, Marilena, *Sommeils et veilles dans le conte merveilleux grec*, Helsinki: Suomalainen Tiedeakatemia, 2002, p. 175.

5. Györgypal-Eckert, Irma, *Die deutsche Volkserzählung in Hajós, einer schwäbischen Sprachinsel in Ungarn*, Hamburg: Hansischer Gildenverlag, 1941, pp. 105–106.

6. Delarue, Paul, *Le conte populaire français*, vol. 1, Paris: Érasme, 1957, pp. 167–169, no. 306.

7. Liungman, Waldemar, *Weißbär am See: Schwedische Volksmärchen von Bohuslän bis Gotland*, Kassel: Röth, 1965, pp. 60–64, 175.

8. Nicoloff, Assen, *Bulgarian Folktales*, Cleveland: Nicoloff, 1979, pp. 26–31, 211–212, no. 15; see also Haralampieff, Kyrill, *Bulgarische Volksmärchen*, Düsseldorf: Diederichs, 1971, pp. 57–63, 285, no. 15.

9. Chertudi, Susanna, *Cuentos folklóricos de la Argentina*, vol. 1, Buenos Aires: Ed. Univ., 1960, pp. 96–99, no. 37.

10. Pino Saavedra, Yolando, *Cuentos folklóricos de Chile*, vol. 1, Santiago de Chile: Universidad de Chile, 1960, pp. 97–100, no. 15.

11. Cascudo, Luis da Câmara, *Contos tradicionais do Brasil: confrontos e notas*, 2nd ed., Bahia: Progresso, 1955, pp. 129–131.

12. Robe, Stanley L., *Mexican Tales and Legends from Los Altos*, Berkeley: University of California Press, 1970, pp. 137–138, no. 38.

13. Liungman, Waldemar, *Die schwedischen Volksmärchen: Herkunft und Geschichte*, Berlin: Akademie-Verlag, 1961, pp. 54–56, no. 306.

14. Cardigos, Isabel, "Schuh," in *Enzyklopädie des Märchens*, vol. 12 (2007), cols. 212–217, at cols. 214–215.

15. For the following, see Bremond, Claude, "En deçà et au-delà d'un conte: le devenir des thèmes," in Bencheikh, Jamel Eddine, Claude Bremond, and André Miquel, *Mille et un contes de la nuit*, Paris: Gallimard, 1991, pp. 79–258, at pp. 134–142; Marzolph, Ulrich, "Ḥannā Diyāb's Unpublished Tales: The Storyteller as an Artist in His

Own Right," in Bauden, Frédéric, and Richard Waller, eds., *Antoine Galland (1646–1715) et son Journal*, Louvain: Peeters, 2018, pp. 75–92, at pp. 94, 96.

16. Galland, Antoine, *Le Journal d'Antoine Galland (1646–1715): La période parisienne*, ed. Frédéric Bauden and Richard Waller, vol. 1, Leuven: Peeters, 2011, pp. 335–338; Marzolph, Ulrich, with Anne E. Duggan, "Ḥannā Diyāb's Tales, part 1," *Marvels & Tales* 32.1 (2018), pp. 113–154, at pp. 140–143.

17. Somadeva, *The Ocean of Story: Being C.H. Tawney's Translation of Somadeva's Kathā Sarit Sāgara (or Ocean of Streams of Stories)*, ed. N.M. Penzer, (2nd ed. London: privately printed, 1923–1928) reprint Delhi: Motilal Banarsidass, 1968, vol. 2, pp. 171–238, no. 29 (bk. 5, ch. 24); Van Buitenen, Johannes Adrianus Bernardus, *Tales of Ancient India*, Chicago: The University of Chicago Press, 1959, pp. 79–101.

18. Bremond, "En deçà et au-delà," p. 139; see Marzolph, "Ḥannā Diyāb's Unpublished Tales," p. 96.

19. Marzolph and Van Leeuwen, *The Arabian Nights Encyclopedia*, vol. 1, p. 176, no. 13; Chraïbi, Aboubakr, *Les Mille et une nuits: Histoire du texte et Classification des contes*, Paris: L'Harmattan, 2008, p. 103, no. 222.

20. Pinault, David, *Story-Telling Techniques in the* Arabian Nights, Leiden: E.J. Brill, 1992, pp. 31–81.

CHAPTER 7

The Unfaithful Wife Transforms Her Husband into a Dog (ATU 449)

As a rule, the nineteenth- and twentieth-century collectors of folk narratives from European oral tradition avoided publishing tales whose dominant connection to and probable origin from previous literary sources was obvious to them. They would exclude these tales as not resulting from the genuine expression of popular tradition, but rather constituting mere retellings of a literary model that did not have a bearing on the presumed creativity of the anonymous "folk" their publications would celebrate. A famous exception to the rule is the Grimm tale "Simeli Mountain," a version of the tale of Ali Baba from *The Thousand and One Nights*, discussed in essay **30, *The Robbers Hiding Their Treasures in a Magic Cavern***.[1] The present tale, classified as tale type ATU 449: *Sidi Numan*, is another case in point.

The tale of the woman who magically transforms her husband into a dog is a tale of multiple transformations. Initially, the evil woman transforms her husband into a dog. After his disenchantment, the husband would in his turn transform his wife, usually into a mule or a mare. Contrary to the man's transformation, the woman's is a lasting one. A previous study of the tale's numerous versions documented from European oral tradition identified a Western and an Eastern strand of tradition.[2] The Western strand of tradition covers all of Europe except for Eastern Europe and also includes versions collected in the Americas.

In 1937, Ludwig Mühlhausen recorded a Gaelic version from the oral performance of Séamus Ó Casaide (James Cassidy), aged 82, from Teilinn, Tirconell, South Donegal, Ireland.[3] The narrator, who had spent many years of his life as a peddler selling Irish goods in Pennsylvania, Ohio, Kentucky, and Illinois, learned the tale from cooper Pad Long from Tralee, County Kerry.

> An old bachelor in the narrator's village was once approached by a young woman who proposed to marry him. As she promises to work efficiently, they marry. During meals, the woman eats only as much as she sucks up through a straw. Noticing that his wife leaves the bed at night, her husband follows her and observes her devouring a dead body in the cemetery

> together with another man. When he confronts her with his discovery at breakfast the next morning, she transforms him into a dog by striking him with her magic wand.
>
> Chased by the other dogs in the village, he seeks shelter with a butcher but is thrown out. Finding refuge with a baker, he gains attention by identifying counterfeit coins in the baker's shop. The daughter of a woman whom he follows realizes that he is an enchanted human being and disenchants him by spraying him with an unspecified liquid. The young woman happens to know the man's wife, who had been "at school" together with her, and teaches the man how to transform his evil wife by spraying some of the magic liquid on her face.
>
> The man transforms his wife into a mare and punishes her by giving her a heavy beating with his whip. When the police notice him maltreating the mare, he is taken to court. The judge sympathizes with his treatment of the mare and does not condemn him, but orders him to give the mare to somebody else.

In the late nineteenth-century French version recorded in Celles-sur-Nièvre from the oral performance of Joseph Bruère, the cannibal woman is a fairy who only eats a single spoonful of soup at table.[4] When the man confronts his wife with the fact that he saw her dig up and devour a dead body, she transforms him into a dog. He is recognized and disenchanted by a friendly old woman (later called his "godmother") who uses a magic wand to transform the woman into a mare. Nine days later, however, when riding the mare he lets the wand fall to the ground, his wife disenchants herself and transforms him into a midge. After he is almost killed by a cattle drover, the friendly old woman again disenchants him and transforms his sleeping wife into a stove pipe. The tale ends on a humorous note, saying that this way she cannot do any harm unless she falls on somebody's head when there is a great wind. A French version from the Languedoc localizes the events in the city of Narbonne and even specifies the exact place where the "suburban beauty" used to live before her marriage as the area of the brickworks close to the Perpignan gate.[5] In this version, the witch arouses her husband's suspicion by only partaking of clear water and giving him a soporific at night. She takes off for the cemetery astride a broom and through the chimney. The man's disenchantment is effected by sprinkling him with water after the dog identified a counterfeit coin. Once his wife is transformed into a mare, the man has her work hard carrying waste in the city during the day and turning the wheel to draw water from the well at night. Essentially congruent versions, including in particular the episode with the counterfeit money, were recorded from areas as far apart as Germany[6] and New Mexico.[7]

Contrasting with texts from the Western strand of tradition, Eastern European versions[8] do not portray the wife as a cannibal, instead having her entertain a relationship with a lover, thus motivating her to get rid of her husband by transforming him into an animal. Moreover, the man often undergoes several instances of transformation, in addition to being a dog often being transformed into a bird. The imaginative version told by the Wallachian peasant Traila Salitraru introduces the poor peasant Stanshu who cultivates corn on the only field he owns.[9]

> One day, the peasant notices that horses devastate his crop. He keeps watch at night and sees a group of wild horses emerge from a black cloud that touched the ground. Catching one of the horses, he is about to kill it when the horse speaks up and tells him to take a walnut from inside its right ear. The nut fulfills all of his wishes so that he turns rich. His wife soon becomes bored being alone and takes a lover. One day she steals the wish-fulfilling nut and transforms her husband, first into a donkey and then into a dog. As a dog, he renders service to the shepherd and rescues the king's three children who had been abducted by an iron wolf. Learning about his success, his wife transforms him into a pigeon. The bird laments about its fate to the "holy Mother Friday" who advises him how to get hold of the magic nut. Once he regains the nut, he transforms himself back into human shape and his wife and her lover into a pair of oxen.

The Lithuanian version contributed by Kazimierz Dejkus from Staki, district Kaunas, in November 1889, begins when the peasant Juodjonis marries a young woman without knowing that she is a witch.[10] Having started a relationship with their farmhand, the woman transforms her husband into a dog. The dog renders good service to the shepherd and is eventually sold to a rich man. In the rich man's house, the dog chases away robbers who attack the house at night transformed as wolfs and is richly rewarded. Longing to meet his wife, the man transformed into a dog goes to see her and is transformed into a bird. A peasant catches the bird and disenchants the man. The peasant gives the man a magic wand with the help of which he transforms his wife into a cow and the farmhand into an ox, both of whom the man employs to plow his fields. Two Russian texts in Aleksandr Afanasyev's collection introduce the tale by first telling about marvelous events that challenge the listener to find out still more marvelous ones.[11] The structure of the two tales corresponds to the above-sketched pattern in that the man is transformed first into a dog and then into a bird, a woodpecker or a raven. Exceptionally, one of the versions has a happy ending in that the man reforms his wife by first transforming her into a goat and then disenchanting her, following which they live happily ever after.[12]

Both strands of European tradition are ultimately related to the tale's version as published in the tenth volume of Antoine Galland's adapted and enlarged translation of *The Thousand and One Nights*.[13] While the Western strand of tradition consists of more or less close retellings of Galland's version, the Eastern European strand is probably more directly connected to the Middle Eastern context from which Galland's version derives. Galland adapted the text he published from the oral performance of the Syrian Maronite storyteller Ḥannā

Diyāb who had come to Paris in the company of the French traveler Paul Lucas. In his diary, Galland noted for Friday, May 10, 1709, that returning from the Academy he went to see Ḥannā Diyāb who told him the tale whose basic structure he wrote down.[14] The text as written down in Galland's diary begins with a frame tale using the frequent motif of the Caliph Hārūn al-Rashīd and his vizier roaming the city in disguise at night (Mot. K1812.17)[15] in order to distract the caliph from his great melancholy. At first they meet a blind man who grabs the caliph's hand and only lets go when slapped. Next, they see "a young man mounted on a horse that he maltreated cruelly, heavily beating it with a whip." Both men are brought to court the next day to tell their experiences. The blind man's adventure corresponds to tale type ATU 836F*: *The Miser and the Eye Ointment* (see essay **22, *The Greedy Man Is Blinded and Falls into Misery***). When the young man is presented to the caliph, he "could hardly tell his story and only did so when forced."[16]

> Sir, said [he], I had an income to live at ease, and I had gotten married. When we were at the table, my wife did not eat anything but a few grains of rice, so little that it would have fitted onto a single spoon. I did everything I could. . . . One night when we were sleeping together, I realized that she got up and dressed herself without making any noise. I pretended to sleep, got up, and followed her. She left the house and went to the cemetery. With the help of a *ghūla*, she removed the soil from a grave where a dead person had been buried the same day; she ate from the flesh of the dead body. . . . When I saw that she wanted to return to the house I preceded her and went back to bed. The next day when she did not want to eat anything but rice in her usual manner, I told her that it was certainly better to eat good meat than the flesh of dead bodies. She changed colors, went into a fury with her eyes protruding from her head. . . . She took some water [that she had] prepared and cast it in my face while uttering charms. I was transformed into a dog. She took a stick and after almost having beaten me to death she opened the door to the street, and almost crushed me when I passed through. I saved myself at a seller of sheep's heads after having been vigorously chased by the dogs of the neighborhood.
>
> My master had a bad temper. After I had stayed with him for a day, he maltreated me so badly that I saved myself, leaving him for a baker. The baker treated me with utmost kindness, and I did not leave him. . . . A woman who had come to buy some bread wanted to give counterfeit money to the baker, and when she denied doing so, the baker turned to me. He showed me the money, and I indicated with a sign that it was counterfeit. News of my ability to distinguish [counterfeit money] spread, and in order to see for themselves everybody hastened to come from the farthest quarters of the city to buy bread from my master, who could hardly furnish it and who got rich by these means.

> A woman who came looked at me more attentively than the others and in a manner that made me believe that she knew I was not a dog like the other ones. I slipped away and followed her to her home. She made me meet her daughter who was a magician and who recognized my disgrace. She cast some water at me . . . and I became a human being again. She gave me some water in a vessel, telling me to cast it at my wife before she looked at me. I cast it at her uttering the charms that she had taught me, and she was transformed into a mare.

Ḥannā Diyāb originated from the Syrian town of Aleppo, and while he was Christian, his version of the tale relates to a web of tradition that encompasses various other tales documented in Muslim Arabic literature of the classical and postclassical period. First and foremost, the present tale is essentially an enriched and elaborated version of a relatively short tale that is told right at the beginning of *The Thousand and One Nights* in the story of "The Trader and the Jinnī"[17] when a *jinnī* threatens to execute a merchant who had inadvertently killed the *jinnī*'s son. One after the other, three old men appear and ransom a third of the merchant's life each by telling a marvelous tale. The present tale is told by the third old man.[18]

> One day he caught his wife in bed with a black slave, whereupon she cast a spell on him, transforming him into a dog. In the shape of the dog, he became friends with a butcher, whose daughter noticed that he was a transformed human. She disenchanted him and instructed him how to turn his wife into a she-mule by means of a magic spell.

The tale is only contained in the later Arabic manuscripts of the *Nights*. In the fifteenth-century manuscript that served as the basis for Galland's adapted translation, it is not included.[19] Instead of citing the tale, the text here only says "that the third old man told the demon a story that was even stranger and more amazing than the first two." Being "much amazed" and "swaying with delight," "the demon released the merchant and departed."[20] The story of "The Trader and the Jinnī" in the *Nights* that might have supplied a basic model for Ḥannā Diyāb's elaborated version is, in its turn, closely modeled on the tale of Khurāfa that is most elaborately told in the proverb collection compiled by al-Mufaḍḍal ibn Salama (d. after 903).[21] In this tale, Khurāfa tells the Prophet Muḥammad how one night he had been taken prisoner by three *jinns*. As they discussed whether to kill, release, or enslave him, one after the other three men appeared, each of whom suggested sharing the prisoner with him, in return for which he would tell the *jinns* an amazing story. The third story embedded in this frame is a tale of transformation in which the narrator's wicked maid plotted together with one of his slaves to transform him into an animal by means of a magic potion. Instead, he himself tricked the two into drinking the magic potion themselves, so that they were transformed into a mare and a stallion. So the ninth-century tale of Khurāfa already presents the basic structure of the tale that later developed into the tale told by the third old man in the story of "The Trader and the Jinnī" and into the version told by Ḥannā Diyāb.

The transformation into an animal by spraying a human being with water is but a faint echo of a particularly detailed process of magic transformation that would have rung a bell in the mind of the premodern Arab audience. This detailed process is described in the tale of "Jullanār the Sea-Born and Prince Badr Bāsim" that is contained both in the fifteenth-century manuscript of *The Thousand and One Nights*[22] and in the fourteenth-century collection of tales known as *Tales of the Marvelous and News of the Strange*.[23] Although this tale also mentions the capacity of water (in addition to a magic spell) to transform a human being into a bird and disenchant him or her later, the witch Lāb practices a complex procedure to produce a magic porridge or dough that would transform a human man into a donkey. The protagonist sees the witch "open a chest, from which she took five containers, and from each of these she took red sand, which she scattered around, muttering a spell over it. When it was opposite the couch a stream flowed through it, and then from a small box she removed barley, which she sowed there, and it immediately sprouted and ripened. She took it, ground it up and made porridge, which she put in a bowl."[24] A similar procedure is also described in Somadeva's eleventh-century *Kathāsaritsāgara* (The Ocean of Streams of Story) and in a number of Arabic texts dating from the ninth to the thirteenth century.[25]

The weird element of the woman devouring the dead bodies dug up in the cemetery in Ḥannā Diyāb's tale finds an early precursor in the tale of the daughter of the *qāḍī* of the Palestinian town Ramla, a tale that was also read as a prefiguration of tale type ATU 315A: *The Cannibal Sister*.[26] It is contained in both of the large narrative compilations written down by al-Muḥassin al-Tanūkhī (d. 994).[27] Although the woman in al-Tanūkhī's tale does not actually devour the flesh of the dead bodies, she desecrates them by taking away and collecting their shrouds.

Finally, the act of recognizing the man in the shape of a dog as a transformed human being would have reminded the premodern Arab audience of "The Second Qalandar's Tale" that is already contained in the fifteenth-century manuscript of the *Nights*.[28] In this tale, a *jinnī* transforms a prince who has a relationship with a woman the *jinnī* had abducted into a monkey. Since the monkey later turns out to be skilled in calligraphy and playing chess, the king's daughter discovers his true nature and opts to disenchant him. The process of disenchantment is, however, much more complicated and violent than in the present tale, as it involves a dramatic fight between the *jinnī* and the sorceress in the course of which the prince loses an eye from a flying spark, the king's face is partly burned, and the exhausted princess goes up in flames.

There is little doubt that both the Western and Eastern European versions of the tale derive either directly from Ḥannā Diyāb's narration as adapted and published by Galland or from the narrative culture that gave rise to the Syrian narrator's story. In addition to focusing on acts of transformation, the present tale itself bears witness to the transformations narratives experience as they travel through time and space. In short, the tale's hypothetical travel appears to have begun with a simply structured tale in which an evil woman attempts to get rid of her master or husband by transforming him into an animal. The next stage would have been a successful act of transformation followed by a disenchantment and another act of transformation in revenge. And, finally, the extended structure would have been embellished by additional elements such as the transgressive act of cannibalism and the demonstration of the dog's, that is, the transformed man's, intelligence that in their turn also relied on a long history in the narrative universe of Arabic tradition.

Notes

1. Marzolph, Ulrich, "Grimm Nights: Reflections on the Connections Between Grimms' *Household Tales* and the *1001 Nights*," *Marvels & Tales* 28.1 (2014), pp. 75–87, at p. 81.

2. Lox, Harlinda, "Sidi Numan," in *Enzyklopädie des Märchens*, vol. 12 (2008), cols. 642–645.

3. Mühlhausen, Ludwig, *Zehn irische Volkserzählungen aus Süd-Donegal, mit Übersetzung und Anmerkungen*, Halle (Saale): Max Niemeyer, 1939, pp. 23–25, 68–71, 117–118, no. 3.

4. Millien, Achille, "Les goules dans les traditions du Nivernais," in *Congrès internationale des traditions populaires, première session: Paris 1889, compte rendu des séances*, Paris: Imprimerie nationale, 1891, pp. 59–61; quoted in Delarue, Paul, and Marie-Louise Tenèze, *Le conte populaire français*, vol. 2, Paris: Maisonneuve et Larose, 1964, pp. 120–122.

5. Lambert, Louis, *Contes populaires du Languedoc*, Montpellier: Coulet, 1899 (reprint Carcassonne: Garae, 1985), pp. 35–43, no. 5; also in Fabre, Daniel, and Jacques Lacroix, *Histoires et légendes du Languedoc*, Paris: Tchou, 1970, pp. 85–89; summarized in Delarue and Tenèze, *Le conte populaire français*, vol. 2, p. 122.

6. Pröhle, Heinrich, *Kinder- und Volksmärchen*, Leipzig: Avenarius und Mendelssohn, 1853 (reprint ed. Helga Stein, Hildesheim: Georg Olms, 1975), pp. 119–120, no. 35 I; Strackerjahn, Ludwig, *Aberglaube und Sagen aus dem Herzogtum Oldenburg*, 2nd ed., ed. Karl Willoh, Oldenburg: Gerhard Stalling, 1909, vol. 1, pp. 482–484, no. 253d; also in Van der Kooi, Jurjen, and Theo Schuster, *Der Großherzog und die Marktfrau: Märchen und Schwänke aus dem Oldenburger Land*, Leer: Schuster, 1994, pp. 108–109, 401, no. 38.

7. Espinosa, José Manuel, *Spanish Folk-Tales from New Mexico*, New York: American Folk-Lore Society, 1937, pp. 169–170, no. 82 (narrated in 1931 by Rufina Valencia, aged 71, from Santa Cruz).

8. The Eastern strand of tradition is discussed in detail by Horálek, Karel, "Märchen aus Tausend und einer Nacht bei den Slaven," *Fabula* 10 (1969), pp. 155–195, at pp. 169–178.

9. Schott, Arthur, "Neue walachische Märchen," in *Hausblätter*, ed. F.W. Hackländer and Edmund Hoefer, vol. 4, Stuttgart: Dolph Krabbe, 1847, pp. 314–320, no. 4.

10. Dowojna-Sylwestrowicz, Mieczysław, *Podania żmujdzkie*, vol. 1, Warsaw: Arct, 1894, pp. 317–324.

11. Afanasyev, Aleksandr Nikolayevich, *Narodnye russkie skazki*, ed. Vladimir Jakovlevich Propp, Moscow: Gosudarstvennoye Izdatel'stvo Khudozhestvennoy Literatury, 1957, vol. 2, pp. 298–300, no. 254; pp. 300–302, no. 255.

12. Ibid., pp. 298–300, no. 254.

13. Chauvin, *Bibliographie*, vol. 6 (1902), pp. 198–199, no. 371; Marzolph and Van Leeuwen, *The Arabian Nights Encyclopedia*, vol. 1, pp. 380–381, no. 351.

14. Galland, Antoine, *Le journal d'Antoine Galland (1646–1715): La période parisienne*, vol. 1 (1708–1709), ed. Frédéric Bauden and Richard Waller, Leuven: Peeters, 2011, pp. 327–330, particularly at pp. 329–330.

15. Marzolph and Van Leeuwen, *The Arabian Nights Encyclopedia*, vol. 2, p. 806; see also Marzolph, Ulrich, "Hārūn al-Rašīd," in *Enzyklopädie des Märchens*, vol. 6 (1990), cols. 534–537.

16. The following translation is adapted from Marzolph, Ulrich, with Anne E. Duggan, "Ḥannā Diyāb's Tales," part 1, *Marvels & Tales* 32.1 (2018), pp. 113–154, at pp. 137–138.

17. Marzolph and Van Leeuwen, *The Arabian Nights Encyclopedia*, vol. 1, pp. 419–420, no. 3.

18. Chauvin, *Bibliographie*, vol. 7 (1903), p. 130, no. 398; the following summary is quoted from Marzolph and Van Leeuwen, *The Arabian Nights Encyclopedia*, vol. 1, p. 378, no. 7.

19. Chraïbi, Aboubakr, *Les Mille et une nuits: Histoire du texte et Classification des contes*, Paris: L'Harmattan, 2008, p. 100, no. 398. Muhsin Mahdi's edition of the Galland manuscript adds several versions of the tale in an appendix; see Mahdi, Muhsin, ed., *The Thousand and One Nights (Alf Layla wa-Layla) from the Earliest Known Sources*, vol. 1, Leiden: Brill, 1984, pp. 689–701.

20. Haddawy, Husain, transl., *The Arabian Nights*, New York: Alfred A. Knopf, 1990, p. 29. For a discussion of this lacuna in context, see Marzolph, Ulrich, "Making Sense of the 'Nights:' Intertextual Connections and Narrative Techniques in the 'Thousand and One Nights'," *Narrative Culture* 1.2 (2014), pp. 239–258, at pp. 244–245.

21. Mufaḍḍal ibn Salama, *al-Fākhir*, ed. Charles A. Storey, Leiden: Brill, 1915, pp. 138–140; ed. ʿAbd al-ʿAlīm al-Ṭaḥāwī and Muḥammad ʿAlī al-Najjār, Cairo: ʿĪsā al-Bābī al-Ḥalabī, 1380/1960, pp. 169–171, in no. 280; MacDonald, Duncan B., "The Earlier History of the Arabian Nights," *Journal of the Royal Asiatic Society* (1924), pp. 353–397, particularly at pp. 372–376; Drory, Rina, "Three Attempts to Legitimize Fiction in Classical Arabic Literature," *Jerusalem Studies in Arabic and Islam* 18 (1994), pp. 146–164, particularly at pp. 147–157; the tale's summary as given here relies on Marzolph and Van Leeuwen, *The Arabian Nights Encyclopedia*, vol. 2, pp. 616–617.

22. Marzolph and Van Leeuwen, *The Arabian Nights Encyclopedia*, vol. 1, pp. 248–251, no. 227. For the representation of magic in this tale and other tales of *The Thousand and One Nights* see Marzolph, Ulrich, "Magie in den *Erzählungen aus Tausendundeiner Nacht*," in *Die Geheimnisse der oberen und der unteren Welt: Magie im Islam zwischen Glaube und Wissenschaft*, ed. Sebastian Günther and Dorothee Pielow, Leiden: Brill, 2018, pp. 403–422.

23. Marzolph, Ulrich, ed., *Das Buch der wundersamen Geschichten: Erzählungen aus der Welt von 1001 Nacht*, Munich: C.H. Beck, 1999, pp. 163–192, 644–645, no. 6; *Tales of the Marvellous and News of the Strange*, transl. Malcolm C. Lyons, London: Penguin, 2014, pp. 113–134.

24. *Tales of the Marvellous*, transl. Lyons, pp. 129–130.

25. Somadeva, *The Ocean of Story: Being C.H. Tawney's Translation of Somadeva's Kathā Sarit Sāgara*, ed. N.M. Penzer, reprint Delhi: Motilal Banarsidass, 1968, vol. 6, pp. 55, 62–66, no. 163.

26. Katrinaki, Manouela, "Schwester: Die menschenfressende S.," in *Enzyklopädie des Märchens*, vol. 12 (2007), cols. 428–431.

27. Tanūkhī, Abū ʿAlī al-Muḥassin ibn ʿAlī al-, *Kitāb al-Faraj baʿd al-shidda*, ed. ʿAbbūd al-Shālijī, Beirut: Dār Ṣādir, 1398/1978, vol. 3, pp. 378–385, no. 362; Tanūkhī, *Nishwār al-muḥāḍara wa-akhbār al-mudhākara*, ed. ʿAbbūd al-Shālijī, Beirut: Dār Ṣādir, 1392/1972, vol. 3, pp. 236–243, no. 152; Hamori, Andras, "The Collector of Ramlah," *Studia islamica* 71 (1990), pp. 65–75; see also Loosen, Paul, "Tanūchī, seine Art und Kunst," *Zeitschrift für Semitistik und verwandte Gebiete* 10 (1935), pp. 46–73; Tanūkhī, At-, *Ende gut, alles gut: Das Buch der Erleichterung nach der Bedrängnis*, transl. Arnold Hottinger, Zurich: Manesse, 1979, pp. 194–203.

28. Marzolph and Van Leeuwen, *The Arabian Nights Encyclopedia*, vol. 1, pp. 338–340, no. 16.

CHAPTER 8

The Two Hunchbacks (ATU 503)

The tale of the two hunchbacks is a tale of reward and punishment, structurally similar to tale type ATU 480: *The Kind and Unkind Girls* and ATU 613: *The Two Travelers.* In tale type ATU 480, the girl who serves the supernatural being kindly is rewarded, whereas her envious stepsister refuses to be helpful and is punished. In terms of reward and punishment, the girls are recompensed with beauty and ugliness, respectively. In tale type ATU 613, the traveler who was blinded by his companion overhears supernatural beings mention a way to achieve his cure. When his companion tries to imitate his success, the supernatural beings punish him, as they suspect the companion to be the one who revealed their secret.

Classified as tale type ATU 503: *The Gifts of the Little People*, the presently discussed tale adds to the narrative pattern of reward for the good and punishment for the evil by healing the former's affliction and transferring it to the latter.[1] In the tale's standard versions, both characters are hunchbacks. In his chance encounter with a group of supernatural beings (or a single supernatural being), the kind hunchback is unafraid and joins their merrymaking. Consequently, the supernatural beings heal him of his affliction by straightening his back. When the second hunchback envies his companion and tries to imitate his success, the supernatural beings are, for various reasons, annoyed, and add the former's hump to his own. Documented worldwide, the tale was recorded particularly frequently from Gaelic oral tradition in Ireland and Scotland where the supernatural beings encountered are fairies. An "expertly told" version was transcribed by Hamish Henderson from the performance of the Scottish storyteller Bella Higgins in Blairgowrie, Perthshire, in 1955.[2]

> Two hunchbacks living at the opposite ends of a glen (valley) have the habit of paying alternating visits to each other on Sundays. When the hunchback living at the glen's lower end goes to see his companion one Sunday, he hears "a lot of singin going on," with the song going, "Saturday, Sunday; Saturday, Sunday; Saturday, Sunday." Immediately, he joins in, "Saturday, Sunday, Monday, Tyoooosday!" The three kinds of fairies in the wood are so delighted by his addition that they grant him to have

his back made "as straight as a rush," henceforth to be in the best of health, and to "always have plenty, tae he goes tae his grave." When he reaches his companion, the latter has difficulty recognizing him in his new shape.

Told what happened, the second hunchback wants to imitate his companion's success. Going to see his companion the following Sunday, he joins the fairies' song by adding all of the remaining days of the week. The fairies are so annoyed at him "for destroyin our lovely song" that they wish his hump to "be a thousand times bigger," himself to be the ugliest man on earth, and "to be in torture and punishment" for the rest of his life. The envious hunchback's hump grows to such an enormous size that is takes "aboot seventeen pair of blankets tae cover him," and when he dies, it takes "twenty-four coffins to hold him."

In a late nineteenth-century Dutch tale, the supernatural beings are witches who dance transformed as cats.[3] When the first hunchback fearlessly joins their dance, the cats enjoy it so much that they take away his hump, hanging it high up on a nail. When the second hunchback tries to imitate his companion's luck, he dances so poorly that the cats add his companion's hump to his own. Blaming his companion for his misfortune, the second hunchback starts a fight as a result of which he is killed. An early twentieth-century version recorded in Brittany introduces a hunchback tailor who joins the fairies' song by adding Thursday to their song, "Monday, Tuesday, Wednesday."[4] As a reward, the fairies take away his hump. When the hunchback weaver tries to imitate his neighbor's good luck by adding Friday to the fairies' song, they are so annoyed that they add his companion's hump to his own. Grieving about his bad luck, the weaver dies within the course of a year. In the Judaeo-Spanish folktale told by Mérou Lévi, aged 55, in Saloniki, the hunchback goes to the public bath at night.[5] When he adds the Jewish holiday Saturday to the song of "the good ones" (*los buenos*), they are so delighted about him being Jewish that they relieve him of his hump. The wife of his hunchback neighbor urges her husband to copy the experience, although he is reluctant to do so. When the second hunchback adds the Christian holiday Sunday to their song, the supernatural beings are so annoyed at him that they add his companion's hump to his own.

The tale's distribution and history were scrutinized by German folklorist Ina-Maria Greverus in a traditional application of the historic-geographic method.[6] On the basis of the tale's reported geographical distribution, and to a certain extent ignoring historical evidence, the author concludes that the tale likely originated in the Gaelic language area whence it was disseminated to other regions.[7] The tale's oldest European versions date to the seventeenth century.[8] In his *De nuce maga Beneventana* (Of the Magical Walnut Tree in Benevento), published in 1647, the physician Pietro Piperno from Benevento in Campania, Italy, tells of the hunchback cobbler Lomberto who, when walking back to his native village Altavilla one night, witnesses a group of men and women dancing and singing, "Thursday and Friday."[9] As he adds Saturday and Sunday to their song, one of the dancers hits him so hard on the back that his hump moves from the back to the front (implying that his back is straightened). When he exclaims, "Jesus, Mary," in astonishment, the dancers vanish. Returning home, his wife at first does not want to let him in as she does not recognize him without his hump. This version has a single transformation effected by supernatural beings. An unsuccessful imitation resulting in a second transformation is first mentioned in a letter the Italian physician Franceso Redi, the founder of experimental biology, wrote to his colleague Lorenzo Bellini on January 25, 1689.[10] In Redi's tale, the supernatural beings at the walnut tree in Benevento reward the first hunchback's graceful dance by painlessly removing his hump with a saw of butter, sealing the wound with a coating of marzipan. The envious imitator is punished by having the former's hump attached to his own. Irish poet Thomas Parnell's (1678–1718) poem "A Fairy Tale in the Ancient English Style" narrates the events similarly.[11] In Parnell's version, the events take place in King Arthur's days, and the two main characters are hunchback knight Edwin and shapely knight Topaz. Oberon invites Edwin to partake in the fairies' dance, and Robin Goodfellow throws him against the ceiling so that his hump gets stuck there. When his envious rival, Topaz, also wants to dance with the fairies, they throw him against the ceiling so that Edwin's hump sticks to his back. Although the three seventeenth-century versions demonstrate a certain overlap, each of them has a somewhat different action, and the only version with two hunchbacks is the one given by Francesco Redi.

Arabic literature documents a closely corresponding tale featuring two hunchbacks in Egyptian man of letter Shams al-Dīn Muḥammad ibn Ḥasan al-Nawājī's (d. 1455) *Ḥalbat al-kumayt* (The Racecourse of the Bay Horse), a "literary celebration of wine and connected themes."[12] The events narrated by al-Nawājī take place in a public bathhouse, a place that in Arabic popular tradition is known to be an abode of supernaturals.[13] The text introduces two hunchback friends, one of whom is kind (*laṭīf*) whereas the other one is grumpy and ill-tempered (*kathīf*). The text further specifies that, intially, each of the two hunchbacks has a hump on the back and another one on the chest.[14] One day, the kind hunchback retreats into a separate room in the public bathhouse, enjoying wine and food. As he starts singing, suddenly the wall splits and a hideous elephant-shaped demon, an *ʿifrīt*, appears. Notwithstanding the menacing appearance, the hunchback is not afraid, instead inviting the demon to share his company. Reciprocating the man's kindness, the demon relieves him of his humps by rubbing them and attaching them to the room's ceiling. Then he straightens the man's body with his hands. When the former hunchback informs his companion about the events, the latter also wants to get rid of his humps. Having bought wine and food for three *dirhams*, he goes to the separate room in the bathhouse. As soon as the demon hears the hunchback's voice he appears, imagining his friend to have returned. But since the second hunchback is extremely frightened, the demon at first appeases him. Then he takes the first hunchback's two humps stuck to the room's ceiling and attaches them to the second hunchback's body, one on the left, and the other one on the right side. Later someone on the streets asks the hunchback what happened to him. Sulkily (and not without a touch of self-mockery) he responds, "This is God's work. And as for the two humps on my sides, I bought them from the bathhouse for three *dirhams*." Al-Nawājī's tale is without precedence in Arabic literature. It is quoted again with little variation in a nineteenth-century Arabic chapbook.[15] In the twentieth century, the tale was recorded from oral tradition in Arabic[16] and Persian.[17] The high frequency represented by altogether 29 recorded oral versions in Persian by 1978[18] leads one to presume a written intermediary source, probably a nineteenth- or early twentieth-century chapbook, so far unidentified. In Persian, the tale is linked to the proverbial expression "*quz bālā quz*" (Hump upon hump), the Persian equivalent of the English expressions "from the frying pan into the fire," or "from smoke to smother," implying that things go from bad to worse.

Two earlier texts with a similar structure are known from times and regions far apart. The Japanese *Uji shūi monogatari* (A Collection of Tales from Uji), compiled in the thirteenth century, contains a tale introducing an old man "who had a big wen on his right cheek, the size of an orange."[19] Stuck in the mountains one night, the man hides inside a hollow tree. A group of hideous demons arrive, and their chief takes pleasure in watching them dance. When the chief demon wishes for a truly extraordinary dance, the old man takes courage, comes out of his hiding and dances for him. The demons are so pleased by the old man's performance that they ask him to come again. Intending to make sure that the old man will return, they retain his wen as a pledge. When the old man's neighbor, who has a large wen on his left cheek, learns how the old man got rid of his wen, he persuades his neighbor to tell him all the details of what happened. At first, the demons are delighted to welcome once again the person they take for the previous dancer. However, they do not like the man's dance this time and do not want to see him again. They decide to return the pledge, so that now the envious neighbor has a wen on each side of his face. According to Hiroko Ikeda, the tale "is well known throughout Japan since it has been included in elementary school textbooks."[20] Greverus identified two texts from late nineteenth-century oral tradition in Europe in which the action is virtually the same, particularly regarding the motif of the pledge instead of that of reward and punishment. As one version is from Lappish[21] and the other from Wallonian tradition,[22] Greverus regards a direct oral or literary transmission as the only possible explanation for the correspondence.[23]

The most ancient historical text with a similar structure is the legend of Pandarus and Echedorus[24] "found in the third-century BCE Epidaurian miracle tablets."[25] Through a dream vision in which the god wraps a band around his head, Pandaurus is relieved of the tattoos on his forehead that are now fixed to the band. Later, Echedorus who also seeks to be relieved of the tattoos on his forehead takes Pandaurus's money to dedicate it to Asclepius. But Echedorus fails to deliver the money and lies about it in his dream, promising instead to have the god's portrait painted. Consequently, the "quizzical Asclepius" instructs him to fasten the old headband of Pandarus around his own head, as a result of which he not only keeps his own tattoos but also receives those of Pandarus in addition.

The general motif underlying all of the cited tales, the motif of unsuccessful imitation, is apparently ubiquitous.[26] The more specifically the motif is shaped, the more likely are direct relations between versions documented in times and regions far apart. Considering this theoretical stance, the tale's fifteenth-century Arabic version might well constitute an adaptation of the Greek legend to the specific circumstances of Arabic urban culture of the Muslim period. The text given in Francesco Redi's seventeenth-century letter might then read as a further adaptation of the Arabic tale of the two hunchbacks to Italian tradition as specifically linked to the walnut tree in Benevento. And the frequently documented tales from Gaelic tradition in Ireland and Scotland would appear to be versions that were so successfully adapted to their particular context as to gain the extraordinary popularity documented by nineteenth- and twentieth-century folklorist research. Thus, the frequency of a given text's documentation often primarily bespeaks folklorists' collecting activity rather than being indicative of a tale's origin.

Notes

1. Clouston, William Alexander, "The Hunchback and the Fairies," in Clouston, *Popular Tales and Fictions*, ed. Christine Goldberg, Santa Barbara, CA: ABC-Clio, 2002, pp. 172–184.

2. Bruford, Alan, and Donald A. MacDonald, *Scottish Traditional Tales*, Edinburgh: Polygon, 1994, pp. 333–336, 473, no. 65.

3. Cox-Leick, A.M.A., and Heinrich Leonhard Cox, *Märchen der Niederlande*, Düsseldorf: Diederichs, 1977, pp. 92–94, 251, no. 20.

4. Delarue, Paul, and Marie-Louise Tenèze, *Le conte populaire français*, vol. 2, Paris: Maisonneuve et Larose, 1964, pp. 228–230, no. 503.

5. Crews, Cynthia Mary, *Contes judéo-espagnols des Balkans*, ed. A. Angelopoulos, Paris: Corti, 2009, pp. 210–211, 373.

6. Greverus, Ina-Maria, "Die Geschenke des kleinen Volkes, KHM 182 = AT 503: Eine vergleichende Untersuchung," *Fabula* 1 (1958), pp. 263–279.

7. See also Uther, Hans-Jörg, "Gaben des kleinen Volkes," in *Enzyklopädie des Märchens*, vol. 5 (1987), cols. 637–642.

8. For the following, see Bolte and Polívka, *Anmerkungen*, vol. 3, pp. 324–326, no. 182.

9. Piperno, Pietro, *De effectibus magicis libri sex ac de nuce maga beneventana liber unicus*, Naples: Colligni, 1647, p. 41 (casus II); http://reader.digitale-sammlungen.de/en/fs3/object/display/bsb10133198_00005.html (accessed January 24, 2018); Leland, Charles Godfrey, *Etruscan Roman Remains in Popular Tradition*, New York: Charles Scribner's Sons, 1892, pp. 192–193.

10. Imbriani, Vittorio, *La novellaja fiorentina*, Livorno: Vigo, 1877, pp. 561–563, no. 43.

11. Parnell, Thomas, *The Poetical Works*, ed. John Mitford, London: William Pickering, 1833, pp. 25–32.

12. Van Gelder, G.J.H., "al-Nawājī," in Meisami, Julie Scott, and Paul Starkey, eds., *Encyclopedia of Arabic Literature*, London: Routledge, 1998, p. 584; Van Gelder, Geert Jan, "A Muslim Encomium on Wine: *The Racecourse of the Bay (Ḥalbat al-kumayt)* by al-Nawāǧī (d. 859/1455) as a Post-classical Arabic Work," *Arabica* 42 (1995), pp. 222–234.

13. Grotzfeld, Heinz, *Das Bad im arabisch-islamischen Mittelalter*, Wiesbaden: Harrassowitz, 1970, pp. 129–133.

14. Nawājī, Shams al-Dīn Muḥammad ibn Ḥasan, *Ḥalbat al-kumayt*, Cairo 1299/1881, p. 49; French translation by Basset, René, "Les bossus et l'éléphant," *Bulletin de folklore* 2 (1892), pp. 256–257; German summary in Bolte and Polívka, *Anmerkungen*, vol. 3, pp. 328–329.

15. Ālātī, Ḥasan al-, *Tarwīḥ al-nufūs wa-muḍḥik al-ʿabūs*, Cairo: Maṭbaʿa al-Jarīda al-maḥrūsa, 1889, vol. 2, pp. 157–158.

16. El-Shamy, *Types*, p. 253, no. 0503.

17. Marzolph, *Typologie*, pp. 103–104, no. 503.

18. Enjavi Shirāzi, Abol-Qāsem, *Tamsil va masal*, 2nd ed., Tehran: Amir Kabir, 2537/1978, pp. 245–247.

19. Mills, Douglas Edgar, *A Collection of Tales from Uji: A Study and Translation of Uji Shūi Monogatari*, Cambridge: Cambridge University Press, 1970, pp. 137–140, no. 3.

20. Ikeda, Hiroko, *A Type and Motif Index of Japanese Folk-Literature*, Helsinki: Suomalainen Tiedeakatemia, 1971, pp. 128–129, no. 503.

21. Halász, Ignácz, *Svéd-lapp nyelv*, vol. 3: *Ume- és Tornio-Lappmarki nyelvmutatványok*, Budapest: Magyar Tudományos Akadémia, 1887, p. 106.

22. Monseur, Eugène, "Les deux bossus et les nains," *Bulletin de Folklore* 2 (1893), p. 77.

23. Greverus, "Die Geschenke," p. 277.

24. Frazer, James George, *Folk-Lore in the Old Testament: Studies in Comparative Religion, Legend and Law*, vol. 2, London: MacMillan and Co., 1919, pp. 45–46; Wesselski, *Märchen des Mittelalters*, pp. 207–208; Naiden, Fred, "*Hiketai* and *Theōroi* at Apidauros," in Elsner, Jaś, and Ina Rutherford, eds., *Pilgrimage in Graeco-Roman & Early Christian Antiquity: Seeing the Gods*, Oxford: Oxford University Press, 2005, pp. 73–95, at pp. 83–85.

25. Holmes, Brooke, "Aelius Aristides's Illegible Body," in Harris, William Vernon, and Brooke Holmes, eds., *Aelius Aristides Between Greece, Rome, and the Gods*, Leiden: Brill, 2008, pp. 81–113, at p. 103. The summary follows this source.

26. Köhler-Zülch, Ines, "Imitation: Fatale und närrische I.," in *Enzyklopädie des Märchens*, vol. 7 (1993), cols. 92–100.

CHAPTER 9

The Unpromising Rascal Makes His Fortune with the Help of a Magic Object (ATU 561)

The Hungarian "Tale of a Gypsy Boy," originally published in the Hungarian journal *Magyar Nyelvőr* in 1874, has all the features of a typical fairy tale.[1] Essentially, it tells of a lower-class rascal who makes his fortune, in the end being rewarded by the threefold fairy-tale bliss of becoming rich, marrying the princess, and being destined to succeed the ruler.[2]

There once was a gypsy woman whose only son was very handsome. One day, the son said to his mother, "My dear mother! Go to the king and tell him I want to marry his daughter!" His mother refused to go, since it was quite unlikely that the king would give his daughter to a gypsy boy. But the young man would not let go, he went to the king and asked him for his daughter. The king said, "Get lost, you foul gypsy! How would I give my daughter to a gypsy?" But the young man kept on begging, until the king finally said, "All right, I will give her to you if you bring three trees to my courtyard in the morning. One of them is to bear golden figs, the second one golden apples, and the third one golden pears."

After this, the gypsy went to the church and stole everything he could lay his hands on. When he was ready to leave he noticed that he had left a rusty old lock. He thought to himself, "I will also take the lock. Perhaps this will be the most useful thing of all." So he decided to take the lock, too. When he turned it around three times, three beautiful maidens appeared, addressing him, "O king, what is your command?" He told them to plant three trees of such and such a kind in the king's courtyard in the morning, and all three of them disappeared. In the morning, when the king looked into his courtyard, he noticed the three trees, just as he had asked for. Now what was left for him to do? He gave his daughter to the gypsy and also gave them a nasty pigpen to live in. The gypsy's wife was full of grief because of their nasty house. But the man consoled her and said, "Don't worry! It will all change for the better!" Then he turned the lock, and again the three maidens appeared, and the gypsy told them to build a castle in front of the king's castle in the morning, just like the king's castle. They built a beautiful castle, and the gypsy and his wife moved in.

One day, when the gypsy had left his house, a Jew came to his wife offering all kinds of nice goods. The gypsy's wife was fond of a pair of nice shoes and asked the Jew for the price. The Jew said, "I will not give them unless you hand me the rusty lock that is hanging on that nail over there!" Well, the woman gave it to him. When the Jew turned the lock around three times, again the three maidens appeared and asked him, "Master Jew! What is your command?" He ordered them to take the gypsy's wife to a place beyond the seven seas, and they arrived there in a flash. Now the gypsy came home and looked for his wife but could not find her anywhere. He asked everybody whether they had seen his wife. A man told him that he had seen her with a Jew on their way to beyond the seven seas. So the gypsy decided to go there. He walked for three days and three nights, then he suddenly arrived beyond the seven seas. There he saw his wife and was very happy. At once he said, "Dear wife! Throw me the lock, so we can get back home!" The gypsy's wife said to the Jew, "Master Jew, sleep a little!" The Jew fell asleep, the woman threw the lock to her husband, and they got back home. The gypsy became king and said, "Now the princess is mine." And they lived happily ever after. If they have not died, they are still alive.

The tale's fairly rudimentary narrative is predicated on a set of standard fairy-tale elements and actions. The hero is an unpromising outsider from the lower strata of society who makes his fortune by recklessly transgressing the social order in stealing objects from the church. In wooing the king's daughter, the young man ostensibly attempts the impossible, and he uses the magic object he acquires through theft in a matter-of-fact manner without wondering about its origins or qualities. In terms of sociological background, the characters of the thievish gypsy and the rapacious Jew stand out. Both are as politically incorrect as they are frequent stereotypes in historical texts.[3] In terms of cultural history, "beyond the seven seas" as the ultimate faraway region plays on the value of the number seven as indicating perfection, and also constitutes a vague echo of the ancient concept of the seven climes. In folklorist typology, the narrative belongs to a group of fairy tales, tale types ATU 560–649, whose action revolves around a magic object. Probably the best-known Middle Eastern representative of this group is the tale of "Aladdin and the Wonderful Lamp" from *The Thousand and One Nights*[4] that is classified as tale type ATU 561: *Aladdin*.

At first sight, the Hungarian "Tale of a Gypsy Boy" does not seem to be specifically related to a tale from the *Nights*. The gypsy is a typical underdog character of Hungarian popular tradition; the church from which the gypsy steals the lock establishes a Christian context; and the pigpen where the gypsy and his wife are supposed to live clearly demonstrates that the tale's context is not a Muslim one. But even so, the tale can be argued to constitute a version of the tale of Aladdin from the *Nights*, with characteristic details of the Hungarian version resulting from the tale's adaptation to the cultural context of nineteenth-century Hungarian tradition. These details are the outcome of a process of cultural adaptation to which narratives submit when traveling to different cultural contexts, by which they remain culturally valid or acceptable, lest they be otherwise identified as alien, a verdict that would sooner or later lead to their disappearance.[5] It is not always easy to reconstruct the exact nature and characteristics of such a process of adaptation. In the present case, it is possible to identify an item linking the Hungarian "Tale of a Gypsy Boy" to the tale of Aladdin from the *Nights*. Scrutiny of the different qualities of the magic object and the hero's adversary allows us to trace connections and revisions.

The tale of Aladdin is one of the tales in the final volumes of Galland's *Nights* that Mia Gerhardt has dubbed "orphan tales,"[6] since they are not included in the fragmentary fifteenth-century Arabic manuscript that Galland took as the basis for his French translation published between 1704 and 1717.[7] The major source Galland used to fulfill the expectations of his audience for completing his translation, that is, for presenting a text that would actually fill a thousand and one nights, was the oral performance of the young Syrian Maronite storyteller Ḥannā Diyāb who had come to Paris in the company of the French traveler Paul Lucas.[8] Most of the tales Galland owes to Diyāb were originally narrated by the storyteller, taken down by Galland in his diary and elaborated by him for publication at some later point.[9] Diyāb produced the tale of Aladdin for Galland on May 5, 1709. The corresponding note in Galland's diary reads, "le matin, le maronite Hanna d'Alep, acheva de me faire le recit du Conte de La Lampe" (In the morning, the Maronite Hanna from Aleppo finished for me the tale of the lamp).[10] Unlike all of the other tales Diyāb narrated orally, Galland's diary does not contain a summary of the tale. On November 3, 1710, Galland however noted in his diary that he started to read the "Conte Arabe de la Lampe" that "le Maronite de Damas" had written down for him in Arabic more than a year before.[11] Two days later Galland noted that he added three pages and a half to his translation, and on November 15, he again mentioned his work on the tale.[12] The tale's written version produced by Diyāb has not been preserved. The tale's two Arabic manuscript versions identified by Western scholars are later intentional fabrications produced by Arabs residing in Paris, one of them by Michel Sabbagh, the other by Dom Chavis.[13] Galland's adapted and enlarged translation of the *Nights* from the Arabic, praised by historians of French literature as a "belle infidèle,"[14] was soon translated into other European languages including English and German, and eventually the collection's most popular tales were published in cheap "Grub Street" pamphlets and later on in large numbers of popular booklets.[15] Published in the ninth volume of Galland's *Mille et une nuit* (1712), the tale of Aladdin soon became a particular favorite of the European audience. Today, more than three hundred years after the tale's introduction into Western and, subsequently, world literature, its reception in addition to innumerable printed versions, adaptations and literary retellings includes numerous pieces of music, drama, pantomime, and film. One of the last major adaptations is the cartoon version presented in 1992 by the Walt Disney studios.[16]

Similar to the tale of Ali Baba (see essay **30, *The Robbers Hiding Their Treasures in a Magic Cavern***), the tale of Aladdin likely is a learned elaboration of the basic text supplied by Diyāb, adapted to the morals and ethics familiar to the European audience.[17] Consequently, the enthusiastic appreciation of the tales relies partly on the fact that the European audience was presented with tales whose "Oriental" coloring was exotic enough to be appreciated as "authentically Oriental" while at the same time familar enough not to provoke feelings of alienation.[18] Thus it was a matter of course that those two tales became the European (and American) audience's particular favorites.[19] In the eighteenth and nineteenth centuries they were transmitted to the reading and listening audience by way of numerous popular editions, and in the nineteenth and early twentieth centuries they would be retold, often by illiterate narrators, and would subsequently be recorded by folklorists. In this manner, several of the tales from the *Nights* had a considerable impact on European oral tradition.[20]

Regarding the impact of books in historical times, we should keep in mind that the process of reading a book in the eighteenth and early nineteenth centuries did not necessarily imply individual reading in solitude. To the contrary, books were often read aloud as entertainment for a listening (and probably illiterate) audience. This process of semipublic reading opened up numerous ways to transmit to less literate strata of society popular literature such as the booklets with tales from *The Thousand and One Nights*. Although direct testimonies of this process of transmission are rare, the individual situation quoted in the following is probably representative of a larger process. Ulrich Jahn's preface to his *Volksmärchen aus Pommern und Rügen* (Popular Tales from the Region of Pomerania and the Island of Rügen), published in 1891, reports:

> A maid had been presented by her masters with a selection of the narratives of *The Thousand and One Nights* for reading. She liked the well-known tale of "Aladdin and the Magic Lamp" best. She read it again and again until she could reproduce it by heart. Then she would retell the tale occasionally when visiting the neighboring village. A storyteller picked up the tale from her and narrated it a generation after he had heard it himself. Out of the tales he remembered, it was his favorite tale, since it was taken from a printed book and therefore was surely more beautiful than all the other stories he knew.[21]

An early literary reworking of the tale of Aladdin was published in 1739 by German author Johann Leonhard Rost (1688–1727). Rost's tale titled "Eine schöne lesenswerte Historie von dem unschätzbaren Schloß in der afrikanischen

Höhle Xaxa" (A Nice Story Worth Reading about the Unfathomable Lock in the African Cave of Xaxa) is contained in his book *Meleatons Wohlangerichtete und neuerfundene Tugendschule* (Meleaton's Well Prepared and Newly Invented School of Manners).[22] Although modern critics considered Rost's tale to be "long-winded"[23] and "fairly manipulated,"[24] Joseph von Görres, writing about German chapbooks in 1809, was rather enthusiastic. Görres read the tale in a late eighteenth-century edition where it was published together with a "pretty story of a drunken peasant who had been to hell and purgatory." Already the brothers Grimm were fascinated by *The Thousand and One Nights* for "its fervent colors, its fragrance of undisturbed flourishing fantasy, and its constant breath of life."[25] Görres praised Rost's tale even more extravagantly: "As if coming forth from solid flint, in the north the solid power produced the spark of poetry, while in the south it gushes forth in a voluntary discharge. In the thousand nights of Arabic fairy tales the fiery clouds stood under the rays of Canopus, and like a summer-lightning it lit up the northern dark." Following the tale's condensed summary Görres comments, "This is the content of the fairy tale that moves playfully through the elements and rocks above earth and life in the sunshine. It is not a popular book [*Volksbuch*] in the narrow sense, since it did not originate from the people. Nevertheless its ease and graciousness of wonder probably enabled the tale's easy access, and the people adopted this alien with pleasure."[26]

From today's perspective, the most obvious characteristic of the tale of the "unfathomable lock in the African cave of Xaxa" is its anti-Jewish tone. The nameless sorcerer from the Maghreb who acts in the tale of Aladdin has here turned into the malicious and tyrannical Jewish sorcerer Mattetai. Instead of an unnamed town in China, the action takes place in Constantinople, where Mattetai finds the boy Lameth. And besides Mattetai, the merchant to whom Lameth first sells the vessels the *jinnī* had brought him is also a treacherous Jew. The most peculiar trait of Rost's version is the magic object. It is not a lamp as in the tale of Aladdin, but a rusty lock whose wish-fulfilling demon appears when the lock is opened by turning its key. The German word for lock, *Schloß*, also denotes a castle that in some versions is mentioned as the place where the magic object is kept. In order to disambiguate the object, Gustav Schwab in his later rendering of the tale coined the term "key lock" (*Schlüsselschloß*).[27] Rost's tale was published widely in the eighteenth century, so that Görres took it to belong to the genre of *Volksbuch*. Later it was included in standard series of the genre such as Gotthard Oswald Marbach's series *Volksbücher* (1838–1842) where it was published as volume 25.

Since the beginning of the nineteenth century, Rost's version of the tale of Aladdin was also recorded from oral tradition. Probably the earliest recording is attested in the literary estate of the brothers Grimm who received the text from the family Haxthausen living in the Northern German town of Paderborn in 1817. The text is a creative, albeit slightly garbled version titled "Of the Lock Saza in the African Cave." Here, we find the boy as an apprentice of a benevolent sorcerer. The malicious person who makes his appearance somewhat later is again a Jew, whose wickedness is further stressed by the fact that he is black.[28] In a Romansh version recorded in the Swiss region of Bündnerland, a poor peasant boy finds the magic object, a strangely formed ancient key, with his blacksmith godfather, and the object's magic servant is a black man.[29] In a text from the Eastern German region of Silesia the hero's adversary, after abducting his wife, swallows the key, so that—as the text says—"nobody can henceforth summon the seven djinnis;" this act, however, later forces the hero to cut open his adversary's belly.[30] In Heinrich Pröhle's German version titled "The Jew and the Lock" (1835), a strong young man gains his beloved, the castle and imperial rule by proving his worth in three subsequent nights of suffering;[31] the Jew and the magic lock only play a role when the castle is transported to a place behind the mountain "where neither sun nor moon do shine;" the hero's helpers are three giants.[32] Three giants also appear as the servants of the magic lock in the version recorded by Jahn at the end of the nineteenth century in Pomerania; in order to summon the wish-fulfilling demons the lock here has to be shaken.[33] All of the cited texts demonstrate the narrators' diligence in adapting Rost's German tale by introducing typical traits of their regional culture. In addition, the tale was also retold in regions influenced at the time by German culture such as Hungary,[34] Slovakia,[35] and Estonia.[36]

In his encyclopedic survey of the tale of Aladdin, Kurt Ranke analyzed some forty different texts. His analysis confirms the assumption voiced by previous scholars that the majority of versions of the tale of Aladdin recorded from oral tradition derive more or less directly from Galland's text. Ranke states that except for the text contained in the Grimm estate "all variants from oral tradition were recorded after 1850" and concludes that "the processes of evolution and diffusion did not permit the fairy tale to develop notable regional redactions, let alone oicotypical versions."[37] The tale of "The Unfathomable Lock in the African Cave of Xaxa" proves, however, that the tale of Aladdin did, in fact, develop "notable redactions" of its own, albeit deriving from the interference of a literary version. Moreover, the analysis of the popular reception of the tale of Aladdin proper reveals yet more variation.

When we focus on how "popular creativity" adopted[38] what Jahn labeled "the young Oriental intruder,"[39] one of the most obvious points is the fact that next to none of the versions recorded from oral tradition preserve Galland's original ending. In Galland's version the tale could have ended in a "happily ever after" as soon as the malicious sorcerer is killed. Instead, another sorcerer, the brother of the first one, makes his appearance. This sorcerer dresses up as a pious woman and gains the confidence of Aladdin's wife. Seeking to destroy both Aladdin and his wife, he urges the woman to request from the servant of the lamp the egg of the fabulous bird Roc, himself knowing quite well that this presumptuous request will enrage the demon. Obviously, most narrators experienced this ending as redundant, so they did not retain it in their oral retellings of the tale. A rare exception was recorded by Jahn from the above-mentioned narrator in Pomerania who performed the tale he had heard from the maid servant. Jahn said about this version:

> Step by step the tale's performance retold the original, except for the fact that the good man has transformed dirty Aladdin, without knowing why and how, into a red-haired and faithless dumb Jack who could neither read nor write and did not even know how to say the Lord's Prayer. The garden that had been filled by Oriental fantasy with fruit trees bearing pearls and jewels instead of ordinary fruit was transformed into a popular garden of Fehnus. He had kept, however, the egg of the bird Roc [*Rochei*] that plays such an important role in the original tale and that Aladdin should request from the demon of the lamp to be inserted into the cupola of his castle. He deemed this trait to be too important to be changed. Consequently he narrated that in the end red-haired dumb Jack asked the demon to bring king Reckei (literally: Egg of the Roc) and hang him at the top of the vault. When I (says the collector) told him that such as name as Reckei did not exist, he calmly responded, "How do you want me to call him? You are cleverer than I am, so do give him a name that sounds better. His name is King Reckei, and I shall call him by that name as long as I live."[40]

Other recordings of the tale of Aladdin from oral tradition also demonstrate varying degrees of creative adaptation. While in Galland's version, Aladdin is the son of a tailor, his father is sometimes mentioned as practicing another, notably always a humble profession, such as that of a shoemaker,[41] broom maker[42] or swineherd.[43] Instead of the lamp, versions of the tale of Aladdin recorded from oral tradition often mention a magic book or other document—a written document constituting the quintessential representative of unintelligible and thus superior or even supernatural wisdom for the illiterate. For instance, in a Swedish text, an impoverished notable finds a casket in a deserted house in the forest and since, as the tale says, "he was so hungry that his bowels clung to his ribs," he opens the casket hoping to find something he can eat. In the casket the man finds another casket and inside that one yet another one. This continues until he finally opens a tiny box in which he finds the magic object. This object is a piece of paper containing the words "Lasse, my servant." When the man pronounces these words aloud, the bodyless voice of the invisible *jinnī* spellbound to the paper asks for his orders.[44] In a version recorded by Ulrich Knoop in Eastern Pomerania, a sorcerer's young apprentice unintentionally kicks a book from the shelf whose pages open in falling down, "and at once a black man appeared from between the pages, bowed before the boy and asked: 'Your Royal Majesty, what is your command?'"[45] Interestingly, the tale's narrator denied ever having read the story in a book, instead insisting that he learned it from oral performance.[46] This version is, moreover, adapted to the narrator's modest social status in that the hero's prime concern is a simple meal. When his new master asks the hero, the son of a swineherd, what he would like to eat, the answer is, "If I had a plate of potatoes in the skin and herring or a good piece of bread, I would be quite happy." Another fascinating case of the tale's adaptation to the narrator's local context is given in a version recorded in 1895 on Inis Mór, the largest of the Irish Aran islands, in the words of the researcher James Stewart a case of "Aranisation."[47] In the version in the *Nights*, Aladdin transgresses the ban to view the princess on her way to the public bath, and when he sees her, falls immortally in love. On the island, everybody went to the beach in summer. Consequently, the hero hides behind one of the typical stone walls in the vicinity of the beach and, in order to view his beloved without her noticing him, removes a few of the smaller stones to make a loophole.

A version from the region of Siebenbürgen, in today's Romania, is only vaguely connected to the tale of Aladdin in Rost's version. In fact, the only direct relation is constituted by the hero's adversary employing the magic object to transport the hero's castle and wife to a distant land, as the text says, "to the Arabic lands, where the Arabs are."[48] Besides this rather vague reminiscence, this version is a somewhat crowded conglomerate of numerous elements well known in European fairy-tale tradition. The introduction mentions a stereotypical set of three brothers (two of whom, however, soon disappear without leaving any trace). Next the hero has to prove his worth in two subsequent nights of suffering, after which God himself (wandering on earth in human shape) hands him a small booklet as a reward. Whenever the young man takes the booklet in his hands, three soldiers appear asking him, "What just wish do you have, o master?" The hero marries the king's eldest daughter— notably against the standard rule of fairy tales where the hero always marries the youngest daughter, but in harmony with the social rules of the day. The hero's adversary is a doe that consoles the woman during her husband's frequent hunting parties. In the end, when his wife has been abducted, the remorseful hero resolves to search for her using a pair of shoes made of iron and a stick made of steel. Only when the iron shoes are torn and tattered and the steel stick is worn down to the size of his hand does the hero meet a band of twelve robbers. After making friends with the robbers, he steals a pair of magic boots and by asking directions from the sun, moon, and wind finally learns about his wife's whereabouts. Transformed into a fly, he regains command of his magic book. This version is unique in its creative combination of frequently employed fairy-tale elements, although it does not necessarily present a very convincing combination. At any rate, it serves to demonstrate that creative narrators did not refrain from developing their versions of the tale of Aladdin even to the extent that the original tale is almost completely veiled. Moreover, it shows how well some tellers felt the tale fit into the European fairy tale's discursive realm, making it easy to import bits into it from the regional discourses they knew.

The present case demonstrates the extent to which fairy tales as an intercultural narrative genre can be subject to variation and adaptation. The earliest-known version of the tale of Aladdin derives from Middle Eastern narrative tradition, or more specifically the oral performance of a Christian storyteller who had grown up in the cosmopolitan atmosphere of the Syrian town of Aleppo. The tale's best-known form as elaborated by Galland bespeaks the atmosphere at the French court in the early eighteenth century in terms of language, content, and mentality. Its mid-eighteenth-century reworking by Rost documents an early literary adaptation of the tale that, probably due to its language of publication, became highly influential in Germany and the neighboring regions influenced by German culture. And the different versions in nineteenth-century European oral tradition of both the tale of Aladdin and Rost's version demonstrate the ways in which narrators adapted the original "alien" tale to the context they lived in.

Even so, the tale's structure and its basic moral messages remained unchanged. All of the tale's versions celebrate a lower-class protagonist's attainment of happiness. Although the hero's rapid promotion is somewhat unexpected, in the fairy tale's logic it is not altogether undeserved, since his decision to change his status actively guarantees betterment. The tale's model in the *Nights* bears testimony to a distinctly "Oriental" atmosphere, but its characteristic features are easily adaptable to any other context. This capacity is proven by the numerous versions from European popular tradition that adapted the tale to conform with salient moral messages promoted by Western, or maybe even universal, ethics. But even as the narrators of the European versions succeeded in adapting their tales to their own cultural context almost beyond recognition, the ultimate origin of their tales from the influential collection of *The Thousand and One Nights* remains visible.

Notes

1. The present text is an adapted and updated version of Marzolph, Ulrich, "The Tale of Aladdin in European Oral Tradition," in *Les Mille et une Nuits et le récit oriental en Espagne et en Orient*, ed. Aboubakr Chraïbi and Carmen Ramirez, Paris: L'Harmattan, 2009, pp. 401–412; see also Marzolph, "Märchen aus 'Tausendundeine Nacht' in der mündlichen Überlieferung Europas," in *Sichtweisen in der Märchenforschung*, ed. Siegfried Neumann and Christoph Schmitt, Baltmannsweiler: Schneider-Verlag Hohengehren, 2013, 23–41.

2. Sklarek, Elisabet, *Ungarische Volksmärchen*, Leipzig: Diederichs, 1901, pp. 181–183, no. 17.

3. See Erb, Rainer, "Jude, Judenlegenden," in *Enzyklopädie des Märchens*, vol. 7 (1993), cols. 676–686; Köhler-Zülch, Ines, "Zigeuner, Zigeunerin," ibid., vol. 14 (2014), cols. 1345–1358.

4. Marzolph and Van Leeuwen, *The Arabian Nights Encyclopedia*, vol. 1, pp. 82–85, no. 346.

5. See Marzolph, *Arabia ridens*, vol. 1, pp. 234–246; Dégh, Linda, "Akkulturation," in *Enzyklopädie des Märchens*, vol. 1 (1977), cols. 234–239; Honko, Lauri, "Four Forms of Adaptation of Tradition," *Studia Fennica* 26 (1981), pp. 19–33.

6. Gerhardt, Mia I., *The Art of Story-Telling: A Literary Study of the Thousand and One Nights*, Leiden: Brill, 1963, p. 14.

7. Marzolph and Van Leeuwen, *The Arabian Nights Encyclopedia*, vol. 2, pp. 556–560. The travelogue of Ḥannā's journey has now been published as Dyab, Hanna, *D'Alep à Paris: Les pérégrinations d'un chrétien de Syrie au temps de Louis XIV*, transl. Paule Fahmé-Thiéry, Bernard Heyberger, and Jérôme Lentin, Paris: Sindbad, 2015.

8. Dyab, *D'Alep à Paris*, pp. 582–583; Grotzfeld, Heinz, "Hannā Diyāb," in *Enzyklopädie des Märchens*, vol. 6 (1990), cols. 485–487.

9. Abdel-Halim, Mohamed, *Antoine Galland, sa vie et son œuvre*, Paris: Nizet, 1964, pp. 276–287; Larzul, Sylvette, "Les Mille et une Nuits de Galland ou l'acclimation d'une 'belle etrangère'," *Revue de littérature comparée* 69 (1995), pp. 309–323; Larzul, "Further Considerations on Galland's Mille et une Nuits: A Study of the Tales Told by Hanna," in *The Arabian Nights in Transnational Perspective*, ed. Ulrich Marzolph, Detroit: Wayne State University Press, 2007, pp. 16–31; Marzolph, Ulrich, "Les Contes de Hanna," in *les mille et une nuits*, ed. Élodie Bouffard and Anne-Alexandra Joyard, Paris: Institut du Monde Arabe, 2012, pp. 87–91; Bottigheimer, Ruth B., "East Meets West: Ḥannā Diyāb and The Thousand and One Nights," *Marvels & Tales* 28.2 (2014), pp. 302–324; Bottigheimer, and Claudia Ott, "The Case of the Ebony Horse, part 1," *Gramarye* 5 (2014), pp. 8–20; Bottigheimer, "The Case of the Ebony Horse, part 2: Hannā Diyāb's Creation of a Third Tradition," *Gramarye* 6 (2014), pp. 7–16; Marzolph, Ulrich, "Ḥannā Diyāb's Unpublished Tales: The Storyteller as an Artist in His Own Right," in Bauden, Frédéric, and Richard Waller, eds. *Antoine Galland (1646–1715) et son Journal*, Louvain: Peeters, 2018, pp. 75–92.

10. Abdel-Halim, *Antoine Galland*, p. 273; Galland, Antoine, *Le Journal d'Antoine Galland (1646–1715): La période parisienne*, vol. 1 (1708–1709), ed. Frédéric Bauden and Richard Waller, Leuven: Peeters, 2011, p. 321.

11. Galland, *Le Journal d'Antoine Galland*, vol. 2 (1710–1711), pp. 253–254.

12. Ibid., pp. 255, 261.

13. Mahdi, Muhsin, *The Thousand and One Nights (Alf Layla wa-Layla) from the Earliest Known Sources*, vol. 3: *Introduction and Indexes*, Leiden; Brill, 1994, pp. 51–72.

14. See May, Georges, *Les Mille et une nuits d'Antoine Galland*, Paris: Puf, 1986; Larzul, Sylvette, *Les traductions françaises des Mille et une nuits: Étude des versions Galland, Trebutien et Mardrus*, Paris: L'Harmattan, 1996, at pp. 19–116.

15. See Chauvin, *Bibliographie*, vol. 4 (1900), at pp. 25–120.

16. Cooperson, Michael, "The Monstrous Births of 'Aladdin'," *Harvard Middle Eastern and Islamic Review* 1 (1994), pp. 67–86; Marzolph, Ulrich, "Das Aladdin-Syndrom: Zur Phänomenologie des narrativen Orientalismus," in *Hören, Sagen, Lesen, Lernen: Bausteine zu einer Geschichte der kommunikativen Kultur, Festschrift für Rudolf Schenda*, ed. Ursula Brunold-Bigler and Hermann Bausinger, Bern: Lang, 1995, pp. 449–462; Marzolph and Van Leeuwen, *The Arabian Nights Encyclopedia*, vol. 1, pp. 82–85.

17. Galland, *Le Journal d'Antoine Galland*, vol. 1, pp. 88–89.

18. Marzolph, Ulrich, "Der Orient in uns: Die Europa-Debatte aus Sicht der orientalistischen Erzählforschung," *Österreichische Zeitschrift für Geschichtswissenschaft* 15.4 (2004), pp. 9–26, particularly at pp. 14–19.

19. Nance, Susan, *How the Arabian Nights Inspired the American Dream, 1790–1935*, Chapel Hill: The University of North Carolina Press, 2009; Marzolph, Ulrich, "Aladdin

Almighty: Middle Eastern Magic in the Service of Western Consumer Culture," *Journal of American Folklore* 132.525 (2019), pp. 275–290.

20. See, e.g., Horalek, Karel, "Märchen aus Tausend und einer Nacht bei den Slaven," *Fabula* 10 (1969), pp. 156–195; Stewart, James, "Aladdin in Aran: Folktales from Inis Mor, 1895," in *Papers: The 8th Congress for the International Society for Folk Narrative Research, Bergen, June 12th–17th 1984*, vol. 2, ed. Reimund Kvideland and Torunn Selberg, Bergen 1984, pp. 229–237; Cox, Heinrich L., "'L'Histoire du cheval enchante' aus 1001 Nacht in der mündlichen Überlieferung Französisch-Flanderns," in *Volkskultur – Geschichte – Region: Festschrift für Wolfgang Brückner*, ed. Dieter Harmening and Erich Wimmer, Würzburg: Königshausen & Neumann, 1990, pp. 581–596.

21. Jahn, Ulrich, *Volksmärchen aus Pommern und Rügen*, Norden: Soltau, 1891, p. XVI.

22. Rost, Johann Leonhard [= Meleaton], *Die wohlangerichtete neuerfundene Tugendschule in welcher vier und zwanzig anmuthige Historien zu erlaubter Gemüths-Ergötzung der Jugend auf eine erbauliche Art vorgetragen und mit nützlichen Anmerkungen und Lehren begleitet worden*, Frankfurt: Raspe, 1739.

23. Rölleke, Heinz, *Märchen aus dem Nachlaß der Brüder Grimm*, 2nd ed., Bonn: Bouvier, 1979, p. 99.

24. Ranke, Kurt, "Alad(d)in," in *Enzyklopädie des Märchens*, vol. 1 (1977), cols. 240–247, at p. 242.

25. Grimm, Jacob und Wilhelm, *Kinder- und Hausmärchen: Ausgabe letzter Hand*, ed. Heinz Rölleke, Stuttgart: Reclam, 1980 (1993), vol. 3, pp. 348–350, at p. 350 [362].

26. Görres, Joseph von, *Die deutschen Volksbücher*, Heidelberg: Mohr & Zimmer, 1808, pp. 233–234.

27. Schwab, Gustav, *Die deutschen Volksbücher für Jung und Alt wiedererzählt*, vol. 1, Gütersloh: Bertelsmann, s.a., pp. 181–231, at p. 181.

28. Rölleke, *Märchen aus dem Nachlaß*, p. 99.

29. Bundi, Gian, *Märchen aus dem Bündnerland*, Basel: Helbing & Lichtenhahn, 1935, pp. 94–95.

30. Peuckert, Will-Erich, *Schlesiens deutsche Märchen*, Breslau: Ostdeutsche Verlagsanstalt, 1932, pp. 289–292, no. 127.

31. For the motif of "nights of suffering," see Brednich, Rolf Wilhelm, "Qualnächte," in *Enzyklopädie des Märchens*, vol. 11 (2004), cols. 100–103.

32. Pröhle, Heinrich, *Kinder- und Volksmärchen*, Leipzig: Avenarius und Mendelsohn, 1853 (reprint ed. Helga Stein, Hildesheim: Georg Olms, 1975), pp. 37–44, no. 9.

33. Jahn, *Volksmärchen*, pp. 325–331, no. 59.

34. Berze Nagy, János, *Magyar népmesetípusok*, vol. 1–2, Pécs: Baranya Megye Tanácsának Kiadása, 1957, no. 561 (text 1).

35. Polívka, Jiří, *Súpis slovenských rozprávok*, vol. 2, Turciansky sv. Martin: Matica slov., 1924, pp. 417–419, no. 29 A (a).

36. See the Estonian Folklore Archives in Tartu, Estonia.

37. Ranke, "Alad(d)in," p. 244.

38. Görres, *Die deutschen Volksbücher*, p. 234.

39. Jahn, *Volksmärchen*.

40. Jahn, *Volksmärchen*, pp. XVI–XVII; see also Schenda, Rudolf, *Von Mund zu Ohr: Bausteine zu einer Kulturgeschichte volkstümlichen Erzählens in Europa*, Göttingen: Vandenhoeck & Ruprecht, 1993, p. 225.

41. Goyert, Georg, *Vlämische Märchen*, Jena: Diedrichs, 1925, pp. 68–75.

42. Sklarek, *Ungrische Volksmärchen*, pp. 183–189, no. 18.

43. Knoop, Otto, *Volkssagen, Erzählungen, Aberglauben, Gebräuche und Märchen aus dem östlichen Hinterpommern*, Posen: Jolowitz, 1885, pp. 215–223, no. 11; also in Woeller, Waltraud, *Deutsche Volksmärchen von arm und reich*, Berlin: Akademie-Verlag, 1959, pp. 54–63, no. 9.

44. Stroebe, Klara, *Nordische Volksmärchen*, vol. 1, Jena: Diederichs, 1915, pp. 182–196, no. 2.

45. Knoop, *Volkssagen*; Woeller, *Deutsche Volksmärchen*.

46. Knoop, *Volkssagen*, p. XXI.

47. Stewart, "Aladdin in Aran," p. 235.

48. *Archiv für siebenbürgische Landeskunde* 33 (1905/06), pp. 436–441, no. 22.

CHAPTER 10

The Mechanical Flying Gadget (ATU 575)

The manuscript tale "The Wooden Horse" preserved in the literary estate of the brothers Grimm is the earliest instance of the presently concerned tale recorded from European oral tradition.[1] Contributed by historian Franz Joseph Mone (1796–1871) and probably recorded around 1820 in the South-Western German region of Baden, the tale goes as follows.

> A king has the habit of celebrating his name day every year. Artists and artisans from all over his realm would come to present their art, and the king would reward them richly. One day, a young man presents a mechanical wooden horse to the king, claiming that wherever the king wants to send him, he would return within an hour. The king sends him to fetch an item from a city twelve hours away, and the young man mounts his horse, rises into the air, and returns in less than an hour. The king is so pleased that he asks him to come to the castle to receive his reward.
>
> In the meantime, the king's son is curious to find out how the mechanical horse works and eventually turns a screw that makes the horse rise up into the air. Although it takes the prince a while to figure out how to descend, he finally manages to alight on top of a tower in a distant land. Meeting a beautiful young maiden living there, he visits her again the next night, and both of them leave the tower on the third night. As they rest in the forest, the prince falls asleep and robbers steal the horse and abduct the maiden. The prince himself is caught by another band of robbers and is brought to a town of pagans where he has to do menial work. When he learns that the horse and his beloved were brought to that very city, he hires himself out at the castle and finally becomes the valet of his beloved. As the pagans do not know how to work the horse's mechanism, the prince promises to show them, providing that the maiden joins him. Once on horseback, the prince flies away with his beloved and returns to his country. They marry, and after his father's demise, the prince is enthroned as the new king.

In the first edition of their *Kinder- und Hausmärchen* (Children's and Household Tales), the brothers Grimm published the corresponding short tale "The

Carpenter and the Wood Turner."[2] As the Grimms regarded that tale as badly told and incomplete, they replaced it with a different tale from the collection's second edition onward.

> The carpenter and the wood turner produce their masterpieces. The carpenter makes a mechanical fish[3] that swims all by itself, and the turner makes a pair of wings that enable one to fly. As the people like the carpenter's product more, the turner uses his wings to fly to a distant country. In that country, the prince asks the turner to lend him the wings and flies off to another distant country. There he learns that the beautiful princess lives in a secluded tower and visits her using the wings. When their illicit relationship becomes known, the lovers are to be burned at the stake. As the flames already encircle them, the prince escapes together with the princess by flying away with the wings. They return to the prince's native country where the prince is elected as the new king. Soon after, the father of the princess announces that he will cede half his realm to the person who will return his daughter to him. The hero reunites father and daughter and forces the king to keep his promise.

Both of the Grimms' tales are versions of tale type ATU 575: *The Prince's Wings.*[4] In European oral tradition, the tale is mainly attested from central and Eastern Europe. In his dictionary of fairy tales, Walter Scherf chose the German tale "The Prince Who Learned How to Fly" as the "lead version" (*Leitfassung*).[5] This tale was dictated in the first half of the nineteenth century to the collector Johann Friedrich Minssen (1823–1901) by Harm Griep from Scharrel, one of the most renowned storytellers in the Saterland, today a municipality in the district of Cloppenburg in North-Western Germany.[6] In this tale, the king's two sons learn a profession. The eldest son becomes a silversmith and makes a fish. Since his master also taught him magic, he lets the mechanical fish swim in a natural way. The youngest son becomes a carpenter and makes a pair of wings. As the king likes the mechanical fish better, the carpenter flies away to a distant country. There he clandestinely visits the princess who is kept in an inaccessible tower on an island so that no man can make her pregnant. The prince pretends to be the angel Gabriel and has sex with the princess. When the king notices that his daughter is pregnant, he orders her to be burned at the stake. Although the prince insists that he is the one who should be executed, the people do not listen to him. Nevertheless, he joins the princess at the stake. As the people light the fire and heavy smoke rises, the prince flies away together with the princess. Back in his home country the prince marries her and reunites his bride's parents with their daughter during the wedding.

The tale's Czech version, narrated by František Novák from Eastern Bohemia and recorded by Václav Popelka on December 15, 1914, begins with a competition between a goldsmith and a cobbler.[7] The goldsmith produces a golden fish that makes music, and the cobbler makes a pair of wings that enable him to fly. Later, the prince finds the wings and flies away. In a foreign country, the prince stays with a shepherd. Clandestinely, he visits the princess in her secluded castle and has sex with her. When the king finds out about this, the prince is caught and is to be hanged. Just before his execution, he asks to hug the princess a final time and flies away with her. A son is born. The prince returns to his parents, and eventually all of them are reunited. The Belarusian version performed by the peasant Jan Dzežko around the end of the nineteenth century starts with a competition between a goldsmith and a wood turner.[8] The goldsmith makes a mechanical fish, and the turner constructs a mechanical dove that flies. The prince flies away on the dove and lives with a merchant who teaches him how to play the fiddle. He visits the princess in her secluded castle and has sex with her. When the king finds out about their relationship, they detect the prince by smearing the windowsill with tar. As the prince and the princess are about to be executed, they fly away. The princess gives birth to a son. The prince brings them to his father just as the king is about to have the turner hanged. The tale ends with a happy wedding party during which the narrator was generously treated with wine. In the tale's Estonian version as published by Richard Viidalepp, the initial competition is between two goldsmiths.[9] Again the prince acquires the wings. The prince's clandestine visits to the princess in the secluded castle are detected when her old maid finds out that the prince hides in a closet. A lengthy Bulgarian version recorded by Georgi Ruseski and first published in 1891 has the competition take place between two master craftsmen.[10] One makes a music box, the other a mechanical horse that can fly. Although the horse is supposed to be burned after the show, the prince manages to take it for himself. His clandestine visits to the princess in the distant land are found out by smearing tar on the windowsill. Just as the prince is about to be executed, he flies away on the mechanical horse, taking the princess along. When the prince steals a roast from some robbers, the horse's mechanism accidentally burns, and he loses the means to return to the princess. Evading the advances of a robber, a merchant, and a shepherd's son, the princess is eventually chosen as the ruler in another country. One after the other, the robbers, the shepherd, and the merchant pass through the country and receive their due retribution. Finally, the prince comes and the lovers are reunited. The tale ends with a happy wedding. In the tale's Lithuanian version performed by Kasimierz Andriukajtis on December 11, 1889, the prince does not pay attention to the swimming silver fish produced by the smith, instead taking the carpenter's box that turns into a flying chair.[11] Visiting the princess in the secluded castle, the prince is wounded when they try to catch him and is apprehended soon after. Just before being executed, he flies away together with the princess. Back home, he saves the smith and the carpenter from being executed. The German peasant woman Maria Gokesch from Romania performed her version of the tale in 1982.[12] She learned it from her grandmother, in addition to listening to the tale as it was frequently told when the women worked together in the spinning chamber. Here, the prince himself learns a profession. At first, he wants to be a tailor but does not like it. Then he becomes a carpenter and makes a pair of wings. His visits to the princess in the secluded tower are detected when the old maid puts fine sand on the windowsill. As the prince is about to be executed, he asks to do his final prayers, flies away and takes the princess with him. They fly back to his home and live happily ever after.

In European tradition, the tale's history was frequently studied in connection with the metal flying horse mentioned as a gift in Chaucer's unfinished fourteenth-century "Squire's Tale."[13] The tale's oldest full-fledged precursors in Europe are two French verse romances dating to the end of the thirteenth century, Adenet le Roi's *Cléomadès* and Girart d'Amien's *Méliacin*,[14] both of which tell more or less the same story. The following is a short summary of *Cléomadès*.

> The suitors of the three sisters of Prince Cleomades of Sevilla present their gifts to the girls' parents. King Melicandus of Barbary presents a man of gold who warns with his trumpet if treason lurks somewhere. King Bardigans of Armenia presents a hen and six chickens that are so skillfully made as to seem alive. And King Croppart of Hungary presents a wooden horse with which one can mount in the air and travel swiftly. Whereas the two elder sisters are happy with their future husbands, it is young Maxima's lot to marry the ugly and evil Croppart. Imploring her brother to prevent this from happening, the prince challenges Croppart to prove the value of his present. The prince mounts the horse, and although the man of gold sounds his trumpet in warning, the prince moves a steel pin in the horse's forehead, upon which the horse instantly rises into the air. At first not knowing what to do, the prince gradually finds out how to navigate the horse and alights on a lofty tower in the middle of the gardens of a great palace. In the tower, the prince finds beautiful Princess Claremond who has been promised to King Liopatris. Pretending to be that very king, Cleomades falls in love with Claremond, and his feelings are reciprocated. When the princess's father, King Cornuant, finds him there, the prince invents a story to the effect that it was fate that brought him there. Nevertheless, King Cornuant wants to have the stranger executed. The prince asks to receive death while on his horse and flies away. Soon after, he returns and elopes to his native country together with Claremond who consents willingly.
>
> When Cleomades leaves the princess for a while at the summer palace to recover from the fatigues of the journey, Croppart abducts her and urges her to marry him. In the further course of events, Claremond is rescued by Prince Mendulus, and Croppart dies in confinement. Aiming to ward off Mendulus's advances, the princess feigns madness. After a series of adventures, Cleomades finds the princess, poses as a physician who can cure her, and elopes together with her on the flying horse. Cleomades

and Claremond marry, and the noble King Liopatris is wed to Princess Maxima.

Adenet le Roi's narrative is apparently inspired by a tale from Arabic tradition versions of which are encountered in comparatively recent versions of *The Thousand and One Nights*,[15] in the *Nights'* North African sibling collection, *The Hundred and One Nights*, whose earliest preserved manuscript probably dates from as early as the thirteenth century,[16] and in the (lost) second volume of the fourteenth-century anonymous collection translated as *Tales of the Marvellous and News of the Strange*.[17] According to the present state of knowledge, the tale might have reached the French author by way of Spanish oral tradition. To which extent the tale's versions collected from European oral tradition actually derive from Adenet le Roi's romance and its later adaptations or from the context of *The Thousand and One Nights* is difficult to decide, particularly as the version included in Antoine Galland's early eighteenth-century *Mille et une nuit*, adapted from the oral performance of Syrian Maronite storyteller Ḥannā Diyāb, enjoyed a considerable popularity.[18]

Meanwhile, the introductory competition of the two artisans or craftsmen appearing in many of the texts collected from European oral tradition suggests the partial influence of another, independent version of the tale that likewise begins by introducing two craftsmen. This version surfaces in European tradition in *The Thousand and One Days*, the rival collection to the *Nights* similarly published at the beginning of the eighteenth century, by Galland's colleague and competitor François Pétis de la Croix.[19] Instead of three kings bringing presents to the parents of the three princesses they woo, Pétis de la Croix's text introduces a weaver and a carpenter. The text from which Pétis de la Croix adapted his tale is the anonymous Ottoman Turkish collection *Ferec ba'd eş-şidde* (Relief after Hardship) that was probably compiled as early as the late fourteenth century. The Ottoman Turkish collection, in turn, for most of its tales, including the present one, translates a Persian prototype. This prototype is represented in the *Munes-nāme* (The Book as an Intimate Friend) compiled by a certain Abu Bakr ibn Khosrow al-Ostād around the year 1200[20] and a number of later anonymous Persian collections of tales.[21]

Two friends, a weaver and a carpenter, love the same woman. In order to oust his competitor, the carpenter builds a large chest and induces the weaver to get inside and move a particular nail, by virtue of which the chest rises into the air and flies away.

The weaver soon finds out how to navigate the chest. Learning about the beautiful princess of Oman who is locked up in a palace, he visits her at night, masquerading as the archangel Gabriel. The young woman and her maids believe that nobody else but an angel could have visited them in their barred palace, and so she gives in to his advances. From then on, the weaver visits the young woman at night while hiding himself outside the castle in daytime. Finally, the king notices that his daughter is pregnant. He waits for the weaver to arrive, and when he sees him, believes him to be Gabriel and shows his respect.

One day, another king, to whom the princess has been promised, wages war against the king of Oman. The weaver drives the enemy troops away by throwing stones at them from the air. When the enemy troops return, he arms himself with fire bombs. Again, he manages to vanquish the enemy troops, but after his return, one of the bombs accidentally reduces the chest to ashes.

Not being able to visit the princess without his flying chest, the weaver is forced to make a living by working in his original profession. When the king's enemies again prepare to attack the town, the princess happens to recognize the weaver hiding in a corner. As she still considers him to be Gabriel, he pretends that God had punished him for using fire without his permission. In order not to disclose his ruse, the weaver is forced to fight the enemy troops once more. At night, he gallops through the enemy's camp in his wild appearance, and the enemy troops flee in terror.

When the weaver finally confesses his true status to the king, the king asks him to stay, as his purported role as Gabriel will protect the country. From then on, the weaver and his wife live happily together with their son.

If, indeed, the initial setting of this version might have influenced the tale's performances in nineteenth- and twentieth-century oral tradition, the characters of the kings bringing precious presents as in the tale's initially discussed version would have been combined with the characters of the two artisans, a weaver and a carpenter, to produce the amalgamated characters of a goldsmith and a carpenter who actually make the objects that are otherwise presented by the kings. As the initial competition between the two craftsmen appears in a fair number of tales recorded in different regions, one might assume the existence of a literary version that served to stabilize tradition, probably an eighteenth- or early nineteenth-century popular chapbook adaptation of Adenet le Roi's romance. This potential intermediary between the medieval tale and later oral tradition should also be credited with the introduction of the wings as the mechanical gadget enabling the hero to fly, a specific motif that so far is not known from any of the tale's literary versions. Similarly, the Persian version or its adaptations likely influenced later versions of the tale in which the mechanical flying gadget is not a horse but a chest, as for instance in Danish fairy-tale author Hans Christian Andersen's "Den flyvende Kuffert" (The Flying Trunk; 1839),[22] as well as versions in which the mechanical gadget is eventually destroyed by fire.

All of the tale's versions apparently derive from the tale of the weaver posing as God Vishnu that is contained in the ancient Indian mirror for princes, the *Panchatantra* (Five [Books of] Wisdom).[23] This tale introduces a weaver and a carpenter who are friends since childhood. When the weaver falls in love with the princess, the carpenter builds him a mechanical Garuda, the flying steed of

God Vishnu. Equipped with replica of the god's insignia, the weaver visits the princess in her secluded apartments, pretending to be God Vishnu himself, and has sex with her. As the princess's parents detect the relationship, the fact that God Vishnu is his future son-in-law makes the king so arrogant that he gets in trouble with the neighboring rulers who wage war on him. When the weaver sees no choice but to join the king's army in fighting the enemy, the actual God Vishnu is afraid that the weaver's death might be understood as the god's personal defeat and orders Garuda to enter the mechanical Garuda's body while he himself enters the weaver's body. The enemy's army is defeated and from then on, the weaver "enjoyed all known delights with the princess."

The condensed survey of the tale's history and the relation of the tale's European versions recorded from oral tradition to possible precursors cannot do justice to the development of the many narrative motifs creative narrators employed in various ingenious ways. Even so, the fact that oral tradition often feeds on multiple origins is evident. Although all of the tale's documented versions ultimately derive from an ancient Indian model, this model was appropriated in different ways. On the one hand, it generated the Persian and Ottoman Turkish versions that might have influenced European oral tradition either directly or by way of the adaptation published by Pétis de la Croix. On the other hand, the Indian model gave rise to the tale of the mechanical wooden horse with the prince's numerous trials and tribulations that is attested in Arabic and the medieval French adaptations. As both strands of tradition surfaced repeatedly in Europe over the centuries, they might have mingled again in the ingenious adaptations of creative storytellers to create the hybrid versions documented from nineteenth- and twentieth-century European oral tradition.

Notes

1. Bolte and Polívka, *Anmerkungen*, vol. 2, pp. 132–133, no. 77a.
2. Ibid., vol. 2, pp. 131–131, no. 77a.
3. I follow the reading suggested by Bolte who wonders whether the table (German *Tisch*) mentioned in the text is a misreading for fish (German *Fisch*).
4. Horálek, Karel, "Flügel des Königssohnes," in *Enzyklopädie des Märchens*, vol. 4 (1984), cols. 1358–1365.
5. Scherf, Walter, *Das Märchenlexikon*, Munich: C.H. Beck, 1995, vol. 2, pp. 1298–1301.
6. Van der Kooi, Jurjen, and Theo Schuster, *Der Großherzog und die Marktfrau: Märchen und Schwänke aus dem Oldenburger Land*, Leer: Schuster, 1994, pp. 64–67, 393, no. 15.
7. Jech, Jaromir, *Tschechische Volksmärchen*, 2nd ed., Berlin: Akademie-Verlag, 1984, pp. 211–218, 494, no. 40; see also Scherf, *Das Märchenlexikon*, vol. 2, pp. 1312–1316.
8. Barag, Lev G., *Belorussische Volksmärchen*, Berlin: Akademie-Verlag, 1966, pp. 216–221, 602, no. 20.
9. Viidalepp, Richard, *Estnische Volksmärchen*, Berlin: Akademie-Verlag, 1980, pp. 251–253, no. 81.
10. Ognjanowa, Elena, *Märchen aus Bulgarien*, Wiesbaden: Drei Lilien, 1987, pp.

209–221, 494, no. 67; Nicoloff, Assen, *Bulgarian Folktales*, Cleveland: Nicoloff, 1979, pp. 57–66, no. 21.

11. Dowojna-Sylwestrowicz, Mieczysław, *Podania żmujdzkie*, Warsaw: Arct, 1894, vol. 2, pp. 311–314.

12. Stephani, Claus, *Märchen der Rumäniendeutschen*, Munich: Diederichs, 1991, pp. 27–31, 344–345, no. 7.

13. Clouston, William Alexander, "On the Magical Elements in Chaucer's Squire's Tale, with Analogues," in Furnivall, Frederick J., *John Lane's Continuation of Chaucer's 'Squire's Tale'*, London: Kegan Paul, Trench, Trübner & Co., 1888, 1890, pp. 263–476; Jones, H.S.V., "Some Observations upon the Squire's Tale," *Publications of the Modern Language Association* 20.2 (1905), pp. 346–359; DiMarco, Vincent, "The Squire's Tale," in Correale, Robert M., and Mary Hamel, eds., *Sources and Analogues of the Canterbury Tales*, vol. 1, Cambridge: D.S. Brewer, 2002, pp. 169–209; Heffernan, Carol F., *The Orient in Chaucer and Medieval Romance*, Cambridge: D.S. Brewer, 2003, pp. 63–82.

14. Keightley, Thomas, *Tales and Popular Fictions; Their Resemblance and Transmission from Country to Country*, London: Whittaker & Co, 1884, pp. 40–72; Chauvin, Victor, "Pacolet et les mille et une nuits," *Wallonia* 6 (1898), pp. 5–19; Jones, H.S.V., "The Cléomadès, the Méliacin, and the Arabian Tale of the 'Enchanted Horse'," *The Journal of English and Germanic Philology* 6.2 (1907), pp. 221–243; Jones, "The Cléomadès and Related Folktales," *Publications of the Modern Language Association* 23.4 (1908), pp. 577–598; Houdebert, Aurélie, "L'histoire du cheval d'ébène, de Tolède à Paris: propositions sur les modalités d'une transmission," in Egedi-Kovács, Emese, ed., *Byzance et l'Occident: Rencontre de l'Est de de l'Ouest*, Budapest: Collège Eötvös József ELTE, 2013, pp. 143–156; Houdebert, "Le 'Cheval volant:' parcours et métamorphoses d'un motif oriental: Adenet le Roi, Girart d'Amiens, Geoffrey Chaucer," in Egedi-Kovács, Emese, ed., *Littérature et folklore dans le récit médiéval*, Budapest: Collège Eötvös József ELTE, 2011, pp. 149–160; Bottigheimer, Ruth B., and Claudia Ott, "The Case of the Ebony Horse, part 1," *Gramarye* 5 (2014), pp. 8–20; Bottigheimer, "The Case of the Ebony Horse, part 2: Hannā Diyāb's Creation of a Third Tradition," *Gramarye* 6 (2014), pp. 7–16; Houdebert, *Le cheval d'ébène à la cour de France: Cléomadès et Méliacin*, Paris (forthcoming).

15. Chauvin, *Bibliographie*, vol. 5 (1901), pp. 221–231, no. 130; Marzolph and Van Leeuwen, *The Arabian Nights Encyclopedia*, vol. 1, pp. 172–174, no. 103.

16. Fudge, Bruce, ed. and transl., *A Hundred and One Nights*, New York: New York University Press, 2016, pp. 306–343; Ott, Claudia, transl., *101 Nacht*, Zurich: Manesse, 2012, pp. 197–220.

17. Marzolph, Ulrich, ed., *Das Buch der wundersamen Geschichten: Erzählungen aus der Welt von 1001 Nacht*, Munich: C.H. Beck, 1999, pp. 629–630.

18. Bottigheimer, "The Case of the Ebony Horse, part 2;" Marzolph, Ulrich, "The Man Who Made the *Nights* Immortal: The Tales of the Syrian Maronite Storyteller Ḥannā Diyāb," *Marvels & Tales* 32.1 (2018), pp. 114–129.

19. For the following, see Marzolph, *Relief after Hardship*; Pétis de la Croix, François, *Les Mille et un jours: contes persans*, ed. Paul Sebag, Paris: Christian Bourgois, 1980, pp. 269–283, 503.

20. Marzolph, *Relief after Hardship*, p. 48; Askari, Nasrin, "A Mirror for Princesses: *Mūnis-nāma*, A Twelfth-Century Collection of Persian Tales Corresponding to the Ottoman Turkish Tales of the *Faraj ba'd al-shidda*," *Narrative Culture* 5.1 (2018), pp. 121–140.

21. Marzolph, *Relief after Hardship*, pp. 71–73, no. 13.

22. Scherf, *Das Märchenlexikon*, vol. 1, pp. 323–325.

23. Benfey, Theodor, *Pantschatantra: Fünf Bücher indischer Fabeln, Märchen und Erzählungen, aus dem Sanskrit übersetzt mit Einleitung und Anmerkungen*, (Leipzig 1859) reprint Hildesheim: Georg Olms, 1966, vol. 2, pp. 48–56 (bk. 1, no. 5).

CHAPTER 11

The Husband Buried Alive Together with His Deceased Wife (ATU 612)

In the second edition (1819) of their *Kinder- und Hausmärchen* (Children's and Household Tales), the brothers Jacob and Wilhelm Grimm relegated tale number 16 as published in the first edition to the notes of number 62: *The Queen Bee*, instead now (and in subsequent editions) inserting the following tale, titled *The Three Snake-Leaves*.

The son of a poor man leaves his home, fights valiantly for the king, and is richly rewarded. The princess has vowed only to marry a man who would promise to be buried alive together with her, should she die before him. She commits herself to follow the same procedure should her husband die first. The hero and the princess marry, and she dies soon after. When the body of the princess is deposited in the royal crypt, her husband is enclosed together with her, being given a table with four candles, four loaves of bread, and four bottles of wine. As he sees a serpent approach the dead body of his beloved, he cuts the serpent into three pieces with his sword. Soon after, he sees a second serpent resuscitate the first one by placing three green leaves on the dead serpent's properly arranged parts. Applying the same procedure, the man resuscitates his wife. Together, they notify the king's guards and are released from the crypt.

Being alive again, however, the woman's nature has changed, and she is not in love with her husband any more. When they travel by ship to visit his old father, she has the boatman help her drown her sleeping husband by throwing him overboard. The man's faithful servant rescues him and resuscitates him with the help of the three leaves. The man and his servant manage to return to the king sooner than the woman and inform him about her treachery. When she finally returns and pretends that her husband died while travelling, the king shows him to her. The king punishes his daughter and her accomplice by putting them into a boat whose hull is perforated so that they drown.

According to a note in the commentary, the Grimms edited the tale from two texts they had collected that "only differ in insignificant details." The tale corresponds to tale type ATU 612: *The Three Snake-Leaves*, a tale type that regularly consists of two parts.[1] In the first part, the husband would resuscitate his beloved wife, often, but not exclusively, by way of leaves or an herb that he would apply in imitation of the serpent's action. In the second part, the woman would fall in love with another man, desert her husband and either kill him herself or denounce him so that he would be killed for an alleged crime, often the theft of a valuable object. The tale's second part was studied in great detail by Gaston Paris, and Albert Wesselski added numerous additional references.[2] Introduced by the alternative motif of the loving husband giving up a certain number of years of his life in order to bring his wife back to life,[3] the tale's second part is already documented in ancient Indian literature. There are also a fair number of versions from premodern Arabic literature,[4] the oldest one dating to the eleventh century.[5]

The first part of the Grimms' tale is constructed of two elements, namely the motif of the husband being buried alive together with his deceased wife (Mot. S123.2: *Burial of living husband or wife with dead spouse*), and the motif of an animal unintentionally demonstrating the effects of a medicine, usually an herb or some leaves that resuscitate the dead (Mot. B512: *Medicine shown by animal*). Already the brothers Grimm noted that the latter motif is first attested in ancient Greek legend.[6] Both the *Library* (3,3,1), a compendium of myths and heroic legends traditionally attributed to a certain Apollodorus and dated to the first or second centuries CE, and the contemporary *Fabulae* (no. 126) attributed to Hyginus, contain the story of the seer Polyidus who is requested to resuscitate Glaucus, son of Minos and Pasiphae, who was drowned in a jar of honey. Shut up in the crypt with Glaucus's dead body, Polyidus kills a serpent and witnesses another serpent resuscitating it later by placing an herb on its dead body. By applying the same procedure to Glaucus, Polyidus raises him from the dead.[7] In medieval European literature, the motif appears first in Marie de France's twelfth-century *lai Eliduc*, where Eliduc's wife Guildeluec learns from a weasel how to resuscitate her husband's beloved Guilliadun with a certain herb.[8]

Probably the least studied element of the tale's first part is the initial motif of the husband being buried alive together with his deceased wife. Constituting the ultimate expression of love and devotion that outweighs one's own physical existence after the beloved one's death, the motif sounds somewhat strange in view of the burial practice common to the Abrahamic religions. It only appears to make sense either as a practice of nobility, who would bury their deceased ones in a vault or crypt, or as a somewhat unusual custom in far away societies who would dispose of their deceased ones in a natural cave or a cavern. In the first instance, this motif reminded the Grimms of the ancient Nordic legend of Asmund and Aswit. Asmund, son of King Alf in Hethmark, and Aswit, son of King Biorn of Wik, ratify their friendship by making a vow "that whichever of them lived longest should be buried with him who died. For their fellowship and love were so strong, that each determined he would not prolong his days when the other was cut off by death." When Asmund is consigned to the cavern where his dead friend is buried, he takes some provisions along, obviously avoiding to starve or, maybe, not even intending to stay for good. As a matter of fact, when sometime later, the passing Swedes explore the cavern by lowering a man in a basket, Asmund takes his chance to leave the burial cavern. As he explains to his rescuers, Aswit had turned into a revenant attacking his friend at night, and the Swedes could still see the blood "flowing forth and spurting over his face." This version of the motif is contained in the Danish history, *Gesta Danorum*, compiled in Latin by Saxo Grammaticus around the year 1200.[9] Although the motif in the *Gesta Danorum* shows a striking resemblance to the Grimms' tale, there are at least two decisive points in which it differs. First, in terms of content, the vow to be buried together is made by two male friends; and second, in terms of dissemination, the vow of two male friends to be buried together remained a singular case in medieval European tradition. Consequently, although the motif's occurrence in the *Gesta Danorum* may or may not be related to that of the Grimms' tale, a version of the motif that corresponds more closely with that in the Grimms' tale should be considered.

In the second place, the Grimms also alluded to "a similar custom between husband and wife" in the tales of Sindbād the seafaring merchant (who is often erroneously labeled "the sailor"). Before discussing this tale and its different versions in detail, it might be useful to remind ourselves that early Nordic literature had some acquaintance with "Oriental" tradition, as studied, for instance, in Marina Mundt's book on "Oriental images" in ancient Nordic epics.[10] Consequently, the occurrence of the motif in the legend of Asmund and Aswit might result from an adaptation of an originally extraneous, and maybe even a Middle Eastern text. At any rate, the Sindbād tales are without any reasonable doubt much more likely to have transmitted the motif to European popular tradition than the *Gesta Danorum*.

The Sindbād tales, originally compiled as a separate booklet in Arabic, were introduced to the European audience by their inclusion in Antoine Galland's adapted and enlarged French translation of the Arabic *Alf layla wa-layla* (A Thousand and One Nights), published in 1704–17. As a matter of fact, only after translating the Sindbād tales had Galland learned about the *Nights* and had then included the originally independent cycle of seven tales in his translation of the larger work. Galland's *Nights* were widely read all over Europe in the eighteenth and nineteenth centuries and had a decisive impact on oral tradition, particularly as for retellings of its most famous tales, those of Aladdin and Ali Baba (see essays **9, *The Unpromising Rascal Makes His Fortune with the Help of a Magic Object*** and **30. *The Robbers Hiding Their Treasures in a Magic Cavern***).[11] The motif under consideration here appears in the narrative of Sindbād's fourth voyage.

> Having escaped the cannibal Magians, Sindbād comes to a city inhabited by civilized people. He earns his living by making saddles and bridles, which had previously been unknown. After a while, he gets married, only to discover soon after that the people customarily deposit the surviving partner in the burial pit together with a deceased spouse. When Sindbād's wife passes away, he is lowered into the pit with some bread and water so as not to starve immediately. He manages to survive by killing other people who are lowered into the pit after him and taking their provisions. In the end, he finds a way out of the cave by following a wild animal and is picked up by a passing ship, taking with him the jewels and valuable clothes of the people in the pit, some of whom he had killed himself.[12]

In addition to the wide-reaching popularity of the Sindbād tales in European tradition in the eighteenth century, two further points support the argument that the motif in the Grimms' tale ultimately owes its presence to "Oriental" influence, most likely the popularity of the Sindbād tales. First, in tale type ATU 612 the motif is but one of the narrators' choices to evidence the strength of the couple's mutual love. Several other variations occur, as will shortly be argued. And second, the motif of husband and wife vowing to be buried alive together with their dead spouse is part and parcel of Middle Eastern tradition at least since the twelfth century. As a matter of fact, it occurs in a variety of narrative contexts, the most popular of which in the West would have been part of the Sindbād tales.

In tale type ATU 612, the essential motif necessary for the tale's further development is the couple's devotion to each other. There is no need for the husband to be buried together with his wife, as the couple may simply vow to mourn intensely at each other's grave. This vow, that would not have to conflict with the regular burial customs, is attested in a large variety of versions from different regions in which the surviving husband wakes at his wife's grave.[13] Likewise in accordance with the regular burial customs is a Mexican version collected in Los Angeles, in which "the husband's enthusiasm for the agreement diminishes; he has himself buried with her but stays alive by breathing through a reed that emerges above ground. As they lie buried the husband observes how a rat revives its dead love with a flower, and he uses the same flower to resuscitate his wife. They call to the gravediggers through the reed and are freed by them."[14] A further integration of European beliefs is evident in a German tale collected in Hungary, in which a rich merchant and the poor cobbler's daughter vow to wake at their spouse's crypt each night between eleven o'clock and midnight. A ghost appears, giving the husband a certain book to read and advising him to place three roses on the dead wife's body in order to resuscitate her.[15]

Meanwhile, several tales prove that the motif of burial in a vault or crypt was widely known in nineteenth-century European tradition. The motif is not necessarily connected with the resuscitation of the dead spouse, as the protagonist may either stay single or find a new spouse. A strong influence of *The*

Thousand and One Nights is evident in a tale collected from nineteenth-century oral tradition that was published in August Ey's collection of tales from the Harz mountains, a region in central Germany.[16]

> The ship on which a young miner travels is attracted by the Magnetic Mountain.[17] The miner offers to sacrifice himself by going ashore and beating a drum on top of the mountain so as to release the ship. Having done so, he falls into an abyss, loses consciousness and upon awakening finds himself in a lavishly decorated room. He takes a necklace shaped like a live serpent. Falling asleep, he dreams that a beautiful maiden shows him the way out of the mountain and hands him a magic crown by which he can summon her. The miner leaves the mountain and comes to a black people who do not wear any clothes. After a while, he marries the ruler's daughter. He learns about the people's custom to bury a dead person together with the living spouse. Soon after, his wife dies, and they are buried together in a cave, he being given a small loaf of bread and a jug of water. By putting on the magic crown, he summons the magic maiden who orders a bear to show him the way out of the cave. As the man finds himself on a deserted island, the miner summons the maiden again, requesting her to bring him back home. Following her advice, he collects some of the precious stones on the beach, and then a ship takes him back home. Many years later, as he is about to die, he summons the magic maiden again. The orphan who had cared for him closes his eyes, the maiden disappears, and he dies peacefully.

A tale from Judeo-Spanish tradition that was told by narrators originating from Tunisia and Turkey, respectively, is even closer to the Sindbād tale.

> "A young man leaves home and comes to an enchanted seaside village, deserted during the day and inhabited at night by water spirits. He abducts one of these creatures of the sea, marries her, and moves to another village where the custom is to bury the surviving mate with the dead spouse. After his wife dies, he is buried with her in a large pit where he encounters a weeping widow. When a seven-headed monster steals the bread they find in the pit and on which they both live, they have the monster pull them out of the pit, and find themselves on an isolated island. With no other means of escape, they throw themselves into the sea but are saved from drowning by the man's three children by his water-spirit wife."[18]

A direct influence of the Sindbād tales is difficult to prove, if only because the nineteenth- and twentieth collectors of tales from oral tradition would rarely document items that they knew or presumed to be adapted from literary sources. At any rate, the motif is widely spread in Middle Eastern tradition. The Sindbād tales as they were introduced to the European public are a fairly recent phenomenon. While many individual motifs in Sindbād's voyages were shown to derive from older tradition,[19] no complete version of the cycle of seven voyages predating the seventeenth century is known.[20] The motif under consideration here relies on a history of at least a thousand years in the literary tradition of the Muslim world. A closely corresponding version is already contained in a Persian historical work dating to the early twelfth century. The anonymous *Mojmal al-tavārikh* (Compendium of Historical Narratives), compiled in 1126/27, includes the tale of a traveler who comes to the country of the horse-headed people and gets married. Realizing that he will be buried with his deceased wife, the man takes precautions by asking a friend to prepare and deliver to him bread, a lamp, and a knife. In the burial cavern, he later marries a widow who is lowered down, and together they escape by digging their way out with his knife.[21] Still older is the motif's first documented occurrence in Arabic author al-Muḥassin al-Tanūkhī's (d. 994) *al-Faraj ba'd al-shidda* (Relief after Hardship), a collection of tales demonstrating the general theme in a large variety of cases. Here, the woman is only seemingly dead and regains her senses when the cord by which the couple were lowered into the burial cave hits her face. Interestingly, when the woman is saved, she at first forgets about her husband and only remembers that he is still in the cave when she sees his portrait at her mother-in-law's place.[22] This strange negligence also occurs in a tale included in an anonymous Persian compilation of tales belonging to the genre of *Jāmeʿ al-ḥekāyāt* (Collection of Tales) that probably dates to the seventeenth century;[23] here, the dead princess is resuscitated in the same manner as in tale type ATU 612.

A more or less continuous chain of tradition proves the burial motif to have been part and parcel of the narrative stock of storytellers in the Muslim world from the tenth century onward. In a tale included in the Ottoman Turkish *Qırq vezīr* (The Forty Viziers), an enlarged adaptation of the originally Persian *Sendbād-nāme* (The Book of Sendbād [the Sage]) whose earliest versions probably date to the fourteenth century, the husband has no previous knowledge of the custom that he is to be buried together with his deceased wife. In the cave, he finds and marries a young woman. They are saved by following a wild beast through a passage to a river. In the fifteenth- or late fourteenth-century Ottoman Turkish collection *Ferec ba'd eş-şidde* (Relief after Hardship), a compendium of marvelous and strange tales the majority of which were translated from a Persian precursor,[24] the tale's protagonist is appointed successor to the recently deceased king. When his wife dies a few days after the marriage, the widow of the previous king, who was entombed with her husband, is still alive. The man and the king's widow manage to survive on food they find in the coffins, and there is water to be found. In the end, they escape by following a large serpent. A summary of that tale documenting an oral performance dated March 3, 1673, is noted in Antoine Galland's Constantinople diary.[25] A *maqāma* composed by sixteenth-century Arabic author al-Sayyid ʿAbd al-Raḥīm al-ʿAbbāsī (d. 1556) tells about a merchant's son whose ship is wrecked at a magnetic mountain.[26] Only after his marriage does he learn about the country's custom. In the cave, he marries the king's widow and together they escape by following a wild animal. Additional versions of the motif are documented in Persian literature. The oldest preserved version of the Persian Ḥamza romance, the *Romuz-e Ḥamze*, is usually dated at least to early in the seventeenth century. It includes an episode in which the warrior ʿOmar Maʿdi arrives at a foreign city where he is elected successor of the recently deceased king by way of an ordeal involving a bird (as elsewhere in Muslim tradition), in this case, a kite. Celebrating his unexpected new position, ʿOmar gets drunk and requests his vizier to procure a woman to marry. Although the vizier warns him about the country's custom that spouses are buried alive with their deceased partners, the hero accepts and is married. At the beginning of the night, he consummates the marriage, but at the end of the night, his wife is dead. The next day, the country's nobles request him to conform with the country's custom to have himself buried alive with his dead wife, and since he refuses, they drug him unconscious so as to execute their plan. As ʿOmar is about to be buried, the romance's main hero arrives and saves him.[27] Nineteenth-century Persian storytellers, probably feeling the need to rationalize the young woman's sudden death, have her die from the hero's brute sexuality in the wedding night. Following the tragic event, the nobles reckon that, should they keep their new king, the country would soon be without women. Consequently, they prepare two graves and pretend to the hero that their custom requests the husband to be buried alive with his dead wife. Although the hero refuses to comply, they pull him down from his horse and are about to bury him alive, when suddenly the romance's main hero arrives and saves him.[28] The motif also appears in the "Tale of Āzādbakht" that is embedded in the Urdu romance *Bāgh o Bahār* (Bāgh and Bahār),[29] an early nineteenth-century adaptation of a work whose Persian original is attributed to Amir Khosrow of Dehli (d. 1325). Here, the protagonist marries the vizier's daughter and lives with her happily for two years until she dies after giving birth to a still-born child. He is deposited in the burial fortress together with provisions for forty days and a chest of jewels whose value is equivalent to that of all his previous possessions. Living on the provisions he acquires from other people he kills, he later marries a young girl, and both invest a whole year's work into widening a drain so as to make their escape. And finally, the motif is encountered in various tales collected from twentieth-century oral tradition in Arabic,[30] Persian,[31] Kurdish,[32] and Turkish,[33] some of them close retellings of the Sindbād tale.

Considering the long and varied tradition over a period of a thousand years, the motif's inclusion in the tale of Sindbād's fourth voyage is but another occurrence of a narrative element that Middle Eastern storytellers obviously regarded as both attractive and applicable to different contexts. As the Sindbād tales were widely read in Europe following their inclusion in Galland's *Mille et une nuit* at the beginning of the eighteenth century, it is quite likely that the motif owes its inclusion in the Grimms' tale and other versions of tale type ATU 612 to the popularity of the *Nights*. At the same time, other tales might have contributed to the motif's transmission to the West, such as in particular the one included in the Ottoman Turkish *Ferec ba'd eş-şidde* that might have been known in the West by way of oral tradition. At any rate, the motif's occurrence in the Grimms' tale of *The Three Snake-Leaves* appears to be a faint echo of an old "Oriental" tradition. In terms of the tale's plot, it would not have been necessary to have the husband buried alive with his dead spouse, as a simple wake at her grave could equally result in him observing the serpent's resuscitation. But certainly the newly introduced element, when creatively merged with the scene of resuscitation deriving from the narrative tradition of Greek and Roman antiquity, added extra attraction, thus emphasizing the tale's marvelous and strange character.

Notes

1. Goldberg, Christine, "Schlangenblätter: Die drei S.," in *Enzyklopädie des Märchens*, vol. 12 (2007), cols. 50–54.

2. Paris, Gaston, "Die undankbare Gattin," *Zeitschrift des Vereins für Volkskunde* 13 (1903), pp. 1–24, 129–150, Wesselski, *Märchen des Mittelalters*, pp. 12–15, 188–192, no. 3.

3. Wesselski, Albert, "Das Geschenk der Lebensjahre," *Archiv orientální* 10 (1938), pp. 79–114, at pp. 90–98.

4. Chauvin, *Bibliographie*, vol. 8 (1904), pp. 119–120, no. 104; Marzolph and Van Leeuwen, *The Arabian Nights Encyclopedia*, vol. 1, p. 79, no. 432; Basset, *Mille et un contes*, vol. 1, pp. 318–320, no. 6.

5. Paret, Rudi, *Früharabische Liebesgeschichten*, Berlin: Paul Haupt, 1927, pp. 71–72, no. 186.

6. Grimm, Jacob and Wilhelm, *Kinder- und Hausmärchen: Ausgabe letzter Hand*, vol. 3, ed. Heinz Rölleke, Stuttgart: Philipp Reclam Jun., 1980, pp. 38–39 (original pagination of the edition Göttingen 1856, p. 26, no. 16).

7. Hansen, William, *Ariadne's Thread*, Ithaca and London: Cornell University Press, 2002, p. 14.

8. Besthorn, Rudolf, *Ursprung und Eigenart der älteren italienischen Novelle*, Gräfenheinichen: Heine, 1935, p. 120–121.

9. Gramaticus, Saxo, *The First Nine Books of Danish History of Saxo Grammaticus*, transl. Oliver Elton, ed. Frederick York Powell, London: David Nutt, 1894, pp. 200–201 (5, 162); Reinhard, John Revell, *Medieval Pageant*, New York: Haskell, 1939 (1970), pp. 227–228; see also Boberg, Inger M., *Motif-Index of Early Icelandic Literature*, Munskaard: Hafniæ, 1966, p. 237, S123.2.1: *Burial of living man with dead blood-brother.*

10. Mundt, Marina, *Zur Adaptation orientalischer Bilder in den Fornaldarsögur Norðrlanda: Materialien zu einer neuen Dimension altnordischer Belletristik*, Frankfurt: Lang, 1993.

11. Marzolph, Ulrich,"Märchen aus 'Tausendundeine Nacht' in der mündlichen Überlieferung Europas," in *Sichtweisen in der Märchenforschung*, ed. Siegfried Neumann and Christoph Schmitt, Baltmannsweiler: Schneider-Verlag Hohengehren, 2013, 23–41; see also Marzolph, "The Tale of Aladdin in European Oral Tradition," in *Les Mille et une Nuits et le récit oriental en Espagne et en Orient*, ed. Aboubakr Chraïbi and Carmen Ramirez. Paris: L'Harmattan, 2009, pp. 401–412.

12. The summary is adapted from Marzolph and Van Leeuwen, *The Arabian Nights Encyclopedia*, vol. 1, p. 386, in no. 179.

13. Karlinger, Felix, and Gertrude Gréciano, *Provenzalische Märchen*, Düsseldorf: Diederichs, 1974, pp. 188–190, no. 41; Mode, Heinz, *Zigeunermärchen aus aller Welt*, vol. 3, Wiesbaden: Drei-Lilien-Verlag, 1984, pp. 347–351, no. 175; Viidalepp, Richard, *Estnische Volksmärchen*, Berlin: Akademie-Verlag, 1980, pp. 255–258, no. 83; Zentralarchiv der deutschen Volkserzählung, no. 142914 (from Totzau, Sudeten German, 1897).

14. Miller, Elaine K., *Mexican Folk Narrative from the Los Angeles Area*, Austin: University of Texas Press, 1973, 265–274, no. 265, quotation p. 265.

15. Henßen, Gottfried, *Ungardeutsche Volksüberlieferungen*, Marburg: Elwert, 1959, pp. 153–160, no. 33.

16. Ey, August, *Harzmärchenbuch*, Stade: Fr. Steudel, 1862, pp. 134–139; Woeller, Waltraud, *Deutsche Volksmärchen von arm und reich*, Berlin: Akademie-Verlag, 1959, pp. 185–188, no. 33. Woeller, publishing in the then German Democratic Republic, adds a socialist interpretation: "Although the protagonist's profession as a miner lacks any motivation, the apparently superficial embedding in a miner's world enables the tale to express a feeling of solidarity that is particularly widespread with miners" (p. 429).

17. Lecouteux, Claude, "Magnetberg," in *Enzyklopädie des Märchens*, vol. 9 (1999), cols. 24–27. The earliest account of the Magnetic Mountain is contained in the *Naturalis historia* of Plinius (first century BCE). The motif also occurs in the tale of the third Qalandar in *The Thousand and One Nights*; see Marzolph and Van Leeuwen, *The Arabian Nights Encyclopedia*, vol. 2, pp. 631–632.

18. Haboucha, Reginetta, *Types and Motifs of the Judaeo Spanish Folktales*, New York: Garland, 1992, no. *996.

19. Marzolph and Van Leeuwen, *The Arabian Nights Encyclopedia*, vol. 1, p. 387.

20. Bellino, Francesca. "I sette Viaggi di Sindbād il marinaio: un romanzo arabo nelle Mille e Una Notte," in *Paradossi delle Notti: Dieci Studi su Le Mille e Una Notte*, ed. Leonardo Capezzone and Elisabetta Benigni, Pisa and Rome: Fabricio Serra editore, 2015, pp. 101–129; Bellino, "Another Manuscript of Pétis de la Croix's *Histoire arabe de Sindabad le marin*: A Possible Sub-family in the Fluid Transmission of the Story," *Quaderni di studi arabi* 12 (2017), pp. 102–132.

21. Marzolph, Ulrich, "An Early Persian Precursor to the Tales of Sindbād the Seafaring Merchant," *Zeitschrift der Deutschen Morgenländischen Gesellschaft* 167 (2017), pp. 127–141.

22. Margoliouth, D.S., "Review of Deliverance after Stress (Al-Faraj baʿd al-shiddah) by Abu ʿAlī Al-Muḥassin Al-Review of. . .]," *Journal of the Royal Asiatic Society of Great Britain and Ireland* (1905), pp. 425–426; Canard, Marius, "Les Aventures d'un prisonier arabe et d'un patrice byzantin à l'époque des guerres bulgaro-byzantines," *Dumbarton Oaks Papers* 9–10 (1956), pp. 51–72, at pp. 59–60. I owe these references to the kindness of Maurice Pomerantz; see his essay "Tales from the Crypt: On Some Uncharted Voyages of Sindbād the Sailor," *Narrative Culture* 3.1 (2015), pp. 250–269. For the Arabic text, see Tanūkhī, Abū ʿAlī al-Muḥassin ibn ʿAlī al-, *Kitāb al-Faraj baʿd al-shidda*, vol. 2, ed. ʿAbbūd al-Shālijī, Beirut: Dār Ṣādir, 1398/1978, pp. 191–205. A German translation of the tale is available in Tanūkhī, At-, *Ende gut, alles gut: Das Buch der Erleichterung nach der Bedrängnis*, transl. Arnold Hottinger, Zurich: Manesse, 1979, pp. 101–119.

23. Khadish, Pegāh, and Moḥammad Jaʿfari (Qanavāti), eds., *Jāmeʿ al-ḥekāyāt bar asās-e noskhe-ye Āstān-e qods-i Rażavi*, Tehran: Māzyār, 1390/2011, pp. 610–612; Haag-

Higuchi, Roxane, *Untersuchungen zu einer Sammlung persischer Erzählungen: Čihil wa-šiš ḥikāyāt yā ǧāmiʿ al-ḥikāyāt*, Berlin: Klaus Schwarz, 1984, pp. 105–106, no. 41.

24. Hazai, György, and Andreas Tietze, eds., *Ferec baʿd eş-şidde: „Freud nach Leid" (Ein frühosmanisches Geschichtenbuch)*, Berlin: Klaus Schwarz, 2006, vol. 1, p. 637–641, no. 42; Marzolph, *Relief after Hardship*, particularly pp. 117–118, commentary to no. 42.

25. *Journal d'Antoine Galland pendant son séjour à Constantinople (1672–1673)*, ed. Charles Schefer, Paris: Ernest Leroux, 1881 (reprint Frankfurt am Main 1994), vol. 2, pp. 45–46; see Marzolph, Ulrich, "A Scholar in the Making: Antoine Galland's Early Travel Diaries (1672–73) In the Light of Comparative Folk Narrative Research," *Middle Eastern Literatures* 18.3 (2015), pp. 283–300.

26. Pomerantz, Maurice, "Tales from the Crypt: On Some Uncharted Voyages of Sindbād the Sailor," *Narrative Culture* 3.1 (2015), pp. 250–269.

27. *Qeṣṣe-ye Ḥamze (Ḥamze-nāme)*, ed. Jaʿfar Shiʿār, Tehran: Enteshārāt-e dāneshgāh-e Tehrān, 1347/1968, pp. 246–248.

28. *Romuz-e Ḥamze*, Tehran 1273–76/1857–59, fol. 91b.

29. Forbes, Duncan, *Bagh o Bahar, or Tales of the Four Dervishes, translated from the Hindustani of Mir Amman of Dihli*, London: Wm. H. Allan & Co., 1874, pp. 240–246.

30. El-Shamy, Hasan M., *Folk Traditions of the Arab World*, Bloomington: Indiana University Press, 1995, vol. 1, p. 336, motif S 123.2; El-Shamy, *Types*, pp. 638–640, no. 0936A§.

31. Mashdi Galin Khānom, *Qeṣṣehā-ye Mashdi Galin Khānom*, ed. Ulrich Marzolph, AzarAmirhosseini-Nithammer, and Aḥmad Vakiliyān, Tehran: Markaz, 1374/1995, pp. 245–249, no. 57.

32. Information kindly supplied by Mohammad Sina Amani, who is currently compiling a type-index of Kurdish narratives.

33. Eberhard and Boratav, *Typen*, pp. 137–138, no. 120.

CHAPTER 12

The Contending Lovers Are Challenged to Acquire the Rarest Thing in the World (ATU 653A)

Published in the second volume of George E. Powell's and Eiríkr Magnússon's English rendering of the *Icelandic Legends* collected by Jón Árnason, "The Story of the Three Princes"[1] is a combination of tale types ATU 653A: *The Rarest Thing in the World*[2] and ATU 465: *The Man Persecuted because of His Beautiful Wife.*[3] In addition to the discussion of the tale's historical development, in the present context the tale serves to illustrate the skepticism often voiced by folklorists regarding possible literary precursors to tales collected from oral tradition, even when historical evidence clearly argues in favor of a literary model or, at the very least, in favor of a "braided" tradition influenced by oral and written transmission alike.

> A king's three sons fall in love with their father's foster daughter. When the king suggests that she choose her husband herself, the young woman feels unable to do so, as they are all "equally dear to her." Consequently, the king commands the princes to travel for a year. He who returns with "the finest thing" should marry the princess.
>
> The first prince acquires a spyglass so fine that one can see all over the world. The second prince meets a dwarf who is "the cleverest maker of curious and cunning things" and who sells him a magic cloth on which one can travel all over the world. And the third and youngest prince buys an apple "of so strange a nature that if it was put into the arm-hole of a dying man he would at once return to life." When the three princes return to their meeting place, the first one sees through the spy-glass that the beloved princess is so sick that she is about to die; with the cloth acquired by the second prince they reach home in a flash; and the youngest prince's magic apple cures the princess. As all gifts had an equal share in the cure, no decision is reached.
>
> Now the king decides that the ablest shooter is to marry to princess. The eldest brother's arrow falls at no great distance from the mark. The

second brother's arrow comes even closer to the mark. And the arrow of the youngest brother goes so far that they cannot find it again. Consequently, the princess is married to the second brother. The youngest brother eventually finds that his arrow "had by far outstripped the mark," but as the king is unwilling to revise his decision, the young man leaves the country. Wandering about in a great forest, the prince happens to meet ten riders in fine attire and bright armor. The riders bring them to their young and beautiful maiden queen who is in love with the prince. Although the prince is still "in a sad and gloomy state of mind" because of the apparent injustice he experienced, he agrees to marry the queen.

In the meantime, his father the king's wife died and the king married a wayfaring woman who had "much knowledge about many things." Meddling in the affairs of the government, the king's new wife convinces him that his youngest son might try to overthrow his rule and advises him to "be the first in throwing this danger off-hand." Consequently, the king invites his son to come and see him. The king then informs his son that according to law he deserves to die for the contempt he has shown in having run away. But instead of executing his son, the king asks him to acquire three specific items within a year, on pain of death. The first item requested is "a tent which will hold one hundred men but can yet be hidden in the closed hand;" the second is "water that cures all ailments;" and the third is "a man who has not his like in the whole world." The tent happens to be in the possession of the prince's fairy wife. The water she undertakes to procure herself in a difficult mission. And the prince manages to invite his wife's one-eyed demon brother who is of "tremendous ugliness" and "bugbear appearance."

When the prince presents the requested items to his father, they find no fault in the tent and the curing water. The princess's demon brother kills the malicious queen, who turns into "the most monstrous troll ever beheld." In the end, the king confesses that "he had acted thus, egged on by the queen." The king resigns and passes the rule on to his son who governs the realm "to a high age, in great glee and happiness."

Although William Alexander Clouston noticed that the Icelandic tale is "suspiciously" similar to the tale of "Prince Ahmad and the Fairy Perī-Bānū"[4] in Antoine Galland's French adaptation of *The Thousand and One Nights*, he could not "conceive how the peasantry [of Iceland] could have got it out of" the *Nights* and preferred to speculate about other "ways by which the story might have reached them independently of Galland's work."[5] Today we know that Árnason received the tale from Jón Sigurðson (1828–1889), although it is not clear whether the contributor actually told the tale himself or whether he relied on somebody else's narration. Sigurðson was by no means a simple peasant, but a land-holding farmer and member of the parliament,[6] and thus a formally educated person. Whoever actually narrated the tale might well have read it in one of the Icelandic editions (translated from the German?) published in the 1850s,[7] so there is no need to speculate about other ways of transmission. Even well before that date, the *Nights* circulated in Icelandic manuscript versions translated from the Danish, probably as early as late in the eighteenth century.[8] A reservation similar to Clouston's is voiced by Daniel J. Crowley in his assessment of a version of tale type ATU 653A from Trinidad.[9] That tale was recorded in 1955 from the illiterate folk artist Israel Paul, known as "La Wa" (French *Le Roi*), aged about 70. Although Crowley conceded that the narrator, a "leading carrier of the local folk culture," practiced a remarkable "narrative artistry whereby foreign themes are reworded to conform to local values in content and in esthetics," he wondered how the tale from the *Nights* might have reached Trinidad, as the narrator was "unlikely to have heard or read *The Arabian Nights*."[10] Likewise, Aurelio M. Espinosa evaluated the tale's eleven Spanish versions as definitely being "traditional" and deriving from regional popular tradition.[11] Although the Spanish versions overlap with the tale from the *Nights* in almost all details, Espinosa was equally unwilling to admit that they might derive from the *Nights*.

Tale type ATU 653A, which is the only one of interest for the present discussion, belongs to a cluster of narratives discussed by Williard Edward Farnham under the heading "The Contending Lovers."[12] Taking into account numerous versions from ancient Indian literature to contemporary European texts, Farnham discussed tales that feature a number of contending lovers who compete for their beloved either by deploying their special supernatural qualities or by using particular marvelous objects at their disposal. Often, the beloved is dead or about to die. Consequently, Farnham identified five essentially different forms, of which the Resuscitation type and the Rescue type are relevant here. Farnham regarded the first part of the tale from *The Thousand and One Nights*, "Prince Ahmad and the Fairy Perī-Bānū," as the "product of a mingling of types" and treated it separately, as it had an "enormous influence on European folk-literature" where it "has attained a surprisingly wide spread."[13] Farnham defined that tale as constituting the Gift type, "because the lovers perform their services by means of magic gifts."[14] Detailing the sequence and character of events in about 20 international versions of the tale published between 1850 and 1918, Farnham clearly identified the tale of "Prince Ahmad and the Fairy Perī-Bānū" as the Gift type's "Oriental prototype."[15] Numerous versions of the tale were published since then. Out of the great number of tales classified as tale type ATU 653A, only a few of those bearing a close resemblance to the tale from the *Nights* will be considered in the following.

A Corsican version of the tale was performed in 1955 by the former shepherd François Castellani, aged 90, who had heard the tale some 70 years earlier during a wake.[16] Here, three young men woo the same young woman. She promises to marry the one who will bring the nicest present to her in the course of a year. The first one finds a flower that has the power to resuscitate, the second acquires a horse that traverses the distance of a year in a single hour, and the third buys a mirror that enables one to see any person on earth. Together they find out that their beloved died, travel to her in a flash and resuscitate her. The tale has an open ending, as the narrator asks the audience whom the young woman should marry. In the French version from Basse-Bretagne narrated by Janton-Meitour at the beginning of the twentieth century, a lord who already has three sons adopts the daughter of a poor cobbler.[17] The three wooers acquire their magic objects in Paris, consisting of a magic carriage, magic glasses, and three curing apples. When they see with the glasses that their father, their mother, and their adopted sister are about to die, they rush home with the carriage and have them each eat an apple. Since the first two brothers still keep their magic objects, the father decides that young Stéphan will marry the young woman, as he spent the apples saving his family members. In the Swiss version narrated by Maria Ludwig, the three sons rescue their moribund father, and in the end their cousin marries the youngest brother whom she loves most.[18] Many of the short forms of tale type ATU 653A are dilemma tales ending with an open question, a feature that is particularly prevalent in the numerous versions documented from sub-Saharan African tradition.[19] Less numerous are versions of tale type ATU 653A that proceed in the same manner as the Icelandic tale with a shooting contest and the continuation with tale type ATU 465.[20] Several versions of tale type ATU 465 even begin right away with the shooting contest.[21]

Although the general history and dissemination of tale type ATU 653A are too complex to be discussed in detail here, there is little doubt that at least those versions documented in Western oral tradition that continue with the shooting contest and tale type ATU 465, and most likely several of the shorter versions as well, derive from Galland's version of the *Nights*. Tales with this structure are too specific to have developed independently, particularly since the *Nights* were read widely all over Europe since the beginning of the eighteenth century. When the tale was first recorded from oral tradition in the middle of the nineteenth century, it had thus been circulating for a century and a half. Although the literary version in the *Nights* was constantly available and likely engendered retellings and variations in oral performance, once the tale entered oral tradition, it might also have been transmitted orally without the storytellers being conscious of its connection to the *Nights*.

The tale's history and dissemination becomes even more complex when one considers the fact that Galland did not invent the story himself. Galland adapted the tale from the oral narration of the Syrian Maronite storyteller Ḥannā Diyāb who performed it for him, presumably in French, on May 22, 1709.[22] Galland thus adapted the tale directly from an "Oriental" tradition that itself developed in the larger context of other "Oriental" tales about contending lovers.[23] Even so, Diyāb's version is the tale's first documented occurrence and is without reasonable doubt the origin of all later versions that display a close correspondence to it in terms of content and structure. Diyāb's version differs only in details from the Icelandic version summarized above. The magic items here are a flying carpet, a magic telescope, and a healing apple. As in the Icelandic version, the second prince wins the shooting context, but contrasting with the Icelandic version, the youngest prince is not disappointed. Searching for his arrow, he happens to come to the fairy's underground palace. The mischievous person is not the king's second wife but a magician who is jealous of the prince and advises the king to have his son killed by sending him on missions that are impossible to achieve. Again, the fairy wife already possesses the requested tent. As for the water, the prince has to procure it himself. In turn, the fairy calls her brother, "one of the maleficent genies, who just happened to be there."

It should not go without mention that Diyāb's version of the tale is not the only one that circulated in European tradition, as there are numerous other versions of tale type ATU 653A that developed differently or that are influenced by motifs common with other tale types. In this respect, Diyāb's version of the tale of the contending lovers is neither as exclusive nor as influential as, for instance, his versions of the tales of Aladdin (tale type ATU 561; see essay **9, *The Unpromising Rascal Makes His Fortune with the Help of a Magic Object***) or Ali Baba (tale type ATU 954; see essay **30, *The Robbers Hiding Their Treasures in a Magic Cavern***). The fair number of versions of tale type ATU 653A that do, however, derive more or less directly from Diyāb's performance as published by Galland, document the narrator's supreme importance as the most influential early modern storyteller a substantial part of whose repertoire is documented with a high degree of reliability.

Notes

1. Árnason, Jón, *Icelandic Legends*, transl. George E. Powell and Eiríkr Magnússon, vol. 2, London: Longman's, Green, and Co., 1866, pp. 348–365; see also Rittershaus, Adeline, *Die neuisländischen Volksmärchen*, Halle: Niemeyer, 1902, pp. 182–187, no. 43.

2. Ranke, Kurt, "Brüder: Die vier kunstreichen B.," in *Enzyklopädie des Märchens*, vol. 2 (1979), cols. 903–912, at cols. 908–910.

3. Pöge-Alder, Kathrin, "Mann wird wegen seiner schönen Frau verfolgt," ibid., vol. 9 (1999), cols. 162–171.

4. Marzolph and Van Leeuwen, *The Arabian Nights Encyclopedia*, vol. 1, pp. 80–82, no. 355.

5. Clouston, William Alexander, "Variants and Analogues of Some of the Tales in the Supplemental Nights, 3," in Burton, Richard F., *Arabian Nights*, (Benares 1885) reprint Beirut: Khayat, 1966, vol. 13, pp. 551–652, at p. 608; see also Clouston, William Alexander, *Popular Tales and Fictions: Their Migrations and Transformations*, ed. Christine Goldberg, Santa Barbara, CA: ABC-Clio, 2002, p. 128.

6. Information kindly supplied by email from Romina Werth, May 6, 2018. The tale was first published by Árnason, Jón, *Íslenzkar þjóðsögur og æfintýri*, vol. 2, Leipzig: J.C. Hinrichs, 1864, pp. 367–375.

7. Chauvin, *Bibliographie*, vol. 4 (1900), p. 70, nos. 183 (published 1852), 184 (published 1857).

8. Information kindly supplied by email from Romina Werth, May 6, 2018. The first

Danish translation of Galland's *Nights* was published in 1745; see Chauvin, *Bibliographie*, vol. 4 (1900), p. 69, no. 180A.

9. Crowley, Daniel J., "'The Greatest Thing in the World:' Type 653A in Trinidad," in Dégh, Linda, Henry Glassie, and Felix J. Oinas, eds., *Folklore Today: A Festschrift for Richard M. Dorson*, Bloomington: Indiana University, 1976, pp. 93–100.

10. Ibid., quotes pp. 94, 100.

11. Espinosa, Aurelio Macedonio, *Cuentos populares españoles recogidos de la tradición oral de España*, Madrid: Consejo Superior de Investigaciones Científicas, 1946, vol. 3, p. 86.

12. Farnham, Williard Edward, "The Contending Lovers," *Publications of the Modern Language Association* 35.3 (1920), pp. 247–323.

13. Ibid., quotes pp. 272, 276, 295.

14. Ibid., p. 276.

15. Ibid., pp. 280–284.

16. Massignon, Geneviève, *Contes corses*, Aix-en-Provence: Ophrys, 1963, pp. 139–140, no. 61.

17. Delarue, Paul, and Marie-Louise Tenèze, *Le conte populaire français*, vol. 2, Paris: Maisonneuve et Larose, 1964, pp. 559–560, no. 653A; Cadic, François, *Contes de Basse-Bretagne*, Paris: Érasme, 1955, pp. 142–150.

18. Büchli, Arnold, *Mythologische Landeskunde von Graubünden: Ein Bergvolk erzählt*, vol. 3, ed. Ursula Brunold-Bigler, Disentis: Desertina, 1990, pp. 482–483.

19. Bascom, William R., *African Dilemma Tales*, The Hague: Mouton, 1975, pp. 45–52, nos. 36.1–37; see also the somewhat polemical article by Jones, Steven S., "'The Rarest Thing in the World:' Indo-European or African?" *Research in African Literature* 7 (1976), pp. 200–210; also in Crowley, Daniel J., ed., *African Folklore in the New World*, Austin: University of Texas Press, 1977, pp. 54–64.

20. See, e.g., Peuckert, Will-Erich, *Schlesiens deutsche Märchen*, Breslau: Ostdeutsche Verlagsanstalt, 1932, pp. 202–209, no. 103; Rael, Juan B., *Cuentos españoles de Colorado y Nuevo Méjico: Spanish Originals with English Summaries*, Stanford: Stanford University Press, 1940, vol. 1, pp. 50–56, no. 224.

21 See, e.g., Dawkins, Richard M., *Modern Greek Folktales*, Oxford: Clarendon, 1953, pp. 96–103, no. 18; Karadžić, Vuk Stefanović, *Srpske narodne pripovetke*, 4th ed., Belgrade, 1937, pp. 174–177, no. 3; Bogdanović, David, *Izabrane narodne pripovijetke hrvatske*, 2nd ed., Zagreb: St. Kugli, 1930, pp. 178–183.

22. Galland, Antoine, *Le Journal d'Antoine Galland (1646–1715): La période parisienne*, ed. Frédéric Bauden and Richard Waller, vol. 1, Leuven: Peeters, 2011, pp. 243–246; Marzolph, Ulrich, "The Man Who Made the *Nights* Immortal: The Tales of the Syrian Maronite Storyteller Ḥannā Diyāb," *Marvels & Tales* 32.1 (2018), pp. 114–129.

23. Farnham, "The Contending Lovers."

CHAPTER 13

The Sensitive Brothers and Their Clever Deductions (ATU 655)

In a letter the English writer, connoisseur, and collector Horatio (Horace) Walpole, fourth Earl of Orford, wrote to his friend Horace Mann on January 28, 1754, he coined the term "serendipity."[1] Today defined by the *Oxford Dictionary* as "the occurrence and development of events by chance in a happy or beneficial way,"[2] Walpole related the term to his reading of "a silly fairy tale, called *the three Princes of Serendip*" in which "their Highnesses," as they traveled, "were always making discoveries, by accidents and sagacity, of things which they were not in quest of."[3] The tale, or rather collection of tales, Walpole referred to was *The Travels and Adventures of Three Princes of Serendip*, a book presenting itself as "translated from the Persian into French, and from thence done into English,"[4] and printed in London for "Will. Chetwode" in 1722. Little did Walpole know (or, for that matter, care) about the historical and geographical dimensions of the "silly fairy tale." These dimensions reach from ancient Indian literature via premodern Jewish, Arabic, Persian, and Turkish intermediaries to medieval and early modern occurrences in the European literatures and, eventually, to documented recordings from nineteenth- and twentieth-century oral tradition in Europe. In comparative folk narrative studies, the tale is classified as tale type ATU 655: *The Wise Brothers*.[5] In its full form, the tale type comprises two episodes, the first one dealing with clever deductions concerning the traces of an unseen animal, and the second one dealing with equally clever deductions at the host's banquet concerning the nature of the food served as well as the host's pedigree. Often, the tale is framed by an introductory episode about a certain conflict that supplies the reason for the brothers to set out traveling and, complementing this, a final episode resolving the conflict.

A Spanish folktale narrated by Ursulita Quintana, aged 36, from Cortillo, New Mexico, presents a short version that only comprises the tale's first episode.[6] The owners of a strayed camel meet a man who "tells them that the camel is loaded with wheat on the left side and honey on the right side, that it is blind in one eye and has a middle tooth missing." The man informs the astonished owners that he made his deductions on the basis of careful observation.

A Finnish folktale adapts the "accidental sagacity"[7] identified by Walpole to a Christian context. The text was recorded from the oral performance of J.P. Söggel in 1900 and only comprises the tale type's second episode.[8]

> When Jesus is born, the three wise men who come to worship him are received by King Herod with great honors. One of the sages does not take off his cap, arguing that he would not do so in the house of a bastard. The second sage refuses to partake in the roast, arguing that he does not eat dog's meat. And the third refrains from drinking wine, arguing that he cannot possibly drink wine from a barrel in which there was the dead body of a child. After the sages have left, Herod inquires with the cook and the cellar man, only to find out that the allegations of the sages correspond to reality. Embarrassed by the possibility that he himself might not be his parents' legitimate child, he roams the country disguised as a beggar. At night he overhears a woman confessing to her distressed pregnant daughter that she once left the child born from her own premarital (or extramarital) affair on the doorstep of a rich and powerful family at night. Later, that child became King Herod. Having heard this, King Herod returns home.

A full-fledged version from Bosnia published in 1905 comprises both episodes, telling about three poor brothers whose only possessions are "a lot of sagacity and an old mare."[9] When the mare is stolen, the brothers know by intuition that the thief is a man of average stature with a blond beard, named Mussa. Traveling around, they happen to find this Mussa, a wealthy merchant who denies knowing anything about the whereabouts of their horse. When the brothers present their case to the local judge, they are invited to the judge's house for dinner. During the meal, one of the brothers remarks that the wheat used for preparing the bread must have grown on the edges of a cemetery. The second brother notices that the roast smacks of pig, as if the lamb had been suckled by a sow. And the third one declares that their host is of illegitimate birth. Overhearing their remarks, the judge puts the brothers to a test by having them divine a lemon and an egg he hides in his pockets. When the brothers correctly guess the contents of his pockets, the judge proceeds to find out that all of the brothers' previous allegations are to the point, including the fact that his own biological father is a man whose name he never heard before. Finally, the brothers happen to find the missing horse in Mussa's stable. As Mussa claims that he found the horse straying, he is happy to return it to its legitimate owners.

In a Catalan folktale narrated in 1922 by Aurora Blai from Barcelona, three brothers travel to the king to ask him to divide their inheritance.[10] On the way, they meet a man who lost his mule. Although the three brothers correctly describe the mule's characteristics as being one-eyed, grey, and limping, they deny having seen the animal. At court, the king first invites the brothers to have breakfast. During the meal, one of the brothers remarks that the piglet they are being served was raised with the milk of a bitch. The second brother senses that the wine was made from the grapes of a young grapevine. And the third states that the king himself is the son of a Moor. Ascertaining that all of their allegations are true, the king has the brothers explain how they knew about the characteristics of the missing mule. They inform him that there had only been tracks from three of the animal's hooves, that they had seen grey hair on the ground, and that the grain growing beside the road had only been eaten away on one side. Following this, the king decides to put the brothers to a test so as to decide how to divide their inheritance. Only the youngest brother refuses to shoot at an image of their father and is recognized as the sole legitimate heir. The tale's final episode corresponds to tale type ATU 920C: *Shooting at the Father's Corpse as a Test of Paternity.*[11]

A late nineteenth-century Greek version from the island of Symi introduces an aged king advising his three sons that he stored his belongings in a sealed chest they are only to open together when the youngest son comes of age.[12] The youngest son secretly empties the chest without destroying the seal and fills it with stones instead. When they later open the chest, he accuses his elder brothers of having stolen the contents. This introduction reads like a reduced version of tale type ATU 1591: *The Three Joint Depositors* that is first documented in the *Facta et dicta memorabilia* (Memorable Deeds and Sayings; 7,3, externa 5) compiled by Latin author Valerius Maximus in the first half of the first century CE.[13] Together, the brothers resolve to go to the judge to get his decision. On the way they meet a man looking for his lost camel and manage to describe the camel in great detail. It was laden with vinegar, and one of its eyes was blind. As the owner suspects the brothers to have stolen his camel, he accompanies them to the judge. Having explained to the judge how they knew about the camel's characteristics, the brothers are invited to stay for dinner. During the meal, one of the brothers remarks that the roast they are being served smells of dog, as the kid was suckled by a bitch. The second brother argues that the grapes on the table have a nasty taste, as the vine grew out of tombs. And the third one asserts that the judge is a bastard. One after the other, the judge finds out that the brothers' allegations are true. Finally, in order to pass judgment among them, the judge tells them the tale of a woman who promises to meet her lover before consummating her marriage in the wedding night. The lover, however, sends the woman away, telling her that she now belongs to another man. At this point, the younger brother comments that he would never have let the woman go, thus revealing himself to be the one who stole the money from the chest. The final episode corresponds to tale type ATU 976: *Which Was the Noblest Act?* (see essay **31, *Whose Was the Noblest Action?***) that often serves to detect a thief.[14]

The tale was frequently discussed in nineteenth- and twentieth-century research,[15] including the exhaustive treatment of the tale's research history and its numerous historical versions in world literature in Josef Schick's *Corpus Hamleticum* that for a long time was considered as the "last word" on the subject.[16]

Recent findings, to be detailed below, add substantially to the tale's historical dissemination.[17]

In European tradition, the tale or single episodes thereof appear in a number of prominent historical examples.[18] In addition to Cristoforo Armeno's Italian *Peregrinaggio di tre giovani figliuoli del re di Serendippo* (1557)[19] whose English translation Walpole had read, these instances include, to name but a few of the more prominent ones, the legend of Amleth in the *Gesta Danorum* (The History of the Danes) compiled by Saxo Grammaticus (ca 1140–ca 1220),[20] the novella "De Sapientia" (Of Wisdom) by Italian novelist Giovanni Sercambi (1348–1424),[21] a tale in the fifteenth-century anonymous *Novellino*, also known as *Cento novelle antiche* (A Hundred Old Novellas),[22] and the third tale in Voltaire's novella *Zadig; ou la Destinée: histoire orientale* (Zadig, or Destiny: An Oriental Tale; 1747).[23] Voltaire's *Zadig*, probably indebted to the French translation of the *Peregrinaggio* (from which the English translation Walpole read was also prepared), tells about the protagonist's astonishing capacity to describe a runaway dog and horse that he had not seen. The *Cento novelle antiche* mentions a total of three clever deductions: a horse was brought up on a donkey's milk; a precious gem has a worm inside; the king is the son of a baker. In the legend of Amleth, the protagonist argues that "the bread was tainted with blood, the drink had the flavour of iron, and the banquet meat was smothered in the odour of a corpse;" moreover, "the king had the eyes of a slave and . . . his queen had displayed three mannerisms of a maidservant." All of Amleth's observations are subsequently found to correspond to reality.

Of the above-named historical instances, only Armeno and Sercambi present the full-fledged narrative with its two episodes. Armeno starts by introducing a conflict between Giaffer, king of Serendippo (present-day Sri Lanka), and his sons. Notably, the conflict is only resolved at the collection's very end when the sons return home to their aged father.

> The king puts the loyalty of his sons to a test by suggesting to them one after the other to succeed him while he is still alive. Although he is highly satisfied to learn that none of his sons dares to replace him, the king feigns anger at their alleged lack of respect for his wishes and sends them away.
>
> On their journey, the sons deduce from the traces they observe that a camel had passed whose one eye was blind; it also lacked a tooth and was limping. When meeting the camel's owner, they add some more observations. The camel was laden with butter and honey; a woman was riding the camel; the woman was pregnant. At court, the ruler is convinced that the brothers are actually robbers and has them imprisoned until the owner happens to find his camel again.
>
> Having been released, one day the brothers comment on their breakfast. The wine is made from grapes that grew on a grave; the roast is from a lamb that was raised on the milk of a bitch; the ruler's vizier plots to kill him, because the king had the vizier's son executed for his crimes. The

king finds the first two statements to be true. In order to verify the third statement, the king makes the vizier's concubine expect his own favor so that she informs him about the vizier's plan to poison him. When the vizier's plot is unveiled, he is pardoned, and the king marries the concubine to one of his officers.

Sercambi's version of the tale displays essentially the same elements, although the introductory, and consequently, the concluding episodes differ.

When the merchant Alvisir feels that his end is near, he distributes the larger part of his wealth among his three sons. In addition, he hides three precious gems, making his sons promise not to touch them. Having spent his money quickly, the youngest son clandestinely takes one of the gems and sells it. When his brothers later suggest that they divide the three gems, they only find two gems, and the youngest brother accuses his siblings of having stolen one of them. Together they decide to go to the Kali (the *qāḍī* or judge) to ask him to decide.

On the way they deduce by observation that a passing camel was one-eyed, that its load consisted of honey and vinegar, and that its tail was cut off. Thinking that the brothers stole the animal, the camel's owner accompanies them to the Kali. In the Kali's presence, the brothers explain their reasoning. Following this, they present their case, and the Kali promises to make a decision.

When dinner is served, the brothers sense that the meat they are being served is from an animal that was nursed by a bitch; that the wine is from grapes growing on a graveyard; and that the Kali is a bastard.

Finding all of their allegations true, the Kali tells them a tale in order to prepare his decision. The tale is about a beautiful maiden who, when traveling to her future husband, passes through a country owned by three young men, each of whom has the power to do with her whatever they wanted to do. The Kali asks the three brothers present what they would do? The oldest brother would protect the maiden at all means. The second brother would ravish her and then send her to her future husband. And the youngest brother would not only ravish her himself but also have all of his servants rape her, keeping her with himself for the rest of her days. Having learned about the youngest brother's detestable character, the Kali reveals that he is the one who committed the theft. Following this disclosure, the brothers return home in harmony and continue to live a peaceful life.

Armeno's work, including the tale under consideration, was identified beyond reasonable doubt as an adapted prose rendering closely following Persian poet Amir Khosrow Dehlavi's *Hasht behesht* (The Eight Paradises), a poem composed at the beginning of the fourteenth century in emulation of Persian poet Neżāmi's (d. 1209) *Haft peykar* (The Seven Portraits).[24] Amir Khosrow's version supplies the model for the Italian translation in a number of specific points, albeit with several different traits. Contrary to Armeno's text, it resolves the feigned conflict between the king and his sons in the introductory episode right at the tale's end. As in the *Peregrinaggio*, the brothers' clever deductions concerning the traces of the unseen camel are sixfold in two series of three deductions each, and the brothers' temporary imprisonment is mentioned. Only the third statement during the banquet scene, in which Armeno's version reveals the vizier's plot, differs from Amir Khosrow's text that parallels numerous other versions in which the king himself was born from the illegitimate relationship with a cook. Although Armeno's version of the third statement has at times been reasoned to result from his catering to the taste of an aristocratic audience that would not have been amused at the motif of the king's illegitimate pedigree, early Indian versions of the tale displaying a similar choice might have been mediated to the author.[25]

Not discussed in previous research, Sercambi's version of the tale displays a close resemblance to the version contained in the contemporary anonymous Ottoman Turkish collection of tales *Ferec ba'd eş-şidde* (Relief after Hardship) whose initial compilation probably dates to the second half of the fourteenth century.[26] The introductory conflict concerning the inheritance of the three brothers is virtually the same in both versions, as are the three deductions concerning the traces of the unseen camel. The deductions at the host's banquet concerning the nature of the food served refer to bread and meat (instead of Sercambi's meat and wine). The final episode resolving the initial conflict again corresponds to tale type ATU 976. Whereas Sercambi presents this episode in a rudimentary form, the *Ferec ba'd eş-şidde* displays a more elaborate version that does not directly involve the brothers in the plot. Here, the husband agrees to let his wife visit her former lover on the wedding night. A robber refrains from robbing her because of her husband's magnanimity, and her former lover does not touch her out of respect for her husband, instead escorting her back home. The question leading to the thief's discovery is who of those three persons is the most noble-minded one. The youngest brother votes in favor of the robber and thus discloses his mean character. The identical structure of the above-quoted version from Greek oral tradition that is geographically close and historically prone to be influenced by Ottoman Turkish tradition serves as an additional argument to hypothesize a genetic relation between Sercambi's Italian version of the tale and that presented in *Ferec ba'd eş-şidde*. The latter version is known to have been translated and/or adapted to Ottoman Turkish from a previous Persian collection of tales generically known as *Jāmeʿ al-ḥekāyāt* (Collection of Tales). Although most of the genre's preserved representatives date at best from the seventeenth-century,[27] the tale is already included in what appears to be the genre's starting point, the *Munes-nāme* (The Book as an Intimate Friend) compiled by a certain Abu Bakr ibn Khosrow al-Ostād around the year 1200.[28] Contemporary with this early thirteenth-century version, Persian literature also knows the tale's ancient Arabic version as given in Sadid al-Din Moḥammad

ʿAwfi's (d. ca. 1232) extensive *Javāmeʿ al-ḥekāyāt* (Collections of Tales).[29] Here, the king is identified as the Arab chieftain Nizār ibn Maʿadd ibn ʿAdnān, one of the Prophet Muḥammad's ancestors, and the clever deductions are attributed to Nizār's four sons Muḍar, Rabīʿa, Iyād, and Anmār.

The Arabic version featuring Nizār's four sons is known from its inclusion in some twenty works of history, entertaining and educative literature, and other genres, ranging from the tenth to the seventeenth centuries.[30] The tale was shaped in tradition by two early works of history, al-Ṭabarī's (d. 923) *Tārīkh al-rusul wa-'l-mulūk* (History of the Prophets and Kings)[31] and al-Masʿūdī's (d. 956) *Murūj al-dhahab wa-maʿādin al-jawhar* (The Meadows of Gold and Mines of Gems).[32] Al-Ṭabarī presents a matter-of-fact version without any embellishing details.

> Having distributed his belongings to his four sons Muḍar, Rabīʿa, Iyād, and Anmār, Nizār ibn Maʿadd advises them to go to the wise Afʿā from the tribe of Jurhum should any dispute arise among them. As the sons later dispute their father's will, they set out to seek Afʿā's advice.
>
> On the way, they deduce that a passing camel they have not seen has only one eye, that it is lame, that it does not have a tail, and that it has gone astray. Meeting the camel's owner, they are able to describe the camel in great detail. The owner suspects them of having stolen the animal and accompanies them on their way. Listening to the brothers' reasoning, Afʿā realizes that they have not seen the camel.
>
> During the meal, each of the brothers makes a particular remark. The grapes for the wine are grown on a grave; the meat is from an animal that was nursed by a bitch; their host is from a different father than he thinks he is; the last brother finally remarks that he never heard comments as useful as theirs. Having listened to their comments, Afʿā finds all of them corresponding to reality. As his father was not able to produce offspring, his mother had decided to secure their lineage by having intercourse with a stranger.
>
> Following these events, Afʿā distributes the inheritance just as their father had decided.

The version presented by al-Masʿūdī, although essentially identical, differs in several details, including the sequence of the brother's allegations and the sequence of their mention during the distribution of their inheritance. When the case of the camel is decided, Afʿā orders one of his servants to listen to the comments his guests make during the meal. The first brother comments that the bees produced the honey they are being served inside the skull of a large animal. When verifying the brother's assertions, Afʿā learns that his mother slept with a guest of royal descent to secure their lineage. Following the events, Afʿā distributes the inheritance just as their father had decided.

Closely similar versions of the tale are given, to name but a few instances, in the collections of proverbs and their stories compiled by al-Mufaḍḍal ibn Salama (d. after 903)[33] and al-Maydānī (d. 1124);[34] in Ibn al-Jawzī's (d. 1201) universal history *al-Muntaẓam* (The Orderly Arrangement)[35] and his book of entertaining stories on clever people, *Akhbār al-Adhkiyā'*;[36] in al-Nuwayrī's (d. 1332) *Nihāyat al-arab fī funūn al-adab* (The Ultimate Ambition in the Arts of Erudition);[37] and al-Damīrī's (d. 1405) zoographical encyclopedia *Ḥayāt al-ḥayawān* (The Lives of Animals).[38] In texts of *The Thousand and One Nights*, versions of the tale are contained in the Wortley-Montague manuscript, compiled in 1764–1765,[39] and in the alleged Tunisian manuscript parts of which inspired Maximilian Habicht's Breslau edition of the *Nights*.[40] In the latter, the tale is embedded in the frame tale of "King Shāh Bakht and His Vizier al-Rahwān," as it is also encountered in the Kayseri manuscript of the *Nights* that probably dates to as early as the fifteenth century.[41]

Neither Arabic authors nor Western researchers studying the tale have taken notice of the earliest documented Arabic version in ʿAbd al-Malik Ibn Hishām's (d. second quarter of the ninth century) *Kitāb al-Tījān fī mulūk Ḥimyar* (The Book of Crowns: On the Kings of Ḥimyar).[42] The recent discovery of this version pushes the "emergence of the complete story in Arabic in written form" back "to the beginning of the ninth or even the end of the eighth century CE."[43] Ibn Hishām's version of the tale is "significantly more voluminous in every respect" than any of the other known early versions; at the same time, it is characterized by "a lack of uniformity in the flow of the narrative, and also some jagged segues between different traditions and materials."[44]

Having divided his inheritance among his four sons, Nizār gives each of them "a clay pot with a sealed mouth" and tells them to go to Afʿā, the ruler of Najrān "who is wise and the judge of the Arabs."[45] Nizār's son Rabīʿa recites a poem in praise of his deceased father.

On their way to Afʿā, the brothers encounter a number of strange scenes. First, they encounter "a bitch and a small suckling pup. The pup barked at them but the bitch remained silent." Next, they come by "a luminous place of droppings." And then they come to a group of "three bent intertwined trees" with two birds flying from the tree on the right to the one on the left, and vice versa, never settling on the tree in the middle. Finally, they see two old men fighting, each grabbing the other's beard. Both Anmār and Rabīʿa try to separate the men but are beaten by them. Only when Muḍar approaches them do they separate and flee in different directions.

The brothers' deductions concerning the unseen camel mention the facts that it is blind in one eye; that it does not have a tail; that it limps; and that it has gone astray. Meeting the camel's owner, the latter accompanies them to Afʿā who learns about the brothers' deductions and decides that they have not seen the animal. Afʿā comments on the events with a proverb that is often cited in connected with the tale, essentially implying that Nizār's sons are as intelligent as their father.

> During the meal, the sons sense that the lamb was suckled by a bitch; that the "wine was made of a vine that grew over a grave;" that their host "is not the son of his father;" and that the servant who served the food "is the son of royalty and of noble birth." Learning that all of the allegations are true, Afʿā hears from his mother that she was raped by her husband's brother when he was so drunk that he did not really know what he was doing. Learning about his deed, Afʿā's uncle decided to refrain from drinking and recited a poem to that effect.
>
> Before passing his judgment in respect to the inheritance, Afʿā explains the enigmatic scenes the brothers had witnessed on their way to him. The brothers explain their father's will to him, following which he opens the sealed jars. In each of the jars he finds an object that induces him to pass judgment essentially as decreed by their father.

Ibn Hishām's book is known to constitute the adaptation of an earlier work ascribed to Wahb ibn Munabbih (d. 728 or 732), "one of a number of early sages who was claimed to have been a Jewish convert to Islam, or the son of a convert."[46] Although the specific tale under consideration apparently "cannot be considered an adaptation of Wahb ibn Munabbih's account," "this part of the book was also influenced by Jewish and Christian traditions that circulated in his days both orally and in writing."

Predating the Arabic versions, probably by as much as several centuries, the tale, and particularly its first episode, is encountered in Hebrew in the *Babylonian Talmud* (*Sanhedrin* 104a–b) and in several *Midrash* collections, including the account in the *Midrash Lamentations* (*Ekha Rabbati*).[47] The tale's oldest documented occurrences are contained in Buddhist literature dating to the first centuries CE, such as a text included in the Buddhist *Tripiṭaka* (Three Baskets)[48] and a version of the *Vetālapañcaviṃśatika* (Twenty-five Stories of a Corpse Demon) contained in Somadeva's eleventh-century *Kathāsaritsāgara* (The Ocean of Streams of Stories).[49]

The tale of the sensitive brothers and their clever deductions is one of those tales from "Oriental" tradition that in addition to numerous versions in written and oral traditions generated a vast body of research literature,[50] culminating in an impressive volume of Schick's monumental, although still incomplete, *Corpus Hamleticum* that devotes more than a thousand pages to discussing the tale's numerous versions and filiations. Considering the tremendous variety of both primary and secondary sources, the survey presented here aims to highlight a few of the major points related to the tale's Middle Eastern versions. Although the tale's dissemination can only be reconstructed with a certain degree of probability, the relative age of its various versions suggests a clear chronology from Buddhist Indian via Jewish Hebrew and Aramaic, Muslim Arabic, Persian, and Ottoman Turkish texts to fifteenth- and sixteenth-century Christian Italian versions and their ramifications in modern European oral tradition. In this way, the tale not only traveled across various geographical and linguistic boundaries.

Moreover, it displays a remarkable adaptability to a variety of religious contexts, demonstrating its timeless expression of a universally adaptable human experience.

Remarkably, in both English and Middle Eastern tradition, the tale has boiled down to condensed references. In Middle Eastern tradition, Walpole's definition of "serendipity," is contrasted by the saying, "When they ask you, 'Have you seen the camel?' say, 'I have not seen it!'"[51] The saying is first documented in a tale of the Ottoman Turkish *Ferec ba'd eş-şidde*, albeit a different one than the tale that actually tells the events alluded to.[52] The related tale concerning the brothers' clever deductions is particularly popular in modern Turkish,[53] Persian,[54] and Arabic[55] oral traditions. Whereas Walpole's coinage serves to express the ultimate combination of cleverness and happenstance, the Middle Eastern saying implies the warning that one should not meddle with issues that are none of one's own concern. These differing developments may or may not bespeak different mental attitudes based on varying historical experiences.

In addition to its narrative dimensions, the present tale left its imprint on world literature as a major historical source of inspiration for the literary genre of the detective story.[56] As a matter of fact, Régis Messac opened his "pioneering study"[57] on the detective novel (1929) with an extensive chapter on the *Peregrinaggio*, its historical roots and its impact on European literature.[58] Even more, the deductive model introduced by the *Peregrinaggio* and popularized by Voltaire's *Zadig* holds an influential position in the development of "the making of retrospective predictions" that is not only a pivotal feature of detective novels à la Sherlock Holmes but also common to a variety of historical disciplines.[59]

Notes

1. Merton, Robert K., and Elinor Barber, *The Travels and Adventures of Serendipity: A Study in Sociological Semantics and the Sociology of Science*, Princeton: Princeton University Press, 2004, pp. 1–21.

2. https://en.oxforddictionaries.com/definition/serendipity (accessed December 20, 2017).

3. Quotations from Lewis, William Stanley, ed., *The Yale Edition of Horace Walpole's Correspondence*, vol. 20: *Horace Walpole's Correspondence with Sir Horace Mann*, New Haven: Yale University Press, 1960, pp. 407–411; apud Merton and Barber, *The Travels*, p. 2.

4. Actually, the book was first published in Italian and then translated into French.

5. Ranke, Kurt, "Brüder: Die scharfsinnigen B.," in *Enzyklopädie des Märchens*, vol. 2 (1979), cols. 874–887.

6. Rael, Juan B., *Cuentos españoles de Colorado y Nuevo Méjico: Spanish Originals with English Summaries*, vol. 2, Stanford: Stanford University Press, 1940, pp. 558–559, 804, no. 473.

7. Ibid.

8. Loorits, Oskar, *Estnische Volkserzählungen*, Berlin: De Gruyter, 1959, pp. 155–156, 221, no. 141.

9. Preindlsberger-Mrazovič, Milena, *Bosnische Volksmärchen*, Innsbruck: Edlinger, 1905, pp. 68–72.

10. Karlinger, Felix, *Inselmärchen des Mittelmeeres*, Düsseldorf: Diederichs, 1960, pp. 280–282, no. 70 (translated from Amades, Joan, *Folklore de Catalunya*, vol. 2, Barcelona: Selecta, 1950, pp. 657–659, no. 367).

11. Stein, Hans Joachim, "Schuß auf den toten König," in *Enzyklopädie des* Märchens, vol. 12 (2007), cols. 255–259.

12. Loukatos, Demetrios, *Neoellenika laographika keimena*, Athens: Zakharopoulos, 1957, pp. 164–167, no. 9; Dawkins, Richard M., *Modern Greek Folktales*, Oxford: Clarendon Press, 1953, pp. 429–434, no. 72. A somewhat more elaborate Greek version was published in Dawkins, *Forty-five Stories from the Dodekanese*, Cambridge: Cambridge University Press, 1950, pp. 318–326, no. 31.

13. Kvideland, Reimund, "Gläubiger: Die drei G.," in *Enzyklopädie des Märchens*, vol. 5 (1987), cols. 1274–1276.

14. Schoenfeld, Elisheva, "Handlung: Die vornehmste H.," ibid., vol. 6 (1990), cols. 459–464.

15. See, e.g., Basset, René, "Une fable de La Fontaine et les contes orientaux," *Mélusine* 2 (1884/85), pp. 508–517; Lévi, Israel, "Contes juifs," *Revue des études juives* 11 (1885), pp. 209–234, at pp. 209–223; Prato, Stanislao, "Zwei Episoden aus zwei tibetanischen Novellen in der orientalischen und occidentalen Überlieferung," *Zeitschrift des Vereins für Volkskunde* 4 (1894), pp. 347–373; Fraenkel, Siegmund, "Die Scharfsinnsproben," *Zeitschrift für vergleichende Litteraturgeschichte* new series 3 (1890), pp. 220–235; Christoforo Armeno, *Die Reise der Söhne Giaffers*, transl. Johann Wetzel, ed. Hermann Fischer and Johannes Bolte, Tübingen: Litterarischer Verein in Stuttgart, 1895, pp. 198–202; Chauvin, *Bibliographie*, vol. 7 (1903), pp. 158–161, no. 438.

16. Schick, Josef, *Corpus Hamleticum: Hamlet in Sage und Dichtung, Kunst und Musik*, 1. Abteilung: *Sagengeschichtliche Untersuchungen*, vol. 5.1–2: *Die Scharfsinnsproben*, Leipzig: Otto Harrassowitz, 1934, 1938; see Merton and Barber, *The Travels*, p. 15, note 35.

17. Most important is Lerner, Amir, *The* Juʿaydiyya *Cycle: Witty Beggar's Stories from the Montague Manuscript—A Late Augmented* Arabian Nights, Dortmund: Verlag für Orientkunde, 2014.

18. For an almost complete survey of sources, see Schick, *Corpus Hamleticum*, vols. 5.1–2.

19. Cristoforo Armeno, *Peregrinaggio di tre giovani figliuoli del re di Serendippo*, ed. Renzo Bragantini, Rome: Salerno, 2000; Bragantini, Renzo, "The Serendipity of the Three Princes of Serendib: Arabic Tales in a Collection of Italian Renaissance Short Stories," in Bauden, Frédéric, Aboubakr Chraïbi, and Antonella Ghersetti, eds., *Le répertoire narratif arabe médiéval: transmission et ouverture*, Geneva: Droz, 2008, pp. 301–308.

20. Saxo Grammaticus, *Gesta Danorum: The History of the Danes*, ed. Karsten Friis-Jensen, transl. Peter Fisher, vol. 1, Oxford: Clarendon Press, 2015, pp. 195–197 (iii.6.17–20).

21. Sercambi, Giovanni, *Il novellieri*, ed. Luciano Rossi, Rome: Salerno, 1972, vol. 1, pp. 13–25, no. 1; Wesselski, *Märchen des Mittelalters*, pp. 100–106, 222–225, no. 37; Schick, *Corpus Hamleticum*, vol. 5.2, pp. 335–345.

22. Jakob, Ulrich, transl., *Die hundert alten Erzählungen*, Leipzig: Deutsche Verlags-Actiengesellschaft, 1905, pp. 4–6, no. 3; Conte, Alberto, ed., *Il Novellino*, Rome: Salerno, 2001, pp. 10–13, no. 3; Schick, *Corpus Hamleticum*, vol. 5.2, pp. 314–326.

23. Voltaire, *Zadig; ou, La Destinée, histoire orientale*, s.l. 1749, pp. 18–28 (ch. 3); Voltaire, *Romans et contes*, vol. 1: *Zadig et autres contes*, ed. Frédéric Deloffre, Paris: Gallimard, 1979, pp. 91–94; Schick, *Corpus Hamleticum*, vol. 5.2, pp. 419–430.

24. Wesselski, Albert, "Quellen und Nachwirkungen der Haft Paikar," *Der Islam* 22 (1935), pp. 165–173; Cammann, Schuyler V.R., "Christopher the Armenian and the Three Princes of Serendip," *Comparative Literature Studies* 4.3 (1967), pp. 229–258; Piemontese, Angelo Michele, *Gli «Otto Paradisi» di Amir Khusrau da Delhi: Una lezione persiana del «Libro di Sindbad» fonte del «Peregrinaggio» di Cristoforo Armeno*, Rome: Accademia nazionale dei Lincei, 1995.

25. Benfey, Theodor, transl., *Die Reise der drei Söhne des Königs von Serendippo*, ed. Richard Fick and Alfons Hilka, Helsinki: Suomalainen Tiedeakatemia, 1932, p. 50, note 1.

26. Marzolph, *Relief after Hardship*, pp. 83–85, no. 22.

27. Jaʿfari Qanavāti, Moḥammad, ed., *Jāmeʿ al-ḥekāyāt: noskhe-ye Ketābkhāne-ye Ganj-Bakhsh-e Pākestān*, Tehran: Qaṭre, 1391/2012, pp. 463–468, no. 22.

28. See Marzolph, *Relief after Hardship*, p. 48; Askari, Nasrin, "A Mirror for Princesses: *Mūnis-nāma*, A Twelfth-Century Collection of Persian Tales Corresponding to the Ottoman Turkish Tales of the *Faraj baʿd al-shidda*," *Narrative Culture* 5.1 (2018), pp. 121–140.

29. Niẓámu'd-dín, *Introduction*, p. 189, no. 1144 (bk. 1, ch. 25); ʿAwfi, Moḥammad, *Pānzdah bāb-e Javāmeʿ al-ḥekāyāt*, ed. Moḥammad Ramażāni, Tehran: Kolāle-ye khāvar, 1335/1956, pp. 369–371, no. 505. This version is already presented in Balʿami's tenth-century Persian translation of al-Ṭabarī's history, to be discussed below; see Schick, *Corpus Hamleticum*, vol. 5.1, pp. 2–17. It is a Turkish translation of ʿAwfi's text, and not a version by the Persian poet Jāmi (d. 1492), that Joseph Freiherr von Hammer-Purgstall translated in his *Rosenöl: oder Sagen und Kunden des Morgenlandes aus arabischen, persischen und türkischen Quellen gesammelt*, vol. 2, Stuttgart and Tübingen: J.G. Cotta, 1813, pp. 277–280, no. 151. The error occurs in Basset, "Une fable," p. 514, note 7.

30. Schick, *Corpus Hamleticum*, vol. 5.1, pp. 302–450; Marzolph, *Arabia ridens*, vol. 2, pp. 103–104, no. 416; Lerner, *The* Juʿaydiyya *Cycle*, pp. 137–143, particularly at p. 139, note 128.

31. Schick, *Corpus Hamleticum*, vol. 5.1, pp. 318–323; Ṭabarī, Abū Jaʿfar Muḥammad ibn Jarīr al-, *Annales auctore Abu Djafar Mohammed ibn Djarir at-Tabari*, vol. 1.3, ed. P. de Jong, Leiden: E.J. Brill, 1882, pp. 1108–1110.

32. Schick, *Corpus Hamleticum*, vol. 5.1, pp. 323–335; Masʿūdī, al-, *Murūj al-dhahab wa-maʿādin al-jawhar*, ed. Barbier de Meynard and Pavet de Courteille, rev. ed. Charles Pellat, vol. 2, Beirut: Université libanaise, 1966, pp. 238–242, nos. 1092–1098.

33. Schick, *Corpus Hamleticum*, vol. 5.1, pp. 335–343; Mufaḍḍal ibn Salama, *al-Fākhir*, ed. Charles A. Storey, Leiden: Brill, 1915, pp. 155–157; ed. ʿAbd al-ʿAlīm al-Ṭaḥāwī and Muḥammad ʿAlī al-Najjār, Cairo: ʿĪsā al-Bābī al-Ḥalabī, 1380/1960, pp. 189–191, no. 310; Weisweiler, Max, *Arabische Märchen*, vol. 2, Düsseldorf: Eugen Diederichs, 1966, pp. 248–250, 304–305, no. 99.

34. Maydānī, Abū 'l-Faḍl Aḥmad ibn Muḥammad ibn Aḥmad ibn Ibrāhīm, *Majmaʿ al-amthāl*, ed. Muḥammad Abū 'l-Faḍl Ibrāhīm, Cairo: ʿĪsā al-Bābī al-Ḥalabī, 1398/1978, vol. 2, pp. 22–24, no. 32.

35. Ibn al-Jawzī, Abū 'l-Faraj ʿAbd al-Raḥmān ibn ʿAlī, *al-Muntaẓam fī tārīkh al-mulūk wa-'l-umam*, ed. Muḥammad ʿAbd al-Qādir ʿAṭā, Muṣṭafā ʿAbd al-Qādir ʿAṭā, Nuʿaym Zarzūr, 2nd ed., vol. 2, Beirut: Dār al-Kutub al-ilmiyya, 1415/1995, pp. 233–235.

36. Schick, *Corpus Hamleticum*, vol. 5.1, pp. 377–382; Ibn al-Jawzī, Abū 'l-Faraj ʿAbd al-Raḥmān ibn ʿAlī, *Akhbār al-Adhkiyāʾ*, ed. Muḥammad Mursī al-Khūlī, Cairo, 1970, pp. 91–93.

37. Schick, *Corpus Hamleticum*, vol. 5.1, pp. 343–344; Nuwayrī, Shihāb al-Dīn Aḥmad ibn ʿAbd al-Wahhāb al-, *Nihāyat al-arab fī funūn al-adab*, vol. 3, Cairo: Dār al-Kutub al-miṣriyya, 1369/1949, pp. 7–9.

38. Schick, *Corpus Hamleticum*, vol. 5.1, pp. 440–441; Damīrī, Kamāl al-Dīn al-, *Ḥayāt al-ḥayawān al-kubrā*, vol. 1, s.l.: al-Maktaba al-islāmiyya, s.a., p. 31; *Al-Damīrī's Ḥayāt al-Ḥayawān (A Zoological Lexicon)*, transl. A.S.G. Jayakar, vol. 1, London: Luzac, 1906, pp. 59–60.

39. Marzolph and Van Leeuwen, *The Arabian Nights Encyclopedia*, vol. 1, pp. 402–403, no. 357; Lerner, *The* Juʿaydiyya *Cycle*.

40. Marzolph and Van Leeuwen, *The Arabian Nights Encyclopedia*, vol. 1, p. 258, no. 289.

41. Ott, Claudia, transl., *Tausendundeine Nacht: Das glückliche Ende*, Munich: C.H. Beck, 2016, pp. 145–152.

42. Ibn Hishām, Abū Muḥammad ʿAbd al-Malik, *Kitāb al-Tījān fī mulūk Ḥimyar*, Hayderabad: Dāʾirat al-maʿārif al-ʿuthmāniyya, 1347/1928, pp. 213–219; on the book and its author, see Retsö, Jan, "Wahb ibn Munabbih, The *Kitāb al-tījān* and the History of Yemen," *Arabia* 3 (2005–2006), pp. 227–236.

43. Lerner, *The* Juʿaydiyya *Cycle*, p. 143.

44. Ibid., pp. 146–147.

45. The summary follows ibid., pp. 147–155.

46. Here and in the following see Lerner, *The* Juʿaydiyya *Cycle*, pp. 143–144.

47. Wünsche, August, *Der Midrasch Echa Rabbati, das ist die haggadische Auslegung der Klagelieder*, Leipzig: Otto Schulze, 1881, pp. 48–49; Schick, *Corpus Hamleticum*, vol. 5.1, pp. 236–302; Lerner, *The* Juʿaydiyya *Cycle*, pp. 104–105, 113–122. On the tale's Jewish (and other) versions, see also Schwarzbaum, Haim, *Studies in Jewish and World Folklore*, Berlin: Walter de Gruyter, 1968, pp. 202–221, no. 251; Hasan-Rokem, Galit, *Web of Life: Folklore and Midrash in Rabbinic Literature*, Stanford: Standford University Press, 2000, pp. 79–82; Ben-Amos, Dan, *Folktales of the Jews*, vol. 1: *Tales from the Sephardic Dispersion*, Philadelphia: The Jewish Publication Society, 2006, p. 316–319.

48. Lerner, *The* Juʿaydiyya *Cycle*, p. 106; Chavannes, Édouard, *Cinq cents contes et apologues extraits du Tripitaka chinois*, vol. 1, Paris: Ernest Leroux, 1910, pp. 379–381, no. 110.

49. Schick, *Corpus Hamleticum*, vol. 5.1, pp. 90–134; Lerner, *The* Juʿaydiyya *Cycle*, p. 106; Somadeva, *The Ocean of Story: Being C.H. Tawney's Translation of Somadeva's Kathā Sarit Sāgara (or Ocean of Streams of Stories)*, ed. N.M. Penzer, (2nd ed. London: privately printed, 1923–1928) reprint Delhi: Motilal Banarsidass, 1968, vol. 6, pp. 286–287.

50. See, recently, Traninger, Anita, "Serendipity und Abduktion: Die Literatur als Medium einer Logik des Neuen (Cristoforo Armeno, Voltaire, Horace Walpole)," in Ammon, Frieder von, Cornelia Rémi, Gideon Stiening, eds., *Literatur und praktische Vernunft*, Berlin: De Gruyter, 2016, pp. 205–230.

51. Dankoff, Robert, and Semih Tezcan, "Seyahet-name'den Bir Atasözü," *Türk Dili Araştırmaları* 8 (1998), pp. 15–28.

52. Marzolph, *Relief after Hardship*, p. 83, no. 21.

53. Eberhard and Boratav, *Typen*, pp. 378–380, no. 348.

54. Enjavi Shirāzi, Abol-Qāsem, *Tamsil va masal*, 2nd ed., Tehran: Amir Kabir, 2537/1978, pp. 219–224 (21 versions); see also Marzolph, *Typologie*, p. 129–130, nos. 655, 655A.

55. El-Shamy, *Types*, pp. 360–363, nos. 0655, 0655A.

56. Shojaei Kawan, Christine, "Kriminalroman," in *Enzyklopädie des Märchens*, vol. 8 (1996), cols. 440–460, at p. 446.

57. Leps, Marie-Christine, *Apprehending the Criminal: The Production of Deviance in Nineteenth-century Discourse*, Durham, NC: Duke University Press, 1992, p. 245, note 4.

58. Messac, Régis, *Le "Detective Novel" et l'influence de la pensée scientifique*, Geneva: Slatkine reprints, 1975, pp. 17–29.

59. Ginzburg, Carlo, and Anna Davin, "Morelli, Freud and Sherlock Holmes: Clues and Scientific Method," *History Workshop* 9 (1980), pp. 5–36, at 22–23.

CHAPTER 14

Years of Experience in a Moment: The Man Is Transformed into a Woman (and Back Again) (ATU 681)

A popular frame tale uniquely germane to Gaelic narrative tradition tells of a man (rarely a woman) looking for night quarters.[1] When the man finally finds a place to stay, he is asked to pay for his lodging by telling a story. Since he claims not to know any story he could tell, he is sent away on an errand during which he happens to experience a series of extraordinary adventures. When he finally manages to return to his lodgings, he is tired and exhausted. But, as his hosts make him understand, at least he now has a story to tell. Classified as Irish tale type 2412B: *The Man Who Had No Story*,[2] the frame tale is also known from oral tradition in Scotland and Newfoundland.[3] Whereas the frame tale is relatively stable, there is a considerable variety concerning the embedded marvelous adventures.[4] A comparatively small number of versions documented from the oral performance of Scottish travellers involves a boat on which the man is magically transformed into a woman. The woman gets married, has children, and lives with her husband for many years until eventually being transformed back into the former man. When the man returns to his house, his wife tells him that he has only been away for a few moments. Although the change of sex involved in this embedded adventure suggests the tale to be similar to tale type ATU 514: *The Shift of Sex*,[5] it is of a different nature. First, tale type ATU 514 involves a change of sex from woman to man, and second, this change is permanent. In contrast, the embedded tale is about the change of sex from man to woman and back again, thus involving a temporary sex change that is often fictional or based on a subjective experience. The additional feature of experiencing a period of many years in the equivalence of a short moment of real time further documents the tale to be one of several tales demonstrating the relativity of time, a feature highlighted in the "miscellaneous" tale type ATU 681: *Relativity of Time*.[6] The version the outstanding Scottish storyteller Betsy (Bessy, Bessie) Whyte, whose grandmother was a native speaker of Gaelic, narrated to John D. Niles in 1986 frames the tale of the change of sex somewhat differently.[7]

> During a social gathering, the host announces a contest of lying. Sandy, "a cattleman on the laird's estate" cannot think of anything to tell and goes off "walking by himself down by the shore of a nearby loch." When, out of curiosity, he steps into a boat drawn up on the shore, the boat takes off, "the two oars moving all by themselves."
>
> As there is nothing he can do, Sandy suddenly notices that instead of his usual clothes he is wearing "a beautiful taffeta dress." And when he pats himself from head to foot, he realizes that he is transformed into a woman. Eventually reaching the shore, the woman Sandy happens to meet a handsome farmer. Before long they are married, and she gives birth to "two of the bonniest bairns that you ever saw."
>
> Taking a walk down at the shore one day, the woman steps into a boat that immediately takes off. Reaching the opposite shore, Sandy finds himself transformed back into the former man.
>
> Walking back up to the house he had previously left, he finds "the same laird as before, entertaining the very same guests." Telling them about his adventure, he wins the contest as having told the biggest lie the congregation ever heard.

An earlier version performed by Whyte for Peter Cooke and Linda Headlee in 1973 adds local color to the tale by characterizing the cattleman as a "stupid lump" who, when asked to tell a story, says, "Ye ken fine I cannae tell stories, I dinnae ken nothing tae tell." (You know well that I cannot tell stories, I don't know nothing to tell).[8] And yet another version performed by the same storyteller for Linda Williamson on April 16, 1987, at Collessie, Fife, invites the listeners into the lively atmosphere of the big *ceilidh* (social gathering) in which the host explains the rules, "that ye tell a story, sing a sang, show yer bum or oot ye gang!" (. . . or out you go!)[9] Additional versions were recorded from the oral performance of Scots traveller storytellers Willie MacPhee (b. 1910), who "having gathered his stories round campfires over more than half a century" told the tale as a first-person narrative,[10] and Belle Stewart (b. 1906) of Blairgowrie in Perthshire.[11] In both of the latter versions, the protagonist has to fulfill a task, either fetch "the bailer for bailin oot the water oot o the boat" in order "tae measure oot the feed for the cattle,"[12] or take "ten minutes tae bail a' the water oot o' the boat and ten minutes tae fill it fu' again."[13] His predicament starts as soon as he gets into the boat.

In Gaelic narrative tradition, the tale finds an early precursor in manuscript versions of the story of the abbot of Druimenaig. Documented in a number of late medieval Irish manuscripts, in terms of linguistic features the tale dates to a period not later than the year 1200.[14] The abbot, a young man, falls asleep on a pleasant hill and when waking up finds himself transformed into a woman.

She marries a "tall soldierly young man" and spends "seven years as his wife and his spouse," bearing him seven children. Having been transformed back into the former man on the same hilltop, the abbot goes back to his wife who claims "that he had not been absent for more than one hour of that day." In this version, however, the experience proves to be true, as the transformed man's husband and their children exist in reality. The man's "case is presented and a judgment made between him" and his former husband. Barbara Hillers opines that the tale was "current in Gaelic folklore in the fifteenth century" and that it "entered the monastic life from oral fairy lore."[15] John D. Niles even links the frame tale of the man who had no story to tell (without the change of sex) to the tale of the late seventh-century English poet Cædmon's poetic inspiration as told by the Venerable Bede (ca. 673–735).[16]

Earlier versions of a tale incorporating a change of sex from male to female and back again, in international research labeled *fons* (The Spring), are encountered in redactions of *The Seven Sages*. This story is a frame tale that originally derives from the Persian *Sendbād-nāme* (The Book of Sendbād [the Sage]) whose earliest preserved text is the one compiled by Moḥammad ʿAli Ẓahiri Samarqandi around the middle of the twelfth century.[17] The Persian text does not comprise the tale in question, which is, however, contained in the collection's Syriac, Greek, Hebrew, Spanish, and Arabic redactions.[18] In the version of *The Seven Sages*, the vizier's cousin falls in love with a certain princess who is to marry the son of the vizier's master. The vizier leads the prince to a spring that transforms the prince into a woman and abandons him there. The prince, however, is aided by the son of the king of demons who brings him to another spring that transforms him back into his former state. The tale ends in a happy marriage. Arabic versions of the tale are embedded in redactions of *The Seven Viziers* contained in both *The Thousand and One Nights*[19] and *The Hundred and One Nights*.[20] Although the latter of these collections might have been compiled as early as the thirteenth century, its earliest preserved manuscript does not contain the tale in question.[21]

The tale's earliest unambiguously dated version is contained in the collection of proverbs and their stories, *al-Fākhir* (The Excellent One), compiled by ninth-century Arabic author al-Mufaḍḍal ibn Salama (d. after 903).[22] It is embedded in the frame tale of Khurāfa, a man whom the Prophet Muḥammad himself (as attested by his wife ʿĀʾisha) quoted as having told him the story how one night he was taken prisoner by three *jinns*. As the *jinns* discussed whether to let him go, kill him, or enslave him, another person appeared and acquired a share of Khurāfa's fate by narrating a marvelous tale.

> The man tells that he once had to flee from his creditors in his hometown. On the way, he drank water from a certain well, although a voice warned him not to do so. After he had quenched his thirst, the voice said that any man drinking water from the well will be transformed into a woman, and vice versa. Having been transformed into a woman, the person went to a certain city, married a man and bore him two children. Later longing to

> return home, the woman came past the same well, drank again, and was transformed back into a man. Back in his hometown, the man married a woman who bore him another two children. He finishes his account by saying that "I have two sons from my loins and two from my womb."[23]

Presented as the experience of several years in a moment, the sex-change motif appears in the tale of "The Warlock and the Young Cook of Baghdad" in the Chavis manuscript of *The Thousand and One Nights*,[24] a tale that is probably modeled on that of Shaykh Shihāb al-Dīn in the Ottoman Turkish *Qırq vezīr* (The Forty Viziers), of unclear date.[25] In both texts, the magician has the king plunge his head into a cauldron filled with water following which the king finds himself in a vast ocean from which he is rescued by a fisherman. But while in the former version he experiences a transformation of sex, in the latter he remains as he is, marrying a woman and in a period of seven years having two sons and a daughter from her. Eventually, he plunges himself into the water again, only to find that he is back in his own palace and just a few moments have passed.

A Persian tale recorded by L.P. Elwell-Sutton from the narration of the Iranian journalist ʿAli Javāher al-Kalām early in the second half of the twentieth century presents the illusionary events as both a punishment and a purifying experience happening to the second of the "righteous caliphs," ʿUmar ibn al-Khaṭṭāb (d. 644) who is said to initially have disbelieved the Prophet Muḥammad's mission.[26] Until the beginning of the twentieth century, this version of the tale was often performed as well as told in the context of Shiʿi rituals denigrating the Sunni Caliph ʿUmar, which have since been banned.[27] In order to "improve children's Shiʿi beliefs in the Qajar period," the tale was popularized with varying characters through its inclusion in Persian poet Shojāʿi Mashhadi's *Meʿrāj-nāme* (Book on the Prophet Muḥammad's Ascension). The book's nineteenth- and early twentieth-century lithographed copies often included illustrations of the tale's key scenes, such as the disbeliever Zaʿfar being approached by a man after having been transformed into a woman.[28] In a similar form, the tale was also documented from other Middle Eastern traditions,[29] such as the tradition of modern Baluchestan[30] and Middle Eastern Jewish tradition.[31]

Tales of sex-change male to female and back predating those from the Muslim world are known from both the ancient Greek and Indian literatures. Ovid's *Metamorphoses* tells of the Theban soothsayer Teiresias who is turned into a woman for killing a female snake, stays female for seven years, and only later is returned to his former state.[32]And in a tale told with some variation in both the Indian *Bāudhyāna Śrāutra Sūtra* and the *Mahābhārata* God Indra transforms a certain king into a woman for some time when he takes a bath in enchanted water.[33] In the latter version, the transformed king prefers to remain a woman, "because, she said, a woman has more pleasure in sexual intercourse than does a man,"[34] an evaluation that is also shared by the Greek Teiresias. In Indian tradition, the temporary change of sex by plunging into a pool also appears in the Urdu romance *The Rose of Bakawali*.[35]

Although stories of sex-changing water can probably not be regarded "as of common occurrence in folk-tales,"[36] in most of the versions discussed above water plays a decisive role, whether the man is transformed when entering a boat in the Scottish versions or whether he drinks water or plunges into the water in most of the Middle Eastern and Indian versions. It is equally striking that the change of male to female is unwanted, temporary and often occurs as a punishment or a test, whereas the change of female to male occurring in tales classified as tale type ATU 514 is longed for, considered a reward and consequently is of a permanent nature.[37] Although the societies in which these tales were told differ in their specifics, they share the feature of male dominance or preference that constitutes a fertile ground for the narrative realization of essentially identical male fantasies.

Notes

1. O'Malley, Elena, "Paying One's Dues: The Storyteller as Mediator in the Irish Fairy Legend 'The Man Who Had No Story'," *Proceedings of the Harvard Celtic Colloquium* 15 (1995), pp. 56–68; Zimmermann, Georges Denis, *The Irish Storyteller*, Dublin: Four Courts Press, 2001, pp. 537–549.

2. Ó Súilleabháin, Seán, and Reidar Th. Christiansen, *The Types of the Irish Folktale*, Helsinki: Suomalainen Tiedeakatemia, 1967, pp. 343–344, no. 2412B.

3. Halpert, Herbert, and J.D.A. Widdowson, *Folktales of Newfoundland: The Resilience of the Oral Tradition*, vol. 2, New York: Garland, 1996, pp. 964–970, no. 143 (narrated by Mike Molloy from Trepassey Bay, Southern Shore, July 9, 1966; collected by Herbert and Nicholas Halpert).

4. Ó Catháin, Séamas, and Bo Almqvist, "An Fear Nach Rabh Scéal ar Bith Aige/ The Man Who Had No Story," *Béaloideas* 37/38 (1969/1970), pp. 51–64; O'Malley, "Paying One's Dues," p. 58.

5. Ready, Psyche Z., *"She Was Really the Man She Pretended to Be": Change of Sex in Folk Narratives*, M.A. Thesis Fairfax: George Mason University, 2016.

6. Ting, Nai-tung, "Years of Experience in a Moment: A Study of a Tale Type in Asian and European Literature," *Fabula* 22 (1981), pp. 183–213, particularly at pp. 198–199; Naithani, Sadhana, "Relativität der Zeit," in *Enzyklopädie des Märchens*, vol. 11 (2004), cols. 532–537.

7. Niles, John D., "True Stories and Other Lies," in *Myth in Early Northwest Europe*, ed. Stephen O. Glosecki, Tempe, Arizona: Arizona Center for Medieval and Renaissance Studies, 2007, pp. 1–30, at pp. 22–26; also published in Niles, *Old English Heroic Poems and the Social Life of Texts*, Turnhout: Brepols, 2006, pp. 279–307. The present version is retold by Niles in his own words.

8. Bruford, Alan, "Some Aspects of the Otherworld," in *Folklore in the Twentieth Century*, ed. Venetia Newall, Woodbridge: Brewer, 1986, pp. 147–151, at 149–150.

9. Philip, Neil, *The Penguin Book of Scottish Folktales*, London: Penguin, 1995, pp. 55–59.

10. Douglas, Sheila, *The King o the Black Art and Other Folk Tales*, Aberdeen: Aberdeen University Press, 1987, pp. 67–69, quote p. 3; see also Douglas, "Willie MacPhee," in Fischer, Frances S., and Sigrid Rieuwerts, eds., *Emily Lyle: The Persistent Scholar*, Trier: Wissenschaftlicher Verlag Trier, 2007, pp. 67–73.

11. MacColl, Ewan, and Peggy Seeger, *Till Doomsday in the Afternoon: The Folklore of a Family of Scots Travellers, the Stewarts of Blairgowrie*, Manchester: Manchester University Press, 1986, pp. 80–83.

12. Douglas, *The King o the Black Art*, p. 67.

13. MacColl and Seeger, *Till Doomsday in the Afternoon*, p. 81.

14. Gaidoz, Henri, "Du changement de sexe dans les contes celtiques," *Revue de l'histoire des religions* 57 (1908), pp. 317–332, at pp. 320–323; original text publ. by Kuno Meyer in Bergin, Osborn Joseph, et al., *Anecdota from Irish Manuscripts*, vol. 1, Halle (Saale): Max Niemeyer, and Dublin: Hodges, Figgis & Co., 1907, pp. 76–79; see also http://www.ucc.ie/celt/online/G201029/ (accessed February 8, 2017); Hillers, Barbara, "The Abbot of Druimenaig: Genderbending in Gaelic Tradition," *Proceedings of the Harvard Celtic Colloquium* 15 (1995), pp. 175–197, at pp. 176–178; Hillers, "The Man Who Became a Woman (ATU 705B§): The Change of Sex Motif in Gaelic Tradition," unpublished working paper, 2016; Ó Síocháin, Tadhg, *The Case of The Abbot of Drimnagh: A Medieval Irish Story of Sex-Change*, Cork: University College Cork, 2017.

15. Hillers, "The Abbot of Druimenaig," pp. 187, 190.

16. Niles, John D., "Bede's Cædmon, 'The Man Who Had No Story' (Irish Tale-Type 2412B)," *Folklore* 117 (2006), pp. 141–155.

17. Ẓahiri Samarqandi, Moḥammad ʿAli, *Sendbād-nāma*, ed. Moḥammad Bāqer Kamāl al-Dini, Tehran 1381/2002.

18. Chauvin, *Bibliographie*, vol. 8 (1904), p. 43, no. 11; see Clouston, William Alexander, *The Book of Sindibād; or The Story of the King, His Son, His Damsel, and the Seven Vazīrs: From the Persian and Arabic*, Glasgow: privately printed, 1884, pp. 80, 156–162, 299–302; Lacarra, María Jesús, "Entre el Libro de los engaños y los Siete visire: las mil y una caras del Sendebar árabe," in *Les Mille et une nuits et le récit oriental en Espagne et en Occident*, ed. Aboubakr Chraïbi and Carmen Ramirez, Paris: L'Harmattan, 2009, pp. 51–73.

19. Marzolph and Van Leeuwen, *The Arabian Nights Encyclopedia*, vol. 1, pp. 175–176, no. 191.

20. *Les Cents et une nuits*, transl. Maurice Gaudefroy-Demombynes, Paris: Sindbad, 1982, pp. 149–150, 291–292, note 13; Fudge, Bruce, ed. and transl., *A Hundred and One Nights*, New York: New York University Press, 2016, pp. 245–246.

21. *101 Nacht*, transl. Claudia Ott, Zurich: Manesse, 2012.

22. Mufaḍḍal ibn Salama, *al-Fākhir*, ed. Charles A. Storey, Leiden: Brill, 1915, pp. 138–140; ed. ʿAbd al-ʿAlīm al-Ṭaḥāwī and Muḥammad ʿAlī al-Najjār, Cairo: ʿĪsā al-Bābī al-Ḥalabī, 1380/1960, pp. 169–171, in no. 280; see MacDonald, Duncan B., "The Earlier History of the Arabian Nights," *Journal of the Royal Asiatic Society* (1924), pp. 353–397, particularly at pp. 372–379; Drory, Rina, "Three Attempts to Legitimize Fiction in Classical Arabic Literature," *Jerusalem Studies in Arabic and Islam* 18 (1994), pp. 146–164, at p. 152; Sato, Michio, "Geschlechtswechsel," in *Enzyklopädie des Märchens*, vol. 5 (1987), cols. 1138–1142, at col. 1140.

23. Quotes from MacDonald, "The Earlier History," p. 373. This tale is classified as tale type 705B§ by El-Shamy, *Types*, pp. 378–379.

24. Marzolph and Van Leeuwen, *The Arabian Nights Encyclopedia*, vol. 1, pp. 443–444, no. 412.

25. Chauvin, *Bibliographie*, vol. 7 (1903), pp. 106–107, no. 94 of *Syntipas*; Sheykh-Zāda, *The History of the Forty Vezirs*, transl. E.J.W. Gibb, London: George Redway, 1886, pp. 16–27, at pp. 20–22.

26. *Die Erzählungen der Mašdi Galin Ḫānom*, ed. Ulrich Marzolph and Azar Amirhosseini-Nithammer, Wiesbaden: Reichert, 1994, vol. 1, pp. 491–497, no. 118; vol. 2, pp. 43–44.

27. Rossi, Ettore, and Alessio Bombaci, *Elenco di drammi religiosi persiani (fondo mss. Vaticani Cerulli)*, Città del Vaticano: Biblioteca Apostolica Vaticana, 1961, p. 349, no. III 4 (nos. 245, 636); Massé, Henri, *Croyances et coutumes persanes, suivies de contes et chansons populaires*, Paris: G. P Maisonneuve, 1938, vol. 1, pp. 168–169.

28. Boozari, Ali, "Persian Illustrated Lithographed Books on the *Miʿrāj*: Improving Children's Shiʿī Beliefs in the Qajar Period," in *The Prophet's Ascension: Cross-Cultural Encounters with the Islamic Miʿrāj Tales*, ed. Christiane Gruber and Frederick Colby, Bloomington: Indiana University Press, 2010, pp. 252–268, at p. 256; Buẕari, ʿAli, *Qażā-ye bi zavāl: negāhi taṭbiqi be taṣāvir-e chāp-e sangi-ye meʿrāj-e payāmbar (ṣ)*, Tehran: Dastān, 1389/2010, pp. 116–123.

29. Mills, Margaret, "Sex Role Reversals, Sex Changes, and Transvestite Disguise in the Oral Tradition of a Conservative Muslim Community in Afghanistan," in *Women's Folklore, Women's Culture*, ed. Rosan A. Jordan and Susan J. Kalčik, Philadelphia: University of Pennsylvania Press, 1985, pp. 187–213; Mills, "It's about Time—Or Is It?: Four Stories of/in Transformation," in *Fields of Folklore: Essays in Honor of Kenneth S. Goldstein*, ed. Roger D. Abrahams, Bloomington: Indiana University Press, 1995, pp. 184–197.

30. Dames, Mansel Longworth, *Popular Poetry of the Baloches*, vol. 1, London: Nutt, 1907, pp. 159–160.

31. Jason, Heda, "Types of Jewish-Oriental Oral Tales," *Fabula* 7 (1964–1965), pp. 115–224, at p. 158, no. 681 *A; Jason, *Types of Oral Tales in Israel*, Jerusalem: Israel Ethnographic Society, 1975, p. 27–28, no. 681 *A.

32. Ovid, *Metamorphoses*, transl. Alan D. Melville, Oxford: Oxford University Press, 1987, pp. 60–61; quoted from Ready, "*She Was Really the Man She Pretended to Be*," p. 68.

33. Brown, W. Norman, "Change of Sex as a Hindu Story Motif," *Journal of the American Oriental Society* 47 (1927), pp. 3–24; see also the extended discussion in Somadeva, *The Ocean of Story: Being C.H. Tawney's Translation of Somadeva's Kathā Sarit Sāgara*, ed. N.M. Penzer, reprint Delhi: Motilal Banarsidass, 1968, vol. 7, pp. 222–233.

34. Brown, "Change of Sex," p. 7.

35. Clouston, William Alexander, *A Group of Eastern Romances and Stories from the Persian, Tamil, and Urdu*, Glasgow: privately printed, 1889, pp. 299–302; Brown, "Change of Sex," pp. 7–8.

36. Somadeva, *The Ocean of Story*, ed. Penzer, vol. 7, p. 225.

37. Sato, "Geschlechtswechsel," col. 1138.

CHAPTER 15

The Chaste Woman Coveted by Her Brother-in-Law (ATU 712)

The tale of the chaste woman who is coveted and, when she refuses to comply, slandered by her brother-in-law and subsequently by several other men, is best known in European tradition by the name of Crescentia. Crescentia is the female protagonist in the tale's earliest attested European version, the German *Kaiserchronik* (The Emperor's Chronicle) compiled around the middle of the twelfth century.[1] In comparative folk narrative research, the tale is classified as tale type ATU 712: *Crescentia.* Attested in numerous literary versions in various European languages since the twelfth century, the tale was treated extensively in scholarly literature.[2] A distinct point of contention argued pro and con by various European scholars was the question whether the tale is of European or of "Oriental" origin. Recently, the chronological priority of the Middle Eastern versions, the oldest of which date to the tenth century, has been established.[3] The tale's strong moral tone often resulted in a dominant Christian texture in its European versions. Probably due to this characteristic, the tale has rarely been recorded from oral tradition. Moreover, many of the texts documented from oral tradition classified as belonging to tale type ATU 712 actually constitute versions of other, vaguely similar tales about innocently persecuted heroines, such as Constanze,[4] Genoveva[5] or Hildegardis,[6] or contain elements germane to those tales. Although there is a certain overlap in all tales of innocently persecuted heroines, every one of them has a specific structure filled with distinctive elements. The tale of Crescentia starts with an initial seduction attempt by a close relative or friend, continues with the chaste woman being slandered and severely injured, and in its most complete form includes a total of three additional seduction attempts often followed by slander—by a servant of the man who rescues her, by a young man whom she saves from the gallows by paying his debts, and by the captain of a ship. In the end, the heroine becomes a model of devotion and purity who pardons the men who did her wrong and heals their afflictions.

A rare recording from oral tradition is the tale *La Moglie fidele* (The Faithful Wife) that German scholar Carl Weber took down in 1884 from the performance of Angiola, the wife of Pietro, who served as a field guard for the Marchesa Altoviti Avila Clarenza, in Casole near Vicchio di Mugello in the vicinity of Florence in Tuscany, Italy.[7] The editor mentions explicitly that the narrator did not know how to read or write, implying that she was not, or at least not directly, influenced by literary tradition.[8]

> A young and beautiful woman does not want to marry. When one day a stranger shows up, they fall in love and marry. As the man returns to his country, he takes his wife along.
>
> The man's brother falls in love with the woman. Since she does not give in to his advances, he accuses her of adultery and has her buried alive. When her husband returns, he becomes very sad, since he loved his wife dearly.
>
> The woman is liberated from the grave by the chief of a gang of robbers who takes her back to his home. The robber's wife wonders why he brought the woman to their house, but as the woman begs them to be allowed to stay (even promising to pay for everything), she consents. The robber has two children and a black servant. The servant falls in love with the woman. Since she does not give in to the servant's advances, he cuts off the head of one of the children and places it in front of her chamber. Although the robber does not believe that the woman he rescued killed the child, he sends her away.
>
> The woman comes to a country of beautiful and rich palaces where she convinces an old woman to let her stay with her. One day she sees a young man being sentenced to death and liberates him by paying his debts. While she takes a walk on the seashore, the young man thanks her and offers his help, but she tells him that she does not need anything. The young man, who has fallen in love with her, gets angry and sells her to the captain of a ship. The captain brings her to the Green Island (Isola Verde), where she works as an adviser (*maestra*).
>
> The fame of her wisdom spreads, and the queen sends for her, inviting her to stay and eventually become her successor. One day, one of the queen's servants asks her why she is always so sad, and she tells her story. The servant gives her an herb that cures all ailments, and the woman becomes successor to the queen.
>
> In the meantime, the woman's brother-in-law lost his eyesight, the black man is crippled, and the young man turned lame. As they heard about the woman's healing powers, they visit her. She recognizes them, but they do not recognize her. Although the men are reluctant at first, she makes them confess their misdemeanor, and she heals them. Her husband realizes that she had been slandered. They are reunited, and he takes her back to his country.

The collector clearly identified the tale as a version of the legend of Crescentia. The considerable amount of overlap with the tale's "Oriental" version as published in Pétis de la Croix's *Les Mille et un jours*[9] made him question whether the narrator was really telling "an old traditional tale." Instead, he wondered whether she could have heard the "Oriental" tale from somebody who recounted it from memory, either directly, or by way of an additional intermediary. In his detailed discussion of the tale's various elements, the collector conceded, however, that the tale contains various elements, such as the healing herb, that are not encountered in the *Mille et un jours* but are found in other European literary versions.[10]

Another version of the tale from oral tradition was recorded by Richard M. Dawkins in Thrace.[11]

> Myrtle is the beautiful and good wife of a great merchant. When her husband is travelling, the friend to whom he entrusted his wife makes advances to her. As she does not comply, he slanders her in a letter to her husband, and the husband instructs him to bury her alive.
>
> Shepherds passing the burial place in the mountains hear her cries and dig her up. Seeing a young man about to be hanged for not paying his debts, Myrtle pays the debts and delivers the man. As Myrtle is about to embark on a ship, the young man sells her to the captain, claiming her to be his slave. When the captain makes advances to the woman, she prays to God, and a heavy storm arises. The ship is wrecked, and Myrtle is cast up on an island. She takes a job as a nurse in a rich man's house. The man's black servant falls in love with her, but as she "would not have him," he strangles the child and blames her. Although the master does not believe the servant's slander, he drives the woman out. Myrtle meets a nun and reveals to her all her sufferings, and the nun advises her to fast and pray.
>
> One after the other, the men who had sinned against the woman learn about her healing powers and arrive at her place without, however, recognizing her. Her husband lost his eyesight, the hands of her husband's friend are paralysed, the man who sold her to the captain is "in a sad state," and the black man walks on crutches. She tells every one of them to fast and pray so that God may pardon them. Finally, she reveals her identity to her husband, and they are reunited.

Yet another Greek version from Epeiros was published by Johann Georg von Hahn.[12] Here, the tale introduces two brothers, the younger of whom is a spendthrift. As his attempt to slander his brother's wife is not successful, he secretly introduces a drunkard into her house so that the woman is to be executed for adultery. Instead of killing her, the compassionate executioners bury her body in the ground with only her head showing. She is saved by the chief of the robbers and suffers the usual series of calamities, first being driven away for allegedly killing the robber's child, then being sold by the young man whose debts she paid, and finally being assaulted by the captain. In a foreign country, she becomes queen and builds a large hospital where she cures the sick with the help of magic medicines prepared by an old woman. When the culprits show up one after the other, she heals them and forgives them.

The first two of the above-quoted versions from oral tradition are somewhat truncated or confused in relation to the tale's standard structure. In the Italian version, the captain's assault is left out, and in the Greek version from Thrace, the sequence of the episodes is reversed. Even so, the texts demonstrate sufficient overlap to argue that they belong to the same tale type.

Several of the tale's Oriental versions were discussed in previous research. These are the versions contained in Nakhshabī's early fourteenth-century Persian *Ṭuṭi-nāme* (Book of the Parrot); in the Arabic *Thousand and One Nights*; and in Pétis de la Croix's *Les Mille et un jours*, the latter adapted from the fifteenth- or late fourteenth-century Ottoman Turkish *Ferec ba'd eş-şidde* (Relief after Hardship) and published in 1710–12. Meanwhile, Ḥeshmat Mo'ayyad identified the tale's oldest version in an Arabic work titled *al-Kāfī (fī 'ilm al-dīn)* (roughly: A Comprehensive Commentary on the Science of Religion).[13] The work is a guide to Shi'i doctrine in theology and Islamic law compiled by Abū Ja'far Muḥammad ibn Ya'qūb al-Kulaynī (or al-Kulīnī), a Shi'i traditionist who died around 940. It is today regarded as the most authoritative of the four canonical collections on which Shi'i law is based. The tale is included in a passage on narratives before the conclusion of the book treating married life (*nikāḥ*), in a chapter whose title may be rendered as "Only Those Who Respect Other People's Possessions Respect Their Own." After presenting a number of exemplary anecdotes, the author cites the tale in question as follows:[14]

> While his brother has been sent away to take care of some matters by the king, the judge (*qāḍī*) makes advances to his brother's chaste wife. As the woman does not give in, he slanders her, and she is sentenced to be stoned to death for alleged adultery.
>
> Although seriously wounded, the woman manages to free herself and reaches the abode of an ascetic who takes her in. The ascetic's male housekeeper makes advances to her. As she does not give in, the housekeeper kills the ascetic's only son and blames her. The ascetic believes in her innocence, but even so sends her away, giving her some money.
>
> The woman uses the money to free a man who had been crucified for not paying his debts. The man promises to stay with her wherever she would go. Coming to the seashore, the man pretends that she is his slave and sells her to the merchants aboard a ship.
>
> The merchants put her on one of their ships together with all of their merchandise while they stay on the second ship. In a storm, the merchants' ship is wrecked. The woman reaches the shore safely and decides to stay and spend her days in devotion.
>
> In the meantime, the king of her country learns about the woman's saintly status and is advised to travel to her together with his subjects.

There, they should confess and repent their sins, and ask her forgiveness. One after the other, the king, her husband, the judge, the ascetic, the housekeeper, and the man who had been crucified present themselves to her repenting their sins, and she forgives them. As she has no more desire for men, she prefers to spend her life in devotion and sends her husband away together with the ship carrying the merchants' goods.

Not discussed in previous research, another text from Arabic literature documents that the tale existed in different versions already in the tenth century, suggesting that it might be considerably older. The second Arabic tenth-century version is given in Muʿāfà ibn Zakariyya al-Nahrawānī's (d. 999) *adab* work *al-Jalīs al-ṣāliḥ al-kāfī wa-'l-anīs al-nāsiḥ al-shāfī* (The Righteous and Able Companion and the Sincere and Beneficial Confidant).[15]

When a man goes on a voyage and entrusts his wife to his brother, the brother makes advances to the woman. As she does not give in, he accuses her of having made advances to him. Without listening to what the woman has to say, the returning husband stabs her and leaves her out in the open, believing her to be dead.

Although seriously wounded, the woman manages to reach the abode of an ascetic who takes her in and cures her. She stays with the ascetic, nursing his little boy. The ascetic's black slave makes advances to her, and when she does not give in, he kills the ascetic's only son and blames her. Although the ascetic believes in the woman's innocence, he sends her away, giving her some money.

The woman uses the money to free a man who is about to be crucified. The man promises to stay with her wherever she will go. Coming to the seashore, the man pretends that she is his slave and sells her to one of the merchants aboard a ship.

When the merchant makes advances to her, the woman assures him that she is not a slave. Due to her prayer, the ship is wrecked, and she alone is saved. The king of the country she reaches asks her to marry him. As she tells him that she is not able to comply, he installs her in a building and visits her whenever he needs her advice. Before his death, the king appoints her as his successor.

Once she rules the country, one after the other her husband, the judge, the man who was about to be crucified, and the ascetic and his black slave arrive. The woman reveals her true identity to her husband and has her brother-in-law, the black slave, and the man who was about to be crucified executed. Then she rules for as long as God wills.

Although the content of both of the early versions differs in several minor deails, the context in which they are presented is remarkably consistent. Kulaynī has the events take place in the country of a king of the Israelites, and al-Nahrawānī likewise presents the woman's husband as an Israelite. Moreover, both versions introduce the tale with a chain of transmitters (*isnād*), a feature that is traditionally used in Arabic literature to authenticate historical or pseudo-historical narratives. The final instance of this chain of transmitters is a certain Abū ʿAbdallāh. This is the name by which Jaʿfar al-Ṣādiq is known, the sixth *imām* venerated by the twelver-Shiʿi branch of the Shiʿi creed who died in 765.[16] Although the chain of transmitters may or may not be invented in order to authenticate the tale, the tale's origin from Jewish tradition appears likely. As a matter of fact, a Hebrew work apparently compiled in tenth-century Iran, although now only preserved in a thirteenth-century manuscript, contains the tale in question.[17] The most remarkable difference between the Hebrew version and the contemporary Arabic versions is the fact that the latter do not mention any afflictions the wrongdoers suffer, whereas in the former all of them have been afflicted by supernaturally caused physical ailments, often paralysis, that both result from and bespeak their transgression against the innocent and unprotected woman.

In texts from Muslim literatures, the physical afflictions appear to be first mentioned in two more or less contemporary Persian versions dating from the beginning of the thirteenth century. A prose version of the tale is given in Sadid al-Din Moḥammad ʿAwfi's (d. ca. 1232) *Javāmeʿ al-ḥekāyāt* (Compilations of Stories),[18] and a version in verse is contained in Farid al-Din ʿAṭṭār's (d. 1221) mystical poem *Elāhi-nāme* (Book of God).[19] At least a dozen additional versions of the tale are documented from the premodern Persian, Arabic, and Ottoman Turkish literatures.[20] These include, above all, the two early fourteenth-century Persian adaptations of the Indian *Śukasaptati* (Seventy [Tales of a] Parrot);[21] al-Nuwayrī al-Iskandarānī's mid-fourteenth-century *Kitāb al-Ilmām* (The Survey), a local history of the Egyptian Alexandria;[22] the fifteenth- or late fourteenth-century Ottoman Turkish *Ferec baʿd eş-şidde* (Relief after Hardship);[23] the corresponding sixteenth- or early seventeenth-century London manuscript of *Jāmeʿ al-ḥekāyāt* (Collection of Stories);[24] the seventeenth-century Persian collection of proverbs and stories connected to them, *Jāmeʿ al-tamsil* (Collection of Proverbs), by Moḥammad-ʿAli Ḥablerudi;[25] and various eighteenth- and nineteenth-century compilations of *The Thousand and One Nights*.[26] In addition, there are numerous versions in medieval and early modern Jewish literature from the thirteenth century onward.[27] Although the tale is strangely absent from modern Persian and Turkish traditions, several versions from both Jewish[28] and Arabic[29] traditions were documented.

The tale's unbroken tradition over a period of more than a thousand years in a variety of literatures from the Muslim, Jewish, and Christian world proves its ability to adapt to different regional as well as religious contexts in meaningful ways. At the same time, its numerous versions demonstrate the impact of the all-embracing value of piety and devotion in the Abrahamic religions that elevated a mundane tale of envy and transgression to a powerful narrative whose structure has remained surprisingly stable over the long period of its existence.

Notes

1. *Deutsche Chroniken und andere Geschichtsbücher des Mittelalters*, vol. 1: *Kaiserchronik eines deutschen Geistlichen*, ed. Edward Schröder, Hannover: Hahnsche Buchhandlung, 1895, at pp. 289–314, verse 11,352–12,8012. For a short, but outdated, survey of the tale's tradition see Uther, Hans-Jörg, "Crescentia," in *Enzyklopädie des Märchens*, vol. 3 (1981), cols. 167–171.

2. See, e.g., Mussafia, Adolfo, *Über eine metrische Darstellung der Crescentiasage*, Vienna: K.K. Hof- und Staatsdruckerei, 1866; Wallensköld, Axel, *Le conte de la femme chaste convoitée par son beau-frère*, Helsingfors: Societatis Scientiarum Fennicae, 1907; Wesselski, *Mönchslatein*, pp. 136–142, 239, no. 116; Stefanovic, Svetislav, "Die Crescentia-Florence-Sage: Eine kritische Studie über ihren Ursprung und ihre Entwicklung," *Romanische Forschungen* 29 (1911), pp. 461–556; Wallensköld, Axel, "L'origine et l'evolution du conte de la femme chaste convoitée par son beau-frère," *Neuphilologische Mitteilungen* (1912), pp. 67–78; Baasch, Karen, *Die Crescentialegende in der deutschen Literatur des Mittelalters*, Stuttgart: Metzler, 1968; Stiller, Frauke, *"Die unschuldig verfolgte und später rehabilitierte Ehefrau": Untersuchung zur Frau im 15. Jahrhundert am Beispiel der Crescentia- und Sibillen-Erzählungen*, Ph.D. Diss. Humboldt-University Berlin 2001.

3. Marzolph, Ulrich, "Crescentia's Oriental Relatives: The 'Tale of the Pious Man and His Chaste Wife' in the *Arabian Nights* and the Sources of *Crescentia* in Near Eastern Narrative Tradition," *Marvels & Tales* 22.2 (2008), pp. 240–258, 299–311; abridged French version see Marzolph, "Le Conte de l'homme pieux et de son épouse chaste dans les *Mille et une nuits* et les sources de *Crescentia* dans les traditions narratives orientales," in *Medioevo romanzo e orientale. Sulle orme di Shahrazàd: le "Mille e una notte" fra Oriente e Occidente*, VI Colloquio Internazionale, Ragusa, 12–14 ottobre 2006, ed. Mirella Cassarino, Rom: Rubbettino, 2009, 183–191; see also Lewis, Frank, "One Chaste Muslim Maiden and a Persian in a Pear Tree: Analogues of Boccaccio and Chaucer in Four Earlier Arabic and Persian Tales," in *Metaphor and Imagery in Persian Poetry*, ed. Ali Asghar Seyed-Gohrab, Leiden: Brill, 2012, pp. 173–203; Santomá Juncadella, Luís, "El milagro de la mujer lapidada: Crítica literaria de la versión en occitano cispirenaico aragonés," *Revista de Filología Románica* 27 (2010), pp. 285–313.

4. Rölleke, Heinz, "Constanze," in *Enzyklopädie des Märchens*, vol. 3 (1981), cols. 130–131; in fact, Lewis, "One Chaste Muslim Maiden," misreads the tale of the chaste maiden as a version of the tale of Constanze.

5. Vanja, Konrad, "Genoveva," in *Enzyklopädie des Märchens*, vol. 5 (1987), cols. 1003–1009.

6. Maaz, Wolfgang, "Hildegardis," ibid., vol. 6 (1990), cols. 1017–1021.

7. Weber, Carl, "Italienische Märchen in Toscana aus Volksmund gesammelt," in *Forschungen zur romanischen Philologie: Festgabe für Hermann Suchier zum 15. März 1900*, Halle: Max Niemeyer, 1900, pp. 309–348, at pp. 328–336.

8. Ibid., p. 309.

9. Pétis de la Croix, François, *Les Mille et un jours: contes persans*, ed. Paul Sebag, Paris: Christian Bourgois, 1980, pp. 450–467, 507–508 (Histoire de Repsima).

10. Ibid., pp. 330–331.

11. Dawkins, Richard M., *Modern Greek Folktales*, Oxford: Clarendon, 1953, pp. 369–372, no. 58.

12. Hahn, Johann Georg von, *Griechische und albanesische Märchen*, part 1, Leipzig: Engelmann, 1918, pp. 140–148, no. 16.

13. Mo'ayyad, Ḥeshmat, "Sar-gozasht-e 'zan-e pārsā'-ye 'Aṭṭār," *Irān-shenāsi* 9.3 (1376/1997), pp. 427–442. The following passage is adapted from Marzolph, "Crescentia's Oriental Relatives," pp. 250–252.

14. Full translations are given in Marzolph, "Crescentia's Oriental Relatives," pp. 300–305, and Lewis, "One Chaste Muslim Maiden," pp. 196–199.

15. Nahrawānī al-Jarīrī, Mu'āfà ibn Zakariyya al-, *al-Jalīs al-ṣāliḥ al-kāfī wa-'l-anīs al-nāsiḥ al-shāfī*, ed. Muḥammad Mursī al-Khūlī, vol. 1, Beyrouth: 'Ālam al-kutub, 1981, pp. 298–301.

16. Not Ḥoseyn, the Prophet Muḥammad's grandson and third *imām* of the Shi'a, as Lewis, "One Chaste Muslim Maiden," p. 196, has it; see Mo'ayyad, "Sar-gozasht," p. 434.

17. Marzolph, "Crescentia's Oriental Relatives," p. 255, note 5.

18. Niẓámu'd-dín, *Introduction*, p. 231, no. 1766 (bk. 3, ch. 23). The tale's summary follows 'Awfi, Sadid al-Din Moḥammad al-, *Matn-e enteqādi-ye Javāme' al-ḥekāyāt wa-lavāme' al-revāyāt*, book 3, part 2, ed. Amir Bānu Moṣaffā and Maẓāher Moṣaffā, Tehran: Bonyād-e Farhang-e Irān, 1353/1974, pp. 674–679; see the translation in Marzolph, "Crescentia's Oriental Relatives," pp. 303–305.

19. Prose summary in Ritter, Hellmut, *The Ocean of the Soul: Man, the World and God in the Stories of Farīd al-Dīn 'Aṭṭār*, transl. John O'Kane, Leiden: Brill, 2003, pp. 366–369; translation in Lewis, Frank, "The Tale of the Righteous Woman (Whose Husband Had Gone on a Journey)," in *Converging Zones: Persian Literary Tradition and the Writing of History, Studies in Honor of Amin Banani*, ed. Wali Ahmadi, Costa Mesa, CA: Mazda, 2012, pp. 200–219.

20. For detailed references not repeated here see Marzolph, "Crescentia's Oriental Relatives."

21. Hatami, *Untersuchungen*, pp. 108–110, no. 52.

22. Nuwayrī al-Iskandarānī al-, *Kitāb al-Ilmām bi-'l-i'lām fīmā jarat bihi al-aḥkām wa-'l-umūr al-maqḍiyya fī waq'at al-Iskandariyya*, vol. 4, ed. 'Azīz Sūriyāl 'Aṭiyya, Haydarabad: Dār al-ma'ārif al-'uthmāniyya, 1390/1970, pp. 278–281; for the work see Brockelmann, Carl, *Geschichte der arabischen Litteratur*, suppl. Vol. 2, Leiden: Brill, 1938, p. 34, no. 2.

23. Rossi, Ettore, "La fonte turca della novella poetica albanese 'Erveheja' di Muhamet Çami (sec. XVIII–XIX) e il tema di 'Florence de Rome' e di 'Crescentia'," *Oriente moderno* 28 (1949), pp. 143–153; Marzolph, *Relief after Hardship*, pp. 95–96, no. 30.

24. French translation in Wallensköld, *Le conte de la femme chaste*, pp. 99–111.

25. Ḥablerudi, Muḥammad 'Ali, *Jāme' al-tamsil*, ed. Ḥasan Ẕol-Faqāri, Tehran: Mo'in 1390/2011, pp. 465–484.

26. See Marzolph and Van Leeuwen, *The Arabian Nights Encyclopedia*, vol. 2, p. 797, no. 712.

27. Bin Gorion, Micha Joseph, *Mimekor Yisrael: Classical Jewish Folktales, Abridged and Annotated*, ed. Emanuel Bin Gorion, prepared by Dan Ben-Amos, Bloomington: Indiana University Press, 1990, pp. 386–388, no. 202.

28. Jason, Heda, "Types of Jewish Oriental Oral Tales," *Fabula* 7 (1964–1965), pp. 115–224, at p. 160, no. 712*A; Jason, *Types of Oral Tales in Israel*, Jerusalem: Israel Ethnographic Society, 1975, p. 29, no. 712.

29. El-Shamy, *Types*, pp. 393–395, no. 0712.

CHAPTER 16

The Three Old Men (ATU 726)

The present tale is essentially a tale about phenomenal longevity. Classified as tale type ATU 726: *The Three Old Men*, the tale occurs in different forms.[1] In the form prevalent in Western tradition, the three old men are usually a man of highly advanced age, his father, and his grandfather. The most often documented group of versions introduces a respected person such as the local priest, a count, or the king traveling around the country. Eventually, that person happens to come across an old man sitting in front of his house weeping bitterly. When asked why he cries, the old man responds, "Because my father has beaten me." Surprised that the old man's father should still be alive and so vigorous that he would give his son a beating, the visitor enters the house and finds an even older man whose rage is still showing. Asking him why he has beaten his son, the visitor is told that the son has been unkind to his grandfather. Sure enough, the old man's grandfather is still alive and well.

Texts following this structure are attested above all from nineteenth- and twentieth-century tradition in Germany,[2] where the tale was popularized by its inclusion in the *Deutsche Sagen* (German Legends) published by the brothers Grimm.[3] The Grimms present a text originally published in 1809 as told by a Mr. Schmidt from Lübeck. It attributes the experience to a certain priest Oest whose parish used to be on the small peninsula of Angeln in the Northern German province of Schleswig-Holstein around the middle of the eighteenth century. German versions of the tale often boost the visitor's astonishment, as even the priest who baptized the grandfather is still alive.[4] Texts with this additional point were collected from oral tradition in Mecklenburg-Vorpommern as told in April 1963 by farmer Pingel in Zieslübbe[5] and in April 1962 by August Rust who claimed to have heard the tale in the 1920s as narrated by August Schröder, station master in Blankensee.[6] Salesman Klaas Gerdes from Jever in Oldenburg, who told the tale in 1974, is said to have entertained his potential customers with this kind of jocular tales.[7] In his version, the first old man is above age 70, his father is 92, and his grandfather 115 years of age. The unnamed narrator of a Ukrainian version recorded in the district of Galicia has the father inform the astonished king that he managed to reach such an old age in good health by avoiding alcoholic beverages and pickles, and having sex with his wife only twice a year.[8] Standard versions of the tale were also collected in Spain from Castilian,[9] Catalonian,[10] and Galician traditions,[11] and from Slavonic tradition in Southern Albania.[12] Several versions add details stressing the tale's implicit jocular qualities. For instance, French narrator M. Basset from Sigottier in the region Hautes-Alpes, who told his version in February 1959, mentioned that the grandfather had taken part in the Hundred Years' War (1337–1453) where he was wounded 90 times. A sword split his tongue in half, enabling him to speak French and English at the same time.[13] Jean Bieder, aged 68, of Dahlonega, Lumpkin County, in the state of Georgia in the United States, whose version was recorded in spring 1975, detailed the age of the three men at 78, 98, and 107.[14] The visitor is informed that the grandfather is presently not there, as he is getting married that evening. And when asking why a man of 107 years would want to get married, the startling response is, "He didn't want to; they're making 'im!" This "lovely variation" was also told by tennis champion Vic Seixas at the 1955 Davis Cup Dinner.[15]

Northern European tradition developed a specific form of the tale in which the standard number of three old men is extended to up to seven persons. Additionally, the visitor is made to experience a series of magic events that mark the old men as supernatural beings. Versions of this form were collected from Irish,[16] English,[17] Norwegian,[18] and Swedish traditions.[19]

Historically, the tale is first documented in European tradition in the second half of the sixteenth century. French author Noël du Fail included it in his *Contes et discours d'Eutrapel* (Tales and Discourses of Eutrapel), originally published in 1585,[20] and German author Michael Neander told his version in a learned Latin treatise on the physical qualities of things, also first published in 1585.[21] In Neander's text, the three old men assume their longevity to be due to their frugal diet, mainly including bread, salt, milk, and cheese. In addition, they would at times consume a puree of elderberries (Latin *sambucus*). Neander's text was reprinted numerous times in German books for gardening and chapbooks of entertaining tales ranging from the seventeenth to the twentieth centuries[22] and lived on in early twentieth-century oral tradition.[23]

Contrasting with the tale's form discussed so far in which the older men are the direct ancestors of the person the visitor first meets, there exists another form in which the three old men are brothers. Additionally, in the latter form the visitor does not encounter the old men by chance but has been actively searching for them in order to ask their advice. Although this form is used as a motif in a variety of tales, apparently particularly in Italian tradition,[24] it is often attested as part of a specific narrative that features an extremely large grain of wheat.

A folktale recorded from Slavonic tradition in Southern Albania introduces a man who finds a pot full of coins on the piece of land he just bought.[25] As he does not feel entitled to keep the money for himself, he offers it to the land's previous owner who equally does not want it. The judge to whom they appeal for a solution suggests that they marry their children and give both the money and the land to them. The following year, the harvest yields a large amount of very good wheat that they put in storage. Time passes, and when many years later the people clean the granary they find the stored grains of wheat large as a chicken's egg. The people ask the advice of the three old men, the hair of the youngest of whom is white, of the second grey, and of the third black. Having informed the people about the nature of their find, owing to the virtuous actions of those who grew and stored it, the eldest brother also demonstrates to them why he is the most youthful. Inviting the people to share a watermelon with him, he sends his wife seven times to fetch a good fruit, although he knows that there is only a single melon in the house. Nevertheless, the man's wife obeys his orders without the least complaint. That way the old man demonstrates that a man's health and well-being depends on the good nature of his wife. His younger brother's wife is neither good nor bad (French *comme ci comme ça*), and his youngest brother's wife is ill-natured, thus explaining the different signs of their advanced age.

Whereas the Slavonic folktale from Albania starts by informing the audience how the large grains came into existence, the audience of a Slovak folktale is as uninformed as the tale's protagonist. The Slovak tale was recorded in October 1905 by S. Czambel from the oral performance of Fr. Vojt, aged 52, in Podbiel. It begins with a man finding a single, strangely large grain in the woods.[26] As the man is curious to identify his find, he presents it to the king who is equally at a loss to tell what it is. When even the king's viziers are not able to explain the grain's nature, one of them suggests asking an old man of 120 years of age who is so frail that he needs two crutches to move. The old man is also unable to help but suggests asking his father. Although the father is 150 years old, he is in better physical shape than his son, only needing a single crutch to move. Unable to identify the object, the father again refers them to his father. Although that man is 180 years of age, he is more vigorous than his offspring. He informs the king that the object is a grain from the kind of wheat that used to grow when he was young. In those days, justice and compassion reigned to such a degree that the farmers would donate their surplus wheat to the poor. But when deceit and falseness spread in the world, the wheat grew smaller, and the life span of people grew shorter. A version similar to the Slovak folktale, including a similar "socialist" moral of justice and peace for everyone, was recorded by Russian folklorist Aleksandr Afanasyev in the Northern Russian district of Arkhangelsk.[27] Afanasyev's tale served as a model for Lev Tolstoy's literary adaptation titled "The Grain as Big as a Hen's Egg," published in 1886.[28]

Although it is impossible to ascertain a genetic link between the tale's various forms as outlined above, a precursor in Middle Eastern narratives is constituted by a lengthy and fairly complex narrative included in the Ottoman Turkish *Ferec ba'd eş-şidde* (Relief after Hardship), an anonymous compilation dating to the fifteenth or the latter half of the fourteenth century.[29] Essentially, that tale is about destiny and the impossibility to change or influence a decreed fate (see also essay 53, ***The Men Realize That They Will Never Manage to Control Women's Sexuality***). This feature is exemplified by the Phoenix challenging King Solomon, claiming that she can prevent the newly born son of the Eastern king from impregnating the newly born daughter of the Western king as decreed by destiny. Of course, the tale's logic requires that the Phoenix fails in her attempt, and once grown up, the boy and the girl meet. A tale with this structure is already attested in ancient Indian Buddhist literature[30] and was known in the Muslim world at least since its inclusion in al-Thaʿlabī's (d. 1038) collection of tales of the prophets (*qiṣaṣ al-anbiyāʾ*).[31] Embedded within the frame tale are the boy's adventures, the first of which has him explore the source of the river Nile. At one point, the boy sees a group of trees whose shiny fruits are covered in bags of cloth. Eventually, he comes to the three brothers, the oldest of whom looks youngest. He informs the young man that the fruits are jewels that grew during the reign of a just king. As neither the person who planted the trees nor the king felt entitled to harvest the fruits, they covered them with cloth bags so that nobody would covet them. As the Ottoman Turkish collection is likely adapted from previous Persian collections of the *Jāmeʿ al-ḥekāyāt* (Collections of Tales) genre, most of them equally anonymous, the tale is also encountered in various later representatives of the genre, including the Mashhad manuscript known as *Chehel va shesh ḥekāyāt* (46 Tales), probably dating from the beginning of the sixteenth century.[32] The version of the present tale included in that manuscript begins with the man finding a treasure in his field, as in the Slavonic folktale from Albania. Instead of tremendously large wheat, the field brings forth trees covered with jewel fruits. Relating to the marvelous wheat, the tale is also told in Żiyāʾ al-Din Nakhshabi's (d. 1350) *Ṭuṭi-nāme* (Book of the Parrot), completed around 1330, as well as the collection's subsequent Ottoman Turkish version.[33] The tale's earliest Persian version, the oldest one identified so far, is contained in Abu Bakr ibn Khosrow al-Ostād's Persian *Munes-nāme* (The Book as an Intimate Friend), compiled around the year 1200.[34]

In addition to the full-fledged Middle Eastern tale, single elements of it are known from a variety of sources. The initial motif of marrying the children of the two contesting parties, one of whom found a treasure on the land previously owned by the other, is present in a tale from ancient Jewish tradition as told in the commentaries on the biblical books Genesis and Leviticus (first and third books Moses), that is, the *Midrash Bereshit Rabba* and the *Midrash Wayikra Rabba*, and other works.[35] Here, the arbiter is King Ḳaẓia whom Alexander the Great visits.[36] On the authority of the Prophet Muḥammad, the tale is cited with an anonymous arbiter in several of the standard Sunni collections of prophetic traditions (*ḥadīth*) compiled in the ninth century, such as those by Bukhāri (d. 870), Muslim (d. 875), and Ibn Ḥanbal (d. 855).[37] Featuring the Sassanian King Kisrā Anūshīrwān as the wise ruler, the tale is contained in al-Ghazzālī's (d. 1111) *Naṣīḥat al-mulūk* (Counsel for Kings).[38] Placing the events during Anūshīrwān's reign as a period of perfect justice, the tale was rendered in verse in Persian poet ʿAbd al-Raḥmān Jāmi's (d. 1492) *Haft owrang* (Seven Thrones).[39] Again with Kisrā Anūshīrwān as the wise arbiter, the tale is given in Arabic prose by al-Qalyūbī (d. 1658).[40] The texts usually end with the peaceful solution without mentioning any further consequences. The gradual shrinking of wheat grain size in times of degenerating justice and growing human depravity appears in a tale told by Kaʿb al-Aḥbār (d. ca. 654), "a learned Jew converted to Islam, and the greatest authority on Jewish legendary lore,"[41] that is cited in Arabic author Muḥammad ibn ʿAbdallāh al-Kisāʾī's twelfth-century compilation of tales of the prophets (*qiṣaṣ al-anbiyāʾ*). According to Kaʿb al-Aḥbār's narration, grains of wheat were originally as big as an ostrich's egg. Gradually, they shrunk to the size of a hen's egg, then to the size of a hazelnut and of peas. And "finally, in the days of Jesus, when the Christians claimed him to be Allah's son . . . and his mother was regarded by them as Allah's spouse, the grain assumed its present (tiny) size."[42] In this manner, the introduction to the tale's full-fledged Middle Eastern versions appears as the combination of motifs that together serve to arouse curiosity and initiate the quest that eventually leads to the meeting with the three old men.

Notes

1. Lixfeld, Hannjost, "Alten: Die drei Alten," in *Enzyklopädie des Märchens*, vol. 1 (1977), cols. 383–387.

2. Henßen, Gottfried, *Volk erzählt: Münsterländische Sagen, Märchen und Schwänke*, Münster: Aschendorf, 1935, pp. 349–350; Ranke, Kurt, *Schleswig-holsteinische Volksmärchen*, vol. 3, Kiel: Hirt, 1962, pp. 82–85, no. 726; Uther, *Deutscher Märchenkatalog*, p. 165, no. 726.

3. Grimm, Jacob and Wilhelm, *Deutsche Sagen*, ed. Hans-Jörg Uther and Barbara Kindermann-Bieri, Munich: Diederichs, 1993, vol. 1, pp. 291–292, 316, no. 363; see also Müllenhoff, Karl, *Sagen, Märchen und Lieder der Herzogthümer Schleswig Holstein und Lauenburg*, Kiel: Schwers, 1845, pp. 98, 594, no. 116.

4. Ranke, *Schleswig-holsteinische Volksmärchen*, vol. 3, pp. 84–85.

5. Neumann, Siegfried, *Plattdeutsche Schwänke: Aus den Sammlungen Richard Wossidlos und seiner Zeitgenossen sowie eigenen Aufzeichnungen in Mecklenburg*, Rostock: VEB Hinstorff Verlag, 1968, pp. 36, 213, no. 50.

6. Neumann, Siegfried, *Ein mecklenburgischer Volkserzähler: Die Geschichten des August Rust*, Berlin: Akademie-Verlag, 1968, pp. 76–77, 156, no. 77.

7. Van der Kooi, Jurjen, and Theo Schuster, *Der Großherzog und die Marktfrau: Märchen und Schwänke aus dem Oldenburger Land*, Leer: Schuster, 1994, pp. 341–342, 437–438, no. 236.

8. Lintur, Petro V., *Ukrainische Volksmärchen*, Berlin: Akademie-Verlag, 1972, pp. 581–582, 787, no. 90.

9. Sánchez Pérez, Jose A., *Cien cuentos populares*, Madrid: Saeta, 1942, pp. 55–57, no. 35.

10. Oriol, Carme, and Josep M. Pujol, *Index of Catalan Folktales*, Helsinki: Suomalainen Tiedeakatemia, 2008, p. 143, no. 726.

11. Noia Campos, Camiño, *Catálogo tipolóxico do conto galego de tradición oral: clasificación, antoloxía e bibliografía*, Vigo: University of Vigo, 2010, pp. 324–327, no. 726.

12. Mazon, André, *Documents, contes et chansons slaves de l'Albanie du sud*, Paris: Droz, 1936, p. 219, no. 59.

13. Joisten, Charles, *Contes populaires du Dauphiné*, Grenoble: Musée Dauphinois, 1971, vol. 2, p. 412, no. 285.

14. Burrison, John A., *Storytellers: Folktales and Legends from the South*, Athens: University of Georgia Press, 1989, pp. 194, 247.

15. Dorson, Richard M., *Negro Folktales in Michigan*, Cambridge: Harvard University Press, 1956, p. 220, no. 145.

16. Ó Duilearga, Séamus, *Seán Ó Conaill's Book: Stories and Traditions from Iveragh*, Baile Átha Cliath: Comhairle Bhéaloideas Éireann, 1981, pp. 113–114, 384, no. 22.

17. Briggs, *A Dictionary*, vol. A1, pp. 346–347.

18. Christiansen, Reidar Thoralf, *Folktales of Norway*, London: Routledge & Kegan Paul, 1964, pp. 82–84, no. 34; Kvideland, Reimund, and Hallfreður Örn, *Norwegische und isländische Volksmärchen*, Berlin: Akademie-Verlag, 1988, pp. 157–158, 302, no. 29.

19. Liungman, Waldemar, *Weißbär am See: Schwedische Volksmärchen von Bohuslän bis Gotland*, Kassel: Röth, 1965, pp. 148–150, 188.

20. Bolte, Johannes, "Die drei Alten: Nach Reinhold Köhlers Kollektaneen," *Zeitschrift des Vereins für Volkskunde* 7 (1897), pp. 205–207, at pp. 205–206.

21. Neander, Michael, *Physice, sive potius syllogae physicae rerum eruditarum*, Leipzig: Defner, 1585, pp. 248–250; Bolte, "Die drei Alten," p. 206.

22. Ranke, *Schleswig-holsteinische Volksmärchen*, vol. 3, pp. 82–83; Birlinger, Anton, "Die drei Alten," *Alemannia* 4 (1877), pp. 265–266.

23. Henssen, Gottfried, *Sagen, Märchen und Schwänke des Jülicher Landes: Aus dem Nachlaß Heinrich Hoffmanns herausgegeben und durch eigene Aufzeichnungen vermehrt*, Bonn: Röhrscheid, 1955, p. 307, no. 484.

24. Chauvin, *Bibliographie*, vol. 7 (1903), p. 62, note 4; Wesselski, Albert, "Alters-Sinnbilder und Alters-Wettstreit," *Archiv Orientální* 4 (1932), pp. 1–22, at p. 1; Bolte and Polívka, *Anmerkungen*, vol. 2, p. 400, no. 97.

25. Mazon, *Documents*, pp. 195, 197, no. 51.

26. Polívka, Jiří, *Súpis slovenských rozprávok*, vol. 4, Turciansky sv. Martin: Matica slov., 1930, p. 47.

27. Afanasyev, Aleksandr Nikolaevich, *Narodnyia russkiia legendy*, Moscow 1859, pp. VIII–IX; Ralston, W.R.S., *Russian Folk-Tales*, London: Smith, Elder, & Co., 1873, pp. 328–329.

28. Zhdanov, Vladimir, and Evelina Zaidenshnur, "Khudozhestvennye proizvedeniya," *Literaturnoe nasledstvo*, vol. 69.2, Moscow: Rossiiskaya Akademiia Nauk, Institut Mirovoi Literatury im. A.M. Gorkogo, 1961, pp. 436–471, at p. 469. For an English translation of Tolstoy's tale, see http://www.online-literature.com/tolstoy/2898/ (accessed April 4, 2018).

29. Marzolph, *Relief after Hardship*, pp. 97–99, no. 31.

30. Chavannes, Édouard, *Cinq cents contes et apologues extraits du Tripitaka chinois*, Paris: Ernest Leroux, 1910–1935 (reprint Paris: Maisonneuve, 1962), vol. 1, pp. 376–377, no. 108; see also Chauvin, Victor, "Note sur le Conte de Salomon et le griffon," *Le muséon* 24 (1905), pp. 85–90, at pp. 87–90.

31. Thaʿlabī, Abū Isḥāq Aḥmad ibn Muḥammad ibn Ibrāhīm al-, *ʿArāʾis al-majālis fī qiṣaṣ al-anbiyāʾ*, transl. William M. Brinner, Leiden etc., Brill, 2002, pp. 498–505.

32. Haag-Higuchi, Roxane, *Untersuchungen zu einer Sammlung persischer Erzählungen:*

Čihil wa-šiš ḥikāyāt yā ǧāmiʿ al-ḥikāyāt, Berlin: Klaus Schwarz, 1984, pp. 84–93, nos. 33, 33a; Khadish, Pegāh, and Moḥammad Jaʿfari (Qanavāti), eds., *Jāmeʿ al-ḥekāyāt bar asās-i noskhe-ye Āstān-i qods-i Rażavi*, Tehran: Māzyār, 1390/2011, pp. 533–548, no. 33.

33. Hatami, Mahroo, *Untersuchungen zum persischen Papageienbuch des Naḫšabī*, Freiburg: Klaus Schwarz, 1977, pp. 155–158, no. 79; Nakhshabi, Żiyā' al-Din, *Ṭuṭi-nāme*, ed. Fatḥallāh Mojtabā'i and Gholām-ʿAlī Āryā, Tehran: Manūchehr, 1372/1993, pp. 400–404 (night 49).

34. Askari, Nasrin, "A Mirror for Princesses: *Mūnis-nāma*, A Twelfth-Century Collection of Persian Tales Corresponding to the Ottoman Turkish Tales of the *Faraj baʿd al-shidda*," *Narrative Culture* 5.1 (2018), pp. 121–140.

35. Chauvin, "Note," p. 86; Wünsche, August, *Der Midrasch Bereschit Rabba: das ist die haggadische Auslegung der Genesis*, Leipzig: Schulze, 1881, p. 143; Wünsche, *Der Midrasch Wajikra Rabba: Das ist die haggadische Auslegung des dritten Buches Mose*, Leipzig: Schulze, 1884, p. 184; Kazis, Israel J., *The Book of the Gests of Alexander of Macedon/Sefer Toledot Alexandros ha-Makdoni: A Medieval Hebrew Version of the Alexander Romance by Immanuel Ben Jacob Bonfils*, Cambridge, MA: The Medieval Academy of America, 1962, pp. 20–22.

36. See also Stoneman, Richard, *Alexander the Great: A Life in Legend*, New Haven: Yale University Press, 2008, p. 121.

37. Wensinck, Arent Jan, *Concordance et indices de la tradition musulmane*, 8 vols., Leiden: Brill, 1936–1988 (Reprint Istanbul: Çağrı Yayınları, 1988), vol. 4, p. 296, s.v. ʿaqār.

38. *Ghazālī's Book Counsel for Kings (Naṣīḥat al-mulūk)*, transl. F.R.C. Bagley, London: Oxford University Press, 1964, pp. 61–62.

39. Askari, "A Mirror for Princesses;" Jāmi, Nur al-Din ʿAbd al-Raḥmān ibn Aḥmad, *Masnavi-ye Haft owrang*, ed. Mortażā Modarres Gilāni, Tehran: Saʿdi, 1337/1958, pp. 974–975.

40. Qalyūbī, Aḥmad Shihāb al-Dīn Salāma al-, *al-Nawādir*, 3rd ed., Cairo: Muṣṭafā al-Bābī al-Ḥalabī wa-awlāduhu, 1374/1955, pp. 25–26, no. 34.

41. Schwarzbaum, Haim, *Biblical and Extra-Biblical Legends in Islamic Folk-Literature*, Walldorf: Verlag für Orientkunde, 1982, p. 49.

42. Ibid. Schwarzbaum translates from Kisā'ī, Muḥammad ibn ʿAbdallāh al-, *Qiṣaṣ al-anbiyā'*, ed. Isaac Eisenberg, Leiden: Brill, 1922, p. 65; see also Kisā'ī, Muḥammad ibn ʿAbdallāh al-, *The Tales of the Prophets*, transl. W.M. Thackston, Boston: Twayne, 1978, p. 69.

CHAPTER 17

The Foolish Couple Waste the Three Wishes They Have Been Granted (ATU 750A)

The international tale type ATU 750A: *The Three Wishes* gathers a variety of tales that share the foolish use of wishes the fulfillment of which supernatural characters have granted to humans. The specific tale considered here usually mentions three wishes (rarely two or four) granted to a saintly man and foolishly wasted by the man and his wife, the latter often displaying a distinct sexual ambition. As the man is not sure how best to use the wishes, he asks his wife for advice. The first wish, pronounced either by the man on behalf of his wife or by the woman herself, is meant to realize a long cherished or spontaneous fantasy. The second wish either intends to remedy the previous situation but actually makes it even worse, or it is used in anger to punish the person who made the first wish. In both cases, the third wish is used to restore the original status. In this manner, all three wishes are wasted without any lasting benefit.

The majority of the tale's versions recorded from nineteenth- and twentieth-century European tradition document a trivialized plot whose focus on the satisfaction of alimentary needs betrays the historical condition of European peasant societies for whom meat was a rare luxury. German narrator Franz Voit, who told his version in the Bohemian town of Waidhaus close to the border of the Czech Republic in 1950, heard it from his father.[1]

> One night, a couple living in a small house give shelter to a beggar. As the beggar leaves the next morning, he tells the woman that she will be granted three wishes. When the couple eat potatoes in their jacket, the woman wishes to have a sausage for their meal, and immediately the sausage appears. The man is so enraged about the silly use of the first wish that he wishes for the sausage to be attached to his wife's nose. The couple have to use the third wish to make the sausage disappear.

In a version from the region of Bonn in Western Germany, the wishes are granted by an old woman.[2] The Irish version recorded in 1929 from the traveling chimney sweep Patrick Shearlock in Ennistimon, County Clare, introduces an old man visiting an old couple.[3] The old man grants two wishes to the man and one to the woman, and the man advises his wife to "wish for somethin' good." As they walk around town, the woman sees another woman making pudding and wishes that she had a pudding herself. The old man gets "so vexed to see her wish gone for nothin'" that he wishes for the pudding to hang off of her nose. But since, "of course, he was ashamed to go around through the street with his missis with the puddin' hangin' off o' her nose," he wishes for it to drop off again. In a lengthy nineteenth-century Hungarian version a "pretty little woman," later identified as a fairy, grants three wishes to a poor man for dragging her "beautiful little golden carriage" out of the mud.[4] Informing his wife about the events, the man tells her to "try and wish for something." She immediately wishes to have some sausage, and "no sooner were the words uttered than a frying pan came down the chimney, and in it a sausage of such length that it was long enough to fence the whole garden." As the husband wants to light his pipe, he is "so awkward about it" that he upsets the frying-pan with the sausage in it, and his wife gets so enraged about his clumsiness that she wishes for the sausage to stick to his nose. Quarreling for some time whether or not to cut the sausage off, at last they wish that "the sausage would go back into the pan." Although they are "as poor as ever," at least they make "a hearty meal of the sausage." As the event has taught the couple that they get along with each other much better without quarreling, and being "industrious and thrifty," they eventually manage to acquire a modest fortune. In the excessively didactic Spanish version recorded in 1986 from the oral performance of the mason and painter Belarmino García García, aged 70, from Castrocalbón, a poor woodcutter's wife is granted three wishes for having been kind to an old man.[5] The woman gets excited about her options and wishes for her husband to be there. Her husband is so enraged about his wife's silly waste of the first wish that he wishes for her to have donkey ears. The tale finishes with the "good Christian" husband wishing that their home should be filled with happiness as before, and that his wife's donkey ears should disappear. The old man who had granted the wishes reveals himself to be God's envoy who was sent to demonstrate that poverty is not necessarily an obstacle to happiness. In the end, the old man informs them that they will be granted a male child who will constitute their happiness.

Tales about a similarly silly use of wishes are documented in European tradition since the twelfth century.[6] Considering the present tale's early forms, the sausage mentioned in many recent European texts since Charles Perrault's *Les souhaits ridicules* (The Silly Wishes; 1697) appears to express sublimated (or maybe consciously bowdlerized?) sexuality. The beautiful dress the woman wishes for in the tale's earliest German version, thirteenth-century poet Der Stricker's *Ein Maere von drîen Wünschen* (A Tale of Three Wishes),[7] contains an implication of sexuality, alluding to the woman's wish to be attractive and, implicitly, sexually active.

In contrast to the folktales collected from relatively recent oral tradition, the medieval French *fabliau Les .iv. sohaiz saint Martin* (Saint Martin's Four Wishes),[8] explicitly expresses the sexual character of the wishes. In the rhymed *fabliau*, Saint Martin grants four wishes to a pious and devout peasant. Although the peasant thinks "women all have addled brains," he agrees to let his wife have the first wish. When the woman wishes that her husband's body should be covered with penises, he is so enraged that he likewise wishes "that you had just as many cunts on you as I have pricks." Soon after realizing the futility of their wishes, the couple then wish "that all their cunts and pricks were gone," only to find "her cunt has disappeared, and he, too, had an awful shock to find himself without a cock." In the end, they have to use the fourth wish to return to their original physical shape. The *fabliau* ends with the advice that if men follow their wives' judgment, "calamity often ensues."

Historically, the "amusing and obscene exaggeration"[9] of the *fabliau* reads like a logical elaboration of the tale's first documented occurrence in the oldest preserved version of the Persian *Sendbād-nāme* (The Book of Sendbād [the Sage]) compiled by Moḥammad ʿAli Ẓahiri Samarqandi around the middle of the twelfth century.[10] This version, in international research known as *nomina* (The Names), is told by the sixth vizier.[11] It is presented in a mixture of prose and verse.[12]

> A pious man (*zāhed*) in Kashmir is friends with a supernatural creature, a *pari* (fairy) or *jinnī*, who magically helps him whenever he is in distress. One day, the *jinnī* informs his friend that he has to leave to take care of an errand in Iraq. As he does not know how long he will be gone, he presents the man with three of God's great names (*se nām az nāmhā-e bozorg-e izad*), each one of which has the capacity to fulfill a wish in times of need. When the *jinnī* has left, the man is so sad about his friend's absence that his wife gets concerned. The man tells her what happened and asks her advice on how to best use the three wishes. His wife argues that a woman needs nothing more than a man's member. Accordingly, she suggests that her husband spend the first wish on making his penis increase (in size or quantity).[13] The stupid (*ablah, nādān*) man follows her advice, only to find that penises come forth from every part of his body. When the man reproaches his wife for her stupid suggestion, she consoles him by advising him to use his second wish to make all the penises disappear. The man does so, but now he is left without even his original member. So he is forced to use the third wish to restore his original physical state.
>
> The vizier ends the tale by arguing that this is what happens to men who follow the advice given by women.

The tale is given in almost identical form in the version of the *Sendbād-nāme* included in the Arabic *Hundred and One Nights*.[14] Here, the woman's initial suggestion is, however, motivated somewhat differently, as she says, "All you men think about is women," thus not arguing for her own sex but rather alluding to male wishful thinking. The tale in the Syriac, Greek, Hebrew, and early Spanish versions of the *Sendbād-nāme* develops the second meaning of the double entendre in the Persian text, that is, an increase in penis size.[15] This is also the version in the *Sendbād-nāme* included in *The Thousand and One Nights*.[16] The latter expresses the tale's "islamization," as the man is granted the wishes during the *laylat al-qadr*, the "Eve of Destiny," or "Eve of (Divine) Power." Mentioned in the Koran (97:3), this night (whose exact date during the Muslim lunar calendar nobody knows) in popular Muslim belief is thought to be of particular blessing for those who consciously witness it, as the angels come down to earth and such fortunate persons will have their wishes fulfilled.[17]

In addition to the tale's explicitly sexualized versions, Arabic and Persian literatures also know a version in which the sexual aspect is less pronounced.[18] This version is first documented in Ibn Qutayba's (d. 889) *'Uyūn al-akhbār* (Quintessential Reports).[19]

> Ibn 'Abbās once told an exemplum, a tale about a bad woman (*al-mar'a al-sū'*).
>
> A pious man had a bad (that is, morally corrupt) woman. Once a man appeared to him announcing, "I have been sent to you from God who has granted you three wishes. Now wish for something in this world or the next, whatever you may desire." Then he got up and left.
>
> The pious man went back to his house where his wife asked him why he was so thoughtful and unhappy. The man told her what had happened, whereupon she said, "Am I not your wife, your companion, and the mother of your daughters? So confer one of your wishes on me!" At first the man declined, but then his daughters intervened in favor of their mother. They would not give in until he finally agreed, "You shall have a single wish!" The woman wished, "Lord! Make my face the most beautiful of all people's!" And so it happened.
>
> Soon the woman began to have sexual relations with her servant, and although her husband admonished her, she did not cease. One day he got so angry that he exclaimed, "Lord! Transform her into a pig (*khanzīr*)!" And she was transformed. When their daughters saw what had happened to her mother, they cried, beat their faces, and pulled their hair (in distress). Finally, the man had mercy on her and asked God to transform her back into her original state. In this way, all of his three wishes were wasted because of her.

The tale's telling is attributed to Ibn 'Abbās, the Prophet Muḥammad's cousin 'Abdallāh ibn 'Abbās ibn 'Abd al-Muṭṭalib, who died in 687. Although this attribution need not be taken at face value, it would date the tale at least to the seventh century, that is, to a period before the Persian *Sendbād-nāme* was compiled.[20] In subsequent centuries, the tale is found in a fair number of sources that as a rule also cite it on the authority of Ibn 'Abbās. Sometimes, the tale is told about an Israelite. The plot only manifests minor variations, such as when vanity induces the beautiful woman to request separation from her husband, when instead of a pig she is transformed into a bitch in heat (*kalba nabbāḥa*), or when the couple's children intervening on her behalf are their sons and not their daughters. In addition to *adab* literature, in the Arab Muslim context the tale is frequently cited in exegetical literature (the *tafsīr*) with reference to the Koranic verse "And relate to them the story of him to whom We delivered Our signs, but he detached himself from them" (7:175), alluding to the man's stupid use of the wishes granted by divine grace. An additional attribution links the tale to a woman called Basūs whose mischief (*shuʾm*) became proverbial in Arabic tradition.

In Persian literature, the tale is first rendered in Neẓām al-Molk's (d. 1092) *Siyāsat-nāme* (Book of Government).[21] Here, the name of the Israelite man is given as Yūsuf (Joseph), and his wife is called Kirsuf. Not having committed any sins for forty years, the man is granted three wishes. He asks his loving wife for advice as to how to spend the wishes, and she wishes to become the most beautiful woman on earth so that her husband will be pleased whenever he sees her. When transformed into a ravishing beauty, however, the woman's vanity gains the upper hand. As she disobeys her husband and neglects her duties toward her children, the man spends his second wish asking God to punish her by transforming her into a bear. When in the end he uses his third wish to reestablish the original state, the woman believes that she has been dreaming. Neẓām al-Molk adds the usual moral that men should not seek the advice of women. The tale is similarly cited in one of Farid al-Din ʿAṭṭār's (d. 1221) mystical poetical works,[22] where the man is a wood-gatherer, and in Sadid al-Din Moḥammad ʿAwfi's (d. ca. 1232) *Javāmeʿ al-ḥekāyāt* (Collections of Stories), where the man again is a pious Israelite.[23]

Joseph Bédier, who devoted a lengthy essay to the classification and study of the tale's versions, dismissed the value of studies of comparative literature[24] to such an extent that even recent studies seriously question the general usefulness of "genetic questions."[25] Such doubt is often triggered by lack of knowledge of or access to a given tale's "Oriental" versions. Although the present case does not intend to argue for a revival of studies of a given tale's ultimate origin, the usefulness of which is admittedly limited, it demonstrates several points beyond reasonable doubt. First, the tale of the three wishes wasted by the foolish couple can be shown to have been transmitted in an unbroken line of tradition from the Persian *Sendbād-nāme* via the work's Western derivatives and the medieval French *fabliau* to domesticated trivialized folktale versions of recent written and oral tradition. Second, the tale's explicit sexual content was gradually moderated in later versions both in Western and Muslim tradition. Sexually explicit versions may or may not still exist in modern oral tradition, but they were as unlikely to be narrated to the nineteenth- and early twentieth-century scholarly collectors as the collectors would have ventured to publish them. And third, the inherent misogyny remains embedded in the tale, regardless of a given narrator's context in terms of geographical region, culture, religion, language, or period. Only occasionally mitigated by allusion to the man's stupidity in following his wife's advice or by a depiction of the couple as equally stupid, the misogynist tendency proves to be the strongest lasting message the tale conveys.

Notes

1.Benzel, Ulrich, *Volkserzählungen aus dem nördlichen Böhmerwald*, Marburg: Elwert, 1957, p. 59, no. 220a.

2. Dietz, Josef, *Aus der Sagenwelt des Bonner Landes*, Bonn: Röhrscheid, 1965, p. 203, no. 846.

3. *Béaloideas* 3.4 (1932), p. 434; a similar version is in Briggs, *A Dictionary*, vol. B1, p. 522 (told by Robert Stewart, aged 11, from Fetterangus).

4. Jones, W. Henry, and Lajos L. Kropf, *The Folk-tales of the Magyars*, London: Stock, 1889, pp. 217–219.

5. Camarena Laucirica, Julio, *Cuentos tradicionales de León*, Madrid: Universidad Complutense, Seminario Menendez Pidal, 1991, vol. 1, pp. 291–292, 434, no. 125.

6. Röhrich, Lutz, *Erzählungen des späten Mittelalters und ihr Weiterleben in Literatur und Volksdichtung bis zur Gegenwart*, vol. 1, Bern: Francke, 1962, pp. 62–79, 253–258; Chesnutt, Michael, "Wünsche: Die drei W.," in *Enzyklopädie des Märchens*, vol. 14 (2014), cols. 1076–1083.

7. Grubmüller, Klaus, ed., *Novellistik des Mittelalters: Märendichtung*, Frankfurt am Main: Dt. Klassiker-Verlag, 1996, pp. 56–69, 1044–1047.

8. Bédier, Joseph, "Les quatre souhaits Saint Martin," in *Les Fabliaux: Études de littérature populaire et d'histoire littéraire du Moyen Age*, 2nd ed., Paris: Émile Bouillon, 1895, pp. 212–228; the following quotations are taken from Ned Dubin's English rendering http://myweb.ecu.edu/sidhun/Les%20iv%20sohaiz%20St.%20 Martin.pdf (accessed March 6, 2017).

9. Bédier, "Les quatre souhaits," p. 220.

10. Ẓahiri Samarqandi, Moḥammad ʿAli, *Sendbād-nāme*, ed. Moḥammad Bāqer Kamāl al-Dini, Tehran: Mirāṯ-e maktub, 1381/2002, pp. 163–168.

11. I am not aware of any previous detailed discussion of this version. Notably, it is deemed "unfit to be repeated" by Clouston, William Alexander, *The Book of Sindibād, or The Story of the King, His Son, His Damsel, and the Seven Vazīrs: From the Persian and Arabic*, Glasgow: privately printed, 1884, pp. 72, 190, 253.

12. For this genre in Persian literature, see Meisami, Julie Scott, "Mixed Prose and Verse in Medieval Persian Literature," in Harris, Joseph, and Karl Reichl, eds., *Prosimetrum: Crosscultural Perspectives on Narrative in Prose and Verse*, Woodbridge, Suffolk: D.S. Brewer, 1997, pp. 295–319.

13. The text here has a double entendre, since the "more" (*bishtar*) the woman asks for can imply either an increase in size or an increase in quantity.

14. Gaudefroyes-Demombynes, Maurice, transl., *Les Cent et une nuits*, Paris: Sindbad, 1982, p. 160–161; Fudge, Bruce, ed. and transl., *A Hundred and One Nights*, New York: New York University Press, 2016, p. 271.

15. Chauvin, *Bibliographie*, vol. 8 (1904), pp. 51–52, no. 19.

16. Marzolph and Van Leeuwen, *The Arabian Nights Encyclopedia*, vol. 1, p. 419, no. 199.

17. El-Shamy, Hasan M., *Religion among the Folk in Egypt*, Westport, Connecticut: Praeger, 2009, p. 184.

18. Marzolph, *Arabia ridens*, vol. 2, p. 58, no. 221; vol. 1, pp. 197–203.

19. Ibn Qutayba al-Dīnawarī, Abū Muḥammad ʿAbdallāh ibn Muslim, *ʿUyūn al-akhbār*, 2nd ed., vol. 4, Cairo: al-Muʾassasa al-miṣriyya al-ʿāmma lil-taʾlif wa-ʾl-tarjama wa-ʾl-ṭibāʿa, 1963, p. 117.

20. The following observations rely on Marzolph, *Arabia ridens*, vol. 1, pp. 200–203.

21. Niẓām al-Mulk, *The Book of Government or Rules for Kings: The Siyāsat-nāma or Siyar al-Mulūk of Niẓām al-Mulk*, transl. Hubert Darke, London: Routledge & Kegan Paul, 1960, pp. 189–191.

22. Ritter, Hellmut, *The Ocean of the Soul: Man, the World and God in the Stories of Farīd al-Dīn ʿAṭṭār*, transl. John O'Kane, Leiden: Brill, 2003, pp. 97–98.

23. ʿAwfi, Sadid al-Din Moḥammad al-, *Matn-e enteqādi-ye Javāmeʿ al-ḥekāyāt wa-lavāmeʿ al-revāyāt*, book 3, part 2, ed. Amir Bānu Moṣaffā and Maẓāher Moṣaffā, Tehran: Bonyād-e Farhang-e Irān, 1353/1974, pp. 708–709 (bk. 3, ch. 24, no. 8); Niẓámu'd-dín, *Introduction*, p. 232, no. 1780.

24. Bédier, *Les Fabliaux*, p. 475.

25. Grubmüller, *Novellistik des Mittelalters*, p. 1046.

CHAPTER 18

The Subaltern Does Not Want to Sell the House to the Ruler (ATU 759E)

As a proponent of enlightened absolutism, Frederick II, king of Prussia (r. 1740–1786), considered himself "the first servant of the state." Styled in German popular tradition as the prototype of a just and caring ruler, a German Hārūn al-Rashīd, he is affectionately remembered as "Old Fred" (Der alte Fritz). The anecdote about Frederick II and the miller of Sanssouci demonstrates in an exemplary manner the extent to which the people trusted in the independence of the Prussian judicial system installed by the ruler in which even the sovereign could not consider himself to be above the law.[1]

> Annoyed by the noise of a mill close to his newly constructed palace Sanssouci (Without Worries), Frederick II offers to buy the mill from the miller. The miller, however, does not want to sell the mill, arguing instead that it was his father's and his grandfather's possession, and so it is his legal right to keep it where it is. Getting tired of negotiating, the king finally threatens to take the mill from him by force. At this point, the miller responds bluntly, "You could probably do that, were it not for the court in Berlin!"[2]

This anecdote is stereotypically recounted in relation to the palace Sanssouci in innumerable printed sources. The assertion that the items in the collection from which the above text is quoted were "collected from the mouth of the people" probably constitutes a timely attempt at authentication rather than a reliable proof of the text's recording from contemporary oral tradition. Even so, the anecdote's "constant repetition and the belief of millions of people"[3] in the irrevocable rule of justice in Frederick's Prussia strongly suggests that the anecdote was not only read but also frequently retold. Its well-known presence in written sources might even account for the very fact that it was rarely, if ever, recorded from oral tradition, as collectors would have taken the anecdote's oral performance as constituting a mere retelling from literature that usually was outside of their focus of collecting genuine folklore.[4] Considering this feature, the international system of tale types only includes the anecdote in its most recent edition, where it is now listed as tale type ATU 759E: *The Miller of Sans Souci*.[5]

The attribution of all kinds of anecdotes to Frederick II already began during his lifetime when various publications praised the king of Prussia as "one of the greatest, happiest, and most glorious monarchs that ever lived on earth."[6] Historically, the anecdote relates to a quarrel between the king and the miller, whose mill (after an extensive reconstruction in 1993) still today stands close to the royal residence. The historical argument, however, did not concern the mill's noise. Instead, it was the miller who complained to the ruler about decreasing revenues due to the fact that the palace and the surrounding trees diminished the power of the wind that drove his mill. Consequently, he asked for, and eventually received, considerable subsidies.[7] Other historical anecdotes similarly stress the sovereign's proverbial sense of justice even to his own disadvantage.[8]

The first instance of the anecdote's attribution to "Old Fred" was identified in French author Jean-Charles Lavaux's *Vie de Frederic II, Roi de Prusse*,[9] a work whose initial volumes were published in the year following the king's demise. A year later, the anecdote was republished in German in Georg Ritter von Zimmermann's *Über Friedrich den Großen und meine Unterredungen mit ihm kurz vor seinem Tode* (On Frederick the Great and My Conversations with Him Shortly before His Death).[10] Eventually, it became popular, appearing in a number of publications including Johann Peter Hebel's widely read *Schatzkästlein des rheinischen Hausfreundes* (The Rhenish Family Friend's Treasure Box), originally published in 1811.[11] Although credible in its historical context, the anecdote to all appearance is a migratory legend[12] whose attribution to Frederick II is just one out of several documented attributions the oldest of which are known from Arabic and Persian literatures.

The earliest quotation of the anecdote's old form in a European literature is encountered in Italian author Giovanni Botero's *Detti memorabili di personaggi illustri* (Memorable Facts of Illustrious Persons).[13] Here, the events take place between an old woman and the Persian emperor (*prencipe*), called *Quissera*, Kisrā Anūshīrwān (Arabic; Persian Khosrow Anōsharvān, r. 531–579). A king of the Sasanian dynasty (226–651) that ended with the Arab conquest in the middle of the seventh century, Anūshīrwān became the model of a just ruler in subsequent Arabic and Persian tradition. The story goes that when Anūshīrwān constructed his palace in his capital (Greek Ctesiphon, Arabic al-Madā'in) in Iraq, an old woman refused to sell her house to the king, arguing that she had been living there all her life and also wanted to die there. Instead of dispossessing the old woman by force, the ruler left the house as it was and built the palace around it, causing a peculiar imperfection in the palace's otherwise harmonious construction. Addressed concerning this imperfection, the ruler responds that, as a matter of fact, he regarded this imperfection as a sign of its perfection, since it demonstrated his just regard toward the rights of his subalterns. Translated into German by an anonymous translator in 1620,[14] the anecdote is cited by several compilers of German chapbooks in the seventeenth and eighteenth centuries, including Samuel Gerlach, Christoph Lehmann, Abraham a Sancta Clara, and

Daniel Elias Helmhack.[15] Although a French version of the tale predating Lavaux's attribution to Frederick II has not so far been identified, he likely adapted his version from this tradition.

Botero most probably translated his version from Persian historian Mirkhond's (d. 1498) *Rowżat al-ṣafā* (The Garden of Purity).[16] In addition to the tale's identical wording by both authors, an anecdote immediately following in Botero was argued to indicate this provenance, as in Mirkhond's work the same anecdote is also cited shortly after the tale in question. This second tale is about the consequences of unjustified transgressions and serves as an argument why the king decides to advocate the rule of justice. Also known from Ḥoseyn Vāʿeẓ Kāshefi's Persian adaptation of *Kalila wa-Dimna*, the *Anvār-e Soheyli* (The Lights of Soheyli), it demonstrates the working of talion by telling about a king who sees a dog tearing off the leg of a fox; a man later hits the dog with a stone; a horse kicks the man so that his leg breaks; and, finally, one of the horse's legs gets stuck in a hole in the ground so that it breaks.[17] In this manner, each of the actors is punished for the evil deed committed.

The Persian historian Mirkhond's version of the presently concerned tale, in turn, derives from a long tradition in Arabic literature that is first documented in the ninth century and that has since been cited numerous times, with only minor variations.[18] In his *Murūj al-dhahab* (Meadows of Gold), the Arab historian al-Masʿūdī (d. 956) tells the following.[19]

> When Anūshīrwān installed his capital in Iraq, numerous rulers sent their ambassadors to him with presents. When the ambassador of the Byzantine ruler marveled at the construction of the reception hall (*īwān*), he noticed an anomaly (*iʿwijāj*) in its construction and remarked that the yard was not perfectly square. He was told that close to the place of the anomaly there had been the house of an old woman. Although the king offered her much money to buy the house from her, she had declined, and he had not seized the house from her by force. That was the reason for the anomaly the ambassador noticed. Following this explanation the Byzantine ambassador exclaimed, "This anomaly is better than regularity!"

Many of the later versions culminate in the final exclamation that in Arabic reads *al-iʿwijāj aḥsan min al-istiwāʾ/al-istiqāma*. With only minor variations, essentially the same text is attested in a variety of later works of history, geography, and literature, including Abū ʿUbayd al-Bakrī's (d. 1094) *al-Masālik wa-ʾl-mamālik* (Routes and Countries),[20] Ibn Badrūn's (d. 1211) commentary on Ibn ʿAbdūn's *qaṣīda*,[21] al-Nuwayrī's (d. 1332) *Nihāyat al-arab fī funūn al-adab* (The Ultimate Ambition in the Arts of Erudition),[22] Ibn al-Wardī's (d. 1349) *Kharīdat al-ʿajāʾib wa-farīdat al-gharāʾib* (The Unpierced Pearl of Marvels and the Precious Gem of Strange Things),[23] Ibn Nubāta's (d. 1366) commentary on Ibn Zaydūn's epistle,[24] al-Ḥimyarī's (d. 1494) *al-Rawḍ al-miʿṭār fī khabar al-aqṭār* (The Perfumed Garden: News of [Foreign] Regions),[25] al-Qaramānī's (d. 1610)

Akhbār al-duwal wa-āthār al-uwal (News of the Countries and Traces of the Ancient),[26] and al-Shirwānī's (d. 1840) *Nafḥat al-Yaman* (The Breeze from Yemen).[27] Major variations of the tale are only encountered in the geographical lexicons compiled by Yāqūt (d. 1229)[28] and al-Qazwīnī (d. 1283),[29] respectively. Yāqūt reports having seen the ruins of the building himself and mentions the specific local denomination *qubbat al-ʿajūz* (The Old Woman's Dome). Al-Qazwīnī adds a few picturesque details not mentioned elsewhere. As the smoke from the old woman's abode used to spoil the precious paintings in the audience hall, the ruler gave orders not to keep her from lighting a fire but instead to refurbish the paintings whenever needed. When the old woman's cow needed milking at night, it would walk to her house across the royal hall, and the servants would roll up the carpets until the cow had left for the pasture again.

In addition to the tale's mainstream version, various texts develop a similar situation, thus documenting the tale's quality as a migratory legend at an early stage. Arabic authors al-Zamakhsharī (d. 1144),[30] Ibn al-Jawzī (d. 1201),[31] and Bahā al-Dīn al-ʿĀmilī (d. 1621)[32] mention a rich man in Basra who wants to buy an old woman's nearby house so as to enlarge his own mansion. When the woman refuses to sell the house even for several times its value, the rich man threatens to have her punished. The woman responds that the buyer rather than herself should be punished for offering to pay such a ridiculously high price. Various solutions are offered: The woman refuses to sell even when threatened (Ibn al-Jawzī); she is offered an even higher price and consents (al-Zamakhsharī); the man refrains from acquiring the house (Bahā al-Dīn al-ʿĀmilī). Ibn al-Jawzī has the *qāḍī* Abū Ḥāmid al-Khorāsānī narrate the event as a personal experience. The Iranian scholar Neẓām al-Molk (d. 1092), who served as vizier of the Seljuq Empire for more than thirty years, tells the story of the governor of Azarbaijan during the reign of Anushirvān who forcibly seized an old woman's legally owned property, even refusing to compensate her or offer a substitute. When the matter is brought to the ruler's attention, he gives orders "to strip the skin from that man's body, throw his flesh to the dogs, stuff the skin with straw and hang it upon the palace gate"[33] as a warning to other potential oppressors. The prominent Danish scholar of Iranian studies, Arthur Christensen, regarded this text as the tale's "Urform," and probably the version from which all other versions originate. Already Theodor Nöldeke, however, warned that the author's concern is not so much a depiction of reality but rather the *fabula docet*, the message the tale conveys.[34] The prose version in Sadid al-Din Moḥammad ʿAwfi's (d. ca. 1232) *Javāmeʿ al-ḥekāyāt* (Compilations of Stories) corresponds to the mainstream version.[35] The Persian mystical poet Farid al-Din ʿAṭṭār (d. 1221) elaborated the tale with drastic consequences. As the old woman does not want to sell her house, the ruler has it pulled down. When the woman returns, she "shouts a prayer to heaven and the castle immediately collapses and buries the unjust king beneath it."[36] The tale's quality as a migratory legend attributed to various localities is also evidenced by its attachment to the Ulu Jāmiʿ in Bursa.[37]

Notes

1. The present text is adapted from my entry "Müller von Sanssouci," in *Enzyklopädie des Märchens*, vol. 9 (1999), cols. 993–999. That text, in turn, is heavily indebted to Wesselski, Albert, "Der Müller von Sanssouci," *Mitteilungen des Vereins für die Geschichte Berlins* 44 (1927), pp. 147–152; also in Wesselski, *Erlesenes*, Prague: Gesellschaft deutscher Bücherfreunde in Böhmen, 1928, pp. 46–63. An earlier comprehensive discussion of the anecdote is Brechenmacher, Josef Karlmann, *Friedrich der Große und der Müller von Sanssouci: Schürfungen auf dem Grenzrain von Geschichte und Sage*, Stuttgart: Verlag des katholischen Schulvereins für die Diözese Rottenburg, 1910; see also Brechenmacher, "Friedrich der Große und der Müller von Sanssouci," *Zeitschrift für deutschen Unterricht* 21 (1907), pp. 273–287; Jacob, Georg, "Wandersagen," *Der Islam* 18 (1929), pp. 200–206, at pp. 200–204.

2. Schwartz, Wilhelm, *Sagen und alte Geschichten der Mark Brandenburg: Aus dem Munde des Volkes gesammelt und wiedererzählt*, 7th ed., Berlin: Märkische Verlangsanstalt, 1895, p. 38, no. 18; see also Kügler, Hermann, *Hohenzollernsagen*, Leipzig-Gohlis: Hermann Eichblatt, 1922, pp. 148–149, no. 40.

3. Schneider, L., "Die historische Windmühle bei Sanssouci," *Märkische Forschungen* 6 (1858), pp. 165–193, at p. 183; Brechenmacher, *Friedrich der Große*, p. 18.

4. Neumann, Siegfried, *Der Alte Fritz: Geschichten und Anekdoten*, Schwerin: Demmler, 2003, p. 10 (quoted from Schwartz, *Sagen*). The tale is not quoted in Neumann, Siegfried, *Friedrich der Große in der pommerschen Erzähltradition: Eine volkskundliche Studie und Dokumentation*, Rostock: Wossidlo-Archiv, 1998.

5. According to Uther, *Deutscher Märchenkatalog*, p. 181, no. 759E, this is the tale's only German version collected from oral tradition.

6. Quoted from a collection dated 1758 in Neumann, Siegfried, *Geschichte und Geschichten: Studien zu Entstehung und Gehalt historischer Sagen und Anekdoten*, Rostock: Wossidlo-Archiv, 2001, p. 24.

7. Schneider, "Die historische Windmühle."

8. Wesselski, "Der Müller," pp. 50–52.

9. Laveaux, Jean Charles Thibaut de, *Vie De Frederic II., Roi De Prusse: Accompagnée d'un grand nombre de Remarques, Pièces justificatives & Anecdotes, dont la plupart n'ont point encore été publiées*, vol. 4: *Vie privée & littéraire*, Strasbourg: Treuttel, 1787, p. 308; see Brechenmacher, *Friedrich der Große*, pp. 3–4; Wesselski, "Der Müller," p. 46.

10. Zimmermann, Georg Ritter von, *Über Friedrich den Großen und meine Unterredungen mit ihm kurz vor seinem Tode*, Leipzig: Weidmannische Buchhandlung, 1788, p. 222; see Brechenmacher, *Friedrich der Große*, p. 4; Wesselski, "Der Müller," p. 49.

11. Brechenmacher, *Friedrich der Große*, pp. 6–7.

12. Alzheimer-Haller, Heidrun, *Handbuch zur narrativen Volksaufklärung: Moralische Geschichten 1780–1848*, Berlin: De Gruyter, 2004, p. 186.

13. Botero, Giovanni, *Detti memorabili di personaggi illustri*, Brescia: Bartholomeo Fontana, 1610, pp. 262–266; Wesselski, "Der Müller," p. 56–57.

14. Brechenmacher, *Friedrich der Große*, p. 10; Wesselski, "Der Müller," p. 60–61.

15. Brechenmacher, *Friedrich der Große*, p. 11; Wesselski, "Der Müller," p. 61–62; Uther, *Deutscher Märchenkatalog*, p. 181, no. 759E.

16. Mirkhond, Mir Moḥammad ibn Borhān al-Din Khāvandshāh, *Tārikh-e Roużat al-ṣafā*, vol. 1, Tehran: Ketābkhāne-ye markazi, 1338/1959, pp. 789–790; Mirkhond,

Muhammad Bin Khâvendshâh Bin Mahmûd, *The Rauzat-us-safa; or, Garden of Purity, Containing the Histories of Prophets, Kings, and Khalifs*, transl. E. Rehatsek, ed. F.F. Arbuthnot, vol. 1.2, London: Royal Asiatic Society, 1891, p. 386; Wesselski, "Der Müller," p. 55–60.

17. Chauvin, *Bibliographie*, vol. 2, p. 116, no. 93.

18. Marzolph, *Arabia ridens*, vol. 2, p. 103, no. 415.

19. Mas'ūdī, Abū 'l-Ḥasan 'Alī ibn al-Ḥusayn al-, *Murūj al-dhahab wa-ma'ādin al-jawhar*, ed. Charles Pellat, vol. 1, Beirut: Publications de l'Université libanaise, 1966, p. 306, no. 620.

20. Bakrī, Abū 'Ubayd al-, *Kitāb al-Masālik wa-'l-mamālik*, ed. Adriyān fān Lyūfin and Andrī Fīrī, Tunis: Dār al-'arabī lil-kitāb, 1992, vol. 1, p. 286, no. 446.

21. Ibn Badrūn, *Commentaire historique sur le poème d'Ibn-Abdoun, par Ibn Badroun*, ed. Reinhart Pieter Anne Dozy, Leiden: S. and J. Luchtmans, 1846, p. 42.

22. Nuwayrī, Shihāb al-Dīn Aḥmad ibn 'Abd al-Wahhāb al-, *Nihāyat al-arab fī funūn al-adab*, vol. 15, Cairo: Dār al-Kutub al-miṣriyya, 1369/1949, p. 192.

23. Ibn al-Wardī, Sirāj al-Dīn Abū Ḥafṣ 'Umar, *Kharīdat al-'ajā'ib wa-farīdat al-gharā'ib*, Cairo: al-Maṭba'a al-'āmira, 1324/1906, p. 164.

24. Basset, *Mille et un contes*, vol. 2, p. 109, no. 84.

25. Ḥimyarī, Muḥammad ibn 'Abd al-Mun'im, al-, *al-Rawḍ al-mi'ṭār fī khabar al-aqṭār*, ed. Iḥsān 'Abbās, Beirut: Maktabat Lubnān, 1975, p. 70.

26. Qaramānī, Aḥmad ibn Yūsuf al-, *Akhbār al-duwal wa-āthār al-uwal*, ed. Aḥmad Ḥaṭīṭ and Fahmī Sa'd, vol. 3, Beirut: 'Ālam al-kutub, 1412/1992, pp. 153–154.

27. Shirwānī, Aḥmad ibn Muḥammad al-Anṣārī al-Yamanī al-, *Nafḥat al-Yaman*, Cairo 1356/1937, p. 18; Rescher, Oskar, *Die Geschichten und Anekdoten aus Qaljûbî's Nawâdir und Schirwânî's Nafhat el-Jemen*, Stuttgart: W. Heppeler, 1920, pp. 221, no. 35.

28. Wüstenfeld, Ferdinand, "Jâcût's Reisen, aus seinem geographischen Wörterbuche beschrieben," *Zeitschrift der Deutschen Morgenländischen Gesellschaft* 18 (1864), pp. 397–493, at pp. 406–407; *Jacut's geographisches Wörterbuch*, ed. Ferdinand Wüstenfeld, vol. 1, Leipzig: Deutsche Morgenländische Gesellschaft, 1924, p. 426; Brechenmacher, *Friedrich der Große*, p. 9; Wesselski, "Der Müller," p. 53–54; Jacob, "Wandersagen," p. 201–202.

29. Qazwīnī, Zakariyyā ibn Muḥammad ibn Maḥmūd al-, *Āthār al-bilād wa-akhbār al-'ibād*, Beirut: Dār Ṣādir, 1380/1960, p. 454; Wesselski, "Der Müller," p. 54–55; Jacob, "Wandersagen," p. 202–203.

30. Zamakhsharī, Abū 'l-Qāsim Maḥmūd ibn 'Umar, *Rabī' al-abrār wa-nuṣūṣ al-akhbār*, ed. Salīm al-Nu'aymī, vol. 3, Baghdad: al-'Ānī, 1980, p. 608.

31. Ibn al-Jawzī, Abū 'l-Faraj 'Abd al-Raḥmān ibn 'Alī, *Akhbār al-Adhkiyā'*, ed. Muḥammad Mursī al-Khūlī, Cairo, 1970, pp. 239–240; Wesselski, "Der Müller," p. 55–56, note 1.

32. Basset, *Mille et un contes*, vol. 2, pp. 98–99, no. 72.

33. Niẓām al-Mulk, *The Book of Government or Rules for Kings: The Siyāsat-nāma or Siyar al-Mulūk of Niẓām al-Mulk*, transl. Hubert Darke, London: Routledge & Kegan Paul, 1960, pp. 35–40, quote p. 40 (ch. 5); Wesselski, "Der Müller," p. 56, note 1; Christensen, Arthur, *L'Iran sous les Sassanides*, 2nd ed., Copenhagen: Ejnar Munksgaard, 1944, pp. 376–377.

34. Nöldeke, Theodor, "Review of *Siasset Namèh*, ed. Charles Schefer, Paris.

Ernest Leroux, 1891," *Zeitschrift der Deutschen Morgenländischen Gesellschaft* 46 (1892), pp. 761–768, at p. 767; Wesselski, "Der Müller," p. 56, note 1.

35. Niẓámu'd-dín, *Introduction*, p. 154, no. 369 (bk. 1, ch. 6); see Mordtmann, Andreas David, "Zu Dionys, dem Tyrannen schlich," *Die Gartenlaube* (1869), pp. 151–153, at p. 153.

36. Ritter, Hellmut, *The Ocean of the Soul: Man, the World and God in the Stories of Farīd al-Dīn 'Aṭṭār*, transl. John O'Kane, Leiden: Brill, 2003, p. 122 (*Moṣibat-nāme*, ch. 7).

37. Ibid.

CHAPTER 19

The Treasure Finders Murder One Another (ATU 763)

Classified as tale type ATU 763: *The Treasure Finders Who Murder One Another*, this didactic tale basically tells of several men (a minimum of two) who find a treasure. Before dividing the treasure between themselves, they send one party away to fetch food or drink. In the meantime, both parties plot to kill the other, so as not having to share the treasure. The food carrier is murdered by his companion or companions upon his return, and they are in turn killed by the poison he had put in the food or drink. Many of the tale's versions are presented with an explicit warning against strong attachment to mundane possessions, as that will lead to greed, envy, destruction, and death. First documented in early Indian Buddhist literature,[1] the tale was transmitted to the West by Arabic intermediaries and made its first appearance in Western European literature in the thirteenth century.[2] It is probably best known from Chaucer's fourteenth-century "Pardoner's Tale" that inspired numerous discussions of corresponding versions.[3] Albeit mainly a phenomenon of learned literature, the tale was also documented from oral tradition virtually all over Europe, including versions transmitted by European tradition in Latin America.[4]

A Lithuanian version collected in 1889 from the oral performance of Tadeusz Digajtis from the village of Aleksandria in the district of Rosień frames the core plot with the story of a saintly hermit who equates money with death and is proved correct by the turn of events.[5]

> In the woods, a hermit finds a casket full of money. He shakes it and shouts, "I have found death! I have found death!" Twelve robbers in the vicinity happen to notice this and say to themselves, "What did the hermit find?" As soon as the hermit has left, they go to that place and find money. So they say, "The hermit is a fool. He found money and shouted that he had found death!"
>
> Then they bring the money to their hut in the woods. They decide that six of them should stay at home and six should go to town to fetch liquor. Those who go to town decide, "One ought to take along a bottle of poison so as to poison those who stayed at home, so the money will belong to us!"

But those who stay behind decide, "Let us load our rifles, and every one of us will shoot one of those who will come back from town." This they do. They shoot the returning party and take the liquor from the dead bodies.

When they place the bottle on the table and drink the poisoned liquor, all of them die. So the money is left as before, and when the hermit again walks in the woods, he finds six dead robbers out in the open, and then another six in the hut lying at the side of the casket standing on the table. So the hermit says, "Death it was! And death stayed!"

A Croatian version from Bukovica in Dalmatia tells essentially the same tale about three people, additionally attributing the events to the days of Jesus Christ.[6]

Three travelers go into the world. Traveling around, they find a large piece of gold and carry it one after the other, finding pleasure in looking at it. As they travel, they get hungry, and as they have no food with them, they decide that one of them should go to town to buy bread and bring it back. So one of them goes, and two stay behind to watch the gold. The one who goes to buy bread decides to poison the bread so that the other two will be killed and the gold will remain for him alone. After he has gone to fetch the bread, the two others agree to kill their partner as soon as he returns with the bread, and divide the gold between themselves. That one buys the bread, puts the poison inside and brings it for his companions. Even before starting to eat, they jump up and kill him. Then they eat all of the bread. But the poison starts to cause pain, and they die within a short while. And so all of them remain lying dead with the gold.

At this moment, Christ comes by, finding the piece of gold and around it the three dead men. Being God, he knows all about what had happened. He gives orders to throw the gold into an abyss so that no further people will be killed or lose their senses because of it. And he tells everyone that it is an evil to fall in love with money and wealth.

A version collected from oral tradition in Brazil likewise mentions three treasure finders, fleshing the story out with additional details.[7]

As three robbers are waiting under a tree for the rain to stop, one of them notices the corner of a casket showing from beneath the ground. Quickly they dig it out and pull out a vessel full of gold coins. They are mad with joy. "Let us divide it into three equal parts," says one of them. Another one says, "I want the largest part, because I discovered it!" After an intense discussion they agree on a just division. The eldest of them declares that the youngest had better go and fetch a good workhorse with two baskets and two bags, so as to transport the gold. Soon after, the third one reminds them of their hunger, saying the lad should bring something to eat. They give him money, and the lad goes away.

Then the two of them agree to kill the third one and to divide his share between them. When the lad returns with the animal, they attack their companion and kill him, stabbing him with their knives.—"Let us fill the vessels immediately!"—As soon as one of the (two remaining) robbers bends down to take money from the casket, his companion stabs him in the back with his knife, killing him instantly. He keeps all the money for himself.

Now the remaining robber is tired and hungry. He goes and takes out the roasted meat, flour, sugar, with a bottle of wine. The robber eats and drinks. As soon as he swallows the food, his vision gets blurred, he becomes dizzy and falls dead. The youngest robber had poisoned the drink, so as to have the money for himself.

Because of their greed, none of them was able to enjoy the gold in the casket.

The three quoted texts serve to demonstrate that the tale is defined through a core plot that can be fleshed out in different ways. These variations include different specifications for the treasure, the way in which it is found, the number of people who find it, and the ways in which the two groups of people kill one another. In addition, some versions are framed by the commentary of a saintly person, while others are not.[8] Details such as these help to identify strands of tradition that served to disseminate the tale, first in learned, and then in popular tradition. As this task is beyond the scope of the present condensed discussion, short indications of details will have to suffice.

The tale makes its first appearance in Western European literature in the Italian *Novellino*, also known as *Cento novelle antiche* (A Hundred Old Novellas), compiled toward the end of the thirteenth century.[9] As the tales included in the collection's editions vary to a certain extent, there are two slightly different versions of the present tale.[10] In the first edition, dated 1525, the tale is embedded in a core plot in which Christ admonishes his disciples when they find a "quantity of gold piastres." In the embedded tale, the money is found by two people, and the messenger poisons the bread.[11] In a later edition, dated 1572, a hermit fleeing from a cave in which he found "much gold" encounters "three ruffians," and the messenger poisons both food and drink. Next in chronological sequence come two relatively short texts, one in the anonymous French compilation of *exempla* compiled around 1320 that for want of an existing title is commonly known as *Ci nous dit* (Thus We Were Told; four men, bread),[12] and the other in a collection of sermons attributed to the fourteenth-century Dominican preacher John Bromyard (hermit, three companions, food).[13] Contemporary with Chaucer's version (hermit and three companions) are the Portuguese version in Fra Hermenegildo de Tancos's *Orto do esposo* (four robbers find a treasure in Rome)[14] and in the sermons of the Catalan preacher San Vicente Ferrer (1350–1419; hermit and three robbers).[15] Versions from the sixteenth and seventeenth centuries include Italian novelist Girolamo Morlini's (magician learns of treasure in

Rome, unspecified number of companions)[16] and German author Hans Sachs's poem *Der Dot im Stock* (Death in the Staff; hermit and three companions).[17] As for the modern literary versions, those included in Rudyard Kipling's *The Second Jungle Book* (1895)[18] and in B. Traven's *Der Schatz der Sierra Madre* (The Treasure of the Sierra Madre; 1927)[19] deserve particular mention.

The tale's ultimate origin in Indian Buddhist tradition has been explored since the end of the nineteenth century.[20] The *Vedabbha Jātaka* forms part of the collection of tales relating to the Buddha's previous existences, the *Jātakas*, whose earliest items date from the third or second century BCE.[21] It tells of several hundred treasure-finders murdering one another until only two of them are left. One of them kills his returning companion and is then killed by eating the poisoned rice the other brought back from the village. Similarly framed by a reference to the Buddha and his disciples, a shorter version mentioning three treasure-finders is later encountered in the Chinese translation of the Buddhist canon, the *Tripiṭaka* (Three Baskets).[22] Although it is impossible to identify the exact way in which the tale was transmitted to the West, Arabic versions are more than likely to have acted as intermediaries.

A legend written in Aljamiado (Spanish in Arabic script) includes the tale at the end of a lengthy sequence of events in which Jesus performs various miracles aiming to convince his traveling companion to confess that he secretly ate one of the three breads they had as their joint provisions.[23] Essentially, this part is a version of tale type ATU 785: *Lamb's Heart* (see essay ***20, Greed Makes the Cheater Admit His Misdemeanor***).[24] In the end, Jesus divides a treasure into three parts: one for himself, one for his companion, and the third part for the one who ate the bread. Finally, his companion confesses to having eaten the bread. Soon after, the companion is killed by three robbers who, in turn, kill one another in the usual manner. The Aljamiado legend has a direct precursor in the identical version included in the mirror for princes *Sirāj al-mulūk* (The Lamp of the Rulers), compiled by Spanish Arabic author Abū Bakr Muḥammad ibn al-Walīd al-Ṭarṭūshī (d. 1131).[25]

The oldest-known Arabic version that stands at the beginning of a continuous and extensively documented tradition is contained in the commentary on the Koran (*tafsīr*) compiled by Abū Jaʿfar Muḥammad ibn Jarīr al-Ṭabarī (d. 923).[26] The version given by al-Ṭabarī is attributed to the well-known interpreter of the Koran, Ismāʿīl ibn ʿAbd al-Raḥmān al-Suddī (d. 744).

> The tale starts with Jesus performing miracles. Although Jesus warns against negative consequences, following his prayer the water in the pots is transformed into meat, broth, and bread, and that in the jugs into wine. Again warning against undesired effects, Jesus resuscitates the king's dead son.
>
> Traveling together, Jesus and his mother are joined by a Jew. Jesus suggests they share their provisions, but when the Jew sees that Jesus only has one loaf of bread compared to his two, he repents and secretly eats one

> of them. As he denies ever having possessed a second loaf of bread, Jesus performs several miracles so as to make him confess his deed. Finally, they pass a treasure that was dug up by wild animals. Although the Jew wants to take the treasure, Jesus warns him about its evil effect.
>
> As four men come by, they send two of their group to fetch food and drink as well as a mule to carry the treasure. The two messengers poison the food, while the two men who stay behind decide to kill the messengers on their return. At the end, all four men are dead.
>
> At this point, Jesus divides the treasure into three equal shares, announcing one share to be for himself, one for his companion, and the third share for the one who ate the third bread. Now the Jew confesses to having eaten the bread and takes his two shares of the treasure. As he leaves, he is swallowed by the Earth.

Similar versions, with or without the longer context, and otherwise only differing in only minor details, are given, in chronological order, in al-Thaʿlabī's (d. 1035) *Qiṣaṣ al-anbiyāʾ* (Tales of the Prophets),[27] where the tale is presented as being told by "the famous old Islamic traditional storyteller and folklorist"[28] Wahb ibn Munabbih (d. 728 or 732), in Abū Ṭālib al-Makkī's (d. 996) *Qūt al-qulūb* (The Hearts' Nourishment),[29] in several (Arabic and Persian) works of the polymath al-Ghazzālī (d. 1111),[30] including his monumental *Iḥyāʾ ʿulūm al-dīn* (The Revival of the Religious Sciences),[31] in Saʿd al-Din Varāvini's thirteenth-century redaction of the Persian mirror for princes *Marzbān-nāme*[32] and its fifteenth-century Arabic adaptation *Fākihat al-khulafāʾ* (Fruits of the Caliphs) by Ibn ʿArabshāh,[33] in Persian poet Farid al-Din ʿAṭṭār's (d. 1221) *Moṣibat-nāme*,[34] in Arab historian Ibn Ṣaṣrā's late fourteenth-century chronicle of Damascus,[35] in al-Yāfiʿī's (d. 1367) *Rawḍ al-rayāḥīn fī ḥikāyāt al-ṣāliḥīn* (Garden of the Spirited People: Tales of the Righteous),[36] in al-Damīrī's (d. 1405) zoographical encyclopedia *Ḥayāt al-ḥayawān* (The Lives of Animals),[37] in al-Ibshīhī's widely read fifteenth-century encyclopedia of useful knowledge,[38] in ʿAbd al-Raḥmān al-Saffūrī's entertaining compilation *Nuzhat al-majālis wa-muntakhab al-nafāʾis* (Entertainment of the Learned Gatherings and Choice of Precious Anecdotes"), compiled in 1479,[39] and in Persian historian Mirkhond's fifteenth-century world history *Rowżat al-ṣafā* (The Garden of Purity).[40] Embedded in the narrative cycle of "King Shāh Bakht and His Vizier al-Raḥwān," there is also a version of the tale in *The Thousand and One Nights*.[41] The tale's wide dissemination in literature also gave rise to retellings and adaptations in modern Arabic oral tradition.[42] A short version of the tale's form in Muslim tradition, featuring Jesus in the frame tale, appeared in Antoine Galland's *Paroles remarquables* (1697),[43] albeit without having any noticeable impact on subsequent oral tradition in Europe.

The tale's continuous tradition in Arabic compilations from the tenth century onward, and particularly its quotation in the work of the Spanish Arabic author al-Ṭarṭūshī, leave little doubt that Arabic literature is responsible for mediating the Buddhist narrative to the West. In the Muslim world, the Buddhist moral tale was adapted as an apocryphal legend of Jesus, a character who in Muslim religion contrary to Christianity is not regarded as the son of God, even though he is venerated as a highly esteemed prophet. At any rate, there is no need to presume the tale to originate from "the folk tradition of the early Christian Arabs."[44] Although the above-quoted version from Croatia betrays a certain proximity to Muslim tradition in attributing the tale to the times of Jesus, most Christian versions opted to condense the lengthy framing narrative into a focused warning or to delete it altogether, instead replacing Jesus as an admonisher against mundane possessions with an anonymous hermit serving the same role.

Notes

1. Tawney, C.H., "The Buddhist Original of Chaucer's Pardoner's Tale," *The Journal of Philology* 12 (1883), pp. 203–208.

2. Ulrich, Jakob, transl., *Die hundert alten Erzählungen*, Leipzig: Deutsche Verlags-Actiengesellschaft, 1905, pp. 83–84, no. 83.

3. Chaucer, Geoffrey, *The Complete Poetry and Prose*, ed. John H. Fischer, New York: Holt, Reinhart & Winston, 1977, pp. 221–231; Clouston, William Alexander, *Popular Tales and Fictions: Their Migrations and Transformations*, ed. Christine Goldberg, Santa Barbara, CA: ABC-Clio, 2002, pp. 490–511; Canby, Henry Seidel, "Some Comments on the Sources of Chaucer's 'Pardoner's Tale'," *Modern Philology* 2 (1904–1905), pp. 477–487; Werner, A., "Chaucer's Pardoner's Tale: African Analogue," *Notes and Queries* 11.4 (1911), pp. 82–83; Hart, Walter Morris, "The 'Pardoner's Tale' and 'Der Dot im Stock,' *Modern Philology* 9 (1911–1912), pp. 17–22; Wells, Whitney, "A New Analogue to the Pardoner's Tale," *Modern Language Notes* 40.1 (1925), pp. 58–59; Wells, "An Unnoted Analogue to the 'Pardoner's Tale'," *Modern Philology* 25.2 (1927), pp. 163–164; Kirby, Thomas A., "'The Pardoner's Tale' and 'The Treasure of the Sierra Madre'," *Modern Language Notes* 66 (1951), pp. 269–270; Tupper, Frederick, "The Pardoner's Tale," in *Sources and Analogues of Chaucer's Canterbury Tales*, ed. William Frank Bryan and Germaine Dempster, 2nd ed., London: Routledge & Kegan Paul, 1958, pp. 415–438; Hamer, Douglas, "'The Pardoner's Tale:' A West-African Analogue," *Notes and Queries* 214 (1969), pp. 335–336; Dias-Ferreira, Julia, "Another Portuguese Analogue of Chaucer's 'Pardoner's Tale'," *The Chaucer Review* 11 (1977), pp. 258–260; McKenna, Connan, "The Irish Analogues to Chaucer's *Pardoner's Tale*," *Béaloideas* 45–47 (1977–1979), pp. 63–77; Hamel, Mary, and Charles Merrill, "The Analogues of the *Pardoner's Tale* and a New African Version," *The Chaucer Review* 26 (1991), pp. 175–183; Wenzel, Siegfried, "Another Analogue to *The Pardoner's Tale*," *Notes and Queries* 241 (1996), pp. 134–136.

4. Marzolph, Ulrich, "Schatzfinder morden einander," in *Enzyklopädie des Märchens*, vol. 11 (2004), cols. 1282–1290.

5. Dowojna-Sylwestrowicz, Mieczysław, *Podania żmujdzkie*, vol. 1, Warsaw: Arct, 1894, pp. 52–53.

6. Ardalić, Vladimir, "Narodne pripovijetke (Bukovica u Dalmaciji)," *Zbornik za narodni život i običaje Južnih Slavena* 19 (1914), pp. 350–357, at p. 357, no. 7.

7. Cascudo, Luis da Câmara, *Trinta "estorias" brasileiras*, Lisbon: Portucalense, 1955, pp. 78–79.

8. Hamel and Merrill, "The Analogues of the *Pardoner's Tale*."

9. Rossi, Luciano, "Novellino," in *Enzyklopädie des Märchens*, vol. 10 (2002), cols. 129–134.

10. For the following see Clouston, *Popular Tales and Fictions*, pp. 381–385; Tupper, "The Pardoner's Tale," pp. 416–418.

11. Conte, Alberto, ed., *Il Novellino*, Rome: Salerno, 2001, pp. 139–141, 375–376, no. 83.

12. Blangez, Gérard, ed., *Ci nous dit: recueil d'exemples moraux*, Paris: Société des anciens textes français, 1979, vol. 1, p. 164, no. 160.

13. Wenzel, "Another Analogue."

14. Clouston, *Popular Tales and Fictions*, p. 388; Williams, Frederick G., "Chaucer's The Pardoner's Tale and The Tale of the Four Thieves from Portugal's Orto do esposo compared," *Bulletin des études portugaises et brésiliennes* 44–45 (1983–1985), pp. 93–107; Pedrosa, José Manuel, "Más reescrituras del cuento de El tesoro fatal (AT 763): del Orto do esposo, Vicente Ferrer y Hans Sachs a eça de Queiroz, William Faulkner y Max Aub," *Revista de poética medieval* 5 (2000), pp. 27–43, at 29–30.

15. Sant Vicent Ferrer, *Sermons*, ed. Gret Schib, vol. 3, Barcelona: Barcino, 1975, pp. 294–295; Pedrosa, "Más reescrituras," pp. 30–31; Lacarra, María Jesús, *Cuento y novela corta en España*, Barcelona: Crítica, 1999, pp. 241–243.

16. Clouston, *Popular Tales and Fictions*, p. 389; see also Ruiz Sánchez, Marcos, "Versiones latinas de la historia del tesoro maldito," *Cuadernos de Filología Clásica: Estudios Latinos* 34.2 (2014), pp. 241–265.

17. Hart, "The 'Pardoner's Tale'."

18. Erickson, Jon, "Chaucer's *Pardoner's Tale* as Anti-Märchen," *Folklore* 94.2 (1983), pp. 235–239, at p. 237–238.

19. Kirby, "'The Pardoner's Tale'."

20. Tawney, "The Buddhist Original"; Clouston, *Popular Tales and Fictions*, pp. 400–404; Canby, "Some Comments," p. 477.

21. Laut, Jens Peter, "Jātaka," in *Enzyklopädie des Märchens*, vol. 7 (1993), cols. 500–507.

22. Hinüber, Oskar von, "Tripiṭaka," ibid., vol. 13 (2010), cols. 933–940; Chavannes, Édouard, *Cinq cents contes et apologues extraits du Tripitaka chinois*, Paris: Ernest Leroux, 1910–1935 (reprint Paris: Maisonneuve, 1962), vol. 1, pp. 386–387, no. 115.

23. Grünbaum, Max, *Neue Beiträge zur semitischen Sagenkunde*, Leiden: Brill, 1893, pp. 280–282; Fradejas Lebrero, José, "El tesoro fatal," in *Homenaje a Álvaro Galmés de Fuentes*, vol. 3, Madrid: Universidad de Oviedo-Gredos, 1987, pp. 471–483.

24. Schwarzbaum, Haim, "A Jewish Moses Legend of Islamic Provenance," in *Fields of Offerings: Studies in Honor of Raphael Patai*, ed. Victor D. Sanua, London and Toronto: Associated University Presses, 1983, pp. 99–110.

25. Fradejas Lebrero, "El tesoro fatal," pp. 476–477, quoting from the Spanish translation Abubéquer de Tortosa, *Lámpara de príncipes*, transl. M. Alarcón, Madrid: Instituto de Valencia de Don Juan, 1930, vol. 1, pp. 49–51; Ṭarṭūshī, Muḥammad ibn al-Walīd al-, *Sirāj al-mulūk*, ed. Jaʿfar al-Bayātī, London: Riad el-Rayyes, 1990, p. 79–80; Asin et Palacios, Michaël, "Logia et agraphia domini Jesu apud moslemicos scriptores," in Graffin, René, and François Nau, eds., *Patrologia orientalis*, vol. 13, Paris: Firmin-Didot et Co., 1919, pp. 385–386, no. 54bis.

26. Ṭabarī, Abū Jaʿfar Muḥammad ibn Jarīr al-, *Tafsīr Ṭabarī: Jāmiʿ al-bayān ʿan taʾwīl āy al-Qurʾān*, ed. Maḥmūd Muḥammad Shākir and Aḥmad Muḥammad Shākir, vol.

6, Cairo: Dār al-Ma'ārif bi-Miṣr, 1971, pp. 444–448, no. 7122; Spies, Otto, "Das Grimmsche Märchen 'Bruder Lustig'" in arabischer Überlieferung," *Rheinisches Jahrbuch für Volkskunde* 2 (1951), pp. 48–60; Schwarzbaum, "A Jewish Moses Legend," pp. 100–101.

27. Spies, "Das Grimmsche Märchen 'Bruder Lustig'," pp. 54–55; Schwarzbaum, "A Jewish Moses Legend," pp. 99–100; Tha'labī, Abū Isḥāq Aḥmad ibn Muḥammad ibn Ibrāhīm al-, *'Arā'is al-majālis fī qiṣaṣ al-anbiyā'*, transl. William M. Brinner, Leiden etc., Brill, 2002, pp. 661–663.

28. Schwarzbaum, "A Jewish Moses Legend," p. 99.

29. Asin et Palacios, "Logia et agraphia," pp. 387–388, no. 54[quater]; Abū Ṭālib al-Makkī, *Die Nahrung der Herzen: Abū Ṭālib al-Makkīs Qūt al-qulūb*, transl. Richard Gramlich, vol. 2, Stuttgart: Steiner, 1994, pp. 242–243, no. 365.

30. See Marzolph, "Schatzfinder morden einander," col. 1283. See *Ghazālī's Book Counsel for Kings (Naṣīḥat al-mulūk)*, transl. F.R.C. Bagley, London: Oxford University Press, 1964, p. 38.

31. Ghazzālī, Abū Ḥāmid Muḥammad al-, *Iḥyā' 'ulūm al-dīn*, vol. 3, Cairo: al-Kutub al-'arabiyya al-kubrā, s.a., p. 236 (at the end of book 27); Asin et Palacios, "Logia et agraphia," pp. 383–385, 386–387, no. 54, 54[ter]; Schwarzbaum, "A Jewish Moses Legend," p. 108, note 23.

32. Varāvini, Sa'd al-Din, *Marzbān-nāme*, ed. Khalil Khaṭib Rahbar, 2nd ed., Tehran: Ṣafi 'Alishāh, 1366/1987, pp. 195–196 (ch. 3); Ṣan'atiniyā, Fāṭeme, *Ma'ākheẕ-e qeṣaṣ va tamṡilāt-e maṡnavihā-ye 'Aṭṭār-e Neishāburi*, Tehran: Zavvār, 1369/1990, pp. 195–196.

33. Chauvin, *Bibliographie*, vol. 2 (1897), p. 194, no. 18; vol. 8 (1904), pp. 100–101, no. 73.

34. Rückert, Friedrich, "Eine persische Erzählung," *Zeitschrift der Deutschen Morgenländischen Gesellschaft* 14 (1860), pp. 280–287; Clouston, *Popular Tales and Fictions*, pp. 499–502; Ritter, Hellmut, *The Ocean of the Soul: Man, the World and God in the Stories of Farīd al-Dīn 'Aṭṭār*, transl. John O'Kane, Leiden: Brill, 2003, pp. 95–96; ; Ṣan'atiniyā, *Ma'ākheẕ*, pp. 194–195:

35. Ibn Ṣaṣrā, Muḥammad ibn Muḥammad, *A Chronicle of Damascus 1389–1397*, transl. William M. Brinner, Berkeley and Los Angeles: University of California Press, 1963, p. 276.

36. Yāfi'ī al-Yamanī, Abū Muḥammad 'Abdallāh ibn As'ad al-, *Rawḍ al-rayāḥīn fī ḥikāyāt al-ṣāliḥīn*, Cairo: Aḥmad al-Bābī al-Ḥalabī, 1307/1889, p. 149, no. 322; Ritter, *The Ocean of the Soul*, p. 96.

37. Damīrī, Kamāl al-Dīn al-, *Ḥayāt al-ḥayawān al-kubrā*, vol. 2, s.l.: al-Maktaba al-islāmiyya, s.a., pp. 292–293; *Al-Damīrī's Ḥayāt al-Ḥayawān (A Zoological Lexicon)*, transl. A.S.G. Jayakar, vol. 1, London: Luzac, 1906, p. 676.

38. Ibshīhī, Shihāb al-Dīn Muḥammad ibn Aḥmad Abī al-Fatḥ al-, *al-Mustaṭraf fī kull fann mustaẓraf*, ed. Mufīd Qumayḥa, vol. 2, Beirut: Dār al-Kutub al-'ilmiyya, 1403/1983, pp. 606–607; Ibshīhī, al-, *Al-Mostaṭraf: recueil de morceaux choisis çà et là*, transl. Gustav Rat, vol. 2, Paris: Leroux, 1899, p. 792; Basset, *Mille et un contes*, vol. 2, pp. 302–305, no. 112.

39. See the reference in Ritter, *The Ocean of the Soul*, p. 96.

40. Mirkhond, Muhammad Bin Khâvendshâh Bin Mahmûd, *The Rauzat-us-safa; or, Garden of Purity, Containing the Histories of Prophets, Kings, and Khalifs*, transl. E. Rehatsek, ed. F.F. Arbuthnot, vol. 1, part 2, London: Royal Asiatic Society, 1892, pp. 173–175.

41. Chauvin, *Bibliographie*, vol. 8 (1904), p. 100–101, no. 73; Marzolph and van Leeuwen, *The Arabian Nights Encyclopedia*, vol. 1, pp. 415–416, no. 299.

42. El-Shamy, *Types*, pp. 426–427, no. 763.

43. Marzolph, Ulrich, "The Literary Genre of 'Oriental Miscellany'," in Bauden, Frédéric, Aboubakr Chraïbi, and Antonella Ghersetti, eds., *Le Répertoire narratif arabe médiéval: transmission et ouverture, Actes du colloque international, Université de Liège 15-17 septembre 2005*, Geneva: Droz, 2008, pp. 309–319, at pp. 314–315.

44. Ritter, *The Ocean of the Soul*, p. 96.

CHAPTER 20

Greed Makes the Cheater Admit His Misdemeanor (ATU 785)

In order to convey their message, religious legends sometimes employ the dichotomy between a wise, patient, and sympathetic teacher, and a second, morally deficient, character. The latter's moral deficiencies propel the action and eventually culminate in a timeless instruction addressed at the tale's audience. In Christian contexts, the two characters are often Jesus Christ and Saint Peter.[1] The tale classified as international tale type ATU 785: *Lamb's Heart* is a case in point.[2] Its basic structure is as follows.

> The companion of a saintly character clandestinely eats part of the available food. Asked where the missing part of the food is, he denies having eaten it, instead claiming that the missing part never existed. The saint offers his companion various occasions to admit his misdemeanor by performing miracles, but the companion does not give in. Often, this includes the latter's rescue after an unsuccessful attempt to imitate a resuscitation effected by the saint, an episode that is classified separately as tale type ATU 753A: *Unsuccessful Resuscitation*. In the end, the saint offers to divide a certain amount of money between them. One share is to be for himself, one for his companion, and the third share for the one who ate the missing food. At this point, greed drives the companion to confess.

The legend was recorded from nineteenth- and twentieth-century oral tradition all over the Western (Christian) world in hundreds of versions. Most often specifying the missing food as the heart (or liver) of a lamb the saintly character had asked his companion to prepare, the available texts range from short factual summaries of as little as a hundred words to extensively detailed versions that are at times combined or continued with additional episodes. An example for an extremely short version is the German dialect text told by Josef Salter, Sr.[3] The narrator said he learned the tale from his mother who had been living in the forest regions of Bohemia, today in the Western Czech Republic. The text was recorded in Lollar, as small town in the district of Gießen in Hesse, Germany, on November 1, 1952. It adds an additional character to make a total of three and collates the food and the money into a single item.

> Saint Peter and "our Lord" (*unser Herrgott*) travel on earth in the company of a certain man. Having slaughtered a sheep, they grill it on a spit. As Saint Peter and God go to sleep, they ask their companion to take good care of the roast. When the next day God divides the roast, he notices that the liver is missing. The companion denies having eaten it, instead claiming that the animal did not have a liver. God divides the food into four portions, one for each of them, and the fourth share for the one who ate the liver. At this point, their companion confesses.

The tale's oldest documented Flemish version, recorded in 1888 by Alfons de Cock in Dendereleeuw in the Belgian province of East Flanders, has the action take place between God and a certain cobbler.[4]

> A cobbler joins God in his travels on earth, accepting the condition that he will only eat or sleep when God does so. When God finally gives him money to buy and roast a sheep, the cobbler has grown so hungry that he eats the animal's heart, but later denies having done so. As they have no money when they reach the next town, God decides to do what he can do best. He resuscitates the princess by boiling the dead body and bringing it back to life with a stroke of his staff. Since God does not accept any compensation, the cobbler wants to make money by imitating the action. In the next town, the cobbler tries to resuscitate the recently deceased king. As his attempt is unsuccessful, the enraged people want to hang him, and God arrives just in time to save him and resuscitate the king himself. Having now received a generous compensation, they travel on. While God walks on the water, the cobbler does not admit his fault, although he is about to drown. When God finally suggests they divide their spoils, making three shares, the cobbler admits having eaten the sheep's heart. The tale ends on a happy note with the cobbler returning home during the annual fair. "And if they have not stopped making pancakes, they will still be doing so."

About a hundred different versions of the tale were recorded from Lithuanian oral tradition. The version recorded by B. Buinevičius from the oral performance of J. Zdanavičienė in Kėdainiai introduces three poor brothers, one of whom decides to leave and go begging. On the way, he meets God disguised as an old man.[5] At night, they first share the beggar's two loaves of bread between them. But when God sleeps, the beggar steals God's two loaves and eats them, the next morning denying having done so. Although God tries to make him confess by working miracles such as walking on water and passing through fire unharmed, the man does not give in. When they divide the money God has received for resuscitating the recently deceased daughter of a certain squire, the beggar finally admits his misdemeanor so as to receive the additional share. The tale ends with God admonishing the beggar not to steal or at least to admit when he has stolen. Following this, their ways part.

In the Hungarian version narrated by Josef Janzsó, aged 37, from Schachendorf in the district of Oberwart in Burgenland, South-East Austria, Jesus Christ and Saint Peter hire a peasant to carry their luggage when traveling on earth.[6] At night, the peasant secretly eats the heart of the goose they are roasting. Even though he is twice about to be killed, once when falsely accused of stealing and once when trying to walk on water as Jesus and Saint Peter do, the peasant does not admit having eaten the heart. Only when Jesus suggests to divide the money Saint Peter carries does the peasant confess, claiming the share of the one who has eaten the bird's heart.

In March 1991, folklorist Gianni Gugliotta recorded an Italian version from the peasant Giovanni Abbate, aged 83, in Grazzanise in the province of Caserta in Campagna region.[7] Here, Saint Peter denies having eaten the liver of the lamb that Jesus Christ had explicitly requested be kept for him, pretending that the lamb did not have a liver. Although Saint Peter is about to drown when attempting to cross the water as Jesus Christ does, he does not confess. Only when they divide the money they received for Jesus Christ's resuscitation of the princess does Saint Peter admit having eaten the liver. Saint Peter's unsuccessful attempt at resuscitating another princess follows, and Jesus Christ arrives just in time to save him from being executed.

In Germany and beyond, the tale was popularized by its inclusion in the second edition of the *Kinder- und Hausmärchen* (Children's and Household Tales) published by the brothers Grimm at the beginning of the nineteenth century. The Grimms followed a version that had been recorded by the librarian Georg Passy from the performance of an old woman in Vienna.[8] Here, the events take place between a former soldier and Saint Peter traveling on earth disguised as a beggar. The tale includes the eaten lamb's heart, the walking on water, and a compensation for the resuscitation of the princess. The soldier's unsuccessful imitation of the resuscitation follows the dividing of the money.

The tale's oldest-known European version is contained in the Italian *Novellino*, also known as *Cento novelle antiche* (A Hundred Old Novellas), a collection of tales compiled by an as yet unidentified author at the end of the thirteenth century.[9] In this version, God while traveling on earth joins a certain jester (*giullare*). While God earns money by resuscitating a dead person, the jester joins a wedding and eats his fill. From the money God earned they buy a small buck and prepare it for the two of them. Clandestinely, the jester eats the buck's kidneys, later pretending that in this country bucks do not have kidneys. God then instructs the jester how to successfully resuscitate a dead person and sends him to do so. The dead boy's father, however, thinks that the jester is mocking him in his grief and wants to have him hanged. God arrives just in time to save the jester. Although the jester faces death, he does not want to admit that he ate the kidneys. Only when God suggests dividing the money between them does the jester confess. The tale ends with the insight that money makes people confess deeds they would not have confessed even though they might be facing death.

The vast majority of the tale's versions documented from European written or oral tradition specify the missing food as an inner organ (heart, kidney, liver) of an animal (sheep, buck, goose), only rarely mentioning pieces or loaves of bread.[10] Contrasting with this, bread is the standard disputed item in the tale's versions in the Arabic and Persian literary traditions that otherwise essentially share the same structure.

The tale's oldest version documented so far dates from the end of the ninth or the beginning of the tenth century. It is cited in the commentary on the Koran (*tafsīr*) compiled by Abū Jaʿfar Muḥammad ibn Jarīr al-Ṭabarī (d. 923),[11] serving to interpret the context of the Koranic verse 3:52, where Jesus wonders who is going to assist him on his way to God. Al-Ṭabarī's version is attributed to the well-known interpreter of the Koran, Ismāʿīl ibn ʿAbd al-Raḥmān al-Suddī (d. 744). It presents a highly complex and winding narrative that begins with Jesus and his mother being driven forth from their home.[12]

> Jesus and his mother find shelter with a certain man in a country that is ruled by an oppressive king. When it is their host's turn to feed the king's soldiers for a day, Jesus helps him reluctantly, warning that his action might result in negative consequences. Even so, he asks God to change the water in the pots to meat, broth, and bread, and the water in the jugs to wine. When the king becomes aware of the miracle, he requests Jesus to resuscitate his recently deceased son. Although Jesus again warns him about the possible negative consequences, he insists, and the son is resuscitated through Jesus's intervention. When the people of the country realize that the son of their oppressive king is alive, they start a rebellion. Jesus and his mother leave the country.
>
> They travel on in the company of a Jew. Jesus suggests they share their provisions, but when the Jew sees that Jesus only has one loaf of bread compared to his two loaves, he secretly eats one of them. The next day he denies ever having possessed an additional loaf. The following days, Jesus performs several miracles so as to make the Jew admit his misdemeanor, each time asking him how many loaves of bread he actually possessed. First, Jesus resuscitates a sheep they ate without breaking the bones. Then he repeats the action with a calf. As the Jew imagines that the act of resuscitation is linked to a staff Jesus uses, he takes a similar stick and decides to imitate the action. In the next village he hits the sick king with his stick until the king dies and then tries to resuscitate him by beating him again. Seeing this, the people decide to crucify the man, and Jesus arrives just in time to save him and resuscitate the king. Even after this adventure, the

Jew does not want to admit that he originally possessed a second loaf of bread.

The following episode corresponds to tale type ATU 763: *The Treasure Findes Who Murder One Another* (see essay **19, *The Treasure Finders Murder One Another***). When all of the four treasure finders are dead, Jesus and the Jew return to the place where they had found the treasure, and Jesus decides to divide it between them, making three shares. Finally, the Jew admits having eaten the additional bread and receives the third share. But as he walks away he is swallowed by the Earth.

The version given in al-Thaʿlabī's (d. 1035) book of tales of the prophets (*qiṣaṣ al-anbiyāʾ*) differs in various details.[13] Jesus travels without his mother. The Jew eats his second loaf of bread while Jesus performs his prayers. Jesus performs miracles by making a blind man see again, restoring a cripple to good health, walking on water, and resuscitating an antelope and a calf. After the Jew's unsuccessful attempt at resuscitation, they reach a large ruined town where they find three gold ingots that Jesus suggests they divide between them. Since the treasure is too heavy to carry, they leave it there. Three treasure finders murder one another, and eventually Jesus and the Jew return to the place. Jesus resuscitates the treasure finders. As they do not yearn for the treasure any more, Jesus allows the Jew to take the treasure for himself. But "when the Jew went to carry it, the Earth swallowed him up and Jesus departed."

In al-Ghazzālī's (d. 1111) *Iḥyāʾ ʿulūm al-dīn* (The Revival of the Religious Sciences), the tale is again told with different details.[14] The religion of the man with whom Jesus travels is not specified. Together the two companions have three loaves of bread. Having eaten a loaf each, Jesus goes to the river to drink. When he returns, his companion has eaten the third loaf but denies having done so. Next, Jesus resuscitates the young gazelle they had slaughtered and crosses a river together with his companion by walking on the water. Each time Jesus implores his companion, "by the one who made you witness this miracle," to tell him who ate the third loaf of bread, to no avail. Finally, Jesus works a miracle to transform earth into gold and divides the gold into three shares. Now the man admits having eaten the third loaf, and Jesus lets him have all of the gold. In the following, the companion meets two other men and the three men kill one another. When Jesus late returns to the place, he admonishes his disciples to beware of indulging in mundane pleasures. Ghazzālī's version is retold in al-Yāfiʿī's (d. 1367) collection of educative stories *Rawḍ al-rayāḥīn fī ḥikāyāt al-ṣāliḥīn* (Garden of the Spiritual: Tales of the Righteous) without the miraculous crossing of the river.[15] Ghazzālī's text is quoted again without alterations in al-Damīrī's (d. 1405) zoographical encyclopedia *Ḥayāt al-ḥayawān* (The Lives of Animals) under the heading *al-khashaf*, a term denoting the offspring of a gazelle.[16]

The Spanish Arabic author Abū Bakr Muḥammad ibn al-Walīd al-Ṭarṭūshī (d. 1131) presents an adapted abridgment of al-Ghazzālī's version in his mirror for princes *Sirāj al-mulūk* (The Lamp of the Rulers).[17] Here, Jesus sends his unspecified companion to the village to fetch three loaves of bread. As Jesus performs his prayers when the companion returns, the latter gets tired waiting for him and eats the third loaf, later pretending that he only brought two loaves. Following the resuscitation of the gazelle and the crossing of the river, they happen to find three gold ingots. When the companion departs with the gold he meets three men who kill him, following which the three men kill one another. In his fifteenth-century encyclopedia of all kinds of useful knowledge, Egyptian author al-Ibshīhī more or less renders the same version, albeit with two variations.[18] First, there is no resuscitation of the gazelle, Jesus instead asking his companion to admit his fault referring to a miracle that the gazelle followed Jesus's call to be slaughtered. And second, following this the author inserts another miracle, so far unmentioned. When they travel on, Jesus asks God to let somebody inform him about the fate of a certain village, and God has a brick speak to him. In Andalusia, al-Ṭarṭūshī's version is given with identical content in a legend written in Aljamiado (Spanish in Arabic script),[19] constituting an intermediary between Arabic and Western tradition.

In Persian, the mystical poet Farid al-Din ʿAṭṭār (d. 1221) retold the story in verse, with the content closely following Ghazzālī's version.[20] The only structural variation is that in ʿAṭṭār's version, the episodes of walking on water and of the resuscitation of the gazelle change places.

Like the tale of the treasure finders who murder one another, which is usually attached to the Arabic versions, the present tale appears to have originated in an apocryphal gospel or a kind of "Haggada enlargement of the life story of Jesus."[21] When, why, and by whom the bread of the Arabic versions was changed to the inner organ of an animal is not clear. A jocular tale attributed to the Arabic jester Juḥā in Ibn al-Jawzī's (d. 1201) *Akhbār al-Ḥamqā* (Tales of Stupid People) suggests that this change might already have taken place in Arabic literature, as it has a greedy person argue in a similar manner that the parts of meat he ate never existed.[22] In the tale concerned, Juḥā's father sends his son to fetch the boiled head of a sheep. Returning home, Juḥā starts nibbling at the head, eventually eating the eyes, ears, tongue, and brain. Asked where the missing parts are, he justifies himself by claiming that the sheep never had those parts, as it had been blind, deaf, dumb, and scabby. Since this tale later gained a powerful medium of dissemination by being integrated into the repertoire of the Turkish jester Nasreddin Hodja,[23] creative storytellers might have integrated the motif into the larger tale at some point, thus enhacing the tale's preposterous dimension.

Already by the beginning of the twelfth century, the anti-Jewish bias of the early Arabic versions was abandoned, enabling the tale's adaptation on an international level, although a similar bias was not alien to medieval and early modern European tradition. Given the overall point that lying is sinful and that greed constitutes a powerful motivation for morally unstable persons, the tale has a universal message. And finally, the fact that all of the early Arabic versions attach the tale of the treasure finders who murder one another as a final episode might not be irrelevant. Since the latter tale doubtlessly derives from ancient Indian precursors, the tale of the cheater who only admits his misdemeanor out of greed might also derive from earlier Indian models that are yet to be identified.

Notes

1. Neumann, Siegfried, "Petrusschwänke," in *Enzyklopädie des Märchens*, vol. 10 (2002), cols. 814–824.

2. Schmitt, Christoph, "Lammherz," ibid., vol. 8 (1996), cols. 743–747.

3. Benzel, Ulrich, *Volkserzählungen aus dem nördlichen Böhmerwald*, Marburg: Elwert, 1957, p. 58, no. 218.

4. Lox, Harlinda, *Flämische Märchen*, Munich: Diederichs, 1999, pp. 178–183, no. 38.

5. Range, Jochen D., *Litauische Volksmärchen*, Munich: Diederichs, 1981, pp. 178–180, no. 51.

6. Gaál, Károly, *Volksmärchen der Magyaren im südlichen Burgenland*, Berlin: De Gruyter, 1970, pp. 166–167, 229, no. 39.

7. DeSimone, Roberto, *Fiabe campane*, Torino: Einaudi, 1994, vol. 1, pp. 408–415, vol. 2, 1451, no. 33b.

8. Grimm, Jacob and Wilhelm, *Kinder- und Hausmärchen: Ausgabe letzter Hand mit den Originalanmerkungen der Brüder Grimm*, ed. Heinz Rölleke, Stuttgart: Philipp Reclam Jun., 1980, vol. 1, pp. 392–404, vol. 3, 141–143, no. 81; Bolte and Polívka, *Anmerkungen*, vol. 2, pp. 149–163, no. 81.

9. Jakob, Ulrich, transl., *Die hundert alten Erzählungen*, Leipzig: Deutsche Verlags-Actiengesellschaft, 1905, pp. 78–80, no. 75; Wesselski, Albert, *Italiänischer Volks- und Herrenwitz: Fazetien und Schwänke aus drei Jahrhunderten*, Munich: Georg Müller, 1912, pp. 3–5, 223–224; Wesselski, *Märchen des Mittelalters*, pp. 88–89, 218, no. 30; Keller, Walter, *Italienische Märchen*, Jena: Diederichs, 1929, pp. 15–17, no. 2; Conte, Alberto, ed., *Il Novellino*, Rome: Salerno, 2001, pp. 126–128, 368–370, no. 75.

10. Range, *Litauische Volksmärchen*, pp. 178–180, no. 51 (Lithuanian); Bolte and Polívka, *Anmerkungen*, pp. 150 (German), 156 (Polish, Russian), 157 (Belarusian).

11. Ṭabarī, Abū Jaʿfar Muḥammad ibn Jarīr al-, *Tafsīr Ṭabarī: Jāmiʿ al-bayān ʿan taʾwīl āy al-Qurʾān*, ed. Maḥmūd Muḥammad Shākir and Aḥmad Muḥammad Shākir, vol. 6, Cairo: Dār al-Maʿārif bi-Miṣr, 1971, pp. 444–448, no. 7122.

12. Spies, Otto, "Das Grimmsche Märchen 'Bruder Lustig' in arabischer Überlieferung," *Rheinisches Jahrbuch für Volkskunde* 2 (1951), pp. 48–60, at pp. 50–54.

13. Thaʿlabī, Abū Isḥāq Aḥmad ibn Muḥammad ibn Ibrāhīm al-, *ʿArāʾis al-majālis fī qiṣaṣ al-anbiyāʾ*, transl. William M. Brinner, Leiden etc., Brill, 2002, pp. 661–663; Clouston, William Alexander, *Popular Tales and Fictions: Their Migrations and Transformations*, ed. Christine Goldberg, Santa Barbara, CA: ABC-Clio, 2002, pp. 497–498; Spies, "Das Grimmsche Märchen 'Bruder Lustig'," pp. 54–55; Schwarzbaum, Haim, "A Jewish Moses Legend of Islamic Provenance," in *Fields of Offerings: Studies in Honor of Raphael Patai*, ed. Victor D. Sanua, London and Toronto: Associated University Presses, 1983, pp. 99–110, at pp. 99–100.

14. Ghazzālī, Abū Ḥāmid Muḥammad al-, *Iḥyāʾ ʿulūm al-dīn*, vol. 3, Cairo: al-Kutub al-ʿarabiyya al-kubrā, s.a., p. 236 (at the end of book 27); Schwarzbaum, "A Jewish Moses Legend," p. 108, note 23; Asin et Palacios, Michaël, "Logia et agraphia domini

Jesu apud moslemicos scriptores," in Graffin, René, and François Nau, eds., *Patrologia orientalis*, vol. 13, Paris: Firmin-Didot et Co., 1919, pp. 331–639.

15. Yāfiʿī al-Yamanī, Abū Muḥammad ʿAbdallāh ibn Asʿad al-, *Rawḍ al-rayāḥīn fī ḥikāyāt al-ṣāliḥīn*, Cairo: Aḥmad al-Bābī al-Ḥalabī, 1307/1889, p. 149, no. 322.

16. Damīrī, Kamāl al-Dīn, al-, *Ḥayāt al-ḥayawān al-kubrā*, vol. 2, s.l.: al-Maktaba al-islāmiyya, s.a., pp. 292–293; *Al-Damīrī's Ḥayāt al-Ḥayawān (A Zoological Lexicon)*, transl. A.S.G. Jayakar, vol. 1, London: Luzac, 1906, p. 676.

17. Ṭarṭūshī, Muḥammad ibn al-Walīd al-, *Sirāj al-mulūk*, ed. Jaʿfar al-Bayātī, London: Riad el-Rayyes, 1990, pp. 79–80; Abubéquer de Tortosa, *Lámpara de príncipes*, transl. M. Alarcón, vol. 1, Madrid: Instituto de Valencia de Don Juan, 1930, pp. 49–51; Chauvin, *Bibliographie*, vol. 8 (1904), p. 100, no. 73; Asin et Palacios, "Logia et agraphia," pp. 385–386, no. 54bis; Spies, "Das Grimmsche Märchen'Bruder Lustig'," p. 55.

18. Ibshīhī, Shihāb al-Dīn Muḥammad ibn Aḥmad Abī al-Fatḥ al-, *al-Mustaṭraf fī kull fann mustaẓraf*, ed. Mufīd Qumayḥa, vol. 2, Beirut: Dār al-Kutub al-ʿilmiyya, 1403/1983, pp. 606–607; Ibshīhī, al-, *Al-Mostaṭraf: recueil de morceaux choisis çà et là*, transl. Gustav Rat, vol. 2, Paris: Leroux, 1899, pp. 792–793; Wesselski, *Italiänischer Volks- und Herrenwitz*, pp. 223–224; Basset, vol. 2, pp. 302–305, no. 112.

19. Grünbaum, Max, *Neue Beiträge zur semitischen Sagenkunde*, Leiden: Brill, 1893, pp. 280–282; Spies, "Das Grimmsche Märchen 'Bruder Lustig'," p. 55; Fradejas Lebrero, José, "El tesoro fatal," in *Homenaje a Álvaro Galmés de Fuentes*, vol. 3, Madrid: Universidad de Oviedo-Gredos, 1987, pp. 471–483, at pp. 476–477.

20. Rückert, Friedrich, "Eine persische Erzählung," *Zeitschrift der Deutschen Morgenländischen Gesellschaft* 14 (1860), pp. 280–287; Clouston, *Popular Tales and Fictions*, pp. 499–502; Ritter, Hellmut, *The Ocean of the Soul: Man, the World and God in the Stories of Farīd al-Dīn ʿAṭṭār*, transl. John O'Kane, Leiden: Brill, 2003, pp. 95–96.

21. Ritter, *The Ocean of the Soul*, p. 96; see also Spies, "Das Grimmsche Märchen 'Bruder Lustig'," pp. 57–60.

22. Ibn al-Jawzī, Abū 'l-Faraj ʿAbd al-Raḥmān ibn ʿAlī, *Akhbār al-Ḥamqā wa-'l-mughaffalīn*, ed. Kāẓim al-Muẓaffar, al-Najaf: al-Maktaba al-ḥaydariyya, 1386/1966, p. 32.

23. Marzolph, *Arabia ridens*, vol. 2, p. 260, no. 1208; Wesselski, *Der Hodscha Nasreddin*, vol. 2, pp. 14–15, 188, no. 365.

CHAPTER 21

God Willing! (ATU 830C)

The three Abrahamic religions, Judaism, Christianity, and Islam, share the belief in one God only. In the everyday practice of the pious, this belief finds its expression in the imperative to begin each and every activity with the expression "God willing!" Since God is omnipotent, His inexplicable ways overrule human decisions, so that whatever humans may decide will only happen if God wills (New Testament, James 4:15; Koran 18:23–24).[1] This pious belief is exemplified in the folktale classified as tale type ATU 830C: *"If God Wills."*[2] Although documented in a rare version from Germany, the tale is best known in regions that were historically influenced by Muslim culture, mainly the Iberian Peninsula and the Balkans.

A tale collected by Matthias Zender in the German Eifel region tells of a young woman who is about to finish weaving a piece of cloth.[3] The passing sexton remarks that, "God willing," she will be able to finish that day. To which the young woman responds, "God willing or not, the cloth will be finished." For two weeks, however, she is not able to take the cloth from the loom, for no other reason than her having refused to acknowledge God's superior will. In a tale documented in Serbia and Croatia, the man intending to go to the market the next day refuses to say, "God willing," as he intends to go whether God wills or not. The next day, however, he has fallen ill,[4] or his horse was eaten by wolves,[5] or the horse is so sick that it is about to die.[6] The tale's Portuguese version introduces a man who does not see any connection to God's will when going to chop wood in the forest.[7] When he breaks his leg, however, the man changes his attitude, instructing his passing neighbor, "Tell my wife to harness the oxen, if God wills, and to yoke them, if God wills, so that she can come to fetch me, if God wills!" The protagonist of a Brazilian tale intends to go to the market to buy a pig.[8] Although his wife reminds him to say, "God willing," he responds, "The money is in my pocket, and the pig is on the market. So God willing or not, the pig will be mine." On the way, his horse shies and throws him off its back, so that he returns home aching and without having achieved anything. From now on, whenever the man intends to do anything, he would say, "Tomorrow, God willing, I will ride my horse, God willing, on the road, God willing, to buy bricks for the shed, God willing!" The tale was recorded with similar action several times from Catalan tradition.[9] In Spanish, the everyday expression *¡ojalá!* acquired the meaning of "hopefully" or "perhaps." Its origin is, however, a phonetic adaptation of the Arabic *in shā' Allāh*, meaning "God willing."

In classical Arabic literature, the corresponding tale is first documented in an-Naysābūrī's (d. 1015) book *'Uqalā' al-majānīn* (Wise Fools).[10]

> One day, a certain Abū Jawāliq wants to go to the market to buy a donkey. Although a friend admonishes him to add, "God willing," Abū Jawāliq responds by saying, "This is not the right time to say, 'God willing.' The money is in my pocket, and the donkey is on the market." On the way, however, his money is stolen so that he returns home in a bad mood. When his friend meets him again and asks him whether he bought the donkey, Abū Jawāliq responds, "The money was stolen, God willing!"

The tale is repeated verbatim contemporaneously in al-Ābī's (d. 1030) encyclopedia of jokes and anecdotes, *Nathr al-durr* (Pearls of Prose).[11] As Abū Jawāliq was obviously not a well-known character, his name here appears as Abū Jawālīq. About a century later, al-Rāghib al-Iṣfahānī (d. 1108) attributes the tale to an anonymous protagonist in his book *Muḥāḍarāt al-udabā'* (Conversations of the Educated).[12] Another century later, Ibn al-Jawzī (d. 1201) in his book on stupid people, *Akhbār al-Ḥamqā*, has the friend of the anonymous protagonist add the final line, "Now this is not the right time to say, 'God willing'."[13] In his florilegium *al-Kashkūl* (The Beggar's Bowl), Bahā' al-Dīn al-'Āmilī (d. 1621) has the protagonist explicitly state, "Why should I need to say that?"[14] In the nineteenth century, the jocular tale is given in al-Shirwānī's (d. 1840) *Ḥadīqat al-afrāḥ* (The Garden of Delights).[15] Here, the robbed man's response is seasoned with a repeated expression of "God willing," including the final "and curses upon you, God willing!"

In Persian author 'Obeyd-e Zākāni's (d. 1371) Arabic compilation of jocular tales, the events are for the first time attributed to the popular jester Juḥā, whose final response to his friend is extended to, "I come from the market, God willing, and have not bought the donkey, God willing. Now I go back to my house in a distressed mood, God willing!"[16] Since the comprehensive modern Arabic compilation, published in 1861, the tale has become a standard constituent of Juḥā's jests,[17] thus offering a powerful medium for the tale's dissemination all over the regions of Muslim influence.

The Hebrew *Alphabet of Ben Sira (Sirach)*, an Eastern text compiled before the year 1000, contains a tale with a similar point.[18] Here, a rich man goes to the city to purchase oxen with which to plow his land. Meeting the prophet Elijah on his way, he twice refuses to say, "If His Name decrees." In order to teach him a lesson, Elijah has him lose his money. Only when the man submits to adding the pious formula does the prophet restore the money to him, so that he succeeds in buying the animals. Whereas the tale's Arabic versions mock the foolish man's action in a lighthearted manner, albeit not without a certain didactic intention, the Jewish tale is ruled by a fairly stern religious tone.

Notes

1. Jospe, Raphael, and Yonatan Milo, "God Willing: *Im Yirzeh Hashem—In Sha Allah*," *The Review of Rabbinic Judaism* 16 (2013), pp. 1–27.

2. Masing, Uku, "Gottes Segen," in *Enzyklopädie des Märchens*, vol. 6 (1990), cols. 12–16.

3. Zender, Matthias, *Sagen und Geschichten aus der Westeifel*, 2nd ed., Bonn. Röhrscheid, 1966, p. 181.

4. Vrčević, Vuk, *Srpske narodne pripovijetke, ponajviše kratke i šaljive*, vol. 1, Belgrade: Srpska kraljevska državna štamparija, 1868, pp. 9–10, no. 17.

5. Karadžić, Vuk Stefanović, *Srpske narodne pripovetke*, 4th ed., Belgrade, 1937, p. 275.

6. Stojanović, Mijat, *Pučke pripoviedke i pjesme*, Zagreb, 1867, pp. 27–28, no. 3.

7. Meier, Harri, and Dieter Woll, *Portugiesische Märchen*, Düsseldorf: Diederichs, 1975, p. 220, 271, no. 116.

8. Cascudo, Luís da Câmara, *Trinta "estorias" brasileiras*, Lisbon: Fortucalense, 1955, pp. 69–70.

9. Noia Campos, Camiño, *Catálogo tipolóxico do conto galego de tradición oral: clasificación, antoloxía e bibliografía*, Vigo: University of Vigo, 2010, p. 417, no. 830C.

10. Naysābūrī, Abū 'l-Qāsim al-Ḥasan ibn Muḥammad ibn Ḥabīb, *'Uqalā' al-majānin*, ed. 'Umar al-As'ad, Beirut: Dār al-Nafā'is, 1407/1987, p. 224; Marzolph, *Arabia ridens*, vol. 2, p. 121, no. 481.

11. Ābī, Abū Sa'd Manṣūr ibn al-Ḥusayn al-, *Nathr al-durr*, ed. Muḥammad 'Alī Qarna et al., vol. 2, Cairo: al-Hay'a al-miṣriyya al-'āmma lil-kitāb, 1981, p. 226.

12. Rāghib al-Iṣfahānī, al-Ḥusayn ibn Muḥammad al-, *Muḥāḍarāt al-udabā' wa-muḥāwarāt al-shu'arā' wa-'l-bulaghā'*, vol. 3, Beirut 1961, p. 193.

13. Ibn al-Jawzī, Abū 'l-Faraj 'Abd al-Raḥmān ibn 'Alī, *Akhbār al-Ḥamqā wa-'l-mughaffalīn*, ed. Kāẓim al-Muẓaffar, al-Najaf: al-Maktaba al-ḥaydariyya, 1386/1966, p. 145.

14. 'Āmilī, Bahā' al-Dīn al-, *al-Kashkūl*; consulted at http://www.alwaraq.net, p. 352 (accessed February 8, 2018).

15. Shirwānī, Aḥmad ibn Muḥammad al-Anṣārī al-Yamanī al-, *Ḥadīqat al-afrāḥ*, Cairo: Muṣṭafā al-Bābī al-Ḥalabī, 1320/1902, p. 56; Basset, *Mille et un contes*, vol. 1, p. 248, no. 128.

16. Zākāni, 'Obeydallāh, *Kolliyāt-e 'Obeyd-e Zākāni*, ed. Parviz Atābeki, Tehran 1331/1952, p. 286; Marzolph, Ulrich, "Mollā Naṣroddīn in Persia," *Iranian Studies* 28.3–4 (1995), pp. 157–174, at p. 163.

17. Juḥā, *Hādhihi nawādir al-khūjah Naṣr al-Dīn Afandī Juḥā al-Rūmī*, Būlāq: Mūsā Kāstillī, 1278/1861, p. 7; Wesselski, *Der Hodscha Nasreddin*, vol. 2, pp. 56, 201, no. 394.

18. Bin Gorion, Micha Joseph, *Mimekor Israel: Classical Jewish Folktales, Abridged and Annotated*, ed. Emanuel Bin Gorion, prepared by Dan Ben-Amos, Bloomington: Indiana University Press, 1990, pp. 438–439, no. 224; see also Schwarzbaum, Haim, *Studies in Jewish and World Folklore*, Berlin: Walter de Gruyter, 1968, pp. 271–272.

CHAPTER 22

The Greedy Man Is Blinded and Falls into Misery (ATU 836F*)

A fair number of international folktales of a didactic import warn against the consequences of unabashed greed and stinginess that will lead to misery instead of the desired comfort and luxury.[1] As exemplified in tale type ATU 763: *The Treasure Finders Who Murder One Another* (see essay **19, *The Treasure Finders Murder One Another***), the greedy are not only bound to lose whatever they had sought but moreover risk losing their well-being or even their lives. Punishment is often inflicted by supernatural powers such as divine providence or, in case of a human agent, by misused magic. The presently concerned tale demonstrates this feature in a simple but highly effective manner. Classified as tale type ATU 836F*: *The Miser and the Eye Ointment*, the tale tells of a magician's magic salve. By applying the salve to one's left eye, one is able to see the world's hidden treasures. The greedy man who joins the magician imagines that he will see even more treasures by applying the salve also to his right eye. Although the magician warns him that he will turn blind, he insists on doing so. Consequently, the man turns blind and is reduced to misery.

Particularly richly documented in Latvia,[2] in Europe the tale is also attested with little variation in single versions from nineteenth- and early twentieth-century oral tradition in Flemish,[3] Slovakian,[4] Galician,[5] and Polish.[6] In the Americas, Spanish versions of the tale were collected in Puerto Rico[7] and, from the narration of Félix Pino, aged 35, from Santa Fe, in New Mexico.[8] Whereas most texts are independent versions of the tale, the Flemish text conjoins it with two other tales of magic in which a human is transformed into an animal. A text from late nineteenth-century Bosnian tradition embeds the tale in a lengthy narrative in which the main protagonist is asked to solve the enigma of the queen of England's unfathomable riches.[9] The queen promises to tell him her secret only after he has solved another enigma, and in what follows, the protagonist is requested to solve a succession of enigmas. The last person he meets is finally willing to inform him without further condition, and on his way back he learns the previous persons' secrets one after the other. Finally, the queen of England informs him that she is in possession of Solomon's treasures.

The tale's version embedded in the Bosnian text is similar to that in Galland's *Nights*, although the dervish's magic object is not an ointment but a mirror that blinds the greedy man when he looks at it, first with one eye, and then the other.

The introduction of the present tale to Western tradition can be unambiguously identified. Titled "Histoire de l'aveugle Baba-Abdalla" (The Story of Bābā 'Abdallāh the Blind), the tale was first published in 1712 in the tenth volume of Antoine Galland's *Mille et une nuit*.[10] Galland had learned the tale in Paris from the oral performance of the young Syrian Maronite narrator Ḥannā Diyāb, a summary of whose presumably French narration he had taken down in his diary on Friday, May 10, 1709.[11] At that time, Galland, due to the fragmentary nature of the fifteenth-century Arabic manuscript at his disposal, had run out of tales to publish in his adapted translation of the *Nights*. Consequently, he took liberty to include several tales adapted from Ḥannā Diyāb's oral performance in the final volumes of his *Nights*, including the present one.[12] Both the original tale and Galland's elaborated rendering are embedded in the frame tale of "The Caliph's Night Adventure"[13] that starts out, as do several tales of *The Thousand and One Nights*, with the caliph roaming the nocturnal city in disguise as he cannot find sleep and is curious to learn about the lives of his subjects (Mot. K1812.17).[14] When the caliph and his vizier meet a blind beggar, the beggar asks to receive a slap before accepting the caliph's alms. Wondering about the reason behind this strange request, the caliph has the beggar summoned to the palace the next day where he is made to recount his adventure. Ḥannā Diyāb's original tale as told by the beggar himself goes as follows.

> The man used to be rich, earning a living by renting out his herd of eighty camels. One day, a dervish proposes to load the man's camels with gold and jewels on condition that the dervish may keep forty camels for himself. The man accompanies the dervish to a place in the desert where the latter opens up the ground by way of a conjuration. The dervish lets the owner of the camels load the animals with treasures while taking only a small box with a certain ointment for himself. Following this they separate. No sooner has the dervish left than the man follows him, requesting that the dervish return the camels, as they would be of no use to him. The man also obliges the dervish to hand him the box and informs him what it is good for. The dervish tells the man that if one applies the ointment to the left eye, one will immediately see all of the world's hidden treasures. Testing the dervish's statement, the man finds it true. Out of greed, the man requests that the dervish apply the ointment also to his right eye, although the dervish warns him that he will turn blind. When the man turns blind, the dervish sets out with all of the eighty camels, leaving his companion in the desert. The man is saved by a passing caravan but is now reduced to asking for alms. In the following, he makes it a rule that each time somebody gives him alms, he would ask that person to slap him so as to remind

him of the consequences of his greed. The caliph has pity on the man and grants him a small stipend so that he will no longer have to ask for alms.

Galland embellished the published version of the tale as taken down from the oral performance of Ḥannā Diyāb with several traits, such as naming the beggar and introducing the tale with the popular motif of the rich merchant's profligate son squandering his fortune that appears in several tales of the *Nights* (Mot. W131.1),[15] thus linking the added tale to the collection's previously existing repertoire. Considering the tremendous popularity of the *Nights* ever since the work's introduction to world literature, there is little doubt that the tale's retellings recorded from nineteenth- and early twentieth-century Western oral tradition constitute little more than direct or semidirect retellings. This becomes all the more apparent in oral tales, such as the Flemish one, that combine the present tale with the other tales embedded in Galland's adapted and elaborated published text, such as tale type ATU 449: *Sidi Numan* (see essay **7, *The Unfaithful Wife Transforms Her Husband into a Dog***).[16]

At the same time, Ḥannā Diyāb's tale is apparently part of a larger Middle Eastern tradition that probably links to the origin of some of the versions from South Eastern Europe, that is, the regions that were directly influenced by Middle Eastern tradition. This applies in particular to the Bosnian text featuring a protagonist on his quest to find the solutions to a chain of riddles.[17] A similar quest including the present tale in its third adventure constitutes the frame tale of the Persian romance commonly known as *Haft seyr-e Ḥātem* (Ḥātem's Seven Quests), *Haft so'āl-e Ḥātem* (Ḥātem's Seven Questions), or simply as *Ḥātem-nāme* (The Book of Ḥātem).[18] The romance's hero is a folktale version of the historical Arabian poet Ḥātim al-Ṭā'ī (d. 578) who in popular tradition of the Muslim world is famed for his boundless generosity. Although the romance's hero displays acts of magnanimity every now and then, his main task in the romance is to find the solutions to various riddles posed by the beautiful princess Ḥosn Bānu. The third riddle the princess poses pertains to finding and learning about the fate of a man who continuously exclaims, "Do evil to none; if you do, evil will overtake you."[19]

Ḥātem happens to come across an old man who is imprisoned in a cage hung up in a tree. The old man informs Ḥātem about his experience on condition that Ḥātem will help him later. The old man is the son of a wealthy merchant who squandered his riches after his father's death (Mot. W131.1). Having become destitute, he tried to locate the treasures his father had hidden for him. As he did not succeed, he was helped by a young man to whom he promised to give a quarter of the findings as reward. When they had located the treasures, however, the owner refused to give his helper the promised share, instead driving him away. Some days later, the young man returned and apologized for his previous behavior. Gradually, the two men became friends. One day, the young man made his companion curious about a certain ointment that enabled him to see the world's hidden treasures. Putting the ointment on his eyes, however, the merchant's son immediately turned blind. His companion obliged him to spend his life in the cage and continuously exclaim the above-mentioned words. Ḥātem frees the old man, cures his blindness with a magic flower and returns, having found the solution to the princess's riddle.

The Persian romance of Ḥātem-e Ṭā'i (or Ṭāy, as he is known in Persian) likely derives from the performance of professional Persian storytellers in India.[20] None of the preserved manuscripts bears a date. From stylistic and linguistic criteria, it was surmised that the work was compiled around the seventeenth or eighteenth century, thus placing its compilation vaguely contemporary with Ḥannā Diyāb's Paris performance in 1709. Whereas tales about the loss of happiness and wealth through greed are legion in Arabic and Persian literature, the constitutive motif of the present tale appears to have been used in different contexts at about the same time. Since tales about Ḥātem-e Ṭā'i's generosity were also part of Ottoman Turkish popular tradition as told in *Ferec ba'd eş-şidde* (Relief after Hardship),[21] probably compiled before the end of fourteenth century, the present tale might have been mediated to Bosnian tradition in the Balkans by an Ottoman Turkish version.

Notes

1. Marzolph, Ulrich, "Geiz, Geizhals," in *Enzyklopädie des Märchens*, vol. 5 (1987), cols. 948–957; Uther, *The Types*, vol. 3, pp. 194 (Greed), 221–222 (Miser, Miserly), 263 (Stingy).

2. Arājs, Kārlis, and Alma Medne, *Latviešu pasaku tipu rādītājs*, Riga: Zinātne, 1977, p. 133, no. 836F*.

3. De Meyer, Maurits, *Le conte populaire flamand*, Helsinki: Suomalainen Tiedeakatemia, 1968, p. 86, no. 726**.

4. Tille, Václav, *Soupis českých pohádek*, vol. 1, Prague: České Akademie Věd a Umĕni, 1929, pp. 78–81.

5. Camarena, Julio, and Maurice Chevalier, *Catálogo tipológico del cuento folklórico español*, vol. 3, Alcalá de Henares: Centro de Estudios Cervantinos, 2003, pp. 316–318, no. 836F*; Noia Campos, Camiño, *Catálogo tipolóxico do conto galego de tradición oral: clasificación, antoloxía e bibliografía*, Vigo: University of Vigo, 2010, pp. 421–423, no. 836F*.

6. Krzyżanowski, Julian, *Polska bajka ludowa w układzie systematycznym*, Polska Akad. Nauk. Wydz. Nauk Społecznych, 1963, vol. 1, p. 253, no. 806.

7. Hansen, Terrence Leslie, *The Types of the Folktale in Cuba, Puerto Rico, the Dominican Republic, and Spanish South America*, Berkeley: University of California Press, 1957, p. 102, no. 836**M; Mason, J. Alden, and Aurelio M. Espinosa, "Porto-Rican Folk-lore: Folk-Tales," *Journal of American Folklore* 42 (1929), pp. 85–156, p. 145, no. 111.

8. Robe, Stanley L., *Index of Mexican Folktales*, Berkeley: University of California Press, 1973, p. 133, no. 836F*; Rael, Juan B., *Cuentos españoles de Colorado y Nuevo Méjico: Spanish Originals with English Summaries*, Stanford: Stanford University Press, 1940, vol. 2, pp. 570–572, no. 490.

9. Schütz, Joseph, *Volksmärchen aus Jugoslawien*, Düsseldorf: Diederichs, 1960, pp. 5–13, 308, no. 1.

10. Galland, Antoine, *Les Mille et Une Nuits: Contes arabes*, ed. Jean-Paul Sermain and Aboubakr Chraïbi, Paris: Flammarion, 2004, vol. 3, pp. 125–136; Chauvin, *Bibliographie*, vol. 5 (1901), pp. 146–147, no. 72; Marzolph and Van Leeuwen, *The Arabian Nights Encyclopedia*, vol. 1, pp. 113–114, no. 350.

11. Galland, Antoine, *Le Journal d'Antoine Galland (1646–1715): La période parisienne*, ed. Frédéric Bauden and Richard Waller, vol. 1, Leuven: Peeters, 2011, pp. 327–330.

12. Marzolph, Ulrich, "The Man Who Made the *Nights* Immortal: The Tales of the Syrian Maronite Storyteller Ḥannā Diyāb," *Marvels & Tales* 32.1 (2018), pp. 114–129.

13. Marzolph and Van Leeuwen, *The Arabian Nights Encyclopedia*, vol. 1, p. 134, no. 349.

14. Ibid., vol. 2, p. 806; see also Marzolph, Ulrich, "Hārūn al-Rašīd," in *Enzyklopädie des Märchens*, vol. 6 (1990), cols. 534–537; Marzolph, Ulrich, with Anne E. Duggan, "Ḥannā Diyāb's Tales, part 1," *Marvels & Tales* 32.1 (2018), pp. 113–154, at pp. 136–137.

15. Marzolph and Van Leeuwen, *The Arabian Nights Encyclopedia*, vol. 2, p. 808.

16. De Meyer, *Le conte populaire flamand*, p. 86, no. 726**.

17. Schütz, *Volksmärchen aus Jugoslawien*, pp. 5–13, 308, no. 1.

18. Ethé, Hermann, "Neupersische Literatur," in Geiger, Wilhelm, and Ernst Kuhn, *Grundriss der iranischen Philologie*, vol. 2, Strasburg: Karl J. Trüber, 1896–1914, pp. 212–368, at p. 319; Monzavi, Aḥmad, *Fehrestvāre-ye ketābhā-ye fārsi*, vol. 1, Tehran: Markaz-e Dā'erat al-maʿāref-e bozorg-e eslāmi, 1382/2001, pp. 313–314.

19. *Ḥātem-nāme*, ed. Ḥoseyn Esmāʿili, Tehran: Moʿin, 1386/2007, vol. 1, pp. 216–217; Forbes, Duncan, *The Adventures of Hatim Taï: A Romance, Translated from the Persian*, London: Oriental Translation Fund, 1880, pp. 111–115; Clouston, William Alexander, "Variants and Analogues of Some of the Tales in the Supplemental Nights, 3," in Burton, Richard F., *Arabian Nights*, (Benares 1885) reprint Beirut: Khayat, 1966, vol. 13, pp. 551–652, at pp. 583–585; Schwarz, Rainer, transl., *Die sieben Abenteuer des Prinzen Hatem: Ein iranischer Märchenroman*, Leipzig: Gustav Kiepenheuer, 1990, pp. 150–153.

20. Omidsālār, Maḥmud, "Ḥātem-nāme," in Bojnurdi, Kāẓem Musavi, ed., *Dānesh-nāme-ye farhang-e mardom-e Irān*, vol. 3, Tehran: Markaz-e Dā'erat al-maʿāref-e bozorg-e eslāmi, 1394/2015, pp. 475–477.

21. Marzolph, *Relief after Hardship*, pp. 109–110, no. 37.

CHAPTER 23

Drinking Leads to Committing Serious Crimes (ATU 839)

The demonization of intoxicating substances is probably as old as their use, and both aspects are as ancient as they are internationally relevant. In the Eurasian cultures, wine was historically the most common intoxicant, and its praise as well as its criticism extend to the three Abrahamic religions, Judaism, Christianity, and Islam. Even in Muslim cultures, the positive effects of controlled drinking are at times highly praised, and although Islam strictly prohibits the consumption of wine and, by extension, all alcoholic beverages and other intoxicating substances, historically wine drinking often constituted an, at least implicitly accepted, regular practice of social life.[1] Excessive drinking is unanimously condemned by all of the three Abrahamic religions due to its often disastrous consequences.[2] Probably no tale exemplifies this more drastically than the one classified as tale type ATU 839: *One Vice Carries Others With It.*[3]

A nineteenth-century French tale allegedly often told for nocturnal entertainment tells of a monk who is so dissatisfied with his superior that he wishes him dead.[4] Right after the superior died from a stroke, the devil appears to the monk informing him that he fulfilled the monk's wish. In return, the monk will now have to commit a sin. He is allowed to choose one out of three sins—drinking, fornication, or murder. Pondering a long time what to choose, the monk finally consents to drinking, presuming this the least objectionable deed. As soon as he is drunk, he rapes a woman and, when her husband arrives at the scene, kills him. So instead of just committing one sin, he commits all three. In the tale's Estonian version collected by M. Reimann in 1892, a ghost attempts to seduce a man to either steal, fornicate, or drink hard liquor.[5] The man reasons that if he steals, he will be jailed; if he sleeps with another man's wife, he will receive a heavy beating. But he sees no harm in drinking. Being drunk, the man has sex with another man's wife and later also steals. Consequently, in addition to the heavy beating he receives, he is also jailed.

The Polish folktale narrated by Antoni Ignatawicze from the village Auksztrakiej, district Rosień, on January 24, 1890, introduces a poor peasant who is so desperate about his situation that he decides to hang himself.[6] As the peasant walks around the forest looking for a suitable tree, he meets a nobleman who promises to lend him money, providing that the man repay the money by a given day. The nobleman, who is none other than the devil in disguise, leads the man to a large oak tree inside of which there are lavishly decorated rooms, and gives him as much money as he can carry. The peasant returns home and manages his affairs so well that at the agreed date he has much more money than the devil lent him. When he meets his creditor, the latter suggests that he should keep the money, providing that within the course of a year he will commit one out of three deeds—kill a man, fornicate, or get drunk. Not knowing what to decide, the peasant is advised by his wife to get drunk, as she sees nothing terribly wrong with that. He would simply come home and have a good sleep and that way they would keep the money. On his return from the pub, however, the drunken peasant rapes a young woman. When his wife learns about this, she makes him leave the house. In the end, the peasant kills the young woman, thinking that this is the best way to quell rumors.

In a Slovak folktale, the devil is angry at a pious old man who has never committed a sin in his life.[7] The devil, appearing in his most detestable form, commands the pious man to commit one out of three sins—kill somebody, blaspheme, or get drunk. When the pious man does not want to give in, the devil blackmails him to choose a particular sin, or else he would make him commit all three sins in a row. Pondering about his fate, the pious man finally concedes that all human beings have sinned at least once in their lives. Considering getting drunk as the least harmful, he gets drunk. Back home, he accidentally kills his infant grandchild, following which he curses God in the most abominable ways. The tale's concluding moral attributes the invention of hard liquor to the devil.

A German language version of the tale told by Karl Reiterer in Austrian Styria, and recorded by Hans von der Senn in July 1892, has the devil appear to a pious hermit disguised as a hermit.[8] Discussing between themselves what is the greatest sin, the devil insists that drunkenness is the greatest sin of all. As the pious hermit agrees to test the devil's allegation, the devil takes him to a pub and pays for a number of drinks. On his way back home, the hermit meets a girl to whom he makes "an indecent offer." He then kills the girl so as to get rid of the only witness of his sinful act. Seeking absolution, the hermit confesses his sins to a pious priest who sends him to the pope in Rome. The pope orders the hermit to return to his cell, to live a life of utmost abstinence, and not to speak a word. Some years later, the hermit, now with long hair and long fingernails, looking like a wild creature, is found by a count out hunting in the woods. The count takes the hermit along and puts him on show in his deer park, where everybody is "highly amused with the creature's docile and intelligent behavior." Again many years later, a white apparition announces the hermit's deliverance. He regains his "agreeable human shape" and returns to live a godly life in his cell.

Comparatively scarcely documented from European oral tradition, the tale is often told in eighteenth-century jestbooks[9] whose versions draw on the strong current of medieval exemplum literature.[10] The tale's frequent iterations appear, for instance, in the works of Johannes Pauli in the sixteenth century,[11] John Bromyard (*Summa predicantium*, E 1,3) in the fifteenth,[12] and Stephen of Bourbon (Étienne de Bourbon) in the thirteenth century.[13]

Developed against an intricate backdrop of Jewish and Christian elements,[14] the tale's oldest documented versions date to ninth-century Arabic literature. A concise version told on the authority of the third of the "righteous caliphs," ʿUthmān (d. 656), is given by Ibn Qutayba (d. 889) in his book *al-Ashriba* (Drinks).[15] Introducing the tale, ʿUthmān is cited as quoting the Prophet Muḥammad's prescriptive dictum,[16] "Beware of wine (*al-khamr*), because it is the key to all evils (*miftāḥ kull sharr*)."

> Someone (i.e., the devil) came to a man and said, "Either you rip apart this book (i.e., the Koran), kill this boy, adore this idol, empty this goblet (of wine), or fornicate with this woman." The man considered that drinking from the goblet was the easiest for him. (Having done that,) he had sex with the woman, killed the boy, ripped apart the book, and adored the Cross.

No other citation of this short tale is so far known from Arabic literature. Particularly longer versions of the tale in which the pious man kills the woman he raped are discussed in connection with the ancient legend of the monk Barṣīṣa who lusted for the young woman entrusted to him, killed her, and even succumbed to adoring the devil in return for the latter's vain promise of help.[17] The legend lacks, however, the presently considered tale's constitutive motif of the pious man first getting drunk.

In the ninth century, the series of motifs constituting the present tale also appears as part of the larger legend of Hārūt and Mārūt, the two angels that are mentioned in a somewhat enigmatic passage in the Koran (2:102). Aiming to explain the context of the sentence "They (that is, the devils) taught the people witchcraft and what was revealed in Babylon to Hārūt and Mārūt," the authors of *tafsīr*-literature (commentaries on the Koran) assembled from authoritative transmitters a variety of shorter and longer versions of the related tale whose citation became, as a matter of fact, a standard feature in Koranic commentary. In its elaborate form, of which various versions are given in al-Ṭabarī's (d. 923) *Tafsīr*, this legend adds a misogynous tone as it is a woman who seduces the two male angels to commit the series of sins.[18]

> When the angels argue with God about humankind's sinfulness, God admonishes them that they would behave no better if they possessed a human nature. God charges the angels to name two out of their midst whom he will send to earth to demonstrate this, and Hārūt and Mārūt are chosen. God "explicitly adjures the pair to avoid specific transgressions such as idolatry, theft, bloodshed, fornication, and drinking wine."[19] On earth,

and equipped with a human nature, the angels become infatuated with a beautiful woman who only consents to give in to their advances if they worship the idol she worships and drink wine. Once drunk, the two agree to do whatever the woman asks them to do and end up killing a man so as to cover up their illegitimate sexual adventure.

In the legend's further course, which is of no relevance here, the woman learns from the angels God's supreme name, which enables her to be transformed into a star in heaven. The two angels are punished, according to their wish, in this world, by being hung upside down in a well in Babylon.[20] Although the drinking of wine is not mentioned in one of the legend's earliest textual documentations as contained in the *Tafsīr* compiled by ʿAbd al-Razzāq ibn Hammām al-Ṣanʿānī (d. 827),[21] already in the ninth century its mention became a standard feature, as documented by two other ninth-century commentaries on the Koran.[22] Subsequently, the legend was also integrated into the genre of *qiṣaṣ al-anbiyāʾ* (tales of the prophets), a prominent representative of which is the work of al-Thaʿālibī (d. 1035).[23]

The standard version of the tale of Hārūt and Mārūt was introduced to Persian by way of the translation of al-Ṭabarī's *Tafsīr* prepared in the tenth century.[24] In the fifteenth century, it is cited in Persian historian Mirkhond's (d. 1498) universal history *Rowżat al-ṣafā* (The Garden of Purity).[25] It remained so popular in Persian tradition that still in the nineteenth century, Mirzā ʿAli-Qoli Khoʾi, the illustrator of the first lithographed edition of the Persian translation of al-Qazwīnī's (d. 1286) cosmography *ʿAjāʾib al-makhlūqāt* (The Wonders of Creation) would illustrate the tale with an image depicting the woman offering wine to the two angels, one of whom is about to throw a copy of the Koran into the fire while the other kills a man, although the book's text does not mention any of those details.[26]

In Ottoman Turkish, the tale of Hārūt and Mārūt is contained in *Qırq vezīr* (The Forty Viziers), an adapted version of the originally Persian *Sendbād-nāme* (The Book of Sendbād [the Sage]).[27]

Notes

1. Marzolph and Van Leeuwen, *The Arabian Nights Encyclopedia*, vol. 2, pp. 738–739; Sadan, Joseph, "Vin, fait de civilisation," in Rosen-Ayalon, Myriam, *Studies in Memory of Gaston Wiet*, Jerusalem: Hebrew University, 1977, pp. 129–160.

2. Bimmer, Andreas, "Trunkenheit," in *Enzyklopädie des Märchens*, vol. 13 (2010), cols. 971–977.

3. Pintel-Ginsberg, Idit, "Sünden: Die drei S. des Eremiten," ibid., cols. 43–46.

4. Delarue, Paul, and Marie-Louise Tenèze, *Le conte populaire français*, vol. 4.1, Paris: Maisonneuve et Larose, 1985, pp. 273–274.

5. Loorits, Oskar, *Estnische Volkserzählungen*, Berlin: De Gruyter, 1959, p. 184, no. 168.

6. Dowojna-Sylwestrowicz, Mieczysław, *Podania żmujdzkie*, vol. 1, Warsaw: Arct, 1894, pp. 374–376.

7. Karlinger, Felix, and Bohdan Mykytiuk, *Legendenmärchen aus Europa*, Düsseldorf: Diederichs, 1967, pp. 154–156.
8. Ranke, Kurt, *Folktales of Germany*, Chicago: University of Chicago Press, 1966, pp. 155–156, 224, no. 61.
9. Uther, *Deutscher Märchenkatalog*, p. 216, no. 839.
10. Taylor, Archer, "The Three Sins of the Hermit," *Modern Philology* 20.1 (1922), pp. 61–94, at p. 69.
11. Pauli, Johannes, *Schimpf und Ernst*, ed. Johannes Bolte, Berlin: Herbert Stubenrauch, 1924 (reprint Hildesheim: Olms, 1972), vol. 1, p.155, and vol. 2, p. 318, no. 243.
12. Wesselski, *Mönchslatein*, p. 99, 228, no. 81.
13. Ranke, *Folktales*, p. 224, no. 61. For detailed references and discussion of the medieval European versions, see Taylor, "The Three Sins"; Tubach, *Index exemplorum*, pp. 147–148, no. 1816.
14. Grünbaum, Max, "Beiträge zur vergleichenden Mythologie aus der Hagada," *Zeitschrift der Deutschen Morgenländischen Gesellschaft* 31 (1847), pp. 183–359; Heller, Bernhard, "La chute des anges Schemhazai, Ouzza, et Azaël," *Revue des études juives* 60 (1910), pp. 202–212; Schwarzbaum, Haim, *Studies in Jewish and World Folklore*, Berlin: Walter de Gruyter, 1968, pp. 247–249, no. 293.
15. Ibn Qutayba al-Dīnawarī, Abū Muḥammad ʿAbdallāh ibn Muslim, *Kitāb al-Ashriba*, ed. Muḥammad Kurd ʿAlī, Damascus: al-Majmaʿ al-ʿilmī al-ʿarabī, 1366/1947, pp. 24–25; Marzolph, *Arabia ridens*, vol. 2, p. 31, no. 113.
16. Wensinck, Arent Jan, *Concordance et indices de la tradition musulmane*, vol. 5, Leiden: Brill, 1965 (Reprint Istanbul: Çağrı Yayınları, 1988), p. 55.
17. Chauvin, *Bibliographie*, vol. 8 (1904), pp. 128–129, no. 118; Heller, Bernhard, "Die Legende von den drei Sünden des Einsiedlers und vom Mönch Barṣīṣa," *Ungarische Rundschau* 1 (1912), pp. 653–673.
18. Littmann, Enno, "Hārūt and Mārūt," in *Festschrift für Friedrich Carl Andreas*, Leipzig: Harrassowitz, 1916, pp. 70–87; Ṭabarī, Abū Jaʿfar Muḥammad ibn Jarīr al-, *Tafsīr Ṭabarī: Jāmiʿ al-bayān ʿan taʾwīl āy al-Qurʾān*, ed. Maḥmūd Muḥammad Shākir and Aḥmad Muḥammad Shākir, vol. 2, Cairo: Dār al-Maʿārif bi-Miṣr, 1969, pp. 419–426.
19. Reeves, John C., "Some Parascriptural Dimensions of the 'Tale of Hārūt wa-Mārūt'," *Journal of the American Oriental Society* 135.4 (2015), pp. 817–842, at p. 826.
20. Tottoli, Roberto, " Hārūt and Mārūt," in *Encyclopedia of Islam*, 3rd ed., Leiden: Brill, 2017, fasc. 5, pp. 95–97.
21. Ṣanʿānī, ʿAbd al-Razzāq ibn Hammām al-, *Tafsīr ʿAbd al-Razzāq*, ed. Muḥammad Maḥmūd ʿAbduh, vol. 1, Beirut: Dār al-Kutub al-ʿilmiyya, 1419/1999, pp. 282–283, no. 97.
22. Hūd ibn al-Muḥakkam al-Huwwārī, *Tafsīr Kitāb Allāh al-ʿazīz*, ed. Bālḥājj ibn Saʿīd Sharīfī, Beirut: Dār al-Gharb al-islāmī, 1990, vol. 1, pp. 131–132; Qummī, Abū 'l-Ḥasan ʿAlī ibn Ibrāhīm al-, *Tafsīr*, ed. Muḥammad-Bāqir Muwaḥḥad al-Abṭaḥī al-Iṣfahānī, Qum: Muʾassasat al-imām al-Mahdī, vol. 1, pp. 88–90.
23. Thaʿlabī, Abū Isḥāq Aḥmad ibn Muḥammad ibn Ibrāhīm al-, *ʿArāʾis al-majālis fī qiṣaṣ al-anbiyāʾ*, transl. William M. Brinner, Leiden etc., Brill, 2002, pp. 87–88.
24. Ṭabarī, Abū Jaʿfar Muḥammad ibn Jarīr al-, *Tarjome-ye Tafsīr-e Ṭabarī*, ed. Ḥabib Yaghmāʾi, Tehran: Chāpkhāne-ye dowlati-ye Irān, 1339/1969, vol. 1, pp. 96–97.
25. Mirkhond, Mir Moḥammad ibn Borhān al-Din Khāvandshāh, *Tārikh-e Rouẓat al-ṣafā*, vol. 1, Tehran: Ketābkhāne-ye markazi, 1338/1959, pp. 53–55; Mirkhond,

Muhammad Bin Khâvendshâh Bin Mahmûd, *The Rauzat-us-safa; Or, Garden of Purity, Containing the Histories of Prophets, Kings, and Khalifs*, transl. E. Rehatsek, ed. F.F. Arbuthnot, vol. 1.1, London: Royal Asiatic Society, 1891, pp. 75–77.

26. Qazvini, Zakariyyā ibn Moḥammad al-, *ʿAjāʾeb al-makhluqāt wa-gharāʾeb al-mowjudāt*, Tehran, 1264/1847, fol. 34b.

27. Chauvin, *Bibliographie*, vol. 8 (1904), p. 131, no. 123; Sheykh-Zāda, *The History of the Forty Vezirs*, transl. E.J.W. Gibb, London: George Redway, 1886, pp. 167–170.

CHAPTER 24

The Princess Whose Suitors Will Be Executed if They Fail to Solve Her Riddles (AT 851A)

The oldest folktale documented in Romanian tradition is the "Istoria unui voinic înţălept şi învăţat, întrebându-se din ponturi cu o fată a unui împărat" (Tale of a Wise Hero Who Had a Conversation with a Learned Princess).[1] The tale was written down on March 28, 1797, unfortunately without any details specifying the narrator or the circumstances of performance. It is today preserved in the archives of the Romanian Academy of Sciences in Bucharest. Published by Ion Constantin Chiţimia, the tale, a considerable portion of which concerns the riddles or enigmatic questions posed by the princess, goes as follows.[2]

> An impoverished hero of good breeding decides to sell his parents as slaves in exchange for a horse and a decent dress so that he can set out and find a job with a rich man to make a living. On the way, he meets a gullible man on his way to deliver a letter to the emperor. As the man's horse is exhausted, the hero offers to deliver the letter and sends the man home. Since the hero is curious to learn about the letter's content, he opens it and reads that the person delivering the letter is to be beheaded immediately. He destroys the letter and continues on his way.
>
> At the emperor's palace, the young man sees the decapitated bodies of numerous men. Taking residence with a kind old woman, he learns that the emperor's highly educated daughter will only marry the suitor who can answer her enigmatic questions. Whoever is not able to do so, will be beheaded. Although first the old woman and then the emperor warn the young man not to take the risk, he insists on meeting the princess. In her presence, he consciously disciplines himself not to look at her, persumably so as not to be bedazzled by her beauty. For two days he responds to her questions, most of which concern biblical knowledge. Having successfully passed the second session, the young man proposes in turn to ask the princess a question, "Who is the handsome person who turned his father into a horse and his mother into a dress?" As the princess is at a loss to answer, she is granted one night's respite.

That evening she disguises herself as the blacksmith's daughter and visits the young man, allegedly so as to save him from the murderous princess. Although the young man is aware of her true identity, he pretends not to notice and passes a joyful evening hugging and kissing her. In the end, he is so drunk that he reveals the answer to his riddle, and the young woman returns home.

As the princess is able to supply the answer to the young man's question the next day, the emperor gives orders to execute the young man, allowing him, however, to have a final word. The young man tells the emperor about the nocturnal visit of a little dove from court who lost a feather when leaving, and shows a golden ring as proof. Although the princess denies owning the ring and, in fact, has the goldsmith produce an identical ring overnight, her unfair ruse becomes evident. In order not to be disgraced, she consents to marry the young man.

The tale's concluding comment lauds the young man for defeating the princess, thus restoring the natural superiority of the male sex.

Chiţimia and, following him, the editors of the tale's German translation, were inclined to regard the text as being inspired by traditional booklets popular in Romania.[3] A particularly suitable candidate for comparison is the *Viaţa lui Bertoldo* (The Life of Bertoldo), the Romanian translation of an Italian version of the medieval tale of *Solomon and Marcolf* that contains a similar session in which enigmatic questions have to be solved.[4] Mihai Moraru later noticed the Romanian tale's similarity to the tale of Turandot, first published in François Pétis de la Croix's *Les Mille et un jours* (The Thousand and One Days; 1710–1712), a sibling collection to Antoine Galland's *Les Mille et une nuit* (The Thousand and One Nights; 1704–1717),[5] and Ion Taloş specified the tale's classification as a version of tale type AT 851A: *Turandot*.[6] The recent revision of the tale-type index integrates the subtype AT 851A into tale type ATU 851, thus abolishing a clear distinction between the two originally separate items. Although both tale types share common features, each of them is characterized by specific features and deserves to be classified separately. Tale type ATU 851 features a princess who boasts being able to find the solution to each and every riddle. Accordingly, it is her suitors who pose a question, and the one suitor who asks a question relating to his own experience, whose answer she cannot possibly know, wins her hand. In tale type AT 851A, it is the princess who poses riddles or enigmatic questions to her suitors, and the successful suitor has to answer a certain number of her questions on pain of death. Once the suitor responded to all of the princess's questions, he asks her a question relating to his own identity. The events that follow overlap with tale type ATU 851.

Tale type AT 851A has rarely been documented from European oral tradition. A fairly detailed version is given in the mid-nineteenth-century Italian tale "I tre indovinelli" (The Three Riddles), recorded in South Tyrol.[7] Here, the male hero is a prince whose parents were taken prisoner by an enemy king who conquered their country. Having been brought up by one of his father's subjects, the prince eventually roams the world and is given shelter by a poor old woman whose humble shack lies outside of the walls of the enemy emperor's city. Challenging the princess, the hero gives the correct answers to the three questions she poses. When he notices that the princess is curious to know who he is, he grants her respite for eight days to find the answer to his own riddle, "Who is the king who was expelled from his realm and yet will return?" On the seventh night, one of the princess's servants overhears the prince talking to himself, and so the princess triumphs the next day. Deeply distressed at not being able to conquer his beloved, the prince asks her at least to set his parents free. At this point, the princess confesses her infatuation for him, and all unite happily. The tale ends by mentioning the prince's gratitude for the poor old woman's generosity and concludes with the advice, addressed at the tale's audience, to welcome poor but honest guests, "because you never know who they really are."

A rudimentary Flamish version of the tale was recorded in 1924 from night watchman S.J. in Wechel-ter-Zande, today's Wechelderzande in the Belgian region of Antwerp.[8] This tale introduces the princess and her condition to marry only the suitor who will answer her three questions. The successful suitor is a poor swineherd who spent a full three years in the wilderness living off plants and herbs and thinking about "human beings and things" day and night. He would even keep his eyes open with little sticks so as not to fall asleep, in this way acquiring great wisdom. Following the introduction of the tale's characters, the session of questions passes quickly, and in the end they get married.

Although all of the three tales summarized above feature a princess asking questions, they differ in detail. The Flamish text appears to be heavily truncated, preserving little more than the tale type's constitutive feature. Compared to the Romanian tale, the Italian tale reads like an intermediary version, substituting the introductory motif of the hero selling his parents by the parents' imprisonment, lacking the motif of the deathly letter, and substituting the final scene of seduction by a less compromising overhearing of the hero's secret. Even so, the Romanian and Italian versions overlap in introducing a lonely hero who lost his parents, although for different reasons. Considering this introductory motif, Pétis de la Croix's tale of Turandot appears to be a likely historical precursor of the tale, as it also begins with a hero and his parents being forced to flee their country that has been invaded by enemy forces.[9] When they are totally destitute, the prince wins the favors of the local ruler by finding and returning the ruler's beloved falcon. As the ruler grants him three wishes in return, the prince asks him to take care of his parents before requesting a horse with all necessary equipment and a princely dress and armour. The final scene in which the princess attempts to learn the prince's secret by bewildering him with her female charms also finds its equivalent in de la Croix's tale. Here, one of the princess's beautiful slave girls visits the prince at night, suggesting they flee the country together, as the princess plots to have him killed. Although the prince declines to flee, the slave girl learns about his name and informs the princess accordingly. When the princess solves the prince's riddle the next day, the hero is at first shocked, but then the princess confesses her love for him. In a dramatic scene, the slave girl also professes her infatuation for the prince and, since she will not be able to unite with him, commits suicide in public. In this manner, most elements of the Romanian tale correspond with de la Croix's tale of Turandot. The only element that does not have an equivalent is the motif of the deathly letter mentioned in the introduction of the Romanian tale. Since the motif is widely spread in international tradition,[10] the narrator of the Romanian text or some prior oral source might have added it to de la Croix's tale, thus not necessarily excluding the latter as model for the former.

Meanwhile, de la Croix's *Mille et un jours* is an adapted version of the anonymous fifteenth- or late fourteenth-century Ottoman Turkish collection of tales, *Ferec baʿd eş-şidde* (Relief after Hardship).[11] The Ottoman Turkish source text not only contains the motif of the deathly letter but also embeds it convincingly in the tale's structure as an omen indicating that the prince's period of misfortune is over and that he will prevail in his dispute with the princess.[12] In a similar function, the motif also appears in the Arabic version, of unclear provenance, compiled late in the eighteenth century by Dom Chavis in his effort to add to the tales of *The Thousand and One Nights*.[13]

As the riddles of the Romanian version relate to a dominant Christian context, its relation to the Ottoman Turkish tale in which at least some of the riddles relate to a Muslim context is probably not a direct one. A possible intermediary between the two versions is suggested by the late Byzantine, and thus Christian, literary tale *Alexander and Semiramis*, dating to the late fourteenth or early fifteenth century.[14] This text is preserved in two seventeenth-century manuscripts.[15] As the names indicate, the male hero here is Alexander the Great, and the princess is the legendary queen Semiramis. Some elements of the Ottoman Turkish tale, such as the hero abandoning his parents and the deathly letter, are missing in the Byzantine tale. Even so, the latter is likely indebted to the former as it includes the episode in which the hero finds and restores the ruler's lost falcon, an episode that is otherwise only contained in de la Croix's version and in the Ottoman Turkish tale (and its older Persian model). An additional minor trait also suggests the late Byzantine version as an intermediary between the Ottoman Turkish and the Romanian tales. In the Ottoman Turkish text, the hero looks at the princess and falls hopelessly in love with her. However, he immediately concentrates so as not to let her beauty confuse him. Only in the Byzantine version, Alexander does not look at the princess because he fears to lose his senses because of her beauty. On the one hand, this enables him to concentrate on her questions, but on the other, he thus fails to recognize her during her nocturnal visit.[16] In the Romanian tale, the hero first takes a quick glance at the princess, "but then he lowered his gaze, thinking, 'I must not look at her . . . .'"[17]

The tale's historical development is further complicated by the fact that, as mentioned above, essentially the second half of tale type AT 851A is classified as tale type ATU 851. In this tale type, the princess challenges her suitors to ask her a question or pose a riddle whose answer she will not be able to find. Again, the suitor's question relates to his personal experience. He does not, however, ask the princess to identify his origins. Instead, he constructs a riddle the answer to which is his personal experiences on the way to meeting her.

A lengthy version of tale type ATU 851 was told by C.A. Beckmann in the village Ruddienen in the vicinity of the East Prussian town of Heydekrug, today Šilutė in Lithuania, and published in 1930.[18]

> A haughty princess, her parents' only child, decides to marry only a man cleverer than herself. A tournament in which her suitors are to pose a riddle to her is to decide her fate. Should she find the answer, the suitor is to be killed. One after the other, the three sons of a rich farmer try their luck. When the two elder brothers do not return, Hans, the youngest one, decides to set out, aided by clever Fritz, the coachman's son. As Hans's mother hates the thought of him being killed by the princess, she decides that it is better to kill him herself and prepares a poisonous drink for her son. Fritz, however, warns Hans, so that he spills the drink on the back of his horse. When the horse dies from the poison, three crows eat from the flesh and also die. Hans and Fritz collect the dead birds and use them to prepare a meal for a group of thirteen robbers to whose den they happen to come, hereby killing all of the robbers. Alluding to the events, Hans poses the following riddle, "One killed none and yet killed one. One killed three, and three killed thirteen." When the princess is unable to solve the riddle, she sends first her maid and then her lady-in-waiting to Hans to find out the solution. As both of them return without having succeeded, she is forced to visit him herself. Each time, Fritz takes a token from the women, and when the princess gives Hans her ring, he finally discloses his secret. When the princess is able to give the correct answer the next day, Hans is about to be executed. He is, however, saved by Fritz who discloses the princess's stratagem, following which the princess is forced to confess her ruse and marry Hans. In addition, his two brothers (who have not been killed, after all) are freed and married to the two other women.

Although the three brothers and the younger brother's helper are specific to this version, numerous other versions collected from oral tradition all over Europe display essentially the same structure and events. A small selection of texts include the following: a Finnish version collected in 1882 by A. Lampinen in the town of Mikkeli,[19] a Portuguese version told by S. João de Airão-Minho,[20] a French version performed in January 1957 by the farmer Mrs. Léon Bertrand in Aspres-les-Corps,[21] a Lithuanian version collected by A. Lerhis-Puškaitis in Džūkste, district Jelgava (Zemgale),[22] and a Scottish version narrated by fisherman John Mackenzie near Inverary, who "learned the tale from an old man in Lorn many years ago." [23] The oldest text of this version attested in European tradition is contained in the Latin *Compilatio singularis exemplorum*, a collection of tales compiled in the second half of the thirteenth century, most probably in France.[24] Edited by Alfons Hilka, the relevant tale was presented in translation by Albert Wesselski.[25]

> A knight who lost all of his fortune in armed tournaments learns that a certain king will give half his kingdom to the person who vanquishes his daughter in a tournament of riddles. Meeting the princess, the knight is given the choice to either answer her riddles or pose riddles himself. He choses the latter and asks his first riddle, "On the way I met another knight and proposed that he carry me a mile, and I would carry him the next one." Immediately, the princess guesses correctly that he alludes to storytelling. His second riddle is more difficult, "When I felt cold on the way, I warmed myself by lighting a fire with simple words." As the princess has no idea what this alludes to, she sends her maids to the knight, directing them to find the solution at whatever cost. The knight, however, only discloses the solution when the princess herself visits him, promising not to use it against him. When the next day the princess guesses correctly that his second riddle alluded to the burning of his book of hours, he poses his third riddle, "In the forest, I met several beautiful bitches, all of whom were kind to me. I let all of them go except for one whom I pierced." In order not to be disgraced in public, the princess is forced to give in and marry him.

Two Persian versions of the more detailed tale type AT 851A predate this text by about a century, thus constituting the tale's oldest documented versions presently known.[26] The first of these versions is contained in the *Munes-nāme* (The Book as an Intimate Friend), a collection of wise sayings and entertaining tales compiled by a certain Abu Bakr ibn Khosrow al-Ostād.[27] As the author dedicated his work to the reigning sovereign, Noṣrat al-Din Abu Bakr ibn Moḥammad Ildigiz, Atabeg of Azerbaijan (r. 1194–1210), the work dates from the end of the twelfth or the beginning of the thirteenth century. The *Munes-nāme* is the oldest-known existing specimen of a genre of books that later came to be known under the generic title *Jāmeʿ al-ḥekāyāt* (Collection of Tales). As indicated by their close correspondence in terms of content and structure, either the late twelfth or early thirteenth-century *Munes-nāme* itself or a closely related derivative served as the base text for the late fourteenth- or fifteenth-century Ottoman Turkish compilation *Ferec baʿd eş-şidde* that in turn supplied the tales adapted in de la Croix's early eighteenth-century *Mille et un jours*. The *Munes-nāme*'s list of contents mentions the "Tale of the Prince, His Mother, His Father, and the Emperor of China," thus unambiguously alluding to the tale presently discussed. As several pages in the manuscript are missing, the actual text of the tale has not been preserved.[28] There is, however, good reason to presume that later representatives of the genre *Jāmeʿ al-ḥekāyāt*, such as the manuscript in the Ganj Bakhsh Library in Islamabad whose text is published,[29] present the tale's text in a form similar to that in the *Munes-nāme*. As this Persian version does not differ decisively from the Ottoman Turkish *Ferec baʿd eş-şidde* in terms of content and structure, the latter can reasonably be assumed to constitute a faithful translation of the former.

Another, somewhat shorter, early thirteenth-century Persian version is given in Sadid al-Din Moḥammad ʿAwfi's (d. ca. 1232) encyclopedic compilation *Javāmeʿ al-ḥekāyāt* (Collections of Tales). Lacking the episode of the restored falcon, this version is contained in the twenty-fifth and final chapter of the first book, titled "On the Anecdotes of Sagacious and Acute Persons."[30]

Before agreeing to marry, the highly educated daughter of the Greek emperor submits her suitors to a session of questions. First she will ask nine or ten questions and then her suitor would have the same right. Should she not be able to give the correct answers, she will marry her suitor. Should he not be able to do so, he will lose his life.

At the same time in a town of the country of Irāq, a poor man spent whatever he owned on the education of his clever only son. When they are totally destitute, the young man advises his parents to sell their house, and together they travel to Iran. There the young man proposes that the king buy his parents, whom he presents as his slaves, in exchange for a horse and armor. The king grants the young man's request as a present, and his parents stay on as the king's guests.

Arriving in Greece, the young man enters the service of the vizier, who showers him with marks of respect to such an extent that the king becomes angry. In order to rid himself of the vizier, the king sends him to deliver a letter to his governor, containing the order to execute the bearer immediately. As the vizier considers the letter to be beneficial, he asks the young man to deliver it and collect the presumed presents in his stead. On the way, the young man gets thirsty. When he drinks water from a well, the letter gets wet and he opens it to see whether the message is still legible. As he reads the death order, he destroys the letter and returns to the vizier.

Noticing that the young man's fortune is favorable, the vizier suggests that he face the challenge to answer the princess's questions. Although the princess warns him, the young man faces her, answering nine (or ten) questions to her satisfaction. Following this, the young man is invited to test the princess. His question is, "Who is that person whose father is a horse and whose mother is a suit of armor? He travels toward his ruin, and only a sheet of paper that got wet saved him from destruction." As the princess has no idea what he alludes to she has recourse to a ruse to find the solution to the riddle. Dressing her maids as ladies, and disguising herself as their maid, they visit the young man at night. The young man is not deceived and first requires them to leave their precious dresses and jewelry with him. Having informed the women about his experience, he then rejects the ladies' offer to chose one of them for his pleasure, instead asking for the favors of the alleged maid. At this point, the women make their escape.

The next morning, the princess is able to answer his question. Then the young man asks her to interpret a riddle referring to the nocturnal visit of three doves who left their feathers behind when leaving him. Fearing to be disgraced, the princess requests a night's respite. Asking her mother's advice, she is advised to marry the young man, which she does. They marry, and the king passes his throne on to the young man. The young man immediately demands the king of Persia, who owes him tribute, to release his parents and receives them with great honor.

The tale ends with praise of knowledge and wisdom.

Fritz Meier regarded ʿAwfi's version as the tale's "original" version, the "Ur-Roman."[31] Although tales in which riddles play a major role abound in both Eastern and Western tradition,[32] no version of the tale older than that attested by ʿAwfi has come to light. A heavily abridged version of ʿAwfi's version is contained in an unspecified Ottoman translation of his work, containing little more than the introduction and some eight questions.[33] In the end, the princess is tired of asking questions and marries the young man. In Persian tradition, the full-fledged tale was revitalized in the nineteenth century by its inclusion in the shorter version of the *Ṭuṭi-nāme* (Book of the Parrot), the anonymous chapbook *Chehel ṭuṭi* (Forty Parrots).[34] Although this chapbook was printed numerous times between its first edition in 1848 and modern editions printed until the event of the Iranian revolution in 1979,[35] the tale did not have a noticeable impact on Persian oral tradition.

The above discussion has consciously avoided the specific riddles or enigmatic questions posed by the princess. Although their thorough investigation might supply further clues as to the relation between the tale's various versions, they are of no major relevance for the present discussion. Rather to the contrary, the multitude of varying questions in the tale's different versions risks blurring the clear argument presented here, as there are virtually no two texts employing the same riddles. In terms of intercultural communication, the most salient point of the present tale's tradition is the fact that in both the Byzantine and the Romanian versions, the enigmatic questions relate to the Christian context in which they are presented, constituting a conscious adaptation from the Muslim context of the Ottoman Turkish and Persian versions. For de la Croix's rendering, there was no need to adapt the questions to a changed context, as the author unambiguously presents his text as "alien," that is, not relating to his own cultural context. This conscious alienation or, in other words, "orientalization," also furthered the tale's adaptation in subsequent European drama and opera. Adapted for the stage by Italian playwright Carlo Gozzi (1762), the tale's version by German dramatist Friedrich Schiller (1802) served as the basis for the libretto of Giacomo Puccini's opera *Turandot*. First performed in 1926, this opera continues to enjoy a considerable popularity with modern audiences.

Notes

1. Taloş, Ion, "Rumänien," in *Enzyklopädie des Märchens*, vol. 11 (2004), cols. 886–897, at col. 887, referencing Chiţimia, Ion Constantin, "Un basm necunoscut înregistrat în secolul al XVIII-lea," *Revista de istorie şi teorie literară* 17 (1968), pp. 109–118.

2. Ms. 1344, fol. 1r–11r. German translation by Emanuel Turczynski in Karlinger, Felix, and Ovidiu Bîrlea, *Rumänische Volksmärchen*, Düsseldorf: Diederichs, 1969, pp. 5–14, 297, no. 1.

3. Chiţimia, "Un basm necunoscut," pp. 109–110; Karlinger and Bîrlea, *Rumänische Volksmärchen*, p. 297; see also Moraru, Mihai, "Postfaţă: Cărţile populare—încercare de definire structurală," in Cartojan, Nicolae, *Carţile populare în literatura românească*, vol. 2, Bucharest: Enciclopedică română, 1974, pp. 481–519, at p. 504.

4. Schenda, Rudolf, "Bertoldo, Bertoldino," in *Enzyklopädie des Märchens*, vol. 2 (1979), cols. 165–171; Röcke, Werner, "Salomon und Markolf," ibid., vol. 11 (2004), cols. 1078–1085.

5. Moraru, Mihai, *De nuptiis Mercurii et Philologiae*, Bucharest: Fundaţiei culturale române, 1997, pp. 87–91.

6. Taloş, "Rumänien," col. 887. For the tale type, see Goldberg, Christine, "Rätselprinzessin," in *Enzyklopädie des Märchens*, vol. 11 (2004), cols. 286–294. The most recent study of the tale of Turandot, and especially the name, is Orsatti, Paola, *Materials for a History of the Persian Narrative Tradition: Two Characters: Farhād and Turandot*, Venice: Edizioni Ca'Foscari, 2019, pp. 63–100.

7. Schneller, Christian, *Märchen und Sagen aus Wälschtirol: Ein Beitrag zur deutschen Sagenkunde*, Innsbruck: Wagner'sche Universitätsbuchhandlung, 1867, pp. 132–137, no. 49.

8. De Meyere, Victor, *De Vlaamsche vertelselschat*, vol. 3, Antwerp: De Sikkel, 1929, pp. 191–192, 314, no. 258.

9. Pétis de la Croix, François, *Histoire du prince Calaf et de la princesse de la Chine: Conte des «Mille et un jours»*, ed. Paul Sebag, Paris: L'Harmatan, 2000.

10. Shojaei Kawan, Christine, "Uriasbrief," in *Enzyklopädie des Märchens*, vol. 13 (2010), cols. 1262–1267.

11. Pétis de la Croix, François, *Les Mille et un jours: contes persans*, ed. Paul Sebag, Paris: Christian Bourgois, 1980; rev. ed. Paris: Phébus, 2003.

12. Marzolph, *Relief after Hardship*, pp. 87–89, no. 25. A complete transcript and a German translation of the Ottoman Turkish text are supplied by Anetshofer, Helga, *Temporale Satzverbindungen in altosmanischen Prosatexten*, Wiesbaden: Harrassowitz, 2005, pp. 285–343.

13. Chauvin, *Bibliographie*, vol. 5 (1901), pp. 194–195, no. 114; Marzolph and Van Leeuwen, *Arabian Nights Encyclopedia*, vol. 1, pp. 269–271, no. 411.

14. Moennig, Ulrich, "Eine spätbyzantinische literarische Version des Märchens von der Rätselprinzessin („Turandot") verglichen mit ihrer wahrscheinlich osmanischen Vorlage," in *Akten des 27. Deutschen Orientalistentages (Bonn—28.September bis 2. Oktober*

1998): Norm und Abweichung, ed. Stefan Wild und Hartmut Schild, Würzburg: Ergon, 2001, pp. 705–714; Moennig, *Die Erzählung von Alexander und Semiramis: Kritische Ausgabe mit einer Einleitung, Übersetzung und einem Wörterverzeichnis*, Berlin: Walter de Gruyter, 2004, particularly at pp. 19–34.

15. Moennig, *Die Erzählung*, pp. 7–14.

16. Moennig, "Eine spätbyzantinische literarische Version," p. 711.

17. Karlinger and Bîrlea, *Rumänische Volksmärchen*, p. 7.

18. Plenzat, Karl, *Die goldene Brücke: Volksmärchen*, Leipzig: Eichblat, 1930, pp. 100–110, 162.

19. Simonsuuri, Lauri, and Pirkko-Liisa Rausmaa, *Finnische Volkserzählungen*, Berlin: De Gruyter, 1968, pp. 111–112, no. 68.

20. Meier, Harri, and Dieter Woll, *Portugiesische Märchen*, Düsseldorf and Cologne: Diederichs, 1975, pp. 131–134, no. 65 (from Teófilo Braga, *Contos tradicionais do povo português*, vol. 1, Lisbon: Dom Quixote, 1987, pp. 135–138).

21. Joisten, Charles, *Contes populaires du Dauphiné*, vol. 2, Grenoble: Musée Dauphinois, 1971, pp. 17–18, no. 74.

22. Ambainis, Ojārs, *Lettische Volksmärchen*, Berlin: Akademie-Verlag, 2nd ed. 1979, pp. 286–290, no. 87.

23. Campbell, John Francis, *Popular Tales of the West Highlands*, new ed., Edinburgh and London, 1890, vol. 2, pp. 36–46, no. 22 (quote p. 44).

24. Wolff, Reinhold, "Unterwegs vom mittelalterlichen Predigtmärlein zur Novelle der Frühen Neuzeit: Die Erzählsammlung 'Compilatio singularis exemplorum'," *Mittellateinisches Jahrbuch* 41.1 (2006), pp. 53–76; see also Wollin, Carsten, "Geschichten aus der 'Compilatio singularis exemplorum'," ibid., pp. 77–91.

25. Hilka, Alfons, "Neue Beiträge zur Erzählungsliteratur des Mittelalters (die Compilatio Singularis der Hs. Tours 468, ergänzt durch eine Schwesterhandschrift Bern 679)," *90. Jahresbericht der Schlesischen Gesellschaft für vaterl[ändische] Cultur: Sitzung der Sektion für neuere Philologie vom 5. Dezember 1912* (Breslau 1913), pp. 1–24, at p. 8, no. 2; Wesselski, *Märchen des Mittelalters*, pp. 70–71, no. 25.

26. Meier, Fritz, "Turandot in Persien," *Zeitschrift der Deutschen Morgenländischen Gesellschaft* 95 (1941), pp. 1–27, 415–421; Rossi, Ettore, "La leggenda di Turandot," in *Studi orientalistici in onore di Giorgio Levi della Vida*, ed. Raffaele Ciasca, vol. 2, Rome: Istituto per l'Oriente, 1956, pp. 457–476; see also *Turandot: Die persische Märchenerzählung in zwei Fassungen*, ed. and transl. Youssef Mogtader and Gregor Schoeler, Wiesbaden: Reichert, 2017.

27. For the following see Meredith-Owens, G.M., "An Early Persian Miscellany," in *Iran and Islam: In Memory of the Late Vladimir Minorsky*, ed. Clifford Edmund Bosworth, Edinburgh: Edinburgh University Press, 1971, pp. 435–441; Marzolph, *Relief after Hardship*, pp. 47–48.

28. Meredith-Owens, "An Early Persian Miscellany," p. 438.

29. *Jāmeʿ al-ḥekāyāt: noskhe-ye ketābkhāne-ye Ganj Bakhsh-e Pākestān*, ed. Moḥammad Jaʿfari Qanavāti, Tehran: Qaṭre, 1391/2012, pp. 371–404, no. 18.

30. Niẓámu'd-dín, *Introduction*, p. 190, no. 1165; ʿAwfi, Moḥammad, *Pānzdah bāb-e Javāmeʿ al-ḥekāyāt*, ed. Moḥammad Ramażāni, Tehran: Kolāle-ye khāvar, 1335/1956, pp. 381–389, no. 522; German translation by Behrnauer, Walter, "Der junge Perser und die griechische Prinzessin," *Johannes-Album* (Chemnitz 1857), pp. 57–70.

31. Meier, "Turandot in Persien," p. 7.

32. Goldberg, Christine, *Turandot's Sisters: A Study of the Folktale AT 851*, New York: Garland, 1993.

33. Hammer, Joseph von, *Rosenöl: oder Sagen und Kunden des Morgenlandes aus arabischen, persischen und türkischen Quellen gesammelt*, Stuttgart and Tübingen: J.G. Cotta, 1813, vol. 2, pp. 287–289, no. 156.

34. Meier, "Turandot in Persien," pp. 418–421; Marzolph, Ulrich, *Die vierzig Papageien: Das persische Volksbuch Čehel Ṭuṭi, ein Beitrag zur Geschichte des Papageienbuches*, Walldorf: Verlag für Orientkunde, 1979, pp. 22–27 (analysis), 71–80 (text).

35. Marzolph, Ulrich, *Dāstānhā-ye širin: Fünfzig persische Volksbüchlein aus der zweiten Hälfte des zwanzigsten Jahrhunderts*, Stuttgart: Franz Steiner, 1994, pp. 38–39, no. XII.

CHAPTER 25

The Entrapped Would-Be Seducers Have to Work to Earn Their Food (ATU 882A*)

A Finnish folktale, collected in 1891 from the oral performance of Heikki Makkonen, aged 25, tells of an unequal marriage in which the socially inferior woman proves her worth by protecting her absent husband's interests:[1]

> There was a lord of a castle, who married a nearby lower-class maiden, and then immediately had to go to war for three years. Counts Frederick and Charles wagered with the lord that they would fool his wife out of all his possessions during his absence.
>
> Some time thereafter they went to the castle as guests. The mistress received them with great respect, and they stayed there for two days. Now Count Frederick started to approach this lady in an inept manner, and she understood their naughty goal, that this was mere fraud and deceit. She pretended to agree to their deceptions and gave them permission to come the next day to the same house, where she would be at two o'clock, but she indicated a route they had to take through seven buildings. The doors of the buildings opened by themselves and then shut again. But when they had reached the fifth building, the door did not open, nor the doors of the previous buildings, where they had come in. And the room was about three fathoms wide and had a stone wall five fathoms high. There was only one little window at the top. When they tried to open the doors and they did not open, Fredrick said, "Well, it seems we are prisoners of Rosamunda." An hour after that a servant came who opened a little hole in the wall and gave them food, fish, bread, water and salt, and said, "Better than this you will not be able to earn by spinning!" After that a spinning wheel with tows of the worst possible quality was lowered from the ceiling. And so they earned their poor food by spinning for three years. When the lord came home, they had lost all their property and went away in shame to distant lands.

Finnish folklorist Pirkko-Liisa Rausmaa classified this text, obviously the sole one recorded of its kind in Finnish tradition, as tale type ATU 882A*: *Suitors at* *the Spinning Wheel*. The short summary of this comparatively rarely documented tale type in the third revision of the international tale-type index, ATU, reads as follows: "In the absence of her husband (ship captain) a wife is annoyed by three suitors. She tricks them into a room and makes them spin (work)." The few versions of tale type ATU 882A* known from European tradition, such as the above-quoted Finnish tale, are often either rudimentary on the one hand, or embellished with additional details, some of them alien to the tale type, on the other. As the following discussion will argue, the tale type's most detailed historical versions demonstrate a clearly constructed plot whose constitutive elements are as follows: (1) A man leaves his wife who assures him of her faithfulness, sometimes by giving him a token of chastity whose characteristics will change should she betray him; (2) at times provoked by the husband's declared conviction that his wife will remain faithful to him under all circumstances, several suitors make advances to her, each following the previous one several days or weeks later; (3) although the faithful wife does not always have the time to develop a scheme, she manages to confine the suitors one after the other in a secluded room; (4) there, they have to earn their living by doing typically female work, such as to comb or spin cotton; and (5) the suitors are only released from confinement after the husband's return. As there are several other tale types with a structure similar to tale type ATU 882A*, the history of the latter tale type and its relation to Middle Eastern tradition deserve a detailed consideration.

In terms of structure and content, tale type ATU 882A* is related to tale type ATU 1730: *The Entrapped Suitors* (see essay **87, *The Clever Woman Has the Entrapped Would-Be Lovers Publicly Humiliated***). In this widely attested tale type, several suitors make advances to a faithful wife. At times, the suitors are some of the town's officials who promise to help the woman in exchange for sexual favors. Apparently giving in to their advances, the woman asks all of them to visit her on a specific day, at short intervals. Just as the first suitor makes himself comfortable, the next one arrives, and she asks the first one to hide in a closet where she locks him up. This happens to all of the suitors, usually three or four. When in the end the woman presents her case to the ruler, he advises her to seek help from the town's officials. As none of them is available (since all of them are locked up), the woman suggests the king listen to the closet testifying to the justice of her claim. One after the other, the men in the closet speak up, are released and publicly humiliated as lechers who were tricked by a woman. Tale type ATU 1730 is first identified in Indian tradition and owes its international dissemination to adapted translations of the version included in the Persian *Sendbād-nāme* (The Book of Sendbād [the Sage]).[2] Considering its wide distribution, tale type ATU 1730 often serves as a receptacle for a variety of tales in which a faithful married woman dupes the men trying to seduce her. In terms of general structure, tale type ATU 882A* to which the above-quoted Finnish tale belongs, generally corresponds to tale type ATU 1730. But there are several decisive differences.

First, the most complete versions of tale type ATU 882A* begin with the mention of the index of chastity, thus foregrounding and preordaining the ensuing development. The few European versions of tale type ATU 882A* listed in ATU include a small cluster of versions from the Eastern Slavonic languages (Russian, Ukrainian, Belarusian) whose abstract description in the catalogue of Eastern Slavonic tales explicitly mentions this element:[3] A man leaves his wife in a shirt on which black stains will appear should his wife be unfaithful to him; she shuts up her husband's acquaintances who attempt to seduce her in a cellar (or another room) and forces them to work (spin). The index of chastity is here a white shirt worn by the husband. Meanwhile, the index of chastity also appears prominently in the introductory episode of tale type ATU 888: *The Faithful Wife*. This tale type features a woman whose husband is separated from her (usually having been taken prisoner in Turkey) while wearing a shirt that stays stainless as long as she remains faithful to him.[4] In terms of narrative dynamics, the chastity index challenges an envious person (or several persons) who aim to seduce the faithful woman.[5] The further course of events of tale type ATU 888 develops differently, as the woman sets out to liberate and manages to rescue her husband.

Second, in tale type ATU 1730 the suitors' inept advances are to some extent motivated by the beautiful woman asking for their help, and the men she approaches see an opportunity to extort sex from an unprotected woman in exchange for doing her a favor. The woman's absent husband is of concern for the plot only insofar as he is the one whose affairs the woman aims to straighten. In contrast, in tale type ATU 882A*, the suitors aim to seduce the faithful woman in order to shatter her husband's unfailing confidence in her chastity. The idea behind this motivation is the men's (and, probably, the audience's) firm conviction that weakness and faithlessness are inherent in female character to an equal degree as their own male charm is irresistible. In other words, in the tale's logic, the woman's intended seduction only constitutes a collateral damage, as the prime target of the suitors' action is the man.

Third, in tale type ATU 1730 the woman herself decides when the suitors are to visit her. Accordingly, she has ample time to prepare for the expected visitors. As a matter of fact, she often tells the suitors to come visit her only after a few days during which she has a carpenter build the closet she later uses to trap the men. In contrast, in tale type ATU 882A* the woman's suitors or would-be seducers regularly show up uninvited and without much prior notice. As the woman is taken by surprise, she has to devise a spontaneous strategem to dupe the men. Versions in which she, or her husband, already took precautions against the unforeseen events are probably influenced by the widely more popular tale type ATU 1730.

Fourth, in tale type ATU 1730 the suitors are locked up in separate compartments of the closet and have to stay quiet so as not to be noticed. In tale type ATU 882A* they are not only confined in the same room but are further humiliated by being forced to execute a menial kind of labor in their confinement.[6] This labor is often considered particularly humiliating, as it involves spinning or weaving, both of which in traditional societies were considered typically female tasks.

And fifth, although tale type ATU 882A* overlaps with tale type ATU 1730 in the confinement and the humiliation of the would-be seducers, in the latter they are finally exposed to public ridicule when they have been trapped in the custom-made closet and the woman accused of adultery asks "the closet" to testify to her innocence. In tale type ATU 882A*, the confinement and humiliation of the would-be seducers is not a public act, but rather occurs in the private context of the couple's house, in addition to the married couple usually involving the servants. While the public exposure in tale type ATU 1730 aims at and results in ridiculing the suitors, their humiliation in the private context rather constitutes an act of education aiming to teach them a lesson by making each of them individually understand that their advances were inappropriate.

The Finnish text quoted initially is a somewhat truncated version of the full-fledged tale type ATU 882A*, since it lacks the motif of the chastity index that appears in the Eastern Slavonic (and other) versions. But the further course of events, including the unforeseen attempt at sexual transgression and the clever woman's self-protection as well as the humiliation and education of the transgressors, clearly documents the occurrence of tale type ATU 882A* in a region that is geographically distant from the tale's origins.

Geographically closer to the tale's Middle Eastern region of origin is the tale's version given in Jerre Mangione's *A Memoir of Italian American Life* (1981).[7] The author retells the tale as heard in his youth by his uncle Nino from the Sicilian town of Caltanissetta. The faithful and chaste wife here is "the daughter of a peasant widow who married the richest baron in the province." The original narrator authenticated the tale through the fact that he "had been secretary to the baron's nephew as a young man," thus purporting to narrate events that had actually taken place. Uncle Nino's version also lacks the motif of the chastity index, motivating the men's attempts, as in the Finnish tale, by having them presume that the woman's "inferior blood . . . naturally gives her base instincts which she can't possibly escape, no matter how much education you have pumped into her." One after the other, the woman locks her three would-be seducers up in a secluded room, and her maid communicates with the men through an opening in the room's ceiling. The Sicilian version stands out through its expressed focus on scatological aspects, as the imprisoned men are not even given a container to relieve themselves. When the men are finally set free, they are further humiliated by having to "scrub and clean the room," and their disgrace becomes publicly known when they are requested to "send for their personal physicians to disinfect it."

Probably genetically related to the tale's early Ottoman Turkish version is a text from Greek tradition in Cyprus, originally published in 1961. The tale was performed by the illiterate female storyteller Vassilou Dimitri, aged 70, and originating from the district of Kapouti in Northern Cyprus.[8]

> Since a mason does not find any work where he lives, he and his beautiful wife decide that he should try to earn money elsewhere. Before he leaves, she gives him two roses to take along, telling him that the roses will not wilt as long as she remains faithful to him.
>
> As the man's new companions are curious to learn about the properties of the roses, he unsuspiciously tells them, and one of them sets out to seduce his wife so as to demonstrate that women are not to be trusted. He presents himself to the mason's wife and is hosted by her. Accommodating her guest in a room on the lower floor, the woman herself sleeps in a chamber on the upper floor. In order to protect herself, she removes a plank in the floor and covers it with a carpet. As the guest intends to seduce the woman, he enters her chamber, falls into the trap and finds himself in a secluded room from which he cannot escape. The next morning, the woman hands him a spindle and some cotton, telling him that he has to work in return for being fed by her. When the mason's comrades see that the roses do not wither, another one attempts to seduce his wife. He also falls into the trap and is forced to spin cotton.
>
> As soon as the mason earned enough money, he returns back home. Although his wife is happy to see him, she wonders why he had sent his companions to visit her. Since the mason is not aware of having sent anybody, he has a look and recognizes his former companions. Promising to rescue them, he instead kills them by scalding them with hot water.
>
> A neighbor agrees to discard the first man's corpse. When he returns to collect the agreed remuneration, the mason reproaches him for not having discarded the corpse, and shows him the second corpse in proof. The neighbor also discards the second corpse and then runs away, as he thinks the body might have come to life again. From then on, the mason and his wife live happily ever after.

Finishing with an additional episode that is reminiscent of tale type ATU 1536: *Disposing of the Corpse*, the Greek text from Cyprus has all the elements a full-fledged version of tale type ATU 882A* requires. In particular, the specification of the tale's male protagonist as a mason serves as an additional element to make the tale seem more realistic, as masons would often have been obliged to travel in order to find work.

In European tradition, the tale was known at least as early as the fifteenth century, when English poet Adam of Cobsam, about whose life nothing is known, composed his poem *The Wright's Chaste Wife* sometime before the year 1462.[9] Here, a carpenter marries the beautiful and chaste daughter of a widow, and his mother-in-law gives him a garland of roses that will not wilt as long as his wife remains faithful to him. Before the carpenter sets out to travel for professional reasons, he installs a trapdoor in a room that will deliver any intruders into an enclosed pit. The lord for whom he works learns about the garland's marvelous property and decides to test it. Offering to pay the woman for her love, he falls through the trapdoor into the pit. There, she makes him earn his living by beating flax to separate the fibers. The same happens to the lord's steward, who is made to pull the fibers through a swingel, and to the proctor of the church, who has to use a spindle to spin linen thread. After her husband's return, the woman releases the three imprisoned men only after having called the lord's wife to serve as witness and support her.

Adam of Cobsam's poem was frequently discussed in studies of late medieval English literature, particularly for its sociological import.[10] *The Wright's Chaste Wife* was compared to a tale in the Latin *Gesta Romanorum*, probably compiled in the fourteenth century, that also mentions a carpenter and his wife, the white shirt as a chastity index, and three entrapped suitors.[11] Since the menial tasks the suitors have to execute are not mentioned in that version, previous research has rejected it as an immediate precursor to Adam of Cobsam's poem. Meanwhile, virtually all modern scholars disregard the fact that already soon after Furnivall's first publication of Cobsam's tale in 1865, German scholar Reinhold Köhler in his review of Furnivall's edition pointed out the tale's closely corresponding version in the anonymous Ottoman Turkish compilation of entertaining and instructive tales, *Ferec ba'd eş-şidde* (Relief after Hardship).[12] The oldest unambiguously dated manuscript of this compilation dates from 1451, and the literature mentions an even older manuscript dating from 1382.[13] The Ottoman Turkish compilation is thus older than Adam of Cobsam's poem and likely constitutes the source he drew upon.[14]

> Despite his superb skills, the master builder of Bam in the country of Kerman is not hired by anybody, and so his chaste wife encourages him to look for work somewhere else. As a token of her chastity, she gives him a green twig from a box tree. The man travels to the town of Gavāshīr, constructs a magnificent palace and is greatly honored by the king.
>
> The king's envious viziers aim to spoil the master builder's reputation by calumniating him, but the master builder convinces the king of his innocence. Then the envious viziers make the master builder drunk so that he tells them about the details of his life at home. They forge a letter from his neighbors informing him that his wife engages in debauchery. Although the green twig proves the woman's faithfulness, they succeed in casting doubt into the master builder's heart. They insist that one of them must travel to Bam to investigate the matter, while the master builder remains in Gavāshīr.
>
> In Bam, an old woman helps the vizier arrange a meeting with the master builder's wife. The woman has been informed by her husband about his situation in Gavāshīr and quickly understands the vizier's intention. She invites the vizier to her house at night, drugs him unconscious during a

festive meal, and locks him up in an underground vault. When the vizier wakes up the next morning, a slave girl pretends that the woman's brother arrived and they were forced to hide him; the woman has now gone to a wedding and will only be back to release him after a whole week. Moreover, the slave girl insinuates that the vizier has been sexually abused by a male slave when drunk. Finally, the vizier is so enraged that he curses the master builder and his own scheme, and the woman understands that her suspicions are true. Although the vizier implores the slave girl to set him free, she pretends that this is not possible, as the woman's brother and some of his friends are still in the house. In exchange for giving him some bread, she has him spin cotton.

After a while, the second vizier travels to Bam to find out what happened to the first one. He suffers the same fate as the first vizier, as does the third vizier a little while later. When none of the viziers returns, the king himself travels to Bam. He also visits the woman and dines with her in her house. Out of respect, she does not drug him unconscious. Instead, she pretends that her brothers are about to arrive and offers to hide him in the underground vault. There, the king encounters his three viziers and reproaches them for their vicious scheme that has gotten not only them, but also himself, into trouble. Hearing the king speak, the woman realizes his true position. She releases him and apologizes, and the king admires her cleverness and chastity. Back in Gavāshīr, the king gives orders to execute the three envious viziers. He installs the chaste woman as the head of his family quarters and unites her with her husband.

Since Ottoman Turkish literature of the period was heavily influenced by Persian literature, there is little doubt that the Ottoman Turkish compilation was translated from the Persian. As a matter of fact, an extremely similar version of the tale appears in a Persian representative of the genre *Jāmeʿ al-ḥekāyāt* (Collection of Tales).[15] Although the undated manuscript of this Persian compilation appears to be from a comparatively recent period, probably the eighteenth century, it is but a recent representative of a genre whose historical roots date at least to the late twelfth or early thirteenth century. The *Munes-nāme* (The Book as an Intimate Friend), compiled by a certain Abu Bakr ibn Khosrow al-Ostād and dedicated to the reigning sovereign, Noṣrat al-Din Abu Bakr ibn Moḥammad Ildigiz, Atabeg of Azerbaijan (r. 1194–1210), contains the tale in question in a version that is very similar to the one in the Ottoman Turkish *Ferec baʿd eş-şidde*.[16] Another Persian representative of the same literary genre, likewise of comparatively recent date, contains a slightly different version of the tale in which the male protagonist is a soldier (*mard-e lashkari*) and the two entrapped suitors are kitchen servants (*maṭbakhi*).[17] This version can be traced back to an earlier occurrence in Żiyāʾ al-Din Nakhshabi's *Ṭuṭi-nāme* (Book of the Parrot), compiled in 1329, and its precursor, titled *Javāher al-asmār* (Jewels of Nocturnal Tales), compiled by a certain ʿEmād ibn Moḥammad in 1314.[18] Aiming to trace the origin of the tale's Persian versions, the nineteenth-century scholars Reinhold Köhler and William Alexander Clouston discussed the tale's oldest documented version in Somadeva's eleventh-century *Kathāsaritsāgara* (The Ocean of Streams of Story).[19] Here, the loving couple are the merchant Guhasena and his beautiful wife Devasmitā; the chastity index is twofold, constituted of two red lotuses delivered by god Shiva; the woman's chastity is tested by four envious merchants who are introduced by an old hag who tries to win over the woman by showing her a weeping bitch, allegedly a former woman who was transformed due to her having been over-chaste (an episode corresponding to tale type ATU 1515: *The Weeping Bitch*).[20] Instead of trapping the would-be seducers, the woman drugs them unconscious one after the other, brands their foreheads with a dog's foot of iron and lets them go. In the end, the woman disguises herself in men's clothes and travels to the country of the "young libertines" where she claims them to be her slaves. The merchants are forced to buy their release by paying her a large sum of money. Although this version includes the motifs of the chastity index and the woman's relatively spontaneous action, the further course of events differs from the standard action in tale type ATU 882A* to such an extent that the tale in the *Kathāsaritsāgara* can at best be seen as an early precursor of the tale type whose distinct structure was later developed in Persian literature.

The tale's historical development can thus be traced with a relatively high degree of certainty. The tale's initial motif of the chastity index (and subsequent attempts at seduction) is first documented in ancient Indian literature. Early adaptations include two different tales in Persian literature, the earliest one dating from around the year 1200, and again different fourteenth-century tales in the Latin *Gesta Romanorum* or the "Tale of the Rose" in the French prose romance *Perceforest*.[21] While the Persian tale featuring a soldier left no decisive trace in international tradition, the other one, featuring a mason or a carpenter as its male protagonist, was translated to Ottoman Turkish at the latest by the middle of the fifteenth century. It may have been this version that inspired Adam of Cobsam to write his poem, whose plot closely corresponds to the Ottoman Turkish version. At the same time, the Middle Eastern versions live on in contemporary oral tradition of the region, documented by versions from countries as far apart as Afghanistan[22] and Tajikistan[23] on the one hand, and Tunisia[24] on the other. The tale's versions recorded from oral tradition in Europe are but a faint echo of the original texts. One can only speculate about the reasons why tale type ATU 882A* was relatively seldom documented in popular tradition in comparison to the more popular tale type ATU 1730. Although both tale types stress female agency, maybe the former tale's fairly intricate plot was less appealing to popular storytellers than the drastic dimension of public humiliation practiced in the latter. Or perhaps the female tasks the confined suitors had to do in tale type ATU 882A* were deemed excessively denigrating in contrast to the suitors' confinement in boxes, which even a male audience would have appreciated with a good laugh. But maybe the tale types' differing popularity is simply due to the different channels of distribution, as the *Sendbād-nāme* and its European derivatives were doubtless more influential than less known compilations such as the Persian *Jāmeʿ al-ḥekāyāt* or the Ottoman Turkish *Ferec baʿd eş-şidde.*

Notes

1. Rausmaa, Pirkko-Liisa, *Suomalaiset kansansadut*, vol. 2: *Legenda- ja novellisadut*, Helsinki: Suomalaisen Kirjallisuuden Seura, 1982, pp. 176–177, no. 106.

2. Wehse, Rainer, "Liebhaber bloßgestellt," in *Enzyklopädie des Märchens*, vol. 8 (1996), cols. 1056–1063, particularly at cols. 1058–1059.

3. Barag, Lev G., et al., *Sravnitel'ny ukazatel' syuzhetov vostochnoslavyanska skazka*, Leningrad: Nauka, 1979.

4. For the term "chastity index" see Somadeva, *The Ocean of Story: Being C.H. Tawney's Translation of Somadeva's Kathā Sarit Sāgara*, ed. N.M. Penzer, reprint Delhi: Motilal Banarsidass, 1968, vol. 1, pp. 165–168.

5. Williams-Krapp, Werner, "Frau: Die treue F.," in *Enzyklopädie des Märchens*, vol. 5 (1987), cols. 203–207.

6. Wehse, "Liebhaber bloßgestellt," col. 1059.

7. Mangione, Jerre, *Mount Allegro: A Memoir of Italian American Life*, New York: Harper & Row, 1981, pp. 141–151.

8. Diller-Sellschopp, Inez, *Zypriotische Märchen*, Athens: Akadēmia Athēnōn, 1982, pp. 197–199.

9. Adam of Cobsam, *The Wright's Chaste Wife [. . .]: A Merry Tale, by Adam of Cobsam*, ed. Frederick J. Furnivall, London: Kegan Paul etc., 1865. For a short summary in modern English, see Hanawalt, Barbara A., *The Wealth of Wives: Women, Law, and Economy in Late Medieval London*, Oxford: Oxford Universiy Press, 2007, p. 127–128. A summary of the tale is cited as a folktale in Briggs, *A Dictionary*, vol. A2, pp. 503–504.

10. Hanawalt, Barbara A., "Separation Anxieties in Late Medieval London: Gender in *The Wright's Chaste Wife*," *Medieval Perspectives* 11 (1996), pp. 23–41; reprinted in *"Of Good and Ill Repute": Gender and Social Control in Medieval England*, Oxford: Oxford University Press, 1998, pp. 88–103; Niebrzydowski, Sue, *Bonoure and Buxum: A Study of Wives in Late Medieval English Literature*, Oxford: Peter Lang, 2006, pp. 188–193; Hanawalt, *The Wealth of Wives*, pp. 127–128; Hutson, Lorna, "Probable Infidelities from Bandello to Massinger," in *Staging Early Modern Romance: Prose Fiction, Dramatic Romance, and Shakespeare*, ed. Mary Ellen Lamb, Valerie Wayne, New York: Routledge, 2009, pp. 219–235, at pp. 223–224; Cooper, Lisa H., *Artisans and Narrative Craft in Late Medieval England*, Cambridge: Cambridge University Press, 2011, pp. 88–93.

11. Adam of Cobsam, *The Wright's Chaste Wife*, p. vii; Clouston, William Alexander, "Additional Analogues of 'The Wright's Chaste Wife'," ibid., pp. 25–39, at p. 26.

12. Köhler, Reinhold, "Zu der Erzählung Adams von Cobsam 'The Wright's Chaste Wife'," *Jahrbuch für romanische und englische Litteratur* 8 (1867), pp. 44–65, at pp. 47–49; also in Köhler, *Kleinere Schriften zur erzählenden Dichtung des Mittelalters*, ed. Johannes Bolte, Berlin: Emil Felber, 1900, pp. 444–464.

13. Hazai, György, and Andreas Tietze, eds., *Ferec baʿd eş-şidde: „Freud nach Leid" (ein frühosmanisches Geschichtenbuch)*, Berlin: Klaus Schwarz, 2006, vol. 1, p. 15, 19.

14. For a detailed discussion of the Ottoman Turkish text and its implications see Marzolph, *Relief after Hardship*, pp. 53–55, no. 3. The present summary is a condensed version of the summary given there. For a French translation of the tale see

Decourdemanche, Jean-Adolphe, *Les Ruses des femmes (Mikri-zenan) et extraits du Plaisir après la peine (Feredj bad chiddeh)*, Paris: E. Leroux, 1896, pp. 161–208; a German translation was published by Hazai, György, and Heidi Stein, transl., "Proben aus dem *Ferec ba'd eş-şidde* in der deutschen Übersetzung von Andreas Tietze," *Archivum Ottomanicum* 30 (2013), pp. 49–104, at pp. 86–103. An oral performance of the tale is summarized in Antoine Galland's Istanbul diary under the date January 11, 1673; see *Journal d'Antoine Galland pendant son séjour à Constantinople (1672–1673)*, ed. Charles Schefer, Paris: Ernest Leroux, 1881 (reprint Frankfurt am Main 1994), vol. 2, pp. 7–8.

15. Jaʿfari Qanavāti, Moḥammad, ed., *Jāmeʿ al-ḥekāyāt: noskhe-ye Ketābkhāne-ye Ganj-Bakhsh-e Pākestān*, Tehran: Qaṭre, 1391/2012, pp. 55–94, no. 3.

16. Meredith-Owens, G.M., "An Early Persian Miscellany," in *Iran and Islam: In Memory of the Late Vladimir Minorsky*, ed. Clifford Edmund Bosworth, Edinburgh: Edinburgh University Press, 1971, pp. 435–441.

17. Khadish, Pegāh, and Moḥammad Jaʿfari (Qanavāti), eds., *Jāmeʿ al-ḥekāyāt bar asās-e noskhe-ye Āstān-i qods-e Rażavi*, Tehran: Māzyār, 1390/2011, pp. 436–441, no. 26; see also Haag-Higuchi, Roxane, *Untersuchungen zu einer Sammlung persischer Erzählungen: Čihil wa-šiš ḥikāyat yā ǧāmiʿ al-ḥikāyāt*, Berlin: Klaus Schwarz, 1984, pp. 73–74, no. 26.

18. Nakhshabi, Żiyāʾ al-Din, *Ṭuṭi-nāme*, ed. Fatḥallāh Mojtabāʾi and Gholām-ʿAlī Āryā, Tehran: Manūchehr, 1372/1993, pp. 35–43; ʿEmād ibn Moḥammad [al-S̱aghari], *Ṭuṭi-nāme: Javāher al-asmār*, ed. Shams al-Din Āl-e Aḥmad, Tehran: Bonyād-e farhang-e Irān, 1352/1973, pp. 70–71; Hatami, Mahroo, *Untersuchungen zum persischen Papageienbuch des Naḫšabī*, Freiburg: Klaus Schwarz, 1977, pp. 35–37, no. 4.

19. *The Ocean of Story*, ed. Penzer, vol. 1, pp. 158–164; Köhler, "Zu der Erzählung Adams von Cobsam," pp. 61–63; Clouston, "Additional Analogues," pp. 27–28;

20. Uther, Hans-Jörg, "Hündin: Die weinende H.," in *Enzyklopädie des Märchens*, vol. 6 (1990), cols. 1368–1372.

21. For the latter see Joret, Charles, *La Rose dans l'Antiquité et au Moyen Age: histoire, légendes et symbolisme*, Paris: Emile Bouillon, 1892, pp. 328–329; Paris, Gaston, "Le Conte de la Rose dans le roman de Perceforest," *Romania* 23 (1894), pp. 78–116, at pp. 102ff.; Barchilon, Jacques, "Perceforest," in *Enzyklopädie des Märchens*, vol. 10 (2002), cols. 719–721.

22. Mills, Margaret A., "The Gender of the Trick: Female Tricksters and Male Narrators," *Asian Folklore Studies* 60.2 (2001), pp. 237–258, at pp. 242–249 (summary and analysis); Mills, "Another Locust's Leg: Folktale Types, Subtypes, 'Décor,' and Meaning," in Bendix, Regina F., and Dorothy Noyes, eds., *Terra Ridens—Terra Narrans: Festschrift zum 65. Geburtstag von Ulrich Marzolph*, Dortmund: Verlag für Orientkunde, 2018, pp. 213–238.

23. Amonov, R., and K. Ulughzoda, eds., *Afsonahoi khalqii tojikī*, Stalinobod: Nashriyoti davlatii Tojikiston, 1957, pp. 379–399; Amonov, Raǵab, and Klavdija Ulug-Zade, *Die Sandelholztruhe: Tadshikische Volksmärchen*, Berlin: Kultur und Fortschritt, 1961, pp. 238–241.

24. Cosquin, Emmanuel, "Le Conte du Chat et de la Chandelle dans l'Europe du Moyen Age et en Orient," *Romania* 40 (1911), pp. 371–430, 481–531; also in Cosquin, *Études folkloriques*, Paris: Édouard Champion, 1922, pp. 401–495, particularly at pp. 469–178, quoting Stumme, Hans, *Tunisische Märchen und Gedichte*, 2 vols., Leipzig: Hinrichs, 1893, vol. 2, pp. 80–81, no. 5.

CHAPTER 26

The Prince Learns a Profession (ATU 888A*)

In September 1931, the Royal Irish Academy in collaboration with the Lautabteilung (Sound Department) of the Prussian State Library organized and administered a project of sound recordings in the Irish province of Ulster. Today, the recordings are kept at the Humboldt-University in Berlin, Germany.[1] They are commonly known as the Ulster Doegen recordings, referring to the name of Wilhelm Doegen, the former head of the Lautabteilung. On September 29, 1931, in the Courthouse at Letterkenny, Doegen's assistant Karl Tempel, recorded a "somewhat confused" narrative told by Irish storyteller Pádraig Ó Siadhail (Patrick Shields, ca. 1894–1976) from County Donegal.[2] The tale lasts for just over four minutes and goes as follows.[3]

> A prince wants to marry the daughter of a cobbler. Before consenting to the marriage, the cobbler requires the prince to learn a trade. In the woods, the prince meets an old man cutting sticks. He learns how to make baskets from the old man and marries the cobbler's daughter. A while later, a captain falls in love with the young woman and wants her for himself. He invites the couple to his ship, sails "out on the deep water" on a pretext, and then has his crew throw the man overboard in a closed barrel. The man is washed ashore on an island, breaks open the barrel, and makes a living from producing and selling baskets. Eventually, he comes to a castle where he finds his wife. They recognize each other by way of the rings "they had when they got married." The following day, they will have a feast together with the captain and the mayor the town, and the woman is to disclose the events by telling their story. At this point, the narative breaks off.

Classified as corresponding to the international tale type AT 888A*: *The Basket Maker,* the Irish tale is a representative of the Northern European oicotype of a folktale whose earliest-known versions date from early twelfth-century Persian literature. According to the available data, versions of this oicotype are known (at least) from Russian,[4] Latvian,[5] Lithuanian,[6] Irish,[7] and English language tradition.[8] A faint echo of the tale's constitutive motif, the recognition token, is even encountered in an Icelandic tale in which Frans finds his beloved Úlrikka when he sees the name she stitched into the hat of the man with whom she shared her life (in chastity).[9] A particularly lively version was recorded by Herbert Halpert and J.D.A. Widdowson from storyteller Freeman Bennett in Saint Pauls, Great Northern Peninsula, Newfoundland, on August 31, 1966.[10]

> The farmer's son Jack wants to marry another farmer's daughter whom he has known since childhood, but her father will not let him have her unless he has "a trade." Meeting an old native woman on the street who sells baskets, he pays her for teaching him within a week how to make baskets out of dyed birch rind. When he presents himself to the girl's father the next time, the old man is satisfied, and they marry. Going to the harbor for their honeymoon, a captain invites the couple to board his ship and "off an' away they goes." When the young woman's hat is blown off, Jack gets into a boat to fetch it. But when he is in the boat "they chopped the line" so that he drifts away. Suddenly a man climbs in over the stern of the boat. The man gives him a piece of rope into which he ties three knots. He tells Jack that by untying a knot the boat will move fast and disappears. At first, Jack does not dare to untie a knot, but then he unties first one, and then another one, and the boat is "almost flyin over the water." That day he reaches the same harbor where the ship with his wife anchors. With the little money he has in his pocket, he buys some dye and makes baskets from birch rind. Selling the baskets for several days, he makes a lot of money. Finally, he comes to a big building where he sees a woman "standin up by the window," and the woman passes him a note informing him that she is his wife. When the captain is to marry Jack's wife the next day, Jack dresses up, joins the wedding party, and offers to tell a tale. The tale he tells is his own, and he finishes by pointing to his wife and informing the audience that the captain took her from him. The captain is arrested, and Jack gets his wife back again.

In their commentary, the editors inform us that the "tale has some relevance to the local context in that Indian basket-sellers were well known in Newfoundland." [11] Moreover, birch rind was used for multiple purposes by the local population. In addition, the editors quote from Bo Almqvist's notes to a version of the Irish tale of "The Man Who Had No Story" (see essay **14, *Years of Experience in a Moment: The Man Is Transformed into a Woman [and Back again]***) that "many Irish farmers and fishermen took up [the trade of basketmaker] as a sideline when it was impossible to eke out an existence from their main occupation." Accordingly, basketmakers figure frequently in Irish stories, and the particular tale of the basketmaker classified as tale type ATU 888A* is "extraordinarily popular in Ireland."[12] The least one can conclude from the commentaries to the above-quoted versions of the Northern European oicotype is that these texts were convincingly adapted to their local and regional context.

But the tale's Northern European oicotype is only one side of a coin whose other side is constituted by tale type AT 949*: *Young Gentleman Learns Basketwork*. The catalogue's short description characterizes the tale type as follows: "He falls in love with a common girl, who refuses to marry him until he has learned some trade. He learns basketwork and later is obliged to live by his trade."[13] In Europe, this Southern European (and Middle Eastern) oicotype is documented above all from Slovak,[14] Romanian,[15] Bulgarian,[16] Serbian,[17] Macedonian,[18] and Greek[19] oral tradition. In the tale's different versions, the young woman's suitor is asked to learn one of a variety of professions, such as basketmaking, weaving reed mats, selling fruit, or even begging. The elaborate Romanian version, collected by Ion Dragoslav in 1937, takes particular pleasure in ridiculing the prince's purely intellectual knowledge by pointing out "that he had learned the story of Alexander off by heart and had the Psalter at his finger-tips," or "that he knew ever so many languages and . . . could make fine speeches and take part in discussions."[20] Although in this version, it is a prince asking for a princess in marriage, the young woman's father still asks him to learn a trade before he would give him permission to marry his daughter, and in the end the young man learns how to make rush mats. Virtually all versions agree in that the mere learning and practicing of a trade or craft satisfies the demand of the young woman's father, as the king says at the end of the Romanian version, "Bravo, my lad! . . . That craft of yours is worth more than a kingdom, for now I know that even if you lose your throne your wife won't have to starve because you can earn your living."[21] Although any audience might accept this conclusion based on a theoretical assumption of possibilities as sufficiently convincing, it is obvious that the tale would gain additional appeal if the prince's practical knowledge were put to a successful test. The proof of the usefulness of practical knowledge is found in the tale's older Persian and Ottoman Turkish versions as well as in versions recorded from recent Persian,[22] Kurdish,[23] Turkish,[24] Arabic,[25] and Judeo-Spanish[26] oral tradition.

The tale's oldest documented version is contained in the encyclopedic collection of traditional tales and anecdotes titled *Javāmeʿ al-ḥekāyāt* (Compilations of Stories), compiled by Persian author Sadid al-Din Moḥammad ʿAwfi who was in the central Asian city of Bukhara around 1175 and who, after traveling to and sojourning in numerous other places, died in Delhi around 1232. ʿAwfi's version is included in the third book's fourth chapter that bears the title "On the Contemptibility of Covetousness."[27]

> On his fourteenth birthday (when he is coming of age), the prince of Kermān informs his father that he wants to learn a profession, since his teacher taught him that "a profession saves a man from annihilation and makes an uncompleted voyage perfect." His father objects that a profession is of no use to a ruler, and that he has already mastered all the skills a ruler

needs. But his son is convinced that a ruler's power is not to be trusted. Consequently, the king summons all the craftsmen in the city, and his son choses to learn the craft of weaving straw mats as the apprentice of a man from Gorgān. Soon he has mastered the craft and asks his father for permission to travel. His father sends him to Baghdad together with his annual delegation to the caliph.

Having arrived in Baghdad, the prince and his servant decide to visit the city before paying their respects to the caliph. First, however, they intend to have some food at the restaurant of a famous Jewish cook. Seeing them, the Jew apologizes for the modesty of his restaurant and invites them to his home. As soon as they arrive in the courtyard of the Jew's house, two black men grab them and lower them into a pit with the help of a rope. In the pit, they encounter numerous other men who inform them that the Jew has the habit of imprisoning strangers he would then kill and serve their meat in his restaurant.

Soon after, the Jew hauls the prince up, intending to kill him. The prince, however, argues that instead of killing him, the Jew would make much more profit from selling the magnificent straw mats he can produce. Having been given the necessary material, the prince makes a straw mat that the Jew sells for a good price. Selling the second mat to the vizier, the greedy Jew asks the prince to prepare a mat so beautiful that he could offer it to the caliph himself. The prince weaves a message concerning his present state and whereabouts into the mat's complex pattern. Reading the message, the caliph understands it and asks the Jew from where he acquired the mat. Although the man at first lies, saying that one of his servants acquired the mat in Gorgān, the caliph asks him to send a messenger to his home to bring that servant to his presence. As the Jew makes various other excuses, the caliph sends his own men to the house where they find and free the prince and the other captives. He gives all the Jew's accumulated riches to the prince and sends him back home.

In this way, the Prophet Muḥammad's dictum (*ḥadīth*) "A profession saves you from poverty" (Arabic: *al-ḥirfatu amānun min al-fiqr*)[28] is proved to be true.

Leaving aside the stereotypes of the greedy Jew and the brute black man typical for much of premodern Muslim literature, the tale in addition to learning a craft mentioned in the tale's European versions emphasizes the applicability of practical knowledge. In this manner, it not only puts the theoretical usefulness of having a trade to a practical test but also makes the tale more appealing by demonstrating the practical consequences of the prince's wise decision. Several other versions of the tale are known from the premodern Persian, Ottoman Turkish, and Arabic literatures.

In the version given in the Ottoman Turkish fifteenth- or late fourteenth-century anonymous collection of tales titled *Ferec ba'd eş-şidde* (Relief after

Hardship), prince Chipur suffers the same fate at the hands of a Jew who kills his prisoners to boil them and make soap.[29] This text continues with a version of tale type ATU 978: *The Youth in the Land of Cheaters* (see essay ***32, The Villager in the Town of Rogues***).[30]

In the Persian *Jāmeʿ al-tamsil*, a collection of proverbs and the stories related to them compiled in 1644 by Moḥammad-ʿAli Ḥablerudi,[31] a Persian author resident in India, the tale illustrates the proverb *ḥerfat zinat-e mard ast*, "A profession is a man's decoration." Ḥablerudi follows the content of the earliest version closely, adding a considerable amount of verbiage in the ornate prose style of the day, including numerous proverbial expressions and suitable lines of poetry. In addition, his narration also details some of the scenes so as to rationalize and add verisimilitude to the dramatic action: when captured, the prince of Fārs and his companion are undressed and chained; enticing the Jew to make profit by allowing him to produce mats, the prince pretends to be Jewish himself; saved from being killed, he witnesses the two black men slaughter one of the captives; although the Jew has been living in Baghdad (and conducting his gruesome practice) for thirty years, he does not read the Arabic script; having convinced the Jew to let him live, the prince saves his fellow Muslims by asking the Jew to spare his prisoners for some days so that they can assist him in the arduous task of preparing a mat worthy of being presented to the caliph. Toward the end, the captives are rescued just as the black men are about to slaughter one of them. Finally, the Jew confesses that he was advised by a member of the Jewish community in Baghdad, and his confession leads to a pogrom in which several hundred members of the Jewish community, all of whom had been concealing their true creed, are executed.

The equally "baroque" version in Barkhordār ibn Maḥmud Farāhi's late sixteenth- or early seventeenth-century didactic collection of stories, *Maḥbub al-qolub* (The Hearts' Beloved)[32] presents the story embedded in a frame tale in which the king of Āẕarbāyjān judges in favor of a clever and skillful man, although his vizier thinks the man's opponent to be free from guilt. Explaining his rationale to the vizier, he tells his story. As a young man he learned the art of mat-making. When he was out on a pleasure excursion on the sea, the ship got wrecked, and he and two of his companions managed to save their lives by floating on a broken plank. Having been washed ashore, they reached the city of Baghdad. The king sold one of his rings, and they proceeded to buy some food. The Jewish shopowner invited them to his house where they fell through a trapdoor into a deep well. Arousing the greed of their captor, the king offered to produce mats for sale, and eventually made one for the caliph Hārūn al-Rashīd, "working into the borders of it an account of [his] circumstances in the Arabic language." The king was saved and the criminal punished, and the caliph sent the king back to his father with a lavish set of presents. The king ends his narrative by saying, "it was by the help of a trade that I was saved. I have perfect confidence in skillful men, and decided always to honor men who have a profession and despise those that have none."[33]

The version in the Mashhad manuscript of *Jāmeʿ al-ḥekāyāt*, a unique representative of the genre with a specific repertoire that was probably compiled in the seventeenth century, closely follows the version in ʿAwfi's *Javāmeʿ al-ḥekāyāt*.[34]

Finally, the tale's most recent version in a Middle Eastern literature is included in the eighteenth-century Wortley-Montague manuscript of *The Thousand and One Nights*.[35] The tale of the "Three Princes of China" begins with a heavily anti-Jewish version of tale type ATU 1000: *Contest Not to Become Angry* that is followed by a standard version of the above tale in which the criminals are simply characterized as robbers.[36] The text in the Mardrus translation of the *Nights* was adapted from a contemporary collection of Egyptian tales and reproduces the truncated version known from European tradition.[37]

Notes

1. For the "Ulster Doegen Recordings," see http://www.smo.uhi.ac.uk/~oduibhin/doegen/pearsanta.htm (accessed February 8, 2016).

2. For the storyteller, see http://www.smo.uhi.ac.uk/~oduibhin/doegen/osiadhail_biog.htm (accessed February 8, 2016).

3. A sound recording, transcription, and English translation of the tale are available at http://doegen.ie/LA_1232d1 (accessed February 8, 2016). The tale is also said to be transcribed in Ní Bhaoill, Róise, *Ulster Gaelic Voices: bailúchán Doegen 1931*, Belfast: Iontaobhas Ultach, 2010, pp. 142–147 (not seen).

4. Barag, Lev G., et al., *Sravnitel'ny ukazatel' syuzhetov vostochnoslavyanska skazka*, Leningrad: Nauka, 1979, no. 888A*.

5. Arājs, Kārlis, and Alma Medne, *Latviešu pasaku tipu rādītājs*, Riga: Zinātne, 1977, no. 888A*.

6. Kerbelytė, Bronislava, *Lietuvių liaudies padavimų katalogas*, Vilnius: Lietuvos TSR Moksl ų Akad., 1973, no. 888A*. Lina Būgienė kindly checked the exact content of the six versions listed by Kerbelytė, five of which represent different versions pertaining to the Northern European oicotype. All of the texts were recorded between 1928 and 1965. Some of them introduce elements of magic into the otherwise realistic tales, such as when the woman is abducted by a witch who transforms her into a bird; after recognizing her husband she is released from the magic spell by being placed into his basket.

7. Ó Súilleabháin, Seán, and Reidar Thoralf Christiansen, *The Types of the Irish Folktale*, Helsinki: Suomalainen Tiedeakatemia, 1963, no. 888A*. The large number of references in this catalogue include a variety of tales in which the woman is reunited with her husband "by means of a token (a song she sings, a basket he made that she recognises, and so on). Also, the story of a man who meets his sister in a brothel."

8. For an English language version, see note 10 below. In the present essay, reference is not made to ATU, as the compiler does not distinguish between the two tale types defined by AT. Moreover, he indiscriminately lumps together all kinds of references as ATU 888A*, so that it is not possible to distinguish any particular content.

9. http://www.ismus.is/i/audiokey/id-1000394 (accessed February 8, 2016). The tale (SÁM 86/887 EF) was recorded from Guðríður Finnbogadóttir on January 18, 1967. The Icelandic archive's text classified as AT 949* (SÁM 86/684 EF; see http://www.ismus.is/i/audiokey/id-1000687) is irrelevant for the present discussion, as the only overlap consists in two noble girls learning to do a housewife's work in order to marry the two farmers they love.

10. Halpert, Herbert, and J.D.A. Widdowson, *Folktales of Newfoundland: The Resilience of the Oral Tradition*, vol. 1, New York and London: Garland, 1996, pp. 521–529.

11. Ibid., p. 527.

12. Almqvist, Bo, "Notes," to Ó Catháin, Séamus, "An Fear nach rabh Scéal ar bith aige," *Béaloideas* 37–38 (1969–1970), pp. 51–59, 59–64, at 62.

13. See AT 949*.

14. Gašparíková, Viera, *Katalóg slovenskej ľudovej prózy*, Bratislava: Národopisný ústav SAV, 1991–92, no. 236.

15. Ure, Jean, *Pacala and Tandala and Other Rumanian Folk-Tales*, London: Methuen, 1960, pp. 117–125.

16. Daskalova Perkowski, Liliana, et al., *Typenverzeichnis der bulgarischen Volksmärchen*, ed. Klaus Roth, Helsinki: Suomalainen Tiedeakatemia, 1995, pp. 219–220, no. 949*.

17. Eschker, Wolfgang, *Serbische Märchen*, Munich: Diederichs, 1992, pp. 161–164, no. 32.

18. Cepenkov, Marko K., *Makedonski narodni prikazni*, ed. Kiril Penušliski, Skopje: MK, 1989, vol. 3, pp. 88–90, no. 253; 90–92, no. 254.

19. Puchner, Walter, "Der unveröffentlichte Zettelkasten eines Katalogs der griechischen Märchentypen nach dem System von Aarne-Thompson von Georgios A. Megas," in *Die heutige Bedeutung oraler Traditionen*, ed. Walther Heissig and Rüdiger Schott, Opladen and Wiesbaden: Westdeutscher Verlag, 1988, pp. 88–105, no. 888A*.

20. Ure, *Pacala and Tandala*, p. 117, 123.

21. Ibid., 124.

22. Marzolph, *Typologie*, no. *888B.

23. Wentzel, Luise-Charlotte, *Kurdische Märchen*, Düsseldorf: Diederichs, 1978, pp. 188–191, no. 19.

24. Eberhard and Boratav, *Typen*, p. 278, no. 231.

25. Nowak, Ursula, *Beiträge zur Typologie des arabischen Volksmärchens*, Diss. Freiburg, 1969, pp. 254–255, no. 267; El-Shamy, *Types*, p. 538, no. 0888A*.

26. Haboucha, Reginetta, *Types and Motifs of the Judaeo-Spanish Folktales*, New York: Garland, 1992, pp. 356–358, no. 888A*.

27. Niẓámu'd-dín, *Introduction*, p. 216, no. 1577 (bk. 3, ch. 4). The tale's summary follows ʿAwfi, Sadid al-Din Moḥammad al-, *Matn-e enteqādi-ye Javāmeʿ al-ḥekāyāt wa-lavāmeʿ al-revāyāt*, book 3, part 1, ed. Amir Bānu Moṣaffā and Maẓāher Moṣaffā, Tehran: Bonyād-e Farhang-e Irān, 1352/1973, pp. 86–94.

28. This is obviously a *ḥadīth* germane to Shiʿi (or uncritical popular) tradition, as it is not mentioned in any of the major Sunni works; see Wensinck, Arent Jan, *Concordance et indices de la tradition musulmane*, Leiden: Brill, 1936 (Reprint Istanbul: Çağrı Yayınları, 1988).

29. Marzolph, *Relief after Hardship*, pp. 112–114, no. 40.

30. Goldberg, Christine, "Stadt der Gauner," in *Enzyklopädie des Märchens*, vol. 12 (2008), cols. 1136–1140.

31. Ḥablerudi, Muḥammad ʿAli, *Jāmeʿ al-tamsil*, ed. Ḥasan Zol-Faqāri, Tehran: Moʿin 1390/2011, pp. 291–303. For the author and his collection, see Marzolph, Ulrich, "Illustrated Exemplary Tales: A Nineteenth-Century Edition of the Classical Persian Proverb Collection *Jāmeʿ al-tamsil*," *Proverbium* 16 (1999), pp. 167–191.

32. Farāhi, Barkhordār ibn Maḥmud, *Maḥbub al-qolub*, Bombay 1298/1881, pp. 30/-4–33/-7; Clouston, William Alexander, *A Group of Eastern Romances and Stories from the Persian, Tamil, and Urdu*, Glasgow: privately printed, 1889, pp. 434–441. The text

is an adapted reproduction from Eduard Rehatsek's translation in his *Amusing Stories: Translated from the Persian*, Bombay 1871, pp. 1–7, no. 1. See also Brockett, Eleanor, *Persian Fairy Tales*, (London: Frederick Muller, 1962) reprint Chicago and New York: Follett, 1968, pp. 109–116, no. 13.

33. Clouston adds a note that he has read "an Indian story very similar to this," but did not "recollect the particular story-book in which it occurs."

34. Khadish, Pegāh, and Moḥammad Jaʿfari (Qanavāti), eds., *Jāmeʿ al-ḥekāyāt bar asās-e noskhe-ye Āstān-i qods-e Rażavi*, Tehran: Māzyār, 1390/2011, pp. 320–312, no. 20; Haag-Higuchi, Roxane, *Untersuchungen zu einer Sammlung persischer Erzählungen: Čihil wa-šiš ḥikāyt yā ǧāmiʿ al-ḥikāyāt*, Berlin: Klaus Schwarz, 1984, pp. 60–61, no. 20.

35. For the manuscript, see Lerner, Amir, *The* Juʿaydiyya *Cycle: Witty Beggars' Stories from the "Montague Manuscript"—A Late Augmented* Arabian Nights, Dortmund: Verlag für Orientkunde, 2014; Akel, Ibrahim, "Liste des manuscrits arabes des *Nuits*," in *Arabic Manuscripts of the* Thousand and One Nights, ed. Aboubakr Chraïbi, Paris: espaces & signes, 2016, pp. 65–114, at p. 84.

36. Marzolph and Van Leeuwen, *The Arabian Nights Encyclopedia*, vol. 1, pp. 416–417, no. 390; Chauvin, *Bibliographie*, vol. 6 (1902), pp. 72–72, no. 239; Burton, Richard F., *Arabian Nights*, (Benares 1885) reprint Beirut: Khayat, 1966, vol. 15, pp. 213–228.

37. *The Arabian Nights Encyclopedia*, vol. 1, pp. 140–141, no. 477; Chauvin, *Bibliographie*, vol. 9 (1905), p. 83; Mardrus, Joseph Charles Victor, *Le livre des Mille et une Nuits*, vol. 15, Paris: La Revue Blanche, 1904, pp. 305–310; Spitta-Bey, Guillaume, *Contes arabes modernes*, Leiden: Brill, 1883, pp. 94–104, no. 7.

CHAPTER 27

A Pound of Flesh as Security for a Loan (ATU 890)

Studies on the present tale are so numerous that it is hardly possible to do the tale's history and dissemination justice in a short survey.[1] Without repeating the detailed arguments presented by previous research and aiming to summarize the most important points for the tale's history and dissemination, the present discussion is short. Classified as tale type ATU 890: *A Pound of Flesh*, the tale was most often investigated in relation to the character Shylock in Shakespeare's *Merchant of Venice*. It is essentially about a creditor who when lending money to a person requests a pound of the debtor's flesh as security. Should the debtor not be able to return the money at a mutually agreed date, the creditor will be allowed to cut a pound of flesh from the debtor's body. When the debtor is not able to fulfill his obligation, a clever judge helps him avoid the mutilation by requesting the creditor to cut exactly the stipulated amount of flesh, not any less or more. As the creditor is unable to fulfill the condition, he is forced to forfeit his claim. The tale's versions in both oral and written tradition display a considerable variety.

Told by Mrs. MacGeachy from Islay, the southernmost island of the Inner Hebrides, a late nineteenth-century Scottish version embeds the tale in a lengthy narrative about a prince who gains a bride, is separated from her due to a lost wager, and after various trials and tribulations is finally reunited with his wife.[2] Right at the beginning, the prince takes a loan of fifty pounds from a merchant, with the stipulated condition that if he does not repay the money at the end of the year and a day, the merchant will be entitled to take a strip of skin from the top of the prince's head to the sole of his foot. When the time has come, the prince is not able to return the money. In the meantime, he was separated from his wife following a lost wager with a certain captain, and his wife traveled the world in men's clothing, eventually finding him again without him recognizing her. Now the prince's wife saves him from being mutilated by specifying the condition that the creditor must not spill a single drop of blood during the process, thus making the creditor forfeit his claim. A twentieth-century Italian version from Calabria likewise introduces the son of a rich merchant looking for a bride.[3] As the young man at first wastes his money without reaching his goal, he takes a loan from one of his companions, agreeing to let the creditor cut a pound of flesh from his body should he not be able to repay the money after a period of a year, a month, and a day. When the agreed time has come, the debtor's wife dresses in men's clothing and bribes the judge to let her take his position. She then requests the creditor to cut exactly a pound of flesh, not any less or more, making him forgo his claim. In a similarly structured romantic tale from Chile, performed by Francisco Coronado in Ignao, Valdivia, in January 1951, the suitor's godfather lends him the requested money "on the condition that he would claim a pound of flesh from his godson's rump if the boat (of gold and silver) weren't returned in time."[4] In the tale's Serbian and Croatian versions, the stipulation concerns the debtor's tongue.[5]

The tale's numerous versions in oral and written traditions were classified in six different forms that are distinguished by their respective frames.[6] Embedded in a story about the discovery of the Holy Cross, the earliest attestation of the tale's first and simple form is contained in the English poem "Cursor Mundi," probably written by a priest from Northumbria around 1300 CE.[7] The Italian and Chilean narratives summarized above belong to the tale's third form that is characterized by the fact that the suitor at first oversleeps the rendezvous with his desired fiancée as he was drugged. When he finally realizes that he was drugged, he has already spent all of his funds and needs to borrow money to continue his courting. This form is first attested in the tale "Creditor" in John of Alta Silva's *Dolopathos*, a version of *The Seven Sages* compiled around 1300 CE,[8] and in fourteenth-century versions of the *Gesta Romanorum*.[9] Mediated by William Painter's *Palace of Pleasure* (1566), the text in Italian author Ser Giovanni Fiorentino's late fourteenth-century *Pecorone*[10] exerted a certain influence on Shakespeare's version, which was classified as belonging to the tale's second form. As in the tale's third form, the suitor here takes the loan for his courting. This form lacks, however, the repeated visits during which the suitor is drugged. In the fifth form identified, the tale is embedded in tale type ATU 1534: *Series of Clever Unjust Decisions*. In European tradition, the earliest-known occurrence of this form is encountered in the German Meistergesang "Kaiser Karls Recht" (Emperor Charlemagne's Law), initially printed in 1493.[11] It is this form that is closely related to Middle Eastern tradition.

Predating the German Meistergesang at least by several decades, the tale's version in the anonymous Ottoman Turkish collection of tales *Ferec ba'd eş-şidde* (Relief after Hardship) was celebrated, albeit not without subsequent critical discussions, as "the Oriental origin of Shylock."[12] Whereas the collection's earliest preserved manuscripts date from around the middle of the fifteenth century, its language suggests an original composition in the latter half of the fourteenth century. The collection's tale number 38, titled "The Muslim, the Jew, and the Kadi of Ḥimṣ," is a full-fledged version of tale type ATU 1534.[13] It begins with a Jewish moneylender lending money to a Muslim borrower on the condition that, should the borrower not be able to repay his debt, the creditor will be entitled to cut a clearly defined amount of flesh from his body. When the debtor is not able to repay the money the two men at first argue and finally agree to accept the judgment of the judge in the city of Ḥimṣ. A contemporary Middle Eastern audience would at this point have been aware of the fact that in regional tradition Ḥimṣ is the stereotypical town of fools, and so the judge's series of absurd decisions that follows with regard to a number of unusual accidents they experience on the way would not have come as a surprise. Since the moneylender is not able to cut exactly the stipulated amount of flesh from the creditor's body, he has to forfeit his claim. In addition, he is sentenced to paying a fine so as to compensate for the illegal agreement he had made. Although most of the tales in *Ferec ba'd eş-şidde* are known to have been translated from Abu Bakr ibn Khosrow al-Ostād's Persian *Munes-nāme* (The Book as an Intimate Friend), compiled around the year 1200,[14] the tale in question is not contained in that work. It appears, however, in later Persian compilations of the same genre collectively known as *Jāmeʿ al-ḥekāyāt* (Collection of Tales) that date from the seventeenth century.[15] As these compilations likely preserve tales from the repertoire of earlier works it is not far-fetched to assume that a Persian or Arabic version of the tale predating *Ferec ba'd eş-şidde* might be identified in the future. In order to establish the tale's origin unambiguously from Middle Eastern tradition, this hypothetically existing version would have to date from before the year 1300.

In addition to the tale's fifteenth- or late fourteenth-century occurrence in the Ottoman Turkish *Ferec ba'd eş-şidde*, its inclusion in John of Alta Silva's *Dolopathos* might suggest the existence of an older Middle Eastern version, since the latter work belongs to the narrative cycle known as *The Seven Sages* whose frame (although not necessarily all of the tales included in the cycle's later Western versions) is of Persian origin. Even so, the *Dolopathos* with the tale's specific embedding in a romance of courting was more influential in European oral tradition than the tale's Middle Eastern version with its sequence of absurd judgments that had a distinct impact on modern Arabic, Persian, and Turkish oral traditions.[16]

Notes

1. Wenger, Berta Viktoria, "Shylocks Pfund Fleisch: Eine stoffgeschichtliche Untersuchung," *Shakespeare-Jahrbuch* 65 (1929), pp. 92–174; Schamschula, Eleonore, "Das Fleischpfand: Mot. J1161.2 in Volkserzählung und Literatur," *Fabula* 25 (1984), pp. 277–295; Lixfeld, Hannjost, "Fleischpfand," in *Enzyklopädie des Märchens*, vol. 4 (1984), cols. 1256–1262; Artese, Charlotte, "'You Shall Not Know:' Portia, Power, and the Folktale Sources of The Merchant of Venice," *Shakespeare* 5.4 (2009), pp. 325–337; Artese, *Shakespeare's Folktale Sources*, Newark: University of Delaware Press, 2015, 99–118.

2. Campbell, John Francis, *Popular Tales of the West Highlands*, new ed., Edinburgh and London: Edmonston & Douglas, 1890, vol. 2, pp. 9–23, no. 18; Ehrentreich, Alfred, *Englische Volksmärchen*, Jena: Diederichs, 1938, pp. 249–254.

3. Lombardi Satriani, Raffaele, *Racconti popolari Calabresi*, Naples: De Simone, 1953, pp. 187–192, no. 28.

4. Pino-Saavedra, Yolando, *Folktales of Chile*, Chicago: The University of Chicago Press, 1967, pp. 194–198, 273–274, no. 38.

5. Stojanović, Mijat, *Pučke pripoviedke i pjesme*, Zagreb, 1867, pp. 176–182, no. 37; Chaikanovich, Veselin, *Srpske narodne pripovetke*, Belgrade: Izdaniye knizharnitse Raikovicha i Vukovicha, 1929, p. 283, no. 114.

6. Schamschula,"Das Fleischpfand," pp. 277–278.

7. Wenger, "Shylocks Pfund Fleisch," pp. 139–140;

8. Chauvin, *Bibliographie*, vol. 8 (1904), pp. 200–203, no. 245.

9. Wesselski, *Mönchslatein*, pp. 172–179, 248–250, no. 138; Wesselski, *Märchen des Mittelalters*, pp. 163–168, 252–254, no. 61; Schamschula, "Das Fleischpfand," p. 278; Wenger, "Shylocks Pfund Fleisch," pp. 134–136.

10. Floerke, Hanns, *Der Pecorone des ser Giovanni*, vol. 1, Munich: Georg Müller, pp. 68–97; Fiorentino, Giovanni, *Il Pecorone*, ed. E. Esposito, Ravenna, Longo, 1974, pp. 87–118 (4,1).

11. Schamschula, "Das Fleischpfand," p. 278; Wenger, "Shylocks Pfund Fleisch," pp. 123–124.

12. Vámbéry, Ármin, "Der orientalische Ursprung von Shylock," *Keleti szemle* 2 (1901), pp. 18–29; see also Decourdemanche, Jean-Adolphe, "Le marchand de Venise dans les contes orientaux," *Revue des traditions populaires* 19.11 (1904), pp. 449–460, at pp. 450–454, Basset, René, "L'origine orientale de Shylock," *Keleti szemle* 2 (1901), pp. 182–186.

13. Marzolph, *Relief after Hardship*, pp. 110–111, no. 38.

14. Askari, Nasrin, "A Mirror for Princesses: *Mūnis-nāma*, A Twelfth-Century Collection of Persian Tales Corresponding to the Ottoman Turkish Tales of the *Faraj ba'd al-shidda*," *Narrative Culture* 5.1 (2018), pp. 121–140.

15. Decourdemanche, "Le marchand de Venise," pp. 454–460.

16. El-Shamy, *Types*, pp. 538–540, no. 0890; Marzolph, *Typologie*, pp. 220–221, no. 1534 (3, 7); Eberhard and Boratav, *Typen*, p. 339, no. 297.

CHAPTER 28

The Lowly Man Shrewdly Responds to the King's Unanswerable Questions (ATU 922)

Folklorist Walter Anderson's study *Kaiser und Abt* (The Emperor and the Abbot), published in 1923,[1] demonstrates the application of the historic-geographic method advocated by the Finnish school of historical and comparative folk narrative research in an exemplary manner. The study is devoted to a comprehensive investigation of tale type ATU 922: *The Shepherd Substituting for the Clergyman Answers the King's Questions.*[2] The tale type is essentially about a ruler who, for various reasons, requires a subordinate of high status to answer a set of questions on pain of death. As the potential respondent has no clue how to supply the required answers, he willingly accepts the offer of a man of lowly status to act in his stead, usually in disguise. The man evades giving direct answers to the questions posed that are, in fact, unanswerable. Instead, he shrewdly responds with hilariously absurd claims or clever assertions that are impossible to disprove.

In his study, Anderson surveys a total of almost 600 different texts, of which 167 are documented in written or literary tradition and 428 originate from international oral tradition. He starts by grouping the texts into 62 chronologically arranged versions and proceeds to classify the texts according to their origin from 50 different ethnic groups. The larger part of his study is devoted to a comprehensive comparative analysis in eleven sections whose topics range from surveys of characters and content via a discussion of different redactions or groups of analogous versions, to the reconstruction of the tale's history in terms of chronology and geographical distribution. The study finishes with a discussion of theoretical issues, including the law of "self correction" (*Selbstberichtigung*) that Anderson held responsible for the comparatively strong stability of tales in oral tradition.[3] Although a substantial number of new versions have come to light since then, the main results of Anderson's exemplary study remain valid today.[4] To some extent, Anderson's study was probably inspired by the discovery of the tale's oldest version in an Arabic historical work dating to the ninth century to which American historian Charles C. Torrey drew attention some twenty years before.[5] The following is a short sampling of tales from various European regions published after Anderson's study.

On January 26, 1967, Alan Bruford recorded a Scottish version from Angus Henderson in Tobermory on the Isle of Mull.[6] The narrator, a retired blacksmith and "crofter" (farmer), learned the tale from his father, who also worked as a blacksmith.

> Threatening to execute a priest in Scotland who had offended him, the king offers to free the priest should he know the answers to three questions the king would ask him. As the priest knows that some of the questions might simply be unanswerable, he is happy to accept the offer of his simpleton brother to go in his stead. Dressed as the priest, the brother goes to the king's palace and answers the questions. "Where is the center of the world?"—"Right here where I knock my staff on the floor."—"What am I worth in money?"—"You are not worth more than thirty pieces of silver, since the best man ever born in the world (Jesus) was sold for thirty pieces of silver."—"What am I thinking?"—"You think that you are talking to the priest and not to his foolish brother."
>
> Impressed by the answers, the king decides that "anyone who has a brother like that . . . deserves to get off."

The narrator of the Irish version recorded by Séamus Ó Duilearga in Newcastle, County Wicklow, on February 1, 1930, was Richard Walker, aged 75.[7] He had learned the tale about ten years previously from a man from Rathdrum, in the same county.

> The king of England finds out that the bishop of Drogheda in Ireland is a heavy drinker, although in his sermon he preached that "any man would take too much intoxicatin' liquor would be makin' a glutton o' himself." The king challenges the bishop to answer three questions he poses or else be beheaded. A day before the end of a fortnight's respite, the bishop is offered help by old Jack the fool. The bishop dresses Jack up in his own attire and has him shaved by a barber across the street. Jack answers the first question how many baskets it would take to hold all the sea-gravel around the sea-coast of Ireland by suggesting that one basket could hold it all if it only was big enough. The second and third question and answer are the same as in the Scottish version cited above. Following this, the king is so impressed that he keeps Jack at court for two months and gives him so much money that he "could turn out a gentleman after it."

The short Estonian version recorded in 1932 by Richard Viidalepp from Kaarel Jürjenson, born 1868 in Kodavere, has different questions.[8] There is no substitution of persons, the king instead asking a young man who is famed for being able to give an answer to all kinds of questions nobody else could solve. The first questions is, "How many stars are in heaven?" The young man takes a pencil and makes innumerable dots on a piece of paper, suggesting that the king counts to see whether they correspond to the number of stars as he claims.

The question as to how long eternity lasts is answered by referring to an eagle who whets his beak on a high mountain once a year. When the mountain is worn away, an hour of eternity will have passed.[9] In the Dutch version narrated by Dirk Schuurman from Broek at Waterland to C. Bakker in 1901, the king is annoyed that one of his bodyguards claims to have no worries while he himself has plenty of them.[10]

> Threatening to dismiss his bodyguard, the king gives him the chance to stay if he answers three questions. A friend changes clothes with the bodyguard and answers the questions in his stead. "How many shovels would you need to empty the sea?"—"One, if it is a big one!"— "How many days would it take you to ride round the world?"—"Twenty-four hours, if you sat on the sun!"—"Can you read my thoughts?"—"You think I am your bodyguard, but I am his mate!"
>
> In the end the king laughs and admits to being outwitted.

The French narrator Raoul Pic told his anticlerical version in 1973 in Branoux-Les Taillades.[11] He introduces a bishop who is annoyed about a priest who lives together with a young maid. Aiming to see how the priest lives, he visits him one day. Asking the priest what he does all day long, the bishop receives the answer that the priest produces jewelry. Asking him whose children are all over the house, he is told that they belong to the priest's brother. Finally, in response to the question how much he himself is worth, he is reckoned at 29 pieces of silver, since Jesus was sold for 30 pieces. The bishop's companion later explains how silly the bishop's first and second questions had been. What would the priest possibly do most of the time living together with a beautiful young woman? And, of course, the children were none but his own! In the Romansh tale narrated by Flori Aloisi Zarn in Domat on March 14, 1936, the Austrian emperor is upset about the good life of the abbot of Saint Gall.[12] He challenges the abbot to answer three questions or else be shamed by being led around the country seated backward on a donkey. As none of the country's learned people can think of adequate answers, the monk herding the abbey's sheep offers to answer the questions in the abbot's stead. Maja Bošković-Stulli recorded a Croatian version from Pavo Vajalo, born 1896, in the village Dunace in Dalmatia.[13] In this folktale, Napoleon threatens to kill the senators of Dubrovnik should they not be able to answer his three questions. A shepherd dressed up as the bishop leads the town's delegation and answers the questions. In the Serbian version told by the cleric Nikola Tasić, born 1918, to Dragutin M. Djordjević in Leskovac on August 17, 1953, the sexton answers the tsar's questions in the parson's stead.[14]

Anderson identified the tale's oldest European versions in a number of thirteenth-century works.[15] These include German author Der Stricker's *Pfaffe Âmîs*,[16] a version of French Dominican preacher Stephen of Bourbon's (Étienne de Bourbon's) collection of sermons,[17] and an anonymous world history compiled in the Provençal or Catalan language. In the following centuries cited in influential collections such as John Gobi's *Scala coeli*, Francesco Sacchetti's *Trecentonovelle* (Three Hundred Novellas), the jests attributed to Till Eulenspiegel,[18] Johannes Pauli's *Schimpf und Ernst* (Jocular and Serious Tales),[19] Nicolas de Troyes's *Le grand parangon de nouvelles nouvelles*,[20] Juan de Timoneda's *El Patrañuelo*, the Yiddish *Maasse-Buch*, Antoine d'Ouvilles *L'élite des contes*, the Ottoman Turkish and Arabic collections of Nasreddin Hodja anecdotes,[21] and the Grimm brothers' *Kinder- und Hausmärchen* (Children's and Household Tales),[22] the tale is documented in a steady chain of literary versions until is was recorded in hundreds of versions from nineteenth- and twentieth-century oral tradition all over Europe.

The tale's oldest-known version as identified by Torrey is given in the *Futūḥ Miṣr* (The Conquest of Egypt) compiled by the Arab historian ʿAbd al-Raḥmān ibn ʿAbdallāh Ibn ʿAbd al-Ḥakam (d. 871).[23] Although Torrey judged the author to be "one who possessed few of the qualities of a good historian," he nevertheless conceded that the work is of great importance. Giving a list of the Egyptian kings who ruled Memphis in one of the book's introductory chapters, the author cites the tale in relation to Bawla, son of Manākīl, whom "the historian identifies with Pharaoh Necho, of Old Testament fame (2 Kings xxiii.29–35)."

> The king grudges his viziers their pay and challenges them to answer three questions on pain of death. The questions are: What is the number of the stars in the heavens? What sum of money does the sun earn daily, by his labor for each human being? What does God almighty do every day? As the viziers are granted a month's respite, a potter offers to answer the questions in their stead, provided one of them continues to work in his place. He also requests to be furnished with clothing like their own. Before meeting the king, the potter visits the son of the former king, "whom ill fortune had overtaken," promising him to make the king leave the city so that the prince could regain his rightful position.
>
> Meeting the king, the potter answers the first question by pouring out a bag of sand, inviting the king to have someone count to see whether the potter is right in claiming that the number of grains of sand equals that of the stars. He supplies the answer to the second question by referring to the amount of one *qīrāṭ* (a small coin) as the amount the day laborer who works from sunrise to sunset receives each day. Following this, the potter promises to answer the third question the next day. He takes the king to his workshop outside the city and explains that what God almighty does every day is this, "He humbles men, and exalts men, and ends the life of men." In order to demonstrate the truth of his statement, the potter refers to the vizier who works in a potter's kiln and to himself, now mounted on one of the royal beasts and wearing the garments of the court. In addition, he mentions that the son of the former king "has just barred the gates of Memphis against you!"

> Although the king hastens back to the city, the gates are already barred. Led by the prince, the people depose him. "He went crazy; and used to sit by the gate of the city of Memphis, raving and drivelling."
>
> The narrator ends by saying that the Copts, the Christian Egyptians, refer to King Bawla when addressing a person that displeases them.

As Ibn ʿAbd al-Ḥakam's work "contains one of the oldest and most interesting narratives of the Mohammedan conquest of Spain," Torrey contends that it "was well known, and probably extensively circulated, among the Spanish Arabs from the ninth century on," thus constituting a possible intermediary between Arabic and subsequent European tradition.[24] Considering the biblical nature of many of the questions posed, Anderson considers the tale to originate from a Middle Eastern Jewish community, probably toward the beginning of the seventh century, and suggests that it was likely transmitted to Europe by French crusaders in the thirteenth century.[25] In its region of origin, the tale remained popular well into the twentieth century, as the considerable number of about fifteen versions from a region extending from Kuwayt via Iraq, Palestine, and Lebanon to Egypt, Sudan, and Morocco documents.[26]

Notes

1. Anderson, Walter, *Kaiser und Abt: Die Geschichte eines Schwanks*, Helsinki: Suomalainen Tiedeakatemia, 1923; for a short summary of the results, see Krohn, Kaarle, *Übersicht über einige Resultate der Märchenforschung*, Helsinki: Suomalainen Tiedeakatemia, 1931, pp. 162–164.
2. Nicolaisen, Wilhelm F.H., "Kaiser und Abt," in *Enzyklopädie des Märchens*, vol. 7 (1993), cols. 845–852.
3. Anderson, *Kaiser und Abt*, pp. 397–403; Goldberg, Christine, "Selbstberichtigung," in *Enzyklopädie des Märchens*, vol. 12 (2008), cols. 546–548.
4. Bolte and Polívka, *Anmerkungen*, vol. 3, pp. 214–233, no. 152; Anderson, Walter, "Zwei neuentdeckte Fassungen von 'Kaiser und Abt' (1693)," *Fabula* 4 (1961), pp. 260–263; Entner, Heinz, "Noch eine Variante von 'Kaiser und Abt' (1492)," *Fabula* 8 (1966), pp. 237–240; Nicolaisen, "Kaiser und Abt."
5. Torrey, Charles C., "The Egyptian Prototype of 'King John and the Abbot'," *Journal of the American Oriental Society* 20 (1899), pp. 209–216.
6. Bruford, Alan, and Donald A. MacDonald, *Scottish Traditional Tales*, Edinburgh: Polygon, 1994, pp. 223–225, 458–459, no. 30a.
7. Ó Duilearga, Séamus, "The Three Questions," *Béaloideas* 2.4 (1930), pp. 381–383.
8. Loorits, Oskar, *Estnische Volkserzählungen*, Berlin: De Gruyter, 1959, pp. 202–203, 226, no. 195.
9. For this motif, see Moser-Rath, Elfriede, "Ewigkeit," in *Enzyklopädie des Märchens*, vol. 4 (1984), cols. 588–592, at col. 591–592.
10. Bødker, Laurits, D'Aronco, Gianfranco, and Christina Hole, *European Folktales*, Copenhagen: Rosenkilde and Bagger, 1963, pp. 103–104.
11. Pelen, Jean-Noël, *Le conte populaire en Cévennes*, 2nd ed., Paris: Payot et Rivages, 1994, pp. 639–642, 758, no. 176a.

12. Uffer, Leza, *Rätoromanische Märchen und ihre Erzähler*, Basel: Krebs, 1945, pp. 20–225, 300–301.

13. Bošković-Stulli, Maja, *Kroatische Volksmärchen*, Düsseldorf and Cologne: Diederichs, 1975, pp. 201–202, no. 43.

14. Djordjević, Dragutin M., *Srpske narodne pripovetke i predanja iz leskovačke oblasti*, ed. Nada Milošević-Djordjevič, Belgrade: Srpska Akademija Nauka i Umetnosti, 1988, pp. 284, 524, no. 146.

15. For the following, see Anderson, *Kaiser und Abt*, pp. 6–33.

16. Röhrich, Lutz, *Erzählungen des späten Mittelalters und ihr Weiterleben in Literatur und Volksdichtung bis zur Gegenwart: Sagen, Märchen, Exempel und Schwänke*, vol. 1, Bern: Francke, 1967, pp. 146–149, no. VIII.1.

17. Ibid., pp. 149–150, no. VIII.2.

18. Ibid., pp. 150–151, no. VIII.3.

19. Pauli, Johannes, *Schimpf und Ernst*, ed. Johannes Bolte, Berlin: Herbert Stubenrauch, 1924, vol. 1, pp. 39–40, and vol. 2, pp. 270–271, no. 55.

20. Kasprzyk, Krystyna, *Nicolas de Troyes et le genre narratif en France au XVIe siècle*, Warsaw: Państwowe Wydawnictwo Naukowe, and Paris: Klincksieck, 1963, pp. 93–103, no. 36.

21. Wesselski, *Der Hodscha Nasreddin*, vol. 1, pp. 36–39, 226, no. 70.

22. See Bolte and Polívka, *Anmerkungen*, vol. 3, pp. 214–233, no. 152.

23. Torrey, "The Egyptian Prototype;" Ibn ʿAbd al-Ḥakam, *The History of the Conquest of Egypt, North Africa and Spain Known as the Futūḥ Miṣr*, ed. Charles C. Torrey, New Haven: Yale University Press, 1922, pp. 29–30.

24. Torrey, "The Egyptian Prototype," p. 215.

25. Anderson, *Kaiser und Abt*, pp. 382–384.

26. El-Shamy, *Types*, p. 600–601. The only modern Arabic version considered by Anderson, *Kaiser und Abt*, p. 74 (As Arab 1) is from Meissner, Bruno, "Neuarabische Geschichten aus dem Iraq," *Beiträge zur Assyriologie und Semitischen Sprachwissenschaft* 5 (1903–1906), pp. 1–148, at pp. 88–91, no. 48.

CHAPTER 29

The Treacherous Treasure Hunter (ATU 936*)

In his collection of folktales from Greater Russia, the Russian linguist and ethnographer Dmitriy K. Zelenin (1878–1954) published a version of the tale "The Golden Mountain."[1] The tale was recorded from the oral performance of Mardan Mukhametov (b. 1878). Of Bashkir ethnicity, the talented storyteller could only read or write the Tatar language. He narrated his tales in a somewhat rudimentary Russian that the collector edited to a certain extent. Mukhametov's adapted performance is significant as a fairly recent link between the "Oriental" and Western traditions of a tale whose internationally best-known version probably is the tale of "Hasan of Basra" included in *The Thousand and One Nights*:[2]

> A workman looking for a job on the bazaar in Petropavlovsk is hired by a Tatar. Taken to his employer's home, the workman is well fed that day. The next day, they depart together by carriage, taking an additional horse with them. At the side of a high mountain, they stop, slaughter the horse and have a good meal during which the employer makes the workman drunk. The Tatar sews the unconscious workman into the carcass of the dead horse and waits until a large eagle carries the carcass to the top of the mountain. When the workman awakens, the Tatar has him throw down pieces of golden rock that he finds up there. But when the workman asks how to get down from the mountain, the Tatar bluntly informs him that there is no way down, and that he will be devoured by the eagles. Eventually, the workman finds a trapdoor leading to an underground pathway that gets him back down to the place where he had left his employer.
>
> Several days later, the workman is again hired by the same employer, who does not recognize him, and the sequence of events is repeated. But now the workman makes his employer drunk, fixes him in the carcass of the dead horse and has him lifted up to the mountain top. After the Tatar has thrown pieces of golden rock down to him, the workman leaves him up on the mountain to be eaten by the eagles.

The workman sells the gold and squanders the money until he is reduced to poverty.

The tale's international versions are classified as tale type ATU 936*: *The Golden Mountain*. Although the tale is particularly popular in Middle Eastern and Middle Asian traditions,[3] several versions closely similar to the performance of the Bashkir storyteller are documented from European oral tradition. Zelenin himself mentioned the corresponding version in Aleksandr Afanasyev's large and highly influential collection of Russian folktales, first published in 1855–1867.[4] Afanasyev's version most likely originates from the collection of Vladimir I. Dal' (1801–1872), who apparently recorded it in the region of Orenburg, fairly close to the border of present-day Kazakhstan.[5] Here, the protagonist is a merchant's son who having squandered his wealth (Mot. W131.1) is hired by a rich merchant. The sequence of events is essentially the same, except that the hero's rescue from the mountain is arranged differently. In Afanasyev's version, the merchant's beautiful daughter falls in love with the young man and secretly gives him a magic lighter enabling him to summon helpers who bring him down from the mountain. A short episode with a ship that can only move after taking him aboard, marks the hero as an extraordinary person. Once the rich and evil merchant who hired him is dead, the hero appropriates the merchant's riches, marries his daughter, and moves to the merchant's house with his own family.

A Belarusian version in the collection of Lev G. Barag (1911–1994)[6] was recorded from the oral performance of Roman Saganovich, aged 35, a worker at a brick factory in the village of Turnaya in the region of Pinsk.[7] Here, the treacherous employer is a squire who hires a poor cobbler, promising him a whole year of feasting and only requiring him to work for a single day. The cobbler is made to stay in a cave where a magic wand enables him to summon male attendants feeding him and beautiful girls entertaining him by singing and dancing. On the appointed day, his employer makes the cobbler drunk and stuffs him into a leather bag to which he attached a chunk of meat. Abandoned on the mountain, the hero later uses the same means, bag and meat, to get back down. Although the magical attendants and the enchanted girls want him to stay as their sovereign, he abandons them, instead enjoying a life of leisure in his familiar world. This tale ends without the bad squire being punished.

The Bashkir and Russian versions present the tale clearly structured in two parts, the second of which mirrors the first one by repeating the events with exchanged roles.[8] The treacherous treasure hunter thus suffers his punishment in exactly the same manner as he treated his employee.[9] More often than this two-part narrative, international tradition documents an elaborated version in which the first part of the above narrative merely serves as an introduction for the internationally widespread tale type ATU 400: *The Man on a Quest for His Lost Wife*, such as documented in a Sicilian folktale collected by Laura Gonzenbach (1842–1878).[10] The Sicilian tale begins with Joseph, the son of a poor farmer, leaving home to make his fortune in the world. Joseph is hired by a rich man who invites him to live a life of luxury in his castle for a whole year. Having briefly visited his parents in order to show off his new status, Joseph returns to serve his master and is taken to the top of the mountain whence he throws down bags he filled with the diamonds collected up there. Having been abandoned on the mountain top, he finds a trapdoor leading him to the abode of a friendly (and somewhat stupid) giant who takes him to be his nephew. The giant helps him acquire a wife by having him steal the shirt of a swan maiden. Some time later, when Joseph is giving a party in his house, the swan maiden manages to regain her hidden shirt and leaves him. Joseph has himself hired by the rich man again, but instead of throwing down diamonds, he showers him with rocks. Once more abandoned on the mountain top, he again visits the giant who informs him of a fairly complicated procedure by which he can free his wife, who is held captive by another giant. With the help of several grateful animals, an ant, an eagle, and a lion, he manages to kill the evil giant, frees his wife and several other captive women, and returns home laden with riches that enable him to live a life of ease and happiness.

The tale's various forms share the motif of a man being hidden in a receptacle, usually the carcass of a horse or mule, so as to be lifted by a giant bird to a mountain whose top is strewn with valuables such as gold or diamonds. Stith Thompson classified this motif twice as both Mot. K521.1.1: *Man sewed in animal's hide carried off by birds*, and Mot. K1861.1: *Hero sewed up in animal hide so as to be carried to height by birds*. In European tradition, the motif already appears in medieval narratives, such as the twelfth-century romance *Count Ernst*[11] and the legend of Henry the Lion, Duke of Saxony (d. 1195),[12] both of which current research commonly holds to profit from the adaptation and integration of motifs of an "Oriental" provenance. In Middle Eastern narrative tradition, the motif is comparatively more frequent. Versions of *The Thousand and One Nights* include a total of four narratives in which the motif occurs, including the tales of "Hasan of Basra," "Jūdar and the Moor Maḥmūd," "The Third Qalandar," and the originally independent romance of *Sayf ibn Dhī Yazan*.[13] A strikingly similar incidence occurs in the second voyage of Sindbād the seafaring merchant.[14] In order to escape from a deserted island, Sindbād ties himself to the leg of a giant bird that carries him to a mountaintop strewn with diamonds. He soon realizes that a group of diamond gatherers harvests the gems by having a bird lift a large carcass to the mountain top to which the diamonds would stick. When they later have the bird bring the carcass down, Sindbād holds on to it and is saved. As Richard Burton, the editor of an English translation of the *Nights*, noted, "Epiphanius, archbishop of Salamis in Cyprus" (d. 403), gives "a precisely similar description of the mode of finding jacinths in Scythia."[15]

Although the origin of these Middle Eastern narratives cannot be dated with certainty, the motif of the treacherous treasure hunter is already attested in the tale of "Abū 'l-Favāris the Seaman" that is contained in the late fourteenth- or fifteenth-century Ottoman Turkish compilation *Ferec ba'd eş-şidde* (Relief after Hardship).[16] In that tale, a merchant hires the protagonist's ship in order to bring him to a certain island.[17] There, the merchant sends Abū 'l-Favāris down into some underground caves to harvest large pearls. Although the merchant promised to share the revenue, he leaves Abū 'l-Favāris down in the caves so that the secret be kept, and departs without him. Having escaped from the cave through a narrow tunnel, Abū 'l-Favāris later takes revenge. Not recognizing him, the merchant hires him again, and together they travel to the caves. There, Abū 'l-Favāris pretends to be too stupid to understand what he should do and convinces the merchant to go down first so as to instruct him. When the merchant has done his work, however, Abū 'l-Favāris leaves him down there to die. Similarly documented in a Persian compilation of tales that probably dates from the seventeenth century,[18] the ruthless revenge justified by Abū 'l-Favāris's ethics of violence is reminiscent of the Sindbād tales.[19] This tale of a treacherous treasure hunter offers variant but equivalent content and identical structure.

It is particularly the motif of the hero being sent to an underground cave (rather than to a mountain) that links the tale from the Ottoman Turkish *Ferec ba'd eş-şidde* to a tale in the Indian *Cārudatta-carita*, a romance of travel and adventure in the style of the tales of Sindbād the seafaring merchant that might have belonged to the ancient *Bṛhatkathā* (The Great Narrative).[20] That tale features only the initial scene in which the treacherous employer sends the hero down into the cave to fetch an elixir needed to produce gold and leaves him down there. Another man who was left down in the cave earlier informs the hero about a giant alligator that visits the cave to drink sweet water, and clutching to the alligator's tail the hero manages to leave the cave. Driven by greed, he once again searches for the entrance to the cave. When a wild buffalo attacks him, he is saved by a giant serpent emerging from between the rocks that attacks the buffalo.

The tale's elaborated version such as attested in the Sicilian tale and numerous other texts from Middle Asia, the Middle East, the Balkans, and North Africa reflects the tale of "Hasan of Basra" as included in *The Thousand and One Nights*.[21] This lengthy tale with its numerous digressions and additional adventures can be read as a compilation of various components from different sources that also appear in other tales of the *Nights*.[22] The tale of "Hasan of Basra" is particularly shaped by its constitutive combination with the widely documented motif of the swan maiden, her disappearance and later recovery,[23] to which the motif of the treacherous treasure hunter serves as a mere introduction. In Hasan's tale, the protagonist is drugged and abducted by a wicked Persian magician named Bahrām (as Persians are often named in the *Nights*).[24] Once lifted to the mountaintop sewn inside a camel's hide, Hasan's task is to throw down a special kind of wood the magician needs for the preparation of an elixir that enables him to produce gold. The specific form of the motif under consideration does not allow to establish a direct relation between the tale's Sicilian version and the *Nights*. Rather, the motif's use in a fair variety of forms and contexts reminds one of other motifs such as employed in tale type ATU 612: *The Three Snake-Leaves* (see essay **11, *The Husband Buried Alive Together with His Deceased Wife***) that illustrate a wide range of possible applications when used by talented storytellers.

Versions from Middle Eastern oral tradition were recorded in Arabic,[25] Persian,[26] Kurdish,[27] and Turkish.[28]

Notes

1. Zelenin, Dmitriy Konstantinovich, *Velikorusskie skazki Permskoy gubernii*, Petrograd: Orlov, 1914 (reprint St. Petersburg, 1997), pp. 450–453, 580, no. 98.

2. Marzolph and Van Leeuwen, *The Arabian Nights Encyclopedia*, vol. 1, pp. 207–211, no. 230.

3. Marzolph, Ulrich, "Hasan von Basra," in *Enzyklopädie des Märchens*, vol. 6 (1990), cols. 538–540.

4. Afanasyev, Aleksandr Nikolayevich, *Narodnye russkie skazki*, ed. Vladimir Jakovlevich Propp, Moscow: Gosudarstvennoye Izdatel'stvo Khudozhestvennoy Literatury, 1957, vol. 2, pp. 273–275, no. 243; English translation in Bain, R. Nisbet, *Russian Fairy Tales*, London: Lawrence and Bullen, 1892, pp. 1–7.

5. Zelenin, *Velikorusskie skazki Permskoy gubernii*, p. 580.

6. Novikov, Nikolaj V., "Barag, Lev Grigor'evič," in *Enzyklopädie des Märchens*, vol. 1 (1977), cols. 1209–1210.

7. Barag, Lev G., *Belorussische Volksmärchen*, Berlin: Akademie-Verlag, 1966, pp. 338–341, 613, no. 43.

8. Marzolph, "Hasan von Basra," col. 538.

9. Seidenspinner, Wolfgang, "Talion," in *Enzyklopädie des Märchens*, vol. 13 (2011), cols. 168–172.

10. Gonzenbach, Laura, *Sicilianische Märchen*, ed. Otto Hartwig, Leipzig: Engelmann, 1870, vol. 1, pp. 28–39, 207, no. 6.

11. Lecouteux, Claude, "Herzog Ernst," in *Enzyklopädie des Märchens*, vol. 6 (1990), cols. 939–942.

12. Gerndt, Helge, "Löwentreue," ibid., vol. 8 (1996), cols. 1234–1239.

13. Marzolph and Van Leeuwen, *The Arabian Nights Encyclopedia*, vol. 1, pp. 207–211, no. 230; pp. 245–247, no. 445; pp. 340–341, no. 18; 360–362, no. 536.

14. Ibid., vol. 1, p. 385, in no. 179.

15. Burton, Richard F., *Arabian Nights*, (Benares 1885) reprint Beirut: Khayat, 1966, vol. 5, p. 342, note 1. The motif's further development was sketched by Bremond, Claude, "L'Ascension du monte inaccessible," *Studia Islamica* 76 (1992), pp. 97–118, particularly at pp. 99–101.

16. Hazai, György, and Andreas Tietze, eds., *Ferec baʿd eş-şidde: „Freud nach Leid" (ein frühosmanisches Geschichtenbuch)*, Berlin: Klaus Schwarz, 2006, vol. 1, p. 15, 19.

17. Marzolph, *Relief after Hardship*, pp. 106–107, no. 35.

18. Haag-Higuchi, Roxane, *Untersuchungen zu einer Sammlung persischer Erzählungen: Čihil wa-šiš ḥikāyat yā ǧāmiʿ al-ḥikāyāt*, Berlin: Klaus Schwarz, 1984, pp. 82–84, no. 32.

19. Molan, Peter D., "Sindbad the Sailor: A Commentary on the Ethics of Violence," *Journal of the American Oriental Society* 98 (1978), pp. 237–247; also in *The Arabian*

Nights Reader, ed. Ulrich Marzolph, Detroit: Wayne State University Press, 2006, pp. 327–346.

20. Alsdorf, Ludwig, "Zwei neue Belege zur 'indischen Herkunft' von 1001 Nacht," *Zeitschrift der Deutschen Morgenländischen Gesellschaft* 89 (1935), pp. 275–314, at pp. 279–293.

21. Marzolph, "Hasan von Basra," col. 538.

22. Marzolph and Van Leeuwen, *The Arabian Nights Encyclopedia*, vol. 1, p. 211, no. 230.

23. Bäcker, Jörg, "Schwanjungfrau," in *Enzyklopädie des Märchens*, vol. 12 (2008), cols. 311–318.

24. Marzolph, Ulrich, "The Persian *Nights*: Links between the *Arabian Nights* and Persian Culture," *Fabula* 45 (2004), pp. 275–293; also in *The Arabian Nights in Transnational Perspective*, ed. Ulrich Marzolph, Detroit: Wayne State University Press, 2007, 221–243, at p. 227.

25. El-Shamy, *Types*, pp. 640–641, no. 0936*.

26. Marzolph, *Typologie*, pp. 174–175, no. 936* (8 versions).

27. Wentzel, Luise-Charlotte, *Kurdische Märchen*, Düsseldorf: Diederichs, 1978, pp. 145–146, no. 10.

28. Eberhard and Boratav, *Typen*, pp. 233–235, no. 198.

The Robbers Hiding Their Treasures in a Magic Cavern (ATU 954)

The tale of the robbers who hide their treasure in a magic cavern is one of the rare instances of a tale popular in Western tradition whose first oral performance in the European context is reliably documented in terms of time and space. As a matter of fact, both the original narrator and the exact time of narration are known. The tale was originally performed for Antoine Galland in Paris by the Syrian Maronite narrator Ḥannā Diyāb on Monday, May 27, 1709. Galland took down a condensed version of the performance in his diary, titled "Marjāna's Perspicacity, or The Forty Robbers Extinguished through the Skillfulness of a Slave."[1] Some years later, he elaborated his notes and prepared the tale for publication. It was published posthumously, Galland having died in 1715, in the eleventh volume of Galland's *Mille et une nuit* (1717), now titled "Ali Baba and the Forty Robbers (Extinguished by a Slave)."[2] By way of the numerous complete and selective editions, reprints, and retellings of the *Nights*, the tale became one of the most widely documented tales in Western oral tradition. Kurt Ranke mentions more than six hundred versions recorded from oral tradition as of the middle of the nineteenth century.[3] Although the tale clearly owes its popularity to Galland's literary text, its original version as performed by Ḥannā Diyāb likely derives from an older oral tradition. Its wide international dissemination, in turn, resulted in the tale being recorded in the international system of tale types. Originally split up into two units, tale type AT 676: *Open Sesame* and tale type AT 954: *The Forty Thieves*, the two units were reunited in the third and most recent revision of the international tale-type index as tale type ATU 954: *The Forty Thieves*.[4] Contrary to the tale's original title that acknowledged the pivotal role played by the clever slave girl Marjāna, ever since its publication by Galland the tale is best known by the name of its male protagonist, Ali Baba. In *The Thousand and One Nights*, the tale goes as follows.

> One day, the poor and morally good woodcutter Ali Baba overhears a band of robbers open the cavern where they keep their booty using the magic formula "Open Sesame!" As soon as they have left, Ali Baba opens the cavern with the magic formula, takes some of the treasures, and

returns home. At home, his wife borrows a scale from Ali Baba's rich and morally corrupt brother Cassim. As Cassim's wife is curious to know what Ali Baba needs the scale for, she smears the scale's bottom with grease. A gold coin sticks to the bottom of the scale, and Ali Baba is forced to reveal his secret to his brother. Following this, Cassim enters the cavern to take some gold. Inside, his greed makes him forget the magic formula and he remains locked up. When the robbers return, they cut Cassim to pieces. Ali Baba recovers his brother's corpse, promises to marry Cassim's widow and moves into his brother's house. The clever slave-girl Morgiane hires a cobbler to stitch the dead body's pieces together, following which Cassim is buried.

The robbers find the cobbler who leads them to Ali Baba's house. In order to identify it again, they mark the house, but the clever slave girl puts the same mark on many other houses in the vicinity. Finally, the captain of the robbers asks for shelter in Ali Baba's house, pretending to be a merchant trading in oil. His forty men are hidden in large leather vessels, waiting to be alerted for a night attack. Looking for oil, the slave girl becomes aware of the robbers and kills them one by one by pouring hot oil on top of them. Only the captain manages to make his escape. Some time later, the captain again disguises as a merchant and visits Ali Baba, who entertains him. The slave girl recognizes the captain and stabs him. In the end, the slave girl is married to Ali Baba's son, and all of them live happily.

Versions of the tale documented from Western oral tradition range between faithful retellings of the tale from *The Thousand and One Nights* and inspired adaptations to the teller's local context, sometimes involving the combination of episodes isolated from the original tale with episodes from other, originally unrelated tales. A particularly fanciful version was recorded in the Creole settlements about sixty-five miles south of Saint Louis, Missouri.[5]

This tale begins with a competition between the two suitors of a princess, Adrien and Aladin. In order to decide who is to marry the princess, the king requests them to bring a most unusual object. As Adrien wins the competition, Aladin plots Adrien's death. "He finds lodging in his house with forty soldiers concealed in oil casks. The maid goes out to get oil for her lamp, discovers the plot, and scalds the men to death. Then disguised as a harmless and witless old woman, she plays around Aladin with a knife until she kills him."[6]

Only the final episode, here quoted from the tale's English summary, corresponds to the tale of Ali Baba, in which it also constitutes the final episode. The initial episode of the Creole text corresponds, however, to tale type ATU 653A: *The Rarest Thing in the World* (see essay **12, *The Contending Lovers Are Requested to Acquire the Rarest Thing in the World***), a tale that also figures in Galland's *Nights*, incidentally having been told to Galland by the same narrator who performed "Ali Baba." The name Aladin links to yet another famous tale of the *Nights* (see essay **9, *The Unpromising Rascal Makes His Fortune with the Help of a Magic Object***), again originally told by the same narrator, so that in the end the Creole tale reads like a peculiar concoction of ingredients originating from three different tales. Folk narrative researchers adhering to the concept of pure and unambiguously defined tale types might judge this fanciful narrative as a badly told "contamination,"[7] assuming that the narrator was not capable of retelling Diyāb's "original" tale of Ali Baba faithfully. With adequate consideration of the dynamics of narrative creativity, one might rather credit this version to the imaginative adaptation of the narrator (or a chain of subsequent narrators). Above all, the Creole tale demonstrates that various elements of "Ali Baba" and other tales from the *Nights* were so familiar in the regional popular tradition as to be combined freely, without being restricted to their original sequence and position.

In a similar vein several European versions add the episode of the maid killing the robbers at the end of tale type ATU 956B: *The Clever Maiden Alone at Home Kills the Robbers*, thus creating a particularly conclusive combination.[8] Numerous other versions document a similarly creative attitude, whether changing the number of robbers from originally forty to twelve[9] or seven,[10] having the rich instead of the poor brother discover the cave,[11] or presenting a variety of fanciful contortions of the word "sesame" in the magic formula "Open, Sesame!,"[12] such as Simson,[13] Susanna,[14] Semsi,[15] Simso,[16] or Sanke.[17] While there are versions that mention or integrate the original tale's final episode, the death of the robbers, there are others that end with the greedy man being killed or the discovery of his dead body in the cavern.[18]

The tale "Simeli Mountain," number 142 in the Grimm brothers' *Kinder- und Hausmärchen* (Children's and Household Tales), deserves a special mention.[19] As a rule, the collectors of folk narratives from nineteenth- and twentieth-century European oral tradition would exclude tales they presumed to constitute retellings from literary sources obvious to them. But although Wilhelm Grimm noticed "a strange similarity with an Oriental tale from the *1001 Nights*,"[20] the Grimm brothers opted to include the tale in their collection. Whereas the Grimms refrained from publishing a version of the tale of Aladdin they had received from an unidentified contributor because they recognized its more or less direct origin from the *Nights*, they retained "Simeli Mountain" because they took the name "Simeli" to be an ancient (*uralt*) German name for a mountain, and hence the related tale as a genuinely German one.

Galland's elaborated published version follows Ḥannā Diyāb's performance closely. A minor detail in Galland's summary demonstrates, however, that there was and is an oral tradition independent of his rendering.[21] In his summary of Ḥannā Diyāb's performance, Galland notes that when entering the cave, the protagonist, here named Hogia Baba, "found the table set, and lots of provisions and foodstuff." This detail is not mentioned in the tale's published version. Consequently, any versions mentioning this particular detail cannot possibly derive from Galland's *Nights*, but must relate to an independent tradition to which Ḥannā Diyāb's early eighteenth-century version also belongs. Although the Syrian Christian narrator is the one to whose performance the tale owes its fame, it is thus likely that he had learned it from his local or regional tradition. Whether or not there was a written tradition of the tale independent of Galland was discussed in relation to the Arabic manuscript version prepared by Jean-Georges Varsy in the first half of the nineteenth century.[22]

Exactly how the tale came into existence is not known. What we do know is its particularly ingenious individual combination of motifs, several of which go back to ancient Egyptian tradition.[23] There is the conflict between the needy poor and the greedy rich that is also exemplified in the conflict between the envier and the envied in tale type ATU 613: *The Two Travelers*.[24] The motif of the thief caught in the treasure trove is already known from tale type ATU 950: *Rhampsinitus*.[25] And the tricky way of introducing one's army into the enemy's territory, here Ali Baba's house, is an equally ancient strategem.[26]

The tale of the robbers and the magic cavern demonstrates the tremendously creative potential successful tales in literature possess to exert a lasting impact on subsequent oral tradition. When versions of the tale were recorded from oral tradition as of the nineteenth century, the tale's original publication was already more than a century old. Although storytellers changed various details of the tale in their fanciful retellings, the tale's original structure was usually preserved, demonstrating the storytellers' indebtedness to Galland's highly influential early eighteenth-century publication and the oral performance of the Syrian storyteller to whom Galland owed the tale.

Notes

1. Galland, Antoine, *Le Journal d'Antoine Galland (1646–1715): La période parisienne*, vol. 1 (1708–1709), ed. Frédéric Bauden and Richard Waller, Leuven: Peeters, 2011, pp. 359–363.

2. Chauvin, *Bibliographie*, vol. 5 (1901), pp. 79–84, no. 24; Marzolph and Van Leeuwen, *The Arabian Nights Encyclopedia*, vol. 1, pp. 89–91, no. 353.

3. Ranke, Kurt, "Ali Baba und die vierzig Räuber," in *Enzyklopädie des Märchens*, vol. 1 (1977), cols. 302–311.

4. Uther, *The Types*, vol. 1, p. 592–594.

5. Carrière, Joseph Médard, *Tales from the French Folk-Lore of Missouri*, Evanston, IL: Northwestern University, 1937, pp. 200–204.

6. Ibid., p. 20.

7. Shojaei Kawan, Christine, "Kontamination," in *Enzyklopädie des Märchens*, vol. 8 (1996), cols. 201–217.

8. See, e.g., Haiding, Karl, *Märchen und Schwänke aus Oberösterreich*, Berlin: De Gruyter, 1969, pp. 90–91, no. 72; Massignon, Geneviève, *Contes corses*, Aix-en-Provence: Ophrys, 1963, pp. 55–56, no. 24; Méraville, Marie Aimée, *Contes d'Auvergne*, Paris:

Érasme, 1956, pp. 110–114, no. 16; Piprek, Jan, *Polnische Volksmärchen*, Wien: Verein für Österreichische Volkskunde, 1918, pp. 150–158; Rausmaa, Pirkko-Liisa, *Suomalaiset kansansadut*, vol. 2: *Legenda- ja novellisadut*, Helsinki: Suomalaisen Kirjallisuuden Seura, 1982, pp. 303–307, no. 181.

9. Merkelbach-Pinck, Angelika, *Volkserzählungen aus Lothringen*, Münster: Aschendorff, 1967, pp. 91–94; Neumann, Siegfried, *Mecklenburgische Volkserzählungen*, Berlin: Akademie-Verlag, 1971, pp. 250–252, no. 123.

10. Lemieux, Germain, *Les vieux m'ont conté*, vol. 21, Montréal: Bellarmin, 1984, pp. 197–202.

11. Ibid.

12. See Marzolph, Ulrich, "Märchen aus 'Tausendundeine Nacht' in der mündlichen Überlieferung Europas," in *Sichtweisen in der Märchenforschung*, ed. Siegfried Neumann and Christoph Schmitt, Baltmannsweiler: Schneider-Verlag Hohengehren, 2013, pp. 23–41, at p. 37.

13. Meier, Ernst, *Deutsche Volksmärchen aus Schwaben: Aus dem Munde des Volks gesammelt*, Stuttgart: Scheitlin, 1852, pp. 187–188, no. 53.

14. Bukowska-Grosse, Ewa, and Erwin Koschmieder, *Polnische Volksmärchen*, Düsseldorf: Diederichs, 1967, pp. 173–176, no. 44.

15. Dittmaier, Heinrich, *Sagen, Märchen und Schwänke von der unteren Sieg*, Bonn: Röhrscheid, 1950, pp. 121–122, no. 366.

16. Sirovátka, Oldřich, *Tschechische Volksmärchen*, 2nd ed., Düsseldorf: Diederichs, 1980, pp. 124–135, no. 16.

17. Moser, Dietz-Rüdiger, "Kommentare," in *Ungarndeutsche Märchenerzähler*, vol. 2: *Die "Blinden Madel" aus Gant im Schildgebirge*, Freiburg: Volkskunde Tonarchiv, 1971, pp. 70–103, at pp. 100–103, referring to no. 11, p. 68–69; disk III B.

18. See, e.g., Kindl, Ulrike, *Märchen aus den Dolomiten*, Munich: Diederichs, 1992, pp. 32–36, no. 6; Karlinger, Felix, and Johannes Pögl, *Märchen aus der Karibik*, Cologne: Diederichs, 1983, pp. 39–40, no. 9; Kúnos, Ignaz, *Türkische Volksmärchen aus Stambul*, Leiden: Brill, 1905, pp. 231–234; Loukatos, Demetrios, *Neoellēnika laographika keimena*, Athens: Zakharopulos, 1957, pp. 127–312, no. 19; Rael, Juan B., *Cuentos españoles de Colorado y Nuevo Mějico*, vol. 2, Stanford: Stanford University Press, 1940, pp. 395–397, no. 343; Toschi, Paolo, and Angelo Fabi, *Buonsangue romagnolo: racconti di animali, scherzi, anedotti, facezie*, Bologna: Cappelli, 1960, pp. 185–187, no. 91.

19. Marzolph, Ulrich, "Grimm Nights: Reflections on the Connections Between Grimms' *Household Tales* and the *1001 Nights*," *Marvels & Tales* 28.1 (2014), pp. 75–87, at p. 81.

20. Grimm, Jacob and Wilhelm, *Kinder- und Hausmärchen: Ausgabe letzter Hand*, ed. Heinz Rölleke, Stuttgart: Philip Reclam Jun., 1980, vol. 3, p. 137, note 1.

21. For the following see Chraïbi, Aboubakr, "Galland's 'Ali Baba' and Other Arabic Versions," in *The Arabian Nights in Transnational Perspective*, ed. Ulrich Marzolph, Detroit: Wayne State University Press, 2007, pp. 3–15.

22. Zakharia, Katia, "Jean-Georges Varsy et l'"histoire d'Ali Baba:' révélations et silences de deux manuscrits récemments découverts," *Arabica* 62 (2015), pp. 652–687; Zakharia, "La version arabe la plus ancienne de l'"histoire d'Ali Baba:' si Varsy n'avait pas traduit Galland? Réhabiliter le doute raisonable," *Arabica* 64 (2017), pp. 50–77.

23. Chraïbi, "Galland's 'Ali Baba'," pp. 11–13.

24. Maennersdoerfer, Maria Christa, "Wanderer: Die beiden W.," in *Enzyklopädie des Märchens*, vol. 14 (2014), cols. 476–483; El-Shamy, Hasan, *Folktales of Egypt*, Chicago: The University of Chicago Press, 1980, pp. 96–101, 261–264, no. 14.

25. Van der Kooi, Jurjen, "Rhampsinit," in *Enzyklopädie des Märchens*, vol. 11 (2004), cols. 633–640.

26. Köstlin, Konrad, "Kriegslist," ibid., vol. 8 (1996), cols. 436–440.

CHAPTER 31

Whose Was the Noblest Action? (ATU 976)

Two texts recorded in the nineteenth and twentieth century, respectively, document the occurrence of a tale in Scottish tradition that is otherwise mainly popular in the Middle East. A shorter version was recorded in 1859 by John Francis Campbell (1822–1885)[1] from the oral performance of Donald Macintyre from Benbecula, an island of the Outer Hebrides.[2]

As he feels his end coming, a rich farmer informs his three sons that he deposited a sum of gold for them. When the brothers inspect the location, however, they do not find anything. This makes the youngest son doubt whether their father spoke the truth. In order to clarify the situation, the three brothers decide to ask the advice of their father's old friend. Being sure that their father never told a lie, the father's friend first entertains the brothers for ten days. Then he tells them a tale.

The daughter of a rich man falls in love with the son of her poor neighbor. Although they are not allowed to marry, they pledge themselves to each other. When the young woman finally marries, she confesses the pledge to her husband, and her husband not only agrees with her obligation but even delivers her to her former suitor. With equal magnanimity, the suitor frees her from the pledge and sends the young woman back to her husband. On the way back, the young woman is seized by three robbers. Two of the robbers insist to take the money she offers, whereas the third robber refrains from accepting anything, instead escorting her back home.

Following the tale, the old man asks the three brothers, "Which of all these do you think did best?" The eldest son votes in favor of the woman's husband, the second in favor of her former suitor, and the youngest thinks the robbers were "the wisest of all." Revealing that he had closely watched their character for the past ten days, the old man now is sure that the youngest brother stole the money. The youngest brother confesses, and the money is returned and divided among the three of brothers.

An elaborate version was performed by James MacKinnon from Barra, another island of the Outer Hebrides, and recorded by Calum MacLean in 1947.[3] The tale tells of a farmer on an island of the Uists and his three sons Donald, Neil, and Rory. Before passing away, the farmer shows his sons the sum of 60 pounds, asking them to share the money whenever they are in need. According to their father's wish, the eldest son, Donald, soon gets married but stops working thereafter. Suspecting his brother to have spent the money, Rory insists he receive his share. But when they open the chest, the money is not there. Although Donald insists that he did not take it, Rory has his brother summoned to court in Inverness several times, but even then the situation is not clarified. Finally, the judge advises Rory to sue his brother at the head of the great bridge in Edinburgh. As the brothers do not speak English and none of the people they meet speaks Gaelic, they are about to despair. Finally, a man speaking Gaelic offers his help and tells them a tale. A noble woman falls in love with a farmer. Although she cannot marry him, she promises him that no man should ever possess her before him. When the woman marries a nobleman, she confesses her pledge to her husband on the wedding night. The husband delivers her to her former suitor so that she can keep her promise, assuring her that whatever happens will not affect him. Learning about her husband's magnanimity, the former suitor releases her from her promise. On the way back home, she surprises twelve robbers slaughtering one of her cows. Admonishing the robbers to lead a decent life, the woman gives them some money and asks them to escort her back home. Following the tale, the narrator asks the three sons to vote who of the male characters was the best. Donald votes in favor of the robbers, thus disclosing his mean character. It turns out that Donald's wife had taken the money. He is made to restore his brothers' share and pay all the court fees.

Both of the above texts correspond to the international tale type ATU 976: *Which Was the Noblest Act?*[4] of which the archives of the School of Scottish Studies in Edinburgh hold another three versions that only differ in details.[5] The Scottish texts are the tale's only versions documented from Northern European tradition, except for two Irish tales. The Irish tales differ from all other known versions, as the father here announces that he will give a precious diamond to the one of his three sons who will commit the noblest deed while traveling.[6] Other European versions of the tale are almost exclusively documented from oral tradition in the Balkans. At the end of the nineteenth-century, a Serbian peasant in Bosnia introduced the tale with the father informing his three sons that he buried his savings at the foot of an apple tree in the garden.[7] When the sons later find the money gone and turn to the judge to solve their dispute, the judge tells them the said tale. Except for minor details, the main variation in this version is the fact that the woman encounters the robber on the way to her former suitor. When she informs the robber about her intention and promises to let him have whatever he wants on her way back, the robber lets her pass safely. The tale ends with the second brother confessing the theft. Following this, the judge divides the inheritance among the three brothers, but, as the narrator cynically remarked, "he himself also did not go without his share." Another Bosnian version presents the tale without the frame, leaving the question whose action was the noblest to the audience.[8]

A late nineteenth-century Greek tale from the island of Symi has the brothers go to the judge to settle their dispute over the missing inheritance.[9] The tale continues with a version of tale type ATU 655: *The Wise Brothers* (see essay **13, *The Sensitive Brothers and Their Clever Deductions***). In the version of tale type ATU 976 then following, the woman goes straight to her former suitor who sends her away since she now belongs to another man. There is no mention of a robber on the woman's way to her former suitor, and the woman's return to her husband is not mentioned. As the thief cannot be identified by his solidarity with the robber, the youngest prince is found to be the thief when he says, "If it had been me, I never would have let her go."

The presently concerned tale type relies on a long and varied tradition documented for a span of almost two millennia. Prominently discussed versions in the medieval European literatures include Chaucer's "Franklin's Tale" in his fourteenth-century *Canterbury Tales*,[10] the tale connected with the fourth question, proposed by Menedon, in Boccaccio's (1313–1375) *Filocolo*,[11] and the essentially identical tale of Dianora and Ansaldo narrated on the tenth day by Emilia in the *Decamerone*.[12] As both the tale in the *Decamerone* and Chaucer's "Franklin's Tale" ultimately derive from the earlier *Filocolo*,[13] it is not surprising that the three tales share a number of structural features that both define them as a specific group and delineate them against other groups in the tale's tradition. In all three texts, a married woman is courted by an unwed man, and in all of them she finally consents to give in to his courting, requesting him, however, to fulfill a condition that she deems impossible to achieve. In *Filocolo* and the *Decamerone*, the woman requests her suitor to produce a garden in January that would grow splendidly blossoming flowers as if it were May. In "The Franklin's Tale," the task is to remove all rocks from the coast of Brittany. In all of the three versions, the task is performed through magic by a person whom the suitor hires, promising to compensate him profusely. As the woman never imagined that her request could actually be achieved, she is reluctant to go and needs her husband's urging to meet her former suitor. Her suitor, however, treats her respectfully, apologizes for his folly, and sends her back to her husband. Learning about the suitor's magnanimity, the magician cancels the suitor's debt. The question as to which man's act was the noblest does not expect to be met with any particular answer. Particularly Boccaccio's version was influential in terms of literary impact, in addition to Chaucer's "Franklin's Tale" being adapted in the twelfth chapter of Italian author Matteo Boiardo's late fifteenth-century *Orlando innamorato* (Orlando in Love)[14] and in German theologian Johann Valentin Andreae's (1586–1654) *Chymische Hochzeit Christiani Rosencreutz 1459* (The Chemical Wedding of Christian Rosenkreutz; Strassburg, 1616), one of the founding texts of

Rosicrucianism.[15] None of these texts did, however, have a discernible impact on modern oral tradition, whether in Italy, Germany, or England.

Similar in structure to the late nineteenth-century Greek tale is Italian novelist Giovanni Sercambi's (1348–1424) novella "De Sapientia" (Of Wisdom).[16] Introduced by the dispute over the brothers' inheritance and following a full-fledged version of tale type ATU 655, Sercambi's concluding version of tale type ATU 976 is heavily truncated, although still recognizable. Preparing his decision, the judge tells the brothers the tale of the beautiful maiden who, when traveling to her future husband, passes through a country owned by three young men, each of whom has the power to do with her whatever they wanted to do. The judge asks the three brothers present what they would do. When the youngest brother confesses that he would not only ravish her himself but also have all of his servants rape her, keeping her with himself for the rest of her days, he discloses his detestable character, and the judge is sure that he is the one who committed the theft.

Although the present tale type's variety is quite dazzling, several additional groups in addition to the group constituted by Boccaccio's version and its derivatives can be clearly identified. Placing the woman's encounter with the robber or robbers after the meeting with her former suitor rather than before, the two Scottish versions display a close affinity to Jewish tradition for which this sequence is constitutive.[17] Jewish versions usually introduce three travelers who (for religious reasons) bury their money before the beginning of the Sabbath, only to find it missing when they want to recover it later. The judge is Solomon who gains the travelers' trust by pretending that he wants to solve a riddle somebody else has posed to him. Notably, the Jewish versions are the only ones that consider praising the woman's action. The earliest-known version of this type appears in the *Midrash of the Ten Commandments* (or *Midrash Decalogue*), originating in the tenth century. Another early source is the *Sefer ha-ma'asim* (Book of Tales) compiled in France at the beginning of the thirteenth century. Further told and retold in a variety of sources from the Renaissance onward, the theme unfolds in almost 40 Jewish versions from the tenth century to today.

Sercambi's version belongs to a group in which the introductory dispute over the inheritance and the present tale as the final episode frame tale type ATU 655. A closely similar text is contained in the anonymous Ottoman Turkish collection of tales *Ferec ba'd eş-şidde* (Relief after Hardship) whose initial compilation probably dates to the second half of the fourteenth century, thus predating Sercambi.[18] The earliest documented representative of this group is the Persian *Munes-nāme* (The Book as an Intimate Friend) compiled by a certain Abu Bakr ibn Khosrow al-Ostād around the year 1200.[19] The group is further characterized by the fact that in its version of tale type ATU 976 the only threat to her safety the young woman encounters on her way to her former suitor is a robber. A short version introduced by the dispute over the inheritance but lacking the embedded tale type ATU 655 is contained in the Ottoman Turkish *Qırq vezīr*

(The Forty Viziers), an adaptation of the Persian *Sendbād-nāme* (The Book of Sendbād [the Sage]) attributed to Sheykh-zāda and probably compiled as early as the fourteenth century.[20] Together with the frame tale of the *Qırq vezīr*, this text was later integrated into versions of *The Thousand and One Nights*.[21]

Persian literature from the thirteenth century onward also knows a number of texts in which the said tale serves to detect a thief, the earliest of which attested so far is presented in Sadid al-Din Moḥammad ʿAwfi's (d. ca. 1232) encyclopedia of traditional narratives, *Javāmeʿ al-ḥekāyāt* (Collections of Stories).[22] The author quotes the tale from "a book compiled by the Indian sages" with the intention to demonstrate that people's differing mental dispositions (*ṭabāyeʿ*) become evident through their behavior.

> A man who owns a precious jewel travels together with four companions. When his jewel is missing one day, he suspects one of his companions of having stolen it. Although the king has the four companions imprisoned, none of them confesses. Finally, the princess has them released from prison and treats them kindly for a number of days so as to make them feel comfortable and off their guard. Then she tells them the tale.
>
> When strolling around in the garden, a princess wants to have a beautiful flower blossoming on a tree. The gardener picks the flower for her and, since he is young and does not know proper behavior, jokingly asks her to visit him in her wedding night before even consummating the marriage with her husband, and the princess agrees. Years later, the princess marries, and her husband consents to let her go in order to fulfill her promise. On the way, the princess first meets a lion and then a robber threatening her. She manages to pass unharmed by promising to be at their disposal on her way back. The princess's suitor, however, apologizes for his former inconsiderate wish and sends her back to her husband. The robber whom she meets on her return lets her go because of her faithfulness. The lion discloses his true identity as a spiritual being (*yeki az jomle-ye ruḥāniyān*) who had been sent to test the woman's faithfulness; since she passed the test successfully, he will not harm her.
>
> When the four companions are asked to vote for their different preferences whose act was the noblest one, the jewel's thief is discovered.

Early in the nineteenth century, the royal Persian storyteller Mollā Ādine attached a variant of ʿAwfi's version of the tale to his performance of a tale corresponding to tale type ATU 1641: *Dr. Know-All* (see essay ***79, The Lowly Man Posing as a Soothsayer***).[23] Closely similar versions are contained in the two early Persian adaptations of the Indian *Śukasaptati* (Seventy [Tales of a] Parrot),[24] ʿEmād ibn Moḥammad al-S̱aghari's *Javāher al-asmār* (The Jewels of Nocturnal Stories), compiled in ornate prose in 1314,[25] and Żiyāʾ al-Din Nakhshabi's (d. 1350) *Ṭuti-nāme* (Book of the Parrot).[26] The only major variation in these versions is their mention of the princess encountering a wolf instead of a lion. Since both books warn against women's sexual infidelity, these versions end differently from the ones discussed so far. In *Javāher al-asmār*, the woman when rebuked by her former suitor curses and reviles him out of disappointment before returning to her husband. The version of the *Ṭuṭi-nāme* ends with the gardener admonishing the woman that every action has its consequences, and "each today has its tomorrow" (*har ʿamal-rā jazāʾi ast va har emruzi-rā fardāʾi*).

The above discussed texts are predated by tales in the Indian literatures. In addition to the *Śukasaptati*,[27] the tale is included in the *Vetālapañcaviṃśatika* (Twenty-five Tales of a Corpse Demon),[28] versions of which are contained in Somadeva's eleventh-century *Kathāsaritsāgara* (The Ocean of Streams of Stories)[29] and Kṣemendra's slightly earlier *Bṛhatkathāmañjarī* (A Bouquet of Flowers from the *Bṛhatkathā*),[30] both of them essentially constituting adaptations of Guṇāḍhya's lost *Bṛhatkathā* (The Great Narrative). In the *Vetālapañcaviṃśatika*, the vetāla, a particular kind of demon residing in a dead human body, tells the tales to the king. The version of tale type ATU 976 does not have a particular introduction, starting right away with the young woman promising to visit her suitor in her wedding night. The only threat to her safety the young woman encounters on the way is a robber. In an old Jain version[31] an adaptation of which is contained in Hēmavijaya's *Kathāratnākara* (The Sea of Stories), completed in 1600, the tale is told by the king to "a gathering of gamblers, adulterers, thieves and other vermin" in order to find out who stole the Mango fruits from the king's garden.[32] On her way, the young woman is threatened by both a robber and a cannibal demon.

The tale's oldest version known so far is contained in Kang Seng-Hui's (d. 280) Chinese translation of a collection of tales that form part of the Buddhist canon, the *Tripiṭaka* (Three Baskets).[33]

> The bride is celebrating a party with her female friends on top of a tower. When an orange falls down, the women promise to reward the one who brings it back by giving her food and drink, and the bride herself steps down. The young man who picked up the orange will only cede it if the bride promises to visit him before consummating her marriage in the wedding night. The bride agrees and receives the orange.
>
> Getting married, the bride informs her husband about her promise, and he lets her go. On the way, she convinces a robber and a cannibal demon to let her pass unharmed so that she can fulfill her promise. Finally meeting the young man, the latter does not transgress the boundaries of proper behavior, instead giving her food and drink, and even presenting her with a golden gem.
>
> The tale ends with the Buddha's commentary that each of the four characters involved acted in an exceptionally noble manner, without giving preference to any one of them.

Details of the tale experienced numerous variations over the many centuries of its history, but the tale's basic structure remained surprisingly stable. The tale's constitutive elements comprise not only the young woman's rash promise and her conscious visit to her former suitor but, more than that, the noble action of the tale's characters. Except for the versions in the *Book of the Parrot* that in connection with the book's main argument tend to portray the woman as lecherous, it is her faithful compliance with a promise given long ago under different circumstances that not only propels the action but also causes the tale's other, exclusively male, characters to refrain from acting spontaneously as custom or their personal inclination might require. Even so, in the final evaluation, the woman is reduced to an object of male desire rather than an active agent of her own fate. The last tale in Spanish author Don Juan Manuel's *El conde Lucanor* (1330–1335), that is at times related to the tale under discussion, overlaps inasmuch as a married woman promises to be at her suitor's disposal should he achieve a certain difficult task.[34] As this task is not of a practical but rather a moral nature, it eventually leads to the suitor's reform and repentance rather than to the fulfillment of his original wishes. Moreover, in this tale the woman remains active throughout, instead of victimizing herself managing to change the male partner's attitude. In this respect, Don Juan Manuel's tale is rather close to a specific variation of tale type ATU 891B*: *The King's Glove* in which the king coveting the wife of one of his subordinates repents when reading a book containing pious warnings against adultery as he waits for the woman to get ready. First documented in tenth-century Arabic literature,[35] differing versions of this tale type are included in the various redactions of *The Thousand and One Nights*.[36]

Notes

1. Wehse, Rainer, "Campbell of Islay, John Francis," in *Enzyklopädie des Märchens*, vol. 2 (1979), cols. 1165–1167.

2. Campbell, John Francis, *Popular Tales of the West Highlands: Orally Collected*, Edinburgh, 1890, pp. 24–27; Aitken, Hannah, and Ruth Michaelis-Jena, *Märchen aus Schottland*, Düsseldorf: Eugen Diederichs, 1965, pp. 346–349, 380, no. 69.

3. Aitken and Michaelis-Jena, *Märchen aus Schottland*, pp. 335–342, 380, no. 67. The summary follows the German translation. The English translation made available to me by John Shaw differs in several details.

4. Schoenfeld, Elisheva, "Handlung: Die vornehmste H.," in *Enzyklopädie des Märchens*, vol. 6 (1990), cols. 459–464.

5. John Shaw kindly prepared English summaries of the three versions from the sound recordings. The most remarkable variation occurs in the version narrated by Angus MacLellan, South Uist (SA1960.002.A2), when the robbers actually strip the young woman naked since she has no money, before sending her back to her husband.

6. Ó Súilleabháin, Seán, and Reidar Thoralf Christiansen, *The Types of the Irish Folktale*, Helsinki: Suomalainen Tiedeakatemia, 1963, p. 193, no. 976.

7. Krauss, Friedrich S., "Südslavische Volksüberlieferungen, die sich auf den

Geschlechtsverkehr beziehen, 1: Erzählungen," *Anthropophyteia* 1 (1904), pp. 1–506, at pp. 219–222, no. 179.

8. Ibid., pp. 222–223.

9. Loukatos, Demetrios, *Neoellēnika laographika keimena*, Athens: Zakharopoulos, 1957, pp. 164–167, no. 9; Dawkins, Richard M., *Modern Greek Folktales*, Oxford: Clarendon Press, 1953, pp. 429–434, no. 72.

10. Clouston, William Alexander, "The Damsel's Rash Promise: Indian Original and Asiatic and European Version of the *Franklin's Tale*," in *Originals and Analogues of Some of Chaucer's Canterbury Tales*, ed. F.J. Furnivall, Edmund Brock, and William Alexander Clouston, part 4, London: N. Trübner & Co., 1886, pp. 289–340; Rajna, Pio, "Le origini della novella narrata dal 'Frankeleyn' nei Canterbury Tales del Chaucer," *Romania* 32.126 (1903), pp. 204–267; Aman, Anselm, *Die Filiation der Frankeleynes Tale in Chaucers Canterbury Tales*, Erlangen: Junge & Sohn, 1912; Edwards, Robert, "The Franklin's Tale," in Correale, Robert M., and Mary Hamel, eds., *Sources and Analogues of the Canterbury Tales*, vol. 1, Cambridge: D.S. Brewer, 2002, pp. 211–264; Edwards, *Chaucer and Boccaccio: Antiquity and Modernity*, Houndmills: Palgrave, 2002, pp. 153–172; Bleeth, Kenneth, *Chaucer's Squire's Tale, Franklin's Tale, and Physician's Tale: An Annotated Bibliography 1900–2005*, Toronto: University of Toronto Press, 2017.

11. http://sites.fas.harvard.edu/~chaucer/special/authors/boccaccio/filoc.html (accessed January 3, 2018).

12. Clouston, "The Damsel's Rash Promise," pp. 328–331.

13. Battles, Dominique, "Chaucer's *Franklin's Tale* and Boccaccio's *Filocolo* Reconsidered," *The Chaucer Review* 43.1 (1999), pp. 38–59.

14. Clouston, "The Damsel's Rash Promise," pp. 333–338.

15. Ibid., p. 331, note 1.

16. Sercambi, Giovanni, *Novelle*, ed. Giovanni Sinicropi, Bari: Gius. Laterza & Figli, 1972, pp. 65–79, no. 2 (online edition available at http://www.classicitaliani.it/sercambi/sercambi_novelle_01.htm, accessed December 20, 2017); Wesselski, *Märchen des Mittelalters*, pp. 100–106, 222–225, no. 37; Schick, Josef, *Corpus Hamleticum: Hamlet in Sage und Dichtung, Kunst und Musik*, 1. Abteilung: *Sagengeschichtliche Untersuchungen*, vol. 5.2: *Die Scharfsinnsproben*, Leipzig: Otto Harrassowitz, 1938, pp. 335–345.

17. On the tale's Jewish versions, see Clouston, "The Damsel's Rash Promise," pp. 315–319; Bolte and Polívka, *Anmerkungen*, vol. 4, p. 328, no. 19; Schwarzbaum, Haim, *Studies in Jewish and World Folklore*, Berlin: Walter de Gruyter, 1968, pp. 207–208, 215–216, 474; Elstein, Yoav, Avidov Lipsker, and Rella Kushelevsky, *Encyclopedia of the Jewish Story*, vol. 2, Ramat-Gan: Bar-Ilan University Press, 2009, pp. xxii–xxiii (English summary), 113–128 (Hebrew text); Kushelevsky, Rella, *Tales in Context: Sefer ha ma'asim in Medieval Northern France*, Detroit: Wayne State University Press, 2017, pp. 146–151, 420–425, no. 16.

18. Marzolph, *Relief after Hardship*, pp. 83–85, no. 22.

19. See Marzolph, *Relief after Hardship*, p. 48; Askari, Nasrin, "A Mirror for Princesses: *Mūnis-nāma*, A Twelfth-Century Collection of Persian Tales Corresponding to the Ottoman Turkish Tales of the *Faraj ba'd al-shidda*," *Narrative Culture* 5.1 (2018), pp. 121–140.

20. Sheykh-Zāda, *The History of the Forty Vezirs*, transl. E.J.W. Gibb, London: George Redway, 1886, pp. 105–111; Clouston, "The Damsel's Rash Promise," pp. 322–325; Chauvin, *Bibliographie*, vol. 8 (1904), pp. 123–124, no. 110.

21. Marzolph and Van Leeuwen, *The Arabian Nights Encyclopedia*, vol. 1, pp. 411–412, no. 439.

22. ʿAwfi, Sadid al-Din Moḥammad al-, *Matn-e enteqādi-ye Javāmeʿ al-ḥekāyāt wa-lavāmeʿ al-revāyāt*, book 3, part 1, ed. Amir Bānu Moṣaffā and Maẓāher Moṣaffā, Tehran: Bonyād-e Farhang-e Irān, 1352/1973, pp. 14–22, no. 9; see also Hammer-Purgstall, Joseph von, *Rosenöl, oder Sagen und Kunden des Morgenlandes aus arabischen, persischen und türkischen Quellen gesammelt*, vol. 2, Stuttgart: J.G. Cotta, 1813, pp. 277–280, no. 151.

23. Malcolm, John, *Sketches of Persia*, London: Murray, 1845, pp. 265–270; Clouston, "The Damsel's Rash Promise," pp. 305–310.

24. Hatami, Mahroo, *Untersuchungen zum persischen Papageienbuch des Naḫšabī*, Freiburg: Klaus Schwarz, 1977, pp. 64–67, nos. 23–24.

25. ʿEmād ibn Moḥammad [al-S̱aghari], *Ṭuṭi-nāme: Javāher al-asmār*, ed. Shams al-Din Āl-e Aḥmad, Tehran: Bonyād-e Farhang-e Irān, 1352/1973, pp. 153–165, nos. 22–23.

26. Nakhshabi, Żiyāʾ al-Din, *Ṭuṭi-nāme*, ed. Fatḥallāh Mojtabāʾi and Gholām-ʿAlī Āryā, Tehran: Manūchehr, 1372/1993, pp. 111–119; Clouston, "The Damsel's Rash Promise," pp. 310–312.

27. Hatami, *Untersuchungen*, pp. 64–67, nos. 23–24.

28. Sathaye, Adheesh, "*Vetālapañcaviṃśatika*," in *Enzyklopädie des Märchens*, vol. 14 (2014), cols. 178–183.

29. Somadeva, *The Ocean of Story: Being C.H. Tawney's Translation of Somadeva's Kathā Sarit Sāgara (or Ocean of Streams of Stories)*, ed. N.M. Penzer, (2nd ed. London: privately printed, 1923–1928) reprint Delhi: Motilal Banarsidass, 1968, vol. 7, pp. 199–204.

30. Schick, Josef, "Die ältesten Versionen von Chaucer's Frankeleynes Tale," *Studia Indo-Iranica: Ehrengabe für Wilhelm Geiger zur Vollendung des 75. Lebensjahres*, ed. Walther Wüst, Leipzig: Harrassowitz, 1931, pp. 89–107.

31. Ibid., pp. 103–106.

32. Hēmavijaya, *Kathāratnākara: Das Märchenmeer, eine Sammlung indischer Erzählungen*, transl. Johannes Hertel, Munich: Georg Müller, 1920, vol. 1, pp. 233–237, no. 82.

33. Chavannes, Édouard, *Cinq cents contes et apologues extraits du Tripitaka chinois*, vol. 1, Paris: Ernest Leroux, 1910, pp. 388–389, no. 117.

34. Don Juan Manuel, *Libro del Conde Lucanor*, ed. Reinaldo Ayerbe-Chaux, Madrid: Alhambra, 1983, pp. 445–466, no. 50; see Serrano Reyes, Jesús L., *Didactismo y moralismo en Geoffrey Chaucer y Don Manuel: Un estudio comparativo textual*, Córdoba: Universidad de Córdoba, 1996, pp. 125–251 (quoted from Edwards, "The Franklin's Tale," p. 197, note 1).

35. Marzolph, *Arabia ridens*, vol. 2, p. 118, no. 471.

36. Marzolph and Van Leeuwen, *The Arabian Nights Encyclopedia*, vol. 1, p. 183, no. 285; 257, no. 313; pp. 260–261, no. 138; 261, no. 182.

CHAPTER 32

The Villager in the Town of Rogues (ATU 978)

According to the current state of documentation, the tale classified as tale type ATU 978: *The Youth in the Land of the Cheaters* is exclusively attested, as far as European oral tradition is concerned, in single versions from Macedonia and Bulgaria, respectively.[1] The Macedonian version was narrated by Mikhaila Kostenceva and published in Marko Cepenkov's (1829–1920)[2] seminal collection of Macedonian folktales.[3]

A poor villager collects pieces of a certain precious wood growing in the mountains and takes them to town to sell, hoping to make considerable profit. In town, a rogue makes the villager believe that the townspeople use that particular wood as ordinary firewood and offers to buy it cheaply. On the way, a one-eyed man accuses the villager of having stolen his missing eye and demands one of the villager's own eyes in compensation. Yet another man demands, without any particular reason, that the villager drink up the sea. Frightened by the town's challenges, the villager intends to travel back to his village the next day without even requesting to be paid for his wood.

At night, the villager is taken in by an old woman who pities him. Dressing him in her deceased husband's local clothes so that he would not be recognized as a stranger, the old woman takes him to a place where the town's rogues meet at night. There he clandestinely listens to their talk and figures out a scheme to extricate himself from the difficulties he faces. When the rogue who plans to cheat the villager out of his precious wood brags about his deed, the chief rogue scolds him for not having concluded his business that very day. He might be in great trouble if the next day the villager asked him for three plates full of fleas as payment. The rogue who demanded that the villager give him one of his eyes might equally face difficulties, since the villager might suggest that each of them take out one of their eyes and weigh them so as to find out whether the villager's eye really belongs to the townsman. That way the one-eyed man would lose his remaining eye while the villager would still have one of his eyes. And the third rogue is also severely scolded, since the villager might demand that the rogue stop the water from all the rivers before he attempts to drink up the sea. The three rogues defend themselves by arguing that the villager is unlikely to conceive such tricks, but the villager listened carefully.

The next day, the villager follows the advice inadvertently given by the chief rogue. In order not to be humiliated before their chief, each of the three rogues has to extricate himself by paying the villager lots of money. Happily, the villager returns home.

The tale ends with an old saying to the extent that hard work brings its own reward.

In European literary tradition, the tale appears in a limited number of texts, including the fourteenth-century French prose romance *Bérinus*,[4] the related "Tale of Beryn" contained in a single fifteenth-century manuscript of Chaucer's *Canterbury Tales*,[5] the fourteenth-century icelandic *Hróa Þáttr heimska* (Tale of Hrói the Simple),[6] and Hebrew author Berechiah ha-Nakdan's thirteenth-century *Mishle Shu'alim* (Fox Fables).[7] Although the historical texts differ in various details, all of them ultimately derive from the "Oriental" branch of *The Seven Sages* tradition. In international research labeled *senex caecus* (The Blind Old Man), the tale is contained in the collection's Persian, Syriac, Greek, Hebrew, Spanish, and Arabic versions.[8] Its oldest preserved version is attested in Persian author Ẓahiri Samarqandi's mid-twelfth-century *Sendbād-nāme* (The Book of Sendbād [the Sage]).[9] In this version, a merchant from the Turkish town of Antakya wants to make money by selling sandalwood. After the first rogue tried to swindle him out of his merchandise, the merchant loses in gambling and is requested to drink up the sea. His meeting with the one-eyed man is followed by a meeting with another rogue who challenges him to sew a shirt from stone. Having learned how to outsmart the rogues, the merchant demands the first one to pay him with a pot full of fleas, half of them being male and the other half female. The second and the third rogues are outwitted as in the version from Macedonian oral tradition. Countering the fourth rogue, the merchant asks him to procure a thread of steel. With somewhat different challenges, a version of the tale is also given in the anonymous Ottoman Turkish collection of tales *Ferec ba'd eş-şidde* (Relief after Hardship), probably translated toward the end of the fourteenth century from a Persian source.[10] This text begins with a version of tale type ATU 888A*: *The Basket-Maker* (see essay **26, *The Prince Learns a Profession***). Further, the tale is encountered in seventeenth-century versions of the Persian compilations collectively known as *Jāme' al-ḥekāyāt* (Collection of Tales) that likely draw on older Persian or Arabic tales; and, more recently, in the Arabic version of the *Sendbād-nāme* contained in *The Thousand and One Nights*.[11] A separate short version of the challenge to drink up the sea is also documented in Arab author Ibn al-Jawzī's (d. 1201) *Akhbār al-Adhkiyā'* (Tales of Clever People).[12]

Although the tradition of *The Seven Sages* was highly influential in transmitting tales of Middle Eastern tradition to the West, the tale's occurrence in the Ottoman Turkish *Ferec ba'd eş-şidde* suggests that there were also later, probably equally influential instances of transmission. Since the Balkans were under Ottoman dominion for several centuries, the Turkish version might account more suitably than *The Seven Sages* for the tale's repercussion in Balkan oral tradition.

Notes

1. The present essay relies to a considerable extent on Goldberg, Christine, "Stadt der Gauner," in *Enzyklopädie des Märchens*, vol. 12 (2008), cols. 1136–1140.

2. Matičetov, Marko, "Cepenkov, Marko Kostov," ibid., vol. 2 (1979), cols. 1189–1191.

3. Cepenkov, Marko, K., *Makedonski narodni prikazni*, ed. Kiril Penušliski, Skopje: MK, 1989, vol. 3, pp. 111–118, no. 259.

4. *Bérinus, roman en prose du XIVe siècle*, ed. Robert Bossuat, 2 vols., Paris: Société des anciens textes français, 1931–1933.

5. Burrow, John, "The *Tale of Beryn*: An Appreciation," *The Chauver Review* 49.4 (2015), pp. 499–511.

6. Schier, Kurt, *Märchen aus Island*, Cologne: Diederichs, 1983, pp. 247–248; Strömbäck, Dag, "En orientalisk saga i fornnordisk dräkt," in *Donum Grapeanum: festskrift tillägnad överbibliotekarien Anders Grape*, Uppsala: Almqvist & Wiksell, 1945, pp. 408–444; Strömbäck, "Uppsala, Iceland, and the Orient," in Brown, Arthur, and Peter Foote, eds., *Early English and Norse Studies Presented to Hugh Smith in Honour of His 60th Birthday*, London: Methuen, 1963, pp. 178–190.

7. Schwarzbaum, Haim, *The Mishle Shu'alim (Fox Fables) of Rabbi Berechiah ha-Nakdan*, Kiron: Institute for Jewish and Arab Folklore Research, 1979, pp. 558–567, no. 118.

8. Chauvin, *Bibliographie*, vol. 8 (1904), pp. 60–62, no. 26; Basset, René, "Deux manuscrits d'une version arabe inédite du recueil des Sept Vizirs," *Journal asiatique* 2.2 (1903), pp. 43–83, at pp. 81–82.

9. Clouston, William Alexander, *The Book of Sindibād; or The Story of the King, His Son, His Damsel, and the Seven Vazīrs: From the Persian and Arabic*, Glasgow: privately printed, 1884, pp. 96–105; Ẓahiri Samarqandi, Moḥammad 'Ali, *Sendbād-nāme*, ed. Moḥammad Bāqer Kamāl al-Dini, Tehran 1381/2002, pp. 211–220.

10. Marzolph, *Relief after Hardship*, pp. 112–114, no. 40.

11. Marzolph and Van Leeuwen, *Arabian Nights Encyclopedia*, vol. 1, pp. 359–360, no. 205.

12. Marzolph, *Arabia ridens*, vol. 2, p. 252, no. 1169.

CHAPTER 33

The Dishes of the Same Flavor (ATU 983)

Misogynous tales are part and parcel of international male-dominated narrative tradition, whether historical, modern, or contemporary. One of the most influential collections of tales in this respect is probably the Persian *Sendbād-nāme* (The Book of Sendbād [the Sage]), a collection whose frame tale embeds numerous narratives about women's lewdness, sexual insatiability, fickleness, and unreliability.[1] The present tale, classified in international folk narrative scholarship as tale type ATU 983: *The Dishes of the Same Flavor*,[2] relates to this context as it also appears in the collection's Arabic version. Presented as an educative narrative, the tale essentially represents a male perspective that reduces women to the status of an object lacking individuality. Even so, the tale is ambiguous in its misogynous message, as the woman concerned often displays a remarkable agency.

Tale type ATU 983 comprises two distinct forms. The two forms overlap in the sexually charged context and the narrative motif of dishes of the same flavor being served. Although both forms presumably address a male audience, the respective messages are diametrically opposed. In the more often documented form, a woman wards off the advances of an enamored man by serving him the same food in differing preparations, thus teaching him that all women are essentially the same; or the ruler makes his subaltern understand through a similar trick that even the queen is "just another woman." Whereas this form of the tale probably aims to teach men not to indulge in fancy fantasies, the tale's second form serves as a man's justification to seek distraction and excitement elsewhere, as no man could possibly be expected to relish one and the same dish day after day. Recordings of each of the two forms from European oral tradition are rare.

Karl Stolz from the former German region of Prussia told his dialect version of the tale's second form in the first half of the twentieth century.[3]

> The father of the Prussian King Frederick II (r. 1740–1786), popularly nicknamed "Old Fred" (Der alte Fritz), marries his son to an ugly and stupid woman. After his father's death, the king neglects his wife, instead enjoying the company of female dancers in his castle. When a certain priest annoys the king by criticizing his conduct, the king invites him to

> stay at the fortress in Spandau and gives orders to serve him his favorite dish of trout every day for three months. Finally, the king goes to see the priest and asks him whether he is being treated well. The priest is quite happy with the treatment, but admits that "every day trout and always trout—who can stand that?" Old Fred responds by saying, "Now you see: every day Karoline and always Karoline—who can stand that?" From then on, the priest refrains from criticizing the king.

A closely similar version of the tale in which the king rebukes a pharmacist for neglecting his wife in favor of other women was recorded from Galician tradition in Spain.[4]

A version of the tale's first form is documented in a little booklet purporting to present jocular tales from the tradition of German peasants formerly residing in the forest regions of Bohemia, today part of the Czech Republic.[5]

> Two traveling companions confess their most ardent wishes to each other. The first would like to share a meal with the emperor, and the second would love to have sex with the emperor's wife. Their wishes are overheard by the emperor himself who happens to walk behind them. Soon after, the emperor invites them to his castle.
>
> The first companion is invited to join the emperor's meal at the golden table. The second companion is served three plates of soup poured from one and the same bowl. Following this, he is asked to judge which soup was the best. As he says that the soup from each of the three plates tasted quite the same, the emperor jovially informs him, "Now you see, this is just the same as it is with women, since one of them is just like the other."

A nineteenth-century Albanian version introduces the sultan in disguise (Mot. K1812.17) joining three men who enjoy themselves at night.[6] One of them wishes to marry the sultan's daughter, another wants to have the sultan's best horse; and the third wishes to be rid of his debts. The following day, the sultan has the three men brought to court where they are asked to repeat their wishes. The first one is blindfolded and given three kinds of grapes to eat. Since he is not able to distinguish between the white, red, and black grapes, he is told that he is unfit to marry the sultan's daughter. Instead, he is advised to be happy with his present status. The second man is allowed to choose the sultan's best horse for himself. And the third man is beheaded because of his presumptuous wish, as even the sultan himself has to tolerate having debts.

Historically, the tale's second form is documented in a number of French, Italian, and Spanish sources of the fourteenth to seventeenth centuries.[7] The *Vocabulario de refranes y frases proverbiales* compiled by Spanish author Gonzalo Correas (1571–1631) contains a short version.[8] Here, a nobleman falls in love with the wife of one of his servants. Learning about the situation, the servant invites the nobleman to his house where his wife prepared different dishes of eggplant, thus making the nobleman understand that somebody else's wife is just as good as one's own. A fairly elaborate version is given in Boccaccio's fourteenth-century *Decamerone*, told by Fiametta as the fifth tale on the first day.[9]

> Hearing about the beautiful wife of the Marquis of Monferrato, who is absent on a crusade, King Philip II of France (r. 1180–1223) falls "of a sudden ardently in love with her." When he visits her on his way to join the crusade, the noble lady receives him "with great honour and rejoicing." Although the king enjoys her company, during the meal he soon begins "somewhat to marvel, perceiving that, for all the diversity of the dishes, they were nevertheless of nought other than hens." When the king asks the lady whether there are no roosters around, she responds boldly, "Nay, my lord; but women, albeit in apparel and dignities they may differ somewhat from others, are natheless all of the same fashion here as elsewhere." Understanding "the virtue hidden in her speech," the king thanks her for the honorable entertainment and makes a prompt departure.

Particularly in those versions in which the woman teaches the lecherous man a lesson, the tale's larger context relates to tale type ATU 891B*: *The King's Glove*.[10] In this tale, the enamored ruler is reformed by the woman he covets, sometimes by means of having him read a pious book while she pretends to prepare herself. Various versions of this tale, in international research on *The Seven Sages* labeled *leo* (The Lion), are known from *The Thousand and One Nights*.[11] The particular text from the Arabic version of the *Sendbād-nāme*, known as *The Seven Viziers*,[12] also has the woman argue by means of a large number of dishes, each "of a different colour, but all of the same sort of food."[13]

The occurrence of food in the version of tale type ATU 891B* included in the Arabic *Seven Viziers* is both optional and chronologically fairly recent. At the same time, it stands at one end of a tradition whose oldest appearance is attested in al-Rāghib al-Iṣfahānī's (d. 1108) Arabic work of entertaining and educative literature, *Muḥāḍarāt al-udabā'* (Conversations of the Educated).[14] In a short section devoted to women's chastity and virtue in the book's fifteenth chapter that deals with married life, the author presents the following basic version.

> Once, when separated from his company, a certain prince entered the house of a woman and coveted her. She said, "Let us first have some food." Then she put a table in front of him on which there were twenty bowls all of which contained pickles (*kāmikh*). He tasted it and found it to be from one and the same kind and taste. He understood that she wanted to indicate that all women are of the same kind and that she was loyal to her husband, and so he refrained from (bothering) her.

In contrast to all other studied versions, the man here displays an astonishing acuity that in psychological terms might probably be explained by his intuitive sense that he was transgressing the boundaries of proper behavior. Since the text's author was Iranian and since the tale is cited right after another one whose protagonist is the Sassanian emperor Kisrā Abarwīz or Khosrow II Parviz (r. 591–628), al-Rāghib al-Iṣfahānī might well have adopted the tale from an ancient Persian source that remains to be substantiated.

About a century later, Arabic tradition attributed an extended tripartite version of the tale to al-Rāghib al-Iṣfahānī's Western contemporary Yūsuf ibn Tāshufīn (d. 1106), the founder of the Almoravid dynasty in North Africa.[15] First documented in the "complete" history, *al-Kāmil*, compiled by Iraqi scholar Ibn al-Athīr (d. 1233),[16] the tale introduces the ruler as a devout character renowned for his justice and magnanimity, a "model Islamic prince, virtuous, even-tempered and sober."[17] One day, the ruler happens to be informed about the wishes made by three men. The first man wishes for a thousand *dīnārs* to do business; the second wants to be hired by the ruler so as to work for him; and the third longs for al-Nafzāwiyya, the ruler's beautiful wife. Fulfilling the wishes of the first two men, the ruler scolds the third for aiming to attain the impossible. Then he sends the man to his wife who hosts him in a tent for three days, serving him the same food every day. At the end of this period, she asks him what he had eaten during the past three days. And when he says, "One and the same food," she makes him understand that all women are the same. Following this, she presents him with money and a gown and sends him away.

Without major alterations, the tale is cited in subsequent centuries in Arabic sources mentioning Yūsuf ibn Tāshufīn, including the biographical dictionaries compiled by Ibn Khallikān (d. 1282),[18] al-Ṣafadī (d. 1363),[19] and Ibn al-ʿImād (d. 1679),[20] explicitly referencing Ibn al-Athīr. Having quoted the tale's standard version as attributed to Yūsuf ibn Tāshufīn, the fourteenth-century author al-Yāfiʿī (d. 1367) cites a similar tale he knows from hearsay (*qad samiʿtu*).[21] This version introduces an Indian king. Strolling around his realm at night to learn what the people think of his rule, the king happens to overhear the wishes of three men. The first wants to be king, the second wishes to marry the king's wife, and the third longs to own a horse, sword, and armor to defend the country (literally: to do battle for God's course). The next day the king summons the three men to court. He presents a horse, sword, and armor to the one who longed for it. He seats the one who wanted to be king on his throne with a sharp sword dangling above his head. As the man fears that the sword might harm him, the king demonstrates to him that he is not fit to be a ruler. To the one who wished to marry the king's wife, the king has a number of dishes served, all of them prepared from the same kind of food, albeit in different ways. When the man admits that the dishes all taste the same, the king tells him that this also goes for women. Essentially sharing the same content and structure as the tale's other versions, the tale of the Indian king bears traits of a certain "folklorization," as it incorporates popular motifs such as that of the king wandering around in disguise at night (Mot. K1812.17) and a rare occurrence of the ancient motif of the "Sword of Damocles" (Mot. F833.2)[22] in Arabic literature.[23]

The tale's short version as given by al-Rāghib al-Iṣfahānī is also included in the abridged and adapted Persian translation of his work prepared by seventeenth-century author Moḥammad Ṣāleḥ Qazvini (d. after 1705).[24] Although the short version would thus have been available to a learned Iranian public, the tale's recordings from modern oral tradition in Iran document the tripartite structure.[25] A fair variety of versions was also recorded from oral tradition in the Arab world.[26]

Notes

1. Ranelagh, Elaine L., *The Past We Share*, London: Quartet Books, 1979, p. 226.

2. Moser-Rath, Elfriede, "Essen: das gleiche E.," in *Enzyklopädie des Märchens*, vol. 4 (1984), cols. 469–471.

3. Grannas, Gustav, *Volk aus dem Ordenslande Preussen erzählt Sagen, Märchen und Schwänke*, Marburg: Elwert, 1960, p. 117, no. 76.

4. Noia Campos, Camiño, *Catálogo tipolóxico do conto galego de tradición oral: clasificación, antoloxía e bibliografía*, Vigo: University of Vigo, 2010, pp. 517–519, no. 983.

5. Kubitschek, Rudolf, *Böhmerwäldler Bauernschwänke*, Vienna: Strache, 1920, pp. 64–65; the tale is not listed in Uther, *Deutscher Märchenkatalog.*

6. Jarník, Jan Urban, "Albanesische Märchen und Schwänke," *Zeitschrift für Volkskunde in Sage und Mär* 3 (1891), pp. 296–298, at pp. 296–297.

7. Moser-Rath, "Essen," col. 470.

8. Chevalier, *Cuentos folklóricos*, p. 136, no. 80.

9. Boccaccio, Giovanni, *The Decameron*, transl. John Payne, New York: Walter J. Black, s.a., https://www.gutenberg.org/files/23700/23700-h/23700-h.htm#THE_FIFTH_STORY (accessed January 9, 2018).

10. Wesselski, *Märchen des Mittelalters*, pp. 209–211, commentary for no. 16.

11. Marzolph and Van Leeuwen, *The Arabian Nights Encyclopedia*, vol. 1, p. 183, no. 285; 257, no. 313; pp. 260–261, no. 138; 261, no. 182.

12. Ibid., vol. 1, p. 261, no. 182.

13. Clouston, William Alexander, *The Book of Sindibād; or The Story of the King, His Son, His Damsel, and the Seven Vazīrs: From the Persian and Arabic*, Glasgow: privately printed, 1884, p. 144–147, at p. 146; see also Chauvin, *Bibliographie*, vol. 7 (1903), pp. 122–123, no. 2 de Syntipas.

14. Rāghib al-Iṣfahānī, al-Ḥusayn ibn Muḥammad, *Muḥāḍarāt al-udabāʾ wa-muḥāwarāt al-shuʿarāʾ wa-'l-bulaghāʾ*, Beirut 1961, vol. 3, p. 228; Marzolph, *Arabia ridens*, vol. 2, p. 238, no. 1084.

15. Ferhat, Halima, "Yūsuf ibn Tāshufīn," in *Encyclopaedia of Islam*, 2nd ed., vol. 11, Leiden: Brill, 2002, pp. 355–356.

16. Ibn al-Athīr, ʿIzz al-Dīn Abū 'l-Ḥasan ʿAlī, *al-Kāmil fī 'l-tārīkh*, Cairo: Idārat al-ṭibāʿa, 1348/1929, vol. 8, p. 237. I owe the initial reference to Ibn al-Athīr to Basset, *Mille et un contes*, vol. 1, pp. 324–325, no. 13.

17. Ferhat, "Yūsuf ibn Tāshufīn," p. 356.

18. Ibn Khallikān, Abū 'l-ʿAbbās Shams al-Dīn Aḥmad ibn Muḥammad ibn Abī Bakr, *Wafayāt al-aʿyān*, ed. Iḥsān ʿAbbās, Beirut: Dār Ṣādir, 1977, vol. 7, p. 125.

19. Ṣafadī, Ṣalāḥ al-Dīn Khalīl ibn Aybak al-, *al-Wāfī fī 'l-wafayāt = Das biographische Lexikon des Ṣalāḥaddīn Ḫalīl Ibn Aibak aṣ-Ṣafadī*, vol. 29, ed. Maher Jarrar, Stuttgart: Steiner, 1997, p. 175–176.

20. Ibn al-ʿImād al-Ḥanbalī, Abū ʾl-Falāḥ ʿAbd al-Ḥayy ibn Aḥmad, *Shadharāt al-dhahab fī akhbār man dhahab*, Beirut: al-Maktab al-tijārī lil-ṭibāʿa wa-ʾl-nashr wa-ʾl-tawzīʿ, ca. 1970, vol. 3, pp. 412–413.

21. Yāfiʿī, Abū Muḥammad ʿAbdallāh ibn Asʿad al-, *Mirʾāt al-jinān wa-ʿibrat al-yaqẓān fī maʿrifat mā yuʿtabar min hawādīth al-zamān*, 2nd ed., Beirut: Muʾassasat al-Aʿlamī lil-maṭbūʿāt, 1970, vol. 3, p. 164.

22. Lozar, Angelika, "Leben am seidenen Faden," in *Enzyklopädie des Märchens*, vol. 8 (1996), cols. 813–815.

23. The motif is not listed in El-Shamy, Hasan M., *Folk Traditions of the Arab World: A Guide to Motif Classification*, 2 vols., Bloomington: Indiana University Press, 1995.

24. Rāgheb Eṣfahāni, *Navāder: tarjome-ye ketāb-e Moḥāżarāt al-odabāʾ [. . .]*, transl. Moḥammad Ṣāleḥ Qazvini, ed. Aḥmad Mojāhed, Tehran: Sorush, 1371/1992, p. 257.

25. Marzolph, *Typologie*, pp. 181–182, no. 983 (4 versions).

26. El-Shamy, *Types*, pp. 686–687, no. 0983 (16 versions).

CHAPTER 34

The Fool Guards the Door by Taking It Along (ATU 1009)

Jocular tales use different mechanisms to create a humorous effect. As simple as it is striking is the pattern in which the tale's protagonist executes an everyday instruction by following its literal rather than its commonly accepted meaning.[1] Whether the action results from a foolish misunderstanding or a conscious misinterpretation,[2] the humorous effect is achieved. The present tale demonstrates these points.

The international tale type ATU 1009: *Guarding the Store-Room Door* is both ancient and widely documented internationally, including a rich non-European tradition.[3] When going out of the house, one character instructs another to "guard" or "pull" the door, implying to make sure that the door is closed so that no unauthorized person enters the house. Some time later, and for various reasons, the addressed person pulls the door off its hinges and carries or pulls it along, defending the action as a literal and precise execution of the instruction.

In Western tradition, the tale is documented with little variation in dozens of versions from a fair variety of regions in Europe and the Americas.[4] Often, the tale is embedded in a long cumulative chain of other tales about stupid people.[5] A rare appearance of the tale by itself is documented in a nineteenth-century version from Nottinghamshire in which husband and wife set out for the market.[6] When the husband learns that the wife has not "pulled the door after her, meaning to ask if she had shut it," he beats her and sends her back to execute his original instruction. After a long time she finally returns, having lifted the door from its hinges and actually pulling it after her. A nineteenth-century German version allegedly collected from oral tradition has Jan instruct his wife Griet to take good care of the door as he is leaving.[7] When he returns, he finds that the door is not in its place, as Griet has pulled it off the hinges and placed it in the attic so as to keep it safe.

An early European version is cited as the final tale in the sixteenth-century chapbook *The Sack-Full of Newes*, of which a single copy of the edition of 1673 survives.[8] Here, the action takes place between an English lady and her French lover.

> In the countrey dwelt a Gentlewoman who had a French man dwelling with her, and he did ever use to go to Church with her, and upon a time he and his mistresse were going to church, and she bad him pull the doore after him and follow her to the church, and so he took the doore betweene his armes, and lifted it from the hooks, and followed his mistresse with it. But when she looked behinde her and saw him bring the doore upon his back, Why thou foolish knave, qd she, what wilt thou do with the door? Mary mistresse, qd he, you bad me pull the doore after me. Why whorson qd she, I did command thee that thou shouldest make fast the doore after thee, and not to bring it upon thy back after me. But after this, there was much good sport and laughing at his simplicity and foolishnesse therein.

Apart from the fact that this is the tale's earliest dated version in European tradition, the text is interesting for its language, particularly as regards changing cultural attitudes toward gross language in print. The chapbook's initial reprint is complete and faithful to the original in having the lady address her lover rudely as "whorson." In contrast, and contrary to scholarly editorial procedure, later editors opted for various other terms to avoid the gross address. Likely causing amusement in the period of its original publication, the invective was deemed inappropriate in the Victorian period that was notorious for its prudery. In his 1881 reprint of the chapbook, William Carew Hazlitt bowed to the *Zeitgeist* by suppressing the two previous tales as being "too gross for publication."[9] The first of these tales deals with a man's nocturnal defecation in his dream (and in reality), and the other treats the popular subject of the adopted fart.[10] Hazlitt did, however, retain the word "whorson" in its original spelling. Later editors chose to replace the word by less provocative expressions such as "foolish knave"[11] or simply "fool."[12]

Of particular relevance for the tale's history in European tradition are the versions from Italy and Malta. Contrary to many other European versions in which the foolish character made fun of is female, these versions attribute the events to the regional equivalent of Juḥā, the male protagonist acting in the tale's older versions in Arabic tradition, that is, Giufà (Sicily), Giucco (Siena), or Ġaħan (Malta). While some of the Italian versions likewise integrate the tale into an extended chain of silly actions,[13] the tale was also recorded independently. In both the Sicilian version recorded by Giuseppe Pitrè from the performance of Rosa Brusca, aged 45,[14] and the Maltese version collected from an unspecified narrator by Bertha Ilg,[15] the simpleton's mother instructs her son to keep an eye on the door as she goes to church. Soon after, she sees her son enter the church, dragging the door behind him.

In Arabic literature, the tale is first documented early in the eleventh century. The encyclopedia of jokes and anecdotes, *Nathr al-durr* (Pearls of Prose), compiled by Abū Manṣūr al-Ābī (d. 1030) presents a short and matter-of-fact version in its chapter of anecdotes attributed to Juḥā.[16]

> His mother (once) went to a wedding party and left him at home, telling him, "Watch the door!" (*iḥfaẓ al-bāb*). He sat there until noon. When she was late in returning, he took the door from its hinges and carried it on his shoulders.

About two centuries later, Ibn al-Jawzī (d. 1201) in one of his ethical treatises compares the action of people who do not know right from wrong to that of Juḥā, citing a slightly more embellished version.[17]

> They (the aforementioned people) behaved like the proverbial Juḥā. When his mother (once) told him, "Watch the door!" he took it from the hinges and pulled it along. (Thieves) stole whatever was in the house, and so his mother scolded him. But he argued, "You said, 'Watch the door!' You did not say, 'Watch the house!'"

In the fifteenth century, a certain Abū Muḥammad ʿAbdallāh ibn Naṣr ibn ʿAbd al-ʿAzīz al-Zaydī compiled his *Lubāb Nathr al-durr*, a book whose title advertises it as a choice of the "best pieces" (*lubāb*) from al-Ābī's compilation.[18] The text given here, although identical in structure, is much more elaborated.

> One day (Juḥā's) mother went to a wedding party, instructing him, "My son, watch the door!" He lifted the door from its hinges, took it along and busied himself playing. Thieves entered and emptied the house. When his mother returned and saw the house in such a state, she said to him, "You detestable one! Have I not consigned the door to you?" He responded, "You silly one! The door is well preserved!"

And the version given by the seventeenth-century author Yūsuf ibn al-Wakīl al-Maylāwī in his comprehensive collection of tales about Juḥā is still more embellished.[19]

> His (Juḥā's) mother went to a wedding party and instructed him to watch the door, saying, "Watch the door until I return!" At first, he sat down next to the door. But when his mother was late in returning, he lifted it from its hinges and carried it along, going away and leaving the house. Thieves came and took everything there was in the house. When his mother came and saw the house in a mess, she scolded him. But he responded, "You told me to watch the door. You did not tell me to watch the house!"

A version more compact than the one presented by al-Ābī is contained in the first printed edition of jocular tales attributed to Juḥā in 1861,[20] from which it was later adapted into collections in Persian and a variety of European languages.[21]

The tale's oldest documented version is contained in the Chinese translation of Buddhist canonical scriptures, the *Tripiṭaka* (Three Baskets), compiled in the fifth century CE.[22] Here, a man instructs his slave to take care of the door, his donkey, and the donkey's harness while he himself sets out traveling. After a while, the slave goes to hear music in a neighboring house and fixes the door with the harness on the donkey's back. When the master returns he finds that thieves stole all his valuables. But the slave defends himself, saying that he did exactly as instructed; anything else had been none of his business. With a similar action, the tale is cited again in Somadeva's eleventh-century *Kathāsaritsāgara* (The Ocean of Streams of Stories).[23] Here, the master is specified as a merchant, and the slave takes the door on his shoulder to watch an actor perform. There is no mention of thieves, and the slave argues again that he took care of the door as he had been told.

Building on a simple but highly effective structure, the jocular tale has been around for almost two millennia during which its structure has not changed. Probably the most notable difference between the tale's premodern and many of the modern versions in which the tale is embedded in a chain of foolish actions is the change of its main character from male to female. The misogynist feature appears to be fairly recent and is not germane to European tradition, as it also appears in modern versions recorded in Iran[24] and elsewhere in the Middle East.[25]

Notes

1. Kaplanoglou, Marianthi, "Wörtlich nehmen," in *Enzyklopädie des Märchens*, vol. 14 (2014), pp. 995–1003.

2. Neumann, Siegfried, "Mißverständnisse," ibid., vol. 9 (1999), cols. 707–717; Van der Kooi, Jurjen, "Sprachmißverständnisse," ibid., vol. 12 (2007), cols. 1094–1099.

3. Schröder, Ina, "Tür bewacht," in *Enzyklopädie des Märchens*, vol. 13 (2010), cols. 1024–1027.

4. For versions from the Americas, see, e.g., Dorson, Richard M., *American Negro Folktales*, Greenwich, Conn.: Fawcett, 1967, pp. 341–343, no. 205; Miller, Elaine K., *Mexican Folk Narrative from the Los Angeles Area*, Austin: University of Texas Press, 1973, pp. 324–340, nos. 81–82; Pino Saavedra, Yolando, *Cuentos mapuches de Chile*, Santiago de Chile: Universidad de Chile, 1987, pp. 169–175, no. 46; Stroup, Thomas B., "Two Folk Tales from South Central Georgia," *Southern Folklore Quarterly* 2 (1937), pp. 207–212, at 207–211; reprinted in McCarthy, William Bernard, *Cinderella in America: A Book of Folk and Fairy Tales*, Jackson: University of Mississipi Press, 2007, pp. 232–235, no. 54.

5. Uther, *The Types*, vol. 2, pp. 12–13, no. 1009.

6. Briggs, *A Dictionary*, vol. A2, p. 243.

7. Merkens, Heinrich Ludwig, *Was sich das Volk erzählt: Deutscher Volkshumor*, 2nd ed., vol. 3, Jena: Costenoble, 1900, p. 140.

8. Hazlitt, J.O., ed., *The Sackfull of Newes: An Old Jest-Book, Originally Printed in the Sixteenth Century*, London: The Editor, 1861, pp. 39–40. A facsimile of the 1673 edition is available online by subscription to the database "Early English Books Online"; a facsimile of an edition dated 1700 (?) and titled *The Sack ful of News with a Stone-weight of Recreation* is available online by subscription to the database "Eighteenth-Century Collections online."

9. Hazlitt, W. Carew, ed., *Shakespeare Jest-Books: Reprints of the Early and Very Rare Jest-Books Supposed to Have Been Used by Shakespeare*, London: Willis & Sotheran, 1881, p. 187.

10. Daxelmüller, Christoph, "Furz," in *Enzyklopädie des Märchens*, vol. 5 (1987), cols. 593–600, at col. 596.

11. Ashton, John, *Humour, Wit, & Satire of the Seventeenth Century*, London: Chatto and Windus, 1883, p. 32.

12. Clouston, William Alexander, *The Book of Noodles: Stories of Simpletons; or, Fools and Their Follies*, London: Elliot Stock, 1903, p. 98.

13. Gonzenbach, Laura, *Sicilianische Märchen*, ed. Otto Hartwig, vol. 1, Leipzig: Engelmann, 1870, pp. 249–261, no. 37; Marzocchi, Ciro, *Novelle popolari senesi: raccolte da Ciro Marzocchi, 1978*, ed. Aurora Milillo, Gabriella Aiello, and Florio Carnasecchi, vol. 1, Rome: Bulzoni, 1992, pp. 65–68, no. 21; see also the references in Basset, *Mille et un contes*, p. 277, at no. 173.

14. Pitrè, Giuseppe, *Fiabe, novelle e racconti popolari siciliani*, vol. 1, Palermo: Lauriel, 1875, p. 366, no. 9.

15. Ilg, Bertha, *Maltesische Märchen und Schwänke: aus dem Volksmunde gesammelt*, vol. 2, Leipzig: Schönfeld, 1906, p. 44, no. 93.

16. Ābī, Abū Saʿd Manṣūr ibn al-Ḥusayn al-, *Nathr al-durr*, ed. Muḥammad ʿAlī Qarna et al., vol. 5, Cairo: al-Hayʾa al-miṣriyya al-ʿāmma lil-kitāb, 1987, p. 309; Marzolph, *Arabia ridens*, vol. 1, p. 247, no. 1; vol. 2, p. 200, no. 877; Marzolph, *Nasreddin Hodscha*, p. 32, no. 37.

17. Ibn al-Jawzī, Abū ʾl-Faraj ʿAbd al-Raḥmān ibn ʿAlī, *Ṣayd al-khāṭir*, Miṣr: Dār al-Kutub al-ḥadītha, ca. 1966, p. 116.

18. Zaydī, Abū Muḥammad ʿAbdallāh ibn Naṣr ibn ʿAbd al-ʿAzīz al-, *Lubāb Nathr al-durr*, Paris, Bibliothèque Nationale, ms. arabe 3490, fol. 78a.

19. ʿAnābsa, Ghālib, "Min adab al-nawādir: naẓra fī makhṭūṭāt [Irshād] man naḥā ilā nawādir Juḥā, jamʿ al-faqīr ilā ʾllāh taʿālā Yūsuf ibn al-Wakīl al-Maylāwī," in ʿAnābsa, *Dirāsāt muḍīʾa fī ṣafaḥāt al-turāth*, Zaḥāliqa: Dār al-Hudā, and Jordan: Dār al-Jarīr, 2013, pp. 174–196, at p. 185; see also Basset, *Mille et un contes*, vol. 1, pp. 276–277, no. 173.

20. Juḥā, *Hādhihi nawādir al-khūjah Naṣr al-Dīn Afandī Juḥā al-Rūmī*, Būlāq: Mūsā Kāstillī, 1278/1861, p. 3; see also Farrāj, ʿAbd al-Sattār Aḥmad, *Akhbār Juḥā*, Cairo: Maktabat Miṣr, 1954, p. 92.

21. Christensen, Arthur, "Les sots dans la tradition populaire des Persans," *Acta Orientalia* 1 (1922), pp. 43–75, at p. 47, no. 2; Wesselski, *Der Hodscha Nasreddin*, vol. 2, pp. 6, 182–183, no. 345.

22. Chavannes, Édouard, *Cinq cents contes et apologues extraits du Tripitaka chinois*, Paris: Ernest Leroux, 1910–1935 (reprint Paris: Maisonneuve, 1962), vol. 2, pp. 189–190, no. 281; Hertel, Johannes, *Ein altindisches Narrenbuch*, Leipzig: B.G. Teubner, 1912, p. 33, no. 24.

23. Somadeva, *The Ocean of Story: Being C.H. Tawney's Translation of Somadeva's Kathā Sarit Sāgara (or Ocean of Streams of Stories)*, ed. N.M. Penzer, (2nd ed. London: privately printed, 1923–1928) reprint Delhi: Motilal Banarsidass, 1968, vol. 5, p. 117, no. 128.

24. Marzolph, *Typologie*, p. 185, no. 1009.

25. Dirr, Adolf, *Kaukasische Märchen*, Jena: Diedrichs, 1920, pp. 271–272, no. 78; Stevens, Ethel Stefana, *Folk-tales of Iraq*, London: Milford, 1931, pp. 1–6, no. 1.

CHAPTER 35

The Fools Try to Keep the Bird from Escaping (ATU 1213)

From ancient times, it was common "for the inhabitants of a particular district, town, or village to be popularly regarded as pre-eminently foolish, arrant noodles or simpletons."[1] As the ancient Greeks "had their stories of the silly sayings and doings" of the people of Abdera,[2] so the Arabs localized the epitome of foolishness in the Syrian town of Ḥimṣ and the Persians in Qazvin. In Germany, the inhabitants of the fictional town of Schilda, the Schildburger, and in England those of Gotham were stereotyped by popular tradition as the quintessential fools. Today, these stereotypes are at times used in the service of marketing. As recently as December 30, 2016, the German *Süddeutsche Zeitung* published the following jocular legend.[3]

> Once the people of Dorfen, a small town in Bavaria, marveled at some pewits that had settled on their marketplace. When trying to figure out how to catch the birds, someone suggested closing the town's four gates so as to keep them from flying away. As the people surrounded the birds, they nevertheless flew away, making the people aware of the fact that, after all, their idea had not been so clever.

Originally published in 1926 by writer Rudolf Kirmeyer in the *Dorfener Zeitung* as an "old legend,"[4] the jocular tale corresponds to tale type ATU 1213: *The Pent Cuckoo*, numerous versions of which are known from European tradition. German folklorist Richard Wossidlo (1859–1923) recorded a short tale in the Northern German province of Mecklenburg in which the mayor of Teterow, a town in the district of Rostock, sends his clerk to the gatekeeper instructing him to keep the gates open until his pigeons would return to their loft.[5] A tale recorded in Villingen, a town in the South-eastern German region of Baden-Württemberg, tells how the mayor's favorite pet bird, a crossbill, escaped.[6] Immediately, the mayor gave orders to have the town gates closed. Only after the bird returned, having spent two winter nights outside, did he allow the gates to be opened again. Similarly, the people of Haiterbach in Swabia, who had never seen a cuckoo before,[7] or the people from the Austrian mining town of Hallein one of whose siskins had escaped,[8] tried to keep the bird from flying away. In the Netherlands, the tale is frequently attached to the mayor of Kampen's canary.[9]

In England, the tale appears to be particularly widely spread, although with a slightly different silly attempt to keep the bird from flying away.[10] James Harrison of Low Fell, Crosthwaite, told the tale in April 1936, as heard from a native of Thirlmere, Cumberland, in 1901. In this version, the people of Borrowdale aim to keep a cuckoo from flying away by building a high wall around the place where it had settled.[11] In the text recorded in 1913 by Ruth L. Tongue from L. Wyatt of Crewkerne, Somerset, the "Crewkerne wiseacres" think that the success of their harvest is linked to the coming of the cuckoo.[12] In order to have three harvests in a single year, they build a fence around a young cuckoo whom they bring up. But when the bird fledges, it flies "nice and 'igh." And in another English folktale, the people of "Austwick, near Settler, in the West Riding," "had noticed that when the cuckoo was about the weather was generally fine."[13] Aiming to always have fine weather, they build a wall around a resting cuckoo. When the bird flies away, they blame themselves for not having built the wall high enough.

In European tradition, the tale's oldest reliably dated version appears in the late sixteenth- or early seventeenth-century chapbook *The Merry Tales of the Mad Men of Gottam*, whose oldest preserved copy dates from 1630.[14] Here again, the people try to pen in the cuckoo by building a high hedge and placing the bird inside. When the cuckoo flies away, they regret not having made the hedge high enough. In German, the tale of the mayor who gives orders to have the gates closed so that his pigeons would not escape is contained in a number of seventeenth-century chapbooks; an early eighteenth-century chapbook renders a version in which the canary has escaped.[15]

Probably disseminated to Northern Europe by way of the "joke trade route"[16] that would have passed through either Spain or Italy, the tale's town gate version was known in Arabic literature since the ninth century.[17] First documented in two almost identical texts in Ibn Qutayba's (d. 889) *adab* compilation *'Uyūn al-akhbār* (Quintessential Reports)[18] and his book *al-Ma'ārif* (Useful Knowledge),[19] the fool here is the historical character Abū Bakr Bakkār (d. 750), a son of the fifth Umayyad caliph 'Abd al-Malik ibn Marwān (r. 685–705), who was known for being one of the particularly stupid members of the Quraysh clan. The bird is a falcon, an animal highly valued in traditional (and modern) Arabic culture as a faithful hunting companion, and the order is simply to close the city gates. With two different protagonists—both of them, notably, closely related members of the same family—the tale has remained popular throughout the centuries. Attributed to the same protagonist, Abū Bakr Bakkār ibn 'Abd al-Malik ibn Marwān, the tale is told in al-Ābī's (d. 1030) encyclopedia of jokes and anecdotes, *Nathr al-durr* (Pearls of Prose)[20] and Ibn Abī 'l-Ḥadīd's (d. 1258) *Sharḥ Nahj al-balāgha*, a commentary on the exemplary traditions of 'Alī ibn Abī Ṭālib.[21] In the majority of later texts, the protagonist is Bakkār's uncle

Muʿāwiya ibn Marwān, who was equally known for his stupidity. This applies to Ibn ʿAbd Rabbih's (d. 940) *al-ʿIqd al-farīd* (The Unique Necklace),[22] Abū 'l-Faraj al-Iṣfahānī's (d. 967) *Kitāb al-Aghānī* (Book of Songs),[23] Ibn ʿAbd al-Barr's (d. 1071) *Bahjat al-majālis* (Glory of the Learned Gatherings),[24] al-Qazwīnī's (d. 1258) cosmography *ʿAjāʾib al-makhlūqāt* (The Wonders of Creation),[25] and Ibn ʿĀṣim's (d. 1426) *Ḥadāʾiq al-azāhir* (Flower Gardens).[26] The versions in the works of Ibn ʿAbd Rabbih, Ibn ʿAbd al-Barr, and Ibn ʿĀṣim are likely of particular relevance for the tale's dissemination East to West, as the authors lived and published in Muslim Spain.

In the introductory passage of his book on stupid people, *Akhbār al-Ḥamqā*, Ibn al-Jawzī (d. 1201) presents an anonymous version of the tale as a representative example of utter stupidity.[27] Although the tale continued to be cited by authors of the Mamluk period,[28] by the sixteenth century, and probably earlier, it was solidly integrated into the series of absurd statements and actions attributed to the twelfth-century judge Bahāʾ al-Dīn Qarāqūsh, who in popular tradition became "notorious as a byword for stupidity."[29] This is the only Arabic version in which the two gates mentioned are specified as the Bāb al-Naṣr and the Bāb Zuwayla in Cairo. Different versions of the tale, one of them featuring Qarāqūsh, and the other attributed to an intoxicated consumer of hashish, continue to appear in late nineteenth-century Arabic chapbooks.[30]

An anonymized version of the tale adapted from al-Ābī's encyclopedia is given in the Syriac *Laughable Stories* compiled by the leading authority of the Eastern Jacobite church, Bar Hebraeus (d. 1286),[31] through which it would have been available to a Middle Eastern Christian audience. An early Persian translation, mentioning Bakkār ibn ʿAbd al-Malik ibn Marwān, is contained in Fakhr al-Din ʿAli Ṣafi's (d. 1532) *Laṭāʾef al-ṭavāʾef* (Jocular Tales from the Various Strata of Society).[32] The modern adaptation in Ḥabiballāh Kāshāni's *Reyāż al-ḥekāyāt* (Gardens of Tales) is apparently adapted from a different source as it attributes the event to Muʿāwiya ibn Marwān.[33]

Notes

1. Clouston, William Alexander, *The Book of Noodles: Stories of Simpletons; or, Fools and Their Follies*, London: Elliot Stock, 1903, p. 16; Brednich, Rolf Wilhelm, "Ortsneckereien," in *Enzyklopädie des Märchens*, vol. 10 (2002), cols. 376–382.

2. Bausinger, Hermann, "Abderiten," in *Enzyklopädie des Märchens*, vol. 1 (1977), cols. 10–11.

3. http://www.sueddeutsche.de/muenchen/erding/sz-serie-sagen-und-mythen-folge-gruesse-aus-schilda-1.3315540 (accessed January 29, 2018).

4. https://www.merkur.de/lokales/erding/narren-stehen-schon-startloechern-994447.html (accessed January 29, 2018).

5. Wossidlo, Richard, *Aus dem Lande Fritz Reuters: Humor in Sprache und Volkstum Mecklenburgs*, Leipzig: Wigand, 1910, p. 183.

6. Merkens, Heinrich Ludwig, *Was sich das Volk erzählt: Deutscher Volkshumor*, 2nd ed., vol. 2, Jena: Costenoble, 1892, pp. 27–28, no. 36.

7. Birlinger, Anton, and Michael Richard Buck, *Volksthümliches aus Schwaben*, vol. 1: *Sagen*, Märchen und Aberglauben, Freiburg: Herder, 1861, pp. 443–444.

8. Lang-Reitstätter, Maria, *Lachendes Österreich: Österreichischer Volkshumor*, 2nd ed., Salzburg: Österreichischer Kulturverlag, 1948, p. 31.

9. http://www.verhalenbank.nl/items/show/33024 (accessed January 29, 2018).

10. Field, John Edward, *The Myth of the Pent Cuckoo*, London: Elliot Stock, 1913.

11. Briggs, *A Dictionary*, vol. A2, pp. 25–26; Briggs, Katherine M., and Ruth L. Tongue, *Folktales of England*, 2nd ed., London: Routledge, 1966, pp. 128–129, no. 72.

12. Briggs, *A Dictionary*, vol. A2, pp. 51–52.

13. Addy, Sidney Oldall, *Household Tales with Other Traditional Remains: Collected in the Counties of York, Lincoln, Derby, and Nottingham*, London: Nutt, 1895, p. 112.

14. Hazlitt, W. Carew, ed., *Shakespeare Jest-Books: Reprints of the Early and Very Rare Jest-Books Supposed to Have Been Used by Shakespeare*, vol. 3, London: Willis & Sotheran, 1881, p. 6, no. 3; Wardroper, John, *Jest upon Jest: A Selection of Jestbooks and Collections of Merry Tales Published from the Reign of Richard III to George III*, London: Routledge & Kegan Paul, 1970, pp. 98, 174–175, no. 106.

15. Moser-Rath, *"Lustige Gesellschaft,"* pp. 385, 436, no. 71.

16. Wardroper, *Jest upon Jest*, p. 175.

17. Marzolph, *Arabia ridens*, vol. 1, p. 247, no. 2; vol. 2, pp. 44–45, no. 166.

18. Ibn Qutayba al-Dīnawarī, Abū Muḥammad ʿAbdallāh ibn Muslim, *ʿUyūn al-akhbār*, 2nd ed., vol. 2, Cairo: al-Muʾassasa al-miṣriyya al-ʿāmma lil-taʾlif wa-ʾl-tarjama wa-ʾl-ṭibāʿa, 1963, p. 42.

19. Ibn Qutayba al-Dīnawarī, Abū Muḥammad ʿAbdallāh ibn Muslim, *al-Maʿārif*, ed. Tharwat ʿUkkāsha, 2nd ed., Cairo: Dār al-Maʿrif, 1969, p. 358.

20. Ābī, Abū Saʿd Manṣūr ibn al-Ḥusayn al-, *Nathr al-durr*, ed. Muḥammad ʿAlī Qarna et al., vol. 7, Cairo: al-Hayʾa al-miṣriyya al-ʿāmma lil-kitāb, 1991, p. 362.

21. Ibn Abī ʾl-Ḥadīd, ʿAbd al-Ḥamīd ibn Hibatallāh, *Sharḥ Nahj al-balāgha*, Cairo: Dār Iḥyāʾ al-kutub al-ʿarabiyya, 2nd ed., vol. 18, 1387/1967, p. 162.

22. Ibn ʿAbd Rabbih, Abū ʿUmar Aḥmad ibn Muḥammad, *Kitāb al-ʿIqd al-farīd*, ed. Aḥmad Amīn, Aḥmad al-Zayn, Ibrāhīm al-Abyārī, 3rd ed., vol. 6, Cairo: Lajnat al-taʾlīf wa-ʾl-tarjama wa-ʾl-nashr, 1368/1949, p. 157.

23. Iṣfahānī, Abū ʾl-Faraj al-, *Kitāb al-Aghānī*, vol. 16, Būlāq (reprint Beirut: Ṣaʿb, ca. 1980), p. 93.

24. Ibn ʿAbd al-Barr al-Namarī al-Qurṭubī, Abū ʿUmar Yūsuf ibn ʿAbdallāh ibn Muḥammad, *Bahjat al-majālis wa-uns al-mujālis*, ed. Muḥammad Mursī al-Khūlī, vol. 2, Beirut: Dār al-Kutub al-ʿilmiyya, ca. 1969, p. 554.

25. Qazwīnī, Zakariyyā ibn Muḥammad al-, *ʿAjāʾib al-makhlūqāt wa-gharāʾib al-mawjūdāt*, ed. Fārūq Saʿd, Beirut: al-Āfāq al-jadīda, 1401/1981, p. 382.

26. Ibn ʿĀṣim al-Andalusī, Abū Bakr ibn Muḥammad, *Ḥadāʾiq al-azāhir*, ed. ʿAfīf ʿAbd al-Raḥmān, Beirut: al-Masīra, 1401/1981, p. 270; López Bernal, Desirée, *Los Ḥadāʾiq al-azāhir de Abū Bakr ibn ʿĀṣim al-Garnāṭī: Traducción y estudio de una obra de adab de la Granada nazarí*, vol. 1, Ph.D. thesis University of Granada, 2016, p. 423, no. 1035; López Bernal, "Los cuentos de Ibn ʿĀṣim (m. 1426): precedentes peninsulares de relatos españoles y del folklore universal en el s. XV," *Boletín de literatura oral* 9 (2019), pp. 35–52, at p. 42, no. 36.

27. Ibn al-Jawzī, Abū ʾl-Faraj ʿAbd al-Raḥmān ibn ʿAlī, *Akhbār al-Ḥamqā wa-ʾl-mughaffalīn*, ed. Kāẓim al-Muẓaffar, al-Najaf: al-Maktaba al-ḥaydariyya, 1386/1966, p. 8.

28. See, e.g., ʿIṣāmī, ʿAbd al-Malik ibn al-Ḥusayn ibn ʿAbd al-Malik al-, *Samṭ an-nujūm al-ʿawālī fī anbāʾ al-awāʾil wa-ʾl-tawālī*, ed. ʿĀdil Aḥmad ʿAbd al-Mawjūd and ʿAlī Muḥammad Muʿawwaḍ, vol. 3, Beirut: Dār al-Kutub al-ʿilmiyya, 1419/1998, p. 286.

29. Sobernheim, M. "Ḳarākūsh," in *Encyclopaedia of Islam*, 2nd ed., vol. 4 (1978), pp. 613–614, at p. 613; see Marzolph, *Arabia ridens*, vol. 1, p. 11; see Casanova, Paul, *Ḳaraḳoûch, Mémoires publiés par les members de la Mission Archéologique Français du Caire* 6 (1897), pp. 447–491, at pp. 473, 499 (Arabic text), 485, 499, no. 9 (French translation).

30. Marzolph, *Arabia ridens*, vol. 2, p. 45, no. 166.

31. Bar Hebraeus, Mâr Gregory John, *The Laughable Stories*, transl. E.A. Wallis Budge, London: Luzac and Co., 1897, p. 146, no. 573.

32. Ṣafi, Fakhr al-Din ʿAli, *Laṭāʾef al-ṭavāʾef*, ed. Aḥmad Golchin-Maʿāni, Tehran: Moḥammad Ḥoseyn Eqbāl, 1336/1957, p. 405.

33. Christensen, Arthur, "Les sots dans la tradition populaire des Persans," *Acta Orientalia* 1 (1922), pp. 43–75, at p. 62, no. 24.

CHAPTER 36

Trying to Please Everyone (ATU 1215)

The *Nederlandse Volksverhalenbank* (Dutch Folktale Databank) contains a total of four versions of an ancient tale demonstrating the truism that it is not possible to please each and everyone, since different people have different opinions, preferences, and suggestions.[1] While one of the versions is a pictorial representation documented on Facebook in August 2015,[2] the remaining three are textual renderings in Frisian and Dutch recorded in the years 1972, 1973, and 2000, respectively. The Frisian version documented from the oral performance of the prolific narrator Minke Schaafsma and contributed by Adam Aukes (Dam) Jaarsma (1914–1991), a writer, poet, assistant preacher, and avid collector of folktales,[3] is summarized as follows.[4]

> Once, a grandson and grandfather went with a donkey to the market. The old man was tired and mounted the animal. A man came along and did not find it right that he let the boy walk. The grandfather got off the donkey, and let the boy ride. Moments later, someone observed that such a boy ought be able to walk himself, and so they were all three walking. Someone else opined that it was stupid that they were walking while they had a beast of burden with them, and so the man and the boy mounted the donkey. Then a woman coming by felt sorry for the donkey, and remarked that they might better carry the donkey. Carrying the animal, they came home and realized that it was not easy to please everyone.

Classified as tale type ATU 1215: *The Miller, His Son, and the Donkey*, the tale is richly documented in European tradition, albeit with a clear dominance of written tradition, as versions of the tale collected from oral tradition are comparatively scarce.[5] A unique version recorded in 1977 by Marisa Rey-Henningsen from the Galician fishmonger Malvina Nogueiras, aged 68, in the municipality of Carballo, La Coruña, Spain, introduces a grandmother and her grandson on their way to the cattle market. Initially, both of them ride the animal. Being criticized by some "distinguished people," at first the grandmother dismounts, then she asks the boy to walk, and finally both of them walk. Now being ridiculed as a "dim-witted pair," the grandmother decides again that both of them would ride, saying, "We can't please everybody, so we might as well please ourselves."[6]

The tale's rich tradition in European literary sources reads like an inventory of influential collections ranging from the nineteenth back to the thirteenth century,[7] and including works such as German author Johannes Pauli's *Schimpf und Ernst* (Jocular and Serious Tales) in the sixteenth century,[8] the papal secretary Poggio Bracciolini's Latin collection of facetious stories around the middle of the fifteenth century,[9] and Dominican preacher John Bromyard's extensive compilation of exempla, *Summa predicantium* (J10, 22),[10] in the fourteenth century. Of particular importance for the tale's early history is its occurrence in the *Libro del Conde Lucanor*, compiled around 1330–1335 by the Spanish *infante* Don Juan Manuel (1282–1348).[11] Only preceded by the tale's earliest documented European version in the anonymous *Tabula exemplorum*, compiled in 1277 in France,[12] Don Juan Manuel is known to be strongly influenced by stories from Arab tradition.

The tale's ultimately earliest-known version was identified by Johann Gildemeister[13] in the historical work *al-Mughrib fī ḥulā al-Maghrib* (The Extraordinary Book about the Adornments of the West), compiled by the thirteenth-century Arab geographer and historian Abū 'l-Ḥasan ʿAlī ibn Mūsā ibn Saʿīd al-Maghribī (d. 1286). Although the author's original work is lost, parts of it have been preserved by way of quotations in Aḥmad ibn Muḥammad al-Maqarrī's (d. 1632) history of Muslim Spain, *Nafḥ al-ṭīb min ghuṣn al-Andalus al-raṭīb* (The Breeze of Fragrance from the Green Branch of Andalusia). Al-Maqarrī quotes Ibn Saʿīd as recounting a conversation with his father in which he, the son, wondered why people always have different opinions and never accept others to act in ways those people deem best for themselves.[14] In response, the father advises his son to give up all hopes of not being criticized for his book, the *Mughrib*, illustrating his advice with the following tale. Mirroring their own situation, the tale again begins with a son asking his wise (*ʿāqil*) father if he had not better accept the people's opinions so as to prevent them from criticizing him. The father mildly admonishes his son for his lack of experience, telling him that there is no way to gain each and everyone's approval. In order to demonstrate the truth of his statement, the father tells him to mount the donkey they have with them, and he himself follows on foot. A person they next meet on the way criticizes both the boy for lacking respect, as he is riding and letting his father walk, and the father for allowing his son to do so. When they change places so that the son walks, the father is scolded for lacking parental care. And when the father asks his son to ride the donkey together with him, they are reproached for overstraining the animal's capacity. When both of them end up walking alongside the donkey they are ridiculed for not using the donkey. The father ends his demonstration by saying, "You heard what they said and saw that no one can feel safe from being criticized by the people, whatever one does!"

Although no other early versions of the tale are known from any other tradition, Bill Hansen argues that the tale might "have been in oral circulation in Aristophanes' day,"[15] that is, in the fifth or fourth century BCE. Hansen's argument is connected to a version of a somewhat related tale, tale type ATU 1242A: *Carrying Part of the Load* in Artistophanes' *Frogs* in which two men travel with a donkey, one of them riding and the other walking. The one who walks "suggests more or less that since the present arrangement is not working out, the donkey should be carried." This is exactly what father and son decide to do in some, albeit much later, versions of the above tale.

Discussing some of the tale's early versions, Gaston Paris further suggested that here, as in other instances, the tale's Arab version transmits a tale originating from India. Paris regarded the Buddhist character of this "excellent parable" as "striking,"[16] because father and son are a pair that stereotypically appears in Buddhist tales, in the form of the Buddhist ascetic and his disciple. Since Paris does not supply any hard evidence, his hypothesis is purely speculative.[17]

Notes

1. http://www.verhalenbank.nl/solr-search?facet=49_s%3A%22ATU+1215%22 (accessed November 4, 2016).

2. http://www.verhalenbank.nl/files/show/3831 (accessed November 4, 2016). For the tale's versions in the modern media, see Gonzalo Tobajas, Ángel J., "*El padre, su hijo y el asno* (ATU 1215): la pervivencia de un cuento de raíz medieval en los balbuceos de la era digital (Facebook, Youtube y Whatsapp)," *eHumanística* 31 (2015), pp. 524–538; see http://www.ehumanista.ucsb.edu/sites/secure.lsit.ucsb.edu.span.d7_eh/files/sitefiles / ehumanista/volume31/ehum31.tobajas.pdf (accessed December 8, 2016).

3. https://nl.wikipedia.org/wiki/Dam_Jaarsma (accessed November 4, 2016).

4. http://www.verhalenbank.nl/items/show/33875 (accessed November 4, 2016).

5. Brednich, Rolf Wilhelm, "Asinus vulgi," in *Enzyklopädie des Märchens*, vol. 1 (1977), cols. 867–873, at col. 869.

6. Rey-Henningsen, Marisa, *The Tales of the Ploughwoman*, Helsinki: Suomalainen Tiedeacatemia, 1996, pp. 116–117, no. 59.

7. Holbek, Bengt, "Asinus Vulgi: Om Niels Heldvads oversættelse og dens aner," *Danske Studier* 59 (1964), pp. 32–53.

8. A comprehensive list of versions is given in the annotation to Pauli, Johannes, *Schimpf und Ernst*, ed. Johannes Bolte, Berlin: Herbert Stubenrauch, 1924 (reprint Hildesheim: Olms, 1972), vol. 1, p. 329; vol. 2, pp. 384–385, no. 577.

9. Marzolph, Ulrich, "Poggio Bracciolini, Giovanni Francesco," in *Enzyklopädie des Märchens*, vol. 10 (2002), col. 1101–1106, at col. 1103, no. 100.

10. Rehermann, Ernst Heinrich, and Fritz Wagner, "Bromyard, John," ibid., vol. 2 (1979), cols. 797–802, at col. 800–801.

11. For a comparison of Don Juan Manuel's text with two versions collected from oral tradition in Asturias, see Suárez López, Jesús, *Cuentos medievales en la tradición oral de Asturias*, electronic edition Red de Museos Etnográficos de Asturias, 2009, pp. 161–166.

12. Don Juan Manuel, *Libro del Conde Lucanor*, ed. Reinaldo Ayerbe-Chaux, Madrid: Alhambra, 1983, pp. 80–92, no. 2.

13. Gildemeister, Johann, "Zum Asinus vulgi," *Orient und Occident* 1 (1862), pp. 733–734.

14. Maqarrī, Aḥmad ibn Muḥammad al-, *Nafḥ al-ṭīb min ghuṣn al-Andalus al-raṭīb*, ed. Iḥsān ʿAbbās, vol. 2, Beirut: Dār Ṣādir, 1388/1968, pp. 327–328.

15. Hansen, William, *Ariadne's Thread: A Guide to International Tales Found in Classical Literature*, Ithaca and London: Cornell University Press, 2002, pp. 66–69, quotations at p. 68.

16. Paris, Gaston, *La poésie du moyen age: leçons et lectures*, deuxième série, Paris: Hachette et Cie, 1895, pp. 92–112, at p. 97.

17. Brednich, "Asinus vulgi," col. 871.

CHAPTER 37

The Fool Doubles the Load by Counterbalancing the Wheat with Stones (AT 1242B)

Vance Randolph (1892–1980)[1] was the pioneering folklorist of the Ozarks, a hilly region covering a significant portion of Northern Arkansas and Southern Missouri in the United States of America whose inhabitants are targeted as the stereotypical hillbillies of jocular prose. Randolph published several versions of a popular tale whose most elaborate one he titled "Corn for the Miller."[2] The tale was told by William Hatton, in Columbia, Missouri, in July 1929. The narrator believed that the story originated in Lawrence, Missouri, about 1905.

> A farm boy is riding to the mill "with a grinding of corn in a big old tow-sack." In order to balance the corn contained in one end of the sack, he has put a rock into the other. Meeting a "smart aleck from town," he is advised that "it ain't sensible to put rocks" on the pony's back. The boy justifies his action by saying, "My pappy always done it this way, and so did grandpappy before him. What's good enough for them is good enough for me." Advised by another "smart aleck" that the animal's load is too heavy, he gets down and walks, leading the pony. And when a third person critiques him again, he even takes the animal's load and puts it on his back. When he gets tired of walking, he gets into the saddle again, "still carrying the corn and the rock on his shoulders."
>
> As the miller laughs at him, the boy figures out that "them three smart alecks has made a fool out of me." The next time he goes to the mill, he does as before. This time, he is advised by someone that "carrying extra weight is wasteful; it would be more economical to take the rock out and put half the corn in each end of the sack." "Yes, I reckon it would be a saving," says he, "But when this rock wears out all I got to do is pick up another one. There's plenty of 'em in our pasture, and we don't give a damn for expenses."

In terms of folklorists' analysis, the tale is a combination of three tale types that are also attested independently. The motif of balancing the corn on one side with a rock on the other corresponds to tale type AT 1242B: *Balancing the Meal-sack*;[3] the motif of following everyone's advice relates to tale type ATU 1215: *The Miller, His Son, and the Donkey* (see essay **36, *Trying to Please Everyone***); and the motif of carrying the donkey's load on one's own shoulders while riding the animal corresponds to tale type ATU 1242A: *Carrying Part of the Load.* Only the initial motif is of interest here. A shorter version of the tale published by Randolph focuses only on the initial motif.[4] It is "about an old hillman who was delighted when somebody gave him a watermelon." He put the melon in one end of a gunnysack and a rock in the other end, and threw the sack across the saddle in front of him. A tourist noticed the melon hanging on one side and the rock on the other. "Wouldn't it be more economical," the tourist asked, "to carry another melon instead of that stone?" The mountaineer eyed him coldly. "Yes, I reckon it would be a savin'," he answered. "But I'm eighty year old now, an' I don't figger on livin' till the rocks give out."

Eli J. Hoenshel recorded yet another version as told by "Dr. Compton, an old time physician of Taney County," who presented the event as a personal recollection.[5] "Many times," Dr. Compton is reported to have said, "when visiting [the old settler] have I thought of the boy going to mill horseback, with corn in one end of the sack and a rock in the other end." When advised by a friend to take the rock out and divide the corn equally on both sides, the boy argues, "No, my father and my grandfather have always followed this plan, and they made a good living." Probably the tale's oldest published Ozark version, combining the tale just quoted with tale type AT 1242A, is mentioned by Charles H. Hibler in 1902.[6] Referring to popular tradition of "a few years ago," Hibler says that the "stalwart youth of this wild region rode long distances to mill on horseback," placing their grain in one end of a sack and balancing it behind their saddles with a rock of equal weight in the other. "To relieve their jaded horses while on these tiresome journeys, they humanely shifted the load to their own broad shoulders, while yet astride the animal." In order to prove that the "Hill Billy," "notwithstanding his opposition to innovations," is making undeniable progress, Hibler goes on to say that "latterly," "these hardy sons go forth on a frosty morning," balancing the corn with a jug of local corn whisky instead of the stone. Hilbert thinks the tale to be "hoary with age." As a matter of fact, the tale is not only much older but also known from a wide geographical area.

In a Pennsylvanian German text from Lehigh County, a Swabian goes down a hill to fetch water.[7] "To balance the full pail of water, he took up a heavy object in the other hand. When he came to the top of the hill he wanted to carry the object back, so he carried the pail of water along as balance." A Flemish version published at the end of the nineteenth century is not exactly from popular tradition, instead presented as a rhymed tale authored by Edouard Remouchamps.[8] Yehudah Hermann, born in Warsaw in 1913, told a Jewish version of the tale from Poland, as recorded in 1981 in the Israeli Kibbuz Bet Keshet by Yifreḥ Ḥaviv.[9] The protagonist of the lenghty Jewish tale is the medieval poet Abraham ibn Ezra (d. 1165 or 1176). Ibn Ezra meets a rich man who balances the gems he carries in a purse on his back with another purse full of stones on his chest, tied together with the first one. Ibn Ezra advises the man to divide the gems into two equal parts, so that his burden would be lighter. At first, the rich man appreciates the advice. But when he learns that Ibn Ezra is poor, he scorns the advice, as he himself learned from his ancestors never to heed the advice of a poor man. Later, when their ship encounters a heavy storm, the captain asks each of the passengers to throw half of their belongings overboard. The rich man offers the purse full of rocks, happy not to have followed Ibn Ezra's advice, as he would now have lost half of his wealth.

The tale's oldest documented version is contained in Arabic author Ibn Qutayba's (d. 889) *ʿUyūn al-akhbār* (Quintessential Reports).[10] Here, the foolish man accepts the advice he is given without further ado.

> Once, a hermit came by, carrying a stick on his neck on whose ends there were two baskets that almost crushed him (because of their weight). In one of them was wheat, in the other one soil. They said to him, "What is that?" He responded, "I balanced the wheat with this soil, because it pulled me to one side." So a man took the basket with the soil, emptied it, and divided the wheat in two (equal) halves in the two baskets, saying, "Now carry it!" Thereupon the hermit carried it, and when he found it to be lighter, he exclaimed, "What a clever old man you are!"

In almost identical wording, but attributing the event to an unspecified simpleton, the tale is repeated in al-Ḥuṣrī's (d. 1015) *Jamʿ al-jawāhir* (The Collection of Jewels).[11] In his mystical *summa*, the *Masnavi-ye maʿnavi*, the Persian poet Jalāl al-Din Rumi (d. 1273) supplied the tale with a different twist.[12] Here, a philosopher rebukes an "Arab of the desert" who loaded his camel with two big bags, one of them full of grain, the other one full of sand. At first, the Bedouin praises the philosopher for his "subtle thought and excellent judgment." But when he learns that the philosopher is poor, having got "nothing but phantasy and headache" from all his wisdom and learning, he asks the philosopher to stay away from him, so that he may not be affected by the philosopher's ill-luck. The Bedouin finishes by saying, "My foolishness is a very blessed foolishness, for my heart is well-furnished (with spiritual graces) and my soul is devout." Rumi further elaborates this statement into a praise of spiritual over scholarly learning, and of mystical understanding over mundane power.

Two twentieth-century versions from Jewish-Iranian tradition in Iran and Afghanistan treat the motif in a manner similar to Rumi and the Polish Jewish text.[13] The (apparent) simpleton does not follow the scholar's advice to throw away the stones and divide the flour he is carrying between his two sacks because the scholar is so poor. But here, the tale ends in a surprising lucky twist, since "on arrival to the market it turns out that the people need exactly such a kind of stones as the man carries and he sells them for a good price."

Notes

1. Lindahl, Carl, "Randolph, Vance," in *Enzyklopädie des Märchens*, vol. 11 (2004), cols. 192–194.

2. Randolph, Vance, "Ozark Mountain Tales," *Southern Folklore Quarterly* 16 (1952), pp. 165–176, at pp. 173–174; Randolph, *The Devil's Pretty Daughter and Other Ozark Folk Tales*, New York: Columbia University Press, 1955, pp. 146–148, 221–222; reprinted in McCarthy, William Bernard, *Cinderella in America: A Book of Folk and Fairy Tales*, Jackson: University Press of Mississippi, 2007, pp. 236–237, no. 55.

3. In the most recent revision of the international tale-type index, tale type AT 1242A is incorporated into tale type ATU 1242B, making a clear identification of the contents of the various references impossible; see Uther, *The Types*, vol. 2, p. 85, no. 1242A ("Widespread anecdote with various versions").

4. Randolph, Vance, *We Always Lie to Strangers: Tall Tales from the Ozarks*, New York: Columbia University Press, 1951, p. 27.

5. Hoenshel, Eli J., *Stories of the Pioneers: Incidents, Adventures and Reminiscences as Told by Some of the Old Settlers of Taney County, Missouri*, Point Lookout: School of the Ozarks Press, 1915, p. 36.

6. Hibler, Charles H., *Down in Arkansas*, Kansas City: J.W. Smith, 1902, pp. 32–32.

7. Brendle, Thomas Royce, and William S. Troxell, *Pennsylvania German Folk Tales, Legends, Once-upon-a-time Stories, Maxims, and Sayings, Spoken in the Dialect Popularly Known as Pennsylvania Dutch*, Norristown, Pa.: Pennsylvania German Society, 1944, p. 116.

8. Laport, George, *Les contes populaires wallons*, Helsinki: Suomalainen Tiedeakatemia, 1932, p. 88, no. *1205; the poem was originally published in *Bulletin de la Société liégoise de littérature wallon* 2.8 (1885), p. 271.

9. Ben-Amos, Dan, *Folktales of the Jews*, vol. 2: *Tales from Eastern Europe*, Philadelphia: Jewish Publications Society, 2007, pp. 269–272, no. 36.

10. Ibn Qutayba al-Dīnawarī, Abū Muḥammad ʿAbdallāh ibn Muslim, *ʿUyūn al-akhbār*, 2nd ed., vol. 2, Cairo: al-Mu'assasa al-miṣriyya al-ʿāmma lil-ta'lif wa-'l-tarjama wa-'l-ṭibāʿa, 1963, p. 38; Marzolph, *Arabia ridens*, vol. 1, p. 247–248, no. 3; vol. 2, p. 44, no. 163.

11. Ḥuṣrī al-Qayrawānī, Abū Isḥāq Ibrāhīm ibn ʿAlī al-, *Jamʿ al-jawāhir fī 'l-mulaḥ wa-'l-nawādir*, ed. ʿAlī Muḥamad al-Bijāwī, Cairo: Dār Iḥyā' al-kutub al-ʿarabiyya, 1372/1952, p. 308.

12. Rumi, Jalāl al-Din, *The Mathnawí of Jalálu'ddín Rúmí*, transl. Reynold A. Nicholson, vol. 2, London: Luzac & Co., 1934, pp. 386–388 (bk. 2, verses 3176–3200); Foruzānfar, Badiʿ al-Zamān, *Ma'ākhez-e qeṣaṣ va tamsilāt-e Masnavi*, Tehran: Amir Kabir, 3rd printing. 1362/1983, p. 79, no. 75; Marzolph, Ulrich, "Rumi, Ǧalāloddin," in *Enzyklopädie des Märchens*, vol. 11 (2004), cols. 897–904. A modern prose rendering of Rumi's verse is given by Arberry, Arthur John, *Tales from the Masnavi*, London: Allen & Unwin, 1961, pp. 172–173, no. 58.

13. Soroudi, Sarah Sorour, *The Folktales of Jews from Iran, Central Asia and Afghanistan: Tale-Types and Genres*, ed. Heda Jason, Dortmund: Verlag für Orientkunde, 2008, p. 171, no. 1242B.

CHAPTER 38

Making a Hole in the Ground to Deposit the Soil from the Previous Digging (ATU 1255)

Often attributed to the people of a certain location renowned for their naivete and thorough disregard of logic, the present jocular tale offers a simple solution to the dilemma of what to do with the excavated material of a large hole in the ground, as it suggests to dig another hole and deposit the soil in it. Should the new hole not be large enough to hold both the old and the new material, it would simply have to be made larger.[1] Classified as tale type ATU 1255: *A Hole to Throw the Earth In*, the tale is widely documented in written and oral tradition all over Europe and regions influenced by European tradition.

The above solution is advised by the mayor of Beckum in Germany when the people build a new town hall[2] or by a clever councilman in Zanow in Pomerania or Rátót in Hungary when the people have dug a new well.[3] The people of Fälingen dig a hole to deposit the sand excavated when digging a new well, only to be left with an even larger heap of soil, so their mayor scolds them for not having dug the new hole large enough.[4] Similarly, the people of the Danish town of Molbo, the French town of Villedieu in Normandy, and the Frisian town of Dokkum are advised to dig the new hole large enough to hold both the old and the new material.[5] In a text from Austria, the people of the neighboring towns of Fehring and Feldbach each assert that the event happened not to them, but to those of the other town.[6] As digging a new hole does not solve their problem, they finally accept a stranger's suggestion to make a hill and install a monument on it celebrating the people's wisdom. And in the version told by Virginia Gutiérrez de Casillas in the Mexican town of Valle de Guadalupe on May 9, 1954, the people keep digging new holes one after the other until finally "the original hole reaches the edge of the town where it no longer causes trouble."[7]

From the beginning of the seventeenth century, the tale was popularized in numerous chapbooks such as the German *Grillenvertreiber* (1603)[8] or the English *Wit and Mirth* (1629).[9] In European tradition, the tale's earliest version is attested in Italian author Baldesar Castiglione's manual for courtiers *Il Cortegiano*, written in the first decades of the sixteenth century and first published in 1528.[10]

When Count Federico wonders what to do with the large amount of material excavated for the foundations of the new palace, the abbot present suggests they dig a hole in which to deposit the soil. However much the count argues that this will not work, the abbot insists that one will simply have to make the hole large enough.

The tale's earliest documented version is contained in Ibn al-Jawzī's (d. 1201) *Akhbār al-Ḥamqā* (Tales of Stupid People).[11] Here, the father of the popular prankster Juḥā wonders what to do with the soil that has accumulated next to his house, as his neighbors start complaining and the soil is not good for making bricks. Obviously expecting a reward for his advice, young Juḥā proudly suggest to dig a hole to deposit the soil. A version closely corresponding to Ibn al-Jawzī's is cited in Yūsuf ibn al-Wakīl al-Maylāwī's extensive seventeenth-century compilation of tales attributed to Juḥā,[12] and has been part and parcel of this tradition ever since.[13] A short version attributed to an anonymous protagonist is given in the late nineteenth-century Persian chapbook *Reyāż al-ḥekāyāt* (Gardens of Tales) compiled by Ḥabiballāh Kāshāni.[14]

Notes

1. Huse, Ulrich, "Erdloch für Aushub graben," in *Enzyklopädie des Märchens*, vol. 4 (1994), cols. 164–166.

2. Merkens, Heinrich, *Was sich das Volk erzählt: Deutscher Volkshumor*, 2nd ed., vol. 2, Jena: Costenoble, 1895, p. 18, no. 23.

3. Rosenow, Karl, *Zanower Schwänke: Ein fröhliches Buch*, Rügenwalde: Mewse, 1924, pp. 39–40; Kovács, Ágnes, *König Mátyás und die Rátóter: Ungarische Schildbürgerschwänke und Anekdoten*, Leipzig: Kiepenheuer, 1988, p. 8–9.

4. Kooi, Jurjen van der, and Theo Schuster, *Märchen und Schwänke aus Ostfriesland*, Leer: Schuster, 1993, p. 144, no. 87 (a).

5. Christensen, Arthur, *Molboernes vise gerninger*, Copenhagen: Schønberg, 1939, p. 134, no. 37; Brunet, Victor, "Facéties normandes (1)," in *Revue des traditions populaires* 2 (1887), pp. 183–184; Poortinga, Ype, *De ring fan it ljocht: Fryske folksverhalen*, Baarn: Bosch en Keuning, 1976, pp. 261–262.

6. Lang-Reitstätter, Maria, *Lachendes Österreich: Österreichscher Volkshumor*, 2nd ed. Salzburg: Österreichischer Kulturverlag, 1948, p. 62.

7. Robe, Stanley L., *Mexican Tales and Legends from Los Altos*, Berkeley: University of California Press, 1970, no. 187.

8. Huse, "Erdloch für Aushub graben," col. 164; Uther, *Deutscher Märchenkatalog*, pp. 311–312, no. 1255.

9. Zall, Paul M., *A Nest of Ninnies and Other English Jestbooks of the Seventeenth Century*, Lincoln: University of Nebraska Press, 1970, p. 125, no. 12.

10. Castiglione, Baldesar, *Der Hofmann*, transl. Albert Wesselski, Munich: Georg Müller, 1907, vol. 1, pp. 184, 302.

11. Ibn al-Jawzī, Abū 'l-Faraj ʿAbd al-Raḥmān ibn ʿAlī, *Akhbār al-Ḥamqā wa-'l-mughaffalīn*, ed. Kāẓim al-Muẓaffar, al-Najaf: al-Maktaba al-ḥaydariyya, 1386/1966, p. 32; Marzolph, *Arabia ridens*, vol. 1, p. 248, no. 4; vol. 2, p. 259, no. 1206; Marzolph, *Nasreddin Hodscha*, pp. 38–39, no. 58.

12. ʿAnābsa, Ghālib, "Min adab al-nawādir: naẓra fī makhṭūṭāt [Irshād] man naḥā ilā nawādir Juḥā, jamʿ al-faqīr ilā Allāh taʿālā Yūsuf ibn al-Wakīl al-Maylāwī," in ʿAnābsa, *Dirāsāt muḍīʾa fī ṣafaḥāt al-turāth*, Zaḥāliqa: Dār al-Hudā, and Jordan: Dār al-Jarīr, 2013, pp. 174–196, at p. 191.

13. Farrāj, ʿAbd al-Sattār Aḥmad, *Akhbār Juḥā*, Cairo: Maktabat Miṣr, 1954, p. 72; Wesselski, *Der Hodscha Nasreddin*, vol. 2, pp. 153, 227, no. 480.

14. Christensen, Arthur, "Les sots dans la tradition populaire des Persans," *Acta Orientalia* 1 (1922), pp. 43–75, at p. 64, no. 27.

CHAPTER 39

Warming Oneself on a Distant Fire (ATU 1262)

In the third and most recent revision of the international tale-type index, tale type ATU 1262: *The Effectiveness of Fire* is designed as a cumulative item lumping together two distinct tale types that only overlap in a single constitutive motif.[1] In the elaborate "regular" form, a trickster is refused the reward promised for spending a night out in the cold, as he is reproached with having warmed himself on a distant fire. The trickster later demonstrates the absurdity of this allegation with the similarly absurd attempt to cook food over a distant fire.[2] In the shorter form, the simpleton takes the fishmonger's appraisal literally that the fish he bought is so tender that it only needs to see a fire from the distance to be well-done for consumption. In the end, the simpleton eats the fish raw.[3] The majority of the tale type's European texts document the latter form that corresponds to tale type ATU 65*: *The Fox Catches a Beetle,* albeit with human characters. It is not relevant here, since no Middle Eastern versions of this form are known. Although the general idea of allegedly sensing warmth or even heat over a great distance overlaps in both forms, the idea satirizes a fundamental human experience, so that speculations about a generic connection between the tale type's two forms appear futile. Rare Western versions of the tale type's elaborate form are exclusively attested in what may be called the fringes of Western tradition, as these versions either originate from areas that were strongly influenced by Middle Eastern tradition or were narrated by storytellers originating from a Middle Eastern region.[4]

In his volume of German folktales from Russia and Romania, folklorist Alfred Cammann (1909–2008),[5] whose particular interest was the collection of the folklore of Germans from the Eastern regions they settled in before World War II, published the following tale communicated to him in writing by Traugott Joachim as recorded in an unnamed *kolkhoz* in Tajikistan.[6]

> A rich man constructs a walled area and promises half of his riches to anyone who will spend the night inside the walls completely naked. The two men who initially try this freeze to death. Facing the challenge, another man requests a boulder, allegedly so as to rest on it from time to time.

Actually, he spends the night rolling the boulder around the walled area and thus manages to stay alive. When the rich man finds him alive in the morning, he accuses the man of having warmed himself at a fire burning on a nearby mountain and refuses to give him the reward.

One day the rich man goes hunting with his comrades, and the duped man invites him to his house for tea. When the party arrives, the host hangs the tea pot high up in a tree and lights a fire on the ground below. As the guest wonders how the water could possibly start boiling with the fire so far down below, the duped man shames the rich man by responding that it would start boiling in the same way that he had allegedly warmed himself at a fire burning on a mountain nearby.

Presented as an item relating to "German" tradition, the note to the tale reveals it as having been narrated "after the evening meal by an Uzbek from a Muslim tribe in Asia," thus at best being the German translation of a Middle Eastern tale. A similar caveat applies for a Creole version from the Caribbean island of Guadaloupe published by Elsie Clews Parsons.[7]

A king promises fifty thousand francs to his servant if he manages to spend a night out in the cold completely naked. Although the servant is heavily affected by the cold, he manages to survive. As he later admits to having seen a light at a distance of five kilometers, the king refuses to pay him, claiming that the servant warmed himself by seeing the light.

Some weeks later, the servant invites the king for lunch. As it takes a very long time for the lunch to be ready, the king finally asks the servant to take him to the kitchen. There he sees the fire on the ground while the pot is high up (literally: two kilometers) in the air, and so he reproaches the servant that the food will never get done this way. The servant agrees, pointing out that his way of cooking is as absurd as the king's allegation that he warmed himself at a distant light. The king laughs and awards the servant a thousand francs.

Here, the narrator is identified as a "Syrian merchant in Port au Prince and hotelkeeper at Dolé." So, once more, the tale does not relate to local or regional tradition, as it was told by a Middle Eastern narrator who recently migrated to the region. The Spanish version collected by Juan B. Rael from the performance of Félix Herrera, aged 29, in Española, New Mexico, introduces a rich man who promises to give his daughter in marriage "to any man who can endure being outdoors naked all through a winter night."[8] A shepherd succeeds in doing so, imagining himself to keep warm through the heat of a fire on a distant mountain. When the girl's father refuses to fulfill his promise, arguing that the suitor cheated on the conditions, the young woman demonstrates the absurdity of her father's claim by pretending to prepare meat several feet away from the stove. Although in this case the direct relation to Middle Eastern tradition is not as obvious as in the previously quoted instances, Spanish tradition, here Spanish tradition in the Americas, arguably originates from an area whose narrative culture was historically influenced to a considerable extent by Middle Eastern, specifically Arabic, tradition. Virtually all other known European versions of the tale are similarly documented from regions on the fringes of Western tradition.

An early twentieth-century folktale from Malta introduces a king who promises his daughter to anyone who can spend a full night naked on the palace's roof terrace.[9] Many men die trying to fulfill the condition, including two of three brothers. Only the youngest brother manages to stay alive by watching a small red lantern in the distance. Later, the young man proves the absurdity of the king's claim that he warmed himself at the light of the lantern by preparing food in the kitchen with only a small fire in the middle of the room. In the end, the king gives in and weds the young couple. In the Sicilian version narrated by the porter Gaspare Stinco from Trapani, it is Giucà, the local version of the Arabic jester Juḥā, who demonstrates the absurdity of the rich man's allegation.[10] Here, a man in Trapani is promised a hundred ounces (of gold) if he manages to survive a cold night at the seashore completely naked. The guards in his company notice that he stretches out his hands as if to warm himself when a ship passes in the distance. Giucà helps the duped man gain the promised reward by lighting a fire at the Capuchin monastery (today in ruins) and putting the mutton on the grill at the city's other end. Likewise, in the tale's Bulgarian versions, the protagonist is often a popular trickster character of local tradition, such as Nastradin Hodža, Hităr Petăr (Clever Peter), or a gypsy.[11] In a folktale from Kámpos on the Greek island of Chios, a Christian makes a bet with a Turk and remains naked for a whole night on a hill in January.[12] The Turk watches him from a distance, holding a lantern. Since the local judge at first supports the Turk's allegation that the lantern warmed the Christian, the duped Christian consults Nastradhìn-Chótzas who pretends to prepare food with the kettle hanging from the ceiling and a lit candle on the floor. Only a Romanian text published in 1913 ends tragically.[13] Here, a boyar (a member of the old aristocracy) promises to give all his mills to a gypsy if the latter manages to spend a winter night in the cold water while the boyar watches him from a distance, comfortably seated next to a fire. When at dawn the gypsy appears to win the bet, a passing Turk advises the boyar to extinguish the fire. Having lost his hope to warm up at the fire once the night is over, the gypsy dies from the cold. It is interesting to note how this text develops the psychological effectiveness of seeing the fire.

The tale's tragic version has an early precursor in a narrative introduced as a "widespread tale mentioned in books" in polymath al-Jāḥiẓ's (d. 868) *Kitāb al-Ḥayawān* (Book of Animals).[14] In this tale, a man is thrown into a pool on a cold winter night. The extreme cold is emphasized, mentioning that there was not even any moonlight. With a somewhat critical distance al-Jāḥiẓ quotes ("they say") that the man stayed alive remaining stiff and motionless as long as he was able to look at a fire or a lamp in the distant village. When the light went out, the man passed away.[15] Essentially the same text, albeit introduced by a simple "they said," is cited more than two centuries later in al-Zamakhsharī's (d. 1144) *Rabīʿ al-abrār* (Spring of the Pious).[16] In the light of these early Arabic texts, the tale's bipartite form as documented in nineteenth- and twentieth-century folktales reads like a narrative elaboration of a rather short scientific experiment that counters an absurd allegation with an equally absurd demonstration.

The earliest-known evidence for the bipartite version was recorded early in the second half of the eighteenth century by the German traveler Carsten Niebuhr (1733–1815), the only survivor of the Royal Danish Arabian expedition (1761–1767).[17] In his published travelogue, Niebuhr describes his visit to the grave of Buhlūl, a largely fictional character he introduces as relative and court fool of Caliph Hārūn al-Rashīd.[18] Although Niebuhr quotes the historical assessment of Buhlūl as "Sultan of the Imbeciles," he concedes some bright moments to him. In order to demonstrate this, Niebuhr cites the tale in which a person wagers with another one to pay a certain amount of money if the latter succeeds in swimming across the river Tigris. The second person does so, but since his mother waits for him on the other side with a bright fire, his partner refuses to pay him, arguing that the warming fire contradicts the stipulated condition. As the local judge agrees with the allegation, Buhlūl demonstrates the argument's absurdity by suggesting they boil a stew in a pot hanging high up in a date palm. In the end, the caliph forces the culprit to pay his dues. Although Buhlūl is still mentioned in the late nineteenth-century version recorded by Bruno Meissner,[19] in modern Middle Eastern tradition the tale's trickster role is stereotypically attributed to Nasreddin Hodja or his regional equivalents.[20]

Notes

1. Uther, *The Types*, vol. 2, pp. 92–93, no. 1262.

2. Huse, Ulrich, "Feuer: Fernwirkung des F.s," in *Enzyklopädie des Märchens*, vol. 4 (1984), cols. 1083–1087.

3. Ibid., col. 1085, note 10.

4. The present essay owes some inspiration to Fritz Harkort's two unpublished studies, *Die Schein- und Schattenbußen im Erzählgut*, unpublished Ph.D. dissertation, Kiel 1956, pp. 21–30d (copy in the library of the former Enzyklopädie des Märchens, Göttingen); and *Scheinbußengeschichten*, unpublished typoscript, Göttingen 1967.

5. Brednich, Rolf Wilhelm, "Cammann, Alfred," in *Enzyklopädie des Märchens*, vol. 2 (1979), cols. 1160–1162.

6. Cammann, Alfred, *Deutsche Volksmärchen aus Russland und Rumänien: Bessarabien, Dobrudscha, Siebenbürgen, Ukraine, Krim, Mittelasien*, Göttingen: Schwartz, 1967, pp. 402–403, 446, no. 157.

7. Parsons, Elsie Clews, *Folk-Lore of the Antilles, French and English*, vol. 2, New York: American Folk-Lore Society, 1936, pp. 175–176, no. 96.

8. Rael, Juan B., *Cuentos españoles de Colorado y de Nuevo Mejico*, vol. 2, Stanford: Stanford University Press, ca. 1940, pp. 540–541, 797, no. 438.

9. Ilg, Berta, *Maltesische Märchen und Schwänke: aus dem Volksmunde gesammelt*, vol. 1, Leipzig: G. Schönfeld, 1906, pp. 72–73, no. 20; see also Mifsud-Chircop, Ġorġ, *Type-Index of the Maltese Folktale within the Mediterranean Tradition Area*, unpublished typescript

Malta 1978, vol. 1, pp. 430–431 (copy in the library of the former Enzyklopädie des Märchens, Göttingen).

10. Pitrè, Giuseppe, *Fiabe, novelle e racconti popolari siciliani*, vol. 3, Palermo: Lauriel, 1875, pp. 369–370, no. 13; Wesselski, *Der Hodscha Nasreddin*, vol. 2, pp. 112–114, 212, no. 434.

11. Daskalova Perkowski, Liliana, et al., *Typenverzeichnis der bulgarischen Volksmärchen*, ed. Klaus Roth, Helsinki: Suomalainen Tiedeakatemia, 1995, p. 332, no. *1592C.

12. Argenti, Philip P., and Herbert J. Rose, *The Folk-lore of Chios*, vol. 1, Cambridge: Cambridge University Press, 1949, pp. 570–571, no. 48.

13. Stroescu, *La typologie*, vol. 1, p. 164, no. 3305.

14. Jāḥiẓ, ʿAmr ibn Baḥr al-, *Kitāb al-Ḥayawān*, ed. ʿAbd al-Salām Muḥammad Hārūn, 3rd ed., vol. 4, Beirut: al-Majmaʿ al-ʿilmī al-ʿarabī al-islāmī, 1388/1969, pp. 488–489; see Marzolph, *Arabia ridens*, vol. 1, p. 248, no. 5; vol. 2, pp. 26–27, no. 97.

15. Although the editor amended the tale's last word to "he shivered," both the Bulgarian version and the second version in classical Arabic literature suggest the reading given here.

16. Zamakhsharī, Abū 'l-Qāsim Maḥmūd ibn ʿUmar al-, *Rabīʿ al-abrār wa-nuṣūṣ al-akhbār*, ed. Salīm al-Nuʿaymī, vol. 1, Baghdad: al-ʿĀnī, 1976, pp. 188–189.

17. Niebuhr, Carsten, *C. Niebuhrs Reisebeschreibung nach Arabien und anderen umliegenden Ländern*, vol. 2, Copenhagen: Nicolaus Möller, 1778, pp. 300–302.

18. Marzolph, Ulrich, *Der Weise Narr Buhlūl*, Wiesbaden: Franz Steiner, 1983, p. 60, no. 104.

19. Meissner, Bruno, *Neuarabische Geschichten aus dem Iraq*, Leipzig: J.C. Hinrich, 1903, pp. 77–78, no. 44.

20. Marzolph, *Nasreddin Hodscha*, pp. 192–193, 311, no. 461; Ramażāni, Moḥammad, ed., *Mollā Naṣreddin*, 5th ed., Teheran: Khāvar, 1339/1960, pp. 100–102; Constantin, Gh. I., "18 kirgisische Anekdoten über Nasr Ed-Din Khodja," *Fabula* 14 (1973), pp. 44–70, at pp. 56–57, no. 5.

CHAPTER 40

The Fool Forgets to Count the Donkey He Is Sitting On (ATU 1288A)

American anthropologist Ethelyn G. Orso (1941–1999) conducted her fieldwork in Greece between June 1976 and late May 1977. Having abandoned her original intention to produce a "monograph on some aspect of village life such as folk medicine or women's folklore,"[1] she eventually opted for the more promising venture to collect jokes. Although the material presented in Orso's publication admittedly lacks an adequate discussion of "the surrounding social and political context,"[2] it is of great interest, both for its face value as a collection of humorous texts collected from living oral tradition and for its implications in relation to a young female anthropologist's fieldwork. Although Orso refrains from specifying the names of her informants,[3] she would at times characterize them in a general manner, such as stating that "many of the jokes about dumb villagers were told to me by villagers or peasants."[4] One of the jokes about a dumb villager goes as follows.[5]

> A villager had some work to do, so he borrowed some donkeys from his neighbors. As he was getting ready to leave, he asked his son to count the donkeys.
>
> "One, two, three . . . ten," said the boy.
>
> So the man got his donkey saddled, climbed on top, and decided to check his son's arithmetic. So he counted the donkeys, but there were only nine!
>
> "Son!" he screamed. "You can't count! You told me there were ten donkeys, but there are only nine!"
>
> "But you're sitting on top of the tenth donkey," said the boy.

Corresponding to the international tale type ATU 1288A: *Numskull Cannot Find the Donkey He Is Sitting On*,[6] the short jocular tale about the fool who forgets to count the donkey he is sitting on is documented frequently from oral tradition all over Europe. Around 1980, Marcel Volpilière from the mountainous region north of Montpellier in France told the collectors Nicole Coulomb and Claudette Castell a slightly different version in which the numskull counts eleven donkeys instead of twelve when he is riding one of them. His wife responds that she counts thirteen—including her husband![7] This punch line is also given in a number of other texts, such as those collected from Serbia,[8] from Berber tradition,[9] or from Spanish tradition in Puerto Rico.[10] With little variation, numerous other versions were collected from locations as wide apart as Macedonia,[11] Sicily,[12] or South Africa.[13]

The tale's wide dissemination and continuous popularity is to a considerable extent due to its inclusion in a fair number of European chapbooks published since the sixteenth century,[14] such as the German *Nachtbüchlein* (1559) by Valentin Schumann, the English *Mery Tales and Quicke Answers* (1567), the Latin *Sylva sermonum* (1568) by Johannes Hulsbusch, the French *Recueil des plaisantes nouvelles* (1578), or the Dutch *Groot Klugtboek* (1680).[15] The tale's earliest attestation in European written tradition is contained in the mid-fifteenth-century collection of facetious tales compiled by papal secretary Poggio Bracciolini.[16] In order to authenticate to the event, Poggio mentioned the protagonist by name as a certain Mancinus "from my region." In addition, he localized the event by specifying that the foolish peasant used to sell his wheat at the market in Figlini, today Figline Valdarno, in Tuscany. When the man counts his donkeys on the way back, he appears to notice that one of them is missing (since he is riding it). Delivering the donkeys to his wife, the man sets out again to search for the lost animal. Only when he returns home in great desolation, his wife tells him to dismount, as the donkey he was riding is the one he believed lost.

In Arabic literature, several slightly varying versions of the tale are documented since the beginning of the eleventh century.[17] The oldest of these versions is given in al-Ābī's (d. 1030) comprehensive encyclopedia of jokes and anecdotes, *Nathr al-durr* (Pearls of Prose).[18] It attributes the events to the ninth-century numskull Azhar who is known as "the donkey driver" (*al-ḥammār*), probably because of this very incident.

> This Azhar lived in Sijistān (today's Sistān, a region in South-Eastern Iran) before the (well-known) events happened to (the governor) ʿAmr ibn al-Layth and his brother (that is, before they were executed by order of Caliph al-Muʿtaḍid in 902).
>
> Once he rented ten donkeys to go to a certain place. When he returned, he rode on one of them. He counted the donkeys except for the one he was riding and found them to be nine. Worried, he wanted to reassure himself that he did have ten donkeys. So he dismounted and counted them and found them to be ten. He mounted again and found them to be nine. This he did for a while until he finally said, "I will walk on foot and gain a donkey." So he dismounted and went on foot. For this reason he is known as "The Donkey Driver" (*al-ḥammār*).

Al-Ābī's text was adapted in the selective Syriac translation of his facetious stories compiled by Bar Hebraeus (d. 1286)[19] and in the Persian *Laṭāʾef al-ṭavāʾef*

(Jocular Tales from the Various Strata of Society) compiled by Fakhr al-Din ʿAli Ṣafi (d. 1532).[20] A somewhat shorter Arabic version with the same verbal punch line is attributed to an anonymous inhabitant of Naṣībīn (in Mesopotamia) in al-Rāghib al-Iṣfahānī's (d. 1108) *Muḥāḍarāt al-udabā'* (Conversations of the Educated).[21] The version given in Ibn al-Jawzī's (d. 1201) *Akhbār al-Ḥamqā* (Tales of Stupid People) localizes the events in Dārā in the vicinity of Naṣībīn, explicitly mentioning that the man who left home with ten donkeys was "somewhat stupid" (*kāna fīhi ghafla*).[22] This version has the protagonist say, "I better walk on foot and gain a donkey than ride and lose one!" The narrator authenticates the narrated event by commenting that he himself saw the man walk until he was totally exhausted before finally reaching his village. A version closely related to the one given by Ibn al-Jawzī is included in Ibn Ḥijja al-Ḥamawī's (d. 1434) *Thamarāt al-awrāq* (The Fruits of the [Scattered] Leaves), a book that in the nineteenth century was often printed together with al-Ibshīhī's popular encyclopedia of everything an educated person should know.[23]

In Middle Eastern and general Muslim tradition, the tale enjoyed great popularity at least until the twentieth century. Referring to an anonymous person intoxicated by the consumption of hashish, it is told in a number of early twentieth-century Egyptian chapbooks.[24] In the version given in Ḥabiballāh Kāshāni's *Reyāż al-ḥekāyāt* (Gardens of Tales), a late nineteenth-century Persian chapbook of jocular tales, the fool prefers to walk rather than lose one of his twenty donkeys.[25] In Turkish tradition, the tale is already attested in one of the oldest preserved collections of anecdotes attributed to Nasreddin Hodja, compiled in the sixteenth century.[26] Until the nineteenth and twentieth centuries, a fair number of versions from all over the Muslim world attribute the tale to Nasreddin[27] or his Arabic alter ego Juḥā.[28]

The simple jocular tale is the narrative realization of a basic human experience, the experience that only things one sees "count," and that it takes at least a minimal intellectual effort to take the existence of things into account that are not within a person's immediate visual reach. Even though this feature might serve as an argument for the independent genesis of the tale's numerous versions in regions wide apart, their historical dissemination bespeaks a more or less direct relationship of the numerous recorded versions. There is good reason to presume that, from its oldest documented versions in early eleventh-century Arabic literature, the tale spread both in the Muslim world and, via its adaptation in Poggio's collection, to European chapbook literature and oral tradition, while still considering the possibility of various stages of oral transmission at any time. As donkeys, both in a literal and in a figurative sense, abound both in the Middle East and Europe, the tale proved to be easily adaptable to a large variety of different regional and cultural contexts.

Notes

1. Orso, Ethelyn G., *Modern Greek Humor*, Bloomington: Indiana University Press, 1979, p. ix.
2. Review by Margaret E. Kenna, *Man* 15.4 (1980), pp. 747–748.
3. Orso, *Modern Greek Humor*, p. xii.
4. Ibid., p. 70.
5. Ibid., p. 71, no. 108.
6. Marzolph, Ulrich, "Zählen: Sich nicht z. können," *Enzyklopädie des Märchens*, vol. 14 (2014), cols. 1117–1122.
7. Coulomb, Nicole, and Claudette Castell, *La barque qui allait sur l'eau et sur la terre: Marcel Volpilière, conteur do Mont Lozère*, Carcassonne: Garae/Hesiod, 1986, pp. 145–146, no. 35.
8. Vrčević, Vuk, *Srpske narodne pripovijetke, ponajviše kratke i šaljive*, Belgrade: Srpska kraljevska državna štamparija, 1868, p. 76, no. 171.
9. Frobenius, Leo, *Volksmärchen der Kabylen*, vol. 1, Jena: Eugen Diederichs, 1921, p. 247, no. 46.
10. Mason, J. Alden, and Aurelio M. Espinosa, "Porto-Rican Folk-lore: Folk-Tales," *Journal of American Folklore* 42 (1929), pp. 85–156, at p. 114, no. 29.
11. Eschker, Wolfgang, *Mazedonische Volksmärchen*, Düsseldorf: Diederichs, 1972, p. 258, 276, no. 67.
12. Pitrè, Giuseppe, *Fiabe, novelle e racconti popolari siciliani*, Palermo: Lauriel, 1875, vol. 3, p. 398, no. 192 (narrated by Francesca Amato from Palermo).
13. Coetzee, Abel, Hattingh, S.C., Loots, W.J.G., and P.D. Swart, "Tiperegister van die Afrikaanse Volksverhaal," *Tydskrif vir Volkskunde en Volkstaal* 23 (1967), pp. 1–90, at p. 47, no. 1228A (collected by Abel Coetzee).
14. Bolte and Polívka, *Anmerkungen*, vol. 3, pp. 150–151, note 2.
15. For detailed references see Marzolph, "Zählen," col. 1120.
16. Poggio Bracciolini, Gian-Francesco, *Die Schwänke und Schnurren*, ed. Alfred Semerau, Leipzig: Deutsche Verlags-Actiengesellschaft, 1905, p. 63, 211, no. 55; Marzolph, Ulrich, "Poggio Bracciolini, Giovanni Francesco," in *Enzyklopädie des Märchens*, vol. 10 (2002), cols. 1101–1106.
17. Marzolph, *Arabia ridens*, vol. 1, pp. 221–223; vol. 2, p. 218, no. 977.
18. Ābī, Abū Sa'd Manṣūr ibn al-Ḥusayn al-, *Nathr al-durr*, ed. Muḥammad ʿAlī Qarna et al., vol. 7, Cairo: al-Hay'a al-miṣriyya al-ʿāmma lil-kitāb, 1991, p. 361.
19. Bar Hebraeus, Mâr Gregory John, *The Laughable* Stories, transl. E.A. Wallis Budge, London: Luzac and Co., 1897, pp. 145–146, no. 569.
20. ʿAli Ṣafi, Fakhr al-Din, *Laṭā'ef al-ṭavā'ef*, ed. Aḥmad Golchin-Maʿāni, Tehran: Moḥammad-Ḥoseyn Eqbāl & Co., 1336, p. 411.
21. Rāghib al-Iṣfahānī, al-Ḥusayn ibn Muḥammad, *Muḥāḍarāt al-udabā' wa-muḥāwarāt al-shuʿarā' wa-'l-bulaghā'*, Beirut 1961, vol. 4, p. 722.
22. Ibn al-Jawzī, Abū 'l-Faraj ʿAbd al-Raḥmān ibn ʿAlī, *Akhbār al-Ḥamqā wa-'l-mughaffalīn*, ed. Kāẓim al-Muẓaffar, al-Najaf: al-Maktaba al-ḥaydariyya, 1386/1966, p. 146.
23. Ibn Ḥijja al-Ḥamawī, ʿAlī ibn Muḥammad, *Thamarāt al-awrāq fī 'l-muḥāḍarāt*, ed. Mufīd Qumayḥa, Beirut: Dār al-Kutub al-ʿilmiyya, 1403/1983, p. 137; German translation in Weisweiler, Max, *Von Kalifen, Spaßmachern und klugen Haremsdamen: Arabischer Humor*, Düsseldorf: Eugen Diederichs, 1963, p. 165

24. For detailed references see Marzolph, *Arabia ridens*, vol. 2, p. 218, no. 977.

25. Christensen, Arthur, "Les sots dans la tradition populaire des Persans," *Acta Orientalia* 1 (1922), pp. 43–75, at p. 61, no. 22.

26. Burrill, Kathleen R.F., "The Nasreddin Hoca Stories, 1: An Early Ottoman Manuscript at the University of Groningen," *Archivum Ottomanicum* 2 (1970), pp. 7–114, at p. 47, no. 71; Marzolph, *Nasreddin Hodscha*, p. 89, no. 194.

27. Wesselski, *Der Hodscha Nasreddin*, vol. 1, pp. 152, 267–269, no. 261; Daskalova, Liana, et al., *Narodna proza ot Blagoevgradski okrăg*, Sofia: Bălgarska Akademiya na Naukite, 1985, p. 326, no. 254; Piličkova, Sevim, *Nasradin Oja i Itar Pejo: dukhovni bliznatsi*, Skopje: Posebni izdanija, 1996, p. 136, no. 26.

28. Hanauer, J.E., *Folk-lore of the Holy Land: Moslem, Christian and Jewish*, London: Duckwort & Co., 1907, pp. 84–85; Farrāj, ʿAbd al-Sattār Aḥmad, *Akhbār Juḥā*, Cairo: Maktabat Miṣr, 1954, pp. 109–110; Crews, Cynthia Mary, *Contes judéo-espagnols des Balkans*, ed. A. Angelopoulos, Paris: Corti, 2009, p. 21, 362 (told by Élie Alcheh, aged 23).

CHAPTER 41

The Scholar and the Ferryman (El-Shamy 1293C*)

The jocular tale "The Scholar and the Fisherman on the River Elbe" was originally published in 1943 in a book purporting to contain tales collected from the oral tradition of Germans then living in what is now the Czech Republic.[1] It goes as follows.

> Once, a learned man had a simple fisherman ferry him across the river Elbe. During the passage, the scholar asked various questions. First he asked, "Do you know philosophy?" The fisherman answered, "No. I never heard of that!"—Whereupon the scholar remarked, "Poor man, a quarter of your life has been wasted!" Next he asked, "Do you know geography?"—"No," replied the fisherman, "I don't know that either. People of my trade don't have the time to bother about scholarly issues." At this, the scholar showed great concern and compassionately remarked, "You poor man! Half of your life has been wasted!" After a while, the scholar resumed his questioning, "Do you know mathematics?"—"No," said the fisherman, "I do not even know what that is supposed to be!"—"You very poor man," remarked the scholar, "so three quarters of your life have been wasted!"
>
> He had not even finished talking when suddenly the boat turned over and both men fell into the water. The scholar shouted and screamed as if he were being burned alive. Meanwhile, the fisherman grabbed his jacket and yelled, "Do you know how to swim?"—"No," gasped the scholar, who was so exhausted that his face had already turned blue. "Well then," said the fisherman, "You had better hurry up and hold on to my back or else all four quarters of your life will have been wasted!"

Although the editor does not mention a verifiable source for his rendering, the event is presented as credibly localized and thus authenticated by taking place on the upper section of the river Elbe that rises in the Krkonoš Mountains of the Northern Czech Republic. Since the tale was published in the Nazi period, it might probably be read as implying a message conforming to the contemporary

Zeitgeist, such as a praise of practically oriented working-class people and a critique of fanciful and unworldly intellectuals. If the tale was indeed collected from oral tradition, it might be related to versions documented in contemporary chapbooks for various Romanian regions in the period 1913–1938.[2] Notably, the Romanian versions correspond with the German one in that the scholar asks the ferryman about his knowledge in three fields of science, in this case chemistry, astronomy, and mathematics. As the ferryman responds in the negative each time, the scholar reproaches him that a third of his life has been wasted. A Judaeo-Spanish (Ladino) version, classified as new tale type **1588A,[3] was recorded in 1979 from the collector's mother, Diana Sarano.[4] It differs from the previously mentioned ones insofar as the scholar only pities the ferryman for his lacking competence in the two fields of reading and writing before the storm threatens to turn over the boat.

The tale's oldest attested version is contained in Persian poet Jalāl al-Din Rumi's (d. 1273) mystical *summa*, the *Masnavi-ye ma'navi*,[5] where it is followed by an elaborate interpretation. In the *Masnavi*, the boatman's partner is a grammarian, and the only question he asks is about the boatman's knowledge in his own field of expertise.

> A certain grammarian embarked in a boat. That self-conceited person turned to the boatman and said, "Have you ever studied grammar?"— "No," he replied. The other said, "Half your life is gone to naught." The boatman became heartbroken with grief, but at the time he refrained from answering. The wind cast the boat into a whirlpool. The boatman shouted to the grammarian, "Tell me, do you know how to swim?"— "No," said he, "O fair-spoken good-looking man!" "O grammarian," said he, "Your whole life is naught, because the boat is sinking in these whirlpools."

About a century later, a shorter Persian version in prose appeared in 'Obeyd-e Zākāni's (d. ca. 1371) *Resāle-ye delgoshā* (The Heart-Refreshing Epistle).[6] As Zākāni renders the direct speech in Arabic, and as jokes about grammarians are legion in Arabic literature, the tale's Persian versions might likely derive from an as yet unidentified model in classical Arabic literature.[7]

The tale was also recorded from recent Indian[8] and Arabic[9] oral tradition. The latter was classified as new tale type 1293C*.

Notes

1. Jungbauer, Gustav, *Das Volk erzählt: Sudetendeutsche Sagen, Märchen und Schwänke*, Karlsbad and Leipzig: Adam Kraft, 1943, pp. 331–332. The present essay is an adapted version of the introductory passages of Marzolph, Ulrich, "Persian Humor in the International Context," in Brookshaw, Dominic Parviz, ed., *Ruse and Wit: The Humorous in Arabic, Persian, and Turkish Narrative*, Boston and Washington, DC: Ilex Foundation, 2012, pp. 33–43.

2. Stroescu, *La typologie*, vol. 2, p. 1507, no. 5658 (5 versions).

3. Haboucha, Reginetta, *Types and Motifs of the Judaeo-Spanish Folktales*, New York: Garland, 1992, no. **1588A (1 version).

4. Koen-Sarano, Matilda, *Kuentos del folklor de la famiya djudeo-espanyola*, Jerusalem: Kana, 1986, p. 185.

5. Rumi, Jalāl al-Din, *The Mathnawí of Jalálu'ddín Rúmí*, transl. Reynold A. Nicholson, vol. 1, London: Luzac & Co., 1934, p. 155 (bk. 1, verses 2835–2840); Foruzānfar, Badi' al-Zamān, *Ma'ākhez-e qeṣaṣ va tamṣilāt-e Maṣnavi*, Tehran: Amir Kabir, 3rd printing. 1362/1983, p. 28, no. 23.

6. Zākāni, 'Obeydallāh, *Kolliyāt-e 'Obeyd-e Zākāni*, ed. Parviz Atābeki, Tehran 1331/1952, p. 349.

7. Foruzānfar, *Ma'ākhez*, p. 28. For jokes on grammarians, see Marzolph, *Arabia ridens*, vol. 2, index s.v. "Grammatiker"; Weipert, Reinhard, *Altarabischer Sprachwitz: Abū 'Alqama und die Kunst, sich kompliziert auszudrücken*, Munich: Bayerische Akademie der Wissenschaften, 2009.

8. Thompson, Stith, and Jonas Balys, *The Oral Tales of India*, Bloomington: Indiana University Press, 1958, p. 253, no. J251.1 (1 version).

9. El-Shamy, *Types*, p. 728, no. 1293C*§ (2 versions, from Iraq and Egypt, respectively).

CHAPTER 42

Freeing the Part of the Body Stuck in the Jar by Cutting It Off (ATU 1294)

Simplemindedness and outright stupidity are probably the richest international source for jokes and jests. The present tale demonstrates how jocular tradition offers a variety of solutions for a simple problem.[1] A Greek jest recorded on the island of Chios tells of a man who puts his hand into a jar to take out some figs.[2] As the jar's mouth is narrow, the man cannot withdraw his hand while holding on to the figs. The town's wisest person suggests cutting off the hand so that the pot will remain whole. In a Romanian jest, a child gets its head stuck in a jar of honey while trying to lick the honey from the jar's bottom.[3] Discussing what to do, some of the villagers suggest cutting off the child's head. The wisest man present smashes the jar with a hammer. The hungry guest whose hand is stuck in the pot of soup in a jocular tale from Estonia smashes the pot himself rather than withdraw his hand.[4]

The above jests correspond to tale type ATU 1294A*: *Child with Head Caught in a Jar.* Sparsely documented in European tradition, the tale type appears to constitute a later adaptation of the older tale type ATU 1294: *Getting the Calf's Head Out of the Pot.* In the former, the mischief occurs to a human character. As a consequence, the drastic solution of cutting off a part of the body is only discussed but dismissed in favor of destroying the object. Since in the latter the mischief occurs to an animal, the drastic solution is put to practice, as discussed in a variety of jocular tales documented from popular tradition in Bulgaria[5] and Romania.[6] In a dialect jest from the rural regions of the South of England, the farm-boy alerts his master that the calf got its head stuck in the gate and can't get it out again.[7] The farmer advises the farm boy to get the saw. Doing this, the boy cuts off the calf's head. The farmer scolds him for not sawing the gate, but then turns to his wife, saying, "Never mind, missis, we shall hae plenty o' bif now."

The tale's oldest-known version is documented in the Chinese *Po yu king*, a collection of Buddhist tales dating to the fifth century CE that forms part of the canonical *Tripiṭaka* (Three Baskets).[8] Here, a camel gets its head stuck in a jar of grain. A wise man has the owner first cut off the camel's head and then smash the jar to get the head out.

Arabic literature knows both tale types.[9] The milder consequences occur in a tale contained in Muḥammad ibn Aḥmad ibn (al-)Ilyās al-Ḥanafī's seventeenth-century compilation of amusing tales, *Nuzhat al-udabā'* (Entertainment of the Educated).[10] The events are narrated as having been observed in person by polymath al-Jāḥiz (d. 868) in Ḥimṣ, the Syrian town whose inhabitants constitute the equivalent of the Mad Men of Gotham in classical and premodern Arabic literature. The narrator recounts that when he entered the city, the people were very concerned because the hand of the local ruler's son had got stuck in a jar of walnuts and almonds, and they did not know how to get it out again. The narrator promised the boy to let him have everything the jar contained if only he let go of what he held in his hand. As soon as the boy did that, he was able to withdraw his hand, and al-Jāḥiz poured him the nuts from the jar. The ruler was so pleased with the advice that he rewarded al-Jāḥiz generously with robes of honor and money more than he could carry.

The drastic version about an animal is told by Ibn al-Jawzī (d. 1201) in his *Akhbār al-Ḥamqā* (Tales of Stupid People) as having occurred in a village in the Eastern Iranian province of Khorasan.[11] Here, as in the English version, the animal concerned is a calf whose head is stuck in a pot of water. When the villagers ask the local teacher for advice, the latter takes a knife, cuts off the calf's head and then smashes the pot. The tale ends with a satirical commentary on the problem's "clever" solution.

Versions of both tale types are also documented from modern (oral) tradition in the Arab world,[12] Iran,[13] and Turkey,[14] sometimes as part of a conglomerate of strange or funny events witnessed by a traveler roaming the world in search of clever people.

Notes

1. Marzolph, Ulrich, "Kopf in der Kanne," in *Enzyklopädie des Märchens*, vol. 8 (1996), cols. 257–260.

2. Loukatos, Demetrios, *Neoellēnika laographika keimena*, Athens: Zakharopulos, 1957, pp. 308–309, no. 25.

3. Bîrlea, Ovidiu, *Antologie de Proză Populară Epică*, vol. 3, Bucharest: Editura Pentru Literatură, 1966, pp. 164–165; Stroescu, *La typologie*, vol. 1, p. 486, no. 3852A.

4. Viidalepp, Richard, *Estnische Volksmärchen*, Berlin: Akademie-Verlag, 1980, pp. 377–382, no. 135, at p. 381.

5. Daskalova Perkowski, Liliana, et al., *Typenverzeichnis der bulgarischen Volksmärchen*, ed. Klaus Roth, Helsinki: Suomalainen Tiedeakatemia, 1995, p. 254, no. 1294.

6. Stroescu, *La typologie*, vol. 1, pp. 485–486, no. 3852.

7. Briggs, *A Dictionary*, vol. A2, p. 31 (quoting from Williams, Alfred, *Round about the Upper Thames*, London: Duckworth & Co., 1922, pp. 67–68).

8. Chavannes, Édouard, *Cinq cents contes et apologues extraits du Tripitaka chinois*, vol. 2, Paris: Ernest Leroux, 1910–1935 (reprint Paris: Maisonneuve, 1962), p. 215, no. 311.

9. Marzolph, *Arabia ridens*, vol. 2, p. 262, no. 1221.

10. Basset, *Mille et un contes*, vol. 1, pp. 264–265, no. 151; Ḥanafī, Muḥammad ibn Aḥmad ibn (al-)Ilyās al-, *Nuzhat al-udabā'*, Gotha, Ms. Orient A 2706, fol. 104b–105a.

11. Ibn al-Jawzī, Abū 'l-Faraj 'Abd al-Raḥmān ibn 'Alī, *Akhbār al-Ḥamqā wa-'l-mughaffalīn*, ed. Kāẓim al-Muẓaffar, al-Najaf: al-Maktaba al-ḥaydariyya, 1386/1966, p. 135; Marzolph, *Arabia ridens*, vol. 1, pp. 248–249, no. 6.

12. El-Shamy, *Types*, pp. 728–729, nos. 1294, 1294A*.

13. Marzolph, *Typologie*, p. 195, no. 1294A*; Christensen, Arthur, "Les sots dans la tradition populaire des Persans," *Acta Orientalia* 1 (1922), pp. 43–75, at p. 71, no. 46 (tale type ATU 1294).

14. Eberhard and Boratav, *Typen*, p. 365, no. 331 III (b, c).

CHAPTER 43

The Fox Fears It Might Be Taken for a Camel (El-Shamy 1319N*)

Jocular tales with a straightforward political message have rarely been considered as tale types, whether regional or international. Rather than resulting from neglect or conscious disregard, this decision is mainly due to the fact that the political implications of those tales are more often than not related to specific circumstances, such as individual characters identified by name or references to distinct historical or contemporary situations that prevent a given tale's wide adaptability to changed circumstances. The integration of a given tale into the system of tale types requires a certain independence from specific circumstances that would enable the tale's message to be meaningful for audiences in different periods and different regions. The present tale is a rare exception to the rule. Hasan El-Shamy classified the tale as newly assigned tale types 150A and/or 1319N*, with the heading *Fox Advises Camel Not to Go Near Man (Or to a Certain Country)*.[1] The tale's abstract content is summarized as follows: A man (or animal), often one believed to cause mischief (a Jew; a fox, a rabbit), runs away from town because another species (camels) is being badly treated (punished, killed, drafted to do forced labor). Reminded that he/it does not belong to that species, he/it responds, "I know that. But first they treat you badly, and then they look whether you actually belong to that particular species!"

In a Romanian version allegedly dating from 1937, a man "runs in panic down a Bucharest street."[2] Asked by a friend why he is running like that, he says, "They have decided to shoot all camels." In response to his friend's comment that he is not a camel, the man says, "Yes, but these people shoot first, and then they realize you're not a camel!" In a version current in Nazi Germany, countless rabbits appear at the Belgian border asking for political asylum, since the "Gestapo is arresting all giraffes as enemies of the state."[3] The punchline here is, "We know that (we are not giraffes), but try to make that clear to a member of the Gestapo." A version circulating in Russia at the time of the revolution of 1905 has a rabbit run away because they are killing camels.[4] Numerous similar versions, particularly those from recent Arab[5] and Jewish[6] tradition, testify to the tale's wide adaptability to a variety of different political and social contexts.[7] To be precise, the majority of the tale's published texts lack an unambiguous reference to oral tradition, such as the name of the narrator or the date of recording,[8] and it is mainly the tale's wide circulation in published collections that gives good reason to presume its potential currency in European oral tradition. The tale appears to be particularly popular in contemporary Russia where the punchline, "Try to prove you're not a camel," gained a proverbial status, epitomizing the futility of any attempt to prove something obvious to an obstinate bureaucracy.[9]

The tale's oldest versions are documented in tenth- and eleventh-century Arabic literature.[10] In the short version contained in Ibn Abī ʿAwn's (d. 934) *al-Ajwiba al-muskita* (Quick-Witted Responses), the camel explains to the fox that it runs away because the ruler drafts all donkeys for forced labor. Although the fox knows well that it is not a donkey, it is afraid of the ruler's injustice.[11] The tale is cited almost verbatim in Abū Ḥayyān al-Tawḥīdī's (d. 1023) *al-Baṣāʾir wa-ʾl-dhakāʾir* (Deep Insights and Treasures).[12] In his *Jamʿ al-jawāhir* (The Collection of Jewels), al-Ḥuṣrī (d. 1015) presents a peculiar adaptation attributed to the Egypian poet al-Ḥusayn ibn ʿAbd al-Salām al-Miṣrī (d. 872)[13] nicknamed "The Camel" (*al-jamal*).[14]

> He (once) came by one of his friends at the (locality) "Pass of the Carpenters," running as fast as he could. (His friend) said, "Come to my place," because he feared that some calamity might have occurred to him. So he came to his house, where (the friend) came out (to welcome him) out of view, saying, "What happened to you, Abu ʿAbdallāh?" He answered, "Did you not know that forced labor has been imposed on the camels? What can safeguard me against somebody saying: This is 'the Camel;' so I would be caught and could only be rescued by intercession!"
>
> The tale ends in a short comment that the poet was known for his subtlety.

Iranian authors adapted the story from the Arabic as early as the twelfth century.[15] The prose text in Saʿdi's (d. 1292) *Golestān* (Rose Garden) and the verse text by Anvari (d. ca. 1169) are closely modeled on the shorter Arabic version. The version in Jalāl al-Din Rumi's (d. 1273) mystical *summa*, the *Masnavi-ye maʿnavi*, appears to be modeled on a different source, as both its short prose summary and its rhymed text mention a person "rushing into a house in terror" because "they are seizing asses outside (in the streets) to do forced labour for the tyrannical king." Following the tale proper, Rumi goes into his usual practice of adding mystical elaborations, here about the responsibility of the ruler and the beauty of life on earth, at the end of which he stops himself short, saying, "This discourse hath no end . . . ," following which he returns to the previous tale into which the tale of the fleeing man is embedded.[16] As Rumi composed his work in the cosmopolitan atmosphere of Anatolian Konya, he might have been influenced by local or regional tradition.

Notes

1. El-Shamy, *Types*, p. 58, no. 0150A§/1319N*§.

2. Banc, C., and Alan Dundes, *You Call This Living? A Collection of East European Political Jokes*, Athens and London: The University of Georgia Press, 1990, p. 33.

3. Gamm, Hans-Jochen, *Der Flüsterwitz im Dritten Reich*, Munich: Deutscher Taschenbuchverlag, 1979, p. 20; quoted from Banc and Dundes, *You Call This Living?*, p. 33–34.

4. Quoted from "A. Druyanov, *The Book of Jokes and Wit*, vol. II, No. 1946" in Noy, Dov, *Folktales of Israel*, Chicago: The University of Chicago Press, 1963, pp. 64–65, no. 28 (this version narrated by Shalom Dervish from Iraq; Israel Folktale Archives, no. 581). For Russian versions dating from the 1920s, see https://en.wikipedia.org/wiki/Russian_jokes (accessed March 17, 2016).

5. El-Shamy, Hasan M., *Folktales of Egypt*, Chicago: The University of Chicago Press, 1980, p. 230, no. 66; Kishtainy, Khalid, *Arab Political Humour*, London: Quartet Books, 1985, p. 174; Shehata, Samer S., "The Politics of Laughter: Nasser, Sadat, and Mubarek in Egyptian Political Jokes," *Folklore* 103.1 (1992), pp. 75–91, at pp. 80–81.

6. Schwarzbaum, Haim, *Studies in Jewish and World Folklore*, Berlin: Walter de Gruyter, 1968, p. 92, no. 65.

7. Dundes, Alan, "Six Inches from the Presidency: The Gary Hart Jokes as Public Opinion," *Western Folklore* 48.1 (1989), pp. 43–51, at p. 47; Voigt, Vilmos, "Ergebnisse und Fehler bei der Bearbeitung von 'heutigen' mündlichen Texten," in *Die heutige Bedeutung oraler Traditionen: Ihre Archivierung, Publikation und Index-Erschließung/The Present-Day Importance of Oral Traditions: Their Preservation, Publication and Indexing*, ed. Walther Heissig and Rüdiger Schott, Opladen: Westdeutscher Verlag, 1998, pp. 62–74, at pp. 72–73; Oring, Elliot, *Joking Asides: The Theory, Analysis, and Aesthetics of Humor*, Norman: Utah State University Press, 2016, p. 111.

8. An exception is El-Shamy, *Folktales of Egypt*, p. 230, no. 66 that was "told by a male university student in 1964."

9. According to http://www.talkreason.org/marperak/jokes/party.htm#N_8_ (accessed March 17, 2016), the punch line of this joke, "'Prove that you're not a camel,' has become a widely used part of the Russian vernacular, being applied to many situations when an innocent person becomes a victim of arbitrary persecutions, purges, layoffs, etc." A Google search for "try to prove you are not a camel" yields a considerable number of hits for the use of the proverbial expression in modern Russia.

10. Marzolph, *Arabia ridens*, vol. 2, pp. 88–89, no. 353. The following observations are indebted to my essay "Reconsidering the Iranian Sources of a Romanian Political Joke," *Western Folklore* 47 (1988), pp. 212–216.

11. Yousef, May A., *Das Buch der schlagfertigen Antworten von Ibn Abī ʿAwn*, Berlin: Klaus Schwarz, 1988, pp. 231–232, no. 1385.

12. Tawḥīdī, Abū Ḥayyān al-, *al-Baṣāʾir wa-ʾl-dhakhāʾir*, ed. Wadād al-Qāḍī, Beirut: Dār Ṣādir, 1408/1988, vol. 9, p. 110, no. 356.

13. Ziriklī, Khayr al-Dīn al-, *al-Aʿlām: qāmūs tarājim [. . .]*, Beirut: Dār al-ʿIlm lil-malāyīn, 1980, vol. 2, p. 240.

14. Ḥuṣrī al-Qayrawānī, Abū Isḥāq Ibrāhīm ibn ʿAlī al-, *Jamʿ al-jawāhir fī 'l-mulaḥ wa-'l-nawādir*, ed. ʿAlī Muḥammad al-Bijāwī, Cairo: Dār Iḥyāʾ al-kutub al-ʿarabiyya, 1372/1952, p. 77; see also El-Shamy, *Types*, p. 58, no. 0150A§/1319N*§, reference 1.

15. For references to the following, see Omidsalar, Mahmoud, "A Romanian Political Joke in 12th-Century Iranian Sources," *Western Folklore* 46 (1978), pp. 121–124. The author's conclusions as for the tale's origin and dissemination are amended by Marzolph, " Reconsidering the Iranian Sources."

16. Rumi, Jalāl al-Din, *The Mathnawí of Jalálu'ddín Rúmí*, transl. Reynold A. Nicholson, vol. 3, London: Luzac & Co., 1934, pp. 153–154 (bk. 5, verses 2538–2544); see also Foruzānfar, Badiʿ al-Zamān, *Ma'ākhez-e qeṣaṣ va tamsilāt-e Masnavi*, 3rd printing, Tehran: Amir Kabir, 1362/1983, pp. 179–180, no. 205. A modern prose rendering of Rumi's verse is given by Arberry, Arthur John, *More Tales from the Masnavi*, London: Allen & Unwin, 1963, p. 136, no. 152.

CHAPTER 44

Accidental Cannibalism (ATU 1339G)

In his short essay discussing the motif of "accidental cannibalism" (Mot. X21), Kurt Ranke studied the historical development of the related tale over a period of more than five centuries.[1] Ranke introduced his historical survey with the tale's treatment as a modern legend in the 1950s.

> After World War II, a German family in addition to the usual care packages mailed by their uncle in the United States receives several cans of delicious meat. The meat has, however, a strange taste of ashes and soap. Only after having eaten the meat do they learn that the letter that was supposed to inform them about the content of the cans got lost. The uncle's wife had died, and in order to avoid customs formalities as well as the high cost for transferring the body, the relatives mailed the ashes of her cremated body home for burial in the cans.

Although the modern legend enjoys only an indirect or secondary orality, it is classified in the third revision of the international tale-type index as tale type ATU 1339G: *The Relative in the Urn*. Modern legends regularly owe their occurrence in oral tradition to their frequent publication in popular booklets that often serve to create or at least invigorate oral retellings. Well-known examples of such publications in English include Jan Brunvand's numerous collections and studies, beginning with *The Vanishing Hitchhiker* (1981).[2] Elaborating on Albert Wesselski's notes to a version of the present tale attributed to the Turkish prankster Nasreddin Hodja,[3] Ranke identified the tale's oldest form in the Latin collection of facetious tales compiled by the papal secretary Poggio Bracciolini around the middle of the fifteenth century. Poggio's tale is about two Jews traveling from Venice to Bologna, one of whom dies. In order to circumvent a prohibition and transport the body back to Venice, the surviving comrade cuts it into pieces that he stuffs into a barrel together with honey and odorous spices, presumably so as to cover the rotten smell. Then he asks a Jewish comrade traveling to Venice to take the barrel along. During the journey by ship to Ferrara, a Florentine traveler notices the aromatic smell emanating from the barrel and eats the pieces of meat one after the other without realizing their true nature.

In addition to several quotations of the tale by German authors of the sixteenth and seventeenth centuries, Ranke also discussed two versions originating from Muslim Middle Eastern tradition. Here, a Jew transports his deceased father to be buried in Jerusalem in a similar manner, and the meat is eaten by a Muslim traveler.[4] A seventeenth-century version in Arabic is included in Muḥammad ibn Aḥmad ibn (al-)Ilyās al-Ḥanafī's entertaining compilation *Nuzhat al-udabā'* (Entertainment of the Educated).[5] Another early modern version is attributed to the Turkish prankster Nasreddin Hodja.[6] Ranke interpreted the Muslim versions as a "vicious Muslim satire of Jewish wishful thinking" and concludes that the cans in the care package of twentieth-century European tradition constitute the modern equivalent of the barrel in the earlier versions.

The tale's earliest-known version is contained in al-Rāghib al-Iṣfahānī's (d. 1008) compilation *Muḥāḍarāt al-udabā'* (Conversations of the Educated):[7]

> Embarking on a ship, a man travels together with a Jew who anxiously watches over a basket with some dried meat. The man gets hold of the basket and eats (the meat) until only the bones remain. When the Jew intends to disembark, he notices that the basket is empty. Inquiring about (the situation), he is informed that the man ate its contents. The Jew begins to wail, exclaiming, "He has eaten my father!" And when asked about it, he explains, "My father desired to be buried in Jerusalem. When he died, we cut him up and dried the meat so as to facilitate its transportation. Now that man has eaten him!"

The author presents the events in a passage that assembles a total of three tales in which people accidentally (*ʿalā ghalaṭ*) eat disgusting food (*al-qādhūrāt*). Having drunk milk from from a vessel offered by some Bedouins, the traveling scholar al-Aṣmaʿī (d. 828) wants to ascertain that the vessel is not impure. The Bedouins respond in the affirmative, saying that in daytime they use it for their meals, at night they employ it as a pisspot, and in the morning they would feed the dog from it, who would lick it perfectly clean. This tale corresponds to tale type ATU 1578A*: *The Drinking Cup* (see essay **72, *The Drink Served in the Pisspot***).[8] On another occasion, al-Aṣmaʿī picks small pieces of meat from a suspended cord and eats them. Only when he finished, an old woman informs him that she is responsible for the execution of circumcision (*khatn*) of the young women of her tribe, and that she kept the leftovers of the operation to remind her of the number of operations executed.

In their original context, the above tales served a specific purpose, demonstrating the ignorance and questionable way of life of the Arab Bedouins. On the one hand, Bedouins were famed for the pure Arabic they spoke, which is the reason why there are many tales about the scholar and grammarian al-Aṣmaʿī visiting Bedouins as his informants. On the other hand, the urban elite population regarded Bedouins as thoroughly uncultivated and ridiculed them in numerous jokes.[9] Embedded in the book's tenth chapter dealing with food, the passages of *Muḥāḍarāt al-udabā'* preceding the present tale deal with the ignorance of Bedouins concerning various kinds of food and the dubious character of some of their regular diet. In the associative style of premodern Arabic entertaining and educative literature, the tale about the Jewish traveler is appended to the tales about the Bedouins since its general topic of "eating despicable food" overlaps.

Separating the tale from its original argument, the Arabic version in the *Nuzhat al-udabā'* is presented in the chapter "Whatever Amuses the Spirit in Terms of Tales and Anecdotes" (*Fī-mā yashraḥ al-khāṭir min al-ḥikāyāt wa-'l-nawādir*), thus simply classifying the events as strange and amusing. The tale's anti-Jewish character is pronounced, although the Jewish context, particularly the deceased person's will to be buried in the holy city of Jerusalem, mainly serves to motivate the outrageous decision to cut the dead body into pieces.

Notes

1. Ranke, Kurt, "Zum Motiv 'Accidental Cannibalism'," in *Die Welt der einfachen Formen*, Berlin: De Gruyter, 1978, pp. 286–290.
2. Thursby, Jacqueline, "Brunvand, Jan Harold," in *Enzyklopädie des Märchens*, vol. 14 (2014), cols. 1578–1581.
3. Wesselski, *Der Hodscha Nasreddin*, vol. 1, p. 257, no. 193.
4. Ranke, "Zum Motiv 'Accidental Cannibalism'," pp. 287–288.
5. Basset, *Mille et un contes*, vol. 1, p. 292, no. 200; Ḥanafī, Muḥammad ibn Aḥmad ibn (al-)Ilyās al-, *Nuzhat al-udabā'*, Gotha, Ms. Orient A 2706, fol. 71b.
6. Wesselski, *Der Hodscha Nasreddin*, vol. 1, pp. 105–107, no. 193. Wesselski translated the tale from Decourdemanche, Jean Adolphe, *Sottisier de Nasr-Eddin-Hodja, bouffon de Tamerlan*, Bruxelles: Gay and Doucé, 1878, no. 126, who translated it from an Ottoman Turkish manuscript collection.
7. Rāghib al-Iṣfahānī, al-Ḥusayn ibn Muḥammad, *Muḥāḍarāt al-udabā' wa-muḥāwarāt al-shu'arā' wa-'l-bulaghā'*, Beirut 1961, vol. 2, p. 627; Marzolph, *Arabia ridens*, vol. 2, p. 235, no. 1070.
8. Marzolph, *Arabia ridens*, vol. 2, p. 235, no. 1069; see also vol. 2, p. 228, no. 1031.
9. Marzolph, *Arabia ridens*, p. 316, s.v. "Beduine," Binay, Sarah, *Die Figur des Beduinen in der arabischen Literatur: 9–12. Jh.*, Wiesbaden: Reichert, 2006.

CHAPTER 45

The Thieves Find Nothing to Steal in the Poor Man's House (ATU 1341C)

In his second revision of the international tale-type index, published in 1961,[1] Stith Thompson introduced a considerable number of new items, as additional data had become available since the work's first English edition, published in 1928.[2] In the preface to the second revision, Thompson even admits to frequently breaking his own rule of not including stories attested only once when he "felt that the tale is actually known but not recorded, and when its presence in the index might be useful in the future."[3] This statement is particularly relevant for short jokes. For a variety of reasons, short jokes are a marginal genre in comparative and historical folk narrative research. Although they are told in the thousands, they were rarely recorded, as the interests of most nineteenth- and twentieth-century collectors focused on longer and more complex tales. Further, jokes are often performed in a specific context and many narrators are reluctant to reproduce them out of conversational context with the same ease as complex narratives. In addition, jokes are often so short that they can hardly be considered a "tale," as the related event is boiled down to a single particularly funny scene. Consequently, while several regional catalogues of jokes were compiled,[4] the number of jokes considered in the international tale-type index represent international jocular tradition only to a limited extent. Even so, tale types 1200–1874 list a considerable number of jocular tales and short jokes. The joke under present consideration is listed in the general category of "Numskull Tales" as one of several subtypes detailing an encounter between a fool and thieves or robbers. Thompson's description for tale type AT 1341C: *The Robbers Commiserated* reads as follows.[5]

> A buffoon says to the robbers in his house, "You can't find anything here in the dark, for I can find nothing in broad daylight."

In addition to texts from medieval and early modern literature, the only versions Thompson referenced from oral tradition are Finnish. Although the list of references in the most recent revision of the international tale-type index has considerably increased,[6] the Finnish texts still document the joke's most frequent occurrence in any European oral tradition. The Finnish catalogue of folktales compiled by Pirkko-Liisa Rausmaa lists nine recordings of the joke, with some variations.[7] In the Finnish tales, a pickpocket searches the pockets of a man sleeping on a bench. When the man notices this, he turns around and says, "Go ahead, I did not find anything there either!" The common point between this variation and Thompson's summary is the obvious fact that the man is so penniless that he can be sure the thief will find nothing worth stealing.

Although rarely recorded from oral tradition, the joke enjoyed a certain popularity in European tradition at least since the fourteenth century. It was widely published in jestbooks and other compilations of jocular tales ranging from the twentieth to the sixteenth centuries in Italian,[8] Spanish,[9] English,[10] French,[11] German,[12] Dutch,[13] Danish,[14] Hungarian,[15] Romanian,[16] and probably other European languages.[17] The joke's earliest European versions are attested in two Latin sources, the fifteenth-century anonymous Latin *Mensa philosophica*[18] and John Gobi's fourteenth-century *Scala coeli*.[19] The latter work quotes the joke on the authority of the French preacher Jacques de Vitry, bishop of the Palestinian city of Akka in 1214–1227, suggesting a possible link to previously documented Arabic tradition.

The joke's Arabic dimension is first documented in al-Ābī's (d. 1030) encyclopedia of jokes and anecdotes, *Nathr al-durr* (Pearls of Prose).[20] It is equally short and reads almost exactly like the later European versions.

> Robbers broke into the house of somebody where there was nothing (to steal). As they searched all over the place, the owner of the house woke up, noticed them, and said, "Hey you! What you are looking for at night, I have been searching for in daytime without finding it!"

The joke remained popular in written sources from the Muslim world ever since its first recorded appearance. In the twelfth century, Ibn Ḥamdūn (d. 1167) repeated the joke almost verbatim in his compilation of historical notices, excerpts of literature, entertaining anecdotes, and poetry known as *al-Tadhkira* (The Aide-Mémoire).[21] In the thirteenth century, the head of the Eastern Jacobite Church, Bar Hebraeus (d. 1286), prepared his booklet of amusing stories, largely an adapted selection of tales from *Nathr al-durr* and including the joke in question.[22] In the fourteenth century, the joke appears in Persian translation in satirist ʿObeyd-e Zākāni's (d. 1371) collection of amusing stories.[23] From the sixteenth century onward, the joke was integrated into the collections of anecdotes attributed to the Turkish jester Nasreddin Hodja in a slightly different form. Here, when hearing the robbers search the house, the owner says to his wife, "Don't worry, maybe they'll find something that we can take from them!"[24] The attribution to Nasreddin Hodja supplied the joke with a strong medium for its dissemination in the Muslim world, as the anecdotes were published innumerable times and are available in virtually every region that ever was dominated by or came into close contact with Arabic or Turkish culture. The joke was rarely recorded from modern Middle Eastern oral tradition, probably due to the very circumstances that prevented its recording from oral tradition in Europe. One of the two documented versions from Persian oral tradition originates from Danish scholar of Iranian studies Arthur Christensen's early twentieth-century language teacher Mollā Feyżollāh who was known to have learned much of his narrative repertoire from chapbooks.[25]

Notes

1. Aarne, Antti, *The Types of the Folktale: A Classification and Bibliography. Antti Aarne's Verzeichnis der Märchentypen (FF Communications No. 3) Translated and Enlarged*, ed. Stith Thompson, 2nd Revision, Helsinki: Suomalainen Tiedeakatemia, 1961.

2. Aarne, Antti, *The Types of the Folktale: A Classification and Bibliography. Antti Aarne's Verzeichnis der Märchentypen (FF Communications No. 3) Translated and Enlarged*, ed. Stith Thompson, Helsinki: Suomalainen Tiedeakatemia, 1928.

3. Thompson in Aarne, *The Types*, 1961, p. 8.

4. See, e.g., Raudsep, Loreida, *Antiklerikale estnische Schwänke: Typen- und Variantenverzeichnis*, Tallinn: Institut für Sprach- und Literaturforschung, 1969; Stroescu, *La typologie*; Rausmaa, Pirkko-Liisa, *A Catalogue of Anecdotes: Addenda to the Aarne-Thompson Catalogue of Anecdotes in the Folklore Archives of the Finnish Literature Society*, Turku: Nordic Institute of Folklore, 1973.

5. Aarne, *The Types*, 1961, p. 398, no. 1341C.

6. Uther, *The Types*, vol. 2, p. 143, no. 1341C.

7. Rausmaa, Pirkko-Liisa, *Suomalaiset kansansadut*, vol. 4: *Hölmöläissadut, valhesadut*, Helsinki: Suomalaisen Kirjallisuuden Seura, 1993, p. 134–135, no. 159.

8. Speroni, Charles, *Wit and Wisdom of the Italian Renaissance*, Berkeley: University of California Press, 1964, p. 196, no. 7 (from Ludovico Domenichi's seventeenth-century *Facetie*).

9. Chevalier, *Cuentos folklóricos*, p. 175, no. 105 (from Melchor de Santa Cruz's *Floresta española de apotegmas y sentencias*, 1674).

10. Zall, Paul M., *A Nest of Ninnies and Other English Jestbooks of the Seventeenth Century*, Lincoln: University of Nebraska Press, 1970, pp. 86–87, no. 57 (from *Jests to Make You Merry*, 1607).

11. D'Ouville, Antoine Le Métel, *L'Élite des contes*, ed. G. Brunet, Paris: Librarie des bibliophiles, 1873, vol. 2, p. 319 (originally published in 1641).

12. Bebel, Heinrich, *Schwänke*, ed. Albert Wesselski, Munich: Georg Müller, 1907, vol. 1, pp. 20, 132–133, no. 32; Ranke, Kurt, "Via grammatica," *Fabula* 20 (1979), pp. 160–169, at p. 162, no. 4; Uther, *Deutscher Märchenkatalog*, p. 337, no. 1341C.

13. Overbeke, Arnout van, *Anecdota sive historiae jocosas: Een seventiende-eeuwse verzameling moppen en anekdotes*, ed. Rudolf Dekker and Herman Rodenburg, Amsterdam: Meertens-Institut, 1991, p. 338, no. 2093.

14. See Christensen, Arthur, *Contes persans en langue populaire*, Copenhagen: Det Kgl. Danske Videnskabernes Selskab, 1918, pp. 98–99, no. 38.

15. György, Lajos, *Kónyi János Democritusa*, Budapest: Magyar tudományos akadémia, 1932, pp. 104–105, no. 55.

16. Stroescu, *La typologie*, vol. 2, pp. 980–982, no. 4733.

17. Tubach, *Index exemplorum*, p. 219, no. 2786.

18. Dunn, Thomas Franklin, *The Facetiae of the Mensa Philosophica*, Saint Louis: Washington University, 1934, pp. 29–30, no. 62; Wesselski, *Mönchslatein*, pp. 170, 247, no. 134.

19. Gobi, Jean, *La Scala coeli*, ed. Marie-Anne Polo de Beaulieu, Paris: Centre National de la Recherche Scientifique, 1991, p. 411, no. 572.

20. Ābī, Abū Saʿd Manṣūr ibn al-Ḥusayn al-, *Nathr al-durr*, ed. Muḥammad ʿAlī Qarna et al., vol. 7, Cairo: al-Hayʾa al-miṣriyya al-ʿāmma lil-kitāb, 1990, p. 343; Marzolph, *Arabia ridens*, vol. 1, p. 249, no. 8; vol. 2, pp. 214–215, no. 956.

21. Ibn Ḥamdūn, Muḥammad ibn al-Ḥasan ibn Muḥammad ibn ʿAlī, *al-Tadhkira al-ḥamdūniyya*, ed. Iḥsān ʿAbbās and Bakr ʿAbbās, vol. 8, Beirut: Dār Ṣādir, 1996, p. 109, no. 279.

22. Bar Hebraeus, Mâr Gregory John, *The Laughable Stories*, transl. E.A. Wallis Budge, London: Luzac and Co, 1897, p. 166, no. 658.

23. Zākāni, ʿObeydallāh, *Kolliyāt-e ʿObeyd-e Ẕākāni*, ed. Parviz Atābeki, Tehran 1331/1952, p. 337.

24. Wesselski, *Der Hodscha Nasreddin*, vol. 1, pp. 47, 231–232, no. 83; Marzolph, *Nasreddin Hodscha*, pp. 86, 301, no. 186; Burrill, Kathleen R.F., "The Nasreddin Hoca Stories, 1: An Early Ottoman Manuscript at the University of Groningen," *Archivum Ottomanicum* 2 (1970), pp. 7–114, at p. 45, no. 63; Kut, Günay, "Nasreddin Hoca Hikâyeleri Yazmalarının Kolları Üzerine Bir Deneme," in *IV. Milletlerarası Türk Halk Kültürü Kongresi Bildirileri*, vol. 3: *Halk Edebiyatı*, Ankara, 1992, pp. 147–200, at p. 158, no. 8.

25. Christensen, *Contes persans*, pp. 98–99, no. 38; Marzolph, *Typologie*, pp. 199–200, no. 1341C.

CHAPTER 46

The House Without Food or Drink (ATU 1346)

In this short jocular tale, the euphemism for the grave as a "house without food or drink" causes a funny misunderstanding. In the present context, the tale serves as an example to demonstrate the impact of tales originating from Arabic tradition in regions as far apart as Spain and Iran that, at least at first sight, lack any obvious connection to each other. In the West, the tale appears to be predominantly known in the languages of the Iberian Peninsula.[1] While it is cited in several influential literary texts,[2] versions collected from oral tradition are rarely documented. In September 1997, Margarita Alvarez Cortina, aged 48, told the tale in Beyo (Miranda) in the North-Western Spanish province of Asturias as follows.[3]

> At a wake, the widow of the recently deceased man laments, "By God, Antonio! You are going to a place where there is nothing—no coffee, no firewood, where you even have no tobacco to smoke! There is nothing at all!" One of the people who listened said, "Holy shit![4] They are going to bring him to my house!"

A Judeo-Spanish version was recorded in 1984 from Miriam Raymond (Sarano), born 1945 in Milan into a family who migrated to Israel from Turkey.[5] Here the comment is made by Djohá, the Judeo-Spanish equivalent of the Arabic prankster Juḥā whose jocular tales and anecdotes are known in Arabic literature since the ninth century.[6] When looking out of the window of his house, Djohá overhears a widow lamenting her deceased husband, saying that he is going to a place where there is no light, nothing to eat, where it is cold and where nobody will take care of him. Immediately, Djohá tells his wife to lock the door, as he assumes they are bringing the deceased man to their house. Two other Spanish versions collected from oral tradition have a gypsy (*gitano*) comment on the situation, thus stigmatizing this ethnic minority as living in particularly destitute conditions.[7]

Originally catalogued in Stith Thompson's *Motif-index* as Mot. J2483, the tale was introduced into the tale-type canon in the third revision of the international tale-type index as tale type ATU 1346: *The House Without Food or Drink*. The fairly recent promotion to the status of tale type is probably responsible for the tale's relatively scarce documentation, as the editors of scholarly collections of folktales would rarely have considered classifying the published tales according to the refined and much more complex classification system of the *Motif-index*.

Although the tale is cited by several Spanish authors of the sixteenth and seventeenth centuries,[8] there is little doubt that the oral retellings cited above derive mainly from the tale's most famous rendering in the third chapter (*tratado*) of the Spanish picaresque novel *La vida de Lazarillo de Tormes y de sus fortunas y adversidades* (The Life of Lazarillo de Tormes and of His Fortunes and Adversities), originally published in 1552.[9] It is equally undisputed that the anonymous author of the *Lazarillo* adapted the tale from the Arabic tradition of the Iberian Peninsula, either directly or through an intermediary, probably oral tradition.[10] About a century before the *Lazarillo*, the Andalusian author Ibn ʿĀṣim (d. 1426) presents the tale in the section on quick-witted retorts (*al-ajwiba al-muskita*) of his entertaining compilation *Ḥadāʾiq al-azāhir* (Flower Gardens). Here, an unnamed beggar and his son listen to a woman lamenting her late husband with the words, "They are bringing you to a place (*bayt*) where there is neither blanket (*ghiṭāʾ*) nor bed (?; *waṭāʾ*), neither food (*ghidhāʾ*) nor dinner (*ʿashāʾ*)!" And the beggar's son comments, "By God! They are bringing him to our house!"[11] In Arabic literature, the tale's occurrence dates back at least to the beginning of the tenth century when several authors cite it in differing versions. In his book *al-Maḥāsin wa-ʾl-masāwī* (The Good and the Bad Sides [of Things]), Ibrāhīm ibn Muḥammad al-Bayhaqī cites the tale in relation to the famous party-crasher or sponger (*ṭufaylī*)[12] ʿUthmān ibn Darrāj (misspelled as Ibn Rawāḥ), a person who apparently lived around the beginning of the ninth century.

> They once asked the *ṭufaylī* Ibn Rawāḥ, "How is your son?" He responded, "He is without equal in the world! Once, when following a funeral procession, he overheard a professional wailing woman lament, 'My poor master! They are bringing you to a place where there is no water, nor food, bed, carpet, blanket, lamp, or light!' He said, 'My father! They are bringing him to our house!'"[13]

Contemporary with al-Bayhaqī is the version in the *Kitāb al-Ajwiba al-muskita* (The Book of Quick-Witted Responses) compiled by the Iraqi author Ibn Abī ʿAwn (d. 934)[14] who cites the tale in a wording closely resembling that of Ibn ʿĀṣim. A third early tenth-century version appears in the *Ṭabaqāt al-shuʿarāʾ* (Biographies of Poets) by ʿAbdallāh ibn Muḥammad Ibn al-Muʿtazz, the luckless Abbasid ruler who was murdered by his political opponents less than three weeks after he ascended the throne in December 998.[15] In posterity, Ibn al-Muʿtazz is mainly remembered as an excellent poet. In his version, the protagonist is a little-known poet named Aḥmad ibn ʿAbd al-Salām.

> Al-Khaṣīb ibn Muḥammad al-Asadī narrated: Aḥmad ibn ʿAbd al-Salām told me the following.

> One day I was coming by the Eastern gate of Baghdad together with my little son when a funeral procession approached. It was followed by many people, men and women who wailed and lamented. One of the women cried, "Where are they bringing you to, my poor father! To the abode of decay, the seat of desolation and darkness! (They are bringing you to) where there is neither cheerfulness nor light, neither food nor drink nor happiness!" My son turned to me and said, "My father! They are bringing the dead man to our house!" And when I asked him why he thought so, he replied, "Everything this woman said applies to our house!"

The fact that the three Arabic versions dating from the beginning of the tenth century differ in wording and, to a certain extent, in action as well, leads one to presume that the tale had already been around for some time, probably in oral tradition, thus allowing the development of variations. Although the attribution to the ninth-century *ṭufaylī* Ibn (al-)Darrāj is not historically reliable, the tale might well have originated in or shortly after his time. A conversation between a father and his son corresponding to the one reported by Ibn al-Muʿtazz is narrated in Abū 'l-Faraj al-Iṣfahānī's (d. 967) *Kitāb al-Aghānī* (Book of Songs) in the biography of the aforementioned *ṭufaylī* Abū Saʿīd Uthmān ibn al-Darrāj.[16] Cited in a variety of sources in subsequent centuries,[17] by the beginning of the twentieth century the tale was eventually attached to the narrative repertoire of famous characters of Arabic jocular tradition such as the historical poet Abū Nuwās (d. 815) or the pseudo-historical prankster Juḥā.[18]

In the thirteenth century the tale also made its way into Persian literature that in its turn contributed to spreading the tale into the vernacular tradition of the Indian subcontinent.[19] In his mystical *summa*, the *Mas̱navi-ye maʿnavi*, the Persian poet Jalāl al-Din Rumi (d. 1273) presents the tale in the form of an extensive dialogue between a son and his father, here Juḥi, the Persian equivalent of the Arabic Juḥā.[20] Rumi's rendering of the tale proper is followed by a lengthy mystical application in which Rumi uses the destitute house as a simile for the heart that is unilluminated "by the beams of the sun of the (Divine) Majesty." A century later, the tale is attributed to an unnamed beggar (*darvish*) in the Persian jocular tales of satirist ʿObeyd-e Zākāni's (d. ca. 1371) *Resāle-ye delgoshā* (The Heart-Refreshing Epistle).[21] In the sixteenth century, Fakhr al-Din ʿAli Ṣafi cites it in a conversation between Jūḥi and his daughter in his compilation *Laṭāʾef al-ṭavāʾef* (Jocular Tales from the Various Strata of Society).[22] Eventually, in the nineteenth century, chapbook versions such as those in Ḥabiballāh Kāshāni's *Reyāż al-ḥekāyāt* (Gardens of Tales)[23] or the anonymous *Laṭāʾef-e ʿajibe* (Marvelous Amusing Tales; Bombay 1846)[24] paved the way for the tale to reach a wide audience and thus be retold in and collected from oral tradition in the Persianate world, including the Indian subcontinent. And finally, already in the premodern manuscript tradition of Ottoman Turkey the tale was attached to the repertoire of Nasreddin Hodja[25] that resulted in spreading it into the Balkans and elsewhere in the regions under Ottoman influence.

Altogether, the tale's impact in Western tradition, both written and oral, is apparently limited. Even so, the tale proves to be an interesting case for studying the dissemination of a specific narrative item and the various branches it developed over a period spanning more than a thousand years from its tenth-century Arabic versions to the present. Reaching out to both West and East, the tale thus provides a strong argument for the unifying potential of humor.

Notes

1. Braga, Theophilo, *Contos tradicionaes do povo portuguez: Historias o Exemplos de thema tradicional e fórma litteraria. Litteratura dos Contos populares em Portugal*, 2nd ed. Lisbon: J.A. Rodrigues & C.ª, 1915, vol. 2, pp. 114–155 quotes a Portuguese version of the tale from *Arte de Furtar* by Alexander de Gusmão (1695–1753); the book is, more prominently, attributed to the seventeenth-century author Manuel da Costa (1601–1667).

2. Foulché-Delbosc, Raymond, "Remarques sur *Lazarillo de Tormes*," *Revue hispanique* 7 (1900), pp. 81–97, at 94–95; Lida de Malkiel, María Rosa, "Función del cuento popular en el Lazarillo de Tormes," *Primer Congreso Internacional de Hispanistas, Oxford 1962: Actas*, ed. Frank Pierce and Cyril A. Jones, Madrid 1964, pp. 349–359, at 356–357; Ayala, Francisco, "Fuente árabe de un cuento popular en el Lazarillo," *Boletín de la Real Academia Española* 45 (1965), pp. 493–495; Rumeau, Aristide, "Notes au Lazarillo: La casa lóbrega y oscura," *Les langues neo-latines* 173 (1965), pp. 16–25; Granja, Fernando de la, "Nuevas notas a un episodio del Lazarillo de Tormes," *Al-Andalus* 36 (1971), pp. 223–237; Marzolph, Ulrich, "Das Haus ohne Essen und Trinken: Arabische und persische Belege zu Mot. J 2483," *Fabula* 24 (1983), pp. 215–222; Vilanova, Antonio, "Reminiscencias del *Asno de oro* en 'la casa donde nunca comen ni beben' del *Lazarillo*," *Bulletin hispanique* 92.1 (1990), pp. 627–653.

3. Suárez López, Jesús, *Cuentos del Siglo de Oro en la tradición oral de Asturias*, s.l.: Red de Museos etnográficos de Asturias, 2009, p. 191, no. 54.

4. The original exclamation is "¡Me cago'n la madre que os parió!", literally "I shit on the mother that gave birth to you!"

5. Koen Sarano, Matilda, *Djoha ke dize? Kuentos populares djudeo espanyoles*, Jerusalem: Kana, 1991, p. 345; see Haboucha, Ginette, "The Judeo-Spanish Folktale: A Current Update," *Jewish Folklore and Ethnology Review* 15.2 (1993), pp. 32–38, at p. 36.

6. Marzolph, Ulrich, "Juḥā," in *Encyclopedia of Islam*, 3rd ed., Leiden: Brill, 2017, fasc. 5, pp. 139–141; Marzolph, "Zur Überlieferung der Nasreddin Hoca-Schwänke außerhalb des türkischen Sprachraumes," in *Türkische Sprachen und Kulturen: Materialien der 1. Deutschen Turkologen-Konferenz*, ed. Ingeborg Baldauf, Klaus Kreiser, and Semih Tezcan, Wiesbaden: Harrassowitz, 1991, pp. 275–285.

7. Núñez, P. Jésus, *Historias de curas*, Barcelona: Martínez Roca, 2002, pp. 59–60; Sánchez Ferra, Anselmo, *Un tesoro en el desván: los cuentos de mis padres*, Cabanillas del Campo (Guadalajara): Palabras del candil, 2009, no. 20. Yet another Spanish version was published in the *Revista Murciana de Antropología* 20 (2013): Sánchez Ferra, Anselmo J., *El cuento folklórico en Lorca*, vol. 1 (= *Revista Murciana de Antropología*), p. 301, no. 271.

8. See Marzolph, "Das Haus ohne Essen und Trinken," p. 219, note 22.

9. *La vida de Lazarillo de Tormes*, ed. Joseph V. Ricapito, 3rd ed., Madrid: Cátedra, 1977, p. 170.

10. Ayala, "Fuente árabe;" Shafa, Shojaeddin, *De Persia a la España Musulmana: La Historia Recuperada*, Huelva: Universidad de Huelva, 2000, p. 313.

11. Ibn ʿĀṣim al-Andalusī, Abū Bakr ibn Muḥammad, *Ḥadāʾiq al-azāhir*, ed. ʿAfīf ʿAbd al-Raḥmān, Beirut: Dār al-Masīra, 1401/1981, p. 150; see López Bernal, Desirée, "Los cuentos de Ibn ʿAsim (m. 1426): precedentes en la península ibérica de relatos españoles y del folklore universal en el siglo XV," *Hispanic Review* 85.4 (2017), pp. 419–440, at pp. 434–436.

12. For the phenomenon of the professional party-crasher in classical Arabic culture see Malti-Douglas, Fedwa, "Structure and Organization in a Monographic Adab Work: al-Taṭfīl of al-Khaṭīb al-Baghdādī," *Journal of Near Eastern Studies* 40 (1981), pp. 227–245.

13. Baihaqī, Ibrāhīm ibn Muḥammad al-, *Kitāb al-Maḥāsin val-Masāvī*, ed. Friedrich Schwally, Giessen: J. Ricker'sche Verlagsbuchhandlung, 1902, 340; Basset, *Mille et un contes*, vol. 1, p. 194, no. 46.

14. Ibn Abī ʿAwn al-Kātib, Ibrāhīm ibn Muḥammad, *Kitāb al-Ajwiba al-muskita*, ed. ʿAbd al-Qādir Aḥmad, Cairo 1985, p. 174; Yousef, May A., *Das Buch der schlagfertigen Antworten von Ibn Abī ʿAwn*, Berlin: Klaus Schwarz, 1988, p. 214, no. 1283.

15. Ibn al-Muʿtazz, *ʿAbdallāh* ibn Muḥammad *Ṭabaqāt al-shuʿarāʾ*, ed. ʿAbd al-Sattār Aḥmad Farrāg, Cairo: al-Maʿārif, 1375/1956, pp. 406–407.

16. Iṣfahānī, Abū ʾl-Faraj al-, *Kitāb al-Aghānī*, Būlāq (reprint Beirut: Ṣaʿb, ca. 1980), vol. 15, p. 37.

17. Marzolph, *Arabia ridens*, vol. 2, pp. 85–86, no. 340; Marzolph, "Das Haus ohne Essen und Trinken," p. 218.

18. Marzolph, *Arabia ridens*, vol. 2, p. 85, no. 340.

19. Marzolph, "Das Haus ohne Essen und Trinken," p. 219–221; Thompson, Stith, and Jonas Balys, *The Oral Tales of India*, Bloomington: Indiana University Press, 1958, p. 288, s.v. Mot. J2483.

20. Rumi, Jalāl al-Din, *The Mathnawí of Jalálu'ddín Rúmí*, transl. Reynold A. Nicholson, London: Luzac & Co., 1934, vol. 1, pp. 383–385 (bk. 2, verses 3116–3154), quotation p. 384; see Marzolph, Ulrich, "Mollā Naṣroddīn in Persia," *Iranian Studies* 28.3–4 (1995), pp. 157–174, at p. 161. A modern prose rendering of Rumi's verse is given by Arberry, Arthur John, *Tales from the Masnavi*, London: Allen & Unwin, 1961, p. 171, no. 57.

21. Zākāni, ʿObeydallāh, *Kolliyāt-e ʿObeyd-e Ẓākāni*, ed. Parviz Atābeki, Tehran 1331/1952, p. 348; Omidsālār, Maḥmud, "Molāḥażāti dar bāre-ye Laṭāʾef-e ʿObeyd-e Zākāni dar ʿResāle-ye delgoshāʾ," *Irān-nāme* 6.2 (1988), pp. 228–247, at p. 238.

22. Ṣafi, Fakhr al-Din ʿAli, *Laṭāʾef al-ṭavāʾef*, ed. Aḥmad Golchin-Maʿāni, Tehran: Moḥammad Ḥoseyn Eqbāl, 1336/1957, p. 390.

23. Christensen, Arthur, "Júhí in the Persian Literature," in ʿAǵab-nāma: *A Volume of Oriental Studies Dedicated to Edward G. Browne*, ed. Thomas W. Arnold and Reynold A. Nicholson, Cambridge: Cambridge University Press, 1922, pp. 129–136, at p. 131–132.

24. Marzolph, *Arabia ridens*, vol. 2, p. 86.

25. Wesselski, *Der Hodscha Nasreddin*, vol. 1, p. 127, 262, no. 229; Marzolph, *Nasreddin Hodscha*, p. 42, no. 70; Kut, Günay, "Nasreddin Hoca Hikâyeleri Yazmalarının Kolları Üzerine Bir Deneme," in *IV. Milletlerarası Türk Halk Kültürü Kongresi* Bildirileri, vol. 3: *Halk Edebiyatı*, Ankara, 1992, pp. 147–200, at p. 186, no. 220.

CHAPTER 47

The Liar Sows Discord between a Married Couple (ATU 1353)

The tale of the liar who succeeds in sowing discord between a married couple is both fairly old and widely distributed in Middle Eastern as well as European traditions. Classified as tale type ATU 1353: *The Old Woman as Trouble Maker*, the tale was studied several times since the end of the nineteenth century, resulting in long lists of the numerous corresponding versions identified in European literary sources or collected from nineteenth- and twentieth-century oral tradition.[1] Although the tale's historical dimension in classical Arabic literature has only recently been fully explored,[2] the various stages of the tale's historical development and its adaptations can now be reconstructed with a high degree of plausibility. In short, the tale is first attested in ninth-century Arabic ethical writings and was likely transmitted to the West through the adapted version cited in *Sefer sha'hu'im* (The Book of Delight), a "book-length fantasy of self-discovery"[3] compiled by the twelfth-century Hebrew author Joseph ibn Zabara. The Hebrew text resulted in a fair number of literary versions in Latin compilations of exempla and sermons[4] that in turn gave rise to numerous literary versions in the vernacular languages of both Western and Eastern Europe.[5] These again resulted in an equally large number of versions collected from nineteenth- and twentieth-century oral tradition. In its Arabic context, the tale was a somewhat cynical narrative about the unexpectedly dramatic consequences of a new acquisition, here a male slave who had been advertised as telling a big lie once a year. The Hebrew author adapted the tale as a misogynous narrative of moral and religious import, warning against women being more scheming and mischievous than the devil himself.

Considering the prominent role collections of tales for use in sermons played for the tale's international dissemination in Europe, one of the versions published by Stanislaus Prato as a comment to Hans Sachs's play *The Devil and the Old Woman* (1545) is particularly relevant. Prato mentions that version as having been told to him on April 7, 1896, by university librarian Francesco Prudenzano in Naples. The narrator informed the collector that he had heard the tale in 1839 being told by the preacher Nicolao Tortola in the main church of the town of Manduria in the Italian region of Apulia.[6]

> The devil seeks to sow discord between a loving couple, albeit without success. Meeting an old washerwoman, the devil promises to give her a pair of new shoes should she succeed. First, the washerwoman makes the wife suspect her husband of having a clandestine lover, in addition making her believe that the magic act of cutting three hairs from his beard would make him love her as before. Next the washerwoman makes the husband suspect that his wife is unfaithful and intends to kill him. Following her advice, the husband pretends to be sleeping the next night and catches his wife approaching his throat with a knife. The woman, however, manages to explain her action, and the couple is reconciled. When the devil realizes that the old woman achieved in two days what he had not been able to achieve in thirty years, he fears that she might even do harm to him. In order to keep a safe distance, he hands her the promised pair of shoes across the river, attached to a long pole.

The harmonious way in which the couple solves the situation in this version is fairly, though not extraordinarily, unusual, as more often than not the man kills his wife or gives her a heavy beating, an action traditionally regarded as suitable means to reform an unruly wife.[7] The devil's promise to reward the old woman with a pair of shoes is, however, a later addition to the plot that is first encountered in the late thirteenth- or early fourteenth-century German version of the anonymous jocular poem *Salomon and Morolf* (*Solomon and Marcolf*).[8] Texts following the oldest European version found in the twelfth chapter of Joseph ibn Zabara's *Sefer sha'hu'im* or its derivatives lack the devil's promise and usually have the tale culminate in a tragic ending, as the husband kills his wife for attempted murder. In retaliation, the man is killed by the woman's family, and the ensuing vendetta between the families results in the death of numerous people (more than 200 in *Sefer sha'hu'im*).[9]

Living in Spain, Joseph ibn Zabara in addition to Hebrew and Spanish knew Arabic, and there is little doubt that he adapted the tale from one of the Arabic versions accessible to him.[10] In particular, it was most likely this author who embellished and shaped the tale as a misogynous exemplum, introducing the devil as the instigator and the washerwoman as the prototypical scheming character, both of whom are not encountered in the tale's Arabic versions. The Arabic versions, the earliest of which predates Joseph ibn Zabara by three centuries, present the narrative's core concerning a habitual liar who succeeds in sowing discord between a loving couple. Although the narrative's main action is essentially identical to that of Joseph ibn Zabara, including the violent ending, the Arabic version has a male protagonist, thus lacking Ibn Zabara's misogynous tone.

The Arabic author to provide the tale's oldest version is ninth-century traditionist Ibn Abī 'l-Dunyā (d. 894). In two of his religiously edifying writings, the *Kitāb Dhamm al-ghība wa-'l-namīma* (The Book of Blame of Slander and Calumniation) and the epistle *al-Ṣamt wa ādāb al-lisān* (Silence and the Proper Conduct of the Tongue), he presents slightly diverging versions of a short anecdote that essentially goes as follows:[11]

> A man buys a male slave, notwithstanding the slave's declared fault of being a slanderer. After a while, the slave makes the man's wife believe that her husband loves another woman and intends to divorce her. In order to secure his love, she should cut some hair from his throat while he is asleep. At the same time, he tells the man that his wife intends to kill him, so that he better only pretend to be sleeping in order to be ready to stop her. When the woman approaches her husband at night with a knife in her hand, he suspects her of intending to kill him and kills her instead. Subsequently, the man is killed by the woman's family.

With little variation in content, although with a certain flexibility in wording, the tale is cited in a variety of Arabic works of an ethical, instructive, or simply entertaining character from the ninth to the nineteenth century, at a rate of approximately one attested occurrence per century. So far, the tale is known from al-Bayhaqī's tenth-century moralistic compilation *al-Maḥāsin wa-'l-masāwī* (The Good and the Bad Sides [of Things]),[12] Ibn Ḥibbān al-Bustī's (d. 965) *Rawḍat al-ʿuqalāʾ* (The Garden of the Wise),[13] al-Ghazzālī's (d. 1111) influential *Iḥyāʾ ʿulūm al-dīn* (The Revival of the Religious Sciences),[14] al-Rāfiʿī's (d. 1226) history of the city of Qazwin,[15] al-Dhahabī's (d. 1348) *Kitāb al-Kabāʾir* (The Cardinal Sins),[16] Ibn ʿArabshāh's (d. 1450) mirror for princes *Fākihat al-khulafāʾ* (The Fruits of the Caliphs),[17] Muḥammad ibn Aḥmad ibn (al-)Ilyās al-Ḥanafī's seventeenth-century compilation of amusing tales, *Nuzhat al-udabāʾ* (Entertainment of the Educated),[18] and al-Shirwānī's (d. 1840) *Nafḥat al-Yaman* (The Breeze from Yemen).[19]

The only major deviation from the standard plot is encountered in the version cited by Ibn ʿArabshāh. In terms of language, the usually short and concisely narrated tale is here presented with a somewhat baroque verbosity. In a shift of content, the slave is advertised as telling a lie "once every year." Perhaps due to this specification, in the first year the slave tells a lie that is vaguely reminiscent of tale type ATU 2040: *The Climax of Horrors* (see essay **101, *The Climax of Horrors***). When his master has gone to the public bath, the slave returns home wailing and lamenting, pretending that his master fell from his mule and broke his neck. Returning to his master, he lies to him that the house collapsed, killing all his family. Although the slave's invented news succeed in creating great concern and confusion, he is forgiven, and after a year his master has even forgotten about the slave's fault. Then the present tale's standard version follows, culminating in the husband killing his wife and being sentenced to death in retaliation. Incidentally, the plot of the first section of Ibn ʿArabshāh's version is also told by the second eunuch in the tale of Ghānim ibn Ayyūb in the standard versions of *The Thousand and One Nights*, embedded in the frame tale as the narrator's own adventure.[20] A close retelling of Ibn ʿArabshāh's version is also contained in a nineteenth-century neo-Aramaic manuscript.[21]

Sadid al-Din Moḥammad ʿAwfi's thirteenth-century Persian encyclopedia of traditional stories, *Javāmeʿ al-ḥekāyāt* (Collections of Stories), contains the only old non-Arabic version so far documented.[22] In most of the tale's Arabic versions, the magical procedure of using three hairs from the husband's beard to induce him to love his wife again is only vaguely described. In ʿAwfi's tale, the slave tells the woman explicitly that he knows a sorcerer who is so powerful that he can bring the moon down from the sky and make the fish come out of the sea. This sorcerer would use the three hairs to make a charm (Persian *ṭelesm*) that would induce her husband to fall in love with her again. A similarly elaborate procedure is only given in Ibn ʿArabshāh's version, in which the slave mentions a sorcerer who would induce the husband to love his wife forever by making him inhale the fumes from the burned hairs. Ibn Ḥibbān al-Bustī has the slave advise the woman to cense her husband with the fumes from the hairs, al-Ghazzālī has him inform the woman that he would use the hairs for a magic spell, and al-Rāfiʿī has the slave ask the woman to bring him three hairs from the husband's throat. All remaining versions do not specify the implied magic procedure.[23]

The tale's Arabic versions belongs to a scattered cluster of mainly jocular narratives that reflect a specific principle of Muslim customary law.[24] According to an ancient custom already known from Roman law, "a seller was legally accountable for damages if the slave he sold turned out to be defective."[25] By analogy, any item whose fault had not been explicitly advertised by the seller and acknowledged by the buyer could be returned. This aspect is only developed to some extent in the tale's version in *The Thousand and One Nights*, where the slave's owner is not permitted to return the "faulty" slave and instead has him castrated in punishment. Meanwhile, the legal principle creates a specific context that supplied additional meaning to the tale, particularly in a society whose economic success relied to a considerable extent on commerce. At the same time, virtually all of the Arabic versions leave little doubt that their main point is to rebuke lying, slander, and calumniation as morally detestable acts.

The tale of the liar who sows discord between a married couple shares its pattern of dissemination with numerous other narratives originating from Middle Eastern tradition, particularly those included in the large collections *Sendbād-nāme* (The Book of Sendbād [the Sage]) and *Kalila wa-Dimna*, both of which were transmitted East to West by Hebrew versions. The linguistic criteria mentioned in the above discussion—Arabic, Hebrew, Latin and the European vernacular languages—would usually correlate with religious criteria—Muslim, Jewish, and Christian. Read from a religious angle, the Muslim version takes place in the commercial context of a lay society, and its moralistic tone is so generally applicable that it does not bespeak a particular religious background. Meanwhile, the commercial aspect of possessing and trading human beings as slaves was not practiced in medieval European societies. Of course, the tale could have been translated and transmitted as taking place in a foreign society ruled by different laws and customs. But then it would have remained an exotic oddity lacking the appeal of a narrative from within one's own society. Already al-Dhahabī characterized the working of the slanderer as more harmful (*aḍarr*) than that of the devil, and tales of scheming old women abound in premodern and modern Muslim literatures. But (although oral versions might have served as intermediaries) it was only the Jewish author who, by introducing the devil and the habitually scheming old woman, adapted the tale to a religious and moral context that was perfectly acceptable for Christian standards, thus enabling the tale's wide European distribution as a religiously lined exemplum.

Notes

1. A representative list of documented literary and popular versions was published in Kasprzyk, Krystyna, *Nicolas de Troyes et le genre narratif en France au XVIe siècle*, Warsaw: Państwowe Wydawnictwo Naukowe, and Paris: Klincksieck, 1963, pp. 44–48; see also Lacarra, María Jesús, *Cuento y novela corta en España*, Barcelona: Crítica, 1999, pp. 287–290. For other lists of references see ATU 1353.

2. Marzolph, Ulrich, "Weib: Böses W. schlimmer als der Teufel," in *Enzyklopädie des Märchens*, vol. 14 (2014), cols. 551–555.

3. Brann, Ross, *Power in the Portrayal: Representations of Jews and Muslims in Eleventh- and Twelfth-century Islamic Spain*, Princeton: Princeton University Press, 2002, p. 153.

4. Wesselski, *Mönchslatein*, pp. 27–30, 206, no. 22.

5. Moser-Rath, *"Lustige Gesellschaft,"* p. 107.

6. Prato, Stanislaus, "Vergleichende Mitteilungen zu Hans Sachs Fastnachtspiel Der Teufel mit dem alten Weib," *Zeitschrift des Vereins für Volkskunde* 9 (1899), pp. 189–194, 311–321, at pp. 189–190.

7. See, e.g., Sheyn, Pavel Vasilyevich, *Materiali dlya izuchenija byta i yazika russkogo naseleniya severo-zapadnogo kraya*, Saint Peterburg: Imp. Akad. Nauk, 1893, pp. 135–137, no. 61; Barag, Lev G., *Belorussische Volksmärchen*, Berlin: Akademie-Verlag, 1966, pp. 397–400, no. 63; Kerbelytė, Bronislava, *Litauische Volksmärchen*, Berlin: Akademie-Verlag, 1978, pp. 310–314, no. 105.

8. Kasprzyk, *Nicolas de Troyes*, pp. 52–53, 59.

9. Ibid., pp. 50–51.

10. Schreiber, Eva, "Joseph ibn Sabara," in *Enzyklopädie des Märchens*, vol. 7 (1993), cols. 650–653.

11. Ibn Abī 'l-Dunyā, Abū Bakr ʿAbdallāh ibn Muḥammad, *Dhamm al-ghība wa-'l-namīma*, ed. ʿAbd al-Raḥmān Khalaf, Cairo: Dār al-Iʿtiṣām, 1989, p. 177–178, no. 132; see also p. 72–73; Ibn Abī 'l-Dunyā, *al-Ṣamt wa-ādāb al-lisān*, ed. Muḥammad ʿAbd al-Qādir Aḥmad ʿAṭā, Beirut: Mu'assasa al-kitāb al-thaqāfiyya, 1409/1988, p. 177, no. 270; the Notes to both editions also mention the tale as being quoted (from Ibn Abī 'l-Dunyā) in al-Murtaḍā al-Zabīdī's (d. 1791) *Itḥāf al-sāda* (ch. *al-ghība*).

12. Baihaqī, Ibrāhīm ibn Muḥammad al-, *Kitāb al-Maḥāsin val-Masāvī*, ed. Friedrich Schwally, Giessen: J. Ricker'sche Verlagsbuchhandlung, 1902, p. 614.

13. Ibn Ḥibbān al-Bustī, Abū Ḥātim ibn Muḥammad, *Rawḍat al-ʿuqalāʾ wa-nuzhat al-fuḍalāʾ*, ed. Muḥammad Muḥyī al-Dīn ʿAbd al-Raḥmān, Beirut: Dār al-Kutub al-ʿilmiyya, 1395/1975, p. 179–180.

14. Ghazzālī, Abū Ḥāmid Muḥammad al-, *Iḥyāʾ ʿulūm al-dīn*, Cairo: al-Kutub al-ʿarabiyya al-kubrā, s.a., p. 137 (bk. 4, ch. 16).

15. Rāfiʿī al-Qazwīnī, ʿAbd al-Karīm ibn Muḥammad al-, *Kitāb al-Tadwīn fī akhbār Qazwīn*, ed. ʿAzīzallāh al-ʿAṭāridī, Beirut: Dār al-Kutub al-ʿilmiyya, 1408/1987, vol. 3, p. 332.

16. Dhahabī, Shams al-Dīn Muḥammad ibn Aḥmad al-, *Kitāb al-Kabāʾir*, Cairo: al-Maktaba al-tijāriyya al-kubrā, 1385/1965, p. 156–157 (ch. 43).

17. Ibn ʿArabshāh, Aḥmad ibn Muḥammad, *Fākihat al-khulafāʾ wa-mufākahat al-ẓurafāʾ*, ed. Ayman ʿAbd al-Jabbār al-Buḥayrī, Cairo: Dār al-Āfāq, 1421/2001, pp. 157–159, no. 24 (ch. 4); Chauvin, *Bibliographie*, vol. 2 (1897), p. 195, no. 20.

18. Ḥanafī, Muḥammad ibn Aḥmad ibn (al-)Ilyās al-, *Nuzhat al-udabāʾ*, Gotha, Ms. Orient A 2706, fol. 31b–32a.

19. Shirwānī, Aḥmad ibn Muḥammad al-Anṣārī al-Yamanī al-, *Nafḥat al-Yaman*, Cairo 1356/1937, p. 51; Basset, *Mille et un contes*, vol. 2, pp. 186–187, no. 178; Rescher, Oskar, *Die Geschichten und Anekdoten aus Qaljûbî's Nawâdir und Schirwânî's Nafhat el-Jemen*, Stuttgart: W. Heppeler, 1920, pp. 259–260, no. 98.

20. See Marzolph, Ulrich, "Making Sense of the 'Nights:' Intertextual Connections and Narrative Techniques in the 'Thousand and One Nights'," *Narrative Culture* 1.2 (2014), pp. 239–258, particularly at pp. 247–250.

21. Lidzbarski, Mark, *Geschichten und Lieder aus den neu-aramäischen Handschriften der Königlichen Bibliothek zu Berlin*, Weimar: Felber, 1896, pp. 155–156, no. X (31).

22. Niẓámu'd-dín, *Introduction*, p. 228, no. 1722 (bk. 3, ch. 19). The tale's summary follows ʿAwfi, Sadid al-Din Moḥammad al-, *Matn-e enteqādi-ye Javāmeʿ al-ḥekāyāt wa-lavāmeʿ al-revāyāt*, book 3, part 2, ed. Amir Bānu Moṣaffā and Maẓāher Moṣaffā, Tehran: Bonyād-e Farhang-e Irān, 1353/1974, pp. 561–564.

23. For comments on the magical procedure in the tale's European versions see, e.g., Prato, "Vergleichende Mitteilungen," p. 319; Wesselski, *Märchen des Mittelalters*, p. 196, no. 6; Kuder, Ulrich, "Haar, Haare," in *Enzyklopädie des Märchens*, vol. 6 (1990), cols. 337–343.

24. Marzolph, "Making Sense," pp. 248–249; Marzolph, *Arabia ridens*, vol. 1, pp. 210–211.

25. Baldwin, Barry, *The Philogelos, or Laughter-Lover*, Amsterdam: Gieben, 1983, p. 58.

CHAPTER 48

The Frightened Person Withdraws the Vow to Die Instead of a Close Relative (ATU 1354)

On April 23, 1936, the flutist (*dulzainero*) Juan Pascual Alonso, aged 55, from Aldeonsancho in the province of Segovia in central Spain, narrated the following tale,[1] a version of tale type ATU 1354: *Death for the Old Couple.*[2]

> Both partners of a married couple often confess their unconditional love to each other, vowing that each of them prefers to die sooner than the other, so that the other could live on. The husband, however, mistrusts his wife's repeated vows and decides to test her. At first, he makes her believe that Death is a creature whose skin is totally bare. Soon after he plucks a rooster and one night sets it free in their bedroom, pretending that Death has come. While the man hides himself in a corner of the room, the rooster goes after the woman who is so frightened that she shouts, "Bald Death (*muerte pelada*), you have certainly come for my husband who hides in the corner!" Hearing this, the husband gets out of his hiding place and gives his wife a heavy beating. The next day he eats the rooster without sharing it with her, not even letting her have the bird's tail.

The tale's version performed in November 1983 by Fermín Palomino Fernández, aged 49, from central Spain, introduces a priest and his aged mother, both of whom vow that they want to die sooner than the other if Death should come.[3] Plucking a chicken, the man one day pretends that Death has come, and when his mother sees the creature, she shouts, "You have come for my son!" In May 1985, the housewife Emilia Caballero González, aged 58, from Orallo in the Spanish province of Léon, narrated yet another version.[4] Here, the woman is so sick that she is afraid to die soon. When she sees a chicken with a bald throat she assumes that this must be Death and shouts, "Bald Death, go to the oven, that's where my husband is!" Numerous other versions were recorded from oral tradition of the Iberian Peninsula.[5] German versions of the tale likewise often feature a plucked rooster or a goose as the alleged personified Death.[6] In the early twentieth-century tale told by Alfons Perlick from Rokittnitz in Silesia, the woman denounces her husband.[7] In the tale told by Mrs. Köppen, the wife of a simple laborer from Waren in Mecklenburg-Vorpommern, in the 1890s, the woman asks Death to take her aged father who is sitting by the oven.[8] In tales from Slavonic tradition in the Balkans, Death usually appears in person, and the frightened woman tells Death to take either her husband[9] or her grandson.[10] In corresponding texts from the Americas the married couple is frightened by a trickster.[11]

The tale was disseminated in popular tradition through a fair number of iterations in collections of jocular tales in Italian, Latin, Spanish, French, German (and probably other European languages) since the fourteenth century.[12] The tale's oldest documented European version is the novella "De mulieri adultera" (The Adulterous Woman) in Italian author Giovanni Sercambi's late fourteenth-century *Novelliere*, featuring a man who uses a rooster to frighten his wife who is having an affair with the local priest.[13] The equally influential versions in Italian author Laurentius Abstemius's *Hecatomythion* (1539) and, closely following him, in German author Burkard Waldis' *Esopus* (1548)[14] are short, featuring personified Death.

The tale's oldest version currently known is contained in Persian mystical poet Sanā'i's (d. 1131) *Ḥadiqat al-ḥaqiqa* (The Garden of Truth).[15] The tale introduces an old woman in the village of Takāv[16] and her daughter Mahseti who own three cows. When Mahseti falls seriously ill, her mother is so worried that she frequently wishes her own death to precede her daughter's. One day, one of the cows gets its head jammed in a pot. When the old woman sees the creature running toward her, she assumes it to be ʿAzrā'il, the angel of Death. Fearing that he has come to take her, she cries out, "I am not Mahseti. If it is Mahseti whom you want, she is over there!"

Shortly after Sanā'i and closely following his poem, Abu 'l-Maʿāli Naṣrallāh Monshi integrated the verse narration into his early twelfth-century adapted Persian prose translation of Ibn al-Muqaffaʿ's eighth-century Arabic rendering of the fable collection *Kalīla wa-Dimna*.[17] Following this, the tale was retold in a number of subsequent Persian adaptations of *Kalile va Demne* whose content is based on Naṣrallāh Monshi's version. This includes the widely read elaborate prose version with interspersed lines of poetry in Vāʿeẓ Kāshefi's early sixteenth-century adaptation of the fable collection, *Anvār-e Soheyli* (The Lights of Soheyli)[18] and its derivatives.[19]

Although Sanā'i likely relied on an Arabic source, no occurrence of the tale predating Sanā'i has so far been identified. Meanwhile, classical Arabic literature knows a similarly structured joke attributed to Ibn Abī ʿAtīq, a seventh-century poet who was so renowned for his jocular ways that al-Ābī (d. 1030) devoted a whole chapter to him in his encyclopedia of jokes and anecdotes, *Nathr al-durr* (Pearls of Prose).[20] In addition to al-Ābī,[21] other eleventh-century authors such as al-Ḥuṣrī (d. 1015)[22] and al-Thaʿālibī (d. 1038)[23] cite the following anecdote in identical structure, though different wording. Contrasting with the tale's other versions, in the anecdote both characters are witty and affectionate, not fools. Joking about death and their human fears they are not so obviously victimized by their fears.

> Ibn Abī ʿAtīq visited his paternal aunt, ʿĀʾisha bint Ṭalḥa, when she was mortally ill. Asking her how she was, Ibn Abī ʿAtīq added the common verbiage, "May I be sacrificed in your stead!" (*juʿiltu fidāki*; literally, "May I be your ransom!") ʿĀʾisha asked, "Even in death?" And Ibn Abī ʿAtīq was quick to respond, "In that case, no ransom! I had thought there was still more time left!" Upon which ʿĀʾisha laughed and said, "You never drop your jocular ways, do you?"

In addition to potentially existing oral intermediaries, a possible link between Naṣrallāh Monshi's twelfth-century text and the tale's first occurrence in fourteenth-century Italian literature could, of course, be Sanāʾi's unidentified (and probably Arabic) source. Another link may be suggested by the fact that Naṣrallāh Monshi's Persian adaptation of *Kalile va Demne* enjoyed such a great reputation that it was even translated to Arabic.[24] The translation was prepared by a certain ʿUmar ibn Dāʾūd ibn Shaykh Sulaymān al-Fārisī and dedicated to one of the descendants of the ruler Ṣalāḥ al-Dīn Ayyūbī (d. 1260), better known in European tradition as Saladin. The translation's existing manuscript was copied in 1327. Although this date is a few decades later than the end of the Frankish hold on the East during the Crusades (1291), the early fourteenth-century Arabic translation of the twelfth-century Persian work might nevertheless indicate that the work or the tales it included already enjoyed a certain popularity in the Levantine countries in the thirteenth century and could thus, potentially, have been available to the European crusaders whose narration might eventually have inspired Sercambi.

Once more, it is interesting to witness how European tradition adapted the tale. Originally taking place between two female characters, one of whom is admittedly somewhat simple-minded, European tradition predominantly shaped the events as a misogynist conflict between a married couple, with the wife not only being gullible but also treacherous and faithless. The beating the husband gives his wife in compensation for her faithlessness would likely have added to the amusement of historical (male) audiences in Europe, supporting, as it does, stereotypes of female shortcomings and male superiority. Although the tale's "Oriental" version already plays on old women's gullibility and foolishness, the tale's European versions thus added a whole new layer of interpretation.

Notes

1. Espinosa, Aurelio Macedonio, Jr., *Cuentos populares de Castilla y Leon*, vol. 2, Madrid: Consejo Superior de Investigaciones Científicas, 1988, pp. 149–150, 502, no. 294.

2. Steinbauer, Bernd, "Tod der Alten," in *Enzyklopädie des Märchens*, vol. 13 (2011), cols. 712–715.

3. Lorenzo Vélez, Antonio, *Cuentos anticlericales de tradición oral*, Valladolid: Ámbito, 1997, p. 86–87.

4. Camarena Laucirica, Julio, *Cuentos tradicionales de León*, vol. 2, Madrid: Universidad Complutense, Seminario Menendez Pidal, 1991, pp. 39, 259, no. 170.

5. Meier, Harri, and Dieter Woll, *Portugiesische Märchen*, Düsseldorf: Diederichs, 1975, pp. 219–220, 270–271, no. 15; Cardigos, Isabel, *Catalogue of Portuguese Folktales*, Helsinki: Suomalainen Tiedeakatemia, 2006, pp. 279–280, no. 1354; Noia Campos, Camiño, *Catálogo tipolóxico do conto galego de tradición oral: clasificación, antoloxía e bibliografía*, Vigo: University of Vigo, 2010, pp. 584–586, no. 1354; Raba Saura, Gregorio, and Anselmo J. Sánchez Ferra, "La memoria obstinada: Referencias clásicas de la tradición oral en la región de Murcia," *Mastia: Revista del museo arqueológico de Cartagena* 10.2011 (2017), pp. 121–200, at p. 158.

6. Uther, *Deutscher Märchenkatalog*, p. 346, no. 1354.

7. Peuckert, Will-Erich, *Schlesiens deutsche Märchen*, Breslau: Ostdeutsche Verlagsanstalt, 1932, pp. 506–507, 653, no. 229.

8. Neumann, Siegfried, *Plattdeutsche Schwänke: Aus den Sammlungen Richard Wossidlos und seiner Zeitgenossen sowie eigenen Aufzeichnungen in Mecklenburg*, Rostock: VEB Hinstorff Verlag, 1968, pp. 162, 222, no. 274.

9. Vrčević, Vuk, *Srpske narodne pripovijetke, ponajviše kratke i šaljive*, vol. 2, Belgrade: Srpska kraljevska državna štamparija, 1882, p. 99; Bošković-Stulli, Maja, "Usmene propovijetke i predaje s otoko Brača," *Narodna Umjetnost* 11–12 (1975), pp. 5–150, at pp. 67, 129, no. 21.

10. Vrčević, *Srpske narodne pripovijetke*, vol. 1 (1868), p. 69, no. 154; Karadžić, Vuk Stefanović, *Srpske narodne pripovetke*, 4th ed., Belgrade, 1937, p. 300, no. 67.

11. Parsons, Elsie Clews, *Folk-lore of the Antilles, French and English*, vol. 2, New York: American Folk-lore Society, 1936, pp. 57–58, no. 46; Rael, Juan B., *Cuentos españoles de Colorado y Nuevo Méjico: Spanish Originals with English Summaries*, vol. 1, Stanford: Stanford University Press, 1940, pp. 131, 631, no. 69.

12. Montanus, Martin, *Schwankbücher (1577–1566)*, ed. Johannes Bolte, Tübingen: Litterarischer Verein in Stuttgart, 1899, pp. 105–106, 579, no. 41; Wesselski, Albert, "Das Geschenk der Lebensjahre," *Archiv orientální* 10 (1938), pp. 79–114, at pp. 109–110; Chevalier, *Cuentos folklóricos*, p. 196, no. 119; Uther, *Deutscher Märchenkatalog*, p. 346, no. 1354.

13. Sercambi, Giovanni, *Il novellieri*, ed. Luciano Rossi, vol. 1, Rome: Salerno, 1972, pp. 100–105, no. 13.

14. Burkard Waldis, *Esopus: 400 Fabeln und Erzählungen nach der Erstausgabe von 1548*, ed. Ludger Lieb, Jan Mohr, and Herfried Vögel, vol. 1, Berlin: De Gruyter, 2011, p. 173, no. II 85 (Abstemius, no. 60).

15. Wesselski, "Das Geschenk," p. 109; Kuka, Meherjibhai Nosherwanji, *Wit, Humour and Fancy of Persia*, new impression, Bombay 1937, pp. 124–125, no. 3.

16. Although a village by that name exists, the name was obviously introduced only to rhyme with the second hemistich's final word *gāv* (cow).

17. Naṣrallāh Monshi, Abu 'l-Ma'āli, *Tarjome-ye Kalile va Demne*, ed. Mojtabā Minovi Ṭehrāni, Tehran: Dāneshgāh-e Ṭehrān, 1343/1964, pp. 288–290; Nasrollah Monschi, *Kalila und Dimna: Fabeln aus dem klassischen Persien*, transl. and ed. Seyfeddin Najmabadi and Siegfried Weber, Munich: C.H. Beck, 1996, pp. 237–238.

18. Chauvin, *Bibliographie*, vol. 2 (1897), p. 124, no. 119; Vā'eẓ Kāshefi, Kamāl

al-Din Ḥoseyn ibn ʿAli, *Anvār-e Soheyli yā Kalile va Demne-ye Kāshefi*, Tehran: Amir Kabir, 1362/1983, pp. 406–407; see Grube, Ernst J., "Prolegomena for a Corpus Publication of Illustrated *Kalīlah wa Dimnah* Manuscripts," *Islamic Art* 4 (1990–1991), pp. 301–481, at p. 446 (ch. 12, C.29).

19. See, e.g., Hertel, Johannes, *Indische Märchen*, Düsseldorf: Diederichs, 1953, pp. 351–352, no. 86.

20. Ābī, Abū Saʿd Manṣūr ibn al-Ḥusayn al-, *Nathr al-durr*, ed. Muḥammad ʿAlī Qarna et al., vol. 7, Cairo: al-Hayʾa al-miṣriyya al-ʿāmma lil-kitāb, 1991, pp. 331–340.

21. Ibid., p. 331.

22. Ḥuṣrī al-Qayrawānī, Abū Isḥāq Ibrāhīm ibn ʿAlī al-, *Jamʿ al-jawāhir fī ʾl-mulaḥ wa-ʾl-nawādir*, ed. ʿAlī Muḥammad al-Bijāwī, Cairo: Dār Iḥyāʾ al-kutub al-ʿarabiyya, 1372/1952, p. 55.

23. Thaʿālibī, Abū Manṣūr ʿAbd al-Malik ibn Muḥammad, *Kitāb Laṭāʾif al-ṣaḥāba wa-ʾl-ṭābiʿīn* (selections), in Cool, P., *Brevis Chrestomathia*, in Roorda, T., *Grammatica Arabica*, Leiden: S. and J. Luchtmans, 1835, pp. 1–31 (Arabic text), at p. 2. I owe the reference to Chauvin, *Bibliographie*, vol. 2 (1897), p. 124, no. 119.

24. Omidsalar, Mahmoud, "Kalila wa Demna ii. The translation by Abu'l-Maʿāli Naṣr-Allāh Monši," in *Encyclopædia Iranica* http://www.iranicaonline.org/articles/kalila-demna-ii (accessed March 16, 2018); Ghofrāni, Moḥammad, "Noṣuṣ-e nā-shenākhte az Kelile va Demne," *Maqālāt va bar-resi-hā* 7–8 (1971), pp. 54–97, at pp. 64–65.

CHAPTER 49

The Weighed Cat (ATU 1373)

In his small collection of jocular tales on the stereotypically silly "Wise Men of Mols," the prolific collector of Danish folklore, Evald Tang Kristensen (1843–1929),[1] published a total of three versions[2] of a short tale recorded from Danish oral tradition in which a dog is blamed for eating a certain amount of butter. The tale classifies as a version of tale type ATU 1373: *The Weighed Cat*[3] adapted to the Danish context.

> A skipper who was very stingy would not give his crew any butter. One day, as they landed, the crew took seven pounds of butter stored in a bucket to treat themselves with it, and agreed to blame the dog for having eaten it. The skipper picked up a scale and weighed the dog. When it weighed just seven pounds, he exclaimed indignantly, "Seven pounds of dog and seven pounds of butter—may the devil take the dog if it has eaten my butter!"

The other two versions Kristensen published are equally short but stress the claim's absurdity further by having the dog weigh even less than the amount of butter it is said to have eaten. The tale's versions documented from Southern and South-Eastern Europe (Italy, Hungary, Macedonia, Bulgaria) are geographically close to Middle Eastern tradition from which they probably derive more or less directly. Sparsely documented versions from Northern European tradition in Latvia, Ireland, and the Netherlands might originate from their publication in calendars that would sometimes draw on "Oriental" sources.[4] Two German versions dating from the second half of the seventeenth century are known. In 1669, the tale is cited in a German chapbook.[5]

> Of two neighbors. One woman complained to her neighbor that the latter's cat had eaten her two pounds of veal. "No," said the neighbor, "my cat is well-behaved and gets enough to eat so that it has no need to go hunt anywhere else." And so that everybody should see that the other woman was quarrelsome and false, she took her cat to the street and put it on a scale. It turned out that the cat weighed less than two pounds altogether.

In 1671, Hans Jakob Christoph von Grimmelshausen, in a continuation of the adventures of his picaresque hero Simplicius Simplicissimus, has the hungry children of a stingy notary steal the tripe he bought and blame the cat. The cat, however, weighs just less than the missing tripe.[6] The tale's oldest-known version in a European language is attested in *Las tardes de Alcázar* compiled in 1636 by Spanish author Juan de Robles.[7] In this version, the cat only weighs a pound and a half although the woman claims it has eaten a pound of meat. In Spain, the tale had a certain repercussion in nineteenth- and twentieth-century literature and popular tradition.[8]

The tale's oldest documented version altogether is cited in the book on misers compiled by the Arabic polymath al-Jāḥiẓ (d. 868).[9] Here, the narrator is a nephew of Muslim theologian and ascetic Wāṣil ibn ʿAṭāʾ (d. 748). Wāṣil is particularly known for founding the religious movement known as Muʿtazila, a school of Islamic theology based on reason and rationalist thought that flourished in the cities of Basra and Baghdad during the eighth to tenth centuries. The narrator introduces the tale with the phrase "*qad aḥsana*" (He did well), indicating approval for the protagonist's rational arguing. The tale's punch line is short, as the protagonist simply says, "If this is the meat, then where is the cat?" A somewhat elaborated version in which the amount of meat is specified as being three *raṭl* or pounds is contained in Andalusian author Ibn ʿĀṣim's (d. 1426) *Ḥadāʾiq al-azāhir* (Flower Gardens).[10]

The Persian poet Jalāl al-Din Rumi (d. 1273) adapted the tale in his mystical *summa*, the *Masnavi-ye maʿnavi*, characterizing the man's wife as "sneering, dirty, and rapacious."[11] He also extended the punch line to the later standard reading, "If this is the cat, then where is the meat? Or, if this is the meat, where is the cat?" Whereas in the *Masnavi*, the tale provokes the author to go into lengthy mystical considerations about the ways in which body and spirit are inseparably linked to each other, the chronologically next occurrence in Persian poet ʿAbd al-Raḥmān Jāmi's (d. 1492) *Haft owrang* (Seven Thrones) cites it as a mere, albeit profound, joke.[12]

In nineteenth- and twentieth-century Middle Eastern tradition, the tale is stereotypically attributed to the Arabic jester Juḥā and his Turkish alter ego Nasreddin Hodja. With this attribution, the tale is first documented in the earliest-known printed version of Juḥā's jests in Arabic, published in Cairo by Florentine printer Moshe Castelli in 1861.[13] Here, Juḥā's wife prepares the three pounds (*raṭl*) of meat he bought for their meal and feasts on it with her lover, at her husband's return blaming the cat for having eaten the meat. When Juḥā finds the cat to weigh exactly three pounds, he exclaims, "If this is the cat, then where is the meat? And, if this is the meat, where is the cat?" The attribution to Juḥā/Nasreddin Hodja enabled the tale's wide geographic dissemination in the Islamicate world, extending from North Africa and the Balkans to Middle Asia and China.

Notes

1. Kofod, Else Marie, "Kristensen, Evald Tang," in *Enzyklopädie des Märchens*, vol. 8 (1996), cols. 468–471.

2. Kristensen, Evald Tang, *Molbo- og Aggerbohistorier, samt andre dermed beslægtede fortællinger* [vol. 1], Viborg: backhausen, 1892, p. 112, nos. 352 (translated), 351; [vol. 2], p. 9, no. 15.

3. Marzolph, Ulrich, "Katze: Die gewogene K.," in *Enzyklopädie des Märchens*, vol. 7 (1993), cols. 1109–1111.

4. Brunold-Bigler, Ursula, "Kalender, Kalendergeschichte," ibid., vol. 7 (1993), cols. 861–878; Kooi, Jurjen van der, "Een rechter tie-zaak in Drenthe. Chinese volksverhalen in hest westen; een probleemveld," *Driemaandelijkse Bladen voor taal en volksleven in hest oosten van Nederland* 39 (1987), pp. 133–157; Marzolph, *Arabia ridens*, vol. 1, pp. 76–77.

5. Wolgemuth, Ernst, *500 / Frische und vergüldete / Haupt-Pillen [. . .]*, Warhausen im Warnethal 1669, vol. 1, p. 26, no. 73; the full version of the baroque title is given by Moser-Rath, *"Lustige Gesellschaft,"* p. 475.

6. German Schleifheim von Sulsfort, *Gantz neu eingerichteter allenthalben viel verbesserter abentheuerlicher Simplicius Simplicissismus*, Mompelgart: Fillion, [ca 1671], p. 373 (bk. 3, ch. 24); see Wesselski, Albert, *Das lachende Buch*, Leipzig: Johannes M. Meulenhoff, 1914, pp. 41–42.

7. Gómez Camacho, Alejandro, "Los cuentos en la obra de Juan de Robles," *Etiópicas* 2 (2006), pp. 202–254, at p. 249; López Bernal, Desirée, "Procedencia árabe de un cuentecillo singular en la obra de Juan de Robles," *Hipogrifo* 4.1 (2016), pp. 217–230; López Bernal, *Los Ḥadāʾiq al-azāhir de Abū Bakr ibn ʿĀṣim al-Garnāṭī: Traducción y estudio de una obra de adab de la Granada nazarí*, 2 vols., Ph.D. thesis University of Granada, 2016, vol. 2, pp. 155–156, no. 326.

8. López Bernal, Desirée, "De criadas, sisas y gatos: huellas de un cuento folclórico árabe (ATU 1373) en la España de los siglos XIX y XX," *Boletín de Literatura Oral* 8 (2018), pp. 73–96.

9. Jāḥiẓ, ʿAmr ibn Baḥr al-, *al-Bukhalāʾ*, ed. Ṭāhā al-Ḥājirī, Cairo: Dār al-Maʿārif, 1981, p. 145.

10. Ibn ʿĀṣim al-Andalusī, *Ḥadāʾiq al-azāhir*, ed. ʿAfīf ʾAbd al-Raḥmān, Beirut: Dār al-Maṣīra, 1401/1981, p. 108; López Bernal, *Los Ḥadāʾiq al-azāhir*, vol. 1, p. 184.

11. Rumi, Jalāl al-Din, *The Mathnawí of Jalálu'ddín Rúmí*, transl. Reynold A. Nicholson, vol. 3, London: Luzac & Co., 1934, pp. 204–205 (bk. 5, prose summary and verses 3410–3418); see Schimmel, Annemarie, *The Triumphal Sun: A Study of the Works of Jalāloddin Rumi*, Albany: State University of New York Press, 1993, pp. 98–99; Kuka, Meherjibhai Nosherwanji, *Wit, Humour and Fancy of Persia*, new impression, Bombay 1937, pp. 140–141, no. 11. A modern prose rendering of Rumi's verse is given by Arberry, Arthur John, *More Tales from the Masnavi*, London: Allen & Unwin, 1963, p. 148, no. 160.

12. Jāmi, Nur al-Din ʿAbd al-Raḥmān ibn Aḥmad, *Maṡnavi-ye Haft owrang*, ed. Mortażā Modarres Gilāni, Tehran: Saʿdi, 1337/1958, p. 213; Qeisari, Ebrāhim, "Ma'khaẕ-e barkhi az dāstānhā-ye Haft owrang," *Jostārhā-ye adabi* 20.3 = 78 (1366/1987), pp. 599–644, at p. 616–617; Clouston, William Alexander, *Flowers from a Persian Garden and Other Papers*, London: David Nutt, 1890, p. 80; Kuka, *Wit, Humour and Fancy of Persia*, pp. 141–142. Referring to Paul Horn's essay "Zu Hodža Nasreddin's Schwänken," *Keleti*

Szemle 1 (1900), pp. 66–72, at p. 71, Wesselski, *Der Hodscha Nasreddin*, vol. 2, p. 185, no. 348, erroneously states the tale also to be included in the collection of jokes compiled by Persian author ʿObeyd-e Zākāni (d. 1371).

13. Juḥā, *Hādhihi nawādir al-khūjah Naṣr al-Dīn Afandī Juḥā al-Rūmī*, Būlāq: Mūsā Kāstillī, 1278/1861, p. 7; see Wesselski, *Der Hodscha Nasreddin*, vol. 2, p. 7, 185, no. 348.

Test of Self-Composure: Small Animal Escapes When Lid of Vessel Is Lifted (ATU 1416)

The monumental collection of folktales, *Latviešu pasakas un teikas* (Latvian Fairy Tales and Legends), amassed by Latvian linguist and folklorist Pēteris Šmits (1869–1938),[1] incorporates a vast amount of material from a variety of earlier collections. A tale contributed by J. Lautenbach (1847–1928), of which more than a dozen additional Latvian versions are documented,[2] is about a poor peasant couple blaming the biblical Adam for their misery.

> Toiling to gather wood in the forest, a poor peasant couple blames Adam for being the cause of their misery. When a rich man overhears their complaints, he invites them to join him in his mansion and enjoy a lavish life without having to work. The only condition he sets is that by no means should they ever lift the lid of a bowl placed on the table. For a long time, the couple enjoys the good life. But one day they can no longer contain their curiosity and lift the bowl's lid. No sooner have they done this than a mouse jumps out of the bowl and vanishes. The landlord appears and angrily asks them to leave, telling them from now on to blame themselves for their misery.

The tale is a version of tale type ATU 1416: *The Mouse in the Silver Jug* of which numerous texts were recorded from all over Europe.[3] Whereas the Latvian version holds both characters responsible for not being able to contain their curiosity, most other versions of the tale put the blame on the woman. In a German version recorded by the teacher Hermann Galbach in Gross Jerutten, East Prussia, in 1938, the old man is so happy about his master's invitation that he "would have liked to lie down on the bench by the stove and take a nap."[4] Several times he manages to prevent his wife from uncovering the dish, but finally she succeeds, and the master drives them out of the house with his horsewhip. In another German version from Bavaria collected by Ludwig Aurbacher (1784–1847) and preserved in the unpublished archived materials of the brothers Grimm, the king invites the poor lumberjack and his wife to join him in his palace.[5] On the seventh day, the curious woman finally succeeds in pushing her husband to open the lid, and the king has them dress in their rags again and orders them thrown out of the palace. At times, the woman's insistence on lifting the lid is further emphasized by an explicitly misogynist commentary such as when the narrator of a Ukrainian version says, "Of course, women want to have a look at what is in there, and so she could not restrain herself."[6] Rarely, the poor man is invited all by himself, such as in a late nineteenth-century English tale narrated by E.S. Hartland, as heard by him from his childhood nurse.[7] Most often, the animal escaping from the bowl is a mouse or, as in the French version narrated by Marie Rouzaud from Ariège in South-Western France, a rat.[8]

Primarily in versions recorded from oral tradition in the Iberian Peninsula, the escaping animal is a bird[9] or, as in the folktale narrated by Abelino Ponte, aged 72, from Tenorio, Pontevedra, in North-Western Spain in 1977, a butterfly.[10] The latter tale is explicitly titled "It's the Woman's Fault." The versions mentioning a bird show a somewhat greater variation in plot. In the tale narrated in May 1986 by Ricardo Árias Martínez from Villalibre de Somoza, aged 74, the parrot a man wants to present to the queen is inadvertently set free by the queen's curious court ladies.[11] In a version from Santiponcé, Sevilla, Saint Teresa of Ávila (d. 1582) wonders why she should not be allowed to receive confessions and shrive people. In order to test her, God orders her to keep a box closed for three days. When she opens the lid before the agreed time, the bird contained in the box flies away, and God takes this as a proof that she is not able to keep a secret, even if only for three days.[12] A tediously pedagogical version from Spain introduces a mother admonishing her little daughter not to open a certain box while she is away.[13] When the girl opens the box and the two parrots inside escape, she is advised by an old man to clean herself and dress nicely, following which the parrots are willing to return to the box. In the end, the girl promises to herself from now on always to obey her mother's instructions.

Popularized in European tradition by its publication in historical chapbooks[14] and almanacs,[15] the tale's two strands of tradition are richly documented in medieval and early modern literature.[16] Versions mentioning a flying animal apparently derive from a somewhat younger tradition initiated by Caesarius of Heisterbach (d. after 1240) and Stephen of Bourbon (Étienne de Bourbon; d. 1261),[17] while versions with a mouse are documented slightly earlier, as they are first narrated by Marie de France (d. about 1200)[18] and Jacques de Vitry (d. 1240).[19] Contrary to the paired protagonists in popular tradition, the main character in the two latter versions is a hermit who admonishes a man who resents Adam for having transgressed the prohibition to eat fruits from the tree of knowledge. In Jacques de Vitry's version, the admonished person is another hermit, in Marie de France's he is a layman.

The tale's Arabic versions precede the earliest documented European versions at least by about a century and a half.[20] Apparently first told in Abū Nuʿaym al-Iṣfahānī's (d. 1038) *Ḥilyat al-awliyāʾ wa-ṭabaqāt al-aṣfiyāʾ* (The Adornment of the

Friends of God and the Ranks of the Pure Ones), completed in 1031, the tale is presented as a hagiographic legend attributed to the famous mystic Abū 'l-Fayḍ Thawbān ibn Ibrāhīm, commonly known as Dhū 'l-Nūn al-Miṣrī (d. 859).[21] It is told as a personal experience by Abū Ya'qūb Yūsuf ibn al-Ḥusayn al-Rāzī (d. 916), himself a renowned Sufi.[22]

> When the narrator was in Mecca, he learned that Dhū 'l-Nūn actually knew God's greatest name (*ism Allāh al-a'ẓam*), an arcane knowledge that is considered to grant unlimited powers. When he met Dhū 'l-Nūn in the Egyptian town al-Gizeh, the latter appeared to be irritated by his attire, as Yūsuf looked like a beggar with his long beard, wearing a cloth around his waist and a coat on his shoulders, his bare feet full of weals. Some days later, Yūsuf impressed the mystic by rebutting a theologian who had previously had the better of Dhū 'l-Nūn, so that the latter treated him with respect and kindness from now on. Having stayed in Dhū 'l-Nūn's company for a whole year and assuming to have gained his confidence, Yūsuf finally took courage to inform Dhū 'l-Nūn about his ardent wish to learn God's greatest name from him, as he deemed himself worthy of such a powerful and precious knowledge.
>
> For the following six months, Dhū 'l-Nūn does not mention the affair. Finally, he asks Yūsuf to deliver a closed vessel wrapped in a piece of cloth as a present to one of Dhū 'l-Nūn's friends in Fusṭāṭ (today in Southern Cairo). As the vessel is very light, after a while Yūsuf wonders what is inside. When his curiosity brings him to open the vessel's lid, a mouse jumps out. Furious about the presumed mockery, Yūsuf returns to Dhū 'l-Nūn. But when Dhū 'l-Nūn sees him, he guesses what happened and addresses him with these words, "You fool! I entrusted a mouse to you and you betrayed me. How can I entrust God's greatest name to you? Leave me alone, go away, and never let me see you again!"

As one of the most important sources on the early history of Muslim mystics, or Sufis, Abū Nu'aym al-Iṣfahānī's work exerted a tremendous influence, and the tale under consideration is quoted from his work many times in subsequent centuries in more or less the same words. The range of relevant sources extends from al-Khaṭīb al-Baghdādī's (d. 1071) *Tārīkh Baghdād* (History of Baghdad)[23] via Ibn Abī Ya'lā's (d. 1131) *Ṭabaqāt al-ḥanābila* (The Ranks of the Ḥanbalites, the followers of the legal school initiated by Ibn Ḥanbal),[24] Ibn al-Jawzī's (d. 1201) historical work *al-Muntaẓam* (The Orderly Arrangement),[25] and the same author's compilation of entertaining tales about clever people, *Akhbār al-Adhkiyā'*,[26] al-Qazwīnī's (d. 1283) geographical work *Āthār al-bilād* (Traces of the Countries)[27] and Ibn 'Asakir's (d. 1176) *Tārīkh madīnat Dimashq* (History of Damascus)[28] as well as its abridgment by Ibn Manẓūr (d. 1311)[29] to Ibn Ḥijja al-Ḥamawī's (d. 1434) entertaining anthology *Thamarāt al-awrāq* (The Fruits of the [Scattered] Leaves).[30] An elaborated Persian adaptation of the tale is presented in Farid al-Din ʿAṭṭār's (d. 1221) *Tadhkirat al-awliyā'* (Memorial of God's Friends).[31] Considering its wide publication, the tale is a standard feature in the biography of Yūsuf ibn al-Ḥusayn al-Rāzī.

Another Arabic tale in which the motif of the escaping animal plays a slightly different role is already known from a tenth-century source. The tale attributes the act to the *qāḍī* Jaʿfar ibn ʿAbd al-Wāḥid al-Hāshimī (d. 871) who is otherwise infamous as an unreliable (*kadhdhāb*) transmitter of traditions of the Prophet Muḥammad.[32] In this tale, the small animal kept in a closed vessel is a bee, or rather two bees, and the purpose is not so much a demonstration of a character's overt curiosity or unreliability. Instead, the bees prove to the vessel's recipient whether the person delivering the goods inside opened the vessel unauthorized so as to avail himself of its content. The earliest-known version of this tale is contained in the tenth-century book *al-Tuḥaf wa-'l-hadāyā* (Gifts and Presents) compiled by the two sons of Hāshim al-Khālidī, Abū Bakr Muḥammad (d. 990) and Abū ʿUthmān Saʿīd (d. 981).[33] The tale introduces Jaʿfar ibn ʿAbd al-Wāḥid as a downright stingy (*bakhīl*) character. During the season, one of his friends in Samarra used to send him a basket full of fresh dates every now and then. Since the basket arrived in disorder, the recipient suspected the slave delivering the basket of having touched its contents. At first, Jaʿfar advised his friend to seal the basket's lid. Since the basket still arrived in disorder, as an additional provision he then instructed his friend to put two bees inside the basket before sealing the lid. That way, if the bees flew out when he opened the basket, he would know for certain that nobody had opened it before arrival. In addition to its earliest occurrence, this tale is contained in al-Khaṭīb al-Baghdādī's (d. 1071) book *al-Bukhalā'* (Misers),[34] Ibn ʿAsākir's (d. 1176) *Tārīkh madīnat Dimashq*[35] and its abridgment by Ibn Manẓūr (d. 1311),[36] and Andalusian author Ibn ʿĀṣim's (d. 1426) *Ḥadā'iq al-azāhir* (Flower Gardens).[37] The tale is also cited in a modern anthology of tales from Arabic tradition, *Qiṣaṣ al-ʿarab* (Tales of the Arabs).[38]

Further substantiating the popularity of the latter tale in ninth-century Arabic tradition is a short passage in the famous epistle in praise of stinginess attributed to Sahl ibn Hārūn (d. 830), a character who held important administrative positions during the time of the caliphs Hārūn al-Rashīd and his son al-Ma'mūn.[39] Without developing any action, the author defends himself against the reproach of having sealed a basket full of costly fruits and choice dates so as to protect it against the greed of a gluttonous slave (*ʿabd nahim*) and other characters he considered unreliable, a child, a maidservant, and a stupid wife. First published by polymath al-Jāḥiẓ (d. 868) in his book on stingy people, *al-Bukhalā'*,[40] the epistle containing the said passage is later cited in almost the same wording in Ibn ʿAbd Rabbih's (d. 940) *adab* work *al-ʿIqd al-farīd* (The Unique Necklace)[41] and al-Nuwayrī's (d. 1332) *Nihāyat al-arab fī funūn al-adab* (The Ultimate Ambition in the Arts of Erudition).[42]

Considering the textual evidence presented above, it is tempting to relate the two strands of European tradition, one with a rodent (a mouse or a rat), and the other one with a flying animal (a bird or a butterfly), to the two different strands of tradition documented in premodern Arabic literature, one equally with a mouse, and the other one equally with flying animals (two bees). Both Arabic strands of tradition were available in the period when cultural contacts during the Crusades (1095–1291) might have effected their transmission East to West. Although the two Arabic strands of tradition are distinct in their content, structure, and intention, they overlap in the motif of the fugitive animal or animals enclosed in a vessel, a motif that is somewhat reminiscent of the ancient myth of "Pandora's box."[43] Whereas the context of the bee version is mundane and humorous, actually mocking the miser's precautions, the mouse version is an outright didactic tale in a serious religious and hagiographic context. In Muslim tradition, the knowledge of God's greatest name is equally laden with meaning and as connected with powerful consequences as is Adam's transgression in paradise in Christian tradition, and the acting characters' inappropriate curiosity is equally unacceptable in both the Muslim and the Christian contexts. If the assumption of relating the two European and Arabic strands of tradition to each other is feasible, the mundane context of the Arabic bee version was lost in favor of the religious message that is dominant in the mouse versions, whether Christian or Muslim. The mouse versions (including the adapted Christian European bird version) also overlap to some extent in their underlying ethical message, as the texts from both traditions warn against hubris, instead advocating that one should be conscious of one's own limitations and content with one's own lot. But whereas the Christian tale by implication aims to discipline the poor so that those in power can continue to exploit their labor, the Muslim tale emphasizes the position of the "friends of God," those exceptional characters who through their true devotion and abstention from selfish desires gain a powerful knowledge whose exclusivity also entails that it will rarely, if ever, be put to practice. Incidentally, the present tale is another example of a tale whose misogynist tendency, if the tale indeed migrated East to West, was only introduced when the tale was adapted to the Christian context. All of the characters acting in the older Arabic versions are male, and human foibles such as curiosity and disobedience in the mouse version, and gluttony as well as stinginess in the bee version, are attributed exclusively to these male characters. Only the Christian versions, many of which relate the tale to the biblical story of Adam and Eve from the very beginning, put the blame on the woman's action, and even in versions in which the man opens the vessel's lid, he often does so because his wife pressed him to satisfy her curiosity. In terms of its general structure and narrative dynamics, the tale is ruled by the motif of the interdiction, a motif that in many tales is linked to the prohibition against opening a specific door.[44] Of course, the interdiction arouses curiosity and, in terms of narrative dynamics, serves to propel the tale's action.[45]

Notes

1. Pakalns, Guntis, "Šmits, Pēteris," in *Enzyklopädie des Märchens*, vol. 1 (2007), cols. 798–800.

2. Šmits, Pēteris, "Ādams un Ieva," *Latviešu tautas teikas un pasakas*, ed. Haralds Biezais, 2nd ed., vol. 11, Waverly, Iowa: Latvju Grāmata, 1968, pp. 407–408, no. 90; Arājs, Kārlis, and Alma Medne, *Latviešu pasaku tipu rādītājs*, Riga: Zināne, 1977, p. 184, no. 1416.

3. Schwarz, Paul, "Eva: Die neue E.," in *Enzyklopädie des Märchens*, vol. 4 (1984), cols. 563–569.

4. Ranke, Kurt, *Folktales of Germany*, Chicago: The University of Chicago Press, 1966, pp. 183–184, 230–231, no. 75.

5. Rölleke, Heinz, *Märchen aus dem Nachlaß der Brüder Grimm*, 2nd ed., Bonn: Bouvier, 1979, pp. 45–46, 101, no. 15; Meier, Ernst, *Deutsche Volksmärchen aus Schwaben: Aus dem Munde des Volks gesammelt*, Stuttgart: Scheitlin, 1852, pp. 241–242, 315, no. 67.

6. Lintur, Petro V., *Ukrainische Volksmärchen*, Berlin: Akademie-Verlag, 1972, pp. 606–608, 789, no. 100.

7. Jacobs, Joseph, *More English Fairy Tales*, London: D. Nutt, 1894, pp. 109–110, 231, no. 67; Briggs, *A Dictionary*, vol. A1, p. 279.

8. Joisten, Charles, *Contes populaires de l'Ariège*, Paris: Maisonneuve et Larose, 1965, pp. 160–163, no. 24.

9. See, e.g., Espinosa, Aurelio Macedonio, Jr., *Cuentos populares de Castilla y Leon*, vol. 1, Madrid: Consejo Superior de Investigaciones Científicas, 1987, pp. 38–39.

10. Rey-Henningsen, Marisa, *The Tales of the Ploughwoman*, Helsinki: Suomalainen Tiedeakatemia, 1996, pp. 25–26, no. 9.

11. Camarena Laucirica, Julio, *Cuentos tradicionales de León*, vol. 2, Madrid: Universidad Complutense, Seminario Menendez Pidal, 1991, p. 66, no. 191.

12. Espinosa, Aurelio Macedonio, *Cuentos populares españoles recogidos de la tradición oral de España*, vol. 1, Madrid: Consejo Superior de Investigaciones Científicas, 1946, pp. 136–137; vol. 2, 308–310, no. 76.

13. Jiménez Roberto, Alfonso, *La flor de la florentena: cuentos tradicionales*, ed. Melchor Pérez Bautista and Juan Antonio del Río Cabrera, Sevilla: Fundación Machado, 1990, pp. 203–204, 259, no. 60.

14. Uther, *Deutscher Märchenkatalog*, p. 371, no. 1416.

15. Van der Kooi, Jurjen, and Babs A. Gezelle Meerburg, *Friesische Märchen*, Munich: Diederichs, 1990, pp. 120–122, 349–350, no. 39.

16. Tubach, *Index exemplorum*, pp. 266–267, no. 3427.

17. Wesselski, *Mönchslatein*, pp. 110–111, 233–234, no. 94.

18. Marie de France, *Fables*, ed. and transl. Harriet Spiegel, Toronto: University of Toronto Press, 1987, pp. 156–159, no. 53.

19. Jacques de Vitry, *The Exempla or Illustrative Stories from the Sermones Vulgares*, ed. Thomas F. Crane, London: Nutt, 1890, p. 4, no. 13.

20. Merceron, Jacques, "Des souris et des hommes: pérégrination d'un motif narratif et d'un *exemplum* d'Islam en chrétienté. À propos de la fable de 'L'Ermite' de Marie de France et du fabliau de *La Sorisete des Estopes*," *Cahiers de civilisation médiévale* 46.181 (2003), pp. 53–69. The author ignores important folklorists' contributions to the tale's history, such as Wesselski, Albert, *Klaret und sein Glossator: Böhmische Volks- und Mönchsmärlein im Mittelalter*, Brünn: Rohrer, 1936, pp. 85–87, no. 79, and Schwarz, "Eva: Die neue E."

21. Abū Nuʿaym al-Iṣfahānī, Aḥmad ibn ʿAbdallāh, *Ḥilyat al-awliyāʾ wa-ṭabaqāt al-aṣfiyāʾ*, ed. Ṣāliḥ Aḥmad al-Shāmī, vol. 9, Cairo: Maktabat al-Khānjī, 1938, pp. 386–387. French translation in Merceron, "Des souris," pp. 58–59.

22. Arberry, Arthur J., *Muslim Saints and Mystics: Episodes from the Tadhkirat al-Auliya' (Memorial of the Saints) by Farid al-Din Attar*, London: Routledge & Kegan Paul, 1966, p. 185.

23. Khaṭīb al-Baghdādī, Abū Bakr Aḥmad ibn ʿAlī al-, *Tārīkh Baghdād*, Cairo: Maktabat al-Khānjī, 1931, vol. 14, pp. 316–317.

24. Ibn Abī Yaʿlā, Abū ʾl-Ḥusayn Muḥammad, *Ṭabaqāt al-ḥanābila*, ed. Muḥammad Ḥāmid al-Faqī, Cairo: Maṭbaʿat al-sunna al-muḥammadiyya, 1371/1952, vol. 1, pp. 419–420, in no. 548.

25. Ibn al-Jawzī, Abū ʾl-Faraj ʿAbd al-Raḥmān ibn ʿAlī, *al-Muntaẓam fī tārīkh al-mulūk wa-ʾl-umam*, ed. Muḥammad ʿAbd al-Qādir ʿAṭā, Muṣṭafā ʿAbd al-Qādir ʿAṭā, Nuʿaym Zarzūr, 2nd ed., vol. 13, Beirut: Dār al-Kutub al-ilmiyya, 1415/1995, pp. 171–172, no. 3133.

26. Ibn al-Jawzī, Abū ʾl-Faraj ʿAbd al-Raḥmān ibn ʿAlī, *Akhbār al-Adhkiyāʾ*, ed. Muḥammad Mursī al-Khūlī, Cairo, 1970, pp. 90–91; Marzolph, *Arabia ridens*, vol. 1, pp. 251–252, no. 10; vol. 2, p. 254, no. 1182.

27. Qazwīnī, Zakariyyā ibn Muḥammad ibn Maḥmūd al-, *Āthār al-bilād wa-akhbār al-ʿibād*, Beirut: Dār Ṣādir, 1380/1960, p. 140.

28. Ibn ʿAsākir, Abū ʾl-Qāsim ʿAlī ibn al-Ḥasan ibn Hibat Allāh ibn ʿAbdallāh, *Tārīkh Madīnat Dimashq*, vol. 74, ed. Muḥibb al-Dīn Abū Saʿīd ibn Gharāma al-ʿAmrawī, Beirut: Dār al-Fikr, 1421/2001, pp. 223–224, in no. 10183.

29. Ibn Manẓūr, Muḥammad ibn Mukarram, *Mukhtaṣar Tārīkh Dimashq*, ed. Rūḥiyya al-Naḥḥās, Damascus: Dār al-Fikr, 1984, vol. 28, pp. 73–74.

30. Ibn Ḥijja al-Ḥamawī, ʿAlī ibn Muḥammad, *Thamarāt al-awrāq*, ed. Mufīd Qumayḥa, Beirut: Dār al-Kutub al-ʿilmiyya, 1403/1983, pp. 121–122.

31. ʿAṭṭār, Farid al-Din, *Tadhkirat al-awliyāʾ*, Mirzā Moḥammad-Khān Qazvini, 3rd ed., Tehran: Ketābkhāne-ye markazi, 1336/1957, vol. 1, p. 281–282; English translation by Losensky, Paul, *Farid al-din ʿAṭṭār's Memorial of God's Friends: Lives and Sayings of Sufis*, New York: Paulist Press, 2009, pp. 308–309.

32. Ibn Ḥajar al-ʿAsqalānī, Shihāb al-Dīn Abū ʾl-Faḍl Aḥmad ibn ʿAlī, *Lisān al-mīzān*, ed. ʿAbd al-Fattāḥ Abū Ghadda and Salmān ʿAbd al-Fattāḥ Abū Ghadda, Beirut: Maktabat al-maṭbūʿāt al-islāmiyya, 1423/2002, vol. 2, p. 457, no. 1861.

33. Khālidī, Abū Bakr Muḥammad ibn Hāshim al- and Abū ʿUthmān Saʿīd ibn Hāshim al- (known as al-Khālidīyān, i.e., the two Khālidīs), *al-Tuḥaf wa-ʾl-hidāyā*, ed. Sāmī al-Dahhān, Cairo: Dār al-Maʿārif, 1956, p. 105.

34. Khaṭīb al-Baghdādī, Abū Bakr Aḥmad ibn ʿAlī al-, *al-Bukhalāʾ*, ed. Aḥmad al-Maṭlūb, Khadīja al-Ḥadīthī, and Aḥmad Nājī al-Qaysī, Baghdad: Maṭbaʿat al-ʿĀnī, 1384/1964, p. 75; Marzolph, *Arabia ridens*, vol. 1, p. 251, no. 10.

35. Ibn ʿAsākir, Abū ʾl-Qāsim ʿAlī ibn al-Ḥasan ibn Hibat Allāh ibn ʿAbdallāh, *Tārīkh Madīnat Dimashq*, vol. 72, ed. Muḥibb al-Dīn Abū Saʿīd ibn Gharāma al-ʿAmrawī, Beirut: Dār al-Fikr, 1421/2001, p. 136, no. 9806.

36. Ibn Manẓūr, Muḥammad ibn Mukarram, *Mukhtaṣar Tārīkh Dimashq*, ed. Rūḥiyya al-Naḥḥās, Damascus: Dār al-Fikr, 1984, vol. 6, pp. 75–76.

37. Ibn ʿĀṣim al-Andalusī, Abū Bakr ibn Muḥammad, *Ḥadāʾiq al-azāhir*, ed. ʿAfīf ʿAbd al-Raḥmān, Beirut: Dār al-Masīra, 1401/1981, p. 226; see López Bernal, Desirée, *Los*

Ḥadāʾiq al-azāhir de Abū Bakr ibn ʿĀṣim al-Garnāṭī: Traducción y estudio de una obra de adab de la Granada nazarí, vol. 1, Ph.D. thesis University of Granada, 2016, p. 356, no. 799.

38. Shams al-Dīn, Ibrāhīm, *Qiṣaṣ al-ʿarab*, Beirut: Dār al-Kutub al-ʿilmiyya, 1423/ 2002, p. 335.

39. Malti-Douglas, Fedwa, *Structures of Avarice: The Bukhalāʾ in Medieval Arabic Literature*, Leiden: E.J. Brill, 1985, pp. 47–50.

40. Jāḥiẓ, ʿAmr ibn Baḥr al-, *al-Bukhalāʾ*, ed. Ṭāhā al-Ḥājirī, Cairo: Dār al-Maʿārif, 1981, p. 10; Pellat, Charles, transl., *Le livre des avares de Ǧāḥiẓ*, Paris: G.P. Maisonneuve, 1951, p. 15.

41. Ibn ʿAbd Rabbih, Abū ʿUmar Aḥmad ibn Muḥammad, *Kitāb al-ʿIqd al-farīd*, ed. Aḥmad Amīn, Aḥmad al-Zayn, Ibrāhīm al-Abyārī, 3rd ed., vol. 6, Cairo: Lajnat al-ta'līf wa-'l-tarjama wa-'l-nashr, 1368/1949, p. 200.

42. Nuwayrī, Shihāb al-Dīn Aḥmad ibn ʿAbd al-Wahhāb al-, *Nihāyat al-arab fī funūn al-adab*, vol. 3, Cairo: Dār al-Kutub al-miṣriyya, 1369/1949, p. 318.

43. Bies, Werner, "Pandora," in *Enzyklopädie des Märchens*, vol. 10 (2002), cols. 505–510.

44. Rieken, Bernd, "Zimmer: Das verbotene Z.," ibid., vol. 14 (2014), cols. 1358–1362.

45. Goldberg, Christine, "Verbot," ibid. 3 (2019), cols. 1389–1396.

CHAPTER 51

The Tricky Lover Regains the Gift He Gave for Intercourse (ATU 1420G)

Sexually explicit folktales have rarely received the folklorists' attention they deserve.[1] Historical audiences are known to have derived tremendous joy from reading, listening to, and telling "bawdy" tales, as evidenced by such genres as the French *fabliau*, the German *Märe*, or the Italian Renaissance *novela*. But the scientification of Western scholarly approaches toward natural phenomena advocated by the Enlightenment resulted in a gradual marginalization of sexuality and its eventual relegation to the obscurity of little-explored privacy. Consequently, the stiffy of a medieval tale might be bowdlerized as a sausage, as argued, for instance, in the discussion of tale type ATU 750A: *The Three Wishes* (see essay **17, *The Foolish Couple Waste the Three Wishes They Have Been Granted***). When tales were recorded from living oral tradition in the nineteenth and twentieth centuries, moral standards as to what was deemed suitable for presentation to the general public would at best allow publication of tales of a bawdy or "obscene" nature in special collections "only for scholars, not intended for sale in bookshops."[2] Until the present day, these publications enjoy a somewhat ambiguous status, being at the same time attractive and entertaining as well as morally questionable. Early publications of sexually explicit folklore are due to the efforts of the Austrian folklorist Friedrich Salomo Krauss (1859–1938)[3] and the journals *Anthropophyteia* (1904–1913) and *Kryptádia* (1883–1911). Published around the end of the nineteenth and the beginning of the twentieth century, these ventures were devoted to the study of erotic and explicitly sexual as well as scatological folklore.[4] More recent publications in a similar vein include those of US scholars Vance Randolph (1892–1980)[5] and Gershon Legman (1917–1999).[6] Although often marked by the male chauvinist attitudes of their times, these publications constitute invaluable historical sources supplying a glimpse into a facet of narrative culture that apparently was as popular with the original audiences as it suffered, and continues to suffer, from the scholarly stigma of being morally objectionable.

The above discussion is particularly pertinent for the presently concerned tale type ATU 1420: *The Lover's Gift Regained*.[7] Stith Thompson's content description of the sexually explicit subtype AT 1420G: *Anser Venalis*, now ATU 1420G: *Buying the Goose*, bashfully sums up: "The lover regains his gift by a ruse (obscene)."[8] Essentially, the subtype plays on the different positions the partners practice during intercourse. Specifically, the tricky man claims that when the woman was on top of him, he did not have sex with her but rather she had sex with him. Consequently, he successfully demands another round to fulfill the agreed-upon bargain. Versions of the tale recorded from oral tradition are rare and have exclusively been published from the Slavonic language area.[9] The Ukrainian peasant Vassyl Jupyk from Cherkhava narrated his version in December 1899 in Drohobych to the collector V. Łevynśkyj.[10]

> On the market in Sambir, a farmer proposes to sell a fat rooster to a woman in exchange for "playing with her a little bit." At first, the woman refuses to accept the deal. Soon after, however, she repents and sends her maid to buy the rooster. The maid equally refuses to act according to the man's wishes. The woman then sends the maid to bring the farmer to her house and accepts his offer, on condition that she will have the upper position during intercourse. When leaving, the farmer wants to take his rooster along, arguing that he did not have sex with her, but rather she had sex with him. After a second intercourse, this time with him in the upper position, the farmer again wants to leave with the rooster, arguing that it was in fact the maid who bought the bird. As they start to quarrel, the woman's husband arrives, and the woman is forced to pretend that their quarrel concerned the rooster's price. In order to get rid of the farmer as quickly as possible, she pays him three *gulden*.

Vasjko (Ivan) Dedyk narrated the tale somewhat differently in July 1900 in Morosovychi, district Sambir, as recorded by V. Boberśkyj.[11]

> As Ivan's wife Marynka wants to sell their goose one day on the market in Sambir, her husband tells her to sell the bird only "for the regular market price." A male customer leaves his gown with the woman as a security, taking the bird and her new fur coat along. Promising to pay the following market day, he never returns. Aiming to make up for the loss, Ivan later brings the gander to the market and offers to trade it for a woman's sexual favors. After having sex with the woman, he gets ready to leave together with the bird, demanding to be paid for his efforts since he did all the work while the woman remained passive. Since the woman's husband arrives during their quarrel, he receives two *gulden* for the goose. Returning home, he brags to his wife that not only did he sell the bird for a good price but also fucked his customer.

The Russian version published in Aleksandr Afanasyev's *Russian Secret Tales* introduces a hunter who has had no luck for two days.[12] Promising to sell his next prey for a woman's sexual favors, he catches a grouse. The female customer who is interested to buy the bird on his conditions tells him that her conscience does not allow her to lie under him. Having had sex in that position, the man claims that "It was not I who futtered you, but you who futtered me." After the next round with changed positions, he claims that now they are only just even. But after the third round, he is obliged to let the woman have the bird and returns home empty-handed. An unspecified Croatian narrator from Zagreb added additional scenes in which the tricky peasant first manages to eat and drink his fill without having to part with his hare.[13] When he offers to sell the hare for sex, he shows so little passion in the act that the woman gets on top of him, giving him the opportunity to argue later that she had sex with him, and not he with her. Taking his hare, he leaves, accompanied by the woman's curses. In a Serbian tale, after the peasant had sex with the woman, she volunteers for a second round during which she is on top.[14] This enables him to argue later that she did not fulfil the condition, since now they are only just even.

In the European literatures, numerous versions of the tale are attested over the centuries,[15] the earliest one contained in the collection of facetious tales compiled around the middle of the fifteenth century by papal secretary Poggio Bracciolini.[16] Poggio's version is about a peasant lad who brings a goose to the market in Florence. After his female customer had sex with him twice in different positions, the woman's husband arrives and the woman is forced to pretend that their quarrel concerned the bird's price: they allegedly agreed to a price of twenty *soldi*, but now he asked for two additional *soldi*. The good-natured husband gives him the money, because, as he says, "that little extra money should not keep us from having a good meal."

The tale's oldest documented version is contained in the little-known Arabic collection of proverbs and related stories *Nuzhat al-anfus wa-rauḍat al-majlis* (Entertainment of the Spirits and Garden of the Convivial Gathering) compiled by a certain Raḍiyy al-Dīn al-ʿIrāqī (d. 1166).[17] Here, the tale is told about the popular fool and jester Juḥā.[18]

> One day, Juḥā buys a fine piece of silk cloth on the market. On the way back home, he gets thirsty and rests on the threshold of a certain house. The beautiful wife of the owner notices him, and when she sends her maid to ask him what he wants, he tells her that he is looking for someone to have sex with him in exchange for the silk cloth. Told his answer by her maid, the woman takes him in. Although she tries to evade a direct commitment by offering him any of her maids, he insists on having sex only with her. She is so disgusted by his dirty and smelly dress that she asks him to lie down so that she can get on top of him. He has sex with her a second time to "get even," and leaves the silk cloth with her after the third time.
>
> Once outside, instead of going away, Juḥā asks one of the maids for some water and lets the jug fall to the ground intentionally. When the owner of the house returns, Juḥā pretends that the man's wife took the silk

cloth from him in compensation for the broken jug. As the woman is not in a position to counter his claim, her husband returns the cloth to him.

A shorter version told on the authority of the philologist and historian Abū ʿUbayda Maʿmar ibn al-Muthannā (d. 825) is given in Ibn al-Jawzī's (d. 1201) *Akhbār al-Adhkiyāʾ* (Tales of Clever People).[19] Here, the poet al-Farazdaq (d. ca. 730) gives his gown for a single act of intercourse with the lady of the house who is advised by her maid not to see anything wrong about it, since "that Arab is not known to anybody." Having broken the glass with which he was offered the requested drink, al-Farazdaq manages to regain his gown when the woman's husband returns. In his fifteenth-century erotic manual *al-Rawḍ al-ʿāṭir fī nuzhat al-khāṭir* (The Perfumed Garden for the Entertainment of the Mind), the author al-Nafzāwī presents a lavishly extended version that takes specific delight in embellishing the explicitly sexual scenes.[20] The protagonist of this text is the Wise Fool Buhlūl with whom Ḥamdūna, the sister of Caliph al-Maʾmūn (d. 833) and wife of his grand vizier, has sex because she covets a golden dress the caliph gave Buhlūl as a present. Claiming that his back hurts, Buhlūl has her get on top at first. Other than that, al-Nafzāwī's version closely follows the one given by Raḍiyy al-Dīn al-ʿIrāqī. In the seventeenth century, the latter version is quoted verbatim in the extensive compilation of Arabic stories on Juḥā compiled by Yūsuf ibn al-Wakīl al-Maylāwī.[21] In Persian literature, the tale is first attested by the satirist ʿObeyd-e Zākāni (d. ca. 1371). In his *Resāle-ye delgoshā* (The Heart-Refreshing Epistle), Zākāni tells the tale about an adolescent Juḥā who is sent by his father to sell two fishes.[22] In this version, the woman takes the initiative to suggest sex in exchange first for one of the fishes, and then for the second one. The tale finishes with the episode of the broken glass at the end of which Juḥā regains both of his fishes.

In terms of typological classification, the tale's extended version in the *Nuzhat al-anfus* consists of two sections that have been taken to define two distinct tale subtypes. While the triple (or, in some of the later versions, double) intercourse in the tale's first section corresponds to tale type ATU 1420G, the final section was classified as tale type ATU 1420A: *The Broken (Removed) Article.* Ancient Indian literature, particularly the Sanskrit *Śukasaptati* (Seventy [Tales of a] Parrot), knows various analogous tales mentioning a single act of love making after which the lover employs a ruse to regain the gift he has given for intercourse.[23] These tales are similar in structure to the simple version in Ibn al-Jawzī's *Akhbār al-Adhkiyāʾ*. The ingenious combination of both subtypes as first documented in twelfth-century Arabic literature presents a logically structured tale whose protagonist is victorious not just once but twice, thus creating additional amusement and satisfaction for the tale's audience. Although the male fantasy of the multiple sexual exploitation of a gullible woman together with the added evasion of promised payment offers a great potential for chauvinist identification and entertainment, the woman's willingness to commodify her sexuality is a remarkable aspect of female agency. Although the available documentation on sexually explicit tales such as the present one is inadequate, it is likely that the tale's complex version did not have a marked impact on oral tradition whereas the ancient tale's first half is known to have lived on separately.

Notes

1. Röhrich, Lutz, "Erotik, Sexualität," in *Enzyklopädie des Märchens*, vol. 4 (1984), cols. 234–278; Fährmann, Sigrid, "Obszönitäten," ibid., vol. 10 (2002), cols. 178–183; Zolkover, Adam D., "Bawdy Tale," in Duggan, Anne E., and Donald Haase, eds., *Folktales and Fairy Tales*, Santa Barbara, CA: Greenwood, 2016, vol. 1, pp. 104–105; Seiffert, Lewis C., "Sex, Sexuality," ibid., vol. 3, pp. 907–911; Jorgensen, Jeana, "Erotic Tales," ibid., vol. 1, pp. 303–305.

2. Tarasevśkyj, Pavło, and Hnatjuk, Vołodymyr, *Das Geschlechtleben des ukrainischen Bauernvolkes in Österreich-Ungarn*, vol. 2, ed. Vołodymyr Hnatjuk, Leipzig: Ethnologischer Verlag, 1912.

3. Köhler-Zülch, Ines, "Krauss, Friedrich Salomo," in *Enzyklopädie des Märchens*, vol. 8 (1996), cols. 352–358.

4. Lixfeld, Hannjost, "Anthropophyteia," ibid., vol. 1 (1977), cols. 596–601; Uther, Hans-Jörg, "Kryptádia," ibid., vol. 8 (1996), cols. 528–531.

5. Lindahl, Carl, "Randolph, Vance," ibid., vol. 11 (2004), cols. 192–194.

6. Marzolph, Ulrich, "Legman, Gershon," ibid., vol. 8 (1996), cols. 875–877.

7. Spargo, John Webster, *Chaucer's Shipman's Tale: The Lover's Gift Regained*, Helsinki: Suomalainen Tiedeakatemia, 1930; Nicholson, Peter, "The Medieval Tale of the Lover's Gift Regained," *Fabula* 21 (1980), pp. 200–222; Nicholson, "Pfand des Liebhabers," in *Enzyklopädie des Märchens*, vol. 10 (2002), cols. 842–849.

8. Aarne, Antti, *The Types of the Folktale: A Classification and Bibliography, Antti Aarne's Verzeichnis der Märchentypen [. . .] Translated and Enlarged*, ed. Stith Thompson, Helsinki: Suomalainen Tiedeakatemia, (1961) 1973, p. 420.

9. Moser-Rath, Elfriede, "Anser venalis," in *Enzyklopädie des Märchens*, vol. 1 (1977), cols. 576–577.

10. Tarasevśkyj and Hnatjuk, *Das Geschlechtleben*, pp. 287–288, no. 303.

11. Ibid., pp. 288–290, no. 304.

12. Afanasyev, Aleksandr Nikolaevich, *Russian Secret Tales: Bawdy Tales of Old Russia*, ed. Alan Dundes, Baltimore: Clearfield, 1998, pp. 56–57; Afanas'ev, A.N., "Contes secrets traduits du Russe," *Kryptádia* 1 (1883), pp. 1–292, at pp. 67–68, no. XXIX.

13. Krauss, Friedrich S., "Südslavische Volksüberlieferungen, die sich auf den Geschlechtsverkehr beziehen, 1: Erzählungen," *Anthropophyteia* 1 (1904), pp. 1–506, at pp. 410–412, no. 312.

14. Ibid., pp. 412–413, no. 313.

15. Pitrè, Giuseppe, "Note comparative al I vol. del *Kryptádia*," *Kryptádia* 4 (1888), pp. 192–261, at pp. 200–202; Spargo, *Chaucer's Shipman's Tale.*

16. Poggio Bracciolini, Gian-Francesco, *Die Schwänke und Schnurren*, ed. Alfred Semerau, Leipzig: Deutsche Verlags-Actiengesellschaft, 1905, pp. 69–70, 216, no. 69.

17. Sellheim, Rudolf, "Eine unbeachtet gebliebene Sprichwörtersammlung: Die *Nuzhat al-anfus wa-rauḍat al-maclis* des Raḍīaddīn al-ʿIrāqī (468/1075–561/1166)," *Oriens* 31 (1988), pp. 82–94.

18. Marzolph, *Arabia ridens*, vol. 2, p. 251, no. 1166; translation vol. 1, pp. 252–253, no. 11.

19. Ibn al-Jawzī, Abū 'l-Faraj, *Akhbār al-Adhkiyā'*, ed. Muḥammad Mursī al-Khūlī, Cairo 1970, p. 112; Spargo, *Chaucer's Shipman's Tale*, p. 32.

20. Nafzāwī, al-Shaykh al-, *al-Rawḍ al-'āṭir fī nuzhat al-khāṭir*, ed. Jamāl Jum'a, London: Riad El-Rayyes, 1990, pp. 36–42; Nafzawi, Muhammad ibn Muhammad al-, *The Perfumed Garden of Sensual Delight (ar-rawḏ al-'âṯir fî nuzhati 'l-khâṯir)*, transl. Jim Colville, London, New York: Kegan Paul International, 1999, pp. 12–17; Nafzâwî, *Der duftende Garten: Ein arabisches Liebeshandbuch*, transl. Ulrich Marzolph, Munich: C.H. Beck, 2002, pp. 23–32; Spargo, *Chaucer's Shipman's Tale*, pp. 32–33; for the protagonist Buhlūl, see Marzolph, Ulrich, *Der Weise Narr Buhlūl*, Wiesbaden: Franz Steiner, 1983, p. 50, no. 87; Marzolph, *Bohlul-nāme*, ed. Bāqer Qorbāni-Zarrin, 3rd ed., Tehran: Behnegār, 1392/2013, pp. 149–150, no. 87.

21. 'Anābsa, Ghālib, "Min adab al-nawādir: naẓra fī makhṭūṭāt [Irshād] man naḥā ilā nawādir Juḥā, jam' al-faqīr ilā 'llāh ta'ālā Yūsuf ibn al-Wakīl al-Maylāwī," in 'Anābsa, *Dirāsāt muḍī'a fī ṣafaḥāt al-turāth*, Zaḥāliqa: Dār al-Hudā, and Jordan: Dār al-Jarīr, 2013, pp. 174–196, at pp. 186–187; Marzolph, *Nasreddin Hodscha*, pp. 36–38, no. 54.

22. Zākāni, 'Obeydallāh, *Kolliyāt*, ed. Parviz Atābeki, Tehran 1331/1952, p. 314; ed. Moḥammad Ja'far Maḥjub, New York: Eisenbrauns, 1999, p. 294, no. 129; Christensen, Arthur, "Remarques sur les facéties de 'Ubaïd-i-Zākānī, avec des extraits de la Risālä-i-dilgušā," *Acta Orientalia* 3 (1924), pp. 1–37, at p. 9, no. II.21; Spargo, *Chaucer's Shipman's Tale*, p. 32; Marzolph, Ulrich, "Mollā Naṣroddīn in Persia," *Iranian Studies* 28.3–4 (1995), pp. 157–174, at p. 163, no. 4; Mojāhed, Aḥmad, *Juḥi (60–160 q)*, Tehran: Enteshārāt-e Dāneshgāh-e Tehran, 1382/2003, p. 713, no. 736.

23. Spargo, *Chaucer's Shipman's Tale*, pp. 29–32; Nicholson, "The Medieval Tale," pp. 265–266.

CHAPTER 52

The Enchanted Tree (ATU 1423)

A New Mexican Village" by American anthropologist Helen Zunser is one of the first ethnographic articles to place Mexican-American tradition in context. The lengthy 1935 article provides a detailed and lively ethnographic account of the town of Hot Springs in North-Eastern New Mexico, covering "customs, beliefs about courtship and marriage, children's games, religious holidays, and, of course, narratives."[1] Almost all of the tales Zunser recorded were told either by Antonio Lorenz or his younger brother Fernán, the latter of whom she presents as a "strikingly handsome" character with "a great appetite for women."[2] Considering Fernán's way of life, the short humorous tale titled "The Apple Tree" that Zunser published following his performance, appears to bear autobiographical traits.[3]

Once there was a fellow who go to California to look for work. He get a job with a farmer, picking apples. Now this farmer have a fine daughter, and the boy want to kiss her, but the father never go way, always around. She willing too. So he thinks him a way. One day he way on top of the apple tree picking apples, throwing them down. Farmer and his daughter on bottom, they pick up the apples, put them in baskets. Now all of a sudden the boy runs down from the tree, very fast, very quick.

"What's the matter?" the farmer say.

"O I quit, I no stay here any more."

"Why you quit? What the matter?"

The boy a good worker. Farmer don't want him to go way.

"O I don't like to stay in a place where I see such things."

"What do you see?"

"I look down from the tree and see you kiss your daughter. I not like that."

The farmer say, "O no, that not true."

"Well, if you don't believe me, go see yourself."

So the farmer climb on the top of the tree and look down. The boy and girl kissing. He holler down, "Yes, what you say is true." They two have a good time.

Richard Dorson, who republished the tale in his survey of "regional folklore in the United States,"[4] identified it as a version of tale type ATU 1423: *The Enchanted Pear Tree.*[5] The tale is best known in European literature from the works of the two "giants of world literature,"[6] Boccaccio's *Decamerone* (VII, 9) and Chaucer's *Canterbury Tales* ("The Merchant's Tale"). Consequently, Aurelio M. Espinosa, Sr., qualified the tale's relatively rare versions recorded from oral tradition as "not really popular and traditional versions, but versions of literary origin that have become popular."[7] While one might debate the bearing of this somewhat puritanical statement for any tale's popularity in oral tradition, several extremely lively versions were recorded from international tradition. Espinosa himself published a version narrated in 1913 by Eduardo Martínez Torner in the Asturian village of Llamo. This text adds a further layer of humor by introducing figs as the fruits to be picked, the fig being an ancient and widespread symbol for the vagina in Southern Europe.

> One day, Xuan and Marica take the priest along to pick figs. Marica climbs the fig tree first. When she is up in the tree, she scolds her husband for "letting the priest be on top of him." Xuan tells Marica that she is crazy and asks her to come down. As he climbs the tree instead, she swears that she was telling the truth.
>
> Now the priest, who is Marica's lover, mounts her to fix her up (*a facer el negociu*). When Xuan sees them from the tree, Marica ensures him that he is as crazy as she was when seeing him. In addition, she tells him to take his time picking the fruits, as the priest likes good figs very much (*tiene grandes ganes de figos bonos*).

A Ukrainian tale published by Aleksandr Afanasyev has a peasant watch through the window how a soldier kisses his wife; otherwise the plot of the tale remains much the same.[8] In the end, the gullible peasant concludes that the window is enchanted and should either be smashed or blocked with wooden planks.

The tale's history, literary dissemination, and presumed "Oriental" origin were discussed in considerable detail in the commentaries to Chaucer's "Merchant's Tale" in the *Originals and Analogues of Some of Chaucer's Canterbury Tales*, in particular William Alexander Clouston's contributions.[9] Recent findings complete the picture.[10]

Ultimately, the tale appears to be of Indian provenance, such as documented in the *Śukasaptati* (Seventy [Tales of a] Parrot),[11] the Indian "Book of the Parrot" compiled before or during the twelfth century. In this version, the peasant heard rumors about his wife meeting her lover under a certain tree on the way to bring him his lunch. In order to find out whether the rumors are true, the peasant hides in the tree and sees the two making love. As the tales of the *Śukasaptati* are about tricky women extracting themselves from compromising situations, the woman now has to find a solution to distract her husband's suspicion. Consequently, she claims that the tree is known of old to have the capacity of doubling the vision of those who climb it. In order to substantiate her claim, she also climbs the tree and accuses her husband of committing adultery while she watches from the tree.

Karl Brockelmann discussed what he regards as an "old Arabic version of the tale of the magic tree" in the *Kitāb al-Ḥayawān* (Book of Animals) compiled by the most prolific author of classical Arabic literature, ʿAmr ibn Baḥr al-Jāḥiẓ (d. 868).[12] Here, a Bedouin woman arranges a meeting with her Bedouin lover who is told to hide in a tree close to their dwelling. When the woman's husband notices the man's figure, she reassures him that it is not a man but the ghost of that tree, and both of them pronounce magic formulas for their protection. When the man goes to sleep, the lover meets the woman, "raises her legs and does her until she is satified." Brockelmann argues that a Bedouin narrator would adapt the tale to the conditions of his habitat, now motivating the husband's gullibility by popular belief in demons. Moreover, in having the husband sleep rather than watch the adulterous act in person, Brockelmann feels that the narrator deprived the tale of its "best pun." From a present-day perspective, the tale appears to be only vaguely related to the original one about the allegedly magic tree.

As of the twelfth century, distinct analogues to the tale are known in the literatures of the Muslim world. The earliest of these analogues is attested in the *Akhbār al-Adhkiyāʾ* (Tales of Clever People), one out of three jestbooks[13] compiled by the Arab jurisprudent, traditionist, historian, and preacher Ibn al-Jawzī (d. 1201).[14] At the end of the chapter "On Those Who Outsmarted Others through Their Intellect to Get What They Want,"[15] Ibn al-Jawzī tells the tale of a woman who is challenged by her lover to find a way for them to make love while her husband is watching. The woman climbs a palm tree, allegedly to pluck some dates. Up on the tree, she reproaches her husband for making love to another woman, although he swears that he is all by himself. After she descended, the husband climbs the tree, and the woman starts to make love with her lover. The gullible husband on the tree does not reproach her, for he thinks that "whoever climbs this palm tree sees what you have seen." In exactly the same wording, the tale is quoted in one of the entertaining compilations of the fifteenth-century Arab polymath Jalāl al-Dīn al-Suyūṭī (d. 1505).[16]

Next in chronological sequence after Ibn al-Jawzī, we find both a short prose summary and an elaborate version in verse in Persian poet Jalāl al-Din Rumi's (d. 1273) mystical *summa*, the *Masnavi-ye maʿnavi*.[17] In Rumi's version, the story also begins with the woman scheming "to do it with her beau in full view of her deluded husband."[18] Having climbed on top of the wild pear tree, the woman reviles her husband for allowing another man to make love to him. He protests and at the same time scolds her for having lost her mind. As the man climbs the tree, the woman embraces her lover. When her husband scolds her for doing what she does, she blames the pear tree for causing illusions. Rumi introduces the tale as a parable and appends a mystical exhortation equal in length to the tale itself in which he interprets the wild pear tree as "primal egotism and self-assertion."

Another Persian version of the tale is contained in ʿEnāyatollāh Kanbu's *Bahār-e dānesh* (The Spring of Knowledge), composed in 1651.[19] The story "forms a subordinate member of the eighth of the 'strange tales and surprising anecdotes in debasement of women, and of the inconstancy of that fickle sex,' related to Sultan Jehángír by his courtiers in order to cure him of a passion which he entertained for a princess whose personal charms had been described to him by a wise parrot."[20] Embedded in a frame tale in which several women agree to dupe a simpleton Brahmin, one of the women promises to make love to him in full view of her husband. She mentions to her husband a date tree that produces miraculous visions: "whoever ascends it, sees many wonderful objects." First, the woman makes love to the Brahmin while her husband from the tree curses her as a "shameless Russian-born wretch." Only thereafter does the woman climb the tree, and finally the husband concludes that "such is the property of this tree, that whoever ascends it, sees man or woman below in such situations."

The tale's version in the fifteenth-century Ottoman Turkish *Qırq vezir* (The Forty Viziers) also begins with the woman promising her lover to "make merry" with him before her husband's eyes.[21] Instead of the tree, however, the alleged magic quality is here attributed to the sweetmeat the couple eat before climbing the tree. Putting her plan into practice, the woman takes her husband to a great tree where they eat some sweetmeats that she presents with the words, "They say that he who eats this sweetmeat sees single things as though they were double." First the woman climbs the tree and accuses her husband of making love to a strange woman. As he swears that nobody was there but himself, they both wonder whether this could be "the work of the sweetmeat." In order to verify this assumption, the man climbs the tree, and the woman calls her lover. Although the woman tries to calm her husband, "the fellow could not endure it and began to come down, and the youth ran off." Another Ottoman Turkish version is given in a manuscript copy of an early sixteenth-century sex manual attributed to the author Kemalpaşazade (d. 1533).[22]

The tale's version in the Breslau edition of the Arabic text of *The Thousand and One Nights* is comparatively late, dating at the earliest from the eighteenth century.[23] Another eighteenth-century Arabic version is given in the Wortley-Montague manuscript of the *Nights*.[24]

In contemporary folk narrative of the Muslim world, the tale is rarely documented. The catalogues list one version each for Turkish,[25] Persian,[26] and Arabic[27] traditions. Similar to the Indo-Persian version in the *Bahār-e dānesh*, the Turkish tale is embedded in a frame tale in which several women compete in deceiving their husbands.

Notes

1. Zunser, Helen, "A New Mexican Village," *Journal of American Folklore* 48 (1935), pp. 125–178; see West, John O., *Mexican-American Folklore*, Little Rock, Arkansas: August House, 1988, p. 13.

2. Zunser, "A New Mexican Village," pp. 144, 129–130.

3. Ibid., pp. 177–178, no. 35.

4. Dorson, Richard M., *Buying the Wind: Regional Folklore in the United States*, Chicago: The University of Chicago Press, 1964, pp. 449–450.

5. Bratcher, James T., "Birnbaum: Der verzauberte B.," in *Enzyklopädie des Märchens*, vol. 2 (1979), cols. 417–421.

6. Schwarzbaum, Haim, "International Folklore Motifs in Petrus Alphonsi's 'Disciplina Clericalis'," in Schwarzbaum, *Jewish Folklore between East and West*, ed. Eli Yassif, Beer-Sheva: Ben-Gurion University of the Negev Press, 1989, pp. 239–358, at p. 335.

7. Espinosa, Aurelio Macedonio, *Cuentos populares españoles recogidos de la tradición oral de España [. . .]*, vol. 3, Madrid: Consejo Superior de Investigaciones Cientificas, 1946, p. 240.

8. Afanasyev, Aleksandr Nikolayevich, *Narodnye russkie skazki*, ed. Vladimir Jakovlevich Propp, Moscow: Gosudarstvennoye Izdatel'stvo Khudozhestvennoy Literatury, 1957, vol. 3, pp. 280–281, no. 474.

9. Clouston, William Alexander, "The Enchanted Tree: Asiatic Versions and Analogues of Chaucer's *Merchant's Tale*," in *Originals and Analogues of Some of Chaucer's Canterbury Tales*, ed. F.J. Furnivall, Edmund Brock, and William Alexander Clouston, part 4, London: N. Trübner & Co., 1886, pp. 341–364, 544 (Additional Notes); see also pp. 177–188.

10. Basset, *Mille et un contes*, vol. 1, pp. 408–410, no. 68; Marzolph, *Arabia ridens*, vol. 2, p. 255, no. 1185; Lewis, Frank, "One Chaste Muslim Maiden and a Persian in a Pear Tree: Analogues of Boccaccio and Chaucer in Four Earlier Arabic and Persian Tales," in *Metaphor and Imagery in Persian Poetry*, ed. Ali Asghar Seyed-Gohrab, Leiden: Brill, 2012, pp. 173–203; Lewis, "A Persian in a Pear Tree: Middle Eastern Analogues for Pirro/Pyrrhus," in *Reconsidering Boccaccio: Medieval Contexts and Global Intertexts*, ed. Olivia Holmes and Dana E. Stewart, Toronto: University of Toronto Press, 2018, pp. 305–343; Lacarra, María Jesús, "'The Enchanted Pear Tree' in Hispanic Tradition," in Bendix, Regina F., and Dorothy Noyes, eds., *Terra Ridens—Terra Narrans: Festschrift zum 65. Geburtstag von Ulrich Marzolph*, Dortmund: Verlag für Orientkunde, 2018, pp. 194–211.

11. *Die Śukasaptati (textus ornatior)*, transl. Richard Schmidt, Stuttgart: W. Kohlhammer, 1899, pp. 99–100, no. 36.

12. Brockelmann, Carl, "Eine altarabische Version der Geschichte vom Wunderbaum," *Studien zur vergleichenden Literaturgeschichte* 8 (1908), pp. 237–238; Jāḥiẓ, ʿAmr ibn Baḥr al-, *Kitāb al-Ḥayawān*, ed. ʿAbd al-Salām Muḥammad Hārūn, 3rd ed., Beirut: al-Majmaʿ al-ʿilmī al-ʿarabī al-islāmī, 1388/1969, vol. 6, pp. 168–169. The reference is also mentioned in El-Shamy, *Types*, no. 1423.

13. Marzolph, Ulrich, "'Erlaubter Zeitvertreib'. Die Anekdotensammlungen des Ibn al-Ǧauzī," *Fabula* 32 (1991), pp. 165–180.

14. Basset, *Mille et un contes*, vol. 1, pp. 408–410, no. 68; Marzolph, *Arabia ridens*, vol. 2, p. 255, no. 1185; Lewis, "One Chaste Muslim Maiden," pp. 152–155, 195 (English translation).

15. Lewis, "One Chaste Muslim Maiden," p. 155.

16. Suyūṭī, Jalāl al-Dīn ʿAbd al-Raḥmān al-, *Kitāb Tuḥfat al-mujālis wa nuzhat al-majālis*, ed. Badr al-Dīn al-Naʿsānī, Cairo 1326/1908, p. 281.

17. Rumi, Jalāl al-Din, *The Mathnawí of Jalálu'ddín Rúmí*, transl. Reynold A. Nicholson, London: Luzac & Co., 1934, vol. 2, pp. 467–468 (bk. 4, verses 3544–3557); Lewis, "One Chaste Muslim Maiden," pp. 192–193. A modern prose rendering of Rumi's verse is given by Arberry, Arthur John, *More Tales from the Masnavi*, London: Allen & Unwin, 1963, p. 86, no. 130.

18. Lewis, "One Chaste Muslim Maiden," p. 192.

19. Scott, Jonathan, *Bahar Danush or Garden of Knowledge: An Oriental Romance Translated from the Persic of Einaïatollah*, London, T. Cadell and W. Davies, 1799, vol. 2, pp. 64–68; Clouston, "The Enchanted Tree," pp. 348–349; Lewis, "One Chaste Muslim Maiden," pp. 155–156.

20. Clouston, "The Enchanted Tree," pp. 343–344.

21. Sheykh-Zāda, *The History of the Forty Vezirs*, transl. E.J.W. Gibb, London: George Redway, 1886, pp. 303–306; Clouston, "The Enchanted Tree," pp. 351–352; Lewis, "One Chaste Muslim Maiden," pp. 156–157.

22. Lewis, "One Chaste Muslim Maiden," p. 157, note. 32.

23. Marzolph and Van Leeuwen, *The Arabian Nights Encyclopedia*, vol. 1, pp. 381–382, no. 295; Clouston, "The Enchanted Tree," pp. 353–355.

24. Marzolph and Van Leeuwen, *The Arabian Nights Encyclopedia*, vol. 1, p. 382, no. 388.

25. Eberhard and Boratav, *Typen*, p. 322, no. 271.

26. Marzolph, *Typologie*, p. 213, no. 1423. The second edition of Enjavi Shirāzi, Abol-Qāsem, *Tamsil va masal*, 2nd ed., Tehran: Amir Kabir, 2537/1979, pp. 296–298, lists a total of five versions. In the most recent edition of that work (ed. Aḥmad Vakiliyān, Tehran: Amir Kabir, 1393/2014), the tale was deleted.

27. El-Shamy, *Types*, p. 799, no. 1423.

CHAPTER 53

The Men Realize That They Will Never Manage to Control Women's Sexuality (ATU 1426)

The Thousand and One Nights is by far the internationally best-known collection of tales from the Muslim world. All-encompassing as the collection is in terms of the variety of topics, themes, and genres the contained narratives cover, its monumental character and its dominant presence at times even in learned discussions risk outshining the influence of other similar collections that are less well known. The presently discussed narrative is a case in point.[1]

The Belarusian tale "The Wiles of Women," originally published in 1891 by Vladimir Nikolaevich Dobrovolsky (1856–1920),[2] was recorded from the oral performance of the aged peasant Vasili Mikhailov in the village Berdebyaki in the district of Smolensk in the 1880s.[3]

> The merchant Gulitow in Petersburg has a handsome son. When visiting the kingdom of Saxony, Gulitow sees the king display his own handsome son, claiming that nobody else could possibly be more handsome. Accepting the challenge, Gulitow sends a letter requesting his son to travel to Saxony immediately.
>
> As Gulitow's son never traveled by ship, he is afraid of the voyage. Just as he is about to depart, he remembers that he forgot to take along his pocket watch. Returning home to fetch it and bid a final farewell to his beloved wife, the young man finds his wife in bed with his steward. Although he does not say a word, he is so deeply irritated that when he arrives in Saxony he has turned "all black and ugly." When the king of Saxony sees him, he regards him as an impostor. Only the intercession of the other kings prevents the king from having the merchant's son beheaded. In order to recover from the strains of the voyage, the king hosts the young man for a period of six months.
>
> Strolling around the garden one day, Gulitow's son notices the prince's wife having sex with a lame saddler. As his rival's misfortune appears even

> greater than his own, he starts to feel better. He makes the prince witness the scene some time later, and both of them decide to travel to find out whether they will encounter similar mores elsewhere.
>
> The travelers happen to meet a peasant who carries his wife in a bag on his back while plowing the fields. As soon as the peasant falls asleep after lunch, the woman signals to her young lover hiding in the bushes to join her. When the peasant wakes up again, he quickly puts both his wife and her lover in the bag without even noticing. As the travelers question him about the bag's content, the lover runs away, and the peasant gives his wife a heavy beating.
>
> In a foreign kingdom, the ruler promises to marry his daughter to one of the two travelers. The travelers pretend that according to their own custom both had rather marry the same woman, and the king consents. At night, the three of them sleep in one bed. The princess asserts that when she would want to have sex with one of them, she would touch the other one so as to turn his back on them. After a week, the merchant's son reproaches the prince for having sex every night, only to learn that the prince thinks the same of him. At night, they notice that the princess asks both of them to turn around, following which she is joined by her lover, the cobbler Yurko, who lowers himself into the bed from a window above.

Having realized that women will always find a way to deceive their husbands, the travelers return home and continue their life as usual.

The tale's editor mentions a similar early twentieth-century version from Siberian Russian tradition that also involves the motifs of the beauty contest and the travelers' marriage to a single woman, without giving further details.[4] A total of three Hungarian versions of the tale were recorded from the oral tradition of the Székely population in Romania.[5] A nineteenth-century version was told by Balácz Orbán, who spent fourteen years of his life in Constantinople.[6] This version was classified as Hungarian tale type 977*[7] that corresponds to the international tale type ATU 1426: *The Wife Kept in a Box*. The tale starts with the queen marveling at the beautiful portrait of a young man, disbelieving that any man could possibly be so handsome. When the young man is brought to her presence, his good looks have vanished since he witnessed his wife having sex with "a beardless and puny guy" just after he left her and only returned to pick up the prayer book he had forgotten. The young man's good looks are reestablished when he witnesses the queen's unfaithfulness. Traveling around together with the king, the two men meet a peasant who carries a heavy trunk on his back while working in the fields. Although the peasant's wife claims that the trunk contains her valuables, in reality it conceals her lover. The second Székely version was recorded before 1941 by János Ösz from the oral performance of György Bukló, a farmhand from Kibéd. Here, the king invites the handsome young man to court. When the man returns home to pick up the letter of invitation he forgot to take along, he finds his wife making love to "an ugly black

Gypsy coachman." Later witnessing the queen making love to "an ugly black gardener," the man gets well again. Roaming the world together with the king, they meet a peasant who carries his wife's lover in a trunk on his back. The third Székely version was recorded by Linda Dégh from day laborer György Andrásfalvi from Kakasd in 1948.[8] Although the collector analyzed traits of the aging narrator's forgetfulness[9] and his "clear adherence to reading matter,"[10] the tale corresponds more or less to the two other Székely versions. A special detail is the fact that the handsome man's loss of beauty becomes apparent right after he witnesses his wife's relation with a black servant, so that the king's chamberlain who comes to take him to the king already wonders what might have happened.

The above tales from Eastern European oral tradition overlap in the initial episode of the beauty contest, the two scenes of extramarital sexual relations and their respective consequences, and the two men setting out to learn whether women anywhere in the world are faithful to their men. All of the Székely tales mention the peasant carrying his wife's lover in a trunk on his back. This part of the tale corresponds to tale type ATU 1358B: *Husband Carries Off Box Containing Hidden Lover.*[11] It is vaguely mirrored in the Belarusian version in which the peasant first carries his wife in a bag, and then his wife together with her lover. The Belarusian text extends the action further by having the two travelers get married to a single woman.

In the European literatures, the tale of the beauty contest occurring in the tale's initial section is first documented in *canto* 28 of Italian author Ariosto's (d. 1533) *Orlando furioso.*[12] Ariosto's version takes place between Iocondo and King Astolfo. Having witnessed the queen's adultery with a hideous dwarf, the two men roam the world and eventually get married to the young woman Fiametta, as in the final episode of the Belarusian text. Ariosto's version is altogether characterized by an almost cheerful mood, as the two men in the end give in to the finding that there is nothing they can do to prevent a woman from following her own sexual agenda, so they might as well live with their wives as before. This tale was translated and adapted into various European languages soon after its publication,[13] including Spanish author Juan de Timoneda's (d. 1583) *Patrañuelo* (ch. 8),[14] German author Johann Michael Moscherosch's (d. 1669) collection of satirical narratives, *Wunderliche und Wahrhafftige Gesichte Philanders von Sittewald* (Wondrous and True Visions of Philander von Sittewald),[15] and French fabulist Jean de La Fontaine's (d. 1695) verse narrative *Joconde.*[16] Even before La Fontaine's widely read translation from Ariosto, the tale experienced a total of three versified translations in French, in seventeenth-century bourgeois culture attaining an almost proverbial publicity.[17]

The motif of a man keeping his wife in a container so as to assure her faithfulness, as occurring in the Belarusian text, made its first appearance in a European literature early in the fourteenth century in German author Heinrich Frauenlob's poem "Das weip in der kiste" (The Woman in the Box).[18] Italian author Giovanni Sercambi (d. 1424) joined this motif to an initial episode elaborating the one man's depression after having witnessed his wife's faithlessness, and the return of his health after having seen the faithless action of the queen.[19]

With the exception of Sercambi's text, none of the above-quoted versions, whether in elite literature or popular tradition, corresponds in detail to a tale of *The Thousand and One Nights*. Even so, Ariosto's tale, which appears to resonate in the tales recorded from Eastern European oral tradition, has repeatedly been argued to originate from that collection. The obvious overlap is the motif of the changing looks experienced by Shahriyār's brother Shāhzamān when witnessing the extramarital sexual activities of first his own and then his brother's wife in the frame tale of *Nights*.[20] In the *Nights*, this is followed by the two men roaming the world and their being blackmailed into having sex with a woman whom a demon keeps in a box, only taking her out when he feels safe enough to have some sleep.[21] The motif of the beauty contest that plays such a prominent role in Ariosto's text and its popular repercussions does, however, find a close analogue in the frame tale of the sibling collection to *The Thousand and One Nights*, *The Hundred and One Nights*.[22] While *The Thousand and One Nights* was popular in the Muslim East, *The Hundred and One Nights* is exclusively documented in manuscripts originating from the Muslim West, that is, North Africa and, at least potentially, Muslim Spain. While the translation of the former collection from Persian to Arabic dates from the ninth century or earlier, the date when the latter collection might have been compiled is being debated. Most of the extant manuscripts date to the nineteenth century while a recently discovered manuscript purportedly dates from the thirteenth century.[23] Intricate and difficult to untangle as the relation between the European texts and their counterparts from Arabic literature is, it is further complicated by the fact that a twentieth-century folktale recorded in Syria contains both the episode of the beauty contest and the motif of the gullible man trying to contain his wife by guarding her in a litter on a camel that is always with him, not knowing that his wife's lover also hides inside.[24]

In his extended discussion of a large variety of source texts, Emmanuel Cosquin demonstrated that most of the motifs and episodes discussed above are already known from early Buddhist literature.[25] This assessment pertains, above all, to the motifs of the beauty contest, including the connected series of events, and of the man's attempt to contain his wife. Close analogues for these two elements are documented in the *Ancient Book of Diverse Instructive Stories* compiled by the Chinese monk Seng-Hui (d. 280) that forms part of the Buddhist canonical collection of tales, the *Tripiṭaka* (Three Baskets).[26] In the first tale, the two men finally decide to live as hermits. In the second, a Brahmin keeps his wife in a pot that he magically contains in his belly, not knowing that his wife uses the same procedure to contain her lover in her belly. Although the tales' specific details changed as they traveled to different cultures, the frame tales of both *The Thousand and One Night* and *The Hundred and One Nights* demonstrate that the Buddhist tales met with a creative reception and adaptation in Muslim Arabic literature whence they were eventually transmitted to the West.

In terms of doctrinal context, the two tales in Seng-Hui's compilation, constituting early analogues to the tales later appearing in Arabic literature, frame another tale whose topic is the immutability of destiny (see also essay **16, *The Three Old Men***). Although destiny is not explicitly mentioned in the two framing tales, their use in this context adds an additional dimension to the tales implying that the wiles of women are as constant and as much decreed by destiny as anything else.[27] The additional tale tells of a certain king's attempt to change the destiny decreed for a young girl he intends to marry once she will have grown up. A wise man reading the girl's horoscope predicts that the king will be able to marry her, but only after she had been together with another man. In order to prevent this from happening, the king has the girl brought up by a crane that keeps her in its nest in a tree on a high mountain. Although the crane guards the girl closely, some years later a young man happens to arrive at the tree and impregnate the young woman, without the crane noticing him or being able to prevent the events from happening.[28] In Arabic, a much elaborated adaptation of this tale, in which the Phoenix at Solomon's court claims that he can change destiny, was included in al-Thaʿlabī's (d. 1038) widely read collection of tales of the prophets (*qiṣaṣ al-anbiyāʾ*).[29] In Persian, the tale was adapted in the *Munes-nāme* (The Book as an Intimate Friend) compiled around 1200 by a certain Abu Bakr ibn Khosrow al-Ostād.[30] The tale's version contained in the late fourteenth- or early fifteenth-century Ottoman Turkish compilation *Ferec baʿd eş-şidde* (Relief after Hardship) that constitutes the main source of François Pétis de la Croix's *Les mille et un jours* (The Thousand and One Days) was published in French translation in a collection of tales published by the Comte de Caylus (d. 1765)[31] and eventually found its way into German author Christoph Martin Wieland's "Der Greif vom Gebürge Kaf" (The Griffon from Mount Kaf) in the collection of tales in the "Oriental" manner, *Dschinnistan* (The Land of the Jinns).[32]

Notes

1 The tale has previously been discussed by Solymossy, Sándor, "A 'szép ember' meséje," *Ethnographia* 27 (1916), pp. 257–275; Marzolph, Ulrich, and Aboubakr Chraïbi, "The *Hundred and One Nights*: A Recently Discovered Old Manuscript," in *Zeitschrift der Deutschen Morgenländischen Gesellschaft* 162 (2012), pp. 299–316, at pp. 305–306, 311; Horta, Paulo Lemos, "Beautiful Men and Deceitful Women: the One Hundred and One Nights and World Literature," *Narrative Culture* 2.2 (2015), pp. 190–207.

2. Barag, Lev G., "Dobrovol'skij, Vladimir Nikolaevič," in *Enzyklopädie des Märchens*, vol. 3 (1981), cols. 730–732.

3. Barag, Lev G., *Belorussische Volksmärchen*, Berlin: Akademie-Verlag, 1966, pp. 392–397, 622, no. 62.

4. Ibid., p. 622.

5. Dégh, Linda, *Märchen, Erzähler und Erzählgemeinschaft: Dargestellt an der ungarischen*

Volksüberlieferung, Berlin: Akademie-Verlag, 1962, pp. 298–299, no. 66; Dégh, *Folktales and Society: Story-telling in a Hungarian Peasant Community*, Bloomington: Indiana University Press, 1989, pp. 330–331, no. 70.

6. Solymossy, "A 'szép ember' meséje," pp. 257–258; Katona, Louis, "Le bel homme trompé par sa femme," *Revue des traditions populaires* 4 (1889), pp. 44–46.

7. Berze Nagy, János, *Magyar népmesetípusok*, Pécs: Baranya Megye Tanácsának Kiadása, 1957, vol. 2, pp. 734–438.

8. Dégh, Linda, *Kakasdi népmesék*, vol. 2: *Palkó Józsefné, Andrásfalvi György, Sebestyén Lajosné és Lázló Márton meséi*, Budapest: Akademiai Kiadó, 1960, pp. 201–204, no. 70.

9. Dégh, *Märchen*, p. 226; Dégh, *Folktales and Society*, p. 239.

10. Dégh, *Folktales and Society*, p. 242; Dégh, *Märchen*, p. 228.

11. Wehse, Rainer, "Ehebruch belauscht," in *Enzyklopädie des Märchens*, vol. 3 (1981), cols. 1055–1065, at cols. 1057–1058.

12. Ariosto, Ludovico, *Orlando furioso e Cinque canti*, ed. Remo Ceserani and Sergio Zatti, Torino: Utet, 2006, vol. 2, pp. 991–1023; see Rajna, Pio, *Le fonti dell'Orlando furioso*, ed Francesco Manzoni, Florence: Sansoni, 1975.

13. Mention of the following details is indebted to Wesselski, *Märchen des Mittelalters*, pp. 3–8, 185–187, no. 1.

14. See http://www.cervantesvirtual.com/obra-visor/el-patranuelo--0/html/fedbc64e-82b1-11df-acc7-002185ce6064_1.html (accessed November 24, 2017).

15. Moscherosch, Hanß Michael, *Gesichte Philanders von Sittewald*, ed. Felix Bobertag, Berlin and Stuttgart: W. Speman, (1883?), pp. 220–227 (in part 2).

16. La Fontaine, *Oeuvres complètes*, vol. 1, ed. Jean-Pierre Collinet, Paris: Gallimard, 1991, pp. 559–571, no. 1.

17. Ibid., p. 1346–1349.

18. Bolte, Johannes, "Neuere Märchenliteratur," *Zeitschrift des Vereins für Volkskunde* 15 (1905), pp. 266–230, at p. 229.

19. Wesselski, *Märchen des Mittelalters*, pp. 3–8, 185–187, no. 1; Marzolph and Van Leeuwen, *Arabian Nights Encyclopedia*, vol. 2, p. 698.

20. Marzolph and Van Leeuwen, *Arabian Nights Encyclopedia*, vol. 1, pp.

21. Horálek, Karel, "Frau im Schrein," in *Enzyklopädie des Märchens*, vol. 5 (1987), cols. 186–192.

22. Horta, "Beautiful Men."

23. Marzolph and Chraïbi, "The *Hundred and One Nights*;" Ott, Claudia, transl., *101 Nacht*, Zurich: Manesse, 2012, pp. 252–256; Fudge, Bruce, ed. and transl., *A Hundred and One Nights*, New York: New York University Press, 2016, pp. xxix–xxxiii.

24. Grotzfeld, Heinz und Sophia, *Die Erzählungen aus Tausendundeiner Nacht*, 2nd rev. ed., Dortmund: Verlag für Orientkunde, 2012, pp. 144–148.

25. Cosquin, Emmanuel, "Le prologue-cadre des Mille et une nuits, les légendes perses et le livre d'Esther," in Cosquin, *Études folkloriques*, Paris: Édouard Champion, 1922, pp. 265–347.

26. Chavannes, Édouard, *Cinq cents contes et apologues extraits du Tripiṭaka chinois*, vol. 1, Paris: Maisonneuve, 1962, pp. 374–376, no. 107; pp. 377–379, no. 109.

27. For the most recent treatment of this topic, see Sayers, David Selim, *The Wiles of Women as a Literary Genre: A Study of Ottoman and Azeri Texts*, Wiesbaden: Harrassowitz, 2019.

28. Chavannes, *Cinq cents contes*, vol. 1, pp. 376–377, no. 108; see also Chauvin,

Victor, "Note sur le Conte de Salomon et le griffon," *Le Muséon* 24 (1905), pp. 85–90, at pp. 87–90.

29. Thaʿlabī, Abū Isḥāq Aḥmad ibn Muḥammad ibn Ibrāhīm al-, *ʿArāʾis al-majālis fī qiṣaṣ al-anbiyāʾ*, transl. William M. Brinner, Leiden etc., Brill, 2002, pp. 498–505.

30. Askari, Nasrin, "A Mirror for Princesses: *Mūnis-nāma*, A Twelfth-Century Collection of Persian Tales Corresponding to the Ottoman Turkish Tales of the *Faraj baʿd al-shidda*," *Narrative Culture* 5.1 (2018), pp. 121–140; Marzolph, *Relief after Hardship*, pp. 48, 97–99, no. 31.

31. Chauvin, *Bibliographie*, vol. 6 (1902), pp. 29–30, no. 201.

32. Wieland, Christoph Martin, "Der Greif vom Gebürge Kaf," *Dschinnistan oder auserlesene Feen- und Feister-Märchen*, vol. 3, Winterthur: Heinrich Steiner und Compagnie, 1789, pp. 22–34.

CHAPTER 54

Ignorance Concerning the Use of Flour (ATU 1446)

This anecdotal tale widely known in European tradition serves as the quintessential expression of how well-to-do people disregard the needs of the poor. Informed that the common people are so destitute that they can even not afford to buy bread, an upper-class person, most often a woman, comments, "Then let them eat cake!"[1] In Western European tradition, the cynical remark is often attributed to Marie-Antoinette, the wife of Louis XVI (r. 1774–1792) and the last queen of France before the French Revolution. Although historically unwarranted, the remark's attribution to Marie-Antoinette is particularly apt, as her extravagance and self-centered ignorance contributed to the declining acceptance of the French monarchy that eventually resulted in her execution by the guillotine during the French Revolution.

Classified as international tale type ATU 1446: *"Let Them Eat Cake!,"* variations of the tale attributed to a variety of different characters appear in a wide range of literary sources from the sixteenth century onward. Nineteenth- and twentieth-century recordings of the tale from European oral tradition are rare. There is, however, a notable cluster of some fifteen versions recorded from Latvian oral tradition.[2] In the Latvian texts, the target of the joke is the German gentry who for a long time held the exclusive right to acquire and own land. Even when local peasants were finally allowed to do so in the nineteenth century, most of them were not able to buy enough land to support themselves. In the Latvian texts, the lady of a manor or a baroness tells the hungry peasants to eat white bread and butter or warm up yesterday's leftovers of meat (both of which the poor peasants obviously did not have).

Historically, the anecdote appears to be the narrative elaboration of a short saying that is already known from Spanish tradition of the late Middle Ages. The Spanish saying, first documented in the first half of the fifteenth century in Iñigo López de Mendoza Santillana's (d. 1458) *Refranes que dizen las viejas tras el fuego* (Sayings of Old Women by the Fireside), goes "A mengua de pan, buenas son tortas" (If there is no bread, cake is also good).[3] Whereas the anecdote targets the cynical selfishness of the well-to-do, the saying suggests a good-natured self-critical reading, although there are no "illustrative quotations or interpretative comments"[4] to support an unambiguous interpretation. At any rate, the later anecdote's sarcasm is not present in the early examples, and there is good reason to believe that it arose only much later. The Spanish saying is further related to an ancient Greek saying rendered in Latin by Dutch Renaissance humanist scholar Erasmus of Rotterdam (1466–1536) as "Bona etiam offa post panem." The word "offa" translates the Greek "maza" that Erasmus explains as a poorer kind of barley bread that peasants are accustomed to eat in place of bread prepared from wheat. So the saying translates as "Barley bread is also good when there is no wheat bread." While the saying might thus relate to ancient Mediterranean dietary habits, its essence as expressed in the anecdote can also be understood as a rich person's ignorance that both bread and cake are made from flour; so if bread becomes unaffordable due to its high price, this will also apply to cake.

The same foolish ignorance is expressed in an anecdote documented in Arabic collections of jocular tales compiled toward the beginning of the eleventh century.[5] In al-Ḥuṣrī's (d. 1015) *Jamʿ al-jawāhir* (The Collection of Jewels) a fool (*mughaffal*) is told that flour has become more expensive (*qad ghalā al-daqīq*). The fool responds calmly, "Why should I bother? I buy bread in the market."[6] With little variation, the tale is reproduced in al-Ābī's (d. 1030) *Nathr al-durr* (Pearls of Prose).[7] Here, the poet Abū ʿAbdallāh Muḥammad ibn ʿAmr "al-Jammāz" (d. 864), who was known for his smart remarks, is introduced as informing an unspecified man that the price of flour has risen (*qad zāda siʿr al-daqīq*). To which the man retorts, "I don't bother, because I buy my bread." The tale's Syriac version in Bar Hebraeus's (d. 1286) *Laughable Stories*, although adapted from al-Ābī's work, instead of the initial factual information has the first person ask whether the price of flour has risen.[8] And the tale's reproduction in the passage devoted to al-Jammāz in Mamluk author al-Ṣafadī's (d. 1363) biographical dictionary, while sharing its introduction with al-Ābī's version, introduces yet another minor variation in having the addressed person respond, "I don't bother, because I buy nothing but bread."[9]

Although the tale's Arabic versions are distinct from both the European sentence and its later narrative elaboration, they share a similar ignorance regarding flour as the main ingredient of either bread or cake. But whereas the Arabic tale and the European sentence simply make fun of a fool's ignorance, the sentence's narrative elaboration in later European tradition with its sarcastic tone turned the tale into a bitter comment on the ignorant and unwordly conduct of the ruling classes.

Notes

1. The present essay's assessment of European tradition is indebted to the tale's previous discussions by Taylor, Archer, "And Marie-Antoinette Said . . . ," in *Comparative Studies in Folklore: Asia—Europe—America*, Taipei: The Orient Cultural Service, 1972,

pp. 249–265 (originally published in *Revista de etnografia* 22, 1968, pp. 1–17); Shojaei Kawan, Christine, "Kuchen: Laßt sie K. essen!" in *Enzyklopädie des Märchens*, vol. 8 (1996), cols. 536–541; Campion-Vincent, Véronique, and Christine Shojaei Kawan, "Marie-Antoinette and Her Famous Saying: Three Levels of Communication, Three Modes of Accusation and Two Troubled Centuries," *Fabula* 41 (2000), pp. 13–41.

2. Arājs, Kārlis, and Alma Medne, *Latviešu pasaku tipu rādītājs*, Riga: Zinātne, 1977, p. 184, no. 1446; Campion-Vincent and Shojaei Kawan, "Marie-Antoinette," pp. 19–20.

3. Santillana, Iñigo López de Mendoza, *Refranes que dizen las viejas tras el fuego*, ed. Hugo O. Bizarri, Kassel: Reichenberger, 1995, p. 79, no. 48.

4. Taylor, "And Marie-Antoinette Said . . . ," p. 259. For the following discussion, see ibid.

5. Marzolph, *Arabia ridens*, vol. 2, pp. 124–125, no. 496.

6. Ḥuṣrī al-Qayrawānī, Abū Isḥāq Ibrāhīm ibn ʿAlī al-, *Jamʿ al-jawāhir fī ʾl-mulaḥ wa-ʾl-nawādir*, ed. ʿAlī Muḥammad al-Bijāwī, Cairo: Dār Iḥyāʾ al-kutub al-ʿarabiyya, 1372/1952, p. 161.

7. Ābī, Abū Saʿd Manṣūr ibn al-Ḥusayn al-, *Nathr al-durr*, ed. Muḥammad ʿAlī Qarna et al., vol. 3, Cairo: al-Hayʾa al-miṣriyya al-ʿāmma lil-kitāb, 1983, p. 254.

8. Bar Hebraeus, Mâr Gregory John, *The Laughable Stories*, transl. E.A. Wallis Budge, London: Luzac and Co, 1897, p. 139, no. 529.

9. Ṣafadī, Ṣalāḥ al-Dīn Khalīl ibn Aybak al-, *al-Wāfī bi-ʾl-wafayāt*, vol. 4, ed. Aḥmad al-Arnāwūṭ and Tazkī Muṣṭafā, Beirut: Dār Iḥyāʾ al-turāth al-ʿarabī, 2000, p. 204, no. 1824.

CHAPTER 55

The Burglar's Lame Excuse: The Sound Will Be Heard Tomorrow Morning (Jason 1525*T)

A jocular tale whose Jewish-Iraqi version Heda Jason classified as tale type 1525*T: *Tomorrow's Music* has the detected thief or burglar present a specific lame excuse.[1] In European popular tradition, the tale is exclusively documented from Balkan tradition. It is particularly well attested in a number of early twentieth-century Romanian publications.[2]

> A poor gypsy fiddler takes to stealing so as not to die of hunger. As he is caught red-handed trying to break the padlock of a door, somebody asks him what he is doing. He says that he is singing. When the man wonders why he does not hear the song, the gypsy responds, "Don't worry—you'll hear it tomorrow morning!"

One of the versions listed in the catalogue of Romanian jocular tales names Nastratin, the local equivalent of the Turkish jester Nasreddin Hodja, as the tale's protagonist.[3] Nasreddin also appears in a Croatian version where he pretends to play the fiddle,[4] an excuse he also uses in Turkish, Greek, and Serbian chapbook compilations of his pranks dating to the nineteenth and early twentieth centuries.[5] In modern Arabic and Turkish booklets, Nasreddin and one of his students are on their way back home one night when they pass some burglars trying to break the lock of a house.[6] Instead of interfering, Nasreddin wants to get away from the scene as quickly as possible, so as not to be attacked. His pupil, however, does not understand what is happening and asks him what the men are doing. "Hush," Nasreddin whispers, "they are making music." And when the pupil says that he does not hear anything, Nasreddin responds, "We are going to hear the music tomorrow!" These versions supply sufficient evidence that the tale was disseminated in recent Turkish and Balkan traditions by its attribution to the popular character of Nasreddin. The manuscript repertoire of tales about Nasreddin includes another tale that overlaps in the attempt to cover a misdeed with a lame excuse.[7] Here, Nasreddin climbs into an apricot tree and starts to eat the fruit. When the owner of the garden asks him what he is doing there, he claims to be a nightingale. But when the owner challenges him to sing, he excuses himself that he is a nightingale without much practice.

Italian Renaissance literature documents the tale in sixteenth-century European literature. In his compilation of jocular tales first published in 1562, Italian polymath Lodovico Domenichi (1515–1564) authenticates the events by localizing them in the Banchi Street in Rome. Although the scene is essentially identical, the burglar's lame excuse is linked to a purported bereavement in the house, thereby seasoning the burglar's response with a double entendre that is only accessible to the tale's audience.[8]

> When a band of burglars is about to carry away the merchandise of the shop they have broken into, the chief of police with his men happens to come by. In response to his question about what is going on, one of the burglars comes to the door with a broom in his hand, pretending to be sweeping, and claiming that they are clearing out things because the owner of the store has died. When the chief of police remarks, "It's funny, but I don't hear anybody weeping inside," the burglar replies, "They certainly will weep tomorrow morning!"

Seventeenth-century Italian author Giovanni Sagredo (1616–1691) cites the tale in similar wording, abandoning, however, the scene's specified location.[9] Although both Domenichi's and Sagredo's books were frequently reprinted,[10] there is no documentation of this particular version from subsequent oral tradition in Italy.[11]

The text in an undated early modern Spanish collection of famous dictums (*dichos famosos*) reads like a close translation from the Italian insofar as the events take place in Rome and one of the burglars takes up a broom.[12] In a number of Spanish versions dating from the *siglo de oro*, the Golden Age of Spanish literature in the sixteenth and seventeenth centuries, the conversation between the burglars stealing items from a house and the passing watchman culminates in the punchline "they will weep tomorrow" (*mañana llorarán*). This short and fairly condensed version is contained in the *Floresta española de apotegmas y sentencias* (A Spanish Grove of Apophthegms and Aphorisms) by Melchor de Santa Cruz (1574),[13] the *Miscelánea: Silva de casos curiosos* (Miscellanea: A Forest of Curious Cases) by Luis Zapata (1592), and the *Vocabulario de refranes y frases proverbiales* (Vocabulary of Proverbs and Proverbial Phrases) by Gonzalo Correas (1627).[14] In confirmation of the burglar's statement, in the two sixteenth-century versions the watchman when passing the house the next day notices several women wailing, because they had been robbed the previous night.

The tale's earliest occurrence is attested in the third book of Jalāl al-Din Rumi's (d. 1273) mystical *summa*, the *Masnavi-ye ma'navi*.[15] Here, the burglar is "cutting a hole at the bottom of the wall" at night. When one of the people living in the house wakes up and asks him what he is doing, he replies that he is beating the drum. The burglar's response to the man's question why he does not hear the noise of the drum is exceptionally explicit, actually conjoining the two previously mentioned versions, as the burglar says, "You will hear this noise tomorrow, (namely) cries of 'Oh, alas!' and 'Oh, woe is me!'" Sixteenth-century Persian author Fakhr al-Din ʿAli Ṣafi (d. 1532) in his *Laṭāʾef al-ṭavāʾef* (Jocular Tales from the Various Strata of Society) cites a version similar to the one given by Domenichi.[16] Having stolen a basket from a house, the thief is surprised by some people coming by. Quick-witted, the thief takes a broom and pretends to sweep the doorway, allegedly because someone in the house has died. The tale's punchline is the usual one about weeping. In the baroque wording typical for his time, Persian author Barkhordār ibn Maḥmud Farāhi included the tale in his late sixteenth- or early seventeenth-century *Maḥbub al-qolub* (The Hearts' Beloved).[17]

Although jocular tales about thieves and burglars abound in premodern Arabic literature,[18] no direct model for the tale predating its earliest documented occurrence in Rumi's *Masnavi* has been identified. Meanwhile, the Andalusian Arab author Ibn ʿĀṣim (d. 1426) in his *Ḥadāʾiq al-azāhir* (Flower Gardens) attests a version likely deriving from an older Arabic source upon which Rumi's version might be modeled.[19] As in the *Masnavi*, a burglar is caught making a hole into the wall of a house. The burglar's excuse to the passing watchman is that he makes the hole so that they can carry a recently deceased person from the house. And when asked why one does not hear the usual sounds of mourning, such as crying and wailing, the burglar responds, "You will hear the lamentation at the end of the night!"

Notes

1. Jason, Heda, *Folktales of the Jews of Iraq: Tale-Types and Genres*, Or Yehuda: Babylonian Jewry Heritage Center, 1988, p. 77, no. 1525*T.

2. Stroescu, *La typologie*, vol. 2, pp. 1338–1339, no. 5384 (6 versions, published between 1899 and 1936).

3. Ibid., version 5 (published 1931).

4. Bošković-Stulli, Maja, *Narodne pripovijetke*, Zagreb: Matica Hrvatska, 1963, pp. 262, 332, no. 111 (from the collections of N. Tordinca).

5. Duman, Mustafa, *Nasreddin Hoca ve 1555 fıkrası*, Istanbul: heyamola, 2008, p. 263, no. 353 (quoting from Elçin, Şükrü, "Nasreddin Hoca'nın Lâtifeleri: Letayif-e Hace Nasreddin Aleyhirrahme," *Türk Dili* 533 (1996), pp. 1233–1239, no. 31); Wesselski, *Der Hodscha Nasreddin*, vol. 2, pp. 174, 234, no. 514.

6. Ṭarābulusī, Ḥikmat Sharīf al-, *Nawādir Juḥā*, Beirut: al-Mu'assasa al-muttaḥida lil-nashr, p. 220, no. 317; Marzolph, *Nasreddin Hodscha*, pp. 194, 311, no. 464.

7. Kut, Günay, "Nasreddin Hoca Hikâyeleri Yazmalarının Kolları Üzerine Bir Deneme," in *IV. Milletlerarası Türk Halk Kültürü Kongresi Bildirileri*, vol. 3: *Halk Edebiyatı*, Ankara, 1992, pp. 147–200, at p. 200, no. 325; see also Marzolph, *Typologie*, p. 232, no. *1624* (A thief on the roof of a house pretends to be a nightingale. "My voice will reach you tomorrow.")

8. Speroni, Charles, *Wit and Wisdom of the Italian Renaissance*, Berkeley: University of

California Press, 1964, pp. 199–200, no. 13; Domenichi, Lodovico, *Detti et fatti de diversi signori et persone private, i quali communemente si chiamano Facetie, Motti, & Burle*, Florence: Lorenzo Torrentino, 1562, p. 157 (in bk. 4); ed. Venice: Francesco Lorenzini, 1562, fol. 92b (the text begins "Furono certi ladri in Roma . . . ").

9. Vacalerio, Ginnesio Gavardo (i.e., Sagredo, Giovanni), *L'Arcadia in Brenta, ovvero La Melanchonia Sbandita*, Colonia: Francesco Kinchio, 1667, p. 319 (latter half of day V); ed. Bologna: Giovanni Recaldini, 1693, pp. 217–218 (the text begins "Certi ladri rubbarono in una bottega a mezza notte . . . ").

10. A Google search with the beginnings of the texts yields hits in a considerable number of nineteenth-century editions.

11. The tale is not listed in Rotunda, Dominic Peter, *Motif-Index of the Italian Novella in Prose*, Bloomington: Indiana University Press, 1942.

12. Fradejas Lebrero, José, *Más de mil y un cuentos del siglo de oro*, Madrid: Iberoamericana, 2008, p. 466, p. (892) 155.

13. Santa Cruz, Melchor de, *Floresta española*, ed. María Pilar Cuartero and Maxime Chevalier, Barcelona: Crítica, 1997, p. 121 (4,5,9).

14. Granja, Fernando de la, "Dos cuentos árabes de ladrones en la literatura española del siglo XVI," *Al-Andalus* 33.2 (1969), pp. 459–469, at pp. 461–464; Chevalier, Maxime, *Cuentecillos tradicionales en la España del Siglo de Oro*, Madrid: Gredos, 1975, pp. 100–101, no. D 2; Chevalier, *Cuentos folklóricos*, pp. 319–320, no. 192; Hernández Valcárcel, María del Carmen, *El cuento español en los siglos de oro: siglo XVI*, Murcia: University of Murcia, 2002, p. 268, no. 117; López Bernal, Desirée, *Los Ḥadāʾiq al-azāhir de Abū Bakr ibn ʿĀṣim al-Garnāṭī: Traducción y estudio de una obra de adab de la Granada nazarí*, Ph.D. thesis University of Granada, 2016, vol. 2, pp. 154–155, no. 218.

15. Rumi, Jalāl al-Din, *The Mathnawí of Jalálu'ddín Rúmí*, transl. Reynold A. Nicholson, vol. 2, London: Luzac & Co., 1934, p. 157 (bk. 3, verses 2797–2804); see also Vakiliyān, Aḥmad, *Tams̲il va mas̲al*, vol. 2, Tehran: Sorush, 1366/1987, pp. 143–144; Marzolph, *Arabia ridens*, vol. 1, p. 101.

16. Ṣafi, Fakhr al-Din ʿAli, *Laṭāʾef al-ṭavāʾef*, ed. Aḥmad Golchin-Maʿāni, Tehran: Moḥammmad Ḥoseyn Eqbāl, 1336/1957, p. 365 (12,3,2).

17. Farāhi, Barkhordār ibn Maḥmud, *Maḥbub al-qolub*, Bombay, 1298/1881, p. 136; *Dāstānhā-ye Maḥbub al-qolub*, ed. ʿAli-Reżā Ẕakāvati Qarāgozlu, Tehran: Markaz-e nashr-e dāneshgāhi, 1373/1994, p. 53 (quoted *apud* Jaʿfari Qanavāti, Moḥammad, and Seyyid Aḥmad Vakiliyān, *Mas̲navi va mardom: revāyathā-ye shafāhi-ye qeṣṣehā-ye Mas̲navi*, Tehran: Sorush, 1393/2014, pp. 160–161); Rehatsek, Edward, *Amusing Stories: Translated from the Persian*, Bombay: Price Current Press, 1871, pp. 63–64, no. 16.

18. Marzolph, *Arabia ridens*, vol. 2, index, pp. 322–323 (Dieb), 327 (Einbrecher).

19. Ibn ʿĀṣim al-Andalusī, Abū Bakr ibn Muḥammad, *Ḥadāʾiq al-azāhir*, ed. ʿAfīf ʿAbd al-Raḥmān, Beirut: Dār al-Maṣīra, 1401/1981, p. 91; Granja, "Dos cuentos árabes," pp. 464–465; López Bernal, *Los Ḥadāʾiq al-azāhir*, vol. 1, p. 152, no. 218; López Bernal, "Nuevas versiones literarias de los cuentos tipo ATU 1848 y ATU 1848A en la Península ibérica," *Oceánide* 10 (2017) http://oceanide.netne.net/articulos/art10-4.pdf (accessed March 17, 2018).

CHAPTER 56

The Swindler Leaves an Uninformed Person as Security for His Purchase (ATU 1526)

The prank in which a swindler leaves an uninformed person in a shop as security for the purchase he or she takes along while pretending to go fetch money was studied in great detail by Kurt Ranke.[1] Classified as ATU 1526: *The Old Beggar and the Robbers*, the prank belongs to "the large genre of tales in which people of all times and regions have sympathized with the wit of crafty sharpers."[2] Historically traceable to thirteenth-century German author Der Stricker's *Pfaffe Âmîs*,[3] the prank is well documented in literary versions as of late in the sixteenth century and recent oral tradition all over Europe.[4] Middle Eastern versions date from at least the middle of the fifteenth century.

In the early twentieth-century German dialect version told by a certain Schraeder from Vorhelm in Westfalia, the swindler dresses the uninformed person up as the bishop.[5]

> A swindler happens to see a man who looks like the bishop. Together with his comrades, they dress him up as the bishop and take him to a large shop in the city. There they seat him on a chair, threatening to kill him should he say anything but "Jau, min Här" (Yes, Sir!). They ask the merchant to display numerous bales of precious cloth and when asking the "bishop" whether he likes it, the man would always respond "Jau, min Här!" Finally, the swindler and his companions load the bales on their wagon and leave, pretending to fetch payment. Asking the merchant whether he prefers gold, silver, or paper money, they leave the man dressed up as the bishop with him until they should return. When the swindlers do not return, the merchant finally grows impatient. Talking to the "bishop" he finds out that he has been swindled out of his merchandise. As the uninformed man cannot be held responsible, the merchant lets him go.

The Finnish narrator Ilma Käyhkö from Savonrante, aged 50, told the tale in 1935 adapted to the region's winter conditions.[6]

> An old man has three sons. The two eldest sons promise to work hard and save money, while the youngest wants to become rich by trading. On his

sleigh, he takes along a man of distinguished stature and goes to a large warehouse, instructing the man to respond to questions only by saying "Joo!" (Yes). In the warehouse, the young man pretends that the man in the sleigh is his father who owns a large shop and who sent him into the warehouse to purchase all kinds of goods for him. After all the requested goods are loaded on the sleigh, they request the "father" to come in and sign the receipt. When the owner of the shop asks him whether the man who bought the goods is his son, the "father" says "Yes!" And he continues to say "Yes!" when asked to sign and to pay. But since he does not have any money to pay the bill, the people realize that they have been swindled out of their goods. In the meantime, the swindler has left. He sells the stolen goods and becomes rich.

The French Canadian narrator Achille Fournier from whose oral performance the tale was recorded in Sainte-Anne, Marouraska, Québec, in 1915, learned it from Joseph Ouellet some twenty years earlier.[7] His tale begins by mentioning three young men who want to make money without having to work. They hire a beggar named Lévêque whom they instruct to say only "Yes," whatever he might be asked. Dressing the beggar up as the bishop (French *évêque*), they lodge him in a fine hotel and proceed to buy silk cloth and numerous other goods. Asked to pay, they refer to "the bishop" (*l'évêque* = Lévêque) in the hotel. When the merchant comes to collect his money, however, he finds that the "bishop" does not even know how to read.

The lengthy Maltese tale of Margherita presents an elaborated version in which the female protagonist repeats her ruse several times.[8] Here, the security the woman leaves when going home to fetch money is a recently deceased baby whom the woman has dug up and wrapped so as to make it appear alive. Contrary to the usual turn of events, she does return. But when she notices that the baby is dead, one after the other she accuses the merchants she deals with having killed her child, and the merchants insist on her taking the goods without payment so they will not have to face criminal charges.

In his analysis, Ranke identified a European and an "Oriental" branch of the tale. The former is documented in numerous versions in the European literatures, including French author Noël du Fail's *Contes et discours d'Eutrapel* (Tales and Discourses of Eutrapel; 1586), Spanish author Mateo Alemán's picaresque novel *Guzmán de Alfarache* (Guzmán of Alfarache; 1599) and German author Johann Peter de Memel's *Lustige Gesellschaft* (Joyful Company; 1656). Tales of the European branch are almost exclusively about a male trickster, and the events are often told in a single short tale. In contrast, versions from the "Oriental" branch present the tale as part of a longer chain of similar con games that are usually told about a well-known female trickster character. The earliest occurrence of the present tale in the Middle Eastern Muslim literatures is contained in the anonymous Ottoman Turkish collection of tales, *Ferec ba'd eş-şidde* (Relief after Hardship), whose oldest manuscripts date to the middle of the fifteenth or the end of the fourteenth century. Here, the tale is told about the female trickster Dalle (Dalīla) whose mischievous pranks are known in Persian literature since the eleventh century.[9]

> Noticing that a blind man hides his money in his coat, Dalla pretends to the blind man that she is his wife whom he had left, and instructs her daughters to address him as their father. Although the blind man finds it hard to believe their story, he finally gives in and accepts the situation (as he imagines it might be to his advantage). Dalla dresses him up, exchanging the blind man's old coat for a new one, and leaves him as a security for some precious jewels that she takes from the jeweler. Soon it becomes apparent that Dalla swindled both the blind man and the jeweler out of their possessions.[10]

The tale is not contained in the twelfth-century Persian compilation of tales, the *Munes-nāme*, that served as a model for the majority of tales in the Ottoman Turkish work.[11] It is, however, rendered in a related Persian compilation dating to the end of the sixteenth or the beginning of the seventeenth century that might well preserve the repertoire of an older work.[12] A version in which an unnamed female trickster leaves a "plaster figure enveloped and dressed up like an infant"[13] as a security is included in the late sixteenth- or early seventeenth-century Persian work *Maḥbub al-qolub* (The Hearts' Beloved) composed by Barkhordār ibn Maḥmūd Farāhi. In the compilation of Dalīla's tricks included in *The Thousand and One Nights*, Dalīla sees the handmaid of the provost of the merchants with her master's son.[14] She sends the servant away under a pretext and runs off with the boy. Then she leaves the boy with a jeweler, asking him to take care of the boy while she goes to his sister's wedding. Leaving the boy as a security, she is allowed to take along some precious jewels for the bride. The modern Persian version told in 1967 by Gholām Moḥammad Dāneshvar, a worker from Bidak-ābād, similarly presents a lengthy tale in one of whose episodes the female trickster's clever daughter leaves an uninformed chicken-seller with the jeweler as security for the jewels she takes along pretending to fetch money from her house.[15] Several versions of the tale are also attested from modern Arabic tradition.[16]

The tale's oldest European version, the one in the Stricker's *Pfaffe Âmîs*, is located in Constantinople, modern Istanbul. Although Ranke wondered whether this is sheer coincidence, he is not sure whether the apparent coincidence would not reveal itself to be intentional when one takes into consideration the structural correspondence of the early German version with its "Oriental" counterparts.[17] Moreover, one might argue that the Stricker's mention of Constantinople indicates the tale's Middle Eastern origin similarly to the mention of Balduch (= Baghdad) in the earliest-known European version of tale type ATU 1645: *The Treasure at Home* in the German *Karlmeinet* (see essay **82, *The Dream of***

Finding One's Fortune Somewhere Else). Although Ranke's conjectures as to Persian versions of Dalīla's tricks dating back as far as the tenth century are unfounded,[18] it is tempting to regard the present tale as "part of the ancient cultural relations between the Orient and the Occident."[19]

Notes

1. Ranke, Kurt, "Der Bettler als Pfand: Geschichte eines Schwanks in Occident und Orient," in Ranke, *Die Welt der Einfachen Formen*, Berlin: De Gruyter, 1978, pp. 224–243; previously published in *Zeitschrift für deutsche Philologie* 76 (1957), pp. 149–162, 358–364; see also Ranke, "Bettler als Pfand," in *Enzyklopädie des Märchens*, vol. 2 (1979), cols. 263–268.

2. Ranke, "Der Bettler als Pfand," p. 225.

3. Röhrich, Lutz, *Erzählungen des späten Mittelalters und ihr Weiterleben in Literatur und Volksdichtung bis zur Gegenwart*, Bern: Francke, 1962, vol. 1, pp. 173–179, no. IX,1.

4. For seventeenth- and eighteenth-century German chapbook versions see Uther, *Deutscher Märchenkatalog*, p. 395, no. 1526.

5. Henßen, Gottfried, *Volk erzählt: Münsterländische Sagen, Märchen und Schwänke*, Münster: Aschendorf, 1935, pp. 203–204, no. 147.

6. German translation in the archive of the *Enzyklopädie des Märchens*, Göttingen (collection Veli Käyyhkö KRK 351).

7. Barbeau, C.-Marius, "Contes populaires canadiens, seconde série," *Journal of American Folklore* 30 (1917), pp. 1–140, at pp. 134–135, no. 71.

8. Stumme, Hans, *Maltesische Märchen, Gedichte und Rätsel in deutscher Übersetzung*, Leipzig: Hinrichs, 1904, pp. 61–64, no. XX.

9. Marzolph, *Relief after Hardship*, p. 105; Decourdemanche, Jean-Adolphe, *Les Ruses des femmes (Mikri-zenan) et extraits du Plaisir après la peine (Feredj bad chiddeh)*, Paris: E. Leroux, 1896, pp. 101–108; Decourdemanche, *The Wiles of Women*, transl. J. and S.F. Mills Whitham, London: G. Routledge, 1928, pp. 77ff.

10. Marzolph, *Relief after Hardship*, p. 103, in no. 34.

11. Meredith-Owens, G.M., "An Early Persian Miscellany," in *Iran and Islam: In Memory of the Late Vladimir Minorsky*, ed. Clifford Edmund Bosworth, Edinburgh: University Press, 1971, pp. 435–441; see Marzolph, *Relief after Hardship*, pp. 47–48.

12. Marzolph, *Relief after Hardship*, p. 19 (manuscript A); see also Haag-Higuchi, Roxane, *Untersuchungen zu einer Sammlung persischer Erzählungen: Čihil wa-šiš ḥikāyat yā ǧāmiʿ al-ḥikāyāt*, Berlin: Klaus Schwarz, 1984, pp. 109–110, no. 43.

13. Rehatsek, Edward, *Amusing Stories, Translated from the Persian*, Bombay: Bombay Price Current Press, 1871, pp. 49–50, in no. 13.

14. Marzolph and Van Leeuwen, *The Arabian Nights Encyclopedia*, vol. 1, pp. 163–164, no. 224.

15. Marzolph, *Typologie*, p. 218, no. 1526; Enjavi Shirāzi, Abol-Qāsem, *Gol be-Ṣenoubar che kard: qeṣṣehā-ye irāni*, vol. 1, part 1, 2nd ed., Tehran: Amir Kabir, 2537/1978, pp. 45–48, no. 8.

16. El-Shamy, *Types*, pp. 830–831, no. 1526.

17. Ranke, "Der Bettler als Pfand," p. 242.

18. Ibid., p. 241.

19. Ibid., p. 243.

CHAPTER 57

The Thief Claims to Have Been Transformed into a Donkey (ATU 1529)

Joe Miller's Jests is probably the most successful English chapbook ever published. Loosely attributing jocular tales it contains to the historical English actor Joe Miller (1684–1738), the chapbook's first edition appeared in the year after his demise, in 1739, bearing the baroque title *Joe Miller's Jests / or, the / Wit's / Vade-Mecum / being / A Collection of the most Brilliant Jests; / the Politest Repartees; the most Ele- / gant Bon Mots, and most pleasant short / Stories in the English language. / First carefully collected in the Company, and / many of them transcribed from the Mouth of the Face- / tious Gentleman, whose Name they bear; and now set / forth and published by his lamentable Friend and former / Companion, Elijah Jenkins, Esq. / Most Humbly Inscribed / to those Choice Spirits of the Age, / Captain Bodens, Mr. Alexander Pope, / Mr. Professor Lacy, Mr. Orator Henley, / and Job Baker, the Kettle-Drummer /* London: / Printed and Sold by T. Read, in Dogwell Court, White / Fryars, Fleet Street. MDCCXXXIX.[1]

The chapbook enjoyed a total of three editions in 1739, a fourth edition appeared in the following year, and from then on the chapbook enjoyed an unprecedented popularity at least until the second half of the nineteenth century.[2] As the chapbook was constantly expanded and enlarged with new material, eventually any "time-worn jest" came to be stereotypically called a "Joe Miller," or simply a "Millerism."[3] In addition to later editions bearing titles such as *The New Joe Miller* (London: Joseph Smith, 1826), or *Joe Miller's Complete Jest Book* (London: H.G. Bohn, 1859), some of the jokes were reprinted in other similar publications such as *Democritus: or, The Laughing Philosopher* (London, 1771), *The Balloon Jester, or, Flights of Wit and Humor* (Dublin: S. Colbert, 1784), or the *Facetiae Cantabrigienses* (London, 1825). As of the end of the eighteenth century, texts from *Joe Miller's Jests* were also used for language instruction in textbooks teaching English to a German audience.[4] Although the jestbook's publication history is primarily a phenomenon of literature, the booklet's popularity gave it a strong potential to feed oral tradition, as the items it contained would not only be read over and over, but were doubtlessly also listened to, learned by heart, and then retold from memory numerous times. The tale under consideration here, already included in the first edition, is a case in point.[5]

> Three or four roguish Scholars walking out one Day from the University of Oxford, spied a poor Fellow near Abingdon, asleep in a Ditch, with an Ass by him, loaded with Earthen-Ware, holding the Bridle in his Hand, says one of the Scholars to the rest, if you'll assist me, I'll help you to a little Money, for you know we are bare at present; no doubt of it they were not long consenting; why then, said he, we'll go and sell this old Fellow's Ass at Abingdon, for you know the Fair is To-morrow, and we shall meet with Chapmen enough; therefore do you take the Panniers off, and put them upon my Back, and the Bridle over my Head, and then lead you the Ass to Market, and let me alone with the Old Man. This being done accordingly, in a little Time after the poor Man awaking, was strangely surprized to see his Ass thus metamorphosed; Oh! for God's-sake, said the Scholar, take this Bridle out of my Mouth, and this Load from my Back. Zoons, how came you here, reply'd the old Man, why, said he, my Father, who is a great Necromancer, upon a idle Thing I did to disoblige him, transformed me into an Ass, but now his Heart has relented, and I am come to my own Shape again, I beg you will let me go Home and thank him; by all Means, said the Crockrey Merchant, I don't desire to have any Thing to do with Conjuration, and so let the Scholar at Liberty, who went directly to his Comrades, that by this Time were making merry with the Money they had sold the Ass for: But the old Fellow was forced to go the next Day, to seek for a new one in the Fair, and after having look'd on several, his own was shewn him for a very good one, O, Ho! said he, what have he and his Father quarrelled again already? No, no, I'll have nothing to say to him.

Incidentally, this is the earliest unambiguously dated attestation in a European language of the widespread folktale that in folk narrative research is classified as tale type ATU 1529: *Thief as Donkey*.[6] Although the impact of *Joe Miller's Jests* on the tale's dissemination in English and European traditions can hardly be overestimated, versions of the tale documented from oral tradition show some variation, suggesting either the creative adaptation of the literary model or the influence of a variety of other appearances in writing or in oral performance that in their turn may have given rise to oral retellings. Specific variations in the tale's orally performed versions concern the occupation of the culprits, the animal the thief pretends to have been transformed into, the reason he gives for having been transformed, and the person who is said to have put the spell on him. Although the animal is most often a donkey or a mule, German versions sometimes mention an ox,[7] a Lithuanian version a horse,[8] and a version from French Canadian oral tradition a cow.[9] The misdemeanor for which the thief claims to have been punished is often not mentioned. If specified, he claims having led a sinful life,[10] having beaten his wife,[11] or having played cards during mass.[12] The person who is claimed to have put the spell on him is at times specified as a rich baron,[13] an angel,[14] the priest,[15] or an unnamed sorcerer;[16] almost exclusively, the person is male. The culprits are most often students, as in *Joe Miller's Jests*. Sometimes, they are specified to be monks.[17]

Other literary instances that may have given rise to retellings in oral tradition include, above all, French author Alexis Piron's (1689–1773) poetic rendering *Le moine bridé* (The Bridled Monk)[18] and a "diverting Italian tale, ascribed, on slight grounds," to Italian novelist Michele Colombo (1747–1830)[19] who is said to be the author of the *Novella di Gianni andato al Bosco a far legna* (Tale of Gianni Who Went to the Woods to Cut Wood).[20] Spanish versions collected from oral tradition often end with the proverb "Quien no te conoce, te compre" (Let Him Buy You Who Does Not Know You).[21] This proverb was recorded in Spain since the sixteenth century. Although it has so definitely "become associated with this tale in Hispanic territory that it is found in almost all variants of the story recorded from Spain, Catalunia, Portugal, and Spanish America,"[22] the tale's earliest documented versions from Hispanic oral tradition only date from the nineteenth century.[23] The version narrated by María Pascal, aged 28, in Pedraza, Segovia, on March 25, 1936, differs from Northern European tradition, where the sorcerer is almost exclusively a man, in that here an old woman is said to have punished the student by transforming him into a mule for a period of thirty years.[24] This variation also appears in a Hungarian tale, where it is the mother,[25] and in the Italian tale performed by Vito Cestone, aged 85, in October 1990, where the female character transforming the priest for his sinful love of "vino, juoco, le ffemmene" (wine, gambling, and women) is alleged to have been the Virgin Mary.[26]

The female character links to the tale's Arabic versions.[27] These include a nineteenth-century Algerian text collected from oral tradition[28] as well as versions in the nineteenth-century Arabic editions of *The Thousand and One Nights*,[29] in a late eighteenth-century anonymous collection of jocular tales focusing on the twelfth-century Ayyubid ruler Qarāqūsh (whom later tradition elaborated as a "focusee"[30] of tales dealing with silly juridical decisions),[31] and in Muḥammad ibn Aḥmad ibn (al-)Ilyās al-Ḥanafī's seventeenth-century compilation *Nuzhat al-udabā'* (Entertainment of the Educated).[32] In all of these versions, it is the man's mother who in some way or another is said to have been involved in the act of magical transformation. In the Algerian text, the man claims to have insulted his mother and consequently have been punished by God, in *The Thousand and One Nights* his mother is said have cursed him, and in both the Qarāqūsh anecdote and the *Nuzhat al-udabā'* his maltreated mother allegedly invoked God to assist her against him, following which he was transformed into an ass. Whereas the variations in other elements of the tale mainly illustrate different social contexts or attitudes such as an anticlerical attitude when the thieves are monks in the European versions, the different gender roles alluded to in the European and Arabic versions betray a decisive difference. The European versions predominantly allude to a male character who actively practices magic, wilfully transgressing the boundaries of nature. In contrast, the Arabic texts present a female character, more specifically the thief's mother. On the one hand, she plays the passive role alloted to her in traditional Arabic society by imploring the omnipotent creator for help against her transgressing son. At the same time, her curse implicitly extends into the realm of the supernatural, linking a woman's capacity of creating life to transforming it through magic.

The tale's earliest identified appearance is documented in Ibn al-Jawzī's (d. 1201) *Akhbār al-Ḥamqā* (Tales of Stupid People).[33] The author himself tells the tale as follows:

> One of my comrades told me that a certain stupid man was once leading his donkey. A certain clever person said to one of his comrades, "I can take away his donkey without this stupid man even noticing." The other one asked, "How do you want to do that, since the halter is in his hand?" Thereupon the first one approached, loosened the halter and attached it to his own head. Then he motioned to his comrade to take the donkey and go away. The other one took away the donkey, and his comrade walked behind the stupid man for some time, the halter attached to his head. Then he stopped. The man pulled the rope, but he did not move. The man noticed him and asked, "Where is the donkey?" The thief responded, "It is me!" The stupid man asked, "How can that be?" And the thief explained, "I was disobedient to my mother, so I was transformed into a donkey and have been in your service since then. Now my mother has forgiven me, and so I turned human again." The stupid man exclaimed, "There is no power nor strength except through God! How am I to keep you in my service, since you are a human being?" The thief responded, "That's the way it was!" And the stupid man said, "So go your way, with God's clemency!" The thief went his way, and the stupid man returned home. There he said to his wife, "Have you already heard the news? We had a human being in our service and did not know about it. How should we make amends and repent?" His wife advised him, "Give alms as much as you can!"
>
> For several days, the stupid man stayed at home, then his wife said to him, "It is your profession to lease out (animals). Go and buy a donkey and work with it." The man went to the market. There he found his own donkey which was being offered for sale. He approached it, put his mouth to its ear and whispered, "You schemer! So you disobeyed your mother again?"

Both the European and the Middle Eastern attestations of the tale satirize the naive belief in magic and sorcery that was widely spread in the premodern world. A well-known tale of magic transformation that might have rung a bell in the mind of the premodern Arab audience is the tale of "Jullanār the Sea-Born and Prince Badr Bāsim" as included in the fourteenth-century manuscript of *al-Ḥikāyāt al-ajība* (Marvelous Tales)[34] and the fifteenth-century manuscript of *The Thousand and One Nights* that served as the basis for Antoine Galland's early eighteenth-century translation (see also essay **7, *The Unfaithful Wife Transforms Her Husband into a Dog***).[35] The magic transformation of a human being into a mount is already mentioned in a tale included in the paremiological work compiled by al-Mufaḍḍal ibn Salama (d. after 903). In this tale ʿĀʾisha, the Prophet Mohammed's wife, ascribes the action to the man Khurāfa, whose name later became the generic denomination for marvelous tales.[36] Moreover, the intricate procedure Queen Lāb employs in the tale of Jullanār to prepare the food she uses to transform Prince Badr Bāsim is detailed in Somadeva's eleventh-century Sanskrit *Kathāsaritsāgara* (The Ocean of Streams of Stories).[37] The bridle that the present story mentions only in passing plays a pivotal role as a magic object in tale type ATU 325: *The Magician and His Pupil.*

In Arabic literature, the jocular tale's tradition was constantly invigorated by its repeated quotations over the centuries. This continued until early in the twentieth century when the tale appears, for instance, in the *Nawādir Juḥā* (Tales about Juḥā)[38] and the Egyptian chapbook *Kitāb Ẓarīf al-maʿānī fī 'l-ḥawādīt wa-'l-aghānī* (The Book of Elegant Expressions: Tales and Songs).[39] In this constantly refreshed tradition, the tale was collected from nineteenth- and early twentieth-century oral tradition in Arabic.[40] Arabic tradition likely is also at the roots of the tale's occurrence in the fifteenth- or late fourteenth-century Ottoman Turkish *Ferec baʿd eş-şidde* (Relief after Hardship)[41] as well as in modern Neo-Aramaic,[42] Persian,[43] and Turkish[44] oral tradition.

Notes

1. https://archive.org/stream/joemillersjestsooomott#page/n3/mode/2up (accessed December 15, 2016).

2. For a representative collection of editions, see *Catalog of the Schmulowitz Collection of Wit and Humor (SCOWAH)*, San Francisco: San Francisco Public Library, 1962, pp. 162–164.

3. https://en.wikipedia.org/wiki/Joe_Miller_(actor) (accessed December 15, 2016).

4. Ebeling, Christoph Daniel, *Vermischte Aufsätze in englischer Prose, hauptsächlich zum Besten derer welche diese Sprache in Rücksicht auf bürgerliche Geschäfte lernen wollen*, 4th ed., Hamburg: C. Herolds Wittwe, 1784; Wagner, Karl Fr. Chr., *Vollständige und auf die möglichste Erleichterung des Unterrichts abzweckende Englische Sprachlehre für die Deutschen*, Braunschweig: Schulbuchhandlung, 1802.

5. *Joe Miller's Jests* (1739), pp. 22–24, no. 79; 4th ed. (1740), p. 18, no. 79; 8th ed. (1745), p. 20–21, no. 104; 12th ed.(1750), pp. 18–19, no. 103; *Democritus: or, The Laughing Philosopher*, London [1771], pp. 96–97; *Joe Miller's Jests*, new ed. London: T. Axtel [1775]), p. 22, no. 103; *The Balloon Jester* (Dublin: S. Colbert, [1784]), pp. 4–5; Ebeling, *Vermischte Aufsätze*, pp. 10–11, no. 19; Wagner, *Vollständige [. . .] Englische Sprachlehre*, p. 360, no. 9; Gooch, Richard, *Facetiae Cantabrigienses*, London: William Cole, 1825, p. 10; *The New Joe Miller* (1826), p. 15; *Joe Miller's Jests* (London: Whittaker and Co., 1836), pp. 11–12, no. 67; *Joe Miller's Complete Jest Book* (1859), pp. 42–43, no. 151. All of these items have been viewed at either Google Books or the Internet Archive. See also Clouston, William Alexander, *Popular Tales and Fictions: Their Migrations and Transformations*, ed. Christine Goldberg, Santa Barbara, CA: ABC-Clio, 2002, p. 236; Briggs, *A Dictionary*,

vol. A2, p. 233, see also p. 183–184 (from the *Facetiae Cantabrigienses*, 1825); Wesselski, *Der Hodscha Nasreddin*, vol. 2, p. 229, no. 487.

6. Matičetov, Milko, "Dieb als Esel," in *Enzyklopädie des Märchens*, vol. 3 (1981), cols. 640–643. The entry lacks a historical discussion.

7. Kubitschek, Rudolf, *Böhmerwäldler Bauernschwänke*, Vienna: Strache, 1920, pp. 47–49; Stübs, Hugo, *Ull Lüj vertellen: Plattdeutsche Geschichten aus dem pommerschen Weizacker*, Greifswald: Bamberg, 1938, pp. 143–145, no. 83.

8. Danner, Edmund, *Die Tanne und ihre Kinder: Märchen aus Litauen*, 2nd ed. Berlin: Groszer, 1961, pp. 67–69.

9. Lemieux, Germain, *Les vieux m'ont conté*, vol. 3, Montréal: Bellarmin, 1974, 231–234 (told in 1964 by Télesphore Courchesne, aged 67, who learned the tale from Théophile Brault, aged 45, around 1916).

10. *Aus der Heimat—für die Heimat* 1 (1905), pp. 3–4 (German from Pomerania); Kubitschek, *Böhmerwäldler Bauernschwänke*, pp. 47–49.

11. Gredt, Nikolaus, *Sagenschatz des Luxemburger Landes*, Luxemburg: Buck, 1883, pp. 641–642, no. 1215.

12. Merkens, Heinrich, *Was sich das Volk erzählt: Deutscher Volkshumor*, 2nd ed., vol. 3, Jena: Costenoble, 1900, pp. 222–223, no. 214; Van der Kooi, Jurjen, and Theo Schuster, *Der Großherzog und die Marktfrau: Märchen und Schwänke aus dem Oldenbuerger Land*, Leer: Schuster, 1994, pp. 236–238, no. 142.

13. Merkens, *Was sich das Volk erzählt*, 2nd ed., vol. 1, Jena: 1892, pp. 208–209, no. 250.

14. Gredt, *Sagenschatz*, pp. 641–642, no. 1215.

15. Van der Kooi and Schuster, *Der Großherzog*, pp. 236–238, no. 142.

16. Dittmaier, Heinrich, *Sagen, Märchen und Schwänke von der unteren Sieg*, Bonn: Röhrscheid, 1950, p. 135, no. 378.

17. Dietz, Josef, *Lachende Heimat: Schwänke und Schnurren aus dem Bonner Land*, Bonn: Trapp, 1951, pp. 32–33, no. 76.

18. Toldo, Pietro, "Le Moine bridé: A propos d'un conte de Piron," *Revue de littérature comparée* 2 (1922), pp. 54–59; see also Clouston, *Popular Tales and Fictions*, pp. 234–235.

19. Clouston, *Popular Tales and Fictions*, pp. 232–233, quote p. 232.

20. See *A Catalogue of the Celebrated Library of the Late Count Borromeo, of Padua*, Auction Catalogue by Mr. Evans, London, 1817, pp. 71, no. 250; Clouston, *Popular Tales and Fictions*, p. 233.

21. Boggs, Ralph S., "Let Him Buy You Who Does Not Know You," *Studies in Philology* 32.1 (1935), pp. 22–39. In German tradition, the phrase also appears at the end of versions of ATU 1170: *The Unsalable Woman*; see Rasumny, Alexander: "Weib: Böses W. als schlechte Ware," in *Enzyklopädie des Märchens*, vol. 14 (2014), cols. 556–557.

22. Boggs, "Let Him Buy You," p. 34.

23. Amores, Montserrat, *Catálogo de cuentos folklóricos reelaboradoros por escritores del siglo XIX*, Madrid: Consejo superior de investigaciones científicas, Departemento de antropología de España y América, 1997, pp. 263–265, no. 173: *El ladrón afirma haber sido transformado en un caballo* (quoting Fernán Caballero, 1859).

24. Espinosa, Aurelio Macedonio, Jr., *Cuentos populares de Castilla y Leon*, vol. 2, Madrid: Consejo Superior de Investigaciones Cientificas, 1988, pp. 373–374, 545, no. 439.

25. Ortutay, Gyula, *Ungarische Volksmärchen*, Berlin: Rütten & Loening, 1957, pp. 474–475, no. 35.

26. De Simone, Roberto, and Ugo Vuoso, *Fiabe campane*, Torino: Einaudi, 1994, pp. 326–331, 1449, no. 26, quote p. 328.

27. Marzolph, *Arabia ridens*, vol. 2, p. 266, no. 1240.

28. Certeux, Alphonse, and Emile Henri Carnoy, *L'Algérie traditionelle*, Paris: Maisonneuve & Leclerc, 1884, p. 49; quoted by Toldo, "Le Moine bridé," pp. 56–57.

29. Chauvin, *Bibliographie*, vol. 7 (1903), pp. 136–137, no. 406; Marzolph and Van Leeuwen, *The Arabian Nights Encyclopedia*, vol. 1, pp. 382–383, no. 118.

30. Marzolph, Ulrich, "'Focusees' of Jocular Fiction in Classical Arabic Literature," in *Story-telling in the Framework of Non-fictional Arabic Literature*, ed. Stefan Leder, Wiesbaden: Harrassowitz, 1998, pp. 118–129.

31. Casanova, Paul, *Karakoûch*, *Mémoires publiés par les members de la Mission Archéologique Français du Caire* 6 (1897), pp. 447–491, at 476 (Arabic text), 489–490 (translation). For other tales about this character see Marzolph, *Arabia ridens*, vol. 1, p. 11, note 48.

32. Basset, *Mille et un contes*, vol. 1, pp. 283–285, no. 186; Ḥanafī, Muḥammad ibn Aḥmad ibn (al-)Ilyās al-, *Nuzhat al-udabāʾ*, Gotha, Ms. Orient A 2706, fol. 77b–78a; see also Lecoy, Félix, "La Farce de Cauteleux, Baras, et le Villain," in *Mélanges de langue et littérature du moyen âge et de la Renaissance offerts à Jean Frappier*, vol. 2, Bern: Droz, 595–602; also in Lecoy, *Mélanges de philologie et de littérature romanes*, Geneva: Droz, 1988, pp. 584 [409]–601 [416].

33. German translation in Marzolph, *Arabia ridens*, vol. 1, pp. 254–255, no. 13.

34. *Tales of the Marvellous and News of the Strange*, transl. Malcolm C. Lyons, London: Penguin, 2014, pp. 113–134, no. 6, at p. 130–131; see also Marzolph, Ulrich, ed., *Das Buch der wundersamen Geschichten: Erzählungen aus der Welt von 1001 Nacht*, Munich: C.H. Beck, 1999, pp. 163–192, 644–645, no. 6.

35. Haddawy, Husain, transl., *The Arabian Nights*, New York: Alfred A. Knopf, 1990, pp. 383–428; Marzolph and Van Leeuwen, *The Arabian Nights Encyclopedia*, vol. 1, pp. 248–251.

36. Mufaḍḍal ibn Salama, *al-Fākhir*, ed. Charles A. Storey, Leiden: Brill, 1915, pp. 138–140; ed. ʿAbd al-ʿAlīm al-Ṭaḥāwī and Muḥammad ʿAlī al-Najjār, Cairo: ʿĪsā al-Bābī al-Ḥalabī, 1380/1960, pp. 169–171, in no. 280; MacDonald, Duncan Black, "The Earlier History of the Arabian Nights," *Journal of the Royal Asiatic Society* (1924), pp. 353–397, at pp. 373–374; Drory, Rina, "Three Attempts to Legitimize Fiction in Classical Arabic Literature," *Jerusalem Studies in Arabic and Islam*, 18 (1994), pp. 146–164, at p. 153.

37. Somadeva, *The Ocean of Story: Being C.H. Tawney's Translation of Somadeva's Kathā Sarit Sāgara*, ed. N.M. Penzer, reprint Delhi: Motilal Banarsidass, 1968, vol. 6, pp. 55–56, 59–66, no. 163.

38. Farrāj, ʿAbd al-Sattār Aḥmad, *Akhbār Juḥā*, Cairo: Maktabat Miṣr, 1954, pp. 65–66.

39. *Kitāb Ẓarīf al-maʿānī fī 'l-ḥawādīt wa-'l-aghānī*, Miṣr: Maktabat Aḥmad ʿAlī al-Malījī, [1910], p. 6. For Arabic chapbbooks of the late nineteenth and early twentieth centuries, see Littmann, Enno, *Arabische Märchen und Schwänke aus Agypten: Nach mündlicher Überlieferung gesammelt, übersetzt und erklärt*, Mainz: Akademie der Wissenschaften und der Literatur, 1955; Khayyat, Latif, "The Style and Contents of Arabic Folk Material in Chapbooks in the New York Public Library," *Fabula* 28 (1987), pp. 59–71; Marzolph, Ulrich, "Still the Same Old Jokes: The Continuity of Jocular Tradition in Early Twentieth-Century Egyptian Chapbooks," in *The Other Print Tradition: Essays on*

Chapbooks, Broadsides, and Related Ephemera, ed. Cathy Lynn und Michael J. Preston, New York: Garland, 1995, pp. 161–179.

40. El-Shamy, *Types*, p. 834, no. 1529 (references from Lebanon, Tunisia, and Morocco).

41. Marzolph, *Relief after Hardship*, pp. 103, 105, in no. 34 (7).

42. Sachau, Eduard, *Skizze des Fellichi-Dialekts von Mosul*, Berlin: Königl. Akademie der Wissenschaften, 1895, pp. 68–70, no. 4.

43. Marzolph, *Typologie*, p. 219, no. 1529.

44. Eberhard and Boratav, *Typen*, p. 373, no. 341 III.

CHAPTER 58

The Subaltern Is Made Lord for a Day (ATU 1531)

From Shakespeare's *Taming of the Shrew* (1590/92) and its sources[1] via Calderón de la Barca's *La vida es sueño* (Life Is a Dream; 1634/35)[2] to frequent quotations in German chapbook literature of the seventeenth and eighteenth centuries,[3] the tale of the common man, often a drunkard, who is made lord for a day is richly documented in the European literatures.[4] Classified as tale type ATU 1531: *Lord for a Day*, the tale essentially tells of a lower-class man who, having fallen into a drunken stupor, is taken to the house of a wealthy man where he is made to believe the next day that he actually is the lord himself and that the power and luxury he experiences are part of his regular life. Made drunk again at night, he is taken back to his previous surroundings. When he wakes up the following day, the man thinks he has been dreaming. Sometimes he experiences a severe crisis of consciousness, as he does not know whether the dream world was real or whether reality is just a dream. Contrasting with the richly documented history of literary versions, the tale has had surprisingly little impact in European oral tradition. A nineteenth-century Russian tale collected by A.I. Kritskov narrates the events in a fairly rudimentary manner, set during the first days of the reign of Tsar Alexander I (1777–1825).[5]

> Driving through town, the tsar perceives a drunken soldier lying unconscious at the side of the road. The tsar takes him to the royal palace where his servants dress up as angels and make the soldier believe that he is in paradise. Rather than eat, the soldier asks them for wine and drinks his fill until he falls unconscious again. The tsar's servants take him back to the place where they originally picked him up and leave him there. Although his companions do not believe him, the soldier never forgets his experience and keeps telling people about his one day in paradise.

The protagonist of a mid-nineteenth-century German version recorded in the parish of Visbek in Oldenburg is the poor broom-maker Harms.[6]

> Having sold his brooms in town, Harms has the habit of getting drunk to such an extent that he can hardly find his way back home. His wife Grete's

> admonitions are to no avail. One day on his way back home from town he stumbles and passes out. A rich nobleman who happens to come by decides to amuse himself by playing a trick on him and has Harms taken to his castle.
>
> Placing Harms in a room in the cellar, the nobleman and his servants make him believe that he is in hell. When Harms repents and swears to be pious and never drink liquor again, the nobleman dresses in white clothes and brings him to a splendid hall where Harms is lavishly treated with food and drink. When he falls into a drunken stupor, they take him back to the place where they had picked him up.
>
> Finally back home, Harms tells his wife about his experience in Hell and Heaven and never returns to his former practice of drinking.

In the tale's version in the introduction to Shakespeare's *Taming of the Shrew*, the tinker Christopher Sly is made to believe that "he is in fact a lord who has, because of insanity, believed himself to be a tinker for years and years."[7] While in Shakespeare's play, believed to have been finished by 1592, the plot has no ending, in the anonymous 1594 play *The Taming of a Shrew*, Sly "continues to interject, eventually falls asleep and is deposited back by the tavern. He assumes that his brief life as a lord was just a dream."[8] The two differing late sixteenth-century versions demonstrate that different solutions and interpretations of the tale existed at an early stage. The tale's earliest European version documented so far is contained in a letter the Valencian scholar and humanist, Juan Luis Vives (d. 1540), wrote to the Duke of Béjar.[9] Shakespeare scholarship mainly quotes the letter from the text published by historian Pontus Heuterus in his *Rerum Burgundicarum Libri Sex* (1485), also known as *De Rebus Burgundicis*.[10] In Vives's version, the lord who picks up the sleeping drunkard is Philip the Good, Duke of Burgundy (1396–1467). When the country fellow wakes up in the lord's castle the next morning, he is made to believe that he is a person of high birth. When at night he again falls asleep, he is stripped of his courtly robes, dressed in his old clothes, and placed where he had originally been found. The jest ends with the poor man believing in his vision, however much his friends try to dissuade him.

Discussing the European versions as "variants and analogues" to the tale of "The Sleeper and the Waker" in *The Thousand and One Nights*,[11] William Alexander Clouston, who is often highly sympathetic toward a given tale's "Oriental" origin, does not think "that this is a story imported from the East: the adventure is just as likely to have happened in Bruges as in Baghdád."[12] The elaborate version of the tale in the *Nights* goes as follows.[13]

> Abū 'l-Ḥasan is the son of a rich merchant. When his father dies, he divides the money he inherits into two equal parts. Stowing away one half of the money, he squanders the other half in *dolce vita* together with a group of young people. When his funds are exhausted, he is, however, shocked that none of his presumed friends is willing to help him. He now returns to the

money he wisely stowed away. Instead of spending his time with unreliable friends, he makes a habit of inviting a stranger to his house every night, vowing not to invite the same person twice.

One evening, Abū 'l-Ḥasan happens to invite Caliph Hārūn al-Rashīd who roams the city in disguise (Mot. K1812.17), and entertains him lavishly with food and drink. When the caliph becomes curious as to his host's status, Abū 'l-Ḥasan warns him not to long for things past since mourning for whatever is bygone makes no sense. As the caliph insists, Abū 'l-Ḥasan proceeds to tell the story of the trickster and the cook in order to demonstrate that whatever you do, your action will have consequences.

A trickster (*ḥarfūsh*) is hungry but has no money to buy food. Confident that his tricks will eventually help him find a solution, he goes to a cook's stall, orders food and starts to consume his meal. Looking around the stall, he happens to see the bloody tail of a horse barely hidden under a vessel. Cleverly deducing that the cook illegally mixes his food with horse meat, he gets up intending to walk away. When the cook requests payment, the trickster pretends to have paid already. As the two of them start quarreling, the people on the street gather around them wondering what the quarrel is about. At one point, the trickster mentions "the tail" and the cook immediately understands the allusion. In order to cover up his misdeed, he pretends to remember his customer's payment and even offers to return him some change.

Following this tale, the caliph insists on hearing his host's own story, and when Abū 'l-Ḥasan tells him about his experience, the caliph is amazed at his foresight, good breeding, and magnanimity. Wishing to return his host's kindness, the caliph asks Abū 'l-Ḥasan whether he has any wish he longed for. Abū 'l-Ḥasan informs him that his only wish is to be in the position of the ruler for a single day so as to punish his malevolent neighbors, the *imām* of the nearby mosque and four old men, who keep complaining about his merry-making and even threatened to report him to the authorities. He wants to have his neighbors whipped, paraded through the streets, and finally have them deported to another city. The caliph decides to make his host's wish come true and makes him unconscious by putting a drug in his drink. The caliph's servants then carry Abū 'l-Ḥasan to the palace where everybody receives strict orders to hail him as the caliph as soon as he wakes up the following morning.

As Abū 'l-Ḥasan wakes up, he finds himself in the palace being treated as the caliph. Not trusting his senses, he is reassured by the servants that he truly is the caliph. Finally he decides that his strange experience is not a dream but reality. Holding court with all the nobles, he acts as a just and considerate ruler. Meanwhile, at one point he orders the vizier Jaʿfar to punish his malevolent neighbors, and Jaʿfar executes the order on the spot. In the evening, Abū 'l-Ḥasan wines and dines together with his entourage,

> in particular enjoying the jovial company of a number of female servants whose names he learns. As the evening draws to a close, the caliph—who has been watching everything in secret—has him drugged again, and Abū 'l-Ḥasan is brought back to his house.
>
> Waking up in the morning, Abū 'l-Ḥasan calls for the female servants, and to the great astonishment of his mother informs her that he is not her son but the caliph. Arguing with him, his mother step by step convinces him that his experience was caused by interference of the Devil and that he is none other than her son. In order to console him further, she tells him the good news that his neighbors were punished the day before in exactly the manner he had longed for. This news throws Abū 'l-Ḥasan into a fit, since he remembers having issued the order while being caliph. He now refuses to believe that his experience was a dream and asserts that, in fact, he was and still is the caliph. As the quarrel with his mother turns into a fight, the neighbors come to his mother's rescue and have Abū 'l-Ḥasan confined in the mental asylum. Here, he is chained and given a heavy treatment of lashes for a number of days until he sobers up and his mother takes him back home.
>
> Returning to his previous habit of inviting guests, Abū 'l-Ḥasan once again meets Hārūn al-Rashīd in disguise. The caliph manages to convince Abū 'l-Ḥasan that he did not do him any harm and, contrary to his host's declared intention, is invited again. As on the previous occasion, Abū 'l-Ḥasan treats his guest lavishly before being drugged and carried to the palace another time. When Abū 'l-Ḥasan finds himself in the palace again, he is so confused by the dramatic challenge to his perception that he asks a slave to bite his ear so as to prove to himself that he is not dreaming. The slave does so with such a vigor that Abū 'l-Ḥasan loses whatever is left of his senses, and to the great amusement of those present rips off his clothes and hilariously dances around in the nude. Finally, the caliph shows himself and reveals his stratagem to Abū 'l-Ḥasan. He apologizes for tricking him and makes him one of his boon companions.
>
> Abū 'l-Ḥasan is married to one of the girls belonging to the entourage of the caliph's wife, and together they enjoy their lives until their financial means are exhausted. Wondering what to do, they devise a plan. Each of them is to pretend that the other one has died, hereby enabling both of them to collect money for the other's burial from Hārūn and his wife, respectively. As Hārūn and his wife come to pay respects to the supposedly dead couple, they wonder which one of them died first. The situation is resolved, and everybody lives happily ever after.

Although the tale of the *Nights* has a similar structure, it differs from the European texts in various points.[14] To list only some of the most obvious variations, first, the protagonist of the *Nights'* version is not a lower-class man or peasant but the well-bred hedonist son of a wealthy merchant. The impoverished spendthrift son of a merchant (Mot. W131.1) is a frequent protagonist of the tales of the *Nights*, a work that Aboubakr Chraïbi characterized as addressing a merchant audience to such an extent as to constitute a "mirror for merchants."[15] Second, although drinking is an essential part of the *Nights* tale, the drinking here occurs in the frame of a convivial gathering the protagonist enjoys with Caliph Hārūn al-Rashīd who roams the town in disguise. Third, the protagonist is not made "caliph for a day" so that the actual ruler can make fun of him. Instead, the caliph allows his host to hold the position of power for a single day in order to enable him to fulfill his most ardent wish, that is, punish his malevolent neighbors who spoil his fun by criticizing him for his hedonism. Accordingly, the man does not lose consciousness because of heavy drinking but as a result of the soporific hemp (*banj*) the caliph tricks him into consuming. And fourth, the events are repeated after an interlude in which the protagonist experiences a severe crisis of consciousness and is only brought back to his wits by going through a ruthless treatment at the local lunatic asylum. Only when the events are repeated a second time does the caliph openly enjoy the protagonist's confusion, immediately afterward disclosing his ruse and rewarding him with the position of boon companion.

The tale's elaborate version in the *Nights* consists of several originally independent sections that were ingeniously joined together. First, the embedded tale of the trickster and the cook as told by Abū 'l-Ḥasan appears to be a fairly late addition that is not contained in the tale's version given in Galland's early eighteenth-century translation[16] nor in the tale's earliest attested Arabic version as included in the *Kitāb Laṭā'if akhbār al-uwal* (Book of Subtle Stories from the Forefathers) compiled by Egyptian historian Muḥammad ibn ʿAbd al-Muʿṭī al-Isḥāqī (d. after 1623).[17] Incidentally, the Arabic manuscript used by Galland that had remained unknown for a long time has recently been identified.[18] And second, the tale's ending in which Abū 'l-Ḥasan and his wife alternately pose as dead is an originally independent anecdote whose earlier versions are attributed to Abū Dulāma (d. ca. 777), a poet of the early Abbasid period.[19] This anecdote, classified as tale type ATU 1556: *The Double Pension (Burial Money)*, is first attested in tenth-century Arabic literature.[20] Already in the fourteenth-century Arabic compilation of tales that for want of an existing title is known as *Kitāb al-Ḥikāyāt al-ʿajība* (Book of Marvelous Tales), it serves as an attachment to a version of the international tale type ATU 1641: *Doctor Know-All* (see essay ***79, The Lowly Man Posing as a Soothsayer***).[21] In the *Nights*, Abū 'l-Ḥasan's trick was read as a suitable revenge for the trick the caliph previously played on him.

Although the tale's version in *The Thousand and One Nights* was frequently discussed as an analogue for the tale's European versions in terms of structure, its relatively late date in addition to its distinctly different protagonist, action, and motivations do not allow the unambiguous identification of the former as a direct precursor to the latter. There is, however, another version of the tale in the shorter sibling of *The Thousand and One Nights*, *The Hundred and One Nights*, a Maghrebi (North African) compilation whose frame tale (although not its embedded tales) largely corresponds to that of the larger compilation.[22] Although the oldest manuscript of *The Hundred and One Nights* may or may not date to the thirteenth century, the tale in question is only included in a single manuscript dating from the nineteenth century.[23] In contrast to the well-bred Abū 'l-Ḥasan, the protagonist here is a lower-class character as in the tale's European versions.

> Old Hunchback, who works for a blacksmith, invests the money he earns every day in food and wine and spends his evenings all by himself out in the open, drinking and reciting poetry. When Caliph Hārūn al-Rashīd and his vizier Jaʿfar happen to come by one night, Hārūn enjoys the old man's company so much that he orders him brought to the palace. Being so drunk that he does not realize what is happening, the old man is properly washed, dressed up in the caliph's robes, and installed on the caliph's throne. When the old man is sobered up with the help of a certain potion, he soon comes to enjoy the courtly company so much that he believes himself to be the ruler and trusts the slave girls pretending to be his wives. As he is intent on having sex with one of them, the young woman insists on first having some food. She then profits from the occasion to make him swallow a drug (*banj*) that makes him unconscious. Once he has passed out, the old man is dressed again in his own clothing and taken back to his house. With some variation and a certain increase in tension, the events are repeated on three consecutive nights. On the third night, Hārūn, who has been participating in the scene without being recognized by the old man, discloses his stratagem and rewards the man generously for the pleasant entertainment.

With reference to the lower-class protagonist and his sexual advances, it was argued that this tale is much closer to the European versions.[24] But even if "the thematic parallels between Sly and "The Old Hunchback" are tantalizing, further work is needed to ascertain a connection between the tale from *The Hundred and One Nights*"[25] and the tale's European versions. Although the relatively late dates of all Arabic versions do not suggest them to have served as a source for the European versions, around the year 1600 Arabic literature appears to have known as many differing versions as did the European literatures.

The discussion of possible relations between the tale's various versions becomes even more complex when considering the fact that the Arabic versions might adapt their basic structure from earlier Indian tales. The Chinese translation of the Buddhist *Tripiṭaka* (Three Baskets), more specifically Kang Seng-Hui's (d. 280) *Liudu jijing* (Scriptural Collection on the [Buddha's Cultivation of the] Six Perfections), compiled in the third century, contains a tale in which a king seeks to enlighten his subjects by teaching them that "the spiritual principle keeps transforming itself."[26]

> One day, the king dresses in disguise so as to learn about his subjects' conditions. When the king asks a poor cobbler whom he regards as the happiest person on earth, the cobbler responds that this must surely be the king. In order to teach him a lesson (and have fun), the king has the cobbler drink until he falls unconscious, brings him to the palace, and has him act as the ruler. Having to deal with the affairs of the state, the poor cobbler becomes unhappier from day to day, until finally his principal wife renders him unconscious again and has him returned to his original dwelling. When the king visits the cobbler again some days later, the latter tells him about his "dream" and admits to having been wrong in his evaluation.

In some ways, the story of Old Hunchback in *The Hundred and One Nights* is closer to the tale's version in the *Tripiṭaka* than the one in *The Thousand and One Nights*.[27] In both the *Tripiṭaka* and *The Hundred and One Nights*, the main protagonist is an old man of lowly profession (a cobbler, the blacksmith's assistant) who for a short period experiences the supreme bliss of wealth and power. Meanwhile, being either naive (*Tripiṭaka*) or focused on the immediate fulfillment of sensual pleasures (*The Hundred and One Nights*), in his incompetence he does not constitute a danger to the actual ruler's position. By contrast, although in *The Thousand and One Nights* Abū 'l-Ḥasan proves to be perfectly competent in giving judgment as a ruler, it is his good breeding that guarantees that he will not abuse the power of his temporary position.

The intoxicating effect of wine is one of the tale's essential ingredients in virtually all of the tale's versions. In the *Tripiṭaka* and in *The Hundred and One Nights*, wine—whether offered by the ruler as in the *Tripiṭaka* or consumed on a customary basis as in *The Hundred and One Nights*—serves to intoxicate the protagonist to such a degree that he loses consciousness. In the story of Abū 'l-Ḥasan in *The Thousand and One Nights*, the drinking of wine merely creates a convivial atmosphere in which none of the participants loses control. *The Hundred and One Nights* betray an intermediary position, since the protagonist first drinks himself unconscious while later, when he is posing as caliph, a lump of *banj* serves to knock him out. The *Tripiṭaka* mentions wine on both occasions, and the story of Abū 'l-Ḥasan mentions *banj* as a soporific in an atmosphere of convivial drinking. Both wine as a means of intentional intoxication and the protagonist's lowly status also link the versions of both the *Tripiṭaka* and *The Hundred and One Nights* to the tale's European versions.

The version of the *Tripiṭaka* opens up yet another avenue for the many different ways in which the "lord for a day" pattern can function. In the European versions and in *The Hundred and One Nights*, the ruler employs his ruse for his own entertainment. In *The Thousand and One Nights*, the ruler grants his convivial friend the full rights of his own supreme position for a day to show his gratitude and recompense his host's kindness.[28] In the *Tripiṭaka*, the tale is linked with the didactic intention of teaching the lowly man the lesson that things are not always what they appear to be. Specifically, the ruler demonstrates that wealth and power do not necessarily guarantee happiness. In ancient Indian literature, this message is similarly used in the *Aśokāvadāna* (The Narrative of King Aśoka), a text whose earliest versions were compiled in the second century BCE and whose English translation relies on a Sanskrit text probably compiled in the second century CE. After his own conversion to Buddhism, King Aśoka aims to convert his brother Vitaśoka with a fairly intricate scheme, as part of which Aśoka has Vitaśoka act as the ruler for a number of days. Although Vitaśoka is surrounded with "all the delights of royalty," he is not able to enjoy his position, since his brother has placed "fearsome executioners at his door to remind him every day of exactly how much time he has left to live."[29] In addition to reminding one of the ancient motif of the "Sword of Damocles" (Mot. F833.2),[30] essentially, this lesson also lies at the core of tale type ATU 754: *Lucky Poverty*, in which the poor man loses his former happiness when a rich man gives him money.[31]

Whatever the different implications of the "lord for a day" pattern, it has proved to be extremely effective over a period of some two millennia. The didactic message of the ancient Indian Buddhist versions is somehow retained in modern European folktales where, rather than demonstrating the fragility of human consciousness, it now serves to discipline lower-class protagonists in a hierarchically structured world to "stick to their last." On the other side of the scale, the "lord for a day" pattern turned into the scheme for a prank by which the powerful abuse the uninformed subaltern for their own amusement. Posited in between, the tale of Abū 'l-Ḥasan from *The Thousand and One Nights* is richest in terms of action and its various layers of motivation and consequences, thus serving as a strong argument—if such an argument was needed—that the tales of the *Nights* are not simply entertaining but always contain a serious message that a diligent reading can unravel.

Notes

1. Ghazoul, Ferial J., "*The Arabian Nights* in Shakespearean Comedy: 'The Sleeper Awakened' and *The Taming of the Shrew*," in *The Arabian Nights: A Structural Analysis*, Cairo: Unesco, 1980, pp. 108–120; Burton, Jonathan, "Christopher Sly's Arabian Night: Shakespeare's *The Taming of the Shrew* as World Literature," *Journal for Early Modern Cultural Studies* 14.3 (2014), pp. 3–30; Artese, Charlotte, *Shakespeare's Folktale Sources*, Newark: University of Delaware Press, 2015, pp. 38–42.

2. Olmedo, Felix G., *Las fuentes de "La vida es sueño:" La idea—el cuento—el drama*, Madrid: Voluntad, 1928; González Treviño, Ana Elena, "Fabulous Awakenings: The Ethics of Metafiction in *La vida es sueño* by Calderón de la Barca and Some Tales from the *Arabian Nights*," *Anuario de Letras Modernas* 15 (2009–2010), pp. 13–21.

3. Uther, *Deutscher Märchenkatalog*, p. 399, no. 1531.

4. Blum, Paul, "Die Geschichte vom träumenden Bauern in der Weltliteratur," *Jahresbericht der K.K. Staats-Oberrealschule in Teschen*, Teschen: Karl Prochaska, 1908, pp. 3–36; Frenzel, Elisabeth, *Stoffe der Weltliteratur*, Stuttgart: Kröner, 2005, pp. 78–82.

5. Pomeranceva, Ėrna Vasil'evna, *Pesni i skazki Jaroslavskoy oblasti*, Jaroslav: Jaroslavskoe knizhnoe izdatelstvo, 1958, 53–56, no. 53.

6. Strackerjan, Ludwig, *Aberglaube und Sagen aus dem Herzogtum Oldenburg*, 2nd ed., ed. Karl Willoh, Oldenburg: Stalling, 1909, vol. 2, pp. 507–509.

7. Artese, Charlotte, "'Tell Thou the Tale:' Shakespeare's Taming of Folktales in *The Taming of the Shrew*," *Folklore* 120 (2009), pp. 317–326, at p. 322.

8. Ibid.

9. Clouston, William Alexander, "Variants and Analogues of Some of the Tales in the Supplemental Nights, 1–2: The Sleeper and the Waker," in Burton, Richard F., *Arabian Nights*, (Benares 1885) reprint Beirut: Khayat, 1966, vol. 12, pp. 291–295, at pp. 293–294; Miller, Stephen Roy, ed., *The Taming of a Shrew: The 1594 Quarto*, Cambridge: Cambridge University Press, 1998, pp. 18–19; Chevalier, *Cuentos folklóricos*, pp. 282–283, no. 169.

10. *The Taming of a Shrew*, ed. Miller, pp. 18–19.

11. Gerhardt, Mia I., *The Art of Story-telling: A Literary Study of the Thousand and One Nights*, Leiden: Brill, 1963, pp. 443–449.

12. Clouston, "Variants and Analogues," p. 294.

13. The summary follows Richard Burton's translation that was prepared from the Arabic text of the Breslau edition; see Burton, *Arabian Nights*, vol. 11, pp. 1–35; Marzolph and Van Leeuwen, *The Arabian Nights Encyclopedia*, vol. 1, pp. 392–393, no. 263.

14. The following discussion relies heavily on Marzolph, Ulrich, "The Story of Abū al-Ḥasan the Wag in the Tübingen Manuscript of the Romance of ʿOmar ibn al-Nuʿmān and Related Texts," *Journal of Arabic Literature* 46 (2015), pp. 34–67; Marzolph, "The Tale of the Sleeper Awakened," in *Arabic Manuscripts of the Thousand and One Nights*, ed. Aboubakr Chraïbi, Paris: espaces & signes, 2016, pp. 261–291.

15. Chraïbi, Aboubakr, "Situation, Motivation, and Action in the *Arabian Nights*," in Marzolph and Van Leeuwen, *The Arabian Nights Encyclopedia*, vol. 1, p. 6; [Galland, Antoine,] *Les Mille et Une Nuits: Contes arabes*, ed. Jean-Paul Sermain and Aboubakr Chraïbi, Paris: Flammarion, 2004, vol. 1, pp. VI–VII.

16. Chauvin, *Bibliographie*, vol. 5 (1901), pp. 272–275, no. 155.

17. Marzolph, "The Story of Abū al-Ḥasan," pp. 48–50; for the author, see Marzolph, Ulrich, "Das *Kitāb Laṭāʾif aḫbār al-uwal* des -Isḥāqī als Quelle der Kompilatoren von *1001 Nacht*," in *Orientalistische Studien zu Sprache und Literatur: Festschrift Werner Diem*, ed. Ulrich Marzolph, Wiesbaden: Harrassowitz, 2011, pp. 317–328; Marzolph, "In the Studio of the Nights," *Middle Eastern Literatures* 17.1 (2014), pp. 43–57.

18. Akel, Ibrahim, "Quelques remarques sur la bibliothèque d'Antoine Galland et l'arrivée des *Mille et une nuits* en Occident," in *Antoine Galland et l'orient des savants: Actes du colloque organisé par L'AIBL, la Société Asiatique et l'INALCO, les 3 et 4 décembre 2015*, ed. Pierre-Sylvain Filliozat and Michel Zink. Paris: De Boccard, 2017, pp. 201–218; Marzolph, Ulrich, "The Arabic Source Text for Galland's *Dormeur eveillé*," *Oriente Moderno* 98 (2019), pp. 1–32.

19. Marzolph, *Arabia ridens*, vol. 2, p. 106, no. 427; Marzolph, "Pension: Die doppelte P.," in *Enzyklopädie des Märchens*, vol. 10 (2002), cols. 709–713; Marzolph, "The Tale of the Sleeper Awakened," pp. 267, 289–291.

20. Marzolph, *Arabia ridens*, vol. 2, pp. 106–107, no. 427.

21. *Tales of the Marvellous and News of the Strange*, transl. Malcolm C. Lyons, London: Penguin, 2014, pp. 207–225, no. 9.

22. Marzolph, Ulrich, "The *Hundred and One Nights*: A Recently Acquired Old Manuscript," in *Treasures of the Aga Khan Museum: Arts of the Book & Calligraphy* (Exhibition Catalogue), ed. Margaret S. Graves and Benoît Junod, Istanbul: Aga Khan Trust for Culture, and Sakip Sabancı University and Museum, 2010, pp. 206–215; enlarged version see Marzolph and Aboubakr Chraïbi in *Zeitschrift der Deutschen Morgenländischen Gesellschaft* 162 (2012), pp. 299–316.

23. *Mi'at layla wa-layla*, ed. Maḥmūd Ṭarshūna, Libya and Tunis: al-Dār al-ʿarabiyya lil-kitāb, 1979, pp. 370–410; the spurious tale was deleted in the book's second edition Cologne: al-Kamel, 2005 (see remark on p. 341); Marzolph, "The Story of Abū al-Ḥasan the Wag," pp. 51–52.

24. Horta, Paulo Lemos, "Tales of Dreaming Men: Shakespeare, "The Old Hunchback," and 'The Sleeper and the Waker'," *Journal of World Literature* 2.3 (2017), pp. 276–296; Horta, "Tales of the Dreaming Man: Shakespeare, 'The Sleeper and the Waker,' and World Literature," in Bendix, Regina F., and Dorothy Noyes, eds., *Terra Ridens—Terra Narrans: Festschrift zum 65. Geburtstag von Ulrich Marzolph*, Dortmund: Verlag für Orientkunde, 2018, pp. 168–193.

25. Horta, "Tales of Dreaming Men."

26. Chavannes, Édouard, *Cinq cents contes et apologues extraits du Tripitaka chinois*, Paris: Leroux, 1910–1935 (reprint Paris: Maisonneuve, 1962), vol. 1, pp. 340–344, no. 87.

27. The following section is adapted from Marzolph, "The Story of Abū al-Ḥasan the Wag," pp. 52–53.

28. For a full assessment of the implications of Abū 'l-Ḥasan's action for the ruler, see Marzolph, "The Story of Abū al-Ḥasan the Wag," pp. 54–55; Chraïbi, Aboubakr, "Processus d'individuation dans trois récits de l'islam médiéval," in *Drôles d'individus: De la singularité individuelle dans le Reste-du-monde*, ed. Emmanuel Lozerand, Paris: Klincksieck, 2014, pp. 417–431, at p. 429.

29. Strong, John S., *The Legend of King Aśoka: A Study and Translation of the Aśokāvadāna*, Princeton: Princeton University Press, 1983, pp. 221–225, quotes pp. 135–136. Another version is given by Chavannes, *Cinq cents contes*, vol. 3, pp. 299–302, in no. 493.

30. Lozar, Angelika, "Leben am seidenen Faden," in *Enzyklopädie des Märchens*, vol. 8 (1996), cols. 813–815.

31. Nörtersheuser, Hans-Walter, "Glückliche Armut," ibid., vol. 5 (1987), cols. 1318–1324.

CHAPTER 59

The Clever Man Privileges Himself When Carving the Roast Chicken (ATU 1533)

In folktales, social underdogs often best members of the upper strata of society. Arguing that the tales were often told by and for members of the less privileged strata, research at times suggested that those tales served as an outlet for social frustrations. Tales in which social underdogs fool or vanquish members of the upper strata of society materialize wishful thinking by depicting a world of restorative justice in which the former take revenge on the latter. They thus reverse the social order, if not permanently, then at least in the carnivalesque situation of storytelling. Numerous versions of tale type ATU 1533: *The Wise Carving of the Fowl* imply this reading. From its first documented occurrence some fifteen centuries ago, the tale often continues with a sequel classified as tale type ATU 1663: *Dividing Five Eggs Equally between Two Men and One Woman* that is here discussed separately (see essay **84, *The Clever Man Privileges Himself When Distributing Food Items among Several Persons***). Although versions of tale type ATU 1533 were recorded from European oral tradition in various countries,[1] the tale appears to be particularly well attested from Slavonic tradition.

The tale's version in Aleksandr Afanasyev's influential collection of Russian folktales is set in the feudal society of nineteenth-century Russia.[2]

> A poor peasant with many children is forced to slaughter his only possession, a goose. Possessing neither bread nor salt to have with the poultry, he decides to go to the feudal lord to trick him out of some bread. When the peasant presents the roast goose as a gift, the lord invites him to carve the bird and divide it among those present, that is, the lord, his wife, their two daughters and two sons, and the peasant himself. The peasant gives the goose's head to the lord, arguing that he is the head of the household. The landlord's wife receives "the pope's nose" (the tail), as her "business is to sit in the house and take care of it." The two sons receive the two legs, as they will soon follow their father's path. And the two daughters are given the wings, as they are expected to leave the house sooner or later. For himself, the peasant takes what is left, as he is "just a stupid peasant."

The lord is so amused about the clever carving that he gives the peasant wine to drink and rewards him with some bread before sending him home.

Following this, a rich peasant tries to emulate the poor peasant's success by bringing the lord five geese as a gift. When the rich peasant is not able to distribute the gift among those present, the poor peasant is called and achieves the distribution to his own advantage. This part of the tale corresponds to tale type ATU 1663.

According to Erna Pomeranzewa, the tale was often published in Russian schoolbooks, from where the narrator E.I. Sorokoviko might have learned his version.[3] Sorokoviko's text is essentially the same as the preceding one, except for the fact that both the poor and the rich peasant slaughter their animals with the intention of receiving a reward for their gift to the lord. In another Russian version, the lord invites the peasant to first carve one goose and then distribute five geese among six people, granting him permission to keep a certain part for himself.[4] Before beginning, the peasant has several drinks and then proceeds to act. The lord, however, understands that the clever division is partly owing to the cleverness of the peasant's daughter and asks her to perform an impossible task. She rids herself of the task by first requesting the lord to fulfill an equally impossible condition. This episode corresponds to tale type ATU 875B: *The Clever Girl and the King.* A Ukrainian version details the tale's initial situation.[5] In this tale, the poor peasant's envious rich brother complains about the rooster's crowing, so that the poor peasant decides to kill the bird and present it to the lord. In return for his clever carving, the lord generously gives the poor farmer a piece of land, thus further inciting the rich brother's envy. The late nineteenth-century text narrated by the Belarusian peasant Paul Dzezhko has the peasant bring the goose to the lord asking for some wheat in exchange.[6] In an early twentieth-century Serbian version from Bosnia, the poor peasant has his children fatten his only goose so well that in the end he decides to present it to the tsar.[7] The tsar rewards the peasant richly the first time, and even more richly the second time when he achieves the clever distribution his envious brother was unable to achieve. Essentially corresponding versions were also recorded in Croatia[8] and from the oral performance of Czech storyteller Josef Smolka in Silesia.[9]

The tale was popularized in late medieval, early modern, and modern Europe by an array of jestbooks and similar compilations[10] such as German author Johannes Pauli's *Schimpf und Ernst* (Jocular and Serious Tales; 1522).[11] Medieval European versions date to the fourteenth century. The Norwegian *Mágus-Saga*, compiled around 1300, in its fourth chapter tells how Ermenga, King Húgon of Miklagard's daughter, asks her suitor, King Hlödver, to carve a roasted chicken for five people, including him and herself, her father, and her two brothers.[12] Hlödver gives the head and throat to the king; the wings to her brothers, as they are about to leave the house; and the legs to the princess, as she is the one to support her family. He keeps the breast for himself, as he will be their protector.

John Gobi's *Scala coeli*, compiled between 1323 and 1330, contains the tale of a poor cleric who is hosted by a soldier when returning home from his studies in Paris.[13] Asked what he learned in Paris, the scholar responds that he knows the natural and the divine sciences. In order to test him, the soldier asks him to carve a goose according to the laws of natural science. At first reluctant, the scholar carves the bird by allotting the head to the host, the neck to his wife, the wings to his daughters, the feet to the servants, and the side pieces to the sons. The text continues with an application of divine science through the distribution of five birds, here partridges, among the members of his host's family. The tale included in Franco Sacchetti's *Trecentonovelle* (Three Hundred Novellas) introduces the castellan Vitale in the castle of Pietra Santa in the state of Lucca who sends his only son to study law at Bologna.[14] The young man's stepmother regards his studies as a waste of money. When the student visits home, his stepmother has his father request that he demonstrate his learning by carving the capon. The young man gives the bird's crest to the parson who joined their meal. The father receives the bird's head, the mother the feet, and the two sisters the wings. The rest he keeps for himself. The tale ends on a conciliatory tone, as "before setting out on his return to Bologna, the youth so very humorously explained the meaning of what he had done, that he won the good-will of the whole party, not excepting his stepmother, who only wished he might never live to return."[15]

In Arabic literature, the tale is documented several times since its first appearance in polymath al-Jāḥiẓ's (d. 868) *Kitāb al-Ḥayawān* (Book of Animals).[16] Jāḥiẓ attributes the tale's narration to the historian Abū 'l-Ḥasan al-Madā'inī (d. 843) who quotes it as having being told to him by an unnamed Bedouin who reports it as his personal experience.

> Having settled in the city of Basra, the Bedouin is visited by another Bedouin living in the desert. Preparing a chicken, the family invites their guest to carve the chicken for them, intending to make fun of him. The guest reluctantly says that he does not know how to carve properly, but if they would accept his judgment, he would do his best. He gives the chicken's head to the head (of the household), the wings to the two sons, the legs to the two daughters, and the tail to the mother. He keeps the breast (*al-zawr*) for the visitor (*al-zā'ir*), meaning himself. The story continues the next day when the host has his wife prepare five chickens, requesting the guest to distribute the birds among them. The guest proposes and proceeds to distribute the birds in two different ways, resulting in uneven and even numbers. Both times the guest himself receives more birds than his hosts. In the end, he raises his hands to the sky and thanks God for having taught him the ways of clever division.

In his comprehensive encyclopedia of jokes and anecdotes, *Nathr al-durr* (Pearls of Prose), al-Ābī (d. 1030) repeats the same tale, albeit without mention of a specific transmitter.[17] In both his *Akhbār al-Adhkiyā'* (Tales of Clever People)[18] and his *Akhbār al-Ẓirāf* (Tales of Subtle People),[19] Ibn al-Jawzī (d. 1201) again presents the tale more or less verbatim, here attributing its transmission to a certain Ibrāhīm ibn al-Mundhir al-Khuzāmī who lived before the ninth century.[20] A small but nevertheless important variation is introduced by the fact that the host is not a Bedouin who settled in the city but a "regular" sedentary. Quoting directly from al-Jāḥiẓ, al-Nuwayrī (d. 1332) includes the tale in his *Nihāyat al-arab fī funūn al-adab* (The Ultimate Ambition in the Arts of Erudition).[21] At the end, Nuwayrī adds another version from an unspecified source whose first-person narrator is the famous grammarian al-Aṣmaʿī (d. 828). In this version, the storyteller is in the desert where he has a contest in poetry with a Bedouin. Then comes the carving of the chicken at the meal. Before eventually distributing five chickens among those present, the Bedouin first distributes three chickens, making even groups—father and two sons plus a chicken; mother and daughters plus a chicken; he himself and a chicken. A full-fledged text of this version, including the poetry, but without the additional distribution of three chickens, is included in seventeenth-century author al-Atlīdī's book on the downfall of the Barmakid dynasty of viziers.[22] Another seventeenth-century version in colloquial language, whose protagonist is also al-Aṣmaʿī, is given in Muḥammad ibn Aḥmad ibn (al-)Ilyās al-Ḥanafī's compilation of amusing tales, *Nuzhat al-udabā'* (Entertainment of the Educated).[23]

In Persian, the clever carving of the chicken is first documented in the tale of Lavvāḥa and Beshr (Bashar) in Abu Bakr ibn Khosrow al-Ostād's *Munes-nāme* (The Book as an Intimate Friend), compiled around the year 1200.[24] It appears again in the Ottoman Turkish *Ferec baʿd eş-şidde* (Relief after Hardship), likely translated from the Persian model before the end of the fourteenth century.[25] In both texts, the clever carving of the chicken is but one episode of a complex tale. It is followed by two distinct episodes of distributing food items among several persons. In the seventeenth or eighteenth century, the episode of carving the chicken became a standard constituent of the tale of "The Robber and the Judge," as documented in the Mashhad manuscript of the anonymous Persian *Jāmeʿ al-ḥekāyāt* (Collection of Tales).[26] That tale, whose earlier versions detail a lengthy encounter between a linguistically sophisticated robber and a judge, is first attested in eleventh-century Arabic literature[27] and is included in both the *Munes-nāme* and *Ferec baʿd eş-şidde* as a separate tale.[28] Still more elaborated with the added episode of the distribution of several chickens among a group of persons, the tale was popularized as a chapbook in Persian, Turkish, and Urdu as of the nineteenth century.[29] Even so, the narration of mid-twentieth-century Persian storyteller Mashdi Galin Khānom appears to be independent of the rich Middle Eastern literary tradition, as she has the chicken carving and distributing events take place between the village mayor and the family of a rich lord.[30]

The oldest documented occurrence of the clever carving of the chicken occurs in Hebrew literature.[31] The *Midrash Lamentations* (*Ekha Rabbati*), probably compiled in the fifth century CE, contains the tale of a man from Jerusalem who dies while in Athens. Before dying, the man entrusts his belongings to an innkeeper to deliver to his son, providing that the son performs three acts of cleverness. Arriving in Athens, the son identifies the unknown house in which his father died by paying a local porter to deliver a load of wood to its owner. When the landlord asks the young man to distribute five chickens among the landlord's family and himself, the young man is at first reluctant but then proceeds in the usual manner. And he performs the third clever act, again reluctantly, in carving the chicken and alloting its parts to the landlord, his wife, his two sons and daughters, and himself. Having demonstrated his cleverness, the son finally receives his father's belongings and travels home to Jerusalem.

Although the tale's Hebrew version is most probably older than any Arabic text, it does not appear to have influenced later European tradition decisively. In the vast majority of Middle Eastern and European versions, the action displays a dramatic increase from the carving of one chicken to the distribution of several birds, whereas the Hebrew tale inverts the two episodes. And even though, according to traditional Muslim custom, a man's wife should not be present when a strange man is visiting, the narrative takes place in a fictional space where the presence of all family members is indispensable for the tale's various points. Considering these arguments, the tale's Muslim versions offer themselves as the logical intermediary between the old Jewish and the medieval and modern European tradition. Additionally, the tale displays a fascinating adaptability to a variety of historical contexts. In the fifth-century Jewish tale the heir has to prove his worth in order to receive his lawful inheritance. Eleventh-century Arabic literature displays an encounter between nomad and sedentary in which the former bests the latter who tries to make fun of him. And in the texts told in the context of a feudal society in nineteenth-century Eastern Europe, the intellectual challenge on which the tale is predicated is further embedded in a social conflict. Considering the tale's historical voyage over fifteen centuries, it developed from an unconditional test of cleverness to a competition between rival groups of society or family members to the triumph of the underdog over his socially superior rival. The tale's adaptability to a variety of contexts and implied messages probably also accounts for the lasting popularity of its fairly artificial plot.

Notes

1. Ghersetti, Antonella, "Teilung: Die sinnreiche T. des Huhns," in *Enzyklopädie des Märchens*, vol. 13 (2010), cols. 329–333.

2. Afanasyev, Aleksandr Nikolaevich, *Narodnye russkie skazki*, ed. Vladimir Jakovlevich Propp, Moscow: Gosudarstvennoye Izdatel'stvo Khudozhestvennoy Literatury, 1957, vol. 3, pp. 291, 444, no. 499; Guterman, Norbert, transl., *Russian Fairy Tales*, New York: Pantheon, 1945, pp. 579–581; see also Moldavskii, D., *Russkaia satiricheskaia skazka v zapisyakh seredini 19—nachala 20 v.*, Moscow: Akad., 1955, pp. 134–136.

3. Pomeranzewa, Erna, *Russische Volksmärchen*, 3rd ed., Berlin: Akademie-Verlag, 1966, pp. 559–563, 645–646, no. 87.

4. Moldavskii, *Russkaia satiricheskaia skazka*, pp. 222–224.

5. Chendeĭ, Ivan, *Skazki verkhovini: zakarpatskie ukrainskie narodnye skazki*, Uzhgorod: Zakarpatskoe oblastnoe izdatelstvo, 1959, pp. 77–79.

6. Kabashnikau, Kanstantin P., *Kazki i legendi rodnaga krayu*, Minsk: Akad., 1960, pp. 221–222, 257.

7. Chaikanovich, Veselin, *Srpske narodne pripovetke*, Belgrade: Izdaniye knizharnitse Raikovicha i Vukovicha, 1929, pp. 260–262, 402, no. 98.

8. Bošković-Stulli, Maja, "Narodne pripovijetke i predaje Sinjske Krajine," *Narodna Umjetnost* 5–6 (1967–1968), pp. 303–432, at pp. 367, 420, no. 34.

9. Satke, Antonín, *Hlučinský pohádkář Josef Smolka*, Ostrava: Krajské nakladadelství, 1958, pp. 113–116, no. 7; Jech, Jaromir, *Tschechische Volksmärchen*, Berlin: Rütten & Loening, 1961, pp. 413–417, no. 49.

10. See Bolte and Polívka, *Anmerkungen*, vol. 2, pp. 360–361, note 1.

11. Pauli, Johannes, *Schimpf und Ernst*, ed. Johannes Bolte, Berlin: Herbert Stubenrauch, 1924 (reprint Hildesheim: Olms, 1972), vol. 1, p. 42; vol. 2, pp. 272–273, no. 58.

12. Köhler, Reinhold, *Kleinere Schriften zur Märchenforschung*, ed. Johannes Bolte, Berlin: Emil Felber, 1900, p. 646; Wulff, Fredrik, *Recherches sur les Sagas de Magus et de Geirarđ et leurs rapports aux épopées françaises*, Lund: Gleerup, 1873, p. 15.

13. Gobi, Jean, *La Scala coeli de Jean Gobi*, ed. Marie-Anne Polo de Beaulieu, Paris: Centre National de la Recherche Scientifique, 1991, pp. 253–254, no. 206.

14. Sacchetti, Franco, *Le trecentonovelle*, ed. Valerio Marucci, Rome: Salerno, 1996, pp. 373–379, no. 123.

15. Quoted from http://elfinspell.com/RoscoeSacchetti2.html (accessed February 5, 2018).

16. Marzolph, *Arabia ridens*, vol. 2, p. 24, no. 90; Jāḥiẓ, ʿAmr ibn Baḥr al-, *Kitāb al-Ḥayawān*, ed. ʿAbd al-Salām Muḥammad Hārūn, 3rd ed., Beirut: al-Majmaʿ al-ʿilmī al-ʿarabī al-islāmī, 1388/1969, vol. 2, pp. 357–359. The tale's Arabic versions were studied in detail in Ghersetti, Antonella, "'La division du poulet' ou 'Quand les moquers sont souvent moqués,'" *Middle Eastern Literatures* 10 (2007), pp. 15–33.

17. Ābī, Abū Saʿd Manṣūr ibn al-Ḥusayn al-, *Nathr al-durr*, ed. Muḥammad ʿAlī Qarna et al., vol. 2, Cairo: al-Hay'a al-miṣriyya al-ʿāmma lil-kitāb, 1981, p. 252–253.

18. Ibn al-Jawzī, Abū 'l-Faraj ʿAbd al-Raḥmān ibn ʿAlī, *Akhbār al-Adhkiyā'*, ed. Muḥammad Mursī al-Khūlī, Cairo, 1970, pp. 95–96.

19. Ibn al-Jawzī, Abū 'l-Faraj ʿAbd al-Raḥmān ibn ʿAlī, *Akhbār al-Ẓirāf wa-'l-mutamājinīn*, ed. Muḥammad Baḥr al-ʿulūm, 2nd ed., al-Najaf: al-Maktaba al-ḥaydariyya, 1386/1966, pp. 97–99.

20. Ghersetti, "'La division du poulet'," p. 17.

21. Nuwayrī, Shihāb al-Dīn Aḥmad ibn ʿAbd al-Wahhāb al-, *Nihāyat al-arab fī funūn al-adab*, vol. 10, Cairo: Dār al-Kutub al-miṣriyya, 1351/1933, pp. 223–224; German translation in Weisweiler, Max, *Von Kalifen, Spaßmachern und klugen Haremsdamen: Arabischer Humor*, Düsseldorf: Eugen Diederichs, 1963, pp. 154–156.

22. Atlīdī, Muḥammad ibn Diyāb, *Nawādir al-khulafā' al-musammā Iʿlām al-nās bi-ma waqāʿa lil-Barāmika maʿa Banī al-ʿAbbās*, ed. Ayman ʿAbd al-Jābir al-Buḥayrī, Cairo: Dār al-Āfāq al-ʿarabiyya, 1418/1998, pp. 337–340; Hammer-Purgstall, Joseph von, *Rosenöl, oder Sagen und Kunden des Morgenlandes aus arabischen, persischen und türkischen Quellen*

gesammelt, vol. 2, Stuttgart: J.G. Cotta, 1813, pp. 136–139, no. 74; Sadan, Joseph, "The 'Nomad versus Sedentary' Framework in Arabic Literature," *Fabula* 15 (1974), pp. 57–86, at pp. 77–78.

23. Ḥanafī, Muḥammad ibn Aḥmad ibn (al-)Ilyās al-, *Nuzhat al-udabā'*, Gotha, Ms. Orient A 2706, fols. 30a–b.

24. Askari, Nasrin, "A Mirror for Princesses: *Mūnis-nāma*, A Twelfth-Century Collection of Persian Tales Corresponding to the Ottoman Turkish Tales of the *Faraj ba'd al-shidda*," *Narrative Culture* 5.1 (2018), pp. 121–140.

25. Marzolph, *Relief after Hardship*, pp. 86–87, no. 24.

26. Haag-Higuchi, Roxane, *Untersuchungen zu einer Sammlung persischer Erzählungen: Čihil wa-šiš ḥikāyāt yā ǧāmi' al-ḥikāyāt*, Berlin: Klaus Schwarz, 1984, p. 72, no. 25; Khadish, Pegāh, and Moḥammad Ja'fari (Qanavāti), eds., *Jāme' al-ḥekāyāt bar asās-i noskhe-ye Āstān-i qods-i Rażavi*, Tehran: Māzyār, 1390/2011, pp. 427–435.

27. Marzolph, *Arabia ridens*, vol. 2, p. 214, no. 952.

28. Marzolph, *Relief after Hardship*, p. 79, no. 18.

29. Chauvin, *Bibliographie*, vol. 5 (1901), p. 187, no. 110; Marzolph, Ulrich, *Narrative Illustration in Persian Lithographed Books*, Leiden: Brill, 2001, pp. 238–239; Marzolph, *Dāstānhā-ye širin: Fünfzig persische Volksbüchlein aus der zweiten Hälfte des zwanzigsten Jahrhunderts*, Stuttgart: Franz Steiner, 1994, p. 40, no. XIV.

30. Mashdi Galin Khānom, *Qeṣṣehā-ye Mashdi Galin Khānom*, ed. Ulrich Marzolph, Azar Amirhosseini-Nithammer, and Aḥmad Vakiliyān, Tehran: Markaz, 1374/1995, p. 100, no. 15; Marzolph, Ulrich, transl., *Wenn der Esel singt, tanzt das Kamel: Persische Märchen und Schwänke*, Munich: Diederichs, 1994, pp. 101–102.

31. Wünsche, August, *Der Midrasch Echa Rabbati, das ist die haggadische Auslegung der Klagelieder*, Leipzig: Otto Schulze, 1881, pp. 46–48; Hasan-Rokem, Galit, *Web of Life: Folklore and Midrash in Rabbinic Literature*, Stanford: Standford University Press, 2000, p. 70; Kushelevsky, Rella, *Tales in Context: Sefer ha ma'asim in Medieval Northern France*, Detroit: Wayne State University Press, 2017, pp. 94–97, 384–386, no. 3.

CHAPTER 60

Quoting the Scripture to Gain an Advantage at the Meal (ATU 1533A)

Neither the Christian nor the Muslim scripture are deemed so holy that they could not appear in jocular contexts. Rather to the contrary, quotations from the Bible or the Koran in secular jokes or anecdotes demonstrate the Scripture's embeddedness as a natural constituent of the respective religious community's everyday life.[1] Tale type ATU 1533A: *Hog's Head Divided According to Scripture* is a case in point.

The father-in-law of worker Köppen narrated the following jocular tale to the collector Richard Wossidlo (1859–1939) in the Northern German town of Waren, Mecklenburg.[2]

> At Easter, a tailor serves his staff a pig's head, requesting that before serving themselves, everybody will have to quote from the Scripture. He begins by saying, "And he gave him a box on the ears" (alluding to John 18:22), cutting off a large piece from the head's cheeks. His assistant says, "And he cut off one of his ears" (alluding to John 18:10), cutting off one of the ears. When it is the apprentice's turn, he says, "And he vanished out of their sight" (Luke 24:31). With this, he takes the whole head and goes out through the door.

With little variation, the jocular tale was recorded in numerous versions all over Europe, particularly from German-speaking regions.[3] In addition to the clever adaptation of quotations from the Scripture, the tale's humorous effect often arises from the fact that the more educated person intends to have the better of a person or persons whom he presumes to be less well versed in the Bible. Mecklenburg storyteller August Rust's version featuring master and apprentices was recorded a total of three times in 1959 and 1966.[4] The text narrated by farmer Josef Wasserhess, aged 70, from Meindorf, today part of Sankt Augustin in North Rhine-Westphalia, alters the final quotation by having the invited sexton allude to John 8:59, "He hid himself and went out of the temple," taking the roast with him.[5] This line is likewise found in versions from Austria and East Frisia.[6] Karl Stolz's version from East Prussia features a stingy parson who invites three passing vagabonds (*Wenktiner*) after they finished chopping wood in his yard, trusting that they will not be able to handle the task.[7] Contrary to his expectations, however, each of the three vagabonds cleverly quotes from the Scripture. When his guests finally leave, the parson contends himself with at least having the soup. Featuring a fish dish, a similar tale is frequently included in Latin, Spanish, and German compilations of jocular tales, the earliest one being the *Ioci ac sales* (Augsburg 1524) compiled by Alsatian Catholic Humanist Ottmar Nachtigall (Luscinius).[8]

In the majority of surveyed texts, the food served is pork. As a rare exception, the Mecklenburg narrator Wolter in Gielow mentions a dish of mashed peas, supposedly served on a large plate with liquid fat in the middle.[9] The host, a stingy cobbler, begins by saying, "And Jesus went over the sea" (alluding to John 6:1), making a furrow in the mash with his spoon so that the fat would flow to his side. Doing the same, his assistant continues by saying, "And his followers followed him" (alluding to John 6:2). And the apprentice finally makes all the fat flow to his side. Unfortunately, the narrator had forgotten the final quote. Interestingly, none of the surveyed text quotes the Bible verbatim, and not a single editor has bothered to verify or document the quotations.

An Arabic tale of closely corresponding nature is documented in al-Khaṭīb al-Baghdādī's (d. 1071) book on professional party-crashers, *al-Taṭfīl wa-ḥikāyāt al-ṭufaylīyīn wa-akhbārihim wa-nawādir kalāmihim wa-ash'ārihim* (Party-Crashing, Tales and Stories of Spongers and What They Said in Prose and Poetry).[10] It is particularly noteworthy that the texture and composition of the dish served in this tale corresponds closely to the dish mentioned by Mecklenburg narrator Wolter.[11] The protagonist of the Arabic tale is the prototypical *ṭufaylī* Bunān who narrates an event he experienced himself when once having been invited to join a company of merchants at a friend's place.

> Bunān begins with a detailed description of the ingredients he uses for cooking a dish of 'aṣīda, essentially consisting of flour, date syrup, and mashed white fish. The food is served as a ring of thick mash with molten butter in the middle. When the company gathers to eat, Bunān mentions that some of the people present thought themselves particularly clever, obviously not recognizing him at first, as they tried to get the better of him. The first of these people starts by taking a bite, dipping it in the butter and making a furrow so that the molten butter would flow in his direction. Doing this, he quotes the Koranic verse "Then they shall be pitched into it (hellfire), they and the perverse" (26:94).[12] The next one does the same, quoting "When it (hellfire) sees them from a far place, they shall hear its bubbling and sighing" (25:12). Bunān quotes "How many a ruined well . . ." (22:45), and makes a furrow for the butter in his own direction. Another quotes, "What, hast thou made a hole in it so as to drown its passengers? Thou hast indeed done a grievous thing" (18:71), making the butter flow toward himself. Bunān quotes "therein two fountains of running water . . ."

> (55:50), drawing the butter in his own direction. Another one makes the butter flow to his side, quoting "and made the earth to gush with fountains, and the waters met for a matter decreed" (54:12). Bunān quotes "we drive it to a dead land . . . " (7:57), again drawing the butter to his side. And when he notices that nobody else says anything, he continues, "And it was said, Earth, swallow thy waters; and, Heaven, abate! And the waters subsided, the affair was accomplished, and the Ark settled on (mount) al-Jūdī, and it was said: Away with the people of the evildoers!" (11:44). With that he mixes the butter with the remaining ʿaṣīda, finishing the dish. The people present laugh so hard that a morsel gets stuck in the throat of one of them. The others hit him on the back until the morsel goes down. Multiple praise to God that he is well now!

Essentially the same tale is attributed to an anonymous group of people in the chapter on party-crashing in Ibn al-Jawzī's (d. 1201) *Akhbār al-Adhkiyāʾ* (Tales of Clever People).[13] Bunān's lively account is here boiled down to the tale's basic structure. There is no introductory preparation of the food, the text does not mention Bunān's name, and a few different verses from the Koran are quoted. A dialect version of the tale is presented in the early twentieth-century chapbook *Ẓarīf al-maʿānī fī ʾḥawādīt wa-ʾl-aghānī* (Witty Meanings: Tales and Songs).[14]

Another Arabic tale corresponds closely to the group of early modern European texts mentioned in relation to the East Prussian tale narrated by Karl Stolz,[15] although the mentioned dishes vary. It is contained in Muḥammad ibn Aḥmad ibn (al-)Ilyās al-Ḥanafī's seventeenth-century *Nuzhat al-udabāʾ* (Entertainment of the Educated).[16] This tale introduces a miser preparing a chicken that he intends to eat all by himself. Since the children of his neighbors saw him prepare the chicken, they enter the room as he just settled down to eat so that the miser cannot hide the food from them. Intending to have the better of them, the miser requests that they only eat after quoting a verse from the Koran, arguing that as children of educated parents they ought to be able to do so. Quoting verses that vaguely correspond to their action, the children one after the other take the chicken's flanks, wings, breasts, and body. When the miser realizes that no poultry is left for him, he takes the plate and drinks the sauce, quoting "And when Abraham . . . had raised the foundations of the House" (2:127).

In medieval Arabic culture, the *ṭufaylī* was by no means an uneducated person. Quite to the contrary, these party-crashers would usually be tolerated and earned their share of the meal by being witty entertainers. In this context, another anecdote attributed to the prototypical *ṭufaylī* Bunān has him quote Koranic verses mentioning numbers that correspond to the number of bites he takes. When he reaches the number 10, he proposes to continue with 20, and so forth. And when his partner finally realizes that he cannot have the better of him, Bunān claims that he could continue their competition until reaching the verse, "Then We sent him to a hundred thousand, or more" (37:147).[17] In yet another jocular tale, a *ṭufaylī* admits to knowing a single verse from the Koran, a single *ḥadīth*, and a single poem.[18] Needless to mention, all of the *ṭufaylī*'s knowledge is related to food.

Notes

1. Marzolph, Ulrich, "The Qur'ān and Jocular Literature," *Arabica* 47 (2000), pp. 478–487; Tamer, Georges, "The Qur'ān and Humor," in Tamer, ed., *Humor in der arabischen Kultur/Humor in Arabic Culture*, Berlin: De Gruyter, 2009, pp. 3–28.

2. Wossidlo, Richard, *Aus dem Lande Fritz Reuters: Humor in Sprache und Volkstum Mecklenburgs*, Leipzig: Wigand, 1910, p. 74; Neumann, Siegfried, *Volksschwänke aus Mecklenburg, aus der Sammlung Richard Wossidlos*, Berlin: Akademie-Verlag, 1963, pp. 25–26, no. 79.

3. Uther, *Deutscher Märchenkatalog*, p. 399–400, no. 1533A.

4. Neumann, Siegfried, *Ein mecklenburgischer Volkserzähler: Die Geschichten des August Rust*, Berlin: Akademie-Verlag, 1968, pp. 55–56, 153, no. 36.

5. Dittmaier, Heinrich, *Sagen, Märchen und Schwänke von der unteren Sieg*, Bonn: Röhrscheid, 1950, pp. 165–166, no. 453.

6. Haiding, Karl, *Märchen und Schwänke aus Oberösterreich*, Berlin: De Gruyter, 1969, pp. 139, 225, no. 109; 200, 232, no. 177; Kooi, Jurjen van der, and Theo Schuster, *Märchen und Schwänke aus Ostfriesland*, Leer: Schuster, 1993, p. 187, 342, no. 128a.

7. Grannas, Gustav, *Volk aus dem Ordensland Preussen erzählt Sagen, Märchen und Schwänke*, Marburg: Elwert, 1960, p. 139, no. 98.

8. Bolte and Polívka, *Anmerkungen*, vol. 2, p. 361; Montanus, Martin, *Schwankbücher (1577–1566)*, ed. Johannes Bolte, Tübingen: Litterarischer Verein in Stuttgart, 1899, pp. 649–650, no. 63.

9. Neumann, *Volksschwänke*, p. 25, no. 76.

10. Marzolph, *Arabia ridens*, vol. 1, pp. 255–256, no. 14; vol. 2, p. 229, no. 1035; Khaṭīb al-Baghdādī, Abū Bakr Aḥmad ibn ʿAlī al-, *al-Taṭfīl wa-ḥikāyāt al-ṭufaylīyīn wa-akhbārihim wa-nawādir kalāmihim wa-ashʿārihim*, ed. Kāẓim al-Muẓaffar, al-Najaf: al-Maktaba al-ḥaydariyya, 1386/1966, pp. 108–110; Malti-Douglas, Fedwa, "Structure and Organization in a Monographic Adab Work: al-Taṭfīl of al-Khaṭīb al-Baghdādī," *Journal of Near Eastern Studies* 40 (1981), pp. 227–245; Ḫaṭīb al-Baġdādī, al-, *L'arte dello scrocco: storie, aneddoti e poemi di scrocconi*, transl. and ed. Antonella Ghersetti, Catanzaro: Abramo, 2006; Khatib al-Baghdadi, al-, *Selections from The Art of Party-Crashing in Medieval Iraq*, transl. Emily Selove, Syracuse, NY: Syracuse University Press, 2012; Ostafin, Barbara, *Intruz przy solte: Ṭuyalī w literaturze adabowej di XI wieku*, Kraków: Wydawnictwo Uniwersytetu Jagiellońskiego, 2013.

11. Neumann, *Volksschwänke*, p. 25, no. 76.

12. Quotations from the Koran follow, with minor adaptations, the translation by Arberry, Arthur J., *The Koran Interpreted*, London: Allen & Unwin, 1955.

13. Ibn al-Jawzī, Abū 'l-Faraj ʿAbd al-Raḥmān ibn ʿAlī, *Akhbār al-Adhkiyā'*, ed. Muḥammad Mursī al-Khūlī, Cairo, 1970, pp. 192–193.

14. *Ẓarīf al-maʿānī fī 'ḥawādīt wa-'l-aghānī*, Cairo: Maktabat Multazima, ca. 1910, p. 22, no. 46.

15. Bolte and Polívka, *Anmerkungen*, vol. 2, p. 361; Grannas, *Volk aus dem Ordensland Preussen*, p. 139, no. 98

16. Basset, *Mille et un contes*, vol. 1, p. 270, no. 161; Ḥanafī, Muḥammad ibn Aḥmad ibn (al-)Ilyās al-, *Nuzhat al-udabā'*, Gotha, Ms. Orient A 2706, fol. 53b–54a.

17. Marzolph, *Arabia ridens*, vol. 2, p. 180, no. 766.

18. Ibid., vol. 2, p. 178, no. 755.

CHAPTER 61

Hanging by Proxy (ATU 1534A*)

Thomas W. Jackson's *On a Slow Train through Arkansas* (1903) is a satirical journey presenting "funny railroad stories, sayings of the Southern darkies (and) all the latest and best minstrel jokes of the day."[1] Sold "by 'train butchers,' boys who hawked items to train passengers, for twenty-five cents a copy,"[2] the book "gained wide popularity with millions of passengers headed to the 1904 World's Fair in St. Louis, becoming a bestseller on all trains." During one of his fictional stops, the author cites the following jocular tale.

> In Arkansas, they believe in doing everything right. I stopped at a place where there was one doctor, two shoemakers and a blacksmith. The doctor killed a man. They didn't want to be without a doctor, so they hung one of the shoemakers.

This jocular tale corresponds to tale type ATU 1534A*: *Barber Substituted for Smith at Execution*. It is not exactly well told, because the mention of the blacksmith here is just a "blind motif,"[3] a superfluous relict of the older versions. In the joke's older versions, there usually is no doctor, and the only blacksmith around killed a man. Published at the beginning of the twentieth century, Jackson's joke about "hanging by proxy" had already been popular in the United States for almost three centuries, albeit in different forms and relating to another region.[4] In his *New English Canaan*, first published in London 1632, Thomas Morton relates the "droll doings 'Of a Parliament held at Wessaguscus,'"[5] later also known as the "Wessaguscus Hanging."[6] Morton's story of "how justice was administered at that early day in New England" tells of a man who stole corn from an underground Indian granary. When the native owner complained about the theft, the community agreed that "it was a felony, and by the laws of England punished with death." Since the culprit was a young and strong man, however, they decided to hang an "old and impotent" person in his stead, "a sickly person that cannot escape death." Although, in the end, the community did not put their plan into practice, the narrative motif of hanging or intending to hang an innocent person in the culprit's stead is the same as in the alleged

Arkansas tale. Thirty years later, Samuel Butler employed the same narrative motif in his mock heroic poem *Hudibras*.[7] And at the beginning of the eighteenth century, Captain Nathaniel Uring told the tale again in the travelogue of his voyages in the Caribbean, published in 1726.[8] Narrated by "Governor Dudley," Uring's version tells of a carpenter who accidentally kills a native when cutting down a tree. Since the community does not want to lose the carpenter, who is "a young and lusty fellow, and very useful," they hang "an old bedridden weaver who had not long to live" in his stead. Although the story was doubtless fictional in the beginning, Drake concludes that "in one form or another the story . . . became current as true."[9]

Whereas no versions of the tale recorded from recent oral tradition in the United States are known, the tale was fairly popular in nineteenth- and twentieth-century Europe. A text contained in a mid-nineteenth-century survey of German towns in the region of Posen, today Poznań in Poland, attributes the events to the inhabitants of the small town of Kiszkowo (Kischkowo).[10] The short and matter-of-fact text states that once, the town's only locksmith was sentenced to death. Since there were two blacksmiths in the town, the community decided to hang one of the blacksmiths instead. The event is said to have given rise to the Polish proverb *Ślusarz zawinił, kowala powieszono* (The locksmith was at fault, the blacksmith was hanged), still popular today.[11] In early twentieth-century versions of the tale from Croatia[12] and Hungary,[13] one of the village's two weavers is hanged instead of the only locksmith. Rarely recorded from oral performance in Europe, this version of the tale repeatedly appeared in German jestbooks since the seventeenth century.[14] Its oldest occurrence in central and Northern European sources is attested in Anthony Copley's late sixteenth-century English jestbook *Wits, Fittes and Fancies* (1595)[15] from where Morton might have known it. Copley, a distant relative of Queen Elizabeth and a secret agent for the king of Spain, published his book largely as an adapted translation from the Spanish, his source text being Melchor de Santa Cruz's *Floresta española de apotegmas y sentencias* (A Spanish Grove of Apophthegms and Aphorisms), first published in 1574.[16] Here as well, the people decide to hang one of their two weavers instead of the blacksmith who killed a man. Frequently documented in Spanish literature since the sixteenth century,[17] the tale was also recorded from Spanish oral tradition in the second half of the twentieth century.[18] At some point attributed to the inhabitants of the municipality of Almudévar in the province of Huesca, Aragon, the tale gave rise to the proverbial "justice of Almudévar."[19] The enmity between the people of Almudévar and the neighboring town of Zuera is already flagged as proverbial in Hernán Nuñez's *Refranes o proverbios en romance* (1555) where the corresponding tale is, however, not given.[20]

The tale's oldest-known attestation occurs in the little booklet *al-Fāshūsh fī aḥkam* (or *ḥikam*) *Qarāqūsh* (The Stupidity in the Judgments of Qarāqūsh), compiled around 1200.[21] In this booklet, the Ayyubid official Abū 'l-Makārim Asʿad ibn al-Muhadhdhab Ibn Mammātī (d. 1209) satirized the judgments of his contemporary, Bahā' al-Dīn ibn ʿAbdallāh al-Asadī, known as Qarāqūsh (d. after 1199), who held important positions as chamberlain to Saladin, representative of the sultan, and prime officer of the sultan's son. Many, if not most, of the anecdotes included in the booklet appear to have been part and parcel of popular tradition on stupid judgments. The anecdote relating to the tale in question goes as follows.

> Once they brought Qarāqūsh one of his stable hands who had killed somebody. Qarāqūsh said, "Hang him!" The people objected, saying, "He is your blacksmith and the one who shoes your horses. If you have him hanged, you will lack his services!" Seeing a basketmaker in front of the gate, Qarāqūsh said, "I need this basketmaker," and they fetched him. Then Qarāqūsh said, "Hang this basketmaker and release the blacksmith who shoes my horses!"

Although the professional specification of the characters concerned differs, the tale's structure is identical to the European versions from subsequent centuries. In the Arab world, Ibn Mammātī's satirical portrayal of Qarāqūsh, including the anecdote in question, remained popular until the present day, and the expression *ḥikam Qarāqūsh* (the judgments of Qarāqūsh) became proverbial, as ʿAbd al-Laṭīf Ḥamza's modern book on Qarāqūsh, originally published in 1945, is reprinted time and again.[22] In the larger historical context, Ibn Mammātī's compilation belongs to tale type ATU 1534: *Series of Clever Unjust Decisions*. This tale type is highly complex and varied, some of its components being attested in ancient Indian and Jewish sources.[23]

Notes

1. Jackson, Thomas W., *On a Slow Train through Arkansas: Funny Railroad Stories, Sayings of the Southern Darkies, All the Latest and Best Minstrel Jokes of the Day*, Chicago: Thos. W. Jackson, 1903.

2. This and the following quote from http://www.encyclopediaofarkansas.net/encyclopedia/entry-detail.aspx?entryID=2217 (accessed February 17, 2018).

3. Lüthi, Max, "Blindes Motiv," in *Enzyklopädie des Märchens*, vol. 2 (1979), cols. 469–471

4. For the following, see Drake, Samuel Adams, *A Book of New England Legends and Folk Lore in Prose and Poetry*, Boston: Little, Brown, and Company, 1901, pp. 365–370. I owe the reference to Baughman, Ernest W., *Type and Motive-Index of the Folktales of England and North America*, The Hague, Mouton & Co., 1966, p. 326, motif J2233.1.1.

5. Drake, *A Book*, p. 365; Morton, Thomas, *The New English Canaan*, Boston: Prince Society, 1883, pp. 249–252.

6. Skinner, Charles Montgomery, *Myths and Legends of Our Own Land*, Philadelphia, J.B. Lippincott, 1896, pp. 14–15.

7. Drake, *A Book*, pp. 368–369.

8. Ibid., pp. 369–370; Uring, Nathaniel, *A History of the Voyages and Travels of Captain Nathaniel Uring*, London: J. Peele, 1726, pp. 116–118.

9. Drake, *A Book*, p. 369.

10. Wuttke, Heinrich, *Städtebuch des Landes Posen*, Leipzig: Hermann Fries, 1864, p. 333; see Knoop, Otto, *Sagen und Erzählungen aus der Provinz Posen*, Posen, 1893, pp. 221, 355–356, no. 53.20.

11. Wander, Karl Friedrich Wilhelm, *Deutsches Sprichwörter-Lexikon: Ein Hausschatz für das deutsche Volk* (1867), Augsburg: Weltbild, 1987, vol. 4, col. 247; Krzyżanowski, Julian, *Polska bajka ludowa w układzie systematycznym*, vol. 2, Polska Akad. Nauk. Wydz. Nauk Społecznych, 1963, p. 80, no. 1543A*.

12. Bošković-Stulli, Maja, *Narodne pripovijetke*, Zagreb: Matica Hrvatska, 1963, pp. 235, 330, no. 86.

13. Kovács, Agnes, *Ungarische Volksmärchen*, Düsseldorf: Diederichs, 1966, pp. 28–31, no. 8, at p. 30; Kovács, *König Mátyás und die Rátóter: Ungarische Schildbürgerschwänke und Anekdoten*, Leipzig: Kiepenheuer, 1988, pp. 228–229; see also György, Lajos, *A magyar anekdota története és egyetemes kapcsolatai*, Budapest: Studium, 1934, pp. 115–116, no. 55.

14. Moser-Rath, *"Lustige Gesellschaft,"* pp. 200, 343, note 9; Uther, *Deutscher Märchenkatalog*, p. 401, no. 1534A*.

15. Copley, Anthony, *Wits, Fittes and Fancies, Fronted and Entermedled with Presidentes of Honour and Wisdome*, London: Richard Johnes, 1595, p. 158; *Wits, Fits, and Fancies: Or, A Generall and Serious Collection, of the Sententious Speeches, Answers, Jests, and Behauiours, of All Sortes of Estates, From the Throane to the Cottage*, 2nd ed., London: Edw. Allde, 1614, p. 158; Zall, Paul M., *A Nest of Ninnies and Other English Jestbooks of the Seventeenth Century*, Lincoln: University of Nebraska Press, 1970, pp. 11–12, no. 862.

16. Santa Cruz, Melchor de, *Floresta española*, ed. María Pilar Cuartero and Maxime Chevalier, Barcelona: Crítica, 1997, p. 123 (4,6,6); Chevalier, Maxime, *Cuentecillos tradicionales en la España del Siglo de Oro*, Madrid: Gredos, 1975, p. 96, no. C5; Wesselski, Albert, *Das lachende Buch*, Leipzig: Johannes M. Meulenhoff, 1914, pp. 192–193, no. 110.

17. Amores, Montserrat, *Catálogo de cuentos folklóricos reelaboradoros por escritores del siglo XIX*, Madrid: Consejo superior de investigaciones científicas, Departemento de antropología de España y América, 1997, pp. 265–266, no. 174.

18. González Sanz, Carlos, *Catálogo tipologico de cuentos folklóricos aragoneses*, Zaragoza: Instituto Aragonés de Antropología, 1996, p. 123, no. 1534A*.

19. Chevalier, *Cuentecillos*, p. 97.

20. Chevalier, *Cuentecillos*, p. 97, no. C5; Chevalier, *Cuentos folklóricos*, p. 284, no. 170; Chevalier, "Cuentecillos chistosos en la Sevilla de principios del siglo XVII," *Cuento tradicional, cultura, litteratura (siglos XVI–XIX)*, Salamanca: Universidad de Salamanca, 1999, pp. 55–65, at p. 55.

21. Casanova, Paul, *Ḳaraḳoûch*, *Mémoires publiés par les members de la Mission Archéologique Français du Caire* 6 (1897), pp. 447–491, at pp. 470 (Arabic text), 479–480 (French translation); see also Jahn, Samia al Azharia, *Arabische Volksmärchen*, Berlin: Akademie-Verlag, 1970, pp. 269–273, 535–536, no. 37.

22. Ḥamza, ʿAbd al-Laṭīf, *Ḥikam Qarāqūsh*, Cairo: Muṣṭafā al-Bābī al-Ḥalabī, 1363/1945, p. 50, no. 5.

23. Van der Kooi, Jurjen, "Schemjaka: Die Urteile des S.," in *Enzyklopädie des Märchens*, vol. 11 (2005), cols. 1356–1362.

CHAPTER 62

The Accused Wins the Law Suit by Feigning to Be Dumb (ATU 1534D*)

In the narrative tradition of the island of Malta, the jester Ġaħan (pronounced Jáhan) is the equivalent of the Arabic character Juḥā whose jests were collected in classical Arabic literature since the ninth century.[1] Published in both scholarly and popular editions, Ġaħan's jests overlap with the repertoire of Juḥā's jests to a certain extent while also documenting items germane to the character in Maltese tradition.[2] Some of the jests display an intermediary role between Arabic and European tradition. The earliest preserved collection of Ġaħan's jests was amassed and published by German folklorist Bertha (Kößler-)Ilg (1881–1965)[3] at the beginning of the twentieth century.[4] It contains the following tale that corresponds to tale type ATU 1534D*: *Sham Dumb Man Wins Suit.*[5]

> As Ġaħan was taking his cart to town one day to sell vegetables, there was a nobleman who made no accommodation to let him pass, although Ġaħan shouted several times, "Get out of the way!" Since the road was downward sloping, Ġaħan could not avoid knocking the man over. The man later sued him, and Ġaħan had to appear at court. During the trial, Ġaħan remained silent all the time, so that the judges thought him to be dumb and refused to pass judgment on him. But the plaintiff suspected that Ġaħan was only pretending to be dumb, since that day he shouted loudly, "Get out of the way!" When the judges hear that Ġaħan had actually warned the man, they dismiss the case, and the plaintiff has to pay for the proceedings.

Essentially the same events are told in a tale from the Spanish region of Murcia.[6] Here, two women are knocked down by a driver's cattle. During the trial, the mayor advises the driver to feign being dumb, and when the women insist that he can talk, since he shouted at them several times, the mayor reproaches them for not having reacted properly. In German tradition, the tale was popular in jestbooks of the seventeenth and eighteenth centuries.[7] Even so, it has apparently never been recorded from German oral tradition. The tale's Hungarian version, of unclear origin, presents the tale as a conflict between a peasant carrying a large bundle of firewood on his back and a nobleman whose coat is ripped apart by a piece of wood when he does not get out of the way.[8] The same events occur in the Bulgarian version narrated by Georgi Paunov, born around 1896,[9] and in a mid-nineteenth-century Romanian version.[10]

The tale's earliest versions in European tradition are attested in German author Johannes Hulsbusch's Latin *Sylva sermonum iucundissimorum* (Forest of the Most Amusing Sermons; 1568)[11] and Italian author Tommaso Costo's collection of novellas in the style of Boccaccio, *Le otto giornate del Fuggilozio* (The Eight Days of Fuggilozio; 1596).[12] While Costo localizes the events in Chiavari, a small town in the region of Genoa, Hulsbusch has them take place in Venice, hereby probably indicating that he relied on an earlier Italian source, as yet unidentified.

In Arabic literature, the tale is first attested in al-Ābī's (d. 1030) comprehensive encyclopedia of jokes and anecdotes, *Nathr al-durr* (Pearls of Prose), from where Ibn Ḥamdūn (d. 1167) copied it almost verbatim in his *al-Tadhkira* (The Aide-Mémoire).[13] The Arabic tale tells the events in a condensed factual manner, with the man leading his horse shouting, "Get out of the way (*al-ṭarīq, al-ṭarīq*)!" At court, the man at first pretends to be dumb. When he later wards the plaintiff off by arguing that he had actually warned him, the judge simply says, "He's right (*ṣadaqa*)!"

Notes

1. Marzolph, Ulrich, and Ingeborg Baldauf, "Hodscha Nasreddin," in *Enzyklopädie des Märchens*, vol. 6 (1990), cols. 1127–1151, at col. 1128.

2. Cassar Pullicino, Ġuże, *Stejjer ta' niesna*, Malta: id-Dipartiment ta' l-informazzjoni, 1967, pp. 32–42; Galley, Micheline, "Two Folkloric Articles, 1: A Mediterranean Hero," *Journal of Maltese Studies* 7 (1971), pp. 64–70; Mifsud, Ġorġ, *Ġaħan u ħrejjef oħra*, San Ġwann, Malta: PEG Publications, 1995; Vella Camilleri, Doris, *Il-Ġaħan ta'Madwarna*, Valetta: Colour Image, 2006.

3. Dannemann, Manuel, "Kößler-Ilg, Bertha," in *Enzyklopädie des Märchens*, vol. 8 (1996), cols. 313–314.

4. Ilg, Bertha, *Maltesische Märchen und Schwänke. aus dem Volksmunde gesammelt*, vol. 2, Leipzig: Schönfeld, 1906, pp. 41–47, nos. 91–97; Wesselski, *Der Hodscha Nasreddin*, vol. 2, pp. 99–100, 210, no. 425.

5. Ilg, *Maltesische Märchen*, p. 47, no. 97.

6. Hernández Fernández, Ángel, *Catálogo tipológico del cuento folclórico en Murcia*, Alcalá: Universidad de Alcalá, 2013, p. 227, no. 1534D*; see also Boggs, Ralph S., *Index of Spanish Folktales*, Helsinki: Suomalainen Tiedeakatemia, 1930, p. 134, no. *1587.

7. Wickram, Georg, *Werke*, vol. 3: *Rollwagenbüchlein, Die sieben Hauptlaster*, ed. Johannes Bolte, Tübingen: Litterarischer Verein in Stuttgart, 1903, pp. 41–43, 370–371, no. 35; Moser-Rath, Elfriede, *Predigtmärlein der Barockzeit: Exempel, Sage, Schwank und Fabel in geistlichen Quellen des oberdeutschen Raumes*, Berlin: De Gruyter, 1964, pp. 382–383, 498, no. 229; Moser-Rath, *"Lustige Gesellschaft,"* p. 440, no. 86; Uther, *Deutscher Märchenkatalog*, p. 401, no. 1534D*.

8. Kovács, Ágnes, *König Mátyás und die Rátóter: Ungarische Schildbürgerschwänke und Anekdoten*, Leipzig: Kiepenheuer, 1988, p. 219.

9. Eschker, Wolfgang, *Der Zigeuner im Paradies: Balkanslawische Schänke und lustige Streiche*, Kassel: Erich Röth, 1986, pp. 159–160, 195, no. 102; see also Daskalova Perkowski, Liliana, et al., *Typenverzeichnis der bulgarischen Volksmärchen*, ed. Klaus Roth, Helsinki: Academia Scientiarum Fennica, 1995, pp. 307–308, no. 1534D*.

10. Stroescu, *La typologie*, vol. 2, pp. 1012–1013, no. 4800.

11. Hulsbusch, Johannes, *Sylva sermonum iucundissimorum*, Basel, 1568, pp. 60–61.

12. Costo, Tomaso, *Il Fuggilozio, diviso in otto giornate*, Venice: Mattia Colosini and Barezzo Barezzi, 1601, pp. 91–92; Costo, *Il Fuggilozio*, ed. Corrado Calenda, Rome: Salerno, 1989, pp. 111–112 (2,15).

13. Marzolph, *Arabia ridens*, vol. 1, p. 256, no. 15; vol. 2, p. 189, no. 814; Ābī, Abū Saʿd Manṣūr ibn al-Ḥusayn al-, *Nathr al-durr*, ed. Muḥammad ʿAlī Qarna et al., vol. 4, Cairo: al-Hayʾa al-miṣriyya al-ʿāmma lil-kitāb, 1985, p. 130; Ibn Ḥamdūn, Muḥammad ibn al-Ḥasan ibn Muḥammad ibn ʿAlī, *al-Tadhkira al-ḥamdūniyya*, ed. Iḥsān ʿAbbās and Bakr ʿAbbās, vol. 8, Beirut: Dār Ṣādir, 1996, p. 259, no. 748.

CHAPTER 63

The Exigent Dreamer (ATU 1543A)

In 1929, Richard Wossidlo recorded a total of three short jocular tales from a Mr. Schwiesow in Rostock, including the following one.[1]

> As the local policeman Karl Steffen walks along the village road, he is in a troubled mood. When a friend asks him what happened, Karl tells him that he had a dream that night.
>
> In the dream, God granted him a wish, and Karl wished for a nice grog. God informed him that he could have a cold drink right away. If he wanted it hot, God would have to fetch it from the seventh heaven. As Karl waited for the hot drink to arrive, his wife kicked him and told him to get up and have their farmhand feed the animals.
>
> Now Karl regrets that he had not taken the drink cold so as to have had something at least.

In his *Book of Noodles,* published in 1903, William Alexander Clouston quotes the "well-worn jest" of an Irishman who dreams that the pope offers him a drink.[2] Thinking to himself, "Would a duck swim?" the Irishman gladly accepts. As there is whisky, lemon, and sugar on the sideboard, he requests "a drop of punch." When the pope offers him to have the punch either hot or cold, the Irishman prefers to have it hot, and the pope steps down to the kitchen to fetch some boiling water. But before the pope comes back, the Irishman wakes up. "Now," he says, "it's distressing me that I didn't take it cold!" Two Romanian versions of the joke are known, published in 1901 and 1916, respectively.[3] In the older text, the protagonist dreams that he is offered Turkish coffee either hot or cold; in the more recent one, he dreams of finding a bottle of hard liquor that his godfather, the priest, lost, and thinks of preparing the drink hot and sweetened.

The joke's early twentieth-century distribution in three widely separated European geographical locations suggests a common precursor for the German, English, and Romanian texts. Considering the historical dissemination of numerous jokes through chapbooks, this medium appears to offer itself as the potential common precursor, even though no hard evidence has so far been discussed. The joke's ultimate model is found in a sample translation of Chinese jokes first published in 1824 by Sinologist Stanislas Julien (1797–1873) in the leading Orientalist journal of the day, the French *Journal Asiatique*.[4] The text is extracted from the Chinese booklet 笑裏笑 *Xiao li xiao* (Laughter), a collection of jocular tales compiled by a certain Nian Hua Xiao Shi and published by Shui Xiang Ji Jiu; the latter's preface to the booklet's manuscript copy preserved at the French Bibliothèque Nationale dates to around 1658.[5] The Chinese joke introduces a habitual drinker who dreams of having found a cup of excellent wine. In order to enjoy its full flavor, the drinker heats the wine. But just as he gets ready to drink it, he wakes up and shouts, "What a fool I am! Why was I not content to have it cold!" The joke's subsequent dissemination in Western tradition sheds light on the medium of journals and newspapers whose important role for the spread of narrative items is rarely taken into consideration.[6] In the same year as its initial publication, Julien's article, in which the joke in question is the first one presented, was reprinted in a French journal of literary curiosities addressing a larger readership than the original specialist audience.[7] Again in 1824, an English translation appeared in the English *Asiatic Journal*,[8] and a year later an unnamed critic discussed the original article in *The Oriental Herald*.[9] The critic confessed that he had "been sadly disappointed in (the article's) perusal," finding himself "put off with some dozen of the most 'weary, stale, flat, and unprofitable' *bons mots*, that ever were palmed upon us under that insinuating title." Although he doubted that "the specimens before us could ever have succeeded in discomposing the solemn gravity of a mandarin's physiognomy," he admitted that the joke under discussion here "may pass muster for a tolerable joke, although not altogether new," and proceeded to quote the item in question. Once more in 1824, Julien's article was published in German translation in two journals of an entertaining nature.[10] Some twenty years later, the Sunday supplement of the *Fürther Tagblatt* reprinted the item.[11] In English, the "anecdotes of the Jo Miller of the Celestial Empire" experienced a certain hype toward the end of the nineteenth-century, when a number of local US newspapers published them in 1891.[12] As there was a significant Chinese population of migrant workers in San Francisco, where the joke was first published in the United States, maybe a humorous item about "Chinese" culture was developed from older sources. Earlier in 1891, the joke even made it into the New Zealand *Otago Daily Times*.[13] Whereas the initial English and German translations were close to the original French, the *Otago Daily Times* and, subsequently, the US-American newspapers had the drinker find "a cup of excellent toddy." In addition to adapting the events to a local context, this change eliminates one of the essential problems the Chinese text presents in translation. Whereas Chinese rice wine, a relatively strong liquor, is regularly consumed hot, only specific alcoholic beverages in Western culture are heated, or rather mixed with hot water, such as grog or "toddy." Canonized by its inclusion in a German compilation of the world's most ancient jokes, the joke in question remains available to a modern audience.[14]

The above documented history of the joke's dissemination in Western culture most likely does not account for more than the proverbial tip of the iceberg of tradition. Even so, the joke's European history, beginning in a scientific journal and continuing in popular journals and the entertaining sections of newspapers, documents the important role these media played for the global dissemination of narrative items. An exhaustive search for additional occurrences is likely to achieve the joke's documentation in a wide variety of popular media in various European languages toward the end of the nineteenth century, whence it would potentially pass on to oral tradition so that it could, eventually, be recorded from the oral performance of popular storytellers by twentieth-century folklorists.

Although jokes about drinkers, drunkards, and the use and abuse of alcoholic beverages are legion in classical Arabic literature,[15] the specific joke in question is not documented prior to its Chinese version. Meanwhile, previous research has often compared the Chinese joke to a corresponding text that features a dreamer who wakes up regretting not having accepted a previous offer, instead in his dream having requested more.[16] The most recent revision of the international tale-type index indiscriminately classifies both texts as the newly introduced tale type ATU 1543A: *The Greedy Dreamer*, without specifying the content of the Chinese text.[17] The text the Chinese joke is compared to is an anecdote attributed to the Turkish jester Nasreddin Hodja. Nasreddin dreams that somebody wants to give him nine coins. Instead of accepting the offer, he insists on receiving ten coins and wakes up with nothing at all. Closing his eyes again and stretching out his hands, he says, "I changed my mind, so let me have the nine coins!"[18] This joke is documented in European publications of Nasreddin's jests in the Balkan countries in Greek, Serbian, and Croatian.[19] The joke's attribution to Nasreddin goes back to the earliest preserved Ottoman Turkish compilations of his pranks, which dates to the sixteenth century.[20] The joke is a standard component of the editions of the jests of Nasreddin and his corresponding characters, the Arabic Juḥā or the Persian Mollā Naṣreddin, printed since the nineteenth century,[21] and also appears in the repertoire of jests on Gioha, the corresponding character in the tradition of the Sephardic, that is, originally Spanish, Jewry.[22] As in other instances, the joke's attribution to this character supplied the item with a powerful medium of dissemination throughout the areas of Muslim influence.

A singular recording of another closely corresponding text from late nineteenth-century Portuguese tradition suggests that there is still more to the joke's history. The item in Teófilo Braga's (1843–1924) seminal collection of traditional Portuguese folktales presents a usurer who dreams of Saint Anthony (of Padua; 1195–1231) offering him a vast fortune.[23] Given the choice of receiving the money in banknotes or in gold, the usurer prefers to have it in gold and is asked to wait so that Saint Anthony can go and fetch the gold. Before the giver returns, the usurer wakes up and regrets not having been content with the paper money. This text was obviously adapted to a Christian context in which the legend of Saint Anthony and the deceased usurer's heart in the treasure chest was widely known.[24] In the popular tradition of the Iberian Peninsula, it appears to be modeled after the jocular tale's first occurrence in a Christian European context as documented in Petrus Alfonsus' (d. after 1121) *Disciplina clericalis* (The Scholar's Guide).[25] In this tale, a shepherd wants to sell his sheep to a dealer who offers him a certain price for each animal. While the shepherd keeps negotiating with the dealer to achieve a higher price, he eventually wakes up. Vaguely realizing that the events only happened in his dream, the shepherd agrees to contend himself with whatever is offered. Contrary to several other tales of the *Disciplina clericalis*, this text had no major impact on subsequent European tradition, as only a few citations modeled on the *Disciplina clericalis* in nineteenth- and early twentieth-century Hungarian texts are presently known.[26]

Arabic authors in Muslim Spain published the tale's monetary version both after and prior to Petrus Alfonsus, suggesting that the tale was well known in Arabic tradition of the Iberian Peninsula.[27] The Arabic version given in Ibn ʿAbd Rabbih's (d. 940) *al-ʿIqd al-farīd* (The Unique Necklace)[28] is later also cited in Ibn ʿĀṣim's (d. 1426) *Ḥadāʾiq al-azāhir* (Flower Gardens).[29] The Arabic text introduces a man who approaches the famous interpreter of dreams, Ibn Sīrīn (d. 728). The man had a dream in which he offered to sell his sheep for eight *dirhams* a piece. As he did not see any money when he opened his eyes, he closed them again and said that he would also be content with four *dirhams* per animal. Asked for the dream's meaning, Ibn Sīrīn dryly suggests that the customers probably found a fault in the animals so that they refrained from buying them, and the dreamer comments that this might have been the case. Introduced by a chain of transmitters, this tale's oldest documented version in Arabic literature is contained in Ibn Qutayba's (d. 889) *ʿUyūn al-akhbār* (Quintessential Reports).[30] Here again, the dreamer asks Ibn Sīrīn to interpret his dream, but the interpreter does not give any comment.

The Arabic tale, in turn, appears to be modeled on a text contained in the only preserved collection of jokes from Greek antiquity, the *Philogelos* (Laughter Lover) that probably dates from the fifth century CE.[31] In this text, a man from Abdera, a city whose inhabitants constitute the ancient Greek equivalent of the Mad Men of Gotham, dreamt that he was selling a piglet, asking a price of 100 *denarii*. When he woke up just as he was refusing a bid of half that price, he stretched out his hand and said, "All right, give me the 50!"

The diligent study of each and every single known version of the joke's various occurrences allows the reconstruction of streams of tradition of versions that are closely related to, depending on, or inspired by earlier versions. Even so, it strongly suggests that the two major forms discussed here came into existence independently in regions wide apart from each other, originating as they do from the ubiquitous and fundamental human experience that dreams, although they can be vivid and emotionally engaging, are not true.

Notes

1. Neumann, Siegfried, *Volksschwänke aus Mecklenburg, aus der Sammlung Richard Wossidlos*, Berlin: Akademie-Verlag, 1963, p. 158, no. 571; the two additional items recorded from Mr. Schwiesow are published pp. 49–50, nos. 169–170.

2. Clouston, William Alexander, *The Book of Noodles: Stories of Simpletons; or, Fools and Their Follies*, London: Elliot Stock, 1903, pp. 92–93.

3. Stroescu, *La typologie*, vol. 2, pp. 1257–1258, no. 5240.

4. Julien, Stanislas Aignan, "Contes et bon mots extraits d'un livre chinois titulé Siao li Siao," *Journal Asiatique* 4 (1824), pp. 100–104, at p. 100.

5. Courant, Maurice, *Catalogue des livres chinois, coréens, japonais, . . .*, vol. 1, Paris: Leroux, 1902, p. 436, no. 4292; Gimm, Martin, "Verlorene mandjurische Übersetzungen chinesischer Romane," *Documenta Barbarorum: Festschrift für Walter Heissig zum 70. Geburtstag*, ed. Klaus Sagaster and Michael Weiers, Wiesbaden: Otto Harrassowitz, 1983, pp. 127–141, at p. 138, no. 111; see also http://archivesetmanuscrits.bnf.fr/ark:/12148/cc27023f; a digital copy of the work can be accessed at http://gallica.bnf.fr/ark:/12148/btv1b9006573s/f3.image (accessed February 14, 2018).

6. For a rare exception, see Stitt, J. Michael, and Dodge, Robert K., *A Tale Type and Motif Index of Early U.S. Almanachs*, New York: Greenwood, 1991.

7. *Musée de variétés littéraires* 4 (1824), p. 186. The references for the following discussion of the joke's dissemination were identified by a variety of Google searches. Rather than specifying the respective url, some of which are excessively long, I encourage readers to search for "Siao li Siao" (the original transcription of the Chinese collection's title), as well as the tale's beginning in a variety of languages, such as "Un buveur de profession ayant trouvé en songe une coupe d'excellent vin," "A drunkard having found in his dream a cup of excellent wine," "A confirmed drunkard in his dreams imagined that he had found a cup of excellent toddy," or "Ein Trinker von Profession hatte im Traum einen Becher köstlichen Weines gefunden."

8. Julien, A. "Anecdotes and Bons-Mots from a Chinese Book Entitled Siao Li Siao," *The Asiatic Journal* (October 1824), pp. 363–365, at p. 363.

9. "Labours of the Asiatic Society of Paris," *The Oriental Herald* 4 (April–June 1825), pp. 389–398, at pp. 396–397.

10. "Anekdoten und Charakterzüge aus dem chinesischen Buche Siao li Siao entlehnt," *Der Sammler: Ein Unterhaltungsblatt* issue 71 (June 12, 1824), p. 283; also in *Der Gesellschafter, oder Blätter für Geist und Herz: ein Volksblatt* 8 (1824), pp. 422–423.

11. *Das Sonntagsblatt: Erzähler zum Fürther Tagblatt* 4.39 (1845), p. 156.

12. *San Francisco Call* June 3, 1891; *Arkansas City Daily Traveler* July 14, 1891; *Winfield Tribune* July 17, 1891; *Independence Daily Reporter*, Kansas, July 21, 1891.

13. *Otago Daily Times*, April 25, 1891; see https://paperspast.natlib.govt.nz/newspapers/ODT18910425.2.33 (accessed February 15, 2018).

14. Elbogen, Paul, *Humor seit Homer: Die ältesten Witze der Welt*, Reinbek: Rowohlt, 1980 (1964), p. 35.

15. See Marzolph, *Arabia ridens*, vol. 2, Index, s.v. "Betrunken," "Trinker," "Wein."

16. Clouston, *The Book of Noodles*, pp. 93–94; Wesselski, *Der Hodscha Nasreddin*, vol. 1, p. 206, no. 5; Ellbogen, *Humor seit Homer*, p. 34–35.

17. Uther, *The Types*, vol. 2, p. 283, no. 1543A.

18. See the references in note 16.

19. Wesselski, *Der Hodscha Nasreddin*, vol. 1, p. 206, no. 5.

20. Burrill, Kathleen R.F., "The Nasreddin Hoca Stories, 1: An Early Ottoman Manuscript at the University of Groningen," *Archivum Ottomanicum* 2 (1970), pp. 7–114, at p. 33, no. 8; Kut, Günay, "Nasreddin Hoca Hikâyeleri Yazmalarının Kolları Üzerine Bir Deneme," in *IV. Milletlerarası Türk Halk Kültürü Kongresi Bildirileri*, vol. 3: *Halk Edebiyatı*, Ankara, 1992, pp. 147–200, p. 160, no. 23.

21. *Leṭā'if-i Hoca Naṣreddin*, Istanbul 1253/1837, pp. 3–4; Juḥā, *Hādhihi nawādir al-khūjah Naṣr al-Dīn Afandī Juḥā al-Rūmī*, Būlāq: Mūsā Kāstillī, 1278/1861, p. 5; *Moṭāyebāt-e Mollā Naṣreddin*, [Tehran] 1299/1881, p. 14; see also Kabbani, Sam, *Altarabische Eseleien: Humor aus dem frühen Islam*, Herrenalb: Horst Erdmann, 1965, pp. 180–181, no. 273.

22. Haboucha, Reginetta, *Types and Motifs of the Judaeo-Spanish Folktales*, New York: Garland, 1992, p. 532, no.**1239.

23. Braga, Teófilo, *Contos tradicionais do povo português*, 3rd ed., vol. 1, Lisbon: Dom Quixote, 1987, p. 275; Cardigos, Isabel, *Catalogue of Portuguese Folktales*, Helsinki: Suomalainen Tiedeakatemia, 2006, p. 323, no. 1543A.

24. See, e.g., no. 16 at http://catholicmystics.blogspot.de/2014/04/miracles-of-st-anthony-of-padua.html (accessed February 15, 2018).

25. Chauvin, *Bibliographie*, vol. 9 (1905), p. 37, no. 30; Tubach, *Index exemplorum*, p. 145, no. 1788; Goldberg, Harriet, *Motif-index of Medieval Spanish Folk Narratives*, Tempe, Arizona: Arizona State University, 1998, p. 83, motif J1473.1; Schwarzbaum, Haim, "International Folklore Motifs in Petrus Alphonsi's 'Disciplina clericalis'," in Schwarzbaum, *Jewish Folklore between East and West: Collected Papers*, ed. Eli Yassif, Beer-Sheva: Ben-Gurion University of the Negev Press, 1989, pp. 239–358, at pp. 328–329, no. 31.

26. György, Lajos, *A magyar anekdota története és egyetemes kapcsolatai*, Budapest: Studium, 1934, p. 201–202, no. 211.

27. Marzolph, *Arabia ridens*, vol. 2, p. 43–44, no. 162.

28. Ibn ʿAbd Rabbih, Abū ʿUmar Aḥmad ibn Muḥammad, *Kitāb al-ʿIqd al-farīd*, ed. Aḥmad Amīn, Aḥmad al-Zayn, Ibrāhīm al-Abyārī, 3rd ed., vol 6, Cairo: Lajnat al-ta'līf wa-'l-tarjama wa-'l-nashr, 1368/1949, p. 164; Spies, Otto, "Arabische Stoffe in der Disciplina Clericalis," *Rheinisches Jahrbuch für Volkskunde* 21 (1973), pp. 170–199, at p. 193–194, no. 31; Basset, *Mille et un contes*, vol. 2, p. 53, no. 26.

29. Ibn ʿĀṣim al-Andalusī, Abū Bakr ibn Muḥammad, *Ḥadā'iq al-azāhir*, ed. ʿAfīf ʿAbd al-Raḥmān, Beirut: al-Masīra, 1401/1981, p. 130; López Bernal, Desirée, *Los Ḥadā'iq al-azāhir de Abū Bakr ibn ʿĀṣim al-Garnāṭī: Traducción y estudio de una obra de adab de la Granada nazarí*, vol 1., Ph.D. thesis University of Granada, 2016, p. 214, no. 398.

30. Ibn Qutayba al-Dīnawarī, Abū Muḥammad ʿAbdallāh ibn Muslim, *ʿUyūn al-akhbār*, 2nd ed., vol. 2, Cairo: al-Mu'assasa al-miṣriyya al-ʿāmma lil-ta'lif wa-'l-tarjama wa-'l-ṭibāʿa, 1963, p. 38.

31. Wesselski, *Der Hodscha Nasreddin*, vol. 1, p. 206, no. 5; Baldwin, Barry, *The Philogelos, or Laughter-Lover*, Amsterdam: Gieben, 1983, p. 24, no. 124; Marzolph, Ulrich, "Philogelos arabikos: Zum Nachleben der antiken Witzesammlung in der mittelalterlichen arabischen Literatur," *Der Islam* 64 (1987), pp. 185–230, at p. 212, no. 124; Andreassi, Mario, *Le facezie del Philogelos: Barzellette antiche e umorismo moderno*, Rome: pensa multimedia, 2004, pp. 119–120.

CHAPTER 64

Promising to Sell the Large Farm Animal for a Trifling Amount (ATU 1553)

In 1924, the primary schoolteacher and Frisian writer Teardze Eeltje Holtrop (1865–1925) published his version of a tale that is widely known in both Middle Eastern and European traditions.[1] The tale's main theme is the attempt to evade the fulfillment of a vow or promise made under certain conditions, often in times of danger. This general theme also rules the Aesopic fable classified as tale type ATU 778: *To Sacrifice a Giant Candle*. In the fable, a man in great distress promises to sacrifice a giant candle should he be saved. As the danger diminishes, the man gradually reduces the size of the promised candle and, when he finally feels safe, does not fulfill his vow at all. The present tale's variation on this theme is more complex in that the protagonist does not attempt to evade the vow altogether but consciously employs a clever ruse to fulfill the vow to the letter without, however, incurring an otherwise inevitable financial loss. The present tale corresponds to tale type ATU 1553: *An Ox for Five Pennies*.[2] Holtrop's version is representative of a particular strand of European tradition.

On his way back from an auction at the local pub, farmer Klemmer notices that the weather has changed. In daytime it was cold, but the skies were clear. Now it was not only pitch dark but also snowing heavily. Although he knows the way back to his farm by heart, walking straight through the fields he loses his way in the darkness. Fearing to break through the ice on one of the irrigation ditches and freeze to death, he does not dare to move. In despair, he begins to pray and even vows to sell one of his cows the next day and donate all the profit to church. Soon after, he sees a light in the distance and manages to reach his home safely.

Waking up the next day, he ponders about his dilemma. Either he will have to break his vow so as not to lose his profit, or he would incur a considerable loss and, in addition, have to face his wife's dissatisfaction. Soon, however, he finds a solution for his dilemma. On the market, he offers to sell his cow for half a florin. However, he would only sell it together with a rabbit at the price of two hundred florin. After some bargaining, a customer buys the animals at the requested price and the farmer returns home satisfied. Keeping a little money for himself, he hands most of it to his wife. The next Sunday, he donates half a florin to church, as that is exactly the profit he made from selling the cow.

In European tradition, the tale was probably already known in the twelfth century. The *Fables* of French author Marie de France (d. about 1200) contain the tale of a rich man who offers to sell a horse and a billy goat on condition that the customer acquires both of them together.[3] Marie de France's version, however, does not supply any motivation for the strange offer. Moreover, it lacks the tale's point, as it does not mention the inverted prices for the animals sold together, instead solely commenting on the seller's stupidity. The earliest full-fledged version known in European tradition is the one in the *Summa predicantium* (E 8,17) compiled by fourteenth-century Dominican preacher John Bromyard. This text mentions a widow evading a stipulation of her husband's will by selling a cow cheaply together with an expensively priced rooster.[4] Following the tale's citation in Johannes Pauli's early sixteenth-century *Schimpf und Ernst* (Jocular and Serious Tales), Bromyard's version was particularly popular in German chapbooks of the baroque period.[5] In the following centuries, the tale is richly documented in a fair variety of European literary sources, including its citation in chapbooks and calendars. In the course of the nineteenth and twentieth centuries, it was collected as a "popular tale" from oral tradition in an area ranging from North Africa to the Baltic Sea.[6]

Many of the texts collected from oral tradition more or less faithfully retell the literary version that had been popularized for many centuries.[7] In that respect, Holtrop's version is exceptional as it motivates the sale of the animals by a vow made in times of utter distress. Holtrop's version is matched by a Spanish version collected in July 1985 from barkeeper Isidora Martino García, aged 70, in Soto de Sajambre in the North-Western Spanish province of León. Here, the tale's protagonist is a man who strongly believes in the powers of Saint Anthony (of Padua; 1195–1231). When his only cow falls sick, he vows to offer the cow to the saint should it be cured. And when the cow gets well, he sells it for five *duros*, but only together with a chicken priced at 2,000 *pesetas*. He donates the smaller amount to the saint and keeps the rest as his own profit.[8] Tales such as this one are independent from the European mainstream tradition, instead relating to the older tradition that is already encountered in Arabic texts of the classical period.

While previous research suggested a variety of origins,[9] the tale's oldest versions are documented in eleventh- and early twelfth-century Arabic literature.[10] Two forms are known. The shorter and earlier form is contained in al-Rāghib al-Iṣfahānī's (d. 1108) *Muḥāḍarāt al-udabā'* (Conversations of the Educated),[11] al-Maydānī's (d. 1124) collection of proverbs and their stories, *Majmaʿ al-amthāl*,[12] and the twelfth-century fable collection *al-Asad wa-'l-ghawwāṣ* (The Lion and the Diver).[13] In this form, a Bedouin whose camel has gone astray, vows to sell it for a single *dirham* should he find it again. When he finds it, however, the Bedouin cannot bring himself to sell it so cheaply. So he takes a cat and attaches it to the camel's neck. Then he advertises the camel for a single *dirham*, on condition that it be bought together with the cat priced at 500 *dirham*. An interested customer observes, "How cheap the camel is, were it not for its collar!"

In two of his compilations of jocular and entertaining stories, *Akhbār al-Adhkiyā'* (Tales of Clever People) and *Akhbār al-Ẓirāf* (Tales of Subtle People), the twelfth-century author Ibn al-Jawzī (d. 1201) presents a somewhat elaborated form of the tale.[14] In this form, a woman in the city of Kufa makes her miserable husband leave for Syria to earn money. He manages to earn 300 *dirhams* with which he acquires a camel. Soon after, however, the man realizes the camel's poor quality and vows in anger to sell it for a single *dirham* upon his return, swearing that he would divorce his wife should he break his promise. Back home, he regrets his rash decision and asks his wife's advice. The woman attaches a cat to the camel's neck and advises him to sell both animals together, the cat for 300 *dirhams*, and the camel for a single *dirham*.

In subsequent Middle Eastern tradition, the tale was disseminated widely by various influential collections. In nineteenth-century Arabic, it was incorporated into the first printed collection (1862) of the pranks focusing on the popular jester and trickster Juḥā, the Arabic equivalent of the Turkish character Nasreddin Hoja.[15] In Persian tradition, where the tale first occurs in Jāmi's (d. 1492) *Bahārestān* (The Spring Garden), it is later included in the chapbook *Ḥekāyāt-e laṭif* (Amusing Tales)[16] whose eighteenth- and nineteenth-century versions were also distributed in various languages of the Indian subcontinent.[17]

When tracing the tale's historical dissemination, it proves to be a particularly revealing item to argue for the assimilation of an original foreign narrative into a different cultural context. For the Bedouin in the tale's original Arabic versions, camels are the most important livestock, in fact essential for survival. Camel and cat enjoyed an almost proverbial status in classical Arabic tradition.[18] In the European versions, the camel did not make sense, and so it was exchanged for a large farm animal that has a similar importance for the European farmer, such as a horse, a cow, or an ox. Similarly, although not equally necessary, in the tale's adapted European versions the smaller animal is now a rooster or chicken whose presence on a farm could be taken for granted.

The man's wife as the one who advises him to practice the clever stratagem already appears in the elaborated twelfth-century Arabic versions. In versions relating to the dominant European literary tradition the woman is often a widow aiming to avoid fulfilling her husband's will to donate the revenue from the animal's sale to church as a meritorious act after his death. By having the widow act for her own profit, these versions add a misogynous touch. Although the longer Arabic version already introduced the seller's wife, and although women in Arabic and general Muslim tradition are stereotypically represented as tricky and mischievous, the original versions of the tale rather play on the specific genre of legal tricks (Arabic *ḥiyal*, sg. *ḥīla*) popular in classical Arabic literature.[19]

A further adaptation concerns the context in which the man makes his vow. In both the Arabic and the European versions, the man makes his vow in a situation of utter desperation. Whereas the Bedouin's vow is motivated by anger about the apparently lost animal, his European counterparts make their vow out of concern for their own well-being, similarly to the situation in the Aesopic fable. In addition, the Arabic tales are embedded in a commercial context, implying that the seller would only harm his own interest without anybody else profiting from the situation except the potential buyer of his camel. In contrast, the European versions are usually embedded in a religious (Christian) context, in that the man or his widow vow to donate the profit from selling the animal to church. Consequently, in the European versions the clever evasion of fulfilling the vow may also be read as an implicit critique of the person's religiosity or even of the church's material attitude. Additional adaptations concern the weather conditions typical for a Northern European winter in the Frisian context or the mention of a popular saint in the Spanish version.

Notes

1. Van der Kooi, Jurjen, and Babs A. Gezelle Meerburg, *Friesische Märchen*, Munich: Diederichs, 1990, pp. 199–203, no. 74.

2. See Marzolph, Ulrich, "Ochse für fünf Pfennig," in *Enzyklopädie des Märchens*, vol. 10 (2002), cols. 193–196.

3. Marie de France, *Fables*, ed. and transl. Harriet Spiegel, Toronto: University of Toronto Press, 1987, pp. 174–175, no. 64.

4. Warnke, Karl, *Die Quellen des Esope der Marie de France*, Halle: Niemeyer, 1900, 50–51, no. 64; Rehermann, Ernst Heinrich, and Fritz Wagner, "Bromyard, John," in *Enzyklopädie des Märchens*, vol. 2 (1979), cols. 707–802, at col. 800.

5. Pauli, Johannes, *Schimpf und Ernst*, ed. Johannes Bolte, Berlin: Stubenrauch, 1924 (reprint Hildesheim: Georg Olms, 1972), vol. 1, p. 271, no. 462; vol. 2, p. 364; Moser-Rath, *"Lustige Gesellschaft,"* p. 457, no. 144.

6. See Marzolph, "Ochse für fünf Pfennig."

7. Merkens, Heinrich, *Was sich das Volk erzählt: Deutscher Volkshumor, gesammelt und nacherzählt*, vol. 2, Jena: Costenoble, 1895, p. 162, no. 196; Van der Kooi, Jurjen, "Almanakteljes en folksforhalen; in stikmennich 17de en 18de ieuske teksten," *It Beaken* 41.1–2 (1979), pp. 70–114, at pp. 97–98, no. 2.13; Van der Kooi, Jurjen, and Theo Schuster, *Märchen und Schwänke aus Ostfriesland*, Leer: Schuster, 1993, pp. 185–186, no. 126.

8. Camarena Laucirica, Julio, *Cuentos tradicionales de León*, vol. 2, Madrid: Universidad Complutense, Seminario Menendez Pidal, 1991, pp. 103–104, no. 222.

9. Summarized in Marzolph, *Arabia ridens*, vol. 1, p. 79.

10. Ibid., vol. 1, p. 81; vol. 2, pp. 234–235, no. 1065.

11. Rāghib al-Iṣfahānī, al-Ḥusayn ibn Muḥammad al-, *Muḥāḍarāt al-udabā᾽ wa-muḥāwarāt al-shuʿarā᾽ wa-᾽l-bulaghā᾽*, Beirut 1961, vol. 2, p. 470.

12. Maydānī, Abū ᾽l-Faḍl Aḥmad ibn Muḥammad ibn Aḥmad ibn Ibrāhīm, *Majmaʿ al-amthāl*, ed. Muḥammad Abū ᾽l-Faḍl Ibrāhīm, Cairo: ʿĪsā al-Bābī al-Ḥalabī, 1398/1978, vol. 3, p. 251, no. 3790.

13. *Asad wa-'l-ghawwāṣ, al-*, ed. Riḍwān al-Sayyid, Beirut: Dār al-Ṭalī'a, 1978, p. 158.

14. Ibn al-Jawzī, Abū 'l-Faraj 'Abd al-Raḥmān ibn 'Alī, *Akhbār al-Adhkiyā'*, ed. Muḥammad Mursī al-Khūlī, Cairo, 1970, p. 109; Ibn al-Jawzī, *Akhbār al-Ẓirāf wa-'l-mutamājinīn*, ed. Muḥammad Baḥr al-'ulūm, 2nd ed., al-Najaf: al-Maktaba al-ḥaydariyya, 1386/1966, p. 150.

15. Wesselski, *Der Hodscha Nasreddin*, vol. 2, pp. 16, 188–190, no. 370.

16. Hertel, Johannes, *Zweiundneunzig Anekdoten und Schwänke aus dem modernen Indien: Aus dem Persischen* übersetzt, Leipzig: Haessel 1992, p. 79, no. 80.

17. Marzolph, Ulrich, "'Pleasant Stories in an Easy Style': Gladwin's Persian Grammar as an Intermediary between Classical and Popular Literature," in *Proceedings of the Second European Conference of Iranian Studies*, ed. Bert G. Fragner et al., Rome: Istituto Italiano per il Medio ed Estremo Oriente, 1995, pp. 445–475.

18. Geyer, Rudolf, "Die Katze auf dem Kamel: Ein Beitrag zur altarabischen Phraseologie," in *Orientalische Studien: Festschrift Theodor Nöldeke*, ed. Carl Bezold, vol. 1, Gießen: Töpelmann, 1906, pp. 57–70.

19. Schacht, Joseph, "Die arabische Ḥiyal-Literatur: Ein Beitrag zur Erforschung der islamischen Rechtspraxis," *Der Islam* 15 (1926), pp. 211–232; Schacht, "Ḥiyal," in *Encyclopedia of Islam*, 2nd ed., vol. 3 (1979), pp. 510–513.

CHAPTER 65

The Rogue Trades Water for Wine (ATU 1555B)

A "roving American trickster tale attached to local scalawags all over the country"[1] tells the story of a rogue who manages to acquire an alcoholic beverage without paying for it. The rogue fills half of his vessel with water and asks the dealer to fill it up with an alcoholic beverage, usually whisky or rum. When it turns out that the rogue is not able to pay, he returns the same amount of liquid to the dealer as he was given. That way, he ends up with a mixture of half water and half alcoholic beverage. Proceeding in the same manner several times with different dealers, the rogue ends up with a mixture strong enough to enjoy drinking.

Corresponding to tale type ATU 1555B: *The Wine and Water Business*, the tale was popularized in US-American print media since the middle of the nineteenth century. Usually, the tale is adapted to the local context so convincingly as to look like a typical American trickster tale. Richard Dorson traced the tale's appearance in US-American weeklies and book publications since about 1845.[2] First published in the Saint Louis *Reveille* about a "bruiser" named Bill, the tale was subsequently published in the New York popular weekly *Spirit of Times* on January 25, 1845, and again in a more elaborate version on July 27, 1850, "as an original contribution from Robin Roughead of Greenville, Mississippi." The latter version is attributed to Big Lige Shattuck, "a crew member poling a broadhorn down the Mississippi with other boatmen." First instructed by the captain to fill the whiskey keg half full of river water, Lige then asks the dealer to fill it up with three gallons of whiskey. But on learning "that the boatman lacks ready cash," the dealer has him pour the three gallons of liquid back. Even so, the resulting dilution of whiskey and water is strong enough "to cheer the captain and crew on the remainder of their voyage." Attributed to General Tay of Laconia, the "deceit" was published in the New York *Atlas* in 1860, and told again about Captain Elisha Smart in the *Berkshire Hills*, a regional magazine of Western Massachusetts. Eventually, the tale ended up in a widely read collection of folklore from New York State, Harold W. Thompson's *Body, Boots and Britches*

(1940),[3] where the event is attributed to the "raftsman-hero," songmaker, trickster, and player of practical jokes "Boney" Quillan (1845–1908).[4]

In Europe, the tale was recorded from late nineteenth- and twentieth-century tradition in Catalonia[5] and Bulgaria.[6] The Bulgarian versions feature the wine and water business together with two other deceits in which several tricksters acquire chicken and bread. Portuguese and Polish traditions know a similar tale of deceit.[7] Here, the rogue first has the dealer fill his jar with wine. Then he admits that he cannot pay and returns a previously prepared jar of water to the dealer that looks exactly like the jar of wine he just received.

Both of the above tales are first attested in European tradition in an early seventeenth-century representative of the Spanish literary genre of picaresque novel, Carlos García's *La desordenada codicia de los bienes agenos* (Disorderly Greed for the Property of Others), initially published in Paris in 1619.[8] García's novel presents an account of the author's (fictional) conversation with a prisoner, set in some prison in Paris, who tells him of his experience as a thief.[9] One of the tales the narrator tells is about a group of rascals who fill a wine skin one-fourth full of water and then have the dealer fill it up with wine. On tasting the wine, they complain of its poor quality and have the dealer withdraw the amount she put in.[10] In the following tale, the trickster returns a bottle of water instead of the bottle of wine he just purchased. The fact that both tales appear one after the other suggests García's work as a common source for both of the tales current in oral tradition, although the exact ways of transmission remain unknown.

In classical Arabic literature, a corresponding tale is stereotypically attributed to al-Mughīra ibn Shuʿba (d. 670), a companion of the Prophet Muḥammad who was equally famed for his insatiable lust for women as for his strong craving for wine.[11] The Arabic tale is documented in two versions. An elaborate version is contained in the character's biography in Abū 'l-Faraj al-Iṣfahānī's (d. 965) *Kitāb al-Aghānī* (Book of Songs).[12] The author introduces al-Mughīra ibn Shuʿba as "one of those among the Arabs who embodied shrewdness, resoluteness, judgment and the capacity to deploy effective ruses."[13] The tale is presented as told by al-Mughīra ibn Shuʿba himself.

> When traveling with a caravan to the city of al-Ḥīra (in present-day Iraq), al-Mughīra's companions crave wine (*khamr*), but the only money they have is a counterfeit *dirham*. Al-Mughīra asks them for the coin and two wine skins, assuring them that he knows what to do. At first, he fills some water into one of the wine skins. In town, he asks a wine dealer to fill that skin with wine, subsequently offering the counterfeit *dirham* as payment. When the dealer informs al-Mughīra that he just poured out wine for 20 *dirhams*, al-Mughīra apologizes, explaining that he is just a Bedouin (implying that he does not know the ways business works in the city). The dealer withdraws the same amount of liquid as poured out, leaving a rich mixture of wine and water in the skin to the same amount as the rogue

> had previously filled the skin with water. The rogue pours the mixture into his second skin, again fills water into the first skin, and goes to the next dealer, diverting the latter's potential suspicion by showing him the wine he now has and asking for a wine of the same quality. As al-Mughīra's request challenges the dealer's pride, the dealer assures him that his wine is of an even better quality. Continuing the same procedure, the rogue visits all of the wine dealers in the city. When he eventually returns to his companions, one of the wine skins is completely filled, and the other one is half full. Informed about his stratagem, his companions marvel at his reckless cleverness.

The tale's shorter version is contained in almost identical wording in three compilations dating to the eleventh and twelfth centuries, Abū Ḥayyān al-Tawḥīdī's (d. 1023) *al-Baṣā'ir wa-'l-dhakhā'ir* (Deep Insights and Treasures),[14] al-Ābī's (d. 1030) *Nathr al-durr* (Pearls of Prose),[15] and Ibn Ḥamdūn's (d. 1167) *al-Tadhkira* (The Aide-Mémoire).[16] In the shorter version, al-Mughīra is said to be addicted to drinking wine (*sharāb*). The event is localized in the city of Khaybar whose Jewish population included many wine dealers. It is specified for the day the Muslim army conquered Khaybar in the year 628, thus further accentuating al-Mughīra's recklessness, as being intoxicated during the battle does not seem to have bothered him. Except for the fact that al-Mughīra here possesses two counterfeit *dirhams* instead of only one, the events are told as before, albeit in a condensed manner.

The exact ways through which the tale might have been transmitted from Arabic literature to European and US-American traditions remain unknown. Oral tradition is likely to have played a role at any time, but historically the tale only surfaces in its literary or otherwise available and historically attested versions. In this respect, the supreme relevance of García's early seventeenth-century version as the crucial link between the tale's various versions is hardly questionable. Whereas the Bulgarian texts might derive from Ottoman Turkish adaptations of the Arabic tale, retellings or adaptations of García's version would account for the tale's attestations from oral tradition in Andalusia, and the US-American versions first published in Saint Louis might derive from Spanish American or French adaptations of García's rendering. At any rate, although the US-American versions impress as typically American migratory tales, their origin from European, and ultimately Arabic tradition is hardly to be doubted.

Notes

1. Dorson, Richard M., *American Folklore*, Chicago: The University of Chicago Press, 1959, p. 57.

2. The following discussion of US-American versions is indebted to ibid., pp. 57–58; Dorson, *Jonathan Draws the Long Bough*, Cambridge, MA: Harvard University Press, 1946, p. 226 (with exact references). For additional US-American versions, see

Baughman, Ernest W., *Type and Motif-Index of the Folktales of England and North America*, The Hague, Mouton & Co., 1966, pp. 39–40, no. 1555B; p. 345, s.v. K231.6.2.2.

3. Thompson, Harold W., *Body, Boots and Britches*, Philadelphia: Lippincott 1940, pp. 281–282.

4. Cazden, Norman, Herbert Haufrecht, and Norman Studer, eds., *Folk Songs of the Catskills*, Albany: State University of New York Press, 1982, p. 18. On Boney Quillan, see Fee, Christopher R., and Jeffrey B. Webb, eds., *American Myths, Legends and Tall Tales: An Encyclopedia of American Folklore*, Santa Barbara, CA: ABC-Clio, 2016, vol. 3, pp. 800–802.

5. Oriol, Carme, and Josep M. Pujol, *Index of Catalan Folktales*, Helsinki: Suomalainen Tiedeakatemia, 2008, p. 255, no. 1555B.

6. Daskalova Perkowski, Liliana, et al., *Typenverzeichnis der bulgarischen Volksmärchen*, ed. Klaus Roth, Helsinki: Suomalainen Tiedeakatemia, 1995, p. 318, no. 1555B; p. 305, no. $*1526A_2$ III.

7. Cardigos, Isabel, *Catalogue of Portuguese Folktales*, Helsinki: Suomalainen Tiedeakatemia, 2006, pp. 326–327, no. 1555B; Krzyżanowski, Julian, *Polska bajka ludowa w układzie systematycznym*, Polska Akad. Nauk. Wydz. Nauk Społecznych, 1963, vol. 2, p. 90, no. 1555B.

8. Childers, J. Wesley, *Tales from the Spanish Picaresque Novels: A Motif Index*, Albany: State University of New York Press, 1977, pp. 107–108, s.v. K231.6.2.1 and K231.6.2.3*; see Thacker, Mike J., "'La desordenada codicia de los bienes ajenos'—a 'caso límite' of the picaresque?," *Bulletin of Hispanic Studies* 55 (1978), pp. 33–41.

9. De Haan, Fonger, *An Outline of the History of the Novela Picaresca in Spain*, The Hague: Nijhoff, 1903, p. 32.

10. Quoted from Childers, *Tales*, p. 108; see Chevalier, *Cuentos folklóricos*, p. 299, no. 178.

11. Marzolph, *Arabia ridens*, vol. 2, p. 107, no. 429.

12. Iṣfahānī, Abū 'l-Faraj al-, *Kitāb al-Aghānī*, Būlāq (reprint Beirut: Ṣaʿb, ca. 1980), vol. 14, p. 140; Weisweiler, Max, *Arabische Märchen*, Düsseldorf: Eugen Diederichs, 1966, vol. 2, pp. 256–257, no. 105; Marzolph, *Arabia ridens*, vol. 1, pp. 257–258, no. 16.

13. Kilpatrick, Hilary, *Making the Great Book of Songs: Compilation and the Author's Craft in Abū l-Faraj al-Iṣbahānī's Kitāb al-aghānī*, London: Routledge Curzon, 2003, p. 75.

14. Tawḥīdī, Abū Ḥayyān al-, *al-Baṣā'ir wa-'l-dhakhā'ir*, ed. Wadād al-Qāḍī, Beirut: Dār Ṣādir, 1408/1988, vol. 6, p. 160, no. 500.

15. Ābī, Abū Saʿd Manṣūr ibn al-Ḥusayn al-, *Nathr al-durr*, ed. Muḥammad ʿAlī Qarna et al., vol. 4, Cairo: al-Hay'a al-miṣriyya al-ʿāmma lil-kitāb, 1985, p. 113.

16. Ibn Ḥamdūn, Muḥammad ibn al-Ḥasan ibn Muḥammad ibn ʿAlī, *al-Tadhkira al-ḥamdūniyya*, ed. Iḥsān ʿAbbās and Bakr ʿAbbās, Beirut: Dār Ṣādir, 1996, vol. 2, p. 337, no. 888.

CHAPTER 66

Welcome to the Clothes (ATU 1558)

The Romanian tale "The Rich Man's Dinner Party"[1] is fashioned as a Christian legend forming part of the cycle of tales depicting God (or Jesus, or Saint Peter) wandering on earth, often instructing humanity on questions of a general ethical import.[2]

> A rich man invites some important people to a dinner party. As God happens to be "in the neighborhood," he decides to participate and makes himself appear as a poor man. The rich man, however, refuses to let him in, telling him that "beggars should keep company with beggars."
>
> Without saying anything, God goes away and transforms himself into a rich man with a carriage and some fine horses. Now the rich man invites him in, seats him at the table and offers him a glass of wine. Instead of drinking the wine God takes the glass and spills the wine all over his clothes, informing the astonished host that he was welcomed only on account of his clothes, and so it was "only right that this glass of wine should go to them."

The Romanian tale corresponds to tale type ATU 1558: *Welcome to the Clothes*, numerous versions of which are documented in European literary sources or recorded from oral tradition, mainly in Southern and South-Eastern Europe. Compared to these versions, the Romanian tale presents a unique adaptation to the Christian context. The tale's regular versions usually attribute the event to a distinguished secular person, whether named or anonymous.[3] One of the tale's earliest European attestations, given by the Dominican preacher Stephen of Bourbon (Étienne de Bourbon) around the middle of the thirteenth century, attributes the action to the philosopher and theologian Peter Abelard (d. 1142) who is said to have humiliated some monks by first visiting them in poor clothes and later returning with a pompous entourage.[4] In central and Northern European traditions, the tale is almost exclusively available in literary sources.[5] In the Middle East, at least as of the seventeenth century, the tale was included in manuscript compilations of the pranks attributed to the Turkish jester Nasreddin

Hodja.[6] Resulting from his popularity, the tale stayed alive in Mediterranean oral tradition where it was attributed to the jester's various regional equivalents, such as Ġaħan (Malta),[7] Giufà (Sicily),[8] Hodjas (Greece),[9] or Nastradin Hodja (Bulgaria).[10]

The tale's earliest documented version is contained in Arab author Ibn al-Jawzī's (d. 1201) *Akhbār al-Ẓirāf* (Tales of Subtle People).[11] Ibn al-Jawzī attributes the act to the religious scholar Sulaymān ibn Mihrān al-Aʿmash (d. 765), a person of Iranian background whose sense of humor later made him a stereotype of sorts.[12]

> When invited to a wedding party, al-Aʿmash dons his fur coat, but the gatekeeper refuses to admit him. So he puts on a shirt and a regular coat and goes again. When the gatekeeper now sees him, he lets him in, and he enters. As the food is served, he stretches one of his sleeves toward the food, saying, "Eat, because you have been invited, not me!" Having said that, he gets up and does not eat.

Various adaptations of the tale in the Middle Eastern literatures exist, such as those in the *Bustān* (The Orchard) by thirteenth-century Persian poet Saʿdi,[13] or in Hēmavijaya's Indian *Kathāratnākara* (The Sea of Tales), dating to 1600.[14] In South Asia, the tale was further popularized by way of its inclusion in chapbooks published in Persian and the vernacular Indian languages. These chapbooks derive from the *Ḥekāyāt-e laṭif* (Amusing Tales), originally a reader appended to Francis Gladwin's grammar of the Persian language, *The Persian Moonshee*, first published in 1795.[15] In modern Persian tradition, the tale's gist is framed as a proverb.[16]

The tale's popularity, whether in Middle Eastern or European tradition, is likely connected to the basic social experience it narrates, that is, that people are often judged according to their outward appearance. This experience is limited neither to a specific time nor to a specific place or culture. An Arabic anecdote first attested in the ninth century suggests that the tale's two-part structure constitutes a later development that served to dramatize the tale's basic idea by juxtaposing the differing experiences.[17] The older anecdote, known in at least seven versions in Arabic works up to the twelfth century, presents only the tale's first half as a specific experience. It simply tells of a ruler who ignores the eloquent person who appears before him badly dressed. The man cleverly attracts the ruler's attention by saying, "It is not the coat who speaks to you, but the person wearing it!" An anecdote attributed to the Turkish jester Nasreddin Hodja, of unspecified date, similarly exemplifies the absurdity of judging persons from their outward appearance.[18] This time, however, the context is not one of hospitality, but of service, and Nasreddin employs the (apparently illogical, but actually appropriate) inverse appreciation of service to demonstrate his point. When Nasreddin goes to the public bath badly dressed, the staff affords him only a simple treatment. In return, Nasreddin gives them an extremely generous tip. When he arrives the next time, the staff recognizes him and treats him in a most obliging manner, but Nasreddin's tip this time is meager. Questioned about the reason for his enigmatic action, Nasreddin explains that the first tip was for the second treatment, and the second tip for the previous one.

Notes

1. Ure, Jean, *Pacala and Tandala and Other Rumanian Folk-Tales*, London: Methuen, 1960, pp. 72–73.

2. Lixfeld, Hannjost, "Erdenwanderung der Götter," in *Enzyklopädie des Märchens*, vol. 4 (1984), cols. 155–164.

3. For comparative listings of the tale in European literary sources see, e.g., Wesselski, *Mönchslatein*, p. 226, no. 73; Wesselski, *Der Hodscha Nasreddin*, vol. 1, p. 222, no. 55; Pauli, Johannes, *Schimpf und Ernst*, ed. Johannes Bolte, Berlin: Stubenrauch, 1924 (reprint Hildesheim: Olms, 1972), vol. 2, pp. 353–354, no. 416.

4. Wesselski, *Mönchslatein*, p. 86, in no. 73.

5. Uther, Hans-Jörg, "Kleider machen Leute," in *Enzyklopädie des Märchens*, vol. 7 (1993), cols. 1425–1429.

6. Kut, Günay, "Nasreddin Hoca Hikâyeleri Yazmalarının Kolları Üzerine Bir Deneme," in *IV. Milletlerarası Türk Halk Kültürü Kongresi Bildirileri*, vol. 3: *Halk Edebiyatı*, Ankara, 1992, pp. 147–200, at p. 165, no. 53; see also Marzolph, *Nasreddin Hodscha*, pp. 153–154, no. 356.

7. Ilg, Bertha, *Maltesische Märchen und Schwänke, aus dem Volksmunde gesammelt*, Leipzig: Schönfeld, 1906, p. 44.

8. Gonzenbach, Laura, *Sicilianische Märchen*, ed. Otto Hartwig, Leipzig: Engelmann, 1870, vol. 1, p. 258–259, in no. 37; Crane, Thomas Frederick, *Italian Popular Tales*, Boston: Houghton, 1885, p. 296, no. 102.

9. Orso, Ethelyn G., *Modern Greek Humor*, Bloomington: Indiana University Press, 1979, p. 78, no. 120.

10. Daskalova, Liana, et al., *Narodna proza ot Blagoevgradski okrăg*, Sofia: Bălgarska Akademiya na Naukite, 1985, p. 321, no. 240.

11. Ibn al-Jawzī, Abū 'l-Faraj ʿAbd al-Raḥmān ibn ʿAlī, *Akhbār al-Ẓirāf wa-'l-mutamājinīn*, ed. Muḥammad Baḥr al-ʿulūm, 2nd ed., al-Najaf: al-Maktaba al-ḥaydariyya, 1386/1966, p. 36; Marzolph, *Arabia ridens*, vol. 1, p. 258, no. 17; vol. 2, p. 267, no. 1243.

12. For other anecdotes related to al-Aʿmash, see Marzolph, *Arabia ridens*, vol. 2, nos. 13, 72, 77, 93, 148, 363, 408, 678, 679, 946, 1102, 1135, 1179, and 1244.

13. Saʿdi, *Bustān*, ed. Gholām-Ḥoseyn Yusefi, Tehran: Anjoman-e ostādān-e zabān va adabiyāt-e fārsi, 1359/1980, pp. 104–107 (verses 2071–2121).

14. *Kathāratnākara: Das Märchenmeer. Eine Sammlung indischer Erzählungen von Hēmavijaya*, transl. Johannes Hertel, vol. 2, Munich: Georg Müller, 1920, p. 42–44, no. 123.

15. Marzolph, Ulrich, "'Pleasant Stories in an Easy Style:' Gladwin's Persian Grammar as an Intermediary beween Classical and Popular Literature," in *Proceedings of the Second European Conference of Iranian Studies*, ed. Bert G. Fragner et al., Rome: Istituto Italiano per il Medio ed Estremo Oriente, 1995, pp. 445–475, at p. 464, no. 63; *Ḥekāyāt-e*

laṭif, ed. Seyyid Kamāl Ḥājj Seyyid Javādi, Tehran: Kavir, 1375/1996, pp. 190–191, no. 63.

16. Vakiliyān, Aḥmad, *Tams̱il va mas̱al*, vol. 2, Tehran: Sorush, 1366/1987, pp. 18–21.

17. Marzolph, *Arabia ridens*, vol. 2, p. 1, no. 3.

18. Marzolph, *Nasreddin Hodscha*, p. 185–186, no. 440.

CHAPTER 67

"Think Thrice before You Speak!" (ATU 1562)

The advice to think carefully before speaking out loud gave rise to a small cluster of tales classified as tale type ATU 1562: *"Think Thrice before You Speak!"* Although the tale type's denomination gives preference to a particular plot that focuses on the formulaic number three, various other structurally similar plots were classified as belonging to the tale type.[1] For instance, a tale collected from oral tradition in the lower Rhine region toward the end of the nineteenth century is only loosely connected to the tale type's general message.[2]

> On a cold day, a German traveling in the Netherlands stops in a pub to warm himself close to the open fire. One of the local people sitting nearby sees a spark from the fire settling on the man's coat without him noticing. Since he considers it impolite to address the man without knowing the stranger's name, he calmly asks the man but does not receive a response. Without losing his temper, he continues to smoke his pipe. When after a while he sees that the spark burned quite a hole in the man's coat, he again asks the man for his name, this time with a little more emphasis. In order to get rid of the seemingly obtrusive person, the German responds gruffly, "Peter." "Well then," said the Dutchman, "Peter, your coat is burning."

Although the tale mentions the same situation as the majority of the tale's other versions, that is, a piece of clothing about to burn, it develops the situation as ridicule of ethnic stereotypes. Notably, the joke arises from the ingenious combination of two stereotypes, the stubborn, self-concerned, and rude German and the unhurried, calm, and somewhat unconcerned Dutchman who would rather wait and see what happens than be overtly obtrusive.

Another tale from the same German publication introduces two traveling journeymen who warm themselves at the open fire.[3] As one of them notices a spark settle on the other one's coat, he asks his companion whether he should tell him some news. The companion responds in the affirmative, but since he explicitly only wants to hear good news, the first one keeps silent. When the man finally notices himself that his coat is on fire, his companion tells him that he already noticed it some time ago. But since his partner only wanted to hear good news, he did not say a word. Similar versions of the tale are documented in a number of German chapbooks since the seventeenth century,[4] having been introduced to German tradition in Johannes Pauli's early sixteenth-century compilation *Schimpf und Ernst* (Jocular and Serious Tales; 1522).[5] Pauli's final moral comments on the human foible the tale exemplifies. Although some people might not heed a warning, they would still complain after having suffered the misfortune others previously warned them about. Pauli in turn most likely adapted his version from the short Latin text given in the *Summa predicantium* (A 26,34) compiled by the fourteenth-century Dominican preacher John Bromyard.[6]

The tale's most widespread, though sparsely documented version is built, as the tale type's denomination indicates, on the explicit advice a senior person gives to a junior. The general situation in which a spark is about to set fire to a person's garment is the same as discussed above. Although a rare version has a teacher advise his pupils "to count to one hundred before saying anything important,"[7] the standard version has a senior person tell a junior colleague to think thrice before speaking out loud. In the Swedish text recorded by G.A. Johansson from the oral performance of Johan Eriksson, born 1840, in Norrköping, Östergötland, the communication takes place between a tailor and his apprentice.[8] In a number of essentially similar versions from English, American English, and Pennsylvania German traditions the event happens between a father and his son. The tale told by Norman F. Wilson in March, 1936, "who heard it about sixty years ago, probably from a Kendal nurse-maid,"[9] has the father chide his son for not saying right away that his coattails were on fire. In the text recorded from the oral performance of an unnamed male retired stone mill worker aged 79 in Mitchell, Indiana, in 1970,[10] a string of the mother's apron catches fire and the son justifies his belated information with the advice he previously received. And in the tale told by Julius Lentz from Laurys, Pennsylvania, before 1944,[11] the father later instructs his son that his advice is not valid in case of fire.

The tale's oldest version in Arabic literature is a fairly long-winded jocular text in Ibn al-Jawzī's (d. 1201) *Akhbār al-Ḥamqā* (Tales of Stupid People).[12]

> In the region of Sijistān (today's Sistān, a region in South-Eastern Iran) there lived an old man who occupied himself with the rules of expressing oneself correctly (*naḥw*). He had a son to whom he said, "If you want to talk about something, first submit it to your consideration and think about it carefully until you are able to present it. Only then bring your thought forth in an orderly manner!"
>
> As they were sitting by the fireside one winter day, a spark settled on the father's silk garment without him noticing. His son saw it, but he stayed

> silent for a while thinking. Then he said, "Father, I want to mention something to you. Do you permit me to do so?" His father replied, "If it is true, speak up!" And when the son responded that he thought it true, the father gave him permission to speak. The son said, "I see something red."—"What is it?"—"A spark that settled on your garment." At once the father looked at his garment only to notice that a part of it was already burned. So he chided the son, "Why did you not tell me any sooner?" And his son retorted, "I thought about it as you had advised me to do. Then I arranged my words and told you about it." At this, the father swore to divorce his wife should his speech ever follow the correct rules of expression again.

No other versions from premodern or modern Arabic literature are known. There is, however, a related tale in the Ottoman Turkish compilation *Qırq vezīr* (The Forty Viziers) in which a skillful minstrel is asked to instruct a student in "the science of music."[13] As the student does not succeed in learning, the minstrel tells him to chant whatever he wants to say according to a certain tune, and he himself would respond in the same manner. When the master's turban catches fire, their particular way of communication takes the master some time to understand what has happened. In the end, he admonishes the boy that this had not been the right time for chanting. The Ottoman Turkish compilation is an adapted and enlarged version of the originally Persian *Sendbād-nāme* (The Book of Sendbād [the Sage]).[14] Although the book presents itself as being translated from an Arabic original titled *Forty Morns and Eves*, this claim is a mystification. The oldest manuscripts of the Ottoman Turkish compilation date from the middle of the fifteenth century. But since most of the manuscripts are both undated and offer a variety of content, the value of the tale's occurrence for determining its position in the historical process of dissemination is limited. Two versions from the Persian language area might indicate the existence of older Persian versions. A Tajik tale does not supply any specification concerning its performance.[15] A Persian version was published from the written text supplied by Nāṣer Mosāʿi, a servant from Shahr-e Reżā, Iran, aged 41 in 1973.[16] The text introduces a master who puts great emphasis on correct behavior (*esm va rasm-dāri*) and supplies local color by the master threatening to give his student a thorough beating should he ever again speak rashly.

Notes

1. Moser-Rath, Elfriede, "Denk dreimal, bevor du sprichst!" in *Enzyklopädie des Märchens*, vol. 3 (1981), cols. 420–421.
2. Merkens, Heinrich, *Was sich das Volk erzählt: Deutscher Volkshumor*, 2nd ed., vol. 2, Jena: Costenoble, 1895, pp. 166–167, no. 205.
3. Ibid., vol. 3 (1900), pp. 216–217, no. 203.
4. Uther, *Deutscher Märchenkatalog*, p. 416, no. 1562.

5. Pauli, Johannes, *Schimpf und Ernst*, ed. Johannes Bolte, Berlin: Herbert Stubenrauch, 1924 (reprint Hildesheim: Olms, 1972), vol. 1, pp. 231, 346, no. 387.

6. Bromyard, John, *Summa prædicantivm*, Venice: Dominic Nicolini, 1586, fol. 78a; see also Clouston, William Alexander, *The Book of Noodles: Stories of Simpletons; or, Fools and Their Follies*, London: Elliot Stock, 1903, p. 167, note 1.

7. Briggs, *A Dictionary*, vol. A2, p. 292.

8. Liungman, Waldemar, *Sveriges samtliga folksagor i ord och bild*, vol. 2, Stockholm: Lindfors, 1950, p. 345; Liungman, *Die schwedischen Volksmärchen: Herkunft und Geschichte*, Berlin: Akademie-Verlag, 1961, pp. 313, 377, no. 1562.

9. Briggs, Katherine M., and Ruth L. Tongue, *Folktales of England*, 2nd ed., London: Routledge, 1966, pp. 120–121, no. 64; see also Briggs, *A Dictionary*, vol. A2, p. 85.

10. Baker, Ronald L., *Jokelore: Humorous Folktales from Indiana*, Bloomington: Indiana University Press, 1986, pp. 100–101, 222, no. 164.

11. Brendle, Thomas R., and William S. Troxell, *Pennsylvania German Folk Tales, Legends, Once-upon-a-time Stories, Maxims, and Sayings, Spoken in the Dialect Popularly Known as Pennsylvania Dutch*, Norristown, Pa.: Pennsylvania German Society, 1944, p. 87.

12. Ibn al-Jawzī, Abū 'l-Faraj ʿAbd al-Raḥmān ibn ʿAlī, *Akhbār al-Ḥamqā wa-'l-mughaffalīn*, ed. Kāẓim al-Muẓaffar, al-Najaf: al-Maktaba al-ḥaydariyya, 1386/1966, p. 177; Marzolph, *Arabia ridens*, vol. 1, pp. 258–259, no. 18; vol. 2, p. 265, no. 1233.

13. Sheykh-Zāda, *The History of the Forty Vezirs*, transl. E.J.W. Gibb, London: George Redway, 1886, p. 383; Chauvin, *Bibliographie*, vol. 8 (1904), pp. 169–170, no. 187; see also Clouston, *Book of Noodles*, pp. 166–167.

14. Tezcan, Semih, "Vierzig Wesire," in *Enzyklopädie des Märchens*, vol. 14 (2014), cols. 195–200.

15. Dekhoti, A., *Tadzhikski narodni yumor*, Stalingrad, 1958, p. 74.

16. Vakiliyān, Aḥmad, *Tamṣil va maṣal*, vol. 2, Tehran: Sorush, 1366/1987, p. 17.

CHAPTER 68

The Sham Threat (ATU 1563*)

The jocular tale in which a man employs a sham threat to intimidate his adversaries and make them back down in a certain conflict exists in several versions. Elaborating Albert Wesselski's findings,[1] Kurt Ranke and, following him, the third revision of the international tale-type index at tale type ATU 1563*: *The Terrible Threat,* distinguished four major forms.[2] These forms focus on a stolen horse, the right to pass on a narrow road, a beggar asking for alms, and a stolen bag, respectively. Introduced with the words, "Often a clever thought supplies that which strength could not achieve, and often he who is without strength is a master of artifice," the oldest-known text documenting the tale's basic structure is attested in the third book of the *Carmina* (Poems) compiled by Bishop Theodulf of Orleans (ca 760–821).[3]

> When a soldier's horse is stolen one day, he demands that it be returned, or else he would do what his father once did in Rome. The people are so intimidated by the prospect of what the soldier might possibly do that the thief returns the horse. When asked what it was that his father did in Rome, the soldier responds, "He was forced to carry the saddle and bridle and walk back home—and this is what I would have done!"

No other versions are known from European tradition until, more than eight centuries after Theodulf, a similar narrative is related in the anonymous German chapbook *Exilium melancholiae, das ist Unlust-Vertreiber* (The Expeller of Sadness), published in 1643 in Strassburg. In this text, a soldier's excesses prompt the people of an unnamed city to confiscate his horse. The soldier exclaims that he knows well what to do now, and that the people are going to repent their action. When the intimidated people return his horse, the soldier admits that had he not regained his horse, he would have had to sell the saddle to make some money. Ranke discusses several similar texts from oral tradition in Dalmatia and Ukraine in which either the horse's bridle or the saddle is stolen.[4] Having additionally identified Jewish versions from Northern Europe as well as a Middle Eastern and a North African Berber version, Ranke comes to the conclusion that the tale must have originated in Arabic tradition and that Theodulf, who most likely came from a Spanish Visigothic background, got to know it in Muslim Spain.[5]

The tale's most widespread form in European tradition tells of two people meeting on a narrow road. As neither of them wants to let the other pass first, one of them says that he thinks of doing what he did last time in a similar situation. Intimidated, the other one lets him pass, only to be told afterward, "I would have let you pass first!" First documented in 1604, and frequently attested in German and English[6] chapbooks of the seventeenth and eighteenth centuries,[7] this version was repeatedly recorded from oral tradition. In a German dialect text recorded in 1956 from the oral performance of F. Böhle in the Hessian region of Waldeck, the popular prankster Eulenspiegel plays the part of the braggart.[8] A tale told in 1935 by the Finnish narrator Juho Hämäläinen is localized in the small Finnish town of Pyhäjärvi.[9]

The tale's third form analyzed by Ranke[10] is of particular interest for Middle Eastern tradition, as it is first attested in the *Resāle-ye delgoshā* (The Heart-Refreshing Epistle) compiled by Persian satirist ʿObeyd-e Zākāni (d. 1371).[11] Here, a beggar asking for alms in a certain village threatens to do the same thing he did in the previous village should his request not be fulfilled. Asked what he did, he simply says that he left that village to go to the next one. Ranke argued for a possible relation between this version and a late fifteenth-century Italian tale told by a Spanish envoy to Pope Innocent VIII (d. 1492). In the historical context, the tale likely served to signal support for the Florentines against the threat posed by the French king who intended to involve them in his conflict with Ferrante II, king of Naples.[12] Arguing that Zākāni adapted many of his jocular tales from Arabic tradition, Ranke was not surprised to find the tale in a "largely corresponding" version in Arabic author Muḥammad ibn Aḥmad ibn (al-)Ilyās al-Ḥanafī's seventeenth-century compilation *Nuzhat al-udabaʾ* (Entertainment of the Educated).[13] The content and the outcome of that version differ, however, considerably from ʿObeyd-e Zākāni's and other versions. In the *Nuzhat al-udabaʾ*, a merchant who is about to be robbed approaches one of the assailants exclaiming, "Today! Today!" When the robber asks him why he keeps shouting these words, the merchant says, "Today I am going to lose my clothes, my merchandise, and everything I possess!" The robber laughs about the merchant's clever retort and protects him against his companions. Although this tale shares the structural element of the (implied) sham threat, its outcome rather links it to the genre of quick-witted responses (*al-ajwiba al-muskita*) or clever retorts that enjoyed considerable popularity in classical and premodern Arabic literature.

The tale's fourth form analyzed by Ranke is a short anecdote in which Nasreddin Hodja misplaces his bag. Intimidated by Nasreddin's remark that he knows exactly what to do now, the villagers search and find his bag. Disclosing what he would have done, Nasreddin says that he would have a new bag made for himself. Since this tale is frequently included in printed versions of the Nasreddin tales, their popularity likely resulted in oral retellings of this particular item.[14]

Although no Arabic or other Middle Eastern texts predating Theodulf's *Carmina* are known, a similarly structured text in al-Ḥuṣrī's (d. 1015) *Jamʿ al-jawāhir* (The Collection of the Jewels) demonstrates that at least the tale's structure was already known in tenth-century Arabic literature.[15] Al-Ḥuṣrī's version focuses on a fairly stereotypical situation in the public bathhouse.

> When the clothes of a certain man disappear in the public bath, he shouts, "I know, I know . . . !" The thief hears him and is alarmed thinking that the man knows who he is, and so he returns the clothes with the words, "I have heard you constantly saying, 'I know!' What is it that you know?" The man responded, "I know that—had my clothes remained hidden—I would have died from the cold."

Since the times of antiquity, "losing one's clothes to theft, especially at the baths, is a commonplace of classical life and literature."[16] This holds equally valid for Arab Muslim urban culture in which the public baths held a prominent position.[17] In addition to the above, several jocular tales from premodern Arabic literature treat similar situations in which clothes or shoes are stolen at the baths.[18]

Notes

1. Wesselski, *Der Hodscha Nasreddin*, vol. 2, p. 134, 217–219, no. 450 (from a Croatian collection); Wesselski, *Italiänischer Volks- und Herrenwitz*, Munich: Georg Müller, 1912, pp. 51–52, 244.

2. Ranke, Kurt, "Der Schwank von der schrecklichen Drohung," in *Humaniora: Essays in Literature, Folklore, Biography, Honoring Archer Taylor on His 70th Birthday*, ed. Wayland D. Hand, Locust Valley, New York: Augustin, 1960, pp. 78–96; reprint in *Die Welt der Einfachen Formen*, Berlin: De Gruyter, 1978, pp. 244–261; see also Ranke, Kurt, "Drohung: Die schreckliche D.," in *Enzyklopädie des Märchens*, vol. 3 (1981), cols. 894–901.

3. Migne, Jacques-Paul, ed., *Patrologia cursus completus, series latina*, vol. 105: *Theodulfi Aurelianensis [. . .] opera omnia*, Paris: Migne, 1851, pp. 191–380, at p. 330; quoted hereafter in Wesselski, *Der Hodscha Nasreddin*, vol. 2, p. 218, and Ranke, "Der Schwank," p. 244–245. An English translation is given in Alexandrenko, Nikolai A., *The Poetry of Theodulf of Orleans; A Translation and Critical Study*, Ph.D. New Orleans: Tulane University, 1970, pp. 277–278, quote p. 277.

4. Ranke, "Der Schwank," pp. 246–247.

5. Ibid., p. 249.

6. Wesselski, *Der Hodscha Nasreddin*, vol. 2, p. 218, reproduces the version published in Crouch, Humfrey, *England's Jests Refin'd and Improv'd*, 3rd ed., London: Harris, 1693, quoted from Ashton, John, *Humour, Wit & Satire of the Seventeenth Century*, London: Chatto and Windus, 1883, p. 200.

7. See Moser-Rath, *"Lustige Gesellschaft,"* p. 510, no. 1563*; Moser-Rath, *Predigtmärlein der Barockzeit*, Berlin: De Gruyter, 1964, p. 370, 495, no. 213; Uther, *Deutscher Märchenkatalog*, p. 418, no. 1563*.

8. Grüner, Gustav, *Waldeckische Volkserzählungen*, Marburg: Elwert, 1964, p. 300, no. 556.

9. Rausmaa, Pirkko-Liisa, *Suomalaiset kansansadut*, vol. 6: *Pilasadut ja kaskut*, Helsinki: Suomalaisen Kirjallisuuden Seura, 2000, p. 227, no. 236; see also Simonsuuri, Lauri, and Pirkko-Liisa Rausmaa, *Finnische Volkserzählungen*, Berlin: De Gruyter, 1968, p. 146, no. 114.

10. Ranke, "Der Schwank," pp. 252–256.

11. Christensen, Arthur, "Remarques sur les facéties de 'Ubaïd-i-Zākāni, avec des extraits de la Risālä-i-dilgušā," *Acta Orientalia* 3 (1924), pp. 1–37, at p. 17–18, no. II.277.

12. Ranke, "Der Schwank," p. 253.

13. Basset, *Mille et un contes*, vol. 2, p. 151, no. 134; Ḥanafī, Muḥammad ibn Aḥmad ibn (al-)Ilyās al-, *Nuzhat al-udabā'*, Gotha, Ms. Orient A 2706, fol. 39b.

14. Ranke, "Der Schwank," p. 256–257.

15. Ḥuṣrī al-Qayrawānī, Abū Isḥāq Ibrāhīm ibn 'Alī al-, *Jam' al-jawāhir fī 'l-mulaḥ wa-'l-nawādir*, ed. 'Alī Muḥammad al-Bijāwī, Cairo: Dār Iḥyā' al-kutub al-'arabiyya, 1372/1952, p. 248; Marzolph, *Arabia ridens*, vol. 1, p. 259, no. 19; vol. 2, p. 128, no. 509.

16. Baldwin, Barry, *The Philogelos, or Laughter-Lover*, translated with an introduction and commentary, Amsterdam: Gieben, 1983, p. 57.

17. Grotzfeld, Heinz, *Das Bad im arabisch-islamischen Mittelalter*, Wiesbaden: Harrassowitz, 1970.

18. Marzolph, Ulrich, "Philogelos arabikos: Zum Nachleben der antiken Witzesammlung in der mittelalterlichen arabischen Literatur," *Der Islam* 64 (1987), pp. 185–230, also in Marzolph, *Ex Oriente Fabula: Beiträge zur narrativen Kultur des islamischen Vorderen Orients*, vol. 1, Dortmund: Verlag für Orientkunde, 2005, pp. 57–108, commentary to §16.

CHAPTER 69

The Trickster Relieves His Itching with a Trick (ATU 1565)

Children's folklore is a rich source for popular narratives, particularly if verbal humor is combined with gestures. Generations of children have probably been initiated into this kind of humor by the jocular tale about a guy whose nose is running when he does not have a tissue.[1] He manages to wipe his nose surreptitiously with his sleeve by running his forearm closely under his nostrils, pretending to point at an object or an event on his left or right side. Although by adult standards sanitarily disgusting, the simple trick helps the man avoid his physical discomfort being exposed.

The international folktale classified as tale type ATU 1565: *Agreement Not to Scratch* illustrates a similar stratagem involving a person who feels the urge to scratch.[2] The tale appears in different forms, two of which are particularly relevant here. Both forms concern a wager to resist the urge to scratch. The person concerned wins the wager as he manages to scratch while pretending to point to a particular part of his body. The main difference between the two forms is the number of actors and, if more than one actor is involved, the nature of the action.

The tale's first form involves a single person. A folktale told by a member of the Finnish-American community in the Upper Peninsula in Michigan attributes the event to the folk character Lapatossu, a "knavish railway worker about whom many jests are told."[3] Lapatossu does not keep himself very clean and consequently has some "renters" on his person. As he travels on a boat one day, the captain sees him scratch himself several times and promises to give him a new suit of clothes if he manages to lie still on the deck for just five minutes. Not being able to avoid scratching himself, the trickster pretends that he wants his new suit to have buttons in several places, illustrating his idea by pointing to the respective places while at the same time relieving his itching by pinching his skin. A late nineteenth-century German text contributed by teacher P. Sommer from Posen attributes the tale to the old and disabled former soldier Jan who had survived Napoleon's Russian campaign in 1812.[4] Jan is introduced as a great storyteller. As he is poor and uncleanly, his old sheepskin coat is infested with bugs. In order to teach Jan a lesson, the landlord invites him to the castle one day, promising to give him a hundred ducats if he manages to tell his stories without moving. Jan proceeds to tell his adventures during the battle of Berezina. When he is not able to control himself any more, he starts to illustrate his narration with gestures emulating the blows and strikes, at the same time pinching his body at the places that itch most. In the end, the landlord acknowledges Jan's clever trick and grants him the promised reward.

The tale's second form usually involves three actors such as a man afflicted by a constant fever, a bald-headed man, and a man with a running nose in a Macedonian folktale.[5] The three men wager that the one of them who first succumbs to relieving his physical discomfort will have to pay lunch and dinner for the other two. The feverish man manages to satisfy his urge to move around by telling a tale of hunting. The bald-headed man pretends that he is riding and has to secure his hat, thus enabling him to scratch his head so as to ease the itching. Finally, the man with the running nose informs his companions that he understands their stratagem by pointing to them one after the other while running his sleeve under his nose. The version told in March 1936 by Spanish narrator Benito Gil, aged 40, from Matabuena, Segovia, introduces three mangy characters,[6] and a version from Spanish-American oral tradition features a mangy, a lousy, and a snivelly youth.[7]

A unique historical text from European tradition is included in Martin Montanus's sixteenth-century German jestbook *Wegkürzer* (The Way Shortener).[8] This tale is about two mangy men waiting for the ferry to cross the river Rhine. They stipulate that the one who first scratches himself will have to pay the fee. Both of them, however, manage to scratch themselves pretending to rejoice while seeing the ferry approach. The wager ends in a tie, and the author leaves it up to the audience to decide who should pay the fee.

A closely corresponding tale was current in Arabic literature since the ninth century.[9] Whereas the European texts refer to an itching and scratching of the body on the outside, the Arabic texts differ in that they have the protagonist experience an itching inside, in his throat. Other than that, the Arabic texts also feature a wager, a trick by which the protagonist avoids having to admit that he broke the condition (here not to clear his throat), and a final reward. The Arabic tale is first attested in Ibn Qutayba's (d. 889) *ʿUyūn al-akhbār* (Quintessential Reports).[10]

> Two Bedouins make a bet that one of them should drink fermented milk without clearing his throat (*tanaḥnaḥa*). When that person drinks the milk and feels an itching in his throat, he says, "A well-fed (*amlaḥ*) ram!" His companion remarks, "By God (*wa-rabb al-Kaʿba*), he did it!" Whereupon the other defends himself saying, "May the one who did it not prosper!" The wager concerned a ram.

The joke here relies on the fact that the Arabic phoneme *ḥ* in the word *amlaḥ* is a guttural sound made deep in the throat. Pronouncing the word would allow the person to clear his throat without having to admit that he actually did. The trick is made even more explicit in the version cited in al-Ābī's (d. 1030) encyclopedia of jokes and anecdotes, *Nathr al-durr* (Pearls of Prose), in which the first person criticizes the second one by saying, "You just cleared your throat" (*innaka tanaḥnaḥta*).[11] Ibn al-Jawzī (d. 1201) presents a slightly more elaborate version of the tale in which the second person uses three different words, each one of which enables him to clear his throat. He says, "A well-fed (*amlaḥ*) ram and a spacious (*afyaḥ*) house in which I will enjoy my life (*atabaḥbaḥ*)."[12]

The tale's European forms differ sufficiently from the Arabic texts as to suggest an independent origin. At the same time, the overall idea, structure, and realization of the tale's various forms is so similar that some kind of connection is not unlikely to exist, particularly as the physical element of the Arabic language necessarily had to be lost in translation. Although the medieval literatures might eventually reveal some as yet unknown intermediate versions, in this particular case an oral (and thus undocumented) transmission of the tale appears more likely than a written one. A strong argument in this regard is the fact that the tale is most appealing in live performance that would enable the narrators to enact either the gestures in the European tales or the potential clearing of the throat in the Arabic ones.

Notes

1. Author's personal experience as mediated around 1960 by one of his elder brothers.

2. Lindahl, Carl, "Kratzverbot," in *Enzyklopädie des Märchens*, vol. 8 (1996), cols. 348–352.

3. Dorson, Richard M., *Bloodstoppers and Bearwalkers: Folk Traditions of the Upper Peninsula*, Cambridge, MA: Harvard University Press, 1952, pp. 148–149.

4. Knoop, Otto, *Sagen und Erzählungen aus der Provinz Posen*, Posen, 1893, pp. 216–217, no. 11.

5. Cepenkov, Marko K., *Makedonski narodni prikazni*, ed. Kiril Penušliski, Skopje: MK, 1989, vol. 4, pp. 212–214, no. 479.

6. Espinosa, Aurelio Macedonio, Jr., *Cuentos populares de Castilla y Leon*, vol. 2, Madrid: Consejo Superior de Investigaciones Científicas, 1988, p. 242, 519–520, no. 346.

7. Rael, Juan B., *Cuentos españoles de Colorado y Nuevo Méjico: Spanish Originals with English Summaries*, Stanford: Stanford University Press, 1940, vol. 1, pp. 129–130; vol. 2, pp. 630–631, no. 66.

8. Montanus, Martin, *Schwankbücher (1577–1566)*, ed. Johannes Bolte, Tübingen: Litterarischer Verein in Stuttgart, 1899, pp. 30–31, no. 9.

9. Marzolph, *Arabia ridens*, vol. 2, p. 52, no. 192.

10. Ibn Qutayba al-Dīnawarī, Abū Muḥammad ʿAbdallāh ibn Muslim, *ʿUyūn al-akhbār*, 2nd ed., Cairo: al-Muʾassasa al-miṣriyya al-ʿāmma lil-taʾlif wa-'l-tarjama wa-'l-ṭibāʿa, 1963, vol. 2, p. 209.

11. Ābī, Abū Saʿd Manṣūr ibn al-Ḥusayn al-, *Nathr al-durr*, ed. Muḥammad ʿAlī Qarna et al., vol. 4, Cairo: al-Hayʾa al-miṣriyya al-ʿāmma lil-kitāb, 1980, p. 122.

12. Ibn al-Jawzī, Abū 'l-Faraj ʿAbd al-Raḥmān ibn ʿAlī, *Akhbār al-Ẓirāf wa-'l-mutamājinīn*, ed. Muḥammad Baḥr al-ʿulūm, 2nd ed., al-Najaf: al-Maktaba al-ḥaydariyya, 1386/1966, p. 97; Ibn al-Jawzī, *Akhbār al-Adhkiyāʾ*, ed. Muḥammad Mursī al-Khūlī, Cairo, 1970, p. 95. The latter version has "in which I will be generous (*asmaḥ*)."

CHAPTER 70

The Prankster's Ambiguous Dream (ATU 1572M*)

Classified as tale type ATU 1572M*: *The Apprentice's Dream*, the present jocular tale is a relatively recent arrival to European tradition, whether written or oral. The rare versions documented from nineteenth- and twentieth-century European tradition comprise short texts from Germany,[1] the Frisian language area,[2] and Finland.[3] The tale has a simple bipartite structure and is usually very short. The oldest European version known at present is an exceptionally detailed version in the German dialect of Rudolstadt in Thuringia that authenticates the events by localizing them in a particular street in Rudolstadt and attributing them to a pair of named protagonists.[4]

> Friede, the apprentice of the old shoemaker Silge in the Saalgasse, is a real prankster. One day as they are mending shoes together in the workshop, Friede starts to laugh about a dream he had. Although his master doubts that the apprentice's dream is interesting, he is nevertheless curious to know it, and Friede tells him his dream.
>
> As both of them walked across a bridge, Friede looked down and saw mud and dirt on his side and honey on the master's side. Suddenly they both fell down, the apprentice into the dirt and his master into the honey. Just as his master starts to admonish him, alluding to the apprentice's bad luck as resulting from his constant mischief, Friede mentions that the dream was not yet over: When they finally managed to get back onto the bridge they had to lick each other clean.

A similar version mentioning the bridge in Prague was recorded from Sudeten German tradition.[5] In this text, the master and his apprentice are in the company of the master's wife who naively believes in the veracity of dreams. A shorter version, recorded in 1915 by Dr. S. Barnewitz from Bützow in Mecklenburg has the apprentice mention his dream when he arrives at the workshop in the morning.[6] In the dream, the apprentice was immersed in a barrel of tar and his master in a barrel of honey. When the master remarks how happy he is that it had not been the other way round, the apprentice says, "The best is yet to come: Later we licked each other clean!" A short version from Berlin mentioning master Bolle and his apprentice Lude has the latter placed in a barrel of black soap.[7] And a version from the Northern German region of Schleswig-Holstein adds an elaborate introduction in which the apprentice tells how he dreamt of the master inviting him to have a drink in the local pub, how the master stayed a long time drinking and playing cards and how, on the way back, they both fell into pits full of honey and dirt.[8] The catalogue of Frisian folktales mentions two versions, dated 1880 and 1911, in which the apprentice stands in a barrel of liquid green soap (*groene zeep*).[9] And the catalogue of Finnish anecdotes supplies a total of nine references referring to a version in which the apprentice fell into a manure barrel and his master into a syrup barrel.[10]

The earliest documented Arabic version of the tale dates from the tenth century.[11] It is contained in the biography of Ashʿab in Abū 'l-Faraj al-Iṣfahānī's (d. 965) *Kitāb al-Aghānī* (Book of Songs), a comprehensive documentation and discussion of songs and related poetry.[12] Ashʿab is a pseudohistorical character who probably lived early in the eight century and who came to represent the stereotypical greedy person in classical Arabic literature. This version is introduced by a chain of transmitters (*isnād*) whose oldest authority is the historian al-Madā'inī (d. 843).[13] Ashʿab informs his mother about his dream in which she was covered with honey while he was covered with excrement. At first, his mother interprets the situation as resulting from her son's evil deeds, but in the end she curses him for his sinful tale-telling. In subsequent centuries, the anecdote is most often attributed to the very same character,[14] a tradition kept alive until the tale's citation in Yūsuf ibn al-Wakīl al-Maylāwī's (d. 1689) seventeenth-century compilation of anecdotes on Ashʿab.[15] At the same time, slightly divergent versions already appeared in the eleventh and twelfth centuries. In his *Rabīʿ al-abrār* (Spring of the Pious), al-Zamakhsharī (d. 1144) cites the conversation as taking place between Ashʿab and an unspecified man,[16] and the *Muḥāḍarāt al-udabā'* (Conversations of the Educated) by al-Rāghib al-Iṣfahānī (d. 1008) mentions a pupil and his teacher, a version that is also cited in Muḥammad ibn Aḥmad ibn (al-)Ilyās al-Ḥanafī's seventeenth-century *Nuzhat al-udabā'* (Entertainment of the Educated).[17] About half of the tale's citations, including the oldest one, use the vulgar term *kharā'*, "shit," while the remainder employ the rather neutral term *ʿadhira*, "excrement." Although this does not allow the identification of a clear development in the tale's Arabic attestations, the European texts obviously opt for a certain euphemization by adjusting the tale's revolting scatological element to a somewhat socially more acceptable substance such as dirt, tar, or a sticky detergent. At the same time, there is little doubt that the European versions are closely related to the earlier Arabic texts that have probably been mediated by quotations in collections of "Oriental miscellanies"[18] or in the narrative sections of popular calendars. As in tale type ATU 2040: *The Climax of Horrors* (see essay **101, *The Climax of Horrors***), European tradition adapted the tale to the stereotype couple of master and servant or apprentice, thereby alluding to an implicit or latent social tension in which the underdog usually trumps his superior.

Notes

1. Uther, *Deutscher Märchenkatalog*, p. 426, no. 1572M*.

2. Van der Kooi, Jurjen, *Volksverhalen in Friesland*, Ph.D. thesis Rijksuniversiteit Groningen, 1984, p. 500, no. 1572M*.

3. Rausmaa, Pirkko-Liisa, *A Catalogue of Anecdotes*, Turku: Nordic Institute of Folklore, 1973, p. 29.

4. Firmenich, Johannes Matthias, *Germaniens Völkerstimmen*, vol. 3, Berlin: Schlesinger'sche Buch- und Musikhandlung, 1854, p. 571; republished in Merkens, Heinrich, *Was sich das Volk erzählt: Deutscher Volkshumor*, 2nd ed., vol. 1, Jena: Costenoble, 1892, pp. 238–239, no. 276.

5. Jungbauer, Gustav, *Das Volk erzählt: Sudetendeutsche Sagen, Märchen und Schwänke*, Karlsbad and Leipzig: Adam Kraft, 1943, pp. 367–368.

6. Neumann, Siegfried, *Plattdeutsche Schwänke: Aus den Sammlungen Richard Wossidlos und seiner Zeitgenossen sowie eigenen Aufzeichnungen in Mecklenburg*, Rostock: VEB Hinstorff Verlag, 1968, pp. 71, 216, no. 119a.

7. Ostwald, Hans, *Der Urberliner in Witz, Humor und Anekdote*, Berlin: Paul Franke, ca. 1930, p. 60.

8. Selk, Paul, *Lügengeschichten aus Schleswig-Holstein*, Husum: Husum Druck- und Verlagsanstalt, 1982, p. 43–44.

9. Van der Kooi, *Volksverhalen in Friesland*, p. 500, no. 1572M*.

10. Rausmaa, *A Catalogue of Anecdotes*, p. 29.

11. Marzolph, *Arabia ridens*, vol. 2, p. 108, no. 434.

12. Iṣfahānī, Abū 'l-Faraj al-, *Kitāb al-Aghānī*, Būlāq (reprint Beirut: Ṣaʿb, ca. 1980), vol. 17, p. 91.

13. Rosenthal, Franz, *Humor in Early Islam*, Leiden: Brill 1956 (reprint 2011), p. 64, no. 50.

14. In addition to the sources quoted in Marzolph, *Arabia ridens*, vol. 2, p. 108, no. 434, see the early fifteenth-century version in Ibn ʿĀṣim al-Andalusī, Abū Bakr ibn Muḥammad, *Ḥadāʾiq al-azāhir*, ed. ʿAfīf ʿAbd al-Raḥmān, Beirut: Dār al-Masīra, 1401/1981, p. 135.

15. Maylāwī, Yūsuf ibn Muḥammad "Ibn al-Wakīl" al-, *al-Ṭirāz al-mudhahhab fī nawādir Ashʿab*, ed. Ghālib al-ʿAnābsa and Nādir Maṣārwa, s.l.: Dār al-Hudā, and Jordan: Dār al-Fikr, 2012, p. 47; see also the modern compilation by Qumayḥa, Mufīd, *Nawādir Ashʿab*, Beirut: Dār al-Fikr al-lubnānī, 1990, p. 83.

16. Zamakhsharī, Abū 'l-Qāsim Maḥmūd ibn ʿUmar al-, *Rabīʿ al-abrār wa-nuṣūṣ al-akhbār*, ed. Salīm al-Nuʿaymī, Baghdad: al-ʿĀnī, 1982, vol. 4, p. 338 (the text is missing several words).

17. Rāghib al-Iṣfahānī, al-Ḥusayn ibn Muḥammad, *Muḥāḍarāt al-udabāʾ wa-muḥāwarāt al-shuʿarāʾ wa-'l-bulaghāʾ*, Beirut 1961, vol. 1, p. 151; Ḥanafī, Muḥammad ibn Aḥmad ibn (al-)Ilyās al-, *Nuzhat al-udabāʾ*, Gotha, Ms. Orient A 2706, fol. 11a.

18. For the genre, see Marzolph, Ulrich, "The Literary Genre of 'Oriental Miscellany'," in Bauden, Frédéric, Aboubakr Chraïbi, and Antonella Ghersetti, eds., *Le Répertoire narratif arabe médiéval: transmission et ouverture, Actes du colloque international, Université de Liège 15-17 septembre 2005*, Geneva: Droz, 2008, pp. 309–319; Marzolph, "Jenseits von '1001 Nacht:' Blütenlesen aus den orientalischen Literaturen um 1800," *Blütenstaub: Jahrbuch für Frühromantik* 2 (2009), pp. 39–50.

CHAPTER 71

The Thievish Tailor's Terrifying Dream of the Patchwork Banner (ATU 1574)

A short jocular tale documented above all from European and Middle Eastern traditions tells of a thievish tailor who falls sick. In his delirium he dreams that he is confronted with a colorful patchwork banner joined from all the pieces of cloth he stole from his customers during his long career. Fearing divine punishment for his misdemeanors, the tailor resolves to change his habits and instructs his apprentice to warn him should he ever be tempted to steal again. Some time later, a customer places an order with a precious piece of cloth. Although the apprentice reminds the tailor of his dream, he calmly responds that this particular piece was not included in the patchwork banner. Corresponding to tale type ATU 1574: *The Tailor's Dream*, the tale has most prominently been published in collections relating to Northern German oral tradition, often in dialect.[1]

The narrator Egbert Gerrits introduced the localized tale he performed for Gottfried Henssen in 1935 with a scene in which the tailor Hermann Lüers argues to a customer that contrary to other tailors he does not have a collection of patches because of his dream. In the end, however, he succumbs to his usual temptation.[2] A text from the Rhineland published by Heinrich Merkens localizes the events in the city of Cologne.[3] August Rust from Mecklenburg used the motif of the patchwork banner and the terrifying dream, as a result of which in his telling the tailor dies, to introduce his version of tale type ATU 800: *The Tailor in Heaven*, performed in 1962.[4] The narrator mentioned having heard the tale from his father when he was a child. Additional versions were recorded in Mecklenburg[5] and Oldenburg.[6] In a text contributed by a member of the Holstiege family in Havixbeck in the region of Munster in Westfalia the tailor is about to die and asks the priest to administer the sacrament. Admonished to discontinue his habit of stealing, the tailor advises his assistants to remind him of the banner he dreamt about. This text lacks the final point.[7]

In German tradition, the jest's oral dissemination likely was invigorated by its inclusion in seventeenth- and eighteenth-century compilations of jocular tales, such as Abraham a Sancta Clara's *Der junge Antihypochondriakus oder Etwas zur*

Erschütterung des Zwerchfells und zur Beförderung der Verdauung (The Young Anti-Hypochondriac, or Something to Unsettle the Midriff [that is, Make People Laugh] and Support Digestion; 1773).[8] In the sixteenth century, German *Meistersinger* Hans Sachs composed two different versions of the tale,[9] and English poet Sir John Harrington (1561–1612) made it the subject of humorous verses "in order to gird at the English Puritans."[10] Although the tale might eventually come to light in "some old monkish collection of *exempla*,"[11] the oldest European version presently known dates from early sixteenth-century editions of the jests attributed to the Italian priest Arlotto Mainardi (1396–1484), a character renowned for his ready wit and funny repartee.[12] Although William Alexander Clouston intimates that the "propensity of tailors to appropriate to their own purpose part of their customer's cloth is a frequent subject of satire in the popular literature of Europe,"[13] he assumes the tale "to be of Asiatic extraction."[14]

Clouston's assumption is based on the tale's publication in French author Denis Dominique Cardonne's *Mélanges de littérature orientale* (A Mixture of Tales from the Oriental Literatures), first published in 1770.[15] Cardonne's work belongs to the genre of "Oriental Miscellany," a literary genre denoting anthologies of entertaining and instructive tales extracted from Arabic, Persian, and Ottoman Turkish works that were widely read in seventeenth- and eighteenth-century Europe.[16] Cardonne's version of the tale in question specifically mentions the sick tailor's delirium vision or dream in which the angel of death shows him the patchwork banner. The Turkish jest thus shares the tale's general structure with the textual representatives of the standard European version. At the same time it introduces the angel of death as an element germane to Muslim belief. There are no conclusive arguments to decide whether this element was introduced in an effort to adapt an originally "extraneous" version to the native Muslim context, or whether it was part of the tale in earlier Muslim tradition. Cardonne quotes the source of his translation as "Latifé-Namé, N° 228." Cardonne generally refrained from specifying the exact nature of his sources, but the title he gives is specific enough to identify the book as the *Leṭā'if-nāme* (Book of Subtle Tales) compiled by Turkish author Lāmi'ī Chelebī (d. 1531).[17] Although the Turkish version is slightly younger than the tale's oldest European versions, and although the possibility of its being adapted from a European version cannot be ruled out, two additional arguments support Clouston's assumption that the tale originated in the Middle East. First, the tale is frequently documented in modern Persian tradition where the punchline *"Ostād, 'alam!"—"In yeki-rā be-kesh qalam!"* ("Master, the banner!"—"Cross out that one!") gained a proverbial status.[18] This suggests the existence of an older, as yet unidentified, Persian version that might have been at the origin of Lāmi'ī Chelebī's Ottoman Turkish version. And second, that hypothetical Persian version would likely derive from a previous source in one of the many compilations of entertaining and instructive tales in classical or postclassical Arabic literature, as was argued without reasonable doubt for a fair number of items.[19] Although this hypothetical earlier

Arabic version has not been identified so far, twelfth-century Arabic literature knows a thematically related tale illustrating the stereotype of the thievish tailor. That tale is first documented in an almost identical wording in two of Ibn al-Jawzī's (d. 1201) compilations of jocular tales, *Akhbār al-Adhkiyā'* (Tales of Clever People) and *Akhbār al-Ẓirāf* (Tales of Subtle People).[20] The translation below follows the former work.

> A tailor came to a certain Turk to prepare a coat (*qabā'*) for him. While he was cutting the cloth, the Turk watched him closely so that the tailor did not have an opportunity to steal any. At one point, the tailor farted so that the Turk laughed so intensely that he fell on his back.[21] Quickly, the tailor took from the cloth as much as he wanted. When the Turk was sitting upright again he exclaimed, "Tailor! Let's have another fart!" But the tailor responded, "That is not advisable, or else the coat will be too tight."

In addition to the jocular potential of farting in public[22] and the stereotypical depiction of the Turk as an uneducated, vulgar, and simple-minded character, this tale is an early narrative realization of the stereotype of the thievish tailor. The tale of the farting tailor enjoyed some popularity in subsequent works in both Arabic and Persian. In Arabic, it is included in al-Damīrī's (d. 1405) zoographical encyclopedia *Ḥayāt al-ḥayawān* (The Life of Animals) and in Persian in ʿObeyd-e Zākānī's (d. 1371) collection of jocular tales, the *Resāle-ye delgoshā* (The Heart-Refreshing Epistle).[23] In his mystical *summa*, the *Masnavi-ye maʿnavi*, the Persian poet Jalāl al-Din Rumi (d. 1273) presented a sanitized adaptation in which a garrulous tailor induces the Turk to laugh about his silly tales several times.[24] This leads Rumi to bring home his mystical interpretation "that the idle folk who wish (to hear) stories are like the Turk, and that the deluding and treacherous World is like the tailor, and that lusts and women are (like) this World's telling laughable jokes, and that Life resembles the piece of satin placed before this Tailor to be made into a coat of eternity and a garment of piety." Although the plot of the tale of the farting tailor is distinct from the previously discussed tale type, it builds on the same basic idea, thus in addition to the existence of an established Persian proverb serving as an argument that the premodern literatures of the Muslim world might have known an early version of tale type ATU 1574.

Notes

1. Uther, *Deutscher Märchenkatalog*, pp. 426–427, no. 1574.

2. Henßen, Gottfried, *Überlieferung und Persönlichkeit: Die Erzählungen und Lieder des Egbert Gerrits*, Münster: Aschendorff, 1951, p. 154, no. 75.

3. Merkens, Heinrich, *Was sich das Volk erzählt: Deutscher Volkshumor*, 2nd ed., vol. 2, Jena: Constenoble, 1895, pp. 134–135, 196, no. 164.

4. Neumann, Siegfried, *Ein mecklenburgischer Volkserzähler: Die Geschichten des August Rust*, Berlin: Akademie-Verlag, 1968, pp. 59–60, 153, no. 44.

5. Wossidlo, Richard, *Aus dem Lande Fritz Reuters: Humor in Sprache und Volkstum*

Mecklenburgs, Leipzig: Wigand, 1910, p. 139; see also Neumann, Siegfried, *Volksschwänke aus Mecklenburg, aus der Sammlung Richard Wossidlos*, Berlin: Akademie-Verlag, 1963, p. 36, no. 120.

6. Van der Kooi, Jurjen, and Theo Schuster, *Der Großherzog und die Marktfrau: Märchen und schwänke aus dem Oldenburger Land*, Leer: Schuster, 1994, pp. 224–225, no. 130.

7. Henßen, Gottfried, *Volk erzählt: Münsterländische Sagen, Märchen und Schwänke*, Münster: Aschendorf, 1935, p. 290.

8. Bolte and Polívka, *Anmerkungen*, vol. 1, p. 343, note 1, in no. 35; Uther, *Deutscher Märchenkatalog*, p. 427; the reference to Abraham a Sancta Clara is from Merkens, *Was sich das Volk erzählt*, p. 196.

9. Wesselski, *Der Hodscha Nasreddin*, vol. 1, p. 256, commentary to no. 190.

10. Clouston, William Alexander, "The Tailor's Dream," in *Popular Tales and Fictions: Their Migrations and Transformations*, ed. Christine Goldberg, Santa Barbara, CA: ABC-Clio, 2002, pp. 312–316, quote at p. 312.

11. Ibid., p. 214.

12. Wesselski, Albert, *Die Schwänke und Schnurren des Pfarrers Arlotto*, Berlin: Alexander Duncker, 1910, vol. 1, pp. 151–154, 221–222, no. 65.

13. Clouston, *Popular Tales and Fictions*, p. 312.

14. Ibid., p. 314.

15. Cardonne, Dénis Dominique, *Mêlanges de littérature orientale, traduits de différens Manuscrits Turcs, Arabes & Persans de la Bibliothèque du Roi*, Paris: Hérissant le Fils, 1770, vol. 2, pp. 82–84.

16. For the genre, see Marzolph, Ulrich, "The Literary Genre of 'Oriental Miscellany'," in Bauden, Frédéric, Aboubakr Chraïbi, and Antonella Ghersetti, eds., *Le Répertoire narratif arabe médiéval: transmission et ouverture, Actes du colloque international, Université de Liège 15-17 septembre 2005*, Geneva: Droz, 2008, pp. 309–319; Marzolph, "Jenseits von '1001 Nacht:' Blütenlesen aus den orientalischen Literaturen um 1800," *Blütenstaub: Jahrbuch für Frühromantik* 2 (2009), pp. 39–50.

17. Wesselski, *Der Hodscha Nasreddin*, vol. 1, p. 256; see also Lox, Harlinda, "Schneider mit der Lappenfahne," in *Enzyklopädie des Märchens*, vol. 12 (2007), cols. 149–152. The "*Defter allathaif: Livre de bons mots*" by "Lamai" is listed in Barthélemy d'Herbelots *Bibliothèque orientale*, Maestricht: J.E. Dufour & Ph. Roux, 1776, p. 264.

18. Marzolph, *Typologie*, p. 228, no. 1574; Enjavi Shirāzi, Abol-Qāsem, *Tamsil va masal*, 2nd ed., Tehran: Amir Kabir, 2537/1978, pp. 20–23 (11 versions).

19. See, e.g., the detailed argument in Marzolph, Ulrich, "Reconsidering the Iranian Sources of a Romanian Political Joke," *Western Folklore* 47 (1988), pp. 212–216.

20. Ibn al-Jawzī, Abū 'l-Faraj ʿAbd al-Raḥmān ibn ʿAlī, *Akhbār al-Adhkiyā'*, ed. Muḥammad Mursī al-Khūlī, Cairo, 1970, p. 153; Ibn al-Jawzī, *Akhbār al-Ẓirāf wa-'l-mutamājinīn*, ed. Muḥammad Baḥr al-ʿulūm, 2nd ed., al-Najaf: al-Maktaba al-ḥaydariyya, 1386/1966, p. 132.

21. For the stereotype of excessive laughter in Arabic narrative literature, see Müller, Kathrin, *"Und der Kalif lachte, bis er auf den Rücken fiel:" Ein Beitrag zur Phraseologie und Stilkunde des klassischen Arabisch*, 2 vols., Munich: Bayerische Akademie der Wissenschaften, 1993.

22. For Arabic literature see Marzolph, *Arabia ridens*, vol. 2, p. 333 (index, s.v. "Furz"); for international tradition see Daxelmüller, Christoph, "Furz," in *Enzyklopädie des Märchens*, vol. 5 (1987), cols. 593–600.

23. Marzolph, *Arabia ridens*, vol. 2, p. 255, no. 1188.

24. Rumi, Jalāl al-Din, *The Mathnawí of Jalálu'ddín Rúmí*, transl. Reynold A. Nicholson, vol. 3, London: Luzac & Co., 1934, pp. 351–354 (bk. 6, verses 1665–1726), quote at p. 354; see also Foruzānfar, Badi' al-Zamān, *Ma'ākhez-e qeṣaṣ va tamsilāt-e Masnavi*, 3rd printing, Tehran: Amir Kabir, 1362/1983, p. 207, no. 237. A modern prose rendering of Rumi's verse is given by Arberry, Arthur John, *More Tales from the Masnavi*, London: Allen & Unwin, 1963, pp. 195–197, no. 182.

CHAPTER 72

The Drink Served in the Pisspot (ATU 1578A*)

A short jocular tale documented from nineteenth- and early twentieth-century oral tradition ridicules the poor sanitary conditions that sometimes reigned in the countryside. A traveler comes to a certain house asking for a drink of water. Instead of water, he is offered sour milk (or a similar drink). When he is offered to drink even more, the traveler expresses his surprise. He is told that it does not really matter, because a mouse (or a rat) drowned in the vessel over night. Throwing the vessel to the ground in disgust, he is admonished not to break it, because at night it serves as a pisspot (or as the bowl for dog food). Classified as tale type ATU 1578A*: *The Drinking Cup*, the tale is documented with little variation in a fair number of versions from Finnish,[1] Bulgarian,[2] Spanish, and Caribbean traditions.[3] The Portuguese and Catalan texts classified as tale type ATU 1578A* refer to a similarly repugnant manner of serving drink or food to a guest.[4] A late nineteenth-century Bulgarian folktale from Serbia adds the events to a version of tale type ATU 1834: *The Clergyman with the Fine Voice* (see essay **91, *How the Preacher's Sermon Makes a Member of His Parish Cry***).[5] The tale ends with the priest drinking a strong alcoholic beverage from a pot the people offer to him. When he throws the vessel to the ground in disgust, the people reproach him, as the vessel had served for many years as the pisspot of an old man's wife.

Classical Arabic literature documents two closely corresponding tales. In his book on misers, *al-Bukhalāʾ*, al-Khaṭīb al-Baghdādī (d. 1071) tells the tale in a lively manner, as related to him by one of his companions.[6]

> On a scorching hot day, a man asks for a drink of water at a house in the city of Kufa. As the housemaid claims there is no water in the house, she offers him milk (*laban*) instead and even urges him to drink more. The guest marvels at the generous treatment, since the people of Kufa are stereotypically known for their stinginess. When he drinks, however, he finds a dead mouse in the vessel. Mentioning this to the maid, she shouts in surprise, "What? Yet another mouse?" As the visitor throws the vessel to the ground

> in disgust, the maid shouts to the lady inside the house, "Miss! This man broke your pisspot!"

In a section on people who unwittingly consumed disgusting food (*al-qādhūrāt*) in his *Muḥāḍarāt al-udabā'* (Conversations of the Educated), al-Rāghib al-Iṣfahānī (d. 1108) ridicules the sanitary conceptions prevailing among the Bedouins (see also essay **44, *Accidental Cannibalism***).[7] The tale's narrator is the scholar al-Aṣmaʿī (d. 828) who is famed for his quest in search of the pure Arabic language spoken by the Bedouins.

> In a Bedouin tent, the guest is served milk (*laban*). While drinking, he wants to make sure that the vessel is clean. He receives the following response, "Of course it is! We eat from it during the day and piss in it at night. When we get up, we let the dog drink from it, and the dog licks it clean!" Disgusted, the scholar invokes God's curse on this kind of cleanliness.

The latter version is repeated with a slight variation in Muḥammad ibn Aḥmad ibn (al-)Ilyās al-Ḥanafī's seventeenth-century *Nuzhat al-udabā'* (Entertainment of the Educated), as the Bedouin here uses the vessel to relieve his bowels at night.[8]

A mouse drowned in a liquid intended for human consumption is already mentioned in a joke in the fifth-century *Philogelos* (The Laughter-Lover), the only surviving jokebook from Greek antiquity. In this joke, a man from Kyme sells honey.[9] When his customer remarks on how good it is, the seller says that he also thinks so. In fact, he would never have sold the honey had not a mouse fallen in. The Arabic tale about the drink served in a pisspot, in turn, reads like the enactment of a statement attributed to the Athenian statesman and general Themistocles (d. 459 BCE).[10] As recounted by the Roman author Claudianus Aelianus (d. 235), the Athenians once ostracized Themistocles, but then they recalled him to run the government. Themistocles declined the offer declaring, "I don't think much of people who use the same jar both as their pisspot and as their wine jar."[11]

As the tale's chronological span over two and a half millennia and its geographical distribution from the ancient world to the twentieth-century Caribbean demonstrate, the denigration of allegedly simple people by ridiculing their sanitary practices enjoys a universal applicability. Although similar sanitary conditions might have given rise to similar tales, the closely corresponding details in the majority of recorded versions leaves little doubt that they are genetically connected in some way.

Notes

1. Rausmaa, Pirkko-Liisa, *Suomalaiset kansansadut*, vol. 6, Helsinki: Suomalaisen Kirjallisuuden Seura, 2000, p. 244, no. 1578A*.

2. Daskalova Perkowski, Liliana, et al., *Typenverzeichnis der bulgarischen Volksmärchen*, ed. Klaus Roth, Helsinki: Suomalainen Tiedeakatemia, 1995, p. 329, nos. 1578A*, *1578A*.

3. Hansen, Terrence Leslie, *The Types of the Folktale in Cuba, Puerto Rico, the Dominican Republic, and Spanish South America*, Berkeley: University of California Press, 1957, pp. 140–141, no. **1554.

4. Cardigos, Isabel, *Catalogue of Portuguese Folktales*, Helsinki: Suomalainen Tiedeakatemia, 2006, p. 332, no. 1578A*; Noia Campos, Camiño, *Catálogo tipolóxico do conto galego de tradición oral: clasificación, antoloxía e bibliografía*, Vigo: University of Vigo, 2010, pp. 739–741, no. 1578A*.

5. Krauss, Friedrich S., "Südslavische Volksüberlieferungen, die sich auf den Geschlechtsverkehr beziehen (Fortsetzung)," *Anthropophyteia* 2 (1905), pp. 265–439, at pp. 387–388, no. 438.

6. Khaṭīb al-Baghādī, Abū Bakr Aḥmad ibn ʿAlī al-, *al-Bukhalāʾ*, ed. Aḥmad al-Maṭlūb, Khadīja al-Ḥadīthī, and Aḥmad Nājī al-Qaysī, Baghdad: Maṭbaʿat al-ʿĀnī, 1384/1964, p. 188; Marzolph, *Arabia ridens*, vol. 2, p. 229, no. 1131.

7. Rāghib al-Iṣfahānī, al-Ḥusayn ibn Muḥammad al-, *Muḥāḍarāt al-udabāʾ wa-muḥāwarāt al-shuʿarāʾ wa-ʾl-bulaghāʾ*, Beirut 1961, vol. 2, p. 627; Marzolph, *Arabia ridens*, vol. 2, p. 235, no. 1069.

8. Ḥanafī, Muḥammad ibn Aḥmad ibn (al-)Ilyās al-, *Nuzhat al-udabāʾ*, Gotha, Ms. Orient A 2706, fol. 27a–27b; Hammer-Purgstall, Joseph von, *Rosenöl, oder Sagen und Kunden des Morgenlandes aus arabischen, persischen und türkischen Quellen gesammelt*, Stuttgart: J.G. Cotta, 1813, vol. 2, p. 314, no. 193.

9. Baldwin, Barry, *The Philogelos, or Laughter-Lover*, Amsterdam: Gieben, 1983, p. 32, no. 173.

10. Stemplinger, Eduard, *Antiker Humor: 204 Anekdoten nach antiken Quellen*, Munich: Piper, 1939, p. 84 (from Aelian, *Miscellaneous History* 13.40).

11. McKeown, James C., *A Cabinet of Greek Curiosities: Strange Tales and Surprising Facts from the Cradle of Western Civilization*, Oxford: Oxford University Press, 2013, p. 254.

CHAPTER 73

The Adviser Is Duped with His Own Advice (ATU 1585)

Tale type ATU 1585: *The Lawyer's Mad Client* demonstrates how a simple ruse responds to the exigencies of solving everyday conflicts in such a striking manner as to easily transcend ethnic or linguistic boundaries, adapting itself to a virtually boundless variety of regional contexts. Essentially, the jocular tale is about a man who is threatened to be brought to trial for some misdemeanor. Not knowing how to avoid punishment, he seeks advice from a clever person, often a lawyer. The clever person advises him to feign insanity by consistently responding to the accusations in one and the same nonsensical manner, either by responding in animal sounds or by pronouncing a nonsense word or expression. As the judge considers the accused to be mad, he dismisses the case. When the adviser claims the stipulated compensation for his advice, the client dupes him by continuing to respond in the same nonsensical manner so that the adviser is forced to renounce his claim. The tale type's title is misleading in that the client never is actually mad, instead, as its assignment to the category *The Clever Man* (tale types 1525–1639) indicates, only feigning to be mad.

In oral tradition, the jocular tale is extremely widespread, its dissemination spanning both Middle Eastern and European traditions, the latter also giving rise to versions in the Americas.[1] The carpenter and farmer Valentin Niederkopfler, aged 48, told his German version in Southern Tyrol in 1941.

> A poor farmer borrows the amount of 100 *guilder* from a rich farmer. When he is asked to pay his debt after a year, he does not have any money and asks a clever lawyer for advice, promising to pay him a fraction of that amount later. The lawyer advises the poor farmer not to respond to the charges in court, instead only using his fingers to whistle. The farmer follows the advice and is dismissed as mad (*narrisch*). When the lawyer, however, requests his compensation, he is paid in the same currency.[2]

A particularly fanciful version was recorded from George Jamison in Selkirk, Scotland, in 1974. The narrator presents the events in a first-person narrative picturing himself selling one and the same horse to two different clients, but delivering it only to the second person. When the first client requests his money back, he fends him off by simply saying, "I've naething to dae wi that now." When he is dragged to court, the lawyer at Hawick advises him to respond to the charges solely by humming a short tune (incidentally, the beginning of Johann Strauss's *Blue Danube*). Having been dismissed, the man briefly forgets to play his role when he tells the lawyer that he has "gotten off." But when the lawyer reminds him to pay the agreed fee, he again only responds by humming the tune.[3] In the Bulgarian version collected by Al. Martinov from Georgi Zl. Atanasov in Babitsa village, Pernik County, the peasant Uncle Dimităr also manages to evade punishment by whistling when he has to present himself in court after having sold one and the same rabbit to several clients.[4]

In German versions, the farmer is advised to respond with variations of "Fancy that!" (*Sisoße/Sisatze*;[5] *Sisosit/Sidatsit*,[6] *Sieh einmal an!*;[7] *Na nu/Seh doa!*[8] or "Nothing" (*nicks*),[9] and equally nonsensical words appear in versions from all over Europe, such as "Heblebleblebleb!" (Hungarian),[10] "Puittis, puittis," (Finnish),[11] "Zist!/Zast!" (Catalan),[12] "Pgitt!" (France),[13] or "Pyhy" (Danish).[14] The French Canadian narrator Alexandre Pourdrier has the accused squeak like a pig,[15] the Argentinian narrator Mariano Vergara from Ciudad de Catamarca has him respond with "Finfa y Fanfa,"[16] and a Mexican narrator has him say nothing except "Meeee."[17] Popularized by such means as printed chapbook versions,[18] the tale's variations in European oral tradition ultimately derive from the lasting impact of its inclusion in the French jocular drama, the *Farce de maistre Pathelin*, compiled by an unknown author around 1464–1469. In *Pathelin*, the tale follows an episode in which Thibault d'Aignelet hides a sheep he stole from the clothier Guillaume Joceaulme in a cradle. This episode corresponds to tale type ATU 1525M: *The Sheep in the Cradle*. When Joceaulme summons Aignelet to court, the lawyer Pathelin advises the latter to say nothing but only bleat like a sheep. When Pathelin later wants to collect his fee, he comes to realize that his own ruse is being used against him. Both the sources and the impact of the *Pathelin* were frequently studied since the middle of the nineteenth century, so that the tale's historical roots can be sketched with a fair degree of certainty.[19]

Essentially, the ruse applied in the tale presents itself as the amplified version of a short text contained in the chapter on lawyers (*De Aduocato*) in the Latin *Scala coeli*, compiled by John Gobi, Jr., at the beginning of the fourteenth century.[20] In this text, a peasant promises to give a lawyer some geese if he teaches him the most useful juridical term (*melius verbum iuris*). The lawyer teaches him to say, "By God, this is not true!" But when he asks the peasant to fulfill his promise, the peasant only responds with the words he has just been taught. The *Mensa philosophica*, compiled by an unidentified author at the beginning of the fourteenth century, contains a similar tale in which the lawyer advises his client to deny the charges brought up against him and to drag the case on until he would finally win. Although neither of these two texts is close enough to the plot of the tale under consideration to constitute a direct model, they closely connect the tale to Arabic tradition that supplies the tale's oldest-known version so far.[21] Chapter 67 of al-Zamakhsharī's (d. 1144) *adab* work *Rabīʿ al-abrār* (Spring of the Pious) includes the following jocular tale.[22]

> A man asked another one, "Teach me (how to conduct) a court suit (*al-khuṣūma*)." The other one said, "Deny whatever they present against you; claim whatever is not yours; call the deceased as your witnesses; and delay the final oath until the case has been decided in your favor."

Only a few pages after this advice that closely corresponds to the one given in the *Mensa philosophica*, al-Zamakhsharī's work cites a full-fledged version of the tale.[23]

> Once, a man was so much in debt that he could not pay it back. One of his creditors said to him, "Should I teach you—providing that you will pay me—a ruse with the help of which you will get rid of this [problem]?" The man promised that, so the other one trusted him and said to him, "If any of your creditors or anybody else meets you, bark at them constantly. Because if you will become known by that (characteristic), they will say that you are insane (*muwaswas*) and will let you off." The man did this. When they had let him off, the one who had taught him the ruse came to him and said, "Now fulfill your promise!" But the man barked at him so that he exclaimed (unbelievingly), "And at me (you bark) too?" The other one did not stop barking until he gave up and went away.

Although the Arabic text does not explicitly mention a court suit but rather a situation that might lead to a juridical dispute, both the initial situation of distress and its proposed solution, including the advice to respond only in animal sounds, are so close to the plot of the tale's European versions as to suggest that the latter results from a direct impact of the former. Al-Zamakhsharī's twelfth-century text is the condensed version of a fairly elaborate text cited in the ninth century in polymath al-Jāḥiẓ's (d. 868) *Kitāb al-Ḥayawān* (Book of Animals).[24] Al-Jāḥiẓ's version is localized in the city of Medina. The plot of this version corresponds closely with al-Zamakhsharī's, but the author adds further credibility to the events by embellishing the action with contextual details and a somewhat extended argument. The creditor advises the debtor to have his servant clean the place in front of his house early in the morning, spread some mats in front of the house, seat himself comfortably on a cushion and wait until people start passing in front of his house. From this moment on, he is advised not to speak to anybody, be it passers-by, members of his family, servants, or creditors, instead only barking at them. When finally the governor comes to look into the case, he should again only bark at him so that the governor will not doubt that he is afflicted by some kind of madness. The debtor acts accordingly. Although the judge puts the debtor in jail for several days, he only barks at the people and is finally released. The tale ends as usual with the adviser being duped with the very same ruse.

As is often the case with tales and anecdotes in Arabic literature, the author tells us about the informant from whom he has learned the tale. In the present case, this is a certain Abū 'l-Ḥasan who is none other than the famous historian al-Madā'inī (d. 840); al-Madā'inī is further said to attribute the tale to a certain Abū Miryam, whose identity is not clear. None of al-Madā'inī's preserved works contain the tale in question, but it appears safe to conclude that the tale was known in Arabic literature at the beginning of the ninth century. Although this period is characterized by the intensive reception of literature and thought from classical antiquity,[25] and although we know that in addition to learned culture even the jocular texts of antiquity had an impact on Arabic literature,[26] there is no evidence to document any earlier versions of the tale that might have existed in ancient Greek literature.

The tale's spread to the West is probably due to cultural contacts during or shortly after the period of the Crusades. At the same time, the tale had a comparatively stronger impact on the literatures of the East, particularly Persian literature.[27] In Persian, the tale's punch line gave rise to the proverbial phrase "Even to me . . . " (*bā man ham . . .*), that is cited by poets from the twelfth century onward, including Sanā'i (d. 1131), Anvari (d. 1169), and Jalāl al-Din Rumi (d. 1273). A full-fledged textual version with a barking debtor, as in al-Zamakhsharī's version, is given in ʿAli Ṣafi's (d. 1532) compilation *Laṭā'ef al-ṭavā'ef* (Jocular Tales from the Various Strata of Society).[28] Farāhāni's (d. 1630) commentary to the *Divān* (Collected Poems) of Anvari supplies the first attestation of the tale's "Persianized" version mentioning the nonsense word *palās*. Persian literature also resulted in spreading both the tale and the related proverbial expression at least to the vernacular traditions of the Indian subcontinent and Turkey.[29] Versions of the tale collected from modern oral tradition in the Middle East are relatively scarce.[30]

Notes

1. Marzolph, Ulrich, "Pathelin," in *Enzyklopädie des Märchens*, vol. 10 (2002), cols. 620–624.

2. Zentralarchiv der deutschen Volkserzählung, Marburg, no. 170595 (collected by "Dr. Mai").

3. Bruford, Alan, and Donald A. MacDonald, *Scottish Traditional Tales*, Edinburgh: Polygon, 1994, pp. 209–212, 458, no. 27.

4. Nicoloff, Assen, *Bulgarian Folktales*, Cleveland: Nicoloff, 1979, pp. 178–181, 246–247, no. 69 (originally published in 1958).

5. Stübs, Hugo, *Ull Lüj vertellen: Plattdeutsche Geschichten aus dem pommerschen Weizacker*, Greifswald: Bamberg, 1938, pp. 132–136, no. 80.

6. Asmus, Ferdinand, and Otto Knoop, *Kolberger Volkshumor*, Köslin: Hendeß, 1927, pp. 123–124, no. 107.

7. Peuckert, Will-Erich, *Schlesiens deutsche Märchen*, Breslau: Ostdeutsche Verlagsanstalt, 1932, pp. 566–567, no. 260.

8. Grannas, Gustav, *Volk aus dem Ordensland Preussen erzählt Sagen, Märchen und Schwänke*, Marburg: Elwert, 1960, pp. 130–131, no. 93 (narrated by Karl Stolz).

9. Wossidlo, Richard, *Volksschwänke aus Mecklenburg*, ed. Siegfried Neumann, Berlin: Akademie-Verlag, 1963, p. 62, no. 213.

10. Kovács, Agnes, *Ungarische Volksmärchen*, Düsseldorf: Diederichs, 1966, 228–213, no. 45.

11. Simonsuuri, Lauri, and Pirkko-Luisa Rausmaa, *Finnische Volkserzählungen*, Berlin: De Gruyter, 1968, pp. 150, no. 124.

12. Serra y Boldú, Valerio, *Rondalles populars*, vol. 7, Barcelona: Políglota, 1932, pp. 63–68 (narrated by Carme Castelló from Granadella).

13. Meyrac, Albert, *Traditions, coutumes, légendes et contes des Ardennes*, Charleville: Petit Ardennais, 1890, pp. 420–422.

14. Kristensen, Evald Tang, *Aeventyr fra Jylland*, Copenhagen: Gyldendal, 1884 vol. 2, pp. 206–210, no. 28.

15. Barbeau, C.-Marius, and Gustav Lanctot, "Contes populaires canadiens," *Journal of American Folklore* 36 (1923), pp. 205–272, at pp. 253–255, no. 110.

16. Chertudi, Susanna, *Cuentos folklóricos de la Argentina*, vol. 1, Buenos Aires: Ed. Univ., 1960, pp. 200–202, no. 74.

17. Wheeler, Howard T., *Tales from Jalisco, Mexico*, Philadelphia: American Folklore Society, 1943, pp. 459–461, no. 160.

18. Briggs, *A Dictionary*, vol. A2, pp. 235–236 (quoting the early fifteenth-century chapbook *A Hundred Merry Tales*); Moser-Rath, *"Lustige Gesellschaft,"* see index p. 510.

19. See., e.g., Staehle, Wilhelm, *"La Farce de Pathelin," in literarischer, grammatischer und sprachlicher Hinsicht*, Phil. Diss. Marburg 1862; Schaumburg, Karl, and A. Banzer, "Die Farce Patelin und ihre Nachahmungen," *Zeitschrift für neufranzösische Sprache und Litteratur* 9 (1887), pp. 1–47; 10 (1888), pp. 93–112; Prato, Stanislas, "La scène de l'avocat et du berger de la farce Maître Pathelin dans les rédactions littéraires et populaires, françaises et étrangères," *Revue des traditions populaires* 9 (1894), pp. 537–552; Oliver, Thomas Edward, "Some Analogues of Maistre Pierre Pathelin," *Journal of American Folklore* 22 (1909), pp. 395–420; Rauhut, Franz, "Fragen und Ergebnisse der Pathelin-Forschung," *Germanisch-Romanische Monatsschrift* 19 (1931), pp. 394–407; Marzolph, Ulrich, "Maistre Pathelin im Orient," in *Gottes ist der Orient, Gottes ist der Okzident: Festschrift für Abdoldjavad Falaturi*, ed. Udo Tworuschka, Köln: Böhlau, 1991, pp. 309–312.

20. For the following, see Wesselski, Albert, "Humanismus und Volkstum," *Zeitschrift für Volkskunde*, new series 6 (1934), pp. 1–35, at p. 11; Dunn, Thomas Franklin, *The Facetiae of the Mensa Philosophica*, St. Louis: Washington University, 1934, 43; Tubach, *Index exemplorum*, p. 181, no. 2259; György, Lajos, *A magyar anekdota története és egyetemes kapcsolatai*, Budapest: Studium, 1934, pp. 180–181, no. 170. For the author of the *Scala coeli* see Gobi, Jean, *La Scala coeli*, ed. Marie-Anne Polo de Beaulieu, Paris: Centre National de la Recherche Scientifique, 1991.

21. Marzolph, *Arabia ridens*, vol. 2, p. 23, no. 87.

22. Zamakhsharī, Abū 'l-Qāsim Maḥmūd ibn ʿUmar al-, *Rabīʿ al-abrār wa-nuṣūṣ al-akhbār*, ed. Salīm al-Nuʿaymī, Baghdad: al-ʿĀnī, vol. 3, 1400/1980, p. 617; see Marzolph, "Maistre Pathelin im Orient," pp. 311–312.

23. Zamakhsharī, *Rabīʿ al-abrār*, vol. 3, pp. 620–621.

24. Jāḥiẓ, ʿAmr ibn Baḥr al-, *Kitāb al-Ḥayawān*, ed. ʿAbd al-Salām Muḥammad Hārūn, 3rd ed. Beirut: al-Majmaʿ al-ʿilmī al-ʿarabī al-islāmī, 1388/1969, vol. 3, pp. 171–172; German translation in Weisweiler, Max, *Von Kalifen, Spaßmachern und klugen Haremsdamen: Arabischer Humor*, Düsseldorf: Eugen Diederichs, 1963, pp. 200–202. Parvin-e Gonābādi, Moḥammad, "Rishe-ye maṣal-e 'Bā hame bale, bā mā ham bale?'" in *Gozine-ye maqālehā*, Tehran: Ketābhā-ye jibi, 2536/1977, pp. 186–191.

25. Gutas, Dimitri, *Greek Thought, Arabic Culture: The Graeco-Arabic Translation Movement in Baghdad and Early ʿAbbāsid Society (2nd–4th/8th–10th Centuries)*, London: Routledge, 1988.

26. Marzolph, Ulrich, "Philogelos arabikos: Zum Nachleben der antiken Witzesammlung in der mittelalterlichen arabischen Literatur," *Der Islam* 64 (1987), pp. 185–230.

27. For detailed references to the following discussion, see Marzolph, "Maistre Pathelin im Orient," pp. 314–317.

28. Ṣafi, Fakhr al-Din ʿAli, *Laṭāʾef al-ṭavāʾef*, ed. Aḥmad Golchin-Maʿāni, Tehran: Moḥammad Ḥoseyn Eqbāl, 1336/1957, p. 323–324.

29. Marzolph, "Maistre Pathelin im Orient," pp. 316–317, 313–314.

30. Vakiliyān, Aḥmad, *Tamṣil va maṣal*, vol. 2, Tehran: Sorush, 1366/1987, pp. 72–75; El-Shamy, *Types*, p. 868, no. 1585; for Turkish versions see Marzolph, "Maistre Pathelin im Orient," p. 317, note 57.

CHAPTER 74

The Inanimate Object Allegedly Gives Birth and Dies (ATU 1592B)

Folktales are never, as the romantic approach proposed, the innocent or harmless expressions of a supposedly anonymous and collective "folk" culture. In their original contexts, folktales mainly serve to convey messages of an educative or paedagogical nature. In the form of an entertaining narrative, folktales inherently teach the moral and ethical values of the society in which they are told. As any other cultural expression, folktales have at times been used and misused in the context of outright cultural or political propaganda. In Nazi Germany, being German was propagated as the highest cultural value, since this criterion implied a given superiority. Aiming to unite all Germans in a single nation, the identification and support of Germans outside the political borders of Germany was regarded as being of utmost importance, and their eventual integration into the "Reich" was considered a national duty. The documentation and study of folktales played an inglorious role in this context.[1] Not all of the scholars involved in the process should necessarily be considered as stout supporters of the ideology of National Socialism, particularly since the question of German identity had already played a decisive role in the formation of the German nation in the nineteenth century. Some of them might probably have put their expertise at the disposal of the political powers of the day with scholarly intentions, and from today's perspective it is at times extremely difficult to judge whether they were fully aware of the implications of their efforts.[2] Wilhelm Bodens (1910–2005) is a case in point.

Bodens is today remembered as the politician who played a decisive and esteemed role in reuniting the Saarland with postwar Germany in the 1950s.[3] Born in a German region bordering the Netherlands, Bodens received his scholarly education at the Institut für geschichtliche Landeskunde (Institute of Historical Applied Geography) at the University of Bonn. Having studied Folkloristics (Volkskunde) with Franz Steinbach (1895–1964), he initially tried to make a living as a freelance author and avid collector of folktales, amassing some five thousand legends, droll stories, and fairy tales in the border regions of Germany, the Netherlands, and Belgium.[4] His two published volumes of German folktales are still today cited as reliable scholarly resources.[5] Bodens' volume *Vom Rhein zur Maas* (From the River Rhine to the River Maas) was published in 1936 as the first volume of the newly initiated series *Deutsches Grenzvolk im Westen erzählt* (German Folk of the Western Border Regions Tell Tales).[6] The volume contains a tale that is of particular relevance for the assimilation and appropriation of Middle Eastern narratives in German tradition. The tale is titled *Die Erdmännchen von Dieteren* (The Gnomes of Dieteren).[7]

> An old man in the town of Millen was convinced of the existence of gnomes living inside a specific hill. These gnomes used to come at night to borrow kettles, and when they returned it the following morning, the kettle was shining from polish.
>
> A certain farmer in Millen was reluctant to lend a kettle to the gnomes, until one day an old gnome promised that lending him a kettle would be to his profit. The next morning, the gnome returned the old and rusty kettle shining like silver, with a small kettle inside. Asked about the small kettle, the gnome responded that the farmer's kettle had been pregnant, and that it gave birth during the night.
>
> When the gnome returns soon after, the farmer does not hesitate to lend him the best copper kettle he has. The gnome, however, does not appear again for a long time, until the farmer's wife makes her husband go and look for him. When the man finally encounters the gnome, the farmer asks him what happened to his kettle. The gnome informs him that, sadly, it died. And when the farmer protests that kettles do not die, the gnome reminds him that he believed in a kettle giving birth, so he should also believe in the kettle's demise. And the greedy farmer never receives his kettle back.

Presented as recorded in "Millen-Heinsberg," a region close to the one in which the collector himself was born, the events are localized as having taken place in the nearby village of Dieteren in the Netherlands, and the explicit mention of the local "Sandberg" (Sandy Hill) serves to further authenticate the tale as originating from regional German tradition. In addition, the text introduces the gnomes with the dialect term "Auvermännkes" (Erdmännchen), denoting a species of gnomes residing in a subterraneous realm. Altogether, the specific presentation of Bodens's text takes great care to suggest an indigenous German (or Germanic) tradition firmly rooted in German folk belief. In the introduction to the volume, Bodens revels in praising his narrators for their creativity and talent, and it appears unlikely that he was aware of the tale's international connections. This suggests that his informant (or probably the informant's earlier source) is responsible for the tale's creative adaptation to the Germanic *Zeitgeist*.

A survey of the tale, that in international tradition is classified as tale type ATU 1592B: *The Pot Has a Child and Dies*, shows that the tale's dissemination is almost exclusively restricted to regions that at some time in their history were or still are submitted to Muslim or, more specific, Turkish Muslim influence.[8] Rare exceptions include the tale's mention in Dutch calendars of the first half of the nineteenth century[9] and three versions in the Dutch Folktale Database (Nederlands Volksverhaalenbank) recorded toward the end of the twentieth century in Utrecht.[10] Although the exact content of the nineteenth-century versions is not available, it is well known that calendars constituted an influential medium for the dissemination of folktales to the European audiences, including folktales of "Oriental" origin.[11] All of the recent Dutch versions attribute the tale to the Turkish prankster Nasreddin Hodja, and it is his popularity that supported the distribution of the tale virtually all over the Muslim world.[12]

Distributed in hundreds of editions in a large variety of languages all over the Muslim world and beyond, the pranks of the Turkish trickster Nasreddin Hodja have become part of world literature.[13] The tale under consideration here is already documented in the early modern Ottoman Turkish manuscript compilations of Nasreddin's jests[14] and constitutes a regular ingredient in virtually all larger collections printed since the middle of the nineteenth century.[15] Resulting from its old and widespread tradition, the tale of how Nasreddin dupes his neighbor by first arousing his greed and then forcing him to face the consequences is particularly popular in the oral tradition of the Balkans and the Middle East. Meanwhile, the attribution to Nasredin Hodja constitutes a later stage compared to the tale's early history in Arabic literature.

Already at the beginning of the eleventh century, the tale is attested in two versions that differ slightly in content and wording. The tale's essential plot is, however, identical in all of the early Arabic texts. In particular, the Arabic texts attribute the events to the pseudohistorical character Ashʿab, the stereotypical representative of greed in classical Arabic literature, who is said to have lived in the first half of the eighth century.[16] The shorter version in al-Ḥuṣrī's (d. 1015) *Jamʿ al-jawāhir* (The Collection of Jewels)[17] reads as follows.

> Ashʿab's wife found a *dīnār* and brought it to him. He said, "Give it to me, so that every week it will give birth to two *dirhams* for you." She gave it to him whereupon he paid her two *dirhams* every week. But when she requested the *dīnār* from him in the fourth week, he said, "It died in childbed!" She exclaimed, "Woe upon me because of you! How can a *dīnār* die?" And he said, "Woe upon you because of your family! How can you believe that it gives birth but deny that it dies in childbed?"

A somewhat longer version, documented in closely corresponding forms in two contemporary works, al-Tawḥīdī's (d. 1023) *al-Baṣāʾir wa-ʾl-dhakhāʾir* (Deep Insights and Treasures)[18] and al-Ābī's (d. 1030) *Nathr al-durr* (Pearls of Prose),[19] is presented as having been told by Ashʿab himself.

> Ashʿab said: A girl brought me a *dīnār* and said, "This is a deposit." So I placed it into a fold of the mattress. She came back after a few days and requested, "Give me the *dīnār*!" I responded, "Lift the mattress and take

its child!" I had placed a *dirham* to the side of the *dīnār*. Thereupon she left the *dīnār* in place and took the *dirham*. After several days she came again and found another *dirham* and took it, too. Likewise, she came back a third time. But when I saw her the fourth time, I cried. She asked, "What makes you cry?" I said, "Your *dīnār* has died in childbed!" She exclaimed, "Praise be to God! Does a *dīnār* die in childbed?" I responded, "You slut! You believe that it can give birth, but you do not believe (that it can die) in childbed?"

In subsequent centuries, this version is cited several times in a fair variety of Arabic sources of an entertaining, biographical, and historical nature.[20] However, the first printed edition of the anecdotes attributed to Juḥā, the Arab equivalent of the Turkish jester Nasreddin, tells the events as they were fashioned in Turkish tradition.[21] Critical readers might argue that the tale's two different versions with a pot and a coin, respectively, constitute two different tales that need not necessarily be genetically related to each other. Meanwhile, the later version can be argued to constitute a logical adaptation of the earlier one. Coins are always bound to a specific culture, and without going into details, an audience not acquainted with the medieval Arabic monetary system needs an instruction informing them that a *dirham* is a fraction of a *dīnār* in order to understand the point. When, apparently, Turkish tradition changed the coin to a kettle or a pot, it replaced a plot requisite linked to a particular cultural specificity with one that is universally intelligible. In addition, the attachment to Nasreddin Hodja, a character whose popularity exceeds that of the Arabic character Ashʿab by far, enabled the tale's international dissemination. Considered together, these features succeeded in creating a highly convincing tale that eventually displaced the earlier one. The initially quoted German example further underlines the tale's potential for a variety of adaptations, although some, and particularly those that are closely linked to a special or even unique context, will be less convincing and influential in tradition than others.

Notes

1. Tomkowiak, Ingrid, and Dietmar Sedlaczek, "Nationalsozialismus," in *Enzyklopädie des Märchens*, vol. 9 (1999), cols. 1243–1255.

2. For the larger context, see Dow, James R., *The Nazification of an Academic Discipline: Folklore in the Third Reich*, Bloomington: Indiana University Press, 1994.

3. Elzer, Herbert, *Die deutsche Wiedervereinigung an der Saar: Das Bundesministerium für gesamtdeutsche Fragen und das Netzwerk der prodeutschen Opposition 1949–1955*, St. Ingbert: Röhrig, 2007, p. 936, s.v. Bodens, Wilhelm; Majerus, Benoît, "Vorstellungen von der Besetzung Belgiens, Luxemburgs und der Niederlande (1933–1944), in *Der Zweite Weltkrieg in Europa: Erfahrung und Erinnerung*, ed. Jörg Echternkamp and Stefan Markens, Paderborn: Ferdinand Schöningh, 2007, pp. 35–43, at p. 42; see also https://de.wikipedia.org/wiki/Wilhelm_Bodens (accessed November 21, 2016).

4. Fischer, Helmut, *Erzählen—Schreiben—Deuten: Beiträge zur Erzählforschung*, Münster: Waxmann, 2001, p. 17.

5. See Uther, *Deutscher Märchenkatalog.*

6. Bodens, Wilhelm, *Vom Rhein zur Maas*, Bonn: Röhrscheid, 1936.

7. Ibid., pp. 40–41, no. 10.

8. Marzolph, Ulrich, "Topf hat ein Kind," in *Enzyklopädie des Märchens*, vol. 13 (2010), cols. 762–764.

9. Archive Jurjen van der Kooi, Groningen (index in the archives of the *Enzyklopädie des Märchens*, Göttingen).

10. Nederlands Volksverhaalenbank, LOMBO105, http://www.verhalenbank.nl/items/show/16757; LOMBO125, http://www.verhalenbank.nl/items/show/17419; LOMBO680, http://www.verhalenbank.nl/items/show/19247 (accessed November 21, 2016).

11. Brunold-Bigler, Ursula, "Kalender, Kalendergeschichte," in *Enzyklopädie des Märchens*, vol. 7 (1993), cols. 861–878.

12. Marzolph, "Topf hat ein Kind," col. 763.

13. Marzolph, Ulrich, and Ingeborg Baldauf, "Hodscha Nasreddin," in *Enzyklopädie des Märchens*, vol. 6 (1990), cols. 1127–1151; Marzolph, "Naṣr al-dīn Khōdjah," in *The Encyclopaedia of Islam*, 2nd ed., vol. 7, fasc. 129–130 (1992), pp. 1018–1020.

14. Kut, Günay, "Nasreddin Hoca Hikâyeleri Yazmalarının Kolları Üzerine Bir Deneme," in *IV. Milletlerarası Türk Halk Kültürü Kongresi Bildirileri*, vol. 3: *Halk Edebiyatı*, Ankara, 1992, pp. 147–200, at p. 164, no. 46.

15. Marzolph and Baldauf, "Hodscha Nasreddin," col. 1139, no. 35.

16. Rosenthal, Franz, *Humor in Early Islam*, Leiden: Brill, 1956 (reprint 2011), pass.

17. Ḥuṣrī al-Qayrawānī, Abū Isḥāq Ibrāhīm ibn ʿAlī al-, *Jamʿ al-jawāhir fī ʾl-mulaḥ wa-ʾl-nawādir*, ed. ʿAlī Muḥammad al-Bijāwī, Cairo: Dār Iḥyāʾ al-kutub al-ʿarabiyya, 1372/1952, p. 199.

18. Tawḥīdī, Abū Ḥayyān al-, *al-Baṣāʾir wa-ʾl-dhakhāʾir*, ed. Wadād al-Qāḍī, Beirut: Dār Ṣādir, 1408/1988, vol. 5, p. 195, no. 679.

19. Ābī, Abū Saʿd Manṣūr ibn al-Ḥusayn al-, *Nathr al-durr*, vol. 5, ed. Muḥammad Ibrāhīm ʿAbd al-Raḥmān and ʿAlī Muḥammad al-Bijāwī, Cairo: al-Hayʾa al-miṣriyya al-ʿāmma lil-kitāb, 1987, p. 316.

20. Basset, *Mille et un contes*, vol. 1, pp. 188–189, no. 39; Rosenthal, *Humor in Early Islam*, pp. 126–127, no. 146; Marzolph, *Arabia ridens*, vol. 2, p. 126, no. 502.

21. Juḥā, *Hādhihi nawādir al-khūjah Naṣr al-Dīn Afandī Juḥā al-Rūmī*, Būlāq: Mūsā Kāstillī, 1278/1861, p. 20.

CHAPTER 75

The Courtiers Force the Bearer of a Present to Share His Anticipated Reward (ATU 1610)

Jocular tales have a specific rationale for putting into practice the dichotomy of reward and punishment on which a large variety of folktales and fairy tales is predicated. One of the common mechanisms to create humor in those tales is to fool the audience's expectations by turning the anticipated events upside down. In tale type ATU 1610: *Sharing the Reward*, a man brings a present to the ruler. As the man is expected to receive a considerable reward, the courtiers granting access to the ruler exploit their privileged position by only letting him pass in return for the promise of sharing the anticipated reward with them. Instead of accepting the generous reward offered, however, the man requests that the ruler punish him with a certain number of lashes. Although sometimes the man has to endure some of the punishment himself, usually the larger part goes to the envious courtiers, thus teaching them a lesson not to abuse their position. In European tradition, both literary and oral, the tale is geographically widely spread.[1] In contrast to many other European folktales, there is no single influential historical version. Four different forms represented by different strands of tradition can be identified,[2] distinguished by the nature of the present.

In the first form, the present is a bird. Having escaped its owner, the bird is returned by a person who accidentally found it. This form was recorded from nineteenth-century oral tradition in Lithuania, the Netherlands, and Romania.[3] Its oldest documented version occurs in the *Trecentonovelle* (Three Hundred Novellas) compiled by the fourteenth-century Italian author Franco Sacchetti (d. 1400).[4] Sacchetti presents the tale as the oral account of a French peasant who told him how he had fooled the gatekeeper of the French King Philip VI (r. 1293–1350). One day, the king's favorite falcon does not return, and the king advertises a rich reward for anybody who would bring it back. The peasant, whose two daughters are of marriageable age, is highly pleased to find the falcon and goes to return it to its owner. The king's gatekeeper, whom he meets on the way, at first wants to convince the peasant to let him return the bird in the peasant's stead. But when the peasant does not comply, the gatekeeper makes him promise to split the anticipated reward between them. In the presence of the king, instead of asking for money, the peasant requests a reward of fifty lashes, explaining his strange request by referring to the arrangement he agreed on with the gatekeeper. Instead of punishing the peasant, the king orders the gatekeeper punished and rewards the peasant profusely. The text ends with a reflection on the peasant's cleverness and his successful stratagem to repay the courtier's greed. Sacchetti's text is noteworthy for its detailed description of how the peasant manages to catch the bird and deliver it to the king, particularly since as a peasant he was neither accustomed to keeping a falcon nor was the bird's possession suitable for a person of his social rank. The author even goes into specific details whereby the peasant has a friend send him the special hood used in falcon keeping. At the same time, the power of the royal gatekeeper is not logically conveyed, as the gatekeeper meets the peasant on the way and not, as might be expected, when the latter attempts to gain access to the king's palace.

In the tale's second form, the present is a particularly rare or beautiful fish. A Polish folktale starts by introducing a man who is heavily fined when illegally trying to cross the border to Germany.[5] As the man happens to catch a big fish in the river Olza soon after, he plans to present the fish to the king and request him to remit the fine. When the man attempts to enter the castle, one after the other four gatekeepers request a fourth of his anticipated reward, respectively. In the end, each of the gatekeepers receives 25 of the hundred lashes the man asks for. The fine that induced the man to present the fish is not mentioned again. The nineteenth-century Italian version, written down for folklorist Gherardo Nerucci from memory and in his own hand by the day laborer (*bracciante*) Pietro di Canestrino from Montale Pistoiese in Tuscany, introduces a widow in Genoa and her three sons, Francesco, Tonino, and Angelino.[6] Angelino is so lazy that he sleeps all the time. Even after being married to Carolina, he only gets up to join his brothers at the table. Finally, they throw Angelino and his wife out of the house. When Angelino intends to deliver a large fish to the king, three courtiers demand their share of his anticipated reward, the first one half of it, the second a quarter, and the third one half of what remains. Instead of a hundred gold coins, Angelino requests to be given 200 lashes and has them delivered to the courtiers. As there are still some lashes remaining, Angelino fools a seller of whips into buying them from him (as the terms for whip and whipping are identical). In the end, the king is so highly amused about Angelino's ruse that he grants Angelino a pension of five gold coins per day, and the tale ends with Angelino inviting his mother and brothers to a sumptuous dinner.

In fifteenth- and sixteenth-century German tradition attributed to the legendary priest of Kalenberg (Pfaffe vom Kahlenberg),[7] the oldest documented version of the tale including the fish motif appears in a fifteenth-century English manuscript of the *Gesta Romanorum*,[8] originally an early fourteenth-century compilation whose numerous manuscripts differ considerably in content. The tale in the *Gesta Romanorum* begins with a lengthy introduction about a king's two sons, the elder of whom is destined to succeed the king while the younger is sent to school. As the younger son is a spendthrift, the king limits the amount of money allotted to him. Using all the money he now owns, the young man buys a fish and a basket that he later intends to present to a nobleman whose castle he passes on his way. When the nobleman's doorman requests the fish's head in return for granting him access, the young man promises to give him half of his reward instead. Two other courtiers request a quarter of the reward each. Finally, the young man asks for twelve slaps in the face and has them delivered to the courtiers. Admiring the young man's wise decision, the nobleman gives him his daughter in marriage and passes his rule on to him. The text ends with a lengthy theological interpretation linking the various characters to virtues and vices.

The third strand of tradition mentions a fruit as the present. This form of the tale is documented from oral tradition in Austria, as narrated by Franz Konrath in 1954,[9] and in Sardinia, as dictated to the collector by the peasant Giovanni Matteo Mariotti from Calangius.[10] An early sixteenth-century version is contained in German author Johannes Pauli's collection of jests *Schimpf und Ernst* (Jocular and Serious Tales; 1522),[11] and an early fifteenth-century version is preserved in the Middle English tale of Sir Cleges.[12] The oldest documented occurrence of the fruit version is given in the *Summa predicantium* (J 6,19) of the fourteenth-century Dominican preacher John Bromyard.[13] In Bromyard's short version, a man presenting fruits to an unspecified king Frederick, probably Frederick I Barbarossa (r. 1155–1190), is compelled to share his reward with the janitor.

In a fourth, probably younger form of the tale, the present is a precious object the ruler lost, such as a ring, a watch, or a medal. This form is frequently documented in Slavonic tradition.[14] German versions often attribute the tale to the Prussian King Frederick II (r. 1740–1786), affectionately known as "Old Fred."[15] On November 9, 1954, Karl Haiding recorded an Austrian version from Maria Maringer in Perg who had learned the tale from her grandfather.[16] In this text, a count advertises a reward for the person who will bring him his lost hunting knife.

The above condensed survey barely summarizes the great diversity of the tale's numerous forms and versions. None of the discussed forms ever became dominant in international tradition. To the contrary, even within the identified strands of tradition there are innumerable variations concerning the sequence of action and the exact division of strokes as well as various additions to the main plot. Moreover, in order to do the tale full justice, several other features would have to be discussed, such as a fairly frequent anti-Jewish bias in international versions in which the character requesting the man to share his reward is a Jew.[17] This feature, notably, was popularized by the text published in the brothers Grimm's nineteenth-century *Kinder- und Hausmärchen* (Children's and Household Tales) that are still widely read today.[18]

A short anecdote included in Ibn Abī ʿAwn's (d. 934) book *al-Ajwiba al-muskita* (Quick-Witted Responses) demonstrates that the tale's basic structure was already known in Arabic literature in the first half of the tenth century.[19] The anecdote's main protagonist is the theologian Thumāma ibn Ashras (d. 828) who in later tradition was famed for his wit and liberal irony.

> Thumāma once proposed to a certain judge to split with him whatever the latter would receive, and the judge agreed. Soon after that, a certain man came by, and the judge asked him, "Where is that which you have promised to me?" The man responded, "(I have nothing but) a blow (for you)." And, says Thumāma, the judge said to me, "(You can have) half of that until something else comes up!"

The tale's oldest documented full-fledged version is contained in Arabic author al-Masʿūdī's (d. 956) historical work *Murūj al-dhahab wa-maʿādin al-jawhar* (The Meadows of Gold and Mines of Gems)[20] in the chapter devoted to the Abbasid Caliph al-Muʿtaḍid (r. 892–902). The tale is presented as told by a certain Ibn al-Maghāzilī, a talented storyteller performing on the streets in Baghdad. His tales are said to be so funny that nobody can resist laughing when listening to him.

> One day performing in front of the palace gate reserved for the entry of the nobles, Ibn al-Maghāzilī is informed by one of the ruler's servants that he praised the storyteller's talent to the caliph so much that the caliph gave orders to present the storyteller to him. Before introducing the storyteller to the caliph, however, the servant demands that he be given half of the storyteller's anticipated reward. Although Ibn al-Maghāzilī tries to bargain him down to a sixth or a fourth, the servant insists on receiving half of whatever the storyteller is to receive.
>
> In the caliph's presence, the storyteller promises to make the caliph laugh. They agree that if he succeeds in doing so, he will be given 500 *dirhams*. Should he fail, he is to accept ten strokes with a certain bag. As the storyteller looks at the bag, he imagines it to be soft and empty and so accepts the condition. Following this, the storyteller begins his performance. He does imitations of various characters, including Bedouins, grammarians, transvestites, judges, and gypsies, and tells jokes and funny stories about thieves and other rascals. Finally, he reaches the end of his repertoire and falls silent. The caliph, however, commands him to proceed without showing the slightest signs of amusement, whereas all the servants and pages already left the room, unable to contain their laughter. At this point, the storyteller admits being exhausted and having nothing but a single joke left. When he requests the caliph to double his punishment, the caliph is about to burst into laughter but still manages to control himself.
>
> Being hit with the bag, Ibn al-Maghāzilī painfully realizes that the bag is not empty. Instead, it is filled with pebbles, so that he has a hard time

> to endure ten blows. As the executioner is about to continue with another ten blows, however, the storyteller asks him to stop, as he promised the other half to the caliph's servant. At this point, the caliph cannot control himself any longer and laughs until he falls on his back, waving his feet in the air and clutching his belly.[21] When the servant receives the other half of the strokes, he complains bitterly about his fate, while Ibn al-Maghāzilī reminds him that he had, in fact, asked him to content himself with less.
>
> In the end, the caliph draws a purse with 500 *dirhams* from under his cushion and divides the money evenly between the two claimants.

In the thirteenth century, the tale is cited almost verbatim in al-Sharīshī's (d. 1222) commentary to the *maqāmāt* of al-Ḥarīrī (d. 1122).[22] It is also said to be contained in a specific manuscript copy of the book the seventeenth-century author Muḥammad Diyāb al-Atlīdī compiled on the downfall of the Barmakids, a powerful dynasty of viziers under the early Abbasid rulers.[23] The book's printed editions do not, however, contain the tale. The tale's version in fifteenth-century author al-Ibshīhī's encyclopedia of everything an educated person should know[24] is presented as an integral part of the "Hārūn cycle," the cycle of stories attached to the Abbasid Caliph Hārūn al-Rashīd (r. 786–809) as the epitome of the wise, just, and caring ruler that appears to have developed soon after the caliph's death.[25] The events start with the common scene of Hārūn al-Rashīd informing his vizier Jaʿfar al-Barmakī at night that he has trouble falling asleep. Rather than deciding to roam the city in disguise, the caliph requests to be entertained. The person who informs the ruler about the storyteller's talents is his standard companion, his executioner Masrūr, and the storyteller is the very same Ibn al-Maghāzilī. The splitting of the anticipated reward is negotiated somewhat differently, so that the storyteller is to end up with one-third while the servant is to receive two-thirds. The reward is mentioned as 500 *dirhams* while the punishment is to be three blows with the bag. The storyteller informs the caliph about their arrangement right after receiving the first blow.

In his Latin *Historia incrementorum atque decrementorum Aulae Othmanicae* (History of the Growth and Decay of the Ottoman Empire), the Moldavian statesman and man of letters Dimitrie Cantemir (1673–1723) attributes a tale to the Turkish jester Nasreddin Hodja in which the jester presents cucumbers to the Mongol emperor Timur or Tamerlane (d. 1405).[26] At first, Nasreddin presents ten cucumbers when the vegetable is still rare and is richly rewarded with ten gold coins. When later during the season he brings a whole wagon full of cucumbers, the doorman remembers the previous reward and demands to be given his share. But this time Tamerlane is angry about Nasreddin's untimely gift and orders him to be given 500 lashes that Nasreddin is happy to share with the courtier. The tale's basic situation of bringing vegetables or fruits at the wrong time of the year corresponds to tale type ATU 1689: *"Thank God They Weren't Peaches."* The tale is first documented in Roman historiographical literature and in Middle Eastern tradition is regularly attributed to Nasreddin Hodja.[27]

The present tale's version as given by al-Ibshīhī appears to have served as the model for the tale's inclusion in the later recensions of *The Thousand and One Nights*. The only major variation is the storyteller's name that is here specified as Ibn al-Qāribī.[28] The late nineteenth- or early twentieth-century Arabic chapbook *Nuzhat al-jullās* (Entertainment of the Companions) attributes more or less the same story to the historical poet Abū Nuwās (d. 814), who in later popular tradition gained the status of court fool at Hārūn al-Rashīd's court.[29]

Notes

1. Reinhard, John R., "Strokes Shared," *The Journal of American Folklore* 36.142 (1923), pp. 380–400.

2. Bolte and Polívka, *Anmerkungen*, vol. 1, pp. 63–65, no. 7. The following survey of European tradition is heavily indebted to Van der Kooi, Jurjen, "Teilung von Geschenken und Schlägen," in *Enzyklopädie des Märchens*, vol. 13 (2011), cols. 323–327.

3. Böhm, Max, and Franz Specht, *Lettische Schwänke und verwandte Volksüberlieferungen*, Reval: Kluge, 1911, pp. 289–291, no. 36; Lox, Harlinda, *Van stropdragers en de pot van Olen: Verhalen over Keizer Karel*, Leuven: Davidsfonds/Literair, 1999, pp. 66–69, 187–188, no. 59; Schott, Arthur, and Albert Schott, *Rumänische Volkserzählungen aus dem Banat*, ed. Rolf Wilhelm Brednich and Ion Taloş, Bucarest: Kriterion, 1971, pp. 281–283, no. 49.

4. Sacchetti, Franco, *Le trecentonovelle*, ed. Valerio Marucci, Rome: Salerno, 1996, pp. 669–673, no. 195; Keller, Walter, *Italienische Märchen*, Jena: Diederichs, 1929, pp. 19–23, no. 5.

5. Kapełus, Helena, and Julian Krzyzanowski, *Sto baśni ludowych*, Warsaw, 1957, pp. 357–358, no. 88.

6. Nerucci, Gherardo, *Sessanta novelle popolari montalesi (circondario di Pistoia)*, 2nd ed., Florence, 1891, pp. 233–237, no. 26; Imbriani, Vittorio, *La novellaja fiorentina*, Livorno: Vigo, 1877, pp. 581–586, no. 46; Monnier, Marc, *Contes populaires en Italie*, Paris: Charpentier, 1880, pp. 236–238.

7. Röcke, Werner, "Pfaffe vom Ka(h)lenberg," in *Enzyklopädie des Märchens*, vol. 10 (2002), cols. 831–836; Bebel, Heinrich, *Schwänke*, ed. Albert Wesselski, Munich: Georg Müller, 1907, vol. 1, pp. 71–72, 190–191, no. 56.

8. Herrtage, Sidney J.H., *The Early English Versions of the Gesta Romanorum*, London: N. Trübner & Co., 1879, pp. 413–416, no. 90; Wesselski, *Märchen des Mittelalters*, pp. 41–43, 202, no. 13.

9. Haiding, Karl, *Märchen und Schwänke aus dem Burgenlande*, Graz: Leykam, 1977, pp. 121–122, 237–238, no. 21.

10. Karlinger, Felix, *Das Feigenkörbchen: Volksmärchen aus Sardinien*, Kassel: Röth, 1973, pp. 22–26, 183, no. 2.

11. Pauli, Johannes, *Schimpf und Ernst*, ed. Johannes Bolte, Berlin: Herbert Stubenrauch, 1924 (reprint Hildesheim: Olms, 1972), vol. 1, p. 342; vol. 2, p. 390, no. 614.

12. Reinhard, "Strokes Shared," p. 380; see Laskaya, Anne, and Eve Salisbury, *The Middle English Breton Lays* (1995), http://d.lib.rochester.edu/teams/text/laskaya-and-salisbury-middle-english-breton-lays-sir-cleges-introduction (accessed January 31, 2018).

13. Wright, Thomas, *A Selection of Latin Stories from Manuscripts of the Thirteenth and Fourteenth Centuries: A Contribution to the History of Fiction during the Middle Ages*, London: Percy Society, 1842, p. 122, no. 127.

14. Afanasyev, Aleksandr Nikolaevich, *Narodnye russkie skazki*, ed. Vladimir Jakovlevich Propp, vol. 3, Moscow: Gosudarstvennoye Izdatel'stvo Khudozhestvennoy Literatury, 1957, pp. 303–304, 445, no. 523; Afanasjew, Alexander N., *Der Feuervogel: Märchen aus dem alten Russland*, Stuttgart: Steingrüben, 1960, pp. 288–290.

15. Henßen, Gottfried, *Volk erzählt: Münsterländische Sagen, Märchen und Schwänke*, Münster: Aschendorf, 1935, pp. 278–280, no. 213; Zender, Matthias, *Volksmärchen und Schwänke aus der Westeifel*, Bonn: Röhrscheid, 1935, pp. 110–112, no. 137; Stübs, Hugo, *Ull Lüj vertellen: Plattdeutsche Geschichten aus dem pommerschen Weizacker*, Greifswald: Bamberg, 1938, pp. 105–110, no. 64; Grannas, Gustav, *Plattdeutsche Volkserzählungen aus Ostpreußen*, Marburg: Elwert, 1957, pp. 141–144, no. 41.

16. Haiding, Karl, *Märchen und Schwänke aus Oberösterreich*, Berlin: De Gruyter, 1969, pp. 94, 220, no. 75.

17. Böhm and Specht, *Lettische Schwänke*, pp. 289–291, no. 36; Grannas, *Plattdeutsche Volkserzählungen*, pp. 141–144, no. 41; Haiding, *Märchen und Schwänke*, pp. 94, 220, no. 75; Lox, Harlinda, *Flämische Märchen*, Munich: Diederichs, 1999, pp. 230–234, 325, no. 57.

18. Grimm, Jacob and Wilhelm, *Kinder- und Hausmärchen: Ausgabe letzter Hand mit den Originalanmerkungen der Brüder Grimm*, ed. Heinz Rölleke, vol. 1, Stuttgart: Philipp Reclam Jun., 1980, pp. 63–68, no. 7.

19. Yousef, May A., *Das Buch der schlagfertigen Antworten von Ibn Abī 'Awn: Ein Werk der klassisch-arabischen Adab-Literatur, Einleitung, Edition und Quellenanalyse*, Berlin: Klaus Schwarz, 1988, p. 231, no. 1379; Ibn Abī 'Awn al-Kātib, Ibrāhīm ibn Muḥammad, *Kitāb al-Ajwiba al-muskita*, ed. 'Abd al-Qādir Aḥmad, Cairo 1985, p. 193.

20. Marzolph, *Arabia ridens*, vol. 2, p. 88, no. 351; Mas'ūdī, al-, *Murūj al-dhahab wa-ma'ādin al-jawhar*, ed. Barbier de Meynard and Pavet de Courteille, rev. ed. Charles Pellat, vol. 5, Beirut: Université libanaise, 1966, pp. 155–157, nos. 3300–3304; French translation in Basset, *Mille et un contes*, vol. 1, pp. 195–201, no. 48; German translation in Weisweiler, Max, *Von Kalifen, Spaßmachern und klugen Haremsdamen: Arabischer Humor*, Düsseldorf: Eugen Diederichs, 1963, pp. 36–41; English translation in Mas'udi, *The Meadows of Gold: The Abbasids*, transl. and ed. Paul Lunde and Caroline Stone, London: Routledge, 2010, pp. 351–354.

21. For expressions of excessive laughter in Arabic literature see Müller, Kathrin, *"Und der Kalif lachte, bis er auf den Rücken fiel:" Ein Beitrag zur Phraseologie und Stilkunde des klassischen Arabisch*, 2 vols., Munich: Bayerische Akademie der Wissenschaften, 1993.

22. Sharīshī, Abū 'l-'Abbās Aḥmad ibn al-Mu'min al-Qaysī al-, *Sharḥ Maqāmāt al-Ḥarīrī al-Baṣrī*, ed. Ṣidqī Muḥammad Jamīl, vol. 2, Beirut: Dār al-Fikr, 1429–1430/2009, pp. 490–491 (in the commentary to no. 43).

23. Girgas, Vladimir Fedorovich, and Viktor Romanovich Rozen, *Arabskaia khrestomatiia*, vol. 1, Sanktpeterburg: Tipografia Imperatorskoj Akademii Nauk, 1876, pp. 33–35, no. 19.

24. Ibshīhī, Shihāb al-Dīn Muḥammad ibn Aḥmad Abī al-Fatḥ al-, *al-Mustaṭraf fī kull fann mustaẓraf*, ed. Mufīd Qumayḥa, vol. 2, Beirut: Dār al-Kutub al-'ilmiyya, 1403/1983, pp. 527–528.

25. Gerhardt, Mia I., *The Art of Story-Telling: A Literary Study of the Thousand and One Nights*, Leiden: Brill, 1963, pp. 419–470; Marzolph, Ulrich, "Hārūn ar-Rašīd," in *Enzyklopädie des Märchens*, vol. 6 (1990), cols. 534–537.

26. Wesselski, *Der Hodscha Nasreddin*, vol. 1, pp. 189–190, 280, no. 328; Constantin, Gh. I., "Démètre Cantemir et Nasr ed-Din Khodja," *Türk Kültürü Araştırmaları* 15.1–2 (1976), pp. 289–310, at pp. 308–309 (Latin text).

27. Marzolph, Ulrich, "Übel: Das kleinere Ü.," in *Enzyklopädie des Märchens*, vol. 13 (2010), cols. 1095–1098.

28. Chauvin, *Bibliographie*, vol. 5 (1901), p. 282, no. 166; Marzolph and Van Leeuwen, *The Arabian Nights Encyclopedia*, vol. 1, pp. 293–294, no. 133.

29. *Nuzhat al-jullās fī nawādir Abū [!] Nuwās*, Beirut: Khalīl and Amīn al-Khūrī, s.a., p. 23; see Ingrams, William Harold, *Abu Nuwas in Life and Legend*, Port Louis, Mauritius: M. Gaud & Cie, 1933, pp. 49–50.

CHAPTER 76

The Greedy Banker Is Deceived into Delivering the Disputed Deposit (ATU 1617)

Premodern societies lacked institutions such as banks that offered people the means to deposit money or other valuables for a certain period of time and that guaranteed the retrieval of their property whenever they would need it later. Anybody intending to deposit valuables had to take recourse to specific individuals who were, either as members of one's own family or by virtue of their position or public office, considered as being of good repute. Rich merchants were often regarded as suitable candidates, as their impressive accumulation of wealth ironically suggested fair dealings with the possessions of others. In the Muslim context, a particularly favored candidate for the task of safekeeping was the judge (*qāḍī*), whose official function was to pass judgment concerning observance of the law and whose own morality was consequently presumed to be of a high standard. In stark contrast to the theoretical expectations, numerous narratives deal with the topic of faithless persons to whom valuable deposits were entrusted and who abused the deposit or even denied outright ever having received it. Whether these narratives illustrate the actual experience of being deceived by treacherous bankers or whether they warn against excessive credulity on the part of the depositors, they document a widespread phenomenon in premodern societies. Since women would almost exclusively travel in male company, it was usually men who would entrust their valuables to a trustworthy person. Reasons for men to travel included, above all, trade, craftsmanship, and religious duty. Merchants were required to travel by virtue of their profession, and craftsmen often had to travel to other locations to find employment, such as exemplified in tale type ATU 882A*: *Suitors at the Spinning Wheel* (see essay **25, *The Entrapped Would-Be Seducers Have to Work to Earn Their Food***). Further, the obligation to perform the pilgrimage (*ḥajj*) to the holy sites in Mecca and Medina at least once in a believer's lifetime is one of the five basic tenets of Islam. Prior to the introduction of modern means of travel, Muslim men who could afford the effort were absent from home for several weeks or months, sometimes even years. Female chastity was of pivotal importance for a man's reputation and honor, and given the stereotype concept of female fickleness, a traveling man might decide to leave his wife in the custody of a seemingly trustworthy person, thus probably exposing her to the predatory advances of a covetous lecher, such as in tale type ATU 712: *Crescentia* (see essay **15, *The Chaste Woman Coveted by Her Brother-in-Law***). In general, any traveler in the premodern world might have decided to leave his money or other valuable goods with a trustworthy person (other than his own potentially fickle wife) while away from home. A small cluster of narratives develops its main plot from this cultural fact.[1] Although the Muslim obligation of pilgrimage to Mecca created particularly favorable conditions for the genesis of these narratives, some of them were also adapted to the conditions of premodern European societies.[2] A widespread tale that enjoyed numerous variations is classified as tale type ATU 1617: *Unjust Banker Deceived into Delivering Deposits*. Although the popularity of this tale's numerous literary versions reached as far as Iceland,[3] versions from nineteenth- or twentieth-century oral traditions were recorded mainly from European regions that at some point in history were submitted to Muslim influence.

A Serbian text published by Vuk Vrčević (1811–1882), a collaborator and student of the seminal collector Vuk Karadžić (1787–1864),[4] in the second half of the nineteenth century locates the events in the Turkish town of Istanbul.[5]

> A widowed woman entrusts her valuables to her merchant neighbor. When she later asks him to return the valuables, he denies ever having received anything. As the woman laments her fate, an unknown (and presumably noble-appearing) woman offers her help, telling her to visit the merchant's shop the next day at the very same hour. The second woman prepares a large bundle filled with stones and presents herself to the merchant. There she pretends to be one of the sultan's wives who escaped from the harem. Just as she asks the merchant to keep her valuables for a while, the widow appears (as previously agreed with the other woman) and requests that the merchant return her deposit. As the greedy merchant does not want to forsake his chance to get hold of an even larger profit, he returns the first deposit, apologizing for having made a joke. Only later does he notice that he was tricked with the second deposit.

The collector states that the tale was narrated to him by the judge (*qāḍī*) of Trebinye who wanted to convince him that the events actually happened when the narrator was living in Istanbul. In addition to the narrator's attempt to authenticate the tale, his text is exceptional for its two female characters, giving the narrator the opportunity to end the tale with the fairly traditional misogynist remark that "in comparison to a woman's guile, a man's guile is futile." Ever since the Koranic commentary (12:28) to the tale of Yūsuf and Potiphar's wife that "your [feminine plural] guile is great (*inna kaydukunna ʿaẓīm*)," the treatment of women's wiles was (and still is) a prominent feature in the literatures and folklore of the Muslim world[6] or, as Fedwa Malti-Douglas puts it, in "the centuries-old world of Arabo-Islamic mental structures regarding women."[7]

While the Serbian tale clearly betrays its origin from Muslim tradition, Hispanic versions from Portugal and the Americas locate the tale in a religiously neutral context. A Portuguese tale originally published by Francisco Adolfo Coelho (1847–1919) tells about a father who sends his son away to earn money.[8] As the son intends to return home, he entrusts his money to a rich merchant. When, however, he happens to spend all of his travel money before leaving and requests his deposit back, the merchant denies ever having received anything. The father helps his son regain the money by making the merchant believe that he wants to deposit a large amount of money with him. Just as the father and the merchant are negotiating, the son shows up and demands his deposit. Since the merchant does not want to lose the prospect of an even larger gain, he returns the first deposit. Following this, the father promises the merchant to return with his prospective deposit but, obviously, never does. This version plays on the stereotypes of the cross-eyed merchant as being clever and deceiving, and the bald-headed father as outwitting him. Similarly, a Spanish version from Mexico mentions a young man depositing his purse with a bald-headed clerk in a bank.[9] The father, who is even balder (and thus, by implication, cleverer), regains the deposit by making the clerk believe that he wants to deposit a large bag of money (which is, however, actually filled with "buttons and rusty washers").

Both the bundle filled with stones in the Serbian version and the bag filled with worthless items in the Mexican version are reminiscent of the tale's oldest European version in the twelfth-century *Disciplina clericalis* (The Scholar's Guide) compiled by Petrus Alfonsus.[10] Here, the cheated depositor is advised by an old woman. The old woman suggests that he make a trusted person ask the banker to keep ten large caskets (filled with stones) as a deposit until the owner would return from his pilgrimage to Mecca. Other influential versions in the medieval European literatures that likely contributed to the tale's dissemination are contained in the Latin *Gesta Romanorum* (no. 118), the *Cento novelle antiche* (no. 74), and Boccaccio's *Decamerone* (day 8, no. 10).[11]

The earliest corresponding version in Arabic tradition is encountered in al-Bayhaqī's tenth-century antithetical work *al-Maḥāsin wa-'l-masāwī* (The Good and the Bad Sides [of Things]) in the chapter on "The Advantages of Cleverness and (Legal) Tricks" (*Maḥāsin al-dahā' wa-'l-ḥiyal*).[12] In this tale, the clever advisor is the historical judge Iyās ibn Muʿāwiya (d. about 740) whose perspicacity is praised in numerous anecdotes.

> A man once gave one of the confidants of Iyās money to keep for him and went away on pilgrimage. When he returned, he requested his money back, but the other one denied having received anything. Thereupon, the man went to Iyās and informed him about the matter. Iyās asked, "Does he know that you informed anybody else but himself?" And the man

responded, "No."— "Does he know that you informed me?"—"No."— "Did you quarrel with him when somebody else was present?"— "No." So Iyās said, "Go away and keep your affair secret. Return to me later on."

Then Iyās had his confidant come and said to him, "Presently, I received a large quantity of money. I want to entrust it to you as a deposit and keep it with you. Look for a place to store it and send somebody to carry it away together with you." Thereupon, the intimate went away and the cheated man returned to Iyās. The latter said, "Now go to the person in question and request your property. Maybe he will return it to you; and if not, inform him that you know me." The man went to see the confidant and said, "Give me my money. If you don't, I will go to the *qāḍī* and inform him." So the confidant returned the money to him. The man went back to Iyās and told him, "He returned my money." Then the confidant came to Iyās because of the proposed deposit, but Iyās drove him away with the words, "Go away, you faithless person!"

With closely similar wording and stereotypically attributed to Iyās, the tale is later rendered in al-Rāghib al-Iṣfahānī's (d. 1108) *Muḥāḍarāt al-udabā'* (Conversations of the Educated) and Ibn al-Jawzī's (d. 1201) *Akhbār al-Adhkiyā'* (Tales of Clever People). It remained popular until the present day by way of al-Ibshīhī's fifteenth-century encyclopedia of useful knowledge that cites the tale twice in separate chapters.[13] Various versions of the tale were recorded from nineteenth- and twentieth-century oral tradition in the Arab world.[14] Probably by way of Persian intermediaries, the Arabic versions also appear to be the source of the tale's Indian renderings, such as the one included in Hēmavijaya's late sixteenth-century compilation *Kathāratnākara* (The Sea of Tales).[15] In the Persian tradition of the Indian subcontinent, a version of the tale in which the ruler makes the unfaithful banker believe that the depositor is his close intimate was popularized by way of its inclusion in the chapbook *Ḥekāyāt-e laṭif* (Amusing Tales), originally a reader appended to Francis Gladwin's grammar of the Persian language, *The Persian Moonshee*, first published in 1795.[16]

Notes

1. Marzolph, Ulrich, "Kredit erschwindelt," in *Enzyklopädie des Märchens*, vol. 8 (1996), cols. 375–380.

2. For a survey of European historical texts, see Kasprzyk, Krystyna, *Nicolas de Troyes et le genre narrative en France au XVIe siècle*, Warsaw: Państwowe Wydawnictwo Naukowe, and Paris: Klincksieck, 1963, pp. 223–235, no. 116.

3. Gering, Hugo, *Islendzk æventyri: Isländische Legenden, Novellen und Märchen*, vol. 2, Halle: Buchhandlung des Waisenhauses, 1883, pp. 227–229, no. XCIII. The editor judges this version to have been written down from memory following an oral performance of the version in Petrus Alfonsus's *Disciplina clericalis*.

4. Bošković-Stulli, Maja, "Karadžić (Stefanović), Vuk," in *Enzyklopädie des Märchens*, vol. 7 (1993), cols. 948–952.

5. Vrčević, Vuk, *Srpske narodne propovijetke, ponajviše kratke i šaljive*, Belgrade: Srpska kraljevska državna štamparija, 1868, vol. 1, pp. 109–110, no. 235.

6. Merguerian, Gayane Karen, and Afsaneh Najmabadi, "Zulaykha and Yusuf: Whose 'Best Story?'," *International Journal of Middle East Studies* 29.4 (1997), pp. 485–508; Mills, Margaret A., "The Gender of the Trick: Female Tricksters and Male Narrators," *Asian Folklore Studies* 60.2 (2001), pp. 237–258; Meisami, Julie Scott, "Writing Medieval Women: Representations and Misrepresentations," in Bray, Julia, ed., *Writing and Representation in Medieval Islam: Muslim Horizons*, London: Routledge, 2006, pp. 47–88, at p. 71; Osman, Rawand, *Female Personalities in the Qur'an and Sunna: Examining the Major Sources of Imami Shi'i Islam*, London: Routledge, 2015, pp. 51–54; Sayers, David Selim, *The Wiles of Women as a Literary Genre: A Study of Ottoman and Azeri Texts*, Wiesbaden: Harrassowitz, 2019.

7. Malti-Douglas, Fedwa, *Men, Women, and God(s): Nawal El Saadawi and Arab Feminist Poetics*, Berkeley: University of California Press, 1995, p. 97; see also Malti-Douglas, *Woman's Body, Woman's Word: Gender and Discourse in Arabo-Islamic Writing*, Princeton: Princeton University Press, 1991, particularly at pp. 54–66.

8. Meier, Harri, and Dieter Woll, *Portugiesische Märchen*, Düsseldorf: Diederichs, 1975, pp. 137–139, 264, no. 69.

9. Aiken, Riley, "A Pack Load of Mexican Tales," in *Puro Mexicano*, ed. James Frank Dobie, Austin: Texas Folklore Society, 1935, pp. 1–87, at p. 46–47.

10. Chauvin, *Bibliographie*, vol. 9 (1905), pp. 23–25, no. 13 (also referencing a number of similar tales); Schwarzbaum, Haim, "International Folklore Motifs in Petrus Alphonsi's 'Disciplina clericalis'," in Schwarzbaum, *Jewish Folklore between East and West*, ed. Eli Yassif, Beer-Sheva: Ben-Gurion University of the Negev Press, 1989, pp. 239–358, at pp. 286–287, no. 15; Spies, Otto, "Arabische Stoffe in der Disciplina Clericalis," *Rheinisches Jahrbuch für Volkskunde* 21 (1973), pp. 170–199, at pp. 184–186. For versions of the tale in Jewish tradition see Marmorstein, Abraham, "Das Motiv vom veruntreuten Depositum in der jüdischen Volkskunde," *Monatsschrift für Geschichte und Wissenschaft des Judentums* (1934), pp. 183–195; Schwarzbaum, Haim, *Studies in Jewish and World Folklore*, Berlin: Walter de Gruyter, 1968, pp. 239–241, no. 281.

11. For details, see Schwarzbaum, "International Folklore Motifs," pp. 286–287; Kasprzyk, *Nicolas de Troyes*, p. 223; György, Lajos, *A magyar anekdota története és egyetemes kapcsolatai*, Budapest: Studium, 1934, pp. 149–150, no. 113; Tubach, *Index exemplorum*, p. 376, no. 4969.

12. Baihaqī, Ibrāhīm ibn Muḥammad al-, *Kitāb al-Maḥāsin val-Masāvī*, ed. Friedrich Schwally, Giessen: J. Ricker'sche Verlagsbuchhandlung, 1902, p. 144–145; German translation in Marzolph, *Arabia ridens*, vol. 1, p. 261, no. 23.

13. Marzolph, *Arabia ridens*, vol. 2, p. 130, no. 450.

14. El-Shamy, *Types*, pp. 877–878, no. 1617.

15. Bloomfield, Maurice, "On False Ascetics and Nuns in Hindu Fiction," *Journal of the American Oriental Society* 44 (1924), pp. 202–242, at pp. 223–224; Hēmavijaya, *Kathāratnākara: Das Märchenmeer. Eine Sammlung indischer Erzählungen*, transl. Johannes Hertel, Munich: Georg Müller, 1920, vol. 1, pp. 200–203, no. 69.

16. Marzolph, Ulrich, "'Pleasant Stories in an Easy Style:' Gladwin's Persian Grammar as an Intermediary between Classical and Popular Literature," in Marzolph, *Ex Oriente Fabula*, vol. 2, Dortmund: Verlag für Orientkunde, 2006, pp. 96–130, at p. 107, no. 6.

CHAPTER 77

The Pauper Regains His Buried Money (ATU 1617*)

Previously classified as motif K1667.1.1: *Retrieving the buried treasure*, the last revision of the international tale-type index now includes the present tale as tale type ATU 1617*: *The Blind Man's Treasure*.[1] The protagonist's identification as being blind is only one of several potential specifications, and many of the tale's versions identify him only as a somewhat simple-minded, yet clever pauper. Oral versions of the tale were primarily recorded from the Iberian Peninsula, Italy, and France, where literary versions dating from the Middle Ages and the early modern period helped to popularize the tale.

A Spanish version of the tale was recorded on May 1, 1936, from the oral performance of Lorenzo Monje Rodríguez, aged 14, in Mota del Marqués, Valladolid.[2]

> A blind man buries the five *duros* he has amassed by way of alms under a certain fig tree. A woman passing by wonders what the blind man hides, finds the money, and takes it. When the blind man does not find his money the next day, he grabs his guitar and sings a song, "Five *duros* I had under the fig tree, and five other ones remain that I will put there!" When the woman hears the song, she decides to return the money so as to be able to take the even larger amount later on. The blind man returns the next day, takes his money and sings, "Whoever wants everything, will lose everything!"

In the Spanish-American text published by Juan Rael, the protagonist is an unspecified pauper whose buried 100 *pesos* are stolen by an unnamed man.[3] A friend advises the pauper to take his guitar and sing, "A hundred *pesos* I have buried, and another hundred I will bury." The greedy thief decides to return the money so as to take the larger amount later, and the pauper regains his property. In a Portuguese version recorded in Porto, the blind pauper suspects who stole his money from under the fig tree and bluntly informs his thievish neighbor that he intends to bury still more.[4] The Tuscan version recorded from Maria Pierazzoli in Pratovecchio again mentions a blind pauper and a fig tree.[5] The text further authenticates the plot by referring to the custom of blind beggars singing songs at the Friday market (on the Piazza della Signorina) in Florence. And a Catalan tale specifies that the owner is an old man who keeps his savings in a tree.[6] When his son steals the money, the old man says to himself in a loud voice that he intends to place some more money in the tree, so the son puts the money back. Contrasting with these relatively short and matter-of-fact versions, a French tale Charles Thibault recorded in Laines-aux-Bois in 1917 presents a fairly circumstantial version in which a rich priest keeps his money in a kettle that he buries in his own garden.[7] When the money is stolen one day, the priest at first suspects the good-for-nothing brother of his maid. But the maid informs him that she noticed the neighboring cobbler that night as he left the garden through a hole in the wall, when at night she got up to answer a call of nature. Suspecting that the cobbler took the money, the priest gives the cobbler an order to make him a nice pair of shoes because he intends to travel to Troyes to collect some money from his superior, thus arousing the cobbler's greed. The cobbler returns the money, the owner retrieves it, and from then on keeps it in his house.

Although the tale is frequently cited in German chapbooks of the seventeenth and eighteenth centuries,[8] it did not have a noticeable impact on subsequent German oral tradition.[9] The tale's literary dissemination is documented by numerous versions in a variety of, predominantly, Latin, French and Italian compilations dating from the medieval and early modern periods.[10] These include the mid-fourteenth-century *Mensa philosophica*,[11] Antonio Beccadelli's *Alfonsi regi dicta et facta* (The Statements and Acts of King Alfonsus; 1455),[12] Francesco Sacchetti's late fourteenth-century *Trecentonovelle* (Three Hundred Novellas),[13] Laurentius Abstemius's *Fabulae* (1499), Baptista Fulgosius Genuensis' *De gestis et dictis memorabilibus* (Of Memorable Deeds and Statements; 1509), Girolamo Morlini's *Novellae* (1520),[14] Lodovico Guicciardini's *L'hore di ricreatione* (Recreation Time; 1558), Juan de Timoneda's *El sobremesa* (Table [Talk]; 1563),[15] Lodovico Domenichi's *Historia varia* (Various Histories;1564), and Nicolas de Troyes's *Le grand parangon de nouvelles nouvelles* (The Great Paragon of New Novellaa; 1536).[16] The French author Jean de La Fontaine's *Fables* (1678; book 10, no. 4) includes a particularly well-known version.

The tale's earliest appearance in European tradition is attested in the second chapter of the sixth book of *Felix: de los Maravelles del Mon* (Felix: On the Wonders of the World), originally compiled around 1287 by the Catalan poet, mystic, theologian, and philosopher Ramón Llull (d. 1316).[17] The tale illustrates the philosopher's teaching to Felix.[18] It is embedded into the tale told by a merchant in order to illustrate his own fate. The merchant, after having invested a fortune to be nominated bailiff of the city in which he lived, had turned to injustice to regain his investment. Subsequently, the king had dismissed him, confiscating not only the money he had invested but also the riches the merchant had originally lent him. In the tale told by the merchant, the blind man buries a thousand *libras* under a certain stone. When the money is stolen, the owner correctly suspects his neighbor to be the thief, and tells him that he intends to bury another thousand *libras* soon. When the thief returns the money to its original place, hoping for a larger booty eventually, the blind man regains his possession. In the end, he ridicules the thief for being even blinder, that is, more ignorant, than himself. The philosopher explains the example by saying that "the merchant desired honors to which he was not entitled" and that "the king deceived him with respect to his office, for the merchant did not see that it was through honor and not money that one was entitled to the office."

The tale's Arabic precursors date from early in the eleventh century, thus predating Llull's text by more than two centuries.[19] Seasoned with a scatological flavor, the Arabic tale shares the same basic structure as documented in the European versions. The Arabic tale is stereotypically attributed to the Wise Fool Buhlūl, a character who according to tradition lived in eighth-century Baghdad and who enjoys a particular reputation with the Shiʿi community as having been a faithful follower of the sixth *imām* Jaʿfar al-Ṣādiq.[20] As a Wise Fool, Buhlūl is part of a Middle Eastern tradition of pranksters that enjoyed a jester's license similar to that of the later European court fools.[21] He is particularly well known for his stringent admonitions and condemnation of mundane vanity. A relatively short version of the present tale is cited in al-Ḥuṣrī's (d. 1015) *Jamʿ al-jawāhir fī 'l-mulaḥ wa-'l-nawādir* (The Collection of Jewels: Funny Tales and Stories).[22]

> Once Buhlūl hid twenty *dirhams* in one of the courtyards of Kufa. Without him noticing, he was observed by a certain tailor. When Buhlūl went away, the tailor took the money. Buhlūl returned later and searched for his money. When he did not find it, he suspected that only the tailor could have stolen it. So he went to him and said, "Hey you! Suppose you take ten *dirhams* into your hand, then thirty, then . . ." until it was a hundred *dirhams*. Then he asked, "If you now add another twenty, how much money will it be?" The tailor responded, "A hundred and twenty." Buhlūl said, "Correct," and went away. Thereupon the tailor thought by himself, "He is certainly going to add the money he counted to the twenty *dirhams* and then put it back into its place. And when he added to it, I will take it all." So he did (that is, he replaced the money). Buhlūl returned to the place, took the money and defecated in its place. Then he went away. Quickly, the tailor got up. But when he extended his hand (into the hiding place), it was full of excrement, and he found nothing (that is, no money). Buhlūl addressed him, "Take that and that into your hand. How much will you hold in your hand?" The tailor responded, "A hundred and twenty." But Buhlūl commented, "In your hand is nothing but shit!"
>
> The news of the tailor's adventure spread and the children made fun of him until he left Kufa.

The second, somewhat longer early Arabic version is rendered in al-Ābī's (d. 1030) encyclopedia of jokes and anecdotes, *Nathr al-durr* (Pearls of Prose).[23] Here,

Buhūl is introduced as normally depositing his belongings with a trusted woman from the tribe of Kinda who was like a mother to him. Only at times would he hide his money by burying it in a ruined building. When he buries the sum of ten *dirhams* one day, he happens to notice the person who later steals it. So when the money is stolen, he approaches that person pretending that he hid money in several places and now wants to collect it in the place where he recently buried his ten *dirhams*. He asks his opponent to help him add up the money, mentioning several amounts until the sum reaches 300 *dirhams*. After the greedy thief returned the stolen money, Buhlūl collects it, defecates in its place, and covers the excrements with earth. When he later makes fun of the thief, the man threatens to give him a beating, and so he runs away.

The tale is cited in similar wording in a number of nineteenth- and twentieth-century collections of the anecdotes on Buhlūl in both Arabic and Persian.[24] A fairly recent expurgated Arabic version is embedded in the narrative cycle of "King Shāh Bakht and His Vizier al-Raḥwān" that is included both in the sixteenth-century Kayseri manuscript and the Breslau edition of *The Thousand and One Nights*.[25] The protagonist here is a former rich man who is impoverished. In the Persian tradition of the Indian subcontinent, the tale was further popularized by way of its inclusion in the chapbook *Ḥekāyāt-e laṭif* (Amusing Tales), originally a reader appended to Francis Gladwin's grammar of the Persian language, *The Persian Moonshee*, first published in 1795.[26]

Persian tradition also knows a specific oicotype that is linked to a proverb. A carpenter (*takht-kesh*) has the habit of singing, "Everything I possess is beneath me," while he works. A thief hears his song, searches the place at night and steals the man's money that is kept in a small vessel hidden beneath his seat. When the thief passes the carpenter's shop some days later, he hears the carpenter sing, "Too bad that he did not allow me to fill it up completely!" Out of greed, the thief returns the vessel intending to steal it again later. Some days later, however, he hears the carpenter ridicule him by singing, "The greedy man's beard in the poor man's anus!" (*rish-e por-ṭamaʿ* [or *khām-ṭamaʿ*] *dar kun-e mofles*).[27] Although the imagery of this Middle Eastern vilification may be alien to the modern Western reader, it finds its equivalent in the English colloquial expression, "Kiss my ass!" At any rate, it is not difficult to understand as expressing the poor man's satisfaction at having outsmarted his opponent. While the related tale was only recorded in the twentieth century, the proverb is already documented in Moḥammad ʿAli Ḥablerudi's paroemiological compilations in the seventeenth century.[28]

Comparing the tale's earliest-known European form to its Arabic precursors, one notices a number of closely corresponding features in addition to the general agreement in terms of plot and structure. As in the Arabic form, the protagonist of Llull's text has an idea who stole his money; and in the end, in both forms he ridicules the thief. The considerable period of time that passed between the early eleventh century and Llull's time likely affected the tale's specific form, and it is not necessarily the European author who should be credited with having adapted particular features from the tale's earlier form. The introduction of the blind beggar is an ingenious adaptation to the urban European context where blind and disabled beggars were frequent.[29] The Arabic Wise Fool as a venerated character who showed traits of madness and who was not able to take care of feeding himself would have been alien to late medieval Europe. At the same time, although European authors of the late Middle Ages and Renaissance were certainly not squeamish, they abandoned the tale's scatological element, while Buhlūl already in one of the oldest anecdotes of his repertoire did not shy away from smearing his own neck with excrement so as to keep the people from hitting him.[30]

Notes

1. Uther, Hans-Jörg, *Behinderte in populären Erzählungen*, Berlin: Walter de Gruyter, 1981, pp. 46–50. The author's entry "Schatz des Blinden" in the *Enzyklopädie des Märchens*, vol. 11 (2004), cols. 1259–1263, follows the account of his earlier study.

2. Espinosa, Aurelio Macedonia, Jr., *Cuentos populares de Castilla y Leon*, vol. 2, Madrid: Consejo Superior de Investigaciones Cientificas, 1988, p. 248, no. 354.

3. Rael, Juan, *Cuentos españoles de Colorado y Nuevo Méjico*, vol. 2, Stanford: Stanford University Press, 1940, pp. 546–547, 800, no. 452 (42).

4. Braga, Teófilo, *Contos tradicionais do povo português*, 3rd ed., vol. 1, Lisbon: Dom Quixote, 1987, pp. 239–240. For other Portuguese versions see Cardigos, Isabel, *Catalogue of Portuguese Folktales*, Helsinki: Suomalainen Tiedeakatemia, 2006, no. 1617*.

5. Pitrè, Giuseppe, *Novelle popolari toscane*, vol. 1, Rome: Società Editrice del libro italiano, 1941, pp. 336–338, no. 70; see also p. 342, note 1.

6. Gascón, Francesc, *Rondalles de la Vall d'Albaida i l'Alcoià*, Ontinyent: Ajuntament d'Ontinyent, 1999, pp. 37–38, no. 5; quoted *apud* Oriol, Carme, and Josep M. Pujol, *Index of Catalan Folktales*, Helsinki: Suomalainen Tiedeakatemia, 2008, p. 259, no. 1617*.

7. Thibault, Charles, *Contes de Champagne*, Paris: Quatre jeudis, 1960, pp. 151–156, no. 19; this version is obvously a close retelling of the version contained in Nicolas de Troyes's sixteenth-century *Grand parangon*, for which see Kasprzyk, Krystyna, *Nicolas de Troyes et le genre narrative en France au XVIe siècle*, Warsaw: Państwowe Wydawnictwo Naukowe, and Paris: Klincksieck, 1963, pp. 75–80, no. 19.

8. The archive of the *Enzyklopädie des Märchens* in Göttingen holds some sixteen versions from those chapbooks, the oldest of which dates from 1607.

9. Uther, *Deutscher Märchenkatalog*, p. 435, no. 1617*.

10. For detailed references to the compilations quoted in the following, see Kasprzyk, *Nicolas de Troyes*, pp. 75–80, no. 19; see also Rotunda, Dominic Peter, *Motif-Index of the Italian Novella in Prose*, Bloomington: Indiana University, 1942, p. 120, s.v. K1667.1.1.*; Childers, J. Wesley, *Tales from the Spanish Picaresque Novels: A Motif Index*, Albany: State University of New York Press, 1977, p. 156, s.v. K1667.1.3.*.

11. Tubach, *Index exemplorum*, p. 58, no. 696; Dunn, Thomas Franklin, *The Facetiae of the Mensa Philosophica*, St. Louis: Washington University, 1934, p. 33.

12. Uther, *Behinderte*, p. 48; Uther, "Schatz des Blinden," cols. 1260–1261.

13. Schenda, Rudolf, *Märchen aus der Toskana*, Munich: Eugen Diederichs, 1996, pp. 39–47, 319, no. 9.

14. Wesselski, Albert, *Die Novellen Girolamo Morlinis*, Munich: Georg Müller, 1908, pp. 149–151, 294–297, no. 43.

15. Childers, J. Wesley, *Motif-Index of the Cuentos of Juan Timoneda*, Bloomington: Indiana University, 1948, p. 36, s.v. K1667.1.1.*.

16. Kasprzyk, *Nicolas de Troyes*, pp. 75–80, no. 19.

17. Lull, Ramón, *Llibre de meravelles*, vol. 1: *Llibres I–VII*, ed. Lola Badia, Palma: Patronat Ramon Llull, 2011, p. 212 (6,34); Lull, *Obras*, vol. 1, ed. Jerónimo Rosselló, Palma de Mallorca, 1903, pp. 156–157; Spanish translation in Lulio, Raymundo, *Libro Felix, o maravillas del mundo*, vol. 1, Mallorca: Audiencia, 1750, pp. 174–175; English translation in Llull, Ramon, *Selected Works*, ed. and transl. Anthony Bonner, vol. 2, Princeton: Princeton University Press, 1985, pp. 771–772; German translation in Lull, Ramon, *Felix oder Das Buch der Wunder*, transl. Gret Schib Torra, Basel: Schwabe, 2007, pp. 105–106.

18. Llull, *Selected Works*, vol. 2, p 772.

19. Marzolph, *Arabia ridens*, vol. 2, p. 125, no. 499.

20. Marzolph, Ulrich, *Der Weise Narr Buhlūl*, Wiesbaden: Franz Steiner, 1983, pp. 43–44, no. 60.

21. See Marzolph, Ulrich, "Timur's Humorous Antagonist, Nasreddin Ḫoca," in Marzolph, *Ex Oriente Fabula*, vol. 2, Dortmund: Verlag für Orientkunde, 2006, 159–174, at pp. 170–171.

22. Ḥuṣrī al-Qayrawānī, Abū Isḥāq Ibrāhīm ibn ʿAlī al-, *Jamʿ al-jawāhir fī ʾl-mulaḥ wa-ʾl-nawādir*, ed. ʿAlī Muḥammad al-Bijāwī, Cairo: Dār Iḥyāʾ al-kutub al-ʿarabiyya, 1372/1952, pp. 163–164.

23. Ābī, Abū Saʿd Manṣūr ibn al-Ḥusayn al-, *Nathr al-durr*, vol. 3, ed. Muḥammad ʿAlī Qarna and ʿAlī Muḥammad al-Bijāwī, Cairo: al-Hayʾa al-miṣriyya al-ʿāmma lil-kitāb, 1984, pp. 266–267; Marzolph, *Arabia ridens*, vol. 1, p. 272, no. 45.

24. Marzolph, *Der Weise Narr Buhlūl*, pp. 43–44, no. 60.

25. Chauvin, *Bibliographie*, vol. 8 (1904), p. 103, no. 77; Ott, Claudia, transl., *Tausendundeine Nacht: Das glückliche Ende*, Munich: C.H. Beck, 2016, pp. 194–196; Marzolph and Van Leeuwen, *The Arabian Nights Encyclopedia*, vol. 1, p. 295, no. 304.

26. Marzolph, Ulrich, "'Pleasant Stories in an Easy Style:' Gladwin's Persian Grammar as an Intermediary between Classical and Popular Literature," in Marzolph, *Ex Oriente Fabula*, vol. 2, Dortmund: Verlag für Orientkunde, 2006, pp. 96–130, at p. 117, no. 67; Marzolph, *Arabia ridens*, vol. 2, p. 125, no. 499.

27. Marzolph, *Typologie*, p. 199, no. 1341; see Enjavi Shirāzi, Abol-Qāsem, *Tams̱il va mas̱al*, Tehran: Amir Kabir, 1352/1973, p. 103 (2nd ed. 2537/1979, p. 186); the book's most recent expurgated edition (ed. Aḥmad Vakiliyān, Tehran: Amir Kabir, 1393/2014) includes neither the proverb nor the related tale.

28. Ḥablerudi, Moḥammad ʿAli, *Majmaʿ al-ams̱āl*, ed. Ṣādeq Kiyā, Tehran: Edāre-ye farhang-e ʿāmme, 1344/1965, p. 83; Ḥablerudi, *Jāmeʿ al-tams̱il*, ed. Ḥasan Ẕol-Faqāri, Tehran: Moʿin, 1390/2011, p. 415; see also Shahri, Jaʿfar, *Qand va namak: żarb al-mas̱alhā-ye tehrāni be-zabān-e moḥāvere*, Tehran: Esmāʿiliyān, 1370, p. 403.

29. For versions in which the beggar is not blind, see Wesselski, *Die Novellen Girolamo Morlinis*, pp. 296–297; Uther, *Behinderte*, p. 50.

30. Marzolph, *Der Weise Narr Buhlūl*, p. 27, no. 2.

CHAPTER 78

The Imaginary Tissue (ATU 1620)

The nineteenth- and early twentieth-century collectors of tales from oral tradition in Europe often consciously avoided recording narratives that to their notion obviously derived from literary models. Even before the stage of storytelling and potential recording, narrators might have decided not to perform tales whose indebtedness to literary models would have been obvious to the collectors. Although this agenda was applied in varying degrees, it appears to hold particularly true for the tales Danish author Hans Christian Andersen (1805–1875) published in his *Eventyr, fortalte for Børn* (Tales, Told for Children) in 1835–1848. As a case in point, Anderson's widely read tale "Kejserens nye Klæder" (The Emperor's New Clothes)[1] "failed to catch the popular fancy."[2] Whether the tale was actually orally transmitted and consciously disregarded by collectors or whether storytellers avoided telling the tale to collectors because of their bias against texts from literature, Anderson's tale did not leave any major traces in documentations of oral tradition. A Lithuanian text recorded in Tilsit in 1868 constitutes a rare exception.[3]

> A king is so obsessed by his precious robes that he always looks for more delicate and more refined tissues. One day, a tailor in collusion with the courtiers intends to teach him a lesson. He presents a tissue to the king that is allegedly so fine that only people with extremely clear eyes are able to see it. Although, in fact, he presents nothing at all, the king pretends to see the fine tissue so as not to be exposed as having weak eyesight, as do the courtiers. When the dress is said to be ready, the king parades himself in town on horseback. All of the people are informed about the ruse and, consequently, praise the king's dress. Finally, a child exclaims, "But mother, the king is naked!" As the people break into laughter, the king is put to shame and goes to hide in his bed (where he might still be hiding today).

The short and straightforward Lithuanian text differs from Andersen's embellished tale in various details. Here, there is only one tailor, whereas Andersen mentions two rascals; the fine tissue is to be seen only by people with extremely clear eyes, whereas in Andersen's text it is stupid people for whom the tissue is said to be invisible; and while Andersen presents the plot as a conscious fraud staged by two swindlers who are after money, the Lithuanian text depicts a carefully designed pedagogical deceit in which all adults but the selfish and ignorant king are involved. Even so, the fact that the fraud is exposed by a child clearly betrays the Lithuanian text's relation to Andersen's famous tale. After all, it was Andersen who (in addition to other modifications) introduced the child into the tale whose European tradition goes back more than five centuries. Andersen read the model he adapted for his tale in the fourth volume of Eduard von Bülow's *Novellenbuch* (1836). In this collection of "old tales" from various Romance languages, English, and German, the original tale from Spanish author Don Juan Manuel's *Conde Lucanor* (no. 32) is presented in German translation, titled "So ist der Lauf der Welt" (This Is the Way of the World).[4]

Don Juan Manuel (1282–1348) compiled his *Libro del Conde Lucanor* in 1335. In his version of the tale, three rascals (*burladores*) propose to a Moorish king to weave a tissue that only people of legitimate birth, that is, born in wedlock, would be able to see.[5] As the king is curious to find out about the status of his entourage, he agrees to the rascals' suggestion. When the rascals pretend to weave the tissue, the king sends several messengers to inform him about their progress. Although the messengers do not see anything, they are afraid that their (potentially) illegitimate birth might be exposed and praise the tissue to such an extent that the king prefers to pretend seeing it as well. Only when the king dresses his new robe and parades himself on his horse in town does the king's black groom "who has nothing to lose" speak out that the king is not wearing anything at all, and gradually all the other people agree.

A Portuguese retelling of Don Juan Manuel's version from oral tradition was recorded from the performance of Francisco Cascudo from Rio Grande do Norte in Brazil.[6] As a matter of fact, the text is likely informed by both Andersen and Don Juan Manuel, as it mentions people of illegitimate birth not being able to see the tissue (as in the *Conde Lucanor*) and a boy (*menino*) revealing the truth (as in Andersen). Since Don Juan Manuel lived and wrote in the multicultural and cross-fertilized context of Muslim Spain, researchers frequently discussed the Arabic influence in his work, both in terms of language and content.[7] Even so, previous studies did not succeed in identifying the presumed Arabic precursor for the tale.[8] Even the "Oriental" origin of the tale that corresponds to tale type ATU 1620: *The Emperor's New Clothes* was challenged altogether.[9]

In terms of the tale type's historical development and dissemination, American folklorist Archer Taylor identified two strands of tradition.[10] The earliest strand of tradition, attested since the German author Der Stricker's *Pfaffe Âmîs*, compiled prior to 1236, speaks of a fraud who pretends to paint an image that only people of legitimate birth would be able to see. The second strand of tradition, in which the rascals pretend to weave a special tissue, is first attested in European tradition in the *Conde Lucanor.*

The single motif of a thread that is so fine as to be invisible already appears in the Buddhist *Avadanas* in a short tale in which a spinner presents an invisible thread to a fool who thinks that the thread is "too fine to be seen even by the best workmen."[11] A full-fledged narrative elaboration of the primitive motif documented in the *Avadanas* dates from the beginning of the eleventh century. It is contained in *Līlāvatī-Sāra* (The Epitome of Queen Līlāvatī), composed by the Jain scholar-monk Jinaratna in 1285. Jinaratna's work is a Sanskrit abridgement of the lost Prakrit novel *Nivvāṇa-Līlāvaī-Kahā* (The Story of the Final Emancipation of Līlāvatī), written in 1036 by Jineśvara.[12] Essentially presenting the same plot as in the *Conde Lucanor,* the Indian tale introduces the merchant-banker Dhana as an exemplification of fraud and theft.[13] At the tale's beginning, Dhana is arrested and banished for making counterfeit coins. In another kingdom he then pretends that he can weave a divine garment that "could be neither seen nor touched by anyone whose birth was illegitimate." Generously paid and equipped with everything he requests, Dhana pretends to produce the garment and deludes all of the king's trusted men as well as the king himself. When the king finally puts the dress on, he sees himself "as he was born," but the vassals admire his dress. As the king parades around "resplendent under his sunshade and attended by the court," the citizens, who do not partake in the delusion, shout loudly wondering whether that naked ascetic is their king. The king realizes that he was duped, but the rogue already escaped. The tale continues with Dhana's flight and further deceitful actions, following which he is killed and reborn several times without changing his evil character.

A Middle Eastern version of the tale is contained in the Ottoman Turkish *Qırq vezīr* (The Forty Viziers), an adapted and enlarged version of the Persian *Sendbād-nāme* (The Book of Sendbād [the Sage]). Here, an old man promises to the king to "weave a turban such that one born in wedlock will see it, while the bastard will see it not."[14] When the king is unable to see the turban, he doubts his own legitimacy and consults his viziers. As the viziers are also unable to see the turban, they agree in the end that the tissue does not exist at all and that the "weaver had thus played a trick for the sake of money." An adequate interpretation of the historical position of the text in *The Forty Viziers* must address various problems. First, the Turkish work presents itself as translated from an Arabic book, now lost, titled *Arbaʿīn ṣabāḥ wa-masāʾ* (Forty Nights and Days). This attribution likely constitutes a mystification,[15] probably intended to authenticate the Ottoman Turkish compilation. Second, although the Turkish work might originally have been compiled as early as the fourteenth century, and thus more or less contemporary with the *Conde Lucanor,* its earliest dated manuscript is from the year 1446. And third, the number and content of the tales embedded in the Turkish work's numerous manuscripts differ, so that one cannot be sure that the specific tale under consideration was already included in the earliest manuscripts. The collection's text published by Elias J.W. Gibb is encountered in a manuscript dating from the year 1600. At any rate, the tale's version in *The Forty Viziers* is fairly old and might indicate the existence of an even older

Arabic version. Even so, Taylor argued that the "similarities of these Oriental tales do not permit any dogmatic assertions about their connections with [the] Western story. It is conceivable that Oriental tradition has given rise to the more elaborate Western forms, but such a derivation cannot be insisted on."[16] The tale from *The Forty Viziers* was adapted at the end of the nineteenth century by Turkish author Kaytazzade Mehmet Nazım.[17]

A Persian version of the tale is contained in the prose collection of tales titled *Javāher al-ʿoqul* (Jewels of Wisdom) that is conventionally regarded as the work of the influential Shiʿi scholar Moḥammad-Bāqer Majlesi (d. 1698).[18] The very same tale, cited in a conversation between a cat and a mouse (as in *Javāher al-ʿoqul*), was also attributed to the Shiʿi scholar Bahāʾ al-Dīn al-ʿĀmilī (d. 1621).[19] The tale is told in order to demonstrate that dervishes are not to be trusted, as they constantly try to ensnare gullible people.

> In the Eastern Iranian province of Khorasan, the young and handsome apprentice of a wandering dervish (*qalandar*) happens to meet the king who is out on a riding tour. The apprentice recites a short poem (*ghazal*) for the king and is richly rewarded. As the apprentice later informs his companions about the event, his master decides to recite a long poem (*qaṣide*) for the king so as to receive an even larger reward. When the dervish happens to meet the king, the latter is, however, in an extremely bad mood and orders the master to be executed. In order to save his life, the dervish asks the vizier to inform the king that he is capable of achieving tasks no other human being is able to achieve. In order to demonstrate his capacities, he promises to weave an imaginary turban (*mandil-e khiyāl*) that only people of legitimate birth would be able to see. Having aroused the king's curiosity, the dervish promises to weave the garment on condition that the king pays all expenses. The dervish receives both money for the necessary equipment and a large house outside the city to install his workshop. Given forty days respite to complete his task, the dervish trusts in God that he will eventually find a solution for his dilemma.
>
> After a while, the king wonders about the dervish's progress, and the vizier sends a messenger to inquire. The dervish indignantly informs the messenger that he needs time to achieve his extraordinary task. Then he invites him to have a look at the tissue he wove, praising its intricate design and brilliant colors. Although the messenger does not see anything, he commends the dervish on his achievement, fearing that otherwise his own potentially illegitimate birth might be exposed. Back in the palace, the messenger praises the (invisible) cloth to the vizier to such an extent that the vizier decides to go and look for himself.
>
> As the dervish displays the tissue, the vizier does not see anything. Fearing that his potentially illegitimate birth might be exposed, the vizier pretends to actually see the tissue and praises the dervish's achievement to the king. The scene is repeated with two more of the king's messengers.

Finally, after another three days of respite, the time has come for the dervish to present the tissue to the king.

When the dervish presents the tissue at court with great ado, the king first asks his viziers to describe what they see. Since all of the viziers praise the tissue abundantly, the king does not dare to admit that he does not see anything. Fearing that his suspicion might be true, the king accuses his mother of having had illegitimate sexual contacts, but his mother indignantly defends herself.

In order to find out what is happening, the king has the dervish meet him in private and threatens to have him executed if he does not tell the truth. The dervish informs the king about the chain of events, from his decision to recite poetry for the king to his strategem of proposing to weave the imaginary turban so as to escape being executed. Finishing his story, he appeals to the ruler's mercy.

The king is happy to learn that his suspicions are unfounded and decides to take revenge on the vizier. The next day happens to be an exceptionally cold winter day. The king summons the dervish and all of his viziers to court and donates the imaginary turban to the vizier, arguing that instead of wearing it himself, he would rather enjoy the beautiful tissue all the more by seeing the vizier wear it every day. Upon his orders, the dervish takes the vizier's turban and places the imaginary turban on his head. As the vizier with his bare head shivers from the cold, the king starts to laugh, and the vizier realizes that the king knows the truth. In the end, the king dismisses all of his viziers and awards the position of vizier to the dervish.

Historical evidence contradicts the assumption that the Persian tale served as a direct model for Andersen.[20] Even so, it presents a fascinating adaptation of the Indian tale. The Persian tale is cited again in the mid-nineteenth-century travelogue *Kanz al-mosāferin* (The Travelers' Treasure), compiled by a certain Ibn ʿAli Ashraf ibn ʿAli ʿAbd al-Vahhāb. This book was created in 1270/1853, and the tale's version included therein likely derives from the lithographed edition of the *Javāher al-ʿoqul* published just a few years earlier, in 1265/1848.[21]

The introductory passage of the Persian version is reminiscent of tale type ATU 503: *The Gifts of the Little People* (see essay **8, *The Two Hunchbacks***) in which supernatural beings reward a kind man and punish his envious imitator. First documented in Greek antiquity,[22] a tale with this structure is also known from medieval Arabic literature[23] and has remained popular in modern Arabic,[24] Persian,[25] and Turkish[26] folk-literature. The manner in which the dervish informs the king about the origin of his stratagem in great detail displays the "Oriental" manner of using direct narration instead of indirect speech, although this feature does not necessarily indicate a chronological priority to any of the other known versions. Both the tale's Ottoman Turkish and Persian versions connect to the *Conde Lucanor* in that the inability to perceive the tissue is taken as a sign of illegitimate birth. In the European versions, the king "when he has lied once, he finds himself forced to continue, even to the point of making a public appearance in a garment made of this wonderful cloth."[27] In contrast to this somewhat compulsive action, the king in the Middle Eastern versions is much wiser, as he refrains from any acknowledgment in public, instead seeking the advice of his viziers (as in the Ottoman version), or finding out the truth by himself (as in the Persian version). The European (and Indian) critique of the selfish ruler whose vanity does not prevent him from making a fool of himself thus contrasts with the "Oriental" portrayal of the wise ruler who might be tempted by rash behavior, superficial decisions, and vanity, but who in the end proves worthy of his position.

Although some missing links still remain to be identified, the tale's historical journey from eleventh-century India to fourteenth-century Spain can be traced with relative certainty. The tale's oldest-known version is contained in a work of Indian wisdom literature where it serves to exemplify the consequences of deceit. Separated from its original context, the tale was likely adapted first in Persian, and then in Ottoman Turkish compilations of an edifying and entertaining character. As all of the Middle Eastern versions presently known are attested later than the tale's earliest European versions, they probably derive from an as yet unknown representative of the widespread Middle Eastern literary genre "mirrors for princes" that might have served as an intermediary between the tale's Indian and European versions. Oral tradition is another possible intermediary, particularly since the Indian and early European versions display a similarly gullible ruler, whereas the king of the Middle Eastern tales is somewhat more cautious in trusting the rogue's pretension.

Notes

1. Andersen, Hans Christian, *Märchen und Geschichten*, vol. 1, ed. Gisela Perlet, Munich: Diederichs, 1996, pp. 95–100, no. 7.

2. Taylor, Archer, "The Emperor's New Clothes," *Modern Philology* 25 (1927–28), pp. 17–27, at 17.

3. Jurkschat, Christoph, *Litauische Märchen und Erzählungen*, Heidelberg: Winter, 1898, pp. 97–98, no. 44.

4. Bülow, Eduard von, *Novellenbuch; oder Hundert Novellen, nach alten italienischen, spanischen, französischen, lateinischen, englischen und deutschen bearbeitet*, vol. 4, Leipzig: F.A. Brockhaus, 1836, pp. 40–44, no. 3.

5. Don Juan Manuel, *Libro del Conde Lucanor*, ed. Reinaldo Ayerbe-Chaux, Madrid: Alhambra, 1983, pp. 310–324, no. 32; Chauvin, *Bibliographie*, vol. 2 (1897), p. 156, no. 32.

6. Cascudo, Luis da Câmara, *Contos tradicionais do Brasil: confrontos e notas*, 2nd ed., Bahia: Progresso, 1955, pp. 311–312.

7. See, e.g., Moral Molina, Celia del, "Huellas de la literatura árabe clásica en las literaturas europeas: vías de transmisión," in *Confluencia de culturas en el Mediterráneo*, ed.

Francisco A. Muñoz, Granada: Universidad de Granada, 1993, pp. 193–215; Lacarra, María Jesús, *Don Juan Manuel*, Madrid: Síntesis, 2006, pp. 63–67; Navarro, David, *Interacciones narrativas árabe, cristiana y judía: convivencia literaria en el Medievo peninsular*, Ph.D. thesis The University of Western Ontario, 2013, pp. 208–262, downloaded from http://ir.lib.uwo.ca/cgi/viewcontent.cgi?article=2444&context=etd (accessed August 21, 2016).

8. For *El conde Lucanor*, no. 21, for which there is ample evidence in previous Arabic (and Persian) tradition, see Lacarra, María Jesús, "El adoctrinamiento de los jóvenes en El conde Lucanor," *e-Spania* 21 (June 2015), http://e-spania.revues.org/24727 (accessed August 21, 2016).

9. The tale's most recent treatment by Moner, Michel, "Texto, corpus e hipertexto en la edición crítica de los textos literarios: el caso del ejemplo XXXII de *El Conde Lucanor*," in *Edición y literatura en España (siglos XVI y XVII)*, ed. Anne Cayuela, Zaragoza: Prensas Universitarias de Zaragoza, 2012, pp. 303–318, does not add anything substantial to the knowledge on the tale's possible sources.

10. Taylor, "The Emperor's New Clothes;" Uther, Hans-Jörg, "Kaisers neue Kleider," in *Enzyklopädie des Märchens*, vol. 7 (1993), cols. 852–857.

11. Taylor, "The Emperor's New Clothes," p. 25; quoting Julien, Stanislas, *The Avadanas*, vol. 1, Paris: Duprat, 1859, p. 150, no. 39, and Parker, Henry, *Village Folk-tales of Ceylon*, Dehiwala: Tisara Prakasakayo, 1914, p. 69.

12. Jinaratna, *The Epitome of Queen Līlāvatī*, vol. 1, ed. and transl. Richard C.C. Fynes, New York: New York University Press, 2005, pp. 15–24; Warder, Anthony Kennedy, *Indian Kāvya Literature*, vol. 6: *The Art of Storytelling*, Delhi: Motilal Banarsidass, 1992, pp. 261–262, nos. 4688–4689.

13. Jinaratna, *The Epitome of Queen Līlāvatī*, vol. 1, pp. 217–292, esp. pp. 237–243; Warder, *Indian Kāvya Literature*, vol. 6, pp. 267–270, nos. 4697–4699.

14. Taylor, "The Emperor's New Clothes," p. 23; quoting Sheykh-Zāda, *The History of the Forty Vezirs*, transl. E.J.W. Gibb, London: George Redway, 1886, pp. 148–149; Behrnauer, Walter Friedrich Adolf, *Die vierzig Veziere oder weisen Meister: ein altmorgenländischer Sittenroman*, Leipzig: Teubner, 1851, pp. 155–150; see Chauvin, *Bibliographie*, vol. 8 (1904), p. 130, no. 120.

15. Tezcan, Semih, "Vierzig Wesire," in *Enzyklopädie des Märchens*, vol. 14 (2014), cols. 195–200.

16. Taylor, "The Emperor's New Clothes," p. 26.

17. Yıkık, Ahmet, "A Protagonist in Cyprus' Tanzimat Literature: Kaytazzade Mehmet Nazım," in *Press and Mass Communication in the Middle East: Festschrift for Martin Strohmaier*, ed. Börte Sagaster, Theoharis Stavrides, and Birgitt Hoffmann, Bamberg: University of Bamberg Press, 2017, pp. 151–168, at pp. 156–158.

18. Pseudo-Majlesi, *Javāher al-ʿoqul*, Lithograph Tehran 1265/1848, fol. 48b–50a.

19. Ẕol-Faqāri, Ḥasan, "Andersen va mandil-e khiyāl," *Farhang-e mardom* 13 (1384/2005), pp. 50–54.

20. Ibid.

21. Ṣafā, Navvāb, "Amir-Qoli Amini va farhang-e ʿavāmm," *Kelk* 53 (1373/1994), pp. 223–234, at 232–234.

22. Hansen, William, *Ariadne's Thread: A Guide to International Tales Found in Classical Literature*, Ithaca and London: Cornell University Press, 2002, pp. 147–151.

23. Bolte and Polívka, *Anmerkungen*, vol. 3, pp. 328–329.
24. El-Shamy, *Types*, p. 253, no. 0503.
25. Marzolph, *Typologie*, pp. 103–103, no. 503.
26. Eberhard and Boratav, *Typen*, pp. 136–137, no. 118.
27. Taylor, "The Emperor's New Clothes," p. 24.

CHAPTER 79

The Lowly Man Posing as Soothsayer (ATU 1641)

As in tale type ATU 1641B: *Physician in Spite of Himself* (see essay **80, *The Miracle Cure***), the presently concerned jocular narrative features a man from the lower strata of society, often a farmer or a peasant, who poses as a learned man of extraordinary capacities. But while in the tale of "The Miracle Cure" he acts as a sham physician, the man's acquired role here is that of a clairvoyant, soothsayer, or astrologer who is able to find or find out about hidden things. Classified as tale type ATU 1641: *Doctor Know-All*, several hundred versions recorded from oral tradition all over Asia, Europe, and the Americas attest to the present tale's international popularity.[1] The selective survey below serves to demonstrate the tale's variability, as well as its wide geographical distribution in Western tradition, including Spanish, Portuguese, English, and French versions in the Americas that likely derive from European tradition. Not all texts contain the full range of potentially included motifs, whereas some include rarely used motifs that may or may not document the existence of regional oicotypes.

The Icelandic collector Páll Pálsson wrote down the tale of "The Omniscient Peasant Lad" from the oral narration of the "old woman" Guðriður Eyolfsdóttir in 1863/64.[2]

> The peasant lad Kresent, whom his parents call Kres, falls in love with Princess Ingibjörk. To his host in the city, Kres explains his shyness as connected to his profession as an omniscient soothsayer. Learning about his alleged capacities, the king asks him to divine whether the queen will give birth to a boy or a girl. As he does not know what to say, he responds that at times he appears to see a boy, and at others a girl. When the queen gives birth to twins, a boy and a girl, he is greatly honored.
>
> When the king asks him to guess the name of a rare dish presented, he laments his helplessness by mentioning his given name, Kres, that incidentally also happens to be the name of the dish.
>
> When a precious ring is stolen, the king demands, on pain of death, that he find it. Kres asks for three days' respite, during which he feasts

> sumptuously, as he imagines his life to be over. The three thieves spy on him one after the other on three consecutive days in order to find out whether he knows about their crime. As he counts the days with a loud voice one by one, they fear that they have been discovered and confess to him. Kres has them feed the ring to the king's best ox. The next day, he pretends to have divined who stole the ring and where it is hidden. When the king's ox is slaughtered, the ring is found, Kres is greatly honored, marries the princess, and is installed as the king's future successor.

This Icelandic version is somewhat unusual in that the item to be guessed is not an animal, as in most other versions, but a certain dish. Even so, the text contains the minimal set of standard motifs that are constitutive for the tale type. These motifs are as follows: (1) a man of lowly origins pretends to possess secret knowledge; (2) fearing their exposure, the thieves who stole a precious object confess to him so that the sham soothsayer can pretend having found the object by divination; and (3) lamenting his helplessness, he mentions his own given name that happens to be the name of the hidden animal (or object).

A Finnish tale begins with the cobbler Frog deciding to pose as a physician.[3] The cobbler's decision is motivated by the fact that the doctor in exchange for just a few minutes of examination requests from him to be paid with a pair of boots that took two people two weeks to make. As a physician, the cobbler mainly prescribes purgatives and nauseants. A wagoner whom he treated with a laxative happens to find the horses that were stolen from his master, and the sham physician is richly rewarded. Thieves who robbed the king's treasury confess to him. And when, finally, the cobbler laments his fate in his own name, Frog, the king thinks he correctly guessed the frog he hides. In a Latvian tale, a lazy boy builds up his mother's reputation as a soothsayer by first stealing and hiding an ox and then having his mother "divine" where to find it.[4] In the final scene of guessing, the king hides three eggs under the mother's seat in the coach. When the woman comments that she is seated as comfortably as a hen hatching her eggs, the king is convinced that she knows about the eggs. In a tale from Flemish tradition, the man's name is Cricket.[5] After a night of heavy drinking during which he spends all the money earned from selling the yarn his wife had spun, the man does not dare to go home. By chance, he learns about a prize the mistress of the castle advertised for the one who finds her precious ring. Fearing exposure, the thieves confess to him. The man feeds the ring to a turkey and later "divines" its whereabouts. The animal he is asked to guess is a cricket. The Polish tale told by Agnes Sekowski styles the cobbler Cricket as "doctor," because he always gives good advice to his people.[6] When the local lord looks for his horses, Cricket gives him a paper with scribblings that the lord takes to be a prescription. Having taken the laxative the pharmacist prepared for him, the lord happens to find his horses.

The plot of versions recorded in the Americas is equally consistent. A Mexican version collected by Virginia Rodríguez Rivera in 1951 was told by Manuel

Guevara, aged 50, who learned the tale in San Miguel Allende, Guanajuato, around 1925.[7] The tale begins with a poor drunkard posing as the soothsayer promising to find the king's stolen horse. As the man counts his three days' respite with a loud voice one after the other, the robbers fear exposure and confess. In a scatological extension, instead of having him guess a hidden animal, the king has a pot filled with excrement and then commands the soothsayer to tell its content. In his distress, the man finally says, "Oh, what a crock of shit!" When he should guess a buried sow, he is "completely disheartened" and cites a proverbial phrase that, incidentally, corresponds to the situation, "My God! This is where the sow turned up her tail and died!" Lew Beardson, whose Ozark version, originally heard in the 1890s, Vance Randolph recorded in 1938, "thought it might be a true story."[8] The protagonist's short name is Coon (for Coonrod), and he claims to have second sight. The text is told in a highly realistic style, embellished with local color and a lively atmosphere. One day, as Coon is bragging about his capacity, he gets "into an awful tight place up on Bull Creek," when a group of gamblers demands that he guess the animal hidden in a kettle. As Coonrad "couldn't do nothing but give up and hope for the best," he says, "Well, Mister Jeffers—it looks like you got old Coon this time." And, of course, the hidden animal is "a big old boar coon, with both front feet in a steel trap." The thieves who stole the ring of the princess, in a French folktale from Louisiana, confess to the old man posing as a wizard.[9] As the old man's name is Cricket, he happens to guess the animal caught in a box. A French Canadian version was told by David Ranger, aged 76, in 1980. The narrator learned the tale around 1919 from Jules Perreault, aged 40, on a building site.[10] The tale's hero who happens to find the king's lost diamond is the vagabond Cricket, who is always short of money.

The tale's European tradition goes back to late medieval literature.[11] The motif of guessing the cricket in the questioner's hand already appears in a novel by Italian writer Giovanni Sercambi (1348–1424).[12]

> Grillo is a poor worker in Cora Vecchia, a village in the vicinity of Siena, who makes a living by transporting bricks. When one day he notices the apparently easy way a lawyer gains his living, he decides to work as a lawyer himself, and takes the name of Ser Martino. When plaintiffs present their cases to him, he solves them by asking the advice of the experienced lawyer Cassesepete, sharing the revenue with him. The fame of Ser Martino's wisdom spreads far and wide, so that one day the prefect of Livorno invites him to participate in a scholarly debate concerning the dogmas of the Christian creed. Ser Martino participates in the debate by sign language only, leaving it to his opponent to interpret what he actually means to say. In the end his opponent acknowledges Ser Martino's superior wisdom. This episode corresponds to tale type ATU 924: *Discussion in Sign Language.* Having caught a cricket, the prefect one day wants to test Ser Martino's capacities and asks him what he holds in his hand. Not knowing

> what to say, the poor man thinks of his former name and laments the fact that Grillo (Cricket) has finally been caught. The prefect believes has divined the animal correctly and rewards him richly.

A more developed version that also includes the episodes of the miracle cure is presented in the Italian poem *Grillo medico* (Grillo the Physician), compiled by an unknown author at the beginning of the sixteenth century.[13] Here, the peasant as sham doctor makes the princess laugh by greasing her naked buttocks so that she coughs up the fishbone stuck in her throat. He makes the patients leave the hospital through his miracle cure. The thieves who stole his money confess, and by referring to his own name, he correctly guesses the cricket (*grillo*) in the king's hand. In the end, the laxative he applies helps a man recover his lost donkey. Popular versions that resulted in the tale's wide international dissemination include Sieur d'Ouville's early seventeenth-century prose jest *D'un devin feint* (Of a Sham Soothsayer)[14] and a tale in the Grimms' *Kinder- und Hausmärchen* (Children's and Household Tales), adapting an oral performance by Dorothea Viehmann.[15] The tale's oldest- known version is attested in ancient Indian literature, where Somadeva's eleventh-century *Kathāsaritsāgara* (The Ocean of Streams of Stories) contains the story of the poor and foolish Brahman Hariśarman.[16]

> Hariśarman is annoyed that his master does not give him the attention he thinks he deserves. Hiding one of his master's horses, he pretends to find it by divination the next day and is greatly honored. When the maid Jihvā (whose name means "tongue") and her brother steal gold and jewels from the king's treasury, Hariśarman is summoned to identify the thieves. When he curses his tongue (Sanskrit *jihvā*) for bringing him into these dire straits, the maid Jihvā overhears him. Fearing exposure, the maid confesses her crime. Hariśarman has the maid bury the treasure in the king's garden, pretends to discover it the next day, and is richly rewarded. Incited by the envious vizier, the king wants to test him and hides a frog in a pitcher. Hariśarman, whose childhood nickname was Frog, laments that "Frog" has now been caught. The king is convinced that he possesses secret knowledge and rewards him richly.

Although it appears unlikely that the Indian version should have been passed on to the European literatures of the Middle Ages without any intermediary, previous studies rarely considered versions from the Middle Eastern Muslim literatures.[17] The tale's earliest-known Arabic version is told in the anonymous collection of tales that for want of an existing title is known as *Kitāb al-Ḥikāyāt al-ʿajība wa-'l-akhbār al-gharība* (Book of Tales of the Marvelous and News of the Strange).[18] The collection's unique preserved manuscript apparently dates to the fourteenth century.

> The poor weaver Abū Dīsa in Baghdad, who is known as ʿUṣfūr (Sparrow), sees a Persian fortune-teller make a lot of money with apparently little

effort. When he tells this to his wife Jarrāda (Grasshopper), she makes him pose as a fortune-teller himself, although he does not even know how to read and write.

Having visited the public bath, the king's pregnant daughter has her maid ask him to divine the gender of her children. Pretending to possess secret knowledge, he tells the maid that the king's daughter will give birth to two children who will be born "neither on earth nor in the sky." Having climbed to a resting place on a tree, the king's daughter gives birth to both, a boy and a girl. As this corresponds to the fortune-teller's prediction, the princess intends to reward him generously. The fortune-teller, however, fears that he might be punished and hides in the oven. When is he is found by the king's messengers, he pretends to have been busy conjuring a charm for the queen of the demons. As they parade the fortune-teller on a mule, he acts so foolishly that the people make fun of him. When, however, the master of the king's stable falls from his mount and breaks his foot, he is sure that his misfortune results from his disrespect to the fortune-teller. The queen raises the man to the rank of her official fortune-teller.

When the king's treasury is robbed, none of the regular fortune-tellers and soothsayers have an idea how to identify the robbers. Summoned to the king's presence, the weaver promises to identify the robbers within a period of ten days. As the ten robbers fear to be exposed, they visit him one after the other on consecutive days. Sitting in front of his house, the weaver makes a remark each time that leads the robbers to assume that he identified them. Finally, they decide to return the stolen treasure, adding a certain amount so as to convince the fortune-teller not to expose them. The fortune-teller has the robbers bury the money in a certain place. The next day, he tells the king where to find the money and is again richly rewarded. In addition to his reward, he requests that the king punish the other fortune-tellers who made fun of him.

Some days later the king forgets a precious ring at the side of a water basin, and the ring is swallowed by a lame duck. A servant notices the scene and decides to slaughter the duck and take the ring for himself, eventually. When the weaver is summoned to the king, he pretends to know everything so that the servant confesses to him where to find the ring. Although the king loves the lame duck dearly, the fortune-teller has him slaughter it, and the ring is found in the duck's crop. The fortune-teller is richly rewarded and again requests the other fortune-tellers be punished.

In order to test the capacities of his fortune-tellers, the king hides a sparrow and a grasshopper under his dress. Not a single one of the king's regular fortune-tellers succeeds in divining what the king is hiding. Lamenting his bad luck, the weaver exclaims that had it not been for Grasshopper (his wife), Sparrow (he himself) would not have been caught in the trap.

> Once more he is richly rewarded and requests the other fortune-tellers be punished.
>
> Similar to Sercambi's version, the Arabic tale continues with a discussion in sign language corresponding to tale type ATU 924. It finishes with a version of tale type ATU 1556: *The Double Pension (Burial Money)*, originally an independent anecdote that is first attested in tenth-century Arabic literature (see also essay **58, *The Subaltern Is Made Lord for a Day***).[19]

In particular the overlapping use of the name "Grasshopper," here applied to the protagonist's wife, and the sham soothsayer's name Grillo in the tale's early Italian versions, is tempting evidence to regard the fourteenth-century Arabic tale as a suitable intermediary between the ancient Indian and the medieval European versions. Numerous similar namings were recorded from nineteenth- and twentieth-century oral tradition in the Arab world.[20]

Although no Persian versions of the tale contemporary with or predating the Arabic text have so far been identified, a seventeenth-century Persian text suggests that Persian literature might have served as a further intermediary between the tale's Indian and Arabic versions. This Persian text is contained in the seventeenth-century prose collection of tales titled *Javāher al-ʿoqul* (Jewels of Wisdom) that is conventionally attributed to the influential Shiʿi scholar Moḥammad-Bāqer Majlesi (d. 1698). Framed by a learned debate between a cat and a mouse, the collection embeds numerous narratives that later gained the status of popular tales, such as the present one.[21]

> Visiting the public bath, the wife of a poor man is humiliated by the wife of the ruler's official fortune-teller. Returning home, the poor man's wife insists that her husband become a fortune-teller, although he does not even know how to read. The poor man buys the necessary equipment and places himself in front of the public bath.
>
> When the vizier's wife visits the bath, her maid hides her mistress's precious ring in a small hole in the wall and conceals it with some hair. When leaving, the maid forgot where she hid the ring and turns to the sham fortune-teller for help. As she squats before him, her torn underwear reveals her vulva (mentioned with the euphemism *dar-e ghār-e Afrāsiyāb* = the entrance to Afrāsiyāb's cave). Since the fortune-teller has no other idea, the view inspires him to suggest that she must have hidden the ring in a hole covered by some hair. Immediately, the maid remembers where she hid the ring, and her mistress rewards the fortune-teller.
>
> When a precious jewel from the king's treasury gets lost, the official fortune-teller is unable to find it. They ask the poor man, who pretends to know everything but asks for two days respite. In the meantime, the Georgian maid who stole the jewel confesses to him in secret, asking him not to expose her. The sham fortune-teller has the maid feed the jewel to a white goose that lives in the king's private quarters. The next day, he

has every living being in the private quarters presented to him and takes great pleasure in adoring the beautiful maids at court. Asking for all the animals to also be presented to him, he finally "divines" that the jewel is to be found in the stomach of the white goose. When the jewel is actually found, the king promotes him to the position of official fortune-teller, and his fame spreads.

When the king goes out hunting, the new fortune-teller has to accompany him. In order to test his capacity of clairvoyance, the king catches a grasshopper and asks the fortune-teller what he holds in his hand. Not knowing what to say, the fortune-teller quotes the popular saying, "One time you escaped, grasshopper; the second time you escaped, grasshopper; but the third time you got caught in the trap, grasshopper!" Thinking that the man divined what he held in his hand, the king rewards him richly.

As he is afraid that his luck will run out, the sham fortune-teller decides to feign madness. As the king rests in the public bath one day, the fortune-teller runs to the building stark naked and pulls the king out of the room. No sooner has he done so than the roof collapses. He justifies his strange action by pretending to have divined what would happen, and is again richly rewarded. This episode corresponds to the second and final episode of tale type ATU 1646: *The Lucky Blow.*

John Malcolm's *Sketches of Persia*, originally published in 1828, documents the tale to have been part and parcel of the professional storyteller's stock of tales at the beginning of the nineteenth century.[22] Malcolm narrates how their party was travelling in Northwestern Iran, from Lake Urmia to the town of Maragha, at night. When their leader asked Mollā Ādine, the ruler's storyteller, "to beguile the weariness of the road with a tale," the storyteller at first asked about the distance of travel the tale was expected to cover. Although Malcolm "could not help laughing at this mode of measuring a tale, (. . . he) was assured it was a common custom, arising out of the calculation professed storytellers were compelled to make of the leisure of their hearers."[23] Mollā Ādine's narration was available to the brothers Grimm, as a selection of the tales inluded in Malcolm's travelogue had been published in German in 1829.[24]

At the beginning of the twentieth century, Arthur Christensen published the Persian version as performed by his Iranian language teacher Mollā Feyżollāh. Concurrent with contemporary scholarly custom, Christensen in his translation obscured the sexually explicit passages (in which the fortune-teller cannot avoid but look at the maid's *surākh-e makhṣuṣ*, or "special hole") in Latin.[25] Several versions of the tale were recorded from late nineteenth- and early twentieth-century Persian as well as Turkish oral tradition.[26]

The tale's Persian versions often add the final episode in which the fortune-teller attempts to rid himself of his new obligation by feigning madness, by happenstance saving the ruler's life. This episode might have reminded members of an educated audience of a short jocular tale that is first attested in Iranian author al-Rāghib al-Iṣfahānī's Arabic-language compilation *Muḥāḍarāt al-udabā'* (Conversations of the Educated).[27] The jocular tale introduces the soothsayer (*munajjim*) Naybakht (whose name identifies him as an Iranian) as an intimate companion of the Abbasid Caliph al-Manṣūr (r. 754–775). One day, as the caliph is on the toilet (*al-mustarāḥ*), the soothsayer requests that he get out of there immediately. No sooner has the caliph left the toilet than the roof incidentally collapses. The anecdote is also contained in the work's seventeenth-century Persian translation, where the soothsayer's name is given as Nowbakht.[28]

Notes

1. Dömötör, Ákos, "Doktor Allwissend," in *Enzyklopädie des Märchens*, vol. 3 (1981), cols. 734–742.

2. Rittershaus, Adeline, *Die neuisländischen Volksmärchen*, Halle: Niemeyer, 1902, pp. 408–413, no. 116.

3. Simonsuuri, Lauri, and Pirkko-Liisa Rausmaa, *Finnische Volkserzählungen*, Berlin: De Gruyter, 1968, pp. 152–153, no. 129.

4. Böhm, Max, and Franz Specht, *Lettische Schwänke und verwandte Volksüberlieferungen*, Reval: Kluge, 1911, pp. 73–76, no. 43.

5. Goyert, Georg, *Vlämische Märchen*, Jena: Diederichs, 1925, pp. 37–40; quoted from De Mont, Pol, and Alfons De Cock, *Zo vertellen de Vlamingen*, Gand 1903, pp. 109ff.

6. Coleman, Moore Marion, *A World Remembered: Tales and Lore of the Polish Land*, Cheshire: Cherry Hill Books, 1965, pp. 107–109.

7. Paredes, Américo, *Folktales of Mexico*, Chicago: University of Chicago Press, 1970, pp. 161–162, no. 57.

8. Randolph, Vance, *The Devil's Pretty Daughter and Other Ozark Folk Tales*, New York: Columbia University Press, 1955, pp. 133–135, 216 (quote). For other versions of this "best known of all Old Marster stories" see Dorson, Richard M., *Negro Folktales in Michigan*, Cambridge: Harvard University Press, 1956, pp. 51–53, 209 (quote); Dorson, *Negro Tales from Pine Bluff*, Bloomington: Indiana University Press, 1958, pp. 172–173, no. 11; Dance, Deryl Cumber, *Shuckin' and Jivin': Folklore from Contemporary Black Americans*, Bloomington: Indiana University Press, 1978, pp. 204, 369, no. 362.

9. Fortier, Alcée, *Louisiana Folk-Tales in French Dialect and English Translation*, Boston and New York: Stechert, 1895, p. 116, no. 9.

10. Lemieux, Germain, *Les vieux m'ont conté*, vol. 16, Montréal: Bellarmin, 1981, pp. 118–123, no. 9.

11. For the historical survey, see Clouston, William Alexander, "The Lucky Impostor," in Clouston, *Popular Tales and Fictions: Their Migrations and Transformations*, ed. Christine Goldberg, Santa Barbara, CA: ABC-Clio, 2002, pp. 512–521; Bolte and Polívka, *Anmerkungen*, vol. 2, pp. 401–413, no. 98; Tubach, *Index exemplorum*, p. 106, no. 1323.

12. Sercambi, Giovanni, *Il novellieri*, ed. Luciano Rossi, Rome: Salerno, 1972, vol. 1, pp. 118–125, no. 15.

13. Ulrich, Giacomo, ed., *Opera nuova e da ridere: Grillo medico: poemetto populare di autore ignoto*, Livorno: Raffaelo Giusto, 1901; Ulrich, Jakob, *Volkstümliche Dichtungen der Italiener*, Leipzig: Dt. Verl., 1906, pp. 42–63, no. 4; Keller, Walter, *Italienische Märchen*, Jena: Diederichs, 1929, pp. 95–107, no. 16.

14. D'Ovville, Sievr, *Les contes avx hevres perdves, ou le recviel de tovs les bons mots, reparties, eqvivoques [. . .] & avtres contes facécieux, non encores imprimez*, Paris: Toussaingt Qvinet, 1643, pp. 300–312.

15. Bolte and Polívka, *Anmerkungen*, vol. 2, pp. 401–413, no. 98; Grimm, Jacob and Wilhelm, *Kinder- und Hausmärchen: Ausgabe letzter Hand*, vol. 3, ed. Heinz Rölleke, Stuttgart: Philipp Reclam Jun., 1980, p. 484.

16. Somadeva, *The Ocean of Story: Being C.H. Tawney's Translation of Somadeva's Kathā Sarit Sāgara*, ed. N.M. Penzer, reprint Delhi: Motilal Banarsidass, 1968, vol. 3, pp. 70–74, no. 39a; see also Zachariae, Theodor, "Zum Doktor Allwissend," in *Kleine Schriften: zur indischen Philologie, zur vergleichenden Literaturgeschichte, zur vergleichenden Volkskunde*, Bonn and Leipzig: Kurt Schroeder, pp. 138–145.

17. A rare exception is Christensen, Arthur, *Contes persans en langue populaire*, Copenhagen: Det Kgl. Danske Videnskabernes Selskab, 1918, pp. 54–56 (Persian original), 123–127 (English translation and commentary, no. 52).

18. *Tales of the Marvellous and News of the Strange*, transl. Malcolm C. Lyons, London: Penguin, 2014, 207–225, no. 9.

19. Marzolph, *Arabia ridens*, vol. 2, p. 106–107, no. 427; Marzolph, Ulrich, "The Tale of the Sleeper Awakened," in Chraïbi, Aboubakr, ed., *Arabic Manuscripts of the* Thousand and One Nights, Paris: espaces & signes, 2016, pp. 261–291, at pp. 289–291.

20. El-Shamy, *Types*, pp. 886–888, no. 1641 (59 versions).

21. Pseudo-Majlesi, *Javāher al-ʿoqul*, Lithograph Tehran 1265/1848, fol. 44b–46b.

22. Malcolm, John, *Sketches of Persia*, London: Murray, 1845, pp. 253–272 (ch. 20). A summary of the tale is given by William Alexander Clouston in his "Variants and Analogues of Some of the Tales in the Supplemental Nights," in Burton, *Arabian Nights*, vol. 12, pp. 291–383, at pp. 341–343.

23. Malcolm, *Sketches of Persia*, p. 253.

24. Grimm, *Kinder- und Hausmärchen*, vol. 3, ed. Rölleke, p. 179 [191], no. 98. The reference is to "Kisseh-Khun," that is, Malcolm, John, *Kisseh-Khūn: der persische Erzähler*, Berlin: Nicolai'sche Buchhandlung, 1829, p. 44.

25. Christensen, *Contes persans*, p. 124.

26. Marzolph, *Typologie*, pp. 233–235, no. 1641 (25 versions); Eberhard and Boratav, *Typen*, pp. 349–350, no. 311 (19 versions).

27. Rāghib al-Iṣfahānī, al-Ḥusayn ibn Muḥammad al-, *Muḥāḍarāt al-udabāʾ wa-muḥāwarāt al-shuʿarāʾ wa-'l-bulaghāʾ*, Beirut 1961, vol. 1, p. 146; Marzolph, *Arabia ridens*, vol. 2, p. 232, no. 1049.

28. Rāgheb Eṣfahāni, *Navāder: tarjome-ye ketāb-e Moḥāżarāt al-odabāʾ [. . .]*, transl. Moḥammad Ṣāleḥ Qazvini, ed. Aḥmad Mojāhed, Tehran: Sorush 1371/1992, p. 34.

CHAPTER 80

The Miracle Cure (ATU 1641B)

Eulenspiegel is Germany's traditional prankster.[1] Popularized in innumerable publications since the beginning of the sixteenth century, many of his pranks were over the centuries retold in oral tradition. In literature often presented in a chronological sequence corresponding to the stages of Eulenspiegel's life, many of the pranks attributed to Eulenspiegel were also told individually. The tale of Eulenspiegel's miracle cure appears to have been popular in German tradition at least until the beginning of the twentieth century.[2] The Bohemian narrator Josef Salter originally heard the tale he performed orally in 1952 in the local pub.[3]

> There was a hospital that was overcrowded. Eulenspiegel came by. The senior physician said that he had too many sick people. Eulenspiegel said that he would cure them all. He went into all of the rooms and said to everyone that the sickest person would be slaughtered and burned, and that the others would have to eat the ashes. The next day Eulenspiegel went to the hospital together with the professor. Eulenspiegel said, "Whoever is well should leave." All of them quickly left the hospital. The professor gave much money to Eulenspiegel, and Eulenspiegel left. The next day, all the sick people returned.

Introduced by the tale of the cobbler who boasts having killed seventeen (flies) with a single blow (corresponding to the international tale type ATU 1640: *The Brave Tailor*), a narrative recorded by Bertha Kößler-Ilg in early twentieth-century Malta has the king request the hero on pain of death to cure the hospital's thousand inhabitants.[4] The hero proposes a similar miracle cure as Eulenspiegel's in that one of the oldest patients is to be thrown into a kettle of sizzling hot oil so as to prepare an ointment to heal all the other ones. A tale documented from oral tradition in the Croatian region of Slavonia at the beginning of the twentieth century likewise has the hero propose to prepare an ointment by boiling the fattest patient in a kettle.[5] Both of these versions additionally mention the hero curing the princess. In the Maltese tale, the hero tickles her throat with a feather so that by laughing she coughs up a fishbone that was stuck in her throat. In the Slavonian tale, the hero cures a large ulcer by exposing the princess for three days to the fumes of herbs he boils in a kettle. The latter text is, moreover, introduced by the wife taking revenge on her husband for a beating he gave her by pretending to the king's messengers that the husband is a famous physician. A French tale, told in 1887 by Marie Briffault, aged 37, a farmer's wife at Montigny-aux-Amognes (Nivernais), presents an even more elaborate version.[6] Here, the hero is introduced as an old man who has the habit of beating his young and flirtatious wife. In order to rid herself of her rude husband, the woman pretends to the king's messengers that he is a famous physician who will, however, deny his capacities until given a heavy beating. Finding the man at work in his vineyard, the messengers convince the man to come with them so as to cure the princess in whose throat a big fishbone got stuck. Requesting to be left alone with the princess, the man starts to dance "with his big wooden shoes and his cotton bonnet," producing such a ridiculous sight that the princess bursts into laughter and coughs up the fishbone. This is followed by the episode of the miracle cure in which the man proposes to throw the sickest patient into a large bonfire. The tale concludes with the man's return to his village and the couple's reconciliation. A closely similar dialect version was performed by Barbara Zehetner in Waldneukirchen, Austria, in the summer of 1912; the narrator reported having heard the tale from the farmhand Leopold Hammer.[7] In a French Canadian version recorded in 1960, the farmer's wife wants to get rid of her husband and recommends him to the king as a competent physician when a bone gets stuck in the throat of the princess.[8] As the poor farmer does not know how to cure the princess, he has her swallow a pill he molds from the grease between his dirty toes. Informed about the nature of the pill, the princess is so disgusted that she throws up, clearing the bone from her throat. In the hospital, the farmer advises the incurable patients be burned so as to use their ashes to cure the other patients. This version was told by Charles Allain, aged 72, who had heard it around 1915 from Aimé Essiambe, aged 30 to 35, from New Brunswick.

All of the above-quoted tales ultimately derive from a variety of thirteenth-century sources, the earliest and best studied of which is probably the French *fablel* titled *Le vilain mire* (The Peasant as Physician),[9] a jocular narrative that served as an inspiration for Molière's comedy *Le médécin malgré lui* (The Physician in Spite of Himself; 1666).[10] Carl Zipperling, who studied the *fablel*, particularly as to its origins, its corresponding versions, and its impact on later tradition, identified four constitutive motifs: (1) A woman pretends that her husband is a capable physician; (2) the sham physician happens to cure the princess by provoking her to laugh; (3) he "cures" a large number of sick people by frightening them to such a degree that all of them declare themselves to be well; and (4) he manages to save himself before being exposed.[11] Zipperling discussed ancient Indian analogues to motifs (1) and (2) in great detail, but he never so much as considered Middle Eastern Muslim tradition as a possible intermediary for any of the motifs.[12] Although *Le vilain mire* and corresponding tales are classified as international tale type ATU 1641B: *Physician in Spite of Himself*, the miracle cure (classified by Stith Thompson as Mot. K1955.1: *Sham physician cures people by threatening them with death*) is not included in the tale type's description in the third revision of the international tale-type index.

Historically, the third motif identified by Zipperling, the miracle cure, is also documented in at least two works that are known to reflect Arabic sources.[13] The jocular tales compiled by the papal secretary Poggio Bracciolini around the middle of the fifteenth century root the narrative in history by relating it to the hospital of the cardinal of Bari (probably Landolfo Maramaldo, d. 1415) in the French town of Verceil.[14] One of the cardinal's employees, a certain Petrillo, is said to have driven away the hospital's numerous unprofitable patients through his proposal to prepare a healing ointment by boiling one of them. The early thirteenth-century version contained in Jacques de Vitry's *Sermones vulgares* most probably constitutes the link between the European versions and the tale's previous occurrence in Arabic tradition.[15] Introduced by a somewhat formulaic *audivi*, or "I have heard told," Jacques de Vitry presents his version as linked to an unspecified religious context, whether Christian, Muslim, or Jewish. The tale introduces a large number of sick people gathering at the grave of an unnamed saint where they hope to be cured from their ailments. When the mass of sick people disturb the service, the priest gets rid of them by proposing to burn the sickest patient and use the ashes to cure the others.

The tale's earliest documented version is attested in Arab author Ibn al-Jawzī's (d. 1201) *Akhbār al-Adhkiyā'* (Tales of Clever People).[16] Ibn al-Jawzī's version is presented as told by his contemporary, the grammarian (*al-naḥwī*) Abū Muḥammad al-Khashshāb (d. 1172):

> The tale's protagonist is a weaver, the members of whose profession are traditionally regarded as stupid. When the weaver notices that a physician is well paid for the apparently small effort of prescribing herbal tea or other cures, he is confident that he himself will also be able to practice that profession. Although his wife warns him of the consequences, he starts to prescribe drugs, making a lot of money in a short while. The next day, he is called to treat a certain upper-class woman. It so happens that the lady's affliction is just over, and when the sham doctor has her eat roast chicken, she quickly regains her strength. Soon after, he is summoned to the sultan and incidentally happens to prescribe a helpful medicine.
>
> The weaver's new career soon gives rise to doubt and envy from the side of the people who have long known him. When the sultan does not accept the people's argument that the alleged doctor is only an ignorant weaver, they suggest testing him with a scientific debate. The weaver, however, cleverly argues that only specialists would be able to make sense of his responses, and so a debate with a lay audience would make little sense.

> Instead, he proposes to prove his expertise by curing the long-term, that is, uncurable, patients in the city's hospital.
>
> The weaver enters the hospital only in the company of the warden, requesting that the warden must not disclose to anybody whatever the weaver would do. Then he pours oil into a large pot and heats it, informing the patients that they can only be healed by placing themselves in the boiling oil. In order to escape from the lethal treatment, one after the other the patients confess to feeling well or having been cured, and as they leave the hospital, they report the miracle cure to the people outside.

Although Ibn al-Jawzī's tale has a different beginning, there is a clear correspondence with the tale's European version in both the initial motif of the sham physician and the final motif of the miracle cure. As always, minor divergences should not serve as serious arguments to deny the priority of the Arabic text and the fact that it inspired the European versions, particularly since the sermons of Jacques de Vitry are known to constitute a powerful medium for the transmission of tales East to West.

In passing, it should be mentioned that the initial motif in versions of tale type ATU 1641B, of the sham physician who will only give his advice after having received a thorough beating, is also encountered in Arab tradition, albeit in a comparatively late source. The *Fākihat al-khulafā'* (The Fruits of the Caliphs), compiled by Ibn 'Arabshāh (d. 1450), contains the story of another weaver whom his wife presents as an astrologer who will only respond when beaten;[17] the tale's further plot develops differently.

The motif of the sham physician or rather the poor but clever man posing as a physician "in spite of himself" also occurs prominently in the widely known tale type ATU 1641: *Doctor Know-All* (see essay **79, *The Lowly Man Posing as a Soothsayer***). This tale is first documented in ancient Indian literature whence it was probably transmitted to European tradition by way of Persian and/or Arabic intermediaries that are, however, only documented since about the fourteenth century. Resulting from the common occurrence of the motif in both tales, "The Miracle Cure" and "Doctor Know-All," some texts, such as the Italian poem *Grillo medico*, compiled by an unknown author at the beginning of the sixteenth century,[18] continue the tale after "The Miracle Cure" with elements constitutive of "Doctor Know-All," in particular comprising the motif of guessing the grasshopper or cricket (Italian *grillo*) caught in the questioner's hand.[19]

All of the proposed procedures for the miracle cure correspond in that the sham physician threatens the patients with death. Either he threatens every single one of them, as in Ibn al-Jawzī's version, or he asks for a particular patient to be sacrificed for the welfare of all the other ones in order to prepare healing ashes or an ointment. Ibn al-Jawzī's version reads like a satirical echo of the "Fountain of Youth," a marvelous spring that makes bathers regain their youth, also documented in medieval European sources,[20] thus alluding to and subverting a popular notion. Notably the text of *Grillo medico* is close to Ibn al-Jawzī's Arabic version, although the sham physician here cynically pretends that the king gave orders to boil the patients one after the other with the ultimate goal of eating them. Giuseppe Pitrè recorded a nineteenth-century text closely corresponding to *Grillo medico*, narrated by Rosina Casini in Tuscany.[21]

Notes

1. Hucker, Bernd Ulrich, "Eulenspiegel," in *Enzyklopädie des Märchens*, vol. 4 (1984), cols. 538–555.

2. Fox, Nikolaus, *Saarländische Volkskunde*, Bonn: Klopp: 1927, p. 159; quoted in Debus, Oswald, *Till Eulenspiegel in der deutschen Volksüberlieferung*, (unpublished) Ph.D. dissertation Marburg 1951, p. 173, no. A 17.

3. Benzel, Ulrich, *Volkserzählungen aus dem nördlichen Böhmerwald*, Marburg: Elwert, 1957, p. 64, no. 231.

4. Ilg, Bertha, *Maltesische Märchen und Schwänke: aus dem Volksmunde gesammelt*, 2 vols., Leipzig: Schönfeld, 1906, vol. 1, pp. 113–115, no. 32.

5. Smičiklas, T[adija], "Narodne pripovijetke iz osječke okoline u Slavoniji," *Zbornik za narodni život i običaje Južnih Slavena* 15.2 (1910), pp. 279–305, at pp. 294–295, no. 6.

6. Delarue, Paul, *The Borzoi Book of French Folk Tales*, New York: Knopf, 1956, pp. 332–337, 400, no. 3.

7. Haller, Karl, "Der Arzt wider Willen, ein Volksmärchen aus Ober-Österreich," *Zeitschrift des Vereins für Volkskunde* 26 (1916), pp. 89–91 (with a comparative note by Johannes Bolte).

8. Lemieux, Germain, *Les vieux m'ont conté*, vol. 20, Montréal: Bellarmin, 1984, pp. 65–70, no. 7.

9. Christmann, Hans Helmut, ed., *Zwei altfranzösische Fablels (Auberee, Du Vilain mire)*, Tübingen: Max Niemeyer, 1968, pp. 16–18, 44–57; Noomen, Willem, and Nico van den Boogaard, eds., *Nouveau recueil complet des fabliaux (NRCF)*, vol. 2, Assen: Van Gorcum, 1984, pp. 311–347, 425–431, no. 13.

10. Van der Kooi, Jurjen, "Scharlatan," in *Enzyklopädie des Märchens*, vol. 11 (2004), cols. 1232–1237, at 1234–1236.

11. Zipperling, Carl, *Das altfranzösische Fablel Du Vilain Mire: kritischer Text mit Einleitung, Anmerkungen und Glossar*, Halle a.S.: Max Niemeyer, 1912, p. 6.

12. Ibid., pp. 50–55, reviews the documents for motif (3).

13. Ibid., 50–51, nos. 1 and 7; Marzolph, *Arabia ridens*, vol. 2, pp. 254–255, no. 1184.

14. Poggio Bracciolini, Gian-Francesco, *Die Schwänke und Schnurren*, ed. Alfred Semerau, Leipzig: Deutsche Verlags-Actiengesellschaft, 1905, p. 137, 228, no. 190.

15. Jacques de Vitry, *The Exempla or Illustrative Stories from the Sermones Vulgares*, ed. Thomas F. Crane, London: Nutt, 1890, p. 107, no. 254; Wesselski, *Mönchslatein*, pp. 118–119, 235, no. 99.

16. Ibn al-Jawzī, Abū 'l-Faraj ʿAbd al-Raḥmān ibn ʿAlī, *Akhbār al-Adhkiyā'*, ed. Muḥammad Mursī al-Khūlī, Cairo 1970, pp. 111–112; French translation and commentary in Basset, *Mille et un contes*, vol. 1, pp. 228–230, no. 95; German translation in Weisweiler, Max, *Von Kalifen, Spaßmachern und klugen Haremsdamen: Arabischer Humor*, Düsseldorf: Eugen Diederichs, 1963, pp. 202–205.

17. Chauvin, *Bibliographie*, vol. 2 (1897), p. 205, no. 62.

18. This is not to be confused with Girolamo Baruffaldi's (1675–1755) poem *Grillo*, discussed by Zipperling, *Das altfranzösische Fablel*, pp. 26–27.

19. Ulrich, Giacomo, ed., *Opera nuova e da ridere: Grillo medico: poemetto populare di autore ignoto*, Livorno: Raffaelo Giusto, 1901; Ulrich, Jakob, *Volkstümliche Dichtungen der Italiener*, Leipzig: Dt. Verl., 1906, pp. 42–63, no. 4; Keller, Walter, *Italienische Märchen*, Jena: Diederichs, 1929, pp. 95–107, no. 16.

20. Brednich, Rolf Wilhelm, "Verjüngung," in *Enzyklopädie des Märchens*, vol. 14 (2014), cols. 42–47, at 44–45.

21. Pitrè, Giuseppe, *Novelle popolari toscane*, Florence: G. Barbèra, 1885, pp. 283–288, no. 60; see also Zipperling, *Das altfranzösische Fablel*, pp. 27, 55.

CHAPTER 81

Who Stole?—The Thieves! (ATU 1641B*)

A short jocular tale published in the Romanian journal *Duminica Poporului* in 1929 tells how a clever trickster fools a credulous man by promising to reveal ostensibly special information available to him that, in the end, turns out to be as banal as it is obvious.[1]

> A man complains to the police that somebody stole some of his geese. The policeman promises to inform him who did it, given that the man pay him a round of drinks. When the man furnishes the drinks, the policeman tells him who stole the geese: the thieves!

Corresponding to tale type ATU 1641B*: *Who Stole from the Church*, the Romanian text is an exceptional regional documentation for a tale that is particularly richly attested from twentieth-century oral tradition in Spain. In the Spanish versions, the thieves or burglars stole items from the church. In the version narrated by Señorita de Ercilla, aged 70, in Astudilla, Panecia, on May 14, 1936, a clever fool (*un bobo*) has the people parade him through the village singing, "Tell me Juanillo, Juanillo, who has robbed the church," before he finally gives the banal information.[2] In a version from Montanar de Cerrato, Palencia, the village fool has long claimed to be a soothsayer, so when the church is robbed, the people turn to him for help.[3] In order to find the thief, the version told by José del Río Alonso, aged 80, and recorded by A. Lorenzo and P. Esteban in Valero, Salamanca, in August 1983, has the whole village summoned to confessional until a certain Periquito says that he knows who did it.[4] Numerous other versions from various Spanish regions more or less follow the same structure.[5] Spanish tradition also appears to have transmitted the tale to Argentina where it was published in a collection of children's folklore.[6] Although the tale's particularly rich documentation in Spanish tradition suggests the existence of an as yet unverified early version from the *siglo de oro*, the Golden Age of Spanish literature in the sixteenth and seventeenth centuries, it may at least partly derive from the tale's inclusion in a popular mid-nineteenth-century "complete" collection of all kinds of entertaining and funny tales.[7] In this version, however, the thieves steal from a rich farmer in La Mancha, and the trickster is a man from Andalusia, Spain's southernmost province, who lets himself be entertained for three full days before conveying the obvious information to his host in a mysterious atmosphere.

In Arabic literature, the tale is first attested in al-Ābī's (d. 1030) comprehensive encyclopedia of jokes and anecdotes, *Nathr al-durr* (Pearls of Prose).[8] In a form closely similar to the later Spanish versions, the tale is here attributed to the Wise Fool Buhlūl, a legendary character who is said to have lived during the reign of the Abbasid Caliph Hārūn al-Rashīd (r. 786–809).

> When Buhlūl passes through the bazar of the cloth merchants, he notices that the people gather at a shop whose door was forced open. Asking the people whether they know who did that, Buhlūl claims to know it. As the people imagine that Buhlūl might incidentally have seen the burglars during the night, they pressure him to tell them. But Buhlūl is hungry and demands to be fed first. Having a sumptuous meal consisting of four *raṭl* (pounds) of thin bread together with two sheep's heads, he insists on finishing with some sweets. Finally, he gets back to the shop and again asks the people whether they still cannot figure out who forced the door open. And when they confess to not having the slightest idea, he says, "This is undoubtedly the work of burglars!"

The tale is cited again in Ibn Ḥamdūn's (d. 1167) *al-Tadhkira* (The Aide-Mémoire) in almost identical wording.[9] The version given in Ibn al-Jawzī's (d. 1201) *Akhbār al-Ẓirāf* (Tales of Subtle People) shortens the description of Buhlūl's meal while otherwise repeating the same wording.[10] Al-Ābī's tale was adapted to Christian Syriac literature in the *Laughable Stories* authored by the learned historian Bar Hebraeus (d. 1286). As Bar Hebraeus wrote for a Christian audience whose familiarity with the character of Buhlūl must have been limited, he attributed the tale to an anonymous "lunatic."[11]

Although by referring to a church, the tale's modern Spanish versions localize the events in a distinctly Christian context, many of them expressly attributing the obvious remark to a person introduced as foolish, as in the Arabic versions. In both traditions, the fool, after all, is not as dumb as he might appear at first sight since he displays a remarkable talent to exploit the people's expectations for his own end. In this respect, the short tale's humor is not innocent at all, since the fool's wisdom reveals the people's credulity and thus unmasks the narcissistic hypocrisy of their social differentiation between the wise and the foolish. Although the Spanish versions were at times published in collections of "anticlerical" tales,[12] the tale's general message thus lends itself to a much wider, in fact a universal application.

Notes

1. Stroescu, *La typologie*, vol. 1, p. 684, no. 4170 (*Duminica Poporului*, 1929, nos. 23–24, p. 6).

2. Espinosa, Aurelio Macedonio., Jr., *Cuentos populares de Castilla y Leon*, vol. 2, Madrid: Consejo Superior de Investigaciones Científicas, 1988, pp. 234–235, no. 340.

3. Espinosa, Aurelio Macedonio, *Cuentos populares españoles recogidos de la tradición oral de España*, vol. 1, Madrid: Consejo Superior de Investigaciones Científicas, 1946, p. 98, no. 55; this version is classified in Boggs, Ralph S., *Index of Spanish Folktales*, Helsinki: Suomalainen Tiedeakatemia, 1930, p. 133–134, no. *1550B.

4. Lorenzo Vélez, Antonio, *Cuentos anticlericales de tradición oral*, Valladolid: Ámbito, 1997, pp. 130–132.

5. Rodríguez Pastor, Juan, *Cuentos extremeños obscenos y anticlericales*, Badajoz: Diputación de Badajoz, 2001, pp. 208–209 (narrated by Jesús Azañón del Prado, aged 40, Castilblanco, Badajoz, May 1992, recorded by Alberto Azañón Montero); Asiáin Ansorena, Alfredo, "Narraciones folklóricas navarras: recopilación, clasificación y análisis," *Cuadernos de Etnología y Etnografía de Navarra* 38.81 (2006), pp. 4–289, at pp. 197–198, no. 108 (narrated by Benedicto Martínez Abdigar "Bene" from Legaria); Agúndez García, José Luis, "Límites entre tradición oral y literatura: cuentecillos en autores del XIX y XX," in *El cuento folklórico en la literatura y en la tradición oral*, ed. Rafael Beltrán and Marta Haro, Valencia: University of Valencia, 2006, pp. 17–56, at p. 44; Noia Campos, Camiño, *Catálogo tipolóxico do conto galego de tradición oral: clasificación, antoloxía e bibliografía*, Vigo: University of Vigo, 2010, pp. 759–761, no. 1641B*; Hernández Fernández, Ángel, *Catálogo tipológico del cuento folclórico en Murcia*, Alcalá de Henares: University of Alcalá, 2011, p. 249, no. 1641B*; Atiénzar García, María del Carmen, *Cuentos populares de Chinchilla*, Ph.D. thesis, Universidad Nacional de Educación a Distancia, 2016, pp. 279–280, no. 131 (narrated by José Manuel Doménech Hinarejos).

6. Hansen, Terrence Leslie, *The Types of the Folktale in Cuba, Puerto Rico, the Dominican Republic, and Spanish South America*, Berkeley: University of California Press, 1957, p. 140, no. *1550 **E (referring to Aramburu, Julio, *El folklore de los niños*, Buenos Aires: El Ateneo, 1944, p. 145).

7. Boira, Rafael, *El libro de los cuentos: colección completa de anécdotas, cuentos, gracias, chistes[. . .]*, 2nd ed., Madrid: D. Miguel Arcas y Sanchez, 1862, vol. 2, p. 196.

8. Ābī, Abū Sa'd Manṣūr ibn al-Ḥusayn al-, *Nathr al-durr*, vol. 3, ed. Muḥammad 'Alī Qarna and 'Alī Muḥammad al-Bijāwī, Cairo: al-Hay'a al-miṣriyya al-'āmma lil-kitāb, 1984, p. 267; Marzolph, *Arabia ridens*, vol. 2, p. 185, no. 794; Marzolph, Ulrich, *Der Weise Narr Buhlūl*, Wiesbaden: Franz Steiner, 1983, p. 46, no. 69; Marzolph, *Bohlul-nāme*, ed. Bāqer Qorbāni-Zarrin, 3rd ed. Tehran: Behnegār, 1392/2013, pp. 132–133, no. 69.

9. Ibn Ḥamdūn, Muḥammad ibn al-Ḥasan ibn Muḥammad ibn 'Alī, *al-Tadhkira al-ḥamdūniyya*, ed. Iḥsān 'Abbās and Bakr 'Abbās, Beirut: Dār Ṣādir, vol. 8, 1996, p. 266, no. 768.

10. Ibn al-Jawzī, Abū 'l-Faraj 'Abd al-Raḥmān ibn 'Alī, *Akhbār al-Ẓirāf wa-'l-mutamājinīn*, ed. Muḥammad Baḥr al-'ulūm, 2nd ed., al-Najaf: al-Maktaba al-ḥaydariyya, 1386/1966, p. 81.

11 Bar-Hebraeus, Mâr Gregory John, *The Laughable Stories*, transl. E.A. Wallis Budge, London: Luzac and Co, 1897, p. 161–162, no. 644; see Marzolph, Ulrich, "Die Quelle der Ergötzlichen Erzählungen des Bar Hebräus," *Oriens Christianus* 69 (1985), pp. 81–125.

12. Lorenzo Vélez, *Cuentos anticlericales*, pp. 130–132; Rodríguez Pastor, *Cuentos extremeños*, pp. 208–209.

CHAPTER 82

The Dream of Finding One's Fortune Somewhere Else (ATU 1645)

The English legend "The Pedlar of Swaffham" is first recorded in the diary entry of the English antiquarian Abraham de la Pryme (1671–1704) dated November 10, 1699.[1]

> A poor man in Swaffham (Soffham, Sopham), later sometimes identified as a John Chapman, a pedlar by profession, dreams three nights in a row that he "should hear joyful news" if he goes to London. As he stands in London "on the great bridge" for three days waiting for something to happen, finally a man asks him why he was waiting there. When the pedlar tells the man about his dream, the other calls him a fool, as he himself has been dreaming that under a certain oak tree in a garden in Swaffham he would find a great treasure. Realizing that the mentioned garden is none other than his own, the pedlar travels back home, digs in his garden, finds the treasure, and grows exceedingly rich. Not forgetting "his duty in the pride of his riches," he rebuilds the church at Swaffham, "and when he died they put a statue of him therein all in stone with his pack at his back and his dog at his heels."

Still today, the legend is remembered in Swaffham, a small market town in the English county of Norfolk, where the pedlar is also commemorated with a town sign.[2] Meanwhile, Swaffham is just one of a number of places in England and several other European countries where the migratory legend, corresponding to tale type ATU 1645: *The Treasure at Home*, was localized.[3] European versions of the legend are mainly documented from oral tradition of the nineteenth and twentieth centuries. A rare version of European origin in the Americas was recorded in Spanish as narrated by Salvador González Quesada in Yahualica in the federal state of Jalisco, Mexico, on July 10, 1960.[4] Here, a "resident of Río Colorado near Yahualica dreams that a merchant in the town of Aguascalientes will reveal to him great wealth." The legend is particularly richly documented in nineteenth- and early twentieth-century German language collections, where its versions were localized in a great variety of places, such as—to name but the internationally best known—Berlin, Bremen, Dresden, Flensburg, Frankfurt, Hamburg, Hameln, Kassel, Magdeburg, Mainz, Mannheim, Munich, and Regensburg.[5]

In European tradition, the tale's genealogy ultimately goes back to its earliest-known rendition right at the beginning of the German *Karlmeinet*, a history of Charlemagne compiled soon after 1300.[6]

> A dwarf appears at midnight at the bedside of a certain Hoderich who lives in the village Balduch near Paris. Three nights in a row the dwarf urges Hoderich to go to a bridge in Paris where he will find both joy and sorrow. As Hoderich rests on the bridge, he is met by a money-changer who scolds him for foolishly following the dwarf's advice. The dwarf also appeared to the money-changer informing him that in the village of Balduch he would find a great treasure under a certain willow tree. The money-changer thinks it so foolish to follow the dwarf's advice that he slaps Hoderich in the face. Returning home, however, Hoderich and his brother Hanfrat (Haenfrait) dig up a leaden pot full of gold, silver, and jewels, and become exceedingly rich. In this manner, Hoderich found both sorrow and joy in Paris.

The version in the *Karlmeinet* is exceptional in that it is the only one in which, in terms of structure, the advice of the dwarf serves the same purpose as the dream in virtually all other known versions. Chronologically the next European version is a Latin text contained in the *Mensa philosophica*, an anonymous collection of table talk probably compiled in the late fourteenth or early fifteenth century.[7] Manuscript versions of the *Mensa philosophica* do not exist, and its earliest printed copy dates to the second half of the fifteenth century. This version is extremely short, comprising just under a hundred words.

> A peasant (*rusticus*) dreams that he would find a great sum of money (*magnam pecuniam*) on the bridge in the German city of Regensburg (*Ratispona*). Meeting another man on the bridge, the peasant tells him about his dream. The man slaps him and scolds him for foolishly following his dream, because he himself dreamt of finding a large treasure (*thesaurum magnum*) under a willow tree in a certain village. The peasant immediately recognizes the village to be his own, returns home, and digs up the treasure.

About half a dozen additional versions are known from German works of the sixteenth, seventeenth, and eighteenth centuries, some of them written in Latin, including one in Johannes Agricola's sixteenth-century collection of proverbs that was later incorporated into the German legends of the Grimm brothers.[8]

In most versions, the legend was ingeniously adapted to a specific local or regional context, leaving no trace of an extraneous origin. But two details of the earliest-known European version in the *Karlmeinet* clearly betray the fact that the legend ultimately derives from Middle Eastern, and more specifically Arabic, tradition. The first detail is the name Balduch that Victor Chauvin identified as a common medieval contortion of the name Baghdad, or Baldac in Marco Polo's (1254–1324) spelling.[9] The second is the mention of the "joy and sorrow" the dreamer would find. Whereas the "joy" is evident, the "sorrow" appears to be introduced somewhat artificially, as the dreamer receives a mere slap for foolishly believing his dream to be true. Since this trait is without consequence for the tale's further events, it rarely appears in the tale's later standard versions. However, the mention of "joy and sorrow" constitutes an unambiguous reference to, or maybe better a reflection of, the genre of Arabic literature from which the tale was most likely adapted.

The tale is first attested in Arabic author al-Muḥassin al-Tanūkhī's (d. 994) *al-Faraj baʿd al-shidda* (Relief after Hardship, or: Joy after Sorrow). This work is the major representative of a specific literary genre popular in Arabic and other Middle Eastern literatures.[10] The tales of Tanūkhī's extensive compilation structurally share the agenda advertised in the book's title in that their protagonists undergo a number of trials and tribulations before attaining final peace and happiness.[11] In the book's chapter on auspicious dreams and authenticated by a chain of transmitters mentioned by name, Tanūkhī tells the tale of a man in Baghdad who after having been poor for a long time suddenly became rich. Following this, the man proceeds to tell his own story.

> Having inherited from my father considerable wealth, I squandered it rapidly until I was obliged to sell the doors and (paneled) ceilings of my house and had nothing left in the world to make a living. For some time I was left with no other food than that which my mother gained by spinning, and I wanted to die.
>
> One night, I dreamt that someone said to me, "Your fortune is in Cairo, so go there!" Early in the morning I went to the *qāḍī* Abū ʿUmar, to whom I had access as his neighbor and because of a service my father had rendered to his father. I asked him to write a letter of reference to Cairo for me, so that I could find a position there. He did so, and I left. When I arrived in Cairo, I delivered the letter applying for a position. But God prevented me from securing an official position, and I found no other job.
>
> Having exhausted my provisions, I remained at a loss for what to do. I thought of begging from the people, extending my hand on the streets, but my pride did not allow that. So I said to myself, "I will go begging at night." I went out between the two evening prayers and loitered around in the streets. My pride did not allow me to beg, though hunger impelled me to do so. I did nothing until the night was half over. A guard met me and arrested me. As he saw that I was a stranger and did not know my state of affairs, he asked me where I was from. I said, "I am a destitute man." He did not believe me, threw me to the ground and gave me a beating with his stick, until I cried, "I will tell you the truth!"—"Let's have it!"

he said. So I told him my story from beginning to end, including the tale of the dream.

In response, he said to me, "I never met anybody more stupid than you! By God, several years ago I had a dream in which a man said to me, 'In Baghdad, in thingamabob street, in thingamabob neighborhood . . .'"—and he mentioned my street and my neighborhood, while I remained silent and appeared not to pay attention. Finishing his story, the guard said, "there is a house whose name is thingamabob house . . ."—and he mentioned my house and my name—"with a garden in which there is a lotus tree . . ."—and in my house there was a lotus tree—"and buried beneath the lotus tree there are thirty thousand *dīnārs*. Go there and take it!' I never believed in that story and did not pay attention to it. But you, you fool, left your country and came to Egypt because of a dream!"

(Hearing this,) my heart regained its strength. And when the guard had released me, I spent the night in one of the mosques. Early in the morning I left Cairo. Back in Baghdad, I cut down the lotus tree, dug in the soil under it and found a vessel holding thirty thousand *dīnārs*. I took it and restored my affairs. Until today, I have been living from those *dīnārs*, by virtue of the estates and plots of land I bought with it.

More or less the same version is cited in Andalusian author Ibn ʿĀṣim's (d. 1426) *Ḥadāʾiq al-azāhir* (Flower Gardens),[12] constituting a possible precursor to subsequent Christian tradition on the Iberian Peninsula that is first attested in the work of Spanish historian Lope García de Salazar (1399–1476).[13] Citing al-Tanūkhī's (d. 994) *al-Faraj baʿd al-shidda* as his source, Ibn Ḥijja al-Ḥamawī (d. 1434) also retells the tale in his popular anthology *Thamarāt al-awrāq* (The Fruits of the [Scattered] Leaves).[14]

Already in the context of Arabic literature, the tale proved its ability to adapt to various characters and locations.[15] A fourteenth-century manual for pilgrims cites the events as establishing the great wealth displayed by the historical character ʿAffān ibn Sulaymān (d. 935), a person who was famed for his extraordinary generosity.[16] Although his story essentially has the same plot as Tanūkhī's version, instead of traveling from Baghdad to Cairo, ʿAffān travels from his native Cairo to Baghdad where he first finds a job as a tailor. Twice cited in fifteenth-century Arabic literature, a slightly modified version of Tanūkhī's text was integrated into the seventeenth-century history of Egypt compiled by ʿAbd al-Muʿṭī al-Isḥāqī (d. after 1623), from which the compilers of the more recent manuscripts of *The Thousand and One Nights* apparently copied it more or less verbatim.[17]

By the first half of the eleventh century, the tale appears to have migrated to Persian literature, as one may surmise from the allusion to a certain "owner of Zahman" in a verse that is commonly attributed to the Persian poets Farrokhi (d. 1073) or Asjadi (d. 1040).[18] The related tale is first attested in the collection of mirabilia and marvelous tales compiled by twelfth-century Persian author

Moḥammad ibn Maḥmud Hamadāni.[19] It refers to a house called Zahman in the town of Rey, today a suburb of Iran's capital Tehran. The poor owner of the house dreams that he will find a treasure in Damascus. Only after having had the same dream for several nights does he leave for Damascus. When asked in Damascus what he came there for, he thinks himself stupid because he believed in a dream. Following this, the other person tells him about his own dream concerning a treasure in the house called Zahman. The man travels back home and finds a golden anvil weighing almost 100 kilos. Rather than following this early Persian text, the version in Persian poet Jalāl al-Din Rumi's (d. 1273) mystical *summa*, the *Masnavi-ye maʿnavi*,[20] instead derives from Tanūkhī's version that had been translated into Persian around the middle of the thirteenth century by Ḥoseyn ibn Asʿad Dahestāni.[21]

Whereas several versions of the tale were recorded from twentieth-century oral tradition in Egypt,[22] a small number of Turkish versions document only a vague reflection of the original story, as the dreamer either finds a treasure or a valuable object in Baghdad or is told in a direct manner that he will find a treasure in his house.[23] No versions are documented from twentieth-century oral tradition in Iran.

The tale's versions from the historical literatures of the Muslim world derive their attraction to a certain extent from the inherent ambiguity between a believed prophetic quality of dreams and the Koranic dictum of "false dreams" (*aḍghāth al-aḥlām*; 21:5), an ambiguity that is similarly evident in the European versions. The Arabic and Persian versions often have the destitute man spend the night in a mosque and thus add a dimension of religiously motivated charity that is typical for the regional context. Contrasting with this, but structurally similar, virtually all of the European texts follow the earliest version in the *Karlmeinet* in that the man is to find his fortune on a bridge in a major town. As Johannes Bolte remarked, a major bridge in any city would see the most dense human traffic,[24] and so, if the dreamer was to meet his fortune anywhere, the bridge would be the most likely place. In addition to rationalizing the tale's action, the tale's localization in the European audiences' familiar regional and social landscape likely added to the tale's credibility and thus favored its wide international distribution.

Notes

1. Jacobs, Joseph, *More English Fairy Tales*, London, D. Nutt, 1894, pp. 91–93, 229, no. 63; Briggs, *A Dictionary*, vol. B2, pp. 298–301, 301–303.

2. See https://en.wikipedia.org/wiki/Pedlar_of_Swaffham (accessed May 22, 2018).

3. For other English versions see Briggs, *A Dictionary*, vol. B2, pp. 234–235, 364–365, 385–386.

4. Robe, Stanley L., *Mexican Tales and Legends from Los Altos*, Berkeley: University of California Press, 1970, 461–463, no. 130; for older Spanish versions see Chevalier, *Cuentos folklóricos*, pp. 346–347, no. 211; Pedrosa, José Manuel, "El cuento de *El tesoro*

soñado (AT 1645) y el complejo leyendístico de *El becerro de oro*," *Estudos de literatura oral* 4 (1998), pp. 127–157.

5. For a general survey of the tale in German and international tradition see Bolte, Johannes, "Zur Sage vom Traum vom Schatz auf der Brücke," *Zeitschrift des Vereins für Volkskunde* 19 (1909), pp. 189–198; Röhrich, Lutz, *Erzählungen des späten Mittelalters und ihr Weiterleben in Literatur und Volksdichtung bis zur Gegenwart*, Bern: Francke, 1967, vol. 2, pp. 121–155, 429–438, no. IV, here at p. 430–431.

6. The summary follows Röhrich, *Erzählungen*, vol. 2, p. 434 (original text pp. 122–128).

7. Wesselski, *Mönchslatein*, pp. 120, 235, no. 101; Röhrich, *Erzählungen*, vol. 2, p. 129, 435.

8. Röhrich, *Erzählungen*, vol. 2, p. 429; Grimm, Jacob and Wilhelm, *Deutsche Sagen*, 3 vols., ed. Hans-Jörg Uther and Barbara Kindermann-Bieri, Munich: Diederichs, 1993, vol. 1, pp. 193–194, 307, no. 212.

9. Chauvin, Victor, "Le Reve du trésor sur le pont," *Revue des Traditions Populaires* 13 (1898), pp. 193–196; see also Leclerf, Jean, "The Dream in Popular Culture: Arabic and Islamic," in *The Dream and Human Societies*, ed. Gustav Edmund van Grunebaum and Roger Caillois, Berkeley: University of California Press, 1966, pp. 364–380, at p. 371–372.

10. Wiener, Alfred, "Die Farağ ba'd aš-šidda-Literatur," *Der Islam* 4 (1913), pp. 270–298, 387–420.

11. Tanūkhī, Abū 'Alī al-Muḥassin ibn 'Alī al-, *Kitāb al-Faraj ba'd al-shidda*, 5 vols., ed. 'Abbūd al-Shālijī, Beirut: Dār Ṣādir, 1398/1978, vol. 2, pp. 268–269, no. 212; German translation Tanūkhī, At-, *Ende gut, alles gut: Das Buch der Erleichterung nach der Bedrängnis*, transl. Arnold Hottinger, Zurich: Manesse, 1979, pp. 132–134: see also Scheiber, Alexander, "Traum vom Schatz auf der Brücke," in *Essays on Jewish Folklore and Comparative Literature*, Budapest: Akad. Kiadó, 1985, pp. 392–392 (previously published in *Fabula* 25, 1984, pp. 91–93); French translation in Galtier, Édouard, "Fragments d'une étude sur les Mille et une Nuits," *Mémoires de l'Institut français du Caire* 27 (1912), pp. 135–194, at 187–189.

12. Ibn 'Āṣim al-Andalusī, Abū Bakr ibn Muḥammad, *Ḥadā'iq al-azāhir*, ed. 'Afīf 'Abd al-Raḥmān, Beirut: al-Masīra, 1401/1981, pp. 383–384; López Bernal, Desirée, *Los Ḥadā'iq al-azāhir de Abū Bakr ibn 'Āṣim al-Garnāṭī: Traducción y estudio de una obra de adab de la Granada nazarí*, 2 vols., Ph.D. thesis University of Granada, 2016, vol. 1, p. 464–465, no. 1136; vol. 2, pp. 165–166, 170.

13. Fradejas Lebrero, José, "Sobre un cuento de Ambrosio de Salazar," *Murgetana* 107 (2002), pp. 53–63, at pp. 55–56.

14. Ibn Ḥijja al-Ḥamawī, 'Alī ibn Muḥammad, *Thamarāt al-awrāq fī 'l-muḥāḍarāt*, ed. Mufīd Qumayḥa, Beirut: Dār al-Kutub al-'ilmiyya, 1403/1983, pp. 310–311.

15. Marzolph, Ulrich, "Traum vom Schatz auf der Brücke," in *Enzyklopädie des Märchens*, vol. 13 (2010), cols. 877–882.

16. Muwaffaq al-Dīn ibn 'Uthmān, *Murshid al-zuwār ilā qubūr al-abrār* (Guide of the Pilgrims to the Graves of the Pious), ed. Muḥammad Fatḥī Abū Bakr, Cairo: al-Dār al-miṣriyya al-lubnāniyya, 1995, pp. 656–657.

17. Marzolph, Ulrich, "Das *Kitāb Laṭā'if aḫbār al-uwal* des -Isḥāqī als Quelle der Kompilatoren von *1001 Nacht*," in *Orientalistische Studien zu Sprache und Literatur: Festschrift Werner Diem*, ed. Ulrich Marzolph, Wiesbaden: Harrassowitz, 2011, pp. 317–328.

18. Dehkhodā, ʿAli-Akbar, *Loghat-nāme*, 30 vols., Tehran: Sāzmān-e Loghat-nāme, vol. 20, 6 (1350/1971), p. 577.

19. Hamadāni, Moḥammad ibn Maḥmud, *ʿAjāʾeb-nāme*, ed. Jaʿfar Modarres Ṣādeqi, Tehran: Markaz 1375/1996, p. 197.

20. Rumi, Jalāl al-Din, *The Mathnawí of Jalálu'ddín Rúmí*, transl. Reynold A. Nicholson, London: Luzac & Co., 1934, vol. 3, pp. 490–500 (bk. 6, verses 4206–4385). A modern prose rendering of Rumi's verse is given by Arberry, Arthur John, *More Tales from the Masnavi*, London: Allen & Unwin, 1963, pp. 227–229, no. 197.

21. Foruzānfar, Badiʿ al-Zamān, *Maʾākheẕ-e qeṣaṣ va tams̱ilāt-e Mas̱navi*, Tehran: Amir Kabir, 3rd printing, 1362/1983, p. 220, no. 260; Dahestāni, Ḥoseyn ibn Asʿad, *Faraj baʿd al-shidde*, 3 vols., ed. Esmāʿil Ḥākemi, Tehran: Eṭṭelāʿāt, 1364–1364/1985–1986, vol. 1, pp. 503–506.

22. El-Shamy, *Types*, p. 892.

23. Eberhard and Boratav, *Typen*, p. 150–151, no. 133; see also Marzolph, *Relief after Hardship*, pp. 62–65, no. 8.

24. Bolte, "Zur Sage vom Traum," p. 296.

CHAPTER 83

The Dreamer Marks the Treasure with His Excrements (ATU 1645B)

Telling of a dreamer who defecates in his sleep when dreaming of a treasure, this widespread scatological tale is classified as tale type ATU 1645B: *Dream of Marking the Treasure*, mainly with reference to the tale's European versions. The tale's European versions, on the one hand, and its earlier Arabic and Middle Eastern ones, on the other, are clearly distinguished by the reasons given for this involuntary mishap that in the societies in which the tale was told must have served to create a certain *Schadenfreude*, a joy that arose from amusement over the teller's misfortune. Although the tale's European versions are mainly encountered in literary sources of the fourteenth to nineteenth centuries, a few versions were recorded from oral tradition in Europe and the Americas. In his extensively annotated edition of "Thirty Brazilian tales," Brazilian folklorist Luís da Câmara Cascudo (1898–1986)[1] published a version that he reports to have been told as a personal narrative by the brother of his paternal grandmother, Martinho Ferreira de Melo.[2]

> A man always said that nobody should believe in dreams. A dream is a lie. But then a terrible event happened to him. He dreamt that his grandfather appeared to him telling him that he left behind a buried jar full of gold. He took him along to below a tree and showed him the place. He began to dig, and the man saw the coins. The apparition hid the jar and disappeared. The man did not know how to mark the position where the gold was buried. Suddenly he felt his bowels move and relieved himself on the spot, on top of the jar. This should have been the best mark in the world. At this moment, he woke up, all dirty and smelly.

Cascudo cites another version from Portugal in which a man in despair invokes the help of the devil.[3] The devil appears and shows him a treasure. As they are in the middle of a deserted area, without a tree or even a stone, the devil advises the man to mark the place with his excrements. As he does so, he is woken by his wife who scolds him for soiling the bed sheets.

The tale collected in 1901 from the oral performance of Ukrainian narrator

Mykoła Šklarj in the district of Drohobych, then belonging to the Austro-Hungarian Empire, offers a slightly different plot whose main elements are, however, identical.[4]

> A man slept together with his wife in bed. At night he had a dream of three piles of money that were lying there somewhere in the mountains, in a field. And he began to wake up. He gathered his wits, still half asleep, and wanted to mark the money. He took his shirt down and placed it on one spot. He thought, "This is one pile of money." He took his underpants down and placed them on the second spot; that would be the second. But he did not have anything to mark the third spot. What to do? So he squatted and pressed with all his might. But his wife woke up, saw it, and shouted, "What are you doing?"—And he said, "Silent, wife, silent! This is going to be for us and for our children."

In European tradition, the tale makes its first appearance in the *summa theologica* or didactic theological work *Lo Crestià* (*The Christian*; bk. 12, ch. 150) compiled by Catalan author Francesc Eiximenis (d. 1409) in 1385/86.[5] This text is introduced by an episode corresponding to tale type ATU 778*: *Two Candles*. At church, a man lights a candle not only for the saints but also for the devil. In order to thank him for the honor, the devil appears in his dream and shows him a treasure. As there is no object to mark the place where the treasure is hidden, the man marks it with his excrements. The tale ends with the cynical remark, "This is the kind of treasure the devil gives" (*aquest es lo thesor qui dona lo diable*).

Chronologically the second and, probably, the more influential version in European tradition is contained in the collection of short jocular tales, the *Facetiae* compiled by the papal secretary Giovanni Francesco Poggio Bracciolini around the middle of the fifteenth century.[6] Poggio authenticates his tale as being told by a friend in a social gathering. The friend attributes the dream to his neighbor. Without further introduction, the man is said to have dreamt that the devil led him to a field to dig for gold. After the standard culmination of the tale, Poggio adds a "comedy topper"[7] in which the man soils himself by putting on his cap into which the cat had emptied its bowels at night. The author ends by saying, "Thus the golden dream had turned to turd" (*Ita aureum somnium in merdam rediit*).[8]

In more or less identical versions, the tale was popularized in fifteenth- and sixteenth-century chapbooks that in turn might have given rise to later versions, including the tale's retellings in oral tradition. In Italian, the tale is attested in Girolamo Morlini's *Novellae*,[9] in English in the "Shakespeare Jest-Book" *Mery Tales and Quicke Answers*,[10] and in German in Johannes Pauli's influential *Schimpf und Ernst* (Jocular and Serious Tales; 1522)[11] as well as the compilations by Georg Wickram,[12] Jakob Frey,[13] and Hans-Wilhelm Kirchhof.[14]

The tale's Arabic tradition goes back to the second half of the ninth century, when it was included in Ibn Qutayba's (d. 889) *ʿUyūn al-akhbār* (Quintessential Reports).[15]

> Dāwūd the madman (*al-muṣāb*) said: I once had a dream half of which was true, and half of which was untrue. I dreamt that I was a carrying a treasure on my back und soiled myself because of the weight. This made me wake up. I saw the shit, but not the treasure.

Subsequent works of Arabic literature cite the tale in closely similar wording.[16] The texts in al-Ābī's (d. 1030) *Nathr al-durr* (Pearls of Prose)[17] and Abū Ḥayyān al-Tawḥīdī's (d. 1023) *al-Baṣāʾir wa-ʾl-dhakhāʾir* (Deep Insights and Treasures),[18] attribute the tale to the said Dāwūd *al-muṣāb*. In his *al-ʿIqd al-farīd* (The Unique Necklace), Andalusian author Ibn ʿAbd Rabbih (d. 940) is the first to attribute the tale to Ashʿab, a historical character who lived in Medina at the beginning of the eighth century and whom tradition developed as the stereotype of the greedy and stingy person.[19] Ibn ʿAbd Rabbih's text is repeated almost verbatim in Andalusian author Ibn ʿĀṣim's (d. 1426) *Ḥadāʾiq al-azāhir* (Flower Gardens)[20] and again, in a heavily abridged form, in Ibn al-Jawzī's (d. 1201) *Akhbār al-Ẓirāf* (Tales of Subtle People).[21] In his *Muḥāḍarāt al-udabāʾ* (Conversations of the Educated), al-Rāghib al-Iṣfahānī (d. 1108) attributes the tale to an anonymous protagonist.[22] Here, another unnamed character starts a casual conversation by stating that dreams usually are only partly true, following which his companion tells about his own experience as a case in point. The head of the Eastern Jacobite Church, Bar Hebraeus (d. 1286), adapted al-Ābī's text in his *Laughable Stories* somewhat bashfully (but less pointed) to a sexual context that was probably deemed less offensive.[23] In his version, the unnamed protagonist dreams of having intercourse with a beautiful maid. On waking up, he realizes that he did, in fact, have intercourse, but not with a maid. With the traditional scatological pun, an extended version of the tale is encountered in ʿAbd al-Muʿṭī al-Isḥāqī's seventeenth-century Arabic history of Egypt whose historical discourse according to the taste of the contemporary audience is interspersed with "local cultural practices and beliefs"[24] as well as numerous anecdotes and entertaining stories.[25] Here, the scatological joke appears in the context of an associative sequence of tales that starts with the tale of a talented interpreter of dreams who identifies and interprets the ruler's forgotten dream. It is followed by the migratory legend classified as tale type ATU 1645: *The Treasure at Home* (see essay **82, *The Dream of Finding One's Fortune Somewhere Else***) that in turn is followed by the present jocular tale. The author then dwells on tales about farts and farting before eventually calling himself back to order so as to return to the more serious historical matter of his discussion.[26]

A Persian version of the tale is included in the fourteenth-century collection of jocular tales compiled by ʿObeyd-e Zākāni, where the dream is attributed to the court jester Ṭalḥak.[27] Fakhr al-Din ʿAli Ṣafi (d. 1532) again cited the tale in his *Laṭāʾef al-ṭavāʾef* (Jocular Tales from the Various Strata of Society), attributed to an anonymous character.[28]

The compilation of jokes related to the popular Arabic jester Juḥā compiled by seventeenth-century Arabic author al-Maylāwī documents a rare variation of the plot.[29] Here Juḥā dreams of being led to a treasure in an underground den. When his helper intends to pull him back up with a rope around his belly, Juḥā suddenly feels somebody holding onto his foot and is advised to shit on that person so as to get rid of him. The version attributed to the Turkish jester Nasreddin Hodja in Ottoman manuscript tradition is close to European mainstream tradition in that Nasreddin simply defecates to mark the place where he found the treasure.[30]

There is little doubt that the tale's European versions constitute adaptations of the Arabic tale, even though the latter constitute a distinct form or oicotype whose plot is characterized by specific elements. The tale's three constitutive elements—dream, treasure, excrement—are identical in both forms, and only the frame as well as the motivation differ. By introducing the devil as the one who deludes the dreamer, European authors, first of all, adapted the tale to the European Christian context. But while the dreamer in the Arabic version dreams of a real treasure whose weight causes him to defecate, the introduction of the devil characterizes the treasure imagined in the dream as a delusion, and the figure of the devil reveals itself as the ultimate enticer. The final "moral" added to several of the European versions further elaborates this point by literally equating the devil's gift with shit.

The present tale also supplies an illustrative example for the interlocking of Arabic and Romance traditions on the Iberian Peninsula. Introduced to Arabic tradition in Spain by Ibn ʿAbd Rabbih at the beginning of the tenth century, the tale is again cited by Ibn ʿĀṣim in the fifteenth century, and the latter instance would often suggest itself as documenting a potential intermediary to subsequent tradition in the Romance languages. In the present case, however, Romance tradition as attested by fourteenth-century Catalan author Francesc Eiximenis predates Ibn ʿĀṣim. The chronological priority strongly suggests a current of the tale in Romance oral tradition before Ibn ʿĀṣim invigorated it again in Arabic literary tradition, although his rendering might have inspired retellings in oral tradition of the Iberian Peninsula.

Notes

1. De Mélo, Verissimo, "Cascudo, Luís da Câmara," in *Enzyklopädie des Märchens*, vol. 2 (1979), col. 1177; Souto Maior, Mário, *Dicionário de folcloristas brasileiros*, Recife: Fundarpe, 1999, pp. 116–117 (not seen; 2nd ed. Goiânia: Kelps, 2000).

2. Cascudo, Luís da Câmara, *Trinta "estorias" brasileiras*, Lisbon: Fortucalense, 1955, pp. 56–57.

3. The quoted reference is Oliveira, F. Xavier d'Ataide, *Contos tradicionais do Algarve*,

vol. 2, Porto, 1905, pp. 455–456. See also Cardigos, Isabel, *Catalogue of Portuguese Folktales*, Helsinki: Suomalainen Tiedeakatemia, 2006, no. 1645B.

4. Tarasevśkyj, Pavło, and Hnatjuk, Vołodymyr, *Das Geschlechtleben des ukrainischen Bauernvolkes in Österreich-Ungarn*, vol. 2, ed. Vołodmyr Hnatjuk, Leipzig: Ethnologischer Verlag, 1912, p. 53, no. 107.

5. Eiximenis, Francesc, *Contes i faules*, ed. Marçal Olivar, Barcelona: Barcino, 1925, pp. 68–70, no. 22; Eiximenis, Francesc, *Aquest es lo Dotzen libre de regiment dels princeps e de comunitats appellat Crestia*, [València:] Lambert Palmart, 1484, fol. 67v; quoted from http://mdc.cbuc.cat/cdm/compoundobject/collection/incunableBC/id/32079 (accessed June 29, 2016). See also Chevalier, *Cuentos folklóricos*, no. 212.

6. Marzolph, Ulrich, "Poggio Bracciolini, Giovanni Francesco," in *Enzyklopädie des Märchens*, vol. 10 (2002), col. 1101–1106.

7. Legman, Gershon, *Rationale of the Dirty Joke: An Analysis of Sexual Humor*, vol. 2, New York: Breaking Point, 1975, p. 918.

8. Quoted from http://www.hs-augsburg.de/~harsch/Chronologia/Lspost15/Poggio/pog_fac1.html#130 (accessed June 30, 2016).

9. Wesselski, Albert, *Die Novellen Girolamo Morlinis*, Munich: Georg Müller, 1908, pp. 52–53, no. 10 (this text begins with a version of ATU 778*).

10. Hazlitt, W. Carew, ed., *Shakespeare Jest-Books: Reprints of the Early and Very Rare Jest-Books Supposed to Have Been Used by Shakespeare*, London: Willis & Sotheran, 1881, pp. 40–41, no. 28 (ending with the man putting on his cap).

11. Pauli, Johannes, *Schimpf und Ernst*, ed. Johannes Bolte, Berlin: Stubenrauch, 1924 (reprint Hildesheim: Olms, 1972), vol. 2, pp. 57, 428, no. 789; pp. 85–86, 438, no. 846 (introduced by tale type ATU 778*).

12. Wickram, Georg, *Werke*, vol. 3: *Rollwagenbüchlein, Die sieben Hauptlaster*, ed. Johannes Bolte, Tübingen: Litterarischer Verein in Stuttgart, 1903, pp. 44, 371–372, no. 37 (introduced by ATU 778*).

13. Frey, Jakob, *Gartengesellschaft*, ed. Johannes Bolte, Tübingen: Litterarischer Verein in Stuttgart, 1896, pp. 92–93, 243–245, no. 77 (ending with the man putting on his cap); see also Stiefel, Abraham Ludwig, "Zur Schwankdichtung im 16. und 17. Jahrhundert, 1: Quellen und Stoffgeschichtliches zu Jakob Frey's 'Gartengesellschaft'," *Zeitschrift für vergleichende Litteraturgeschichte* 12 (1898), pp. 164–180, at 173–174.

14. Kirchhof, Hans Wilhelm, *Wendunmuth*, vol. 3, ed. Hermann Österley, Tübingen: Laupp, 1869, pp. 463–464, no. 189 (introduced by tale type ATU 778*; the dreamer has to lift a heavy stone).

15. Ibn Qutayba al-Dīnawarī, Abū Muḥammad ʿAbdallāh ibn Muslim, *ʿUyūn al-akhbār*, Cairo: al-Mu'assassa al-miṣriyya al-ʿāmma lil-ta'lif wa-'l-tarjama wa-'l-ṭibāʿa, 2nd ed., 1963, vol. 2, p. 51.

16. Marzolph, *Arabia ridens*, vol. 1, pp. 220–221, and vol. 2, p. 46, no. 171.

17. Ābī, Abū Saʿd Manṣūr ibn al-Ḥusayn al-, *Nathr al-durr*, ed. Muḥammad ʿAlī Qarna et al., vol. 3, Cairo: al-Hay'a al-miṣriyya al-ʿāmma lil-kitāb, 1984, p. 263.

18. Tawḥīdī, Abū Ḥayyān al-, *al-Baṣā'ir wa-'l-dhakhā'ir*, ed. Wadād al-Qāḍī, Beirut: Dār Ṣādir, 1408/1988, vol. 4, pp. 46–47, no. 88.

19. Ibn ʿAbd Rabbih, Abū ʿUmar Aḥmad ibn Muḥammad, *Kitāb al-ʿIqd al-farīd*, ed. Aḥmad Amīn, Aḥmad al-Zayn, Ibrāhīm al-Abyārī, 3rd ed., Cairo: Lajnat al-ta'līf wa-'l-tarjama wa-'l-nashr, 1372/1952, vol. 6, p. 431; Rosenthal, Franz, *Humor in Early Islam*, Leiden: Brill, 1956 (reprint 2011), pp. 120–121, no. 132.

20. Ibn ʿĀṣim al-Andalusī, Abū Bakr ibn Muḥammad, *Ḥadāʾiq al-azāhir*, ed. ʿAfīf ʿAbd al-Raḥmān, Beirut: Dār al-Masīra, 1401/1981, p. 135; López Bernal, Desirée, *Los Ḥadāʾiq al-azāhir de Abū Bakr ibn ʿĀṣim al-Garnāṭī: Traducción y estudio de una obra de adab de la Granada nazarí*, Ph.D. thesis University of Granada, 2016, vol. 1, pp. 220–221, no. 421.

21. Ibn al-Jawzī, Abū ʾl-Faraj ʿAbd al-Raḥmān ibn ʿAlī, *Akhbār al-Ẓirāf wa-ʾl-mutamājinīn*, ed. Muḥammad Baḥr al-ʿulūm, 2nd ed., al-Najaf: al-Maktaba al-ḥaydariyya, 1386/1966, p. 30.

22. Rāghib al-Iṣfahānī, al-Ḥusayn ibn Muḥammad al-, *Muḥāḍarāt al-udabāʾ wa-muḥāwarāt al-shuʿarāʾ wa-ʾl-bulaghāʾ*, vol. 1, Beirut 1961, p. 151.

23. Bar Hebraeus, Mâr Gregory John, *The Laughable Stories*, transl. E.A. Wallis Budge, London: Luzac and Co, 1897, p. 159, no. 635.

24. Hanna, Nelly, *In Praise of Books: A Cultural History of Cairo's Middle Class, Sixteenth to Eighteenth Century*, Syracuse, NY: Syracuse University Press, 2003, pp. 115–116.

25. Hanna, Nelly, "The Chronicles of Ottoman Egypt: History or Entertainment?" in *The Historiography of Islamic Egypt (c. 950–1800)*, ed. Hugh Kennedy, Leiden: Brill, 2001, pp. 237–250, at 247–248.

26. Isḥāqī, Muḥammad ibn ʿAbd al-Muʿṭī al-, *Kitāb Laṭāʾif akhbār al-uwal*, ed. Muḥammad Riḍwān Muhannā, al-Manṣūra: Maktabat al-Īmān, 1420/2000, p. 182; Marzolph, Ulrich, "Das *Kitāb Laṭāʾif aḫbār al-uwal* des -Isḥāqī als Quelle der Kompilatoren von *1001 Nacht*," in *Orientalistische Studien zu Sprache und Literatur: Festschrift Werner Diem*, ed. Ulrich Marzolph, Wiesbaden: Harrassowitz, 2011, pp. 317–328, at pp. 322–323.

27. Christensen, Arthur, "Remarques sur les facéties de ʿUbaïd-i-Zākānī, avec des extraits de la Risālä-i dilgušā," *Acta Orientalia* 3 (1924), pp. 1–37, at p. 19 (II. 160).

28. Ṣafi, Fakhr al-Din ʿAli, *Laṭāʾef al-ṭavāʾef*, ed. Aḥmad Golchin-Maʿāni, Tehran: Moḥammad Ḥoseyn Eqbāl, 1336/1957, pp. 325–326.

29. Marzolph, *Nasreddin Hodscha*, p. 61, no. 117; ʿAnābsa, Ghālib, "Min adab al-nawādir: naẓra fī makhṭūṭāt [Irshād] man naḥā ilā nawādir Juḥā, jamʿ al-faqīr ilā Allāh taʿālā Yūsuf ibn al-Wakīl al-Maylāwī," in ʿAnābsa, *Dirāsāt muḍīʾa fī ṣafaḥāt al-turāth*, Zaḥāliqa: Dār al-Hudā, and Jordan: Dār al-Jarīr, 2013, pp. 174–196, at p. 187.

30. Wesselski, *Der Hodscha Nasreddin*, vol. 1, pp. 178, 278, no. 314.

CHAPTER 84

The Clever Man Privileges Himself When Distributing Food Items among Several Persons (ATU 1663)

The title and content description of tale type ATU 1663: *Dividing Five Eggs Equally between Two Men and One Woman* relate to a rarely documented tale with sexual allusions that is apparently inspired by the trivialities of the male genitals.[1] Instead of privileging this comparatively rare variation, the tale type is here discussed in relation to what should be regarded as its dominant form. Not even mentioned in the second revision of the international tale-type index,[2] in the most recent revision this dominant form is relegated to the status of "continuation" of or "conclusion" to tale type ATU 1533: *The Wise Carving of the Fowl* (see essay **59, *The Clever Man Privileges Himself When Carving the Roast Chicken***).[3] In his index of Arabic folktales, Hasan El-Shamy proposed the new tale type 1533B: *The Division: "Odd or Even?"*[4] Analytically abstracted, tale type ATU 1663 deals with the distribution of a specified amount of food items among several persons. In the tale type's dominant form, these food items are birds such as geese, chicken, or partridges, whether alive or prepared for consumption. As tale type ATU 1663 occurs most often as a sequel to tale type ATU 1533, only seldom as a prelude to the latter tale type or independently, the actors include the same array of persons, that is, in addition to the clever distributor there is a man, his wife, and their two daughters and two sons.

First documented in the *Midrash Lamentations* (*Ekha Rabbati*), probably compiled in the fifth century CE,[5] the clever distribution of the birds in European oral tradition is mainly attested from Slavonic countries, as discussed in detail for tale type ATU 1533. The Slavonic versions regularly stage the events in the context of a nineteenth-century rural society in which feudal structures were still alive. The tale's main protagonist is a poor peasant who is richly rewarded by the lord for his clever carving of a single roast bird. His rich antagonist, who is sometimes his brother, aims to outrival him by presenting a total of five birds to the lord. As the rich man is unable to comply with the lord's wish for a sensible distribution of the birds to the members of the lord's family, the lord asks the poor peasant to perform. The poor peasant suggests that they make groups of two family members, each of whom is to receive one bird to constitute a group of three—parents, daughters, and sons. That leaves two birds for himself to constitute another group of three. The lord is so amused about the clever distribution that he rewards the poor peasant again and punishes the peasant's rich antagonist. In addition to the frequently recorded versions from Slavonic regions, the same procedure is also documented in versions from the Baltic countries[6] and other European regions. Whereas in most versions recorded from European oral tradition the distribution of the birds follows the carving of a single bird, in the tale's ancient Hebrew version it precedes the latter. This enables the ancient Hebrew version to proceed from the distribution of live birds to the carving of a single bird prepared for consumption. The historical version in the anonymous fourteenth-century *Compilatio singularis exemplorum* (An Unmatched Compilation of Exemplary Tales) presents a somewhat different scene and set of characters, while staying in accordance with the established manner of distribution.[7]

> A poor scholar returning from university requests the hospitality of a certain farmer. Reluctantly, the farmer hosts him. When asking the scholar about the achievement of his studies, the latter responds that he learned about God and the Trinity. At the table, the farmer insists that the scholar distribute five partridges among the seven persons present, including the farmer, his wife, their son and daughter, two farmhands, and the scholar himself. The scholar constitutes three groups of two persons—parents, children, and farmhands—to form three with a single bird alloted to each of them. That leaves himself and two partridges to constitute another group of three. When the farmer objects to the distribution the scholar argues that his action is in accordance with the true principle of Trinity.

In the version given in John Gobi's *Scala coeli*, compiled between 1322 and 1330, the distribution follows the carving of a roast bird.[8] The tale's main character is a poor cleric who is hosted by a soldier. Whereas the cleric carved the bird according to the laws of natural science, he performs the distribution of five partridges according to the rules of divine science by putting to practice the principle of the Trinity. Although in the previous episode of carving the bird, the scholar had to take into account two servants present, the distribution takes place among himself and the four members of the family only.

In Arabic literature, the tale is first documented in polymath al-Jāḥiẓ's (d. 868) *Kitāb al-Ḥayawān* (Book of Animals),[9] followed by a variety of other attestations ranging from the eleventh to the seventeenth centuries.[10] The distribution of the birds is essentially the same as in the versions recorded from European oral tradition, albeit with an additional point. Following the clever carving of the roast bird, the story continues the next day when the host has his wife prepare five chicken, asking the guest to distribute the birds among them. Before beginning, the guest asks his host whether he should distribute the birds to result in groups of uneven or even numbers. As he is first requested to form groups of uneven numbers, he distributes the birds in the established manner, himself receiving two birds to constitute the final group of three. When his host is not satisfied with the result, he asks his guest to distribute the birds to result in even numbers. The clever Bedouin proceeds to form two groups of three human characters—husband and two sons, wife and two daughters—plus a bird each. That leaves a final group of himself plus three birds, thus augmenting his share. In his *Nihāyat al-arab fī funūn al-adab* (The Ultimate Ambition in the Arts of Erudition), al-Nuwayrī (d. 1332) adds yet another way of distribution in which the host asks his guest to distribute three chickens among all of those present.[11] Announcing that he will form groups of even numbers, the guest gives a bird each to the man and two sons, the wife and two daughters, and himself.

In Persian literature, the tale of the clever distribution is included in Sadid al-Din Moḥammad ʿAwfi's (d. ca. 1232) *Javāmeʿ al-ḥekāyāt* (Collections of Stories).[12] As the tale's full text has not been published, the exact nature of the distribution is not clear.

The description of tale type ATU 1663 proper reads like a sexualized version of the tale, although the only point both tales have in common is the distribution of food items among a certain number of people. In particular, the distributor does not take advantage of his position to privilege himself. Instead, he employs a crude allusion to the physical characteristics of the male genitals to make his point. In the sexualized tale, a man is requested to distribute five eggs among two men and one woman without breaking them.[13] He gives one egg each to the two men, and three to the woman. Requested to explain his decision, he argues that the men already possess two eggs (their testicles), so having received one more they now have three. Awarding three eggs to the woman leaves her with the same number as the men, implying that she had no "eggs" previously.

In European tradition, this distribution occurs first in Cristoforo Armeno's Italian *Peregrinaggio di tre giovani figliuoli del re di Serendippo* (The Travels of the Three Young Sons of the King of Serendip), initially published in 1557.[14] Here, the queen poses the task to one of the three clever young men, promising to acknowledge him as the cleverest of all should he succeed in solving the task in a satisfactory manner. Since the queen invites the young man to join her in privacy, only accompanied by one of her trusted courtiers, the scene suggests an intimate context from the very beginning. The queen's blushing when being presented with the solution to her task underlines the young man's transgression of decent behavior, although the intimate set-up would already have prepared the tale's audience for something unusual to happen, thus contributing an additional seasoning to an already unusual tale. Armeno modeled his book in large parts on Persian poet Amir Khosrow Dehlavi's *Hasht behesht* (The Eight Paradises), a poem composed at the beginning of the fourteenth century in emulation of Neżāmi's (d. 1209) famous *Haft peykar* (The Seven Portraits).[15] The distribution of the eggs is, however, not mentioned in Armeno's model. In Persian literature, it is first documented in the tale of Lavvāḥa and Beshr (Bashar) in Abu Bakr ibn Khosrow al-Ostād's *Munes-nāme* (The Book as an Intimate Friend), compiled around the year 1200.[16] This is chronologically followed by the book's Ottoman Turkish adaptation *Ferec ba'd eş-şidde* (Relief after Hardship), likely translated from the Persian before the end of the fourteenth century.[17] In both texts, the distribution of the eggs is a sequel to the carving of the roast bird and the distribution of four chicken among the host's family, here consisting of husband, wife, and two sons. On the third occasion, the host requests his guest to distribute seven eggs among himself and the members of the family. The four men receive one egg each, and the woman three eggs.

Versions of the tale from nineteenth- and twentieth-century European oral traditions were recorded in Bulgaria, Greece, Italy, and Finland.[18] Referring to Armeno's *Peregrinaggio*, a short summary is quoted in Rudolph von Sinnersberg's German jestbook *Belustigung vor Frauenzimmer und Junggesellen* (Amusement for Maidens and Bachelors), published in 1747.[19] Moreover, German chapbooks of the sixteenth and seventeenth centuries adapted the distribution of eggs to a still more explicitly sexualized context.[20] In a different setting, a father promises to get the one of his three daughters married who is able to invest three eggs in the most profitable manner. The oldest daughter boils the eggs and gives one of them to her father (who already has two), so as to make it a total of three. Her mother receives another egg, since she will get another two when enjoying sex with her husband at night. The final egg she keeps for herself, as she soon hopes to have sex with her future husband. Since in this manner she manages to turn three eggs into a potential of nine, the father acknowledges her cleverness and gets her married.

Notes

1. Marzolph, Ulrich, "Teilung der Eier," in *Enzyklopädie des Märchens*, vol. 13 (2010), cols. 315–319.

2. Aarne, Antti, *The Types of the Folktale*, ed. Stith Thompson, 2nd rev., Helsinki: Suomalainen Tiedeakatemia, 1961, pp. 438–439, no. 1533.

3. Uther, *The Types*, vol. 2, p. 261–262, no. 1533.

4. El-Shamy, *Types*, p. 837, no. 1533B§.

5. Wünsche, August, *Der Midrasch Echa Rabbati, das ist die haggadische Auslegung der Klagelieder*, Leipzig: Otto Schulze, 1881, pp. 46–48; Hasan-Rokem, Galit, *Web of Life: Folklore and Midrash in Rabbinic Literature*, Stanford: Stanford University Press, 2000, p. 70.

6. Ambainis, Ojārs, *Lettische Volksmärchen*, 2nd ed., Berlin: Akademie-Verlag, 1979, pp. 320–321, 436, no. 103; Viidalepp, Richard, *Estnische Volksmärchen*, Berlin: Akademie-Verlag, 1980, pp. 334–336, no. 116.

7. Wesselski, *Märchen des Mittelalters*, p. 229, relating to no. 40.

8. Gobi, Jean, *La Scala coeli*, ed. Marie-Anne Polo de Beaulieu, Paris: Centre National de la Recherche Scientifique, 1991, pp. 253–254, no. 206.

9. Jāḥiẓ, 'Amr ibn Baḥr al-, *Kitāb al-Ḥayawān*, ed. 'Abd al-Salām Muḥammad Hārūn, 3rd ed., Beirut: al-Majma' al-'ilmī al-'arabī al-islāmī, 1388/1969, vol. 2, pp. 357–359.

10. Marzolph, *Arabia ridens*, vol. 2, p. 24, no. 90. The tale's Arabic versions were studied in detail in Ghersetti, Antonella, "'La division du poulet' ou 'Quand les moquers sond souvent moqués,'" *Middle Eastern Literatures* 10 (2007), pp. 15–33.

11. Nuwayrī, Shihāb al-Dīn Aḥmad ibn ʿAbd al-Wahhāb al-, *Nihāyat al-arab fī funūn al-adab*, vol. 10, Cairo: Dār al-Kutub al-miṣriyya, 1351/1933, pp. 223–224.

12. Niẓámu'd-dín, *Introduction*, p. 190, no. 1164 (bk. 1, ch. 25).

13. Marzolph,"Teilung der Eier."

14. Cristoforo Armeno, *Peregrinaggio di tre giovani figliuoli del re di Serendippo*, ed. Renzo Bragantini, Rome: Salerno, 2000, pp. 49–50; Christoforo Armeno, *Die Reise der Söhne Giaffers*, transl. Johann Wetzel, ed. Hermann Fischer and Johannes Bolte, Tübingen: Litterarischer Verein in Stuttgart, 1895, pp. 49–50, 207.

15. Wesselski, Albert, "Quellen und Nachwirkungen der Haft Paikar," *Der Islam* 22 (1935), pp. 165–173; Cammann, Schuyler V.R., "Christopher the Armenian and the Three Princes of Serendip," *Comparative Literature Studies* 4.3 (1967), pp. 229–258; Piemontese, Angelo Michele, *Gli «Otto Paradisi» di Amir Khusrau da Delhi: Una lezione persiana del «Libro di Sindbad» fonte del «Peregrinaggio» di Cristoforo Armeno*, Rome: Accademia nazionale dei Lincei, 1995.

16. Askari, Nasrin, "A Mirror for Princesses: *Mūnis-nāma*, A Twelfth-Century Collection of Persian Tales Corresponding to the Ottoman Turkish Tales of the *Faraj baʿd al-shidda*," *Narrative Culture* 5.1 (2018), pp. 121–140.

17. Marzolph, *Relief after Hardship*, pp. 86–87, no. 24.

18. Marzolph,"Teilung der Eier," col. 316, notes 5 and 6. Several of the references listed under ATU 1663 correspond to tale type ATU 1533B: *The Third Egg* that is neither semantically nor genetically related.

19. Sinnersberg, Rudolph von, *Belustigung Vor Frauenzimmer und Junggesellen*, Rothenburg: Caspar Friedrich Hoffmann, 1747, pp. 80–81, no. 216.

20. Marzolph,"Teilung der Eier," col. 316; Montanus, Martin, *Schwankbücher (1577–1566)*, ed. Johannes Bolte, Tübingen: Litterarischer Verein in Stuttgart, 1899, pp. 275–276, 595, no. 14; Uther, *Deutscher Märchenkatalog*, p. 455, no. 1633.

CHAPTER 85

Anticipatory Beating (ATU 1674*)

The collection of folklore in Poland at the end of the nineteenth century resulted in the recording and subsequent publication of three different texts corresponding to tale type ATU 1674*: *Anticipatory Whipping*.[1] The three texts overlap in the fact that a person receives a beating even before committing an offense. In the first text, a Kashubian and a Pomeranian mock a soldier, arguing that the beating will be too late once the offense will have been committed. In the second, the father gives his son a beating for saying that he wants to ride the foal of a mare his father is yet to buy. The third text tells of a gypsy who beats his child so that it will not break a jar. Except for these three Polish texts, the presently concerned tale was only recorded from oral tradition in the Balkans where it is usually attributed to the popular jester Nasreddin Hodja. In the Bulgarian versions, Nastradin beats his apprentice or son when he sends him off to fetch water with the jar, since a punishment will be useless once the jar is broken (or so that he remembers to come back quickly).[2] The tale is attested with the same protagonist and identical structure from late nineteenth-century Serbian oral tradition.[3] It is likewise documented in Greek and Serbian chapbook versions of Nasreddin's pranks[4] and the corresponding jests of the Judaeo-Arabic prankster Djohá.[5] A Romanian jocular tale published in 1926 attributes the act to a gypsy giving his son a beating so that he will not break the jar.[6] Criticized by a passing Romanian who argues that the father should rather admonish his son than beat him, the gypsy says that words have little effect, whereas "the beating will stick to his skin."

Historical text versions of the tale are as rare in Europe as the tale's recordings from oral tradition. In his German anthology of entertaining events and instructive sentences compiled from a variety of sources, *Ars apophthegmatica*, published in 1655, Georg Philipp Harsdörffer relates the tale of a judge or *alcalde* in Spain who administers a heavy beating to a red-haired man.[7] When asked why he does that, the judge responds, "Although he might not deserve it now, he will certainly deserve it later!" The very same text is repeated in Harpagiander's *Lexicon apophthegmaticum* in 1718.[8] As Harsdörffer's tale explicitly refers to a Spanish context, even foreignizing the text by mentioning the Spanish term *alcalde* (from Arabic *al-qāḍī*), it likely derives from an older Spanish source. Apparently, this source is the *Floresta espagnola de apotegmas y sentencias* (A Spanish Grove of Apophthegms and Aphorisms; 1574) compiled by Melchor de Santa Cruz.[9] In the *Floresta*'s short version, the judge is explicitly sure that the punished man will commit an offense in the future, simply because he has red hair. The Spanish tale predicated on the stereotype of the red-haired culprit[10] is repeated verbatim in Gerærdo Tuningia's Latin *Apophthegmata* (1609).[11] Two Spanish picaresque novels contain structurally similar tales whose specific action, however, differs. In Luis Vélez de Guevara y Dueñas's *El diablo cojuelo* (The Limping Devil; 1641), a sleepwalking man beats his wife and comforts her upon waking.[12] The man justifies the beating as anticipatory punishment for later when his wife might deserve it. In Jerónimo de Alcalá Yáñez y Ribera's *El donado hablador: Alonso mozo de muchos amos* (The Talkative Donor: Alonzo, the Servant of Many Masters; 1624), a mother gives her children nightly whippings so as to remind them to be good when they get too big for her to punish them.[13]

In classical Arabic literature, a tale closely resembling the version in *El donado hablador* is attributed to the fool ʿAynāwa in al-Ābī's (d. 1030) encyclopedia of jokes and anecdotes, *Nathr al-durr* (Pearls of Prose).[14] It is repeated almost verbatim in Ibn Ḥamdūn's (d. 1167) *al-Tadhkira* (The Aide-Mémoire).[15] Here, ʿAynāwa runs away from the children tormenting and teasing him on the street. Encountering a mother and her infant child, ʿAynāwa gives the infant a beating so heavy that it almost dies. When the mother curses him for his action, he justifies himself, arguing, "Your child will grow up to be even worse than those rascals." Toward the end of the thirteenth century, an anonymized version of the tale as given by al-Ābī is included in Syriac author Bar Hebraeus's (d. 1286) *Laughable Stories*.[16] Contemporary with al-Ābī, al-Naysābūrī (d. 1015) in his book on Wise Fools, *ʿUqalāʾ al-majānīn*, attributed a similar tale to the Wise Fool Buhlūl.[17] When encountering small children without their parents, Buhlūl would attack the children, arguing that now he can beat them, while later, when they grow up, they will most certainly beat him.

In his book on stupid people, *Akhbār al-Ḥamqā*, Ibn al-Jawzī (d. 1201) presented a version that closely corresponds to the jest about Nasreddin admonishing his child not to break the jar.[18] Here, a teacher argues that he beats the innocent pupil "before he does something wrong, so that he will not do it." Classical Arabic literature stereotypically represents teachers as ignorant and foolish. Even so, the teacher's action here is not devoid of a certain, albeit distorted, logic.

Both the tale's early attributions to the Wise Fool Buhlūl and to the numskull ʿAynāwa did not have a lasting effect and were abandoned in later Arabic tradition. Instead, the tale was at some point, probably as late as early in the twentieth century, integrated into the repertoires of the Arabic jester Juḥā[19] and his Turkish and Balkan alter ego Nasreddin Hodja. This context supplied a medium that enabled the tale's wide distribution, primarily in South-Eastern

European tradition, and might eventually have given rise to the tale's Polish versions.

Notes

1. Krzyżanowski, Julian, *Polska bajka ludowa w układzie systematycznym*, Polska Akad. Nauk. Wydz. Nauk Społecznych, 1963, vol. 2, p. 122, no. 1674*.

2. Daskalova Perkowski, Liliana, et al., *Typenverzeichnis der bulgarischen Volksmärchen*, ed. Klaus Roth, Helsinki: Suomalainen Tiedeakatemia, 1995, p. 352, no. 1674*.

3. Panić-Surep, Milorad, *Srpske narodne pripovetke*, 2nd ed., Belgrade: Nolit, 1964, p. 328, no. 97.

4. Wesselski, *Der Hodscha Nasreddin*, vol. 2, pp. 167, 231–232, no. 499.

5. Haboucha, Reginetta, *Types and Motifs of the Judaeo-Spanish Folktales*, New York: Garland, 1992, pp. 656–657, no. 1674*; Koén-Sarano, Matilda, *Folktales of Joha: Jewish Trickster*, Philadelphia: The Jewish Publication Society, 2003, p. 130 (narrated by Jeannette Ben-Nae).

6. Stroescu, *La typologie*, vol. 1, p. 646, no. 4101.

7. Harsdörffer, Georg Philipp, *Ars Apophthegmatica: Das ist: Kunstquellen Denckwürdiger Lehrsprüche und Ergötzlicher Hofreden*, Nuremberg: Wolffgang der Jüng. and Joh. Andrae Endtern, 1655, p. 400, no. 1904.

8. Harpagiander, *Compendieuses Lexicon Apophthegmaticum*, Nuremberg: Wolffgang Moritz Endter, 1718, p. 384, no. 1904; Uther, *Deutscher Märchenkatalog*, p. 455, no. 1674*.

9. Santa Cruz, Melchor de, *Floresta española*, ed. María Pilar Cuartero and Maxime Chevalier, Barcelona: Crítica, 1997, p. 107 (4,1,7).

10. Brednich, Rolf Wilhelm, "Rothaarig," in *Enzyklopädie des Märchens*, vol. 11 (2005), cols. 850–854, at col. 852.

11. Tuningio, Gerærdo, *Apophthegmata: græca, latina, italica, gallica, hispanica*, Leiden: Officina Plantiniana Raphelengii, 1609, Spanish pp. 25–26.

12. Childers, J. Wesley, *Tales from the Spanish Picaresque Novels: A Motif Index*, Albany: State University of New York Press, 1977, p. 97, no. J2175.1.2*.

13. Ibid., p. 97, no. J2175.1.3*.

14. Ābī, Abū Sa'd Manṣūr ibn al-Ḥusayn al-, *Nathr al-durr*, ed. Muḥammad 'Alī Qarna et al., vol. 3, Cairo: al-Hay'a al-miṣriyya al-'āmma lil-kitāb, 1984, p. 267; Marzolph, *Arabia ridens*, vol. 2, p. 185, no. 795.

15. Ibn Ḥamdūn, Muḥammad ibn al-Ḥasan ibn Muḥammad ibn 'Alī, *al-Tadhkira al-ḥamdūniyya*, ed. Iḥsān 'Abbās and Bakr 'Abbās, Beirut: Dār Ṣādir, 1996, vol. 9, p. 457, no. 1190 (the name is here misspelled as Ghabāwa).

16. Bar Hebraeus, Mâr Gregory John, *The Laughable Stories*, transl. E.A. Wallis Budge, London: Luzac and Co, 1897, p. 162, no. 645.

17. Naysābūrī, Abū 'l-Qāsim al-Ḥasan ibn Muḥammad ibn Ḥabīb, *'Uqalā' al-majānin*, ed. 'Umar al-As'ad, Beirut: Dār al-Nafā'is, 1407/1987, p. 146, no. 251; Marzolph, Ulrich, *Der Weise Narr Buhlūl*, Wiesbaden: Franz Steiner, 1983, p. 38, no. 25.

18. Ibn al-Jawzī, Abū 'l-Faraj 'Abd al-Raḥmān ibn 'Alī, *Akhbār al-Ḥamqā wa-'l-mughaffalīn*, ed. Kāẓim al-Muẓaffar, al-Najaf: al-Maktaba al-ḥaydariyya, 1386/1966, p. 133; Marzolph, *Arabia ridens*, vol. 2, p. 262, no. 1219.

19. Farrāj, 'Abd al-Sattār Aḥmad, *Akhbār Juḥā*, Cairo: Maktabat Miṣr, 1954, p. 108.

CHAPTER 86

The Animal Will Not Know How to Make Proper Use of the Meat (ATU 1689B)

A folktale from the Swiss canton of Grisons in Graubünden tells how the people from the mountain village of Medel send one of them to the town of Disentis to buy meat for a wedding.[1] The man buys the meat, and the butcher gives him a piece of paper with instructions for how to prepare it. On his way back, the man puts down his basket at the old chapel to get some rest. Suddenly a raven grabs the meat and flies away with it. Without even moving, the numskull calls after the bird, "You might have the meat! But I hold the paper with instructions how to prepare it!"

Corresponding to tale type ATU 1689B: *The Inedible Meat*, the Swiss folktale is similarly known all over Europe. All of the tale's versions overlap in the point that when an animal snatches the numskull's meat, he is not concerned since he is sure that the animal will not know how to prepare the meat properly for consumption.[2] The bird appearing in the Swiss tale is, however, an exceptional actor, as the majority of European versions of the tale mention a dog, occasionally a cat. In addition to its wide dissemination, the tale is remarkable for the feature that some of its narrators attribute it to a clearly identified regional context, thus aiming to authenticate the event as actually having taken place.

The late nineteenth-century Danish tale told by a teacher from Rendbæk in Northern Jutland has the numskull rest on his way back from Sønder-Saltum to Rendbæk when a dog snatches the meat.[3] An early twentieth-century French version from the region Hautes-Alpes introduces a man from Ristolas going to the butcher in Abriès.[4] In an Austrian tale that, judging from its language, has probably been reworked by its editor, a man from the Little Walser Valley in Vorarlberg marvels at the previously unseen sausages in a butcher's shop in Oberstdorf.[5] Wanting to introduce the novelty to his fellows, he spends all his money buying sausages. Since there is no paper, the butcher writes the instructions for preparing the sausages with a piece of chalk on the man's black leather trousers. When a large dog snatches the sausages from the top of the stick the man attached them to, the numskull quickly wipes the recipe from his trousers and rejoices that the dog will not know how to make proper use of the food. A

Hungarian version attributes the event to a certain Pista Bácsi who buys salami in town as the most unusual surprise for his daughter's wedding party.[6] And a Greek folktale has a man from Anogeia on Crete buy dried fish in Heraklion.[7]

In German tradition, the tale is included in a variety of chapbooks since the middle of the seventeenth century.[8] The earliest one of these is the *Exilium melancholiae* (1643) whose compilation is at times attributed to German teacher and politician Christoph Lehmann.[9] In this text, the protagonist is a simple-minded cook originating from the Basque region in Northern Spain whose inhabitants popular tradition regularly marks as numskulls. This is the only German version in which the animal snatching the meat is a cat. Both the cat and the Basque cook already feature in Spanish author Juan de Timoneda's (d. 1583) *Sobremesa y alivio de caminantes* (Table [Talk] and Travelers' Relief; 1563), a collection of jocular tales compiled to entertain the audience, as the title indicates, at table and while traveling.[10]

Arabic narrative tradition knows the tale since the beginning of the eleventh century.[11] The tale's Arabic form differs from the European form insofar as the fool mocks the animal not for lacking the recipe mentioning the spices and instructions how to prepare the meat, but for lacking the spices themselves. The tale's essential point is, however, the same. Since its earliest attested occurrence in al-Ābī's (d. 1030) comprehensive encyclopedia of jokes and anecdotes, *Nathr al-durr* (Pearls of Prose), the tale is regularly attributed to the popular Arabic jester Juḥā.[12]

> One day, Juḥā bought some sausages. An eagle attacked him, snatched some of the sausages, and flew away. Juḥā looked at the eagle and shouted, "You miserable one! Now where will you get the mustard to have with the sausages?"

In subsequent centuries, the tale is cited in the entries on Juḥā in the biographical dictionaries compiled by Muḥammad Ibn Shākir al-Kutubī (d. 1361)[13] and his contemporary Khalīl ibn Aybak al-Ṣafadī (d. 1363)[14] as well as in the collections of Juḥā's pranks in polymath Jalāl al-Dīn al-Suyūṭī's (d. 1505) *Tuḥfat al-mujālis* (The Companion's Present)[15] and in Yūsuf ibn al-Wakīl al-Maylāwī's extensive seventeenth-century compilation.[16] In twentieth-century Balkan tradition, the tale is attributed to Juḥā's Turkish equivalent, Nasreddin Hodja.[17]

Several centuries prior to the Arabic texts, a similar situation is attested in the *Philogelos* (The Laughter-Lover), the only surviving jokebook from Greek antiquity, probably dating from the fifth century CE.[18] Although the overall situation is the same, the numskull's reaction is different. Here, a hawk snatches the meat a man takes home. Enraged, the numskull shouts at the bird, "May I become a thieving creature like you if I don't go and do the same to somebody else!"

A similar logic as discussed above is also evident in a short jocular tale recorded from late nineteenth-century oral tradition in the Northern German region Mecklenburg-Vorpommern.[19] Here, the cashier of the town of Marlow brings the town's money to the bank. On the way, he climbs up a tree intending to support the local cuckoo against a newly arrived one. In the meantime, thieves steal the man's cash box. The numskull is confident that the box will be of no use to the thieves, as he still has the key. This text is similarly attested in a number of seventeenth- and eighteenth-century German chapbooks.[20] Its oldest-known version is presented in a somewhat lengthy tale in Ibn al-Jawzī's (d. 1201) *Akhbār al-Ḥamqā* (Tales of Stupid People).[21] Here, a merchant is depressed to find that burglars robbed his shop, stealing a strongbox full of money and other precious items. Learning about the events, the merchant's stupid son laughs confidently, assuring the people that nothing is lost. As the people imagine him to have an idea about how to recover the stolen items, they comfort his father. But when the father asks his son, the son simply responds, "The key is with me, so the thieves will not be able to open the box!"

Notes

1. Büchli, Arnold, *Mythologische Landeskunde von Graubünden: Ein Bergvolk erzählt*, vol. 2, 3rd ed., ed. Ursula Brunold-Bigler, Disentis: Desertina, 1989, p. 599.

2. Marzolph, Ulrich, "Rezept gerettet," in *Enzyklopädie des Märchens*, vol. 11 (2005), cols. 622–625.

3. Kristensen, Evald Tang, *Molbo- og aggerbohistorier samt andre dermed beslægtede fortællinger*, vol. 2, Århus: Forfatterens Forlag, 1903, pp. 23–24, no. 74.

4. Joisten, Charles, *Contes populaires du Dauphiné*, Grenoble: Musée Dauphinois, 1971, vol. 2, p. 227, no. 157.1.

5. Lang-Reitstätter, Maria, *Lachendes Österreich: Österreichischer Volkshumor*, 2nd ed., Salzburg: Österreichischer Kulturverlag, 1948, p. 45.

6. Kovács, Ágnes, *König Mátyás und die Rátóter: Ungarische Schildbürgerschwänke und Anekdoten*, Leipzig: Kiepenheuer, 1988, pp. 170–171.

7. Orso, Ethelyn G., *Modern Greek Humor: A Collection of Jokes and Ribald Tales*, Bloomington: Indiana University Press, 1979, pp. 64–65, no. 100.

8. Moser-Rath, *"Lustige Gesellschaft,"* p. 245, 357, note 83.

9. Lehmann, Christoph, *Exilium melancholiae*, Straßburg: Lazari Zetzners Erben, 1643, p. 286, no. 54; Graf, Klaus, "Lehmann, Christoph," in *Enzyklopädie des Märchens*, vol. 8 (1996), cols. 881–883.

10. Chevalier, *Cuentos folklóricos*, p. 363, no. 220; Amores, Montserrat, *Catálogo de cuentos folklóricos reelaboradoros por escritores del siglo XIX*, Madrid: Consejo superior de investigaciones científicas, Departemento de antropología de España y América, 1997, pp. 303–304, no. 204; Hernández Valcárcel, María del Carmen, *El cuento español en los siglos de oro: siglo XVI*, Murcia: University of Murcia, 2002, p. 192, no. 84.

11. Marzolph, *Arabia ridens*, vol. 2, p. 202, no. 889.

12. Ābī, Abū Saʿd Manṣūr ibn al-Ḥusayn al-, *Nathr al-durr*, ed. Muḥammad ʿAlī Qarna et al., vol. 5, Cairo: al-Hayʾa al-miṣriyya al-ʿāmma lil-kitāb, 1987, p. 313.

13. Ibn Shākir al-Kutubī, Muḥammad, *ʿUyūn al-tawārīkh*, Ms. Istanbul, Ahmet III 2922/6, fol. 75b.

14. Ṣafadī, Ṣalāḥ al-Dīn Khalīl ibn Aybak al-, *al-Wāfī bi-'l-wafayāt = Das biographische Lexikon des Ṣalāḥaddīn Ḫalīl Ibn Aibak aṣ-Ṣafadī*, vol. 27, ed. Otfried Weintritt, Beirut: Deutsche Morgenländische Gesellschaft, 1997, p. 184 (s.v. Nūḥ).

15. Suyūṭī, Jalāl al-Dīn ʿAbd al-Raḥmān al-, *Kitāb Tuḥfat al-mujālis wa nuzhat al-majālis*, ed. Badr al-Dīn al-Naʿsānī, Cairo 1326/1908, p. 349.

16. ʿAnābsa, Ghālib, "Min adab al-nawādir: naẓra fī makhṭūṭāt [Irshād] man naḥā ilā nawādir Juḥā, jamʿ al-faqīr ilā Allāh taʿālā Yūsuf ibn al-Wakīl al-Maylāwī," in ʿAnābsa, *Dirāsāt muḍīʾa fī ṣafaḥāt al-turāth*, Zaḥāliqa: Dār al-Hudā, and Jordan: Dār al-Jarīr, 2013, pp. 174–196, at p. 186.

17. Wesselski, *Der Hodscha Nasreddin*, vol. 2, pp. 166–167, 231, no. 498.

18. Baldwin, Barry, *The Philogelos, or Laughter-Lover*, Amsterdam: Gieben, 1983, p. 49, no. 259; Marzolph, Ulrich, "Philogelos arabikos: Zum Nachleben der antiken Witzesammlung in der mittelalterlichen arabischen Literatur," *Der Islam* 64 (1987), pp. 185–230, at pp. 222–223, no. 259.

19. Uther, *Deutscher Märchenkatalog*, pp. 462–463, no. 1689B; Neumann, Siegfried, *Plattdeutsche Schwänke: Aus den Sammlungen Richard Wossidlos und seiner Zeitgenossen sowie eigenen Aufzeichnungen in Mecklenburg*, Rostock: VEB Hinstorff Verlag, 1968, p. 25, no. 39.

20. Moser-Rath, *"Lustige Gesellschaft,"* p. 357, note 83.

21. Ibn al-Jawzī, Abū ʾl-Faraj ʿAbd al-Raḥmān ibn ʿAlī, *Akhbār al-Ḥamqā wa-ʾl-mughaffalīn*, ed. Kāẓim al-Muẓaffar, al-Najaf: al-Maktaba al-ḥaydariyya, 1386/1966, p. 176.

CHAPTER 87

The Clever Woman Has the Entrapped Would-Be Lovers Publicly Humiliated (ATU 1730)

In international narrative tradition, tales about female sexual agency display a great variety. Whether this variety applies to chaste women who ingeniously evade the advances of lecherous men or to licentious women who scheme to practice extramarital sex without being exposed, it is often difficult to identify narratives or clusters of narratives belonging to the same strands of tradition and distinguish them from others. Tales classified as tale type ATU 1730: *The Entrapped Suitors* are a case in point.[1] Previous discussions of this tale type often tend to lump together indiscriminately all kinds of narratives about a clever woman, coveted by more than one man at the same time, who manages to evade the advances of her unwanted suitors by entrapping them.[2] The most recent revision of the international tale-type index even lists tale type ATU 1730 as a "miscellaneous type," implying that it is neither possible nor worth the effort to clearly identify and distinguish the tale's different variations. In particular, this tale type must be distinguished from tale type ATU 882A*: *Suitors at the Spinning Wheel* (see essay **25, *The Entrapped Would-Be Seducers Have to Work to Earn Their Food***) in which the would-be lovers are made to perform menial tasks and at the end of which they are humiliated in the private atmosphere of the woman's household. The title coined for the presently discussed tale type, *The Clever Woman Has the Entrapped Would-Be Lovers Publicly Humiliated*, stresses the element common to the majority of the tale's oldest, and "Oriental," versions in which the female protagonist's lecherous adversaries suffer public humiliation. Admittedly, this constitutive element is neither very specific nor is it necessarily germane only to this tale type, since the numerous versions, whether documented in written sources or recorded from oral tradition, display an impressive range of creative and playful variations. The following versions from European oral tradition are but a small selection of possible variations.

The version told to Al. Martinov by G. Ignatov from Golyama Buchino in the region of Pernik in Western Bulgaria and originally published in 1958 introduces a furrier whose wife is coveted by the town's important men.[3]

> The tanner's wife complains to her husband about the improper advances of the priest, the mayor, and the tax collector, and her husband promises her to remedy the situation. In the pub, he tells the men that he intends to leave home to find a better life somewhere else. Each of the men gives him some money to assist him, and he pretends to leave. That evening, when the men happen to come by the woman's house one after the other, she invites them to visit her at specific times, arguing that she feels lonely. Just as the first visitor makes himself comfortable, the second one arrives, and the woman asks the previous one to hide. Finally, her husband arrives, pretending to have lost the money the men had given him. When the husband leaves again, the men get out of their hiding-places, but since one of them fell into the tanning vat, he has to be rescued by his fellows, and the hair and clothes of all of them stick together. The next morning, the tanner claims that his furs were stolen and blackmails the three men into giving him money so that he will not accuse them of theft.

A tanner's wife is also the main character of the Ukrainian version collected by O. Krasnoluts'kyi from the narration of the boy Yarmokha in Semenovka in 1898.[4] Here, the tale's main action is preceded by a long introduction in which the poor tanner Ivan tricks his rich neighbor into letting him marry his daughter by making him believe that Ivan is actually rich. Once they are married, the tanner's wife Marfa invites the priest, the deacon, and the cantor one after the other to visit her in private. Lasciviously sprawling on the bed, she has her would-be lovers one after the other undress and then hide in a barrel full of tanning agent as her husband arrives home. When all three of them are trapped, her husband loads the barrel on his wagon and on the way suggests to a curious rich man to show him three devils. The rich man pays him generously as he opens the barrel and the three men frantically run away.

The Norwegian narrator Anne Sundbøhaugen from Hjartdal in Telemark performed her version for collector Rikard Berge around 1924.[5] The farmer's beautiful wife is coveted by the reeve, the clerk, and the priest. In order to teach them a lesson, the couple decides that the woman should invite them one after the other to her house where they clandestinely prepared three barrels, one containing tar, the other feathers, and the third one water. When the would-be lovers arrive, the woman first requests the men to take a bath and has them jump into the tar, then the feathers, and finally the water, so that the feathers stick firmly to their body. When each suitor arrives, she has the previous one hide in the oven. When finally her husband comes home, he prepares to heat the oven and makes each of the would-be lovers pay a considerable sum of money in exchange for sparing them.

Several versions from widely dispersed European regions culminate in a scatological point, such as the Frisian one recorded in 1969 from the oral performance of Jan de Vries (b. 1888), a farmhand from Boelenslaan known for his hefty jests.[6] The sculptor's beautiful wife is coveted by the priest, the teacher, and the butcher. Having invited them to her house, the woman induces them to undress and hide in a closet one after the other as the next suitor arrives. Finally the sculptor arrives in the company of some visitors wanting to inspect his art. Opening the closet, they see the three nude "statues." As they need to place the candle somewhere, they stick it into the butcher's arse. In church the following day, the would-be lovers allude to their adventure in verse, with the butcher complaining about his particular misfortune.

Similar versions were told in Spanish by Ecequiela Manero, aged 50, from Burgos (province Burgos) in 1936[7] and in French by Maria Giraud, aged 61, from La Plaine-de-Chabottes (Dauphiné) in 1953.[8] The last man's rhymed lament about his hilarious misfortune was sure to make the audience burst into uproarious laughter. In German, it reads, "*Mit jedem schlief sie, aber / mein Arschloch war ihr Kandelaber.*"[9] In the Spanish tale, the poor organist, from whom the man was not able to extract any money, recites, "*Yo que no tuve dinero, / ¡puse el culo por candelero!*" In French, the sexton, equally unable to buy his way out of the situation, says, "*Et moi qui n'avais pas de quoi payer, / Mon trou du cul a servi de chandelier!*"[10] The Scottish version told to Calum MacLean by traveller Alasdair Stewart in 1955 has an equally provocative sexually nuanced climax.[11] Here, the tailor decides to travel to make more money. While he is away, his wife pretends to offer her favors to several suitors one after the other. Just as each of the would-be lovers gets into bed, a knock on the door announces the arrival of the next suitor, so the woman tells the previous one to hide in the cupboard. When the husband finally arrives, she tells him that she has been "taking pictures," that is, making sculptures. While the husband inspects her work, the men in the cupboard at first do not move. But when he criticizes his wife's work representing the doctor saying that she made "that bit of him just slightly . . . a little too long," suggesting to "snip a bit off" with his scissors, all three of them "made a dash for the door."[12]

Although the above summaries suggest a considerable variety of individual solutions, the general plot of texts corresponding to tale type ATU 1730 is relatively stable. The stunningly beautiful and faithful married woman is coveted by a number of men, often three. Together with her husband she plots to invite the would-be lovers at short intervals one after the other. Just as the men's fantasies are about to come true, the next suitor arrives, forcing the previous one to hide in an uncomfortable and often disagreeable place. When all of the would-be lovers are trapped, they are either punished, forced to buy their freedom, killed, or exposed to ridicule.[13] Although numerous versions from the medieval and early modern European literatures exist,[14] the tale's literary development and the different branches that gave rise to the varying schemes documented from oral tradition in Europe have never been studied in detail. The tale's earliest-known

European version is encountered in the *Constant du Hamel*, a French *fabliau* commonly dated to the first half of the thirteenth century.[15]

> Constant du Hamel's beautiful wife Isabeau is coveted by the priest, the chief warden of the prisons, and the forest warden. Since Isabeau does not give in to the men's advances, they cause her husband misfortune by claiming that he owes each of them a considerable sum of money. In order to teach them a lesson, the woman has them called to her house one after the other. While the first suitor is taking a bath, she takes his clothes and money and sends her maid to invite the second one. When the second suitor arrives, she tells the first one to hide in a barrel filled with feathers. The same happens to the second and third of her would-be lovers. Finally, the husband arrives and lights a fire under the barrel. As the men try to escape, naked and covered in feathers, they are pursued by Constant's dogs. In the end, they are given a good beating and promise not to molest the woman any more.

Although the exact stages of the tale's transmission East to West have not been identified, the considerable number of ancient "Oriental" versions leave little doubt that the tale's Western versions were adopted from one or several Middle Eastern models. The tale's oldest Arabic version, and incidentally the oldest-known version that can be dated with a certain degree of reliability, is encountered in the work *al-Maḥāsin wa-'l-aḍdād* (The Good Side of Things and Their Opposites). Although often attributed to the polymath al-Jāḥiẓ (d. 868), the work was apparently compiled in the aftermath of al-Bayhaqī's similarly antithetical early tenth-century work *al-Maḥāsin wa-'l-masāwī* (The Good and the Bad Sides [of Things]).[16] The text presents itself as being told to the governor al-Ḥajjāj ibn Yūsuf (d. 714) by the allegedly illiterate Bedouin Abū Sulaymān Ayyūb ibn Zayd (d. 703), a person whose eloquence was proverbial.[17]

> The virtuous ʿAmr ibn ʿĀmir in Basra has a beautiful wife named Jamīla (The Beautiful). One day, he deposits a thousand *dīnār*s with one of his pious friends to keep for his wife, should she ever be in need. After her husband's demise, Jamīla is forced to send one of her handmaids to sell a precious ring. The maid happens to meet her late husband's friend who informs her about her master's deposit. When the friend arrives to deliver the money to the widow, he is so enraptured by her beauty that he voices his feelings, and the woman sends him away in disgust without having received the money. One after the other she complains about him to the chamberlain, the chief of police, and the *qāḍī*, each of whom makes advances to her. Now she devises a scheme to both receive her money and rid herself of the importunate suitors.
>
> She has a carpenter make a large closet with three separate compartments. Then she invites the men to visit her one after the other at short intervals. She receives them politely, but just as the men are immersed in

conversation with her, the next man happens to arrive, so that the woman tells the previous one to hide in the closet where she locks him up. When the chamberlain, the chief of police, and the judge are trapped, she promises the pious man to give in to his desire if he solemnly promises to return her husband's deposit to her, and he does so. Immediately, the woman sends her maid to the king to pass judgment on her complaint against the pious man. Since the king is not able to locate any of his officers in charge, he is forced to take care of the matter himself. The woman requests that the king admit the testimonial of the closet and it is brought into the king's presence. She requests the closet to testify whether her demand is justified, or else she will burn it, and the three men trapped in the closet testify that the pious man admitted to owing her the money. When the king expresses his astonishment about the procedure, she argues that these were the most trustworthy persons she could find. She releases the three men from the closet, informs the king of all the details of her scheme, and receives her money.

Having listened to the account, al-Ḥajjāj expresses his admiration for the woman's cleverness.

Two other distinct Arabic versions of the tale, in international research labeled *4 amatores* (The Four Lovers), were identified in *The Seven Viziers*, an undated relatively recent adaptation of the originally Persian *Sendbād-nāme* (The Book of Sendbād [the Sage]) whose contents differs from that of its Persian precursor.[18] In the first version, the married woman requests the release of her lover from the chief of police (the *wālī*), the judge, the vizier, and the governor. Having shut all of them up in separate compartments of a large cabinet, she leaves town with her released lover. Later, the shamefaced officials come forth from the closet amidst the derision of the whole court.[19] In the second version, which is included in the nineteenth-century Wortley-Montague manuscript of *The Thousand and One Nights*,[20] a virtuous married woman invites the judge, the tax collector, the chief of the butchers, and the wealthy merchant. Before trapping them she has them put on dresses of different colors. When her husband returns, the men are forced to tell stories and make a fool of themselves.

An elaborate version of the tale is also included in the Ottoman Turkish compilation *Ferec baʿd eş-şidde* (Relief after Hardship) whose oldest manuscript dates from the last quarter of the fourteenth century.[21]

A goldsmith has a faithful wife, whom a scholar covets for a long time. When the goldsmith gets old and is reduced to poverty, his wife goes to the scholar asking him to return a deposit her husband entrusted to him a long time ago. Instead of returning the deposit, the scholar makes advances to the woman, promising her additional money should she give in. The wife is outraged at the scholar's indecent proposal and informs her husband about the events. Her husband sends her one after the other to the headman of the bazaar, the judge, the town's prefect, and the governor, but each one of them makes an equally inappropriate proposal to the woman. Finally, the woman orders a carpenter to make her a large closet with four single compartments.

The woman visits her suitors one after the other and invites them to come to her house, the scholar being the first. While the scholar gets ready to seduce her, she pretends that her brother just arrived, and he is forced to hide himself. In the following, she has the headman of the bazaar, the judge, the prefect, and the governor hide in one of the closet's compartments, whose door she locks. She then makes the scholar leave his hiding and confess his debt toward her as the four locked would-be lovers listen from inside the closet. Following his confession, she excuses herself and has her servants beat up the scholar, pretending that he is a burglar.

The next day, she complains to the king about the scholar not wanting to pay his debt, but the king advises her to ask the judgment of his chief officers. As none of the officers is available, the king finally consents to pass judgment himself, and the woman brings the closet as witness. As the closet does not speak, she prepares to burn it, and one after the other the men in their compartments testify to her claim and are released. The king makes the scholar pay his debt, punishes the culprits, and has their houses looted. From then on, he regularly invites the goldsmith's wife to tell her story to the women of his household.

The Ottoman Turkish version is a fairly faithful translation of the tale as encountered in the twelfth-century Persian *Munes-nāme* (The Book as an Intimate Friend).[22] The *Munes-nāme*, in turn, constitutes the archetype of the Persian genre *Jāme' al-ḥekāyāt* (Compilation of Tales), later representatives of which[23] likely affected at least some of the tale's retellings in contemporary Persian oral tradition.[24]

The existence of two eleventh-century Indian versions leaves little doubt that the tale's oldest written version is to be sought in the lost Indian *Bṛhatkathā* (The Great Narrative), compiled by Guṇāḍhya some time between the second century BCE and the third century CE. These versions are contained in Kṣemendra's *Bṛhatkathāmañjarī* (A Bouquet of Flowers from the *Bṛhatkathā*)[25] and Somadeva's eleventh-century *Kathāsaritsāgara* (The Ocean of Streams of Story).[26] The latter version, more or less identical to the former, goes as follows.

Having deposited his wealth in the hands of the merchant Hiraṇyagupta "for the maintenance of my house," Vararuchi temporarily leaves his wife Upakośā. Upakośā is seen bathing by the king's domestic chaplain, the head magistrate, and the prince's minister. The men make advances to her and are told to come visit her at night one after the other. When Upakośā asks the merchant Hiraṇyagupta for some of the money her husband deposited with him "in order that she might honour the Brāhmans," the merchant also propositions her. She has her handmaids prepare four pieces of rag anointed with soot mixed with oil, and a large trunk with an external latch. As her suitors arrive one after the other, she at first requests them to take a bath, following which the maids smear them with the lotion and bundle them into the trunk. When the merchant arrives, the woman makes him confess that he owes her the money, and she asks the "gods" in the trunk to listen. After the merchant has taken a bath, he is also smeared with soot and thrown out of the house.

The next day the woman complains about the merchant to the king. When the merchant denies having received anything from her, she has the trunk brought. The "gods" testify to the justice of her claim, the men are released, the "whole assembly burst out laughing," and Upakośā explains everything: "The virtuous behaviour of women of good family who are protected by their own excellent disposition only, is remarkable." The culprits are punished and banished from the country. The king shows his great regard for Upakośā and accepts her as his (spiritual) sister.

Alexander Cunningham identified a bas-relief on the *stūpa* of Barhut dating from the third century BCE[27] as a visual representation of the tale at the time of its presumably oldest textual appearance.[28] Although the *Yava-Majhakiya Jātaka* (Young Woman Jātaka?) to which the visual representation relates is not part of the standard collections of *Jātakas*, stories about Buddha's previous births, a closely related tale was identified in the Tibetan Buddhist compilation *Kanjūr* (The Translation of the Word).[29] In this version, Mahaushadha's beautiful wife Viśākhā is constantly harassed by the king's six viziers. In order to teach them a lesson, she spreads news that her husband is seriously sick and invites the would-be lovers to her house where she traps them one after the other in separate caskets. When she later exposes the men in front of the king, it becomes obvious that they have additionally been humiliated by having "their hair and beards shorn, and their hands and feet tied together." The king laughs and marvels at the woman's "acuteness and resolution." The major difference between the visual representation and the majority of textual versions appears to be the fact that the would-be lovers are not entrapped in (separate compartments of) a single closet but in separate caskets, four in the bas-relief, and six in the Tibetan text.

Contrasting with the numerous tales about the alleged unrestrained lust of women, the present tale presents a challenging model in which the woman's cleverness is unconditionally applauded. Although the woman exposes and ridicules high authorities, her action is not only seen as perfectly justified but even as deserving unconditional praise. As a woman, she does not have the social power to challenge or avert the sexual aggression of the male lechers directly and is forced to resort to a ruse. Instead of criticizing her duplicity, the tale's end leaves no doubt that her action is regarded as justified and that the male suitors are themselves responsible for the misfortune they suffer. In this manner, the tale warns both against female ingenuity and unrestrained indulgence of male lust. The tale's relative stability over a period of more than two millennia and across the whole Indo-European tradition area suggests that the tale's message has a universal bearing.

Notes

1. Wehse, Rainer, "Liebhaber bloßgestellt," in *Enzyklopädie des Märchens*, vol. 8 (1996), cols. 1056–1063, at cols. 1058–1060.

2. See, e.g., Clouston, William Alexander, "The Lady and Her Suitors," in Clouston, *Popular Tales and Fictions: Their Migrations and Transformations*, ed. Christine Goldberg, Santa Barbara, CA: ABC-Clio, 2002, pp. 436–451.

3. Haralampieff, Kyrill, *Bulgarische Volksmärchen*, Düsseldorf: Diederichs, 1971, pp. 206–209, 290, no. 43.

4. Mykytiuk, Bohdan, *Ukrainische Märchen*, Düsseldorf: Diederichs, 1979, pp. 170–177, no. 37.

5. Kvideland, Reimund, and Hallfreður Örn, *Norwegische und isländische Volksmärchen*, Berlin: Akademie-Verlag, 1988, pp. 258–260, 206, no. 61.

6. Van der Kooi, Jurjen, and Babs A. Gezelle Meerburg, *Friesische Märchen*, Munich: Diederichs, 1990, pp. 243–247, 373–374, no. 97.

7. Espinosa, Aurelio M., Jr., *Cuentos populares de Castilla y Leon*, vol. 2, Madrid: Consejo Superior de Investigaciones Cientificas, 1988, pp. 319–320, no. 394.

8. Joisten, Charles, *Contes populaires du Dauphiné*, vol. 2, Grenoble: Musée Dauphinois, 1971, pp. 368–369, no. 251.

9. Van der Kooi and Gezelle Meerburg, *Friesische Märchen*, p. 246.

10. Joisten, *Contes populaires*, vol. 2, p. 369.

11. Bruford, Alan, and Donald A. MacDonald, *Scottish Traditional Tales*, Edinburgh: Polygon, 1994, pp. 212–214. no. 28.

12. Ibid., p. 214.

13. Wehse, "Liebhaber bloßgestellt," col. 1059.

14. Wesselski, Albert, *Die Novellen Girolamo Morlinis*, Munich: Georg Müller, pp. 222–227, 314–317, no. 73.

15. Noomen, Willem, and Nico Van den Boogaard, *Nouveau recueil complet des fabliaux (NRCF)*, Assen: Van Gorcum, vol. 1, 1983, pp. 29–126, no. 2; the summary follows Tegethoff, Ernst, *Französische Volksmärchen*, Jena: Diederichs, vol. 1, 1923, pp. 182–189. See also Toldo, Pietro, "Pel fableau di Constant du Hamel," *Romania* 32.128 (1903), pp. 552–564; Galmés de Fuentes, Álvaro, "Un cuento de 'Las mil y una noches,' el 'Fabliau Constant de Hamel' y la farsa 'Les deulx gentilz hommes et la mounyere.'" *Revista del Instituto egipcio de estudios islamicos en Madrid* 27 (1995), pp. 41–51; also in *Romania arabica*, vol. 2, Madrid: Real Academia de Historia, 2000, pp. 89–100. For a recent interpretation of the *fabliau* in the context of contemporary economic considerations, see Murtaugh, Daniel M., "Constant du Hamel: Women, Money, and Power in an Old French *fabliau*," in *Women and Wealth in Late Medieval Europe*, ed. Theresa Earenfight, New York: Palgrave Macmillan, 2010, pp. 13–32.

16. (Pseudo-)Jāḥiẓ, *Le livre des beautés et des antithèses, attribué à al-Djahiz*, ed. Gerlof von Vloten, Leiden: Brill, 1898 (reprint Amsterdam: Oriental Press, s.a.), pp. 363–367; (Pseudo-)Ǧāḥiẓ, *Das kitâb al-maḥâsin wa 'l-masâwî (Über die guten und schlechten Seiten der Dinge)*, transl. Oskar Rescher, Stuttgart, 1922, pp. 75–79. See also Cosquin, Emmanuel,

"Le conte du chat et de la chandelle. Excursus III: Le conte de l'honnête femme et des galants," in Cosquin, *Études folkloriques*, Paris: Édouard Champion, 1922, pp. 457–473, at p. 460.

17. Pellat, Charles, "Ibn al-Ḳirriya," in EI², vol. 3, pp. 841–842.

18. For the content of the book's different versions, see Clouston, William Alexander, *The Book of Sindibād; or The Story of the King, His Son, His Damsel, and the Seven Vazīrs: From the Persian and Arabic*, Glasgow: privately printed, 1884, foldout after p. xvi; Hilka, Alfons, *Historia septem sapientium*, vol. 1: *Eine bisher unbekannte lateinische Übersetzung einer orientalischen Fassung der Sieben weisen Meister (Mischle Sendabar)*, Heidelberg: Carl Winter's Universitätsbuchhandlung, 1912, pp. XXIV–XXV.

19. Clouston, *Popular Tales and Fictions*, p. 442; Clouston, *Sindibād*, pp. 181–190, commentary pp. 311–322; Cosquin, *Études folkloriques*, p. 462; Marzolph and Van Leeuwen, *The Arabian Nights Encyclopedia*, vol. 1, p. 266, no. 198.

20. Clouston, *Popular Tales and Fictions*, p. 443; Clouston, *Sindibād*, p. 312; Basset, René, "Deux manuscrits d'une version arabe inédite du recueil des Sept Vizirs," *Journal asiatique* 2.2 (1903), pp. 43–83, at pp. 73–75; Chauvin, *Bibliographie*, vol. 6 (1902), pp. 11–12, no. 185; Marzolph and Van Leeuwen, *The Arabian Nights Encyclopedia*, vol. 1, pp. 196–197, no. 393; Burton, Richard F., *Arabian Nights*, (Benares 1885) reprint Beirut: Khayat, 1966, vol. 15, pp. 253–259; Tauer, Felix, *Tausendundeine Nacht: Neue Erzählungen*, Frankfurt am Main: Insel, 1995, pp. 557–579.

21. Marzolph, *Relief after Hardship*, pp. 70–71, no. 12.

22. Meredith-Owens, G.M., "An Early Persian Miscellany." In *Iran and Islam: In Memory of the Late Vladimir Minorsky*, ed. Clifford Edmund Bosworth, Edinburgh: Edinburgh University Press, 1971, pp. 435–441.

23. Jaʿfari Qanavāti, Moḥammad, ed., *Jāmeʿ al-ḥekāyāt: noskhe-ye Ketābkhāne-ye Ganj-Bakhsh-e Pākestān*, Tehran: Qaṭre, 1391/2012, pp. 287–303, no. 12.

24. Marzolph, *Typologie*, pp. 246–247, no. *1730, particularly version 2.

25. Cunningham, Alexander, *The Stūpa of Bharhut: A Buddhist Monument Ornamented with Numerous Sculptures Illustrative of Buddhist Legend and History in the Third Century B.C.*, London: W.H. Allen & Co, 1879, pp. 53–55; Toldo, "Pel fableau di Constant du Hamel," pp. 557–559.

26. Somadeva, *The Ocean of Story: Being C.H. Tawney's Translation of Somadeva's Kathā Sarit Sāgara*, ed. N.M. Penzer, reprint Delhi: Motilal Banarsidass, 1968, vol. 1, pp. 32–36 and commentary pp. 42–44: "The 'Entrapped Suitors' Motif;" see also Cunningham, *The Stūpa*, pp. 55–56; Clouston, *Sindibād*, pp. 314–317; Cosquin, *Études folkloriques*, pp. 459–460.

27. Cunningham, *The Stūpa of Bharhut*.

28. Ibid.

29. Cosquin, *Études folkloriques*, pp. 457–458; Schiefner, Anton von, transl., *Tibetan Tales Derived from Indian Sources: Translated from the Tibetan of the Kah-gyur*, transl. William Ralston Shedden Ralston, London: Kegan Paul, Trench, Trübner & Co., 1906, pp. 165–167, quotations at p. 167.

CHAPTER 88

The Clever Culprit Pretends That His Sword Has Been Transformed to Wood (ATU 1736A)

In July 2017, the Drama Factory in Antioch, California, performed "The Tale of Basim the Blacksmith and His Battle of Wits with the Shah of Isfahan," written by John Ballesteros, at the Nick Rodriguez Community Theater.[1] Advertised as "adapted from an age-old Persian tale," the "play is fun and colorful harking back to the days of Aladdin full of music and laughter. As the story goes, Basim is a happy man who wants nothing more than to be able to feast every evening with his friends, singing and dancing. When the Shah is in disguise he discovers that Basim will stop at nothing to make his festivities happen." Stimulating the audience's curiosity, the advertisement culminates in the open question, "What obstacles will the Shah put in his path?"

Classified as tale type ATU 1736A: *Sword Turns to Wood*, the tale of the blacksmith Bāsim and his encounter with the ruler is indeed a well-known folktale in modern Persian tradition.[2] The Persian folktale consists of two parts. The initial set of events starts with the ruler exploring the city in disguise (Mot. K1812.17). Meeting a poor but happy craftsman, most often a blacksmith or a cobbler, the ruler wants to find out whether the man's trust that God will always provide his livelihood is justified. In order to test the man's allegation, the ruler bans his profession. But each time he does so, the man manages to make a living in some other profession, for instance as a porter or a water-carrier. In the tale's second and final part, the happy man is hired as an executioner. As he is to receive his salary only later, he sells his sword and puts a wooden one in the sheath instead. When ordered to execute a convict, he cleverly avoids an exposure of his misdemeanor by stating that the person must be innocent, since the blade of his sword miraculously turned to wood. The tension dissolves in laughter as the ruler discloses his true identity and generously rewards the man. Although marketing claims such as the existence of an "age-old" version on which the Drama Factory's play is modeled need not be taken literally, the tale is known in Arabic versions dating at least from the early modern period.

First turning to the tale's European versions, the tale's second part is richly documented in nineteenth- and twentieth-century European tradition, often attributing the events to a well-known national ruler.[3] German versions of the tale are stereotypically attributed to the Prussian king Frederick II (r. 1740–1786), who is affectionately remembered in German popular tradition as "Old Fred" (Der alte Fritz).[4] A representative version was told in 1869 by the retired forester Pet. Borquoi in Birlinghoven, today a district of Sankt Augustin in North Rhine-Westphalia.[5]

> Old Fred in disguise mistrusts a soldier who hangs around in the pubs more than anybody else. The king learns that a soldier's life is miserable, were it not for the "Prussian trick" (*preussischer Pfiff*). As Old Fred is curious to know what this trick is, the soldier tells him that he secretly sold his saber, keeping a wooden saber instead. Aiming to expose the treacherous soldier, Old Fred some days later orders him to execute one of his companions. The soldier, however, claims that the alleged culprit is innocent. If his claim were correct, the Lord should transform his saber to wood. He then draws the wooden blade, and the king acknowledges the soldier's supreme command of the "Prussian trick."

Farm hand Wilhelm Kanzenbach, aged 72, told his dialect version of the tale in Lettnin in the former county of Pyritz in Pomerania before 1938, supplying a motivation for the king's order to the soldier.[6] In the pub, the king notices that one of the soldiers pawns his badge for liquor, putting on a paper badge instead, while another pawns his sword and replaces it with a wooden one. When inspecting the troops that day, the king orders the second soldier to execute his companion for charges of disorder. As the soldier cannot refuse the king's command, he invokes the Lord to transform his sword to wood. Another dialect version bricklayer Johann Hünike from Neustadt, born in 1825, narrated to collector Wilhelm Wisser details the amount for which the soldier pawns his sword at eight *groschen*.[7] In the end, good-natured Old Fred gives the soldier a full *taler* with which to reclaim his sword.

The Hungarian version performed by Péter Szergenyi, aged 69, a farmer of Kisvárda, Szabolcs County, and recorded by collector Bálint Bodnár in 1957, begins with a lengthy introduction in which the king in disguise is tricked by some soldiers into spending his money for liquor.[8] When the king later wants to take revenge by exposing the one soldier who left his sword in pledge with the innkeeper, the soldier pretends that his sword was miraculously transformed to wood. The tale's editor mentions that the narrator picked up his stories some fifty years earlier during his military service. At that time, "when the light was put out in the barracks, each soldier had to tell a tale at the command of the barracks sergeant." Predating the tale's recordings from oral tradition is a text contained in the Italian chapbook *Il compagno del passeggio campestre* (Companion for the Countryside Walk), first published in 1816, that attributes essentially the same events to an unspecified ruler named Federico.[9] Unlike these versions that exclusively contain the longer tale's second part, a Greek text from Rhodos[10] and the Sicilian folktale narrated by Antonina Basile from Salaparuta[11] reproduce the tale's two-part version.

Although the specific version of the tale's second part as an independent tale is only attested since the latter half of the nineteenth century, a tale similarly playing on the motif of the wooden sword appears in German chapbooks of the eighteenth century. The third volume of the chapbook series *Vade Mecum für lustige Leute* (Vade Mecum for Cheerful People), originally published in 1767, presents the tale as "an alleged miracle."[12]

> When the city of Naples was once severely besieged, the governor gave orders that each and every able-bodied man should on pain of death at least be armed with a rapier when out on the streets. One day, the guards caught a man disobeying the order and wanted to hang him on the spot. At first trying all kinds of excuses to get away, the man finally realized that he could not escape his punishment. But instead of accepting to die in such a disreputable manner, he convinced the guards that the first man coming by should kill him with his rapier. It so happened that the first man coming by was a gallant young man who had put a wooden rapier into his sheath, as this weighed less, and as he never intended to use it. Pressed to perform the execution, the gallant young man at first tried to evade. When the guards did not let him go, he finally laid his cloak aside, knelt down and invoked the Lord to transform his rapier to a wooden one should He not desire the man's execution. As the man pulled his rapier from the sheath, the people marveled at the alleged miraculous transformation. The culprit was pardoned, and the wooden rapier was henceforth kept in the city's main church.

This tale is quoted verbatim in a late nineteenth-century German chapbook bearing the colorful title *Eine Dose voll attisches Salz, um sich nach dem Essen den Schlaf zu vertreiben* (A Box Full of Attic Salt Serving to Dispel Sleep after the Meal).[13] The tale's localization in Naples might indicate its translation from an Italian source that has so far not been verified.

In his learned discussion of the tale's regional distribution and possible origins, Albert Wesselski identified the oldest occurrence of the motif of the sword or saber that allegedly turned to wood in early sixteenth-century Italian literature. In his *Della fortuna libri sei* (Six Books of Fortune), first published in 1547, Girolamo Garimberto tells the following tale.[14] When Galeotto della Rovere, cardinal of San Pietro in Vincula and a renowned supporter of artists and scholars, died, Pope Julius II (r. 1503–1513) installed Sisto Gara della Rovere, a person "of contrarian character" as successor of his deceased half-brother. The Portuguese Cardinal Jorge da Costa is said to have commented on this decision with the satirical remark that the pope acted like the peasant who, having lost his knife, put a wooden knife into the sheath. The anecdote is also cited in sixteenth-century French literature. At least by early in the seventeenth century, it gave rise to the Italian proverb *Fa come il villano,* "to act like the peasant."[15]

In Arabic literature, the tale is exclusively documented in the complex two-part version. Although more recent than the Italian reference to the peasant's knife, the Arabic version is considerably older than any of the tale's full-fledged versions recorded from European oral tradition. The earliest reliable documentation of the tale of "The Blacksmith Bāsim and Caliph Hārūn al-Rashīd" is contained in an Arabic manuscript that polymath naturalist Patrick Russell (1727–1805), the owner of a manuscript of *The Thousand and One Nights,*[16] acquired in the Syrian town of Aleppo.[17] Translated into English, the tale was published in the third volume of William Beloe's *Miscellanies* (1795). Soon after, it was included in German translation in both the volume dedicated to "new Arabic and Persian tales" in the *Blaue Bibliothek aller Nationen* (Blue Library of All Nations; 1797)[18] as well as the eleventh volume of the enlarged edition of *The Thousand and One Days* published by Friedrich Heinrich von der Hagen (1832).[19]

> When Caliph Hārūn al-Rashīd is unable to find rest one night, he decides to roam the city, together with his vizier Jaʿfar al-Barmakī and his executioner Masrūr, all of them disguised as merchants. Passing a house whose owner spends his time at merrymaking, they are permitted to join him on condition that they not ask any questions. Eventually, their host, the blacksmith Bāsim, tells the three listeners about his life. Earning a mere five *dirhams* each day, he spends all of his money on food and drink, having confidence that God will always provide his livelihood.
>
> Aiming to put the blacksmith's trust in God to a test, the next day the caliph prohibits the practice of his profession for three days to come. Although Bāsim is enraged about the caliph's order, he finds work as an attendant in the public bath and spends the money he earns on food and drink as usual. As the caliph and his companions in disguise visit him again at night, they are amazed to see him enjoy his life as ever. The events are repeated several times in a similar vein. When the caliph has the public baths closed, Bāsim earns money as a counselor. But the next day, the caliph has all recently practicing counselors submitted to a bastinado, so Bāsim cannot continue his practice. The following day, he decides to equip himself with a piece of wood as a sword and see whether he can find a job. In the marketplace, he successfully intervenes in a violent fight between two men. Taking Bāsim as an officer acting on behalf of some high-ranking personality, the market supervisor pays him to present the culprits to the caliph for punishment. Although the people in the marketplace insist that Bāsim must let the culprits go, he proceeds to the palace where he makes such an impression that he is given a job that earns him a

> substantial income. Again the caliph and companions witness that Bāsim's unfaltering trust in God earns him a living.
>
> When the caliph musters his officers the following day, three of them and Bāsim are ordered to behead a group of four robbers with their swords. As the three other officers execute the command, Bāsim fears that his fraud might be revealed. He secretly induces the fourth culprit to claim that he is innocent and pretends to the caliph that his sword will transform to wood if he tries to execute an innocent person. The caliph is so amused about Bāsim's trick that he awards him rich presents and hires him permanently.

Although no Middle Eastern version of the tale reliably predating the eighteenth century is known, the tale's wide distribution in Middle Eastern oral tradition appears to argue for an older tradition.[20] In addition to Arabic oral tradition,[21] the tale is documented in a fair number of Persian,[22] Turkish,[23] Georgian,[24] and Jewish Oriental (Arabic and Persian) versions.[25] The character of the hedonist blacksmith also appears in the tale of "Old Hunchback," a version of the international tale type ATU 1531: *Lord for a Day* (see essay **58, *The Subaltern Is Made Lord for a Day***) included in a nineteenth-century manuscript of the Arabic collection *The Hundred and One Nights*.[26] Moreover, a Judaeo-Arabic manuscript version of the tale in the Cambridge Genizah collection,[27] of unclear date, supports the tale's high profile in Middle Eastern oral tradition, at least of the modern period.

Notes

1. For the following quotations, see http://www.eastbaytimes.com/2017/07/16/on-tap-italian-american-classics-at-music-show-july-29/ (accessed December 11, 2017) and other websites advertising the play.

2. Marzolph, *Typologie*, p. 152, no. *844B.

3. Hauschild, Christiane, "Säbel: Der hölzerne S.," in *Enzyklopädie des Märchens*, vol. 11 (2004), cols. 964–967.

4. Uther, *Deutscher Märchenkatalog*, p. 477, no. 1736A.

5. Dittmaier, Heinrich, *Sagen, Märchen und Schwänke von der unteren Sieg*, Bonn: Röhrscheid, 1950, 150–151, no. 418.

6. Stübs, Hugo, *Ull Lüj vertellen: Plattdeutsche Geschichten aus dem pommerschen Weizacker, nach dem Volksmunde gesammelt und aufgezeichnet*, Greifswald: Bamberg, 1938, p. 122, no. 70; republished in Neumann, Siegfried, *Friedrich der Große in der pommerschen Erzähltradition: Eine volkskundliche Studie und Dokumentation*, Rostock: Wossidlo-Archiv, 1998, pp. 119–120, 143 (with a list of other German versions).

7. Wisser, Wilhelm, *Plattdeutsche Volksmärchen: Neue Folge*, Jena: Eugen Diederichs, 1927, pp. 143–144.

8. Dégh, Linda, *Folktales of Hungary*, Chicago: The University of Chicago Press, 1965, pp. 161–168, 321–322, no. 15.

9. Pezzi, Carlo Antonio, *Il compagno del passeggio campestre, ossia raccolta piacevole di fatti*

storici e di anedotti veri, Naples: Raffaele de Stefano e Socii, 1835, pp. 144–146, no. 15 (first edition Milan: A.F. Stella, 1816).

10. Hallgarten, Paul, *Rhodos: Die Märchen und Schwänke der Insel*, Frankfurt am Main: Frankfurter Societäts-Druckerei, 1929, pp. 169–172.

11. Pitrè, Giuseppe, *Fiabe, novelle e racconti populari siciliani*, vol. 3, Palermo: Lauriel, 1875, pp. 198–204, no. 158.

12. Uther, *Deutscher Märchenkatalog*, p. 477, no. 1736A (reference to the edition 1767, p. 143, no. 190); *Vade Mecum für lustige Leute, enthaltend eine Sammlung angenehmer Scherze, witziger Einfälle und spaßhafter kurzer Historien, aus den besten Schriftstellern zusammengetragen*, vol. 3, Berlin: August Mylius, 1781, pp. 143–144, no. 190.

13. *Eine Dose voll attisches Salz, um sich nach dem Essen den Schlaf zu vertreiben*, 2nd ed., Vienna: Joseph Gerold, 1781, pp. 161–162, no. 267.

14. Wesselski, Albert, *Erlesenes*, Prague: Gesellschaft Deutscher Bücherfreunde in Böhmen, 1928, pp. 115–119, at p. 118; Garimberto, Girolamo, *Della fortuna libri sei*, Venice, 1547, fol. 24b.

15. Buoni, Tomaso, *Nuovo thesoro de' proverbij italiani*, Venice: Giovanni Battista Ciotti Senese, 1604, p. 305.

16. Chauvin, *Bibliographie*, vol. 4 (1900), p. 209, no. CC; Akel, Ibrahim, "Liste des manuscrits arabes des *Nuits*," in Chraïbi, Aboubakr, ed., *Arabic Manuscripts of the* Thousand and One Nights, Paris: espaces & signes, 2016, pp. 65–114, at pp. 83–84, no. Ar 18.

17. Van den Boogert, Maurits H., "'Antar Overseas: Arabic Manuscripts in Europe in the Late 18th and Early 19th Century," Vrolijk, Arnold, and Jan P. Hogendijk, eds., *O Ye Gentlemen: Arabic Studies on Science and Literary Culture in Honour of Remke Kruk*, Leiden: Brill, 2007, pp. 339–352, at p. 348; see also Muehlhaeusler, Mark, "Oriental Tales in 18th-Century Manuscripts . . . and in English Translation," *Middle Eastern Literatures* 16.2 (2013), pp. 189–202 (ms. Cambridge Add. 3495); Browne, Edward G., A *Hand-List of the Muḥammadan Manuscripts, Including all Those Written in the Arabic Character Preserved in the Library of the University of Cambridge*, Cambridge: University Press, 1900, p. 335, no. 1490.

18. Bertuch, Friedrich Justin, et al., eds., *Die Blaue Bibliothek aller Nationen*, vol. 11: *Neue Arabische und Persische Mährchen*, Weimar: Verlag des Industrie-Comptoirs, 1797, pp. 8–96.

19. Chauvin, *Bibliographie*, vol. 5 (1901), pp. 171–174, no. 96; Ernst, Paul, *Erzählungen aus Tausendundein Tag, vermehrt um andere morgenländische Geschichten*, vol. 2, Frankfurt am Main: Insel, 1963, pp. 462–522.

20. Uther, *The Types*, vol. 2., pp. 403–404, no. 1736A.

21. El-Shamy, *Types*, pp. 925–926, no. 1736A.

22. Marzolph, *Typologie*, p. 152, no. *844B.

23. Eberhard and Boratav, *Typen*, pp. 346–347, no. 309.

24. See Tietze, Andreas, review of Eberhard and Boratav, *Typen*, *Oriens* 7 (1954), pp. 141–152, at p. 151; Sobḥi, Fażlallāh, *Dāstānhā-ye melal*, Tehran: Anjoman-e ravābeṭ-e farhangi-ye Irān bā Etteḥād-e jamāhir-e shouravi-e susyālisti, s.a., pp. 101–107.

25. Jason, Heda, *Folktales of the Jews of Iraq: Tale-Types and Genres*, Or Yehuda: Babylonian Jewry Heritage Center, 1988, p. 87, no. 1736A; Soroudi, Sarah Sorour, *The Folktales of Jews from Iran, Central Asia and Afghanistan: Tale-Types and Genres*, ed. Heda Jason, Dortmund: Verlag für Orientkunde, 2008, p. 199, no. 1736A.

26. Marzolph, Ulrich, "The Story of Abū al-Ḥasan the Wag in the Tübingen Manuscript of the Romance of ʿOmar ibn al-Nuʿmān and Related Texts," *Journal of Arabic Literature* 46 (2015), pp. 34–67, at pp. 51–52.

27. Baker, Colin F., and Meira Polliack, *Arabic and Judaeo-Arabic Manuscripts in the Cambridge Genizah Collections: Arabic Old Series (T-S Ar. 1a–54)*, Cambridge: Cambridge University Press, 2001, p. 33, ms. T-S Ar.6.16.

CHAPTER 89

The Preacher Cleverly Avoids Delivering a Sermon (ATU 1826)

In 1935, Kustaa Lahtinen from the municipality of Kuhmalahti, about 60 kilometers east of Tampere in Finland, narrated a short jocular tale to the Finnish folklorists who recorded it for their archives.[1] The tale is about a priest who is to deliver a sermon on Saint Stephen's Day (Finnish Tapaninpäivä; December 26). Instead of preaching, the priest only says that he already mentioned everything he knew about the saint during last year's sermon, and nothing new has happened since then. Corresponding to the international tale type ATU 1826: *The Clergyman Has No Need to Preach*, the tale likely derives from a more elaborately structured tripartite Middle Eastern narrative, most of whose versions recorded from European oral tradition are fragmentary in some way or another.[2]

The particular form evident in the Finnish text is first documented in the collection of jocular tales compiled by papal secretary Poggio Bracciolini around the middle of the fifteenth century.[3] Poggio localizes the tale in a small mountain city in the vicinity of Florence. He further introduces the events by stating that the other clerics present urged the one designated to deliver the sermon on Saint Stephen's Day to make it short as it was late and they were getting hungry. So the preacher begins the sermon by saying that he already mentioned everything he knew about the saint the year before and that he is sure the congregation would remember. Since then, nothing new has happened, so it is time to make the sign of the cross, pronounce the *confiteor*, and that is all. A version identical in content is attributed to the facetious preacher Arlotto Mainardi (d. 1484) in Florence who is asked to deliver the sermon on Saint Lawrence's Day (August 10).[4] The only minor, albeit significant, additional element in this version is Arlotto's concluding advice that those who were not present last year should ask to be informed by those who had been present.

A small group of Eastern European versions preserves the bipartite structure suggested by the final joke in the version attributed to Arlotto. The Belarusian text recorded at the end of the nineteenth century from the oral performance of Marysya Gorbachykha from Dvorchany in the Grodno (Hrodna) region tells about a peasant who wants his son to become a priest.[5] Instead of studying, the hedonist son fools around for some years, spends all of the money his father gave him, gets married, and returns home eventually. Obviously he pretends to have finished his studies, although the text does not mention this explicitly. When the sham preacher is asked to hold a sermon on Sunday, he presents "his book," presumably the Bible, to the congregation, asking them whether they know what the book contains. As the people respond in the negative, he scolds them saying that due to their ignorance, it will be of no use to preach to them. Perplexed about the priest's reaction, the people decide to answer in the positive the next Sunday. But when they do so, the priest again refuses to preach, arguing that there is no need for him to make an effort since they already know what he is going to say. Similar versions, at times with an inverted sequence of the audience's reaction or with additional events, are attested from Russian,[6] Ukrainian,[7] and Lithuanian[8] traditions. A German language version of tale type ATU 1641: *Doctor Know-All* (see essay **79, *The Lowly Man Posing as a Soothsayer***) narrated by Resi Klemm from the Hungarian Almáskamarás in the 1950s in its initial passages contains a vague echo of both versions mentioned so far.[9] First, the uneducated man posing as priest refuses to preach to the "ignorant" congregation twice. And when the people complain to the bishop about him, the bishop justifies his action by arguing that all priests share the same education. Consequently, if they had listened to the previous sermons regularly, there was nothing new he could tell them. While the first element corresponds to the bipartite version, the argument in the second is similar to that of Poggio's version.

The full-fledged text from which the previously mentioned versions likely derive repeats the same scene three times, with the preacher each time asking the congregation whether they know what he is going to say. When the people first respond in the positive, the preacher says that since they already know there is no need to tell them. When they answer in the negative the second time, he refuses to instruct them because of their ignorance. Twice disappointed, the congregation then decides that next time some of them should say they know while others would say they don't. "All the better," responds the preacher, "so now those who know can tell those who don't." And, again, he leaves without delivering his sermon. The tripartite version was recorded in the twentieth century from oral traditions as far apart as Hungarian,[10] Greek,[11] and Catalan.[12] It appears to be quite popular in Bulgaria.[13] In 1890, British folklorist William Alexander Clouston mentioned a version, presumably in oral tradition, that "within comparatively recent years" was credited to an Irish priest.[14] The Spanish literary version in Luis de Pinedo's sixteenth-century *Libro de chistes* (Book of Jokes) preserves only the final joke.[15]

Luis de Pinedo's text dates from about two centuries after the tale's full-fledged text was included in Andalusian Arab author Ibn ʿĀṣim's (d. 1426) compilation *Ḥadāʾiq al-azāhir* (Flower Gardens).[16] Here, the tale is attributed to Abū 'l-ʿAnbas al-Ṣaymarī (d. 888), a poet and boon companion of the Abbasid caliphs al-Mutawakkil (r. 847–861) and al-Muʿtamid (r. 870–892).[17] In Arabic tradition, Abū 'l-ʿAnbas was known as a jester to such an extent that al-Ābī (d. 1030) devoted a whole chapter to him in his comprehensive encyclopedia of jokes and anecdotes, *Nathr al-durr* (Pearls of Prose).[18]

> Once, Abū 'l-ʿAnbas ascended a certain pulpit in (the town of) al-Ṭā'if (in Yemen). He praised and glorified God. Then he said, "As for what follows . . . ," and paused. Then he continued, "Do you know what I want to say to you?" (The audience) answered, "No!" Whereupon he said, "Then that which I want to say to you will be of no use." Thereupon he descended (from the pulpit).
>
> The next Friday he ascended the pulpit, said, "As for what follows . . . ," paused, and continued to say, "Do you know what I want to say to you?" The people answered, "Yes!" He responded, "So what use is there in telling you what you already know?" Then he descended.
>
> The third Friday he said again, "As for what follows . . . ," paused and asked, "Do you know what I want to say to you?" They answered, "Some of us know it while others don't!" So he said, "Then those who know it shall inform those who don't!" Then he descended.

Ibn ʿĀṣim's version is an almost verbatim rendition of the tale's oldest-known version as given in the *Kitāb al-ʿIqd al-farīd* (Book of the Unique Necklace) by Ibn ʿAbd Rabbih (d. 940),[19] notably also an Andalusian author whose lifetime overlapped with that of the tale's protagonist. The tale's only other occurrence in Arabic literature before the Mongol invasion is contained in al-Ābī's (d. 1030) *Nathr al-durr.*[20] It is, however, not given in the chapter devoted to Abū 'l-ʿAnbas, but toward the end of the following chapter that deals with jokes about sermons, the call for prayer, and prayer itself. Here, the tale is told with only minor variations about an anonymous governor (*baʿḍ al-wulāt*) in an unnamed location. Ābī's text is cited again in the sixteenth-century *Tuḥfat al-mujālis* (The Companion's Present) compiled by polymath Jalāl al-Dīn al-Suyūṭī (d. 1505).[21]

Already in the sixteenth century, the tale's tripartite version was integrated into the repertoire attributed to the Turkish jester Nasreddin Hodja as documented in its oldest preserved manuscript collections.[22] The tale's inclusion in the enlarged editions printed in the nineteenth century in Ottoman Turkish,[23] Arabic,[24] and Persian[25] firmly anchored the tale in the repertoire of Nasreddin Hodja and his equivalents, including the Arabic Juḥā and the Persian Mollā Naṣreddin.[26] This attribution constituted a powerful medium for the tale's further dissemination.

The present tale is an instructive example for the hypothetical dissemination of tales East to West. The tale's oldest documented Western version as included in Poggio's *Facetiae* appears to be only vaguely related to the Arabic texts or, maybe, as the application of a similar joke in the Christian context. The second medieval Italian version as attributed to Arlotto with its final punch line that "those who were present should inform those who were not" makes it appear likely that the tripartite version was known in fifteenth-century Italy, and its final joke is proved to have been current in sixteenth-century Spain. How exactly the tale might have reached Italian tradition is unclear, although Poggio's work contains several tales adapted from the Arabic. Considering the fact that all of the tale's early European versions only correspond to parts of the older Arabic jest, oral tradition is a more likely avenue of transmission than written tradition. In Andalusia, Ibn ʿĀṣim's compilation probably transmitted the tale to the Spanish non-Muslim audience. The tale's nineteenth- and twentieth-century versions, particularly those in the Balkans and in East European traditions, likely owe their existence to Nasreddin Hodja's popularity and the numerous editions of his jests that were read and retold innumerable times. The Greek and Bulgarian versions constitute exact equivalents to the Nasreddin tale, but the farther the tale traveled from its origins to the North, the more it was fractured and fragmented so that only single elements survived in vaguely similar contexts. Jokes such as the one about the Irish priest quoted by Clouston that closely correspond to the version attributed to Nasreddin probably owe their existence to more or less direct retellings from written sources. After all, the tale's first publication of Nasreddin's jests in English dates to as early as 1854,[27] so it could potentially have been known to the British audience in Clouston's days.

Notes

1. Rausmaa, Pirkko-Liisa, *Suomalaiset kansansadut*, vol. 6, Helsinki: Suomalaisen Kirjallisuuden Seura, 2000, p. 415, no. 474.

2. Fährmann, Sigrid, "Predigtschwänke," in *Enzyklopädie des Märchens*, vol. 10 (2002), cols. 1280–1291, at cols. 1285–1286.

3. Poggio Bracciolini, Gian-Francesco, *Die Schwänke und Schnurren*, ed. Alfred Semerau, Leipzig: Deutsche Verlags-Actiengesellschaft, 1905, pp. 54, 207, no. 38; György, Lajos, *A magyar anekdota története és egyetemes kapcsolatai*, Budapest: Studium, 1934, pp. 105–106, no. 56.

4. Wesselski, Albert, *Die Schwänke und Schnurren des Pfarrers Arlotto*, 2 vols., Berlin: Alexander Duncker, 1910, pp. 27–28, 188, no. 8; Arlotto, Piovano, *Motti e facezie del Piovano Arlotto*, ed. Gianfranco Folena, Milano: Riccardo Ricciardi, 1995, pp. 23–24, no. 9.

5. Barag, Lev G., *Belorussische Volksmärchen*, Berlin: Akademie-Verlag, 1966, pp. 437–438, 627, no. 78.

6. Afanasyev, Aleksandr Nikolaevich, *Narodnye russkie skazki*, ed. Vladimir Jakovlevich Propp, Moscow: Gosudarstvennoye Izdatel'stvo Khudozhestvennoy Literatury, 1957, vol. 3, pp. 293, 445, no. 516; Chendeĭ, Ivan, *Skazki Verkhoviny: zakarpatskie ukrainskie narodnye skazki*, Uzhgorod: Zakarpatskoe oblastnoe izdatelstvo, 1959, pp. 52–53.

7. Krauss, Friedrich Salomo, "Folklore de l'Ukraine: Usages, contes et légendes, chansons, proverbes et jurons," *Kryptádia* 8 (1902), pp. 303–398, at 391–395, no. 12.

8. Capeller, Carl, *Litauische Märchen und Geschichten*, Berlin: De Gruyter, 1924, pp. 104–105, no. 35.

9. Künzig, Johannes, and Werner-Künzig, Waltraut, eds., *Lied- und Erzählgut der*

Resi Klemm aus Almáskamarás im ungarischen Banat. Authentische Tonaufnahmen 1952–1961, Freiburg 1980, pp. 85–88, 113.

10. Kovács, Ágnes, *König Mátyás und die Rátóter: Ungarische Schildbürgerschwänke und Anekdoten*, Leipzig: Kiepenheuer, 1988, pp. 230–231.

11. Hallgarten, Paul, *Rhodos: Die Märchen und Schwänke der Insel*, Frankfurt am Main: Frankfurter Societäts-Druckerei, 1929, p. 71.

12. Oriol, Carme, and Josep M. Pujol, *Index of Catalan Folktales*, Helsinki: Suomalainen Tiedeakatemia, 2008, p. 279, no. 1826.

13. Daskalova Perkowski, Liliana, et al., *Typenverzeichnis der bulgarischen Volksmärchen*, ed. Klaus Roth, Helsinki: Suomalainen Tiedeakatemia, 1995, p. 375, no. 1826.

14. Clouston, William Alexander, *Flowers from a Persian Garden and Other Papers*, London: David Nutt, 1890, pp. 65–66.

15. Chevalier, *Cuentos folklóricos*, p. 384, no. 232.

16. Ibn ʿĀṣim al-Andalusī, Abū Bakr ibn Muḥammad, *Ḥadāʾiq al-azāhir*, ed. ʿAfīf ʿAbd al-Raḥmān, Beirut: al-Masīra, 1401/1981, p. 269. For the following, see Granja, Fernando de la, "Tres cuentos españoles de origen árabe," *Al-Andalus* 33,1 (1968), pp. 123–141, at pp. 131–136; Marzolph, *Arabia ridens*, vol. 2, pp. 94–95, no. 378; López Bernal, Desirée, *Los Ḥadāʾiq al-azāhir de Abū Bakr ibn ʿĀṣim al-Garnāṭī: Traducción y estudio de una obra de adab de la Granada nazarí*, Ph.D. thesis University of Granada, 2016, vol. 2, pp. 163–165, no. 1027; López Bernal, "Los cuentos de Ibn ʿĀṣim (m. 1426): precedentes peninsulares de relatos españoles y del folklore universal en el s. XV," *Boletín de literatura oral* 9 (2019), pp. 35–52, at pp. 36–37, no. 27.

17. Meisami, Julie Scott, and Paul Starkey, eds., *Encyclopaedia of Arabic Literature*, 2 vols., London and New York: Routledge, 1998, p. 26.

18. Ābī, Abū Saʿd Manṣūr ibn al-Ḥusayn al-, *Nathr al-durr*, ed. Muḥammad ʿAlī Qarna et al., vol. 7, Cairo: al-Hayʾa al-miṣriyya al-ʿāmma lil-kitāb, 1990, pp. 299–303.

19. Ibn ʿAbd Rabbih, Abū ʿUmar Aḥmad ibn Muḥammad, *Kitāb al-ʿIqd al-farīd*, ed. Aḥmad Amīn, Aḥmad al-Zayn, Ibrāhīm al-Abyārī, 3rd ed., vol. 4, Cairo: Lajnat al-taʾlīf wa-ʾl-tarjama wa-ʾl-nashr, 1381/1962, p. 148; German translation in Marzolph, *Arabia ridens*, vol. 1, pp. 262–263, no. 25.

20. Ābī, *Nathr al-durr*, vol. 7, pp. 314–315.

21. Suyūṭī, Jalāl al-Dīn ʿAbd al-Raḥmān al-, *Kitāb Tuḥfat al-mujālis wa nuzhat al-majālis*, ed. Badr al-Dīn al-Naʿsānī, Cairo 1326/1908, p. 341.

22. Burrill, Kathleen R.F., "The Nasreddin Hoca Stories, 1: An Early Ottoman Manuscript at the University of Groningen," *Archivum Ottomanicum* 2 (1970), pp. 7–114, at pp. 32, nos. 4–6; see also Kut, Günay, "Nasreddin Hoca Hikâyeleri Yazmalarının Kolları Üzerine Bir Deneme," in *IV. Milletlerarası Türk Halk Kültürü Kongresi Bildirileri*, vol. 3: *Halk Edebiyatı*, Ankara, 1992, pp. 147–200, at pp. 159–160, nos. 19–21.

23. *Leṭāʾif-i Hoca Naṣreddin*, Istanbul 1253/1837, p. 2.

24. Juḥā, *Hādhihi nawādir al-khūjah Naṣr al-Dīn Afandī Juḥā al-Rūmī*, Būlāq: Mūsā Kāstillī, 1278/1861, p. 5.

25. *Moṭāyebāt-e Mollā Naṣreddin*, [Tehran] 1299/1881, p. 14.

26. Wesselski, *Der Hodscha Nasreddin*, vol. 1, p. 5, 205, no. 1; Basset, *Mille et un contes*, vol. 1, p. 271, no. 162; Marzolph, *Nasreddin Hodscha*, pp. 7, 291, no. 1.

27. Barker, William Burckhardt, *Reading Book of the Turkish Language, with a Grammar and Vocabulary*, London: James Madden, 1854, pp. 27–30 of the Turkish text.

CHAPTER 90

The Numskull Thinks That a Name Ages (ATU 1832N*)

One way to generate humor in numskull tales is to ridicule foolish people for their apparent inability to accept the unchanging and timeless validity of commonly acknowledged facts. In the present tale, corresponding to tale type ATU 1832N*: *Lamb of God Becomes Sheep of God*, this inability concerns the fact that a given name or denomination is not subject to the usual process of aging. The tale is documented in two distinct forms, a Christian and a Muslim one.[1] The tale's Christian form, common in European tradition, toys with the aging of the title "Lamb of God" (Latin *agnus dei*). The term, appearing in the New Testament at John 1:29, is commonly used to denote Jesus who sacrificed himself to take away the sins of the world. Most of the relatively few versions recorded from European oral tradition in the nineteenth and twentieth centuries are short, such as the following one from an unspecified region in Germany.[2]

> A year after finishing his religious instruction, young shepherd Hans in his prayer does not pronounce, "O Lamb of God, have mercy on us!" but rather, "O Sheep of God, . . . !" When the parson criticizes him, the shepherd responds that after a year, the lamb will certainly have grown up to be a sheep.

In the Finnish version recorded from Martti Kangas in Kankaanpää in 1938, the simpleton cannot read but only sing.[3] When the parson prompts him to sing, the man sings, "O Sheep of God, who takes away the sins . . . ," explaining his willful interpretation by the fact that the original "Lamb of God" will by now have grown up to be a sheep. In a German dialect text from Loosen in the region of Mecklenburg, the parson sees a young boy pray to the Lord for protection from thunderstorms by jumping back and forth across a ditch,[4] a motif corresponding to the international tale type ATU 827: *A Pious Innocent Man Knows Nothing of God*.[5] The parson teaches the boy to pray, "Christ, Thou Lamb of God!" When they meet again a year later, the "lamb" has turned into a "sheep," and the parson scolds the boy for being really dumb. The Spanish version narrated by Mota del Marqués from Valladolid in April 1936 is identical in terms of structure.[6] A somewhat elaborated version documented from the region of Aquitaine in South-Western France introduces Jean "of the herds," the dumb son of a rich father who is just clever enough to herd the sheep.[7] Jean has fallen in love with the miller's daughter. One evening, as she fetches water from the well, he jumps at her from behind, hugging and kissing her. Although the girl is not particularly shocked, she outwardly reprimands Jean and tells him to go to confession the next day. The parson is amused at Jean's confession and has him do penance by saying each morning and night for two years, "O Lamb of God, who takes away the sins of the world, have mercy on me!" Although, after two years, the "lamb" has grown to be a "sheep," the parson then absolves him. The miller's daughter not only pardons him but also marries him since, as the text says, "She said to herself that a rich man who is a little dumb serves her better than a clever man without a penny."

In a variety of European languages, including English, French, Dutch, and German, the tale was popularized in jestbooks as of the sixteenth century.[8] It is first attested in the English chapbook *A C Mery Talys*, published in 1526.[9] No versions of the tale from European medieval sources are known so far.

The tale's corresponding form in Arabic tradition is first documented in Ibn al-Jawzī's (d. 1201) *Akhbār al-Ḥamqā* (Tales of Stupid People).[10]

> An astrologer asked a man from Ṭarsūs (in Southern Turkey), "What is your sign of the zodiac?" The man replied, "The Billy Goat (*at-tays*)." Those present laughed and said, "There is no sign of the zodiac or stellar constellation called 'The Billy Goat'!" But the man replied, "Twenty years ago when I was still a boy, they told me that my sign of the zodiac was The Kid (*al-jady*). Doubtlessly it has grown up to be a billy goat by now!"

No other versions of the tale from premodern Arabic literature are known. Persian versions of the tale are contained in Sadid al-Din Moḥammad ʿAwfi's (d. ca. 1232) encyclopedic compilation *Javāmeʿ al-ḥekāyāt* (Collections of Tales)[11] and Fakhr al-Din ʿAli Ṣafi's (d. 1532) *Laṭāʾef al-ṭavāʾef* (Jocular Tales from the Various Strata of Society).[12] Although the tale is not attested in the manuscript repertoire of jocular tales attributed to the Muslim world's most popular trickster character,[13] in the nineteenth century, it was incorporated into the printed collections of tales about Nasreddin Hodja (Turkish), Juḥā (Arabic), or Mollā Naṣreddin (Persian),[14] thus opening up a large avenue for its adaptation in oral tradition all over the Muslim world.

Whether or not the tale's European Christian versions constitute adaptations of the Middle Eastern Muslim ones remains open to speculation,[15] as documents proving the adaptation beyond reasonable doubt are lacking. If, however, the former constitute adapted versions of the latter, then the change of key detail is not coincidental, but rather imperative. The Muslim sign of the zodiac, "The Kid," corresponds to the Western Capricorn, denoting an emblematic animal whose age is irrelevant. Thus, a simple translation of the Middle Eastern jest would not have made sense in the Western context. Similarly, the title "Lamb of God" does not make sense in a Muslim context that does not share the same concept. At the same time, the Christian "Lamb of God" like the Muslim "Kid," denotes a young animal that the foolish person can imagine to grow up. The adaptation of a fair number of originally Arabic Muslim jocular tales from al-Ābī's (d. 1030) comprehensive encyclopedia of jokes and anecdotes, *Nathr al-durr* (Pearls of Prose), to Syriac Christian ones by Bar Hebraeus (d. 1286) to such an extent as to completely obscure their origin, not only attests that similar adaptations occurred[16] but also suggests that the like adaptations were common in other less solidly documented cases. The eventual identification of medieval Christian versions from a Latin, Andalusian, Italian, or Greek context might serve to strengthen this argument.

Notes

1. Van der Kooi, Jurjen, "Hammel Gottes," in *Enzyklopädie des Märchens*, vol. 6 (1990), cols. 425–427.

2. Merkens, Heinrich, *Was sich das Volk erzählt: Deutscher Volkshumor*, 2nd ed., vol. 1, Jena: Costenoble, 1892, p. 251, no. 297. The short commentary on p. 277 describes the tale as "of great antiquity, but still often alive in popular oral tradition."

3. Rausmaa, Pirko-Liisa, *Suomalaiset kansansadut*, 6: *Pilasadut ja kaskut*, Helsinki: Suomalaisen Kirjallisuuden Seura, 2000, p. 424, no. 491.

4. Wossidlo, Richard, *Volksschwänke aus Mecklenburg*, ed. Siegfried Neumann, Berlin: Akademie-Verlag, 1963, p. 90, no. 307.

5. Barag, Lev G., "Heiligkeit geht über Wasser," in *Enzyklopädie des Märchens*, vol. 6 (1990), cols. 694–698.

6. Espinosa, Aurelio Macedonio, Jr., *Cuentos populares de Castilla y Leon*, vol. 2, Madrid: Consejo Superior de Investigaciones Cientificas, 1988, p. 349, no. 419.

7. Perbosc, Antonin, *Contes licencieux de l'Aquitanie*, (Paris, 1907) reprint Carcassonne: Garae, 1984, pp. 37–39, no. XVII.

8. Wickram, Georg, *Werke*, vol. 3: *Rollwagenbüchlein, Die sieben Hauptlaster*, ed. Johannes Bolte, Tübingen: Litterarischer Verein in Stuttgart, 1903, pp. 45–46 (text), 372 (references), no. 39; Uther, *Deutscher Märchenkatalog*, p. 503, no. 1832N*.

9. Briggs, *A Dictionary*, vol. A2, 1970, p. 263 (quoting from Zall, Paul M., *A Hundred Merry Tales and Other English Jestbooks of the Fifteenth and Sixteenth Centuries*, Lincoln: University of Nebraska Press, 1977, p. 124); Hazlitt, W. Carew, ed., *A Hundred Merry Tales: The Earliest English Jestbook*, London: J.W. Jarvis & Son, 1887, fol. 19a.

10. Ibn al-Jawzī, Abū 'l-Faraj ʿAbd al-Raḥmān ibn ʿAlī, *Akhbār al-Ḥamqā wa-'l-mughaffalīn*, ed. Kāẓim al-Muẓaffar, al-Najaf: al-Maktaba al-ḥaydariyya, 1386/1966, p.182; Marzolph, *Arabia ridens*, vol. 2, p. 265–266, no. 1237.

11. Niẓámu'd-dín, *Introduction*, p. 260, no. 2097 (bk. 4, ch. 25).

12. ʿAli Ṣafi, Fakhr al-Din, *Laṭā'ef al-ṭavā'ef*, ed. Aḥmad Golchin-Maʿāni, Tehran: Moḥammad-Ḥoseyn Eqbāl & Co., 1336, p. 409.

13. Kut, Günay, "Nasreddin Hoca Hikâyeleri Yazmalarının Kolları Üzerine Bir Deneme," in *IV. Milletlerarası Türk Halk Kültürü Kongresi Bildirileri*, vol. 3: *Halk Edebiyatı*, Ankara, 1992, pp. 147–200, at p. 198, no. 311.

14. Ottoman Turkish ed., *Leṭā'if-i Hoca Naṣreddin*, Istanbul 1253/1837, p. 34; Arabic ed., Juḥā, *Hādhihi nawādir al-khūjah Naṣr al-Dīn Afandī Juḥā al-Rūmī*, Būlāq: Mūsā Kāstillī, 1278/1861, p. 34–35; Persian ed., *Moṭāyebāt-e Mollā Naṣreddin* [Tehran] 1299/1881, p. 31; for the early publication history of the jests, see Marzolph, Ulrich, and Ingeborg Baldauf, "Hodscha Nasreddin," in *Enzyklopädie des Märchens*, vol. 6 (1990), cols. 1127–1151, at col. 1128–1130; see also Wesselski, *Der Hodscha Nasreddin*, vol. 1, pp. 55, 235, no. 105.

15. Van der Kooi, "Hammel Gottes;" Marzolph, *Arabia ridens*, vol. 1, pp. 239–240.

16. Marzolph, Ulrich, "Die Quelle der Ergötzlichen Erzählungen des Bar Hebräus," *Oriens Christianus* 69 (1985), pp. 81–125; see also Marzolph, *Arabia ridens*, vol. 1, pp. 236–237.

CHAPTER 91

How the Preacher's Sermon Makes a Member of His Parish Cry (ATU 1834)

The jocular tale about a preacher who makes a member of his parish cry, albeit for other reasons than impressing that person with his sermon, is classified as tale type ATU 1834: *The Clergyman with the Fine Voice.*[1] It exists in two forms. In the tale's Western form that covers most of European tradition, the person in the congregation is regularly a woman who usually cries because the preacher's miserable singing reminds her of the braying of her recently perished donkey. The tale's second form is prevalent in Middle Eastern tradition and regularly features a man whom the preacher's beard reminds of his recently perished goat. The latter form is also attested from the Balkans. Hybrid forms exist.

A Norwegian text, collected in 1879 from Seljord, Telemark, from an unnamed narrator presents a tale in which the woman's goat was eaten by a wolf.[2] The woman listening to the priest's sermon in a tale recorded in 1971 from Julien Mondet, aged 87, from La Vachette in the French region Hautes-Alpes is likewise reminded of her goat.[3] The narrator of a late nineteenth-century Frisian version tells the tale as the personal experience of his grandmother who cried because the priest's loud bellowing reminded her of her perished bull.[4]

Some versions of the tale mention altogether other reasons for the woman's crying. A late nineteenth-century German dialect tale narrated by day laborer Bergholz in Solzow, Mecklenburg-Pomerania, introduces a priest who is frustrated because he never manages to impress his congregation so much that they cry.[5] As one day, an old woman cries during his sermon, he asks her for the reason. Although the woman is at first reluctant to tell him, she subsequently informs him that her son studies to become a priest. Hearing the priest's poor sermon, the woman cried because she was afraid that her son might become an equally futile babbler.

A hybrid version from the Swiss region of Valais in the uppermost Rhône valley introduces a monk from the Capuchin order who wonders why a certain woman cries and laughs alternately during the sermon.[6] She explains that at times his beard reminded her pleasantly of her billy goat when "he was dealing with the nanny goats," whereas at other times she missed her billy goat dearly.

European versions of the tale's second form are documented from Bulgarian tradition. A lengthy text from Panajot Dinovski's late nineteenth-century collection of tales introduces a priest who is shocked by the irreligious attitude of his parish, as one of the peasants even dares to smoke his pipe during the sermon.[7] When he sees one of the people present crying, the priest is happy that there is at least one devout person, only to learn later that his beard reminded the peasant of a recently perished goat. The tale ends with the priest drinking a strong alcoholic beverage from a pot the people offer to him. When he throws the vessel to the ground in disgust, the people reproach him, as the vessel had served for many years as the pisspot of an old man's wife. The tale's final motif corresponds to tale type ATU 1578A*: *The Drinking Cup* (see essay **72, *The Drink Served in the Pisspot***). A Macedonian version features a bishop who asks the shepherd in his congregation why he cried although he did not understand a word of the sermon given in Greek.[8] The peasant responds in detail how the bishop's head resembles the head of his perished goat.

The tale's first form, alluding to the preacher's voice, was popularized in European tradition by chapbooks and other collections of jocular tales published in a variety of languages.[9] In English, it was included in the chapbook *Tales and Quick Answers*, first printed around 1535.[10] For German tradition, Johannes Pauli's *Schimpf und Ernst* (Jocular and Serious Tales in 1522) constituted a powerful medium of dissemination.[11] In the fifteenth century, the tale was included in Poggio Bracciolini's Latin collection of facetious tales, featuring a woman crying for her perished donkey.[12] This version is first attested in the thirteenth-century sermons of the French preacher Jacques de Vitry.[13]

Although no Middle Eastern versions predating Jacques de Vitry are known so far, three arguments strongly suggest that his text derives from Middle Eastern, and most probably from Arabic tradition.[14] First, Jacques de Vitry was ordained bishop of the Palestinian town of Acre in 1217 and stayed in the Middle East for a considerable number of years. Although the author's affirmation that he heard the tale (*audivi*) is somewhat formulaic, there is little doubt that the tale might have been current in Palestinian oral tradition in his day. Second, already in the fourteenth century the tale was included in the *Resāle-ye delgoshā* (Heart-Refreshing Epistle) compiled by Persian satirist ʿObeyd-e Zākāni (d. 1371),[15] many of whose jocular tales were adapted from Arabic literature. And third, the tale is contained in Muḥammad ibn Aḥmad ibn (al-)Ilyās al-Ḥanafī's seventeenth-century *Nuzhat al-udabā'* (Entertainment of the Educated),[16] a compilation of jocular tales dating from the Ottoman period most of whose tales are taken from older Arabic sources, some of them not preserved today. Both historical Middle Eastern texts feature a preacher and a man whom the preacher's beard reminds of his recently perished goat.

The tale's general structure proved to be adaptable to a variety of regional and religious contexts, in addition to Christian and Muslim traditions also including Jewish tradition.[17] Whether or not Jacques de Vitry adapted an earlier Middle Eastern tale, there is a distinct shift of aggressiveness between the Middle Eastern and Balkan form on the one side, and the standard European form on the other. In the former, the crying person is a man whom the preacher's physical characteristics remind of a perished beloved animal. In the latter, the crying person is a woman who, while also lamenting a lost animal, comments critically on the preacher's attitude or skills. In both forms the joke's victim is the preacher. While one might argue that a weeping man appears sillier, as men are supposed to be more restrained in grief, the latter form with its focus on the woman's unrestrained behavior binds in well with an increased level of misogyny that is often encountered in medieval European Christian and Jewish versions of tales originating from Muslim Middle Eastern tradition.

Notes

1. Marzolph, Ulrich, "Pfarrer mit der feinen Stimme," in *Enzyklopädie des Märchens*, vol. 10 (2002), cols. 887–891.

2. Kvideland, Reimund, and Hallfreður Örn, *Norwegische und isländische Volksmärchen*, Berlin: Akademie-Verlag, 1988, pp. 266, 307, no. 64.

3. Joisten, Charles, *Contes populaires du Dauphiné*, Grenoble: Musée Dauphinois, 1971, vol. 2, p. 360, no. 246.

4. Van der Kooi, Jurjen, *Volksverhalen uit Friesland*, Utrecht: Uitgeverij het spectrum, 1979, pp. 209, 276, no. 77m.

5. Neumann, Siegfried, *Volksschwänke aus Mecklenburg, aus der Sammlung Richard Wossidlos*, Berlin: Akademie-Verlag, 1963, p. 64, no. 220.

6. Jegerlehner, Johannes, *Sagen und Märchen aus dem Oberwallis*, Basel: Helbig & Lichtenhahn, 1913, pp. 140–141.

7. Krauss, Friedrich S., "Südslavische Volksüberlieferungen, die sich auf den Geschlechtsverkehr beziehen (Fortsetzung)," *Anthropophyteia* 2 (1905), pp. 265–439, at pp. 387–388, no. 438.

8. Cepenkov, Marko K., *Makedonski narodni prikazni*, ed. Kiril Penušliski, Skopje: MK, 1989, vol. 4, p. 206, no. 473.

9. Overbeke, Arnout van, *Anecdota sive historiae jocosas: Een seventiende-eeuwse verzameling moppen en anekdotes*, ed. Rudolf Dekker and Herman Rodenburg, Amsterdam: Meertens-Institut, 1991, p. 151, no. 850.

10. Zall, Paul M., *A Hundred Merry Tales and Other English Jestbooks of the Fifteenth and Sixteenth Centuries*, Lincoln: University of Nebraska Press, 1977, pp. 266–267, no. 31.

11. Pauli, Johannes, *Schimpf und Ernst*, ed. Johannes Bolte, Berlin: Herbert Stubenrauch, 1924 (reprint Hildesheim: Olms, 1972), vol. 1, p. 328, vol. 2, pp. 383–384, no. 576.

12. Poggio Bracciolini, Gian-Francesco, *Die Schwänke und Schnurren*, ed. Alfred Semerau, Leipzig: Deutsche Verlags-Actiengesellschaft, 1905, pp. 155–156, no. 230.

13. Crane, Thomas Frederick, *The Exempla or Illustrative Stories from the Sermones Vulgares of Jacques de Vitry*, London: Nutt, 1890, p. 22, no. 56; Wesselski, *Mönchslatein*, pp. 8, 197–198, no. 2; see also Tubach, *Index exemplorum*, p. 336, no. 4395.

14. Marzolph, *Arabia ridens*, vol. 1, p. 113; Marzolph, "Pfarrer," col. 888.

15. Zākāni, ʿObeydallāh, *Kolliyāt-e ʿObeyd-e Zākāni*, ed. Parviz Atābeki, Tehran 1331/1952, p. 347.

16. Basset, *Mille et un contes*, vol. 1, p. 191, no. 43; Ḥanafī, Muḥammad ibn Aḥmad ibn (al-)Ilyās al-, *Nuzhat al-udabā'*, Gotha, Ms. Orient A 2706, fol. 20b.

17. Schwarzbaum, Haim, *Studies in Jewish and World Folklore*, Berlin: Walter de Gruyter, 1968, pp. 257–258.

CHAPTER 92

The Simpleton Is Not Able to Perform a Seemingly Easy Mental Task (ATU 1835D*)

The jocular tale classified as tale type ATU 1835D*: *Wager: Clergyman to Read Prayer without Thinking of Anything Else*[1] illustrates the difficulty of concentrating on a particular mental task, however easy it may seem, without having one's mind stray and get occupied with other thoughts. In Christian European tradition, the tale's versions are embedded in a religious context, as they ridicule the human foible of being unable to concentrate on religious duty when mundane gain is involved. "Old Caraux" together with Françoise Lallan from Lectoure in Gascony dictated their elaborate version of the tale to French folklorist Jean-François Bladé in the second half of the nineteenth century.[2]

The Lord is bored with staying in paradise all the time. He decides to visit earth together with Saint Peter and chooses two good horses for travel. As they do not have any money with them, Saint Peter suggests they return to paradise to fetch money, but the Lord only laughs about Saint Peter's anxiety. When they hear beggars requiting their benefactors' alms with the blessing, "May God give to you!" Saint Peter is so embarrassed about God not having anything to give that he intends to return to paradise by himself. In order to teach him a lesson, the Lord transforms some blossoms into coins, and now that they have money, Saint Peter decides to stay with him. In order to punish Saint Peter for his lack of confidence, the Lord has him give away his horse and walk on foot.

After having traveled several miles, the Lord has pity on Saint Peter and offers to give him a horse if he manages to say the Lord's Prayer without thinking of anything else. Saint Peter starts to recite the prayer, but suddenly asks whether he is also to receive saddle and bridle as with the horse he had previously. Although Saint Peter failed the test, the Lord still has pity on him and gives him a horse.

Following this, the two travelers meet two peasants, one after the other, whose wagons have overturned. The Lord refuses to assist the first one, as he makes no effort to help himself. He helps the second one, as the man does his best to help himself, although cursing viciously in the process. A third peasant they meet reciprocates their friendly greeting with a rude retort to mind their own business, so the Lord makes his wagon overturn. Later having pity on the third peasant, the Lord has Saint Peter help him. But when Saint Peter's efforts are requited with the simple remark, "A little help goes a long way," the Lord is so angry that he makes the trolley overturn again and leaves the peasant alone.

In this version the task to say the Lord's Prayer without thinking of anything else is embedded in a lengthy structured narrative that presents itself as part of the cycle of tales in which God and Saint Peter travel on earth.[3] The tale's various elements essentially serve to educate the audience by demonstrating the consequences of disbelief and false pride. In most other versions known, whether from oral or written traditions, the presently concerned task is usually told as a separate short tale. In the late nineteenth-century Flemish version published by Amaat Joos, the action takes place between an abbot and a simple-minded peasant.[4] As the abbot mentions how difficult he finds it to devote himself to devout prayer without having his thoughts stray, the peasant brags that this is an easy task for him, and the abbot promises his horse to the peasant if he can say the Lord's Prayer without occupying his thoughts with anything else. Predictably, the peasant interrupts his prayer after a few lines by asking whether he will also get the saddle, and the abbot is proven right. In terms of structure, the tale's versions documented from European oral tradition show little variation, whether they originate from Denmark,[5] Finland,[6] Germany,[7] or Portugal.[8] In an unusual German dialect version told by Mr. Wilsecker from Schwinnen in March 1934, a woman is promised a litter of piglets. She interrupts her prayer to ask for a barrow in addition.[9]

Historically, the tale was popularized in Europe by collections of jocular tales in the sixteenth and seventeenth centuries,[10] such as the English chapbook *Tales and Quick Answers*, first published around 1535.[11] In the Middle Ages, the tale was disseminated in a variety of collections of exempla,[12] such as John Gobi's fourteenth-century *Scala coeli*.[13] In European tradition, it first appears in Jacques de Vitry's *Sermones feriales et communes*.[14] As Jacques de Vitry, who was ordained bishop of the Palestinian city of Acre in 1217, spent a considerable time in Arab lands, and as he introduces his version of the tale with the somewhat formulaic *audivi*, or "I have heard told," he likely adapted the tale from Arabic oral tradition.

The tale's Arab equivalent is first documented in polymath al-Jāḥiẓ's (d. 868) *Kitāb al-Ḥayawān* (Book of Animals).[15] The author cites his older contemporary, the historian Abū 'l-Ḥasan al-Madā'inī (d. 843), as informant.

Someone used to make fun of the people by claiming that he could conjure away a toothache. If somebody came to him to complain of a toothache,

> he would tell him during the conjuration, "When you go to bed, beware of thinking of a monkey. Because if you think of monkeys, the conjuration will not be effective." When that person would go to bed, the first thing he would think of was monkeys, and he would spend the night with his usual pain. In the morning, he would go to the conjurer who would ask him, "How did you fare yesterday?" Informed that the person had spent the night in pain, the conjurer would suggest, "Maybe you thought of monkeys." And since the response was in the affirmative, he would reply, "That is why you could not profit from the conjuration."

An almost verbatim quotation from al-Jāḥiẓ is contained in al-Iskāfī's (d. 1030) *Luṭf al-tadbīr fī siyāsat al-mulūk* (The Delicateness of Management: The Politics of Kings).[16] With reference to al-Jāḥiẓ, Ibn al-Jawzī (d. 1201) includes a condensed version in his *Akhbār al-Adhkiyā'* (Tales of Clever People).[17] Although the Arab tale is not attested in more recent versions, it appears to have stayed alive in popular tradition in the Muslim world, since Russian author Leonid Solov'ev (born 1906 in Lebanon) integrated a lively adaptation into the novel he wrote about the Uzbek hero Nasreddin as a feerless fighter for social justice.[18]

It is impossible to prove that the Arabic tale constitutes a direct precursor for Jacques de Vitry's text. Although both versions of the tale involve different characters in different situations, they demonstrate striking structural similarities. Whereas in the tale's Arabic version, a person is requested to perform a fairly unspecific task (fall asleep) while not thinking of a specific item (monkeys), the European versions request the person to perform a specific task (recite the Lord's Prayer) while not thinking of an unspecified item (anything else but the prayer). Both versions include a tempting challenge, either by specifying the forbidden object or by raising particular expectations, and both offer a material gain for the successful performance of the task, that is, relief from pain or the gift of a horse. In addition, both failing characters are simpletons who succumb to a strongly suggestive challenge. The Arabic tale is situated in the context of a society believing in the working of magic and sorcery. As the alleged sorcerer does not expect the cure to succeed, he protects himself against accusations of fraud by making a self-fulfilling injunction. Jacques de Vitry adapted, if indeed he did, the tale to advocate Christian standards, all the while making the same point of spoiling the simpleton's expectations by challenging him to perform a seemingly easy task whose successful performance the challenger himself jeopardizes by temptation.

Notes

1. Hubrich-Messow, Gundula, "Vaterunser beten, ohne an anderes zu denken," in *Enzyklopädie des Märchens*, vol. 13 (2011), cols. 1358–1360.

2. Bladé, Jean-François, *Contes populaires de Gascogne*, Paris: Maisonneuve, 1886, vol. 2, pp. 158–162, no. 5.

3. Lixfeld, Hannjost, "Erdenwanderung der Götter," in *Enzyklopädie des Märchens*, vol. 4 (1984), cols. 155–164.

4. Joos, Amaat, *Vertelsels van het Vlaamsche volk*, vol. 1, Brugge: Standaard, 1889, pp. 72–73, no. 42.

5. Kristensen, Evald Tang, *Vore fædres Kirketjeneste: belyst ved exempler, optegnede efter folkemunde*, Århus: Forfatterns Forlag, 1899, p. 21, no. 46.

6. Rausmaa, Pirkko-Liisa, *Suomalaiset kansansadut*, vol. 6, Helsinki: Suomalaisen Kirjallisuuden Seura, 2000, p. 432–433, no. 512.

7. Merkens, Heinrich Ludwig, *Was sich das Volk erzählt: Deutscher Volkshumor*, 2nd ed., vol. 2, Jena: Costenoble, 1895, pp. 131–131, no. 158; Zaunert, Paul, *Deutsche Märchen aus dem Donaulande*, Jena: Diederichs, 1926, pp. 156–157.

8. Cardigos, Isabel, *Catalogue of Portuguese Folktales*, Helsinki: Suomalainen Tiedeakatemia, 2006, p. 371, no. 1835D*.

9. Zender, Matthias, *Volksmärchen und Schwänke aus der Westeifel*, Bonn: Röhrscheid, 1935, p. 122, no. 153.

10. Overbeke, Arnout van, *Anecdota sive historiae jocosas: Een seventiende-eeuwse verzameling moppen en anekdotes*, ed. Rudolf Dekker and Herman Rodenburg, Amsterdam: Meertens-Institut, 1991, p. 378, no. 2360; Uther, *Deutscher Märchenkatalog*, p. 510, no. 1835D*.

11. Zall, Paul M., *A Hundred Merry Tales and Other English Jestbooks of the Fifteenth and Sixteenth Centuries*, Lincoln: University of Nebraska Press, 1977, p. 263, no. 27; Briggs, *A Dictionary*, vol. A2, p. 237.

12. Tubach, *Index exemplorum*, p. 280, no. 3615.

13. Gobi, Jean, *La Scala coeli*, ed. Marie-Anne Polo de Beaulieu, Paris: Centre National de la Recherche Scientifique, 1991, p. 210, no. 255.

14. Frenken, Goswin, *Die Exempla des Jacob von Vitry: Ein Beitrag zur Geschichte der Erzählungsliteratur des Mittelalters*, Munich: C.H. Becksche Verlagsbuchhandlung, 1914, p. 122, no. 48; Greven, Joseph, *Die Exempla aus den Sermones feriales et communes*, Heidelberg: Carl Winter's Universitätsbuchhandlung, 1914, p. 34, no. 49.

15. Jāḥiẓ, ʿAmr ibn Baḥr al-, *Kitāb al-Ḥayawān*, ed. ʿAbd al-Salām Muḥammad Hārūn, 3rd ed., Beirut: al-Majmaʿ al-ʿilmī al-ʿarabī al-islāmī, 1388/1969, vol. 4, p. 65; Marzolph, *Arabia ridens*, vol. 1, p. 156.

16. Iskāfī, Muḥammad ibn ʿAbdallāh al-, *Kitāb Luṭf al-tadbīr*, ed. Aḥmad ʿAbd al-Bāqī, 2nd ed., Beirut: Dār al-Kutub al-ʿilmiyya, 1399/1979, p. 227–228.

17. Ibn al-Jawzī, Abū 'l-Faraj ʿAbd al-Raḥmān ibn ʿAlī, *Akhbār al-Adhkiyāʾ*, ed. Muḥammad Mursī al-Khūlī, Cairo, 1970, p. 110.

18. See Marzolph, *Arabia ridens*, vol. 1, pp. 149, 156.

CHAPTER 93

The Illiterate Fool's Reckoning of Time Is Ruined (ATU 1848A)

In popular tradition, the ignorance of religious authorities constitutes a rich field for ridicule. In the international tale-type index, a large section of jokes and anecdotes is devoted to "jokes about clergymen and religious figures" (tale types ATU 1725–1849). Of particular relevance for the proper execution of religious duties is the reckoning of time, a task that in Christian tradition pertains to the days of the week or the determination of the religious holidays whose exact dates change over the course of the years. A clergyman lacking the basic capacity to determine those days serves as the epitome of stupidity. This feature is exemplified by tale type ATU 1848A: *The Clergyman's Calendar.*[1] The tale type covers texts of a considerable variety.

In Balkan tradition of various regions, the illiterate and simple-minded priest reckons the duration of the Lenten season by keeping a specific number of beans or peas in his pocket, discarding one of them every day. That way he would know when to celebrate Easter. In a Slavonic tale collected by Kuzman Šapkarev in the Macedonian town of Okhrid, the priest's wife notices the peas in the pocket of her husband's coat.[2] Not knowing what they are good for, she thinks that her husband likes to eat them and fills the pocket completely with peas. As Easter arrives, there are still many peas left, and when the priest counts the peas, he informs the people of his parish that according to the number of peas in his pocket there will be no Easter this year or the following. Only when on the way back home the priest sees some discarded colored eggshells does he realize that it must be Easter right now. In a Greek version from Cyprus, the priest realizes that it is Easter when the people in the neighboring parish ring their bells.[3] A Serbian text introduces the illiterate priest's wife wishing to fix her husband's coat.[4] Not realizing the function of the beans her husband keeps to reckon the days remaining until Christmas, the woman at first throws them away. Later she randomly gives him half a handful of beans, so that when only ten days are left until Christmas, the priest still counts more than 40 beans.

Versions from central and Northern Europe tell about a priest whose parish is so poor that he is forced to earn an additional living, usually by making wheels[5] or brooms.[6] Each day of the week he would produce one item, so that when he produced six items altogether, he would know that the next day is Sunday again. The lively tale narrated in 1963 by glassworker Georg Balk, aged 68, from the Bavarian municipality of Moosbach, features the simple-minded priest in a chain of episodes, the first of which concerns the priest's reckoning of the days of the week from the brooms he made.[7] Since the miller steals one of the brooms, the priest does not realize when it is Sunday, and his cook has to alert him that the people already congregated for service in the church. Historically, this tale is documented in the seventeenth-century English chapbook *The Sack-Full of Newes* (1673).[8] In this text, the priest simply forgets that he produced six baskets and has to be reminded that it is already Sunday while he is about to make another one. The broom version is first attested in sixteenth-century German author Georg Wickram's *Rollwagenbüchlein* (The Cart Booklet), localizing the events in the village of Langenwasen in French Lorraine.[9] Here, a peasant plays a trick on the priest by hiding one of his brooms that is rediscovered only later. In the end, the peasant apologizes to the priest for having jeopardized his authority. The priest promises to the sexton that he seriously intends to learn how to read the calendar, and all of them spend the evening in the local pub where the good-natured priest invites them for drinks. The author concludes by reassuring his readers that "we do not have similarly inept priests in the German lands."

More than a century prior to Wickram, a comparably silly reckoning of time, here the reckoning of times of the day, is attested in Andalusian author Ibn ʿĀṣim's (d. 1401) Arabic compilation *Ḥadāʾiq al-azāhir* (Flower Gardens).[10] Since that text relates to a Muslim religious context, the stupid person is a muezzin who is responsible for the daily calls to prayer. In traditional Arabic jocular tradition this character often serves as the subject of ridicule.[11]

> A certain muezzin took a dried pumpkin, made two holes in it and then filled it with water. When (so much water had dropped out of the two holes that) the (level of) water came down to the first hole, he made the call for the noon prayer (*al-ẓuhr*), and when it came down to the second hole, he made the call for the afternoon prayer (*al-ʿaṣr*). Another muezzin noticed that and enlarged the first hole so that the flow of water accelerated. The first muezzin inspected the pumpkin as usual and found that the water had reached the first hole, although it was not yet (the) time (of day) for the call for prayer. Even so he called for prayer, and (consequently) the people scolded him. But he said, "Calm down! I know this by way of my pumpkin!"

Ibn ʿĀṣim's text is somewhat enigmatic. On the one hand, its protagonist is allegedly so stupid as to trust the physical evidence of an instrument that has been tampered with rather than evidence that is supported by the observation of natural phenomena such as the position of the sun. On the other, the muezzin is apparently quite ingenious, as he is able to design and construct a simple but very effective instrument that, if handled correctly, appears to function with a high degree of reliability. In modern terms, one might regard him as a technical nerd who refuses to admit that the correct functioning of his gadget has been sabotaged, rather than apply his common sense. As no additional Arabic versions of the tale are known, the tale presumably derives from oral tradition in the Iberian Peninsula.[12]

An interesting intermediary that might eventually shed further light on the relationship between the Arabic text and the tale's later European versions is contained in the jests attributed to the Italian priest Piovano Arlotto as attested in a manuscript compiled around the second half of the sixteenth century.[13] In this tale, Arlotto makes an opening in a dried pumpkin. For every good day he experiences, he puts a bean into the pumpkin, and for every day with a bad experience, he takes a bean out. At the end of the year, he is thus able to say that he enjoyed a surplus of so many good days as there are beans inside the pumpkin. This tale combines the pumpkin as container, as in Ibn ʿĀṣim's Arabic tale, with the reckoning of days by way of beans, as in the European texts. It lacks, however, the sabotage of the calculating device that functions as the core motif in tale type ATU 1848A.

Notes

1. Schmidt, Andreas, "Kalender des Pfarrers," in *Enzyklopädie des Märchens*, vol. 7 (1993), cols. 878–879.
2. Haralampieff, Kyrill, *Bulgarische Volksmärchen*, Düsseldorf: Diederichs, 1971, pp. 251–252, 292, no. 62.
3. Diller-Sellschopp, Inez, *Zypriotische Märchen*, Athens: Akadēmia Athēnōn, 1982, pp. 268–269, 283, no. 86.
4. Vrčević, Vuk, *Srpske narodne pripovijetke, ponajviše kratke i šaljive*, vol 1, Belgrade: Srpska kraljevska državna štamparija, 1868, p. 62, no. 139.
5. Wrasman, Adolf, *Die Sagen der Heimat: Sagenschatz des Regierungsbezirks Osnabrück*, Osnabrück: Pillmeyer, 1908, pp. 75–76; Van der Kooi, Jurjen, and Theo Schuster, *Der Großherzog und die Marktfrau: Märchen und Schwänke aus dem Oldenburger Land*, Leer: Schuster, 1994, pp. 283–284, 430, no. 181j.
6. Benzel, Ulrich, *Volkserzählungen aus dem oberpfälzisch-böhmischen Grenzgebiet*, Münster: Aschendorff, 1965, pp. 134–136, no. 157.
7. Ibid.
8. Hazlitt, W. Carew, ed., *Shakespeare Jest-Books: Reprints of the Early and Very Rare Jest-Books Supposed to Have Been Used by Shakespeare*, London: Willis & Sotheran, 1881, vol. 2, p. 186.
9. Wickram, Georg, *Werke*, vol. 3: *Rollwagenbüchlein, Die sieben Hauptlaster*, ed. Johannes Bolte, Tübingen: Litterarischer Verein in Stuttgart, 1903, pp. 61–63, 375, no. 47.
10. Ibn ʿĀṣim al-Andalusī, Abū Bakr ibn Muḥammad, *Ḥadāʾiq al-azāhir*, ed. ʿAfīf ʿAbd al-Raḥmān, Beirut: al-Masīra, 1401/1981, pp. 268–269; López Bernal, Desirée, *Los Ḥadāʾiq al-azāhir de Abū Bakr ibn ʿĀṣim al-Garnāṭī: Traducción y estudio de una obra de adab de la Granada nazarí*, Ph.D. thesis University of Granada, 2016, vol. 1, p. 420, no. 1022; see also López Bernal, "Nuevas versiones literarias de los cuentos tipo ATU 1848 y ATU

1848A en la Península ibérica," *Oceánide* 10 (2017) http://oceanide.netne.net/articulos/art10-4.pdf (accessed March 19, 2018); López Bernal,"Los cuentos de Ibn ʿĀṣim (m. 1426): precedentes peninsulares de relatos españoles y del folklore universal en el s. XV," *Boletín de literatura oral* 9 (2019), pp. 35–52, at pp. 37–38, no. 29.

11. Marzolph, *Arabia ridens*, vol. 2, Index, s.v. "Gebetsrufer."

12. López Bernal, "Nuevas versiones."

13. Wesselski, Albert, *Die Schwänke und Schnurren des Pfarrers Arlotto*, Berlin: Alexander Duncker, 1910, vol. 2, pp. 98, 233, no. 98.

CHAPTER 94

The Rider Goes Where His Bolting Mount Takes Him (ATU 1849*)

The short jocular tale classified as tale type ATU 1849*: *The Clergyman on the Cow's Tail* is exclusively documented from oral tradition in the Baltic countries and the Balkans. The Croatian version narrated by the literate worker Mile Milanović, born 1915, from the village of Glavice tells of a priest who mounts his petulant cow so that his servant can milk her with greater ease.[1] The cow breaks loose, and the priest grabs her horns so as not to fall off her back. When the peasants ask him whether he is going somewhere far, he shouts in response, "Only the devil and the cow know that!" The tale's Hungarian version supplies a detailed localization for the event.[2] Here, the parson of Akali brings a cow to the market in Keszi. In the area of Köveskáll the animal bolts, dragging along the parson holding the rope. Asked by some peasants working on the fields where he is going, the parson responds, "Only God and this stupid cow know that!" A Serbian text begins with an elaborate introduction featuring the lively depiction of the (Orthodox) priest and his wife as they try to milk the cow that keeps overturning the bucket as she wags her tail to ward off the numerous flies.[3] Finally, the priest mounts the cow to calm her down, but instead she breaks loose. As the priest does not manage to stop the cow even as they are about to leave the village, he shouts to the villagers, "If am not back by tomorrow, tell everybody that next Thursday is Ascension Day!" The tale's three oldest versions known so far were recorded from Romanian tradition around 1900, two of them mentioning the protagonist to be a Swabian or a Saxon, respectively.[4]

Featuring a priest and his only cow as she is being milked, the tale is naturally grounded in the social and religious environment of rural societies in Christian Europe. Particularly the image of the priest sitting astride the bolting cow must have been experienced as hilariously funny, all the more so since the cow is not a regular mount. As historical references to the tale are lacking, the form quoted above likely constitutes the adaptation of an earlier form featuring a donkey or a mule as a regularly used mount.[5] The German chapbook *Fasciculus facetiarum*, published in 1670, introduces a priest who is called to visit a sick person in a neighboring village.[6] On his way, the priest notices that the footbridge crossing a creek is broken and asks a nearby miller to let him cross the water on the miller's donkey. Although the miller warns the priest that the donkey is not to be trusted, the priest insists upon riding it. Having crossed the water, the donkey picks up speed beyond the priest's control as it knows that the mill, its usual destination, is close-by. When the priest is not able to stop the donkey as they pass through the village, the people shout at him asking where he is going, and the priest responds, "Only God and the donkey know that!" In the collection of sermons compiled by German preacher Conrad Purselt (1644–1706), the event is similarly attributed to a doctor in Palermo whose donkey runs amok.[7] The doctor's response to the people's question is given in Latin as "Nescitur, pepite a mulo!" (I don't know, ask the mule!) The tale's oldest European version is contained in Italian author Francesco Sacchetti's fourteenth-century collection of novellas, *Le trecentonovelle* (Three Hundred Novellas), here attributed to the fictional character Alberto in Siena, obviously a stereotype character of jocular tales in contemporary Italian tradition.[8] To the people's question where he is going, Alberto simply responds, "Where the mule takes me!"

Prior to European tradition, the tale is attested in early eleventh-century Arabic literature.[9] In his comprehensive encyclopedia of jokes and anecdotes, *Nathr al-durr* (Pearls of Prose), al-Ābī (d. 1030) attributes the tale to the popular jester Juḥā.[10]

> One day, Juḥā's mule bolted, taking another way than the one he intended. One of his friends met him and asked, "Where are you going, Abū 'l-Ghuṣn?" And Juḥā responded, "Wherever the mule has an affair to settle."

With little variation and the stereotype attribution to Juḥā, the tale is included in Ibn Ḥamdūn's (d. 1167) *al-Tadhkira* (The Aide-Mémoire)[11] and the entries on Juḥā in the biographical dictionaries compiled by Muḥammad Ibn Shākir al-Kutubī (d. 1361)[12] and his contemporary Khalīl ibn Aybak al-Ṣafadī (d. 1363).[13] It is subsequently cited in the collections of Juḥā's pranks in al-Zaydī's fifteenth-century florilegium of "the best" from al-Ābī's encyclopedia, *Lubāb Nathr al-durr*,[14] in polymath Jalāl al-Dīn al-Suyūṭī's (d. 1505) *Tuḥfat al-mujālis* (The Companion's Present),[15] in Muḥammad ibn Aḥmad ibn (al-)Ilyās al- Ḥanafī's seventeenth-century *Nuzhat al-udabā'* (Entertainment of the Educated),[16] in Yūsuf ibn al-Wakīl al-Maylāwī's compilation dedicated to Juḥā's pranks that equally dates from the seventeenth century,[17] and in al-Ḥafnāwī's eighteenth-century *Bughyat al-jalīs* (The Companion's Desire).[18] In the nineteenth century, the tale is included in the earliest printed Arabic edition (1861) of Juḥā's pranks[19] and remained a constant ingredient ever since.

The tale's ultimately oldest occurrence so far known is included in the ancient Greek *The Cynic*, a dialogue that is commonly attributed to the second-century BCE author Lucian.[20] In the course of conversation, the cynic compares his opponent's situation to that of people washed about by a flood who simply drift with the current. As a further illustration, he cites the tale of a person who mounts a mad (or vicious) horse that runs off together with him. When asked where he is going to, the man replies, "Wherever this fellow decides," pointing to the horse. Whereas the tale's ancient Greek version is thus embedded in the context of a particular argument, Gustave Edmund von Grunebaum took the tale's Arabic version as an apt example for the ways "striking elements survived apart from their true context."[21]

Sigmund Freud (1856–1939), the founder of psychoanalysis, probably knew the jocular tale from Jewish tradition. As he cited the item a total of three times in the course of 23 years, it appears to have been one of his favorite jokes.[22]

Notes

1. Bošković-Stulli, Maja, "Narodne pripovijetke i predaje Sinjske Krajine," *Narodna Umjetnost* 5–6 (1967–1968), pp. 303–432, at pp. 369, 421, no. 37.

2. Kovács, Ágnes, *König Mátyás und die Rátóter: Ungarische Schildbürgerschwänke und Anekdoten*, Leipzig: Kiepenheuer, 1988, p. 53.

3. Chaikanovich, Veselin, *Srpske narodne pripovetke*, vol. 1, Belgrade: Izdaniye knizharnitse Raikovicha i Vukovicha, 1927, pp. 379–380, 538, no. 130.

4. Stroescu, *La typologie*, vol. 1, p. 784, no. 4348.

5. Marzolph, *Arabia ridens*, vol. 1, pp. 56–59.

6. *Fasciculus facetiarum*, vol. 1, Schnatterberg im Waschland, 1670, pp. 33–34, no. 23.

7. Moser-Rath, Elfriede, *Predigtmärlein der Barockzeit: Exempel, Sage, Schwank und Fabel in geistlichen Quellen des oberdeutschen Raumes*, Berlin: De Gruyter, 1964, pp. 281–282, 472, no. 129.

8. Sacchetti, Franco, *Le trecentonovelle*, ed. Valerio Marucci, Rome: Salerno, 1996, pp. 38–39, no. 12.

9. Marzolph, *Arabia ridens*, vol. 2, p. 198–199, no. 869.

10. Ābī, Abū Sa'd Manṣūr ibn al-Ḥusayn al-, *Nathr al-durr*, ed. Muḥammad 'Alī Qarna et al., vol. 5, Cairo: al-Hay'a al-miṣriyya al-'āmma lil-kitāb, 1987, p. 308; Marzolph, *Nasreddin Hodscha*, p. 31, no. 30.

11. Ibn Ḥamdūn, Muḥammad ibn al-Ḥasan ibn Muḥammad ibn 'Alī, *al-Tadhkira al-ḥamdūniyya*, ed. Iḥsān 'Abbās and Bakr 'Abbās, Beirut: Dār Ṣādir, 1996, vol. 9, p. 455, no. 1177.

12. Ibn Shākir al-Kutubī, Muḥammad, *'Uyūn al-tawārīkh*, Ms. Istanbul, Ahmet III 2922/6, fol. 74b–75a.

13. Ṣafadī, Ṣalāḥ al-Dīn Khalīl ibn Aybak al-, *al-Wāfī bi-'l-wafayāt = Das biographische Lexikon des Ṣalāḥaddīn Ḫalīl Ibn Aibak aṣ-Ṣafadī*, vol. 27, ed. Otfried Weintritt, Beirut: Deutsche Morgenländische Gesellschaft, 1997, p. 182 (s.v. Nūḥ).

14. Zaydī, Abū Muḥammad 'Abdallāh ibn Naṣr ibn 'Abd al-'Azīz al-, *Lubāb Nathr al-durr*, Paris, Bibliothèque Nationale, ms. arabe 3490, fol. 78a.

15. Suyūṭī, Jalāl al-dīn 'Abd al-Raḥmān al-, *Kitāb Tuḥfat al-mujālis wa nuzhat al-majālis*, ed. Badr al-dīn al-Na'sānī, Cairo 1326/1908, p. 348.

16. Basset, *Mille et un contes*, vol. 1, pp. 299–300, no. 211.

17. 'Anābsa, Ghālib, "Min adab al-nawādir: naẓra fī makhṭūṭāt [Irshād] man naḥā ilā nawādir Juḥā, jam' al-faqīr ilā Allāh ta'ālā Yūsuf ibn al-Wakīl al-Maylāwī,"

in ʿAnābsa, *Dirāsāt muḍīʾa fī ṣafaḥāt al-turāth*, Zaḥāliqa: Dār al-Hudā, and Jordan: Dār al-Jarīr, 2013, pp. 174–196, at p. 188.

18. Ḥafnāwī, Shihāb al-Dīn Aḥmad al-Bashshārī al-, *Bughyat al-jalīs wa-ʾl-musāmir wa-nuzhat al-arwāḥ wa-ʾl-khawāṭir*, Ms. Paris, Biliothèque Nationale Or. 3448/51, fol. 69b.

19. Juḥā, *Hādhihi nawādir al-khūjah Naṣr al-dīn Afandī Juḥā al-Rūmī*, Būlāq: Mūsā Kāstillī, 1278/1861, p. 3; Wesselski, *Der Hodscha Nasreddin*, vol. 2, pp. 6, 181–182, no. 343.

20. Basset, *Mille et un contes*, vol. 1, pp. 299–300, no. 211; Lucian: With an English translation by M.D. MacLeod, vol. 8, Cambridge, MA: Harvard University Press, 1967, p. 409.

21. Grunebaum, Gustave Edmund, "Greek Form Elements in the Arabian Nights," *Journal of the American Oriental Society* 62 (1942), pp. 277–292, at p. 279, note 21.

22. Oring, Elliot, *The Jokes of Sigmund Freud: A Study in Humor and Jewish Identity*, Philadelphia: University of Pennsylvania Press, 1984, pp. 52–53.

CHAPTER 95

The Greater Bribe Wins (ATU 1861A)

Collected by prominent folklorist Richard Wossidlo (1859–1939),[1] a short jocular tale recorded from oral tradition in the local dialect of the North-Eastern German region of Mecklenburg-Vorpommern tells of two litigants presenting their case to the lawyer whom they have chosen to arbitrate between them.[2] The plaintiff, whose claim is justified, presents the lawyer with a ram, and the defendant sends him an ox. When the lawyer has a look at the animals in his stable, he says to the plaintiff, "You are certainly right, but the ox puts you down!" Classified as tale type ATU 1861A: *The Greater Bribe*, varying versions of the tale were documented from European oral and literary traditions.[3] All versions concur in the fact that the arbiter or judge rules in favor of the person who presents him with the more valuable gift, regardless of which of the two opponents may or may not be right. As a matter of fact, most texts do not even bother to detail the nature of the conflict nor do they mention whose claim is justified or not. In a late nineteenth-century dialect version from the Haverland in Northern Germany, the conflict takes place between a butcher and a furrier.[4] The butcher presents the lawyer with the leg of an ox he has slaughtered for the occasion, and the furrier sends the lawyer a valuable fur. When the two opponents finally meet at the lawyer's, the butcher reminds the lawyer of his gift by saying, "Ox, let us hear you bellow!" At this point, the furrier remarks, "Well, it is not going to bellow, since I crammed a fur down its throat." A twentieth-century version from Northern Bavaria introduces the owner of an oil mill who presents the judge with several jugs of oil.[5] His opponent is a peasant who sends the judge a fat pig. When the miller is disappointed that judgment is ruled against him, the judge comments, "Well, the pig simply toppled the jugs!"

The tale is richly documented in European literary tradition since the late Middle Ages and was frequently published in Latin collections of exempla[6] as well as early modern and modern chapbooks in a fair variety of languages, including German,[7] English,[8] Dutch,[9] Hungarian,[10] and Romanian.[11] Influential early versions include those in the anonymous *Mensa philosophica*, compiled around 1400, and in the collection of facetious tales compiled by papal secretary Poggio Bracciolini around 1450. The *Mensa philosophica* has two versions. In one of them, a man bribes the judge with a wagon and his opponent with two horses.[12] The latter wins the lawsuit, since the horses pull the wagon. In the other, the litigants bribe the judge with a bull and a cow.[13] The judge does not rule in favor of the donor of the bull because the cow would not permit it. Poggio's version corresponds to the Bavarian text cited above.[14] In the tradition of the Iberian Peninsula, the tale was known since its inclusion in the sermons of the Catalan preacher San Vicente Ferrer (1350–1419)[15] and is attested from both written and oral traditions in a variety of Iberian languages.[16]

In Arabic tradition, a tale displaying essentially the same plot is attested since the ninth century.[17] Two features distinguish the Arabic tale from the European narratives. First, the mentioned bribes differ, and second, the Arabic tale associates the action with a specific historical protagonist, whereas the European versions usually feature anonymous characters. The tale's earliest Arabic version is documented in Ibn Qutayba's (d. 889) *ʿUyūn al-akhbār* (Quintessential Reports),[18] quoting the renowned transmitter of prophetic traditions (*ḥadīth*), Isḥāq ibn Rāhawayh (d. 852), as informant. The event is said to have taken place during the period when al-Ḥajjāj ibn Yūsuf served as governor of Iraq (694–714).

> Al-Ḥajjāj installed al-Mughīra ibn ʿAbdallāh al-Thaqafī as judge in Kufa. Once, someone presented al-Mughīra with a brass lamp. When his opponent learned about this, he presented the judge with a female mule. As the opponents met in the judge's presence, al-Mughīra judged against the donor of the lamp, although the latter repeatedly claimed, "My affair is clearer than the lamp!" Finally, al-Mughīra said, "Stop it! The mule toppled the lamp so that it broke!"

This tale is repeated with little variation in al-Rāghib al-Iṣfahānī's (d. 1108) *Muḥāḏarāt al-udabāʾ* (Conversations of the Educated)[19] and Andalusian author Ibn ʿĀṣim's (d. 1426) *Ḥadāʾiq al-azāhir* (Flower Gardens).[20]

Although it is tempting to regard the tale's European versions as deriving or adapted from the Arabic, a consideration of ancient Jewish sources adds complexity.[21] In its sixteenth chapter, the Aggadic tractate *Sabbath* contains a tale illustrating the consequences of bribery.[22] The tale is told in relation to historical characters living at the end of the first and the beginning of the second century CE.

> Imma Shalom and Rabbi Gamaliel, her brother, want to expose a judge who has a reputation for being unsusceptible to bribery. Presenting him with a golden candle, the woman pretends that her father died and that she wishes to inherit some of his possessions. Although Jewish law decrees that wherever there is a son, a daughter cannot inherit, the judge rules in her favor arguing that since the Israelites are currently in exile, the law

> given by Moses has been revoked, and a new law has been given by which daughters may inherit equally with sons. The next day, Rabbi Gamaliel brings a Libyan ass, informing the judge that he does not want his sister to share the inheritance. Now the judge argues that he consulted the law again and found that the Mosaic law has not been abolished. When the woman remarks to the judge, "May God make your light as bright as a candle," her brother adds, "An ass came along and extinguished your candle."

As the tale's Arabic versions display essentially the same bribes, they are likely modelled on the earlier Jewish tradition. None of the later European versions mentions the very same items, although there is a certain overlap in that most versions involve some animal of daily use in traditional societies. The oil mentioned in Poggio's version might constitute a reflection or adaptation of the candle or lamp in the previous Middle Eastern versions, but it is impossible to decide whether Poggio's text was adapted, if indeed it was, from Arabic Muslim or from Hebrew Jewish tradition. At any rate, the tale's historical travel across cultural, regional, linguistic, and religious boundaries over a period of two millennia convincingly demonstrates its applicability to a variety of contexts, as both the institution of the judge and the human foible of a socially responsible character's receptiveness to personal gain constitute universally known features.

Notes

1. Neumann, Siegfried, "Wossidlo, Richard," in *Enzyklopädie des Märchens*, vol. 14 (2014), cols. 1015–1018.

2. Neumann, Siegfried, *Volksschwänke aus Mecklenburg, aus der Sammlung Richard Wossidlos*, Berlin: Akademie-Verlag, 1963, p. 58, no. 201.

3. Moser-Rath, Elfriede, "Bestechung," in *Enzyklopädie des Märchens*, vol. 2 (1979), cols. 209–214, at col. 211.

4. Merkens, Heinrich Ludwig, *Was sich das Volk erzählt: Deutscher Volkshumor*, 2nd ed., vol. 1, Jena: Costenoble, 1892, pp. 246–247, no. 288.

5. Kapfhammer, Günther, *Bayerische Schwänke "dastunka und dalogn,"* Düsseldorf: Diederichs, 1974, p. 118.

6. Tubach, *Index exemplorum*, pp. 223–224, no. 2851; p. 235, no. 2998.

7. Uther, *Deutscher Märchenkatalog*, pp. 523–524, no. 1861A.

8. Hazlitt, W. Carew, ed., *Shakespeare Jest-Books: Reprints of the Early and Very Rare Jest-Books Supposed to Have Been Used by Shakespeare*, London: Willis & Sotheran, 1881, vol. 1, pp. 33–34, no. 22 (from *Mery Tales, Wittie Questions and Quick Answers*, 1567).

9. Overbeke, Arnout van, *Anecdota sive historiae jocosas: Een seventiende-eeuwse verzameling moppen en anekdotes*, ed. Rudolf Dekker and Herman Rodenburg, Amsterdam: Meertens-Institut, 1991, p. 280, no. 1632; p. 298, no. 1773.

10. György, Lajos, *Kónyi János Democritusa*, Budapest: Magyar tudományos akadémia, 1932, pp. 98–101, no. 52; György, *A magyar anekdota története és egyetemes kapcsolatai*, Budapest: Studium, 1934, pp. 161–162, no. 137.

11. Stroescu, *La typologie*, vol. 2, p. 1105, no. 4972.

12. Tubach, *Index exemplorum*, pp. 223–224, no. 2851; Pauli, Johannes, *Schimpf und Ernst*, ed. Johannes Bolte, Berlin: Herbert Stubenrauch, 1924 (reprint Hildesheim: Olms, 1972), vol. 1, p. 85; vol. 2 pp. 290–291, no. 125.

13. Tubach, *Index exemplorum*, p. 235, no. 2998; Dunn, Thomas Franklin, *The Facetiae of the Mensa Philosophica*, Saint Louis: Washington University, 1934, pp. 42–43, no. 144; *Mensa philosophica: Faksimile und Kommentar*, ed. Erwin Rauner and Burghart Wachinger, Tübingen: Max Niemeyer, 1995, p. 302, no. IV, 33a.

14. Poggio Bracciolini, Gian-Francesco, *Die Schwänke und Schnurren*, ed. Alfred Semerau, Leipzig: Deutsche Verlags-Actiengesellschaft, 1905, pp. 171–172, no. 256.

15. Neugaard, Edward J., *Motif-Index of Medieval Catalan Folktales*, Binghamtpon, New York: Medieval & Renaissance Texts & Studies, 1993, p. 53, no. J1192.1; Sant Vicent Ferrer, *Sermons*, ed. Josep Sanchis Sivera and Gret Schib, vol. 1, Barcelona: Barcino, 1971, pp. 151–152.

16. Cardigos, Isabel, *Catalogue of Portuguese Folktales*, Helsinki: Suomalainen Tiedeakatemia, 2006, p. 373, no. 1861A; Noia Campos, Camiño, *Catálogo tipolóxico do conto galego de tradición oral: clasificación, antoloxía e bibliografía*, Vigo: University of Vigo, 2010, pp. 894–895, no. 1861A; see also López Bernal, Desirée, *Los Ḥadāʾiq al-azāhir de Abū Bakr ibn ʿĀṣim al-Garnāṭī: Traducción y estudio de una obra de adab de la Granada nazarí*, Ph.D. thesis University of Granada, 2016, vol. 2, pp. 167–168.

17. Marzolph, *Arabia ridens*, vol. 2, p. 33, no. 121.

18. Ibn Qutayba al-Dīnawarī, Abū Muḥammad ʿAbdallāh ibn Muslim, *ʿUyūn al-akhbār*, 2nd ed., Cairo: al-Muʾassasa al-miṣriyya al-ʿāmma lil-taʾlif wa-ʾl-tarjama wa-ʾl-ṭibāʿa, 1963, vol. 1, p. 52; Marzolph, *Arabia ridens*, vol. 1, p. 263, no. 26.

19. Rāghib al-Iṣfahānī, al-Ḥusayn ibn Muḥammad al-, *Muḥāḍarāt al-udabāʾ wa-muḥāwarāt al-shuʿarāʾ wa-ʾl-bulaghāʾ*, Beirut 1961, vol. 1, p. 197.

20. Ibn ʿĀṣim al-Andalusī, Abū Bakr ibn Muḥammad, *Ḥadāʾiq al-azāhir*, ed. ʿAfīf ʿAbd al-Raḥmān, Beirut: al-Masīra, 1401/1981, p. 219; López Bernal, *Los Ḥadāʾiq al-azāhir*, vol. 1, p. 346, no. 765; vol. 2, pp. 165, 167–168; López Bernal, "Los cuentos de Ibn ʿĀṣim (m. 1426): precedentes peninsulares de relatos españoles y del folklore universal en el s. XV," *Boletín de literatura oral* 9 (2019), pp. 35–52, at p. 38, no. 30.

21. Schwarzbaum, Haim, *Studies in Jewish and World Folklore*, Berlin: Walter de Gruyter, 1968, pp. 347–348, no. 477.

22. The following text is adapted from http://www.jewishvirtuallibrary.org/tractate-shabbat-chapter-16 (accessed March 28, 2018).

CHAPTER 96

Diagnosis by Observation (ATU 1862C)

In April 1951, Vance Randolph, the pioneering folklorist of the Ozarks,[1] recorded the tale "Too Much Church Work" from the oral performance of George Head at Eureka Springs, Arkansas. The events are told as having taken place in the storyteller's own settlement.[2]

> Arriving at the settlement, the new doctor has an older colleague show him around his patients, so as to get acquainted with the people. Twice, the experienced doctor pronounces his diagnosis apparently without any thorough examination. He scolds a woman for having eaten too many sweets, only later justifying his diagnosis to his young colleague by the fact that he noticed the many candy-wrappings in the fireplace. And he criticizes a man for smoking too much, later pointing out to his younger colleague that there were cigarette butts all over the floor. Finally, he asks his new colleague to take the next case so as to see how he will be doing. The young doctor admonishes the sick woman to cut down on her church work for a while. When the old doctor is surprised that he could have made a diagnosis so easily, the young colleague responds, "Didn't you see that preacher under the bed?"

The commentary to this tale mentions another slightly earlier version from the Ozarks that is "credited to a traveling salesman."[3] Yet another, equally contemporary version has "political activity" instead of "church work," and the governor taking the preacher's place under the bed. Herbert Halpert's comparative annotation points to the tale's international dimension, as it is, in fact, a sexualized version of tale type ATU 1862C: *Diagnosis by Observation* that is widely spread in European tradition. Examples collected from oral tradition are rare, as the tale is mainly encountered in chapbooks and other compilations of jocular and entertaining tales.[4] A nineteenth-century German version credits the events to a doctor and his simple-minded apprentice in Cologne.[5] Since the experienced doctor sees the apple peels under the sick man's bed and correctly diagnoses that the patient ate too many apples, the apprentice scolds another patient for having eaten raw potatoes, as he noticed potato peels under the bed.

And in an English version told by Manivel Smith in Burton-on-Trent on January 20, 1922, the apprentice "gravely offended the squire of the place, who was suffering from gout, by telling him that he had been eating too much fox-pie," arguing to his colleague that "there were a lot of foxes' heads and tails hanging on the walls just as you go into the house."[6] While all of the above versions differ both from one another and from their historical models, the Welsh version told in 1967 by the retired teacher Isaac Herriman, aged 73, from Rhymni, Monmouthsire, is closer to the tale's traditional form discussed in the following.[7]

> The doctor scolds his patient for having eaten things that he should not eat, instructing his assistant that he must always keep his eyes open. In fact, there had been shells of fresh cockles all over the place, so the patient's bad health resulted from having eaten too many cockles. When the assistant comes to see "Mr. Jones" the next day, he likewise scolds him for having eaten the wrong food. Arguing to the doctor, he says that the patient must have eaten a horse, since he saw the bridle and saddle under the bed.

A medieval text in the anonymous *Mensa philosophica*, compiled in the fourteenth or fifteenth century, tells of a female healer who is advised by the bishop to pay attention to the items around the sick person's bed that would inform her about the patient's diet.[8] When the bishop himself is sick one day, the healer cannot see anything of relevance but cushions and admonishes him for having eaten "too much cushion." As the bishop bursts into laughter, the ulcer in his throat breaks open so that he is healed. More influential than the text in the *Mensa philosophica* was, however, the version in the Latin collection of *Facetiae* compiled by Italian author Poggio Bracciolini around the middle of the fifteenth century.[9] Poggio presents the tale with a distinct critical perspective not only on the foolish apprentice, but also on the experienced doctor who makes his patients believe that he possesses the capacity of clairvoyance that would enable him to know exactly whatever they had eaten. From a donkey's packsaddle under the patient's bed, the apprentice deduces that the man must have eaten the donkey. Poggio served as the papal secretary, and the numerous international contacts he must have had make it appear perfectly natural that his collection of jocular tales also includes several items deriving or adapted from Arabic tradition.

The tale is first documented in Ibn al-Jawzī's (d. 1201) *Akhbār al-Ḥamqā* (Tales of Stupid People).[10] The text is cited as told by the poet Ibn al-Rūmī (d. 896) and thus claims to relate to ninth-century tradition.

> A doctor said to his student, "When you visit a sick person, have a good look at the leftovers of food and drink that are with him, because they will inform you about what is not good for him." One day the young man came to a sick man. Noticing the pillion of a camel's saddle in the house, he scolded the sick man, "By God, I will not write you a prescription!" When asked why, he responded, "Because you have eaten a camel." And

when the sick man exclaimed, "By God, I have definitely not eaten camel meat!" he said, "So where is that pillion from?"

Roughly a century later, the cosmography *ʿAjāʾib al-makhlūqāt* (The Wonders of Creation) by Zakariyyā ibn Muḥammad al-Qazwīnī (d. 1283) contains a considerably extended version in which the doctor appears to determine the sick man's diet purely from feeling his pulse and inspecting his urine.[11] Explaining the rationale of his action to his son, the doctor tells him that he made his diagnosis partly from examining the sick man and inspecting his urine, but in addition taking into account the fruit peels and chicken feathers in the room. Even so, he had been prudent enough to say, "Maybe you have eaten . . . " Having listened to his father, the son aims to put the lesson into practice. But when called to a sick man, he asks the patient whether he ate donkey meat and is put to shame by the man's resolute protest. Later he argues to his father that he saw a donkey's packsaddle in the room, thinking that if the donkey was alive, it would be carrying the saddle; and since the saddle was not in use, the donkey must surely be dead, slaughtered, and eaten. The tale ends with the rhymed "moral", "Of no use will a lesson be, if there is no capacity" (*fa-lā yanfaʿu masmūʿ idhā lam yaku maṭbūʿ*).

No other versions of the tale from premodern Arabic, Persian, or Turkish literature are known so far. Although nineteenth-century Middle Eastern literature of the chapbook kind might have served as a medium for transmitting the tale from classical literature to oral tradition, in Middle Eastern oral tradition the tale was only recorded from twentieth-century Persian storytellers[12] and from Jewish narrators originating from Iraq and Bukhara.[13] Although the above-quoted Arabic texts strongly suggest the tale's origin from Arabic tradition, they remain a rare phenomenon in comparison to the richly documented European tradition that was continuously refreshed by the tale's repeated quotation in a fair number of publications from the fifteenth century onward. Together with the creative adaptations in Western oral tradition, they bear witness to the rich afterlife of a tale from the Muslim world that met with Western interest to such an extent as to be accepted, adapted, and transformed in multiple ways.

Notes

1. Lindahl, Carl, "Randolph, Vance," in *Enzyklopädie des Märchens*, vol. 11 (2004), cols. 192–194.

2. Randolph, Vance, *The Devil's Pretty Daughter and Other Ozark Folk Tales*, New York: Columbia University Press, 1955, pp. 164–165.

3. Ibid., p. 225.

4. Moser-Rath, Elfriede, "Diagnose: Die einfältige D.," in *Enzyklopädie des Märchens*, vol. 3 (1981), cols. 573–575; Pauli, Johannes, *Schimpf und Ernst*, ed. Johannes Bolte, Berlin: Stubenrauch, 1924 (reprint Hildesheim: Olms, 1972), vol. 2, pp. 59, 429, no. 792; Moser-Rath, *"Lustige Gesellschaft,"* pp. 196–197 and p. 341, note 50; Chevalier, *Cuentos folklóricos*, p. 407, no. 245 (from Juna de Timoneda's sexteenth-century *Portacuentos*, no. 53).

5. Merkens, Heinrich Ludwig, *Was sich das Volk erzählt: Deutscher Volkshumor*, 2nd ed., vol. 3, Jena: Costenoble, 1900, pp. 127–128, no. 103.
6. Briggs, *A Dictionary*, vol. A2, p. 59.
7. Ranke, Kurt, *European Ancedotes and Jests*, transl. Timothy Buck, Copenhagen: Rosenkilde and Bagger, 1972, pp. 28–29, no. 13.
8. Wesselski, *Mönchslatein*, pp. 19–20, no. 13.
9. Poggio Bracciolini, Gian-Francesco, *Die Schwänke und Schnurren*, ed. Alfred Semerau, Leipzig: Deutsche Verlags-Actiengesellschaft, 1905, pp. 220–221, no. 109.
10. Ibn al-Jawzī, Abū 'l-Faraj ʿAbd al-Raḥmān ibn ʿAlī, *Akhbār al-Ḥāmqā wa-'l-mughaffalīn*, ed. Kāẓim al-Muẓaffar, al-Najaf: al-Maktaba al-ḥaydariyya, 1386/1966, p. 183; see also Marzolph, *Arabia ridens*, vol. 1, p. 215, and vol. 2, p. 266, no. 1238.
11. Qazwīnī, Zakariyyā ibn Muḥammad al-, *ʿAjāʾib al-makhlūqāt wa-gharāʾib al-mawjūdāt*, ed. Fārūq Saʿd, Beirut: al-Āfāq al-jadīda, 1401/1981, p. 381.
12. Marzolph, *Typologie*, p. 250, no. 1862 C.
13. Jason, Heda, *Folktales of the Jews of Iraq: Tale-Types and Genres*, Or Yehuda: Babylonian Jewry Heritage Center, 1988, p. 88, no. 1862 C; Soroudi, Sarah Sorour, *The Folktales of Jews from Iran, Central Asia and Afghanistan: Tale-Types and Genres*, ed. Heda Jason, Dortmund: Verlag für Orientkunde, 2008, p. 201, no. 1862 C.

CHAPTER 97

The Liar Reduces the Size of His Lie (ATU 1920D)

In the international system of tale types, tall tales occupy their own slot, ranging from tale type ATU 1875 to 1999. Tale type ATU 1920: *Contest in Lying* and its numerous subtypes often deal with a conversation between two people telling hilariously untrue facts. Tales classified as tale type ATU 1920D: *The Liar Reduces the Size of His Lie* have another person challenge the liar to reduce the object he lies about at least to a somewhat credible size. These tales appear in two different forms. In the first form the liar reduces his lie gradually, as in the following text recorded from Albanian tradition.[1]

> When a habitual liar takes part in a dinner party, his servant admonishes him to refrain from lying excessively. As his master finds it impossible to forego his habit, the servant proposes to warn him by pulling a cord attached to his body should his lie exceed reasonable dimensions. The master tells of a fox whose tail was 150 feet in length, and the servant pulls the cord, so that the master gradually reduces his lie, first to 100 feet, then to 50 feet. When the servant still pulls the cord, the master finally shouts at him aggressively, protesting that he could not possibly say that the fox had no tail at all.

In a tale attributed to Bohemian German peasant tradition, the liar is the priest, and the person admonishing him is the sacristan.[2] In his sermon, the priest talks of Saint Martin's horse having had a tale five fathoms in length. Admonished by the sacristan, he gradually reduces the size to four, three, and two fathoms. When the sacristan keeps admonishing him, he finally exclaims, "What the devil! The horse must have had a tail, after all!"

In the tale's second form, the liar reduces the size of the item he lies about in a single drastic step, so that the second size given is as implausible as the first one.[3] A version collected in Indiana in the 1930s goes as follows.[4]

> A man who attended a barn raising was prone to stretch the truth. His brother reminded him one morning when they started a new job not to tell

stories that no one would believe. "All right, when you think I am making the story too big just step on my toes."

They were all telling of their biggest building, and this man said, "The largest barn I ever raised was 300 feet long and three (his brother stepped on his toes) . . . wide." The story brought a laugh.

Similarly, the liar in the Danish text told by A.C. Anderson from Tollestrup and published by Evald Tang Kristensen in the journal *Skattegraveren* tells of a church a hundred cubits long and a single cubit wide.[5] An Austrian version goes at great lengths to authenticate the tall tale by adding local color.[6] The tale is presented as told by a traveling journeyman who is given shelter at a farmer's place in the Gölsen valley in Lower Austria. The farmer is quite satisfied to have the journeyman and his companion with him that evening, since, as the text argues, "it is well known that they are a wandering newspaper," thus bringing news of the world to the farmer's remote dwelling. As the company sits on the bench in front of the house having a drink, the visitor starts to tell of a new church they are building in England, "a truly big one, right!" He claims the church to be three hundred fathoms in length, but when his companion steps on his foot to remind him not to lie excessively, he has the church be only two fathoms wide. When the farmer wonders why the church is so narrow, the narrator says that it would have been wider had his companion not stepped on his foot. In the German language area (and probably beyond), the tale type's second form was popularized from the middle of the seventeenth century by its publication in a fair number of chapbooks,[7] which further resulted in its inclusion as narrative material in baroque-era sermons.[8]

The oldest currently known attestation of the tale's second form is documented in Ibn al-Jawzī's (d. 1201) *Akhbār al-Ḥamqā* (Tales of Stupid People).[9] It is told as part of a small cluster of anecdotes about the numskull Azhar who was known as "the donkey driver" (*al-ḥammār*),[10] probably relating to his silly counting of donkeys in tale type ATU 1288A: *Numskull Cannot Find the Donkey He Is Sitting On* (see essay **40, *The Fool Forgets to Count the Donkey He Is Sitting On***). The event takes place in the presence of ʿAmr ibn al-Layth (r. 879–902), the second ruler (*amīr*) of the Ṣaffārid dynasty that administered large parts of Iran.

Once, a messenger from the sultan came to ʿAmr ibn al-Layth and dined with him. The ruler said to Azhar, "Today it is befitting that you practice silence." So Azhar remained silent for a long time. But then he could not stand it any longer and said, "In the village they built a tower a thousand measures (*khaṭwa*) in height." The chamberlain indicated that he should stay silent, but the messenger asked him, "And how wide (is it)?" Azhar replied, "A single measure in width." The messenger asked him again, "If its hight was a thousand measures how could a single measure in width be enough?" And Azhar responded, "I wanted to add more, but this chap kept me from doing so!"

Whereas no additional citations in Arabic sources of subsequent centuries are documented, the tale is included in the modern editions of the anecdotes attributed to the Arabic prankster Juḥā.[11] Exactly how the twelfth-century Arabic version is related to the European versions attested as of the seventeenth century can only be hypothesized. The most likely potential candidates for the tale's transmission East to West are early Spanish or Italian versions such as they exist for the tale type's first form.[12] For the second form, any such intermediary versions are not attested. Even so, the close correspondence of the tale's Arabic versions to the Western ones in terms of structure and content suggests a close relation rather than an independent genesis of the latter versions.

Notes

1. Jarník, Jan Urban, "Albanesische Märchen und Schwänke," *Zeitschrift für Volkskunde in Sage und Mär* 2 (1890), pp. 421–424, at p. 424; reprinted in Holzinger, Michael, *Märchen aus Albanien*, 3rd ed., Berlin: Zeno, 2014, p. 135.

2. Kubitschek, Rudolf, *Böhmerwäldler Bauernschwänke*, Vienna: Strache, 1920, p. 25.

3. Rausmaa, Pirkko-Liisa, "Lügenwette," in *Enzyklopädie des Märchens*, vol. 8 (1996), cols. 1274–1279, at col. 1276.

4. Baker, Ronald L., *Jokelore: Humorous Folktales from Indiana*, Bloomington: Indiana University Press, 1986, pp. 3, 210, no. 2.

5. *Skattegraveren* 8 (1887), pp. 72–73, no. 220.

6. Lang-Reitstätter, Maria, *Lachendes Österreich: Österreichischer Volkshumor*, 2nd ed., Salzburg: Österreichischer Kulturverlag, 1948, pp. 148–149.

7. Uther, *Deutscher Märchenkatalog*, p. 539, no. 1920D.

8. Moser-Rath, Elfriede, *Predigtmärlein der Barockzeit*, Berlin: De Gruyter, 1964, pp. 368–369, 494, no. 209; see also Müller-Fraureuth, Karl, *Die deutschen Lügendichtungen bis auf Münchhausen*, Halle: Niemeyer, 1881, p. 79 and p. 140, note 277.

9. Ibn al-Jawzī, Abū 'l-Faraj ʿAbd al-Raḥmān ibn ʿAlī, *Akhbār al-Ḥamqā wa-'l-mughaffalīn*, ed. Kāẓim al-Muẓaffar, al-Najaf: al-Maktaba al-ḥaydariyya, 1386/1966, p. 34; a slightly different version from an unidentified (Arabic?) source was translated by Kabbani, Sam, *Altarabische Eseleien: Humor aus dem frühen Islam*, Herrenalb: Horst Erdmann, 1965, p. 74, no. 94; see also Marzolph, *Arabia ridens*, vol. 2, p. 260, no. 1210.

10. For other jocular tales attributed to this character see Marzolph, *Arabia ridens*, vol. 2, p. 218, no. 977; p. 220, no. 988.

11. Farrāj, ʿAbd al-Sattār Aḥmad, *Akhbār Juḥā*, Cairo: Maktabat Miṣr, 1954, pp. 65–66.

12. Chevalier, *Cuentos folklóricos*, pp. 423–424, no. 255.

CHAPTER 98

The Trickster Forces His Challenger to Admit that He Is Telling a Lie (ATU 1920F)

In a specific group of tall tales the actual tales are embedded in the frame of a contest or a wager that introduces a rich or powerful person challenging the narrator to tell lies to win a specific reward.[1] Although the narrator does his best to perform tales about hilariously exaggerated or unbelievable objects or events, his challenger refuses to acknowledge the tales as lies, instead arguing that they could potentially be true, so as not to lose the wager. Finally, the narrator exceeds all previous bounds by directly involving his counterpart in a tall tale, insinuating the challenger's lowly descent or claiming that the challenger owes him an amount of money larger than the promised reward. Only then does the challenger admit that the narrator actually told a lie, and the trickster receives the promised reward. An unambiguous classification of these tales is often difficult, as both the frame tales and the nature of the embedded lies display a great variety. Essentially, most of the presently concerned tales correspond to tale type ATU 1920F: *He Who Says, "That's a Lie," Must Pay a Fine.*

Tales in which the liar insinuates his challenger's lowly descent usually depict the events as taking place between a nobleman and a peasant. In the German dialect folktale recorded in 1963 from the performance of glassworker Georg Balk, aged 68, and originating from the border region between Southern Germany and former Czechoslovakia, the nobleman challenges the peasant as to which of them can tell the greater lie.[2] The nobleman tells a tale about absurdly large animals such as a deer whose antlers are so large that the nobleman was able to use them as a ladder to climb to heaven. Acknowledging the nobleman's tale as potentially true, the peasant tells a tale about a tree growing into the skies. As he climbed the tree, the peasant saw the nobleman's father herding pigs down below. At this point, the nobleman protests that this cannot be true and loses the wager. With different embedded tall tales but essentially displaying the same structure and final point, the tale was also recorded from Lithuanian,[3] Ukrainian,[4] and Austrian[5] traditions. In the German version told by Mr. Reckmann from Vellern, a tailor claims to have seen the father of "Old Fred," that is, Prussian King Frederick II (r. 1740–1786), herding geese.[6] In an

Estonian folktale, the nobleman tells about a pumpkin whose skin was so large that they used it to build a carriage.[7] The peasant reciprocates by claiming that a beanstalk grew so high that he climbed to heaven on it, from above seeing the nobleman's father working as a blacksmith.

Sometimes, the frame tale includes the promise of marrying the liar to the rich man's daughter should he succeed.[8] This specific form corresponds to tale type ATU 852: *Lying Contest*. An early twentieth-century text from Northern Russia also mentions the partner's humiliation, as the peasant claims to have seen his own father in hell riding on the back of the nobleman's father.[9] More often, however, the liar consciously avoids denigrating his future father-in-law, and so the narrative simply ends with the latter acknowledging the former's superiority in telling tale tales. The Bulgarian folktale told around 1954 by B.M. Tabakova from Teteven introduces a man who loses the nine mules he intended to sell in a lying contest with a certain priest.[10] The man's clever son challenges the priest with a tall tale about a walnut tree growing from a wounded mule's back and is married to the priest's daughter. In a Portuguese tale, the landlord promises to waive the peasant's rent if he can tell him a lie "as big as today and tomorrow together."[11] The peasant's clever son receives the landlord's respect for a tall tale about a beanstalk growing from the ear of a donkey, resulting in a huge harvest of beans. Similarly, a Slovenian folktale has the youngest of three servants win the contest by telling a tall tale about a bear that ate so much honey that the people harvested nine barrels of honey from the bear's belly.[12]

As for the tale's form mentioning the counterpart's alleged debt, a Karelian tale recorded in 1941 by A. Leonteva tells of the tsar demanding his storyteller on pain of death to come up with a new tale each time.[13] Twice, the clever boy manages to tell tales the tsar acknowledges never having heard before. In order to shame the storyteller, the tsar orders his courtiers to assert the next time that they already heard the performed tale before, no matter what the boy would tell. The storyteller claims that the tsar's father owed his own father forty barrels of gold. Since the tsar ordered his courtiers to acknowledge the tale as true at all events, they do so, and the storyteller takes all the tsar's gold, thus, as the story says, teaching the tsar a lesson that he should stop killing innocent people. The tale's two Judaeo-Spanish versions as performed by Nahman Halevy, aged 75, and Yoshoa Graziani, aged 72, in Monastir, Tunisia, are identical. Both texts have the king jail all storytellers whose tall tales he does not accept as lies.[14] At one point, the king offers a golden scepter to the one who can tell a great lie. A clever man asks the king to lend him a cart, fetches a large barrel from his house, and claims that the king's father owed his own father as many gold coins as the barrel would hold. The king is forced to acknowledge the claim as a lie and gives the clever man the scepter rather than pay the alleged debt.

In Arabic literature, the tale's latter form is first attested early in the eleventh century.[15] Abū Ḥayyān al-Tawḥīdī (d. 1023) in his *al-Baṣāʾir wa-'l-dhakhāʾir* (Deep Insights and Treasures)[16] and Abū Manṣūr al-Ābī (d. 1030) in his *Nathr al-durr*

(Pearls of Prose)[17] tell the tale in essentially identical wording. Both authors cite the tale on the authority of the historian al-Madā'inī (d. 843) who attributed it to a certain Dīnārwayh in the city of al-Madā'in, the ancient Seleucia-Ctesiphon.

> Dīnārwayh is said to have been a mischievous and tricky (*khabīth*) character. One day, the city's governor promises Dīnārwayh to reward him with wine (*sharāb*), money, and more if he managed to tell a tall tale (*kadhba*) never heard before. Dīnārwayh tells three hilariously exaggerated tales that allegedly happened to himself, but the governor acknowledges them as true. The first tale is about a slave who runs away and is found much later inside a watermelon (*baṭṭīkh*) where he works as a shoemaker. In the second tale, a large pomegranate tree grows from a pomegranate seed on the back of a horse. The third tale features the narrator's slave who had a fur coat that was so infested with fleas that when the fleas jumped they jumped for two miles together with the coat and its bearer. When Dīnārwayh fears that the governor is going to credit all of his tall tales as true, he claims that in his father's books he found a certificate documenting that the governor owed his father four thousand *dirhams*. Finally, the governor admits that he never heard such a tale and is asked to grant the promised reward.

About a century later, Ibn Ḥamdūn (d. 1167) in his *al-Tadhkira* (The Aide-Memoire)[18] repeats the tale in almost identical wording. A shorter version mentioning a slave girl as reward and containing only the first two lies is attested in al-Rāghib al-Iṣfahānī's (d. 1108) *Muḥāḍarāt al-udabā'* (Conversations of the Educated).[19] Here, the tricky narrator is the poet Ru'ba ibn ʿAbdallāh al-ʿAjjāj (d. 762) whom an anonymous person asks to tell tall tales. When, in the end, the narrator claims that his challenger's deceased father owed him a thousand *dīnār*s, his challenger exclaims, "You son of a whore, that is a lie!" In his seventeenth-century *Nuzhat al-udabā'* (Entertainment of the Educated), Muḥammad ibn Aḥmad ibn (al-)Ilyās al-Ḥanafī includes a short text with unnamed characters in Medina, including the first and third tall tales from the oldest-known Arabic version.[20]

Predating the Arabic texts by more than a thousand years, a similar event is attributed to the wise Ahiqar in a text presumably dating from around 500 BCE.[21] In that tale's Syriac and Arabic versions, Pharaoh requests Ahiqar to tell him something he never heard before, at the same time instructing his nobles to acknowledge as true whatever Ahiqar would say. Ahiqar forges a letter to the effect that Sennacherib, king of Assyria and Niniveh, asks Pharaoh to lend him 900 talents of silver (or gold). When Pharaoh is confronted with the letter, he marvels at Ahiqar's cleverness.[22] In the tale's corresponding Greek version, Aesop presents a forged letter to the Egyptian king Nectanebo in which the latter admits to owing a thousand talents to Lykeros, king of Babylon.[23] The *Babylonian Talmud* attributes another similar tale to the famous Rabbi Joshua Ben Hanania who claims that the newly born offspring of a mule had a note around its neck documenting that his father was entitled to receive the payment of a large debt.[24] Here, the claim's absurdity is further underlined by the well-known physical fact that mules do not produce offspring.

Notes

1. Rausmaa, Pirkko-Liisa, "Lügenwette," in *Enzyklopädie des Märchens*, vol. 8 (1996), cols. 1274–1279.
2. Benzel, Ulrich, *Volkserzählungen aus dem oberpfälzisch-böhmischen Grenzgebiet*, Münster: Aschendorff, 1965, pp. 118–119, no. 140.
3. Böhm, Max, and Franz Specht, *Lettische Schwänke und verwandte Volksüberlieferungen*, Reval: Kluge, 1911, pp. 293–295, no. 39.
4. Mykytiuk, Bohdan, *Ukrainische Märchen*, Düsseldorf: Diederichs, 1979, pp. 232–233, no. 62.
5. Haiding, Karl, *Märchen und Schwänke aus Oberösterreich*, Berlin: De Gruyter, 1969, pp. 115–116, 222, no. 86.
6. Henßen, Gottfried, *Volk erzählt: Münsterländische Sagen, Märchen und Schwänke*, Münster: Aschendorf, 1935, pp. 345–346, no. 294.
7. Viidalepp, Richard, *Estnische Volksmärchen*, Berlin: Akademie-Verlag, 1980, pp. 322–323, no. 110.
8. Goldberg, Christine, "Redekampf mit der Prinzessin," in *Enzyklopädie des Märchens*, vol. 11 (2004), cols. 436–443, at cols. 436–438.
9. Propp, Vladimir, ed., *Severnorusskie skazki v zapisiakh A.I. Nikiforov*, Moscow: Izdatel'stvo Akademii Nauk SSSR, 1961, pp. 60–61, no. 23.
10. Haralampieff, Kyrill, *Bulgarische Volksmärchen*, Düsseldorf: Diederichs, 1971, pp. 219–220, 290, no. 47.
11. Meier, Harri, and Dieter Woll, *Portugiesische Märchen*, Düsseldorf: Diederichs, 1975, pp. 29–30, 256, no. 13.
12. Bolhar, Alojzij, *Slovenske narodne právljice*, 7th ed., Ljubljana: Mladinska knjiga, 1974, pp. 168–169.
13. Konkka, Unelma Semenovna, *Karel'skie narodnye skazki*, Moscow: Izdatel'stvo Akademii Nauk SSSR, 1963, pp. 498–500.
14. Crews, Cynthia Mary, *Contes judéo-espagnols des Balkans*, ed. A. Angelopoulos, Paris: Corti, 2009, pp. 65–66, 354; see also Haboucha, Reginetta, *Types and Motifs of the Judaeo-Spanish Folktales*, New York: Garland, 1992, pp. 716–719, no. 1920F–*A.
15. Marzolph, *Arabia ridens*, vol. 2, p. 143, no. 578.
16. Tawḥīdī, Abū Ḥayyān al-, *al-Baṣā'ir wa-'l-dhakhā'ir*, ed. Wadād al-Qāḍī, Beirut: Dār Ṣādir, 1408/1988, vol. 5, p. 194, no. 674.
17. Ābī, Abū Sa'd Manṣūr ibn al-Ḥusayn al-, *Nathr al-durr*, ed. Muḥammad 'Alī Qarna et al., vol. 6.2, Cairo: al-Hay'a al-miṣriyya al-'āmma lil-kitāb, 1990, p. 531.
18. Ibn Ḥamdūn, Muḥammad ibn al-Ḥasan ibn Muḥammad ibn 'Alī, *al-Tadhkira al-ḥamdūniyya*, ed. Iḥsān 'Abbās and Bakr 'Abbās, Beirut: Dār Ṣādir, 1996, vol. 3, pp. 84–85, no. 195.
19. Rāghib al-Iṣfahānī, al-Ḥusayn ibn Muḥammad al-, *Muḥāḍarāt al-udabā' wa-muḥāwarāt al-shu'arā' wa-'l-bulaghā'*, Beirut 1961, vol. 1, pp. 124–125.
20. Basset, *Mille et un contes*, vol. 1, pp. 249–250, no. 131; Ḥanafī, Muḥammad ibn Aḥmad ibn (al-)Ilyās al-, *Nuzhat al-udabā'*, Ms. Gotha, fol. 52a–b.

21. Schwarzbaum, Haim, *Studies in Jewish and World Folklore*, Berlin: Walter de Gruyter, 1968, pp. 198–202, no. 245, at p. 199.

22. Charles, Robert Henry, *The Apocrypha and Pseudepigraphia of the Old Testament*, Oxford: Clarendon Press, 1913, vol. 2, pp. 761–762.

23. Ibid., p. 784.

24. Schwarzbaum, *Studies*, p. 200.

A Nonsense Introduction to the Fairy-Tale World (ATU 1965)

The tale "Knoist un sine dre Sühne" (Knoist and His Three Sons), number 138 in the Grimms' *Kinder- und Hausmärchen* (Children's and Household Tales), is a short nonsense tale narrated in the Western German dialect of the Sauerland, today a region in the federal state of North Rhine-Westphalia. Corresponding to tale type ATU 1965: *The Disabled Comrades*,[1] the tale tells of Knoist's three sons, one of whom was blind, the second one lame, and the third naked. Crossing a field, the blind son shot a hare, the lame son caught it, and the naked son put it in his pocket. Coming to a great body of water, they found three boats, one of which was leaking, the second one was about to sink, and the third did not have a bottom. They continued their travel with the last boat, as all three of them fitted into it. Eventually they reached a forest with a tall tree in whose top there was a chapel in which the parson and the sexton distributed holy water with cudgels. The tale was contributed by a sister of August von Haxthausen, according to whose note the text is usually narrated in singing and with drawn-out syllables.[2]

Similar nonsense tales are known from all over Europe.[3] An English folktale from Yorkshire attributes an equally absurd sequence of events to five men.[4] The blind man sees a bird, the dumb man says that he is going to shoot it, the man without legs is going to run after it, the man without arms will pick it up, and the naked man will put it in his pocket. In the French tale narrated by Jean Testas, aged 75, from Gascony, three men go hunting.[5] Two of them are naked, and the third one does not wear any clothes. Two of their rifles are not loaded, and the third one does not have a bullet inside. They shoot at three hares missing two of them while the third one escapes. Looking into the pocket of the naked man they wonder how they will cook the hare. Reaching a house that has no walls, no doors, no windows, in fact nothing at all, they knock at the door. A person who is not there asks them what they want. And when told that the three men want a pot to cook the hare that escaped, that person says that he only has three pots, two of which have no bottom and the third one is totally useless. An Italian folktale begins in a similar manner.[6] When the three hunters ask their grandmother for a pot to cook the hare they have not caught, she tells them that she has three pots in the kitchen, two of which are broken and one has no bottom. When asked whether she has anything in her garden (to cook with the hare), the hunters are told that there are three walnut trees, two of which are dead, and the third one never bears nuts. Later, the three men take their soup to a village where there are many sick people and distribute the broth with a skimmer. When one of the people consumes so much broth that he is on the point of death, they send for three physicians. The blind physician wants to have a look at the sick man's tongue, the deaf physician inquires how he feels, and the mute physician asks for paper, pen, and ink, and writes down a nonsense prescription.

In German literature, the hunt of the three "disabled comrades" first appears in a rhymed nonsense sermon dating from the fifteenth century and is also documented in two sixteenth-century sources.[7] Similar nonsense tales enjoy a considerable popularity in Turkish tradition. Today known as *tekerleme*, the numerous documented versions of this nonsense tale draw on a fair variety of motifs.[8] Historically, one of the earliest examples of a similar nonsense tale in Ottoman Turkish literature appears in the poetry of the early fourteenth-century poet Yunus Emre.[9] In Emre's poem, a man defending the food he cooked in his pot fights against a paralyzed man, and a man without arms grabs him by the feet. A deaf man hears the words he whispers to a blind man, and a dumb man wants to be shown what he said.

The earliest occurrence of this kind of nonsense tale is attested in the mystical *summa*, the *Masnavi-ye ma'navi*, compiled by Jalāl al-Din Rumi (d. 1273), a Persian poet who spent the greater part of his life in the Anatolian town of Konya.[10] Rumi uses the nonsense tale to introduce his version of the story of the Sabaeans, an ancient people mentioned in the Koran (2:62, 5:69, 22:17) as true believers. He introduces the city of Sabā as an enormously large settlement the size of a saucer or an onion.[11] Although the people of ten cities gathered in Sabā, its population comprised only three "beggarly fools." One of them was far-sighted and blind, the second sharp of hearing and extremely deaf, and the third naked and wearing long garments. The blind man sees an army approach, the deaf man hears the soldiers' voices, and the naked man is afraid that they will cut something off his shirt. Fleeing from the approaching army, the three men find a fat fowl, "but not a mite of flesh on it." Eating the fowl, each of the men grows fat like an elephant. Notwithstanding their enormous size, the three men "sprang forth through a chink in the door and departed."

Rumi introduces the tale by referring to the stories children tell. Although those stories mention, as Rumi says, "many ridiculous things," the author advises his audience to seek the treasure "in all ruined places," as "in their tales there is enfolded many a mystery and a moral lesson." Following his usual procedure, Rumi supplies a mystical interpretation for the three characters.[12] The far-sighted blind man represents hope, as he is perfectly aware of humanity's mortality but does not consider his own death; the blind man represents greed, as he sees other people's faults without perceiving "one mote of his own fault;" and the naked man stands for humanity's general "anxiety on account of the thief," even though "bare he came and naked he goes." In addition to suggesting the tale's origin in oral tradition, Rumi's introductory statement links to modern Turkish tradition where the formulaic nonsense tale often serves to introduce the audience to the never-never-land in which the ensuing fairy tale would take place.[13] Often in rhyme, the Turkish *tekerleme* is a specific folk narrative genre that serves as a lead into a prose story performance, as a marker and a disclaimer for the fiction to follow.

Although it was surmised that Rumi's mention of the elephant suggests an Indian model for his rendering of the tale,[14] no similar narrative has yet been discussed for the ancient Indian literatures. Moreover, tale type ATU 1965 is conspicuously absent from modern Indian oral tradition.[15]

Notes

1. Boratav, Pertev Naili, "Gesellen: Die schadhaften G.," in *Enzyklopädie des Märchens*, vol. 5 (1987), cols. 1147–1151.

2. Grimm, Jacob and Wilhelm, *Kinder- und Hausmärchen: Ausgabe letzter Hand mit den Originalanmerkungen der Brüder Grimm*, ed. Heinz Rölleke, Stuttgart: Philipp Reclam Jun., 1980, vol. 3, pp. 232–233, no. 138.

3. Bolte and Polívka, *Anmerkungen*, vol. 3, pp. 115–119, no. 138.

4. Briggs, *A Dictionary*, vol. A2, p. 542.

5. Bladé, Jean-François, *Contes populaires de Gascogne*, Paris: Maisonneuve, 1886, pp. 254–255, no. 8.

6. Crane, Thomas Frederick, *Italian Popular Tales*, Boston: Houghton, 1885, pp. 263–264, no. 84.

7. See Bolte and Polívka, *Anmerkungen*, vol. 3, pp. 116, no. 138.

8. Boratav, Pertev Naili, *Le "Tekerleme:" Contribution à l'étude typologique et stylistique du conte populaire turc*, Paris: Société Asiatique, 1963.

9. Boratav, Pertev Naili, "Les trois compagnons infirmes," *Fabula* 2 (1959), pp. 231–253, at p. 245.

10. Ibid., pp. 242–244; Spies, Otto, "Die orientalische Herkunft des Stoffes 'Knoist und sine dre Sühne'," *Rheinisches Jahrbuch für Volkskunde* 12 (1961), pp. 47–52, at pp. 50–51.

11. Rumi, Jalāl al-Din, *The Mathnawí of Jalálu'ddín Rúmí*, transl. Reynold A. Nicholson, London: Luzac & Co., 1934, vol. 2, pp. 146–147 (bk. 3, verses 2600–2627). A modern prose rendering is given in Arberry, Arthur John, *Tales from the Masnavi*, London: George Allen & Unwin, 1961, pp. 243–244, no. 84.

12. Rumi, *The Mathnawí*, pp. 147–149 (bk. 3, verses 2628ff.).

13. Spies, "Die orientalische Herkunft," p. 49.

14. Ibid., p. 52.

15. Uther, *The Types*, vol. 2, p. 509, no. 1965.

CHAPTER 100

Mouse-Maid Marries Mouse (ATU 2031C)

The narrative genre of the clock tale[1] was proposed by Joan Ruman Perkal in 1960.[2] A "particularly unusual formula tale," the clock tale is defined by "a common interaction, namely: the burden of guilt for an accident is successively shifted from one animal character to another, each denying its own blame in the matter, and each pointing an accusing finger at a fellow creature;" eventually, "the ultimate responsibility for the crime comes back to rest with the original accuser."[3] As the "closest example of a tale with a clock-like pattern," Perkal identified the "Indian tale of the Mouse-Maiden who was looking for the strongest person in the world to become her husband, and who, after various inquiries and tasks, ultimately ends up with another mouse as her mate."[4] This tale is classified as tale type ATU 2031C: *The Mightiest Being as Husband for the Daughter.*[5] In European oral tradition, the tale was recorded exclusively from the Iberian Peninsula and the Balkans.[6] The only central European version known is listed for German writer and collector of folktales Ludwig Bechstein's (1801–1860) *Neues deutsches Märchenbuch* (New German Fairy-Tale Book), containing the author's retelling that is closely modeled on the tale's late medieval German literary version.[7] Although Bechstein's publication was popular in its day, it did not have a noticeable impact on German oral tradition.[8]

The tale's Catalan version as narrated in 1919 by Teresa Bernat from Reus introduces an aged couple ardently longing for a child.[9] Finding a little mouse one day, the old woman wishes for the mouse to be a little girl. No sooner has she finished her wish than the mouse is transformed into a maid. When the girl grows up, they make great efforts to find her a suitable husband. Thinking that there can be no better husband for his daughter than the sun, the old man asks the sun. The sun visits the mouse maid for three days. As the sun does not show up on the fourth day, it later admits that the clouds kept it from visiting. Disappointed by the sun's limitations, the old man goes to ask the cloud. When the cloud admits that the wind kept it from visiting, the old man asks the wind. And when the wind is hindered by the mountain, he asks the mountain. Finally, on the fourth day of its visit, the mountain admits to being bothered by a mouse. As soon as the old man realizes that the mouse is stronger than the mountain, he wonders why they ever wished the mouse to be a maid. No sooner has he said that than the mouse maid is transformed into a mouse again and vanishes through the same hole in the wall whence it had come.

The tale's Greek version has essentially the same chain of events, here entailing the sun, the clouds, the wind, and a tower.[10] Instead of a mouse turned maid, however, the tale's characters are mice only. Likewise, there is no framing transformation in the Serbian version narrated by Vojko Miljanović from Podvori, a village in the district of Mostar, as recorded on tape by Vlajko Palavestra on June 29, 1963.[11] Here, the male mouse starts looking for a bride for himself, visiting the sun, the cloud, the wind, and an old oak tree. In the end, the mouse marries the daughter of another mouse gnawing at the oak tree's roots. Versions of the tale's Bulgarian oicotype were told by Angel Mizhorkov from Ratsigovo as recorded at the end of the nineteenth century by Georgi Ruseski,[12] and by Vasilka Stoilkova Mitovska from the village Dăbrava as recorded by Dorotea Dobreva on November 16, 1978.[13] The chain of potential suitors for the male mouse here entails sun, cloud, wind, valley, river, and riverbank. In the end, they find the modest mole with its den in the riverbank to be the most powerful being of all, and the mouse is married to the daughter of the mole.

The tale is included in the numerous European and Middle Eastern versions of the Arabic collection of fables and animal tales known by the names of two jackals that play a prominent role in its frame tale as *Kalīla wa-Dimna* (Kalīla and Dimna).[14] Bechstein adapted the tale from Anton von Pforr's late fifteenth-century German translation *Buch der Beispiele der alten Weisen* (Book of Exemplary Tales of the Ancient Sages),[15] itself a German rendering of the thirteenth-century Latin version *Directorium vitae humanae* (A Guide for Human Life) by John of Capua that in turn was based on Rabbi Joël's twelfth-century Hebrew translation from the Arabic. John of Capua's rendering was highly influential as the basis of most of the book's translations and adaptations in various European languages that enabled their audience to read the tales in the vernacular, thus potentially generating retellings in oral tradition. A second Latin translation was prepared in the fourteenth century by Raymond of Béziers,[16] based on a mid-thirteenth-century Spanish translation.[17] The texts of the present tale in these translations are closely related to Middle Eastern tradition in that they preserve the frame of double transformation. This is also the case in the short version included in the seventh book of *Felix: de los Maravelles del Mon* (Felix: On the Wonders of the World), originally compiled around 1287 by the Catalan poet, mystic, theologian, and philosopher Ramón Llull (d. 1316)[18] from which the quoted Catalan example might have been adapted.

Another strand of tradition influential in European tradition does not mention a transformation but has a mouse itself look for a partner. This strand of tradition, to which most of the folktales recorded from European oral tradition are related, is historically documented by the versions included in Marie de France's late twelfth-century French *Fables*,[19] Berechiah ha-Nakdan's thirteenth-century

Hebrew *Mishle Shu'alim* (Fox Fables),[20] and Odo of Cheriton's thirteenth-century Latin *Liber parabolarum* (Book of Instructive Tales).[21]

Mediated through a pre-Islamic, Middle Persian translation of the Indian *Panchatantra* (Five [Books of] Wisdom),[22] now lost, the book's internationally most influential version is the Arabic *Kalīla wa-Dimna*.[23] In *Kalīla wa-Dimna*, the tale starts by introducing a hermit who is so pious that God answers his prayers. The hermit saves a mouse from a bird of prey and takes it home to take care of it. Intending to avoid trouble, the hermit asks the Lord to transform the mouse into a girl whom he presents to his wife to bring up as their daughter. When the girl comes of age, the hermit suggests that she should choose a husband, be it a human or a supernatural being, and the girl expresses her wish to marry the most powerful being on earth. The hermit then goes to ask the sun, the clouds, the wind, and the mountain, each of which admits that another entity is more powerful. Finally, the rat is willing to marry the girl, objecting only to the girl's size in comparison to its own small home. Following the girl's wish, the hermit asks God to transform her back into a mouse.

Notes

1. Bulang, Tobias, "Ringerzählung," in *Enzyklopädie des Märchens*, vol. 11 (2004), cols. 700–702.

2. Perkal, Joan Ruman, "A 'Clock' Tale and Its Related Motif-Complex," *Fabula* 3 (1960), pp. 254–269.

3. Ibid., pp. 254–255.

4. Ibid., p. 255.

5. Hansen, William, "Stärkste Dinge," in *Enzyklopädie des Märchens*, vol. 12 (2007), cols. 1188–1194, at cols. 1191.

6. Uther, *The Types*, vol. 2, p. 5252, no. 2031C lists versions from oral traditions in Catalan, Portuguese, Hungarian, Bosnian, Bulgarian, and Greek.

7. Bechstein, Ludwig, *Neues Deutsches Märchenbuch*, ed. Hans-Jörg Uther, Munich: Eugen Diederichs, 1997, pp. 249–252, no. 43.

8. Uther, *Deutscher Märchenkatalog*, does not list the tale type.

9. Schulte-Kemminghausen, Karl, and Hüllen, Georg, *Märchen der europäischen Völker*, vol. 7, Münster: Aschendorff, 1967, pp. 49–51, 62–64.

10. Megas, Georgios A., *Griechische Volksmärchen*, Cologne: Diederichs, 1965, p. 18, no. 8.

11. Eschker, Wolfgang, *Der Zigeuner im Paradies: Balkanslawische Schwänke und lustige Streiche*, Kassel: Erich Röth, 1986, pp. 78–80, 187, no. 53.

12. Nicoloff, Assen, *Bulgarian Folktales*, Cleveland: Nicoloff, 1979, pp. 5–7, 206–207, no. 5; Ognjanowa, Elena, *Märchen aus Bulgarien*, Wiesbaden: Drei Lilien, 1987, pp. 182–184, 488–489, no. 49.

13. Daskalova, Liana, et al., *Narodna proza ot Blagoevgradski okrăg*, Sofia: Bălgarska Akademiya na Naukite, 1985, p. 37, 415, no. 17; see also Daskalova Perkowski, Liliana, et al., *Typenverzeichnis der bulgarischen Volksmärchen*, ed. Klaus Roth, Helsinki: Suomalainen Tiedeakatemia, 1995, p. 397, no. 2031C.

14. Chauvin, *Bibliographie*, vol. 2 (1897), p. 97–98, no. 55; Schwarzbaum, Haim,

The Mishle Shu'alim (Fox Fables) of Rabbi Berechiah ha-Nakdan, Kiron: Institute for Jewish and Arab Folklore Research, 1979, pp. 167–178, no. 28; see also Bin Gorion, Micha Joseph, *Mimekor Israel: Classical Jewish Folktales, Abridged and Annotated*, ed. Emanuel Bin Gorion, prepared by Dan Ben-Amos, Bloomington: Indiana University Press, 1990, pp. 467–468, no. 252; Grotzfeld, Heinz and Sophia, and Ulrich Marzolph, "Kalila und Dimna," in *Enzyklopädie des Märchens*, vol. 7 (1993), cols. 888–895.

15. Bechstein, *Neues Deutsches Märchenbuch*, p. 295, no. 43; Pforr, Anton von, *Das Buch der Beispiele der alten Weisen*, ed. Friedmar Geißler, Berlin: Akademie-Verlag, 1964, vol. 1, p. 95–96 (ch. 5, no. 8).

16. Luyster, Amanda, "The Conversion of Kalila and Dimna: Raymond de Béziers, Religious Experience, and Translation at the Fourteenth-Century French Court," *Gesta* 56.1 (2017), pp. 81–104.

17. *Calila e Dimna*, ed. Juan Manuel Cacho Blecua and María Jesús Lacarra, Madrid: Castalia, 2004.

18. Llull, Ramon, *Selected Works*, ed. and transl. Anthony Bonner, vol. 2, Princeton: Princeton University Press, 1985, pp. 789–790.

19. Marie de France, *Fables*, ed. and transl. Harriet Spiegel, Toronto: University of Toronto Press, 1987, pp. 198–203.

20. Schwarzbaum, *The Mishle Shu'alim*, pp. 167–178, no. 28.

21. Wesselski, *Mönchslatein*, pp. 82–85, 224–225, no. 71; Odo of Cheriton, *The Fables*, transl. John C. Jacobs, Syracuse, NY: Syracuse University Press, 1985, pp. 141–142, no. 94.

22. Benfey, Theodor, *Pantschatantra: Fünf Bücher indischer Fabeln, Märchen und Erzählungen, aus dem Sanskrit übersetzt mit Einleitung und Anmerkungen*, (Leipzig 1859) reprint Hildesheim: Georg Olms, 1966, vol. 2, pp. 262–266 (3.12); Vishnusharma, *The Panchatantra*, transl. Arthur W. Ryder, Chicago: Chicago University Press, 1925, pp. 353–359; Hertel, Johannes, *Indische Märchen*, Düsseldorf: Diederichs, 1953, pp. 54–55, 403, no. 17 (from the *Tantrākhyāyika*).

23. Cheikho, Louis, *La version arabe de Kalîlah et Dimnah ou Les fables de Bipai*, (Beirut 1905) reprint Amsterdam: Philo Press, 1981, pp. 159–160.

CHAPTER 101

The Climax of Horrors (ATU 2040)

In a volume of popular tales and jests collected in the Western Eifel, a rural region in Western Germany adjacent to Belgium and Luxemburg, German folklorist Matthias Zender (1907–1993) published the following short jocular tale titled *Everything in Best Order.*[1] The original German text is in local dialect, reproducing or at least emulating the original performance.

> There was a count who had been travelling for a long time. As he returns home, his servant comes to pick him up at the train station. He asks the servant how things are at home. "Oh," says the servant, "everything is in best order."
>
> The count had a dog whose name was Bello that was very dear to him. So the count asks the servant, "How is Bello doing?"—"Oh," says he, "Bello is dead." How could it be that Bello was dead? He ate too much horse flesh. How could it be that he ate the horse flesh? Oh, recently, when the castle burned down, the seven best horses also burned, and so he ate too much horse flesh. How could it be that the castle burned down? Oh, when the count's mother died, they forgot to put out the lights, and so the castle burned down. How could it be that his mother died? The count's wife eloped with another man, and that grieved her so much that she died. So Bello died, the seven best horses are dead, the castle burned down, the count's mother died, and the wife eloped with another man—that is what you call: everything is in best order.

The tale was recorded from a certain Nober in Plütscheid in 1934. The narrator himself added, "I heard the little piece (German *Steckelchen*) when I was going to school, and I have only thought of it recently. An old man from Kopsched, Matth[ias] Denter, had told it."[2] Several other versions of the tale were recorded from early twentieth-century German local tradition, all of them notably published in regional dialect.[3] The tale, corresponding to the international tale type ATU 2040: *The Climax of Horrors*, enjoyed a certain popularity in Germany since early in the nineteenth century, when a version was included in Johann Peter Hebel's *Schatzkästlein des rheinischen Hausfreunds* (The Rhenish Family Friend's

Treasure Box), originally published in 1811.[4] Here, the setting and sequence of events differ only slightly. The son of a rich man in Swabia returns home after having studied in Paris. The news the servant breaks one after the other are as follows: the raven died from eating too much horse flesh; the horses died from working too hard fetching water to extinguish the fire; the house burned because they had buried the man's father at night, and sparks from the torches set the house on fire; the father died from grief because the young man's sister had given birth to a son from an unknown father. As in the other versions, this one ends with the servant saying, "Other than that, there is not much news." Hebel's version can be traced to a precursor in the late eighteenth-century German chapbook *Vademecum*. The introduction of a raven instead of the usually mentioned dog might possibly be explained through the author's misreading of the word *canis* (dog) in his Latin source as *corvus* (raven).[5]

Commenting on one of the tale's oldest European version in the sermons of the French preacher Jacques de Vitry (d. 1240),[6] Thomas Frederick Crane quotes an English version of the tale, "translated, with a few changes" from Hebel, mentioning that it "was once a favourite dialogue for school speakers."[7]

Mr. G.: Ha! Steward, how are you, my old boy? How do things go on at home?
Steward: Bad enough, you honour; the magpie's dead.
Mr. G.: Poor Gam! So he's gone. How came he to die?
Steward: Overate himself, sir.
Mr. G.: Did he, indeed? A greedy dog! Why, what did he get that he liked so well?
Steward: Horse flesh, sir; he died of eating horse flesh.
Mr. G.: How came he to get so much horse flesh?
Steward: All your father's horses, sir.
Mr. G.: What, are they dead, too?
Steward: Ay, sir; they died of overwork.
Mr. G.: And why were they overworked, pray?
Steward: To carry water, sir.
Mr. G.: To carry water! And what were they carrying water for?
Steward: Sure, sir, to put out the fire.
Mr. G.: Fire! What fire?
Steward: Oh! Sir, your father's house is burned down to the ground.
Mr. G.: My father's house burnt down! And how came it on fire?
Steward: I think, sir, it must have been the torches.
Mr. G.: Torches! What torches?
Steward: At your mother's funeral.
Mr. G.: My mother dead!
Steward: Ah! Poor lady, she never looked up after it.
Mr. G.: After what?
Steward: The loss of our father.

Mr. G.: My father gone too?
Steward: Yes, poor gentleman, he took to his bed as soon as he heard of it.
Mr. G.: Heard of what?
Steward: The bad news, sir, an' please your honor.
Mr. G.: What? More miseries? More bad news?
Steward: Yes, sir; your bank has failed, and your credit is lost; and you are not worth a shilling in the world. I made bold, sir, to come to wait on you about it; for I thought you would like to hear the news!

In addition to reading "Magpie" not as the bird, but as the dog's name, and adding the mother's death, the most decisive alteration in this English version is the change of loss of honor (referring to the daughter's illegitimate offspring) in Hebel's version to a loss of social reputation based on wealth. Joseph Jacobs, the editor of a widely read series of English fairy tales, published virtually the same text in his volume *More English Fairy Tales* (1894),[8] quoting from "Bell's *Speaker*," that is, *The Modern Reader and Speaker: A Selection of Poetry and Prose from the Writings of Eminent Authors, with Copious Extracts for Recitation [. . .]* compiled by David C. Bell. First published in Dublin in 1850, this book was extremely popular in the second half of the nineteenth century, as it went through more than fifty editions in the following 30 years, its fifty-fourth edition appearing in 1881. Also known from a slightly more condensed version in the folklore collection amassed by James D. Carpenter in the first half of the twentieth century,[9] the tale was finally canonized as part of English language tradition (from Jacobs) by its inclusion in Katherine M. Briggs's *A Dictionary of British Folk-Tales in the English Language*.[10]

In terms of its historical dissemination, the tale constitutes one of the rare cases for which a consecutive chain of instances transmitting the tale can be reconstructed. As the English versions relied on Hebel, so Hebel relied on the *Vademecum*. The *Vademecum*, in turn, ultimately relies on the earliest European version as given in the *Disciplina Clericalis* (The Scholar's Guide), a collection of entertaining and moralizing tales in Latin compiled by Petrus Alfonsus, a Jew converted to Christianity who lived in the multicultural context of late eleventh- and early twelfth-century Spain.[11] Petrus Alfonsus includes the tale in a little conglomerate of tales about the lazy servant Maimundus. The chain of events mentioned there is as follows: the dog Bispella died as it was kicked by the mule; the mule balked when the son fell to his death from the balcony; the boy's mother died from grief; the house burned down when the maid forgot to extinguish the lamp; and the maid died when a falling beam crushed her head. As is well known, Petrus Alfonsus adapted a considerable part of his narrative material from Arabic tradition.[12]

In Arabic tradition, already in the eleventh century the tale exists in different versions, and so its actual origin might even date earlier.[13] The earliest-known version, mentioning the poet Abū 'l-Aswad al-Du'alī (d. 689) as protagonist, is included in al-Ābī's (d. 1030) comprehensive encyclopedia of jokes and anecdotes, *Nathr al-durr* (Pearls of Prose).[14]

> A Bedouin came to Abū 'l-Aswad as he was just eating. He greeted him, and Abū 'l-Aswad returned the greeting. Then he began to eat without inviting the Bedouin. The Bedouin said, "I came by your family." Abū 'l-Aswad remarked, "That was a long way!"—"All of them are healthy."—"That is how I left them."— "Your wife is pregnant."—"That I entrusted to her."—"She gave birth."—"Of course she had to give birth."— "She gave birth to two boys."— "The same way her mother did."— "One of them died."— "She could not nourish both of them."— "Then the other one died."— "He did not want to live on after his brother."— "Then the mother died."— "Grieving for her children."— "What a good meal you have!"— "That is what inspires me to eat it."— "Ugh! How stingy you are."— "Whosoever wants to do it, may insult the person with whom he speaks."

In this rudimentary version, the character of the news develops according to the (lacking) degree of hospitality. In Arabic tradition, Bedouins are stereotypically considered greedy, and hospitality is a highly valued moral obligation. So when the hungry Bedouin realizes that his counterpart does not invite him, nor do his flattering remarks produce a positive effect to that end, he changes the character of the news from good to bad so as to harm at least. But even so, the aggressive adjustment of the news leaves no impression on the stingy man who remains firm in his decision not to share his meal. In his book *al-Bukhalā'* (Stingy People), al-Khaṭīb al-Baghdādī (d. 1071) in addition to the tale's rudimentary version presents a more elaborate text.[15] The chain of transmitters supplied for this tale extends to the famous scholar al-Aṣmaʿī (d. 828) as the one who originally told the tale.

> Visiting another tribe, a Bedouin met a member of his own tribe and sat down with him. His host asked, "How did you leave my dog Bulayq?" He responded, "He fills all the tribe's territory with his barking!"— "That is good news! And how did you leave my red camel?"— "It carries water for the whole tribe."— "That is good news! And how did you leave my son ʿAmr?"— "He is in good spirits and fills the whole tribe with his kindness."— "That is good news! And what about the house?"— "It is richly filled with the family."— "That is good news!" Then the host called the maidservant to serve dinner. The Bedouin started to eat with great appetite, so that the host became angry and wanted to keep him from eating by making him talk.
>
> So he said, "Continue the news!" The Bedouin responded, "Ask me for what you want to know!" The host asked, "What about my dog Bulayq?"—"It would be good, were it alive."—"Did it die?"—"Yes."—"How come?"—"He ate from the flesh of the red camel."—"So the red camel died?"—"Yes."—"How come?"—"It died from carrying water to the grave of ʿAmr's mother."—"So my wife died?"—"Yes."—"How come

she died?"—"Grieving the death of her son."—"So ʿAmr died?"—"Yes."—"What brought about his death?"—"The house crashed on top of him."—"So the house crashed?"—"Yes."

Thereupon the host called out, "Maid! Clear the meal and bring a stick!" Upon which the Bedouin ran away so that the other one could not catch him.

While the general structure of the rudimentary version was retained, the elaborate version not only has the guest change his tactics in order to be invited to share the meal but also details the events in much the same manner as they appear in later European tradition. Yet another variation of the tale is documented in al-Zamakhsharī's (d. 1144) *Rabīʿ al-abrār* (Spring of the Pious).[16] This time, the guest gets the better of the host. Two Bedouins meet, and the newcomer is asked about news from the tribe. Since the news is positive, the inquirer sits down to eat without inviting the visitor. When a dog passes, the visitor starts to lament, and recounts the commonly narrated chain, now with a disastrous impact. The dog died from eating too much camel flesh; the camel died from tripping over the grave of the man's wife; the woman died grieving the death of her son; and the son died from falling from the top of the house. As the eater starts to lament his misfortune, scattering the meal, the newcomer calmly assembles the food and curses people who are stingy.

In Arabic literature, the tale was repeatedly cited in works of subsequent centuries,[17] such as al-Nuwayrī's (d. 1332) *Nihāyat al-arab fī funūn al-adab* (The Ultimate Ambition in the Arts of Erudition),[18] Ibn Ḥijja al-Ḥamawī's (d. 1434) *Thamarāt al-awrāq* (The Fruits of the [Scattered] Leaves),[19] or Muḥammad ibn Aḥmad ibn (al-)Ilyās al-Ḥanafī's seventeenth-century *Nuzhat al-udabāʾ* (Entertainment of the Educated).[20] Probably most important for the tale's dissemination in popular tradition was its inclusion in al-Ibshīhī's fifteenth-century encyclopedia *al-Mustaṭraf fī kulli fann mustaẓraf* (The Exquisite Elements from Every Art Considered Elegant), a compilation that enjoyed a tremendous popularity in Arabic households well into the twentieth century.[21] The elaborate version presented by al-Khaṭīb al-Baghdādī found its way into the pranks attributed to the Arabic jester Juḥā compiled early in the second half of the nineteenth century.[22]

In Persian literature, the tale was rendered in prose in Fakhr al-Din ʿAli Ṣafi's (d. 1532) anecdotal compilation *Laṭāʾef al-ṭavāʾef* (Jocular Tales from the Various Strata of Society)[23] and turned into poetry by Lavāʾi, a poet who lived in Esfahan during the time of the Safavid ruler Shāh ʿAbbās I (1571–1629).[24] The tale's Persian prose version was later included in the anthology of entertaining texts in Francis Gladwin's *Persian Moonshee*, originally published in 1801. From there, it passed on into the anthology's numerous separate chapbook versions distributed in the Indian subcontinent in Persian and in a variety of local languages.[25]

The Arabic and Persian versions hinge their humour on the Bedouin custom of news sharing en route by travelers and on stereotypes of greed and stinginess, both of which are commonly attributed to Bedouins. In contrast, the European master-to-servant versions as first documented in the *Disciplina clericalis* adopt the tale to the context of a sedentary culture, and their humor may be read to turn on implicit or latent social tension.

In terms of rhetorics, the tale illustrates the strategy of blunting, already known in antiquity as *amblysia*, an early version of which is given by Plutarch (*Solon* 6). Visiting Thales in Milet, Solon wonders why Thales lives without wife and children. In order to demonstrate his motivation, Thales arranges for a fictive envoy to arrive. When questioned by Solon about news from Athens, the envoy says, as previously agreed with Thales, that there is no big news, except for the burial of a certain young man whose eminent father is currently travelling. Further questions reveal that the travelling father is nobody but Solon himself. As Solon laments his bad fortune, however, his host reveals the news to be part of his strategy to demonstrate his motivation to live a life of celibacy.[26] In this way, the technique of blunting "pretends to dull the edge of dire news while really sharpening it."[27] Whether or not the tale's Arabic versions derive from antique models remains to be studied.

Notes

1. Zender, Matthias, *Volksmärchen und Schwänke aus der Westeifel*, Bonn: Röhrscheid, 1935, pp. 67–68, no. 54.

2. Ibid., 68.

3. Findeisen, Hans, *Sagen, Märchen und Schwänke von der Insel Hiddensee*, Stettin: Saunier, 1925, p. 32, no. 33; Tewaag, F., *Erzählungen, Märchen, Sagen und Mundarten aus Hessen*, Marburg, Friedrich: 1885 (1888), p. 94; Wossidlo, Richard, *Volksschwänke aus Mecklenburg*, ed. Siegfried Neumann, Berlin: Akademie-Verlag, 1963, p. 10, no. 26 (told by the blacksmith Grospitz in Waschow); different, but with the same punchline, in Van der Kooi, Jurjen, and Theo Schuster, *Märchen und Schwänke aus Ostfriesland*, Leer: Schuster, 1993, pp. 284–285, no. 219.

4. Hebel, Johann Peter, *Schatzkästlein des rheinischen Hausfreunds*, ed. Winfried Theiss, Stuttgart: Reclam, 1981, pp. 170–171.

5. Marzolph, Ulrich, "Häufung des Schreckens," in *Enzyklopädie des Märchens*, vol. 6 (1990), cols. 576–581.

6. Wesselski, *Mönchslatein*, pp. 25–26, 206, no. 20.

7. Crane, Thomas Frederick, *The Exempla or Illustrative Stories from the Sermones Vulgares of Jacques de Vitry*, London: Nutt, 1890 (reprint Nendeln: Kraus, 1967), pp. 216–217, no. 205. Crane quotes from Noble Butler's *The Common School Speaker*, Louisville, KY: Morton & Griswold, 1856, p. 57.

8. Jacobs, Joseph, *More English Fairy Tales*, London: D. Nutt, 1894, pp. 168–169.

9. Carpenter, James M., "Two Versions of a Hard-luck Story. I: Soft-peddling Sorrowful News," *North Carolina Folklore* 2 (1954), p. 16. This is followed pp. 16–17 by a slightly different version "clipped from a Texas newspaper [. . .] by Professor Floyd Stovall, of the University of North Carolina, in June 1954." For the Carpenter Collection of Folklore, see Bishop, Julia C., "'Dr Carpenter from the Harvard College in America:' An Introduction to James Madison Carpenter and His Collection," *Folk Music Journal* 7.4 (1998), pp. 402–420.

10. Briggs, *A Dictionary*, vol. A2, pp. 199–200.

11. Lacarra Ducay, María Jesús, "Petrus Alfonsus," in *Enzyklopädie des Märchens*, vol. 10 (2002), cols. 797–802.

12. Schwarzbaum, Haim, "International Folklore Motifs in Petrus Alphonsi's 'Disciplina Clericalis'," in Schwarzbaum, *Jewish Folklore between East and West*, ed. Eli Yassif, Beer-Sheva: Ben-Gurion University of the Negev Press, 1989, pp. 239–358, at pp. 315–322, no. 27; see also Spies, Otto, "Arabische Stoffe in der Disciplina Clericalis," *Rheinisches Jahrbuch für Volkskunde* 21 (1973), pp. 170–199, p. 193.

13. Marzolph, *Arabia ridens*, vol. 2, p. 188, no. 811. An early twentieth-century survey of the sources is given by Tardel, Hermann, "Das Motiv des Gedichtes 'Botenart' von Anastasius Grün," in *Festschrift zum 16. Neuphilologentag in Bremen vom 1. bis 4. Juni 1914*, Heidelberg 1914, pp. 163–201.

14. Ābī, Abū Sa'd Manṣūr ibn al-Ḥusayn al-, *Nathr al-durr*, ed. Muḥammad 'Alī Qarna et al., vol. 3, Cairo: al-Hay'a al-miṣriyya al-'āmma lil-kitāb, 1984, p. 291.

15. Khaṭīb al-Baghdādī, Abū Bakr Aḥmad ibn 'Alī al-, *al-Bukhalā'*, ed. Aḥmad al-Maṭlūb, Khadīja al-Ḥadīthī, and Aḥmad Nājī al-Qaysī, Baghdad: Maṭba'at al-'Ānī, 1384/1964, pp. 146–147.

16. Zamakhsharī, Abū 'l-Qāsim Maḥmūd ibn 'Umar al-, *Rabī' al-abrār wa-nuṣūṣ al-akhbār*, ed. Salīm al-Nu'aymī, vol. 4, Baghdad: al-'Ānī, 1982, p. 171.

17. Hammer-Purgstall, Joseph Freiherr von, *Rosenöl, oder Sagen und Kunden des Morgenlandes aus arabischen, persischen und türkischen Quellen gesammelt*, vol. 2, Stuttgart: J.G. Cotta, 1813, pp. 274–275, no. 147, translates from a comparatively recent work falsely attributed to the eighth-century alchemist Jābir ibn Ḥayyān.

18. Nuwayrī, Shihāb al-Dīn Aḥmad ibn 'Abd al-Wahhāb al-, *Nihāyat al-arab fī funūn al-adab*, vol. 3, Cairo: Dār al-Kutub al-miṣriyya, 1369/1949, pp. 304–305 (2 versions).

19. Ibn Ḥijja al-Ḥamawī, 'Alī ibn Muḥammad, *Thamarāt al-awrāq fī 'l-muḥāḍarāt*, ed. Mufīd Qumayḥa, Beirut: Dār al-Kutub al-'ilmiyya, 1403/1983, p. 363.

20. Ḥanafī, Muḥammad ibn Aḥmad ibn (al-)Ilyās al-, *Nuzhat al-udabā'*, Gotha, Ms. Orient A 2706, fol. 27b–28a, 29a (2 versions).

21. Ibshīhī, Shihāb al-Dīn Muḥammad ibn Aḥmad Abī al-Fatḥ al-, *al-Mustaṭraf fī kull fann mustaẓraf*, ed. Mufīd Qumayḥa, Beirut: Dār al-Kutub al-'ilmiyya, 1403/1983, vol. 1, p. 382; Marzolph, Ulrich, "Medieval Knowledge in Modern Reading: A 15th Century Arabic Encyclopedia of *omni re scibili*," in *Pre-modern Encylopaedic Texts: Proceedings of the Second COMERS Congress, Groningen, 1–4 July 1996*, ed. Peter Binkley, Leiden: Brill, 1997, pp. 407–419. Gustave Rat's French translation is quoted by Tardel, "Das Motiv," p. 167.

22. Juḥā, *Hādhihi nawādir al-khūjah Naṣr al-Dīn Afandī Juḥā al-Rūmī*, Būlāq: Mūsā Kāstillī, 1278/1861, pp. 11–12.

23. Ṣafi, Fakhr al-Din 'Ali, *Laṭā'ef al-ṭavā'ef*, ed. Aḥmad Golchin-Ma'āni, Tehran: Moḥammmad Ḥoseyn Eqbāl, 1336/1957, pp. 147–148.

24. Kuka, Meherjibhai Noosherwanji, *The Wit and Humor of the Persians*, Bombay 1894, pp. 83–84; Kuka, *The Wit, Humor and Fancy of Persia*, Bombay 1937, pp. 126–129. See also the review of Falconer, Forbes, *Extracts from Some of the Persian Poets*, London 1843 in the *Journal Asiatique* (July and August 1843), pp. 124ff., with a French prose translation of the tale that is also quoted by Tardel, "Das Motiv," pp. 168–169.

25. Marzolph, Ulrich, "'Pleasant Stories in an Easy Style:' Gladwin's Persian Grammar as an Intermediary between Classical and Popular Literature," in *Proceedings of the*

Second European Conference of Iranian Studies, ed. Bert G. Fragner et al., Rome: Istituto Italiano per il Medio ed Estremo Oriente, 1995, pp. 445–475, at p. 465, no. 66. Gladwin's text is also quoted by Tardel, "Das Motiv," pp. 167–168.

26. Tardel, Hermann, "Motivgeschichtliches," *Niederdeutsche Zeitschrift für Volkskunde* 14 (1936), pp. 216–221, at p. 219.

27. Esar, Evan, *The Humor of Humor*, London: Phoenix, 1954, pp. 42–44, quote p. 42.

WORKS CITED

Tale types are regularly cited in the text as ATU (Aarne, Thompson, and Uther = Uther, *The Types*) or AT (Aarne and Thompson = Aarne, *The Types of the Folktale*, 2nd rev.) and occasionally mentioned narrative motifs as Mot. (= Thompson, *Motif-Index*). Studies in Western languages appearing in the notes to ten or more different essays are cited in an abbreviated manner giving the author's name and a short title.

A Catalogue of the Celebrated Library of the Late Count Borromeo, of Padua, Auction Catalogue by Mr. Evans, London, 1817.

Aarne, Antti, *The Types of the Folktale: A Classification and Bibliography. Antti Aarne's Verzeichnis der Märchentypen (FF Communications No. 3) Translated and Enlarged*, ed. Stith Thompson, Helsinki: Suomalainen Tiedeakatemia, 1928.

Aarne, Antti, *The Types of the Folktale: A Classification and Bibliography. Antti Aarne's Verzeichnis der Märchentypen (FF Communications No. 3) Translated and Enlarged*, ed. Stith Thompson, 2nd rev., Helsinki: Suomalainen Tiedeakatemia, 1961 (reprint 1973).

Aarne, Antti Amatus, *Verzeichnis der Märchentypen, mit Hülfe von Fachgenossen ausgearbeitet*, Helsinki: Suomalainen Tiedeakatemia, 1910.

Abdel-Halim, Mohamed, *Antoine Galland, sa vie et son œuvre*, Paris: Nizet, 1964.

Ābī, Abū Saʿd Manṣūr ibn al-Ḥusayn al-, *Nathr al-durr*, ed. Muḥammad ʿAlī Qarna, ʿAlī Muḥammad al-Bijāwī, Ḥusayn Naṣṣār, Muḥammad Ibrāhīm ʿAbd al-Raḥmān, Ḥāmid ʿAbd al-ʿĀl, Munīr Muḥammad al-Madanī, 7 vols., Cairo: al-Hayʾa al-miṣriyya al-ʿāmma lil-kitāb, 1980–1991.

Abubéquer de Tortosa, *Lámpara de príncipes*, transl. M. Alarcón, 2 vols., Madrid: Instituto de Valencia de Don Juan, 1930.

Abū Nuʿaym al-Iṣfahānī, Aḥmad ibn ʿAbdallāh, *Ḥilyat al-awliyāʾ wa-ṭabaqāt al-aṣfiyāʾ*, ed. Ṣāliḥ Aḥmad al-Shāmī, 9 vols., Cairo: Maktabat al-Khānjī, 1932–1938.

Abū Nuwās, see *Nuzhat al-jullās fī nawādir Abū [!] Nuwās*.

Abū Ṭālib al-Makkī, *Die Nahrung der Herzen: Abū Ṭālib al-Makkīs Qūt al-qulūb*, transl. Richard Gramlich, 4 vols., Stuttgart: Steiner, 1992–1995.

Adam of Cobsam, *The Wright's Chaste Wife [...]: A Merry Tale, by Adam of Cobsam*, ed. Frederick J. Furnivall, London: Kegan Paul etc., 1865.

Addy, Sidney Oldall, *Household Tales with Other Traditional Remains: Collected in the Countries of York, Lindoln, Deby, and Nottingham*, London: Nutt, 1895.

Adrados, Francisco Rodríguez, *History of the Graeco-Latin Fable*, vol. 3, *Inventory and Documentation of the Graeco-Latin Fable*, Leiden: Brill, 2003.

Afanas'ev, A.N., "Contes secrets traduits du Russe," *Kryptádia* 1 (1883), pp. 1–292.

Afanasjew, Alexander N., *Der Feuervogel: Märchen aus dem alten Russland*, Stuttgart: Steingrüben, 1960.

Afanas'ev, Aleksandr Nikolaevich, *Narodnyia russkiia legendy*, Moscow 1859.

Afanasyev, Aleksandr Nikolaevich, *Russian Secret Tales: Bawdy Tales of Old Russia*, ed. Alan Dundes, Baltimore: Clearfield, 1998.

Afanasyev, Aleksandr Nikolaevich, *Narodnye russkie skazki*, ed. Vladimir Jakovlevich Propp, 3 vols., Moscow: Gosudarstvennoye Izdatel'stvo Khudozhestvennoy Literatury, 1957.

Agúndez García, José Luis, "Límites entre tradición oral y literatura: cuentecillos en autores del XIX y XX," in *El cuento folklórico en la literatura y en la tradición oral*, ed. Rafael Beltrán and Marta Haro, Valencia: University of Valencia, 2006, pp. 17–56.

Aiken, Riley, "A Pack Load of Mexican Tales," in *Puro Mexicano*, ed. James Frank Dobie, Austin: Texas Folklore Society, 1935, pp. 1–87.

Aitken, Hannah, and Ruth Michaelis-Jena, *Märchen aus Schottland*, Düsseldorf: Eugen Diederichs, 1965.

Akel, Ibrahim, "Liste des manuscrits arabes des *Nuits*," in Chraïbi, Aboubakr, ed., *Arabic Manuscripts of the* Thousand and One Nights, Paris: espaces & signes, 2016, pp. 65–114.

Akel, Ibrahim, "Quelques remarques sur la bibliothèque d'Antoine Galland et l'arrivée des *Mille et une nuits* en Occident," in *Antoine Galland et l'orient des savants: Actes du colloque organisé par L'AIBL, la Société Asiatique et l'INALCO, les 3 et 4 décembre 2015*, ed. Pierre-Sylvain Filliozat and Michel Zink, Paris: De Boccard, 2017, pp. 201–218.

Ālātī, Ḥasan al-, *Tarwīḥ al-nufūs wa-muḍḥik al-ʿabūs*, 3 vols., Cairo: Maṭbaʿa al-Jarīda al-maḥrūsa, 1889–1891.

Albertus Magnus, *Beati Alberti Magni, Ratisbonensis Episcopi, Ordinis Prædicatorum, Opera*, vol. 6: *De Animalibus lib. XXVI*, ed. Pierre Jammy, Lugduni: Claude Prost, 1651.

Albertus Magnus, *On Animals: A Medieval Summa Zoologica*, transl. and ed. Kenneth F. Kitchell Jr. and Irven M. Resnick, 2 vols., Baltimore: Johns Hopkins University Press, 1999.

Albertus Magnus, *Thierbuch*, transl. Walther Hermann Ryff, Frankfurt: Jacob, 1545.

Alexandrenko, Nikolai A., *The Poetry of Theodulf of Orleans; A Translation and Critical Study*, Ph.D. New Orleans: Tulane University, 1970.

Allardt, Anders, and Selim Perklén, *Nyländska folksagor och -sägner*, Helsingfors: Nyländska afdelningen, 1896.

Allen, Roger, and D.S. Richards, eds., *Arabic Literature in the Post-Classical Period* (*The Cambridge History of Arabic Literature*), Cambridge: Cambridge University Press, 2006.

Almqvist, Bo, "Notes," to Ó Catháin, Séamus, "An Fear nach rabh Scéal ar bith aige," *Béaloideas* 37–38 (1969–1970), pp. 51–59, 59–64.

Alsdorf, Ludwig, "Zwei neue Belege zur 'indischen Herkunft' von 1001 Nacht," *Zeitschrift der Deutschen Morgenländischen Gesellschaft* 89 (1935), pp. 275–314.

Alzheimer-Haller, Heidrun, *Handbuch zur narrativen Volksaufklärung: Moralische Geschichten 1780–1848*, Berlin: De Gruyter, 2004.

Amades, Joan, *Folklore de Catalunya*, 3 vols., Barcelona: Selecta, 1950–1969.

Aman, Anselm, *Die Filiation der Frankeleynes Tale in Chaucers Canterbury Tales*, Erlangen: Junge & Sohn, 1912.

Allen, Roger, and D.S. Richards, eds., *Arabic Literature in the Post-Classical Period* (*The Cambridge History of Arabic Literature*), Cambridge: Cambridge University Press, 2006.

Amani, Mohammad Sina, *Typologie des kurdischen Volksmärchens*, Ph.D. dissertation University of Göttingen (forthcoming).
Ambainis, Ojārs, *Lettische Volksmärchen*, 2nd ed., Berlin: Akademie-Verlag, 1979.
ʿĀmilī, Bahāʾ al-Dīn al-, *al-Kashkūl*; consulted at http://www.alwaraq.net (accessed February 8, 2018).
Amonov, R., and K. Ulughzoda, eds., *Afsonahoi khalqii tojikī*, Stalinobod: Nashriyoti davlatii Tojikiston, 1957.
Amonov, Raǵab, and Klavdija Ulug-Zade, *Die Sandelholztruhe: Tadshikische Volksmärchen*, Berlin: Kultur und Fortschritt, 1961.
Amores, Montserrat, *Catálogo de cuentos folklóricos reelaboradoros por escritores del siglo XIX*, Madrid: Consejo superior de investigaciones científicas, Departemento de antropología de España y América, 1997.
ʿAnābsa, Ghālib, "Min adab al-nawādir: naẓra fī makhṭūṭāt [Irshād] man naḥā ilā nawādir Juḥā, jamʿ al-faqīr ilā Allāh taʿālā Yūsuf ibn al-Wakīl al-Maylāwī," in ʿAnābsa, *Dirāsāt muḍīʾa fī ṣafaḥāt al-turāth*, Zaḥāliqa: Dār al-Hudā, and Jordan: Dār al-Jarīr, 2013, pp. 174–196 (previously published as "Min nawādir al-makhṭūṭāt: wa-hādhā Kitāb [Irshād] man naḥā ilā nawādir Juḥā," in *In the Oasis of Pens: Studies in Arab Literature and Culture in Honour of Professor Joseph Sadan*, ed. Abdullah Sheikh Musa, Nader Masarwah, and Ghaleb Anabseh, Cologne: al-Jamal, 2011, vol. 1, pp. 183–208).
Andersen, Hans Christian, *Märchen und Geschichten*, ed. Gisela Perlet, 2 vols., Munich: Diederichs, 1996.
Anderson, Walter, "Zwei neuentdeckte Fassungen von 'Kaiser und Abt' (1693)," *Fabula* 4 (1961), pp. 260–263.
Anderson, Walter, *Kaiser und Abt: Die Geschichte eines Schwanks*, Helsinki: Suomalainen Tiedeakatemia, 1923.
Andreassi, Mario, *Le facezie del Philogelos: Barzellette antiche e umorismo moderno*, Rome: pensa multimedia, 2004.
"Anekdoten und Charakterzüge aus dem chinesischen Buche Siao li Siao entlehnt," *Der Sammler: Ein Unterhaltungsblatt* issue 71 (June 12, 1824), p. 283; also in *Der Gesellschafter, oder Blätter für Geist und Herz: ein Volksblatt* 8 (1824), pp. 422–423.
Anetshofer, Helga, *Temporale Satzverbindungen in altosmanischen Prosatexten*, Wiesbaden: Harrassowitz, 2005.
Apu, Sato, "Aarne, Antti," in Duggan, Anne E., and Donald Haase, eds., *Folktales and Fairy Tales*, Santa Barbara, CA: Greenwood, 2016, vol. 1, pp. 1–2.
Apu, Sato, "Historic-Geographic Method," in Duggan, Anne E., and Donald Haase, eds., *Folktales and Fairy Tales*, Santa Barbara, CA: Greenwood, 2016, vol. 2, pp. 453–455.
Arājs, Kārlis, and Alma Medne, *Latviešu pasaku tipu rādītājs*, Riga: Zinātne, 1977.
Aramburu, Julio, *El folklore de los niños*, Buenos Aires: El Ateneo, 1944.
Arberry, Arthur John, *More Tales from the Masnavi*, London: Allen & Unwin, 1963.
Arberry, Arthur John, *Muslim Saints and Mystics: Episodes from the Tadhkirat al-Auliyaʾ (Memorial of the Saints) by Farid al-Din Attar*, London: Routledge & Kegan Paul, 1966.
Arberry, Arthur John, *Tales from the Masnavi*, London: George Allen & Unwin, 1961.
Arberry, Arthur John, *The Koran Interpreted*, London: Allen & Unwin, 1955.
Archive Jurjen van der Kooi, Groningen (index in the archives of the *Enzyklopädie des Märchens*, Göttingen).
Ardalić, Vladimir, "Narodne pripovijetke (Bukovica u Dalmaciji)," *Zbornik za narodni život i običaje Južnih Slavena* 19 (1914), pp. 350–357.

Argenti, Philip P., and Herbert J. Rose, *The Folk-lore of Chios*, 2 vols., Cambridge: Cambridge University Press, 1949.
Ariosto, Ludovico, *Orlando furioso e Cinque canti*, 2 vols., ed. Remo Ceserani and Sergio Zatti, Torino: Utet, 2006.
Arlotto, Piovano, *Motti e facezie del Piovano Arlotto*, ed. Gianfranco Folena, Milano: Riccardo Ricciardi, 1995.
Arlotto see Wesselski, *Die Schwänke und Schnurren*.
Árnason, Jón, *Icelandic Legends*, transl. George E. Powell and Eiríkr Magnússon, vol. 2, London: Longman's, Green, and Co., 1866.
Árnason, Jón, *Íslenzkar þjóðsögur og æfintýri*, vol. 2, Leipzig: J.C. Hinrichs, 1864.
Artese, Charlotte, "'Tell Thou the Tale:' Shakespeare's Taming of Folktales in *The Taming of the Shrew*," *Folklore* 120 (2009), pp. 317–326.
Artese, Charlotte, "'You Shall Not Know:' Portia, Power, and the Folktale Sources of The Merchant of Venice," *Shakespeare* 5.4 (2009), pp. 325–337.
Artese, Charlotte, *Shakespeare's Folktale Sources*, Newark: University of Delaware Press, 2015.
Asad wa-'l-ghawwāṣ, al-, ed. Riḍwān al-Sayyid, Beirut: Dār al-Ṭalīʿa, 1978.
Ashʿab, see Qumayḥa, *Nawādir Ashʿab*.
Ashtiany, Julia, T.M. Johnstone, J.D. Latham, R.B. Serjeant, and G. Rex Smith, eds., *ʿAbbasid Belles-Lettres (The Cambridge History of Arabic Literature)*, Cambridge: Cambridge University Press, 1990.
Ashton, John, *Humour, Wit & Satire of the Seventeenth Century*, London: Chatto and Windus, 1883.
Asiáin Ansorena, Alfredo, "Narraciones folklóricas navarras: recopilación, clasificación y análisis," *Cuadernos de Etnología y Etnografía de Navarra* 38.81 (2006), pp. 4–289.
Asin et Palacios, Michaël, "Logia et agraphia domini Jesu apud moslemicos scriptores," in Graffin, René, and François Nau, eds., *Patrologia orientalis*, vol. 13, Paris: Firmin-Didot et Co., 1919, pp. 331–639.
Askari, Nasrin, "A Mirror for Princesses: *Mūnis-nāma*, A Twelfth-Century Collection of Persian Tales Corresponding to the Ottoman Turkish Tales of the *Faraj baʿd al-shidda*," *Narrative Culture* 5.1 (2018), pp. 121–140.
Asmus, Ferdinand, and Otto Knoop, *Kolberger Volkshumor: neue Sagen, Erzählungen und Märchen, Schwänke, Scherze und Ortsneckereien aus dem Kreise Kolberg-Körlin*, Köslin: Hendeß, 1927.
Atiénzar García, María del Carmen, *Cuentos populares de Chinchilla*, Ph.D. thesis, Universidad Nacional de Educación a Distancia, 2016.
Atlīdī, Muḥammad ibn Diyāb, *Nawādir al-khulafāʾ al-musammā Iʿlām al-nās bi-ma waqāʿa lil-Barāmika maʿa Banī al-ʿAbbās*, ed. Ayman ʿAbd al-Jābir al-Buḥayrī, Cairo: Dār al-Āfāq al-ʿarabiyya, 1418/1998.
ʿAṭṭār, Farid al-Din, *Tadhkirat al-awliyāʾ*, Mirzā Moḥammad-Khān Qazvini, 3rd ed., Tehran: Ketābkhāne-ye markazi, 1336/1957.
ʿAwfi, Moḥammad, *Pānzdah bāb-e Javāmeʿ al-ḥekāyāt*, ed. Moḥammad Ramażāni, Tehran: Kolāle-ye khāvar, 1335/1956.
ʿAwfi, Sadid al-Din Moḥammad, *Gozide-ye Javāmeʿ al-ḥekāyāt*, ed. Jaʿfar Sheʿār, Tehran: Sāzmān-e enteshārāt va āmuzesh-e enqelāb-e eslāmi, 1363/1984.
ʿAwfi, Sadid al-Din Moḥammad al-, *Matn-e enteqādi-ye Javāmeʿ al-ḥekāyāt wa-lavāmeʿ*

al-revāyāt, book 3, part 1–2, ed. Amir Bānu Moṣaffā and Maẓāher Moṣaffā, Tehran: Bonyād-e Farhang-e Irān, 1352–1353/1973–1974.

Ayala, Francisco, "Fuente árabe de un cuento popular en el Lazarillo," *Boletín de la Real Academia Española* 45 (1965), pp. 493–495.

Baasch, Karen, *Die Crescentialegende in der deutschen Literatur des Mittelalters*, Stuttgart: Metzler, 1968.

Bäcker, Jörg, "Schwanjungfrau," in *Enzyklopädie des Märchens*, vol. 12 (2008), cols. 311–318.

Baihaqī, Ibrāhīm ibn Muḥammad al-, *Kitāb al-Maḥāsin val-Masāvī*, ed. Friedrich Schwally, Giessen: J. Ricker'sche Verlagsbuchhandlung, 1902.

Bain, R. Nisbet, *Russian Fairy Tales*, London: Lawrence and Bullen, 1892.

Baker, Colin F., and Meira Polliack, *Arabic and Judaeo-Arabic Manuscripts in the Cambridge Genizah Collections: Arabic Old Series (T-S Ar. 1a–54)*, Cambridge: Cambridge University Press, 2001.

Baker, Ronald L., *Jokelore: Humorous Folktales from Indiana*, Bloomington: Indiana University Press, 1986.

Bakrī, Abū 'Ubayd al-, *Kitāb al-Masālik wa-'l-mamālik*, ed. Adriyān fān Lyūfan (Adrian Van Leeuwen) and Andrī Fīrī, 2 vols., Tunis: al-Dār al-ʿarabiyya lil-kitāb, 1992.

Baldauf, Ingeborg, "Freude nach Bedrängnis? Literarische Geschichten zwischen Osmanisch, Persisch und Tatarisch," in *Armağan: Festschrift für Andreas Tietze*, ed. Ingeborg Baldauf, Suraiya Faroghi, and Rudolf Veselý, Prague: enigma, 1994, pp. 29–46.

Baldwin, Barry, *The Philogelos, or Laughter-Lover*, transl. with an introduction and commentary, Amsterdam: Gieben, 1983.

Banc, C., and Alan Dundes, *You Call This Living? A Collection of East European Political Jokes*, Athens and London: The University of Georgia Press, 1990.

Barag, Lev G., "Dobrovol'skij, Vladimir Nikolaevič," in *Enzyklopädie des Märchens*, vol. 3 (1981), cols. 730–732.

Barag, Lev G., "Heiligkeit geht über Wasser," in *Enzyklopädie des Märchens*, vol. 6 (1990), cols. 694–698.

Barag, Lev G., *Belorussische Volksmärchen*, Berlin: Akademie-Verlag, 1966.

Barag, Lev G., I.P. Berezovskiy, K.P. Kabashnikov, and N.V. Novikov, *Sravnitel'ny ukazatel' syuzhetov vostochnoslavyanska skazka*, Leningrad: Nauka, 1979.

Barbeau, C.-Marius, "Contes populaires canadiens, seconde série," *Journal of American Folklore* 30 (1917), pp. 1–140.

Barbeau, C.-Marius, and Gustav Lanctot, "Contes populaires canadiens," *Journal of American Folklore* 36 (1923), pp. 205–272.

Barchilon, Jacques, "Perceforest," in *Enzyklopädie des Märchens*, vol. 10 (2002), cols. 719–721.

Barker, William Burckhardt, *Reading Book of the Turkish Language, with a Grammar and Vocabulary*, London: James Madden, 1854.

Bar Hebraeus, Mâr Gregory John, *The Laughable Stories*, transl. E.A. Wallis Budge, London: Luzac and Co., 1897.

Bascom, William R., *African Dilemma Tales*, The Hague: Mouton, 1975.

Başgöz, İlhan, and Pertev Boratav, *I, Hoca Nasreddin, Never Shall I Die: A Thematic Analysis of Hoca Stories*, Bloomington: Indiana University Press, 1998.

Basset, René, "Deux manuscrits d'une version arabe inédite du recueil des Sept Vizirs," *Journal asiatique* 2.2 (1903), pp. 43–83.

Basset, René, "Les bossus et l'éléphant," *Bulletin de folklore* 2 (1892), pp. 256–257.
Basset, René, "L'origine orientale de Shylock," *Keleti szemle* 2 (1901), pp. 182–186.
Basset, René, "Une fable de La Fontaine et les contes orientaux," *Mélusine* 2 (1884/85), pp. 508–517.
Basset, René, *Mille et un contes, récits et légends arabes*, ed. Aboubakr Chraïbi, 2 vols. Paris: José Corti, 2005 (previously published in 3 vols., Paris: Maisonneuve, 1924–26).
Battles, Dominique, "Chaucer's *Franklin's Tale* and Boccaccio's *Filocolo* Reconsidered," *The Chaucer Review* 43.1 (1999), pp. 38–59.
Bauden, Frédéric, Aboubakr Chraïbi, and Antonella Ghersetti, eds., *Le Répertoire narratif arabe médiéval: transmission et ouverture, Actes du colloque international, Université de Liège 15–17 septembre 2005*, Geneva: Droz, 2008.
Bauden, Frédéric, and Richard Waller, eds., *Antoine Galland (1646–1715) et son Journal: Actes du colloque international organisé à l'Université de Liège (16–18 janvier 2015) à l'occasion du tricentenaire de sa mort.* Louvain: Peeters, 2019.
Baughman, Ernest W., *Type and Motif-Index of the Folktales of England and North America*, The Hague, Mouton & Co., 1966.
Baum, Paul Franklin, "The Fable of Belling the Cat," *Modern Language Notes* 34 (1919), pp. 462–470; also in Carnes, Pack, ed., *Proverbia in Fabula*, Bern: Lang, 1988, pp. 37–46.
Bausinger, Hermann, "Abderiten," in *Enzyklopädie des Märchens*, vol. 1 (1977), cols. 10–11.
Bebel, Heinrich, *Schwänke*, ed. Albert Wesselski, 2 vols., Munich: Georg Müller, 1907.
Bechstein, Ludwig, *Neues Deutsches Märchenbuch*, ed. Hans-Jörg Uther, Munich: Eugen Diederichs, 1997.
Bédier, Joseph, *Les Fabliaux: Études de littérature populaire et d'histoire littéraire du Moyen Age*, 2nd ed., Paris: Émile Bouillon, 1895.
Behrnauer, Walter Friedrich Adolf, *Die vierzig Veziere oder weisen Meister: ein altmorgenländischer Sittenroman*, Leipzig: Teubner, 1851.
Behrnauer, Walter, "Der junge Perser und die griechische Prinzessin," *Johannes-Album* (Chemnitz 1857), pp. 57–70.
Belcher, Stephen, "Benfey, Theodor," in Duggan, Anne E., and Donald Haase, eds., *Folktales and Fairy Tales*, Santa Barbara, CA: Greenwood, 2016, vol. 1, p. 118.
Belcher, Stephen, "The Diffusion of the Book of Sindbad," *Fabula* 28 (1987), pp. 34–58.
Bell, David C., *The Modern Reader and Speaker: A Selection of Poetry and Prose from the Writings of Eminent Authors, with Copious Extracts for Recitation [. . .]*, Dublin: MacGlashan & Gill, 1850.
Bellino, Francesca. "I sette Viaggi di Sindbād il marinaio: un romanzo arabo nelle Mille e Una Notte," in *Paradossi delle Notti: Dieci Studi su Le Mille e Una Notte*, ed. Leonardo Capezzone and Elisabetta Benigni, Pisa and Rome: Fabricio Serra editore, 2015, pp. 101–129.
Bellino, Francesca, "Another Manuscript of Pétis de la Croix's *Histoire arabe de Sindabad le marin*: A Possible Sub-family in the Fluid Transmission of the Story," *Quaderni di studi arabi* 12 (2017), pp. 102–132.
Ben-Amos, Dan, *Folktales of the Jews*, vol. 1: *Tales from the Sephardic Dispersion*, Philadelphia: The Jewish Publication Society, 2006.
Ben-Amos, Dan, *Folktales of the Jews*, vol. 2: *Tales from Eastern Europe*, Philadelphia: Jewish Publications Society, 2007.

Bendix, Regina, *In Search of Authenticity: The Formation of Folklore Studies*, Madison: University of Wisconsin Press, 1997.

Bendix, Regina F., and Dorothy Noyes, eds., *Terra Ridens – Terra Narrans: Festschrift zum 65. Geburtstag von Ulrich Marzolph*, Dortmund: Verlag für Orientkunde, 2018.

Benfey, Theodor, transl., *Die Reise der drei Söhne des Königs von Serendippo*, ed. Richard Fick and Alfons Hilka, Helsinki: Suomalainen Tiedeakatemia, 1932.

Benfey, Theodor, *Pantschatantra: Fünf Bücher indischer Fabeln, Märchen und Erzählungen, aus dem Sanskrit übersetzt mit Einleitung und Anmerkungen*, 2 vols., (Leipzig 1859) reprint Hildesheim: Georg Olms, 1966.

Bentham, Jeremy, *The Book of Fallacies*, ed. Philip Schofield, Oxford: Clarendon Press, 2015.

Benzel, Ulrich, *Volkserzählungen aus dem nördlichen Böhmerwald*, Marburg: Elwert, 1957.

Benzel, Ulrich, *Volkserzählungen aus dem oberpfälzisch-böhmischen Grenzgebiet*, Münster: Aschendorff, 1965.

Bergin, Osborn Joseph, R.I. Best, Kuno Meyer, and J.G. O'Keefe, eds., *Anecdota from Irish Manuscripts*, 5 vols. Halle (Saale): Max Niemeyer, and Dublin: Hodges, Figgis & Co., 1907–13.

Bérinus, roman en prose du XIVe siècle, ed. Robert Bossuat, 2 vols., Paris: Société des anciens textes français, 1931–1933.

Berlioz, Jacques, "Odo of Cheriton," in *Enzyklopädie des Märchens*, vol. 10 (2002), cols. 219–225.

Bertuch, Friedrich Justin, ed., *Die Blaue Bibliothek aller Nationen*, 12 vols. Weimar: Verlag des Industrie-Comptoirs, 1790–1800.

Berze Nagy, János, *Magyar népmesetípusok*, 2 vols., Pécs: Baranya Megye Tanácsának Kiadása, 1957.

Besthorn, Rudolf, *Ursprung und Eigenart der älteren italienischen Novelle*, Gräfenheinichen: Heine, 1935.

Bies, Werner, "Pandora," in *Enzyklopädie des Märchens*, vol. 10 (2002), cols. 505–510.

Bimmer, Andreas, "Trunkenheit," in *Enzyklopädie des Märchens*, vol. 13 (2010), cols. 971–977.

Binay, Sarah, *Die Figur des Beduinen in der arabischen Literatur: 9 – 12. Jh.*, Wiesbaden: Reichert, 2006.

Bin Gorion, Micha Joseph, *Mimekor Israel: Classical Jewish Folktales, Abridged and Annotated*, ed. Emanuel Bin Gorion, prepared by Dan Ben-Amos, Bloomington: Indiana University Press, 1990.

Bîrlea, Ovidiu, *Antologie de Proză Populară Epică*, 3 vols., Bucharest: Editura Pentru Literatură, 1966.

Birlinger, Anton, "Die drei Alten," *Alemannia* 4 (1877), pp. 265–266.

Birlinger, Anton, and Michael Richard Buck, *Volksthümliches aus Schwaben*, vol. 1: Sagen, *Märchen und Aberglauben*, Freiburg: Herder, 1861.

Bishop, Julia C., "'Dr Carpenter from the Harvard College in America:' An Introduction to James Madison Carpenter and His Collection," *Folk Music Journal* 7.4 (1998), pp. 402–420.

Blackburn, Stuart, "The Brahmin and the Mongoose: The Narrative Context of a Well-Travelled Tale," *Bulletin of the School of Oriental and African Studies* 57 (1996), pp. 494–507.

Bladé, Jean-François, *Contes populaires de Gascogne*, Paris: Maisonneuve, 1886.

Blangez, Gérard, ed., *Ci nous dit: recueil d'exemples moraux*, 2 vols., Paris: Société des anciens textes français, 1979.
Bleeth, Kenneth, *Chaucer's Squire's Tale, Franklin's Tale, and Physician's Tale: An Annotated Bibliography 1900–2005*, Toronto: University of Toronto Press, 2017.
Bloomfield, Maurice, "On False Ascetics and Nuns in Hindu Fiction," *Journal of the American Oriental Society* 44 (1924), pp. 202–242.
Blum, Paul, "Die Geschichte vom träumenden Bauern in der Weltliteratur," *Jahresbericht der K.K. Staats-Oberrealschule in Teschen*, Teschen: Karl Prochaska, 1908, pp. 3–36.
Boberg, Inger M., *Motif-Index of Early Icelandic Literature*, Munskaard: Hafniæ, 1966.
Boccaccio, Giovanni, *The Decameron*, transl. John Payne, New York: Walter J. Black, s.a.
Boden, Doris, "Urform," in *Enzyklopädie des Märchens*, vol. 13 (2011), cols. 1259–1262.
Bodens, Wilhelm, *Vom Rhein zur Maas*, Bonn: Röhrscheid, 1936.
Bødker, Laurits, D'Aronco, Gianfranco, and Christina Hole, *European Folktales*, Copenhagen: Rosenkilde and Bagger, 1963.
Bogdanović, David, *Izabrane narodne pripovijetke hrvatske*, 2nd ed., Zagreb: St. Kugli, 1930.
Boggs, Ralph S., "Let Him Buy You Who Does Not Know You," *Studies in Philology* 32.1 (1935), pp. 22–39.
Boggs, Ralph S., *Index of Spanish Folktales*, Helsinki: Suomalainen Tiedeakatemia, 1930.
Böhm, Max, and Franz Specht, *Lettische Schwänke und verwandte Volksüberlieferungen*, Reval: Kluge, 1911.
Boira, Rafael, *El libro de los cuentos: colección completa de anécdotas, cuentos, gracias, chistes [...]*, 2nd ed., Madrid: D. Miguel Arcas y Sanchez, 1862.
Bolhar, Alojzij, *Slovenske narodne právljice*, 7th ed., Ljubljana: Mladinska knjiga, 1974.
Bolte, Johannes, "Die drei Alten: Nach Reinhold Köhlers Kollektaneen," *Zeitschrift des Vereins für Volkskunde* 7 (1897), pp. 205–207.
Bolte, Johannes, "Neuere Märchenliteratur," *Zeitschrift des Vereins für Volkskunde* 15 (1905), pp. 266–230.
Bolte, Johannes, "Zur Sage vom Traum vom Schatz auf der Brücke," *Zeitschrift des Vereins für Volkskunde* 19 (1909), pp. 189–198.
Bolte, Johannes, and Georg Polívka, *Anmerkungen zu den Kinder- und Hausmärchen der Brüder Grimm*, 2nd ed., 5 vols., Leipzig: Dietrich, 1918 (reprint Hildesheim: Olms, 1963).
Boozari, Ali, "Persian Illustrated Lithographed Books on the *Miʿrāj*: Improving Children's Shiʿī Beliefs in the Qajar Period," in *The Prophet's Ascension: Cross-Cultural Encounters with the Islamic Miʿrāj Tales*, ed. Christiane Gruber and Frederick Colby, Bloomington: Indiana University Press, 2010, pp. 252–268.
Boratav, Pertev Naili, "Gesellen: Die schadhaften G.," in *Enzyklopädie des Märchens*, vol. 5 (1987), cols. 1147–1151.
Boratav, Pertev Naili, "Les trois compagnons infirmes," *Fabula* 2 (1959), pp. 231–253.
Boratav, Pertev Naili, *Le "Tekerleme:" Contribution à l'étude typologique et stylistique du conte populaire turc*, Paris: Société Asiatique, 1963.
Bošković-Stulli, Maja, "Karadžić (Stefanović), Vuk," in *Enzyklopädie des Märchens*, vol. 7 (1993), cols. 948–952.
Bošković-Stulli, Maja, "Narodne pripovijetke i predaje Sinjske Krajine," *Narodna Umjetnost* 5–6 (1967–1968), pp. 303–432.
Bošković-Stulli, Maja, "Usmene propovijetke i predaje s otoko Brača," *Narodna Umjetnost* 11–12 (1975), pp. 5–150.
Bošković-Stulli, Maja, *Kroatische Volksmärchen*, Düsseldorf and Cologne: Diederichs, 1975.

Bošković-Stulli, Maja, *Narodne pripovijetke*, Zagreb: Matica Hrvatska, 1963.
Botero, Giovanni, *Detti memorabili di personaggi illustri*, Brescia: Bartholomeo Fontana, 1610.
Bottigheimer, Ruth B., "East Meets West: Ḥannā Diyāb and The Thousand and One Nights," *Marvels & Tales* 28.2 (2014), pp. 302–324.
Bottigheimer, Ruth B., "Flying Carpets in the Arabian Nights: Disney, Dyab . . . and d'Aulnoy?" *Gramarye* 13 (2018), pp. 19–34.
Bottigheimer, Ruth B., "Ḥannā Diyāb's Tales in Antoine Galland's Mille et une nuit(s): I. New Perspectives on Their Recording; II. New Conclusions about Western Sources within Nights Texts," in Bauden, Frédéric, and Richard Waller, eds., *Antoine Galland (1646–1715) et son Journal*, Louvain: Peeters, 2019, pp. 53–74.
Bottigheimer, Ruth B., "The Case of the Ebony Horse, part 2: Hannā Diyāb's Creation of a Third Tradition," *Gramarye* 6 (2014), pp. 7–16.
Bottigheimer, Ruth B., and Claudia Ott, "The Case of the Ebony Horse, part 1," *Gramarye* 5 (2014), pp. 8–20.
Bowen, Barbara C., *One Hundred Renaissance Jokes*, Birmingham, Alabama: Summ Publications, 1988.
Braga, Teófilo, *Contos tradicionais do povo português*, 3rd ed., 2 vols., Lisbon: Dom Quixote, 1987.
Braga, Theophilo, *Contos tradicionaes do povo portuguez: Historias o Exemplos de thema tradicional e fórma litteraria. Litteratura dos Contos populares em Portugal*, 2nd ed., 2 vols., Lisbon: J.A. Rodrigues & C.ª, 1914–1915.
Bragantini, Renzo, "The Serendipity of the Three Princes of Serendib: Arabic Tales in a Collection of Italian Renaissance Short Stories," in Bauden, Frédéric, Aboubakr Chraïbi, and Antonella Ghersetti, eds., *Le répertoire narratif arabe médiéval: transmission et ouverture*, Geneva: Droz, 2008, pp. 301–308.
Brann, Ross, *Power in the Portrayal: Representations of Jews and Muslims in Eleventh- and Twelfth-century Islamic Spain*, Princeton: Princeton University Press, 2002.
Bratcher, James T., "Birnbaum: Der verzauberte B.," in *Enzyklopädie des Märchens*, vol. 2 (1979), cols. 417–421.
Brechenmacher, Josef Karlmann, "Friedrich der Große und der Müller von Sanssouci," *Zeitschrift für deutschen Unterricht* 21 (1907), pp. 273–287.
Brechenmacher, Josef Karlmann, *Friedrich der Große und der Müller von Sanssouci: Schürfungen auf dem Grenzrain von Geschichte und Sage*, Stuttgart: Verlag des katholischen Schulvereins für die Diözese Rottenburg, 1910.
Brednich, Rolf Wilhelm, "Asinus vulgi," in *Enzyklopädie des Märchens*, vol. 1 (1977), cols. 867–873.
Brednich, Rolf Wilhelm, "Cammann, Alfred," in *Enzyklopädie des Märchens*, vol. 2 (1979), cols. 1160–1162.
Brednich, Rolf Wilhelm, "Ortsneckereien," in *Enzyklopädie des Märchens*, vol. 10 (2002), cols. 376–382.
Brednich, Rolf Wilhelm, "Qualnächte," in *Enzyklopädie des Märchens*, vol. 11 (2004), cols. 100–103.
Brednich, Rolf Wilhelm, "Rothaarig," in *Enzyklopädie des Märchens*, vol. 11 (2005), cols. 850–854, at col. 852.
Brednich, Rolf Wilhelm, "Verjüngung," in *Enzyklopädie des Märchens*, vol. 14 (2014), cols. 42–47.

Brednich, Rolf Wilhelm, *Die Ratte am Strohhalm: Allerneueste sagenhafte Geschichten von heute*, Munich: C.H. Beck, 1996.
Bremond, Claude, "En deçà et au-delà d'un conte: le devenir des thèmes," in Bencheikh, Jamel Eddine, Claude Bremond, and André Miquel, *Mille et un contes de la nuit*, Paris: Gallimard, 1991, pp. 79–258.
Bremond, Claude, "Jacques de Vitry," in *Enzyklopädie des Märchens*, vol. 7 (1993), cols. 387–394.
Bremond, Claude, "L'Ascension du monte inaccessible," *Studia Islamica* 76 (1992), pp. 97–118.
Brendle, Thomas R., and William S. Troxell, *Pennsylvania German Folk Tales, Legends, Once-upon-a-time Stories, Maxims, and Sayings, Spoken in the Dialect Popularly Known as Pennsylvania Dutch*, Norristown, Pa.: Pennsylvania German Society, 1944.
Briesemeister, Dietrich, "Juan Manuel, Infante Don," in *Enzyklopädie des Märchens*, vol. 7 (1993), cols. 668–671.
Briggs, Katherine M., *A Dictionary of British Folk-Tales in the English Language*, 4 vols. London: Routledge & Kegan Paul, 1970–71.
Briggs, Katherine M., and Ruth L. Tongue, *Folktales of England*, 2nd ed., London: Routledge, 1966.
Brockelmann, Carl, "Eine altarabische Version der Geschichte vom Wunderbaum," *Studien zur vergleichenden Literaturgeschichte* 8 (1908), pp. 237–238.
Brockelmann, Carl, "Fabel und Tiermärchen in der älteren arabischen Literatur," *Islamica* 2 (1926), pp. 96–128.
Brockelmann, Carl, *Geschichte der arabischen Litteratur*, 2 vols. and 3 supplement vols., Leiden: Brill, 1937–1949.
Brockett, Eleanor, *Persian Fairy Tales*, (London: Frederick Muller, 1962) reprint Chicago and New York: Follett, 1968.
Bromyard, John, *Summa prædicantivm*, Venice: Dominic Nicolini, 1586.
Brown, W. Norman, "Change of Sex as a Hindu Story Motif," *Journal of the American Oriental Society* 47 (1927), pp. 3–24.
Browne, Edward G., A *Hand-List of the Muḥammadan Manuscripts, Including all Those Written in the Arabic Character Preserved in the Library of the University of Cambridge*, Cambridge: University Press, 1900.
Bruford, Alan, "Some Aspects of the Otherworld," in *Folklore in the Twentieth Century*, ed. Venetia Newall, Woodbridge: Brewer, 1986, pp. 147–151.
Bruford, Alan, and Donald A. MacDonald, *Scottish Traditional Tales*, Edinburgh: Polygon, 1994.
Brunet, Victor, "Facéties normandes (1)," in *Revue des traditions populaires* 2 (1887), pp. 183–184.
Brunold-Bigler, Ursula, "Kalender, Kalendergeschichte," in *Enzyklopädie des Märchens*, vol. 7 (1993), cols. 861–878.
Brunvand, Jan Harold, *The Choking Doberman and Other "New" Urban Legends*, New York: W.W. Norton & Company, 1984.
Brunvand, Jan Harold, *The Vanishing Hitchhiker*, New York: Norton, 1981.
Büchli, Arnold, *Mythologische Landeskunde von Graubünden: Ein Bergvolk erzählt*, vol. 2, 3rd ed., vol. 3, ed. Ursula Brunold-Bigler, Disentis: Desertina, 1989, 1990.
Bukowska-Grosse, Ewa, and Erwin Koschmieder, *Polnische Volksmärchen*, Düsseldorf: Diederichs, 1967.

Bulang, Tobias, "Ringerzählung," in *Enzyklopädie des Märchens*, vol. 11 (2004), cols. 700–702.
Bülow, Eduard von, *Novellenbuch; oder Hundert Novellen, nach alten italienischen, spanischen, französischen, lateinischen, englischen und deutschen bearbeitet*, 4 vols., Leipzig: F.A. Brockhaus, 1834–36.
Bundi, Gian, *Märchen aus dem Bündnerland: Nach dem Rätoromanischen erzählt*, Basel: Helbing & Lichtenhahn, 1935.
Buoni, Tomaso, *Nuovo thesoro de' proverbij italiani*, Venice: Giovanni Battista Ciotti Senese, 1604.
Burkard Waldis, *Esopus: 400 Fabeln und Erzählungen nach der Erstausgabe von 1548*, ed. Ludger Lieb, Jan Mohr, and Herfried Vögel, vol. 1, Berlin: De Gruyter, 2011.
Burrill, Kathleen R.F., "The Nasreddin Hoca Stories, 1: An Early Ottoman Manuscript at the University of Groningen," *Archivum Ottomanicum* 2 (1970), pp. 7–114.
Burrison, John A., *Storytellers: Folktales and Legends from the South*, Athens: University of Georgia Press, 1989.
Burrow, John, "The *Tale of Beryn*: An Appreciation," *The Chauver Review* 49.4 (1015), pp. 499–511.
Burton, Jonathan, "Christopher Sly's Arabian Night: Shakespeare's *The Taming of the Shrew* as World Literature," *Journal for Early Modern Cultural Studies* 14.3 (2014), pp. 3–30.
Burton, Richard F., *Arabian Nights*, 16 vols. (10 vols. and 6 supplement vols.) (Benares 1885) reprint Beirut: Khayat, 1966.
Butler, Noble, *The Common School Speaker*, Louisville, KY: Morton & Griswold, 1856.
Buẕari, ʿAli, *Qażā-ye bi zavāl: negāhi taṭbiqi be taṣāvir-e chāp-e sangi-ye meʿrāj-e payāmbar (ṣ)*, Tehran: Dastān, 1389/2010.
Cadic, François, *Contes de Basse-Bretagne*, Paris: Érasme, 1955.
Calila e Dimna, ed. Juan Manuel Cacho Blecua and María Jesús Lacarra, Madrid: Castalia, 2004.
Camaj, Martin, and Uta Schier-Oberdorffer, *Albanische Märchen*, Düsseldorf: Diederichs, 1974.
Camarena Laucirica, Julio, *Cuentos tradicionales de León*, 2 vols., Madrid: Universidad Complutense, Seminario Menendez Pidal, 1991.
Camarena, Julio, and Maurice Chevalier, *Catálogo tipológico del cuento folklórico español*, vol. 3, Alcalá de Henares: Centro de Estudios Cervantinos, 2003.
Cammann, Alfred, *Deutsche Volksmärchen aus Russland und Rumänien: Bessarabien, Dobrudscha, Siebenbürgen, Ukraine, Krim, Mittelasien*, Göttingen: Schwartz, 1967.
Cammann, Schuyler V.R., "Christopher the Armenian and the Three Princes of Serendip," *Comparative Literature Studies* 4.3 (1967), pp. 229–258.
Campbell, John Francis, *Popular Tales of the West Highlands*, new ed., 4 vols., Edinburgh and London: Edmonston & Douglas, 1890.
Campbell, Marie, "The Three Teachings of the Bird," in *Studies in Biblical and Jewish Folklore*, ed. Raphael Patai, Francis Lee Utley, and Dov Noy, Bloomington: Indiana University Press, 1960, pp. 95–107.
Campion-Vincent, Véronique, and Christine Shojaei Kawan, "Marie-Antoinette and Her Famous Saying: Three Levels of Communication, Three Modes of Accusation and Two Troubled Centuries," *Fabula* 41 (2000), pp. 13–41.
Canard, Marius, "Les Aventures d'un prisonier arabe et d'un patrice byzantin à

l'époque des guerres bulgaro-byzantines," *Dumbarton Oaks Papers* 9–10 (1956), pp. 51–72.

Canby, Henry Seidel, "Some Comments on the Sources of Chaucer's 'Pardoner's Tale'," *Modern Philology* 2 (1904–1905), pp. 477–487.

Capeller, Carl, *Litauische Märchen und Geschichten*, Berlin: De Gruyter, 1924.

Cardigos, Isabel, "Schuh," in *Enzyklopädie des Märchens*, vol. 12 (2007), cols. 212–217, at cols. 214–215.

Cardigos, Isabel, *Catalogue of Portuguese Folktales*, Helsinki: Suomalainen Tiedeakatemia, 2006.

Cardonne, Dénis Dominique, *Mêlanges de littérature orientale, traduits de différens Manuscrits Turcs, Arabes & Persans de la Bibliothèque du Roi*, 2 vols. Paris: Hérissant le Fils, 1770.

Carpenter, James M., "Two Versions of a Hard-luck Story. I: Soft-peddling Sorrowful News," *North Carolina Folklore* 2 (1954), p. 16.

Carrière, Joseph Médard, *Tales from the French Folk-Lore of Missouri*, Evanston, IL: Northwestern University, 1937.

Casanova, Paul, *Ḳaraḳoûch*, *Mémoires publiés par les members de la Mission Archéologique Français du Caire* 6 (1897), pp. 447–491.

Cascudo, Luis da Câmara, *Contos tradicionais do Brasil: confrontos e notas*, 2nd ed., Bahia: Progresso, 1955.

Cascudo, Luís da Câmara, *Trinta "estorias" brasileiras*, Lisbon: Fortucalense, 1955.

Cassar Pullicino, Ġuże, *Stejjer ta' niesna*, Malta: id-Dipartiment ta' l-informazzjoni, 1967.

Castiglione, Baldesar, *Der Hofmann*, transl. Albert Wesselski, 2 vols., Munich: Georg Müller, 1907.

Catalog of the Schmulowitz Collection of Wit and Humor (SCOWAH), San Francisco: San Francisco Public Library, 1962.

Cazden, Norman, Herbert Haufrecht, and Norman Studer, eds., *Folk Songs of the Catskills*, Albany: State University of New York Press, 1982.

Cejpek, Jiří, "Iranian Folk-Literature," in Rypka, Jan, ed., *History of Iranian Literature*, ed. Karl Jahn, Dordrecht: D. Reidel, 1968, pp. 607–709.

Cento novelle antiche see Jakob, *Die hundert alten Erzählungen*; Conte, *Il Novellino*

Cepenkov, Marko K., *Makedonski narodni prikazni*, 5 vols., ed. Kiril Penušliski, Skopje: MK, 1989.

Certeux, Alphonse, and Emile Henri Carnoy, *L'Algérie traditionelle*, Paris: Maisonneuve & Leclerc, 1884.

Chaikanovich, Veselin, *Srpske narodne pripovetke*, Belgrade: Izdaniye knizharnitse Raikovicha i Vukovicha, 1929.

Chaikanovich, Veselin, *Srpske narodne pripovetke*, vol. 1, Belgrade: Izdaniye knizharnitse Raikovicha i Vukovicha, 1927.

Charles, Robert Henry, *The Apocrypha and Pseudepigraphia of the Old Testament*, Oxford: Clarendon Press, 1913.

Chaucer, Geoffrey, *The Complete Poetry and Prose*, ed. John H. Fischer, New York: Holt, Reinhart & Winston, 1977.

Chauvin, Victor, "Le Reve du trésor sur le pont," *Revue des Traditions Populaires* 13 (1898), pp. 193–196.

Chauvin, Victor, "Note sur le Conte de Salomon et le griffon," *Le Muséon* 24 (1905), pp. 85–90.

Chauvin, Victor, "Pacolet et les mille et une nuits," *Wallonia* 6 (1898), pp. 5–19.

Chauvin, Victor, *Bibliographie des ouvrages arabes ou relatifs aux arabes [...]*, 12 vols., Liège: H. Vaillant-Carmanne, and Leipzig: O. Harrassowitz, 1892–1922.

Chavannes, Édouard, *Cinq cents contes et apologues extraits du Tripitaka chinois*, 4 vols., Paris: Ernest Leroux, 1910–1935 (reprint Paris: Maisonneuve, 1962).

Cheikho, Louis, *La version arabe de Kalîlah et Dimnah ou Les fables de Bipai*, (Beirut 1905) reprint Amsterdam: Philo Press, 1981.

Chendeĭ, Ivan, *Skazki Verkhoviny: zakarpatskie ukrainskie narodnye skazki*, Uzhgorod: Zakarpatskoe oblastnoe izdatelstvo, 1959.

Chertudi, Susanna, *Cuentos folklóricos de la Argentina*, 2 vols., Buenos Aires: Ed. Univ., 1960–64.

Chesnutt, Michael, "Wünsche: Die drei W.," in *Enzyklopädie des Märchens*, vol. 14 (2014), cols. 1076–1083.

Chevalier, Maxime, "Cuentecillos chistosos en la Sevilla de principios del siglo XVII," *Cuento tradicional, cultura, litteratura (siglos XVI–XIX)*, Salamanca: Universidad de Salamanca, 1999, pp. 55–65.

Chevalier, Maxime, *Cuentecillos tradicionales en la España del Siglo de Oro*, Madrid: Gredos, 1975.

Chevalier, Maxime, *Cuentos folklóricos en la España del Siglo de Oro*, Barcelona: Crítica, 1983.

Childers, J. Wesley, *Motif-Index of the Cuentos of Juan Timoneda*, Bloomington: Indiana University, 1948.

Childers, J. Wesley, *Tales from the Spanish Picaresque Novels: A Motif Index*, Albany: State University of New York Press, 1977.

Chiţimia, Ion Constantin, "Un basm necunoscut înregistrat în secolul al XVIII-lea," *Revista de istorie şi teorie literară* 17 (1968), pp. 109–118.

Chraïbi, Aboubakr, "Galland's 'Ali Baba' and Other Arabic Versions," in Marzolph, Ulrich, ed., *The Arabian Nights in Transnational Perspective*, Detroit: Wayne State University Press, 2007, pp. 3–15.

Chraïbi, Aboubakr, "Processus d'individuation dans trois récits de l'islam médiéval," in *Drôles d'individus: De la singularité individuelle dans le Reste-du-monde*, ed. Emmanuel Lozerand, Paris: Klincksieck, 2014, pp. 417–431.

Chraïbi, Aboubakr, "Situation, Motivation, and Action in the *Arabian Nights*," in Marzolph, Ulrich, and Richard Van Leeuwen, *The Arabian Nights Encyclopedia*, Santa Barbara, CA: ABC-Clio, 2004, vol. 1, pp. 5–9.

Chraïbi, Aboubakr, *Les Mille et une nuits: Histoire du texte et Classification des contes*, Paris: L'Harmattan, 2008.

Chraïbi, Aboubakr, ed., *Arabic Manuscripts of the* Thousand and One Nights, Paris: espaces & signes, 2016.

Christensen, Arthur, "Júhí in the Persian Literature," in *'Ajab-nāma: A Volume of Oriental Studies Dedicated to Edward G. Browne*, ed. Thomas W. Arnold and Reynold A. Nicholson, Cambridge: Cambridge University Press, 1922, pp. 129–136.

Christensen, Arthur, "Les sots dans la tradition populaire des Persans," *Acta orientalia* 1 (1922), pp. 43–75.

Christensen, Arthur, "Remarques sur les facéties de 'Ubaïd-i-Zākāni, avec des extraits de la Risālä-i-dilgušā," *Acta Orientalia* 3 (1924), pp. 1–37.

Christensen, Arthur, *Contes persans en langue populaire*, Copenhagen: Det Kgl. Danske Videnskabernes Selskab, 1918.

Christensen, Arthur, *L'Iran sous les Sassanides*, 2nd ed., Copenhagen: Ejnar Munksgaard, 1944.
Christensen, Arthur, *Molboernes vise gerninger*, Copenhagen: Schønberg, 1939.
Christiansen, Reidar Thoralf, *Folktales of Norway*, London: Routledge & Kegan Paul, 1964.
Christmann, Hans Helmut, ed., *Zwei altfranzösische Fablels (Auberee, Du Vilain mire)*, Tübingen: Max Niemeyer, 1968.
Christoforo Armeno, *Die Reise der Söhne Giaffers*, transl. Johann Wetzel, ed. Hermann Fischer and Johannes Bolte, Tübingen: Litterarischer Verein in Stuttgart, 1895.
Clouston, William Alexander, "Additional Analogues of 'The Wright's Chaste Wife,'" in Adam of Cobsam, *The Wright's Chaste Wife [...]: A Merry Tale, by Adam of Cobsam*, ed. Frederick J. Furnivall, London: Kegan Paul etc., 1865, pp. 25–39.
Clouston, William Alexander, "The Damsel's Rash Promise: Indian Original and Asiatic and European Version of the *Franklin's Tale*," in *Originals and Analogues of Some of Chaucer's Canterbury Tales*, ed. F.J. Furnivall, Edmund Brock, and William Alexander Clouston, part 4, London: N. Trübner & Co., 1886, pp. 289–340.
Clouston, William Alexander, "The Enchanted Tree: Asiatic Versions and Analogues of Chaucer's *Merchant's Tale*," in *Originals and Analogues of Some of Chaucer's Canterbury Tales*, ed. F.J. Furnivall, Edmund Brock, and William Alexander Clouston, part 4, London: N. Trübner & Co., 1886, pp. 341–364.
Clouston, William Alexander, "On the Magical Elements in Chaucer's Squire's Tale, with Analogues," in Furnivall, Frederick J., *John Lane's Continuation of Chaucer's 'Squire's Tale'*, London: Kegan Paul, Trench, Trübner & Co., 1888, 1890, pp. 263–476.
Clouston, William Alexander, "Variants and Analogues of Some of the Tales in the Supplemental Nights, 1–2: The Sleeper and the Waker," in Burton, Richard F., *Arabian Nights*, reprint Beirut: Khayat, 1966, vol. 12, pp. 291–295.
Clouston, William Alexander, "Variants and Analogues of Some of the Tales in the Supplemental Nights, 3," in Burton, Richard F., *Arabian Nights*, reprint Beirut: Khayat, 1966, vol. 13, pp. 551–652.
Clouston, William Alexander, *A Group of Eastern Romances and Stories from the Persian, Tamil, and Urdu*, Glasgow: privately printed, 1889.
Clouston, William Alexander, *Flowers from a Persian Garden and Other Papers*, London: David Nutt, 1890.
Clouston, William Alexander, *Popular Tales and Fictions: Their Migrations and Transformations*, ed. Christine Goldberg, Santa Barbara, CA: ABC-Clio, 2002.
Clouston, William Alexander, *The Book of Noodles: Stories of Simpletons; or, Fools and Their Follies*, London: Elliot Stock, 1903.
Clouston, William Alexander, *The Book of Sindibād; or The Story of the King, His Son, His Damsel, and the Seven Vazīrs: From the Persian and Arabic*, Glasgow: privately printed, 1884.
Cock, Alfons de, "De vogelaar en de nachtigaal," [1904], in *Studien en essays over oude volksvertelsels*, Antwerp: De Sickel, 1919, pp. 51–75.
Coetzee, Abel, Hattingh, S.C., Loots, W.J.G., and P.D. Swart, "Tiperegister van die Afrikaanse Volksverhaal," *Tydskrif vir Volkskunde en Volkstaal* 23 (1967), pp. 1–90.
Coleman, Moore Marion, *A World Remembered: Tales and Lore of the Polish Land*, Cheshire: Cherry Hill Books, 1965.

Constantin, Gh. I., "18 kirgisische Anekdoten über Nasr Ed-Din Khodja," *Fabula* 14 (1973), pp. 44–70.
Constantin, Gh. I., "Démètre Cantemir et Nasr ed-Din Khodja," *Türk Kültürü Araştırmaları* 15.1–2 (1976), pp. 289–310.
Conte, Alberto, ed., *Il Novellino*, Rome: Salerno, 2001.
Cooper, Lisa H., *Artisans and Narrative Craft in Late Medieval England*, Cambridge: Cambridge University Press, 2011.
Cooperson, Michael, "The Monstrous Births of 'Aladdin'," *Harvard Middle Eastern and Islamic Review* 1 (1994), pp. 67–86.
Copley, Anthony, *Wits, Fits, and Fancies: Or, A Generall and Serious Collection, of the Sententious Speeches, Answers, Jests, and Behauiours, of All Sortes of Estates, From the Throane to the Cottage*, 2nd ed., London: Edw. Allde, 1614.
Copley, Anthony, *Wits, Fittes and Fancies, Fronted and Entermedled with Presidentes of Honour and Wisdome*, London: Richard Johnes, 1595.
Cosquin, Emmanuel, "Le Conte du Chat et de la Chandelle dans l'Europe du Moyen Age et en Orient," *Romania* 40 (1911), pp. 371–430, 481–531.
Cosquin, Emmanuel, *Études folkloriques: Recherches sur les migrations des contes folkloriques et leur point de départ*, Paris: Édouard Champion, 1922.
Costo, Tomaso, *Il Fuggilozio, diviso in otto giornate*, Venice: Mattia Colosini and Barezzo Barezzi, 1601.
Costo, Tomaso, *Il Fuggilozio*, ed. Corrado Calenda, Rome: Salerno, 1989.
Coulomb, Nicole, and Claudette Castell, *La barque qui allait sur l'eau et sur la terre: Marcel Volpilière, conteur do Mont Lozère*, Carcassonne: Garae/Hesiod, 1986.
Courant, Maurice, *Catalogue des livres chinois, coréens, japonais, . . .* vol. 1, Paris: Leroux, 1902.
Cox, Heinrich L., "'L'Histoire du cheval enchante' aus 1001 Nacht in der mündlichen Überlieferung Französisch-Flanderns," in *Volkskultur – Geschichte – Region: Festschrift für Wolfgang Brückner*, ed. Dieter Harmening and Erich Wimmer, Würzburg: Königshausen & Neumann, 1990, pp. 581–596.
Cox-Leick, A.M.A., and Heinrich Leonhard Cox, *Märchen der Niederlande*, Düsseldorf: Diederichs, 1977.
Crane, Thomas Frederick, *Italian Popular Tales*, Boston: Houghton, 1885.
Crane, Thomas Frederick, *The Exempla or Illustrative Stories from the Sermones Vulgares of Jacques de Vitry*, London: Nutt, 1890 (reprint Nendeln: Kraus, 1967).
Crews, Cynthia Mary, *Contes judéo-espagnols des Balkans*, ed. A. Angelopoulos, Paris: Corti, 2009.
Crowley, Daniel J., "'The Greatest Thing in the World:' Type 653A in Trinidad," in Dégh, Linda, Henry Glassie, and Felix J. Oinas, eds., *Folklore Today: A Festschrift for Richard M. Dorson*, Bloomington: Indiana University, 1976, pp. 93–100.
Cristoforo Armeno, *Peregrinaggio di tre giovani figliuoli del re di Serendippo*, ed. Renzo Bragantini, Rome: Salerno, 2000.
Cristoforo Armeno, *Peregrinaggio* see Benfey, *Die Reise der drei Söhne des Königs von Serendippo*; see also Christoforo Armeno.
Crouch, Humfrey, *England's Jests Refin'd and Improv'd*, 3rd ed., London: Harris, 1693.
Cunningham, Alexander, *The Stūpa of Bharhut: A Buddhist Monument Ornamented with Numerous Sculptures Illustrative of Buddhist Legend and History in the Third Century B.C.*, London: W.H. Allen & Co, 1879.

Dahestāni, Ḥoseyn ibn Asʿad, *Faraj baʿd al-shidde*, ed. Esmāʿil Ḥākemi, 3 vols., Tehran: Eṭṭelāʿāt, 1364–1364/1985–1986.
Dähnhardt, Oskar, *Natursagen: Eine Sammlung naturdeutender Sagen, Märchen, Fabeln und Legenden*, 4 vols., Leipzig: Teubner, 1907–1912 (reprint Hildesheim: Georg Olms, 1983).
Dames, Mansel Longworth, *Popular Poetry of the Baloches*, 2 vols., London: Nutt, 1907.
Damīrī, Kamāl al-Dīn al-, *Ḥayāt al-ḥayawān al-kubrā*, 2 vols., s.l.: al-Maktaba al-islāmiyya, s.a.
Al-Damīrī's Ḥayāt al-Ḥayawān (A Zoological Lexicon), transl. A.S.G. Jayakar, 2 vols., London: Luzac, 1906–08.
Dance, Deryl Cumber, *Shuckin' and Jivin': Folklore from Contemporary Black Americans*, Bloomington: Indiana University Press, 1978.
Dankoff, Robert, and Semih Tezcan, "Seyahet-name'den Bir Atasözü," *Türk Dili Araştırmaları* 8 (1998), pp. 15–28.
Dannemann, Manuel, "Kößler-Ilg, Bertha," in *Enzyklopädie des Märchens*, vol. 8 (1996), cols. 313–314.
Danner, Edmund, *Die Tanne und ihre Kinder: Märchen aus Litauen*, 2nd ed. Berlin: Groszer, 1961.
Darke, Hubert, transl., *The Book of Government or Rules for Kings: The Siyāsat-nāma or Siyar al-Mulūk of Nizām Al-Mulk*, London: Routledge & Kegan Paul, 1960.
Das Sonntagsblatt: Erzähler zum Fürther Tagblatt 4.39 (1845).
Daskalova, Liana, Doroteja Dobreva, Jordanka Koceva, and Evgenija Miceva, *Narodna proza ot Blagoevgradski okrăg*, Sofia: Bălgarska Akademiya na Naukite, 1985.
Daskalova Perkowski, Liliana, Doroteja Dobreva, Jordanka Koceva, and Evgenija Miceva, *Typenverzeichnis der bulgarischen Volksmärchen*, ed. Klaus Roth, Helsinki: Suomalainen Tiedeakatemia, 1995.
Datcu, Iordan, ed., *Sabina Cornelia Stroescu*, Bucarest: Grai şi suflet, 2011.
Dawkins, Richard M., *Forty-five Stories from the Dodekanese*, Cambridge: Cambridge University Press, 1950.
Dawkins, Richard M., *Modern Greek Folktales*, Oxford: Clarendon, 1953.
Daxelmüller, Christoph, "Furz," in *Enzyklopädie des Märchens*, vol. 5 (1987), cols. 593–600.
De Blois, François, *Burzōy's Voyage to Indian and the Origin of the Book of Kalīlah wa Dimna*, London: Royal Asiatic Society, 1990.
De Haan, Fonger, *An Outline of the History of the Novela Picaresca in Spain*, The Hague: Nijhoff, 1903.
Dégh, Linda, "Erzählen, Erzähler," *Enzyklopädie des Märchens*, vol. 4 (1984), cols. 315–342.
Dégh, Linda, *Folktales and Society: Story-telling in a Hungarian Peasant Community*, Bloomington: Indiana University Press, 1989.
De Mélo, Verissimo, "Cascudo, Luís da Câmara," in *Enzyklopädie des Märchens*, vol. 2 (1979), col. 1177.
De Meyer, Maurits, *Le conte populaire flamand*, Helsinki: Suomalainen Tiedeakatemia, 1968.
De Meyere, Victor, *De Vlaamsche vertelselschat*, 4 vols., Antwerp: De Sikkel, 1925–1933.
De Mont, Pol, and Alfons De Cock, *Zo vertellen de Vlamingen*, Gand, 1903.
De Simone, Roberto, and Ugo Vuoso, *Fiabe campane*, Torino: Einaudi, 1994.
Debus, Oswald, *Till Eulenspiegel in der deutschen Volksüberlieferung*, (unpublished) Ph.D. dissertation Marburg 1951.

Decourdemanche, Jean-Adolphe, "Le marchand de Venise dans les contes orientaux," *Revue des traditions populaires* 19.11 (1904), pp. 449–460.
Decourdemanche, Jean-Adolphe, *Les Ruses des femmes (Mikri-zenan) et extraits du Plaisir après la peine (Feredj bad chiddeh)*, Paris: E. Leroux, 1896.
Decourdemanche, Jean Adolphe, *Sottisier de Nasr-Eddin-Hodja, bouffon de Tamerlan*, Bruxelles: Gay and Doucé, 1878.
Decourdemanche, Jean-Adolphe, *The Wiles of Women*, transl. J. and S.F. Mills Whitham, London: G. Routledge, 1928.
Dégh, Linda, "Akkulturation," in *Enzyklopädie des Märchens*, vol. 1 (1977), cols. 234–239.
Dégh, Linda, *Folktales and Society: Story-telling in a Hungarian Peasant Community*, Bloomington: Indiana University Press, 1989.
Dégh, Linda, *Folktales of Hungary*, Chicago: The University of Chicago Press, 1965.
Dégh, Linda, *Kakasdi népmesék*, 2 vols., Budapest: Akademiai Kiadó, 1960.
Dégh, Linda, *Märchen, Erzähler und Erzählgemeinschaft: Dargestellt an der ungarischen Volks*überlieferung, Berlin: Akademie-Verlag, 1962.
Dehkhodā, ʿAli-Akbar, *Loghat-nāme*, 30 vols., Tehran: Sāzmān-e Loghat-nāme, 1337–1352/1958–1973.
Dekhoti, A., *Tadzhikski narodni yumor*, Stalingrad, 1958.
Delarue, Paul, and Marie-Louise Tenèze, *Le conte populaire français*, 4 vols., Paris: Maisonneuve et Larose, 1957–2000.
Delarue, Paul, *The Borzoi Book of French Folk Tales*, New York: Knopf, 1956.
Democritus: or, The Laughing Philosopher, London [1771].
DeSimone, Roberto, *Fiabe campane*, 2 vols., Torino: Einaudi, 1994.
Deutsche Chroniken und andere Geschichtsbücher des Mittelalters, vol. 1: *Kaiserchronik eines deutschen Geistlichen*, ed. Edward Schröder, Hannover: Hahnsche Buchhandlung, 1895.
Dhahabī, Shams al-Dīn Muḥammad ibn Aḥmad al-, *Kitāb al-Kabāʾir*, Cairo: al-Maktaba al-tijāriyya al-kubrā, 1385/1965.
D'Herbelot, Barthélemy, *Bibliothèque orientale*, Maestricht: J.E. Dufour & Ph. Roux, 1776.
Dias-Ferreira, Julia, "Another Portuguese Analogue of Chaucer's 'Pardoner's Tale'," *The Chaucer Review* 11 (1977), pp. 258–260.
Dicke, Gerd, and Klaus Grubmüller, *Die Fabeln des Mittelalters und der frühen Neuzeit: Ein Katalog der deutschen Versionen und ihrer lateinischen Entsprechungen*, Munich: Fink, 1987.
Dietz, Josef, *Aus der Sagenwelt des Bonner Landes*, Bonn: Röhrscheid, 1965.
Dietz, Josef, *Lachende Heimat: Schwänke und Schnurren aus dem Bonner Land*, Bonn: Trapp, 1951.
Digby, Kenelm, *Two Treatises: In the One of Which the Nature of Bodies; In the Other, the Nature of Man's Soule, Is Looked Into: In Way of Discovery of the Immortality of Reasonable Soules*, London: Iohn Williams, 1645.
Digby, Kenelm, *Two Treatises: Of Bodies and of Man's Soul*, ed. Paul S. MacDonald, s.l.: The Gresham Press, 2013.
Diller-Sellschopp, Inez, *Zypriotische Märchen*, Athens: Akadēmia Athēnōn, 1982.
DiMarco, Vincent, "The Squire's Tale," in Correale, Robert M., and Mary Hamel, eds., *Sources and Analogues of the Canterbury Tales*, vol. 1, Cambridge: D.S. Brewer, 2002.
Dittmaier, Heinrich, *Sagen, Märchen und Schwänke von der unteren Sieg*, Bonn: Röhrscheid, 1950.Dirr, Adolf, *Kaukasische Märchen*, Jena: Diedrichs, 1920.
Djordjević, Dragutin M., *Srpske narodne pripovetke i predanja iz leskovačke oblasti*, ed. Nada Milošević-Djordjevič, Belgrade: Srpska Akademija Nauka i Umetnosti, 1988.

Domenichi, Lodovico, *Detti et fatti de diversi signori et persone private, i quali communemente si chiamano Facetie, Motti, & Burle*, Florence: Lorenzo Torrentino, 1562.

Domenichi, Lodovico, *Detti et fatti*, Venice: Francesco Lorenzini, 1562.

Dömötör, Ákos, "Doktor Allwissend," in *Enzyklopädie des Märchens*, vol. 3 (1981), cols. 734–742.

Don Juan Manuel, *Libro del Conde Lucanor*, ed. Reinaldo Ayerbe-Chaux, Madrid: Alhambra, 1983.

Dorson, Richard M., *American Folklore*, Chicago: The University of Chicago Press, 1959.

Dorson, Richard M., *American Negro Folktales*, Greenwich, Conn.: Fawcett, 1967.

Dorson, Richard M., *Bloodstoppers and Bearwalkers: Folk Traditions of the Upper Peninsula*, Cambridge, MA: Harvard University Press, 1952.

Dorson, Richard M., *Buying the Wind: Regional Folklore in the United States*, Chicago: The University of Chicago Press, 1964.

Dorson, Richard M., *Jonathan Draws the Long Bough*, Cambridge, MA: Harvard University Press, 1946.

Dorson, Richard M., *Negro Folktales in Michigan*, Cambridge: Harvard University Press, 1956.

Dorson, Richard M., *Negro Tales from Pine Bluff*, Bloomington: Indiana University Press, 1958.

Dorson, Richard M., *The British Folklorists: A History*, London 1968.

Douglas, Sheila, "Willie MacPhee," in Fischer, Frances S., and Sigrid Rieuwerts, eds., *Emily Lyle: The Persistent Scholar*, Trier: Wissenschaftlicher Verlag Trier, 2007, pp. 67–73.

Douglas, Sheila, *The King o the Black Art and Other Folk Tales*, Aberdeen: Aberdeen University Press, 1987.

D'Ouville, Antoine Le Métel, *L'Élite des contes*, ed. G. Brunet, Paris: Librarie des bibliophiles, 1873.

D'Ovville, Sievr, *Les contes avx hevres perdves, ou le recviel de tovs les bons mots, reparties, eqvivoques [...] & avtres contes facécieux, non encores imprimez*, Paris: Toussaingt Qvinet, 1643.

Dow, James R., *The Nazification of an Academic Discipline: Folklore in the Third Reich*, Bloomington: Indiana University Press, 1994.

Dowojna-Sylwestrowicz, Mieczysław, *Podania żmujdzkie*, 2 vols., Warsaw: Arct, 1894.

Drake, Samuel Adams, *A Book of New England Legends and Folk Lore in Prose and Poetry*, Boston: Little, Brown, and Company, 1901.

Drory, Rina, "Three Attempts to Legitimize Fiction in Classical Arabic Literature," *Jerusalem Studies in Arabic and Islam* 18 (1994), pp. 146–164.

Duggan, Anne E., "Oriental Tales," in Duggan, Anne E., and Donald Haase, eds., *Folktales and Fairy Tales*, Santa Barbara, CA: Greenwood, 2016, vol. 2, pp. 747–751.

Duggan, Anne E., and Donald Haase, eds., *Folktales and Fairy Tales: Traditions and Texts from around the World*, 4 vols., Santa Barbara, CA: Greenwood, 2016.

Duman, Mustafa, *Nasreddin Hoca ve 1555 fıkrası*, Istanbul: heyamola, 2008 (second enl. ed. *Nasreddin Hoca ve 1616 fıkrası*, Istanbul: Everest, 2018).

Dundes, Alan, "Six Inches from the Presidency: The Gary Hart Jokes as Public Opinion," *Western Folklore* 48.1 (1989), pp. 43–51.

Dunn, Thomas Franklin, *The Facetiae of the Mensa Philosophica*, St. Louis: Washington University, 1934.

Dyab, Hanna, *D'Alep à Paris: Les pérégrinations d'un chrétien de Syrie au temps de Louis XIV*, transl. Paule Fahmé-Thiéry, Bernard Heyberger, and Jérôme Lentin, Paris: Sindbad, 2015.

Ebeling, Christoph Daniel, *Vermischte Aufsätze in englischer Prose, hauptsächlich zum Besten derer welche diese Sprache in Rücksicht auf bürgerliche Geschäfte lernen wollen*, 4th ed., Hamburg: C. Herolds Wittwe, 1784.

Eberhard, Wolfram, and Pertev Naili Boratav, *Typen türkischer Volksmärchen*, Wiesbaden: Steiner, 1953.

Edwards, Robert, "The Franklin's Tale," in Correale, Robert M., and Mary Hamel, eds., *Sources and Analogues of the Canterbury Tales*, vol. 1, Cambridge: D.S. Brewer, 2002, pp. 211–264.

Edwards, Robert, *Chaucer and Boccaccio: Antiquity and Modernity*, Houndmills: Palgrave, 2002.

Ehrentreich, Alfred, *Englische Volksmärchen*, Jena: Diederichs, 1938.

Eine Dose voll attisches Salz, um sich nach dem Essen den Schlaf zu vertreiben, 2nd ed., Vienna: Joseph Gerold, 1781.

Eiximenis, Francesc, *Aquest es lo Dotzen libre de regiment dels princeps e de comunitats appellat Crestia*, [València:] Lambert Palmart, 1484.

Eiximenis, Francesc, *Contes i faules*, ed. Marçal Olivar, Barcelona: Barcino, 1925.

Elbogen, Paul, *Humor seit Homer: Die ältesten Witze der Welt*, Reinbek: Rowohlt, 1980 (1964).

Elçin, Şükrü, "Nasreddin Hoca'nın Lâtifeleri: Letayif-e Hace Nasreddin Aleyhirrahme," *Türk Dili* 533 (1996), pp. 1233–1239.

El-Shamy, Hasan, *A Motif-Index of "The Thousand and One Nights,"* Bloomington: Indiana University Press, 2006.

El-Shamy, Hasan M., *Folk Traditions of the Arab World: A Guide to Motif Classification*, 2 vols., Bloomington: Indiana University Press, 1995.

El-Shamy, Hasan M., *Folktales of Egypt*, Chicago: The University of Chicago Press, 1980.

El-Shamy, Hasan, *Motific Constituents of Arabic-Islamic Folk Tradition: A Cognitive Systemic Approach*, 2 vols., IUScholarWorks;https://scholarworks.iu.edu/dspace/handle/2022/20938; (accessed July 23, 2018).

El-Shamy, Hasan M., *Religion among the Folk in Egypt*, Westport, Connecticut: Praeger, 2009.

El-Shamy, Hasan M., *Types of the Folktales in the Arab World: A Demographically Oriented Tale-Type Index*, Bloomington: Indiana University Press, 2004.

Elstein, Yoav, Avidov Lipsker, and Rella Kushelevsky, *Encyclopedia of the Jewish Story*, vol. 2, Ramat-Gan: Bar-Ilan University Press, 2009.

Elzer, Herbert, *Die deutsche Wiedervereinigung an der Saar: Das Bundesministerium für gesamtdeutsche Fragen und das Netzwerk der prodeutschen Opposition 1949–1955*, St. Ingbert: Röhrig, 2007.

ʿEmād ibn Moḥammad [al-S̱aghari], *Ṭuṭi-nāme: Javāher al-asmār*, ed. Shams al-Din Āl-e Aḥmad, Tehran: Bonyād-e farhang-e Irān, 1352/1973.

Emerson, Peter Henry, *Welsh Fairy-Tales and Other Stories*, London: D. Nutt, 1894.

Enjavi Shirāzi, Abol-Qāsem, *Gol be-Ṣenoubar che kard: qeṣṣehā-ye irāni*, vol. 1, 2 parts, 2nd ed., Tehran: Amir Kabir, 2537/1978.

Enjavi Shirāzi, Abol-Qāsem, *Tams̱il va mas̱al*, ed. Aḥmad Vakiliyān, Tehran: Amir Kabir, 1393/2014.

Enjavi Shirāzi, Abol-Qāsem, *Tams̱il va mas̱al*, 2nd ed., Tehran: Amir Kabir, 2537/1978.

Entner, Heinz, "Noch eine Variante von 'Kaiser und Abt' (1492)," *Fabula* 8 (1966), pp. 237–240.
Enzyklopädie des Märchens, vols. 1–15. Berlin: Walter de Gruyter, 1977–2015.
Erb, Rainer, "Jude, Judenlegenden," in *Enzyklopädie des Märchens*, vol. 7 (1993), cols. 676–686.
Erickson, Jon, "Chaucer's *Pardoner's Tale* as Anti-Märchen," *Folklore* 94.2 (1983), pp. 235–239.
Ernst, Paul, *Erzählungen aus Tausendundein Tag, vermehrt um andere morgenländische Geschichten*, 2 vols., Frankfurt am Main: Insel, 1963.
Esar, Evan, *The Humor of Humor: The Art and Techniques of Popular Comedy*, London: Phoenix, 1954.
Eschker, Wolfgang, *Der Zigeuner im Paradies: Balkanslawische Schwänke und lustige Streiche*, Kassel: Erich Röth, 1986.
Eschker, Wolfgang, *Mazedonische Volksmärchen*, Düsseldorf: Diederichs, 1972.
Eschker, Wolfgang, *Serbische Märchen*, Munich: Diederichs, 1992.
Espinosa, Aurelio Macedonio, *Cuentos populares españoles recogidos de la tradición oral de España*, 3 vols., Madrid: Consejo Superior de Investigaciones Científicas, 1946.
Espinosa, Aurelio Macedonio, Jr., *Cuentos populares de Castilla y Leon*, 2 vols., Madrid: Consejo Superior de Investigaciones Científicas, 1987–1988.
Espinosa, José Manuel, *Spanish Folk-Tales from New Mexico*, New York: American Folk-Lore Society, 1937.
Ethé, Hermann, "Neupersische Literatur," in Geiger, Wilhelm, and Ernst Kuhn, *Grundriss der iranischen Philologie*, vol. 2, Strasburg: Karl J. Trüber, 1896–1914, pp. 212–368.
Étienne de Bourbon, *Anecdotes historiques, légendes et apologues tirés du recueil inédit d'Étienne de Bourbon*, ed. A. Lecoy de la Marche, Paris: Renouard, 1877.
Ey, August, *Harzmärchenbuch, oder Sagen und Märchen aus dem Oberharze*, Stade: Fr. Steudel, 1862.
Fabre, Daniel, and Jacques Lacroix, *Histoires et légendes du Languedoc*, Paris: Tchou, 1970.
Fabre, Daniel, and Jacques Lacroix, *La tradition orale du conte occitan*, 2 vols., Paris: Presses Universitaires de France, 1973–1974.
Fährmann, Sigrid, "Obszönitäten," in *Enzyklopädie des Märchens*, vol. 10 (2002), cols. 178–183.
Fährmann, Sigrid, "Predigtschwänke," in *Enzyklopädie des Märchens*, vol. 10 (2002), cols. 1280–1291.
Falk, Harry, "Pañcatantra(m)," in *Enzyklopädie des Märchens*, vol. 10 (2002), cols. 497–505.
Farāhi, Barkhordār ibn Maḥmud, *Dāstānhā-ye Maḥbub al-qolub*, ed. ʿAli-Reżā Ẕakāvati Qarāgozlu, Tehran: Markaz-e nashr-e dāneshgāhi, 1373/1994.
Farāhi, Barkhordār ibn Maḥmud, *Maḥbub al-qolub*, Bombay, 1298/1881.
Farnham, Williard Edward, "The Contending Lovers," *Publications of the Modern Language Association* 35.3 (1920), pp. 247–323.
Farrāj, ʿAbd al-Sattār Aḥmad, *Akhbār Juḥā*, Cairo: Maktabat Miṣr, 1954.
Fasciculus facetiarum, vol. 1, Schnatterberg im Waschland, 1670.
Fee, Christopher R., and Jeffrey B. Webb, eds., *American Myths, Legends and Tall Tales: An Encyclopedia of American Folklore*, 3 vols., Santa Barbara, CA: ABC-Clio, 2016.
Ferhat, Halima, "Yūsuf ibn Tāshufīn," in *Encyclopaedia of Islam*, 2nd ed., vol. 11, Leiden: Brill, 2002, pp. 355–356.

Field, John Edward, *The Myth of the Pent Cuckoo*, London: Elliot Stock, 1913.
Findeisen, Hans, *Sagen, Märchen und Schwänke von de Insel Hiddensee*, Stettin: Saunier, 1925.
Fiorentino, Giovanni, *Il Pecorone*, ed. E. Esposito, Ravenna, Longo, 1974.
Firmenich, Johannes Matthias, *Germaniens Völkerstimmen*, 3 vols., Berlin: Schlesinger'sche Buch- und Musikhandlung, 1843–1866.
Fischer, Helmut, *Erzählen —Schreiben—Deuten: Beiträge zur Erzählforschung*, Münster: Waxmann, 2001.
Floerke, Hanns, *Der Pecorone des ser Giovanni*, 2 vols., Munich: Georg Müller, 1921.
Flügel, Gustav, "Einige bisher wenig oder gar nicht bekannte arabische und türkische Handschriften," *Zeitschrift der Deutschen Morgenländischen Gesellschaft* 14 (1869), pp. 527–546, at pp. 534–538.
Forbes, Duncan, *Bagh o Bahar, or Tales of the Four Dervishes, translated from the Hindustani of Mir Amman of Dihli*, London: Wm. H. Allan & Co., 1874.
Forbes, Duncan, *The Adventures of Hatim Taï: A Romance, Translated from the Persian*, London: Oriental Translation Fund, 1880.
Fortier, Alcée, *Louisiana Folk-Tales in French Dialect and English Translation*, Boston and New York: Stechert, 1895.
Foruzānfar, Badiʿ al-Zamān, *Maʾākhez-e qeṣaṣ va tamṯilāt-e Maṯnavi*, Tehran: Amir Kabir, 3rd printing. 1362/1983.
Foulché-Delbosc, Raymond, "Remarques sur *Lazarillo de Tormes*," *Revue hispanique* 7 (1900), pp. 81–97.
Fox, Baedron, *The Fox and the Fleas*, 2018; available at https://www.storyjumper.com/book/index/29378656/The-Fox-and-the-Fleas# (accessed June 4, 2018).
Fox, Nikolaus, *Saarländische Volkskunde*, Bonn: Klopp: 1927.
Fradejas Lebrero, José, "Apostillas al catálogo tipológico del cuento folklórico español," *Estudos de literatura oral* 11–12 (2005–2006), pp. 113–128.
Fradejas Lebrero, José, "El tesoro fatal," in *Homenaje a Álvaro Galmés de Fuentes*, vol. 3. Madrid: Universidad de Oviedo-Gredos, 1987, pp. 471–483.
Fradejas Lebrero, José, "Sobre un cuento de Ambrosio de Salazar," *Murgetana* 107 (2002), pp. 53–63.
Fradejas Lebrero, José, *Más de mil y un cuentos del siglo de oro*, Madrid: Iberoamericana, 2008.
Fraenkel, Siegmund, "Die Scharfsinnsproben," *Zeitschrift für vergleichende Litteraturgeschichte* new series 3 (1890), pp. 220–235.
Frazer, James George, *Folk-Lore in the Old Testament: Studies in Comparative Religion, Legend and Law*, 3 vols., London: MacMillan and Co., 1919.
Frenken, Goswin, *Die Exempla des Jacob von Vitry: Ein Beitrag zur Geschichte der Erzählungsliteratur des Mittelalters*, Munich: C.H. Becksche Verlagsbuchhandlung, 1914.
Frenzel, Elisabeth, *Stoffe der Weltliteratur*, Stuttgart: Kröner, 2005.
Frey, Jakob, *Gartengesellschaft*, ed. Johannes Bolte, Tübingen: Litterarischer Verein in Stuttgart, 1896.
Frobenius, Leo, *Volksmärchen der Kabylen*, 3 vols., Jena: Eugen Diederichs, 1921–1922.
Fröhlich, Ida, "Heller, Bernhard," in *Enzyklopädie des Märchens*, vol. 6 (1990), cols. 799–802.
Fudge, Bruce, ed. and transl., *A Hundred and One Nights*, New York: New York University Press, 2016.
Gaál, Károly, *Volksmärchen der Magyaren im südlichen Burgenland*, Berlin: De Gruyter, 1970.

Gaidoz, Henri, "Du changement de sexe dans les contes celtiques," *Revue de l'histoire des religions* 57 (1908), pp. 317–332.
Galland, Antoine, *Journal d'Antoine Galland pendant son séjour à Constantinople (1672–1673)*, ed. Charles Schefer, 2 vols., Paris: Ernest Leroux, 1881 (reprint Frankfurt am Main 1994).
Galland, Antoine, *Le Journal d'Antoine Galland (1646–1715): La période parisienne*, ed. Frédéric Bauden and Richard Waller, 4 vols., Leuven: Peeters, 2011–2015.
Galland, Antoine, *Les Mille et Une Nuits: Contes arabes*, ed. Jean-Paul Sermain and Aboubakr Chraïbi, 3 vols., Paris: Flammarion, 2004.
Galley, Micheline, "Two Folkloric Articles, 1: A Mediterranean Hero," *Journal of Maltese Studies* 7 (1971), pp. 64–70.
Galmés de Fuentes, Álvaro, "Un cuento árabe y el *Lai* francés del *Oiselet*," in *Homenaje al profesor Jacinto Bosch Vilá*, vol. 2, Granada: Universidad de Granada, 1991, pp. 729–737; also in *Romania arabica: Estudios de literatura comparada árabe y romance*, vol. 2, Madrid: Real Academia de la Historia, 2000, pp. 57–69.
Galmés de Fuentes, Álvaro, "Un cuento de 'Las mil y una noches,' el 'Fabliau Constant de Hamel' y la farsa 'Les deulx gentilz hommes et la mounyere.'" *Revista del Instituto egipcio de estudios islamicos en Madrid* 27 (1995), pp. 41–51; also in *Romania arabica*, vol. 2, Madrid: Real Academia de Historia, 2000, pp. 89–100.
Galtier, Édouard, "Fragments d'une étude sur les Mille et une Nuits," *Mémoires de l'Institut français du Caire* 27 (1912), pp. 135–194.
Gamm, Hans-Jochen, *Der Flüsterwitz im Dritten Reich*, Munich: Deutscher Taschenbuchverlag, 1979.
Garimberto, Girolamo, *Della fortuna libri sei*, Venice 1547.
Gascón, Francesc, *Rondalles de la Vall d'Albaida i l'Alcoià*, Ontinyent: Ajuntament d'Ontinyent, 1999.
Gašparíková, Viera, *Katalóg slovenskej l'udovej prózy*, Bratislava: Národopisný ústav SAV, 1991–92.
Gaudefroyes-Demombynes, Maurice, transl., *Les Cent et une nuits*, Paris: Sindbad, 1982.
Gerhardt, Mia I., *The Art of Story-Telling: A Literary Study of the Thousand and One Nights*, Leiden: Brill, 1963.
Gering, Hugo, *Islendzk æventyri: Isländische Legenden, Novellen und Märchen*, vol. 2, Halle: Buchhandlung des Waisenhauses, 1883.
German Schleifheim von Sulsfort, *Gantz neu eingerichteter allenthalben viel verbesserter abentheuerlicher Simplicius Simplicissismus*, Mompelgart: Fillion, [ca 1671].
Gerndt, Helge, "Löwentreue," in *Enzyklopädie des Märchens*, vol. 8 (1996), cols. 1234–1239.
Gervase of Tilbury, "Gervasii Tilberensis Otia imperialia [...]." in *Scriptores rerum Brunsvicensium*, vol. 1, ed. Gottfried Wilhelm Leibniz, Hannover: Förster, 1707, pp. 881–1005.
Gervase of Tilbury, *Otia imperialia: Recreation for an Emperor*, ed. and transl. S.E. Banks and J.W. Binns, Oxford: Clarendon Press, 2002.
Gesner, Conrad, *Historia animalium*, 2 vols., Zurich: Froschover, 1551 (reprint ed. Olaf Breidbach, Hildesheim: Olms-Weidmann, 2012).
Geyer, Rudolf, "Die Katze auf dem Kamel: Ein Beitrag zur altarabischen Phraseologie," in *Orientalische Studien: Festschrift Theodor Nöldeke*, ed. Carl Bezold, vol. 1, Gießen: Töpelmann, 1906, pp. 57–70.
Ghazālī, *Ghazālī's Book Counsel for Kings (Naṣīḥat al-mulūk)*, transl. F.R.C. Bagley, London: Oxford University Press, 1964.

Ghazoul, Ferial J., *The Arabian Nights: A Structural Analysis*, Cairo: Unesco, 1980.
Ghazzālī, Abū Ḥāmid Muḥammad al-, *Iḥyā' 'ulūm al-dīn*, 4 vols., Cairo: Dār al-Kutub al-'arabiyya al-kubrā, s.a.
Ghazzālī, al-, *Kīmiyā-ye sa'ādat*, ed. Aḥmad Ārām, Tehran: Ketābkhāne va chāpkhāne-ye markazi, 1319/1940.
Ghersetti, Antonella, "'La division du poulet' ou 'Quand les moquers sont souvent moqués,'" *Middle Eastern Literatures* 10 (2007), pp. 15–33.
Ghersetti, Antonella, "Teilung: Die sinnreiche T. des Huhns," in *Enzyklopädie des Märchens*, vol. 13 (2010), cols. 329–333.
Ghofrāni, Moḥammad, "Noṣuṣ-e nā-shenākhte az Kelile va Demne," *Maqālāt va barresi-hā* 7–8 (1971), pp. 54–97.
Gier, Albert, "Marie de France," in *Enzyklopädie des Märchens*, vol. 9 (1999), cols. 332–336.
Gildemeister, Johann, "Zum Asinus vulgi," *Orient und Occident* 1 (1862), pp. 733–734.
Gimm, Martin, "Verlorene mandjurische Übersetzungen chinesischer Romane," *Documenta Barbarorum: Festschrift für Walter Heissig zum 70. Geburtstag*, ed. Klaus Sagaster and Michael Weiers, Wiesbaden: Otto Harrassowitz, 1983, pp. 127–141.
Ginzburg, Carlo, and Anna Davin, "Morelli, Freud and Sherlock Holmes: Clues and Scientific Method," *History Workshop* 9 (1980), pp. 5–36, at 22–23.
Girgas, Vladimir Fedorovich, and Viktor Romanovich Rozen, *Arabskaia khrestomatiia*, vol. 2, Sanktpeterburg: Tipografia Imperatorskoj Akademii Nauk, 1876.
Gobi, Jean, *La Scala coeli de Jean Gobi*, ed. Marie-Anne Polo de Beaulieu, Paris: Centre National de la Recherche Scientifique, 1991.
Goldberg, Christine, "Rätselprinzessin," in *Enzyklopädie des Märchens*, vol. 11 (2004), cols. 286–294.
Goldberg, Christine, "Redekampf mit der Prinzessin," in *Enzyklopädie des Märchens*, vol. 11 (2004), cols. 436–443.
Goldberg, Christine, "Schlangenblätter: Die drei S.," in *Enzyklopädie des Märchens*, vol. 12 (2007), cols. 50–54.
Goldberg, Christine, "Selbstberichtigung," in *Enzyklopädie des Märchens*, vol. 12 (2008), cols. 546–548.
Goldberg, Christine, "Stadt der Gauner," in *Enzyklopädie des Märchens*, vol. 12 (2008), cols. 1136–1140.
Goldberg, Christine, "Thompson, Stith," in *Enzyklopädie des Märchens*, vol. 13 (2010), cols. 515–519.
Goldberg, Christine, "Tubach, Frederic (Fritz) Christian," in *Enzyklopädie des Märchens*, vol. 13 (2011), cols. 996–998.
Goldberg, Christine, "Verbot," in *Enzyklopädie des Märchens* 3 (2019), cols. 1389–1396.
Goldberg, Christine, *Turandot's Sisters: A Study of the Folktale AT 851*, New York: Garland, 1993.
Goldberg, Harriet, *Motif-index of Medieval Spanish Folk Narratives*, Tempe, AZ: Arizona State University, 1998.
Gómez Camacho, Alejandro, "Los cuentos en la obra de Juan de Robles," *Etiópicas* 2 (2006), pp. 202–254.
González Sanz, Carlos, *Catálogo tipologico de cuentos folklóricos aragoneses*, Zaragoza: Instituto Aragonés de Antropología, 1996.
González Treviño, Ana Elena, "Fabulous Awakenings: The Ethics of Metafiction in *La*

vida es sueño by Calderón de la Barca and Some Tales from the *Arabian Nights*," *Anuario de Letras Modernas* 15 (2009–2010), pp. 13–21.

Gonzalo Tobajas, Ángel J., "*El padre, su hijo y el asno* (ATU 1215): la pervivencia de un cuento de raíz medieval en los balbuceos de la era digital (Facebook, Youtube y Whatsapp," *eHumanística* 31 (2015), pp. 524–538.

Gonzenbach, Laura, *Sicilianische Märchen*, ed. Otto Hartwig, 2 vols. Leipzig: Engelmann, 1870.

Gooch, Richard, *Facetiae Cantabrigienses*, London: William Cole, 1825.

Görres, Joseph von, *Die deutschen Volksbücher: Nähere Würdigung der schönen Historien, Wetter, und Arzneibüchlein, welche theils inneren Werth, theils Zufall, Jahrhunderte hindurch bis auf unsere Zeit erhalten hat*, Heidelberg: Mohr & Zimmer, 1808.

Goyert, Georg, *Vlämische Märchen*, Jena: Diederichs, 1925.

Graf, Klaus, "Lehmann, Christoph," in *Enzyklopädie des Märchens*, vol. 8 (1996), cols. 881–883.

Granja, Fernando de la, "Dos cuentos árabes de ladrones en la literatura española del siglo XVI," *Al-Andalus* 33.2 (1969), pp. 459–469.

Granja, Fernando de la, "Nuevas notas a un episodio del Lazarillo de Tormes," *Al-Andalus* 36 (1971), pp. 223–237.

Granja, Fernando de la, "Tres cuentos españoles de origen árabe," *Al-Andalus* 33.1 (1968), pp. 123–141.

Granja, Fernando de la, *Precedentes y reminiscencias de la literatura y el folklore árabes en nuestro Siglo de Oro*, Madrid: Real Academia de la Historia, 1996.

Grannas, Gustav, *Plattdeutsche Volkserzählungen aus Ostpreußen*, Marburg: Elwert, 1957.

Grannas, Gustav, *Volk aus dem Ordensland Preussen erzählt Sagen, Märchen und Schwänke*, Marburg: Elwert, 1960.

Gredt, Nikolaus, *Sagenschatz des Luxemburger Landes*, Luxemburg: Buck, 1883.

Greven, Joseph, *Die Exempla aus den Sermones feriales et communes*, Heidelberg: Carl Winter's Universitätsbuchhandlung, 1914.

Greverus, Ina-Maria, "Die Geschenke des kleinen Volkes, KHM 182 = AT 503: Eine vergleichende Untersuchung," *Fabula* 1 (1958), pp. 263–279.

Grimm, Jacob and Wilhelm, *Deutsche Sagen*, ed. Hans-Jörg Uther and Barbara Kindermann-Bieri, 3 vols., Munich: Diederichs, 1993.

Grimm, Jacob and Wilhelm, *Kinder- und Hausmärchen: Ausgabe letzter Hand mit den Originalanmerkungen der Brüder Grimm*, ed. Heinz Rölleke, 3 vols., Stuttgart: Philipp Reclam Jun., 1980.

Grotzfeld, Heinz, "Hannā Diyāb," in *Enzyklopädie des Märchens*, vol. 6 (1990), cols. 485–487.

Grotzfeld, Heinz, *Das Bad im arabisch-islamischen Mittelalter*, Wiesbaden: Harrassowitz, 1970.

Grotzfeld, Heinz and Sophia, *Die Erzählungen aus Tausendundeiner Nacht*, 2nd rev. ed., Dortmund: Verlag für Orientkunde, 2012.

Grotzfeld, Heinz and Sophia, and Ulrich Marzolph, "Kalila und Dimna," in *Enzyklopädie des Märchens*, vol. 7 (1993), cols. 888–895.

Grube, Ernst J., "Prolegomena for a Corpus Publication of Illustrated *Kalīlah wa Dimnah* Manuscripts," *Islamic Art* 4 (1990–1991), pp. 301–481.

Grubmüller, Klaus, ed., *Novellistik des Mittelalters: Märendichtung*, Frankfurt am Main: Dt. Klassiker-Verlag, 1996.

Grünbaum, Max, "Beiträge zur vergleichenden Mythologie aus der Hagada," *Zeitschrift der Deutschen Morgenländischen Gesellschaft* 31 (1847), pp. 183–359.
Grünbaum, Max, *Neue Beiträge zur semitischen Sagenkunde*, Leiden: Brill, 1893.
Grunebaum, Gustave Edmund, "Greek Form Elements in the Arabian Nights," *Journal of the American Oriental Society* 62 (1942), pp. 277–292.
Grüner, Gustav, *Waldeckische Volkserzählungen*, Marburg: Elwert, 1964.
Gutas, Dimitri, *Greek Thought, Arabic Culture: The Graeco-Arabic Translation Movement in Baghdad and Early 'Abbāsid Society (2nd–4th/8th–10th Centuries)*, London: Routledge, 1988.
Guterman, Norbert, transl., *Russian Fairy Tales*, New York: Pantheon, 1945.
György, Lajos, *A magyar anekdota története és egyetemes kapcsolatai*, Budapest: Studium, 1934.
György, Lajos, *Kónyi János Democritusa*, Budapest: Magyar tudományos akadémia, 1932.
Györgypal-Eckert, Irma, *Die deutsche Volkserzählung in Hajós, einer schwäbischen Sprachinsel in Ungarn*, Hamburg: Hansischer Gildenverlag, 1941.
Haag-Higuchi, Roxane, *Untersuchungen zu einer Sammlung persischer Erzählungen: Čihil wa-šiš ḥikāyāt yā ǧāmiʿ al-ḥikāyāt*, Berlin: Klaus Schwarz, 1984.
Ḥablerudi, Moḥammad ʿAli, *Jāmeʿ al-tamsil*, ed. Ḥasan Ẕol-Faqāri, Tehran: Moʿin, 1390/2011.
Ḥablerudi, Moḥammad ʿAli, *Majmaʿ al-ams*āl, ed. Ṣādeq Kiyā, Tehran: Edāre-ye farhang-e ʿāmme, 1344/1965.
Haboucha, Ginette, "The Judeo-Spanish Folktale: A Current Update," *Jewish Folklore and Ethnology Review* 15.2 (1993), pp. 32–38.
Haboucha, Reginetta, *Types and Motifs of the Judaeo-Spanish Folktales*, New York: Garland, 1992.
Haddawy, Husain, transl., *The Arabian Nights*. New York: Alfred A. Knopf, 1990.
Ḥafnāwī, Shihāb al-Dīn Aḥmad al-Bashshārī al-, *Bughyat al-jalīs wa-'l-musāmir wa-nuzhat al-arwāḥ wa-'l-khawāṭir*, Ms. Paris, Biliothèque Nationale Or. 3448/51.
Hahn, Johann Georg von, *Griechische und albanesische Märchen*, 2 vols., Leipzig: Engelmann, 1918.
Haiding, Karl, *Märchen und Schwänke aus dem Burgenlande*, Graz: Leykam, 1977.
Haiding, Karl, *Märchen und Schwänke aus Oberösterreich*, Berlin: De Gruyter, 1969.
Halász, Ignácz, *Svéd-lapp nyelv*, vol. 3: *Ume- és Tornio-Lappmarki nyelvmutatványok*, Budapest: Magyar Tudományos Akadémia, 1887.
Haller, Karl, "Der Arzt wider Willen, ein Volksmärchen aus Ober-Österreich," *Zeitschrift des Vereins für Volkskunde* 26 (1916), pp. 89–91.
Hallgarten, Paul, *Rhodos: Die Märchen und Schwänke der Insel*, Frankfurt am Main: Frankfurter Societäts-Druckerei, 1929.
Halpert, Herbert, and J.D.A. Widdowson, *Folktales of Newfoundland: The Resilience of the Oral Tradition*, 2 vols., New York: Garland, 1996.
Hamadāni, Moḥammad ibn Maḥmud, *'Ajā'eb-nāme*, ed. Jaʿfar Modarres Ṣādeqi, Tehran: Markaz 1375/1996.
Hamel, Mary, and Charles Merrill, "The Analogues of the *Pardoner's Tale* and a New African Version," *The Chaucer Review* 26 (1991), pp. 175–183.
Hamer, Douglas, "'The Pardoner's Tale:' A West-African Analogue," *Notes and Queries* 214 (1969), pp. 335–336.
Hammer-Purgstall, Joseph von, *Rosenöl, oder Sagen und Kunden des Morgenlandes aus arabischen, persischen und türkischen Quellen gesammelt*, 2 vols., Stuttgart: J.G. Cotta, 1813.

Hammer-Purgstall, Joseph von, *Geschichte der schönen Redekünste Persiens, mit einer Blütenlese persischer Dichter*, Vienna, 1818.
Hamori, Andras, "The Collector of Ramlah," *Studia islamica* 71 (1990), pp. 65–75.
Ḥamza, ʿAbd al-Laṭīf, *Ḥikam Qarāqūsh*, Cairo: Muṣṭafā al-Bābī al-Ḥalabī, 1363/1945.
Ḥamze-nāme, see *Qeṣṣe-ye Ḥamze*; *Romuz-e Ḥamze*.
Ḥanafī, Muḥammad ibn Aḥmad ibn (al-)Ilyās al-, *Nuzhat al-udabāʾ*, Gotha, Ms. Orient A 2706.
Hanauer, J.E., *Folk-lore of the Holy Land: Moslem, Christian and Jewish*, London: Duckwort & Co., 1907.
Hanawalt, Barbara A., *"Of Good and Ill Repute": Gender and Social Control in Medieval England*, Oxford: Oxford University Press, 1998.
Hanawalt, Barbara A., "Separation Anxieties in Late Medieval London: Gender in *The Wright's Chaste Wife*," *Medieval Perspectives* 11 (1996), pp. 23–41.
Hanawalt, Barbara A., *The Wealth of Wives: Women, Law, and Economy in Late Medieval London*, Oxford: Oxford University Press, 2007.
Hanna, Nelly, "The Chronicles of Ottoman Egypt: History or Entertainment?" in *The Historiography of Islamic Egypt (c. 950–1800)*, ed. Hugh Kennedy, Leiden: Brill, 2001, pp. 237–250.
Hanna, Nelly, *In Praise of Books: A Cultural History of Cairo's Middle Class, Sixteenth to Eighteenth Century*, Syracuse, NY: Syracuse University Press, 2003.
Hansen, Terrence Leslie, *The Types of the Folktale in Cuba, Puerto Rico, the Dominican Republic, and Spanish South America*, Berkeley: University of California Press, 1957.
Hansen, William, "Stärkste Dinge," in *Enzyklopädie des Märchens*, vol. 12 (2007), cols. 1188–1194.
Hansen, William, *Ariadne's Thread: A Guide to International Tales Found in Classical Literature*, Ithaca and London: Cornell University Press, 2002.
Haralampieff, Kyrill, *Bulgarische Volksmärchen*, Düsseldorf: Diederichs, 1971.
Harkort, Fritz, *Die Schein- und Schattenbußen im Ezählgut*, unpublished PhD dissertation, Kiel 1956.
Harkort, Fritz, *Scheinbußengeschichten*, unpublished typoscript, Göttingen 1967.
Harpagiander, *Compendieuses Lexicon Apophthegmaticum*, Nuremberg: Wolffgang Moritz Endter, 1718.
Harsdörffer, Georg Philipp, *Ars Apophthegmatica: Das ist: Kunstquellen Denckwürdiger Lehrsprüche und Ergötzlicher Hofreden*, Nuremberg: Wolffgang der Jüng. and Joh. Andrae Endtern, 1655.
Hart, Walter Morris, "The 'Pardoner's Tale' and 'Der Dot im Stock,' *Modern Philology* 9 (1911–1912), pp. 17–22.
Hasan-Rokem, Galit, *Web of Life: Folklore and Midrash in Rabbinic Literature*, Stanford: Standford University Press, 2000.
Hatami, Mahroo, *Untersuchungen zum persischen Papageienbuch des Naḫšabī*, Freiburg: Klaus Schwarz, 1977.
Ḥātem-nāme, ed. Ḥoseyn Esmāʿili, 2 vols., Tehran: Moʿin, 1386/2007.
Ḫaṭīb al-Baġdādī, al-, *L'arte dello scrocco: storie, aneddoti e poemi di scrocconi*, transl. and ed. Antonella Ghersetti, Catanzaro: Abramo, 2006.
Hauschild, Christiane, "Säbel: Der hölzerne S.," in *Enzyklopädie des Märchens*, vol. 11 (2004), cols. 964–967.

Hazai, György, and Andreas Tietze, eds., *Ferec baʿd eş-şidde: „Freud nach Leid" (ein frühosmanisches Geschichtenbuch)*, 2 vols., Berlin: Klaus Schwarz, 2006.

Hazai, György, and Heidi Stein, transl., "Proben aus dem *Ferec baʿd eş-şidde* in der deutschen Übersetzung von Andreas Tietze," *Archivum Ottomanicum* 30 (2013), pp. 49–104.

Hazlitt, J.O., *The Sackfull of Newes: An Old Jest-Book, Originally Printed in the Sixteenth Century*, London: The Editor, 1861.

Hazlitt, W. Carew, *Shakespeare Jest-Books: Reprints of the Early and Very Rare Jest-Books Supposed to Have Been Used by Shakespeare*, 3 vols., London: Willis & Sotheran, 1881.

Hazlitt, W. Carew, ed., *A Hundred Merry Tales: the Earliest English Jestbook*, London: J.W. Jarvis & Son, 1887.

Hebel, Johann Peter, *Schatzkästlein des rheinischen Hausfreunds*, ed. Winfried Theiss, Stuttgart: Reclam, 1981.

Heffernan, Carol F., *The Orient in Chaucer and Medieval Romance*, Cambridge: D.S. Brewer, 2003.

Ḥekāyāt-e laṭif see Javādi, Seyyid Kamāl Ḥājj Seyyid

Heller, Bernhard, "Arabische Motive in deutschen Märchen und Märchendichtungen," in *Handwörterbuch des deutschen Märchens*, ed. Lutz Mackensen, vol. 1, Berlin: De Gruyter, 1930, pp. 93–108.

Heller, Bernhard, "Das hebräische und arabische Märchen," in *Anmerkungen zu den Kinder- und Hausmärchen der Brüder Grimm*. ed. Johannes Bolte and Georg Polívka, 2nd ed., vol. 4, Leipzig: Dietrich, 1929 (reprint Hildesheim: Olms, 1963), pp. 315–418.

Heller, Bernhard, "Die Legende von den drei Sünden des Einsiedlers und vom Mönch Barṣīṣa," *Ungarische Rundschau* 1 (1912), pp. 653–673.

Heller, Bernhard, "La chute des anges Schemhazai, Ouzza, et Azaël," *Revue des études juives* 60 (1910), pp. 202–212.

Hēmavijaya, *Kathāratnākara: Das Märchenmeer. Eine Sammlung indischer Erzählungen*, transl. Johannes Hertel, 2 vols., Munich: Georg Müller, 1920.

Henssen, Gottfried, *Sagen, Märchen und Schwänke des Jülicher Landes: Aus dem Nachlaß Heinrich Hoffmanns herausgegeben und durch eigene Aufzeichnungen vermehrt*, Bonn: Röhrscheid, 1955.

Henßen, Gottfried, *Überlieferung und Persönlichkeit: Die Erzählungen und Lieder des Egbert Gerrits*, Münster: Aschendorff, 1951.

Henßen, Gottfried, *Ungardeutsche Volksüberlieferungen*, Marburg: Elwert, 1959.

Henßen, Gottfried, *Volk erzählt: Münsterländische Sagen, Märchen und Schwänke*, Münster: Aschendorf, 1935.

Hernández Fernández, Ángel, *Catálogo tipológico del cuento folclórico en Murcia*, Alcalá: de Henares: University of Alcalá, 2013.

Hernández Valcárcel, María del Carmen, *El cuento español en los siglos de oro: siglo XVI*, Murcia: University of Murcia, 2002.

Herrtage, Sidney J.H., *The Early English Versions of the Gesta Romanorum*, London: N. Trübner & Co., 1879.

Hertel, Johannes, "Altindische Parallelen zu Babrius 23," *Zeitschrift für Volkskunde* 22 (1912), pp. 244–252.

Hertel, Johannes, *Ein altindisches Narrenbuch*, Leipzig: B.G. Teubner, 1912.

Hertel, Johannes, *Indische Märchen*, Düsseldorf: Diederichs, 1953.

Hertel, Johannes, *Zweiundneunzig Anekdoten und Schwänke aus dem modernen Indien: Aus dem Persischen übersetzt*, Leipzig: Haessel 1992.
Hibler, Charles H., *Down in Arkansas*, Kansas City: J. W Smith, 1902.
Hilka, Alfons, "Neue Beiträge zur Erzählungsliteratur des Mittelalters (die Compilatio Singularis der Hs. Tours 468, ergänzt durch eine Schwesterhandschrift Bern 679)," *90. Jahresbericht der Schlesischen Gesellschaft für vaterl[ändische] Cultur: Sitzung der Sektion für neuere Philologie vom 5. Dezember 1912* (Breslau 1913), pp. 1–24.
Hilka, Alfons, *Historia septem sapientium*, vol. 1: *Eine bisher unbekannte lateinische Übersetzung einer orientalischen Fassung der Sieben weisen Meister (Mischle Sendabar)*, Heidelberg: Carl Winter's Universitätsbuchhandlung, 1912.
Hillers, Barbara, "The Abbot of Druimenaig: Genderbending in Gaelic Tradition," *Proceedings of the Harvard Celtic Colloquium* 15 (1995), pp. 175–197.
Hillers, Barbara, "The Man Who Became a Woman (ATU 705B§): The Change of Sex Motif in Gaelic Tradition," unpublished working paper, 2016.
Ḥimyarī, Muḥammad ibn ʿAbd al-Munʿim, al-, *al-Rawḍ al-miʿṭār fī khabar al-aqṭār*, ed. Iḥsān ʿAbbās, Beirut: Maktabat Lubnān, 1975.
Hinüber, Oskar von, "Tripiṭaka," in *Enzyklopädie des Märchens*, vol. 13 (2010), cols. 933–940.
Hoenshel, E.J., *Stories of the Pioneers: Incidents, Adventures and Reminiscences as Told by Some of the Old Settlers of Taney County, Missouri*, Point Lookout: School of the Ozarks Press, 1915.
Holbek, Bengt, "Asinus Vulgi: Om Niels Heldvads oversættelse og dens aner," *Danske Studier* 59 (1964), pp. 32–53.
Holbek, Bengt, *Interpretation of Fairy-Tales: Danish Folklore in a European Perspective*, Helsinki: Suomalainen Tiedeakatemia, 1987.
Holmes, Brooke, "Aelius Aristides's Illegible Body," in Harris, William Vernon, and Brooke Holmes, eds., *Aelius Aristides Between Greece, Rome, and the Gods*, Leiden: Brill, 2008, pp. 81–113.
Holzinger, Michael, *Märchen aus Albanien*, 3rd ed., Berlin: Zeno, 2014.
Hommel, Fritz, *Die älteste arabische Barlaam-Version*, Vienna: Alfred Hölder, 1887.
Honko, Lauri, "Four Forms of Adaptation of Tradition," *Studia Fennica* 26 (1981), pp. 19–33.
Horálek, Karel, "Flügel des Königssohnes," in *Enzyklopädie des Märchens*, vol. 4 (1984), cols. 1358–1365.
Horálek, Karel, "Frau im Schrein," in *Enzyklopädie des Märchens*, vol. 5 (1987), cols. 186–192.
Horálek, Karel, "Märchen aus Tausend und einer Nacht bei den Slaven," *Fabula* 10 (1969), pp. 156–195.
Horn, Paul,"Zu Hodža Nasreddin's Schwänken," *Keleti Szemle* 1 (1900), pp. 66–72.
Horta, Paulo Lemos, "Beautiful Men and Deceitful Women: The One Hundred and One Nights and World Literature," *Narrative Culture* 2.2 (2015), pp. 190–207.
Horta, Paulo Lemos, "Tales of Dreaming Men: Shakespeare, "The Old Hunchback," and 'The Sleeper and the Waker'," *Journal of World Literature* 2.3 (2017), pp. 276–296.
Horta, Paulo Lemos, "Tales of the Dreaming Man: Shakespeare, 'The Sleeper and the Waker,' and World Literature," in Bendix, Regina F., and Dorothy Noyes, eds., *Terra Ridens—Terra Narrans: Festschrift zum 65. Geburtstag von Ulrich Marzolph*, Dortmund: Verlag für Orientkunde, 2018, pp. 168–193.

Horta, Paulo Lemos, *Marvellous Thieves: Secret Authors of The Arabian Nights*, Cambridge: Harvard University Press, 2017.
Houdebert, Aurélie, "L'histoire du cheval d'ébène, de Tolède à Paris: propositions sur les modalités d'une transmission," in Egedi-Kovács, Emese, ed., *Byzance et l'Occident: Rencontre de l'Est de de l'Ouest*, Budapest: Collège Eötvös József ELTE, 2013, pp. 143–156.
Houdebert, Aurélie, "Le 'Cheval volant:' parcours et métamorphoses d'un motif oriental: Adenet le Roi, Girart d'Amiens, Geoffrey Chaucer," in Egedi-Kovács, Emese, ed., *Littérature et folklore dans le récit médiéval*, Budapest: Collège Eötvös József ELTE, 2011, pp. 149–160.
Houdebert, Aurélie, *Le cheval d'ébène à la cour de France: Cléomadès et Méliacin*, Paris (forthcoming).
Hubrich-Messow, Gundula, "Vaterunser beten, ohne an anderes zu denken," in *Enzyklopädie des Märchens*, vol. 13 (2011), cols. 1358–1360.
Hucker, Bernd Ulrich, "Eulenspiegel," in *Enzyklopädie des Märchens*, vol. 4 (1984), cols. 538–555.
Hūd ibn al-Muḥakkam al-Huwwārī, *Tafsīr Kitāb Allāh al-ʿazīz*, ed. Bālḥājj ibn Saʿīd Sharīfī, Beirut: Dār al-Gharb al-islāmī, 1990.
Hulsbusch, Johannes, *Sylva sermonum iucundissimorum*, Basel, 1568.
Hundred and One Nights see Fudge; Gaudefroyes-Demombynes; Ott; Ṭarshūna.
Huse, Ulrich, "Erdloch für Aushub graben," in *Enzyklopädie des Märchens*, vol. 4 (1994), cols. 164–166.
Huse, Ulrich, "Feuer: Fernwirkung des F.s," in *Enzyklopädie des Märchens*, vol. 4 (1984), cols. 1083–1087.
Ḥuṣrī al-Qayrawānī, Abū Isḥāq Ibrāhīm ibn ʿAlī al-, *Jamʿ al-jawāhir fī 'l-mulaḥ wa-'l-nawādir*, ed. ʿAlī Muḥammad al-Bijāwī, Cairo: Dār Iḥyā' al-kutub al-ʿarabiyya, 1372/1952.
Hutson, Lorna, "Probable Infidelities from Bandello to Massinger," in *Staging Early Modern Romance: Prose Fiction, Dramatic Romance, and Shakespeare*, ed. Mary Ellen Lamb, Valerie Wayne, New York: Routledge, 2009, pp. 219–235.
Ibn ʿAbd al-Barr al-Namarī al-Qurṭubī, Abū ʿUmar Yūsuf ibn ʿAbdallāh ibn Muḥammad, *Bahjat al-majālis wa-uns al-mujālis*, ed. Muḥammad Mursī al-Khūlī, 3 vols., Beirut: Dār al-Kutub al-ʿilmiyya, ca. 1969.
Ibn ʿAbd al-Ḥakam, *The History of the Conquest of Egypt, North Africa and Spain Known as the Futūḥ Miṣr*, ed. Charles C. Torrey, New Haven: Yale University Press, 1922.
Ibn ʿAbd Rabbih, Abū ʿUmar Aḥmad ibn Muḥammad, *Kitāb al-ʿIqd al-farīd*, ed. Aḥmad Amīn, Aḥmad al-Zayn, Ibrāhīm al-Abyārī, 3rd ed., 7 vols., Cairo: Lajnat al-ta'līf wa-'l-tarjama wa-'l-nashr, 1372/1953–1385/1965.
Ibn Abī 'l-Dunyā, Abū Bakr ʿAbdallāh ibn Muḥammad, *al-Ṣamt wa-ādāb al-lisān*, ed. Muḥammad ʿAbd al-Qādir Aḥmad ʿAṭā, Beirut: Mu'assasa al-kitāb al-thaqāfiyya, 1409/1988.
Ibn Abī 'l-Dunyā, Abū Bakr ʿAbdallāh ibn Muḥammad, *Dhamm al-ghība wa-'l-namīma*, ed. ʿAbd al-Raḥmān Khalaf, Cairo: Dār al-Iʿtisām, 1989.
Ibn Abī 'l-Ḥadīd, ʿAbd al-Ḥamīd ibn Hibatallāh, *Sharḥ Nahj al-balāgha*, Cairo: Dār Iḥyā' al-kutub al-ʿarabiyya, 2nd ed., 20 vols., 1385/1965–1387/1967.
Ibn Abī ʿAwn al-Kātib, Ibrāhīm ibn Muḥammad, *Kitāb al-Ajwiba al-muskita*, ed. ʿAbd al-Qādir Aḥmad, Cairo 1985.
Ibn Abī Yaʿlā, Abū 'l-Ḥusayn Muḥammad, *Ṭabaqāt al-ḥanābila*, ed. Muḥammad Ḥāmid al-Faqī, 2 vols., Cairo: Maṭbaʿat al-sunna al-muḥammadiyya, 1371/1952.

Ibn al-Athīr, ʿIzz al-Dīn Abū ʾl-Ḥasan ʿAlī, *al-Kāmil fī ʾl-tārīkh*, 9 vols., Cairo: Idārat al-ṭibāʿa, 1348/1929.

Ibn al-ʿImād al-Ḥanbalī, Abū ʾl-Falāḥ ʿAbd al-Ḥayy ibn Aḥmad, *Shadharāt al-dhahab fī akhbār man dhahab*, 8 vols., Beirut: al-Maktab al-tijārī lil-ṭibāʿa wa-ʾl-nashr wa-ʾl-tawzīʿ, ca. 1970.

Ibn al-Jawzī, Abū ʾl-Faraj ʿAbd al-Raḥmān ibn ʿAlī, *Akhbār al-Adhkiyāʾ*, ed. Muḥammad Mursī al-Khūlī, Cairo 1970.

Ibn al-Jawzī, Abū ʾl-Faraj ʿAbd al-Raḥmān ibn ʿAlī, *Akhbār al-Ḥamqā wa-ʾl-mughaffalīn*, ed. Kāẓim al-Muẓaffar, al-Najaf: al-Maktaba al-ḥaydariyya, 1386/1966.

Ibn al-Jawzī, Abū ʾl-Faraj ʿAbd al-Raḥmān ibn ʿAlī, *Akhbār al-Ẓirāf wa-ʾl-mutamājinīn*, ed. Muḥammad Baḥr al-ʿulūm, 2nd ed., al-Najaf: al-Maktaba al-ḥaydariyya, 1386/1966.

Ibn al-Jawzī, Abū ʾl-Faraj ʿAbd al-Raḥmān ibn ʿAlī, *al-Muntaẓam fī tārīkh al-mulūk wa-ʾl-umam*, ed. Muḥammad ʿAbd al-Qādir ʿAṭā, Muṣṭafā ʿAbd al-Qādir ʿAṭā, Nuʿaym Zarzūr, 2nd ed., 19 vols., Beirut: Dār al-Kutubal-ilmiyya, 1415/1995.

Ibn al-Jawzī, Abū ʾl-Faraj ʿAbd al-Raḥmān ibn ʿAlī, *Ṣayd al-khāṭir*, Miṣr: Dār al-Kutub al-ḥadītha, ca. 1966.

Ibn al-Muʿtazz, *ʿAbdallāh* ibn Muḥammad *Ṭabaqāt al-shuʿarāʾ*, ed. ʿAbd al-Sattār Aḥmad Farrāg, Cairo: al-Maʿārif, 1375/1956.

Ibn al-Wardī, Sirāj al-Dīn Abū Ḥafṣ ʿUmar, *Kharīdat al-ʿajāʾib wa-farīdat al-gharāʾib*, Cairo: al-Maṭbaʿa al-ʿāmira, 1324/1906.

Ibn ʿArabshāh, Aḥmad ibn Muḥammad, *Fākihat al-khulafāʾ wa-mufākahat al-ẓurafāʾ*, ed. Ayman ʿAbd al-Jabbār al-Buḥayrī, Cairo: Dār al-Āfāq, 1421/2001.

Ibn ʿAsākir, Abū ʾl-Qāsim ʿAlī ibn al-Ḥasan ibn Hibat Allāh ibn ʿAbdallāh, *Tārīkh Madīnat Dimashq*, vol. 72, 74, ed. Muḥibb al-Dīn Abū Saʿīd ibn Gharāma al-ʿAmrawī, Beirut: Dār al-Fikr, 1421/2001.

Ibn ʿĀṣim al-Andalusī, Abū Bakr ibn Muḥammad, *Ḥadāʾiq al-azāhir*, ed. ʿAfīf ʿAbd al-Raḥmān, Beirut: Dār al-Masīra, 1401/1981.

Ibn Badrūn, *Commentaire historique sur le poème d'Ibn-Abdoun, par Ibn Badroun*, ed. Reinhart Pieter Anne Dozy, Leiden: S. and J. Luchtmans, 1846.

Ibn Ḥajar al-ʿAsqalānī, Shihāb al-Dīn Abū ʾl-Faḍl Aḥmad ibn ʿAlī, *Lisān al-mīzān*, ed. ʿAbd al-Fattāḥ Abū Ghadda and Salmān ʿAbd al-Fattāḥ Abū Ghadda, vol. 2, Beirut: Maktabat al-maṭbūʿāt al-islāmiyya, 1423/2002.

Ibn Ḥamdūn, Muḥammad ibn al-Ḥasan ibn Muḥammad ibn ʿAlī, *al-Tadhkira al-ḥamdūniyya*, ed. Iḥsān ʿAbbās and Bakr ʿAbbās, 10 vols., Beirut: Dār Ṣādir, 1996.

Ibn Ḥibbān al-Bustī, Abū Ḥātim ibn Muḥammad, *Rawḍat al-ʿuqalāʾ wa-nuzhat al-fuḍalāʾ*, ed. Muḥammad Muḥyī al-Dīn ʿAbd al-Raḥmān, Beirut: Dār al-Kutub al-ʿilmiyya, 1395/1975.

Ibn Ḥijja al-Ḥamawī, ʿAlī ibn Muḥammad, *Thamarāt al-awrāq fī ʾl-muḥāḍarāt*, ed. Mufīd Qumayḥa, Beirut: Dār al-Kutub al-ʿilmiyya, 1403/1983.

Ibn Hishām, Abū Muḥammad ʿAbd al-Malik, *Kitāb al-Tījān fī mulūk Ḥimyar*, Hayderabad: Dāʾirat al-maʿārif al-ʿuthmāniyya, 1347/1928.

Ibn Iyās al-Ḥanafī, Muḥammad ibn Aḥmad, *Badāʾiʿ al-zuhūr fī waqāʾiʿ al-duhūr*, see Suyūṭī, Jalāl al-Dīn ʿAbd al-Raḥmān.

Ibn Khallikān, Abū ʾl-ʿAbbās Shams al-Dīn Aḥmad ibn Muḥammad ibn Abī Bakr, *Wafayāt al-aʿyān*, ed. Iḥsān ʿAbbās, 8 vols., Beirut: Dār Ṣādir, 1977.

Ibn Manẓūr, Muḥammad ibn Mukarram, *Mukhtaṣar Tārīkh Dimashq*, 31 vols., ed. Rūḥiyya al-Naḥḥās, Damascus: Dār al-Fikr, 1984–1996.
Ibn Qutayba al-Dīnawarī, Abū Muḥammad ʿAbdallāh ibn Muslim, *Kitāb al-Ashriba*, ed. Muḥammad Kurd ʿAlī, Damascus: al-Majmaʿ al-ʿilmī al-ʿarabī, 1366/1947.
Ibn Qutayba al-Dīnawarī, Abū Muḥammad ʿAbdallāh ibn Muslim, *al-Maʿārif*, ed. Tharwat ʿUkkāsha, 2nd ed., Cairo: Dār al-Maʿrif, 1969.
Ibn Qutayba al-Dīnawarī, Abū Muḥammad ʿAbdallāh ibn Muslim, *ʿUyūn al-akhbār*, 2nd ed., 4 vols., Cairo: al-Muʾassasa al-miṣriyya al-ʿāmma lil-taʾlif wa-ʾl-tarjama wa-ʾl-ṭibāʿa, 1963.
Ibn Ṣaṣrā, Muḥammad ibn Muḥammad, *A Chronicle of Damascus 1389–1397*, transl. William M. Brinner, Berkeley and Los Angeles: University of California Press, 1963.
Ibn Shākir al-Kutubī, Muḥammad, *ʿUyūn al-tawārīkh*, Ms. Istanbul, Ahmet III 2922/6.
Ibshīhī, Shihāb al-Dīn Muḥammad ibn Aḥmad Abū ʾl-Fatḥ al-, *al-Mustaṭraf fī kull fann mustaẓraf*, ed. Mufīd Qumayḥa, 2 vols., Beirut: Dār al-Kutub al-ʿilmiyya, 1403/1983.
Ibshīhī, al-, *Al-Mostaṭraf: recueil de morceaux choisis çà et là*, transl. Gustav Rat, 2 vols., Paris: Leroux, 1899.
Ikeda, Hiroko, *A Type and Motif Index of Japanese Folk-Literature*, Helsinki: Suomalainen Tiedeakatemia, 1971.
Ilg, Bertha, *Maltesische Märchen und Schwänke: aus dem Volksmunde gesammelt*, 2 vols., Leipzig: Schönfeld, 1906.
Imbriani, Vittorio, *La novellaja fiorentina*, Livorno: Vigo, 1877.
Ingrams, William Harold, *Abu Nuwas in Life and Legend*, Port Louis, Mauritius: M. Gaud & Cie, 1933.
Irwin, Robert, *For Lust of Knowing: The Orientalists and Their Enemies*, London: Allen Lane, 2006.
Irwin, Robert, *Ibn Khaldun: An Intellectual Biography*, Princeton: Princeton University Press, 2018.
Irwin, Robert, *The Arabian Nights: A Companion*, London: Allen Lane, 1994.
ʿIṣāmī, ʿAbd al-Malik ibn al-Ḥusayn ibn ʿAbd al-Malik al-, *Samṭ an-nujūm al-ʿawālī fī anbāʾ al-awāʾil wa-ʾl-tawālī*, ed. ʿĀdil Aḥmad ʿAbd al-Mawjūd and ʿAlī Muḥammad Muʿawwaḍ, 4 vols., Beirut : Dār al-Kutub al-ʿilmiyya, 1419/1998.
Iṣfahānī, Abū ʾl-Faraj al-, *Kitāb al-Aghānī*, 21 vols., Būlāq (reprint Beirut: Ṣaʿb, ca. 1980).
Isḥāqī, Muḥammad ibn ʿAbd al-Muʿṭī al-, *Kitāb Laṭāʾif akhbār al-uwal*, ed. Muḥammad Riḍwān Muhannā, al-Manṣūra: Maktabat al-Īmān, 1420/2000.
Iskāfī, Muḥammad ibn ʿAbdallāh al-, *Kitāb Luṭf al-tadbīr*, ed. Aḥmad ʿAbd al-Bāqī, 2nd ed., Beirut: Dār al-Kutub al-ʿilmiyya, 1399/1979.
Ibn Iyās al-Ḥanafī, *Badāʾiʿ al-zuhūr fī waqāʾiʿ al-duhūr*, see Suyūṭī, Jalāl al-Dīn ʿAbd al-Raḥmān al-.
Jackson, Thomas W., *On a Slow Train through Arkansas: Funny Railroad Stories, Sayings of the Southern Darkies, All the Latest and Best Minstrel Jokes of the Day*, Chicago: Thos. W. Jackson, 1903.
Jacob, Georg, "Wandersagen," *Der Islam* 18 (1929), pp. 200–206.
Jacobs, Joseph, *More English Fairy Tales*, London: D. Nutt, 1894.
Jacques de Vitry, *The Exempla or Illustrative Stories from the Sermones Vulgares*, ed. Thomas F. Crane, London: Nutt, 1890.

Jaʿfari Qanavāti, Moḥammad, ed., *Jāmeʿ al-ḥekāyāt: noskhe-ye Ketābkhāne-ye Ganj-Bakhsh-e Pākestān*, Tehran: Qaṭre, 1391/2012.
Jaʿfari Qanavāti, Moḥammad, and Seyyid Aḥmad Vakiliyān, *Masnavi va mardom: revāyathā-ye shafāhi-ye qeṣṣehā-ye Masnavi*, Tehran: Sorush, 1393/2014.
Jāḥiẓ, ʿAmr ibn Baḥr al-, *al-Bukhalāʾ*, ed. Ṭāhā al-Ḥājirī, Cairo: Dār al-Maʿārif, 1981.
Jāḥiẓ, ʿAmr ibn Baḥr al-, *Kitāb al-Ḥayawān*, ed. ʿAbd al-Salām Muḥammad Hārūn, 3rd ed., 7 vols., Beirut: al-Majmaʿ al-ʿilmī al-ʿarabī al-islāmī, 1388/1969.
Jahn, Samia al Azharia, *Arabische Volksmärchen*, Berlin: Akademie-Verlag, 1970.
Jahn, Ulrich, *Volksmärchen aus Pommern und Rügen*, Norden: Soltau, 1891.
Jakob, Ulrich, transl., *Die hundert alten Erzählungen*, Leipzig: Deutsche Verlags-Actiengesellschaft, 1905.
Jāmeʿ al-ḥekāyāt see Jaʿfari Qanavāti; Khadish and Jaʿfari (Qanavāti)
Jāmi, Nur al-Din ʿAbd al-Raḥmān ibn Aḥmad, *Masnavi-ye Haft owrang*, ed. Mortażā Modarres Gilāni, Tehran: Saʿdi, 1337/1958.
Jarisch, Hieronymus Anton, *Heimatsklänge: Gedichte in der Mundart der Deutschen in verschiedenen Gegenden Nordböhmens und des Egerlandes, dann in Mähren, Schlesien und Sachsen*, Warnsdorf: Ambr. Opitz, 1910.
Jarník, Jan Urban, "Albanesische Märchen und Schwänke," *Zeitschrift für Volkskunde in Sage und Mär* 2 (1890), pp. 421–424; 3 (1891), pp. 296–298.
Jason, Heda, "Types of Jewish-Oriental Oral Tales," *Fabula* 7 (1964–1965), pp. 115–224.
Jason, Heda, *Folktales of the Jews of Iraq: Tale-Types and Genres*, Or Yehuda: Babylonian Jewry Heritage Center, 1988.
Jason, Heda, *Types of Oral Tales in Israel*, Jerusalem: Israel Ethnographic Society, 1975.
Javādi, Seyyid Kamāl Ḥājj Seyyid, ed., *Ḥekāyāt-e laṭif*, Tehran: Kavir, 1375/1996.
Jech, Jaromir, *Tschechische Volksmärchen*, Berlin: Rütten & Loening, 1961, pp. 413–417, no. 49.
Jegerlehner, Johannes, *Sagen und Märchen aus dem Oberwallis*, Basel: Helbig & Lichtenhahn, 1913.
Jiménez Roberto, Alfonso, *La flor de la florentena: cuentos tradicionales*, ed. Melchor Pérez Bautista and Juan Antonio del Río Cabrera, Sevilla: Fundación Machado, 1990.
Jinaratna, *The Epitome of Queen Līlāvatī*, vol. 1, ed. and transl. Richard C.C. Fynes, New York: New York University Press, 2005.
Joe Miller's Complete Jest Book (1859).
Joe Miller's Jests, London: T. Read, 1739; 4th ed. (1740); 8th ed. (1745); 12th ed. (1750).
Joe Miller's Jests, London: Whittaker and Co., 1836.
Joe Miller's Jests, new ed., London: T. Axtel [1775].
Joisten, Charles, *Contes populaires de l'Ariège*, Paris: Maisonneuve et Larose, 1965.
Joisten, Charles, *Contes populaires du Dauphiné*, 2 vols., Grenoble: Musée Dauphinois, 1971.
Jones, H.S.V., "Some Observations upon the Squire's Tale," *Publications of the Modern Language Association* 20.2 (1905), pp. 346–359.
Jones, H.S.V., "The Cléomadès and Related Folktales," *Publications of the Modern Language Association* 23.4 (1908), pp. 577–598.
Jones, H.S.V., "The Cléomadès, the Méliacin, and the Arabian Tale of the 'Enchanted Horse'," *The Journal of English and Germanic Philology* 6.2 (1907), pp. 221–243.
Jones, Steven S., "'The Rarest Thing in the World:' Indo-European or African?" *Research in African Literature* 7 (1976), pp. 200–210; also in Crowley, Daniel J., ed., *African Folklore in the New World*, Austin: University of Texas Press, 1977, pp. 54–64.

Jones, W. Henry, and Lajos L. Kropf, *The Folk-tales of the Magyars*, London: Stock, 1889.
Joos, Amaat, *Vertelsels van het Vlaamsche volk*, 2 vols., Brugge: Standaard, 1889–1890.
Joret, Charles, *La Rose dans l'Antiquité et au Moyen Age: histoire, légendes et symbolisme*, Paris: Emile Bouillon, 1892.
Jorgensen, Jeana, "Erotic Tales," in Duggan, Anne E., and Donald Haase, eds., *Folktales and Fairy Tales*, Santa Barbara, CA: Greenwood, 2016, vol. 1, pp. 303–305.
Jospe, Raphael, and Yonatan Milo, "God Willing: *Im Yirzeh Hashem—In Sha Allah*," *The Review of Rabbinic Judaism* 16 (2013), pp. 1–27.
Juḥā, *Hādhihi nawādir al-khūjah Naṣr al-Dīn Afandī Juḥā al-Rūmī*, Būlāq: Mūsā Kāstillī, 1278/1861.
Julien, A. "Anecdotes and Bons-Mots from a Chinese Book Entitled Siao Li Siao," *The Asiatic Journal* (October 1824), pp. 363–365.
Julien, Stanislas Aignan, "Contes et bon mots extraits d'un livre chinois titulé Siao li Siao," *Journal Asiatique* 4 (1824), pp. 100–104.
Julien, Stanislas, *The Avadanas: contes et apologues Indiens inconnus jusqu' à ce jour suivis de fables et de poésies Chinoises*, 3 vols., Paris: Duprat, 1859–1860.
Jungbauer, Gustav, *Das Volk erzählt: Sudetendeutsche Sagen, Märchen und Schwänke*, Karlsbad and Leipzig: Adam Kraft, 1943.
Jurkschat, Christoph, *Litauische Märchen und Erzählungen*, Heidelberg: Winter, 1898.
Kabashnikau, Kanstantin P., *Kazki i legendi rodnaga krayu*, Minsk: Akad., 1960.
Kabbani, Sam, *Altarabische Eseleien: Humor aus dem frühen Islam*, Herrenalb: Horst Erdmann, 1965.
Kapełus, Helena, and Julian Krzyzanowski, *Sto baśni ludowych*, Warsaw, 1957.
Kapfhammer, Günther, *Bayerische Schwänke "dastunka und dalogn,"* Düsseldorf: Diederichs, 1974.
Kaplanoglou, Marianthi, "Wörtlich nehmen," in *Enzyklopädie des Märchens*, vol. 14 (2014), pp. 995–1003.
Karadžić, Vuk Stefanović, *Srpske narodne pripovetke*, 4th ed., Belgrade, 1937.
Karlinger, Felix, *Das Feigenkörbchen: Volksmärchen aus Sardinien*, Kassel: Röth, 1973.
Karlinger, Felix, *Inselmärchen des Mittelmeeres*, Düsseldorf: Diederichs, 1960.
Karlinger, Felix, and Ovidiu Bîrlea, *Rumänische Volksmärchen*, Düsseldorf: Diederichs, 1969.
Karlinger, Felix, and Gertrude Gréciano, *Provenzalische Märchen*, Düsseldorf: Diederichs, 1974.
Karlinger, Felix, and Bohdan Mykytiuk, *Legendenmärchen aus Europa*, Düsseldorf: Diederichs, 1967.
Karlinger, Felix, and Johannes Pögl, *Märchen aus der Karibik*, Cologne: Diederichs, 1983.
Kasprzyk, Krystyna, *Nicolas de Troyes et le genre narratif en France au XVIe siècle*, Warsaw: Państwowe Wydawnictwo Naukowe, and Paris: Klincksieck, 1963.
Katona, Louis, "Le bel homme trompé par sa femme," *Revue des traditions populaires* 4 (1889), pp. 44–46.
Katrinaki, Manouela, "Schwester: Die menschenfressende S.," in *Enzyklopädie des Märchens*, vol. 12 (2007), cols. 428–431.
Kazis, Israel J., *The Book of the Gests of Alexander of Macedon/Sefer Toledot Alexandros ha-Makdoni: A Medieval Hebrew Version of the Alexander Romance by Immanuel Ben Jacob Bonfils*, Cambridge, MA: The Mediaeval Academy of America, 1962.
Keightley, Thomas, *Tales and Popular Fictions; Their Resemblance and Transmission from Country to Country*, London: Whittaker & Co, 1884.

Keller, Walter, *Italienische Märchen*, Jena: Diederichs, 1929.
Kerbelytė, Bronislava, *Lietuvių liaudies padavimų katalogas*, Vilnius: Lietuvos TSR Moksl ų Akad., 1973.
Kerbelytė, Bronislava, *Litauische Volksmärchen*, Berlin: Akademie-Verlag, 1978.
Khadish, Pegāh, and Moḥammad Ja'fari (Qanavāti), eds., *Jāme' al-ḥekāyāt bar asās-i noskhe-ye Āstān-i qods-i Rażavi*, Tehran: Māzyār, 1390/2011.
Khālidī, Abū Bakr Muḥammad ibn Hāshim al- and Abū 'Uthmān Sa'īd ibn Hāshim al- (known as al-Khālidīyān, i.e. the two Khālidīs), *al-Tuḥaf wa-'l-hidāyā*, ed. Sāmī al-Dahhān, Cairo: Dār al-Ma'ārif, 1956.
Khaṭīb al-Baghdādī, Abū Bakr Aḥmad ibn 'Alī al-, *al-Bukhalā'*, ed. Aḥmad al-Maṭlūb, Khadīja al-Ḥadīthī, and Aḥmad Nājī al-Qaysī, Baghdad: Maṭba'at al-'Ānī, 1384/1964.
Khaṭīb al-Baghdādī, Abū Bakr Aḥmad ibn 'Alī al-, *al-Taṭfīl wa-ḥikāyāt al-ṭufaylīyīn wa-akhbārihim wa-nawādir kalāmihim wa-ash'ārihim*, ed. Kāẓim al-Muẓaffar, al-Najaf: al-Maktaba al-ḥaydariyya, 1386/1966.
Khaṭīb al-Baghdādī, Abū Bakr Aḥmad ibn 'Alī al-, *Tārīkh Baghdād*, 14 vols., Cairo: Maktabat al-Khānjī, 1931.
Khaṭīb al-Baghdādī, Abū Bakr Aḥmad ibn 'Alī al-, see also Ḫaṭīb al-Baġdādī, al-.
Khatib al-Baghdadi, al-, *Selections from The Art of Party-Crashing in Medieval Iraq*, transl. Emily Selove, Syracuse, NY: Syracuse University Press, 2012.
Khayyat, Latif, "The Style and Contents of Arabic Folk Material in Chapbooks in the New York Public Library," *Fabula* 28 (1987), pp. 59–71.
Kiefer, Emma Emily, *Albert Wesselski and Recent Folktale Theories*, Bloomington: Indiana University Press, 1947.
Kilpatrick, Hilary, *Making the Great Book of Songs: Compilation and the Author's Craft in Abū l-Faraj al-Iṣbahānī's Kitāb al-aghānī*, London: Routledge Curzon, 2003.
Kindl, Ulrike, *Märchen aus den Dolomiten*, Munich: Diederichs, 1992.
Kirby, Thomas A., "'The Pardoner's Tale' and 'The Treasure of the Sierra Madre'," *Modern Language Notes* 66 (1951), pp. 269–270.
Kirchhof, Hans Wilhelm, *Wendunmuth*, ed. Hermann Österley, 5 vols., Tübingen: Laupp, 1869
Kisā'ī, Muḥammad ibn 'Abdallāh al-, *Qiṣaṣ al-anbiyā'*, ed. Isaac Eisenberg, Leiden: Brill, 1922.
Kisā'ī, Muḥammad ibn 'Abdallāh al-, *The Tales of the Prophets*, transl. W.M. Thackston, Boston: Twayne, 1978.
Kishtainy, Khalid, *Arab Political Humour*, London: Quartet Books, 1985.
Kitāb Ẓarīf al-ma'ānī fī 'l-ḥawādīt wa-'l-aghānī, Miṣr: Maktabat Aḥmad 'Alī al-Malījī, [1910].
Knoop, Otto, *Ostmärkische Sagen, Märchen und Erzählungen*, Lissa i. P.: Eulitz, 1909.
Knoop, Otto, *Sagen und Erzählungen aus der Provinz Posen*, Posen, 1893.
Knoop, Otto, *Volkssagen, Erzählungen, Aberglauben, Gebräuche und Märchen aus dem östlichen Hinterpommern*, Posen: Jolowitz, 1885.
Koen Sarano, Matilda, *Djoha ke dize? Kuentos populares djudeo espanyoles*, Jerusalem: Kana, 1991.
Koén-Sarano, Matilda, *Folktales of Joha: Jewish Trickster*, Philadelphia: The Jewish Publication Society, 2003.

Koen-Sarano, Matilda, *Kuentos del folklor de la famiya djudeo-espanyola*, Jerusalem: Kana, 1986.

Kofod, Else Marie, "Kristensen, Evald Tang," in *Enzyklopädie des Märchens*, vol. 8 (1996), cols. 468–471.

Köhler, Reinhold, "Zu der Erzählung Adams von Cobsam 'The Wright's Chaste Wife'," *Jahrbuch für romanische und englische Litteratur* 8 (1867), pp. 44–65.

Köhler, Reinhold, *Kleinere Schriften zur erzählenden Dichtung des Mittelalters*, ed. Johannes Bolte, Berlin: Emil Felber, 1900.

Köhler, Reinhold, *Kleinere Schriften zur Märchenforschung*, ed. Johannes Bolte, Berlin: Emil Felber, 1900.

Köhler, Ines, and Rudolf Schenda, "Alexander der Große," in *Enzyklopädie des Märchens*, vol. 1 (1977), cols. 272–291.

Köhler-Zülch, Ines, "Imitation: Fatale und närrische I.," in *Enzyklopädie des Märchens*, vol. 7 (1993), cols. 92–100.

Köhler-Zülch, Ines, "Krauss, Friedrich Salomo," in *Enzyklopädie des Märchens*, vol. 8 (1996), cols. 352–358.

Köhler-Zülch, Ines, "Schuhe: Die zertanzten S.," in *Enzyklopädie des Märchens*, vol. 12 (2008), cols. 221–227.

Köhler-Zülch, Ines, "Zigeuner, Zigeunerin," in *Enzyklopädie des Märchens*, vol. 14 (2014), cols. 1345–1358.

Konkka, Unelma Semenovna, *Karel'skie narodnye skazki*, Moscow: Izdatel'stvo Akademii Nauk SSSR, 1963.

Kooi, Jurjen van der, "Een rechter tie-zaak in Drenthe. Chinese volksverhalen in hest westen; een probleemveld," *Driemaandelijkse Bladen voor taal en volksleven in hest oosten van Nederland* 39 (1987), pp. 133–157.

Kooi, Jurjen van der, and Theo Schuster, *Märchen und Schwänke aus Ostfriesland*, Leer: Schuster, 1993.

Köstlin, Konrad, "Kriegslist," in *Enzyklopädie des Märchens*, vol. 8 (1996), cols. 436–440.

Kovács, Ágnes, *König Mátyás und die Rátóter: Ungarische Schildbürgerschwänke und Anekdoten*, Leipzig: Kiepenheuer, 1988.

Kovács, Agnes, *Ungarische Volksmärchen*, Düsseldorf: Diederichs, 1966.

Krauss, Friedrich Salomo, "Folklore de l'Ukraine: Usages, contes et légendes, chansons, proverbes et jurons," *Kryptádia* 8 (1902), pp. 303–398.

Krauss, Friedrich S., "Südslavische Volksüberlieferungen, die sich auf den Geschlechtsverkehr beziehen, 1: Erzählungen," *Anthropophyteia* 1 (1904), pp. 1–506; 2 (1905), pp. 265–439.

Kristensen, Evald Tang, *Aeventyr fra Jylland*, 4 vols., Copenhagen: Gyldendal, 1881–1897.

Kristensen, Evald Tang, *Molbo- og aggerbohistorier samt andre dermed beslægtede fortællinger*, 2 vols., Viborg: backhausen, 1892, and Århus: Forfatterens Forlag, 1903.

Kristensen, Evald Tang, *Vore fædres Kirketjeneste: belyst ved exempler, optegnede efter folkemunde*, Århus: Forfatterns Forlag, 1899.

Krohn, Kaarle, *Übersicht über einige Resultate der Märchenforschung*, Helsinki: Suomalainen Tiedeakatemia, 1931.

Krönung, Bettina, "The Wisdom of the Beasts: The Arabic *Book of Kalīla and Dimna* and the Byzantine *Book of Stephanites and Ichnelates*," in Cupane, Carolina, and Bettina

Krönung, eds., *Fictional Storytelling in the Medieval Eastern Mediterranean World and beyond*, Berlin: De Gruyter, 2016.
Krzyżanowski, Julian, *Polska bajka ludowa w układzie systematycznym*, 2 vols., Polska Akad. Nauk. Wydz. Nauk Społecznych, 1963.
Kubitschek, Rudolf, *Böhmerwäldler Bauernschwänke*, Vienna: Strache, 1920.
Kuder, Ulrich, "Haar, Haare," in *Enzyklopädie des Märchens*, vol. 6 (1990), cols. 337–343.
Kügler, Hermann, *Hohenzollernsagen*, Leipzig-Gohlis: Hermann Eichblatt, 1922.
Kühne, Udo, "Johannes von Capua," in *Enzyklopädie des Märchens*, vol. 7 (1993), cols. 580–583.
Kuka, Meherjibhai Nosherwanji, *The Wit and Humor of the Persians*, Bombay 1894.
Kuka, Meherjibhai Nosherwanji, *The Wit, Humour and Fancy of Persia*, new impression, Bombay 1937.
Kúnos, Ignaz, *Türkische Volksmärchen aus Stambul*, Leiden: Brill, 1905.
Künzig, Johannes, and Werner-Künzig, Waltraut, eds., *Lied- und Erzählgut der Resi Klemm aus Almáskamarás im ungarischen Banat. Authentische Tonaufnahmen 1952–1961*, Freiburg 1980.
Kushelevsky, Rella, *Tales in Context: Sefer ha ma'asim in Medieval Northern France*, Detroit: Wayne State University Press, 2017.
Kut, Günay, "Nasreddin Hoca Hikâyeleri Yazmalarının Kolları Üzerine Bir Deneme," in *IV. Milletlerarası Türk Halk Kültürü Kongresi Bildirileri*, vol. 3: *Halk Edebiyatı*, Ankara, 1992, pp. 147–200.
Kvideland, Reimund, "Gläubiger: Die drei G.," in *Enzyklopädie des Märchens*, vol. 5 (1987), cols. 1274–1276.
Kvideland, Reimund, and Hallfreður Örn, *Norwegische und isländische Volksmärchen*, Berlin: Akademie-Verlag, 1988.
"Labours of the Asiatic Society of Paris," *The Oriental Herald* 4 (April–June 1825), pp. 389–398.
Lacarra Ducay, María Jesús, "Petrus Alfonsus," in *Enzyklopädie des Märchens*, vol. 10 (2002), cols. 797–802.
Lacarra, María Jesús, "El adoctrinamiento de los jóvenes en El conde Lucanor," *e-Spania* 21 (June 2015).
Lacarra, María Jesús, "Entre el Libro de los engaños y los Siete visire: las mil y una caras del Sendebar árabe," in *Les Mille et une nuits et le récit oriental en Espagne et en Occident*, ed. Aboubakr Chraïbi and Carmen Ramirez, Paris: L'Harmattan, 2009, pp. 51–73.
Lacarra, María Jesús, "'The Enchanted Pear Tree' in Hispanic Tradition," in Bendix, Regina F., and Dorothy Noyes, eds., *Terra Ridens—Terra Narrans: Festschrift zum 65. Geburtstag von Ulrich Marzolph*, Dortmund: Verlag für Orientkunde, 2018, pp. 194–211..
Lacarra, María Jesús, *Cuento y novela corta en España*, Barcelona: Crítica, 1999.
Lacarra Ducay, María Jesús, *Cuentos de la edad media*, Madrid: Castalia, 1986.
Lacarra Ducay, María Jesús, *Cuentos medievales: de Oriente a Occidente*, Madrid: Fundación José Antonio de Castro, 2016.
Lacarra, María Jesús, *Don Juan Manuel*, Madrid: Síntesis, 2006.
Lackner, Irmgard, "Barlaam and Josaphat," in *Enzyklopädie des Märchens*, vol. 1 (1977), cols. 1243–1252.
Lacoste-Dujardin, Camille, "Basset, René," in *Enzyklopädie des Märchens*, vol. 1 (1977), cols. 1319–1322.

La Fontaine, *Oeuvres complètes*, 2 vols., ed. Jean-Pierre Collinet, Paris: Gallimard, 1991.
Lambert, Louis, *Contes populaires du Languedoc*, Montpellier: Coulet, 1899 (reprint Carcassonne: Garae, 1985).
Lang-Reitstätter, Maria, *Lachendes Österreich: Österreichischer Volkshumor*, 2nd ed., Salzburg: Österreichischer Kulturverlag, 1948.
Laport, George, *Les contes populaires wallons*, Helsinki: Suomalainen Tiedeakatemia, 1932.
Larzul, Sylvette, "Further Considerations on Galland's Mille et une Nuits: A Study of the Tales Told by Hanna," in Marzolph, Ulrich, ed., *The Arabian Nights in Transnational Perspective*, Detroit: Wayne State University Press, 2007, pp. 16–31.
Larzul, Sylvette, "Les Mille et une Nuits de Galland ou l'acclimation d'une 'belle etrangère'", *Revue de littérature comparée* 69 (1995), pp. 309–323.
Larzul, Sylvette, *Les traductions françaises des Mille et une nuits: Étude des versions Galland, Trebutien et Mardrus*, Paris: L'Harmattan, 1996.
Laskaya, Anne, and Eve Salisbury, *The Middle English Breton Lays* (1995), http://d.lib.rochester.edu/teams/text/laskaya-and-salisbury-middle-english-breton-lays-sir-cleges-introduction (accessed January 31, 2018).
Laut, Jens Peter, "Jātaka," in *Enzyklopädie des Märchens*, vol. 7 (1993), cols. 500–507.
Laveaux, Jean Charles Thibaut de, *Vie De Frederic II., Roi De Prusse: Accompagnée d'un grand nombre de Remarques, Pièces justificatives & Anecdotes, dont la plupart n'ont point encore été publiées*, 4 vols., Strasbourg: Treuttel, 1787.
Lazarillo de Tormes see Ricapito, Joseph V.
Leclerf, Jean, "The Dream in Popular Culture: Arabic and Islamic," in *The Dream and Human Societies*, ed. Gustav Edmund van Grunebaum and Roger Caillois, Berkeley: University of California Press, 1966, pp. 364–380.
Lecouteux, Claude, "Herzog Ernst," in *Enzyklopädie des Märchens*, vol. 6 (1990), cols. 939–942.
Lecouteux, Claude, "Magnetberg," in *Enzyklopädie des Märchens*, vol. 9 (1999), cols. 24–27.
Lecoy, Félix, "La Farce de Cauteleux, Baras, et le Villain," in *Mélanges de langue et littérature du moyen âge et de la Renaissance offerts à Jean Frappier*, vol. 2, Bern: Droz, pp. 595–602; also in Lecoy, *Mélanges de philologie et de littérature romanes*, Geneva: Droz, 1988, pp. 584 [409]–601 [416].
Legman, Gershon, *Rationale of the Dirty Joke: An Analysis of Sexual Humor*, 2 vols., New York: Breaking Point, 1975.
Lehmann, Christoph, *Exilium melancholiae*, Straßburg: Lazari Zetzners Erben, 1643.
Leland, Charles Godfrey, *Etruscan Roman Remains in Popular Tradition*, New York: Charles Scribner's Sons, 1892.
Lemieux, Germain, *Les vieux m'ont conté*, 33 vols., Montréal: Bellarmin, 1973–1993.
Leps, Marie-Christine, *Apprehending the Criminal: The Production of Deviance in Nineteenth-century Discourse*, Durham, NC: Duke University Press, 1992.
Lerner, Amir, "Two Amalgamated Ancient Bird Fables in Classical Arabic Literature and Their Shape in Later Popular Prose Tradition: A Comparative Study and Critical Edition," *Al-Qantara* 39.2 (2018), pp. 321–351.
Lerner, Amir, *The* Juʿaydiyya *Cycle: Witty Beggars' Stories from the "Montague Manuscript"—A Late Augmented* Arabian Nights, Dortmund: Verlag für Orientkunde, 2014.
Leṭāʾif-i Hoca Naṣreddin, Istanbul 1253/1837.
Lévi, Israel, "Contes juifs," *Revue des études juives* 11 (1885), pp. 209–234.

Lewis, Frank, "One Chaste Muslim Maiden and a Persian in a Pear Tree: Analogues of Boccaccio and Chaucer in Four Earlier Arabic and Persian Tales," in *Metaphor and Imagery in Persian Poetry*, ed. Ali Asghar Seyed-Gohrab, Leiden: Brill, 2012, pp. 173–203.

Lewis, Frank, "The Tale of the Righteous Woman (Whose Husband Had Gone on a Journey)," in *Converging Zones: Persian Literary Tradition and the Writing of History, Studies in Honor of Amin Banani*, ed. Wali Ahmadi, Costa Mesa, CA: Mazda, 2012.

Lewis, Franklin, "A Persian in a Pear Tree: Middle Eastern Analogues for Pirro/Pyrrhus," in *Reconsidering Boccaccio: Medieval Contexts and Global Intertexts*, ed. Olivia Holmes and Dana E. Stewart, Toronto: University of Toronto Press, 2018, pp. 305–343.

Lewis, William Stanley, ed., *The Yale Edition of Horace Walpole's Correspondence*, vol. 20: *Horace Walpole's Correspondence with Sir Horace Mann*, New Haven: Yale University Press, 1960.

Lida de Malkiel, María Rosa, "Función del cuento popular en el Lazarillo de Tormes," *Primer Congreso Internacional de Hispanistas, Oxford 1962: Actas*, ed. Frank Pierce and Cyril A. Jones, Madrid 1964, pp. 349–359.

Lidzbarski, Mark, "Ein Desideratum," *Der Islam* 8 (1918), pp. 300–301.

Lidzbarski, Mark, *Geschichten und Lieder aus den neu-aramäischen Handschriften der Königlichen Bibliothek zu Berlin*, Weimar: Felber, 1896.

Lindahl, Carl, "Kratzverbot," in *Enzyklopädie des Märchens*, vol. 8 (1996), cols. 348–352.

Lindahl, Carl, "Randolph, Vance," in *Enzyklopädie des Märchens*, vol. 11 (2004), cols. 192–194.

Lintur, Petro V., *Ukrainische Volksmärchen*, Berlin: Akademie-Verlag, 1972.

Littmann, Enno, "Alf laila wa-laila," in *Encyclopaedia of Islam*, 2nd ed., vol. 1, Leiden: Brill, 1960, pp. 358–364.

Littmann, Enno, "Hārūt and Mārūt," in *Festschrift für Friedrich Carl Andreas*, Leipzig: Harrassowitz, 1916, pp. 70–87.

Littmann, Enno, *Arabische Märchen und Schwänke aus Ägypten: Nach mündlicher Überlieferung gesammelt, übersetzt und erklärt*, Mainz: Akademie der Wissenschaften und der Literatur, 1955.

Liungman, Waldemar, *Die schwedischen Volksmärchen: Herkunft und Geschichte*, Berlin: Akademie-Verlag, 1961.

Liungman, Waldemar, *Sveriges samtliga folksagor i ord och bild*, 3 vols., Stockholm: Lindfors, 1949–1952.

Liungman, Waldemar, *Weißbär am See: Schwedische Volksmärchen von Bohuslän bis Gotland*, Kassel: Röth, 1965.

Lixfeld, Hannjost, "Alten: Die drei Alten," in *Enzyklopädie des Märchens*, vol. 1 (1977), cols. 383–387.

Lixfeld, Hannjost, "Anthropophyteia," in *Enzyklopädie des Märchens*, vol. 1 (1977), cols. 596–601.

Lixfeld, Hannjost, "Bolte, Johannes," in *Enzyklopädie des Märchens*, vol. 2 (1979), cols. 603–605.

Lixfeld, Hannjost, "Erdenwanderung der Götter," in *Enzyklopädie des Märchens*, vol. 4 (1984), cols. 155–164.

Lixfeld, Hannjost, "Fleischpfand," in *Enzyklopädie des Märchens*, vol. 4 (1984), cols. 1256–1262.

Llull, Ramon, *Selected Works*, ed. and transl. Anthony Bonner, 2 vols., Princeton: Princeton University Press, 1985.

Lombardi Satriani, Raffaele, *Racconti popolari Calabresi*, Naples: De Simone, 1953.
Loorits, Oskar, *Estnische Volkserzählungen*, Berlin: De Gruyter, 1959.
Loosen, Paul, "Tanūchī, seine Art und Kunst," *Zeitschrift für Semitistik und verwandte Gebiete* 10 (1935), pp. 46–73.
López Bernal, Desirée, "De criadas, sisas y gatos: huellas de un cuento folclórico árabe (ATU 1373) en la España de los siglos XIX y XX," *Boletín de Literatura Oral* 8 (2018), pp. 73–96.
López Bernal, Desirée, "Los cuentos de Ibn 'Asim (m. 1426): precedentes en la península ibérica de relatos españoles y del folklore universal en el siglo XV," *Hispanic Review* 85.4 (2017), pp. 419–440.
López Bernal, Desirée, "Los cuentos de Ibn 'Āṣim (m. 1426): precedentes peninsulares de relatos españoles y del folklore universal en el s. XV," *Boletín de literatura oral* 9 (2019), pp. 35–52.
López Bernal, Desirée, "Nuevas versiones literarias de los cuentos tipo ATU 1848 y ATU 1848A en la Península ibérica," *Oceánide* 10 (2017); http://oceanide.netne.net/articulos/art10-4
López Bernal, Desirée, "Procedencia árabe de un cuentecillo singular en la obra de Juan de Robles," *Hipogrifo* 4.1 (2016), pp. 217–230.
López Bernal, Desirée, *Los Ḥadā'iq al-azāhir de Abū Bakr ibn 'Āṣim al-Garnāṭī: Traducción y estudio de una obra de adab de la Granada nazarí*, 2 vols., Ph.D. thesis University of Granada, 2016.
Lorenzo Vélez, Antonio, *Cuentos anticlericales de tradición oral*, Valladolid: Ámbito, 1997.
Losensky, Paul, *Farid al-din 'Aṭṭār's Memorial of God's Friends: Lives and Sayings of Sufis*, New York: Paulist Press, 2009.
Loukatos, Demetrios, *Neoellēnika laographika keimena*, Athens: Zakharopulos, 1957.
Lowry, Joseph E., and Devin J. Stewart, eds., *Essays in Arabic Literary Biography, 1350–1850*, Wiesbaden: Harrassowitz, 2009.
Lox, Harlinda, "Schneider mit der Lappenfahne," in *Enzyklopädie des Märchens*, vol. 12 (2007), cols. 149–152.
Lox, Harlinda, "Sidi Numan," in *Enzyklopädie des Märchens*, vol. 12 (2008), cols. 642–645.
Lox, Harlinda, *Flämische Märchen*, Munich: Diederichs, 1999.
Lox, Harlinda, *Van stropdragers en de pot van Olen: Verhalen over Keizer Karel*, Leuven: Davidsfonds/Literair, 1999.
Lozar, Angelika, "Leben am seidenen Faden," in *Enzyklopädie des Märchens*, vol. 8 (1996), cols. 813–815.
Lucian: With an English translation by M.D. MacLeod, vol. 8, Cambridge, MA: Harvard University Press, 1967.
Lulio, Raymundo, *Libro Felix, o maravillas del mundo*, 2 vols., Mallorca: Audiencia, 1750.
Lull, Ramon, *Felix oder Das Buch der Wunder*, transl. Gret Schib Torra, Basel: Schwabe, 2007.
Lull, Ramón, *Llibre de meravelles*, vol. 1: *Llibres I–VII*, ed. Lola Badia, Palma: Patronat Ramon Llull, 2011.
Lull, Ramón, *Obras*, 4 vols., ed. Jerónimo Rosselló, Palma de Mallorca, 1903.
Lundt, Bea, "Sieben weise Meister," in *Enzyklopädie des Märchens*, vol. 12 (2008), cols. 654–660.
Lüthi, Max, "Blindes Motiv," in *Enzyklopädie des Märchens*, vol. 2 (1979), cols. 469–471.
Luyster, Amanda, "The Conversion of Kalila and Dimna: Raymond de Béziers,

Religious Experience, and Translation at the Fourteenth-Century French Court," *Gesta* 56.1 (2017), pp. 81–104.
Maaz, Wolfgang, "Hildegardis," in *Enzyklopädie des Märchens*, vol. 6 (1990), cols. 1017–1021.
Mac Giollarnáth, Seán, "Trí sgéal ar an sionnach," *Béaloideas* 2.1 (1929), pp. 90–94.
MacColl, Ewan, and Peggy Seeger, *Till Doomsday in the Afternoon: The Folklore of a Family of Scots Travellers, the Stewarts of Blairgowrie*, Manchester: Manchester University Press, 1986.
MacDonald, Duncan B., "The Earlier History of the Arabian Nights," *Journal of the Royal Asiatic Society* (1924), pp. 353–397.
Maennersdoerfer, Maria Christa, "Wanderer: Die beiden W.," in *Enzyklopädie des Märchens*, vol. 14 (2014), cols. 476–483.
Magnus, Olaus, *Historia de gentibus septentrionalibus*, ed. Peter Foote, 3 vols., London: Hakluyt Society, 1996–1998.
Mahdi, Muhsin, ed., *The Thousand and One Nights (Alf Layla wa-Layla) from the Earliest Known Sources*, 3 vols., Leiden; Brill, 1884–1994.
Majerus, Benoît, "Vorstellungen von der Besetzung Belgiens, Luxemburgs und der Niederlande (1933–1944), in *Der Zweite Weltkrieg in Europa: Erfahrung und Erinnerung*, ed. Jörg Echternkamp and Stefan Markens, Paderborn: Ferdinand Schöningh, 2007, pp. 35–43.
Malcolm, John, *Kisseh-Khūn: der persische Erzähler*, Berlin: Nicolai'sche Buchhandlung, 1829.
Malcolm, John, *Sketches of Persia*, London: Murray, 1845.
Malti-Douglas, Fedwa, "Structure and Organization in a Monographic Adab Work: al-Taṭfīl of al-Khaṭīb al-Baghdādī," *Journal of Near Eastern Studies* 40 (1981), pp. 227–245.
Malti-Douglas, Fedwa, *Men, Women, and God(s): Nawal El Saadawi and Arab Feminist Poetics*, Berkeley: University of California Press, 1995.
Malti-Douglas, Fedwa, *Structures of Avarice: The Bukhalāʾ in Medieval Arabic Literature*, Leiden: E.J. Brill, 1985.
Malti-Douglas, Fedwa, *Woman's Body, Woman's Word: Gender and Discourse in Arabo-Islamic Writing*, Princeton: Princeton Universit Press, 1991.
Mangione, Jerre, *Mount Allegro: A Memoir of Italian American Life*, New York: Harper & Row, 1981, pp. 141–151.
Maqarrī, Aḥmad ibn Muḥammad al-, *Nafḥ al-ṭīb min ghuṣn al-Andalus al-raṭīb*, ed. Iḥsān ʿAbbās, 8 vols., Beirut: Dār Ṣādir, 1388/1968.
Mardrus, Joseph Charles Victor, *Le livre des Mille et une Nuits*, 16 vols., Paris: La Revue Blanche, 1899–1904.
Margoliouth, D.S., "Review of Deliverance after Stress (Al-Faraj baʿd al-shiddah) by Abu ʿAlī Al-Muḥassin Al-Tanūkhī [...]," *Journal of the Royal Asiatic Society of Great Britain and Ireland* (1905), pp. 51–72.
Marie de France, *Fables*, ed. and transl. Harriet Spiegel, Toronto: University of Toronto Press, 1987.
Marmorstein, Abraham, "Das Motiv vom veruntreuten Depositum in der jüdischen Volkskunde," *Monatsschrift für Geschichte und Wissenschaft des Judentums* (1934), pp. 183–195.
Marzocchi, Ciro, *Novelle popolari senesi: raccolte da Ciro Marzocchi, 1978*, ed. Aurora Milillo, Gabriella Aiello, and Florio Carnasecchi, vol. 1, Rome: Bulzoni, 1992.
Marzolph, Ulrich, "A Scholar in the Making: Antoine Galland's Early Travel Diaries

(1672–73) in the Light of Comparative Folk Narrative Research," *Middle Eastern Literatures* 18.3 (2015), pp. 283–300.
Marzolph, Ulrich, "An Early Persian Precursor to the Tales of Sindbād the Seafaring Merchant," *Zeitschrift der Deutschen Morgenländischen Gesellschaft* 167 (2017), pp. 127–141.
Marzolph, Ulrich, "'Ceci n'est point une fable:' Tale Type ATU 63, *The Fox Rids Himself of Fleas*, from Popular Tradition to Natural History (and Back Again)," in *Contexts of Folklore: Festschrift for Dan Ben-Amos*, ed. Simon Bronner and Wolfgang Mieder, Frankfurt: Lang, 2019, pp. 193–204.
Marzolph, Ulrich, "Crescentia's Oriental Relatives: The 'Tale of the Pious Man and His Chaste Wife' in the *Arabian Nights* and the Sources of *Crescentia* in Near Eastern Narrative Tradition," *Marvels & Tales* 22.2 (2008), pp. 240–258, 299–311.
Marzolph, Ulrich, "Das Aladdin-Syndrom: Zur Phänomenologie des narrativen Orientalismus," in *Hören, Sagen, Lesen, Lernen: Bausteine zu einer Geschichte der kommunikativen Kultur, Festschrift für Rudolf Schenda*, ed. Ursula Brunold-Bigler and Hermann Bausinger, Bern: Lang, 1995, pp. 449–462.
Marzolph, Ulrich, "Das Haus ohne Essen und Trinken: Arabische und persische Belege zu Mot. J 2483," *Fabula* 24 (1983), pp. 215–222.
Marzolph, Ulrich, "Das *Kitāb Laṭāʾif aḫbār al-uwal* des -Isḥāqī als Quelle der Kompilatoren von *1001 Nacht*," in *Orientalistische Studien zu Sprache und Literatur: Festschrift Werner Diem*, ed. Ulrich Marzolph, Wiesbaden: Harrassowitz, 2011, pp. 317–328.
Marzolph, Ulrich, "Der Orient in uns: Die Europa-Debatte aus Sicht der orientalistischen Erzählforschung," *Österreichische Zeitschrift für Geschichtswissenschaft* 15.4 (2004), pp. 9–26.
Marzolph, Ulrich, "Die Quelle der Ergötzlichen Erzählungen des Bar Hebräus," *Oriens Christianus* 69 (1985), pp. 81–125.
Marzolph, Ulrich, "'Erlaubter Zeitvertreib': Die Anekdotensammlungen des Ibn al-Ǧauzī," *Fabula* 32 (1991), pp. 165–180.
Marzolph, Ulrich, "Fable," in *Encyclopaedia of Islam*, 3rd ed., Leiden: Brill, 2016, fasc. 1, pp. 100–106.
Marzolph, Ulrich, "'Focusees' of Jocular Fiction in Classical Arabic Literature," in *Story-telling in the Framework of Non-fictional Arabic Literature*, ed. Stefan Leder, Wiesbaden: Harrassowitz, 1998, pp. 118–129.
Marzolph, Ulrich, "Geiz, Geizhals," in *Enzyklopädie des Märchens*, vol. 5 (1987), cols. 948–957.
Marzolph, Ulrich, "Grimm Nights: Reflections on the Connections Between the Grimms' *Household Tales* and the *1001 Nights*," *Marvels & Tales* 28.1 (2014), pp. 75–87.
Marzolph, Ulrich, "Ḥannā Diyāb's Unpublished Tales: The Storyteller as an Artist in His Own Right," in Bauden, Frédéric, and Richard Waller, eds., *Antoine Galland (1646–1715) et son Journal*, Louvain: Peeters, 2019, pp. 75–92.
Marzolph, Ulrich, "Hārūn al-Rašīd," in *Enzyklopädie des Märchens*, vol. 6 (1990), cols. 534–537.
Marzolph, Ulrich, "Hasan von Basra," in *Enzyklopädie des Märchens*, vol. 6 (1990), cols. 538–540.
Marzolph, Ulrich, "Häufung des Schreckens," in *Enzyklopädie des Märchens*, vol. 6 (1990), cols. 576–581.
Marzolph, Ulrich, "Ibn al-Ǧauzī," in *Enzyklopädie des Märchens*, vol. 7 (19939, cols. 1–7).

Marzolph, Ulrich, "Ibšīhī," in *Enzyklopädie des Märchens*, vol. 7 (1993), cols. 6–10.
Marzolph, Ulrich, "Illustrated Exemplary Tales: A Nineteenth-Century Edition of the Classical Persian Proverb Collection *Jāmeʿ al-tamsil*," *Proverbium* 16 (1999), pp. 167–191.
Marzolph, Ulrich, "In the Studio of the Nights," *Middle Eastern Literatures* 17.1 (2014), pp. 43–57.
Marzolph, Ulrich, "Jenseits von '1001 Nacht': Blütenlesen aus den orientalischen Literaturen um 1800," *Blütenstaub: Jahrbuch für Frühromantik* 2 (2009), pp. 39–50.
Marzolph, Ulrich, "Juḥā," in *The Encyclopaedia of Islam*, 3rd ed., Leiden: Brill, 2017, fasc. 5, pp. 139–141.
Marzolph, Ulrich, "Katze: Die gewogene K.," in *Enzyklopädie des Märchens*, vol. 7 (1993), cols. 1109–1111.
Marzolph, Ulrich, "Katze mit der Kerze," in *Enzyklopädie des Märchens*, vol. 7 (1993), cols. 1113–1117.
Marzolph, Ulrich, "Katze mit der Schelle," in *Enzyklopädie des Märchens*, vol. 7 (1993), cols. 1117–1121.
Marzolph, Ulrich, "Kopf in der Kanne," in *Enzyklopädie des Märchens*, vol. 8 (1996), cols. 257–260.
Marzolph, Ulrich, "Kredit erschwindelt," in *Enzyklopädie des Märchens*, vol. 8 (1996), cols. 375–380.
Marzolph, Ulrich, "Le Conte de l'homme pieux et de son épouse chaste dans les *Mille et une nuits* et les sources de *Crescentia* dans les traditions narratives orientales," in *Medioevo romanzo e orientale. Sulle orme di Shahrazàd: le "Mille e una notte" fra Oriente e Occidente*, VI Colloquio Internazionale, Ragusa, 12–14 ottobre 2006, ed. Mirella Cassarino, Rom: Rubbettino, 2009, pp. 183–191.
Marzolph, Ulrich, "Legman, Gershon," in *Enzyklopädie des Märchens*, vol. 8 (1996), cols. 875–877.
Marzolph, Ulrich, "Lehren: Die drei L. des Vogels," in *Enzyklopädie des Märchens*, vol. 8 (1996), cols. 883–889.
Marzolph, Ulrich, "Les Contes de Hanna," in *les mille et une nuits*, ed. Élodie Bouffard and Anne-Alexandra Joyard, Paris: Institut du Monde Arabe, 2012, pp. 87–91.
Marzolph, Ulrich, "Magie in den *Erzählungen aus Tausendundeiner Nacht*," in *Die Geheimnisse der oberen und der unteren Welt: Magie im Islam zwischen Glaube und Wissenschaft*, ed. Sebastian Günther and Dorothee Pielow, Leiden: Brill, 2018, pp. 403–422.
Marzolph, Ulrich, "Maistre Pathelin im Orient," in *Gottes ist der Orient, Gottes ist der Okzident: Festschrift für Abdoldjavad Falaturi*, ed. Udo Tworuschka, Köln: Böhlau, 1991, pp. 309–312.
Marzolph, Ulrich, "Making Sense of the 'Nights': Intertextual Connections and Narrative Techniques in the 'Thousand and One Nights', *Narrative Culture* 1.2 (2014), pp. 239–258.
Marzolph, Ulrich, "Märchen aus 'Tausendundeine Nacht' in der mündlichen Überlieferung Europas," in *Sichtweisen in der Märchenforschung*, ed. Siegfried Neumann and Christoph Schmitt, Baltmannsweiler: Schneider-Verlag Hohengehren, 2013, pp. 23–41.
Marzolph, Ulrich, "Medieval Knowledge in Modern Reading: A Fifteenth-Century Arabic Encyclopedia of *omni re scibili*," in *Pre-modern Encylopaedic Texts: Proceedings of the Second COMERS Congress, Groningen, 1–4 July 1996*, ed. Peter Binkley, Leiden: Brill, 1997, pp. 407–419.

Marzolph, Ulrich, "Mollā Naṣroddīn in Persia," *Iranian Studies* 28.3–4 (1995), pp. 157–174.
Marzolph, Ulrich, "Müller von Sanssouci," in *Enzyklopädie des Märchens*, vol. 9 (1999), cols. 993–999.
Marzolph, Ulrich, "Naṣr al-dīn Khōdjah," in *The Encyclopaedia of Islam*, 2nd ed., vol. 7, fasc. 129–130 (1992), pp. 1018–1020.
Marzolph, Ulrich, "Nuzhat al-udabā'," in *Enzyklopädie des Märchens*, vol. 10 (2002), cols. 166–169.
Marzolph, Ulrich, "Ochse für fünf Pfennig," in *Enzyklopädie des Märchens*, vol. 10 (2002), cols. 193–196.
Marzolph, Ulrich, "Orientalisches Erzählgut in Europa," in *Enzyklopädie des Märchens*, vol.10 (2002), cols. 362–373.
Marzolph, Ulrich, "Papageienbuch," in *Enzyklopädie des Märchens*, vol. 10 (2002), cols. 526–531.
Marzolph, Ulrich, "Pathelin," in *Enzyklopädie des Märchens*, vol. 10 (2002), cols. 620–624.
Marzolph, Ulrich, "Pension: Die doppelte P.," in *Enzyklopädie des Märchens*, vol. 10 (2002), cols. 709–713.
Marzolph, Ulrich, "Persian Humor in the International Context," in Brookshaw, Dominic Parviz, ed., *Ruse and Wit: The Humorous in Arabic, Persian, and Turkish Narrative*, Boston and Washington, DC: Ilex Foundation, 2012, pp. 33–43.
Marzolph, Ulrich, "Pfarrer mit der feinen Stimme," in *Enzyklopädie des Märchens*, vol. 10 (2002), cols. 887–891.
Marzolph, Ulrich, "Philogelos arabikos: Zum Nachleben der antiken Witzesammlung in der mittelalterlichen arabischen Literatur," *Der Islam* 64 (1987), pp. 185–230; also in Marzolph, *Ex Oriente Fabula: Beiträge zur narrativen Kultur des islamischen Vorderen Orients*, vol. 1, Dortmund: Verlag für Orientkunde, 2005, pp. 57–108.
Marzolph, Ulrich, "'Pleasant Stories in an Easy Style.' Gladwin's Persian Grammar as an Intermediary between Classical and Popular Literature," in *Proceedings of the Second European Conference of Iranian* Studies, ed. Bert G. Fragner, Christa Fragner, Gherardo Gnoli, Roxane Haag-Higuchi, Mauro Maggi, and Paola Orsatti, Rome: Istituto Italiano per il Medio ed Estremo Oriente, 1995, pp. 445–475; also in Marzolph, *Ex Oriente Fabula*, vol. 2, Dortmund: Verlag für Orientkunde, 2006, pp. 96–130.
Marzolph, Ulrich, "Poggio Bracciolini, Giovanni Francesco," in *Enzyklopädie des Märchens*, vol. 10 (2002), col. 1101–1106.
Marzolph, Ulrich, "Prodesse et delectare," in *Enzyklopädie des Märchens*, vol. 14 (2014), cols. 1800–1803.
Marzolph, Ulrich, "Reconsidering the Iranian Sources of a Romanian Political Joke," *Western Folklore* 47 (1988), pp. 212–216.
Marzolph, Ulrich, "Rezept gerettet," in *Enzyklopädie des Märchens*, vol. 11 (2005), cols. 622–625.
Marzolph, Ulrich, "Rumi, Ǧalāloddin," in *Enzyklopädie des Märchens*, vol. 11 (2004), cols. 897–904.
Marzolph, Ulrich, "Schatzfinder morden einander," in *Enzyklopädie des Märchens*, vol. 11 (2004), cols. 1282–1290.
Marzolph, Ulrich, "Spies, Otto," in *Enzyklopädie des Märchens*, vol. 12 (2008), cols. 1048–1051.
Marzolph, Ulrich, "Still the Same Old Jokes: The Continuity of Jocular Tradition in Early Twentieth-Century Egyptian Chapbooks," in *The Other Print Tradition: Essays*

on Chapbooks, Broadsides, and Related Ephemera, ed. Cathy Lynn und Michael J. Preston, New York: Garland, 1995, pp. 161–179.

Marzolph, Ulrich, "Teilung der Eier," in *Enzyklopädie des Märchens*, vol. 13 (2010), cols. 315–319.

Marzolph, Ulrich, "The Arabic Source Text for Galland's *Dormeur eveillé*," *Oriente Moderno* 98 (2019), pp. 1–32.

Marzolph, Ulrich, "The *Hundred and One Nights*: A Recently Acquired Old Manuscript," in *Treasures of the Aga Khan Museum: Arts of the Book & Calligraphy* (Exhibition Catalogue), ed. Margaret S. Graves and Benoît Junod, Istanbul: Aga Khan Trust for Culture, and Sakip Sabancı University and Museum, 2010, pp. 206–215.

Marzolph, Ulrich, "The Literary Genre of 'Oriental Miscellany'," in Bauden, Frédéric, Aboubakr Chraïbi, and Antonella Ghersetti, eds., *Le répertoire narratif arabe médiéval: transmission et ouverture*, Geneva: Droz, 2008, pp. 309–319.

Marzolph, Ulrich, "The Man Who Made the *Nights* Immortal: The Tales of the Syrian Maronite Storyteller Ḥannā Diyāb," *Marvels & Tales* 32.1 (2018), pp. 114–129.

Marzolph, Ulrich, "The Muslim Sense of Humor," in *Humour and Religion: Challenges and Ambiguities*, ed. H. Geybels and W. Van Herck, London: Continuum, 2011, pp. 169–187.

Marzolph, Ulrich, "The Persian *Nights*: Links between the *Arabian Nights* and Persian Culture," *Fabula* 45 (2004), pp. 275–293.

Marzolph, Ulrich, "The Qurʾān and Jocular Literature," *Arabica* 47 (2000), pp. 478–487.

Marzolph, Ulrich, "The Story of Abū al-Ḥasan the Wag in the Tübingen Manuscript of the Romance of ʿOmar ibn al-Nuʿmān and Related Texts," *Journal of Arabic Literature* 46 (2015), pp. 34–67.

Marzolph, Ulrich, "The Tale of Aladdin in European Oral Tradition," in *Les Mille et une Nuits et le récit oriental en Espagne et en Orient*, ed. Aboubakr Chraïbi and Carmen Ramirez, Paris: L'Harmattan, 2009, pp. 401–412.

Marzolph, Ulrich, "The Tale of the Sleeper Awakened," in Chraïbi, Aboubakr, ed., *Arabic Manuscripts of the* Thousand and One Nights, Paris: espaces & signes, 2016, pp. 261–291.

Marzolph, Ulrich, "Timur's Humorous Antagonist, Nasreddin Ḫoca," in Marzolph, *Ex Oriente Fabula*, vol. 2, Dortmund: Verlag für Orientkunde, 2006, pp. 170–171.

Marzolph, Ulrich, "Topf hat ein Kind," in *Enzyklopädie des Märchens*, vol. 13 (2010), cols. 762–764.

Marzolph, Ulrich, "Traum vom Schatz auf der Brücke," in *Enzyklopädie des Märchens*, vol. 13 (2010), cols. 877–882.

Marzolph, Ulrich, "Übel: Das kleinere Ü.," in *Enzyklopädie des Märchens*, vol. 13 (2010), cols. 1095–1098.

Marzolph, Ulrich, "Weib: Böses W. schlimmer als der Teufel," in *Enzyklopädie des Märchens*, vol. 14 (2014), cols. 551–555.

Marzolph, Ulrich, "Wesselski, Albert," in Duggan, Anne E., and Donald Haase, eds., *Folktales and Fairy Tales*, Santa Barbara, CA: Greenwood, 2016, vol. 3, pp. 1100–1101.

Marzolph, Ulrich, "Wesselski, Albert," in *Enzyklopädie des Märchens*, vol. 14 (2014), cols. 652–656.

Marzolph, Ulrich, "Zählen: Sich nicht z. können," *Enzyklopädie des Märchens*, vol. 14 (2014), cols. 1117–1122.

Marzolph, Ulrich, "Zur Überlieferung der Nasreddin Hoca-Schwänke außerhalb des türkischen Sprachraumes," in *Türkische Sprachen und Kulturen: Materialien der 1. Deutschen Turkologen-Konferenz*, ed. Ingeborg Baldauf, Klaus Kreiser, and Semih Tezcan, Wiesbaden: Harrassowitz, 1991, pp. 275–285.

Marzolph, Ulrich, *Arabia ridens: Die humoristische Kurzprosa der adab-Literatur im internationalen Traditionsgeflecht*, 2 vols., Frankfurt: Klostermann, 1992.

Marzolph, Ulrich, *Bohlul-nāme*, ed. Bāqer Qorbāni-Zarrin, 3rd ed., Tehran: Behnegār, 1392/2013.

Marzolph, Ulrich, ed., *Das Buch der wundersamen Geschichten: Erzählungen aus der Welt von 1001 Nacht*, Munich: C.H. Beck, 1999.

Marzolph, Ulrich, *Dāstānhā-ye širin: Fünfzig persische Volksbüchlein aus der zweiten Hälfte des zwanzigsten Jahrhunderts*, Stuttgart: Franz Steiner, 1994.

Marzolph, Ulrich, *Der Weise Narr Buhlūl*, Wiesbaden: Franz Steiner, 1983.

Marzolph, Ulrich, *Die vierzig Papageien: Das persische Volksbuch Čehel Ṭuṭi, ein Beitrag zur Geschichte des Papageienbuches*, Walldorf: Verlag für Orientkunde, 1979.

Marzolph, Ulrich, *Narrative Illustration in Persian Lithographed Books*, Leiden: Brill, 2001.

Marzolph, Ulrich, *Nasreddin Hodscha: 666 wahre Geschichten*, Munich: C.H. Beck, 1996.

Marzolph, Ulrich, *Relief after Hardship: The Ottoman Turkish Model for* The Thousand and One Days, Detroit: Wayne State University Press, 2017.

Marzolph, Ulrich, ed., *The Arabian Nights in Transnational Perspective*, Detroit: Wayne State University Press, 2007.

Marzolph, Ulrich, ed., *The Arabian Nights Reader*, Detroit: Wayne State University Press, 2006.

Marzolph, Ulrich, *Typologie des persischen Volksmärchens*, Beirut: Deutsche Morgenländische Gesellschaft, 1984.

Marzolph, Ulrich, transl., *Wenn der Esel singt, tanzt das Kamel: Persische Märchen und Schwänke*, Munich: Diederichs, 1994.

Marzolph, Ulrich, and Ingeborg Baldauf, "Hodscha Nasreddin," in *Enzyklopädie des Märchens*, vol. 6 (1990), cols. 1127–1151.

Marzolph, Ulrich, and Aboubakr Chraïbi, "The *Hundred and One Nights*: A Recently Discovered Old Manuscript," in *Zeitschrift der Deutschen Morgenländischen Gesellschaft* 162 (2012), pp. 299–316.

Marzolph, Ulrich, with Anne E. Duggan, "Ḥannā Diyāb's Tales," part 1, *Marvels & Tales* 32.1 (2018), pp. 133–154.

Marzolph, Ulrich, and Richard van Leeuwen, *The Arabian Nights Encyclopedia*, 2 vols., Santa Barbara, CA: ABC-Clio, 2004.

Mašdi Galin Ḫānom, *Die Erzählungen der Mašdi Galin Ḫānom*, ed. Ulrich Marzolph and Azar Amirhosseini-Nithammer, 2 vols. Wiesbaden: Reichert, 1994.

Mashdi Galin Khānom, *Qeṣṣehā-ye Mashdi Galin Khānom*, ed. Ulrich Marzolph, Azar Amirhosseini-Nithammer, and Aḥmad Vakiliyān, Tehran: Markaz, 1374/1995.

Masing, Uku, "Gottes Segen," in *Enzyklopädie des Märchens*, vol. 6 (1990), cols. 12–16.

Mason, J. Alden, and Aurelio M. Espinosa, "Porto-Rican Folk-lore: Folk-Tales," *Journal of American Folklore* 42 (1929), pp. 85–156.

Massé, Henri, *Croyances et coutumes persanes, suivies de contes et chansons populaires*, 2 vols., Paris: G.P. Maisonneuve, 1938.

Massignon, Geneviève, *Contes corses*, Aix-en-Provence: Ophrys, 1963.

Mas'udi, *The Meadows of Gold: The Abbasids*, transl. and ed. Paul Lunde and Caroline Stone, London: Routledge, 2010.

Masʿūdī, Abū 'l-Ḥasan ʿAlī ibn al-Ḥusayn al-, *Murūj al-dhahab wa-maʿādin al-jawhar*, ed. Charles Pellat, 7 vols., Beirut: Université libanaise, 1966–1979.

Matičetov, Marko, "Cepenkov, Marko Kostov," in *Enzyklopädie des Märchens*, vol. 2 (1979), cols. 1189–1191.

Matičetov, Milko, "Dieb als Esel," in *Enzyklopädie des Märchens*, vol. 3 (1981), cols. 640–643.

Maxwell, William Hamilton, *The Field Book: Or, Sports and Pastimes of the United Kingdom*, London: Effingham Wilson, 1833.

May, Georges, *Les Mille et une nuits d'Antoine Galland*, Paris: Puf, 1986.

Maydānī, Abū 'l-Faḍl Aḥmad ibn Muḥammad ibn Aḥmad ibn Ibrāhīm, *Majmaʿ al-amthāl*, ed. Muḥammad Abū 'l-Faḍl Ibrāhīm, 4 vols., Cairo: ʿĪsā al-Bābī al-Ḥalabī, 1398/1978.

Maylāwī, Yūsuf ibn Muḥammad "Ibn al-Wakīl" al-, *Irshād man naḥā ilā nawādir Juḥā*, see ʿAnābsa, "Min adab al-nawādir."

Maylāwī, Yūsuf ibn Muḥammad "Ibn al-Wakīl" al-, *al-Ṭirāz al-mudhahhab fī nawādir Ashʿab*, ed. Ghālib al-ʿAnābsa and Nādir Maṣārwa, s.l.: Dār al-Hudā, and Jordan: Dār al-Fikr, 2012.

Mazon, André, *Documents, contes et chansons slaves de l'Albanie du sud*, Paris: Droz, 1936.

McCarthy, William Bernard, *Cinderella in America: A Book of Folk and Fairy Tales*, Jackson: University Press of Mississipi, 2007.

McKenna, Connan, "The Irish Analogues to Chaucer's *Pardoner's Tale*," *Béaloideas* 45–47 (1977–1979), pp. 63–77.

McKeown, James C., *A Cabinet of Greek Curiosities: Strange Tales and Surprising Facts from the Cradle of Western Civilization*, Oxford: Oxford University Press, 2013.

Megas, Georgios A., *Griechische Volksmärchen*, Cologne: Diederichs, 1965.

Mehl, Dieter, "Chaucer, Geoffrey," in *Enzyklopädie des Märchens*, vol. 2 (1979), cols. 1255–1268.

Mehner, Maximilian, *Märchenhaftes Indien: Theodor Benfey, die indische Theorie und ihre Rezeption in der Märchenforschung*, Munich: Kirchheim, 2012.

Meier, Ernst, *Deutsche Volksmärchen aus Schwaben: Aus dem Munde des Volks gesammelt*, Stuttgart: Scheitlin, 1852.

Meier, Fritz, "Turandot in Persien," *Zeitschrift der Deutschen Morgenländischen Gesellschaft* 95 (1941), pp. 1–27, 415–421.

Meier, Harri, and Dieter Woll, *Portugiesische Märchen*, Düsseldorf: Diederichs, 1975.

Meisami, Julie Scott, "Mixed Prose and Verse in Medieval Persian Literature," in Harris, Joseph, and Karl Reichl, eds., *Prosimetrum: Crosscultural Perspectives on Narrative in Prose and Verse*, Woodbridge, Suffolk: D.S. Brewer, 1997, pp. 295–319.

Meisami, Julie Scott, "Writing Medieval Women: Representations and Misrepresentations," in Bray, Julia, ed., *Writing and Representation in Medieval Islam: Muslim Horizons*, London: Rouledge, 2006, pp. 47–88.

Meisami, Julie Scott, and Paul Starkey, eds., *Encyclopaedia of Arabic Literature*, 2 vols., London and New York: Routledge, 1998.

Meissner, Bruno, *Neuarabische Geschichten aus dem Iraq*, Leipzig: J.C. Hinrich, 1903.

Meleaton see Rost, Johann Leonhard

Mensa philosophica: Faksimile und Kommentar, ed. Erwin Rauner and Burghart Wachinger, Tübingen: Max Niemeyer, 1995.

Méraville, Marie Aimée, *Contes d'Auvergne*, Paris: Érasme, 1956.

Merceron, Jacques, "Des souris et des hommes: pérégrination d'un motif narratif et d'un *exemplum* d'Islam en chrétienté. À propos de la fable de 'L'Ermite' de Marie de France et du fabliau de *La Sorisete des Estopes*," *Cahiers de civilisation médiévale* 46.181 (2003), pp. 53–69.

Meredith-Owens, G.M., "An Early Persian Miscellany," in *Iran and Islam: In Memory of the Late Vladimir Minorsky*, ed. Clifford Edmund Bosworth, Edinburgh: Edinburgh University Press, 1971, pp. 435–441.

Merguerian, Gayane Karen, and Afsaneh Najmabadi, "Zulaykha and Yusuf: Whose 'Best Story?'," *International Journal of Middle East Studies* 29.4 (1997), pp. 485–508.

Merkel, Johannes, *Hören, Sehen, Staunen: Kulturgeschichte des mündlichen Erzählens*, Hildesheim: Olms, 2015.

Merkelbach-Pinck, Angelika, *Volkserzählungen aus Lothringen*, Münster: Aschendorff, 1967.

Merkens, Heinrich Ludwig, *Was sich das Volk erzählt: Deutscher Volkshumor*, 2nd ed., 3 vols., Jena: Costenoble, 1892–1900.

Merton, Robert K., and Elinor Barber, *The Travels and Adventures of Serendipity: A Study in Sociological Semantics and the Sociology of Science*, Princeton: Princeton University Press, 2004.

Messac, Régis, *Le "Detective Novel" et l'influence de la pensée scientifique*, Geneva: Slatkine reprints, 1975.

Meyrac, Albert, *Traditions, coutumes, légendes et contes des Ardennes*, Charleville: Petit Ardennais, 1890.

Mi'at layla wa-layla see Fudge; Gaudefroy-Demombynes; Ott; Ṭarshūna.

Mifsud, Ġorġ, *Ġaħan u ħrejjef oħra*, San Ġwann, Malta: PEG Publications, 1995.

Mifsud-Chircop, Ġorġ, *Type-Index of the Maltese Folktale within the Mediterranean Tradition Area*, 2 vols. unpublished typoscript Malta 1978.

Migne, Jacques-Paul, ed., *Patrologia cursus completus, series latina*, vol. 105: *Theodulfi Aurelianensis [...] opera omnia*, Paris: Migne, 1851.

Miller, Elaine K., *Mexican Folk Narrative from the Los Angeles Area*, Austin: University of Texas Press, 1973.

Miller, Stephen Roy, ed., *The Taming of a Shrew: The 1594 Quarto*, Cambridge: Cambridge University Press, 1998.

Millien, Achille, "Les goules dans les traditions du Nivernais," in *Congrès internationale des traditions populaires, première session: Paris 1889, compte rendu des séances*, Paris: Imprimerie nationale, 1891, pp. 59–61.

Mills, Douglas Edgar, *A Collection of Tales from Uji: A Study and Translation of Uji Shūi Monogatari*, Cambridge: Cambridge University Press, 1970.

Mills, Margaret, "Another Locust's Leg: Folktale Types, Subtypes, 'Décor,' and Meaning," in Bendix, Regina F., and Dorothy Noyes, eds., *Terra Ridens – Terra Narrans: Festschrift zum 65. Geburtstag von Ulrich Marzolph*, Dortmund: Verlag für Orientkunde, 2018, pp. 213–238.

Mills, Margaret, "It's about Time—Or Is It?: Four Stories of/in Transformation," in *Fields of Folklore: Essays in Honor of Kenneth S. Goldstein*, ed. Roger D. Abrahams, Bloomington: Indiana University Press, 1995, pp. 184–197.

Mills, Margaret, "Sex Role Reversals, Sex Changes, and Transvestite Disguise in the Oral Tradition of a Conservative Muslim Community in Afghanistan," in *Women's Folklore, Women's Culture*, ed. Rosan A. Jordan and Susan J. Kalčik, Philadelphia: University of Pennsylvania Press, 1985, pp. 187–213.

Mills, Margaret A., "The Gender of the Trick: Female Tricksters and Male Narrators," *Asian Folklore Studies* 60.2 (2001), pp. 237–258.
Mirkhond, Mir Moḥammad ibn Borhān al-Din Khāvandshāh, *Tārikh-e Rouẓat al-ṣafā*, 7 vols., Tehran: Ketābkhāne-ye markazi, 1338–1339/1959–1960.
Mirkhond, Muhammad Bin Khâvendshâh Bin Mahmûd, *The Rauzat-us-safa; Or, Garden of Purity, Containing the Histories of Prophets, Kings, and Khalifs*, transl. E. Rehatsek, ed. F.F. Arbuthnot, 5 vols., London: Royal Asiatic Society, 1891–94.
Mo'ayyad, Ḥeshmat, "Sar-gozasht-e 'zan-e pārsā'-ye 'Aṭṭār," *Irān-shenāsi* 9.3 (1376/1997), pp. 427–442.
Mode, Heinz, *Zigeunermärchen aus aller Welt*, 4 vols., Wiesbaden: Drei-Lilien-Verlag 1983–1985.
Moennig, Ulrich, "Eine spätbyzantinische literarische Version des Märchens von der Rätselprinzessin ("Turandot") verglichen mit ihrer wahrscheinlich osmanischen Vorlage," in *Akten des 27. Deutschen Orientalistentages (Bonn—28.September bis 2. Oktober 1998): Norm und Abweichung*, ed. Stefan Wild und Hartmut Schild, Würzburg: Ergon, 2001, pp. 705–714.
Moennig, Ulrich, *Die Erzählung von Alexander und Semiramis: Kritische Ausgabe mit einer Einleitung, Übersetzung und einem Wörterverzeichnis*, Berlin: Walter de Gruyter, 2004.
Mogtader, Youssef, and Gregor Schoeler, *Turandot: Die persische Märchenerzählung: Edition, Übersetzung, Kommentar*. Wiesbaden: Reichert, 2017.
Mojāhed, Aḥmad, *Juḥi (60–160 q)*, Tehran: Enteshārāt-e Dāneshgāh-e Tehran, 1382/2003.
Molan, Peter D., "Sindbad the Sailor: A Commentary on the Ethics of Violence," *Journal of the American Oriental Society* 98 (1978), pp. 237–247.
Moldavskii, D., *Russkaia satiricheskaia skazka v zapisyakh seredini 19—nachala 20 v.*, Moscow: Akad., 1955.
Mollā Naṣreddin, see *Moṭāyebāt-e Mollā Naṣreddin*; Ramażāni.
Moner, Michel, "Texto, corpus e hipertexto en la edición crítica de los textos literarios: el caso del ejemplo XXXII de *El Conde Lucanor*," in *Edición y literatura en España (siglos XVI y XVII)*, ed. Anne Cayuela, Zaragoza: Prensas Universitarias de Zaragoza, 2012, pp. 303–318.
Monnier, Marc, *Contes populaires en Italie*, Paris: Charpentier, 1880.
Monseur, Eugène, "Les deux bossus et les nains," *Bulletin de Folklore* 2 (1893), p. 77.
Montanus, Martin, *Schwankbücher (1577–1566)*, ed. Johannes Bolte, Tübingen: Litterarischer Verein in Stuttgart, 1899.
Monzavi, Aḥmad, *Fehrestvāre-ye ketābhā-ye fārsi*, vol. 1, Tehran: Markaz-e Dā'erat al-ma'āref-e bozorg-e eslāmi, 1382/2001.
Moral Molina, Celia del, "Huellas de la literatura árabe clásica en las literaturas europeas: vías de transmisión," in *Confluencia de culturas en el Mediterráneo*, ed. Francisco A. Muñoz, Granada: Universidad de Granada, 1993, pp. 63–67.
Moraru, Mihai, "Postfaţă: Cărţile populare—încercare de definire structurală," in Cartojan, Nicolae, *Carţile populare în literatura românească*, vol. 2, Bucharest: Enciclopedică română, 1974, pp. 481–519.
Moraru, Mihai, *De nuptiis Mercurii et Philologiae*, Bucharest: Fundaţiei culturale române, 1997.
Mordeglia, Caterina, "Sacchetti, Franco," in *Enzyklopädie des Märchens*, vol. 11 (2005), cols. 967–971.

Mordtmann, Andreas David, "Zu Dionys, dem Tyrannen schlich," *Die Gartenlaube* (1869), pp. 151–153.
Morlini see Wesselski, *Die Novellen Girolamo Morlinis*.
Morton, Thomas, *The New English Canaan*, Boston: Prince Society, 1883.
Moscherosch, Hanß Michael, *Gesichte Philanders von Sittewald*, ed. Felix Bobertag, Berlin and Stuttgart: W. Speman, (1883?).
Moser, Dietz-Rüdiger, "Kommentare," in *Ungarndeutsche Märchenerzähler*, vol. 2: *Die "Blinden Madel" aus Gant im Schildgebirge: Authentische Tonaufnahmen 1958 und 1960 von Johannes Künzig und Waltraut Werner*, Freiburg: Volkskunde Tonarchiv, 1971, pp. 70–103.
Moser-Rath, Elfriede, "Anser venalis," in *Enzyklopädie des Märchens*, vol. 1 (1977), cols. 576–577.
Moser-Rath, Elfriede, "Bestechung," in *Enzyklopädie des Märchens*, vol. 2 (1979), cols. 209–214.
Moser-Rath, Elfriede, "Denk dreimal, bevor du sprichst!" in *Enzyklopädie des Märchens*, vol. 3 (1981) cols. 420–421.
Moser-Rath, Elfriede, "Diagnose: Die einfältige D.," in *Enzyklopädie des Märchens*, vol. 3 (1981), cols. 573–575.
Moser-Rath, Elfriede, "Essen: das gleiche E.," in *Enzyklopädie des Märchens*, vol. 4 (1984), cols. 469–471.
Moser-Rath, Elfriede, "Ewigkeit," in *Enzyklopädie des Märchens*, vol. 4 (1984), cols. 588–592.
Moser-Rath, Elfriede, *"Lustige Gesellschaft:" Schwank und Witz des 17. und 18. Jahrhunderts in kultur- und sozialgeschichtlichem Kontext*, Stuttgart: J.B. Metzler, 1984.
Moser-Rath, Elfriede, *Predigtmärlein der Barockzeit: Exempel, Sage, Schwank und Fabel in geistlichen Quellen des oberdeutschen Raumes*, Berlin: De Gruyter, 1964.
Moṭāyebāt-e Mollā Naṣreddin, [Tehran] 1299/1881.
Muehlhaeusler, Mark, "Oriental Tales in 18th-Century Manuscripts … and in English Translation," *Middle Eastern Literatures* 16.2 (2013), pp. 189–202.
Mufaḍḍal ibn Salama, *al-Fākhir*, ed. Charles A. Storey, Leiden: Brill, 1915.
Mufaḍḍal ibn Salama, *al-Fākhir*, ed. ʿAbd al-ʿAlīm al-Ṭaḥāwī and Muḥammad ʿAlī al-Najjār, Cairo: ʿĪsā al-Bābī al-Ḥalabī, 1380/1960.
Muhanna, Elias, *The World in a Book: Al-Nuwayri and the Islamic Encyclopedic Traditon*, Princeton: Princeton University Press, 2018.
Mühlhausen, Ludwig, *Zehn irische Volkserzählungen aus Süd-Donegal, mit Übersetzung und Anmerkungen*, Halle (Saale): Max Niemeyer, 1939.
Müllenhoff, Karl, *Sagen, Märchen und Lieder der Herzogthümer Schleswig Holstein und Lauenburg*, Kiel: Schwers, 1845.
Müller, Kathrin, *"Und der Kalif lachte, bis er auf den Rücken fiel:" Ein Beitrag zur Phraseologie und Stilkunde des klassischen Arabisch*, 2 vols., Munich: Bayerische Akademie der Wissenschaften, 1993.
Müller-Fraureuth, Karl, *Die deutschen Lügendichtungen bis auf Münchhausen*, Halle: Niemeyer, 1881.
Mundt, Marina, *Zur Adaptation orientalischer Bilder in den Fornaldarsögur Norðrlanda: Materialien zu einer neuen Dimension altnordischer Belletristik*, Frankfurt: Lang, 1993.
Murtaugh, Daniel M., "Constant du Hamel: Women, Money, and Power in an Old French *fabliau*," in *Women and Wealth in Late Medieval Europe*, ed. Theresa Earenfight, New York: Palgrave Macmillan, 2010, pp. 13–32.

Mussafia, Adolfo, *Über eine metrische Darstellung der Crescentiasage*, Vienna: K.K. Hof- und Staatsdruckerei, 1866.

Muwaffaq al-Dīn ibn ʿUthmān, *Murshid al-zuwār ilā qubūr al-abrār* (Guide of the Pilgrims to the Graves of the Pious), ed. Muḥammad Fatḥī Abū Bakr, Cairo: al-Dār al-miṣriyya al-lubnāniyya, 1995.

Mykytiuk, Bohdan, *Ukrainische Märchen*, Düsseldorf: Diederichs, 1979.

Nafzāwī, al-Shaykh al-, *al-Rawḍ al-ʿāṭir fī nuzhat al-khāṭir*, ed. Jamāl Jumʿa, London: Riad El-Rayyes, 1990.

Nafzâwî, *Der duftende Garten: Ein arabisches Liebeshandbuch*, transl. Ulrich Marzolph, Munich: C.H. Beck, 2002.

Nafzawi, Muhammad ibn Muhammad al-, *The Perfumed Garden of Sensual Delight (ar-rawḏ al-ʿâṯir fî nuzhati 'l-khâṯir)*, transl. Jim Colville, London, New York: Kegan Paul International, 1999.

Nahrawānī al-Jarīrī, Muʿāfà ibn Zakariyya al-, *al-Jalīs al-ṣāliḥ al-kāfī wa-'l-anīs al-nāsiḥ al-shāfī*, ed. Muḥammad Mursī al-Khūlī and Iḥsān ʿAbbās, 3 vols., Beyrouth: ʿĀlam al-kutub, 1981–1987.

Naiden, Fred, "*Hiketai* and *Theōroi* at Apidauros," in Elsner, Jaś, and Ina Rutherford, eds., *Pilgrimage in Graeco-Roman & Early Christian Antiquity: Seeing the Gods*, Oxford: Oxford University Press, 2005, pp. 73–95.

Naithani, Sadhana, "Relativität der Zeit," in *Enzyklopädie des Märchens*, vol. 11 (2004), cols. 532–537.

Nakhshabi, Ẕiyāʾ al-Din, *Ṭuṭi-nāme*, ed. Fatḥallāh Mojtabāʾi and Gholām-ʿAlī Āryā, Tehran: Manūchehr, 1372/1993.

Nance, Susan, *How the Arabian Nights Inspired the American Dream, 1790–1935*, Chapel Hill: The University of North Carolina Press, 2009.

Naṣrallāh Monshi, Abu 'l-Maʿāli, *Tarjome-ye Kalile va Demne*, ed. Mojtabā Minovi Ṭehrāni, Tehran: Dāneshgāh-e Ṭehrān, 1343/1964.

Nasreddin Hodja, see Başgöz and Boratav; Burrill; Duman; Elçin; Horn; Kut; *Leṭāʾif-i Hoca Naṣreddin;* Marzolph, *Nasreddin Hodscha*; Marzolph and Baldauf; Wesselski, *Der Hodscha Nasreddin.*

Nasrollah Monschi, *Kalila und Dimna: Fabeln aus dem klassischen Persien*, transl. and ed. Seyfeddin Najmabadi and Siegfried Weber, Munich: C.H. Beck, 1996.

Navarro, David, *Interacciones narrativas árabe, cristiana y judía: convivencia literaria en el Medievo peninsular*, Ph.D. thesis The University of Western Ontario, 2013.

Nawādir Juḥā see Juḥā, *Hādhihi nawādir al-khūjah Naṣr al-Dīn Afandī Juḥā al-Rūmī*

Nawājī, Shams al-Dīn Muḥammad ibn Ḥasan, *Ḥalbat al-kumayt*, Cairo 1299/1881.

Naysābūrī, Abū 'l-Qāsim al-Ḥasan ibn Muḥammad ibn Ḥabīb, *ʿUqalāʾ al-majānin*, ed. ʿUmar al-Asʿad, Beirut: Dār al-Nafāʾis, 1407/1987.

Neander, Michael, *Physice, sive potius syllogae physicae rerum eruditarum*, Leipzig: Defner, 1585.

Nerucci, Gherardo, *Sessanta novelle popolari montalesi (circondario di Pistoia)*, 2nd ed., Florence 1891.

Neugaard, Edward J., *Motif-Index of Medieval Catalan Folktales*, Binghamtpon, New York: Medieval & Renaissance Texts & Studies, 1993.

Neumann, Siegfried, "Mißverständnisse," in *Enzyklopädie des Märchens*, vol. 9 (1999), cols. 707–717.

Neumann, Siegfried, "Petrusschwänke," in *Enzyklopädie des Märchens*, vol. 10 (2002), cols. 814–824.
Neumann, Siegfried, "Wossidlo, Richard," in *Enzyklopädie des Märchens*, vol. 14 (2014), cols. 1015–1018.
Neumann, Siegfried, *Der Alte Fritz: Geschichten und Anekdoten*, Schwerin: Demmler, 2003.
Neumann, Siegfried, *Ein mecklenburgischer Volkserzähler: Die Geschichten des August Rust*, Berlin: Akademie-Verlag, 1968.
Neumann, Siegfried, *Friedrich der Große in der pommerschen Erzähltradition: Eine volkskundliche Studie und Dokumentation*, Rostock: Wossidlo-Archiv, 1998.
Neumann, Siegfried, *Geschichte und Geschichten: Studien zu Entstehung und Gehalt historischer Sagen und Anekdoten*, Rostock: Wossidlo-Archiv, 2001.
Neumann, Siegfried, *Mecklenburgische Volkserzählungen*, Berlin: Akademie-Verlag, 1971.
Neumann, Siegfried, *Plattdeutsche Schwänke: Aus den Sammlungen Richard Wossidlos und seiner Zeitgenossen sowie eigenen Aufzeichnungen in Mecklenburg*, Rostock: VEB Hinstorff Verlag, 1968, pp. 162, 222, no. 274.
Neumann, Siegfried, *Volksschwänke aus Mecklenburg, aus der Sammlung Richard Wossidlos*, Berlin: Akademie-Verlag, 1963
Newall, Venetia, "Clouston, William Alexander," in *Enzyklopädie des Märchens*, vol. 3 (1981), cols. 79–80.
Ní Bhaoill, Róise, *Ulster Gaelic Voices: bailúchán Doegen 1931*, Belfast: Iontaobhas Ultach, 2010.
Nicholson, Peter, "The Medieval Tale of the Lover's Gift Regained," *Fabula* 21 (1980), pp. 200–222.
Nicholson, Peter, "Pfand des Liebhabers," in *Enzyklopädie des Märchens*, vol. 10 (2002), cols. 842–849.
Nicolaisen, Wilhelm F.H., "Kaiser und Abt," in *Enzyklopädie des Märchens*, vol. 7 (1993), cols. 845–852.
Nicoloff, Assen, *Bulgarian Folktales*, Cleveland: Nicoloff, 1979.
Niebrzydowski, Sue, *Bonoure and Buxum: A Study of Wives in Late Medieval English Literature*, Oxford: Peter Lang, 2006.
Niebuhr, Carsten, *C. Niebuhrs Reisebeschreibung nach Arabien und anderen umliegenden Ländern*, 2 vols., Copenhagen: Nicolaus Möller, 1774–1778.
Nicoloff, Assen, *Bulgarian Folktales*, Cleveland: Nicoloff, 1979.
Niles, John D., "Bede's Cædmon, 'The Man Who Had No Story' (Irish Tale-Type 2412B)," *Folklore* 117 (2006), pp. 141–155.
Niles, John D., "True Stories and Other Lies," in *Myth in Early Northwest Europe*, ed. Stephen O. Glosecki, Tempe, Arizona: Arizona Center for Medieval and Renaissance Studies, 2007, pp. 1–30.
Niles, John D., "True Stories and Other Lies," in *Old English Heroic Poems and the Social Life of Texts*, Turnhout: Brepols, 2006, pp. 279–307.
Niles, John D., *Homo narrans: The Poetics and Anthropology of Oral Literature*, Philadelphia: University of Pennsylvania Press, 1999.
Niẓámu'd-dín, Muḥammad, *Introduction to the Jawámiʿu'l-ḥikáyát wa lawámiʿu'r-riwáyát of Sadídu-dín Muḥammad al-ʿAwfí*, London: Luzac & Co., 1929.
Noia Campos, Camiño, *Catálogo tipolóxico do conto galego de tradición oral: clasificación, antoloxía e bibliografía*, Vigo: University of Vigo, 2010.
Nöldeke, Theodor, "Das Gleichnis vom Aufziehen eines jungen Raubtiers," in ʿAǧab

nāma: *A Volume of Oriental Studies Presented to Edward G. Browne*, ed. Thomas W. Arnold and Reynold A. Nicholson, Cambridge: University Press, 1922, pp. 371–382.
Nöldeke, Theodor, "Die Erzählung vom Mäusekönig und seinen Ministern: Ein Abschnitt der Pehlewî-Bearbeitung des altindischen Fürstenspiegels," *Abhandlungen der Königlichen Gesellschaft der Wissenschaften zu Göttingen* 25.3 (1879), pp. 1–68.
Nöldeke, Theodor, "Review of *Siasset Namèh*, ed. Charles Schefer, Paris. Ernest Leroux, 1891," *Zeitschrift der Deutschen Morgenländischen Gesellschaft* 46 (1892), pp. 761–768.
Noomen, Willem, and Nico van den Boogaard, eds., *Nouveau recueil complet des fabliaux (NRCF)*, 10 vols., Assen: Van Gorcum, 1983–1998.
Nörtersheuser, Hans-Walter, "Glückliche Armut," in *Enzyklopädie des Märchens*, vol. 5 (1987), cols. 1318–1324.
Novellino see Jakob, *Die hundert alten Erzählungen*; Conte, *Il Novellino*
Novikov, Nikolaj V., "Barag, Lev Grigor'evič," in *Enzyklopädie des Märchens*, vol. 1 (1977), cols. 1209–1210.
Nowak, Ursula, *Beiträge zur Typologie des arabischen Volksmärchens*, Diss. Freiburg, 1969.
Noy, Dov, *Folktales of Israel*, Chicago: The University of Chicago Press, 1963.
Núñez, P. Jésus, *Historias de curas*, Barcelona: Martínez Roca, 2002.
Nuwayrī al-Iskandarānī al-, *Kitāb al-Ilmām bi-'l-i'lām fīmā jarat bihi al-aḥkām wa-'l-umūr al-maqḍiyya fī waq'at al-Iskandariyya*, 7 vols., ed. 'Azīz Sūriyāl 'Aṭiyya, Haydarabad: Dār al-ma'ārif al-'uthmāniyya, 1968–76.
Nuwayrī, Shihāb al-Dīn Aḥmad ibn 'Abd al-Wahhāb al-, *Nihāyat al-arab fī funūn al-adab*, 27 vols., Cairo: Dār al-Kutub al-miṣriyya, 1929–1985.
Nuwayri, Shihab al-Din al-, *The Ultimate Ambition in the Arts of Erudition: A Compendium of Knowledge from the Classical Islamic World*, transl. and ed. Elias Muhanna, New York: Penguin, 2016.
Nuzhat al-jullās fī nawādir Abū [!] Nuwās, Beirut: Khalīl and Amīn al-Khūrī, s.a.
Ó Catháin, Séamas, and Bo Almqvist, "An Fear Nach Rabh Scéal ar Bith Aige/The Man Who Had No Story," *Béaloideas* 37/38 (1969/1970), pp. 51–64.
Odo of Cheriton, *The Fables*, transl. John C. Jacobs, Syracuse, NY: Syracuse University Press, 1985.
Ó Duilearga, Séamus, "The Three Questions," *Béaloideas* 2.4 (1930), pp. 381–383.
Ó Duilearga, Séamus, *Seán Ó Conaill's Book: Stories and Traditions from Iveragh*, Baile Átha Cliath: Comhairle Bhéaloideas Éireann, 1981.
Oestrup, Johannes, "Alf laila wa-laila," in *Encyclopaedia of Islam*, vol. 1, Leiden: Brill, 1913, pp. 252–256.
Ognjanowa, Elena, *Märchen aus Bulgarien*, Wiesbaden: Drei Lilien, 1987.
Oliveira, F. Xavier d'Ataide, *Contos tradicionais do Algarve*, 2 vols., Porto 1905.
Oliver, Thomas Edward, "Some Analogues of Maistre Pierre Pathelin," *Journal of American Folklore* 22 (1909), pp. 395–420.
Olmedo, Felix G., *Las fuentes de "La vida es sueño". La idea—el cuento—el drama*, Madrid: Voluntad, 1928.
O'Malley, Elena, "Paying One's Dues: The Storyteller as Mediator in the Irish Fairy Legend 'The Man Who Had No Story'," *Proceedings of the Harvard Celtic Colloquium* 15 (1995), pp. 56–68.
Omidsalar, Mahmoud, "A Romanian Political Joke in 12th-Century Iranian Sources," *Western Folklore* 46 (1978), pp. 121–124.
Omidsālār, Maḥmud, "Ḥātem-nāme," in Bojnurdi, Kāẓem Musavi, ed., *Dāneshnāme-ye*

farhang-e mardom-e Irān, vol. 3, Tehran: Markaz-e Dā'erat al-ma'āref-e bozorg-e eslāmi, 1394/2015, pp. 475–477.
Omidsalar, Mahmoud, "Kalila wa Demna ii. The translation by Abu'l-Ma'āli Naṣr-Allāh Monši," in *Encyclopædia Iranica online* http://www.iranicaonline.org/articles/kalila-demna-ii
Omidsālār, Maḥmud, "Molāḥażāti dar bāre-ye Laṭā'ef-e 'Obeyd-e Zākāni dar 'Resāle-ye delgoshā'," *Irān-nāme* 6.2 (1988), pp. 228–247.
Oring, Elliot, *Joking Asides: The Theory, Analysis, and Aesthetics of Humor*, Norman: Utah State University Press, 2016.
Oring, Elliot, *The Jokes of Sigmund Freud: A Study in Humor and Jewish Identity*, Philadelphia: University of Pennsylvania Press, 1984.
Oriol, Carme, and Josep M. Pujol, *Index of Catalan Folktales*, Helsinki: Suomalainen Tiedeakatemia, 2008.
Orsatti, Paola, *Materials for a History of the Persian Narrative Tradition: Two Characters: Farhād and Turandot*, Venice: Edizioni Ca'Foscari, 2019.
Orso, Ethelyn G., *Modern Greek Humor: A Collection of Jokes and Ribald Tales*, Bloomington: Indiana University Press, 1979 (review by Margaret E. Kenna, *Man* 15.4 (1980).
Ortutay, Gyula, *Ungarische Volksmärchen*, Berlin: Rütten & Loening, 1957.
Ó Síocháin, Tadhg, *The Case of The Abbot of Drimnagh: A Medieval Irish Story of Sex-Change*, Cork: University College Cork, 2017.
Osman, Rawand, *Female Personalities in the Qur'an and Sunna: Examining the Major Sources of Imami Shi'i Islam*, London: Routledge, 2015.
Ostafin, Barbara, *Intruz przy solte: Ṭuyalī w literaturze adabowej di XI wieku*, Kraków: Wydawnictwo Uniwersytetu Jagiellońskiego, 2013.
Ostwald, Hans, *Der Urberliner in Witz, Humor und Anekdote*, Berlin: Paul Franke, ca. 1930.
Ó Súilleabháin, Seán, and Reidar Thoralf Christiansen, *The Types of the Irish Folktale*, Helsinki: Suomalainen Tiedeakatemia, 1967.
Ott, Claudia, transl., *101 Nacht*, Zurich: Manesse, 2012.
Ott, Claudia, transl., *Tausendundeine Nacht: Das glückliche Ende*, Munich: C.H. Beck, 2016.
Overbeke, Arnout van, *Anecdota sive historiae jocosas: Een seventiende-eeuwse verzameling moppen en anekdotes*, ed. Rudolf Dekker and Herman Rodenburg, Amsterdam: Meertens-Institut, 1991.
Ovid, *Metamorphoses*, transl. Alan D. Melville, Oxford: Oxford University Press, 1987.
Pakalns, Guntis, "Šmits, Pēteris," in *Enzyklopädie des Märchens*, vol. 1 (2007), cols. 798–800.
Panić-Surep, Milorad, *Srpske narodne pripovetke*, 2nd ed., Belgrade: Nolit, 1964.
Papachristophorou, Marilena, *Sommeils et veilles dans le conte merveilleux grec*, Helsinki: Suomalainen Tiedeakatemia, 2002.
Paredes, Américo, *Folktales of Mexico*, Chicago: University of Chicago Press, 1970.
Paret, Rudi, *Früharabische Liebesgeschichten*, Berlin: Paul Haupt, 1927.
Paris, Gaston, "Die undankbare Gattin," *Zeitschrift des Vereins für Volkskunde* 13 (1903), pp. 1–24, 129–150.
Paris, Gaston, "Le Conte de la Rose dans le roman de Perceforest," *Romania* 23 (1894), pp. 78–116.
Paris, Gaston, *La poésie du moyen age: leçons et lectures*, deuxième série, Paris: Hachette et Cie, 1895.
Paris, Gaston, *Légendes du moyen âge*, Paris: Hachette, 1903.
Parker, Henry, *Village Folk-tales of Ceylon*, Dehiwala: Tisara Prakasakayo, 1914.

Parnell, Thomas, *The Poetical Works*, ed. John Mitford, London: William Pickering, 1833.
Parsons, Elsie Clews, *Folk-lore of the Antilles, French and English*, vol. 2, New York: American Folk-lore Society, 1936.
Parvin-e Gonābādi, Moḥammad, "Rishe-ye ma̱sal-e 'Bā hame bale, bā mā ham bale?'" in *Gozine-ye maqālehā*, Tehran: Ketābhā-ye jibi, 2536/1977, pp. 186–191.
Pauli, Johannes, *Schimpf und Ernst*, ed. Johannes Bolte, 2 vols., Berlin: Herbert Stubenrauch, 1924 (reprint Hildesheim: Olms, 1972).
Paxton, Tom, and Robert Rayevsky, *Belling the Cat and Other Aesop's Fables*, New York: Morrow Junior Books, 1990.
Pedrosa, José Manuel, "El cuento de *El tesoro soñado* (AT 1645) y el complejo leyendístico de *El becerro de oro*," *Estudos de literatura oral* 4 (1998), pp. 127–157.
Pedrosa, José Manuel, "Más reescrituras del cuento de El tesoro fatal (AT 763): del Orto do esposo, Vicente Ferrer y Hans Sachs a eça de Queiroz, William Faulkner y Max Aub," *Revista de poética medieval* 5 (2000), pp. 27–43.
Pelen, Jean-Noël, *Le conte populaire en Cévennes*, 2nd ed., Paris: Payot et Rivages, 1994.
Pellat, Charles, "Ibn al-Ḳirriya," in *The Encyclopaedia of Islam*, 2nd ed., vol. 3, Leiden: Brill, 1979, pp. 841–842.
Pellat, Charles, "Seriousness and Humour in Early Islam," *Islamic Studies* 3 (1963), pp. 353–362.
Pellat, Charles, transl., *Le livre des avares de Ǧāḥiẓ*, Paris: G.P. Maisonneuve, 1951.
Perbosc, Antonin, *Contes licencieux de l'Aquitanie*, (Paris, 1907) reprint Carcassonne: Garae, 1984.
Perkal, Joan Ruman, "A 'Clock' Tale and Its Related Motif-Complex," *Fabula* 3 (1960), pp. 254–269.
Perry, Ben Edwin, "The Origin of the Book of Sindbad," *Fabula* 3 (1960), pp. 1–94.
Perry, Ben Edwin, *Babrius and Phaedrus: Newly Edited and Translated into English, Together with an Historical Introduction and a Comprehensive Survey of Greek and Latin Fables in the Aesopic Tradition*, Cambridge: Harvard University Press, 1965.
Pétis de la Croix, François, *Histoire du prince Calaf et de la princesse de la Chine: Conte des «Mille et un jours»*, ed. Paul Sebag, Paris: L'Harmatan, 2000.
Pétis de la Croix, François, *Les Mille et un jours: contes persans*, ed. Paul Sebag, Paris: Christian Bourgois, 1980; rev. ed. Paris: Phébus, 2003.
Peuckert, Will-Erich, *Schlesiens deutsche Märchen*, Breslau: Ostdeutsche Verlagsanstalt, 1932.
Pezzi, Carlo Antonio, *Il compagno del passeggio campestre, ossia raccolta piacevole di fatti storici e di anedotti veri*, Naples: Raffaele de Stefano e Socii, 1835.
Pforr, Anton von, *Das Buch der Beispiele der alten Weisen*, 2 vols., ed. Friedmar Geißler, Berlin: Akademie-Verlag, 1964.
Philip, Neil, *The Penguin Book of Scottish Folktales*, London: Penguin, 1995.
Piemontese, Angelo Michele, *Gli «Otto Paradisi» di Amir Khusrau da Delhi: Una lezione persiana del «Libro di Sindbad» fonte del «Peregrinaggio» di Cristoforo Armeno*, Rome: Accademia nazionale dei Lincei, 1995.
Piličkova, Sevim, *Nasradin Oja i Itar Pejo: dukhovni bliznatsi*, Skopje: Posebni izdanija, 1996.
Pinault, David, *Story-Telling Techniques in the* Arabian Nights, Leiden: E.J. Brill, 1992.
Pino Saavedra, Yolando, *Cuentos folklóricos de Chile*, vol. 1, Santiago de Chile: Universidad de Chile, 1960.

Pino Saavedra, Yolando, *Cuentos mapuches de Chile*, Santiago de Chile: Universidad de Chile, 1987.
Pino-Saavedra, Yolando, *Folktales of Chile*, Chicago: The University of Chicago Press, 1967.
Pintel-Ginsberg, Idit, "Sünden: Die drei S. des Eremiten," in *Enzyklopädie des Märchens*, vol. 13 (2010), cols. 43–46.
Piperno, Pietro, *De effectibus magicis libri sex ac de nuce maga beneventana liber unicus*, Naples: Colligni, 1647.
Piprek, Jan, *Polnische Volksmärchen*, Wien: Verein für Österreichische Volkskunde, 1918.
Pitrè, Giuseppe, "Note comparative al I vol. del *Kryptádia*," *Kryptádia* 4 (1888), pp. 192–261.
Pitrè, Giuseppe, *Fiabe, novelle e racconti popolari siciliani*, 4 vols., Palermo: Lauriel, 1875.
Pitrè, Giuseppe, *Novelle popolari toscane*, Florence: G. Barbèra, 1885.
Pitrè, Giuseppe, *Novelle popolari toscane*, 2 vols., Rome: Società Editrice del libro italiano, 1941.
Plenzat, Karl, *Die goldene Brücke: Volksmärchen*, Leipzig: Eichblat, 1930.
Pöge-Alder, Kathrin, "Mann wird wegen seiner schönen Frau verfolgt," in *Enzyklopädie des Märchens*, vol. 9 (1999), cols. 162–171.
Poggio Bracciolini, Gian-Francesco, *Die Schwänke und Schnurren*, ed. Alfred Semerau, Leipzig: Deutsche Verlags-Actiengesellschaft, 1905.
Polaschegg, Andrea, *Der andere Orientalismus: Regeln deutsch-morgenländischer Imagination im 19. Jahrhundert*, Berlin: De Gruyter, 2005.
Polívka, Jiří, *Súpis slovenských rozprávok*, 5 vols., Turciansky sv. Martin: Matica slov., 1923–1931.
Polo de Beaulieu, Marie Anne, "Johannes Gobi Junior," in *Enzyklopädie des Märchens*, vol. 7 (1993), cols. 596–601.
Pomeranceva, Ėrna Vasil'evna, *Pesni i skazki Jaroslavskoy oblasti*, Jaroslav: Jaroslavskoe knizhnoe izdatelstvo, 1958.
Pomerantz, Maurice "Tales from the Crypt: On Some Uncharted Voyages of Sindbād the Sailor," *Narrative Culture* 3.1 (2015), pp. 250–269.
Poortinga, Ype, *De ring fan it ljocht: Fryske folksverhalen*, Baarn: Bosch en Keuning, 1976.
Popov, Pavel Nikolayevich, *Ukraïns'ki narodni kazky, legendy, anekdoty*, Kyïv: Vid. Khudozhno i literaturi, 1957.
Portnoy, Ethel, *Broodje aap met*, Amsterdam: de Harmonie, 1992.
Prato, Stanislao, "Zwei Episoden aus zwei tibetanischen Novellen in der orientalischen und occidentalen Überlieferung," *Zeitschrift des Vereins für Volkskunde* 4 (1894), pp. 347–373.
Prato, Stanislas, "La scène de l'avocat et du berger de la farce Maître Pathelin dans les rédactions littéraires et populaires, françaises et étrangères," *Revue des traditions populaires* 9 (1894), pp. 537–552.
Prato, Stanislaus, "Vergleichende Mitteilungen zu Hans Sachs Fastnachtspiel Der Teufel mit dem alten Weib," *Zeitschrift des Vereins für Volkskunde* 9 (1899), pp. 189–194, 311–321.
Preindlsberger-Mrazovič, Milena, *Bosnische Volksmärchen*, Innsbruck: Edlinger, 1905.
Pröhle, Heinrich, *Kinder- und Volksmärchen*, Leipzig: Avenarius und Mendelssohn, 1853 (reprint ed. Helga Stein, Hildesheim: Georg Olms, 1975).
Propp, Vladimir, ed., *Severnorusskie skazki v zapisiakh A.I. Nikiforov*, Moscow: Izdatel'stvo Akademii Nauk SSSR, 1961.

(Pseudo-)Ǧāḥiẓ, *Das kitâb al-maḥâsin wa 'l-masâwî (Über die guten und schlechten Seiten der Dinge)*, transl. Oskar Rescher, Stuttgart, 1922.
(Pseudo-)Jāḥiẓ, *Le livre des beautés et des antithèses, attribué à al-Djahiz*, ed. Gerlof von Vloten, Leiden: Brill, 1898 (reprint Amsterdam: Oriental Press, s.a.).
Pseudo-Majlesi, *Javāher al-ʿoqul*, Lithograph Tehran 1265/1848.
Puchner, Walter, "Der unveröffentlichte Zettelkasten eines Katalogs der griechischen Märchentypen nach dem System von Aarne-Thompson von Georgios A. Megas," in *Die heutige Bedeutung oraler Traditionen*, ed. Walther Heissig and Rüdiger Schott, Opladen and Wiesbaden: Westdeutscher Verlag, 1988, pp. 88–105.
Qalyūbī, Aḥmad Shihāb al-Dīn Salāma al-, *al-Nawādir*, 3rd ed., Cairo: Muṣṭafā al-Bābī al-Ḥalabī wa-awlāduhu, 1374/1955.
Qaramānī, Aḥmad ibn Yūsuf al-, *Akhbār al-duwal wa-āthār al-uwal*, ed. Aḥmad Ḥaṭīṭ and Fahmī Saʿd, 3 vols., Beirut: ʿĀlam al-kutub, 1992.
Qazvini, Zakariyyā ibn Moḥammad al-, *ʿAjāʾeb al-makhluqāt wa-gharāʾeb al-mowjudāt*, Tehran, 1264/1847.
Qazwīnī, Zakariyyā ibn Muḥammad al-, *ʿAjāʾib al-makhlūqāt wa-gharāʾib al-mawjūdāt*, ed. Fārūq Saʿd, Beirut: al-Āfāq al-jadīda, 1401/1981.
Qazwīnī, Zakariyyā ibn Muḥammad ibn Maḥmūd al-, *Āthār al-bilād wa-akhbār al-ʿibād*, Beirut: Dār Ṣādir, 1380/1960.
Qeisari, Ebrāhim, "Maʾkhaẕ-e barkhi az dāstānhā-ye Haft owrang," *Jostārhā-ye adabi* 20.3 = 78 (1366/1987), pp. 599–644.
Qeṣṣe-ye Ḥamze (Ḥamze-nāme), ed. Jaʿfar Shiʿār, Tehran: Enteshārāt-e dāneshgāh-e Tehrān, 1347/1968.
Qumayḥa, Mufīd, *Nawādir Ashʿab*, Beirut: Dār al-Fikr al-lubnānī, 1990.
Qummī, Abū 'l-Ḥasan ʿAlī ibn Ibrāhīm al-, *Tafsīr*, ed. Muḥammad-Bāqir Muwaḥḥad al-Abṭaḥī al-Iṣfahānī, Qum: Muʾassasat al-imām al-Mahdī.
Raba Saura, Gregorio, and Anselmo J. Sánchez Ferra, "La memoria obstinada: Referencias clásicas de la tradición oral en la región de Murcia," *Mastia: Revista del museo arqueológico de Cartagena* 10.2011 (2017), pp. 121–200.
Rael, Juan B., *Cuentos españoles de Colorado y Nuevo Méjico: Spanish Originals with English Summaries*, 2 vols., Stanford: Stanford University Press, 1940.
Rāfiʿī al-Qazwīnī, ʿAbd al-Karīm ibn Muḥammad al-, *Kitāb al-Tadwīn fī akhbār Qazwīn*, ed. ʿAzīzallāh al-ʿAṭāridī, 4 vols., Beirut: Dār al-Kutub al-ʿilmiyya, 1408/1987.
Rāgheb Eṣfahāni, *Navāder: tarjome-ye ketāb-e Moḥāẓarāt al-odabāʾ [...]*, transl. Moḥammad Ṣāleḥ Qazvini, ed. Aḥmad Mojāhed, Tehran: Sorush 1371/1992.
Rāghib al-Iṣfahānī, al-Ḥusayn ibn Muḥammad al-, *Muḥāḍarāt al-udabāʾ wa-muḥāwarāt al-shuʿarāʾ wa-'l-bulaghāʾ*, 4 vols., Beirut 1961.
Rajna, Pio, "Le origini della novella narrata dal 'Frankeleyn' nei Canterbury Tales del Chaucer," *Romania* 32.126 (1903), pp. 204–267.
Rajna, Pio, *Le fonti dell'Orlando furioso*, ed Francesco Manzoni, Florence: Sansoni, 1975.
Ralston, W.R.S., *Russian Folk-Tales*, London: Smith, Elder, & Co., 1873.
Ramażāni, Moḥammad, ed., *Mollā Naṣreddin*, 5th ed., Teheran: Khāvar, 1339/1960.
Randolph, Vance, "Ozark Mountain Tales," *Southern Folklore Quarterly* 16 (1952), pp. 165–176.
Randolph, Vance, *The Devil's Pretty Daughter and Other Ozark Folk Tales*, New York: Columbia University Press, 1955.

Randolph, Vance, *We Always Lie to Strangers: Tall Tales from the Ozarks*, New York: Columbia University Press, 1951.
Ranelagh, Elaine L., *The Past We Share: The Near Eastern Ancestry of Western Folk Literature*, London: Quartet Books, 1979.
Range, Jochen D., *Litauische Volksmärchen*, Munich: Diederichs, 1981.
Ranke, Kurt, "Alad(d)in," in *Enzyklopädie des Märchens*, vol. 1 (1977), cols. 240–247.
Ranke, Kurt, "Ali Baba und die vierzig Räuber," in *Enzyklopädie des Märchens*, vol. 1 (1977), cols. 302–311.
Ranke, Kurt, "Anderson, Walter," in *Enzyklopädie des Märchens*, vol. 1 (1977), cols. 493–494.
Ranke, Kurt, "Brüder: Die scharfsinnigen B.," in *Enzyklopädie des Märchens*, vol. 2 (1979), cols. 874–887.
Ranke, Kurt, "Brüder: Die vier kunstreichen B.," in *Enzyklopädie des Märchens*, vol. 2 (1979), cols. 903–912, at cols. 908–910.
Ranke, Kurt, "Bettler als Pfand," in *Enzyklopädie des Märchens*, vol. 2 (1979), cols. 263–268.
Ranke, Kurt, "Der Bettler als Pfand: Geschichte eines Schwanks in Occident und Orient," *Zeitschrift für deutsche Philologie* 76 (1957), pp. 149–162, 358–364.
Ranke, Kurt, "Der Schwank von der schrecklichen Drohung," in *Humaniora: Essays in Literature, Folklore, Biography, Honoring Archer Taylor on His 70th Birthday*, ed. Wayland D. Hand, Locust Valley, New York: Augustin, 1960, pp. 78–96.
Ranke, Kurt, "Drohung: Die schreckliche D.," in *Enzyklopädie des Märchens*, vol. 3 (1981), cols. 894–901.
Ranke, Kurt, "Via grammatica," *Fabula* 20 (1979), pp. 160–169.
Ranke, Kurt, "Zum Motiv 'Accidental Cannibalism'," in *Die Welt der einfachen Formen*, Berlin: De Gruyter, 1978, pp. 286–290.
Ranke, Kurt, *Die Welt der Einfachen Formen*, Berlin: De Gruyter, 1978.
Ranke, Kurt, *European Ancedotes and Jests*, transl. Timothy Buck, Copenhagen: Rosenkilde and Bagger, 1972.
Ranke, Kurt, *Folktales of Germany*, Chicago: University of Chicago Press, 1966.
Ranke, Kurt, *Schleswig-holsteinische Volksmärchen*, 3 vols., Kiel: Hirt, 1955–1962.
Rasumny, Alexander: "Weib: Böses W. als schlechte Ware," in *Enzyklopädie des Märchens*, vol. 14 (2014), cols. 556–557.
Raudsep, Loreida, *Antiklerikale estnische Schwänke: Typen- und Variantenverzeichnis*, Tallinn: Institut für Sprach- und Literaturforschung, 1969.
Rauhut, Franz, "Fragen und Ergebnisse der Pathelin-Forschung," *Germanisch-Romanische Monatsschrift* 19 (1931), pp. 394–407.
Rausmaa, Pirkko-Liisa, "Aarne, Antti Amatus," in *Enzyklopädie des Märchens*, vol. 1 (1977), cols. 1–4.
Rausmaa, Pirkko-Liisa, "Lügenwette," in *Enzyklopädie des Märchens*, vol. 8 (1996), cols. 1274–1279.
Rausmaa, Pirkko-Liisa, *A Catalogue of Anecdotes: Addenda to the Aarne-Thompson Catalogue of Anecdotes in the Folklore Archives of the Finnish Literature Society*, Turku: Nordic Institute of Folklore, 1973.
Rausmaa, Pirkko-Liisa, *Suomalaiset kansansadut*, 6 vols., Helsinki: Suomalaisen Kirjallisuuden Seura, 1972–2000.
Ready, Psyche Z., *"She Was Really the Man She Pretended to Be": Change of Sex in Folk Narratives*, M.A. Thesis Fairfax: George Mason University, 2016.

Reeves, John C., "Some Parascriptural Dimensions of the 'Tale of Hārūt wa-Mārūt'," *Journal of the American Oriental Society* 135.4 (2015), pp. 817–842.

Rehatsek, Edward, *Amusing Stories, Translated from the Persian*, Bombay: Price Current Press, 1871.

Rehermann, Ernst Heinrich, "Chytraeus, Nathanael," in *Enzyklopädie des Märchens*, vol. 3 (1981), cols. 25–29.

Rehermann, Ernst Heinrich, and Fritz Wagner, "Bromyard, John," in *Enzyklopädie des Märchens*, vol. 2 (1979), cols. 797–802.

Reinhard, John R., "Strokes Shared," *The Journal of American Folklore* 36.142 (1923), pp. 380–400.

Reinhard, John Revell, *Medieval Pageant*, New York: Haskell, 1939 (1970).

Rescher, Oskar, *Die Geschichten und Anekdoten aus Qaljûbî's Nawâdir und Schirwânî's Nafhat el-Jemen, in gekürzter freier Wiedergabe aus dem Arabischen übersetzt*, Stuttgart: W. Heppeler, 1920.

Retsö, Jan, "Wahb ibn Munabbih, The *Kitāb al-tījān* and the History of Yemen," *Arabia* 3 (2005–2006), pp. 227–236.

Review of Falconer, Forbes, *Extracts from Some of the Persian Poets, Edited from Manuscripts in the Library of the East-India Company,* London 1843, *Journal Asiatique* (July and August 1843), pp. 124 ff.

Rey-Henningsen, Marisa, *The Tales of the Ploughwoman*, Helsinki: Suomalainen Tiedeacatemia, 1996.

Ricapito, Joseph V., ed., *La vida de Lazarillo de Tormes*, 3rd ed., Madrid: Cátedra, 1977.

Rieken, Bernd, "Zimmer: Das verbotene Z.," in *Enzyklopädie des Märchens*, vol. 14 (2014), cols. 1358–1362.

Río Cabrera, Juan Antonio del, and Melchor Pérez Bautista, *Cuentos populares de animales de la Sierra de Cádiz*, Cádiz: Universidad de Cádiz, 1998.

Ritter, Hellmut, *The Ocean of the Soul: Man, the World and God in the Stories of Farīd al-Dīn ʿAṭṭār,* transl. John O'Kane, Leiden: Brill, 2003.

Rittershaus, Adeline, *Die neuisländischen Volksmärchen*, Halle: Niemeyer, 1902.

Robe, Stanley L., *Index of Mexican Folktales*, Berkeley: University of California Press, 1973.

Robe, Stanley L., *Mexican Tales and Legends from Los Altos*, Berkeley: University of California Press, 1970.

Röcke, Werner, "Pfaffe vom Ka(h)lenberg," in *Enzyklopädie des Märchens*, vol. 10 (2002), cols. 831–836.

Röcke, Werner, "Salomon und Markolf," in *Enzyklopädie des Märchens*, vol. 11 (2004), cols. 1078–1085.

Rodríguez Pastor, Juan, *Cuentos extremeños obscenos y anticlericales*, Badajoz: Diputación de Badajoz, 2001.

Röhrich, Lutz, "Erotik, Sexualität," in *Enzyklopädie des Märchens*, vol. 4 (1984), cols. 234–278.

Röhrich, Lutz, "Geographisch-historische Methode," in *Enzyklopädie des Märchens*, vol. 5 (1987), cols. 1012–1030.

Röhrich, Lutz, *Erzählungen des späten Mittelalters und ihr Weiterleben in Literatur und Volksdichtung bis zur Gegenwart: Sagen, Märchen, Exempel und Schwänke*, 2 vols., Bern: Francke, 1967.

Rölleke, Heinz, "Constanze," in *Enzyklopädie des Märchens*, vol. 3 (1981), cols. 130–131.

Rölleke, Heinz, *Märchen aus dem Nachlaß der Brüder Grimm*, 2nd ed., Bonn: Bouvier, 1979.

Romuz-e Ḥamze, Lithograph Tehran 1273–76/1857–59.

Rosenow, Karl, *Zanower Schwänke: Ein fröhliches Buch*, Rügenwalde: Mewse, 1924.
Rosenthal, Franz, "A Small Collection of Aesopic Fables in Arabic Translation," in Macuch, Maria, Christa Müller-Kessler, and Bert Fragner, eds., *Studia semitica necnon Iranica: Rudolpho Macuch septuagenario ab amicis et discipulis dedicata*, Wiesbaden: Harrassowitz, 1989, pp. 233–256.
Rosenthal, Franz, *Humor in Early Islam*, Leiden: Brill 1956 (reprint 2011).
Rossi, Ettore, "La fonte turca della novella poetica albanese 'Erveheja' di Muhamet Çami (sec. XVIII–XIX) e il tema di 'Florence de Rome' e di 'Crescentia'," *Oriente moderno* 28 (1949), pp. 143–153.
Rossi, Ettore, "La leggenda di Turandot," in *Studi orientalistici in onore di Giorgio Levi della Vida*, ed. Raffaele Ciasca, vol. 2, Rome: Istituto per l'Oriente, 1956, pp. 457–476.
Rossi, Ettore, and Alessio Bombaci, *Elenco di drammi religiosi persiani (fondo mss. Vaticani Cerulli)*, Città del Vaticano: Biblioteca Apostolica Vaticana, 1961.
Rossi, Luciano, "Novellino," in *Enzyklopädie des Märchens*, vol. 10 (2002), cols. 129–134.
Rossi, Luciano, "Sercambi, Giovanni," in *Enzyklopädie des Märchens*, vol. 12 (2008), cols. 594–598.
Rost, Johann Leonhard [i.e. Meleaton], *Die wohlangerichtete neuerfundene Tugendschule in welcher vier und zwanzig anmuthige Historien zu erlaubter Gemüths-Ergötzung der Jugend auf eine erbauliche Art vorgetragen und mit nützlichen Anmerkungen und Lehren begleitet worden*, Frankfurt: Raspe, 1739.
Rotunda, Dominic Peter, *Motif-Index of the Italian Novella in Prose*, Bloomington: Indiana University, 1942.
Rückert, Friedrich, "Eine persische Erzählung," *Zeitschrift der Deutschen Morgenländischen Gesellschaft* 14 (1860), pp. 280–287.
Ruiz Sánchez, Marcos, "Versiones latinas de la historia del tesoro maldito," *Cuadernos de Filología Clásica: Estudios Latinos* 34.2 (2014), pp. 241–265.
Rumeau, Aristide, "Notes au Lazarillo: La casa lóbrega y oscura," *Les langues neo-latines* 173 (1965), pp. 16–25.
Rumi, Jalāl al-Din, *The Mathnawí of Jalálu'ddín Rúmí*, transl. Reynold A. Nicholson, 3 vols., London: Luzac & Co., 1934.
Rypka, Jan, "History of Persian Literature Up to the Beginning of the 20th century," in Rypka, Jan, ed., *History of Iranian Literature*, ed. Karl Jahn, Dordrecht: D. Reidel, 1968, pp. 69–351.
Rypka, Jan, ed., *History of Iranian Literature*, ed. Karl Jahn, Dordrecht: D. Reidel, 1968.
Sacchetti, Franco, *Le trecentonovelle*, ed. Valerio Marucci, Rome: Salerno, 1996.
Sachau, Eduard, *Skizze des Fellichi-Dialekts von Mosul*, Berlin: Königl. Akademie der Wissenschaften, 1895.
Sadan, Joseph, "The 'Nomad versus Sedentary' Framework in Arabic Literature," *Fabula* 15 (1974), pp. 57–86.
Sadan, Joseph, "Vin, fait de civilisation," in Rosen-Ayalon, Myriam, *Studies in Memory of Gaston Wiet*, Jerusalem: Hebrew University, 1977, pp. 129–160.
Saʿdi, *Bustān*, ed. Gholām-Ḥoseyn Yusefi, Tehran: Anjoman-e ostādān-e zabān va adabiyāt-e fārsi, 1359/1980.
Ṣafā, Navvāb, "Amir-Qoli Amini va farhang-e ʿavāmm," *Kelk* 53 (1373/1994), pp. 223–234.
Ṣafadī, Ṣalāḥ al-Dīn Khalīl ibn Aybak al-, *al-Wāfī bi-'l-wafayāt*, vol. 4, ed. Aḥmad al-Arnāwūṭ and Tazkī Muṣṭafā, Beirut: Dār Iḥyā' al-turāth al-ʿarabī, 2000.

Ṣafadī, Ṣalāḥ al-Dīn Khalīl ibn Aybak al-, *al-Wāfī bi-'l-wafayāt = Das biographische Lexikon des Ṣalāḥaddīn Ḫalīl Ibn Aibak aṣ-Ṣafadī*, vol. 27, ed. Otfried Weintritt, Beirut: Deutsche Morgenländische Gesellschaft, 1997.
Ṣafadī, Ṣalāḥ al-Dīn Khalīl ibn Aybak al-, *al-Wāfī bi-'l-wafayāt = Das biographische Lexikon des Ṣalāḥaddīn Ḫalīl Ibn Aibak aṣ-Ṣafadī*, vol. 29, ed. Maher Jarrar, Stuttgart: Steiner, 1997.
Ṣafi, Fakhr al-Din ʿAli, *Laṭāʾef al-ṭavāʾef*, ed. Aḥmad Golchin-Maʿāni, Tehran: Moḥammmad Ḥoseyn Eqbāl, 1336/1957.
Sagredo, Giovanni, see Vacalerio, Ginnesio Gavardo.
Salustius, Hilarius, *Melancholini wohl-aufgeraumter Weeg-Gefärth*, s.l., 1717.
Samarqandi, Moḥammad ʿAli Ẓahiri, *Sendbād-nāme*, ed. Moḥammad Bāqer Kamāl al-Dini, Tehran: Mirāṯ-e maktub, 1381/2002.
Ṣanʿānī, ʿAbd al-Razzāq ibn Hammām al-, *Tafsīr ʿAbd al-Razzāq*, ed. Muḥammad Maḥmūd ʿAbduh, 3 vols., Beirut: Dār al-Kutub al-ʿilmiyya, 1419/1999.
Ṣanʿatiniyā, Fāṭeme, *Maʾākheẕ-e qeṣaṣ va tamṯilāt-e maṯnavihā-ye ʿAṭṭār-e Neishāburi*, Tehran: Zavvār, 1369/1990.
Sánchez Ferra, Anselmo J., *El cuento folklórico en Lorca*, vol. 1. *Revista Murciana de Antropología* 20 (2013).
Sánchez Ferra, Anselmo, *Un tesoro en el desván: los cuentos de mis padres*, Cabanillas del Campo (Guadalajara): Palabras del candil, 2009.
Sánchez Pérez, Jose A., *Cien cuentos populares*, Madrid: Saeta, 1942.
Sándor, István, "György, Lajos," in *Enzyklopädie des Märchens*, vol. 6 (1990), cols. 334–336.
Sant Vicent Ferrer, *Sermons*, ed. Josep Sanchis Sivera and Gret Schib, 6 vols., Barcelona: Barcino, 1971–88.
Santa Cruz, Melchor de, *Floresta española*, ed. María Pilar Cuartero and Maxime Chevalier, Barcelona: Crítica, 1997.
Santillana, Iñigo López de Mendoza, *Refranes que dizen las viejas tras el fuego*, ed. Hugo O. Bizarri, Kassel: Reichenberger, 1995.
Santomá Juncadella, Luís, "El milagro de la mujer lapidada: Crítica literaria de la versión en occitano cispirenaico aragonés," *Revista de Filología Románica* 27 (2010), pp. 285–313.
Sathaye, Adheesh, "*Vetālapañcaviṃśatika*," in *Enzyklopädie des Märchens*, vol. 14 (2014), cols. 178–183.
Satke, Antonín, *Hlučínský pohádkář Josef Smolka*, Ostrava: Krajské nakladadelství, 1958.
Sato, Michio, "Geschlechtswechsel," in *Enzyklopädie des Märchens*, vol. 5 (1987), cols. 1138–1142.
Saxo Gramaticus, *The First Nine Books of Danish History of Saxo Grammaticus*, transl. Oliver Elton, ed. Frederick York Powell, London: David Nutt, 1894.
Saxo Grammaticus, *Gesta Danorum: The History of the Danes*, ed. Karsten Friis-Jensen, transl. Peter Fisher, 2 vols., Oxford: Clarendon Press, 2015.
Sayers, David Selim, *The Wiles of Women as a Literary Genre: A Study of Ottoman and Azeri Texts*, Wiesbaden: Harrassowitz, 2019.
Schacht, Joseph, "Die arabische Ḥiyal-Literatur: Ein Beitrag zur Erforschung der islamischen Rechtspraxis," *Der Islam* 15 (1926), pp. 211–232.
Schacht, Joseph, "Ḥiyal," in *The Encyclopaedia of Islam*, 2nd ed., vol. 3, Leiden: Brill, 1979, pp. 510–513.

Schamschula, Eleonore, "Das Fleischpfand: Mot. J1161.2 in Volkserzählung und Literatur," *Fabula* 25 (1984), pp. 277–295.
Schaumburg, Karl, and A. Banzer, "Die Farce Patelin und ihre Nachahmungen," *Zeitschrift für neufranzösische Sprache und Litteratur* 9 (1887), pp. 1–47; 10 (1888), pp. 93–112.
Scheiber, Alexander, "Traum vom Schatz auf der Brücke," in *Essays on Jewish Folklore and Comparative Literature*, Budapest: Akad. Kiadó, 1985, pp. 392–392.
Schenda, Rudolf, "Bertoldo, Bertoldino," in *Enzyklopädie des Märchens*, vol. 2 (1979), cols. 165–171.
Schenda, Rudolf, "Etienne de Bourbon," in *Enzyklopädie des Märchens*, vol. 4 (1984), cols. 511–519.
Schenda, Rudolf, *Märchen aus der Toskana*, Munich: Eugen Diederichs, 1996.
Schenda, Rudolf, *Von Mund zu Ohr: Bausteine zu einer Kulturgeschichte volkstümlichen Erzählens in Europa*, Göttingen: Vandenhoeck & Ruprecht, 1993.
Scherf, Walter, *Das Märchenlexikon*, Munich: C.H. Beck, 1995.
Schick, Josef, "Die ältesten Versionen von Chaucer's Frankeleynes Tale," *Studia Indo-Iranica: Ehrengabe für Wilhelm Geiger zur Vollendung des 75. Lebensjahres*, ed. Walther Wüst, Leipzig: Harrassowitz, 1931, pp. 89–107.
Schick, Josef, *Corpus Hamleticum: Hamlet in Sage und Dichtung, Kunst und Musik*, 1. Abteilung: *Sagengeschichtliche Untersuchungen*, vol. 5.1–2: *Die Scharfsinnsproben*, Leipzig: Otto Harrassowitz, 1934, 1938.
Schiefner, Anton von, transl., *Tibetan Tales Derived from Indian Sources: Translated from the Tibetan of the Kah-gyur*, transl. William Ralston Shedden Ralston, London: Kegan Paul, Trench, Trübner & Co., 1906.
Schier, Kurt, *Märchen aus Island*, Cologne: Diederichs, 1983.
Schier, Kurt, *Schwedische Volksmärchen*, 2nd ed., Düsseldorf and Cologne: Diederichs, 1971.
Schimmel, Annemarie, *The Triumphal Sun: A Study of the Works of Jalāloddin Rumi*, Albany: State University of New York Press, 1993.
Schmidt, Andreas, "Kalender des Pfarrers," in *Enzyklopädie des Märchens*, vol. 7 (1993), cols. 878–879.
Schmidt, Richard, transl., *Die Śukasaptati (textus ornatior)*, Stuttgart: W. Kohlhammer, 1899.
Schmitt, Christoph, "Lammherz," in *Enzyklopädie des Märchens*, vol. 8 (1996), cols. 743–747.
Schmitt, Jean-Claude, "Hundes Unschuld," in *Enzyklopädie des Märchens*, vol. 6 (1990), cols. 1362–1368.
Schmitt, Jean-Claude, *Der heilige Windhund*, Stuttgart: Klett-Cotta, 1982.
Schneider, L., "Die historische Windmühle bei Sanssouci," *Märkische Forschungen* 6 (1858), pp. 165–193.
Schneller, Christian, *Märchen und Sagen aus Wälschtirol: Ein Beitrag zur deutschen Sagenkunde*, Innsbruck: Wagner'sche Universitätsbuchhandlung, 1867.
Schoenfeld, Elisheva, "Handlung: Die vornehmste H.," in *Enzyklopädie des Märchens*, vol. 6 (1990), cols. 459–464.
Schott, Arthur, "Neue walachische Märchen," in *Hausblätter*, ed. F.W. Hackländer and Edmund Hoefer, vol. 4, Stuttgart: Dolph Krabbe, 1847, pp. 314–320.
Schott, Arthur, and Albert Schott, *Rumänische Volkserzählungen aus dem Banat*, ed. Rolf Wilhelm Brednich and Ion Taloş, Bucarest: Kriterion, 1971.

Schreiber, Eva, "Joseph ibn Sabara," in *Enzyklopädie des Märchens*, vol. 7 (1993), cols. 650–653.
Schröder, Ina, "Tür bewacht," in *Enzyklopädie des Märchens*, vol. 13 (2010), cols. 1024–1027.
Schulte-Kemminghausen, Karl, and Hüllen, Georg, *Märchen der europäischen Völker*, vol. 7, Münster: Aschendorff, 1967.
Schütz, Joseph, *Volksmärchen aus Jugoslawien*, Düsseldorf: Diederichs, 1960.
Schwab, Gustav, *Die Deutschen Volksbücher für Jung und Alt wiedererzählt*, vol. 1, Gütersloh: Bertelsmann, s.a.
Schwartz, Wilhelm, *Sagen und alte Geschichten der Mark Brandenburg: Aus dem Munde des Volkes gesammelt und wiedererzählt*, 7th ed., Berlin: Märkische Verlangsanstalt, 1895.
Schwarz, Paul, "Eva: Die neue E.," in *Enzyklopädie des Märchens*, vol. 4 (1984), cols. 563–569.
Schwarz, Rainer, transl., *Die sieben Abenteuer des Prinzen Hatem: Ein iranischer Märchenroman*, Leipzig: Gustav Kiepenheuer, 1990.
Schwarzbaum, Haim, "A Jewish Moses Legend of Islamic Provenance," in *Fields of Offerings: Studies in Honor of Raphael Patai*, ed. Victor D. Sanua, London and Toronto: Associated University Presses, 1983, pp. 99–110.
Schwarzbaum, Haim, "International Folklore Motifs in Petrus Alphonsi's 'Disciplina clericalis'," in Schwarzbaum, *Jewish Folklore between East and West: Collected Papers*, ed. Eli Yassif, Beer-Sheva: Ben-Gurion University of the Negev Press, 1989, pp. 239–358.
Schwarzbaum, Haim, *Biblical and Extra-Biblical Legends in Islamic Folk-Literature*, Walldorf: Verlag für Orientkunde, 1982.
Schwarzbaum, Haim, *Studies in Jewish and World Folklore*, Berlin: Walter de Gruyter, 1968.
Schwarzbaum, Haim, *The Mishle Shu'alim (Fox Fables) of Rabbi Berechiah ha-Nakdan: A Study in Comparative Folkore and Fable Lore*, Kiron: Institute for Jewish and Arab Folklore Research, 1979.
Scott, Jonathan, *Bahar Danush or Garden of Knowledge: An Oriental Romance Translated from the Persic of Einaïatollah*, 3 vols., London, T. Cadell and W. Davies, 1799.
Seidenspinner, Wolfgang, "Talion," in *Enzyklopädie des Märchens*, vol. 13 (2011), cols. 168–172.
Seiffert, Lewis C., "Sex, Sexuality," in Duggan, Anne E., and Donald Haase, eds., *Folktales and Fairy Tales*, Santa Barbara, CA: Greenwood, 2016, vol. 3, pp. 907–911.
Selk, Paul, *Lügengeschichten aus Schleswig-Holstein*, Husum: Husum Druck- und Verlagsanstalt, 1982.
Sellheim, Rudolf, "Eine unbeachtet gebliebene Sprichwörtersammlung: Die *Nuzhat al-anfus wa-rauḍat al-maclis* des Raḍīaddīn al-ʿIrāqī (468/1075–561/1166)," *Oriens* 31 (1988), pp. 82–94.
Sercambi, Giovanni, *Il novellieri*, ed. Luciano Rossi, 3 vols., Rome: Salerno, 1972.
Sergeant, D.S., "al-Jāḥiẓ," in Meisami, Julie Scott, and Paul Starkey, eds., *Encyclopaedia of Arabic Literature*, London: Routledge, 1998, vol. 1, pp. 408–409.
Serra y Boldú, Valerio, *Rondalles populars*, 18 vols., Barcelona: Políglota, 1932–1933.
Serrano Reyes, Jesús L., *Didactismo y moralismo en Geoffrey Chaucer y Don Manuel: Un estudio comparativo textual*, Córdoba: Universidad de Córdoba, 1996.

Shafa, Shojaeddin, *De Persia a la España Musulmana: La Historia Recuperada*, Huelva: Universidad de Huelva, 2000.
Shahri, Jaʿfar, *Qand va namak: żarb al-maṡalhā-ye tehrāni be-zabān-e moḥāvere*, Tehran: Esmāʿiliyān, 1370.
Shams al-Dīn, Ibrāhīm, *Qiṣaṣ al-ʿarab*, Beirut: Dār al-Kutub al-ʿilmiyya, 1423/2002.
Sharīshī, Abū ʾl-ʿAbbās Aḥmad ibn al-Muʾmin al-Qaysī al-, *Sharḥ Maqāmāt al-Ḥarīrī al-Baṣrī*, ed. Ṣidqī Muḥammad Jamīl, 2 vols., Beirut: Dār al-Fikr, 1429–1430/2009.
Shaykhū, Lūwīs, *Majānī al-adab fī ḥadāʾiq al-ʿarab*. available at al-waraq.net (accessed March 1, 2017).
Shehata, Samer S., "The Politics of Laughter: Nasser, Sadat, and Mubarek in Egyptian Political Jokes," *Folklore* 103.1 (1992), pp. 75–91.
Sheykh-Zāda, *The History of the Forty Vezirs, or the Story of the Forty Morns and Eves*, transl. E.J.W. Gibb, London: George Redway, 1886.
Sheyn, Pavel Vasilyevich, *Materiali dlya izuchenija byta i yazika russkogo naseleniya severo-zapadnogo kraya*, Saint Peterburg: Imp. Akad. Nauk, 1893.
Shirwānī, Aḥmad ibn Muḥammad al-Anṣārī al-Yamanī al-, *Ḥadīqat al-afrāḥ*, Cairo: Muṣṭafā al-Bābī al-Ḥalabī, 1320/1902.
Shirwānī, Aḥmad ibn Muḥammad al-Anṣārī al-Yamanī al-, *Nafḥat al-Yaman*, Cairo 1356/1937.
Shojaei Kawan, Christine, "Kontamination," in *Enzyklopädie des Märchens*, vol. 8 (1996), cols. 201–217.
Shojaei Kawan, Christine, "Kriminalroman," in *Enzyklopädie des Märchens*, vol. 8 (1996), cols. 440–460.
Shojaei Kawan, Christine, "Kuchen: Laßt sie K. essen!" in *Enzyklopädie des Märchens*, vol. 8 (1996), cols. 536–541.
Shojaei Kawan, Christine, "Uriasbrief," in *Enzyklopädie des Märchens*, vol. 13 (2010), cols. 1262–1267.
Simonsuuri, Lauri, and Pirkko-Liisa Rausmaa, *Finnische Volkserzählungen*, Berlin: De Gruyter, 1968.
Simson, Georg von, "Benfey, Theodor," in *Enzyklopädie des Märchens*, vol. 2 (1979), cols. 102–109.
Sinnersberg, Rudolph von, *Belustigung Vor Frauenzimmer und Junggesellen*, Rothenburg: Caspar Friedrich Hoffmann, 1747.
Sirovátka, Oldřich, *Tschechische Volksmärchen*, 2nd ed., Düsseldorf: Diederichs, 1980.
Skinner, Charles Montgomery, *Myths and Legends of Our Own Land*, Philadelphia, J.B. Lippincott, 1896.
Sklarek, Elisabet, *Ungarische Volksmärchen*, Leipzig: Diederichs, 1901.
Smičiklas, T[adija], "Narodne pripovijetke iz osječke okoline u Slavoniji," *Zbornik za narodni život i običaje Južnih Slavena* 15.2 (1910), pp. 279–305.
Šmits, Pēteris, "Ādams un Ieva," *Latviešu tautas teikas un pasakas*, ed. Haralds Biezais, 2nd ed., vol. 11, Waverly, Iowa: Latvju Grāmata, 1968, pp. 407–408.
Sobernheim, M. "Ḳarākūsh," in *Encyclopaedia of Islam*, 2nd ed., vol. 4 (1978), pp. 613–614.
Sobḥi, Fażlallāh, *Dāstānhā-ye melal*, Tehran: Anjoman-e ravābeṭ-e farhangi-ye Irān bā Etteḥād-e jamāhir-e shouravi-e susyālisti, s.a.

Solymossy, Sándor, "A 'szép ember' meséje", *Ethnographia* 27 (1916), pp. 257–275.
Somadeva, *The Ocean of Story: Being C.H. Tawney's Translation of Somadeva's Kathā Sarit Sāgara (or Ocean of Streams of Stories)*, ed. Norman M. Penzer, 10 vols., (2nd ed. London: privately printed, 1923–1928) reprint Delhi: Motilal Banarsidass, 1968.
Soroudi, Sarah Sorour, *The Folktales of Jews from Iran, Central Asia and Afghanistan: Tale-Types and Genres*, ed. Heda Jason, Dortmund: Verlag für Orientkunde, 2008.
Souto Maior, Mário, *Dicionário de folcloristas brasileiros*, Recife: Fundarpe, 1999 (2nd ed. Goiânia: Kelps, 2000).
Spargo, John Webster, *Chaucer's Shipman's Tale: The Lover's Gift Regained*, Helsinki: Suomalainen Tiedeakatemia, 1930.
Speroni, Charles, *Wit and Wisdom of the Italian Renaissance*, Berkeley: University of California Press, 1964.
Spies, Otto, "Arabische Stoffe in der Disciplina Clericalis," *Rheinisches Jahrbuch für Volkskunde* 21 (1973), pp. 170–199.
Spies, Otto, "Arabisch-islamische Erzählstoffe," in *Enzyklopädie des Märchens*, vol. 1 (1977), cols. 685–718.
Spies, Otto, "Damīrī," in *Enzyklopädie des Märchens*, vol. 3 (1981), cols. 219–223.
Spies, Otto, "Das Grimmsche Märchen 'Bruder Lustig' in arabischer Überlieferung," *Rheinisches Jahrbuch für Volkskunde* 2 (1951), pp. 54–55.
Spies, Otto, "Die orientalische Herkunft des Stoffes 'Knoist und sine dre Sühne'," *Rheinisches Jahrbuch für Volkskunde* 12 (19619, pp. 47–52.
Spies, Otto, and Nabila Salem, "Ägypten," in *Enzyklopädie des Märchens*, vol. 1 (1977), cols. 175–227.
Spinette, Alberte, "Boccaccio, Giovanni," in *Enzyklopädie des Märchens*, vol. 2 (1979), cols. 549–561.
Spitta-Bey, Guillaume, *Contes arabes modernes*, Leiden: Brill, 1883.
Staehle, Wilhelm, *"La Farce de Pathelin," in literarischer, grammatischer und sprachlicher Hinsicht*, Phil. Diss. Marburg 1862.
Stein, Hans Joachim, "Schuß auf den toten König," in *Enzyklopädie des* Märchens, vol. 12 (2007), cols. 255–259.
Steinbauer, Bernd, "Tod der Alten," in *Enzyklopädie des Märchens*, vol. 13 (2011), cols. 712–715.
Stemplinger, Eduard, *Antiker Humor: 204 Anekdoten nach antiken Quellen*, Munich: Piper, 1939.
Stephani, Claus, *Märchen der Rumäniendeutschen*, Munich: Diederichs, 1991.
Stevens, Ethel Stefana, *Folk-tales of Iraq*, London: Milford, 1931.
Stewart, James, "Aladdin in Aran: Folktales from Inis Mor, 1895," in *Papers: The 8th Congress for the International Society for Folk Narrative Research, Bergen, June 12th–17th 1984*, ed. Reimund Kvideland and Torunn Selberg, vol. 2, Bergen 1984, pp. 229–237.
Stiefel, Abraham Ludwig, "Zur Schwankdichtung im 16. und 17. Jahrhundert, 1: Quellen und Stoffgeschichtliches zu Jakob Frey's 'Gartengesellschaft'," *Zeitschrift für vergleichende Litteraturgeschichte* 12 (1898), pp. 164–180.
Stiller, Frauke, *"Die unschuldig verfolgte und später rehabilitierte Ehefrau": Untersuchung zur Frau im 15. Jahrhundert am Beispiel der Crescentia- und Sibillen-Erzählungen*, Ph.D. Diss. Humboldt-University Berlin 2001.
Stitt, J. Michael, and Dodge, Robert K., *A Tale Type and Motif Index of Early U.S. Almanachs*, New York: Greenwood, 1991.

Stohlmann, Jürgen, "Orient-Motive in der lateinischen Exempla-Literatur des 12. und 13. Jahrhunderts," in Zimmermann, Alfred, and Ingrid Craemer-Ruegenberg, eds., *Orientalische Kultur und lateinisches Mittelalter*, Berlin: De Gruyter, 1985, pp. 123–150.

Stojanović, Mijat, *Pučke pripoviedke i pjesme*, Zagreb, 1867.

Stoneman, Richard, *Alexander the Great: A Life in Legend*, New Haven: Yale University Press, 2008.

Strackerjan, Ludwig, *Aberglaube und Sagen aus dem Herzogtum Oldenburg*, 2nd ed., ed. Karl Willoh, 2 vols., Oldenburg: Gerhard Stalling, 1909.

Stroebe, Klara, *Nordische Volksmärchen*, 2 vols., Jena: Diederichs, 1915.

Stroescu, Sabina Cornelia, *La typologie bibliographique des facéties roumaines*, 2 vols., Bucharest: Académie de la République Socialiste de Roumanie, 1969.

Strömbäck, Dag, "En orientalisk saga i fornnordisk dräkt," in *Donum Grapeanum: festskrift tillägnad överbibliotekaarrrien Anders Grape*, Uppsala: Almqvist & Wiksell, 1945, pp. 408–444.

Strömbäck, Dag, "Uppsala, Iceland, and the Orient," in Brown, Arthur, and Peter Foote, eds., *Early English and Norse Studies Presented to Hugh Smith in Honour of His 60th Birthday*, London: Methuen, 1963, pp. 178–190.

Strong, John S., *The Legend of King Aśoka: A Study and Translation of the Aśokāvadāna*, Princeton: Princeton University Press, 1983.

Stroup, Thomas B., "Two Folk Tales from South Central Georgia," *Southern Folklore Quarterly* 2 (1937), pp. 207–212.

Stübs, Hugo, *Ull Lüj vertellen: Plattdeutsche Geschichten aus dem pommerschen Weizacker*, Greifswald: Bamberg, 1938.

Stumme, Hans, *Maltesische Märchen, Gedichte und Rätsel in deutscher Übersetzung*, Leipzig: Hinrichs, 1904.

Stumme, Hans, *Tunisische Märchen und Gedichte*, 2 vols., Leipzig: Hinrichs, 1893.

Suárez López, Jesús, *Cuentos del Siglo de Oro en la tradición oral de Asturias*, s. l.: Red de Museos etnográficos de Asturias, 2009.

Suárez López, Jesús, *Cuentos medievales en la tradición oral de Asturias*, electronic edition Red de Museos Etnográficos de Asturias, 2009.

Suyūṭī, Jalāl al-Dīn ʿAbd al-Raḥmān al- [attributed to Ibn Iyās al-Ḥanafī], *Badāʾiʿ al-zuhūr fī waqāʾiʿ al-duhūr*, Cairo: ʿIsā al-Bābī al-Ḥalabī, s.a.

Suyūṭī, Jalāl al-Dīn ʿAbd al-Raḥmān al-, *Kitāb Tuḥfat al-mujālis wa nuzhat al-majālis*, ed. Badr al-Dīn al-Naʿsānī, Cairo 1326/1908.

Ṭabarī, Abū Jaʿfar Muḥammad ibn Jarīr al-, *Annales auctore Abu Djafar Mohammed ibn Djarir at-Tabari*, 13 vols., ed. P. de Jong, Leiden: E.J. Brill, 1880–1890.

Ṭabarī, Abū Jaʿfar Muḥammad ibn Jarīr al-, *Tafsīr Ṭabarī: Jāmiʿ al-bayān ʿan taʾwīl āy al-Qurʾān*, ed. Maḥmūd Muḥammad Shākir and Aḥmad Muḥammad Shākir, 9 vols., Cairo: Dār al-Maʿārif bi-Miṣr, 1969–1972.

Ṭabarī, Abū Jaʿfar Muḥammad ibn Jarīr al-, *Tarjome-ye Tafsīr-e Ṭabarī*, ed. Ḥabib Yaghmāʾi, Tehran: Chāpkhāne-ye dowlati-ye Irān, 1339/1969.

Tales of the Marvellous and News of the Strange, transl. Malcolm C. Lyons, London: Penguin, 2014.

Taloş, Ion, "Rumänien," in *Enzyklopädie des Märchens*, vol. 11 (2004), cols. 886–897.

Tamer, Georges, "The Qurʾān and Humor," in Tamer, ed., *Humor in der arabischen Kultur/ Humor in Arabic Culture*, Berlin: De Gruyter, 2009, pp. 3–28.

Tanūkhī, Abū ʿAlī al-Muḥassin ibn ʿAlī al-, *Kitāb al-Faraj baʿd al-shidda*, ed. ʿAbbūd al-Shālijī, 5 vols., Beirut: Dār Ṣādir, 1398/1978.

Tanūkhī, Abū ʿAlī al-Muḥassin ibn ʿAlī al-, *Nishwār al-muḥāḍara wa-akhbār al-mudhākara*, ed. ʿAbbūd al-Shālijī, 6 vols., Beirut: Dār Ṣādir, 1392/1972.
Tanūkhī, At- *Ende gut, alles gut: Das Buch der Erleichterung nach der Bedrängnis*, transl. Arnold Hottinger, Zurich: Manesse, 1979.
Ṭarābulusī, Ḥikmat Sharīf al-, *Nawādir Juḥā*, Beirut: al-Mu'assasa al-muttaḥida lil-nashr.
Tarasevśkyj, Pavło, and Hnatjuk, Vołodymyr, *Das Geschlechtleben des ukrainischen Bauernvolkes in Österreich-Ungarn*, vol. 2: *Folkloristische Erhebungen in Österreich-Ungarn: 400 Schwänke und novellenartige Erzählungen, die in Ostgalizien und Ungarn gesammelt worden*, ed. Vołodmyr Hnatjuk, Leipzig: Ethnologischer Verlag, 1912.
Tardel, Hermann, "Das Motiv des Gedichtes 'Botenart' von Anastasius Grün," in *Festschrift zum 16. Neuphilologentag in Bremen vom 1. bis 4. Juni 1914*, Heidelberg 1914, pp. 163–201.
Tardel, Hermann, "Motivgeschichtliches," *Niederdeutsche Zeitschrift für Volkskunde* 14 (1936), pp. 216–221.
Ṭarshūna, Maḥmūd, ed., *Mi'at layla wa-layla*, Libya and Tunis: al-Dār al-ʿarabiyya lil-kitāb, 1979.
Ṭarṭūshī, Muḥammad ibn al-Walīd al-, *Sirāj al-mulūk*, ed. Jaʿfar al-Bayātī, London: Riad el-Rayyes, 1990.
Ṭarṭūshī, Muḥammad ibn al-Walīd al- see Abubéquer de Tortosa
Tauer, Felix, *Tausendundeine Nacht: Neue Erzählungen*, Frankfurt am Main: Insel, 1995.
Tawḥīdī, Abū Ḥayyān al-, *al-Baṣā'ir wa-'l-dhakhā'ir*, ed. Wadād al-Qāḍī, 10 vols., Beirut: Dār Ṣādir, 1408/1988.
Tawney, C.H., "The Buddhist Original of Chaucer's Pardoner's Tale," *The Journal of Philology* 12 (1883), pp. 203–208.
Taylor, Archer, "And Marie-Antoinette Said …," in *Comparative Studies in Folklore: Asia—Europe—America*, Taipei: The Orient Cultural Service, 1972, pp. 249–265 (originally published in *Revista de etnografia* 22, 1968, pp. 1–17).
Taylor, Archer, "The Emperor's New Clothes," *Modern Philology* 25 (1927–28), pp. 17–27.
Taylor, Archer, "The Three Sins of the Hermit," *Modern Philology* 20.1 (1922), pp. 61–94.
Tegethoff, Ernst, *Französische Volksmärchen*, 2 vols., Jena: Diederichs, 1923.
Tenberg, Reinhard, "Kreuzzüge," in *Enzyklopädie des Märchens*, vol. 8 (1996), cols. 413–419.
Tewaag, F., *Erzählungen, Märchen, Sagen und Mundarten aus Hessen*, Marburg, Friedrich: 1885 (1888).
Tezcan, Semih, "Vierzig Wesire," in *Enzyklopädie des Märchens*, vol. 14 (2014), cols. 195–200.
Thacker, Mike J., "'La desordenada codicia de los bienes ajenos'—a 'caso límite' of the picaresque?," *Bulletin of Hispanic Studies* 55 (1978), pp. 33–41.
Thaʿālibī, Abū Manṣūr ʿAbd al-Malik ibn Muḥammad, *Kitāb Laṭā'if al-ṣaḥāba wa-'l-tābiʿīn* (selections), in Cool, P., *Brevis Chrestomathia*, in Roorda, T., *Grammatica Arabica*, Leiden: S. and J. Luchtmans, 1835, pp. 1–31.
Thaʿlabī, Abū Isḥāq Aḥmad ibn Muḥammad ibn Ibrāhīm al-, *ʿArā'is al-majālis fī qiṣaṣ al-anbiyā'*, transl. William M. Brinner, Leiden etc., Brill, 2002.
The Balloon Jester. Dublin: S. Colbert, [1784].
The New Joe Miller (1826).
Thibault, Charles, *Contes de Champagne*, Paris: Quatre jeudis, 1960.
Thompson, Harold W., *Body, Boots and Britches*, Philadelphia: Lippincott, 1940.

Thompson, Stith, *Motif-Index of Folk-Literature: A Classification of Narrative Elements in Folktales, Ballads, Myths, Fables, Mediaeval Romances, Exempla, Fabliaux, Jest-Books and Local Legends*, 6 vols., (Helsinki, 1932–1936) rev. and enl. ed. Copenhagen: Rosenkilde and Bagger, 1955–1958 (reprint Bloomington: Indiana University Press, 1965).
Thompson, Stith, and Jonas Balys, *The Oral Tales of India*, Bloomington: Indiana University Press, 1958.
Thursby, Jacqueline, "Brunvand, Jan Harold," in *Enzyklopädie des Märchens*, vol. 14 (2014), cols. 1578–1581.
Tietze, Andreas, "Das türkische Ferec ba'd eş-şidde als Medium der Wanderung orientalischer Stoffe ins Abendland," in *Proceedings of the Twenty-Second Congress of Orientalists held in Istanbul, September 15th to 22nd, 1951*, ed. Zeki Velidi Togan, vol. 2, Leiden: E.J. Brill, 1957, pp. 412–420.
Tietze, Andreas, review of Eberhard and Boratav, *Typen türkischer Volksmärchen*, *Oriens* 7 (1954), pp. 141–152.
Tille, Václav, *Soupis českých pohádek*, vol. 1, Prague: České Akademie Věd a Uměni, 1929.
Ting, Nai-tung, "Years of Experience in a Moment: A Study of a Tale Type in Asian and European Literature," *Fabula* 22 (1981), pp. 183–213.
Toldo, Pietro, "Le Moine bridé: A propos d'un conte de Piron," *Revue de littérature comparée* 2 (1922), pp. 54–59.
Toldo, Pietro, "Pel fableau di Constant du Hamel," *Romania* 32.128 (1903), pp. 552–564.
Tomkowiak, Ingrid, "Moser-Rath, Elfriede," in *Enzyklopädie des Märchens*, vol. 9 (1999), cols. 939–943.
Tomkowiak, Ingrid, and Dietmar Sedlaczek, "Nationalsozialismus," in *Enzyklopädie des Märchens*, vol. 9 (1999), cols. 1243–1255.
Torrey, Charles C., "The Egyptian Prototype of 'King John and the Abbot'," *Journal of the American Oriental Society* 20 (1899), pp. 209–216.
Toschi, Paolo, and Angelo Fabi, *Buonsangue romagnolo: racconti di animali, scherzi, anedotti, facezie*, Bologna: Cappelli, 1960.
Tottoli, Roberto, "Hārūt and Mārūt," in *The Encyclopaedia of Islam*, 3rd ed., Leiden: Brill, 2017, fasc. 5, pp. 95–97.
Traninger, Anita, "Serendipity und Abduktion: Die Literatur als Medium einer Logik des Neuen (Cristoforo Armeno, Voltaire, Horace Walpole)," in Ammon, Frieder von, Cornelia Rémi, Gideon Stiening, eds., *Literatur und praktische Vernunft*, Berlin: De Gruyter, 2016, pp. 205–230.
Tubach, Frederic C., *Index exemplorum: A Handbook of Medieval Religious Tales*, Helsinki: Suomalainen tiedeakatemia, 1969.
Tuningio, Gerærdo, *Apophthegmata: græca, latina, italica, gallica, hispanica*, Leiden: Officina Plantiniana Raphelengii, 1609.
Tupper, Frederick, "The Pardoner's Tale," in *Sources and Analogues of Chaucer's Canterbury Tales*, ed. William Frank Bryan and Germaine Dempster, 2nd ed., London: Routledge & Kegan Paul, 1958, pp. 415–438.
Tuttle, Kelly, "al-Ibshīhī," in Lowry, Joseph E., and Devin J. Stewart, eds., *Essays in Arabic Literary Biography, 1350–1850*, Wiesbaden: Harrassowitz, 2009, pp. 236–242.
Tyroller, Franz, *Die Fabel von dem Mann und dem Vogel in ihrer Verbreitung in der Weltliteratur*, Berlin: Felber, 1912.
Uffer, Leza, *Rätoromanische Märchen und ihre Erzähler*, Basel: Krebs, 1945, pp. 20–225, 300–301.

Ulrich, Giacomo, ed., *Opera nuova e da ridere: Grillo medico: poemetto populare di autore ignoto*, Livorno: Raffaelo Giusto, 1901.
Ulrich, Jakob, *Volkstümliche Dichtungen der Italiener*, Leipzig: Dt. Verl., 1906.
Ulrich Jakob, transl., *Die hundert alten Erzählungen*, Leipzig: Deutsche Verlags-Actiengesellschaft, 1905.
Ure, Jean, *Pacala and Tandala and Other Rumanian Folk-Tales*, London: Methuen, 1960.
Uring, Nathaniel, *A History of the Voyages and Travels of Captain Nathaniel Uring*, London: J. Peele, 1726.
Uther, Hans-Jörg, "Crescentia," in *Enzyklopädie des Märchens*, vol. 3 (1981), cols. 167–171.
Uther, Hans-Jörg, "Fuchs und Flöhe," in *Enzyklopädie des Märchens*, vol. 5 (1987), cols. 484–486.
Uther, Hans-Jörg, "Gaben des kleinen Volkes," in *Enzyklopädie des Märchens*, vol. 5 (1987), cols. 637–642.
Uther, Hans-Jörg, "Hündin: Die weinende H.," in *Enzyklopädie des Märchens*, vol. 6 (1990), cols. 1368–1372.
Uther, Hans-Jörg, "Kaisers neue Kleider," in *Enzyklopädie des Märchens*, vol. 7 (1993), cols. 852–857.
Uther, Hans-Jörg, "Kleider machen Leute," in *Enzyklopädie des Märchens*, vol. 7 (1993), cols. 1425–1429.
Uther, Hans-Jörg, "Kryptádia," in *Enzyklopädie des Märchens*, vol. 8 (1996), cols. 528–531.
Uther, Hans-Jörg, "Schatz des Blinden" in *Enzyklopädie des Märchens*, vol. 11 (2004), cols. 1259–1263.
Uther, Hans-Jörg, *Behinderte in populären Erzählungen*, Berlin: Walter de Gruyter, 1981.
Uther, Hans-Jörg, *Deutscher Märchenkatalog: Ein Typenverzeichnis*, Münster: Waxmann, 2015.
Uther, Hans-Jörg, *The Types of International Folktales: A Classification and Bibliography, Based on the System of Antti Aarne and Stith Thompson*, 3 vols., Helsinki: Suomalainen Tiedeakatemia, 2004.
Vacalerio, Ginnesio Gavardo [i.e. Sagredo, Giovanni], *L'Arcadia in Brenta, ovvero La Melanchonia Sbandita*, Colonia: Francesco Kinchio, 1667.
Vacalerio, Ginnesio Gavardo [i.e. Sagredo, Giovanni], *L'Arcadia in Brenta*, ed. Bologna: Giovanni Recaldini, 1693.
Vade Mecum für lustige Leute, enthaltend eine Sammlung angenehmer Scherze, witziger Einfälle und spaßhafter kurzer Historien, aus den besten Schriftstellern zusammengetragen, 10 vols., Berlin: August Mylius, 1764–1792.
Vā'eẓ Kāshefi, Kamāl al-Din Ḥoseyn ibn 'Ali, *Anvār-e Soheyli yā Kalile va Demne-ye Kāshefi*, Tehran: Amir Kabir, 1362/1983.
Vakiliyān, Aḥmad, *Tamsil va masal*, vol. 2, Tehran: Sorush, 1366/1987.
Vámbéry, Ármin, "Der orientalische Ursprung von Shylock," *Keleti szemle* 2 (1901), pp. 18–29.
Van Buitenen, Johannes Adrianus Bernardus, *Tales of Ancient India*, Chicago: The University of Chicago Press, 1959.
Van den Boogert, Maurits H., "'Antar Overseas: Arabic Manuscripts in Europe in the Late 18th and Early 19th Century," Vrolijk, Arnold, and Jan P. Hogendijk, eds., *O Ye Gentlemen: Arabic Studies on Science and Literar Culture in Honour of Remke Kruk*, Leiden: Brill, 2007, pp. 339–352.
Van der Kooi, Jurjen, "Almanakteljes en folksforhalen; in stikmennich 17de en 18de ieuske teksten," *It Beaken* 41.1–2 (1979), pp. 70–114.

Van der Kooi, Jurjen, "Hammel Gottes," in *Enzyklopädie des Märchens*, vol. 6 (1990), cols. 425–427.
Van der Kooi, Jurjen, "Rhampsinit," in *Enzyklopädie des Märchens*, vol. 11 (2004), cols. 633–640.
Van der Kooi, Jurjen, "Scharlatan," in *Enzyklopädie des Märchens*, vol. 11 (2004), cols. 1232–1237.
Van der Kooi, Jurjen, "Schemjaka: Die Urteile des S.," in *Enzyklopädie des Märchens*, vol. 11 (2005), cols. 1356–1362.
Van der Kooi, Jurjen, "Sprachmißverständnisse," in *Enzyklopädie des Märchens*, vol. 12 (2007), cols. 1094–1099.
Van der Kooi, Jurjen, "Teilung von Geschenken und Schlägen," in *Enzyklopädie des Märchens*, vol. 13 (2011), cols. 323–327.
Van der Kooi, Jurjen, *Volksverhalen in Friesland: Lectuur en mondelinge overlevering. Een typencatalogus*, Ph.D. thesis Rijksuniversiteit Groningen, 1984.
Van der Kooi, Jurjen, *Volksverhalen uit Friesland*, Utrecht: Uitgeverij het spectrum, 1979.
Van der Kooi, Jurjen, and Babs A. Gezelle Meerburg, *Friesische Märchen*, Munich: Diederichs, 1990.
Van der Kooi, Jurjen, and Theo Schuster, *Der Großherzog und die Marktfrau: Märchen und Schwänke aus dem Oldenburger Land*, Leer: Schuster, 1994.
Van der Kooi, Jurjen, and Theo Schuster, *Märchen und Schwänke aus Ostfriesland*, Leer: Schuster, 1993.
Van Gelder, G.J.H., "al-Nawājī," in Meisami, Julie Scott, and Paul Starkey, eds., *Encyclopedia of Arabic Literature*, London: Routledge, 1998, p. 584..
Van Gelder, Geert Jan, "A Muslim Encomium on Wine: *The Racecourse of the Bay (Ḥalbat al-kumayt)* by al-Nawāǧī (d. 859/1455) as a Post-classical Arabic Work," *Arabica* 42 (1995), pp. 222–234.
Vanja, Konrad, "Genoveva," in *Enzyklopädie des Märchens*, vol. 5 (1987), cols. 1003–1009.
Varāvini, Sa'd al-Din, *Marzbān-nāme*, ed. Khalil Khaṭib Rahbar, 2nd ed., Tehran: Ṣafi 'Alishāh, 1366/1987.
Vella Camilleri, Doris, *Il-Ġaħan ta'Madwarna*, Valetta: Colour Image, 2006.
Viidalepp, Richard, *Estnische Volksmärchen*, Berlin: Akademie-Verlag, 1980.
Vishnusharma, *The Panchatantra*, transl. Arthur W. Ryder, Chicago: University of Chicago Press, 1925.
Voltaire, *Romans et contes*, vol. 1: *Zadig et autres contes*, ed. Frédéric Deloffre, Paris: Gallimard, 1979.
Voltaire, *Zadig; ou, La Destinée, histoire orientale*, s.l. 1749.
Vilanova, Antonio, "Reminiscencias del *Asno de oro* en 'la casa donde nunca comen ni beben' del *Lazarillo*," *Bulletin hispanique* 92.1 (1990), pp. 627–653.
Voigt, Vilmos, "Ergebnisse und Fehler bei der Bearbeitung von 'heutigen' mündlichen Texten," in *Die heutige Bedeutung oraler Traditionen: Ihre Archivierung, Publikation und Index-Erschließung/The Present-Day Importance of Oral Traditions: Their Preservation, Publication and Indexing*, ed. Walther Heissig and Rüdiger Schott, Opladen: Westdeutscher Verlag, 1998.
Von Sydow, Carl Wilhelm, *Selected Papers on Folklore*, ed. Laurits Bødker, Copenhagen: Rosenkilde & Bagger, 1948.
Vrčević, Vuk, *Srpske narodne pripovijetke, ponajviše kratke i šaljive*, 2 vols., Belgrade: Srpska kraljevska državna štamparija, 1868–1882.

Wagner, Karl Fr. Chr., *Vollständige und auf die möglichste Erleichterung des Unterrichts abzweckende Englische Sprachlehre für die Deutschen*, Braunschweig: Schulbuchhandlung, 1802.
Wallensköld, Axel, "L'origine et l'evolution du conte de la femme chaste convoitée par son beau-frère," *Neuphilologische Mitteilungen* (1912), pp. 67–78.
Wallensköld, Axel, *Le conte de la femme chaste convoitée par son beau-frère: étude de littérature comparée*, Helsingfors: Societatis Litterariae Fennicae, 1907.
Wander, Karl Friedrich Wilhelm, *Deutsches Sprichwörter-Lexikon: Ein Hausschatz für das deutsche Volk* (1867), 4 vols., Augsburg: Weltbild, 1987.
Warder, Anthony Kennedy, *Indian Kāvya Literature*, vol. 6: *The Art of Storytelling*, Delhi: Motilal Banarsidass, 1992.
Wardroper, John, *Jest upon Jest: A Selection of Jestbooks and Collections of Merry Tales Published from the Reign of Richard III to George III*, London: Routledge & Kegan Paul, 1970.
Warnke, Karl, *Die Quellen des Esope der Marie de France*, Halle: Niemeyer, 1900.
Waṭwāṭ, Muḥammad ibn Ibrāhīm al-, *Mabāhij al-fikar wa-manāhij al-ʿibar*, ed. ʿAbd al-Razzāq Aḥmad al-Ḥarbī, Beirut: al-Dār al-ʿarabiyya lil-mawsūʿāt, 1420/2000.
Weber, Carl, "Italienische Märchen in Toscana aus Volksmund gesammelt," in *Forschungen zur romanischen Philologie: Festgabe für Hermann Suchier zum 15. März 1900*, Halle: Max Niemeyer, 1900, pp. 309–348.
Wehr, Hans, "Chauvin, Victor," in *Enzyklopädie des Märchens*, vol. 2 (1979), cols. 1268–1271.
Wehse, Rainer, "Campbell of Islay, John Francis," in *Enzyklopädie des Märchens*, vol. 2 (1979), cols. 1165–1167.
Wehse, Rainer, "Ehebruch belauscht," in *Enzyklopädie des Märchens*, vol. 3 (1981), cols. 1055–1065, at cols. 1057–1058.
Wehse, Rainer, "Liebhaber bloßgestellt," in *Enzyklopädie des Märchens*, vol. 8 (1996), cols. 1056–1063.
Weipert, Reinhard, *Altarabischer Sprachwitz: Abū ʿAlqama und die Kunst, sich kompliziert auszudrücken*, Munich: Bayerische Akademie der Wissenschaften, 2009.
Weisweiler, Max, *Arabische Märchen*, 2 vols., Düsseldorf: Eugen Diederichs, 1966.
Weisweiler, Max, *Von Kalifen, Spaßmachern und klugen Haremsdamen: Arabischer Humor*, Düsseldorf: Eugen Diederichs, 1963.
Wells, Whitney, "A New Analogue to the Pardoner's Tale," *Modern Language Notes* 40.1 (1925), pp. 58–59.
Wells, Whitney, "An Unnoted Analogue to the 'Pardoner's Tale'," *Modern Philology* 25.2 (1927), pp. 163–164.
Wenger, Berta Viktoria, "Shylocks Pfund Fleisch: Eine stoffgeschichtliche Untersuchung," *Shakespeare-Jahrbuch* 65 (1929), pp. 92–174.
Wensinck, Arent Jan, *Concordance et indices de la tradition musulmane*, 8 vols., Leiden: Brill, 1936–1988 (Reprint Istanbul: Çağrı Yayınları, 1988).
Wentzel, Luise-Charlotte, *Kurdische Märchen*, Düsseldorf: Diederichs, 1978.
Wenzel, Siegfried, "Another Analogue to *The Pardoner's Tale*," *Notes and Queries* 241 (1996), pp. 134–136.
Werner, A., "Chaucer's Pardoner's Tale: African Analogue," *Notes and Queries* 11.4 (1911), pp. 82–83.
Wesselski, Albert, "Alters-Sinnbilder und Alters-Wettstreit," *Archiv Orientální* 4 (1932), pp. 1–22.
Wesselski, Albert, "Das Geschenk der Lebensjahre," *Archiv orientální* 10 (1938), pp. 79–114.

Wesselski, Albert, "Der Müller von Sanssouci," *Mitteilungen des Vereins für die Geschichte Berlins* 44 (1927), pp. 147–152.

Wesselski, Albert, "Humanismus und Volkstum," *Zeitschrift für Volkskunde*, new series 6 (1934), pp. 1–35.

Wesselski, Albert, "Quellen und Nachwirkungen der Haft paikar," *Der Islam* 22 (1935), pp. 165–173.

Wesselski, Albert, *Das lachende Buch*, Leipzig: Johannes M. Meulenhoff, 1914.

Wesselski, Albert, *Der Hodscha Nasreddin*, 2 vols., Weimar: Duncker, 1911.

Wesselski, Albert, *Die Novellen Girolamo Morlinis*, Munich: Georg Müller, 1908.

Wesselski, Albert, *Die Schwänke und Schnurren des Pfarrers Arlotto*, 2 vols., Berlin: Alexander Duncker, 1910.

Wesselski, Albert, *Erlesenes*, Prague: Gesellschaft Deutscher Bücherfreunde in Böhmen, 1928.

Wesselski, Albert, *Italiänischer Volks- und Herrenwitz: Fazetien und Schwänke aus drei Jahrhunderten*, Munich: Georg Müller, 1912.

Wesselski, Albert, *Klaret und sein Glossator: Böhmische Volks- und Mönchsmärlein im Mittelalter*, Brünn: Rohrer, 1936.

Wesselski, Albert, *Märchen des Mittelalters*, Berlin: Herbert Stubenrauch, 1925.

Wesselski, Albert, *Mönchslatein: Erzählungen aus geistlichen Schriften des XIII. Jahrhunderts*, Leipzig: Wilhelm Heims, 1909.

West, John O., *Mexican-American Folklore*, Little Rock, Arkansas: August House, 1988.

Wheeler, Howard T., *Tales from Jalisco, Mexico*, Philadelphia: American Folklore Society, 1943.

Whittaker, Gareth, "William Alexander Clouston (1843–96), Folklorist: Introduction and Bibliography," *Folklore* 115.3 (204), pp. 348–362.

Wickram, Georg, *Werke*, vol. 3: *Rollwagenbüchlein*, *Die sieben Hauptlaster*, ed. Johannes Bolte, Tübingen: Litterarischer Verein in Stuttgart, 1903.

Wieland, Christoph Martin, "Der Greif vom Gebürge Kaf," *Dschinnistan oder auserlesene Feen- und Feister-Märchen*, vol. 3, Winterthur: Heinrich Steiner und Compagnie, 1789, pp. 22–34.

Wiener, Alfred, "Die Farağ baʿd aš-šidda-Literatur," *Der Islam* 4 (1913), pp. 270–298, 387–420.

Williams, Alfred, *Round about the Upper Thames*, London: Duckworth & Co., 1922.

Williams, Frederick G., "Chaucer's The Pardoner's Tale and The Tale of the Four Thieves from Portugal's Orto do esposo compared," *Bulletin des études portugaises et brésiliennes* 44–45 (1983–1985), pp. 93–107.

Williams-Krapp, Werner, "Frau: Die treue F.," in *Enzyklopädie des Märchens*, vol. 5 (1987), cols. 203–207.

Wisser, Wilhelm, *Plattdeutsche Volksmärchen: Neue Folge*, Jena: Eugen Diederichs, 1927.

Woeller, Waltraud, *Deutsche Volksmärchen von arm und reich*, Berlin: Akademie-Verlag, 1959.

Wolff, Reinhold, "Unterwegs vom mittelalterlichen Predigtmärlein zur Novelle der Frühen Neuzeit: Die Erzählsammlung 'Compilatio singularis exemplorum'," *Mittellateinisches Jahrbuch* 41.1 (2006), pp. 53–76.

Wolfgang, Lenora D., *Le Lai de l'oiselet: An Old French Poem of the Thirteenth Century*, Philadelphia: American Philosophical Society, 1990.

Wolgemuth, Ernst, *500 / Frische und vergüldete / Haupt-Pillen* [...], Warhausen im Warnethal 1669.

Wollin, Carsten, "Geschichten aus der 'Compilatio singularis exemplorum'," *Mittellateinisches Jahrbuch* 41.1 (2006), pp. 77–91.

Wossidlo, Richard, *Aus dem Lande Fritz Reuters: Humor in Sprache und Volkstum Mecklenburgs*, Leipzig: Wigand, 1910.

Wossidlo, Richard, *Volksschwänke aus Mecklenburg*, ed. Siegfried Neumann, Berlin: Akademie-Verlag, 1963.

Wrasman, Adolf, *Die Sagen der Heimat: Sagenschatz des Regierungsbezirks Osnabrück*, Osnabrück: Pillmeyer, 1908.

Wright, Thomas, *A Selection of Latin Stories from Manuscripts of the Thirteenth and Fourteenth Centuries: A Contribution to the History of Fiction during the Middle Ages*, London: Percy Society, 1842.

Wulff, Fredrik, *Recherches sur les Sagas de Magus et de Geirard et leurs rapports aux épopées françaises*, Lund: Gleerup, 1873.

Wünsche, August, *Der Midrasch Bereschit Rabba: das ist die haggadische Auslegung der Genesis*, Leipzig: Schulze, 1881.

Wünsche, August, *Der Midrasch Echa Rabbati, das ist die haggadische Auslegung der Klagelieder*, Leipzig: Otto Schulze, 1881.

Wünsche, August, *Der Midrasch Wajikra Rabba: Das ist die haggadische Auslegung des dritten Buches Mose*, Leipzig: Schulze, 1884.

Wüstenfeld, Ferdinand, "Jâcût's Reisen, aus seinem geographischen Wörterbuche beschrieben," *Zeitschrift der Deutschen Morgenländischen Gesellschaft* 18 (1864), pp. 397–493.

Wuttke, Heinrich, *Städtebuch des Landes Posen*, Leipzig: Hermann Fries, 1864.

Yāfiʿī, Abū Muḥammad ʿAbdallāh ibn Asʿad al-, *Mirʾāt al-jinān wa-ʿibrat al-yaqẓān fī maʿrifat mā yuʿtabar min hawādīth al-zamān*, 2nd ed., 4 vols., Beirut: Muʾassasat al-Aʿlamī lil-maṭbūʿāt, 1970.

Yāfiʿī al-Yamanī, Abū Muḥammad ʿAbdallāh ibn Asʿad al-, *Rawḍ al-rayāḥīn fī ḥikāyāt al-ṣāliḥīn*, Cairo: Aḥmad al-Bābī al-Ḥalabī, 1307/1889.

Yāqūt, *Jacut's geographisches Wörterbuch*, ed. Ferdinand Wüstenfeld, 6 vols., Leipzig: Deutsche Morgenländische Gesellschaft, 1924.

Yıkık, Ahmet, "A Protagonist in Cyprus' Tanzimat Literature: Kaytazzade Mehmet Nazım," in *Press and Mass Communication in the Middle East: Festschrift for Martin Strohmaier*, ed. Börte Sagaster, Theoharis Stavrides, and Birgitt Hoffmann, Bamberg: University of Bamberg Press, 2017, pp. 151–168.

Yousef, May A., *Das Buch der schlagfertigen Antworten von Ibn Abī ʿAwn: Ein Werk der klassisch-arabischen Adab-Literatur, Einleitung, Edition und Quellenanalyse*, Berlin: Klaus Schwarz, 1988.

Zachariae, Theodor, "Zum Doktor Allwissend," in *Kleine Schriften: zur indischen Philologie, zur vergleichenden Literaturgeschichte, zur vergleichenden Volkskunde*, Bonn and Leipzig: Kurt Schroeder, pp. 138–145.

Ẓahiri Samarqandi, Moḥammad ʿAli, *Sendbād-nāme*, ed. Moḥammad Bāqer Kamāl al-Dini, Tehran 1381/2002.

Zākāni, ʿObeydallāh, *Kolliyāt-e ʿObeyd-e Zākāni*, ed. Parviz Atābeki, Tehran 1331/1952.

Zākāni, ʿObeydallāh, *Kolliyāt*, ed. Moḥammad Jaʿfar Maḥjub, New York: Eisenbrauns, 1999.

Zakharia, Katia, "Jean-Georges Varsy et l''histoire d'Ali Baba:' révélations et silences de deux manuscrits récemments découverts," *Arabica* 62 (2015), pp. 652–687.

Zakharia, Katia, "La version arabe la plus ancienne de l''histoire d'Ali Baba:' si Varsy

n'avait pas traduit Galland? Réhabiliter le doute raisonable," *Arabica* 64 (2017), pp. 50–77.
Zall, Paul M., *A Hundred Merry Tales and Other English Jestbooks of the Fifteenth and Sixteenth Centuries*, Lincoln: University of Nebraska Press, 1977.
Zall, Paul M., *A Nest of Ninnies and Other English Jestbooks of the Seventeenth Century*, Lincoln: University of Nebraska Press, 1970.
Zamakhsharī, Abū 'l-Qāsim Maḥmūd ibn ʿUmar al-, *Rabīʿ al-abrār wa-nuṣūṣ al-akhbār*, ed. Salīm al-Nuʿaymī, 4 vols., Baghdad: al-ʿĀnī, 1976–1982.
Ẓarīf al-maʿānī fī 'ḥawādīt wa-'l-aghānī, Cairo: Maktabat Multazima, ca. 1910.
Zaunert, Paul, *Deutsche Märchen aus dem Donaulande*, Jena: Diederichs, 1926.
Zaydī, Abū Muḥammad ʿAbdallāh ibn Naṣr ibn ʿAbd al-ʿAzīz al-, *Lubāb Nathr al-durr*, Paris, Bibliothèque Nationale, ms. arabe 3490.
Zedler, Johann Heinrich, *Grosses vollständiges Universal-Lexicon Aller Wissenschaften und Künste*, vol. 51, Halle: Zedler, 1747.
Zelenin, Dmitriy Konstantinovich, *Velikorusskie skazki Permskoy gubernii*, Petrograd: Orlov, 1914 (reprint St. Petersburg, 1997).
Zender, Matthias, *Sagen und Geschichten aus der Westeifel*, 2nd ed., Bonn. Röhrscheid, 1966.
Zender, Matthias, *Volksmärchen und Schwänke aus der Westeifel*, Bonn: Röhrscheid, 1935.
Zhdanov, Vladimir, and Evelina Zaidenshnur, "Khudozhestvennye proizvedeniya," *Literaturnoe nasledstvo*, vol. 69.2, Moscow: Rossiiskaya Akademiia Nauk, Institut Mirovoi Literatury im. A.M. Gorkogo, 1961, pp. 436–471.
Zimmermann, Georg Ritter von, *Über Friedrich den Großen und meine Unterredungen mit ihm kurz vor seinem Tode*, Leipzig: Weidmannische Buchhandlung, 1788.
Zimmermann, Georges Denis, *The Irish Storyteller*, Dublin: Four Courts Press, 2001.
Zipperling, Carl, *Das altfranzösische Fablel Du Vilain Mire: Kritischer Text mit Einleitung, Anmerkungen und Glossar*, Halle a. S.: Max Niemeyer, 1912.
Ziriklī, Khayr al-Dīn al-, *al-Aʿlām: qāmūs tarājim [...]*, Beirut: Dār al-ʿIlm lil-malāyīn, 1980.
Ẕol-Faqāri, Ḥasan, "Andersen va mandil-e khiyāl," *Farhang-e mardom* 13 (1384/2005), pp. 50-54.
Zolkover, Adam D., "Bawdy Tale," in Duggan, Anne E., and Donald Haase, eds., *Folktales and Fairy Tales*, Santa Barbara, CA: Greenwood, 2016, vol. 1, pp. 104–105.
Zunser, Helen, "A New Mexican Village," *Journal of American Folklore* 48 (1935), pp. 125–178.

INDEX OF NARRATORS AND COLLECTORS

Abbate, Giovanni (Italy), 172
Afanasyev, Aleksandr (Russia), 142
Alcheh, Élie (Judaeo-Spanish), 291n28
Allain, Charles (French Canadian), 492
Alonso, Juan Pascal (Spain), 320
Alonso, José del Río (Spain), 497
Álvarez, Celia (Mexico), 54
Amato, Francesca (Sicily), 290n12
Anderson, A.C. (Denmark), 575
Andrásfalvi, György (Hungarian from Romania), 351
Andriukajtis, Kasimierz (Lithuania), 88
Angiola, wife of Pietro (Italy), 133
Árnason, Jón (Iceland), 105, 106
Atanasov, Georgi Zl. (Bulgaria), 445
Aurbacher, Ludwig (Germany), 329

Bakker, C. (Dutch from The Netherlands), 227
Balk, Georg (Germany), 559, 577
Barag, Lev G. (Belarus), 232
Barnewitz, S. (Germany), 433
Basile, Antonina (Sicily), 536
Basset, M. (France), 141
Beardson, Lew (Ozarks, USA), 484
Beckmann, C.A. (German from East Prussia), 196
Bernat, Teresa (Catalonia), 585
Bertrand, Léon (France), 197
Bieder, Jean (Georgia, USA), 141
Blai, Aurora (Catalonia), 112
Berberśkyj, V. (Ukraine), 338
Berge, Rokard (Norway), 526
Bergholz (Germany), 550
Bladé, Jean-François (France), 554
Bodens, Wilhelm (Germany), 450
Bodnár, Bálint (Hungary), 535
Böhle, F. (Germany), 427
Borquoi, Pet. (Germany), 535
Bošković-Stulli, Maja (Croatia), 227
Braga, Teófilo (Portugal), 405
Brauner, Bohuslav (Prague), 30
Briffault, Marie (France), 492
Bruère, Joseph (France), 60
Buinevičius, B. (Lithuania), 171
Bruford, Alan (Scotland), 226
Brusca, Rosa (Sicily), 262
Bukló, György (Hungarian from Romania), 350

Camaj, Martin (Albania), 39
Cammann, Alfread (Germany), 282
Campbell, John (Scotland), 29–30, 243
Canestrino, Pietro di (Italy), 456
Carpenter, James D. (England), 591
Cascudo, Francisco (Brazil), 475
Castell, Claudette (France), 287
Castellani, François (Corsica), 107
Castelló, Carme (Catalonia), 448n12
Cestone, Vito (Italy), 369
Christensen, Arthur (Iran), 307, 488
Cock, Alfons de (Flemish from Belgium), 171
Coetzee, Abel (South Africa), 290n13
Compton, Dr. (Ozarks, USA), 276
Cooke, Peter (Scotland), 126
Coronado, Francisco (Chile), 54, 222
Cortina, Margarita Alvarez (Spain), 309
Coulomb, Nicole (France), 287
Czambel, S. (Slovakia), 142

Dal', Vladimir I. (Russia), 232
Dawkins, Richard M. (Greece), 134
Dedyk, Vasjko (Ukraine), 338
Dégh, Linda (Hungarian from Romania), 351
Dejkus, Kazimierz (Lithuania), 61
Denter, Matthias (Germany), 589
Digajtis, Tadeusz (Lithuania), 161
Dimitri, Vassilou (Greece), 207
Dinovski, Panajot (Bulgarian), 551
Diyāb, Ḥannā (Syria), 9, 14–15, 54–55, 57, 61–63, 64, 76, 90, 108–109, 182–184, 237, 239–240
Djordjević, Dragutin M. (Serbia), 227
Dobreva, Dorotea (Bulgaria), 586
Dragoslav, Ion (Romania), 215
Droste-Hölshoff, Jenny von (Germany), 52
Dzežko, Jan (Belarus), 88
Dzheshko, Paul (Belarus), 386

Elwell-Sutton, L.P. (Iran), 128
Ercilla, Señorita de (Spain), 497
Eriksson, Johan (Sweden), 423
Essiambe, Aimé (French Canadian), 492
Esteban, P. (Spain), 497
Eyolfsdóttir, Guðriður (Iceland), 482

Fernández, Fermín Palomino (Spain), 320
Ferreira, Martinho (Brazil), 507
Finnbogadóttir, Guðriður (Iceland), 218n9
Fournier, Chille (French Canadian), 364

Gagnepain, François (France), 53
Galbach, Hermann (German from East Prussia), 329
García, Belarmino García (Spain), 148
García, Isidora Martino (Spain), 410
Gerdes, Klaas (Germany), 140
Gerrits, Egbert (Germany), 436
Gerstenberger, Irma (German from Bessarabia), 46
Gil, Benito (Spain), 431
Giraud, Maria (France), 527
Gokesch, Maria (German from Romania), 88
González, Emilia Caballero (Spain), 320
Gonzenbach, Laura (Sicily), 232
Gorbachykha, Marysya (Belarus), 541
Griep, Harm (Germany), 87
Graziani, Yoshoa (Judaeo-Spanish from Tunisia), 578
Guevara, Manuel (Mexico), 484
Gugliotta, Gianni (Italy), 172
Gutiérrez de Casillas, Virginia (Mexico), 279

Haiding, Karl (Austria), 457
Halevy, Nahman (Judaeo-Spanish from Tunisia), 578
Halpert, Herbert (Newfoundland), 129n3, 214
Halpert, Nicholas (Newfoundland), 129n3
Hämäläinen, Juho (Finland), 427
Hammer, Leopold (Austria), 492
Harrison, James (England), 267
Hartland, E.S. (England), 330
Hatton, William (Ozarks, USA), 275
Haxthausen (Germany), 78, 582
Head, George (Ozarks, USA), 570
Headlee, Linda (Scotland), 126
Henderson, Angus (Scotland), 226
Henderson, Hamish (Scotland), 68
Henssen, Gottfried (Germany), 436
Hermann, Yehudah (Jewish from Poland), 277
Herrera, Félix (Spanish from New Mexico, USA), 283
Herriman, Isaac (Wales), 571
Hibler, Charles H. (Ozarks, USA), 276
Higgins, Bella (Scotland), 68
Hinarejos, José Manuel Doménech (Spain), 499n5
Hoenshel, Eli J. (Ozarks, USA), 276
Holstiege (Germany), 436
Holtrop, Teardze Eeltje (Friesland), 409

Ignatawicze, Antoni (Polish from Lithuania), 186
Ignatov, G. (Bulgaria), 525
Ilg, Bertha (Malta), 262, 400, 491

Jaarsma, Adam Aukes (The Netherlands), 271
Jamison, George (Scotland), 444
Janton-Meitour (France), 108
Janzsó, Josef (Hungary), 171
Javāher al-Kalām, ʿAli (Iran), 128
Joachim, Traugott (German from Tajikistan), 282
João de Airão-Minho, S. (Portugal), 196
Johansson, G.A. (Sweden), 423
Jonson, Emelie (Sweden), 53
Jupyk, Vassyl (Ukraine), 338
Jürjenson, Kaarel (Estonian), 226

Kangas, Martti (Finland), 546
Kanzenbach, Wilhelm (Germany), 535
Karadžić, Vuk (Serbia), 464
Käyhkö, Ilma (Finland), 363
Khashshāb, Abū Muḥammad al-, 493
Klemm, Resi (German from Hungary), 542
Knoop, Ulrich (German from Pommerania), 80
Konrath, Franz (Austria), 457
Köppen (Germany), 321, 392
Kößler-Ilg, Bertha. *See* Ilg, Bertha
Kostenceva, Mikhaila (Macedonia), 252
Krasnoluts'kyi, O. (Ukraine), 526
Kritskov, A.I. (Russia), 375
Kühn, Angelika (Germany), 45

Lahtinen, Kustaa (Finland), 541
Lallan, Françoise (France), 554
Lampinen, A. (Finland), 196
Lautenbach, J. (Latvia), 329
Lemke, Christoph (Germany), 29
Lentz, Julius (German from Pennsylvania, USA), 423
Leonteva, A. (Karelia), 578
Lerhis-Puškaitis, A. (Lithuania), 197
Lévi, Mérou (Judaeo-Spanish from Greece), 69
Łevynśkyj, V. (Ukraine), 338
Lorenz, Antonio (New Mexico), 343
Lorenz, Fernán (New Mexico), 343
Lorenzo, A, (Spain), 497
Ludwig, Maria (Switzerland), 108

MacGeachy, Mrs. (Hebrides), 221
Macintyre, Donald (Hebrides), 243
Mackenzie, John (Scotland), 197
MacKinnon, James (Hebrides), 244
MacLean, Calum (Hebrides), 244, 527
MacPhee, Willie (Scotland), 126
Makkonen, Heikki (Finland), 203
Manero, Ecequiela (Spain), 527
Maringer, Maria (Austria), 457
Mariotti, Giovanni Matteo (Sardinia), 457
Marqués, Mota del (Spain), 547
Martínez, Ricardo Árias (Spain), 330
Martinov, Al. (Bulgarian), 445, 525
Merkens, Heinrich (Germany), 436
Mikhailov, Vasili (Belarus), 349
Milanović, Mile (Croatia), 562
Miljanović, Vojko (Serbian from Bosnia), 586
Minssen, Johann Friedrich (Germany), 87
Mitovska, Vasilka Stoilkova (Bulgaria), 586
Mizhorkov, Angel (Bulgaria), 586
Mollā Ādine (Iran), 488
Mollā Feyżollāh (Iran), 307, 488
Molloy, Mike (Newfoundland), 129n3
Mondet, Julien (France), 550
Mone, Franz Joseph (Germany), 86
Mühlhausen, Ludwig, 59
Mukhametov, Mardan (Bashkir from Russia), 231

Nerucci, Gherrdo (Italy), 456
Niederkopfler, Valentin (German from Southern Tyrol), 444
Niles, John D. (Scotland), 126
Nilsson, Anna Charlotte (Sweden), 53
Nober (Germany), 589
Nogueiras, Malvina (Galicia), 271
Novák, František (Czech from Bohemia), 87
Nünike, Johann (Germany), 535

Ó Casaide, Séamus (Ireland), 59
Ó Duilearga, Séamus (Ireland), 226
Ó Loideáin, Máirtín (Ireland), 30

Ó Siadhail, Pádraig (Ireland), 213
"Old Caraux" (France) 554
Orbán, Balácz (Hungarian from Romania), 350
Orso, Ethelyn G. (Greece), 287
Ostwald, Maria (German from Hungary), 53
Ösz, János (Hungarian from Romania), 350
Ouellet, Joseph (French Canadian), 364

Palavestra, Vlajko (Serbian from Bosnia), 586
Pálsson, Páll (Iceland), 482
Parsons, Elsie Clews (Guadaloupe), 283
Pascal, María (Spain), 369
Passy, Georg (Austria), 172
Paul, Israel (Trinidad), 107
Paunov, Georgi (Bulgarian), 401
Perlick, Alfons (German from Silesia), 320
Pernía, Antonio (Spain), 46
Perreault, Jules (French Canadian), 484
Pic, Raoul (France), 227
Pierazzoli, Maria (Italy), 468
Pingel (Germany), 140
Pino, Félix (Spanish from New Mexico, USA), 181
Pitrè, Giuseppe (Sicily), 262
Ponte, Abelino (Spain), 330
Popelka, Václav (Czech from Bohemia), 87
Pourdrier, Alexande (French Canadian), 445
Prudenzano, Francesco (Italy), 314

Quesada, Salvador González (Mexico), 500
Quintana, Ursulita (Spanish from New Mexico, USA), 111

Rael, Juan B. (Spanish from New Mexico, USA), 283
Randolph, Vance (Ozarks, USA), 275–276, 337, 484, 570
Ranger, David (French Canadian), 484
Raymond (Sarano), Miriam (Judaeo-Spanish from Turkey), 309
Reckmann (Germany), 577
Reimann, M. (Estonia), 186
Reiterer, Karl (Austria), 187
Rey-Henningsen, Marisa (Galicia), 271
Rivera, Virginia Rodríguez (Mexico), 483
Rodríguez, Lorenzo Monje (Spain), 468
Rouzaud, Marie (France), 330
Ruseski, Georgi (Romania, Bulgaria), 53, 88, 586
Rust, August (Germany), 140, 392, 436

Saganovich, Roman (Belarus), 232
Salitraru, Traila (Romania), 61
Salter, Josef (German from Bohemia), 170, 491
Sánchez, Adela Aguilar (Argentina), 54
Šapkarev, Kuzman (Macedonian), 558
Sarano, Diana (Juaeo-Spanish), 293
Schaafsma, Minke (Friesland), 271
Schmidt (Germany), 140
Schraeder (Germany), 363
Schröder, August (Germany), 140
Schuurman, Dirk (Dutch from The Netherlands), 227
Schwebe, J. (Germany), 29
Schwiesow (Germany), 403
Seixas, Vic (USA), 141
Sekowski, Agnes (Poland), 483
Senn, Hans von der (Austria), 187
Shala, Halit (Albania), 39
Shearlock, Patrick (Ireland), 147
Sigurðson, Jón (Iceland), 106
Šklarj, Mykoła (Ukraine), 508
Smith, Manivel (England), 571
Šmits, Pēteris (Latvia), 329
Smolka, Josef (Czech from Silesia), 386
Söggle, J.P. (Finland), 112
Sommer, P. (German from Posen), 430
Sorokoviko, E.I. (Russia), 386
Stewart, Alasdair (Scotland), 527
Stewart, Belle (Scotland), 126
Stinco, Gaspare (Sicily), 284
Stolz, Karl (German from Prussia), 255, 392, 394, 448n8

Sundbøhaugen, Anne (Norway), 526
Szergenyi, Péter (Hungary), 535

Tabakova, B.M. (Bulgaria), 578
Tasić, Nikola (Serbia), 227
Tempel, Carl (Ireland), 213
Testas, Jean (France), 582
Thibault, Charles (France), 469
Thibault, Georges (France), 39
Thuathaláin, Mac (Ireland), 30
Tongue, Ruth L. (England), 267
Tordinca, N. (Croatia), 361n4
Torner, Eduardo Martínez (Spain), 344
Tortola, Nicolao (Italy), 315

Vajalo, Pavo (Croatia), 227
Valencia, Rufina (New Mexico), 65n7
Vergara, Mariano (Argentina), 445
Viidalepp, Richard (Estonia), 226
Voigt, Fr. (Slovakia), 142
Voit, Franz (German from Bohemia), 147
Volpilière, Marcel (France), 298
Vrčević, Vuk (Serbia), 464
Vries, Jan de (Friesland), 527

Walker, Richard (Ireland), 226
Wasserhess, Josef (Germany), 392
Weber, Carl (Italy), 132
Whyte, Betsy (Scotland), 125, 126
Widdowson, J.D.A. (Newfoundland), 214
Williamson, Linda (Scotland), 126
Wilsecker (Germany), 555
Wilson, Norman F. (German from Pennsylvania, USA), 42
Wisser, Wilhelm (Germany), 535
Wolter (Germany), 393
Wossidlo, Richard (Germany), 266, 392, 403, 566
Wyatt, L. (England), 267

Yarmokha (Ukraine), 526

Zarn, Flori Alisi (Romansh from Switzerland), 227
Zdanavičienė, J. (Lithuania), 171
Zehentner, Barbara (Austria), 492
Zender, Matthias (Germany), 178, 589
Zunser, Helen (USA), 343

INDEX OF NAMES AND MOTIFS IN THE TALES

ʿAbd al-Malik ibn Marwān, 267
Abdera, 266, 406
absurd attempt to change animal nature, 50
Abū Dīsa, 485–486
Abū Dulāma, 379
Abū 'l-ʿAnbas, 542–543
Abū 'l-Aswad al-Du'alī, 591–592
Abū Nuwās, 311, 460
Abū Jawāliq, 179
accidental cannibalism, 302–304
accused: feigns to be dumb, 400–401; feigns to be mad, 444–447
action, noblest, 243–249
Adam and Eve, 329–330, 333
advice: adviser duped with own, 444–447; by dwarf, 501; by fool, 280, 296; by vizier not followed, 50; by woman is foolish, 147, 149–152; by woman is clever, 411; from everybody is useless, 275–278; from three old men, 141–143; illustrated with tale, 272; inadvertently given, 253; only given after heavy beating, 494; promised by bird, 38–41; to think thrice before you speak, 422–424
Aesop, 579
affair, princess has secret, 52–57
ʿAffān ibn Sulaymān, 503
agency: female, 203–211, 337–341, 525–532
Ahiqar, 579
ʿĀ'isha (bint Abī Bakr), 127, 371
ʿĀ'isha bint Ṭalḥa, 322
Aladdin, 75–77, 79, 238, 239
alcoholic beverage. *See* wine
Alexander, 195
Ali Baba, 237–238
Aʿmash, Sulaymān ibn Mihrān al-, 419
ambiguous dream, 433–434
Amleth, 114
ʿAmr ibn ʿĀmir, 528
ʿAmr ibn al-Layth, 575
animal: carcass, man hidden in, 231; demonstrates effects of medicine, 96; escapes when lid of vessel is lifted, 329–333; faithful, rashly killed, 45–47; grateful, 233; has no proper use for stolen meat, 521–523; head of, caught in jar, 295–296, 321; hidden, to be guessed, 482–489; nature cannot be changed, 50; shows way to escape, 98, 101; to be sold cheaply, 409–412; transformation into, 59–65, 150, 181, 371
Antakya, 253
Anthony, Saint, of Padua, 405, 410
Anūshīrwān, 143–144, 155–156
apple: magic, resuscitates, 105, 108
Arlotto Mainardi, 49, 437, 541, 543, 560
Ashʿab, 434, 452, 453, 509
Asinus vulgi, 271–273
Aṣmaʿī, al-, 303, 388, 442, 592
Asmund and Aswit, 96–97
Aśoka, 382
astrologer. *See* soothsayer
Athens, 389
attempt, absurd: to change animal's nature, 50; to keep bird from escaping, 266–268
ʿAynāwa, 519

Ayyūb ibn Zayd, Abū Sulaymān, 528
Azhar al-ḥammār, 288, 575

Baghdad, 216–217, 311, 365, 458, 485, 502–504
baker: dog finds refuge with, 60, 62; king is son of, 114
Bakkār ibn ʿAbd al-Malik, Abū Bakr, 267, 268
Balduch, 365, 501
Bam, master builder of, 208–209
banker: denies having received deposit, 463–466; makes counterfeit money, 476
barley: bread, 357; magic, 64
barrel: dead body transported in, 302; dream of falling into, 433; would-be lover made to hide in, 526, 528
Bāsim, 534, 537–538
basket maker: hanged instead of blacksmith, 398; wooer as, 213–214
Basra, 157, 387, 528
bastard. *See* birth, illegitimate
Basūs, 151
bath, public: clothes stolen in, 428; demons in, 69–71; Nasreddin in, 419–420; object forgotten in, 486–487; princess on her way to, 81
beating: anticipatory, 518–519; as punishment for wife, 60, 315, 320, 322, 349, 492; man will only give advice after, 492, 494
beauty: bedazzling, 192, 195; contest, 349–352; woman wishes for, 151
Bedouin: advised to bell lion, 35; carves roast chicken 387–388; clears throat with trick, 431–432; contest in poetry with, 388; despises poor philosopher, 277; distributes food items, 515; hospitality, 592–594; lovers, 345; poor sanitary conditions of, 303–304, 442; pretends to be ignorant of city life, 415; raises wolf cub on sheep's milk, 50; sells camel only together with cat, 410–412; storyteller, 528
bee escapes from vessel, 332, 333
being, mightiest, 585–587
belling the cat, 34–36
Benevento, 69, 70, 72
best is yet to come, 433
Beth-Gelert, 46
Bible, 392–393
bird: escapes from vessel, 330; ; kept from escaping, 266–268; promises three pieces of advice, 38–41. *See also* chicken
bird, giant: lifts man to mountain top, 231–233; saves man, 56. *See* Roc
birth, illegitimate, 111–120, 474–479
bishop, 226, 227, 363–364, 571
black man as lecher (or lover), 55, 63, 133–134, 136, 349–351
blacksmith: basketmaker hanged instead of, 398; clever, 534, 537–538; disguise as daughter of, 193; godfather, 79; hanged instead of locksmith, 397; hedonist, 380–381; nobleman's father alledgedly worked as, 578
blind: greedy man turns, 181–184; man asks to be slapped in the face, 62, 182; man buries his money, 468–470, 472; man hides money in clothes, 365
boat: as place of magic transformation, 125–126; moves through untying of knots, 214; scholar in, does not know how to swim, 292–293
body: of deceased, cut to pieces, 302–303; part of, cut off, 295–296
Bologna, 302, 387
branding of would-be lovers, 210
bribe: greater, wins, 566–568
bride allowed to visit former lover, 243–249
bread: and water for husband buried alive, 95, 98–100; clandestinely eaten, 164, 171, 173–175; expensive price of, 356; poisoned, 162–163. *See also* baker
bridge, treasure to be found at, 501
Buhlūl, 285, 340, 470–472, 498, 519
Bunān, 393–394
burglar: has lame excuse, 359–361; has no key for stolen srongbox, 523; stole from church, 497–498
burial money collected twice, 379

buried alive, 95–102
Burzōe, 35
butcher, 60, 63

Cairo, 268, 331, 502–503
Caithness hills, 30
calendar: foolish reckoning of, 558–559
calligraphy: monkey practices, 64
Caltanissetta, 206
camel: fox fears it might be taken for a, 298–300; head of, cut off, 295–296; sick person accused of eating, 572; stray, cleverly identified, 111, 113–118, 120; to be sold together with cat, 410–412
candle: held by cat, 49–50; stuck in arse, 527
cannibal: demon, 248; woman, 60, 62; Magians, 98
cannibalism by accident, 302–304
Capricorn, Western, 547
care package (after World War II), 302
carpenter: accidentally kills man, 397; has chaste wife, 205, 207–208, 210; makes closet, 528, 530; makes flying object, 87–91; sings of his possessions, 471
carving the roast chicken, 385–389
casting pearls before swine, 41
cat: and camel to be sold together, 410–412; and candle, 49–50; empties its bowels into cap, 508; steals meat, 522; to be belled, 34–36; weighed, 325–326
cavern: magic, 237–240
cemetery, 59, 62
center of the world: where is it?, 226
Chandraprabhā, 56
change: of animal nature, attempted, 50; of destiny, attempted, 142–143, 353; of sex, 125–129
Chapman, John, 500
chaste wife, 132–137
chastity. *See* index of chastity, token of chastity
cheater admits out of greed, 170–176
cheaters: town of, 252–254. *See also* rogue; swindler; trickster
chess: monkey plays, 64
Chiavari, 401
chicken: distributed, 513–516; roast, carved, 385–389. *See also* rooster
children: given a beating, 519; play with bird, 41
Christ. *See* Jesus
Christian holiday Sunday, 69
City of Gold, 54–55, 56
Claremond, 89–90
Cleomades, 89
clever: deductions, 111–120; man carves the roast chicken, 385–389; man distributes food items, 513–516
climax of horrors, 589–594
closet: would-be lovers trapped in, 205, 525–532
clothes: made from invisible tissue, 474–479; spark sets fire to, 423–424; stolen in public bath, 428; welcome instead of person wearing them, 418–420
coat: infested with bugs, 430–431; invited to eat, 419; magic, makes invisible, 52, 53
cobbler: hedonist, 534; hired by treacherous employer, 232; killed seventeen (flies) with a single blow, 491; made king for a day, 381; poses as soothsayer, 483; requires prince to learn trade, 213; steals buried money, 469; stitches dead body's pieces together, 238; travels with God on earth, 171
coin gives birth and dies, 452–453
coin, counterfeit: banker arrested for making, 476; identified by dog, 60, 62; payment with, 415–416
cold night survived by rolling around boulder, 283
Cologne, 570
commonplace advice, 38
competition: between craftsmen, 86–92; between suitors, 238. *See also* contest
Constant du Hamel, 528

Constantinople, 78, 365
Constanze, 132
contest: beauty, 349–352; in poetry with Bedouin, 388; shooting arrows, 106–107. *See also* competition
corpse: discarded, 207; pieces of, stitched together, 238
couple: liar sows discord between married, 314–318
cow: and rooster (chicken) to be sold together, 409–410; man riding, 562
creditor: asks for debtor's flesh as security, 221–223; duped by debtor, 444–447
Crescentia, 132
craftsmen: competition between, 86–92
cricket, 483, 485–486, 488, 494
crimes committed after drinking, 186–189
Ctesiphon, 155, 579
cure: miracle, 491–493; through laughter, 491, 492, 571

Dalle (Dalīla), 365
Damascus, 503
Damocles: sword of, 258, 382
dancing: in the nude, 378; ridiculous, 492; shoes to pieces, 52–54; of man entertains supernatural creatures, 69–71
days of the week: song with names of, 68–69
death: rooster as personified, 320
deductions: clever, 111–120
deformation magically removed, 68–71
detection of intruder by ruse, 88
Davasmitā, 210
Dāwūd al-muṣāb, 509
debtor: feigns to be mad, 444–447; requested to offer his flesh as security, 221–223
defecation in dream, 26, 507–510
deposit denied, 463–466
depression because of wife's unfaithfulness, 351–353
dervish: has magic ointment, 182; produces allegedly invisible tissue, 477–478
devil: blamed for causing strange adventure, 378; makes dreamer defecate, 507–508, 510; makes pious man drink, 186–188; seeks to sow discord between married couple, 314–315, 318
Dhū 'l-Nūn al-Miṣrī, 331
diagnosis by observation, 570–572
Dīnārwayh, 579
disbeliever punished, 128
discord between married couple, 314–318
dishes of the same flavor, 255–259
disenchantment, 53, 59–65
disguise: as bishop, 363–364; man as woman, 79; ruler as subject, 62, 256, 258, 377, 381, 534; Saint Peter as beggar, 172
Djohá. *See* Juḥā
dog: blamed to have eaten butter, 325; faithful, 45–47, 589, 590–591; fox refuses to deliver letter to, 35; in Bedouin camp, 303, 442, 592–593; snatches meat, 521–522; transformation into, 59–65; (transformed man) identifies counterfeit coins, 60, 62
donkey: alleged transformation into, 367–371; father and son with, 271–273; man wants to buy, 179; not counted, 287–289; punishment: seated backwards on, 227; stupid man compared to, 39; transformation into, 61, 64
door foolishly guarded, 261–264
dream: ambiguous, 433–434; defecation in, 262, 507–510; extraordinary experience believed to have been, 375–382; of finding one's fortune, 500–504; of hot drink, 403–404; of money, 405–406; of patchwork banner, 436–438
dreamer: exigent, 403–406
drink: dream of hot, 403–404; served in pisspot, 441–442

drinking leads to committing crimes, 186–189
drunk soldier believes he is in paradise (or hell), 375
drug makes unconscious, 56, 377–379. *See also* soporific
Druimenaig, abbot of, 126–127
Dubrovnik, 227
dumb: accused feigns to be, 400–401
dwarf informs about treasure, 501

easier said than done, 34
Echedorus, 71
Edinburgh, 244
education: of princes, in secluded atmosphere, 54; of women is useless, 206; princess has good, 192, 198; Scripture part of, 392–394; trumps natural inclination, 49–50; useless for stupid people, 41
eggs distributed, 515–516
Eliduc, 96
elderberries responsible for longevity, 141
enchanted tree, 343–346
England, 181, 226
enigma solved, 52–57
Ermenga (King Húgon of Miklagard's daughter), 386
eternity: definition of, 227
Eulenspiegel, 491
excrements: person soiled with, 434; buried money replaced with, 470–471; treasure marked with, 507–510
excuse: burglar has lame, 359–361
execution: at the stake, 87; by hanging, 88, 396–398
executioner, compassionate, 134

fairy rewards kindness, 53, 68
faithful animal rashly killed, 45–47
falcon lost and returned, 455–456
Farazdaq, al-, 340
fart: adopted, 262; of tailor, 438
father and son and donkey, 271–273
fence shall keep bird from escaping, 267
ferryman and scholar, 292–293
fig as symbol for vagina, 344
fire: distant, supplies warmth, 282–285; spark sets, to clothes, 423–424
fish: cooked on far-away fire, 282; presented to ruler, 456–457; swallows shipwrecked person, 56
fishbone stuck in throat, 491, 492
flavor: dishes of the same, 255–259
fleas: fox rids itself of, 29–31
flesh: pound of, as security, 221–223
Florence, 469, 541
flour: ignorance concerning use of, 356–357
flying mechanical object, 86–92
food: disgusting, 303–304
fool: does not count donkey he is sitting on, 287–289; doubles the load, 275–278; guards the door, 261–264
fortune teller. *See* soothsayer
forty: days respite, 54, 477; robbers, 237–240
fountain of youth, 494
fox: fears it might be taken for a camel, 298–299; refuses to deliver letter to dog, 35; rids itself of fleas, 29–31
Frederick II ("Old Fred"), 49, 154–156, 255–256, 457, 535, 577
frog, 483, 485
fruit presented to ruler, 457, 459

Gabriel, 87, 90–91
Ġaħan. *See* Juḥā
Garuda, 91–92
gates closed to keep bird from escaping, 266–268
Gelert (faithful dog), 46
generosity, 183–184, 193, 503
Genoveva, 132
German: rude, 422
ghūla (female demon), 62
gift: lover regains, 337–341; untimely, of fruits or vegetables, 459
Giucco. *See* Juḥā
Giufà. *See* Juḥā
Glaucus, 96
God walks on earth, 81, 171–173, 418, 554–555

"God willing!", 178–180
gold made with specific elixir, 234
Golden City. *See* City of Gold
Gorgān, 216
Gotham, 266, 296
grain: large, 142–144
grasshopper. *See* cricket
grave: euphemism, 309–312
Greece, 198
greed: leads to disaster, 161–166, 181–184; makes cheater admit his misdemeanor, 170–176; makes thief return stolen money, 468–472
greedy man: is blinded, 181–184; is stupid, 38–41
Guhasena, 210
Guinefort, Saint, 46
gypsy: as trickster, 284; beats child prior to misdeed, 518; boy steals from church, 74; fiddler, 359; lives in destitute conditions, 309

hair: needed for magic procedure to induce love, 314–318
Ḥajjāj ibn Yūsuf, al, 528–529, 567
Ḥamdūna, 340
hand: caught in jar, 295–296
hanging by proxy, 396–398
Hariśarman, 485
Hārūn al-Rashīd, 62, 459, 460, 537
Hārūt and Mārūt, 188–189
hashish: consumer of, 268, 289
Ḥātim al-Ṭā'ī, 183–184
hawk steals the meat, 522
heart: (inner organ) of animal eaten, 170–173, 175; of usurer in treasure chest, 405
hedonist: son of merchant, 376–378; blacksmith, 380–381, 537–538; cobbler, 534; student, 542
hell: man believes he is in, 78, 375–376; opponent's father allegedly seen in, 578
helper: magic, 60, 61; supernatural, 68–72
herb: healing, 95–96
hermit: admonishes against mundane possessions, 161–164, 166; commits sins, 187
Herod, 112
Hildegardis, 132
Ḥimṣ, 222, 266, 296
Hiraṇyagupta, 530
Hităr Petăr, 284
Hodjas. *See* Nasreddin Hodja
hole in the ground to deposit soil, 279–280
horse: bolting, 564; flings man back into real world, 56; flying, 86–92; magic, 61; maltreated, 62; stolen, 426
hospital: miracle cure in, 491–495
house: not sold to ruler, 155–157; without food or drink, 309–312
humiliation: of would-be lovers, 203–211
hunchback, 68–71

Ibn Abī 'Atīq, 322
Ibn (al-)Darrāj, Abū Sa'īd 'Uthmān, 311
Ibn al-Maghāzilī, 458–459
Ibn al-Qāribī, 460
Ibn Sīrīn, 406
'ifrīt, 70
ignorance concerning use of flour, 356
imaginary tissue, 474–479
imitation: of stereotype characters, 458; of serpent's cure, 96; unsuccessful, 68–72, 170–173
index of chastity, 205, 208
Indra, 128
inheritance: quarrel over, 112–113, 115–119, 243–246, 389, 567–568
intellectual knowledge is of no practical use, 213–218, 292–293
intercourse, sexual. *See* sex
invisible: coat makes, 52, 53; *jinnī* spellbound to paper, 80; tissue or thread, 474–479
Irāq, 198
Israelite, 40, 43n19, 136–137, 151
itching relieved with trick, 420–432
Iyās ibn Mu'āwiya, 465–466

Ja'far al-Barmakī, 459, 537
Ja'far ibn 'Abd al-Wāḥid al-Hāshimī, 332

Jamal, al-Ḥusayn ibn ʿAbd al-Salām al-Miṣrī al-, 299
Jan and Griet, 261
jar: hand caught in, 295–296; animal's head caught in, 295–296, 321; used for storing dead body, 302–304
Jerusalem, 389: traveling Jew to be buried in, 303–304
Jesus: and treasure finders, 162, 164–166; and greedy person, 170, 172–175; as Lamb of God, 546; sold for 30 pieces of silver, 226–227
Jewel: alleged, in bird's body, 38–41
jinnī, 63, 64, 80
joy and sorrow, 501–502
Juḥā, 16, 175, 179, 262–263, 280, 284, 289, 309, 311–312, 326, 339–340, 371, 400, 405, 411, 453, 510, 519, 522, 547, 563, 576, 593
Juḥi. *See* Juḥā
justice as prerequisite for good life, 142–143

Kampen, 267
Kanakarekhā, 56
kettle. *See* pot
Khaybar, 416
Khurāfa, 63–64, 127, 371
kindness rewarded, 53
king: and vizier, 50; of the mice, 35
Kion, 49
knowledge: intellectual, is of little practical use, 213–218, 292–293
Koran, 393–395

Lāb (magician), 64, 371
Lamb of God, 546–547
language of birds: man understands, 56
laughter: cure through, 491, 492, 571
Lavvāḥa and Beshr, 388
law: Muslim customary, 317
letter ordering execution of bearer, 192, 195, 198
liar: forces his opponent to admit he is telling a lie, 577–580; gradually reduces size of lie, 574–576; sows discord, 314–318
lion is to belled, 35
liquid disenchants, 60
Llewellyn of Carnavonshire, 46
load: doubled by fool, 275–278
London, 500
Longevity, 140–144
lord for a day, 375–382
Lord's Prayer without thinking of anything else, 555
lover: regains his gift, 337–341; woman has, 56, 59–61
lovers: contending, 105–109. *See also* suitors

Madāʾin, al-, 155, 579
madness: feigned, 89, 444–447, 488
maelstrom, 56
magic: book (written object), 80; boots, 53; cavern, 237–240; charm, 62, 317; formula, 239; healing, 68–71, 95; lock, 74, 78–79; objects acquired by trick, 53; objects requested from wooers, 105–109; ointment (salve), 181–184; procedure to induce love, 314–318. *See also* transformation
magician: female, 55, 56, 64; Jewish, 75, 78–79
magnetic mountain, 99
Mahaushadha, 531
Mahseti, 321
Maimonides, 49
Maimundus, 591
male supremacy endangered, 55
mason travels to find work, 207
master and apprentice (servant, slave), 264, 316–318, 434, 570–572
mat: prince learns how to weave, 215–217
Mattetai, 78
meal: cooked on far-away fire, 283–285; Scripture quoted at, 392–395
mechanically moving object, 86–92
Medina, 446, 579
Memphis, 228–229
mental asylum, 378
merchant denies having received deposit, 465

mice want to bell the cat, 34–36
miller of Sanssouci, 154–156
miracle: cure, 491–495; performed by Jesus, 164–165, 173–175; performed by God traveling on earth, 170–171
mirror: magic, 108, 182
misunderstanding: foolish: door guarded, 261–264; funny: house without food or drink, 309–312; tragic: faithful dog killed, 45–47
Mollā Naṣreddin. *See* Nasreddin Hodja
money: buried, regained, 468–472; dream of, 405–406; gives birth and dies, 452–453; for burial collected twice, 379. *See also* coin; deposit
monkey: knows how to play chess, 64; task: not to think of, 555–556
mount: bolting, 562–564. *See also* donkey; horse; mule
mountain: magnetic, 99; treasure on, 231–233. *See also* cave
mouse: escapes from vessel, 329–330, 331, 333; drowned in milk (honey), 441–442; marries mouse-maid, 585–587
Muʿāwiya ibn Marwān, 268
muezzin uses pumpkin to reckon time, 559
Mughīra ibn ʿAbdallāh al-Thaqafī, al-, 567
Mughīra ibn Shuʿba, al-, 415–416
Muḥammad (the Prophet), 63, 127, 128
mule: bolting, 562; offspring of, 580; topples lamp (bribe), 567
Muʿtaḍid, al-, 458

Nafzāwiyya, al-, 258
name: God's supreme, 150, 189, 331; presumed to age, 546–548
name day celebrated, 86
Napoleon, 227
Naṣībīn, 289
Nasreddin Hodja, 15–16, 175, 228, 285, 289, 302, 303, 306, 311, 326, 359, 405, 411, 418, 419–420, 427–428, 452–453, 459, 510, 518, 519, 522, 543–544, 547, 556
Nastradhìn-Chótzas. *See* Nasreddin Hodja
Nastratin Hodža. *See* Nasreddin Hodja
natural inclination trumped by education, 49–50
Naybakht, 489
Nectanebo, 579
neighbors: malevolent, punished, 377
news: change according to hospitality, 592–593; companion wants to hear only good, 422–423
night out in the open survived, 282–285
Nizār ibn Maʿadd ibn ʿAdnān, 117–118
nocturnal adventure, 52
nonsense: debtor speaks, 444–447; introduction to fairy-tale world, 582–584
nose: running, cleaned, 430, 431
Nowbakht, 489

object gives birth and dies, 450–453
observation: diagnosis by, 570–572
ointment: magic, 181–184; to be prepared by boiling a patient, 493
old: men, 140–144; woman does not want to sell her house, 155–157
Oxford, University of, 368

Pandaurus, 71–72
paradise: drunk soldier believes he is in, 375
Paris, 387, 501
patient: sickest, to be sacrificed for the others, 491–495
Patapsco river, 30
Pathelin, 44
pauper regains his buried money, 468–472
pearls: harvesting of, 234
peas used for reckoning time, 558
peasant poses as soothsayer, 482–483
penis, 149–150
Perpignan gate in Narbonne, 60
Peter, Clever. *See* Hităr Petăr
Peter, Saint, 170–172, 418, 554–555
Peter Abelard, 418
Pharaoh, 579
Philip VI (French king), 455

Philip the Good (Duke of Burgundy), 376
Phoenix, 143, 353
physician: cures madness, 89; makes diagnosis from observation, 570–572; sham, 483, 491–495
pickpocket finds nothing to steal, 306
piety: value of, 132–137, 178–180, 249, 257
pilgrimage, 46, 463–465
pisspot: drinked served in, 441–442
poison, 161–165, 196
Polyidus, 96
pot: gives birth and dies, 451–453; with money buried in garden, 469. *See also* jar
potter answers unanswerable questions, 228
poverty and happiness, 150
Prague, 433
prayer: as ruse to flee, 89; book forgotten, 349; innocent foolish, 546; Jesus works miracles with, 164; old woman's, makes castle collapse, 157; pious woman's, makes ship wreck, 136; reckoning time of day for, 559; silly: O Sheep of God, 546; without thinking of anything else, 555. *See also* Lord's Prayer
preacher: avoids giving sermon, 541–544; sermon of, makes listener cry, 550–552
present to be shared, 455–460
prince learns profession, 213–218
princess: has secret affair, 52–57; puts suitors to a test, 54
profligate son, 232, 376, 379
proxy: hanging by, 396–398
Prussian trick, 535
pumpkin used to reckon time, 559, 560
punishment: for unjust governor, 157; seated backwards on donkey as, 227. *See* beating

Qarāqūsh, Bahā' al-Dīn, 268, 369, 397–398
Qazvin, 266
queen of England's riches, 181
questions: unanswerable, 225–229
Rabbi Gamaliel, 567–568
Rabbi Joshua Ben Hanania, 580
ransom: of prisoner, by telling tales, 63
rape, 119, 186–188, 246
rarest thing in the world, 105–109
rascal makes his fortune, 74–82
rash killing of faithful animal, 45–47
raven steals meat, 521
recipe: animal lacks, 521–523
recognition of transformed human, 59–65
red-haired man, 518
Regensburg, 501
resuscitation: of brothers, 55; of dead partner by serpent (man), 95–96, 98, 102; of princess, 100; of princess with magic object, 107–108; of king's dead son by Jesus, 164; of dead person by saintly man (Jesus, God), 170–175
reward: and punishment, 129; for telling a lie, 577–580; to be shared, 455–460
Rey, 503
Rhine (river), 431
rider goes where mount takes him, 562–564
riddle. *See* task
ring: stolen, found by chance, 482–484, 486–487
robber: and judge, 388; threatens merchant, 427
robbers hide treasure in magic cavern, 237–240
Robin Goodfellow, 70
Roc, 45–46, 79–80
rogue: dupes ruler with allegedly invisible tissue, 474–479; trades water for wine, 414–416. *See also* cheaters; swindler; trickster
rogues try to cheat simpleton, 252–254
Rome, 163, 164, 187, 360, 426
rooster: as personified death, 320; to be sold together with cow, 409–410. *See also* chicken
Rudolstadt, 433
ruler, just. *See* Anūshīrwān; Frederick II; Hārūn al-Rashīd
ruler: covets subject's wife, 256, 257;

gullible, 474–479; in disguise roams the city at night, 62, 256, 258, 377, 534

Sabā, 583
Sahl ibn Hārūn, 332
Śaktideva, 55–56
Śaktivega, 55–56
sandalwood, 253
Saturday (Sabbath), 69, 246
Schilda, 266
scholar: clever, distributes birds, 514; gives unpractical advice, 423–424; ridiculed, 277–278; and ferryman, 292–293. *See also* student
scholars: roguish, dupe simpleton, 368
Scripture quoted at meal, 392–395
security: uninformed person as, 363–366
sea: challenge to drink up, 253
seduction: attempted, 132–137, 203–211. *See also* lover; lovers; suitors
Semiramis, 195
Serendippo, 114
sermon: avoided by preacher, 541–544; makes a listener cry, 550–552
serpent: attacks young Rocs, 54; demonstrates miraculous cure, 95–96; shows way out of burial cave, 100; saves hero from attacking buffalo, 234
sex: change of, 125–129; gift for, 337–341; illicit, 54–56; seen from person on tree, 343–346; wish for, with ruler's wife, 256
sexuality: women's, cannot be controlled, 351–353
sham: healer, 555–556; physician, 482–483, 485, 491–495; soothsayer, 482–489; threat, 426–428
ship moves only when specific passenger is on board, 232
shipwreck, 56, 100, 134–136, 217
shit. *See* excrements
Shiva, 210
shoes danced to pieces, 52
singing: carpenter has habit of, 471; entertains supernatural creatures, 68–70
Shahriyār, 352
Shāhzamān, 352
shrouds: woman collects, 64
Shylock, 221
sign language, debate in, 484, 487
Sijistān, 288, 423
Sindbād, 97–98
slander: by slave, 316–317; of chaste woman, 132–137
slave: gluttonous, 332; slanderous, 316–317. *See* master and slave
social order reversed, 385–389
soldier: clever, carves roast chicken, 387; drunk, believes he is in paradise (hell) 375; finds out princesses' secret, 52–53; has faithful wife, 209, 210; hosts poor cleric, 387, 514; horse of, stolen, 426; kisses peasant's wife, 344; knows "Prussian trick," 535; mocked for anticipatory beating, 518; travels on earth with Saint Peter in disguise, 172
soldiers: forty, hidden in oil casks; Jesus reluctantly performs miracle to feed, 173; three, as wish-fulfilling characters bound to book, 81
Solomon, 143, 181, 246, 353
Solon, 594
soothsayer, sham, 482–489
soporific drug, 56, 60, 375–382
sorcerer. *See* magician
sparrow: caught, has to be guessed, 486; gives advice, 39, 41
speak only after thinking thrice, 422–424
spell, magic. *See* transformation
spices: animal lacks, 522
spinning, 204–209
stars in heaven: how many? 226, 228
Stephen, Saint, 541
stepmother, 106, 387
stone used to counterbalance wheat, 275–278; man's lower body transformed to, 56
story: man cannot tell, 125–126
storyteller: Bedouin, 528; professional, 458–460, 488; ransoms life, 63
student: clever, carves roast chicken, 387. *See also* scholar

stupid: advice, 295–296; bird mocks man for being, 38–41; clergyman, 558; hero pretends to be, 234, 385; husband follows wife's advice, 149, 151; judgment, 396–398; man believes donkey was transformed person, 367–371; muezzin, 559; people cannot be educated, 41; people want to keep bird from flying away, 266–268; weaver, 493
subaltern: does not want to sell house to ruler, 154–157; is made lord for a day, 375–382
suitor: bride allowed to visit former, 243–249; must bring unusual object, 105–109; must find solution to enigmatic question (riddle), 52–57, 192–200; must learn profession, 213–218; must spend night in the cold, 283; unwanted, humiliated, 203–211, 525–532. *See also* lover; lovers
supernatural creatures. *See* fairy; *ghūla; ʿifrīt; jinnī*; Roc; swan maiden
swan maiden, 233
swindler: leaves security, 363–366; presents unvisible tissue, 474–479. *See also* cheaters; rogue; trickster
sword: allegedly transformed to wood, 534–538. *See also* Damocles

Ṭāʾif, al-, 543
tailor: dreams of patchwork banner, 436–438; teaches king a lesson, 474; thievish, 470
Ṭalḥak, 510
talion: working of, 156
Tamerlane, 459
Ṭarsūs, 547
task: set for princess's suitors, 52–57, 183, 192–200; impossible, set for cheaters, 252–253; not to think of anything else, 554–556
teacher: beats child prior to misdeed, 519; stupid, 296; suggests prince to learn a profession, 215
Teiresias, 128
test: of self-composure, 329–333; princess puts suitors to test, 54
Thales, 594
thief: blamed for stealing, 497–498; claims to have been transformed donkey, 367–371; confesses to presumed soothsayer, 483–487; discovered through story, 243–249; finds nothing to steal, 305–307; in tree claims to be nightingale, 359–360; lacks key for stolen cash box, 523
think thrice before you speak, 422–424
threat: sham, 426–428
three: giants tricked out of magic objects, 53; hairs from husband's beard for magic procedure, 315, 317; men in nonsense tale, 582–584; narrators ransom man threated by demon, 63, 127; nights of suffering, 79; old men (brothers), 140–144; pieces of advice, 38–41; princes brought up in secluded atmosphere, 54; princes must bring rarest thing in the world, 105–109; princes of Serendip, 111–120, 515; rogues try to cheat villager, 252–254; sins, man must choose one of, 186–187; sons quarrel over inheritance, 243–249; times to think before speaking, 422–424; unanswerable questions, 225–229; unwanted suitors trapped, 203–211; wishes, 147–142.
throat: cleared with trick, 431–432; fishbone stuck in, 485, 491–492; ulcer in, breaks by laughing, 571
Thumāma ibn Ashras, 458
time: foolish reckoning of, 558–560
Timur. *See* Tamerlane
tip inverse to service, 420
tissue: imaginary, 474–479
token: of chastity, 204, 205, 207–208; of life, 54
tomorrow: sound will be heard, 359–361
toothache healed if man does not think of monkeys, 555–556
town of rogues, 252–254
transformation: alleged, of man into

donkey, 367–371; alleged, of sword to wood, 534–538; handsome into ugly, 351; human being into animal (or object) 59–65, 150, 181, 371; man into woman (and back), 125–129; mouse into girl (and back), 585–587
trapdoor, 53, 207–208, 217, 231, 233
treacherous: cook, 231–238; employer (treasure-hunter), 231–235; wife, 95–96
treasure: buried under tree, 41, 500–504; divided between children, 142, 143; finders murder one another, 161–166; kept in magic cavern, 237–240; marked with excrements, 507–510. *See also* money
tree: enchanted, 343–346; treasure buried under, 41, 500–504
trickster: answers unanswerable questions, 228; female, 364–365; finds a way to eat food without paying, 377; knows who stole: the thieves!, 497–498; relieves his itching, 420–432. *See also* cheaters; rogue; swindler
Trinity, 514
trying to please everyone, 271–273
ṭufaylī, 393–395
Turandot, 193–195, 200
turban made from invisible tissue, 476, 477–478
Turk, 284, 438

ʿUmar ibn al-Khaṭṭāb, 128
underdog trumps superior, 385–389, 433–434, 513–516
Upakośā, 530–531

vagina: fig as symbol for, 344
Venice, 302, 401
Verceil, 493
vessel. *See* jar; pisspot
Viśākhā, 531
Vishnu, 91–92
Vitaśoka, 382
vizier and king, 50
vow: not to invite same person twice, 377; to be buried alive with dead spouse, 95–102; to sell animal cheaply, 409–412; to die instead of close relative withdrawn, 320–322
vulva, 487, 488

wager: lost, 221; to fool wife out of possessions, 203; to resist itching, 430–432; to tell lie, 577–580
wake, 98, 102, 309
warming oneself on distant fire, 282–285
warning: against adultery, 249; against greed, 38–41, 161–166; against hasty action, 45–47; against scheming women, 314; not to meddle with other people's affairs, 120
washerwoman sows discord, 314–318
Wāṣil ibn ʿAṭāʾ, 326
water: involved during magic transformation, 64, 129; traded for wine, 414–416
weaver: and carpenter compete, 90–92; as sham soothsayer, 485–486: as sham physician, 493–494; hanged instead of culprit, 397; hunchback, 69; pretends to weave invisible tissue, 474–479
wedding night: wife dies in, 101; wife visits its former suitor in, 113, 116, 243–249
welcome to the clothes, 410–412
wife: eats suspiciously little, 59, 62; chaste, 132–137; clever, forces would-be suitors to work, 203–211; faithless, 351–353; obedient, 142; of ruler coveted, 255–258; of subject coveted, 249; reformed, 61; punished, 59–65; should not be in presence of visitors, 389; supernatural, 99; treacherous, 95–96. *See also* woman
wiles of women: 203–211, 351–353, 464–465, 525–532
wine. *See* drinking
wish: have sex with ruler's wife, 256
wishes foolishly wasted, 147–152
witch. *See* magician
wolf cub raised on sheep's milk, 50

woman: accused of adultery, 206; beaten by husband, 60, 315, 320, 322, 349, 492; cannibal, 60, 62; chaste, 525–532; coveted by her brother-in-law, 132–137; kept in a container, 352; lecherous, 249. *See also* wife
women: are all the same, 255–259; sexuality of, cannot be controlled, 351–353; *See also* wiles of women
wood: precious, 252–253; sword allegedly transformed to, 534–538
years of experience in a moment, 125–12
youth, fountain of, 494
Yūsuf ibn al-Ḥusayn al-Rāzī, Abū Yaʿqūb, 331–332
Yūsuf ibn Tāshufīn, 258

Zaʿfar, 128
Zahman, 503–504
zodiac, 547

GENERAL INDEX

Aarne, Antti, 6, 7
ʿAbbāsī, al-Sayyid ʿAbd al-Raḥīm al-, 100–101
Ābī, al-. See *Nathr al-durr*
Abraham a Sancta Clara, 155, 436
Abstemius, Laurentius, 321, 469
Abu Bakr ibn Khosrow al-Ostād. See *Munes-nāme*
Abū ʾl-Najm, 35
Abulpharagius. See *Laughable Stories*
Abū Miryam, 447
Abū Nuʿaym al-Iṣfahānī. *See* Iṣfahānī, Abū Nuʿaym al-
adab literature, 11–12, 13–14
Adam of Cobsam, 207–208, 210
adaptation, 76–77, 81–82, 92, 215, 345, 411, 451, 453, 471; "Aranisation," 81
Adenet le Roi. See *Cléomadès*
Aelianus, Claudius, 442
Aesopic fables, 31, 34–37, 50
Afanasyev, Aleksandr, 61, 232, 338, 344, 385
Aghānī, Kitāb al- (by Iṣfahānī), 268, 311, 415, 434
Agreement Not to Scratch (ATU 1565), 430–432
Agricola, Johannes, 501
Ahiqar, 579
ʿĀʾisha, 127, 371
ʿAjāʾib al-makhlūqāt (by Qazwīnī), 14, 189, 268, 572
ʿAjjāj, Ruʾba ibn ʿAbdallāh al-, 579
Ajwiba al-muskita, al- (by Ibn Abī ʿAwn), 299, 310, 458
Akhbār al-Adhkiyāʾ (by Ibn al-Jawzī), 13, 40, 118, 253, 331, 340, 345, 388, 394, 411, 438, 466, 493–494, 556
Akhbār al-duwal (by Qaramānī), 157
Akhbār al-Ḥamqā (by Ibn al-Jawzī), 13, 175, 179, 268, 280, 289, 296, 370, 423, 519, 523, 547, 571, 575
Akhbār al-Ẓirāf (by Ibn al-Jawzī), 13, 388, 411, 418, 438, 498, 509
Aladdin (ATU 561), 74–85, 109
Albertus Magnus, 30
Alemán, Mateo. See *Guzmán de Alfarache*
Alexander, Romance of, 1
Alexander and Semiramis, 195
Alf layla wa-layla. See *Thousand and One Nights, The*
Aljamiado manuscript, 164, 175
almanacs, 330
Almquist, Bo, 214
Alphabet of Ben Sira (Sirach), 179
amalgamation, 91
ambiguity of dreams, 504
Amblysia, 594
ʿĀmilī, Bahāʾ al-Dīn, 157. See *Javāher al-ʿoqul*; *Kashkūl, al-*
Amir Khosrow of Dehli. See *Bāgh o Bahār*; *Hasht behesht*
Andalusia: Arabic literature. See *Ḥadāʾiq al-azāhir*; *ʿIqd al-farīd, al-*; *Sirāj al-mulūk*; Jewish literature. See *Sefer shaʾshuʿim*
Andersen, Hans Christian, 91, 474–475, 478
Anderson, Walter, 6, 225
Andreae, Johann Valentin. See *Chymische Hochzeit Christiani Rosenkreutz 1459*
animal tales, 29
Anser Venalis (AT 1420G), 337–342
Anthropophyteia, 337

Anticipatory Beating (ATU 1674*), 518–520
anticlerical narratives, 227, 498
anti-Jewish narratives, 74–76, 78, 164–165, 170–177, 213–220, 302–304, 457
antiquity, Greek and Roman, 2, 9, 71–72, 96, 102, 266, 478
Anton von Pforr. See *Buch der Beispiele der alten Weisen, Das*
Anvār-e Soheyli (by Kāshefi), 156, 321
Anvari, 299, 447
apochryphal legend of Jesus, 166
Apollodorus. See *Library*
Apprentice's Dream, The (ATU 1572M*), 433–435
Arabia ridens, 7
'Arā'is al-majālis (by Tha'labī). See *Qiṣaṣ al-anbiyā'*
Ariosto. See *Orlando furioso*
Aristophanes, 273
Armeno, Cristoforo. See *Peregrinaggio di tre giovanni figliuoli del re di Serendippo*
Asad wa-'l-ghawwāṣ, al-, 410
Ashriba, al- (by Ibn Qutayba), 188
Asiatic Journal, 404
Asjadi, 503
Aśokāvadāna, 382
Āthār al-bilād (by Qazwīnī), 157, 331
Atlīdī, al-. See *I'lām al-nās*
'Aṭṭār, 15, 151, 157. See *Elāhi-nāme*; *Moṣibat-nāme*; *Tadhkirat al-awliyā'*
ATU: critique of, 218n8, 237, 282, 405, 525. *See also* tale-type classification
authentication. *See* credibility; localization
Avadanas, 476
'Awfi. See *Javāme' al-ḥekāyāt*

Babylonian Talmud, 119, 579
Bāgh o Bahār (by Amir Khosrow), 101
Bahār-e dānesh (by 'Enāyatollāh Kanbu), 346
Bahārestān (by Jāmi), 411
Bahjat al-majālis (by Ibn 'Abd al-Barr), 268
Bakrī, Abū *'Ubayd al-*. See *Masālik wa-'l-mamālik, al-*
Bal'ami, 122n29
Balancing the Mealsack (ATU 1242B), 275–278
Baltimore Sun, 29
Bar Hebraeus. See *Laughable Stories*
Barber Substituted for Smith at Execution (ATU 1534A*), 396–399
Barhut, 531
Barlaam and Josaphat, 39–41
Baṣā'ir wa-'l-dhakhā'ir, al- (by Tawḥīdī), 13, 299, 416, 452, 509, 578
Basket-Maker, The (ATU 888A*), 213–220, 253
basket-making, 214
Basset, René, 5, 7
Bāudhyāna Śrāutra Sūtra, 128
bawdy tales, 337
Bayhaqī. See *Maḥāsin wa-'l-masāwī, al-*
Beach, Rex, 45
Beccadelli, Antonio, 469
Bechstein, Ludwig, 585
Bede, The Venerable, 127
Bédier, Joseph, 151
Belling the Cat (ATU 110), 34–37
Bellini, Lorenzo, 70
Bell's *Speaker*, 591
Beloe, William, 537
Benfey, Theodor, 5
Berechiah ha-Nakdan. See *Mishle Shu'alim*
Bérinus, 253
Bertoldo. See *Viaţa lui Bertoldo*
Bible. See *New Testament*; *Old Testament*
Blind Man's Treasure, The (ATU 1617*), 468–471
Boccaccio, Giovanni, 17. See *Decamerone*; *Filocolo*
Bodens, Wilhelm, 450–451
Boiardo, Matteo. See *Orlando innamorato*
Bolte, Johannes, 7, 17, 504
Botero, Giovanni, 156. See *Detti memorabili di personaggi illustri*
Boundaries, 119–120, 317–318
Braga, Teófilo, 405
Brave Tailor, The (ATU 1640), 491
Bṛhatkathā, 16, 234, 248, 530
Bṛhatkathāmañjarī, 248, 530

Briggs, Katherine M., 591
Brockelmann, Carl, 345
Broken (Removed) Article, The (ATU 1420A), 340
Bromyard, John, 163, 188. See *Summa predicantium*
Brunvand, Jan, 302
Buch der Beispiele der alten Weisen (by Anton von Pforr), 47, 586
Buddhist literature, 273. See *Avadanas*; *Jatakas*; *Tripiṭaka*
Bughyat al-jalīs (by Ḥafnāwī), 563
Bukhalā', al- (by Jāḥiẓ), 12, 326, 332
Bukhalā', al- (by al-Khaṭīb al-Baghdādī), 332, 441, 592–593
Bülow, Eduard von, 475
burial practices, 96, 98
Burton, Richard, 233
Burzōe, 35
Bustān (by Sa'di), 419
Butler, Samuel, 397
Buying the Goose (ATU 1420G), 337–342

Caesarius of Heisterbach, 330
Calderón de la Barca: *La vida es sueño*, 375
calendar, 2, 17, 325, 410, 434, 452
Cannibal Sister, The (ATU 315A), 64
Cantemir, Dimitrie, 459
Canterbury Tales (by Chaucer), 17: "Franklin's Tale," 245; "Merchant's Tale," 344; "Pardoner's Tale," 161, 163; "Squire's Tale," 89; "Tale of Beryn," 253
Cardonne, Denis Dominique, 437
Carrying Part of the Load (ATU 1242A), 273, 276
Cārudatta-carita, 234
Cascudo, Luís da Câmara, 507
Castelli, Moshe, 326
Castiglione, Baldesar. See *Cortegiano, Il*
Cat with the Candle, The (ATU 217), 49–51
Caussin de Perceval, Jean Jacques Antoine, 5
Cento novelle antiche, 17, 114, 163, 172, 465
Cepenkov, Marko, 252
chapbooks, 18, 288, 330, 593: Arabic, 71, 263, 371, 394, 460; Dutch, 566; English, 279, 367, 566; German, 78, 155–156, 279, 325, 375, 469, 516, 536, 562, 566; Hungarian, 566; Italian, 535; Persian, 199, 388; Romanian, 293, 566; Turkish, 388; Urdu, 388. See *Joe Miller's Jests*; *Merry Tales of the Mad Men of Gottam, The*; *Mery Tales, A C*; *Mery Tales and Quicke Answers*; *Sack-Full of Newes, The*; *Tales and Quick Answers*; *Wit and Mirth*. *See also* jestbooks
Chaucer, Geoffrey. See *Canterbury Tales*
Chauvin, Victor, 5, 7, 502
chauvinism, male, 337, 340
Chavis, Dom, 76, 128, 195
Chehel ṭuṭi, 199
Chevalier, Maxime, 8
Child with Head Caught in a Jar (ATU 1294A*), 295–297
children's books, 31
children's folklore, 430, 583
Chiţimia, Ion Constantin, 192–193
Chraïbi, Aboubakr, 19, 379
Christensen, Arthur, 157, 488
Christian context, 75, 112, 132, 170, 195, 199, 225–230, 318, 333, 392–395, 405–406, 412, 418–421, 498, 508, 510, 543, 546–548, 554, 558, 562
Chymische Hochzeit Christiani Rosenkreutz 1459 (by Andreae), 245
Ci nous dit, 163
Cléomadès (by Adenet le Roi), 89–90
Clergyman Has no Need to Preach, The (ATU 1826), 541–545
Clergyman on the Cow's Tail, The (ATU 1849*), 562–565
Clergyman with the Fine Voice, The (ATU 1834), 441, 550–553
Clergyman's Calendar, The (ATU 1848A), 558–561
Clever Girl and the King, The (ATU 875B), 386
Clever Maiden Alone at Home Kills the Robbers, The (ATU 956B), 239
Climax of Horrors, The (ATU 2040), 316, 589–596

clock tale, 585
Clouston, William Alexander, 5, 106, 210, 344, 376, 403, 437, 542, 544
Coelho, Francisco Adolfo, 465
collector's agenda, 59, 99, 105–107, 154, 344, 474
Colombo, Michele, 369
Compagno del passeggio campestre, Il, 535
Compilatio singularis exemplorum, 197, 514
Conde Lucanor, El (by Don Juan Manuel), 17, 249, 272, 475–476, 479
Constant du Hamel, 528
contamination, 19, 55, 239
Contes et discours d'Eutrapel (by Noël du Fail), 141, 364
Contest in Lying (ATU 1920), 574
Contest Not to Become Angry (ATU 1000), 218
Copley, Anthony, 397
Correas, Gonzalo. See *Vocabulario de refranes*
Cortegiano, Il (by Castiglione), 279
Costa, Jorge da, 536
Cosquin, Emmanuel, 49, 352
Costo, Tommaso. See *Fuggilozio, Le otto giornate del*
Count Ernst, 233
court fool (or jester), 49, 285, 470
Crane, Thomas Frederick, 590
credibility, 45–46
Crescentia (ATU 712), 132–139, 464
Crowley, Daniel J., 107
Crusades, The, 2, 16, 229, 322, 333, 447
"Cursor Mundi," 222

Dahestāni, 504
Damīrī, al-. See *Ḥayāt al-ḥayawān*
Danced-Out Shoes, The (ATU 306), 52–58
De nuce maga Beneventana (by Piperno), 69
Death for the Old Couple (ATU 1354), 320–324
Decamerone (by Boccaccio), 245, 257, 344, 465
Desordenada codicia de los bienes agenos, La (by García), 415
detective novel, 120
Detti memorabili di personaggi illustri (by Botero), 155
Deutsche Sagen (by Grimm), 140, 501
Dhahabī, al-, 316, 318
Diagnosis by Observation (ATU 1862C), 570–573
Digby, Sir Kenelm, 30
dilemma tale, 108
Directorium vitae humanae (by John of Capua), 1, 47, 586
Disabled Comrades, The (ATU 1965), 582–584
Disciplina clericalis (by Petrus Alfonsus), 1, 16, 39, 41, 406, 465, 591
Discussion in Sign Language (ATU 924), 484, 487
Dishes of the Same Flavor, The (ATU 983), 255–260
Disposing of the Corpse (ATU 1536), 207
Dividing Five Eggs Equally between Two Men and One Woman (ATU 1663), 385, 386, 513–517
Division: "Odd or Even?", The (ATU 1533B), 513
Diyāb, Ḥannā, 9, 14–15, 54–55, 57, 61–64, 76–77, 90, 108–109, 182–184, 237, 239–240
Dobrovolsky, Vladimir Nikolaevich, 349
Doctor Know-All (ATU 1641), 379, 482–490, 494, 541
Dolopathos (by John of Alta Silva), 222, 223
Domenichi, Lodovico, 360, 469
domestication, 54, 57
Don Juan Manuel. See *Conde Lucanor, El*
Dorson, Richard, 344, 414
Double Pension (Burial Money), The (ATU 1556), 379, 487
Dream of Marking the Treasure (ATU 1645B), 507–512
dreams, ambiguity of, 504
Drinking Cup, The (ATU 1578A*), 303, 441–443, 551
Droste-Hülshoff, Annette von, 52

Effectiveness of Fire, The (ATU 1262), 282–286

Egyptian tradition, ancient, 240
Eiximenis, Francesc: *Lo Crestià*, 508
Elāhi-nāme (by ʿAṭṭār), 41, 137
Élite des contes, L' (by Ouville), 228, 485
El-Shamy, Hasan, 8, 298, 513
ʿEmād ibn Moḥammad al-Saghari. See *Javāher al-asmār*
Emperor's New Clothes, The (ATU 1620), 474–481
Emre, Yunus, 583
ʿEnāyatollāh Kanbu. See *Bahār-e dānesh*
Enchanted Pear Tree, The (ATU 1423), 343–348
Encyclopaedia of Islam, 6
ending: happy, 61; humorous, 60; open, 108
Entrapped Suitors, The (ATU 1730), 204–206, 210, 525–533
Enzyklopädie des Märchens, 7–8, 18, 19
Epidaurian miracle tablets, 71–72
Epiphanius, archbishop, 233
Erasmus of Rotterdam, 357
Esopus (by Waldis), 321
Espinosa, Aurelio M., 107, 344
Étienne de Bourbon. *See* Stephen of Bourbon
Eulenspiegel, Till, 228, 491
Exilium melancholiae, 426, 522
Ey, August, 99

fables and animal tales, 29–33, 34–37, 38–44, 45–48. *See* Aesopic fables
fabliau, 149
Fabulae (by Hyginus), 96
Facebook, 271
factual report, 30
fairy-tale logic, 82
Fākhir, al- (by al-Mufaḍḍal ibn Salama), 127
Fākihat al-khulafā' (by Ibn ʿArabshāh), 165, 316–317, 494
Farahāni, 447
Farāhi. See *Maḥbub al-qolub*
Faraj baʿd al-shidda, Al- (by Tanūkhī), 100, 502–503
Fārisī, ʿUmar ibn Dā'ūd ibn Shaykh Sulaymān al-, 322
Farnham, Williard Edward, 107
Farrokhi, 503
Fasciculus facetiarum, 562
Faithful Wife, The (ATU 888), 205
Fāshūsh fī aḥkam Qarāqūsh, al- (by Ibn Mammātī), 397–398
Felix: de los Maravelles del Mon (by Llull), 469–471, 586
Ferec baʿd eş-şidde, 1, 9, 15, 90, 100, 116, 120, 135, 137, 142, 184, 195, 197–198, 208–209, 216, 222–223, 234, 246, 253–254, 353, 364–365, 371, 388, 516, 529–530
Ferrer, San Vicente, 16, 163, 567
Fieldwork, 287, 343
Filocolo (by Boccaccio), 245
Fiorentino, Ser Giovanni. See *Pecorone*
first person narrative, 296, 311, 317, 331, 370, 387, 388, 444–445
Floresta española (by Santa Cruz), 360, 397, 519
foaf-tale, 45
"folk" literature, 18–19
folklorization, 258
Forty Thieves, The (ATU 954), 109, 237–242
Forty Viziers, The. See *Qırq vezīr*
Fox Advises Camel Not to Go Near Man (El-Shamy 1319N*), 298–301
Fox Catches a Beetle (ATU 65*), 282
Fox Rids Himself of Fleas, The (ATU 63), 29–33
Frauenlob, Heinrich, 351
Freud, Sigmund, 564
Frey, Jakob, 508
Fuggilozio, Le otto giornate del (by Costo), 401
Fulgosius Genuensis, Baptista, 469

Gaelic narratives, 125–127
Galland, Antoine, 1, 54, 62–63, 76, 90, 97, 108–109, 182–183, 237, 239, 379; Constantinople diary of, 100. See *Paroles remarquables*; *Thousand and One Nights*
García, Carlos. See *Desordenada codicia de los bienes agenos, La*

Garimberto, Girolamo: *Della fortuna*, 536
genitals, male, 513, 516
Genizah collection, Cambridge, 538
Gerhardt, Mia, 76
Gerlach, Samuel, 155
Gervase of Tilbury. See *Otia imperialia*
Gesner, Conrad, 30
Gesta Danorum (by Saxo Grammaticus), 97, 114
Gesta Romanorum, 208, 210, 222, 456–457, 465
Getting the Calf's Head Out of the Pot (ATU 1294), 295–297
Ghazzālī, al-, 165. See *Iḥyā' ʿulūm al-dīn*; *Kimiyā-ye saʿādat*, *Naṣīḥat al-mulūk*
Gibb, Elias J.W., 476
Gildemeister, Johann, 272
Girart d'Amien. See *Méliacin*
Gladwin, Francis: *The Persian Moonshee*, 419, 466, 471, 593
Golden Mountain, The (ATU 936*), 231–236
Golestān (by Saʿdi), 299
Görres, Joseph von, 78
Gotham, Mad Men of, 266, 406
Gozzi, Carlo, 199–200
Granja, Fernando de la, 8
Greater Bribe, The (ATU 1861A), 566–569
Greedy Dreamer, The (ATU 1543A), 403–408
Greverus, Ina-Maria, 69, 71
Grillenvertreiber, Der, 279
Grillo medico, 485, 494–495
Grimm, Jacob and Wilhelm, 78, 86–87, 95–97, 488. See *Deutsche Sagen*; *Kinder- und Hausmärchen*
Grimmelshausen, Hans Jakob Christoph von, 326
Groot Klugtboek, 288
gross language, 262
Grunebaum, Gustave Edmund, 564
Guarding the Store-Room Door (ATU 1009), 261–265
Guevara y Dueñas, Luis Vélez de: *El diablo cojuelo*, 519
Guicciardini, Lodovico, 469
Guzmán de Alfarache (by Alemán), 364
György, Lajos, 17

Habicht, Maximilian, 118
Ḥablerudi. See *Jāmeʿ al-tamsil*
Ḥadā'iq al-azāhir (by Ibn ʿĀṣim), 12, 40, 50, 268, 310, 326, 332, 361, 406, 503, 509, 542, 559, 567
Ḥadīqat al-afrāḥ (by Shirwānī), 179
Ḥadiqat al-ḥaqiqa (by Sanā'i), 321
ḥadīth (Prophetic traditions), 143, 188, 216, 332
Ḥafnāwī, al-. See *Bughyat al-jalīs*
Haft owrang (by Jāmi), 144, 326
Haft seyr-e (or *so'āl-e*) *Ḥātem*. See *Ḥātem-nāme*
Hagen, Friedrich Heinrich von der, 537
Haggada, 175, 567
Ḥalbat al-kumayt (by Nawājī), 70–71
Hahn, Johann Georg von, 134
Halpert, Herbert, 570
Hamadāni, 504
Ḥamza, ʿAbd al-Laṭīf, 398
Ḥanafī, al-. See *Nuzhat al-udabā'*
Hans Sachs, 164, 314, 437
Hansen, William, 273
Harpagiander: *Lexicon apophthegmaticum*, 518
Harrington, Sir John, 437
Harsdörfer, Georg Philipp: *Ars apophthegmatica*, 518
Hasht behesht (by Amir Khosrow), 115–116, 515
Ḥātem-nāme, 183
Ḥayāt al-ḥayawān (by Damīrī), 8, 14, 31, 40, 118, 165, 174, 438
Ḥayawān, al- (by Jāḥiẓ), 12, 30–31, 284, 345, 387, 446, 514, 555
Hazlitt, William Carew, 262
He Who Says, "That's a Lie," Must Pay a Fine (ATU 1920F), 577–581
Hebel, Johann Peter. See *Schatzkästlein des rheinischen Hausfreundes*
Ḥekāyāt-e laṭif, 411, 419, 466, 471
Heller, Bernhard, 7
Helmhack, Daniel Elias, 155
Hēmavijaya. See *Kathāratnākara*

Henry the Lion, 233
Hermenegildo de Tancos. See *Orto de esposo*
Hertel, Johannes, 50
Hezār afsān, 15
Ḥikāyāt al-ajība, (*Kitāb*) *al-*, 64, 90, 370, 379, 485–487
Hilka, Alfons, 197
Hillers, Barbara, 127
Ḥilyat al-awliyā' (by Iṣfahānī), 40, 330–331
Ḥimyarī, al-. See *Rawḍ al-mi'ṭār fī khabar al-aqṭār, al-*
historic-geographic method, 6, 69, 225
Hog's Head Divided According to Scripture (ATU 1533A), 392–395
Hole to Throw the Earth In, A (ATU 1255), 279–281
Horace, 12
House Without Food or Drink, The (ATU 1346), 309–313
Hróa Þáttr heimska, 253
Hulsbusch, Johannes. See *Sylva sermonum*
Hundred and One Nights, The, 47, 90, 127, 149–150, 352, 380–381, 538
hunters' tale, 30
Husband Carries Off Box Containing Hidden Lover, The (ATU 1358B), 351
Ḥuṣrī, al-, 321. See *Jam' al-jawāhir*
Hyginus. See *Fabulae*

Iberian Peninsula, 2, 510
Ibn 'Abbās, 150
Ibn 'Abd al-Barr. See *Bahjat al-majālis*
Ibn 'Abd Rabbih. See *'Iqd al-farīd, al-*
Ibn 'Abd al-Ḥakam, 228–229
Ibn Abī 'Awn. See *Ajwiba al-muskita, al-*
Ibn Abī 'l-Dunyā, 316
Ibn Abī 'l-Ḥadīd. See *Sharḥ Nahj al-balāgha*
Ibn Abī Ya'lā. See *Ṭabaqāt al-ḥanābila*
Ibn al-Athīr. See Kāmil, *al-*
Ibn al-'Imād, 258
Ibn al-Jawzī, 12, 157, 263, 432. See *Akhbār al-Adhkiyā'*; *Akhbār al-Ḥamqā*; *Akhbār al-Ẓirāf*; *Muntaẓam, al-*;
Ibn al-Muqaffa', 16. See *Kalīla wa-Dimna*
Ibn al-Mu'tazz. See *Ṭabaqāt al-shu'arā'*
Ibn al-Rūmī, 571
Ibn al-Wardī. See *Kharīdat al-'ajā'ib*
Ibn 'Arabshāh. See *Fākihat al-khulafā'*
Ibn 'Asakir. See *Tārīkh madīnat Dimashq*
Ibn 'Āṣim al-Gharnāṭī. See *Ḥadā'iq al-azāhir*
Ibn Bābawayh (Bābōyah) al-Ṣaddūq. See *Kamāl al-dīn wa-tamām al-ni'ma*
Ibn Badrūn, 156
Ibn Ḥamdūn. See *Tadhkira al-ḥamdūniyya, al-*
Ibn Ḥanbal, 143
Ibn Ḥibbān al-Bustī. See *Rawḍat al-'uqalā'*
Ibn Ḥijja al-Ḥamawī. See *Thamarāt al-awrāq*
Ibn Hishām. See *Kitāb al-Tījān fī mulūk Ḥimyar*
Ibn Khallikān, 14, 258
Ibn Mammātī. See *al-Fāshūsh fī aḥkam Qarāqūsh*
Ibn Manẓūr, 331, 332
Ibn Nubāta, 156
Ibn Qutayba. See *Ashriba, al-*; *Ma'ārif, al-*; *'Uyūn al-akhbār*
Ibn Sa'īd al-Maghribī, 272
Ibn Ṣaṣrā, 165
Ibn Shākir al-Kutubī, 14, 522, 563
Ibn Zabara, Joseph. See *Sefer sha'shu'im*
Ibshīhī, al-. See *Mustaṭraf fī kull fann mustaẓraf, al-*
Icelandic narratives, 2, 105–107, 464
"If God Wills" (ATU 830C), 178–180
Iḥyā' 'ulūm al-dīn (by Ghazzālī), 14, 40, 165, 174, 316–317
Ikeda, Hiroko, 71
I'lām al-nās (by Atlīdī), 388, 459
Ilmām, Kitāb al- (by al-Nuwayrī al-Iskandarānī), 137
Indian theory, 5
Inedible Meat, The (ATU 1689B), 521–524
Innocent VIII, Pope, 427
Innocent Dog, The (ATU 178A), 45–48
internet, 31
'Iqd al-farīd, al- (by Ibn 'Abd Rabbih), 12, 40, 50, 268, 332, 406, 509, 543

ʿIrāqī, Raḍiyy al-Dīn al-. See *Nuzhat al-anfus*
Iṣfahānī, Abū ʾl-Faraj al-. See *Aghānī, Kitāb al-*
Iṣfahānī, Abū Nuʿaym al-. See *Ḥilyat al-awliyāʾ*
Isḥāqī, al-. See *Laṭāʾif akhbār al-uwal*
Iskāfī, al-. See *Lutf al-tadbīr*
isnād (chain of transmitters), 137, 434
Itḥāf al-sāda (by Zabīdī), 318n11

Jackson, Thomas W., 396
Jacobs, Joseph, 591
Jacques de Vitry, 16, 306, 330, 493, 551–552, 555–556, 590
Jaʿfar al-Ṣādiq, 137, 470
Jāḥiẓ, al-, 12, 30–31. See *Bukhalāʾ, al-*; *Ḥayawān, al-*
Jahn, Ulrich, 77, 79–80
Jain narrative literature, 50
Jalīs al-ṣāliḥ al-kāfī, al- (by Nahrawānī), 136
Jamʿ al-jawāhir (by Ḥuṣrī), 277, 299, 357, 428, 452, 470
Jāmeʿ al-ḥekāyāt, 15, 100, 116, 137, 143, 197–198, 209, 218, 223, 253, 388, 530
Jāmeʿ al-tamsil (by Ḥablerudi), 137, 217, 471
Jāmi. See *Bahārestān*; *Haft owrang*
Jāmiʿ al-bayān fī tafsīr āy al-Qurʾān (by Ṭabarī), 164, 173, 188–189
Jason, Heda, 359
Jātakas, 164, 531
Javāher al-asmār (by ʿEmād ibn Moḥammad), 15, 41, 209, 247–248
Javāher al-ʿoqul (ʿĀmilī or Majlesi), 477–478, 487–488
Javāmeʿ al-ḥekāyāt (by ʿAwfi), 15, 41, 117, 137, 151, 157, 198, 215, 218, 247, 317, 515, 547
jestbooks, 188, 306, 397. *See also* chapbooks
Jesus as a prophet of Islam, 166
Jewish tradition, 40
jidd wa-ʾl-hazl, al-, 12, 13
Jinaratna: *Līlāvatī-Sāra*, 476
Jineśvara: *Nivvāṇa-Līlāvaī-Kahā*, 476
Joe Miller's Jests, 17, 367–369
John Bromyard, 16
John Gobi, 16. See *Scala coeli*
John of Capua. See *Directorium vitae humanae*
John of Alta Silva, See *Dolopathos*
joke trade route, 267
jokes and anecdotes, 8–9, 287, 298, 305, 404
Joos, Amat, 555
Juan de Robles: *Las tardes de Alcázar*, 326
Julien, Stanislas, 404

Kaʿb al-Aḥbār, 144
Kāfī (fī ʿilm al-dīn), al- (by Kulaynī), 135
Kaiserchronik, 132
"Kaiser Karls Recht," 222
Kalīla wa-Dimna (by Ibn al-Muqaffaʿ and others), 1, 5, 16, 35, 46–47, 321–322, 586–587
Kamāl al-dīn wa-tamām al-niʿma (by Ibn Bābawayh), 40
Kāmil fī ʾl-tārīkh, al- (by Ibn al-Athīr), 258
Kang Seng-Hui. See *Tripiṭaka*
Kanz al-mosāferin (by Ibn ʿAli Ashraf ibn ʿAli ʿAbd al-Vahhāb), 478
Karlmeinet, 365, 501, 504
Kāshāni, Ḥabiballāh. See *Reyāż al-ḥekāyāt*
Kāshefi. See *Anvār-e Soheyli*
Kashkūl, al- (by ʿĀmilī), 179
Kathāratnākara (by Hēmavijaya), 49, 248, 419, 466
Kathāsaritsāgara (by Somadeva), 5, 16, 47, 55–56, 64, 119, 210, 248, 264, 371, 485, 530
Kaytazzade Mehmet Nazım, 477
Kemalpaşazade, 346
Khālidī, al-. See *al-Tuḥaf wa-ʾl-hadāyā*
Kharīdat al-ʿajāʾib (by Ibn al-Wardī), 156
Khaṭīb al-Baghdādī, al-. See *Bukhalāʾ, al-*; *Taṭfīl, al-*; *Tārīkh Baghdād*
Khoʾi, Mirzā ʿAli-Qoli, 189
Kimiyā-ye saʿādat (by Ghazzālī), 41
Kind and Unkind Girls, The (ATU 480), 68
Kinder- und Hausmärchen, 4, 7; #7, 457;

#16, 95, 102; #81, 172; #98, 485; #133, 52–53; #138, 582; #142, 239; #152, 228
King's Glove, The (ATU 891B*), 257
Kipling, Rudyard, 164
Kirchhof, Hans-Wilhelm, 508
Kirmeyer, Rudolf, 266
Kisā'ī, al-. See *Qiṣaṣ al-anbiyā'*
Köhler, Reinhold, 208, 210
Konya, 300, 583
Koran, 392–395; 2:62, 583; 2:102, 188; 2:127, 394; 3:52, 173; 5:69, 583; 7: 57, 394; 7:175, 151; 11:44, 394; 12:28, 464; 18:23–24, 178; 18:71, 393; 21:5, 504; 22:17, 583; 22:45, 393; 25:12, 393; 26:94, 393; 37:147, 394; 38:86, 50; 54:12, 394; 55:50, 394; 97:3, 150
Kößler-Ilg, Bertha, 400
Krauss, Friedrich Salomo, 337
Kristensen, Evald Tang, 325, 575
Kryptádia, 337
Kulaynī (or Kulīnī), al-. See *al-Kāfī (fī ʿilm al-dīn)*

Lacarra Ducay, María Jesús, 8, 19
La Fontaine, Jean de, 351, 469
Lamb of God Becomes Sheep of God (ATU 1832N*), 546–549
Lamb's Heart (ATU 785), 170–177
Lāmiʿī Chelebī, 437
Laṭā'ef al-ṭavā'ef (by Ṣafī), 15, 268, 288–289, 311, 361, 447, 510, 547, 593
Laṭā'ef-e ʿajibe, 311
Laṭā'if akhbār al-uwal (by Isḥāqī), 379, 503, 509
Latvian narratives, 181, 356
Laughable Stories (by Bar Hebraeus), 13, 39–40, 268, 288, 306, 357, 498, 509, 548
Lavā'i, 593
Lavaux, Jean-Charles, 144
Law, customary, 317
Lawyer's Mad Client, The (ATU 1585), 444–449
Laylat al-qadr (Eve of Divine Power), 150
Lazarillo de Tormes, La vida de, 310
legend, migratory, 155
legend, modern. *See* modern legend
Legman, Gershon, 337
Lehmann, Christoph, 155, 522
"Let Them Eat Cake!" (ATU 1446), 356–358
Levant, The, 2
Liar Reduces the Size of His Lie, The (ATU 1920D), 574–576
Liber parabolorum (by Odo of Cheriton), 34–35, 587
Library (by Apollodorus), 96
Lidzbarski, Mark, 5, 7
literature: Arabic, periods of, 11; Ottoman and modern Turkish, 15–16; Sanskrit, 16
Lithuanian narratives, 171
Littmann, Enno, 6
Llull, Ramón. See *Felix: de los Maravelles del Mon*
Localization, 60, 266, 268, 288, 289, 292, 360, 365, 401, 416, 427, 433, 436, 446, 451, 464, 469, 493, 498, 500–501, 536, 541, 559, 562
Lord for a Day (ATU 1531), 375–384, 538
Lover's Gift Regained, The (ATU 1420), 337
Lubāb Nathr al-durr (by Zaydī), 263, 563
Lucas, Paul, 76
Lucian, 563
Lucky Blow, The (ATU 1646), 488
Lucky Poverty (ATU 754), 382
Lustige Gesellschaft (by Memel), 364
Luṭf al-tadbīr (by Iskāfī), 556
Lying Contest (ATU 852), 578

Maʿārif, al- (by Ibn Qutayba), 267
Maasse-Buch, 228
Madā'inī, al-, 387, 434, 447, 555, 579
Magnus, Olaus, 30
Magnússon, Eiríkr, 105
Mágus-Saga, 386
Magyar Nyelvőr, 74
Mahābhārata, 128
Maḥāsin wa-'l-aḍdād, al- (by Pseudo-Jāḥiẓ), 528

Maḥāsin wa-'l-masāwī, al- (by Bayhaqī), 310, 316, 465, 528
Maḥbub al-qolub (by Farāhi), 40, 217, 361, 365
Majlesi. See *Javāher al-ʿoqul*
Majmaʿ al-amthāl (by Maydānī), 410
Makkī, Abū Ṭālib al-. See *Qūt al-qulūb*
Malcolm, John: *Sketches of Persia*, 488
Malti-Douglas, Fedwa, 465
Man Persecuted because of His Beautiful Wife, The (ATU 465), 105, 108
Man Who Had no Story (Ó Súilleabháin/ Christiansen 2412B), 125
Mangione, Jerry, 206
Maqarrī, al-, 272
Marbach, Gotthard Oswald, 78
Marco Polo, 502
Mardrus translation of the *Nights*, 218
Marie de France, 17, 96, 330, 410, 586
Marzbān-nāme (by Varāvini), 165
Masālik wa-'l-mamālik, al- (by Bakrī), 156
Masnavi-ye maʿnavi (by Rumi), 41, 277, 293, 299–300, 311, 326, 345–346, 360–361, 438, 504, 583–584
Masʿūdī, al-. See *Murūj al-dhahab wa-maʿādin al-jawhar*
Maxwell, William Hamilton, 30
Maydānī, al-, 14, 35, 118. See *Majmaʿ al-amthāl*
Maylāwī, al-, 263, 280, 340, 434, 510, 522, 563
Meier, Fritz, 199
Meistergesang, 222
Meleatons [...] Tugendschule (Rost), 77
Méliacin (by Girart d'Amien), 89
Memel, Johann Peter de. See *Lustige Gesellschaft*
Mensa philosophica, 306, 445–446, 469, 501, 566–567, 571
Meʿrāj-nāme (by Shojāʿi Mashhadi), 128
Merry Tales of the Mad Men of Gottam, The, 267
Mery Tales, A C, 547
Mery Tales and Quicke Answers, 288, 508
Metamorphoses (by Ovid), 128
Mi'at layla wa-layla. See *Hundred and One Nights, The*
Midrash, 119, 143, 246, 388–389, 513
Mightiest Being as Husband for the Daughter, The (ATU 2031C), 585–588
Mīlāwī. *See* Maylāwī, al-
Mille et un jours, Les. See *Thousand and One Days, The*
Mille et une nuit, Les, 9. See *Thousand and One Nights, The*
Miller, His Son, and the Donkey, The (ATU 1215), 271–274, 276
Miller of Sans Souci, The (ATU 759E), 154–160
Mills, Margaret, 19
Mirkhond. See *Rowżat al-ṣafā*
mirror for merchants, 379
mirror for princes. See *Fākihat al-khulafā'*; *Marzbān-nāme*; *Panchatantra*; *Sirāj al-mulūk*
mirror for princesses. See *Munes-nāme*
Miser and the Eye Ointment, The (ATU 836F*), 181–185
Mishle Shu'alim (by Berechiah ha-Nakdan), 253, 586–587
misogyny, 151–152, 255–260, 264, 314–319, 322, 330, 333, 552
Mo'ayyad, Ḥeshmat, 135
modern legend, 45, 47, 302
Mojmal al-tavārikh (anonymous), 100
Molière, 492
Moraru, Mihai, 193
Morlini, Girolamo, 163–164, 469, 508
Morton, Thomas, 396
Moscherosch, Johann Michael. See *Philanders von Sittewald Wunderliche und Wahrhafftige Gesichte*
Moser-Rath, Elfriede, 18
Moṣibat-nāme (by *ʿAṭṭār), 165*
motif: blind, 396; redundant, 79–80; ubiquitous, 36, 72, 289, 406, 419
motifs (Mot., unless specified otherwise) **B512**, 96; **F833.2**, 258, 382; **J251.1**, 294n8; **J1161.2**, 223n1; **J1908**, 50; **J2483**, 309; **K231.6.2.2**, 417n2; **K521.1.1**, 233; **K1667.1.1.*** (Rotunda), 472n10, 473n15; **K1667.1.3*** (Childers), 472n10; **K1812.17**, 62,

182, 256, 258, 377, 534; **K1861.1**, 233: **K1955.1**, 493; **S123.2**, 96; **W131.1**, 183, 232, 379; **X21**, 302
Mouse in the Silver Jug, The (ATU 1416), 329–336
muʿtazila, 326
Mufaḍḍal ibn Salama, al-, 14, 35, 63, 118, 371. See Fākhir, al-
Muḥāḍarāt al-udabāʾ (by al-Rāghib al-Iṣfahānī), 13, 179, 257, 289, 303, 410, 434, 442, 466, 489, 509, 567, 579
Muḥammad, The Prophet, 127, 216, 415
Muʿjam al-udabāʾ (by Yāqūt al-Ḥamawī), 40, 157
Mundt, Marina, 97
Munes-nāme (by Abu Bakr ibn Khosrow), 15, 90–91, 116, 143, 197–198, 209, 223, 246, 353, 365, 388, 516, 530
Muntaẓam, al- (by Ibn al-Jawzī), 118, 331
Murūj al-dhahab (by Masʿūdī), 14, 117, 156, 458–459
Muslim, 143
Mustaṭraf fī kull fann mustaẓraf, al- (by Ibshīhī), 13–14, 31, 165, 459, 466, 593
Muʿtazila, 326
mystical application, 277, 299, 311, 326, 346, 438

Nachtigall, Ottmar, 393
Nachtbüchlein (by Schumann), 288
Nafḥat al-Yaman (by Shirwānī), 50, 157, 316
Nafzāwī, al-. See *al-Rauḍ al-ʿāṭir fī nuzhat al-khāṭir*
Nahrawānī, al-. See *al-Jalīs al-ṣāliḥ al-kāfī*
Nakhshabi. *See Ṭuṭi-nāme*
Naples, 536
narrator, 18–19. *See also* soldier; teacher
Naṣīḥat al-mulūk (by Ghazzālī), 143
Nasreddin Hodja, 7, 15–16, 175, 228
Naṣrallāh Monshi. See *Kalīla wa-Dimna*
Nathr al-durr (by Ābī), 12–13, 40, 179, 262, 267, 288, 306, 321, 357, 387, 401, 416, 432, 452, 470–471, 498, 509, 519, 522, 543, 548, 578, 591. *See also Lubāb Nathr al-durr*
Nawājī, al-. See *Ḥalbat al-kumayt*
Naysābūrī, al-. *See ʿUqalāʾ al-majānīn*
Nazi period narratives, 292–294, 450–454
Neander, Michael, 141
Nederlandse Volksverhalenbank, 271, 452
newspapers, folktales in, 30, 45, 266, 404, 414
New Testament: James 4:15, 178; John 6:1–2, 393; John 18:10, 392; Luke 24:31, 392; Matthew 7:6, 41
Neẓām al-Molk. See *Siyāsat-nāme*
Nicolas de Troyes. See *Parangon de nouvelles nouvelles, Le grand*
Niebuhr, Carsten, 285
Nihāyat al-arab (by Nuwayrī), 13, 118, 156, 332, 388, 515, 593
Niles, John D., 126–127
Noël du Fail. See *Contes et discours d'Eutrapel*
Nöldeke, Theodor, 157
nonsense tale, 582–588
Nordic literature, 97
Novellino. See *Cento novelle antiche*
Noṣrat al-Din Abu Bakr ibn Moḥammad Ildigiz, 197, 209
Numskull Cannot Find the Donkey He Is Sitting On (ATU 1288A), 287–291, 575
Nuñez, Hernán. See *Refranes o proverbios en romance*
Nuwayrī, al-. See *Nihāyat al-arab*
Nuwayrī al-Iskandarānī, al-. See *Kitāb al-Ilmām*
Nuzhat al-anfus (by ʿIrāqī), 339–340
Nuzhat al-jullās, 460
Nuzhat al-majālis (by Saffūrī), 165
Nuzhat al-udabāʾ (by Ḥanafī), 14, 31, 296, 303–304, 316, 369, 388, 394, 427, 434, 442, 551, 563, 579, 593

Odo of Cheriton, 16, 34–35. See *Liber parabolorum*
Oestrup, Johannes, 6
Oicotype, 79, 213, 215, 471, 482, 510, 586
Oiselet, L', 39
Old Beggar and the Robbers, The (ATU 1526), 363–366

Old Testament, 2 Kings 23:29–35, 228
Old Woman as Trouble Maker, The (ATU 1353), 314–319
One Vice Carries Others With It (ATU 839), 186–191
Open Sesame (ATU 676), 237
oral tradition, 2, 9–10, 18–19, 90, 92, 299, 307–308
orality, alleged ("*audivi*"), 493, 551, 555
"Orient," implications of the term, 1, 4
Oriental Herald, The, 404
"Oriental Miscellany," 2, 17, 434, 437
"Oriental" tales, study of, 3–8
orientalism, 1
Orlando furioso (by Ariosto), 351–352
Orlando innamorato (by Boiardo), 245
orphan tales, 76
Orso, Ethelyn G., 287
Orto de esposo (by Hermenegildo de Tancos), 163
Otago Daily Times, 404
Otia imperialia (by Gervase of Tilbury), 30
Ottoman Empire, 2
Ouville, Antoine d'. See *élite des contes, L'*
Ovid. See *Metamporphoses*
Ox for Five Pennies, An (ATU 1553), 409–413
Ozarks, 275–276, 570

Pacific Rural Times, 2
Painter, William: *Palace of Pleasure*, 222
Panchatantra, 1, 5, 16, 34, 47, 91; Greek version, 35; Syriac version, 35
Parangon de nouvelles nouvelles, Le grand (by Nicolas de Troyes), 228, 469
Paris, Gaston, 96, 273
Parnell, Thomas, 70
Paroles remarquables, Les (by Galland), 165
Parrot, Book of the, 249. See *Chehel ṭuṭi*; *Javāher al-asmār*; *Śukasaptati*; *Ṭuṭi-nāme*
party-crasher, 394
Pathelin, Farce de maistre, 445
Patrañuelo, El (by Timoneda), 228, 351
Pauli, Johannes, 46, 188. See *Schimpf und Ernst*
Pecorone (by Fiorentino), 222
Pent Cuckoo, The (ATU 1213), 266–270
Perceforest, 210
Peregrinaggio di tre giovanni figliuoli del re di Serendippo (by Armeno), 114–116, 120, 515–516
performer. *See* narrator
Perkal, Joan Ruman, 585
Perrault, Charles, 148
personal experience. *See* first person narrative
Pétis de la Croix, François, 1. See *Thousand and One Days*
Petrus Alfonsus, 1. See *Disciplina clericalis*
Pfaffe Âmîs, Der (by Der Stricker), 227, 363, 365, 475
Pharaoh, 228, 579
Philanders von Sittewald, Wunderliche und Wahrhafftige Gesichte (by Moscherosch), 351
Philogelos, 13, 406, 442, 522
Physician in Spite of Himself (ATU 1641B), 482, 491–496
Pinedo, Luis de: *Libro de chistes*, 542
Pious Innocent Man Knows Nothing of God, A (ATU 827), 546
Piperno, Pietro. See *De nuce maga Beneventana*
Piron, Alexis, 369
Pitrè, Giuseppe, 495
Plutarch, 594
Po yu king, 295
Poggio Bracciolini, Giovanni Francesco, 272, 288, 302, 338, 493, 508, 541, 543–544, 551, 567–568, 571
Polish narratives, 518
political implications, 298–301
Polívka, Georg (Jiří), 7
Pomeranzewa, Erna, 386
Pontus Heuterus: *De Rebus Burgundicis*, 376
popular tradition, ancient Arab, 30
Pot Has a Child and Dies, The (ATU 1592B), 450–454
Pound of Flesh, A (ATU 890), 221–224
Powell, George E., 105
Prato, Stanislaus, 314
Prince's Wings, The (ATU 575), 86–94
prodesse et delectare, 12

Pröhle, Heinrich, 79
Prophets, Tales of the. See *Qiṣaṣ al-anbiyā'*
proverbs and proverbial phrases, 34–36, 71, 120, 151, 217, 299, 369, 397, 398, 411, 419, 437, 447, 471, 484, 537
Pryme, Abraham de la, 500
Puccini, Giacomo, 200
Purselt, Conrad, 563

Qalyūbī, al-, 144
Qaramānī, al-. See *Akhbār al-duwal wa-āthār al-uwal*
Qazvini, 259
Qazwīnī, al-, 157. See *'Ajā'ib al-makhlūqāt*; *Āthār al-bilād*
Qırq vezīr (by Sheykh-zāda?), 100, 128, 189, 246, 346, 424, 476–477
Qiṣaṣ al-anbiyā' (by Tha'labī), 14, 143, 165, 174, 189, 353; (by Kisā'ī), 14, 144
Qiṣaṣ al-'arab, 332
Qūt al-qulūb (by Makkī), 165

Rabbi Joël, 47, 586
Rabī' al-abrār (by Zamakhsharī), 285, 434, 446, 593
Rael, Juan, 468
Rāfi'ī al-Qazwīnī, al-, 316–317
Rāghib al-Iṣfahānī. See *Muḥāḍarāt al-udabā'*
railroad stories, 396
Randolph, Vance, 275–276, 337, 484, 570
Ranke, Kurt, 18, 79, 302–303, 363–366, 426–427
Rarest Thing in the World, The (ATU 653A), 105–110, 238
Rausmaa, Pirkko-Liisa, 203, 306
Rawḍ al-'āṭir, al- (by Nafzāwī), 340
Rawḍ al-mi'ṭār, al- (al-Ḥimyarī), 156
Rawḍ al-rayāḥīn (by Yāfi'ī), 165, 174
Rawḍat al-'uqalā' (by Ibn Ḥibbān al-Bustī), 316–317
Raymond of Béziers, 586
Reader's Digest, 45
reading habits, historical, 77
reconquista, 17
Recueil de plaisantes nouvelles, 288
Redi, Francesco, 70, 72
Refranes que dizen las viejas (by Santillana), 356
Refranes o proverbios en romance (by Nuñez), 397
Relative in the Urn, The (ATU 1339G), 47, 302–308
Relativity of Time (ATU 681), 125–131
Remouchamps, Edouard, 276
Resāle-ye delgoshā (by Zākāni), 293, 311, 340, 427, 438, 551
reward and punishment, 68–73, 129, 455–462
Reyāż al-ḥekāyāt (by Kāshāni), 268, 280, 289, 311
Rhampsinitus (ATU 950), 240
Robbers Commiserated, The (ATU 1341C), 305–308
Romanian, oldest documented folktale in, 192
romanticism, 18, 450
Romuz-e Ḥamze, 101
Rose of Bakawali, The, 128
Rosicrucianism, 246
Rost, Johann Leonhard. See *Meleatons [. . .] Tugendschule*
Rovere, Galeotto and Sisto Gara della, 536
Rowżat al-ṣafā (by Mirkhond), 156, 165, 189
Royal Irish Academy, 213
Rumi, 15, 447. See *Masnavi-ye ma'navi*
Russell, Patrick, 537
Rypka, Jan, 15

Sabbagh, Michel, 76
Sacchetti, Franco, 17. See *Trecentonovelle*
Sack-Full of Newes, The, 261–262
Sa'di. See *Bustān*; *Golestān*
Ṣafadī, al-, 14, 258, 357, 522, 563
Saffūrī, al-. See *Nuzhat al-majālis wa-muntakhab al-nafā'is*
Ṣafi, Fakhr al-Din 'Ali. See *Laṭā'ef al-ṭavā'ef*
Sagredo, Giovanni, 360
Sahl ibn Hārūn, 332

Said, Edward, 4
Saint Guinefort, 46
Saint Martin, Les .iv. sohaiz, 149
Saladin, 322, 398
Salazar, Lope García de, 503
Salustius, Hilarius, 30
Sanā'i, 447. See *Ḥadiqat al-ḥaqiqa*
Ṣanʿānī, al-, 189
Santa Cruz, Melchor de. See *Floresta española*
Santillana, Iñigo López de Mendoza. See *Refranes que dizen las viejas*
Sari ʿAbdallāh Efendi, 12
satire, 303
Saxo Grammaticus. See *Gesta Danorum*
Sayf ibn Dhī Yazan, 233
Scala coeli (by John Gobi), 228, 306, 387, 445, 514, 555
scatological narrratives, 206, 337, 434–435, 441–443, 468–473, 484, 507–512, 527
Schadenfreude, 507
Schatzkästlein des rheinischen Hausfreundes (Hebel), 155, 589–590
Scherf, Walter, 87
Schick, Joseph, 113, 119
Schiller, Friedrich, 200
Schimpf und Ernst (by Pauli), 228, 272, 386, 410, 423, 457, 508, 551
Schmitt, Jean-Claude, 47
School of Scottish Studies, 244
Schoolbooks, 71, 386
Schumann, Valentin. See *Nachtbüchlein*
Schwab, Gustav, 78
Schwarzbaum, Haim, 50
scientific observation, 30, 284
Scotland, 2
Scottish travellers, 125–126
sedentary cultural setting, 50
Sefer ha-ma'asim, 246
Sefer sha'shu'im (by Ibn Zabara), 314–315
Selbstberichtigung, 225
Sendbād-nāme (by Ẓahiri Samarqandi and others), 1, 46–47, 127, 149–151, 204, 246, 253, 255
Sercambi, Giovanni, 17, 114–116, 246, 321, 351–352, 484–485, 487
Serendip, The Travels and Adventures of Three Princes of, 111
Serendipity, 111–120
Series of Clever Unjust Decisions (ATU 1534), 222
sermons, 18, 314, 583. *See also* Bromyard, John; Hulsbusch, Johannes; Jacques de Vitry; Stephen of Bourbon
Seven Sages, Story of the, 1, 5: *canis*, 47; *creditor*, 222; *fons*, 127; *leo*, 257; *nomina*, 149; *4 amatores*, 529; *senex caecus*, 253
Seven Viziers, The, 127, 257, 529
sexually explicit narratives, 149–151, 337–342, 488, 513, 516
Shaʿbī, al-, 40
Shakespeare, William, 17, 222; *Merchant of Venice*, 221; *Taming of the Shrew*, 375
Sham Dumb Man Wins Suit (ATU 1534D*), 400–402
Sharḥ Maqāmāt al-Ḥarīrī (by Sharīshī), 40, 50, 459
Sharḥ Nahj al-balāgha (by Ibn Abī 'l-Ḥadīd), 40, 267
Sharing the Reward (ATU 1610), 455–462
Sharīshī, al-. See *Sharḥ Maqāmāt al-Ḥarīrī*
Sheep in the Cradle, The (ATU 1525M), 445
Shepherd Substituting for the Clergyman Answers the King's Questions, The (ATU 922), 225–230
Sherlock Holmes, 120
Sheykh-zāda. See *Qırq vezīr*
Shiʿa, 135
Shift of Sex, The (ATU 514), 125, 129
Shirwānī, al-. See *Ḥadīqat al-afrāḥ*; *Nafḥat al-Yaman*
Shoes, fancy, as euphemism for sex, 54
Shojāʿi Mashhadi. See *Meʿrāj-nāme*
Sicily, 2
Sidi Numan (ATU 449), 59–67, 183
Siglo de oro, 360, 497
Silva de casos curiosos (by Zapata), 360
"Simeli Mountain," 59, 239
Sindbād the seafaring merchant, 97–99, 101, 233
Sinnersberg, Rudolph von, 516
Sir Cleges, 457

Sirāj al-mulūk (by Ṭarṭūshī), 164–165, 174–175
Siyāsat-nāme (by Neẓām al-Molk), 151
Sobremesa y alivio de caminantes, El (by Timoneda), 469, 522
socialist interpretation, 103n16
soldier as narrator, 430, 535
Solomon and Marcolf (or *Morolf*), 49, 193, 315
Solov'ev, Leonid, 556
Somadeva. See *Kathāsaritsāgara*
Spies, Otto, 7–8
spinning chamber, 88–89
Spirit of Times, 414
Steinbach, Franz, 450
Stephen of Bourbon, 16, 46, 188, 227, 330, 418
stereotypes: Bedouin, 592, 593; black man, 216; Dutchman, 422; father and son, 273; German, 422; gypsy, 75; gender roles, 322, 411, 464; hillbillies, 275; Jew, 75, 216; master and servant, 434; merchant, cross-eyed, 465; people of Kufa, 441; red-haired person, 519; tailor, 434; teacher, 519; town of fools, 223, 266, 325; Turk, 438
storyteller. *See* narrator
storytellers, professional Persian, 101, 184
Strauss, Johann, 445
Stricker, Der, 148. See *Pfaffe Âmîs, Der*
Stroescu, Sabina Cornelia, 17
Suddī, al-, 164, 173
Suitors at the Spinning Wheel (ATU 882A*), 203–212, 463, 525
Śukasaptati, 5, 15–16, 41, 137, 247–248, 340, 344
Summa predicantium (by John Bromyard), 272, 410, 423, 457
Suyūṭī, al-, 40, 345, 522, 543, 563
Swords Turns to Wood (ATU 1736A), 534–540
Sydow, Carl Wilhelm von, 29
Sylva sermonum (by Hulsbusch), 288, 401
Syntipas. See *Seven Sages, Story of the*

Ṭabaqāt al-ḥanābila (by Ibn Abī Ya'lā), 331
Ṭabaqāt al-shu'arā' (by Ibn al-Mu'tazz)
Ṭabarī, al-. See *Jāmi' al-bayān fī tafsīr āy al-Qur'ān*; *Tārīkh al-rusul wa-'l-mulūk*
Tabula exemplorum, 272
Tadhkira al-ḥamdūniyya, al- (by Ibn Ḥamdūn), 40, 306, 401, 416, 498, 519, 563, 579
Tadhkirat al-awliyā' (by 'Aṭṭār), 332
tafsīr (Exegesis of the Koran), 151, 164, 188–189. See *Jāmi' al-bayān fī tafsīr āy al-Qur'ān*
Tailor in Heaven, The (ATU 800), 436
Tailor's Dream, The (ATU 1574), 436–440
Tales and Quick Answers, 551, 555
Tales of the Marvelous and News of the Strange. See *Ḥikāyāt al-ajība*, (*Kitāb*) *al-*
tale-type classification, 8, 305
tale types (ATU, unless specified otherwise), **63**, 29–33, 34; **65***, 282; **110**, 34–37; **150**, 38–44; **150A§** (El-Shamy), 298; **178A**, 45–48; **217**, 49–51; **306**, 52–58; **315A**, 64; **325**, 371; **400**, 232; **449**, 59–67, 183; **465**, 105, 108; **480**, 68; **503**, 68–73, 478; **514**, 125, 129; **561**, 74–85, 109; **575**, 86–94; **612**, 95–104, 235; **613**, 68; **653A**, 105–110, 238; **655**, 111–124, 245, 246; **676** (AT), 237; **681**, 125–131; **681 *A** (Jason), 131n31; **705B§** (El-Shamy), 130n14; **712**, 132–139, 464; **712 *A** (Jason), 139n28; **726**, 140–146; **750A**, 147–153, 337; **753A**, 170; **754**, 382; **759E**, 154–160; **763**, 161–169, 174, 181; **778**, 409; **778***, 508; **785**, 164, 170–177; **827**, 546; **830C**, 178–180; **836F***, 62, 181–185; **839**, 186–191; ***844B** (Marzolph), 538n2; **851**, 193, 196; **851A** (AT), 192–202; **852**, 578; **875B**, 386; **882A***, 203–212, 463, 525; **888**, 205; **888A***, 213–220, 253; **890**, 221–224; **891B***, 249, 257; **920C**, 113; **922**, 225–230; **924**, 484; **936***, 231–236; **949*** (AT), 215, 218n9; **954**, 109, 237–42; **956B**, 239; **976**, 113, 116, 243–251; **977*** (Berze Nagy), 350; **978**, 217, 252–254; **983**, 255–260; **1000**, 218; **1009**, 261–265;

1213, 266–270; **1215**, 271–274, 276; **1228A** (Coetzee), 290n13; **1242A**, 273, 276; **1242B** (AT), 275–279; **1255**, 279–281; **1262**, 282–286; **1288A**, 287–291, 575; **1293C*** (El-Shamy), 292–294; **1294A**, 295–297; **1294A***, 295–297; **1319N*** (El-Shamy), 298–301; **1339G**, 47, 302–304; **1341C**, 305–308; **1346**, 309–313; **1353**, 314–319; **1354**, 320–324; **1358B**, 351; **1373**, 325–328; **1416**, 329–336; **1420**, 337; **1420A**, 340; **1420G**, 337–342; **1423**, 343–348; **1426**, 349–355; **1446**, 356–358; **1515**, 210; **1525M**, 445; **1525*T** (Jason), 359–362; **1526**, 363–366; **1529**, 367–374; **1531**, 375–384, 538; **1533**, 385–391, 513; **1533B** (El-Shamy), 513; **1533A**, 392–395; **1534**, 222, 398; **1534A***, 396–399; **1534D***, 400–402; **1536**, 207; **1543A**, 403–408; **1543A*** (Krzyżanowski), 399n11; ***1550B** (Boggs), 499n3; **1553**, 409–413; ****1554** (Hansen), 443n3; **1555B**, 414–417; **1556**, 379, 487; **1558**, 418–421; **1562**, 422–425; **1563***, 426–429; **1565**, 430–432; **1572M***, 433–435; **1574**, 436–440; **1578A***, 303, 441–443, 551; ***1578A*** (Daskalova), 442n2; **1585**, 444–449; ***1587** (Boogs), 401n6; ****1588A** (Habboucha), 294n3; **1591**, 113; **1592B**, 450–454; **1610**, 455–462; **1617**, 463–467; **1617***, 468–473; **1620**, 474–481; **1640**, 491; **1641**, 247, 379, 482–490, 494, 542; **1641B**, 482, 491–496; **1641B***, 497–499; **1645**, 500–506, 509; **1645B**, 507–512; **1646**, 488; **1663**, 385, 386, 513–517; **1674***, 518–520; **1689**, 459; **1689B**, 521–524; **1730**, 204–26, 210, 525–533; **1736A**, 534–540; **1826**, 541–545; **1832N***, 546–549; **1834**, 441, 550–553; **1835D***, 554–557; **1848A**, 558–561; **1849***, 562–565; **1861A**, 566–569; **1862C**, 570–573; **1920**, 574; **1920D**, 574–576; **1920F**, 577–581; **1965**, 582–584; **2031C**, 585–588; **2040**, 434, 589–596; **2412B** (Ó Súilleabháin and Christiansen), 125

tall tales, 574–576, 577–581

Talmud, Babylonian. See *Babylonian Talmud*

Taloş, Ion, 193

Taming of the Shrew, The, 376

Tanūkhī, al-, 64. See *Faraj ba'd al-shidda, al-*

Tārīkh al-rusul wa-'l-mulūk (by Ṭabarī), 14, 117

Tārīkh Baghdād (by al-Khaṭīb al-Baghdādī), 331

Tārīkh madīnat Dimashq (by Ibn 'Asakir), 14, 331, 332

Ṭarṭūshī, al-. See *Sirāj al-mulūk*

Taṭfīl wa-ḥikāyāt al-ṭufaylīyīn, al- (by al-Khaṭīb al-Baghdādī), 393

Tawḥīdī, al-. See *Baṣā'ir wa-'l-dhakhā'ir, al-*

Taylor, Archer, 475

teacher as narrator (collector), 305, 329, 409, 430, 488, 521, 571

Tekerleme, 583

Terrible Threat, The (ATU 1563*), 426–429

Tha'ālibī, al-, 321

Tha'labī, al-. See *Qiṣaṣ al-anbiyā'*

Thamarāt al-awrāq (by Ibn Ḥijja al-Ḥamawī), 289, 331, 503, 593

theater, 534

Theodulf of Orleans, 426

Thief as Donkey (ATU 1529), 367–374

"Think Thrice before You Speak!" (ATU 1562), 422–425

Thompson, Harold W., 414

Thompson, Stith, 7, 233, 305

Thousand and One Days, The, 1, 15, 90, 134–135, 193–195, 537

Thousand and One Nights, The, 1, 14–15, 17, 41, 54, 90, 99, 135, 137, 182, 247, 249, 349–355, 369, 471; "Aladdin and the Wonderful Lamp," 74–85; "Ali Baba," 237–242; Breslau edition, 118, 346, 471; Chavis manuscript,

76, 128, 195; "Dalīla," 365; edition by Caussin de Perceval, 5; entry in the *Encyclopaedia of Islam*, 6; "Ghānim ibn Ayyūb," 317; "Hasan of Basra," 231–236; "Jūdar and the Moor Maḥmūd," 233; "Jullanār the Sea-Born," 64, 370–371; Kayseri manuscript, 118, 471; "King Shāh Bakht and His Vizier al-Rahwān," 118, 165, 471; Mardrus translation, 218; "Masrūr the Eunuch and Ibn al-Qāribī," 460; "Prince Ahmad and the Fairy Perī Bānū," 105–109; "Ruined Man Who Became Rich Again through a Dream," 503; "Second Qalandar's Tale," 64; *Seven Sages (Sendbād-nāme)*, 127, 150, 253, 257; "Sīdī Nuʿmān," 59–67; "Sindbād," 97; "The Ensorcelled Prince," 56; "The Sleeper and the Waker," 375–380; "The Third Calendar," 233; "The Trader and the Jinnī," 63; Wortley-Montague manuscript, 118, 218, 346, 529
Three Old Men, The (ATU 726), 140–146
Three Snake-Leaves, The (ATU 612), 95–104, 235
Three Teachings of the Bird (ATU 150), 38–44
Three Wishes, The (ATU 750A), 147–153, 337
Tījān fī mulūk Ḥimyar, Kitāb al- (by Ibn Hishām), 118–119
Till Eulenspiegel. *See* Eulenspiegel, Till
Timoneda, Juna de. See *Patrañuelo, El*; *Sobremesa, El*
To Sacrifice a Giant Candle (ATU 778), 409
Tolstoy, Lev, 142
Tomorrow's Music (Jason 1525*T), 359–362
Torrey, Charles C., 225, 228
traveling: storytelling while, 488
Traven, B., 164
Treasure at Home, The (ATU 1645), 365, 500–506, 509
Treasure Finders Who Murder One Another (ATU 763), 161–169, 174, 181
Trecentonovelle by (Sacchetti), 228, 387, 455–456, 469, 563
Trinidad, 107
Tripiṭaka, 119, 145n30, 164, 248, 263, 295, 352–353, 380–381
Tubach, Frederic (Fritz) Christian, 18
Tuḥaf wa-'l-hadāyā, al- (by Khālidī), 332
Tuningia, Gerærdo: *Apophthegmata*, 519
Turandot (ATU 851A), 192–202
Ṭuṭi-nāme (by Nakhshabi), 15, 41, 135, 143, 209, 247–248
Two Candles (ATU 778*), 508
Two Travelers, The (ATU 503), 68–73, 240, 478

Uji shūi monogatari, 71
Ulster Doegen recordings, 213
Unjust Banker Deceived into delivering Deposits (ATU 1617), 463–467
Unsuccessful Resuscitation (ATU 753A), 170
ʿUqalāʾ al-majānīn (by Naysābūrī), 179, 519
"Ur": *uralt*, 239; Urform, 157; Ur-Roman, 199
Uring, Nathaniel, 397
ʿUthmān ibn ʿAffān, 188
ʿUyūn al-akhbār (by Ibn Qutayba), 12, 150, 267, 277, 406, 431, 509, 567

Vade Mecum für Lustige Leute, 536, 590–591
Valerius Maximus: *Facta et dicta memorabilia*, 113
Varāvini. See *Marzbān-nāme*
Varsy, Jean-Georges, 240
Vetālapañcaviṃśatika, 119, 248
Viaţa lui Bertoldo, 193
Viidalep, Richard, 88
Vilain mire, Le, 492–493
Vives, Juan Luis, 376
Vocabulario de refranes (by Correas), 256, 360
Volksbuch, 78
Voltaire, 114
Vrčević, Vuk, 464
Wager: Clergyman to Read Prayer without Thinking of Anything Else (ATU 1835D*), 554–557

Wahb ibn Munabbih, 119, 165
wake, 107
Waldis, Burkard. See *Esopus*
Walt Disney Studios, 77
Walpole, Horatio (Horace), 111, 120
weeklies, 414
Weeping Bitch, The (ATU 1515), 210
Wegkürzer, Der, 431
Weighed Cat, The (ATU 1373), 325–328
Welcome to the Clothes (ATU 1558), 418–421
Wessaguscus hanging, 396
Wesselski, Albert, 6–7, 96, 197, 302, 426, 536
Which Was the Noblest Act? (ATU 976), 243–251
Who Stole From the Church?—The Thieves! (ATU 1641B*), 497–499
Wickram, Georg, 508, 559
Wieland, Christoph Martin, 353
Wife Kept in a Box, The (ATU 1426), 349–355
wine, 181–191, 381, 414–417
Wine and Water Business, The (ATU 1555B), 414–417
Wise Brothers, The (ATU 655), 111–124, 245, 246
Wise Carving of the Fowl, The (ATU 1533), 385–391, 513
Wit and Mirth, 279

Xiao li xiao, 404

Yāfiʿī, al-, 258
Yáñez y Ribera, Alcalá: *El donado hablador: Alonso mozo de muchos amos*, 519
Yāqūt al-Ḥamawī. See *Muʿjam al-udabāʾ*
Young Gentleman Learns Basketwork (ATU 949*), 215
Youth in the Land of the Cheaters, The (ATU 978), 217, 252–254
Yūsuf and Potiphar's wife, tale of, 464

Zabīdī, al-. See *Itḥāf al-sāda*
Zadig (by Voltaire), 114, 120
Ẓahiri Samarqandi. See *Sendbād-nāme*
Zākāni, ʿObeyd, 179, 306, 510. See *Resāle-ye delgoshā*
Zamakhsharī, al-, 157. See *Rabīʿ al-abrār*
Zapata, Luis. See *Silva de casos curiosos*
Ẓarīf al-maʿānī, 371, 394
Zaydī, al-. See *Lubāb Nathr al-durr*
Zedler, Johann Heinrich, 30
Zeitgeist, 262, 292, 451
Zelenin, Dmitriy K., 231–232
Zimmermann, Georg Ritter von, 155
Zipperling, Carl, 492–493

Lightning Source UK Ltd.
Milton Keynes UK
UKHW041353300421
382903UK00001B/13

9 780814 347737